CAMBRIDGE LIBRARY

Books of enduring scholar

Classics

From the Renaissance to the nineteenth century, Latin and Greek were compulsory subjects in almost all European universities, and most early modern scholars published their research and conducted international correspondence in Latin. Latin had continued in use in Western Europe long after the fall of the Roman empire as the lingua franca of the educated classes and of law, diplomacy, religion and university teaching. The flight of Greek scholars to the West after the fall of Constantinople in 1453 gave impetus to the study of ancient Greek literature and the Greek New Testament. Eventually, just as nineteenth-century reforms of university curricula were beginning to erode this ascendancy, developments in textual criticism and linguistic analysis, and new ways of studying ancient societies, especially archaeology, led to renewed enthusiasm for the Classics. This collection offers works of criticism, interpretation and synthesis by the outstanding scholars of the nineteenth century.

Bacchylides: The Poems and Fragments

Sir Richard Jebb's edition of Bacchylides' *Odes*, published in 1905, remains an authoritative work today. Jebb (1841–1905) was the most distinguished classicist of his generation, a Fellow of Trinity College, Cambridge, and University Orator, subsequently Professor of Greek at Glasgow University and finally Regius Professor of Greek at Cambridge, and a Member of Parliament for the University. This edition contains an introductory essay describing the poet's life, his literary context and his influence on later writers, especially Pindar and Horace. It also includes a section on metre. The text itself is given with a parallel English translation, textual collation and explanatory notes. An appendix discusses conjectural reconstructions of the odes, and there is a vocabulary list and index.

Cambridge University Press has long been a pioneer in the reissuing of out-of-print titles from its own backlist, producing digital reprints of books that are still sought after by scholars and students but could not be reprinted economically using traditional technology. The Cambridge Library Collection extends this activity to a wider range of books which are still of importance to researchers and professionals, either for the source material they contain, or as landmarks in the history of their academic discipline.

Drawing from the world-renowned collections in the Cambridge University Library, and guided by the advice of experts in each subject area, Cambridge University Press is using state-of-the-art scanning machines in its own Printing House to capture the content of each book selected for inclusion. The files are processed to give a consistently clear, crisp image, and the books finished to the high quality standard for which the Press is recognised around the world. The latest print-on-demand technology ensures that the books will remain available indefinitely, and that orders for single or multiple copies can quickly be supplied.

The Cambridge Library Collection will bring back to life books of enduring scholarly value (including out-of-copyright works originally issued by other publishers) across a wide range of disciplines in the humanities and social sciences and in science and technology.

Bacchylides: The Poems and Fragments

EDITED BY RICHARD CLAVERHOUSE JEBB

CAMBRIDGE
UNIVERSITY PRESS

CAMBRIDGE UNIVERSITY PRESS

Cambridge, New York, Melbourne, Madrid, Cape Town, Singapore,
São Paolo, Delhi, Dubai, Tokyo

Published in the United States of America by Cambridge University Press, New York

www.cambridge.org
Information on this title: www.cambridge.org/9781108008983

© in this compilation Cambridge University Press 2010

This edition first published 1905
This digitally printed version 2010

ISBN 978-1-108-00898-3 Paperback

BACCHYLIDES

THE POEMS AND FRAGMENTS

CAMBRIDGE UNIVERSITY PRESS WAREHOUSE,
C. F. CLAY, Manager.
London: FETTER LANE, E.C.
Glasgow: 50, WELLINGTON STREET.

Leipzig: F. A. BROCKHAUS.
New York: THE MACMILLAN COMPANY.
Bombay and Calcutta: MACMILLAN AND CO., Ltd.

BACCHYLIDES

THE POEMS AND FRAGMENTS

EDITED

WITH INTRODUCTION, NOTES, AND PROSE TRANSLATION

BY

Sir RICHARD C. JEBB

REGIUS PROFESSOR OF GREEK AND FELLOW OF TRINITY COLLEGE
IN THE UNIVERSITY OF CAMBRIDGE

CAMBRIDGE :
at the University Press
1905

NOTE.

The Syracusan coin known as the Damareteion, struck in 479 B.C., is reproduced on the cover from the example in the British Museum. Damareta, wife of Gelon, caused this commemorative medal to be issued in silver, defraying the cost from a large gift of gold made to her by the Carthaginians, whom she had helped to obtain favourable terms of peace after their defeat at Himera in 480. The Damareteion weighed ten Attic drachms, or fifty Sicilian litrae (Diod. XI. 26); which is precisely the weight,—found in no other early Sicilian coin,—of the piece in our Museum.

Obverse. A laurel-wreathed head, probably that of Nike. The dolphins, emblems of the sea (cp. Bacchylides XVI. 97 f.), perhaps suggest the maritime city. *Reverse.* A quadriga, crowned by a winged Nike, with allusion to Gelon's victory at Olympia in 488 B.C. It recalls the phrase in which Bacchylides addresses Hieron as Συρακοσίων ἱπποδινάτων στραταγέ (V. 1 f., 476 B.C.). Below, a lion, the symbol of Africa, *i.e.* of vanquished Carthage.

PREFACE.

THE Bacchylides papyrus was brought from Egypt to the British Museum in the autumn of 1896; and the *editio princeps*, by Dr F. G. Kenyon, appeared in 1897. We have thus acquired a large body of work by an author previously known only through scanty fragments; and the value of that acquisition is enhanced by the class to which it belongs. Of all the poets who gave lyric expression to Greek feeling and fancy in the interval between the age of Epos and the age of Drama, Pindar alone, before this discovery, could be estimated in the light of considerable remains. The fragments of the rest, exquisitely beautiful as they sometimes are, afford little more than glimpses of the genius and the art which produced them. Now there is a second representative of Greek song who can be judged by a series of complete compositions. Bacchylides has, of course, no pretension to be a poet of the same order as Pindar; it might rather be said that part of the interest which he possesses for us arises from the marked difference of poetical rank. In reading his odes, so elegant, so transparently clear, so pleasing in their graceful flow of narrative, often so bright in their descriptive touches, and at moments so pathetic, we feel that this is a singer who, moving in a lower sphere than Pindar, must also have been more immediately intelligible to the common Hellenic sense. The great Theban master makes no concealment of a haughty consciousness that his inmost appeal is to the few. This Ionian, if once he likens himself to an eagle —using a conventional simile germane to the style of an epinikion,—is truer to his own spirit when he describes himself as 'the nightingale of Ceos.' He brings home to us the existence and acceptance in Pindar's time of a lyric poetry which, without attaining or attempting the loftier heights, could give a quiet pleasure to the average Greek hearer or reader. There is reason to suppose that, if the fame of Bacchylides in his own day was not conspicuous, at least his popularity was extensive; and it is known that he continued to be widely read down to the sixth century of our era.

He certainly deserves to find readers in the modern world also. Not only is his work attractive in itself; it is a good introduction to the study of Greek lyric poetry: in particular, I believe that students would find it helpful in facilitating the approach to Pindar. The text of Bacchylides is uniformly easy, except in those places where the manuscript is defective or corrupt. The contents abound in matter of poetical and mythological interest;—Croesus, saved from the pyre to which he had doomed himself, and carried by Apollo to the Hyperboreans; Heracles meeting the shade of Meleager in the nether world, listening to the story of that hero's fate, and forming the resolve which is to seal his own; the daughters of Proetus driven by the Argive Hera from Tiryns, and healed by Artemis at Lusi; Theseus, diving after the ring of Minos, and welcomed by Amphitrite in the halls of Poseidon.

It is by considerations such as these that the scope of the present edition has been determined. I have endeavoured to combine criticism and interpretation with a treatment of the poems as literature; and thus to contribute, though it be only a little, towards obtaining for them that place in our Greek studies which they appear well fitted to hold. For such a purpose it was not enough to explain and illustrate the odes themselves; it was necessary also to aim at conveying some idea of the surroundings amidst which the poet worked, of his relation to contemporaries, and of his place in the historical development of the Greek lyric.

Owing to mutilations of the papyrus, gaps of various sizes are frequent in the text. Sometimes there is no clue to the sense of the lost words or verses, and conjecture would be vain; as in Ode VIII. 56–61, XIV. 7–14, 32–36, and elsewhere. Again, there are numerous instances in which a small defect can be supplied with certainty, as in I. 31 ἔπλε[το καρτε]ρόχειρ, or XIX. 5 θρασυκάρ[διος Ἴδας. But there are also two other classes of lacuna, intermediate between these. (1) In some passages, where a few verses have been lost or greatly mutilated, traces remain, which, with the context, sufficed to indicate the general sense of the lost portions. See, *e.g.*, Ode XII., note on 168–174. There are several cases of this class in which the evidence is sufficiently clear and precise to justify an attempt at showing how the defective text could be completed. But it should be clearly understood that wherever, in this edition, a supplement is suggested under such conditions, it is offered only as an *illustration* of the sense to which the evidence points, and not as a restoration of the text[1]. Such a supplement is merely an adjunct of interpretation, giving a definite and coherent form to the presumable meaning of the passage as a whole. The following are examples :—III. 41–43, 72–74 ; IV. 7–12 ; VIII. 89–96; IX. 1–8, 20–26, 54–56. (2) Another class of lacuna is that in which only a few syllables are wanting, while the limits within which a supplement can be sought appear to be narrowly defined alike by the sense and by the metre. A typical example will be found in Ode XV. 1, and another in VIII. 20. See also I. 32, 34 ; VI. 3 ; XII. 226 f. ; XVIII. 33, 35, 36, 38, 50. Small problems of this nature may be said to form a characteristic feature of the Bacchylidean text as it now exists.

Among those to whom my acknowledgments are due, the first is Dr F. G. Kenyon, to whose *editio princeps* of Bacchylides I had the privilege of contributing some suggestions. It would be difficult for me adequately to express how much I have been indebted to him for help during the progress of this book. In places where the papyrus is defective, the lines on which any tentative restoration can proceed must often depend on exceedingly minute indications, perhaps on the ambiguous traces of a single letter. It has frequently happened that, when working with the autotype facsimile published in 1897, I have had to consult Dr Kenyon with regard to the possible interpretations of some faint vestige as it appears in the original papyrus, or to re-examine it in his company at the British Museum.

---

[1] To make this clear, in the few instances where such supplements are suggested they are printed in a Greek type smaller than that of the text.

For the invariable kindness with which he has given me the benefit of his acute and skilled judgment, I cannot too cordially thank him. He has further done me the signal favour of reading large portions of the proofs; and, more especially in the critical notes on the text, several corrections or modifications of detail have been due to him. To Professor Butcher also my warm thanks are due for his great kindness in reading the proofs of text, translation, and commentary.

I desire gratefully to acknowledge here the courtesy of several distinguished scholars, who, at various times from 1897 onwards, have sent me copies of their writings on Bacchylides; among whom are Professors U. von Wilamowitz-Moellendorff, Otto Crusius, L. A. Michelangeli, E. Piccolomini, and Paul Maas. References will be found in several places to notes which from time to time have been communicated to me by Dr Walter Headlam. To Mr R. C. Bosanquet, Director of the British School at Athens, I have been indebted for information respecting the agonistic inscription from Iulis in Ceos, now in the Athenian Museum (p. 182); and to Mr G. F. Hill, of the British Museum, for advice as to the reproduction of the Sicilian coin which appears on the cover of the book.

The literature which has grown around the study of Bacchylides since 1896 is of no inconsiderable volume, a good deal of it being contained in the philological journals of various countries, or in the transactions of learned societies. A contribution to the bibliography is subjoined.

The Bacchylides of Professor Blass, a third edition of which was issued by Teubner in 1904, demands a special notice. It is a work to which every student of this poet must be a debtor; and my own debt is not diminished by the fact that, on many particular points of criticism or interpretation,—as will appear from the following pages,—I have been unable to accept the views of the eminent critic. After the first editor, no one has done so much as Dr Blass towards completing the text by assigning places to small detached fragments of the papyrus.

There is another tribute which I would render before closing this preface; it is to the memory of my friend Alexander Stuart Murray, sometime Keeper of Greek and Roman Antiquities in the British Museum. He was interested in that passage of Bacchylides (III. 17–21) which alludes to the offerings of the Deinomenidae at Delphi (p. 452). In December, 1903, a few months before his lamented death, he sent me a drawing, in which, using ancient data, he showed how a high tripod, such as the poet indicates, might have served as pedestal for a winged Victory ; the total height of the monument, as he conceived it, being about 18 feet 3 inches. A paragraph on page 456, relating to the probable significance of Hieron's tripod at Delphi, embodies the view of that question which was held by Dr Murray.

My best thanks are due to the staff of the Cambridge University Press.

R. C. JEBB.

CAMBRIDGE, *May*, 1905.

CONTENTS.

BIBLIOGRAPHY[1].

I. EDITIONS.

Frederic G. Kenyon. *The Poems of Bacchylides, from a Papyrus in the British Museum.* Printed by Order of the Trustees of the British Museum. 1897. (Editio princeps.)
The Poems of Bacchylides. Facsimile of Papyrus DCCXXXIII in the British Museum. Printed by Order of the Trustees. 1897.

Friederich Blass. *Bacchylidis Carmina cum Fragmentis.* Leipzig, Teubner. 1898. (Second edition, 1899 : third, 1904.)

Niccola Festa. *Le odi e i frammenti di Bacchilide, testo greco, traduzione e note.* Firenze, Barbèra, 1898.

Hugo Jurenka. *Die neugefundenen Lieder des Bakchylides. Text, Übersetzung und Commentar.* [The translation is in verse.] Wien, Holder, 1898.

Editions of Selections.

E. Buchholz. *Anthologie aus den Lyrikern der Griechen.* Vol. II, 4th ed., revised by **J. Sitzler.** Leipzig, Teubner, 1898. The following portions of Bacchylides are included (text and commentary, pp. 139—172) : Odes 2, 5, 17 (18 Ken.), 16 (17) : frag. 13 (Bergk, = 3 in my ed.), 19 (7), 27 (16).

D. Nessi. *Bacchilide: odi scelti* [1, vv. 13—46 ; 2 ; 3, vv. 23—62 ; 5 ; 8 (9), vv. 1—52 ; 10 (11) ; 14 (15), vv. 37—63 ; 16 (17) ; 17 (18) ; 18 (19), vv. 1—25 ; with commentary]. Milan, Allrighi, 1900.

---

[1] This list does not claim to be complete ; and I should be obliged to any reader who would aid me in supplying omissions. The object is to furnish students with a clue to the literature of Bacchylides since the discovery of the papyrus in 1896. A few books of earlier date are also mentioned. In the course of my work, I have read or consulted many of the writings enumerated here, including (I think) most of the more important ; but there are many others which have not been accessible to me.

Herbert Weir Smyth. *Greek Melic Poets.* London, Macmillan, 1900. The following portions of Bacchylides are included (text, pp. 90—131 ; commentary, 381—453) :—Odes 3 ; 5 ; 6 ; 8 (=9 Ken.), vv. 1—52 ; 10 (11) ; 12 (13), vv. 104—207 ; 13 (14) ; 14 (15), vv. 36—end ; 16 (17) ; 17 (18) : also frag. 7 (Bergk, = Ode 1. 13 f. Blass, see below, p. 437) ; 11 (=2 in my ed.) ; 13 (3) ; 14 (4) ; 19 (7) ; 22 (10) ; 27 (16) ; 28 (17) ; 36 (20) ; 40 (23).

II. TRANSLATIONS.

H. von Arnim. *Vier Gedichte des Bakchylides* [3, 5, 16 (17), 17 (18), with introductory article]. Deutsche Rundschau, Apr. 1898, pp. 42—61.

A. M. Desrousseaux. *Les poèmes de Bacchylide de Céos, traduits du Grec.* Paris, Hachette, 1898.

Eugène d'Eichthal et **Théodore Reinach.** *Poèmes choisis de Bacchylide, traduits en vers. Texte grec revisé et notices par Th. Reinach.* Paris, Leroux, 1898.

G. Fraccaroli. *L' ode V di Bacchilide.* Biblioteca delle scuole italiane, Feb. 1900.

R. Garnett. *Theseus and Minos.* Literature, Dec. 25, 1897.

L. Pinelli. *Due nuovi inni di Bacchilide* [*viz.* 10 (11) and 12 (13)]. Treviso, Zoppelli, 1898.

E. Poste. *Bacchylides : A Prose Translation.* [Ten odes are translated, in this order ;—5, 10 (=11 K.), 16 (17), 17 (18), 8 (9), 12 (13), 18 (19), 3, 14 (15), 15 (16); also the fragment on Peace (fr. 13 Bergk, = fr. 3 in this ed.).] London, Macmillan, 1898.

E. Romagnoli. *L' epinicio X di Bacchilide.* Atene e Roma, 1899, pp. 278—283.

F. Vivona. *Due odi di Bacchilide.* Palermo, Reber, 1898.

A. Wolff. *Il terzo epinicio di Bacchilide.* Padova, Randi, 1901.

III. OTHER WRITINGS, CRITICAL, EXEGETICAL, AND ILLUSTRATIVE.

L. D. Barnett. Notes communicated to Blass : 2nd ed., p. LXXII.

H. Bergstedt. *Backylides.* Svenska Humanistika, Förbundet Skrifter no. 3. Stockholm, P. A. Nanstedt & Söners, 1900.

F. Blass. Litterarisches Centralblatt, 1897, nr. 51/2 : 1898, nr. 3, nr. 5 (p. 175). Rheinisches Museum, 1898, pp. 283-307. Hermes, 1901, pp. 272-286.

K. Brandt. *De Horatii studiis Bacchylideis.* Festschrift Johannes Vahlen, 1900, pp. 297—315.

Ewald Bruhn. Zeitschrift f. das Gymnasialwesen, 1898, pp. 691—698. ['Idem antea per litteras mecum sua communicaverat, quibus litteris inerant etiam Ant. Funck et Caroli Niemeyer quaedam coniecturae': Blass, 2nd ed., p. LXXIII.]

J. B. Bury. Classical Review, vol. XIII, pp. 98 f., March, 1899; p. 272, June, 1899; XIV, p. 62, Feb. 1900.

W. Christ. *Zu den neuaufgefundenen Gedichten des Bakchylides.* Sitzungsberichte d. bayer. Akademie, 1898, I, pp. 3—52; 597--98.

G. M. Columba. *Bacchilide.* Rassegna di antichità classica, parte bibliografica, 1898, pp. 81—103.

D. Comparetti. *Les dithyrambes des Bacchylide.* Mélanges Weil, pp. 25—28. Paris, A. Fontemoing, 1898.

A. Croiset. *Les Poèmes de Bacchylide.* Revue Bleue, 1898, p. 705 ff.

Maurice Croiset. *Sur les origines du récit relatif à Méléagre dans l'ode V. de Bacchylide.* Mélanges Weil, pp. 73—80, 1898.

Otto Crusius. *Aus den Dichtungen des Bakchylides.* Philologus, v. LVII (N. F. XI), pp. 150—183.—*Die Dichtungen des B.*, Münch. Allg. Zeitung, Feb. 7, 1898.

A. M. Desrousseaux. *Notes sur Bacchylide*, Revue de Philologie 1898, pp. 184—195. (Also in Revue Universitaire, févr. 1898, p. 179.)

P. Dessoulavy. *Bacchylide et la IIIme ode.* Acad. de Neuchâtel, 1903.

A. Drachmann. Nordisk Tidskrift f. Filologi, 1898.

S. N. Dragumis. 'Αθηνᾶ, X. 4, pp. 413—425, 556 f.

V. Dukat. *Bakhilid* [with Croatian version of odes 5 and 16 (17)]. *Nastavni Vjesnik*, 1898, pp. 233—255, 356—370.

Mortimer L. Earle. Classical Review, vol. XII, p. 394, Nov. 1898.

Robinson Ellis. Class. Rev. XII, pp. 64—66, Feb. 1898.

L. R. Farnell. Class. Rev. XII, 343—346, Oct. 1898.

C. A. M. Fennell. Athenaeum, Feb. 12, May 21, 1898.—Class. Rev. XIII, p. 182, Apr. 1899.

Niccola Festa. *Per l' onore del re di Creta.* Miscellanea per nozze Rostagno-Cavazza, pp. 5—11. Firenze, Carnesecchi, 1898.

G. Fraccaroli. *Bacchilide.* Rivista di Filologia, XXVI. I. pp. 1—44; XXVII. IV., 513—586.

W. A. Goligher. Class. Rev. XII, p. 437, Dec. 1898.

Th. Gomperz. *Beiträge zur Kritik und Erklärung griechischen Schriftsteller VI.*, Sitzungsberichte der Wiener Akad., Bd. CXXXIX, pp. 1—4, 1897. —Also in Wiener Neue Freie Presse, Dec. 24, 1897.

F. Groh. Paper in the Hungarian Listy filologické : Blass, 2nd ed., p. LXXIII.

C. Haeberlin. Wochenschrift f. klass. Philologie, 1898, nr. 25; 1899, nr. 7.

Jane E. Harrison. Class. Rev. XII, pp. 85 f., Feb. 1898.

Walter Headlam. Class. Rev. XII, pp. 66—68, Feb. 1898.—Remarks on metre in Journal of Hellenic Studies, vol. XXII, pp. 214 n. 10, and p. 217. [Also notes communicated to Blass: 3rd ed., p. LXXVI.]

O. Hense. Rheinisches Museum, 1898, pp. 318 ff.; 1901, pp. 305 ff.

H. van Herwerden. Berliner Philologische Wochenschrift, 1898, nr. 5.— Class. Rev. XII, pp. 210 f., May, 1898.—Mnemosyne, XXVII, 1, pp. 1—46. —Museum, nr. 12, 1899. [Also notes communicated to Blass: 2nd ed., p. LXXIII.]

A. E. Housman. Athenaeum, Dec. 25, 1897; Jan. 15, 1898.—Class. Rev. XII, pp. 68—74, Feb. 1898; 134—140 (chiefly on Ode XVI), March, 1898; 216—218, May, 1898.

V. Inama. Rendiconti del R. Instituto Lombard. di scienze e lettere, serie II., vol. XXXI, 1898.

R. C. Jebb. Class. Rev. XII, pp. 123—133, March, 1898; 152—158, Apr. 1898.—*Bacchylidea*, Mélanges Weil, pp. 225—242, 1898.—*Bacchylides* in Encyclopaedia Britannica, 10th ed., vol. XXVI, 1902.—*Bacchylides*, a paper read before the British Academy, June 29, 1904.

H. Stuart Jones. Class. Rev. XII, p. 84, Feb. 1898.

Hugo Jurenka. Zeitschr. f. österr. Gymn., 1898, pp. 878 ff., 982—990.— *Die Dithyramben des Bakchylides*, Wien. Studien, XXI, pp. 216—224.— Festschrift für Th. Gomperz, pp. 220—224 [on Odes VI, VII].

F. G. Kenyon. Class. Rev. XII, p. 133, March, 1898.

Lionello Levi. Notes communicated to N. Festa (see above).

J. H. Lipsius. Neue Jahrbücher f. d. klass. Alterth., 1898, pp. 225—247.

Arthur Ludwich. Verzeichniss der Vorlesungen, Sommer 1898, Königsberg, p. 12 f., 42.

Paul Maas. *Kolometrie in den Daktyloepitriten des Bakchylides.* Philologus, vol. LXIII, pp. 297—309, 1904.

L. Mallinger. *Le caractère, la philosophie et l'art de Bacchylide.* Extrait du 'Musée Belge.' Louvain, C. Peeters, 1899.

L. A. Michelangeli. *Della Vita di Bacchilide, e particolarmente delle pretese allusioni di Pindaro a lui e a Simonide.* (48 pp.) Rivista di Storia antica, Anno II. 3—4. Messina, 1897. [This work appeared before the newly-found poems of Bacchylides had been published. After that publication, the same author wrote further in the Rivista di Storia antica, Anno III. n. 1, pp. 5—22.]

J. A. Nairn. Class. Rev. XI, pp. 449—453, Dec. 1897: XIII, pp. 167 f., Apr. 1899.

P. V. Nikitin. See Blass, 2nd ed., p. LXXV.

U. Pestalozza. Rassegna Nazionale, 16 Apr. 1898, pp. 697—730.

A. C. Pearson. Class. Rev. XII, pp. 74—76, Feb. 1898.

E. Piccolomini, Atene e Roma, I, pp. 3—15, 1898.—*Le odi di Bacchilide* (23 pp.). Firenze-Roma, Bencini, 1898.—*Osservazioni sopra le odi di Bacchilide,* Rendiconti della R. Accad. dei Lincei, VIII. fasc. 3--4.

V. Pingel. Notes communicated to Blass : 2nd ed., p. LXXIII.

Arthur Platt. Athenaeum, Dec. 25, 1897 ; Jan. 15, 1898.—Class. Rev. XII, pp. 58—64, Feb. 1898 ; 133 f., March ; 211—216, May.

A. Poutsma, Mnemosyne, XXVI, p. 339.

W. K. Prentice. *De Bacchylide Pindari artis socio et imitatore.* Halle, 1900. (Blass, 3rd ed., p. LXXII.)

Alexander Pridik. *De Cei Insulae rebus.* Berlin, Mayer & Mueller, 1892.

T(héodore) R(einach). *Notes sur Bacchylide,* Revue des études grecques, pp. 17—30, 1898.

Beatrice Reynolds. Class. Rev. XII, p. 254, June, 1898.

Herbert Richards. Class. Rev. XII, pp. 76 f., Feb. 1898 ; p. 134, March.

Carl Robert. Hermes, XXXIII, 1898, pp. 130—159. [Also Arch. Anzeiger, 1889, p. 141.]

O. Rossbach (quoted by A. Ludwich, p. 13 : see above).

J. E. Sandys. Literature, Dec. 18, 1897 ; Athenaeum, Dec. 25, 1897 : Class. Rev. XII, pp. 77 f.

J. Schöne. *De dialecto Bacchylidea.* Leipzig, Hirschfeld, 1899.

O. Schröder. Berliner Philologische Wochenschrift, 1898, nr. 11, nr. 28.

Arthur Hamilton Smith. *Illustrations to Bacchylides,* Journ. of Hellenic Studies, vol. XVIII, pp. 267—280, 1898. [This article brings together the monuments which illustrate themes treated by Bacchylides in Odes III, V, VIII, XII, XV, XVI, XVII, with full references to the archaeological literature. Ten vases are figured in the text. At the end of the volume, Plate XIV reproduces the picture of Theseus welcomed by Amphitrite, from the cup of Euphronius : see below, p. 225.]

Herbert Weir Smyth. Transactions of the American Philological Association, vol. XXIX, pp. 86—96, 1898.

J. M. Stahl. Rheinisches Museum, 1898, pp. 332 ff.

F. W. Thomas. Class. Rev. XII, pp. 78 f., Feb. 1898.

V. Tommasini. *Imitazioni e reminiscenze omeriche in Bacchilide.* Studi italiani di Filologia classica, VII, 1899, pp. 415—439.

R. Y. Tyrrell. Class. Rev. XII, pp. 79—83, Feb. 1898 ; 412—414, Nov. ; XIII, pp. 44—46, Feb. 1899.

J. Wackernagel. Notes communicated to Blass : 2nd ed., p. LXXVIII.

C. Waldstein. Class. Rev. XII, pp. 473 f., Dec. 1900.

H. Weil. Journal des Savants, Mar. 1898, pp. 174—184.

U. von Wilamowitz. *Bacchylides.* Berlin, Wiedmann, 1898 (33 pp.).— Götting. gelehrte Anzeigen, 1898, pp. 125—160.—Götting. Nachr., 1898, pp. 228—236.

A. Wolff. *Bacchylidea.* Patavii, 1901.

A. Zuretti. *Spigolature Bacchilidee,* Rivista di Filologia, XXVI, pp. 134—149.

Before the discovery of the Egyptian papyrus, those fragments of Bacchylides which are preserved by ancient writers had long been the subject of critical study. The following editions of them deserve especial mention :—

C. F. Neue. *Bacchylidis Cei Fragmenta.* (76 pp.) Berlin, 1822.

F. G. Schneidewin. In *Delectus Poesis Graecorum,* sect. III. (*Poetae Melici*). Göttingen, 1839.

J. A. Hartung. *Die griechischen Lyriker* [with metrical translation and notes], vol. VI. Leipzig, 1857.

Th. Bergk. *Poetae Lyrici Graeci,* 4th ed., vol. III, pp. 569—588. Leipzig, 1882.

GENERAL INTRODUCTION.

I. The Life of Bacchylides.

BACCHYLIDES was born at Iulis, the chief town of *Parentage.*
Ceos. His father's name is given as Medon, Meilon
(clearly an error for Meidon), or Meidylus[1]. His paternal
grandfather Bacchylides had been distinguished as an
athlete[2]. His mother was a younger sister[3] of the poet
Simonides, who, like his nephew, was a native of Iulis.

Simonides was born in 556 B.C.; Pindar, probably in *Date of*
518[4]: and ancient tradition said that Bacchylides was *birth.*

[1] (1) Μέδων is the form given by
Suidas s.v. Βακχυλίδης. It is fairly
frequent as a proper name, particularly
in Attica. (2) Μείλων (in two MSS.
Μίλων) appears in an epigram on the
nine lyric poets quoted by Boeckh,
Pindar vol. II. p. xxxi. The form
Μείλων occurs nowhere else : and in
Μίλων the ι is regularly short (though
long in *Anthol. Planud.* 24 and ap-
pend. 20). (3) Μειδύλος stands in the
Etym. Magn. 582. 20 (where it is
accented Μείδυλος). This is the only
example of it given by Pape-Benseler.
Μειδυλίδης, however, occurs as an
Athenian name, and is related to
Μειδύλος as Βακχυλίδης to Βακχύλος
(which is extant as an Athenian
name).

[2] Suidas s.v.: Βακχυλίδου τοῦ ἀθλη-
τοῦ.

[3] Strabo 10. p. 486 : ἐκ δὲ τῆς
Ἰουλίδος ὅ τε Σιμωνίδης ἦν ὁ μελοποιὸς
καὶ Βακχυλίδης ἀδελφιδοῦς ἐκείνου.
The word ἀδελφιδοῦς must here mean

ἀδελφῆς (not ἀδελφοῦ) υἱός, since Meidon (or Medon) was the son of the
athlete Bacchylides, while Simonides
was the son of Leoprepes (Simon. 146,
147: Her. VII. 228, etc.). If Bacchylides was born about 512–505 B.C.,
his mother may have been some 15 or
20 years younger than her brother.
—By Suidas (s.v.), as by Eudocia
(*Violar.* 93), Bacchylides is merely
termed συγγενής of Simonides.

[4] Pindar was born at the time of a
Pythian festival (fr. 193), and therefore in the third year of an Olympiad ;
and Suidas places his birth in the
65th Olympiad (520–517). Boeckh,
following Pausanias (10. 7 § 3) in
dating the Pythiads from 586 B.C.,
had to place Pindar's tenth Pythian
in 502 B.C. (the Pythiad to which it
related being, as the scholiast says,
the 22nd) ; and thus was led to infer
that Pindar was born not later than
522 B.C. But it is now established (see
Otto Schröder, Prolegom. to Pindar,

younger than Pindar[1]. The earliest work of Bacchylides
which can be approximately dated may belong to 481 or
479. The date of his birth cannot be precisely fixed, but
may probably be placed somewhere within the period from
512 to 505 B.C.

Notices in the Chronicle of Eusebius.—(1) ἤκμαζεν.   According to the Chronicle of Eusebius, he 'was in his
prime' (ἤκμαζεν) in Ol. 78. 2, 467 B.C.[2]. The physical
prime denoted by the word ἤκμαζεν was usually placed at
about the fortieth year. If such a reckoning could be
assumed in the present case, we should have 507 B.C. as
the approximate date of birth; and that is probably not
far from the truth. But, seeing how little appears to have
been known as to this poet's life, it is unlikely that
Eusebius had found a record of the birth-year, from which
he computed the date of the prime. It is more likely that
the choice of the year 467 was an inference from some
other fact or facts. It was known that Bacchylides wrote
odes for Hieron of Syracuse. Now the year 467 was the
date of Hieron's death. If Eusebius, or his authority,
assumed (or had reason to believe) that Bacchylides was
still young when first introduced, not long after 478, to

pp. 48 ff.) that Bergk was right in
preferring the authority of the Pindaric scholia to that of Pausanias,
and in reckoning the Pythiads from
582 B.C. The date of *Pyth.* x. is
therefore 498 B.C.

[1] Eustathius, Life of Pindar in the
Πρόλογος τῶν Πινδαρικῶν παρεκβολῶν
(printed in Christ's ed. of Pindar, p.
103): Thomas Magister, Πινδάρου
γένος (*ib.* p. 108). Pindar was
'younger than Simonides, but older
than Bacchylides.'

[2] Apollodorus of Athens (*circ.*
140 B.C.) was the author of Χρονικά,
or 'Annals,' in four books of iambic
trimeters, beginning from the fall of
Troy, and going down to his own
time. (The fragments are collected
by Müller, *Frag. Hist.*, vol. I. pp.
435 ff.) In this work he gave the
principal events, not only of political,

but also of literary, history; and for
literary history he was the chief
authority of later writers. Eusebius
is not believed to have had any direct
knowledge of that work; he seems
to have based his chronology on later
compendia: but Apollodorus may
have been the principal ultimate
source from which the literary dates
of Eusebius were derived. (See W.
Christ, *Gesch. d. Griech. Litt.*, pp. 608
and 920.)

The Byzantine *Chronicon Paschale*,
p. 162, places the ἤκμαζεν of Bacchylides Ol. 74 (484–481 B.C.): a statement
which (if the ἀκμή is to be placed at
about the 40th year) puts his birth
back to 524–521 B.C. But this, as
L. A. Michelangeli observes (*Della
Vita di Bacchilide*, p. 5), is incompatible with the tradition that Bacchylides was younger than Pindar.

Hieron, his prime may have been conjecturally placed about a decade later. The selection of the year 467 was the more natural, since the end of Hieron's reign might be regarded as closing a chapter in the fortunes of the poet.

Eusebius gives also another indication. Under Ol. 87. 2 (431 B.C.) he notes that Bacchylides was then 'well-known' or 'eminent' (ἐγνωρίζετο). The phrase might be taken as denoting the full maturity of a long-established reputation[1]. But, even on that view, it is surprising to find the epoch placed so late. As early (probably) as 481 or 479[2], Bacchylides had written an important ode for Pytheas, the son of the Aeginetan Lampon, whose victory was also celebrated by Pindar. Lampon would scarcely have given a commission to the Cean poet, if the latter had not already gained some distinction. It is true that, in youth and in middle life, the name of Bacchylides must have been overshadowed by those of the two greater lyric poets. The vigorous old age of Simonides was prolonged to about 467 ; Pindar survived the year 446, and may have lived till 438. It is also true that the gifts of Bacchylides were not such as conquer a swift renown by a few brilliant strokes; they were better fitted to achieve a gradual success, as the elegance and the quiet charm of his work became more widely known among those who could appreciate them. It is easy to conceive that his modest fame may have become brighter towards the evening of life than it had been in the morning or in the meridian. But it is more difficult to suppose that a chronicler, who placed the poet's prime in 467, can have intended to give the year 431 as marking the period at which his reputation culminated.

It may be observed, however, that the phrase ἐγνωρίζετο is susceptible of an interpretation which avoids that difficulty. Eusebius, or the authority on whom he relied, may have found some indication that in 431 Bacchylides was still alive. The indication may have been an ancient

(2) ἐγνωρίζετο.

---

[1] L. A. Michelangeli, *Della Vita di Bacchilide* etc. (1897), p. 6.   [2] Introd. to Ode XII, § 2.

mention of him, which the context made it possible to place at about the beginning of the Peloponnesian War. Or it may have been some work of his, now lost, containing *Probable* an allusion which yielded an approximate date. The *meaning of* chronicler's word, ἐγνωρίζετο, would then be a concise *ἐγνωρίζετο.* mode of saying that the poet 'was still alive and in repute.' The Byzantine chronographer Georgius Syncellus uses the same word ἐγνωρίζετο, but varies from Eusebius in giving Ol. 88 (428–425 B.C.) instead of Ol. 87. 2[1]. We cannot tell whether he was here following an authority distinct from that on which Eusebius relied. If the authority followed by both writers was the same, it is possible that Eusebius, in giving 431 B.C., meant to indicate 'the beginning of the Peloponnesian war' as an approximate date, while Georgius Syncellus found it more accurate to say that Bacchylides was still living in the Olympiad which began in the year 428 B.C. One conclusion, at least, appears warranted. The statement that the poet survived the beginning of the Peloponnesian War must have rested on some definite *Result.* ground which the chroniclers deemed satisfactory. We cannot fix the date of the poet's birth, or of his death. But it is probable that the period from about 507 to 428 was comprised in his lifetime.

Ceos. The surroundings and associations amidst which the boyhood and youth of Bacchylides were passed can in some measure be inferred from the traces which they have left in his work, and from what is known of his native Ceos. The 'lovely isle' of which he speaks, the 'land of rocky heights,' 'nursing vines' on the sunny slopes of its hills[2], was the outermost of the Cyclades towards the north-west. East and south of it lay the islands which

[1] *Chron.* p. 257 (ed. Par.). Georgius, a learned monk, was known as the Σύγκελλος, because he had been syncellus, or attendant, of Tarrasius patriarch of Constantinople (on whom see Finlay, *Hist. Gr.* II. 75 ff.). His Ἐκλογὴ Χρονογραφίας, beginning from Adam, extends to the accession of Diocletian in 284 A.D. He died in 800 A.D., the year to which he had intended to bring down his work. It was continued to 813 A.D. in the chronicle of his friend Theophanes.

[2] Ode V. 10 f. ζαθέας νάσου: I. 11 πολύκρημνον χθόνα: VI. 5 ἀμπελοτρόφον Κέον.

cluster around Delos, the central sanctuary of the Ionian race, whither (as Bacchylides shows us[1]) the people of Ceos were wont to send their tribute of choral paeans for the festivals of Apollo. A saga, which was narrated by *Legends of* Bacchylides in the first ode of our series, made a link of *Ceos.* mythical ancestry between Ceos and the greatest of the Ionian colonies on the coast of Asia Minor. Dexithea, who in her island-home had entertained gods unawares, became by Minos the mother of Euxantius, lord of Ceos, father of Miletus, and progenitor of the Milesian clan of the Euxantidae[2]. Like so many other Ionian communities, Ceos claimed also a tie with the Achaeans of the heroic age. Nestor had landed in the island on his homeward voyage from Troy, and had founded a shrine of Athena[3].

More important than any such legendary kinships were *Ceos and* the affinities and sympathies bred of frequent intercourse *Athens.* with Attica. Only some thirteen miles of sea lay between Ceos and Cape Sunium. From the days of the Peisistratidae onwards, the intellectual and artistic progress of Athens must in some degree have affected the little island, inhabited by men of the same race, which was so close to the Attic shores. A poetical and musical culture had long existed in Ceos. Iulis possessed a temple of the Pythian *Cean cult* Apollo[4]. Another Pythion stood at Carthaea, a prosperous *of Apollo.* seaport on the south-eastern coast of the island; and near it was a choregeion, a building in which choruses were trained for the festivals. Simonides, in his earlier years, *Early life* had taught there[5]. He must soon have made his mark at *of Simon- ides.*

---

[1] Ode XVI. 130. See Introduction to that Ode, § 1.

[2] Introduction to Ode I, § 3.

[3] Strabo 10. p. 486. See Appendix on Ode X. 119 f.

[4] This appears from an inscription (of 363 B.C.) found at Iulis (Köhler, *C. I. A.* II. p. 142), lines 20—22 τοὺς στρατηγ[οὺς] τοὺς [’Iου]λιητῶν...συνεισπράττειν τὰ χρήματα ἐν στήλῃ λιθίνῃ καὶ στῆσαι ἐν τῷ ἱερῷ ’Απόλλωνος τοῦ Πυθίου.

[5] Athenaeus 10. p. 456 F. We there learn that on a wall of the temple of Apollo at Carthaea there was a painting of Epeius, son of Panopeus, toiling as a drawer of water for the Atreidae; when Athena inspired him with skill to make the wooden horse. The incident occurred in the cyclic ’Ιλίου Πέρσις, and was treated by Stesichorus (fr. 18). Simonides wrote these verses (fr. 173):

the Cean school. It was probably about 52⅞ B.C. that Hipparchus invited him to Athens, where, at the age of thirty or a little more, he found himself placed in rivalry, as a chorus-trainer, with the celebrated Lasus of Hermione[1].

Attic influence. It would be unreasonable to take Simonides as a normal example of Attic influence on Ceos. No poet, perhaps, not of Attic birth, ever had so much of the Attic genius: the Danaë fragment is a witness. But his nephew also occasionally manifests a quality which is rather Attic than merely Ionian, especially in verses of the lighter and gayer kind[2]. It may well be supposed that, in the education and in the social life of Ceos, the characteristics and tendencies of eastern Ionia were tempered with elements due to Athens.

Folk-lore of Ceos. We have one specimen of primitive Cean folk-lore which breathes the old spirit of free Ionian fancy, the bright, naïve, sometimes playful spirit which reveals itself in the wonderland of the *Odyssey.* The story relates to the far-off memory of a great drouth which once parched the island, blighting the labours of husbandman and vine-dresser. The Nymphs of Ceos, it was said, had been scared from their haunts in the valleys and on the hills by the apparition of a lion[3]. They fled across the sea to Carystus in Euboea. An illustration of this story can still be seen. Not far from Iulis on the east, a colossal lion, some twenty feet in length, has been rudely carved from a rock, whose natural shape assisted, or suggested, the design[4]. The Nymphs, frightened into exile by the lion,

---

φημὶ τὸν οὐκ ἐθέλοντα φέρειν τέττιγος
    ἄεθλον
τῷ Πανοπηϊάδῃ δώσειν μέγα δεῖπνον
    Ἐπειῷ.

Athenaeus explains them as follows. At Carthaea, water was carried from a fountain up to the chorus-school, over which Simonides presided, by a donkey who was called Epeius; and, if a chorister played truant, the fine was a feed for the donkey. φέρειν τέττιγος ἄεθλον meant ᾄδειν.

[1] [Plat.]*Hipparch.* p. 228C: Aelian *V. H.* 8. 2: Ar. *Vesp.* 1410 f.

[2] As in the fragment (from one of the παροίνια) beginning γλυκεῖ' ἀνάγκα (no. 16 in this ed.).

[3] Heraclides Ponticus *Polit.* 9: Apoll. Rhod. 2. 498 ff. (with the scholia): Hyginus *Poet. Astronomica* II. 4.

[4] Bröndsted, *Reisen und Untersuchungen in Griechenland* I. pp. 31 ff. (Paris, 1826). Bröndsted's work,

were, of course, the water-springs dried up by the torrid heat. Then Aristaeus, the god who prospers all works of the field[1], came from Arcadia to Ceos, where his worship endured. Taught by him, the people raised an altar to Zeus Ikmaios, the Sky-father who sends rain and dew.

With its legends, its cult of Apollo, and its folk-lore, Ceos can have been no uncongenial home for a boy of quick imagination. Another feature in the life of the *Cean athletes.* island was the successful practice of athletics. Cean athletes were especially strong in boxing and in running[2]. The young Bacchylides, whose grandfather and namesake had been an athlete, might naturally follow with interest the growing number of Cean victories. Those victories were recorded at Iulis on slabs of stone, under the festivals to which they severally pertained[3]. In commemorating the success of Argeius, Bacchylides is able to tell us that precisely seventy wreaths had previously been won by Ceans at the Isthmian games[4].

As he grew towards early manhood, events were passing around him which may well have stimulated all his powers of thought and fancy. The overthrow of the *The Persian Wars.* Persians at Marathon in September, 490 B.C., must have brought a thrill of relief to the islanders of the Aegean, most of whom, in their helplessness, had given earth and water to the heralds of Dareius[5]. A few months later the news would reach the people of Iulis that their townsman Simonides had gained the prize offered by Athens for an elegy on those who fell in the great battle[6]. Eleven years later, after that repulse of Xerxes in which the mariners of

---

which was not completed, contains a most careful and minute description of Ceos. See also A. Pridik, *De Cei Insulae rebus,* p. 20 (Berlin, 1892). A very valuable feature of this monograph is the *Appendix epigraphica,* giving references to inscriptions (1) found in Ceos, or (2) relating to Ceos, but found at Athens, Delos, Delphi, or Paros. In some instances the text of the inscription is added.

[1] See note on fragment 44.
[2] Ode VI, verse 7.
[3] See Introd. to Ode I, § 2.
[4] Ode II, 9 f.
[5] Herod. VI. 49.
[6] Aeschylus is said in the Βίος Αἰσχύλου to have been an unsuccessful competitor: ἐν τῷ εἰς τοὺς ἐν Μαραθῶνι τεθνηκότας ἐλεγείῳ ἡσσηθεὶς Σιμωνίδῃ.

Ceos bore their part[1], it was again the Cean poet who rendered the most effective tributes to the heroes of Thermopylae and Artemisium, of Salamis and Plataea[2].
Panhel-lenic repute of Simon-ides. In those days of patriotic enthusiasm and joy, Ceos, and more especially Iulis, must have been proud of the man who had thus become the voice of Hellas. Bacchylides himself had now entered on his poetical career. He could have desired no better introduction, at home or abroad, than the fame of his kinsman.

Hieron of Syracuse. In 478 B.C. Hieron succeeded his brother Gelon in the rule of Syracuse. Gelon, a fine soldier, a capable states-man, and the founder of Syracusan greatness, figured in tradition as one who cared nothing for letters or art, being, indeed, almost ostentatiously scornful of the accomplish-ments which Greeks of his day associated with a liberal education. Once at a banquet, when the lyre was being passed round in order that each guest should play and sing in turn, Gelon ordered his horse to be brought in, and showed the company how lightly he could vault upon its back[3]. Such a story indicates the conception which had been formed of him. Hieron, it was said, had at first resembled his brother in this respect; but after an illness, in which his enforced leisure had been solaced by music
Hieron's patronage of letters. and poetry, he became devoted to the Muses[4]. It is certain that, from the outset of his reign, men of letters found a welcome at his court. The encouragement of literary and musical culture was, indeed, an historical attribute of the Greek tyrannis. It was at the Corinth of Periander that the dithyramb had been invested with a new significance by Arion. Polycrates had entertained Ibycus and Anacreon in Samos. Anacreon, Simonides and Lasus had been honoured sojourners in the Athens of the Peisistratidae. A power which rested on no constitutional basis could derive popularity, and therefore strength, from the presence

---

[1] Herod. VIII. 1 (Artemisium), 46 (Salamis). (Bergk).
[2] Simonides 1—4, 91—101
[3] Plut. *Apophth. Gel.* 4. 175.
[4] Aelian *Var. Hist.* 4. 15.

of men whose gifts and attainments enabled them to increase the attractions of the festivals. Since, moreover, Greek lyric poetry, and now drama, stood in close and manifold relations with Greek religion, the ruler who was visited and extolled by eminent poets not merely enhanced the respectability of his despotism, but obtained for it, so far, something akin to a religious sanction. The patronage of renascent humanism by such men as the Borgias and the Medici was predominantly a matter of personal inclination or of personal pride. The patronage of poets by a Hieron partook, doubtless, of both those motives, but it was also largely an affair of policy. Despite all that was vicious in the atmosphere of a tyrant's court, such patronage was, at that moment, a gain to letters, in so far as it gave a stimulus to poetical genius, and afforded splendid opportunities for its public manifestation. Athens was in process of becoming, but had not yet become, the intellectual centre of Hellas. Meanwhile Greek literature would have been poorer had it not acquired the odes which Pindar and Bacchylides wrote for Hieron, the odes which Pindar wrote for Theron of Acragas and for Arcesilas of Cyrene.

Pindar's first Olympian was composed for the ruler of *Pindar* Syracuse in 476, and the poet seems to have been present *(Olymp.1).* when it was performed. In the same year Hieron founded the new city of Aetna on the site of Catana. The first visit of Aeschylus to Sicily was made at that period. It *Aeschylus.* was then that he rendered to Hieron a tribute greater than any lyric epinikion. In his play, the *Women of Aetna*, he *His* referred to the new city, 'drawing auguries of happiness for *Aetnaeae.* the founders of the settlement[1],' perhaps in the form of a prophecy uttered by some god or semi-divine person. One passage in that drama must have thrilled the Sicilian audience. Aeschylus spoke of the Palikoi, the dread Twin Brethren of the old Sikel faith, the dwellers at the boiling lake[2]; and, using a myth which the Greek settlers in Sicily

---

[1] *Vit. Aeschyl.*: Ἱέρωνος τότε τὴν Αἴτνην κτίζοντος ἐπεδείξατο τὰς Αἰτναί-ας, οἰωνιζόμενος ἐντεῦθεν βίον ἀγαθὸν τοῖς συνοικίζουσι τὴν πόλιν.

[2] Aesch. fr. 6:
τί δῆτ᾽ ἐπ᾽ αὐτοῖς ὄνομα θήσονται βροτοί;
σεμνοὺς Παλικοὺς Ζεὺς ἐφίεται καλεῖν.

had woven on to the mysterious name, he described those
deities as sons borne to Zeus by Thaleia, daughter of
Hephaestus[1]. The trilogy to which the *Persae* belonged,
and which was brought out at Athens in 472, is said to have
been reproduced, by Hieron's request, in Sicily, and to have
won much applause[2]. The third piece of that trilogy, the
Glaucus, brought Heracles from the west of Sicily to its
northern coast,—from Mount Eryx to 'the lofty hill of
Himera[3].' Hieron had borne arms, under the leadership of
his brother Gelon, when the Syracusans and their allies
repulsed the Carthaginian invaders at Himera ; on the
same day, it was said, that Greek defeated Persian at
Salamis. It is easy to imagine the effect that would have
been made in the theatre where Hieron presided if the
Aeschylean Heracles, in prophetic strain, alluded to that
great deliverance.

ἦ καὶ Παλικῶν εὐλόγως μενεῖ φάτις ;
πάλιν γὰρ ἥξουσ' (ἵκουσ' edd.) ἐκ σκότου τόδ' εἰς φάος.
This is the earliest extant mention of
the Palikoi. The seat of their cult
was a small lake, usually about 490 ft.
in circumference, still called the *Lago
de' Palici*, in the province of Catania,
near Favorotta. Apertures in the
bed of the lake, near its centre, emit
a marsh gas, which forces up the
water (to a height of two feet in
places). The whole surface then
seems to boil. See Baedeker's *S.
Italy and Sicily*, p. 298 : and a very
full description in Freeman's *Sicily*,
I. 529 ff. The Palikoi were chthonian
and volcanic daemons and, like Styx,
an inviolable ὅρκος.
  [1] Steph. Byz. p. 496, 9, s.v.
Παλική (the town of Ducetius, whose
name survives in Palagonia). In the
Greek story used by Aeschylus, *Thaleia*
is probably a shortened form of
Αἰθάλεια (= Αἴτνη). Thaleia, preg-
nant by Zeus, hid herself beneath the
earth, to escape Hera's wrath ; and
there bore two sons (the Palikoi).

The myth was suggested by the
Greek fancy which derived Παλικοί
from πάλιν ἵκουσι (!), 'they come
back' to the light of the upper world.
In the fourth verse of the Aeschylean
fragment quoted above, which indicates this derivation, the true reading
(I suspect) is the traditional ἥξουσ',
and not that which modern editors
have preferred, ἵκουσ' : for, as θήσονται in v. 1 shows, it is a prophecy ;
and it was like a poet to *suggest* ἵκουσ'
as the second element in the name,
rather than to give it. The real
etymology is unknown. The Sikels
being of Italic stock, Michaelis proposes *pal* (πολιός) and the *-ic-* of *am-
ic-us*, *Labr-ic-us*, *Mar-ic-a*, etc. ; the
reference would then be to the dirty
greyish colour of the lake's water.
See Block's art. Palikoi in Roscher's
Lexikon.
  [2] *Vit. Aeschyl. ad fin.* : φασὶν ὑπὸ
Ἱέρωνος ἀξιωθέντα ἀναδιδάξαι τοὺς
Πέρσας ἐν Σικελίᾳ, καὶ λίαν εὐδοκιμεῖν.
  [3] Aesch. fr. 32 εἰς ὑψίκρημνον
Ἱμέραν δ' ἀφικόμην. See Freeman,
Sicily vol. I. p. 414.

While Tragedy was thus represented at Hieron's court by the eldest of the Attic masters, the other but less mature branch of drama was also welcomed in the person of Epicharmus. One of his comedies, the *Islands* (Νᾶσοι), alluded to Hieron having sent his brother-in-law Chromius, in 477, to Anaxilas of Rhegium ; a mission which secured the independence of the Epizephyrian Locrians. It is noticeable that the stories of Hieron which were current in later times often imply that he lived on terms of more or less familiar intercourse with the men of letters who were admitted to his circle. Epicharmus, in particular, was credited with a biting answer to an invitation from the tyrant[1]. Granting that some or most of these stories may have been late figments, it seems probable that Hieron's disposition was of a kind which made such intercourse possible, even if, as a rule, it was somewhat perilous. We should have wished to know whether the Sicilian historian Timaeus, who ought to have been well-versed in Syracusan tradition, had any good authority for his statement that Xenophanes of Colophon survived to the days of Hieron[2]. There is a certain piquancy in the thought that the veteran castigator of Homer and Hesiod may have met Pindar and Aeschylus under the roof of a common host. Homer is, indeed, the subject of a remark which, according to Plutarch, Hieron addressed to Xenophanes[3].

Such was the Syracusan court to which Simonides came soon after the beginning of the new reign. He was then seventy-eight years of age. It is remarkable that, among

Epicharmus.

Xenophanes.

Hieron and Simonides.

---

[1] Plut. *De Adul. et amic.*, c. 27. Hieron had put to death some of their common acquaintances, and a few days afterwards asked Epicharmus to dinner. Epicharmus made this unpunctuated reply :—ἀλλὰ πρῴην θύων τοὺς φίλους οὐκ ἐκάλεσας. [The ambiguity would be represented by the following sentence, though it is far less neat than the Greek :—'The other day when you held a sacrifice of your friends I alone was not asked.']

[2] Timaeus fr. 92 (Müller I. p. 215) : Ξενοφάνης...ὅν φησι Τίμαιος κατὰ ῾Ιέρωνα τὸν Σικελίας δυνάστην καὶ Ἐπίχαρμον τὸν ποιητὴν γεγονέναι. From Xenophanes himself (fr. 7) we know that he was still writing at the age of ninety-two.

[3] Plut. *Apophth. Hieron.* 4 : πρὸς δὲ Ξενοφάνην τὸν Κολοφώνιον εἰπόντα μόλις οἰκέτας δύο τρέφειν, ᾽Αλλ᾽ Ὅμηρος, εἶπεν, ὅν σὺ διασύρεις, πλείονας ἢ μυρίους τρέφει τεθνηκώς.

all the fragments or notices of writings ascribed to Simonides, the sole trace of Hieron is a mention of his name, along with those of his brothers, in the epigram on the battle of Himera[1],—an epigram probably written before Hieron had succeeded Gelon at Syracuse. The qualities by which the poet won the tyrant's regard seem to have been personal rather than professional. The friend of Hipparchus, the guest of Thessalian Scopadae and Aleuadae, was not without experience in the life of courts. Not long after his arrival in Sicily,—at some time in the years 478–476,—his Ionian tact achieved a task which must have demanded fine diplomacy. He reconciled Hieron to Theron of Acragas, at a moment when war had almost broken out

Their friendship. between them[2]. From that day until he died, not long after his patron, in Sicily, the relations of Simonides with the master of Syracuse appear to have been those of an intimate and confidential friendship[3]. At this period Bacchylides had already gained a certain measure of distinction. That is sufficiently proved by the epinikion (Ode XII) which he wrote, probably in 481 or 479, for Pytheas, son of Lampon, an eminent citizen of Aegina. The same victory is the subject of Pindar's fifth Nemean. Simonides took an early opportunity of presenting his nephew to Hieron at Syracuse.

The poems of Bacchy- lides for Hieron. The first poem which Bacchylides wrote for Hieron (Ode V) was sent from Ceos in 476 B.C. But a previous visit to Syracuse is indicated, since he is already Hieron's 'guest-friend' (ξένος, V. 11). Six years later, when Hieron's victory in the chariot-race (470 B.C.) elicited Pindar's first Pythian, Bacchylides sent merely a little congratulatory song of twenty verses (Ode IV); he may have been precluded, by some cause unknown to us, from doing more.

---

[1] Simon. 141 (Bergk).

[2] Diodorus Siculus XI. 48. Schol. Pind. *O.* II. 29 (15).

[3] Xenophon's *Hieron*, a dialogue between the tyrant and Simonides, attests the author's belief that the poet enjoyed in the fullest measure a friend's privilege of παρρησία. For other illustrations of the almost proverbial intimacy between Simonides and Hieron, see Arist. *Rhet.* II. 16. § 2 : [Plat.] *Epist.* II. p. 311 A : Cic. *De Nat. Deor.* I. xxii. 60.

In 468 Hieron gained the most important of such successes by winning the chariot-race at Olympia. The poet who celebrated this event was Bacchylides. Pindar did not write. A cordial tribute to Hieron occurs in his sixth Olympian, written in 472 (or, as some think, in 468) for Agesias of Syracuse (vv. 93 ff.). It would, of course, be unwarrantable to suppose that, in 468, Pindar had lost Hieron's favour. Pindar's silence may have been due to some other cause of which we know nothing. But, in the light of so much as is known, that silence is noteworthy. These are, briefly, the facts as to the work of Bacchylides for Hieron. His attitude towards that ruler, as compared with Pindar's, is discussed in another place[1].

In the course of the years 476–468 Pindar and Bacchylides must have met at Syracuse, probably on several occasions. A number of passages in Pindar's odes are interpreted by the scholiasts as containing hostile allusions to Bacchylides, or Simonides, or both. The question is sufficiently curious and interesting to merit some examination. *Supposed allusions of Pindar to the Cean poets.*

A preliminary observation should be made. Some of the Pindaric scholia which give these interpretations add statements to the effect that a jealousy existed between Pindar and Bacchylides ; that Bacchylides disparaged him to Hieron ; and that Hieron preferred the poems of Bacchylides to those of Pindar[2]. It has sometimes been assumed or implied that the Alexandrian commentators had no warrant for such statements except such as they discovered in Pindar's own words. But it is to be remembered that they may have found other evidence in books which are now lost, or of which only fragments remain. Among such books were the histories of Sicily by

---

[1] Introd. to Ode V, § 3.

[2] (1) Schol. Pind. *N.* III. 143 (82) δοκεῖ δὲ ταῦτα τείνειν εἰς Βακχυλίδην· ἦν γὰρ αὐτοῖς καὶ ὑφόρασις πρὸς ἀλλήλους. (2) Schol. *P.* II. 97 (53) αἰνίττεται δὲ εἰς Βακχυλίδην· ἀεὶ γὰρ αὐτὸν τῷ Ἱέρωνι διέσυρεν. (3) Schol. *P.* II. 166 (90) ἡ ἀναφορὰ πάλιν εἰς Βακχυλίδην· εἴληπται δὲ οὕτως ἡ διάνοια διὰ τὸ παρὰ Ἱέρωνι τὰ Βακχυλίδου ποιήματα προκρίνεσθαι.

Antiochus of Syracuse, Philistus of Syracuse, and Timaeus
of Tauromenion.   Those histories included Hieron's reign,
and may have noticed Syracusan traditions relating to
celebrated visitors at his court.   There was also a large
literature of memoirs and anecdotes concerning famous
writers.   Some idea of its abundance can be formed from
Plutarch, Diogenes Laertius, and Athenaeus.   Almost the
whole of that literature has perished.   But at least two
authors can be named, either of whom might well have
touched on Pindar's relations with the poets whom he met
at Syracuse.   One is Chamaeleon of Heracleia in Pontus
(*fl. c.* 310 B.C.), a pupil of Aristotle; the other is Istrus of
Cyrene (*fl. c.* 240 B.C.), a pupil of Callimachus.   These
were the two oldest sources for the biography of Pindar[1].
Timaeus wrote a work on lyric poets (Μελοποιοί).   It is
from Chamaeleon that Athenaeus derives certain particulars respecting the life of Simonides when he was
Hieron's guest[2].   Chamaeleon and Istrus, however, are but
two out of many writers who preserved reminiscences of
the classical poets.   It would be very rash to assume that
the Alexandrians can have had no warrant, beyond Pindar's
text, for their view of his attitude towards the poets of
Ceos.

Again, moderns naturally approach this question with
some reluctance to believe that a great poet could have
dealt in such innuendo.   But it is hardly needful to say
that modern standards of feeling cannot safely be applied
to an age of which the tone in such matters was so different.
It is indisputable that several passages of Pindar express
scorn for some people who are compared to crows or daws,
to apes or foxes[3].   The only question is, are all such utterances merely general, referring to classes of persons, such,
for instance, as the vulgar herd of inferior poets?   Or is
the allusion in such places, or in any of them, to indi-
viduals?   Here the probabilities depend in some measure

[1] Leutsch, *Die Quellen für die Biographien des Pindar*, in *Philolog.* XI. 1 ff.

[2] Athen. 14. p. 656 c, D.

[3] Pind. *O.* II. 96; *N.* III. 82; *P.* II. 72, 77.

on the estimate which may be formed of Pindar's temperament. It is clear, at least, that he intimates his own
superiority to all contemporary masters of lyric song.
Confidence in his own poetical power is joined to a marked
pride of race, and to that sense of an intimate communion
with Delphi which so often lends the note of authority to
his precepts. The disposition suggested by the general
spirit of his work is ardent, strenuous, impetuous : it is also
haughty, and such as would probably have been impatient
of competition.

In considering the passages, then, where the Alexandrians saw hostile references by Pindar to the poets of
Ceos, it is well to bring a mind unbiased by either of two
presumptions; that the Alexandrians can have had nothing
to go upon except Pindar's words ; or that Pindar cannot
have intended such allusions.

The most important of these passages,—that, indeed, *Passage in*
on which the issue primarily turns,—occurs in the second *the second*
Olympian ode, composed for Theron of Acragas in 476 B.C. *Olympian.*
That was the year in which Bacchylides first wrote for
Hieron, celebrating the same victory which is the subject
of Pindar's first Olympian. Simonides had then been in
relations with Hieron for more, at least, than a year.
After a magnificent description of the elysium in the Islands
of the Blest, Pindar abruptly turns to speak of his own
art. '*Many swift arrows are there in the quiver beneath
my arm, shafts with a message for the wise; but for the
crowd they need interpreters*'; and then come these words
(vv. 86—88) :—

> σοφὸς ὁ πολλὰ ϝειδὼς φυᾷ·
> μαθόντες δὲ λάβροι
> παγγλωσσίᾳ, κόρακες ὥς, ἄκραντα γαρύετον
> Διὸς πρὸς ὄρνιχα θεῖον.

The σοφός, the man of intellectual attainment, is here,
as the context shows, specially the poet. The true poet is he
who 'knows much,'—whose mind and fancy are fertile,—'by
nature's gift' (φυᾷ). 'But they who have merely *learned*,'—

the disciples and imitators of others,—'boisterous (λάβροι) with their torrent of words, vainly chatter (the pair of them) like crows, against the godlike bird of Zeus.' To the dual γαρύετον we shall return presently: but first let us consider the general purport of the passage. The 'bird of Zeus' is, of course, Pindar. He again likens himself to an eagle, and other singers to inferior birds, in the third Nemean (probably of 469 B.C.), vv. 80 ff. :—

> ἔστι δ' αἰετὸς ὠκὺς ἐν ποτανοῖς...
> κραγέται δὲ κολοιοὶ ταπεινὰ νέμονται.

'The eagle is swift among the birds of the air,...but the clamorous daws haunt the lower regions of the sky.' The word λάβροι suggests noisy braggarts, as in the *Iliad* (XXIII. 478 f.),—

> ἀλλ' αἰεὶ μύθοις λαβρεύεαι· οὐδέ τί σε χρὴ
> λαβραγόρην ἔμεναι.

The term παγγλωσσία occurs nowhere else. It denotes readiness to utter *anything* (compare παρρησία and πανουργία),—a loquacity not restrained by discernment or by taste. These creatures of mere lore are garrulous, without that discriminating instinct which chastens and refines the language of the born poet. Their utterances are also ἄκραντα: they achieve nothing, they make no abiding impression. In brief, these 'taught' men are pretentious, noisy, strangers to distinction of style, and ineffectual. But the fundamental thing is the contrast between original genius (φυά) and imitative accomplishment (μάθησις). This contrast is habitual with Pindar; we have it again in the third Nemean (vv. 40—42):—

> συγγενεῖ δέ τις εὐδοξίᾳ μέγα βρίθει·
> ὃς δὲ διδάκτ' ἔχει, ψεφηνὸς ἀνὴρ
> ἄλλοτ' ἄλλα πνέων οὔποτ' ἀτρεκεῖ
> κατέβα ποδί, μυριᾶν δ'
> ἀρετᾶν ἀτελεῖ νόῳ γεύεται.

'Born with him is the power that gives weight to a man's fame: but whoso has the fruits of lore alone, he remains in the shade. His spirit veers with every breeze: in no field of trial is his foothold sure: he nibbles at excellence in countless forms, but his mind achieves nothing.' The proximate occasion of this general reflection is the inspired valour of Heracles, to whom Pindar has just referred; but it is obvious that he is thinking also of the born poet. The same remark applies to some verses in the ninth Olympian (of 456 B.C.?), where the immediate contest relates to athletes (vv. 100—102):—

$$\text{τὸ δὲ φυᾷ κράτιστον ἅπαν· πολλοὶ δὲ διδακταῖς}$$
$$\text{ἀνθρώπων ἀρεταῖς κλέος}$$
$$\text{ὤρουσαν ἀρέσθαι.}$$

'Nature's gift is ever best; but many men have strained to win renown by feats to which they had been schooled.'

Such, then, is the general scope of the passage in the second Olympian. Let us next examine a crucial point in it, the use of the dual γαρύετον. *The dual verb.* Emendations have been attempted: but there is a strong presumption that the word is sound[1]. It will be remembered that the use of the dual

---

[1] Bergk (4th ed.) suggested γαρυέτων, which Otto Schröder adopts in his edition of Pindar (1900); a defiant imperative, like οἱ δ' οὖν γελώντων in Soph. *Ai.* 961. Schröder takes it as plural, not dual. Now such a form as γαρυέτων, instead of γαρυόντων, is most rare. The evidence is exhaustively stated in Kühner-Blass, *Ausführliche Gr. Gramm.*, 3rd ed., vol. II. p. 50. (1) ἔστων is 3rd pers. imperat. plural in *Od.* I. 273: also in Plato, Xenophon, Doric and Ionic inscriptions etc. (2) ἴτων in Aesch. *Eum.* 32 is 3rd pers. imperat. plural. (3) ἀνεστακόντων is cited by Kühner-Blass (*l.c.*) as occurring once in Archimedes, who elsewhere uses forms in -ντων: ' but that should certainly be corrected, with Ahrens, to ἀνεστακόντων: cp. Heiberg, Suppl. Fl. Jahr. XIII. 561.' (4) In *Il.* 8. 109, τούτω μὲν θεράποντε κομείτων, that form of the verb was

written by Aristarchus (but κομείτην by Zenodotus: Bergk says, 'alii forte κομεύντων '). κομείτων is usually and naturally taken as dual. In Kühner-Blass (p. 51) it is cited as the only example of the 3rd pers. of the imperative dual in -των which occurs in classical literature. Schröder, however, on Pind. *O.* II. 87 (96), suggests that κομείτων is 3rd pers. plural: I do not know why. It will be seen that the probabilities are very strong against a form of such extreme rarity as γαρυέτων. Schröder thinks that the imperative here is a great improvement to the sense. To me it does not seem so. The clause σοφὸς κ.τ.λ. is opposed to the clause μαθόντες δὲ κ.τ.λ. The verb to be supplied in the first clause is ἐστί: the verb of the second clause would also naturally be in the indicative mood, γαρύετον.

The other proposed emendations

verb implies not merely that there are two agents, but also that they are somehow associated in action. If, for example, it were desired to say in ancient Greek, 'Adams and Leverrier independently discovered the planet Neptune,' the verb would be εὗρον, not εὑρέτην : but in saying, 'Erckmann and Chatrian wrote the book,' it would be ἐγραψάτην. The usage of classical writers frequently illustrates the fine expressiveness of the dual verb. It can lightly emphasise a close comradeship, as when Heracles, in the Sophoclean play, says of Philoctetes and Neoptolemus,

ἀλλ' ὡς λέοντε συννόμω φυλάσσετον
οὗτος σὲ καὶ σὺ κεῖνον.

Or it can convey a shade of mockery, as when the Platonic Socrates says to Euthydemus and his brother, the professors of eristic, χαρίσασθον...ἐπιδείξατον...εἴπετον. In Pindar's γαρύετον the tone of the dual is scornful. These two persons are leagued in a futile competition with their superior. Can the dual be explained without assuming that it indicates two definite persons? No, unless by regarding it as merely incidental to the imagery; *i.e.*, as meaning that an indefinite number of bad poets behave 'like crows chattering in pairs': but that would be pointless, and, indeed, absurd. Who, then, are these two persons?

The scholiast's view. According to an Alexandrian commentator, they are Simonides and Bacchylides[1].

Other explanations. Only two other explanations (so far as I know) have been offered. One is that Pindar alludes to Capys and Hippocrates, kinsmen of Theron, who levied war against

of γαρύετον demand less discussion. (1) Dawes, γαρύεμεν. This is accepted by Michelangeli (p. 27), who, with that candour which marks the whole of his excellent discussion, recognizes the gravity of γαρύετον as an obstacle to his view that Pindar was guiltless of allusion to the Cean poets. The construction then is, λάβροι...γαρύεμεν (ἐντί), 'are fierce in chattering.' I cannot think that this has any proba-

bility. (2) Tycho Mommsen, γαρύεται ('schema Pindaricum '). (3) Herwerden, γαρύετε. (4) Hartung, γαρύεται (plur. of γαρύέτης) : when ἄκραντα must be either an adv., or an acc. governed by the verbal notion (ἄπορα πόριμος).

[1] Schol. Pind. *O.* II. 158 (96), on ἄκραντα γαρύετον.—εἰ δέ πως πρὸς Βακχυλίδην καὶ Σιμωνίδην αἰνίττεται, καλῶς ἄρα ἐξείληπται τὸ γαρύετον δυϊκῶς· καὶ οὕτως ὄντως ἔχει ὁ λόγος.

him, but were defeated. The 'bird of Zeus' will then be Theron: an eagle appears on coins of Acragas[1]. But this hypothesis is clearly incompatible with Pindar's words, and with the context: he is speaking of himself as a poet, and of his art. The other explanation finds in κόρακες an allusion to Corax, the author of the earliest Greek treatise on rhetoric, and supposes that his associate is the rhetorician Teisias. Corax and Teisias (it is suggested) had collaborated, shortly before 476 B.C., in a work which was known to Pindar[2]. Now Corax, indeed, is said to have had influence with Hieron, though his activity as a rhetorician belonged chiefly to the period of democracy which followed the fall of the Deinomenid house. But Teisias is traditionally represented as a man of a younger generation, a pupil of Corax, and afterwards the teacher of Lysias and of Isocrates. The chronological difficulty is not, however,

---

[1] This explanation was suggested by Freeman, *Hist. of Sicily*, II. p. 531. As to the war made on Theron by his two kinsmen, see *ib.* p. 147.

[2] This view was first put forward by Dr A. W. Verrall in an article on Aesch. *Cho.* 935—972 (*Journ. of Philology* IX. 114 ff.), and afterwards developed in his paper on 'Korax and Tisias,' *ib.* 197 ff. To those articles the reader is referred for a full and able statement of all that can be advanced in favour of the hypothesis. It should be noted that παγγλωσσία is explained by Verrall (p. 129) as 'the sum of all γλῶσσαι' (obscure words), and then (p. 130) 'the science of such words and their interpretations.' He thinks that, before 476, the two men, afterwards famous as rhetoricians, 'had published some work, doubtless fanciful enough, upon etymology.' Professor Gildersleeve, who regards the suggestion as ingenious, adds this comment (*Pindar*, p. 153): 'See P. I, 94; where the panegyric side of oratory is recognised. If we must have rivalry, why not rivalry between the old art of poetry (φυᾷ) and the new art of rhetoric (μαθόντες)?' The work on etymology, however, which Dr Verrall supposes, would have been published, as he rightly says (p. 197), at least ten years before Corax published his 'Art of Rhetoric,'—the earliest recorded book of its kind. Pindar, in Dr Verrall's view, represents, not poetry *versus* rhetoric, but the poet's insight into words *versus* the etymological treatment of words 'in prose, cold, crude, and quasi-scientific' (p. 131). The words in *P.* I. 94, to which Prof. Gildersleeve refers, are καὶ λογίοις καὶ ἀοιδαῖς: where λογίοις seems to mean 'chroniclers' (like the logographers). So in *N.* VI. 31 the memorials of fame are ἀοιδαὶ καὶ λόγοι, 'poems and chronicles' (surely not 'speeches'). In *N.* VI. 52 λογίοισιν seem to be 'men versed in tradition,' whether poets or prose-writers. It is more than doubtful whether there is any reference in Pindar to panegyric oratory; and it seems certain that there is none to the art of rhetoric.

the only one. Pindar, in the second Olympian, seems
clearly to point at other poets, the 'crows' of this passage,
the 'daws' of another, who vainly compete with the
sovereign eagle. It is hard to see how, in 476, the art of
rhetoric can have been in any such competition with the
art of poetry as would explain Pindar's words.

Pindar's
relations to
Simonides
and Bac-
chylides.
On the other hand, a reference to Simonides and Bacchylides is perfectly intelligible. Let us briefly recall the
circumstances. Simonides and Pindar, the Ionian and
the Theban, men of contrasted types alike in genius and in
personal character, had now for many years been the two
foremost representatives of lyric poetry. Shortly before
Pindar began to write for Hieron, Simonides came to
Sicily, and soon became established in Hieron's confidence.
Pindar and Bacchylides had already been brought into a
kind of indirect competition, when Lampon of Aegina
(probably in 481 or 479) commissioned both poets to
write for him on the same occasion. Simonides now
introduces Bacchylides to Hieron, whose Olympian victory
in 476 is celebrated by Bacchylides as well as by Pindar.
When account is taken of the temperament which has left
its impress on Pindar's work, it seems probable that
(however unjustly) he would have considered Simonides
as his inferior. He might with more justice take that view
of Bacchylides, whose real excellences, besides being of a
wholly different kind from his own, were on a lower plane.
The nephew was probably regarded by Pindar as a feebler
copy of the uncle. This, then, is the first element in the
situation. As formerly at Aegina, so now in a more
conspicuous manner at Syracuse, Pindar's work has been
set side by side with the work of Bacchylides. The other
element is furnished by the personal relations of Pindar
on the one part, and of the Cean poets on the other, with
Hieron. Pindar, we may be sure, would not have been a
successful courtier. It is hard to conceive of him as
retaining, for any long time, the good graces of an exacting
despot, who must have made continual demands on deference, tact, and pliancy. When asked why, unlike

Simonides, he was little disposed to visit the courts of Sicilian princes, Pindar is said to have replied, 'Because I wish to live my own life, and not that of another[1].' Pindar, one may believe, was too proud a man to care if the poets of Ceos outstripped him in Hieron's personal favour. But Pindar had the passionate love and reverence of a supreme artist for his art. His tribute to Hieron in the first Olympian is no mere conventional piece, written to order: it is one of the most splendid of his odes, showing that his imagination had really been fired by the grandeur of Hieron's position; not simply by the power which clothed the ruler of Syracuse, but also, as is still more evident from the first and second Pythians, by Hieron's place as the champion of Hellene against barbarian in the West. The third Ode of Bacchylides, linked by its occasion with the first Olympian, is a poem of great interest; but it cannot, of course, for a moment be ranked in the same class with Pindar's. Whether Hieron, however, was a good judge of their relative merits, may be doubted: and it seems very possible that, as the Alexandrian scholiast affirms, he preferred the simpler, clearer verse of Bacchylides to that of Pindar. If Pindar saw that, and felt that it was largely due to the personal influence of the Ionians,—an influence won by social gifts which he himself did not possess, and rather despised,—he may have resented it as a slight, not to himself, but to the art for which he lived. Such a feeling would go far to account for the tone of the utterance in the second Olympian. The things said there could not fairly be said either of Simonides or of Bacchylides. But resentment is not apt to be a fair critic. That γαρύετον refers to Simonides and Bacchylides, seems, then, exceedingly probable: though I should welcome a proof that this impression is erroneous. But the reader can now form

---

[1] One of the Πινδάρου ἀποφθέγματα (given in W. Christ's *Pindar* p. CI). 'Επερωτηθεὶς πάλιν, διὰ τί Σιμωνίδης πρὸς τοὺς τυράννους ἀπεδήμησεν εἰς Σικελίαν, αὐτὸς δὲ οὐ θέλει, ὅτι Βούλομαι, εἶπεν, ἐμαυτῷ ζῆν, οὐκ ἄλλῳ.

his own judgment.   The aim of these pages has not been
to advocate an opinion, but to exhibit the evidence.

*Other
passages of
Pindar.*   The other passages of Pindar, in which the Alexandrians
traced similar allusions, are of less moment.   (1) In the
second Pythian, written for Hieron after 477 B.C.,—perhaps
in 475,—Pindar refers to the mischief of 'slander,'—to the
slanderer's disposition as resembling that of 'the crafty
fox,'—and to an 'ape' who is admired by 'children.'   Here
the scholiast finds a reference to Bacchylides; he is the
'ape,' and he disparages Pindar to their common patron
(vv. 52 ff.; and 72 ff.).   This seems at least dubious.   If
Bacchylides was the ape, Pindar must have counted on
Hieron failing to identify himself with the child.   (2) In
the second Isthmian, for Xenocrates of Acragas (*circa*
470 B.C.), verse 6, Pindar refers to the olden days when
'the Muse was not yet covetous, nor a hireling.'   This is
taken by the Alexandrian commentator as glancing at the
avarice of Simonides; and there is some reason for
supposing that Callimachus thought so[1].   (3) In the fourth
Nemean, for Timasarchus of Aegina (*c.* 467–463 B.C.),
vv. 37—41, the poet expresses his assurance of triumphing
over certain foes; though there is 'a man of envious eye'
(φθονερὰ...βλέπων), who 'revolves in darkness a vain
purpose that falls to the ground.'   The scholiast takes this
man to be Simonides: but that seems questionable.

Result.   In no one of these three passages can the Alexandrian
interpretation be regarded as more than possible.   So far
as these are concerned, the net result of the scholia is
merely to illustrate the firmness of the Alexandrian belief
in Pindar's propensity to deal thrusts at the Cean poets.

[1] Pindar's words (*I.* II. 6) are:
ἁ Μοῖσα γὰρ οὐ φιλοκερδής πω τότ'
ἦν οὐδ' ἐργάτις.   The schol. there
says:—ἔνθεν καὶ Καλλίμαχος·
      οὐ γὰρ ἐργάτιν τρέφω
τὴν Μοῦσαν, ὡς ὁ Κεῖος Ὑλλίχου νέπους.
[Callim. fr. 77. Michelangeli p. 4
takes Ὑλλιχος to be the grandfather
of Simonides.   But Rost in Pape-

Benseler s.v. Ὑλιχίδης supposes
Ὑλλίχου νέπους to mean δημότης
Ὑλιχίδης.]   It certainly looks as if
the scholiast was right in taking
Pindar's verse to be the source from
which Callimachus derived his phrase.
That does not prove, but it suggests,
that Callimachus understood Pindar
as alluding to Simonides.

An opinion so fixed tends, however, to strengthen the probability that the belief rested, not solely on Pindar's text, but also on a tradition.

The recently recovered poems of Bacchylides contain not a word which could be construed as reflecting on Pindar. But among the previously known fragments there are two which deserve notice as presenting a curiously marked contrast with Pindaric utterances. (1) Pindar says (*Ol.* II. 85 f.) that his shafts of song are φωνάεντα συνετοῖσιν· ἐς δὲ τὸ πὰν¹ ἑρμηνέων χατίζει. Bacchylides says (XIV. 30f.): *Bacchylides nowhere alludes to Pindar. But there are marked contrasts of sentiment.*

> οὐ γὰρ ὑπόκλοπον φορεῖ
> βροτοῖσι φωνάεντα λόγον σοφία·

'There is nothing furtive'—nothing that is not frank and open—'in the clear utterance that wisdom brings to mortals.' Here σοφία might well be the poet's art. The word φωνάεντα decidedly suggests that the author was thinking of the Pindaric passage, where σοφός (said of the poet) occurs just afterwards. Bacchylides would then be saying, in effect:—'True art does not speak in forms which have a voice only for the select few, but require interpreters for the many: it does not take refuge in riddles: its utterance has a clear sound for all men.' The pellucid character of his own work illustrates that sentiment. (2) Still more remarkable, perhaps, is the other contrast. We have just seen how Pindar heaps scorn on the μαθόντες, the men of διδακταὶ ἀρεταί, the poets who are mere disciples or imitators. Bacchylides mildly observes (fr. 4):—

> ἕτερος ἐξ ἑτέρου σοφὸς τό τε πάλαι καὶ τὸ νῦν·
> οὐδὲ γὰρ ῥᾷστον ἀρρήτων ἐπέων πύλας
> ἐξευρεῖν·

'Poet is heir to poet, now as of old; for in sooth 'tis no light task to find the gates² of virgin song.' 'Can any lyric poet of our day'—so we might expand his thought—'confidently affirm that he owes nothing to the old poets from Homer onwards, the shapers of heroic myth, the

¹ On the shortening of πᾶν, see Schröder, *Prolegom.* to Pindar, p. 34.

² The image is Pindar's: *O.* VI. 27 πύλας ὕμνων ἀναπιτνάμεν.

earliest builders of lyric song, in whose footsteps Pindar
himself has followed?' The words of Bacchylides are (to
my ear) suggestive of such a reply; and that view of them
is not necessarily invalid merely because Pindar would, in
fact, have had a sound rejoinder; viz., that in its essence,
in all that constitutes its distinctive character, his own
work is eminently original. But, at any rate,—and this is
the main point,—in all the extant writings of Bacchylides
there is no polemical utterance. If certain asperities of
Pindar were indeed directed against Simonides and Bacchylides, the Cean poets may have profited by a quality
which was not rare among men of their race. They were
Ionians, and may have been protected from serious annoy-
ance by a sense of humour.

*Banish-
ment of
Bacchyli-
des from
Ceos.*

Apart from the Sicilian chapter, the only recorded
event in the external life of Bacchylides is one which is
noticed by Plutarch in his tract *On Exile*. The authen-
ticity of that piece is not liable to any well-grounded
suspicion. It is a discourse of a consolatory kind
(παραμυθητικός), addressed to a friend who had been
banished from his country. The following passage occurs
in it (§ 14):—

'In the best and most approved compositions of the
ancients, exile, it would seem, was a fellow-worker with
the Muses. Thucydides of Athens wrote his history of the
Peloponnesian War at Scapte-Hyle in Thrace. Xenophon
wrote at Scillus in Elis; Philistus, in Epeirus; Timaeus of
Tauromenion, at Athens; the Athenian Androtion, at
Megara; the poet Bacchylides, in Peloponnesus.

'All these, and several others, were banished from their
respective countries; but they did not despair, or throw
their lives away. They used their gifts of genius, taking
banishment as a travelling-grant[1] made to them by Fortune.
Thanks to such exile, their memories survive in all lands;
while of the men who drove them out, the men whose

[1] ἐφόδιον παρὰ τῆς τύχης τὴν φυγὴν λαβόντες.

faction triumphed, there is not one who is not utterly forgotten.'

Two conclusions may with certainty be drawn from this passage. The first is that, in Plutarch's belief, the departure of Bacchylides from Ceos was not voluntary, but due to a sentence of banishment. The second is that Plutarch supposed him to have resided in Peloponnesus for a considerable time, and to have composed there some appreciable portion of his works. Plutarch had access to a large literature containing memoirs or reminiscences of the older poets, a product characteristic of the whole period between Aristotle and the Augustan age. Somewhere, doubtless, in that literature he found authority for his statement concerning Bacchylides. He gives us no clue to the cause of the banishment, and conjecture would be idle. Nor can the date be determined. But facts deducible *Period to which his* from the poet's odes create certain probabilities respecting *exile* the period of his life to which the event belonged. *probably belonged.* (1) Ode V was sent to Hieron from Ceos in 476. The poet had not then been banished. (2) Odes VI and VII are for Lachon of Ceos. The date of these two poems is fixed by the new fragment of the Olympic register[1] to 452 B.C. The last verses of Ode VI rather suggest that the poet was then in Ceos. At any rate these odes would not have been written by a man who had been driven out of Ceos by a sentence of banishment. If that sentence was passed in the interval between 476 and 452, in 452 it had been cancelled. But it is perhaps more probable that the poet's exile began after 452. As we have seen, there is reason to think that he survived the beginning of the Peloponnesian War. In 452 he cannot have been much more than fifty-five. After 452 there was still room for a chapter of life fruitful in poetical work, such as Plutarch indicates.

It is pertinent to inquire whether any traces of a residence *Traces of* in Peloponnesus can be discerned in the poems or fragments *Peloponnesus in his* of Bacchylides. There is much, undoubtedly, that relates *work.*

[1] *Oxyrhynchus Papyri* II. 85.

J. B. 3

to Peloponnesus. Ode VIII (the only one for a Peloponnesian victor) shows his intimate acquaintance with the legends and cults of Phlius. He knows also the local legends of the neighbouring Nemea (Odes VIII and XII). In Ode X we have the Argive story of Proetus and Acrisius, the offence given by the Proetides to the Argive Hera, and the cult of Artemis Hemera at Lusi in Arcadia. The poet knew that the Mantineians bore the trident of Poseidon on their shields (frag. 6). He told how the centaur Eurytion was slain by Heracles at the house of Dexamenus in Elis (frag. 48). His poem on Idas and Marpessa (XIX) was written for the Spartans. Some of his 'Dorian partheneia' (frag. 40) may also have been for Sparta, a place with which that form of lyric was especially associated.

Limit to inference from such traces.   When, however, we scrutinise these facts, we can scarcely say that, in themselves, they would afford a presumption of residence in Peloponnesus. The knowledge shown in respect to Phlius is noteworthy; yet, after all, it is not more than might have been acquired in the course of a short visit. On the whole, there is nothing that could not be explained by a poet's study of mythology, supplemented, perhaps, by occasional visits to certain localities. That, however, is no reason for doubting the tradition preserved by Plutarch, that the home of the exiled Bacchylides was, for some considerable time, in Peloponnesus.

Geographical distribution of the poems.   The geographical distribution of his extant poems bears witness to a fairly wide-spread repute. Of his thirteen Epinikia, four (I, II, VI, VII) were for Ceos; two (XI, XII) for Aegina; one (IX) for Athens; one (XIII) for Thessaly; one (X) for Metapontion in Magna Graecia; and three (III, IV, V) for Syracuse. Of his six so-called Dithyrambs, the local destination of one (XIV) is unknown. One (XVI) was to be performed by a Cean chorus at Delos; one (XV) was for Delphi. Two probably (XVII, XVIII) were for Athens; and one (XIX) was for Sparta. It is likely that, as at Syracuse, so also at Athens, in Thessaly, and in Magna Graecia, the name of Simonides may have helped to recommend his nephew.

II. The Place of Bacchylides in the History of Greek Lyric Poetry

The work of Bacchylides, well worthy of study in itself, derives a further interest from the peculiar place which he holds in the history of the Greek Lyric. He is the latest of the nine poets whom the Alexandrians included in their lyric canon, the others being Alcman, Alcaeus, Sappho, Stesichorus, Ibycus, Anacreon, Simonides and Pindar. In his youth, all the types of the lyric had been fully developed ; and the life of lyric poetry was still vigorous. Before his death, a decline had begun. In the last third of the fifth century, exquisite lyrics continued to adorn the plays of Sophocles, of Euripides, and of Aristophanes; but, after Bacchylides, no purely lyric poet attained to a high rank. From the commencement of the Peloponnesian War onwards, the only kinds of lyric which remained fertile and popular were such as attested the degradation alike of poetical and of musical art, such productions as the dithyrambs of Philoxenus and the nomes of Timotheus.

The history of the classical Greek Lyric is comprised *Period of* *the* in a period of some two hundred years, from the early or *classical* middle part of the seventh century B.C. to about the middle *Lyric.* of the fifth. The rise of a lyric poetry was necessarily preceded by a development of music, which was traditionally associated with two principal names. The Phrygian Olympus, a dim figure, represented some marked improve- *Olympus.* ment in the music of the double flute ($a\vec{v}\lambda\eta\tau\iota\kappa\acute{\eta}$), soon followed by an advance in the art of singing to that instrument ($a\vec{v}\lambda\wp\delta\iota\kappa\acute{\eta}$). Terpander of Lesbos, whose *Terpander.* activity may be placed about 710–670 B.C., improved the cithara, and was regarded as having founded the art of the 'citharode' who sings to it. The kind of song which Terpander more particularly cultivated was that called the

The nome. 'nome' (νόμος), a general term for a musical strain[1], but one which early acquired a technical sense. A 'nome' was a solo, chanted to the cithara in honour of a god, especially of Apollo, and divided into parts according to a traditional scheme. Only about a dozen genuine lines of Terpander are extant[2]. Some of these are short verses composed wholly of spondees, which suggest a solemn liturgical effect. He also used the hexameter. In Lesbos he founded a citharodic school which maintained his tradition for,

Terpander at Sparta. centuries. He visited Delphi. He established the citharodic art at Sparta, where he is said to have gained a prize at the festival of the Carneia in 676 B.C. The first epoch[3] in the Spartan culture of poetry and music is associated by Plutarch with Terpander's name. The second such epoch

Thaletas at Sparta. was made by Thaletas[4], a native of Gortyn in Crete, who flourished about 670–640 B.C. He brought to Sparta certain kinds of choral song in which the Cretans excelled. These were the *paean* and the *hyporcheme*, both belonging

The paean. to the Cretan cult of Apollo. The paean was usually, though not always, accompanied by dancing, an art which had been elaborately developed in Crete. The kindred,

The hyporcheme. but livelier, hyporcheme was, as the term imports, inseparable from dancing. The Spartan festival of the *Gymnopaediae*, founded (according to Eusebius) in 665 B.C., was that with which, in early times, the performance of paeans was more especially associated.

Thaletas was said to have composed paeans; but

---

[1] The musical sense of νόμος is doubtless derived from that of 'custom,' 'law.' Weir Smyth compares τρόπος, οἴμη, Germ. *Weise*, French and English *air*. See his *Greek Melic Poets*, p. lix, where other explanations are also noticed.

[2] Bergk[4] III. pp. 8–12.

[3] Plut. *De Mus.* 9: ἡ μὲν οὖν πρώτη κατάστασις τῶν περὶ τὴν μουσικὴν ἐν τῇ Σπάρτῃ, Τερπάνδρου καταστήσαντος, γεγένηται. The sense of ἡ πρώτη κατάστασις κ.τ.λ. is indicated by καταστήσαντος. It means

'the first phase in the establishment' of musical and poetical art at Sparta.

[4] Plut. *l.c.* associates with Thaletas, as founders of the δευτέρα κατάστασις at Sparta, Xenodamus of Cythera and Xenocritus of the Epizephyrian Locri, both writers of paeans; also Polymnestus of Colophon, known especially as a writer of ὄρθιοι νόμοι for flutes; and Sacadas of Argos (*fl. c.* 580 B.C.?), who is described by Plutarch as a ποιητὴς ἐλεγείων.

Plutarch observes that the tradition was not undisputed[1]. Some verses, at least, of Terpander were still extant in the second century A.D.; one of our scanty fragments is due to Clement of Alexandria[2]. But the Alexandrians did not include Terpander in their list. He was regarded rather as an early pioneer of lyric song, a 'singer' who was primarily a musician, while his poetical work was of a comparatively archaic kind. The fame which he enjoyed in *Ancient* antiquity is proudly attested in the verse, written perhaps *repute of Terpan-* within a century after his death, by his countrywoman *der.* Sappho:—

$$\pi\acute{\epsilon}\rho\rho o\chi o\varsigma,\ \dot{\omega}\varsigma\ \ddot{o}\tau'\ \ddot{a}o\iota\delta o\varsigma\ \dot{o}\ \Lambda\acute{\epsilon}\sigma\beta\iota o\varsigma\ \dot{a}\lambda\lambda o\delta\acute{a}\pi o\iota\sigma\iota\nu^{3}.$$

There is a remarkable contrast in respect to their history between the two principal branches of the Greek lyric, the Aeolian song for one voice, and the Dorian choral ode. The Aeolian song is suddenly revealed, as a mature *The* work of art, in the spirited stanzas of Alcaeus. It is raised *Aeolian monody.* to a supreme excellence by his younger contemporary Sappho, whose melody is unsurpassed, perhaps unequalled, among all the relics of Greek verse. With those two lives, —contained, probably, within some such limits as the years 640 and 550 B.C.,—the Aeolian lyric begins and ends. In a later generation (*c.* 550–500 B.C.) Anacreon of Teos wrote, indeed, lyric monodies on themes of festivity or of love: but his Ionian grace was not joined to the Lesbian fire; and his metrical forms owed little or nothing to the Lesbian models. His contemporary, Ibycus of Rhegium, in the fragments of love-poems which remain, shows a passion which gives him some measure of spiritual kinship with Alcaeus and Sappho; but his odes, so far as we can now judge, were of a kind wholly distinct from theirs, being choral, and composed in the large Dorian strophes. When Alcaeus and Sappho passed away, the moulds of their song were broken. No third Greek poet, in any age, created similar masterpieces of lyric monody.

---

[1] Plut. *De Mus.* 10.
[2] *Strom.* VI. 784 (Terpander fr. 1).
[3] Fr. 92.

The Dorian choral lyric.

The history of the Dorian choral ode, on the other hand, is that of a series of lyric types gradually developed by successive poets in connexion with religious cults and public festivals. The Dorian state, as represented by Sparta, was based on the education of a warrior caste, trained to arms from boyhood, proud of their heroic ancestry, and imbued with a deep reverence for the institutions and customs of their race. 'The Dorian sons of Pamphylus and of the Heracleidae,' says Pindar, 'dwelling under the cliffs of Taÿgetus, are ever content to abide by the ordinances of Aegimius[1].' In a military aristocracy of this compact kind, the sense of corporate life was peculiarly strong; and that was the sense to which the Dorian choral lyric appealed. It was an act of worship, performed at a gathering of the citizens. The gods of the city, the heroes of racial or local legend, the common beliefs and sentiments, were its normal themes. Choral dancing, in which the Dorians of Crete were so accomplished, was not less congenial to Spartans. The gymnastic training, in which Spartan maidens participated, would confer ease and precision in rhythmic movement. It is easy to understand, then, why the choral lyric, in its earlier phases, was distinctively associated with Dorians. The closeness of that early tie explains the fixed convention which arose from it. A Dorian colouring remained obligatory for the dialect of the choral lyric, even when the composer was Boeoto-Aeolian, like Pindar, or Ionian, like Simonides and Bacchylides.

Alcman. The partheneion.

Both Pindar and Bacchylides, according to Plutarch, wrote 'many Dorian partheneia[2].' The 'virginal song,' or partheneion, was first perfected by Alcman (*c.* 640–600 B.C.), the earliest choral poet known in Greek literature. His parents were probably Aeolian Greeks resident in Lydia.

---

[1] Pind. *P.* 1, 62 ff.

[2] Plut. *De Mus.* 17.—The fragments of Pindar's Παρθένεια are very scanty (fr. 95–104c in Schröder's ed.). But a new fragment, of some 80 verses, from a partheneion, is ascribed by Blass to Pindar (*Oxyrhynchus Papyri* IV. 1904). If the ascription is correct, these verses illustrate the remark of Dionysius, that Pindar's style in his partheneia was simpler and easier than in other classes of his poems. No fragment of a partheneion by Bacchylides is extant.

From Sardis he was brought in boyhood to Sparta, where he lived and died. He wrote hymns, paeans, hyporchemes, drinking-songs, love-songs. But his fame rested chiefly on his partheneia. Few fragments of Greek poetry are more interesting than the passage of about ninety verses by which one of these 'virginal songs' is represented[1]. A chorus of Spartan maidens is offering a robe to Artemis Orthria, goddess of the dawn, and is competing for the musical prize with another Chorus. The time seems to be night,—perhaps shortly before daybreak. Their song begins with the myth of Hippocoon, the wicked king of Sparta, who drove out his brother Tyndareus, but was slain, with his sons, by Heracles. Then it glides into a lighter strain,—praising the beauty of Agido (a prominent member of the Chorus), which is as 'a vision of winged dreams,'—and the vocal skill of the leader Hagesichora, in whom they chiefly trust for victory. The playful grace and airy charm of these stanzas are inimitable. In another fragment[2] of a partheneion, the chorus seems to defend Alcman against detractors; in a third[3], it is he who addresses them, 'the sweet-voiced maidens, who delight with song,' and laments that he is growing too old to take part in their dance. It is a pity that nothing remains from the partheneia of Bacchylides, which must have given scope for his elegance of fancy and lightness of touch. Ionian and Athenian manners did not permit such virginal choruses. The partheneia of Bacchylides may have been written for Sparta, or other Dorian cities, during his residence in Peloponnesus.

Alcman was a fine and versatile artist; but, for the later history of Greek lyric poetry, he is less significant than Stesi- *Stesi-* chorus of Himera (*c.* 610–550 B.C.), the creator of the epic *chorus.* *The epic* hymn. Terpander, Alcman, Alcaeus and Sappho had written *hymn.* hymns; but only in honour of gods, or of such semi-divine

---

[1] Fr. 23 (Bergk). The papyrus was found in 1855 by Mariette in a tomb near the second pyramid. Cp. Weir Smyth, *Greek Melic Poets*, pp. 175 ff.

[2] Fr. 24.

[3] Fr. 26.

persons as the Dioscuri. Stesichorus, taking the material
furnished by epos, recast it in a lyric form. He drew on all
the great cycles of myth, Trojan, Theban, Argive, Thessalian, Aetolian. The hymn became in his hands mainly a
narrative, epic in general style, yet differing from epos by
a fuller expression of characters and feelings. He boldly
modified the old legends, as in his ' Palinode ' concerning
Helen ; and he also added to them. He seems to have
been the first who spoke of Athena as springing full-armed
from the head of Zeus, and the first who sent Aeneas on a
Festivals voyage to Italy. The epic hymns of Stesichorus were
of the intended for choral performance at those festivals of the
heroes. heroes which were numerous in the western colonies ; thus
there was a cult of Philoctetes at Sybaris, of Diomedes at
Thurii, of the Atreidae at Tarentum[1]. Such observances
linked the new homes with the memories of the old : and
at such festivals the hymns of Stesichorus would doubtless
have been popular. In addition to hymns, Stesichorus
wrote paeans, mentioned by Athenaeus as sung at
banquets[2]. He was also the author of lyric romances or
love-stories[3] drawn from folk-lore, and thus was a far-off
precursor of the Greek novel[4]. The volume of his writings
was exceptionally large. In the Alexandrian age, Alcman
was represented by six books of poems, Sappho by nine,
Alcaeus by ten, Pindar by seventeen, and Stesichorus by
twenty-six. A ' book' was, of course, a variable quantity ;
but at any rate this number indicates a great mass of work.
Influence No other Greek poet had so wide or so varied an influence
of Stesi- as Stesichorus on the poetry which came after him. The
chorus. artificial dialect which he employed, Doric in basis but with
a large infusion of epic forms, was the general prototype of
that which prevailed thenceforward in the choral lyric. It
was he, too, who established the norm of choral composition
in strophe, antistrophe, and epode; though whether he was
the inventor of the epode is disputed. His original treat-

---

[1] [Arist.] *De mirabil. auscult.*
106–110. Strabo 6. 262–264.

[2] Athen. 6. p. 250 B.

[3] Athen. 13. p. 601 A.

[4] E. Rohde, *Der griech. Roman,*
p. 29.

ment of the myths furnished a mine of material to Attic
Tragedy. He was also influential in Greek art. The
vase-painters of the sixth and fifth centuries were often
indebted to him. His hymn, 'The Capture of Troy'
('Ιλίου Πέρσις), provided Polygnotus with subjects for his
paintings in the Lesche of Delphi, and can be traced in
those episodes of the Trojan War which some artist in the
first century of our era depicted on the *Tabula Iliaca.*

Among the poems of Bacchylides, there is one (Ode *Stesichorus*
XIV, the *Antenoridae*) which may well have been influenced *and Bac-*
chylides.
by the method of Stesichorus in the lyric handling of an
epic theme. The hymn of Stesichorus on the Calydonian
Boar-hunters (Συοθῆραι) may not improbably have been a
source used by Bacchylides for the story of that hunt as
told by Meleager (Ode V). In writing of the Centaur
Eurytion, slain by Heracles in Elis (fr. 48), Bacchylides was
again on ground traversed by Stesichorus, one of whose
hymns (the Γηρυονηΐς) included the adventures of Heracles
in Peloponnesus on his way home from the abode of
Geryoneus (or Geryon) in the far west. More generally,
a study of Stesichorus may have helped to form that epic
manner of narrating myths which is characteristic of
Bacchylides, as in the story of the Proetides (Ode X), and
in the episode of Ajax at the ships (Ode XII).

Simonides was the last of the classical poets who *Simonides.*
created new types of choral lyric. Those of which he may
be considered the inventor are the enkomion and the
epinikion. An 'enkomion,' or 'song at a revel' (ἐν κώμῳ), *The*
was, in the technical sense, an ode in praise of a distin- *enkomion.*
guished man, intended to be sung by a chorus at or after
a banquet. Strictly speaking, then, the enkomion was a
genus of which the epinikion was a species : and sometimes
the line between the two was not clearly drawn. The ode
of Euripides for Alcibiades, properly an epinikion, is also
called an enkomion[1]. Pindar's encomion for Aristagoras

---

[1] Bergk⁴ II. p. 266. By Athen.   'Ολυμπίασι ἱπποδρομίας εἰς 'Αλκιβιάδην
I. 3 E it is called an ἐπινίκιον: by   ἐγκώμιον. Cp. Plut. *Alcib.* c. 11.
Plut. *Dem.* c. 1, τὸ ἐπὶ τῇ νίκῃ τῆς

of Tenedos, on the occasion of his being installed as president of the Council, stands appended to the Nemean epinikia[1], although in the Alexandrian collection of Pindar's writings the enkomia formed a distinct book. The poem of Simonides on Scopas is an example of the enkomion proper. Among the subjects of Pindar's enkomia were Alexander the son of Amyntas, king of Macedon, and Theron of Acragas.

Hymns to living men. The enkomion and the epinikion represent a further extension in the province of the hymn. Hymns were dedicated by the elder poets to gods or demigods alone ; by Stesichorus, to the heroes also ; and now, by Simonides, to living men. Ibycus might be regarded as having set the example, though only in a limited sense, when he wrote choral hymns in praise of youths at the court of Polycrates. But it was Simonides who first led the Greeks to feel that such a tribute might properly be paid to any man who was sufficiently eminent in merit or in station. We must remember that, in the time of Simonides, the man to whom a hymn was addressed would feel that he was receiving a distinction which had hitherto been reserved for gods and heroes. That chord is touched by Pindar in his enkomion for Alexander :—

$$\pi\rho\acute{\epsilon}\pi\epsilon\iota \; \delta' \; \acute{\epsilon}\sigma\lambda o\hat{\iota}\sigma\iota\nu \; \acute{\upsilon}\mu\nu\epsilon\hat{\iota}\sigma\theta a\iota$$
$$...\kappa a\lambda\lambda\acute{\iota}\sigma\tau a\iota\varsigma \; \acute{a}o\iota\delta a\hat{\iota}\varsigma\cdot$$
$$\tau o\hat{\upsilon}\tau o \; \gamma\grave{a}\rho \; \acute{a}\theta a\nu\acute{a}\tau o\iota\varsigma \; \tau\iota\mu a\hat{\iota}\varsigma \; \pi o\tau\iota\psi a\acute{\upsilon}\epsilon\iota \; \mu\acute{o}\nu o\nu[2].$$

This is the only tribute to human worth that 'verges on the honours rendered to immortals.'

The epinikion. Simonides is the first recorded author of epinikia. It may well be that, before his day, the praises of athletes had been sung to their fellow-townsmen or kinsfolk ; but, if it was so, the songs have left no trace. An epinikion, though appealing in the first instance to the victor's city and family, was also, like his renown, Panhellenic. It was an elaborate and stately work of art ; and the earliest artist in that kind was Simonides. The advent of the

---

[1] [*Nem.* XI.]   [2] Pind. fr. 121.

epinikion at that particular period was not an accident, due to the special bent of one poet's genius: it was con- *Develop-* nected with that new era in the history of the national *ment of the* national games which dated from the earlier part of the sixth *games.* century.

In 582[1] B.C. the ancient Pythian festival in honour of *The* Apollo, which had been held in every ninth year, became *Pythia.* a pentaeteris, to be held in the third year of each Olympiad. Hitherto the contests had been only in music, instrumental and vocal. To these were now added the most important of such athletic and equestrian contests as were then in use at Olympia. The Pythian festival took place in August. The agonothetae, or presidents, were the Amphictyons; the prize was a wreath of laurel.

Two years later, in 580 B.C., the Isthmian festival of *The* Poseidon was reconstituted as a trieteris, to be held in the *Isthmia.* second and in the fourth year of each Olympiad. The celebration was in spring. The presidency belonged, in the fifth century, to the Corinthians. In the earliest times, as again in the Roman age, the Isthmian prize was a wreath of pine (πίτυς), symbolising the cult of Poseidon. In the fifth century it was a wreath of parsley (σέλινον), which had a funereal significance, referring to the legend that the Isthmia had been founded in memory of Ino and her son Melicertes, who, after death in the waves, became re- spectively the Nereid Leucothea and the sea-deity Palaemon.

The festival of the Nemean Zeus was remodelled in *The* 573 B.C. Thenceforth it was a trieteris, held at the *Nemea.* beginning of the second and of the fourth year of each

---

[1] This is the date given for the first Pythiad by the Pindaric scholia, and accepted by Bergk. Pausanias (x. 7. §3) gives 586, which was adopted by Boeckh. The date 582 is confirmed by the fragment of the Olympic register, which shows that Hieron had been victorious at Olympia in 476 and 472. Bacchylides (Ode IV) attests that Hieron, when he won his victory at the Pythian games, had already won twice at Olympia. Now the Pythiad in which Hieron won was the 29th (Schol. Pind. *P.* I.). If the Pythiads were reckoned from 582, the 29th falls in 470. But if they had been reckoned from 586, it would fall in 474.

Olympiad, probably in the month of July. Down to about 460 B.C. the agonothetae were apparently the Cleonaeans; but the presidency afterwards passed to the Argives. The prize was a wreath of parsley, signifying that the festival had originated from the funeral games held by Adrastus and his comrades in memory of Archemorus.

The Olympia.

The Olympian festival of Zeus—said to have been founded by Heracles, and renewed or enlarged by Oxylus, Iphitus, and Pheidon—dated its historical era from 776 B.C. Since then, it had been held in every fourth year. The time of celebration varied within certain limits, according to a cycle of lunar months, so as to coincide either with the second or with the third full moon after the summer solstice. The Eleans were the presidents, and appointed the judges called Hellanodikai. The prize was a wreath of wild olive (κότινος).

Epinikia for minor festivals.

The games at these four great festivals were distinguished as sacred (ἱεροὶ ἀγῶνες). But numerous minor festivals existed in every part of Hellas; and epinikia were often written for these also. Thus the ode which is known as Pindar's 'second Pythian' was for a Theban festival, perhaps the Heracleia or Iolaia. The so-called 'ninth Nemean' was for the Pythia at Sicyon; and the 'tenth Nemean,' for the Hecatombaia at Argos. The thirteenth ode of Bacchylides was for the Petraia in Thessaly. When the custom of writing epinikia had once been established, the demand for them must have been considerable.

Records of victories.

At Olympia the names of victors had been recorded on stone from an early date. When the three other great festivals were reconstituted, a similar practice was doubtless observed. Cities, too, kept local registers of the successful athletes[1]. Nor had a poetical tribute been wholly wanting at Olympia. Before the days of the epinikion, an Olympic victor used to be greeted with that song of Archilochus which Pindar calls 'the triumphal hymn, with

Tributes to victors.

---

[1] See Introd. to Ode I.

threefold loud refrain' (καλλίνικος ὁ τριπλόος κεχλαδώς)[1], *The old*
The refrain was τήνελλα καλλίνικε, in which the first word *καλλίνικος.*
represented the sound of the lyre. Two of the verses
remain :—

Χαῖρ' ἄναξ Ἡράκλεες,
αὐτός τε καὶ Ἰόλαος, αἰχμητὰ δύο.

This song was still used in Pindar's age by a comos escorting an athlete on the day when his victory was announced.

The earliest epinikia of Simonides belonged to the *Epinikia*
latter years of the sixth century. In mentioning Eualcidas *Simonides.*
of Eretria, who was killed at Ephesus, fighting against the
Persians, soon after the burning of Sardis in 499, Herodotus
describes him as a famous athlete, whose victories had been
'much praised' by Simonides[2]. It is clear, then, that the
poet's epinikia gained a wide repute. Another of his early
odes was for Glaucus of Carystus, a famous boxer, of whom
Simonides said that not even Polydeuces or Heracles could
stand up against him :—

οὐδὲ Πολυδεύκεος βία
χεῖρας ἀντείναιτ' ἂν ἐναντίον αὐτῷ,
οὐδὲ σιδάρεον Ἀλκμήνας τέκος[3].

To Alcman that would have sounded very like an impiety ;
but times were changing. Simonides wrote also for Xenocrates of Acragas (brother of Theron), a winner at the
Pythian festival of 490 B.C. ; for Astylus of Croton ; and
for Anaxilas, tyrant of Rhegium[4].

At the date when poetry first brought a tribute to *The poet's*
victors in the games, sculpture was already beginning to *tribute,*
honour them. The earliest sculptors who are known to *sculptor's.*
have made statues of athletes, Eutelidas and Chrysothemis
of Argos, were active from about 520 B.C. ; but there were
some archaic statues of victors which claimed a higher age[5].

---

[1] Pind. *O.* IX. 1 f.: Bergk[4] II.
p. 418.
[2] Herod. V. 102: στεφανηφόρους
τε ἀγῶνας ἀναραιρηκότα καὶ ὑπὸ
Σιμωνίδεω τοῦ Κηΐου πολλὰ αἰνεθέντα.
[3] Simon. fr. 8 (Bergk[4]).

[4] Simon. 6, 7, 10. His epinikia
were classed by contest, as πένταθλοι
(fr. 12), τέθριπποι (fr. 14), etc.
[5] Prof. Ernest Gardner, *Handbook
of Greek Sculpture,* pp. 191 f.

Among the sculptors who commemorated athletes at Olympia, or elsewhere, between 520 and 450 B.C., were the Argive Ageladas, the Sicyonian Canachus, and the greatest representative of the Attic school in this kind, Myron[1]. It is well to remember that, when the epinikion was a new thing, the artist in verse might naturally compare himself with the artist in marble or in bronze. His ode was not to be merely an ephemeral compliment; it was to be an enduring record for the victor's city, and an heirloom for his house[2]. Pindar, to whom Poetry and Sculpture are sisters in the bestowal of fame, contrasts the immovable statue with the poem which travels far and wide[3].

Elements of the epinikion. In all the larger specimens of the epinikion, three elements are normally present;—a reference to the victory, at the beginning ánd at the end,—a mythical episode, linked in some way with the occasion,—and a reflective or gnomic element, leavening the whole. This general pattern *A trait in the epini- kia of Simonides;* was doubtless set by Simonides. The fragments of his epinikia, scanty as they are, warrant the belief that he differed from Pindar in sometimes describing more fully the circumstances of the particular victory. This verse belonged to a description of a chariot-race :—

κονία δὲ παρὰ τροχὸν μεταμώνιος ἄρθη[4]·

'Dust was lifted on the wind beside the chariot-wheel,'— another chariot being just in front. A second verse seems to speak of some precaution taken by a charioteer,—perhaps that of passing the reins round his waist, lest they should slip from his hands ;—

μὴ βάλῃ φοίνικας ἐκ χειρῶν ἱμάντας[5].

and of Bac- chylides. This Simonidean trait recurs in some epinikia of Bac- chylides.

Dithy- rambs of Simonides. The dithyramb, which in the time of Archilochus had been distinctively a song to Dionysus, was afterwards applied to themes unconnected with that god. This en-

---

[1] Prof. Ernest Gardner, *Handbook of Greek Sculpture*, p. 192 (Ageladas): p. 195 (Canachus) : p. 238 (Myron).
[2] Pindar's aim (*N.* IV. 81) is στάλαν

θέμεν Παρίου λίθου λευκοτέραν.
[3] Pind. *N.* v. 1 ff.
[4] Simon. fr. 16.
[5] Simon. fr. 17.

largement of its scope must have taken place before the
days of Simonides; but he is the earliest poet for whom it
is attested. One of his dithyrambs was entitled *Memnon*,
and another *Europa*[1]. The only dithyramb of Pindar from
which a considerable fragment remains (fr. 75) was strictly
Dionysiac: but we do not know whether that was true of
the dithyrambs in which he referred to Orion (fr. 74) and
to Geryon (fr. 81). In the latter part of the fifth century
B.C., dithyrambists of the new school exercised a complete
freedom in their choice of subjects. The Alexandrians *Alexandrian
sense of
'dithy-
ramb.'*
seem to have applied the name 'dithyramb' to any poem
which contained a narrative concerning the heroes.
Speaking of Xenocritus, a native of the Epizephyrian Locri
who was contemporary with Thaletas, Plutarch remarks
that it was disputed whether he wrote paeans[2]. 'They say
that he was the author of poems on heroic subjects,
containing narratives; and that therefore his pieces are by
some called dithyrambs.' In the phrase used here,
ἡρωϊκῶν ὑποθέσεων πράγματα ἐχουσῶν, the word πράγματα
appears to mean 'events' (*res gestas*) set forth in historical
sequence. It recalls the use by Polybius of the term
πραγματεία to denote his own work (I. 2 § 2); and of the
phrase, ὁ τῆς πραγματικῆς ἱστορίας τρόπος (*ib.* § 8), to
express 'the method of systematic history.' Of the poems
in the Bacchylides papyrus, six (XIV—XIX) were classed *The'dithyrambs' of
Bacchy-
lides.*
by the Alexandrians as 'dithyrambs.' One of these (XV)
was so far a dithyramb in the old sense, that it was
intended for performance at Delphi in connexion with the
winter-cult of Dionysus, though the subject (Heracles) did
not relate to the god himself. Another (XVIII) is also
Dionysiac, the point of it being the god's descent from Io.
Of the four others, one (XIV, *Antenoridae*), which concerns
the embassy of Menelaus and Odysseus to Troy, may have
been produced with a dithyrambic chorus, as is suggested
by the fact that, according to Bacchylides, the sons of

---

[1] Simon. fr. 27 and 28 (Bergk[4]
III. pp. 398 f.).

[2] Plut. *De Mus.* 10: ἡρωϊκῶν γὰρ

ὑποθέσεων πράγματα ἐχουσῶν ποιητὴν
γεγονέναι φασὶν αὐτόν· διὸ καί τινας
διθυράμβους καλεῖν αὐτοῦ τὰς ὑποθέσεις.

Antenor were fifty in number. It would then have been
a dithyramb in the same sense as the *Memnon* or the
Europa of Simonides. A like remark applies to no. XVII,
on the adventures of Theseus between Troezen and Athens,
—the only extant specimen of a dithyramb in dialogue.
But the two remaining poems (XVI and XIX) could be called
'dithyrambs' in no further sense than as 'containing heroic
narratives.' One of them (XVI), on the voyage of Theseus
to Crete, is, in fact, a choral paean for Delos. The other
(XIX, *Idas*), though not technically an epithalamion or a
hymenaeus, is of a hymeneal character. In one of his lost
'dithyrambs,' Bacchylides described the warlike array of
the Mantineans; in another, he told the story of Philoctetes[1].

Hypor-
chemes of
Simonides;   Plutarch notes the excellence of Simonides in treating
the hyporcheme, and quotes examples of his marvellous
skill in writing verses of which the rhythm suits a lively
and of Bac- dance[2]. His nephew's poems of this class were also in
chylides. repute. One hyporcheme of Bacchylides,—a verse of
which became proverbial,—was for the cult of the Itonian
Athena, perhaps at her chief Boeotian shrine, that temple
on the banks of the Coralius, near Coroneia, which is
mentioned by Alcaeus[3].

Simonides
as a writer   Lastly, it was Simonides who first established the choral
of dirges; dirge as a recognised form of lyric art[4]. 'The tributes of
the Cean dirge' are, for Horace, typical of their kind; and
Quintilian recognises their author's pre-eminence in pathetic
power[5]. The Danae fragment is an example of that

---

[1] See fragment 6 (=41 Bergk)
and fragment 39 (=16 Bergk).

[2] Plut. *Quaest. conviv.* IX. 15. 2.
Bergk's fragments 29, 30, 31 of
Simonides are passages quoted by
Plutarch as illustrations.

[3] Bacch. fr. 11 (=23 Bergk):
Alcaeus fr. 9.

[4] The rhetor Aristeides (I. 127)
says:—Ποῖος ταῦτα Σιμωνίδης θρηνή-
σει; τίς Πίνδαρος; ποῖον μέλος ἢ λόγον
τοιοῦτον ἐξευρὼν Στησίχορος ἄξιον
φθέγξεται τοιούτου πάθους; In the

20th 'Letter of Phalaris,' we hear of
Stesichorus being asked to write a
funeral elegy. But, though Stesichorus may have been famed for
pathetic verse, there is no evidence
that he had preceded Simonides in
the artistic development of the lyric
θρῆνος.

[5] Hor. *C.* II. i. 38. Quint. X. I.
64: *praecipua tamen eius in com-
movenda miseratione virtus, ut quidam
in hac eum parte omnibus eius operis
auctoribus praeferant.*

power; though it is uncertain whether the poem to which those exquisite verses belonged was a *threnus*. The dirges of Simonides appear to have dealt chiefly with such topics of consolation as could be drawn from the merits and the fame of the departed. In the fragments of Pindar's dirges *compared* the key-note is rather the survival of the soul[1]; the *with* *Pindar.* happiness of him who, having seen the Mysteries, 'understands the end of mortal life, and the beginning' of a new life 'given by Zeus[2]'; the bright and tranquil abode of the blest,

αἰεὶ θύα μειγνύντων πυρὶ τηλεφανεῖ παντοῖα θεῶν ἐπὶ βωμοῖς[3].

The kinds of choral lyric represented by Pindar's *Pindar.* remains are more numerous than in the case of any other poet. But he was not the creator of any new kind, as Simonides of the epinikion ; nor, again, was he the first who gave a new artistic value to any old form of song, as *Character* Simonides gave it to the dirge. What Pindar did was to *of his* *genius.* set the stamp of an original and strongly individual genius on every lyric form in which he composed. He has that force of imagination which can bring clear-cut and dramatic figures of gods and heroes into vivid relief, as when Apollo finds Cyrene ; when Iason suddenly appears in the market-place of Iolcus ; or when Heracles, in Aegina, prays that a son may be given to Telamon : he has that peculiar and inimitable splendour of style, which, though sometimes aided by magnificent novelties of diction, is not dependent on them, but can work magical effects with simple words : he has also, at frequent moments, a marvellous swiftness, alike in the succession of images, and in transitions from thought to thought : and his tone is that of a prophet, who can speak with a voice as of Delphi. But the place to analyse his qualities is not here, where we are dealing with

---

[1] Pind. fr. 131.
[2] fr. 137.
[3] fr. 129, 130. So Tennyson, at the end of *Tiresias*:—
    and every way the vales

Wind, clouded with the grateful incense-fume
Of those who mix all odour to the Gods
On one far height in one far-shining fire.

the development of the choral lyric in its several forms:
what concerns us is to note that, in respect to one of those
forms, the only extant fragments belonging to the fifth
century B.C. are those of Pindar and of Bacchylides.

The prosodion.   This form is the prosodion, or 'song of approach'; a
very old kind of processional hymn, chanted by a chorus
in moving towards the temple or altar of a god, for the
purpose of supplication or of thanksgiving. The earliest
prosodion on record was written by Eumelus of Corinth
(*c.* 740 B.C.) for a chorus which the Messenians sent to the
Delian temple of Apollo[1]. Prosodia are ascribed to Clonas
(*c.* 675 B.C.), variously described as a Boeotian or an
Arcadian, the chief founder of vocal flute-music (αὐλῳδία).

Prosodia of Pindar;   Of Pindar's prosodia, one was for the Delian, and another
for the Pythian, Apollo; a third, which mentioned Latona,
was for the Aeginetan shrine of Aphaea, a goddess akin to
Artemis[2]. So far, the evidence points to Apollo and his
sister as the deities with whose cults the prosodion was
more especially associated; though doubtless it was not
and of Bac-chylides. confined to them. Three fragments from the prosodia of
Bacchylides have been preserved by Stobaeus: but their
contents, which are ethical, afford no clue to the occasion[3].

Love-songs and drink-ing-songs.   Most of the lyric poets wrote love-songs (ἐρωτικά), or
songs meant to be sung over the wine at a banquet (παροίνια
or σκόλια). Some fragments of Alcaeus are classed as
erotica, and others as *skolia*: these were for a single voice,
as were the songs with which wine or love inspired
Anacreon. But the erotic hymns written by Ibycus at the
Pindar's skolia. court of Polycrates seem to have been choral. The skolia
of Pindar also were choral. With reference to his writings,
the term 'skolion' appears to have been used in a large
sense, so as to include 'erotica': the skolion to Theoxenus,
for example, was of the latter kind[4]. All those fragments

---

[1] Paus. IV. 33 §2 quotes from this prosodion two verses, one a hexameter, the other a dactylic pentapody (Bergk⁴ III. p. 6).
[2] Plut. *De Mus.* 3. Pind. fr. 87, 88 (εἰς Δῆλον): fr. 90 (εἰς Δελφούς): fr. 89 (εἰς Ἀφαίαν).
[3] Bacch. fr. 7, 8, 9 (=19, 20, 21 Bergk).
[4] Pind. fr. 123.

of Pindar, indeed, which are classed as 'skolia' are erotic.
But among his fragments of uncertain class there is one
(no. 218), on the fancies inspired by wine, which might
have belonged to a choral drinking-song. The parallelism
with a like fragment of Bacchylides is so close as almost
to suggest that one of the two poets was vying with the
other[1]. In the case of Bacchylides, a class of *erotica* is
attested by Athenaeus[2]. To that class three of his
fragments belong. One of these is curious: it is the refrain
of a love-song, given, probably in chorus, after a single
voice had sung a strophe[3]. It is not on record that
Bacchylides wrote drinking-songs; but two of his fragments seem referable to that class[4].

*Bacchy-
lides.*

Next to Pindar, Bacchylides is the poet who is known
to have written in the largest variety of lyric forms; but
it is possible or probable that Simonides composed lyrics
of other classes besides those of which, in his case, we have
a record. Pindar's remains represent ten species: epinikia;
enkomia; hymns for the gods; paeans; hyporchemes;
dithyrambs; prosodia; partheneia; skolia; and dirges.
The 'erotica' of Bacchylides, and those of his fragments
which may be ranked under the head of 'paroinia,' correspond in class with Pindar's 'skolia.' Of the other nine
forms in which Pindar wrote, only two are absent from the
record of Bacchylides. These are the enkomion and the
dirge.

*Classes of
lyric re-
corded for
Pindar;
and for
Bacchy-
lides.*

The extant works of Pindar and of Bacchylides prove
that, for at least a generation after the Persian Wars, the
choral lyric maintained its prestige, not only in the form of
the epinikion, but in several others also. The period from
about 478 to 446 B.C. was, indeed, that during which Pindar's
fame was at its zenith. Yet with Bacchylides the series of
classical lyric poets ended.

*The classi-
cal lyric
ends with
Bacchy-
lides.*

In the history of Greek poetry from 500 to 450 B.C. the
central fact is the rise of the Attic drama. The year 534 B.C.

*Rise of
Attic
drama.*

---

[1] See n. on Bacch. fr. 16 (=27 Bergk).
[2] Athen. 15. p. 667 C.
[3] See n. on Bacch. fr. 14 (=25 Bergk).
[4] Fr. 16, 17 (=Bergk 27, 28).

is given by the Parian chronicle as that in which Thespis first exhibited at Athens. The official recognition of tragedy as a permanent feature of the Athenian Dionysia, with a State subsidy in the form of a choregia, dated from 508. Aeschylus, born in 525, first competed for the tragic prize in the spring of 499, and gained it for the first time in 484. When, in 456, after writing some ninety plays, Aeschylus died in Sicily, twelve years had passed since Sophocles had begun to exhibit. Attic Tragedy had still another half-century of creative work before it; but it was already mature: nor did it ever touch a higher point than that which Aeschylus had reached in the *Oresteia*. In 456, at least ten years of activity remained to Pindar; and Bacchylides was still in early middle life.

Lyrics in Tragedy.   Attic Tragedy, the offspring of the dithyramb, demanded other gifts beside the lyric; but, in every phase of its development, some measure of lyric faculty was indispensable. In the earlier phase, the lyric element was either actually predominant, or, at least, very large. In the latest phase, represented by Euripides, the choral songs were, indeed, less important; but, on the other hand, they were now exempt from the necessity of being relevant to the action, and thus offered a free field to lyric fancy. During the youth of Bacchylides, an aspirant to purely lyric distinction might have drawn noble inspirations from the *The lyrics of Phryni-chus.* work of dramatists. The *Capture of Miletus* and the *Phoenissae* of Phrynichus would, as dramas, have been sufficiently interesting to a young Ionian of Ceos. But there he would have found also some of those lyrics which, after the lapse of two generations, still commanded the admiration of Athens ; and of which Aristophanes, himself a lyric master, says that their pure melodies seemed to have been caught from the songs of the birds :—

ἔνθεν ὡσπερεὶ μέλιττα
Φρύνιχος ἀμβροσίων ἐπέων ἀπεβόσκετο καρπόν[1].

Aeschylus, apart from his qualities as a dramatist, was

---

[1] Ar. *Av.* 749 f.

one of the greatest lyric writers, comparable, in mastery of *Aeschylus as a lyric poet.* metre and of rhythm, to Pindar, but with a grandeur and an intensity altogether his own. When, in the *Frogs* of Aristophanes, Euripides undertakes to show that Aeschylus is 'a bad lyric composer,' the Chorus wonder what fault he will be able to find with the man whose lyrics (μέλη) are, as they boldly affirm, unsurpassed[1]. The date of the Aeschylean *Supplices* is uncertain, but may perhaps be placed *c.* 491/90. A student of the lyric art could scarcely find more beautiful examples than are furnished by the five great choral odes of that play, which interpret successive and varied emotions. Traces of Aeschylean influence appear, as will be seen later, in the diction of Bacchylides.

There was no reason, then, why the rise of Attic *No reason why drama should depress the Dorian lyric.* drama should have been adverse to the continued cultivation of the higher lyric poetry. It might rather have been expected to favour it. The demand made by Tragedy on lyric accomplishment tended to maintain those studies of music, rhythm, and metre by which the older lyric poets had been formed. A theatre in which choruses sang the lyrics of Phrynichus and of Aeschylus was a school in which large audiences might acquire or improve a lyric taste. On the other hand, the sphere of drama was so distinct from that of the Dorian choral lyric that the attractiveness of the one would not suffice to account for a withdrawal of public favour from the other. We have seen that, in fact, the choral lyric continued to flourish for many years after the drama was mature. The national games still afforded material for epinikia; the worship of the gods still demanded hymns, paeans, prosodia, hyporchemes; the festivals of Dorian cities could still be graced with partheneia. But, in the latter part of the fifth century, one form of choral song, the dithyramb, received a new *The new dithyramb.* development, fraught with far-reaching consequences to the whole lyric art. That development was beginning just as the life of Bacchylides must have been drawing to an end,

---

[1] Ar. *Ran.* 1249—1256.

History of the dithyramb from c. 527 B.C.   In the second half of the sixth century, the new importance given by Peisistratus and his sons to the Athenian festivals of Dionysus had stimulated the demand for dithy-

Dithyrambs of Lasus.   rambs. Lasus of Hermione, who worked at Athens between 527 and 514, modified the older style of dithyrambic composition. The music which accompanied the choral song became more elaborate. From his time, apparently, dated the tendency to enhance the significance of the musical accompaniment relatively to that of the poetical text. As

Protest of Pratinas.   early as c. 500 B.C., Pratinas is found vigorously protesting against the encroachments of the flute-player. The Muse, he says, has ordained that the song shall be mistress, and the flute servant[1]. Still, even in days when, as Pratinas complains, the flute was tending to become master, no serious mischief could be done, so long as the writers of dithyrambs were men loyal to the best traditions of lyric

Simonides and the dithyramb.   poetry. Down to c. 476 B.C. Simonides was a frequent author of dithyrambs for Athenian festivals; he could point to no fewer than fifty-six victories won by him with cyclic choruses[2].

Bacchylides.   The seventeenth poem of Bacchylides, a dithyramb in the form of a dialogue, shows no trace of those faults which disfigure the diction and style of a later school. Bacchylides also maintains the tradition that a dithyramb should be composed in strophes.

The new school:— Melanippides.   The innovator with whom a new school began was Melanippides, a Dorian of Melos[3]. His life was spent

---

[1] Pratinas 5f. (Bergk[4] III. p. 558):
τὰν ἀοιδὰν κατέστασε Πιερὶς βασίλειαν·
ὁ δ᾽ αὐλὸς
ὕστερον χορευέτω· καὶ γὰρ ἐσθ᾽ ὑπηρέτας.

[2] Simon. 145. As Simon. 147 shows, one of these victories was gained in the spring of 476 B.C., when Adeimantus was archon (Bergk[4] III. 495 f.).

[3] Two dithyrambic poets named Melanippides are distinguished by Suidas. (1) The elder, a Melian, son of Criton, was born about 520 B.C. (2) The younger was a maternal

grandson of the elder: his father also was named Criton: his native place is not mentioned. Rohde, in *Rhein. Mus.* 33. 213, holds that Suidas made a mistake. There was only one dithyrambic poet named Melanippides, and he was a Dorian of Melos. Weir Smyth (*Greek Melic Poets*, p. 453) comes to the same conclusion. It was the tendency of Suidas to duplicate personalities, as in the cases of Sappho, the tragic poets Nicomachus and Phrynichus, and the comic poet Crates.

partly at Athens, partly at the court of Perdiccas II of Macedon, who died in 413 B.C. Melanippides wrote his dithyrambs, not in strophes, but in 'free verse' (ἀπολελυμένα). This change was intimately connected with another. He gave greater prominence to a mimetic or dramatic element in the performance of the dithyramb, an element which gained in freedom by the absence of the old strophic framework. He also introduced musical preludes (ἀναβολαί), by which the choral song was broken up into sections. A passage in the *Memorabilia* curiously illustrates his popularity. Xenophon's Aristodemus names three poets whom he regards as supreme in their respective kinds. They are Homer, Sophocles, and Melanippides[1].

The next writer after Melanippides who left a mark on the dithyramb was his pupil Philoxenus, who was born in 435 and died in 380 B.C. He was a native of Cythera. When the Spartans recovered that Dorian island (probably about 413 B.C.) he was sold as a slave, and bought by the poet Melanippides[2]. Philoxenus gave prominence to the solos (μονῳδίαι) which he interspersed between the choral parts. These solos afforded free scope to the florid music which was coming into fashion,.full of those affectations and false ornaments which are ridiculed by Aristophanes. The dramatic side of the performance was now still further developed. The dithyramb of Philoxenus, with acting, dancing, music, and scenery, must have borne some resemblance to an operetta. Among the recorded titles of his pieces are the *Cyclops* and the *Reveller* (Komastes). Philoxenus had a great reputation. His contemporary, the comic poet Antiphanes, who had sometimes made merry with his phrases, paid a generous tribute to his memory[3]. It is instructive to find that, as older and better poets had been contrasted by Aristophanes with the school to which Philoxenus belonged, so Philoxenus himself was extolled by Antiphanes at the expense of worse poets who came after him.

Philoxenus.

[1] Xen. *Mem.* I. iv. 3.
[2] Suidas s.v. Φιλόξενος.

[3] Antiphanes fr. 209 (Kock), from the Τριταγωνιστής.

Timotheus.   Timotheus of Miletus, who flourished at the end of the fifth century and in the earlier part of the fourth, carried the new tendencies still further. The ancient 'nome,' sung to the cithara by one voice, had long ceased to enjoy the vogue given to it by Terpander. Timotheus revived it, but in a form which was essentially new. To the solo he added choral singing ; he made the performance in some measure dramatic, and thus assimilated the nome to the new dithyramb. Alone among the writers of his class in that age, Timotheus can now be judged by a large specimen of his work. In 1902 a fragment containing 253 consecutive verses was found near Memphis[1]. It belongs to one of his *His* most celebrated nomes, the *Persae.* The three principal *'Persae.'* parts of a nome were called 'exordium' (ἀρχή), 'omphalos' (the central portion), and 'seal' (σφραγίς). In our fragment, the exordium is wanting ; the first 214 verses belong to the 'omphalos,' and describe a naval victory of Greeks over Persians, probably that at Salamis ; the last 39 verses are the 'seal,' in which Timotheus speaks of himself, and, as it were, sets his signature to his work. The style is that *The 'di-* which, in its general characteristics, was common to the *thyrambic'* dithyrambic poets of the new school. One trait was a *style.* love for portentous compound words, especially adjectives[2]. Another was the use of grand and round-about phrases for common things[3]. When Timotheus wishes to say that the rowers dropped their oars, he expresses it thus :—

[1] A photographic facsimile was published in 1903 by the Deutsche Orient-Gesellschaft (Leipzig, Hinrichs), with a preface by Prof. v. Wilamowitz-Möllendorf, who has also edited the fragment.

[2] Thus in Plato's *Cratylus* (p. 409), when the words σέλας, ἔνον, νέον, and ἀεί have been rolled into σελαενονεάεια, — denoting the moon's 'light-ever-old-and-new,'—this is pronounced a truly διθυραμβῶδες ὄνομα.

[3] Dithyrambic periphrasis was a fertile source of jest to the Middle Comedy : thus Antiphanes fr. 52:—

πότερ', ὅταν μέλλω λέγειν σοι τὴν
    χύτραν, χύτραν λέγω,
ἢ τροχοῦ ῥύμαισι τευκτὸν κοιλοσώματον
    κύτος;

This feature of the dithyrambic style might be illustrated by many of those examples which Pope culled from his contemporaries in the discourse of Martinus Scriblerus on the ' Art of sinking in poetry'; for some resources of that art are the same in every age. Thus the following mode of saying, 'Shut the door,' is quite in the manner of Timotheus:—

'The wooden guardian of our privacy
    Quick on its axle turn.'

μακραυχενόπλους
χειρῶν δ' ἔκβαλλον ὀρείους
πόδας ναός.

But, owing to the length of the new fragment, our knowledge of his style is not limited to such details: we can judge of its general texture. As an example, we may take the speech in which a drowning Persian upbraids the sea :—

ἤδη θρασεῖα καὶ πάρος
λάβρον αὐχέν' ἔσχες ἐν
πέδᾳ καταζευχθεῖσα λινοδέτῳ τεόν.
νῦν δέ σ' ἀναταράξει
ἐμὸς ἄναξ, ἐμός,
πεύκαισιν ὀριγόνοισιν, ἐγ-
κλήσει δὲ πεδία πλόϊμα νομάσιν αὐγαῖς,
οἰστρομανὲς παλεομί-
σημ' ἄπιστόν τ' ἀγκάλι-
σμα κλυσιδρομάδος αὔρας.
φάτ' ἄσθματι στρευγόμενος,
βλοσυρὰν δ' ἐξέβαλλεν
ἄχναν, ἐπανερευγόμενος
στόματι βρύχιον ἅλμαν.

'Bold as thou art, ere now thou hast had thy boisterous throat bound fast in hempen bonds' [alluding to the bridge over the Hellespont]. 'And now my king,—aye, mine,—will plough thee with hill-born pines, and will encompass thy navigable plains with his far-roaming rays' [*i.e.* the Persian king's power, radiant as the sun, will close round the Aegean on all its coasts]: 'O thou frenzied thing, hated from of old, who treacherously embracest me, while the breeze sweeps over thy surges!' So spake he, panting with strangled breath, as he spat forth the grim sea-dew, belching from his mouth the brine of the deep.

The absurdity, alike of style and of matter, could scarcely be exceeded: but the poet is serious. In a later passage, however, he seems to be designedly comic. A Phrygian prisoner, bewailing himself, speaks fourteen verses of broken Greek.

In the *Cheiron* of Pherecrates, the goddess of Poetry
denounces certain poets by whom she has been injured.
Melanippides was the earliest; but the worst, as she
declares, has been Timotheus[1]. Especial stress is there
laid on his debasement of music. His master in music,
Phrynis, had been trained in the Lesbian school of
citharodes,—a hereditary guild claiming to derive their art
from Terpander,—but had broken with its better traditions;
and the innovations of Timotheus went beyond those of
Phrynis. It is, indeed, hard to conceive how such verses
as those which have just been quoted can have won
applause, unless the music had become so far more important than the words that a musical display in the
newest fashion could carry off the most grotesque libretto.
Yet the compositions of Philoxenus and Timotheus were
still popular in the days of Polybius[2].

Rapid decline in lyric taste. It may seem extraordinary that the first Greeks who
admired such writers were men for whose fathers lyric
poetry had been represented by Simonides, Pindar, and
Bacchylides; and that the earliest successes of the new
dithyrambists were gained when Sophocles and Euripides
Plato's account of that decline. were still living. The most instructive of all commentaries
on this fact is supplied by Plato. In a striking passage of
the *Laws* (written probably not long before 350 B.C.), the
Athenian says that the limited freedom enjoyed by Athens
at the time of the Persian Wars had been better than the
unlimited freedom of his own day. In that older time the
people were 'the willing servants of the laws.' 'Of what
laws?' asks the Lacedaemonian Megillus. An illustra-

[1] Pherecrates fr. 145, verses 3 and 19 ff.

[2] Polybius (IV. 20) describes the education of boys and youths in Arcadia, as he remembers it. They are trained from an early age to sing hymns and paeans on the gods and heroes of their native towns. Next they learn the musical compositions (νόμους) of *Philoxenus* and *Timotheus*, and dance with spirit to the strains of 'the Dionysiac flutists.' [The word νόμους is here used in a large sense which includes both dithyrambs and nomes proper.] When Philopoemen presided at the Nemean festival of 207 (or 205) B.C., the very nome from which we have quoted, the *Persae* of Timotheus, was given in the theatre (Plut. *Philop.* 11).

tion is then given from the province of poetry and
music[1].

Lyric poetry, says the Athenian, was formerly divided
into several distinct species, such as the hymn, the dirge,
the paean, the citharodic nome.   Each species had its own
laws of style and of rhythm.   The judges of merit in each
species were experts.   But in the course of years a new
race of poets arose, men who had no sense of what is 'just
and lawful in the work of the Muse.'   They broke down
the old distinctions of style and rhythm, mingling hymns
with dirges, and paeans with dithyrambs, while they forced
the cithara to mimic the notes of the flute.   Denying that
there was any such thing as correctness (ὀρθότης) in poetry
or in music, they made the pleasure of the hearer their sole
test, without caring whether he was or was not competent
to judge.   'Raging like Bacchanals,' these new poets
brought in a reign of 'uncultured lawlessness' (τῆς ἀμούσου
παρανομίας).   The audiences, formerly silent, now began
to indulge in noisy cries and clapping of hands ; for the
new poetry had taught the multitude to think themselves
connoisseurs.   The old 'aristocracy' in music and poetry,
—the rule of experts and good judges,—was at an end.
An evil 'theatrocracy' took its place[2].

From Alcman to Bacchylides, the distinctive feature in
the evolution of the Greek lyric had been, as Plato indicates,
the adaptation of different species to different themes and
occasions.   In each species the poetical and musical tact
of the Greeks had achieved an artistic harmony between
form and matter.   That harmony depended on the nice
observance of certain rules appropriate to each kind.   The
dividing lines between the several kinds were traced with
a light and delicate touch : to the many those lines might
seem faint ; but for the artist they were distinct ; and they
were also sacred, because they had the sanction of an
intimate fitness which the Greek mind could apprehend.
But, in the latter part of the fifth century, a new lyric

[1] Plat. *Legg.* 700 A–701 B.
[2] Plat. *Legg.* 701 A ἀντὶ ἀριστο-
κρατίας ἐν αὐτῇ [*sc.* τῇ μουσικῇ]
θεατροκρατία τις πονηρὰ γέγονεν.

school cast off that loyalty to the best Greek traditions and instincts. The Attic drama, unrivalled among contemporary forms of poetry in the splendour and variety of its attractions, drew vast audiences to the theatre. Next in popularity, but at an interval, came the *agon* of cyclic choruses at the Great Dionysia, and on certain other occasions. The new dithyrambist felt impelled to bid for popular applause by sensational novelties. A tasteless license broke down the discriminating canons of the older school. Nothing in Plato's sketch of the process is more

Signifi-cance of the decline in musical taste.

instructive than his reminder that such license meant more than a new bent of poetical or musical fashion. It was connected with political and social changes, with the growth of license in every department of civic life, and with new manners which were impatient of decorous restraint. For the Greeks, who, as Plato and Aristotle teach us[1], were so keenly sensitive to the moral effects of music, and to its consequent importance in education, the new corruption of music was, in a sense which we can hardly realise, a grave symptom of moral decay. The difference between Simonides and Timotheus was analogous to the difference between the Athens of Themistocles and the Athens of Cleon.

A further question.

But a further question remains. It must be asked whether the new development at Athens suffices to account for the fact that the classical literature of the Greek lyric ends with Bacchylides. The epinikion, for instance, might have been expected to remain in demand; but the ode of Euripides for Alcibiades (420 B.C.)[2] is the last recorded example of such a composition by an eminent writer. The literary influence of Athens reached far. But a poet who could follow in the steps of the old choral masters ought still to have been secure of appreciative audiences at the festivals of Dorian cities, and at the chief centres of worship, such as Delphi and Delos. Some allowance should doubtless be made for the effects of the Pelopon-

---

[1] *e.g.*, Plat. *Rep.* 398 c—399 c: [2] See above, p. 33.
Arist. *Pol.* v [VIII]. 5—7.

nesian War; for the drain upon those funds which the
Dorians of Peloponnesus could apply to their festivals; for
the interruptions of that elaborate training which the choral
performances at those festivals demanded; and, generally,
for the concentration of thought and interest on the great
struggle. It may be added that the intellectual and the
literary tendencies of the age, its scepticism and its rhetoric,
were unfavourable to ideal art in every kind. But choral
lyric poetry had been zealously cultivated for generations;
it was highly organised; it touched Greek religion and
Greek life at many points; it had hitherto given delight to
multitudes. The complete cessation of higher work in that
province is a phenomenon which only one cause seems
adequate to explain. We are forced to the conclusion that *The inevitable inference.*
those influences, which at Athens were represented by the
new dithyrambic school, speedily became dominant in
Hellas at large. It is significant in this connexion that
Melanippides and Philoxenus were Dorians, that Phrynis
came from Lesbos, and that Timotheus, the pupil who
outdid him, was an Ionian of Miletus. All these men
enjoyed a wide popularity. As to Philoxenus in particular,
it is known that he was well received in Dorian Syracuse
and Tarentum. But wherever the music and the verse of
that school became established in popular favour, the cause
of classical lyric poetry was lost.

We know, however, that there was at least one Dorian
community which upheld the ancient standards, and met
the new depravations with a strenuous protest. Timotheus *Timotheus and the 'old Muse.'*
had openly vaunted the superiority of the 'new songs' to
the 'old':—

οὐκ ἀείδω τὰ παλαιά,
καὶ τὰ καινὰ γὰρ ἅμα κρείσσω·
νέος ὁ Ζεὺς βασιλεύει,
τὸ πάλαι δ' ἦν Κρόνος ἄρχων·
ἀπίτω Μοῦσα παλαιά[1].

'I do not sing the old songs, for the new are also the better.

[1] Timotheus fr. 12 (Bergk[4] III. 624).

Zeus reigns in his young prime : the rule of Cronus is overpast. Away with the old Muse !'

The Spartan protest.

And now, in the fragment of his *Persae* (219—225), he is found invoking Apollo to protect him against the strong censure of Sparta :—

ὁ γάρ μ' εὐγενέτας μακραί-
ων Σπάρτας μέγας ἀγεμών,
βρύων ἄνθεσιν ἤβας,
δονεῖ λαὸς ἐπιφλέγων
ἐλᾷ τ' αἴθοπι μώμῳ,
ὅτι παλαιοτέραν νέοις
ὕμνοις. Μοῦσαν ἀτιμῶ.

' For that noble and ancient folk, mighty lord of Sparta, rich in the flower of youth, storms against me in hot anger, and lashes me with fiery reproach, because in my new songs I dishonour the elder Muse.'

It has been conjectured[1] that Timotheus produced this poem, about 397 B.C., at the Panionia, the festival of the Ionian dodecapolis, held on the promontory of Mycale. Sparta was then dominant in Greece ; and it was the interest of the Ionians to stimulate her warfare against the Persian satraps. I may observe that, if this hypothetical date be accepted, the words βρύων ἄνθεσιν ἤβας are significant. In the Spartan army then on the coasts of Asia Minor, 'the flower of youth' must have included many who, in choruses at the Gymnopaediae, had sung the paeans of lyric poets very unlike Timotheus.

Singular indeed is the contrast thus disclosed. The creative period of Greek poetry is just over, and already the Athenian public has acquiesced in fashions which condemn lyric poetry to a swift and irremediable decay. It is from Sparta that the remonstrance comes. It is at Sparta that a purer taste survives, guarded by laws prohibiting licentious change in the old music of Apollo's festivals, and animated by a tradition dating from the

[1] By Prof. v. Wilamowitz, introd. to the facsimile, p. 11.

far-off days when Spartan youths and maidens danced and sang under the direction of Alcman. More than a generation later, Aristotle could say of his Spartan contemporaries that, if their musical education was defective, at any rate they had a true perception of the difference between good music and bad[1].

We have now traced in outline the evolution and the decay of the Greek lyric. In such a development the relation of a poet to his predecessors is of peculiar moment for a right estimate of his significance. We have seen how the paean and the hyporcheme came down to Bacchylides from Thaletas, how the first models of those 'Dorian partheneia' which he is said to have written had been set by Alcman, and how the influence of Stesichorus may probably be recognised in his treatment of heroic legend. We have also seen how Simonides created the epinikion, and is the first recorded author of dithyrambs on subjects other than Dionysiac ; being thus the precursor of Bacchylides in each of the two kinds to which his extant writings chiefly belong. Lastly, we have sought to elucidate the principal causes which, immediately after the time of Bacchylides, led to the rapid and final decay of Greek lyric art ; thus enabling us to understand why his name is the last in the series of those Greek lyric poets who attained to classical rank. After this endeavour to mark his place in lyric history, we may turn to a brief consideration of the qualities which distinguish his work.

Bacchylides and his predecessors.

----

[1] Arist. *Pol.* v [viii]. 5. § 7.

III. CHARACTERISTICS OF BACCHYLIDES AS A POET.

Extant work of Bacchylides. The poems, or fragments of poems, in the Bacchylides papyrus are of two general kinds. The first thirteen pieces are epinikia. The remaining six, all relating to episodes in the story of heroes and heroines, were collectively classed by the Alexandrians as 'dithyrambs,' in that large sense of the term which was explained above[1]. The number of verses represented by the continuous portions of the papyrus (including verses lost in *lacunae* of which the length can be determined) is 1392. If we suppose, with Blass, that the part lost at the beginning (of which small fragments remain) represents 110 verses[2], the total is 1502. The fragments preserved by ancient writers, and not found in the papyrus, give about 95 verses more, thus raising the approximate total to 1597. That number is only about 150 less than half the total in Pindar's extant odes and fragments, which is (roughly) about 3500.

His treatment of the epinikion. In considering the poetical qualities of Bacchylides, we may set out from his treatment of the epinikion. A trait in which he differs from Pindar, and probably follows Simonides, is the tendency which he sometimes shows to *Details of the victory.* dwell on the circumstances of the particular victory. An illustration is furnished by his fifth ode, as compared with Pindar's first Olympian, which was written on the same occasion. Bacchylides describes the running of the horse Pherenicus in a passage of thirteen verses (vv. 37—49); while Pindar's allusion to the race is very slight and brief (*O.* I. 20—22). The eighth ode depicts the manner in which the victor roused the plaudits of the spectators at Nemea by his performance with the quoit, with the javelin, and in wrestling (VII. 27—39). The ninth ode celebrates an athlete who, at the Isthmus, won two consecutive foot-races. Immediately after his first success, he returns to the starting-place, 'still breathing a storm of hot breath';

[1] See p. 39.　　　[2] See Appendix to Ode I.

and when, for the second time, he rushes past the goal a winner, the olive-oil from his body sprinkles the clothes of the spectators who press around him (IX. 21—26).

Six of the thirteen epinikia are embellished with mythical narratives: these are odes I, III, V, VIII, X, and XII. There is no myth in ode IX ; and there cannot have been space for one in the now multilated ode VII. Odes II, IV, and VI are merely short songs. In regard to XI and to XIII, the scanty remains leave it uncertain whether myths were used. *Myths in the epinikia.*

The choice of the myth for an epinikion was a good test of poetical tact. In some cases, the task was a simple one,—namely, when the traditions of the victor's city or family supplied a suitable legend. Thus in his first ode, for the Cean Argeius, Bacchylides related the myth of Dexithea and Euxantius, which seems to have been specially connected with the victor's native town[1]. The eighth ode, for Automedes of Phlius, glances at the story concerning the origin of the Nemean games ; but the chief mythical ornament is furnished by the local legends of the river Asopus. The twelfth ode, for Pytheas of Aegina, opens with a prophecy inspired by the spectacle of Heracles strangling the Nemean lion ; and the central portion of the poem renders a tribute to the glories of the Aeacidae. *Ode I.* *Ode VIII.* *Ode XII.*

But Odes III, V, and X are those by which we can best measure the skill of Bacchylides in this department. The subject of the third ode is Hieron's victory in the chariot-race at Olympia (468 B.C.). Sacrifice is being offered in the temples of Syracuse, and its streets are alive with hospitable festivities. Thence the poet glides to a mention of the golden tripods which Gelon and Hieron had dedicated, several years before, at Delphi. ' Be generous to the god, and he will prosper you. Apollo saved Croesus of old ';—and then the story is told. The transition from Syracuse to Delphi is lightly and smoothly made ; but the attentive reader experiences a mild surprise at the sudden reference to the tripods, and is left with a suspicion that the myth has been dragged in. Pindar, we might con- *Ode III.*

jecture, would have managed the matter differently. Possibly he would not have attempted to veil the transition by a smooth and swift juncture. The festivities at Syracuse would have led him to speak directly of Hieron's munificence in general. Then there would have been some bold and brilliant utterance of the maxim that the gods reward munificent votaries, followed by the Croesus-myth,—an illustration which would thus have come in naturally. At all events the art of Bacchylides leaves something to be

Ode V. desired here. In the fifth ode, the meeting of Heracles with Meleager in the shades is linked to the poet's immediate subject,—the greatness of Hieron,—by the reflection that 'no man is blest in all things' (v. 53 ff.). Heracles and Meleager, like Hieron, were men in whose lot victory and glory were mingled with suffering. The poet does not expressly indicate this link: he leaves it to be inferred.

Ode X. The tenth ode, for Alexidamus of Metapontion, is another instance in which the link between theme and myth is somewhat slender. At Metapontion there was a temple of Artemis; and the poet assumes that it is Artemis who, by giving the athlete his victory at Delphi, has consoled him for a former disappointment at Olympia. This gracious deed of 'the soothing goddess' suggests the story of the Proetides whom she healed in Arcadia[1]. As these examples indicate, Bacchylides had not all the deftness of Pindar in weaving a legend into the texture of the poem. It is sometimes too apparent that the myth is more or less far-fetched,—an ornamental adjunct, rather than an illustration which seems to spring spontaneously from the poetical motive.

Treatment of the myths by Bacchylides: The simple and direct manner of heroic epos is that in which Bacchylides treats mythology. He gives a continuous narrative, sometimes of considerable length[2]. There is often a genuine charm in the pellucid and easy flow of these passages. At the same time this employment of

---

[1] See Introduction to Ode x, §3.
[2] The story of the Proetides occupies 72 verses (x. 40—112); the passage on the Aeacidae, 74 (XII. 100—174); the legend of Heracles and Meleager, 119 (v. 56—175).

epic style tends to mark off the myth as a distinct section of the ode. Pindar's method is wholly different. He selects from the myth a single episode or scene which he depicts with vivid power, but not, as a rule, at much length; as, for instance, the birth of Iamus (*O.* VI. 35— 57); Athena's gift to Bellerophon (*O.* XIII. 63—92); the infant Heracles strangling the serpents (*N.* I. 35—61); Heracles praying that a son may be born to Telamon (*I.* V. 35—56); the death of Castor (*N.* X. 55—90). Even the story of the Argonauts, which fills so large a space in the fourth Pythian, is told in a few dramatic scenes,— Iason at Iolcus,—the sailing of the Argo,—the hero ploughing with the brazen bulls of Aietes:—and then Pindar breaks off, with a swift glance at the sequel (*P.* IV. 70—254). Bacchylides, if he had devoted an equal space to the same subject, would have told the story straight through, with an equable flow of quasi-epic verse.

compared with Pindar's.

An ode of victory was expected to contain maxims of life and conduct. With Pindar, this 'gnomic' strain is almost always impressive by sheer force or beauty of expression, even when the thought is merely some commonplace of Greek belief or sentiment.

The gnomic element.

Take, for example, the opening of the sixth Nemean :—

'One race is there of men, one race of gods, and from one mother we both have our being; but in our power we are wholly separate: for the race of men is naught; but the brazen heaven abides, a dwelling-place steadfast for ever. Yet withal we have some likeness to the Immortals, perchance in lofty mind, perchance in form; though we know not what line Fate hath marked for the goal of our course, whether in the day-time or in the watches of the night.'

Bacchylides has nothing of this kind. When he moralises, it is in the quiet and simple manner of Ionian elegy. One such passage, concerning the various pursuits of men, is, in fact, a paraphrase from Solon[1]. At other moments we are reminded of Mimnermus or of Theognis.

---

[1] Ode IX. 39—45.

The following extract from the first ode will serve as a specimen :—

'If a mortal is blest with health, and can live on his own substance, he vies with the most fortunate. Joy attends on every state of life, if only disease and helpless poverty be not there. The rich man yearns for great things, as the poorer for less ; mortals find no sweetness in opulence, but are ever pursuing visions that flee before them.'

If the utterances scattered through the poems warrant a conjecture, Bacchylides was of a placid temper; amiably tolerant; satisfied with a modest lot; not free from some tinge of that pensive melancholy which was peculiarly Ionian : but with good sense, and resolute in acting on this precept of his own,—

'One canon is there, one sure way of happiness for mortals,— if one can keep a cheerful spirit throughout life[1].'

He often insists on the duty of giving praise where it is due. Truth, candour (ἀλάθεια), urges men to do so, and 'is wont to prevail' in the end; though envy may strive to keep them mute. He has a vivid conception of φθόνος as a power to be repelled 'with might and main[2].' Who can tell whether his own career had not given him some knowledge of that power?

Ode I.
49—74.   It is remarkable that the first ode ends with twenty-five verses which are wholly 'gnomic.' They contain no reference to the victor or to his victory, such as Pindar would have introduced before the close. Such an ending was ill-suited to an epinikion : it suggests a certain immaturity in the poet's art,—so far as this province of the epinikion was concerned,—at the time when that ode was composed.

Traces of
Pindar's
influence.   On the other hand, the fifth ode (written in 476 B.C.) approximates to Pindar's method in its general structure, and has one especially Pindaric trait,—the abrupt return from myth to theme[3]. An imitation of Pindaric style may

---

[1] Fragment 7.
[2] Ode v. 187 ff.: cp. VII. 42 ff.: VIII. 85 ff.: XII. 199—207. Φθόνος

is εὐρυβίας (XV. 31).
[3] See on Ode v. 176 ff.

also be traced in one passage of the third ode (468 B.C.)[1]. Simonides was probably his nephew's earliest master in the epinikion. But at any rate Bacchylides, while still young, felt also the influence of Pindar.

The six poems in the latter part of the papyrus, *The 'di-* collectively classed as 'dithyrambs' in the Alexandrian *thyrambs.'* sense, show the art of Bacchylides in another phase. The ode on the embassy of Menelaus and Odysseus to Troy (XIV) seems to end abruptly; so also does the 'Heracles' *Ode XIV.* (XV). But each, doubtless, is complete as it stands. The *Ode XV.* aim of each is to present a critical moment in the story, a moment fraught with consequences which are hinted, but left untold. A like purpose appears in the poem (XVII) *Ode XVII.* on the journey of Theseus to Athens. The finest piece *Ode XVI.* in this series is, of course, the choral paean for Delos (XVI),—'Theseus, or the Athenian youths and maidens.' It is one of the two examples which best illustrate the poet's gift for narrative, while they illustrate it in different aspects. The story of Heracles and Meleager, in the fifth ode, moves 'the sense of tears in mortal things': this paean excels in spirited and rapid description. The short *Speeches of* speeches of Theseus and Minos are also dramatically effec- *heroes.* tive in a high degree[2]. Bacchylides, we may note, makes heroes speak in the epic style; whereas Pindar makes them speak in a lyric fashion which is often, indeed, dramatic, but always his own.

All the work of Bacchylides is marked by a skilful use *Pictu-* of picturesque detail: he knows how to apply the small *resque detail.* touches which give life and colour. We have already referred to some places in the fifth, eighth, and ninth odes, where he depicts the circumstances of a victory. Another good example is the scene in the palace of Poseidon beneath the waves, where Theseus is welcomed by Amphi-trite[3]. The fragment on the blessings of peace is also characteristic in this respect: sacrifices blaze 'in the yellow

---

[1] III. 85—87.
[2] XVI. 20—46 (Theseus): 52—66,
and 74—80 (Minos).
[3] XVI. 96—116.

Imagery. flame on carven altars'; 'the webs of red-brown spiders are on the iron-bound handles of shields[1].' Imagery is sparingly employed by Bacchylides; but his images are often impressive and beautiful. The wavering multitudes of ghosts on the banks of Cocytus are compared to 'leaves quivering in the wind, where flocks graze on the gleaming headlands of Ida[2].' There is something of Homeric vividness and force in the simile of the mariners who, after a tempestuous night, see the billows subside at dawn, and are wafted to the haven for which they had ceased to hope: even so the Trojans, when Achilles retired from the battlefield, 'lifted up their hands to the gods; for now they saw a bright gleam of sunshine from under the shadow of the storm[3].'

Use of epithets. The use of epithets by Bacchylides is noteworthy in several respects. His deities and heroes are usually characterized in epic fashion (Διὸς ἀργικεραύνου, Κουρῆσι μενεπτολέμοις, etc.); but he is peculiarly prone to bestow two or more epithets on the same person. In particular, he loves to associate the word σεμνός with other attributes of a deity; thus we have σεμνοῦ Διὸς εὐρυβία (X. 52): ἁ χρυσάρματος | σεμνὰ μεγάθυμος 'Αθάνα (XII. 194 f.): καλυκοστεφάνου | σεμνᾶς χόλον 'Αρτέμιδος λευκωλένου (V. 98 f.): σεμνάν τε πατρὸς ἄλοχον φίλαν | ἴδε βοῶπιν ἐρατοῖσιν 'Αμφιτρίταν δόμοις (XVI. 109 ff.). It will be observed that, in the second of these examples, χρυσάρματος denotes a conventional attribute, and μεγάθυμος a personal quality. In the third example, a like remark applies to καλυκοστεφάνου and λευκωλένου respectively. The most remarkable instance of such accumulation occurs in X. 37 ff.:—

> νῦν δ' "Αρτεμις ἀγροτέρα
> χρυσαλάκατος λιπαρὰν
> ἡμέρα τοξόκλυτος νίκαν ἔδωκε.

Here, ἀγροτέρα, 'the huntress,' denotes a general aspect

---

[1] Fragment 3.
[2] v. 63—67.
[3] XII. 124—140. The Homeric style of the simile is illustrated by the use of the epic δέ τε in v. 129 (where see note).

of Artemis: ἡμέρα, 'the soother,' is a special title given to her in the local cult at Lusi in Arcadia ; χρυσαλάκατος means, 'with golden shaft,' and τοξόκλυτος, 'famed for archery.' Each of the four epithets, then, is significant: the poet's intention, too, is manifest ; he wishes to emphasize the divine attributes of Artemis, for it is this mention of her which gives him his cue for the story of the Proetides. But the crowd of adjectives actually impairs the force of each. In the verse, εὐρυσθενέος φραδαῖσι φερτάτου Διός (XVIII. 17), the second epithet, φερτάτου, is analogous to σεμνοῦ in the first example quoted above (X. 52) ; but it has a much weaker effect. A similar instance is παραπλῆγι φρένας | καρτερᾷ ζεύξασ' ἀνάγκᾳ (X. 45 f.). On the other hand, in αἰθέρα ξουθαῖσι τάμνων | ὑψοῦ πτερύγεσσι ταχείαις αἰετός (V. 17 ff.) neither epithet is otiose.

Another trait, which sometimes lends an air of conventionality to the poet's style, is the frequency of non-distinctive epithets for goddesses and heroines. Thus βαθύζωνος is applied to Dexithea, Latona, Theano, and the Graces ; ἰοστέφανος, to Persephone, Thetis, and the Muses ; κυανοπλόκαμος, to Nike, Thebe, and the daughters of Proetus ; λευκώλενος, to Hera, Artemis, Calliope, Europa, and Iole ; χρυσέα, to Aphrodite, Artemis, and Io.

But it should also be noted that, in many instances, the epithet chosen by Bacchylides is novel, felicitous, and expressive. The following are examples :—δόξαν...πεισίμ-βροτον (VIII. 1 f.) : θερσιεπὴς φθόνος (XII. 199 f.) : λειρίων... ὀμμάτων (XVI. 95) : μελαμφαρέϊ...σκότῳ (III. 13 f.) : πρῶνας ἀργηστάς (V. 67) : κυανανθέϊ...πόντῳ (XII. 124 f.) : πυρι-έθειραν ἀστραπάν (XVI. 56).

The influence of earlier or contemporary poetry has left traces in the work of Bacchylides ; but, so far as we can judge, his debts to it were neither large nor important. Though he was familiar with the style of Homeric epos, there are some slight indications which might suggest that

Influence of other poets on Bacchylides. Homer.

his study of the *Iliad* had not been very close or observant[1].
His version of Meleager's story owes but little to the ninth

Hesiod. book of the *Iliad*[2]. From Hesiod, the only poet whom he
mentions, he cites a sentiment which cannot be identified
with anything extant under Hesiod's name, but tallies
with a verse of Theognis[3]. In a poem of unknown class,

The Cypria. he treated a story told by Hesiod in Κήϋκος γάμος[4]. The
Cypria was doubtless his source in Ode XIV; where there

Stesi-chorus. is also a small touch which suggests the influence of Stesichorus, and another which may be a reminiscence of

Ibycus. Ibycus[5]. In the earlier part of Ode XV there is a probable

Alcaeus. trace of Alcaeus[6]; the source of the latter part may be
the epic *Capture of Oechalia.* Some words in Ode V are

Theognis. paraphrased from Theognis[7]. The ἀγλαὰν ἥβαν of Bacchylides (V. 154, 476 B.C.) may be a reminiscence of ἀγλαὸς
ἥβη in Theognis (985): but not of ἀγλαὸν..ἥβην in
pseudo-Simonides 105. I, written in or after 466 B.C.
The phrase is not epic; and Pindar has only ἀγλαόγυιον
Ἥβαν (*N.* VII. 4: 467 B.C.?). The transcript from Solon in
Ode IX has already been mentioned (p. 59).

Simonides.   Among the poets contemporary with Bacchylides whose
influence we should expect to trace in him, the first is,
of course, Simonides. Unfortunately the fragments of
Simonides are too scanty to afford adequate material
for an estimate of his part in shaping the style of
Bacchylides. As a matter of fact, there are only two or
three words or phrases which the nephew seems to have
borrowed from the uncle. In the Homeric poems ἐραννός
is an epithet of places only: but Simonides has ἐραννὸν
ὕδωρ, and Bacchylides has ἐραννὸν φάος (XVI. 42 f.). If in
Ode VIII. 13 R. A. Neil's ἀωτεύοντα be (as it certainly seems)
a true emendation of ἀσαγευοντα, then the use of ἀωτεύειν,
without the Homeric addition of ὕπνον, in the sense of
'sleeping,' may well have been suggested to the younger

---

[1] See notes on v. 75 f. and XII.
146.
[2] See Appendix on v. 56—175.
[3] See note on v. 191.

[4] Fragment 18.
[5] See notes on XIV. 48 and 58.
[6] See note on XV. 5.
[7] See note on v. 160.

poet by the elder's similar use of ἀωτεῖς (fr. 37. 6). Simonides (fr. 37. 1) has λάρνακι...δαιδαλέα̣ : Bacchylides (V. 140 f.), δαιδαλέας | ἐκ λάρνακος. On the other hand, it may be noted that, while Simonides (156) has Πίσῃ with ῑ, Bacchylides (V. 182) follows Pindar (O. III. 9, etc.) in shortening the first syllable. With regard to mythological material, there are three known instances of themes common to Simonides and Bacchylides. These are, the death of Archemorus ; the voyage of Theseus to Crete ; and the story of Idas and Marpessa[1].

A collation of Bacchylides with Pindar discloses only *Pindar.* one passage which proves verbal imitation on the part of the younger poet. In *Isthm.* III. 19 ff. (IV. 1 ff.), an ode of which the date may be 478 B.C., Pindar says :—

> Ἔστι μοι θεῶν ἕκατι μυρία παντᾷ κέλευθος,
> ὦ Μέλισσ᾽, εὐμαχανίαν γὰρ ἔφανας Ἰσθμίοις,
> ὑμετέρας ἀρετὰς ὕμνῳ διώκειν.

Bacchylides (V. 31 ff., 476 B.C.) has :—

> τὼς νῦν καὶ ἐμοὶ μυρία παντᾷ κέλευθος
> ὑμετέραν ἀρετὰν
> ὑμνεῖν.

There is another parallelism which (as it seems to me) affords a presumption, not indeed of direct imitation, but of reminiscence. Pindar says in *Olymp.* X. 78 ff. (484 B.C.) :—

> ἀρχαῖς δὲ προτέραις ἑπόμενοι καὶ νῦν ἐπωνυμίαν χάριν
> νίκας ἀγερώχου κελαδησόμεθα βροντὰν
> καὶ πυρπάλαμον βέλος
> ὀρσικτύπου Διός.

'Following the beginnings made of yore ' [*i.e.* the tradition of hymning Zeus at Olympia], 'now also, in a tribute of song (χάριν) named after proud victory [*i.e.*, in an ἐπινίκιον], will we celebrate the thunder and the fire-sped bolt of loud-pealing Zeus.'

---

[1] Note on VIII. 11 f. : Introduction to XVI, § 5, n. 3 : Introd. to XIX, § 3, n. 2.

Bacchylides writes thus in XIII. 19 ff. (of unknown date):—

Κλεοπτολέμῳ δὲ χάριν
νῦν χρὴ Ποσειδᾶνος Πετραίου τέμενος κελαδῆσαι.

'Now, in tribute to Cleoptolemus, 'tis meet to celebrate the sacred domain of Poseidon Petraios.'

It will be observed that the points of resemblance between these passages are three :—(1) the peculiar sense of χάριν : (2) the construction of χάριν as accusative in apposition with the sentence : (3) the use of the verb κελαδεῖν.

Pindar in [*Pyth.*] II. 55 f. (475 B.C. ?) describes Archilochus as βαρυλόγοις ἔχθεσιν | πιαινόμενον. Bacchylides (III. 67 f., 468 B.C.) has, εὖ λέγειν πάρεστιν, ὅσ|τις μὴ φθόνῳ πιαίνεται. The stamp of the phrase is Pindaric. Pindar (fr. 90. 5) calls himself Πιερίδων προφάταν : and Bacchylides in VIII. 3 is Μουσῶν...προφάτας. This phrase, which is not epic, may have been first used by Pindar : it has a Delphic tone. Pindar, in *Isthm.* V (VI). 12, has σύν τέ οἱ δαίμων φυτεύει δόξαν : Bacchylides, in XVI. 68 f. (Ζεὺς) Μίνωϊ φύτευσε τιμάν : but this is less significant. We should be cautious in assuming a debt on either part, where the phrase is of a commonplace lyric character. Thus Bacchylides V. 9 (476 B.C.) has σὺν Χαρίτεσσι βαθυζώνοις : Pindar *Pyth.* IX. 1 (of 474 B.C.) has σὺν βαθυζώνοισιν... Χαρίτεσσι : where, if either was a debtor, the chronology points to Pindar ; but as the epithet is so conventional and obvious, it is needless to suppose any borrowing. Again, the phrase of Bacchylides in V. 196 f., εὐκλέα...γλῶσσαν ...πέμπειν Ἱέρωνι, has boldness of a Pindaric kind : but, as a matter of fact, the passages of Pindar which show a like use of γλῶσσα occur in odes probably subsequent in date to the ode of Bacchylides, namely *N.* IV. 86 (456 B.C. ?), and *O.* IX. 44 (464 B.C.).

Apart from any question of verbal imitation, we find some noteworthy coincidences of thought and sentiment

between the two poets. Both deprecate scepticism as to
marvels by the remark that 'nothing is incredible' when
gods are at work (Pind. *Pyth.* X. 48 ff.: Bacch. III. 57 f.,
XVI. 117 f.). Both regard fame and opulence as the two
main factors of ὄλβος, wherewith a mortal should be content (Pind. *Isthm.* IV (V). 13 f.: Bacch. V. 50—55). Both,
when celebrating victories in the chariot-race, praise the
man who 'does not keep his wealth hidden' (Pind. *Nem.*
I. 31, *Isthm.* I. 67: Bacch. III. 13 f.). Both speak of just
praise as a benign dew which fosters the tender plant of
ἀρετά (Pind. *Nem.* VIII. 40 ff.: Bacch. V. 197 f.).

The influence of Aeschylus on the diction of Bacchylides *Aeschylus.*
is shown by a number of traces.

Supplices (*c.* 491–490 B.C.?). 555. βαθύπλουτος. This
word, which first occurs here, is used by Bacchylides (III.
82), but not by Pindar.—104 f. νεάζει πυθμὴν | ...τεθαλώς.
Compare Bacch. V. 198 πυθμένες θάλλουσιν ἐσθλῶν.—
973 f. πᾶς τις ἐπειπεῖν ψόγον ἀλλοτρίοις | εὔτυκος. The
construction of εὔτυκος with an infinitive recurs in Bacch.
VIII. 4 ff.

Persae (472 B.C.). 104. πολέμους πυργοδαϊκτους. Compounds of δαΐζω are Aeschylean: *Theb.* 735 αὐτοδάϊκτοι:
Cho. 1071 λουτροδάϊκτος. Bacchylides (VIII. 6) has μηλοδαΐκταν. [In *Pers.* 104 should we read πυργοδαΐκτας?]—
111. πόντιον ἄλσος. The phrase first occurs in this
place: it is not epic or Pindaric. Bacchylides has it in
XVI. 84 f.—731. κἀπικουρίας στρατοῦ. This is the first
occurrence of ἐπικουρία: the word is used by Bacchylides
(XVII. 13), but by no other poet of the classical age except
Euripides.—1072. ἁβροβάται. The word occurs in Bacch.
III. 78 (468 B.C.), but nowhere else.

Septem contra Thebas (467 B.C.). The rare word ἀργηστής, found in verse 80 (and in *Eumenides* 181), is used by
Bacchylides in V. 67 (476 B.C.). It occurs nowhere else,
except in Theocritus XXV. 131. If it was from the mint of
Aeschylus, Bacchylides must have found it in some lost
play of which the date was earlier than 476 B.C.—882.
ἐρειψίτοιχοι. This is the only extant compound with

ἐρειψι-, except the ἐρειψιπύλαν of Bacchylides in V. 56, and his ἐρειψ[ιλάοις?] in XII. 167.

Prometheus Vinctus (later than 468 B.C.). In 588 Io has the form of a maiden, with the horns of an ox (βούκερως παρθένος). This was probably the conception adopted by Bacchylides (see Introduction to XVIII, § 1). The word οἰστρόπληξ, an epithet of Io which occurs first in *P.V.* 681, is restored with certainty in Bacchylides XVIII. 40.—In 724 f. Prometheus speaks of the Amazons, αἳ Θεμίσκυράν ποτε | κατοικιοῦσιν ἀμφὶ Θερμώδονθ᾽, ἵνα κ.τ.λ.: compare Bacchylides VIII. 42 f. ταί τ᾽ ἐπ᾽ εὐναεῖ πόρῳ | οἰκεῦσι Θερμώδοντος.

Choephori (458 B.C.). 362. πεισιβρότῳ...βάκτρῳ (πισίμβροτον...βάκτρον cod. Laur.). The only other occurrence of the adjective is in Bacchylides VIII. 1 f. δόξαν...πεισίμβροτον (where see n.).—In 1071 f. Agamemnon is Ἀχαιῶν | πολέμαρχος ἀνήρ. (In *Theb.* 828 πολεμάρχους refers to the sons of Oedipus.) Compare Bacchylides XVI. 39 πολέμαρχε Κνωσίων. These are our only examples of the word πολέμαρχος used in a non-technical sense, with the exception of the phrase πολέμαρχος...συνεφήβων in an inscription of the second century (Kaibel, *Epigr. Graeca* 960. 2).

Vocabulary of Bacchylides.   Upwards of a hundred words otherwise unknown are found in the poems of Bacchylides. The nouns substantive are ἄθυρσις (XII. 93), θατήρ (XI. 8), μουνοπάλα (XI. 8). If in XVI. 112 αἰόνα were sound, we should have to assume αἰών as the name for some kind of garment: but the word is probably corrupt. In V. 110 εἰσάνταν is a novel substitute for the Homeric adverb εἴσαντα. The new verbs are γελανόω (V. 80), εὐμαρέω (I. 65), καταχραίνω (V. 44), ὀλιγοσθενέω (V. 139), πεδοιχνέω (XV. 9); to which ἀωτεύω (VIII. 13) may safely be added. But the vast majority of the new words,—more than ninety,—are compound adjectives. Some of these, doubtless, though previously strange to us, had been used by poets before Bacchylides; but many, if not most, of them may well have been his own inventions. The general character of this considerable accession to the lexicons may best, perhaps, be illustrated by a selection of groups.

I. One set of such groups may be arranged according to the first element in the compound. 1. Thus we have the following new compounds beginning with ἀναξι-:— ἀναξίαλος (XIX. 8), ἀναξιβρόντας (XVI. 66), ἀναξίμολπος (VI. 10). 2. With εὐρυ-:—εὐρυάναξ (V. 19), εὐρυδίνας (III. 7), εὐρυνεφής (XV. 17). 3. With μεγιστο-:—μεγιστοπάτωρ (V. 199), μεγιστοάνασσα (XVIII. 21),—meaning μέγιστος πατήρ, μεγίστη ἄνασσα. 4. With ὀρσι-:—ὀρσίαλος (XV. 19), ὀρσιβάκχας (XVIII. 49), ὀρσίμαχος (XIV. 3). 5. With ὑψι-:—ὑψαυχής (XII. 85), ὑψιάγυια (XII. 71), ὑψιδαίδαλτος (XIII. 18), ὑψίδειρος (IV. 4). 6. With χαλκεο- or χαλκο-:[1]— χαλκεόκρανος (V. 74), χαλκεόκτυπος (XVII. 59), χαλκόκτυπος (? XIII. 16), χαλκοκώδων (XVII. 3), χαλκοτειχής (III. 32). II. Other small groups are indicated by the second element in the composite word. 1. New compounds with ἔπος:—θελξιεπής (XIV. 48), θερσιεπής (XII. 199), τερψιεπής (XII. 230). 2. With ὄνομα:—ἐρατώνυμος (XVI. 31), χαριτώνυμος (II. 2). III. We note also a group of which the common characteristic is that the compound adjective is formed by combining the stems of two substantives:— ἀρέταιχμος (XVI. 47), ἀστύθεμις (IV. 3), θερσιεπής (XII. 199), κεραυνεγχής (VII. 48), πολεμαιγίς (XVI. 7), πυργοκέρας (frag. 31, = 51 Bergk), χαριτώνυμος (II. 2). IV. If the new adjectives of Bacchylides are considered in regard to their meaning, we observe that the following are expressive of *colour* or of *splendour*:—κυανανθής (XII. 124), μελαμφαρής (XIII. 13), ξανθοδερκής (VIII. 12), πορφυροδίνας (VIII. 39), πυριέθειρα (XVI. 56), πυρσόχαιτος (XVII. 51), φοινίκασπις (VIII. 10), φοινικόθριξ (X. 105), φοινικοκράδεμνος (XII. 97), φοινικόνωτος (V. 102), χρυσεόπλοκος (XVI. 106), χρυσεόσκαπτρος (VIII. 100), χρυσόπαχυς (V. 40). V. Lastly, from the metrical point of view, it may be noted how many of the poet's new words have the form

---

[1] In compounds Pindar uses only χαλκεο- and χρυσεο-. χαλκο-, χρυσο-: Bacchylides, also

∪–∪∪–:—ἀελλοδρόμας (V. 39), ἀερσίμαχος (XII. 100), ἀμετρόδικος (X. 68), ἀναιδομάχας (v. 195), ἀναξίαλος (XIX. 8), ἀριστοπάτρα (X. 196), ἀταρβομάχας (XV. 28), ἐρειψιπύλας (V. 56), μεγιστοπάτωρ (V. 199).

Besides the adjectives included in the groups just noted, there are more than forty others, also peculiar to Bacchylides, which scarcely call for special remark. They are enumerated below[1].

Adjectives common to Pindar and Bacchylides.

It is instructive to compare Bacchylides and Pindar in respect to their choice of poetical epithets. Many such words are common to both; as ἀγλαόθρονος: δαμασίμβροτος (epithet of sword or spear): διχόμηνις: ἐρισφάραγος (epithet of Zeus): θεόδματος: θεόδοτος: θεότιμος: θρασυμήδης: ἰοβλέφαρος: ἰόπλοκος: ἰοστέφανος: μεγαλοσθενής: μελίφρων: ὀρθόδικος (or -δίκας): πλάξιππος: πολυώνυμος: τηλαυγής: τοξόκλυτος: φαυσίμβροτος: φιλάγλαος: φιλάνωρ: χάλκασπις: χρυσαλάκατος: χρυσάμπυξ: χρυσάρματος:

Analogies in the two vocabularies.

χρυσάωρ (-άορος? Bacch. III. 28): χρύσασπις: χρυσοκόμας: χρυσόπεπλος. Further, we note a large number of instances in which the word of Bacchylides is not used by Pindar, but finds some analogy of form in the Pindaric vocabulary. The following are examples:—

BACCHYLIDES.		PINDAR.
ἀμετρόδικος.	. . .	ἀϊδροδίκας.
ἀναξιβρόντας.	. . .	αἰολοβρόντας.
ἀκαμαντορόας.	. . .	ἀκαμαντόπους (etc.).

[1] ἀκαμαντορόας (V. 183): ἀριστ-αλκής (VII. 7): ἀριστοπάτρα (III. 1): βαθυδείελος (I. 139): βροτωφελής (XII. 191): δᾳδοφόρος (fr. 23): δνόφεος (XV. 32, otherwise known only from Hesych.): δυσμάχητος (if fr. 32 belongs to Bacch.): ἐλικοστέφανος (VIII. 62): ἐρειψίλαος (? XII. 167): ἐρειψιπύλας (V. 56): εὐαίνετος (XVIII. 11): εὔγυιος (X. 10): εὐεγχής (XII. 147): εὐναής (VIII. 42): θελημός (XVI. 85): θρασύχειρ (II. 4): ἰδρώεις (XII. 57): ἱμεράμπυξ (XVI. 9): ἱμερόγυιος (XII. 137): ἱπποδίνητος (V. 2): ἱππώκης (X. 101): καλλιρόας (X. 26, 96): λεπτόπρυμνος (XVI. 119): λιγυκλαγγής

(V. 73, XIII. 14): μεγαίνητος (III. 64): μεγαλοκλεής (VII. 49): μελαγκευθής (? III. 55, fr. 25): μελαμφαρής (III. 13): μελανόκολπος (? fr. 23): μηλοδαΐκτας (VIII. 6): νεόκριτος (see Appendix on VII. 14): νεόκροτος (V. 48): ὀβριμοδερκής (XV. 20): ὀβριμόσπορος (XVIII. 32): ὀλυμπιόδρομος (III. 3): οὔλιος as = οὖλος (XVII. 53): πάμφθερσις (fr. 20): πανθαλής (XII. 229): πάννικος (X. 21): πλείσταρχος (III. 12): πολύφαντος (XII. 61): πρώθηβος (XVII. 57): πυργοκέρας (fr. 31): σεμνοδότειρα (II. 1): ὑμνοάνασσα (XI. 1): φερεκυδής (XII. 182): φρενοάρας (XVI. 118).

BACCHYLIDES.	PINDAR.
ἀναιδομάχας.	ἀπειρομάχας.
ἀριστοπάτρα.	ἀριστόγονος.
βαρύβρομος.	βαρύκτυπος.
δαμασίχθων (of Poseidon).	ἐλασίχθων (do.).
ἑλικοστέφανος.	ἑλικάμπυξ.
εὐρυνεφής (of Zeus).	ὀρσινεφής.
θερσιεπής.	θρασύμυθος.
θρασυμέμνων.	θρασυμάχανος.
θρασύχειρ.	θρασύγυιος.
ἱμερόγυιος.	ἀγλαόγυιος.
ἱπποδίνητος.	ὠκυδίνατος (of chariot-races).
καρτερόχειρ.	καρτεραίχμας.
κεραυνεγχής.	ἐγχεικέραυνος.
κυανανθής ('of dark hue')	λευκανθής (of corpses).
λιπαρόζωνος.	λιπαράμπυξ.
μελίγλωσσος.	μελίγαρυς, μελίφθογγος.
νεόκτιτος.	νεόκτιστος.
ὀρσίαλος (of Poseidon).	ὀρσοτρίαινα (do.).
παλίντροπος.	παλιντράπελος.
πανθᾱλής.	εὐθᾱλής.
πυργοκέρας.	ὑψικέρας.
τανύθριξ.	ταννέθειρα.
ὑψίδειρος.	ὑψίλοφος.
χαλκεόκρανος (ἰός).	χαλκότοξος.
ὠκύπομπος.	ὠκύπορος.

A few notes on special points may be added. (1) Pindar has a remarkable number of adjectives compounded with παμ- or παν-:—παμβίας, παμπειθής, παμποίκιλος, παμπόρφυρος, πάμπρωτος, παμφάρμακος, παμφόρος, πάμφωνος, πανδαίδαλος, πάνδοκος, πανέτης, πάντολμος. Bacchylides has the following (of which those marked with * are peculiar to him):—*πάμφθερσις, πανδαμάτωρ, πανδερκής, πανθᾱλής and *πανθᾱλής, *πάννικος. (2) Very characteristic of Pindar are the compounds of ἀγλαός:—ἀγλαόγυιος, ἀγλαόδενδρος, ἀγλαόθρονος, ἀγλαόκαρπος, ἀγ-

λαόκολπος (probable in *N*. III. 56), ἀγλαόκουρος, ἀγλαο-
τρίαινα. Bacchylides has ἀγλαόθρονος, but no other.
(3) Pindar also loves compounds with ποικίλος :—ποικιλ-
άνιος, ποικιλόγαρυς, ποικιλόνωτος, ποικιλοφόρμιγξ. Bacchylides has no such compound. (4) The Pindaric φοινικο-
group consists of φοινικάνθεμος, φοινικόκροκος, φοινικόπεζα,
φοινικόροδος, φοινικοστερόπας. [In *N*. IX. 28 it is better
to write Φοινικοστόλων, 'sent by the Phoenicians,' than,
with Mezger, φοινικοστόλων.] Not one of these words
occurs in the φοινικο-group of Bacchylides (see above, p.
69). (5) The word λιπαρός is a favourite with Pindar, who
applies it especially to opulent cities, but never to persons.
Here he follows the Homeric rule. (In *Od*. 15. 332, where
youths are λιπαροὶ κεφαλάς, the reference is to anointing
with oil.) But Bacchylides in V. 169 has λιπαρὰν...ἄκοιτιν,
where the notion is that of rich adornment and stately
surroundings; it may be expressed by 'queenly.' This
un-Homeric use may have been suggested by the *Theogony*,
v. 901 : δεύτερον ἠγάγετο λιπαρὴν Θέμιν.

The general result of the foregoing survey is to show
that the diction of Bacchylides, though influenced in
several particulars by earlier or contemporary poets, has a
well-marked character of its own, which comes out when
we examine his mintage of new words. His work in this
kind often shows the bent of his own fancy. Certain
traits of his style which belong to the province of dialect
and of grammar are reserved for separate treatment.

*Bacchyli-
des and
Greek art.* The relation of Bacchylides to Greek art is a subject
which no student of his poetry can ignore. Vase-paintings
illustrate the story of Croesus as told in the third ode;
the struggle of Heracles with the Nemean lion, at the
beginning of the twelfth; the reception of Theseus by
Amphitrite, in the sixteenth ode; and the account of
that hero's deeds on his way from Troezen to Athens, in
the seventeenth. Details as to these vases will be found in
the Introductions to the several poems, and in the commentary on the text. But a few words must be said here

on the general import of such coincidences. It is known
that the epic hymns of Stesichorus furnished themes to
Greek painters in the fifth century B.C.; and it might seem
natural to suppose that, in some cases, Bacchylides
exercised a similar influence. But the relation of Bac- *Stesichorus*
chylides to the vase-painters was, in fact, wholly different *and Bacchylides:*
from that of the older poet. Stesichorus, by an original *their re-*
treatment of the myths, popularised versions which became *spective
relations to*
established in tradition, and which the vase-painters *the vase-
painters.*
adopted[1]. Bacchylides did not innovate, like Stesichorus,
or boldly recast his material, like Pindar. He adhered to
the forms of the myths generally current in his own day.
When he and the vase-painters concur, it certainly is not
because they have followed him. In at least two instances,
his poem is later than the vase which supplies an illustration of it[2]. The cause is either that the same poetical
tradition has been their common source, or that Bacchylides
has followed the vase-painters, who, in the fifth century,
had a large influence in popularising mythical scenes and
situations. A case in which the latter explanation seems
highly probable is that passage of the seventeenth ode
which mentions two heroes as accompanying Theseus on
his journey to Athens[3].

The series of references to Bacchylides in ancient *Repute of
Bacchyli-*
writers extends from the Alexandrian age to the sixth *des in*
century of the Christian era. He is not mentioned in any *antiquity.*
extant book of the fifth or fourth century B.C. But it
would be very unwarrantable to infer from such silence
that his work was then held in slight esteem. We know
that a prominent citizen of Aegina, when he wished his
son's victory at Nemea to be worthily commemorated,
coupled Bacchylides with Pindar in the commission. We
know also that Bacchylides alone celebrated the latest and
highest distinction won at Olympia by the Syracusan

[1] See on this subject C. Robert in
Hermes, vol. XXXIII, p. 130 (1898).
[2] See Introd. to Ode III, §2 (the
Croesus amphora): and Introd. to

XVI, §2 (the kylix of Euphronius).
[3] Introd. to XVII, §3: also the
note on XVII. 46.

prince for whom Pindar had previously written. Among those who, in the fifth century, felt the charm of Bacchylides, we may probably count Euripides. The sixteenth ode would have had some interest for a dramatist whose *Theseus* dealt with the adventure in Crete[1]. A lyric passage in the *Bacchae* (862 ff.) seems to be reminiscent of some beautiful verses in the twelfth ode (83—90). But it is needless to say that in the highest regions of lyric poetry, and in those lyric qualities which pass triumphantly through the test of choral performance, Bacchylides could not vie with Simonides or with Pindar. The distinctive merits of Bacchylides, his transparent clearness, his gift of narrative, his felicity in detail, the easy flow of his elegant verse, rather fitted him to become a favourite with readers. Like Horace, who sometimes imitated him, he was a poet who gave pleasure without demanding effort, a poet with whom the reader could at once feel at home. This, we may well believe, was the secret of his popularity; as would perhaps be still more apparent if time had spared some of his partheneia, and of those lighter compositions, such as the convivial songs, in which a bright fancy and a delicate touch peculiarly qualified him to excel. The earliest mentions of his name, the earliest quotations from his work, occur in the Alexandrian scholia. This is precisely what might have been anticipated ; for the Alexandrian age was an age of readers.

An idea of the vogue which Bacchylides enjoyed in the ancient world may best be formed by considering the sources to which we were indebted for such knowledge of his poetry as existed before the discovery of the Egyptian papyrus. The fragments and notices of Bacchylides collected at the end of this volume are sixty-one in number. The first thirty-four items (as arranged in this edition) are 'fragments' proper, *i.e.* citations of his words. The remaining items are 'notices,' which do not cite his words[2]. In the following survey of the sources, we indicate the item or items which each source furnishes.

---

[1] See Nauck, *Trag. Graec. Fragmenta* (2nd ed.), p. 477.

[2] Elsewhere in this volume, the term 'fragment' (abbreviated 'fr.') is

The oldest sources are the scholia on Homer, Hesiod, *Sources of the fragments and notices.*
Pindar, Aristophanes, Apollonius Rhodius, and Callimachus.
To these are due fragments 6 and 23; and notices 36, 39,
42, 43, 44, 45, 47, 48, 49, 53, 54, 56, 61. Didymus (*flor. c.*
30 B.C.) wrote a special commentary on the Epinikia of
Bacchylides (see fragment 31).

In the Augustan age, Bacchylides is quoted by Dionysius of Halicarnassus on a point of rhythm (fragment 11);
and Strabo corrects him on a point of geography (notice
57). Towards the end of the first century we find Plutarch
speaking of his partheneia (n. 40), and quoting him more
than once (fr. 29, and fr. 3, verses 6—10). In the second
century, he is cited by the grammarian Apollonius Dyscolus
(fr. 31), by the paroemiographer Zenobius (fr. 5, 24), and by
the metrist Hephaestion (fr. 12, 14, 15), on matters pertaining to their respective subjects. Aulus Gellius mentions
him with reference to a detail of mythology (n. 52).
Athenaeus is thoroughly familiar with his poems (fr. 13,
16, 17, 18, 22 : n. 60). Clement of Alexandria draws on
him for illustrations of general sentiments (fr. 21, 32),
especially such as concern the divine nature, and human
destiny (fr. 19, 20 : see also crit. note on ode XIV. 50). In
the third century, Porphyrion indicates an imitation of
Bacchylides by Horace (n. 46); and the rhetor Menander
refers to a class of his hymns (n. 37).

The fourth century continues the series of witnesses.
Himerius touches on the love of Bacchylides for his native
Iulis (n. 59). The commentary of Didymus on the poet's
Epinikia is noticed in the lexicon of Ammonius (n. 35).
From Ammianus Marcellinus we learn that Julian read
Bacchylides with pleasure, and quoted from him a passage
in which the grace lent by purity to rising manhood
was compared with that which a fine artist can give to a
beautiful countenance (n. 41). Servius, the commentator
on Virgil, was acquainted with the 'dithyrambs' of Bacchylides (n. 38, 51).

used, for purposes of reference, as
including the notices. But in this
passage it is convenient to distinguish
fragments in the proper sense from
mere notices. By 'n.' is here meant
a notice.

6—2

At the close of the fifth century, or early in the sixth, Stobaeus culled a large number of passages from the Cean poet, including the well-known fragment of a paean on the blessings of peace (fr. 1, 2, 3, 7, 8, 9, 10, 20, 28). Our debt to Stobaeüs in this respect is larger than to any other single author. Priscian, in the first quarter of the sixth century, illustrates a point of metre from Bacchylides (fr. 27). A few additional fragments or notices come to us from Byzantine or medieval sources, such as the *Etymologicum Magnum* (fr. 25, 30); Joannes Siceliota (fr. 26); Tzetzes (n. 55); Natalis Comes (n. 50). An elegiac inscription for a tripod (fr. 33), and another for a votive shrine (fr. 34), are ascribed to Bacchylides in the Palatine Anthology.

It appears, then, that his writings remained in repute down to the latest period of the ancient civilisation. He was not merely a subject of learned study to specialists in grammar, metre, or mythology. He continued to find readers in the cultivated world at large, among men of letters such as Stobaeus, and among men of affairs such as Julian.

Estimate of Bacchylides in the Περὶ ὕψους. The only definite estimate of Bacchylides which has come down from antiquity is contained in the famous treatise Περὶ ὕψους, 'On elevation of style[1],' traditionally ascribed to Cassius Longinus (*fl. c.* 260 A.D.), but more probably the work of an unknown writer who lived in the first century of our era[2]. The author's aesthetic criticism, often instructive where traits of classical writers are illustrated in detail, sometimes enlarges rhetorically on propositions which now seem platitudes. Thus he insists at

[1] The traditional rendering, 'On the Sublime,' is altogether misleading. However 'sublimity' be defined, the subject of the Περὶ ὕψους is something much wider. It is a discussion of the qualities which raise style to a high excellence.

[2] From the appearance of the *editio princeps* (Robortello's) in 1554 down to the beginning of the nineteenth century, the ascription to Longinus was practically unchallenged. The turning-point was Amati's discovery (in 1808) of the Vatican MS. 285, with the inscription Διονυσίου ἢ Λογγίνου περὶ ὕψους. The question is reviewed, historically and critically, by Prof. W. Rhys Roberts in the introduction to his excellent edition (1899).

some length on the incontrovertible truth that, in literature, high genius, though attended by some faults or lapses, is preferable to flawless merit on a lower level. From that point of view he contrasts Homer with Apollonius Rhodius, Archilochus with Eratosthenes, Sophocles with Ion of Chios, and Pindar with Bacchylides. What we learn from the passage is how this writer defined the most general characteristic, as he deemed it, of Bacchylides. It is, in his phrase, καλλιγραφία, 'elegance of style,' marked by τὸ γλαφυρόν, 'polish,' and equably maintained[1]. That does not tell us much; it is not a help towards appreciating or analysing the qualities distinctive of the poet. Yet it has at least the interest of showing the broad impression which the essayist had received, and which, as he assumes, would be shared by his contemporaries.

Far more instructive are those traces of Bacchylides *Bacchylides and* which remain in the odes of Horace. Paris is carrying *Horace.* Helen across the Aegean; the sea-god Nereus stills the winds, and, addressing him, prophesies the woes that are to come,—the ruin of Troy, and the doom which awaits the false guest of the Spartan king[2]. After the first stanza, which briefly indicates the occasion, the rest of the little ode, which contains only thirty-six verses, is the speech of Nereus. Here, as Porphyrion tells us, Horace was imitating a poem of Bacchylides in which the fate of Ilium was predicted by Cassandra[3]. The type and the scale of that poem may be inferred from the examples which we now possess in the fourteenth, fifteenth, and seventeenth odes of Bacchylides. Horace had seized the motive and caught the inspiration of such pieces. He had noted the peculiar kind of poetical effect which Bacchylides produces by a small picture taken from the heroic mythology,—a short poem which marks a situation, and then breaks off, after foreshadowing a catastrophe. The prophecy

---

[1] Περὶ ὕψους c. XXXIII. Bacchylides and Ion of Chios are described as ἀδιάπτωτοι ('flawless') καὶ ἐν τῷ γλαφυρῷ πάντῃ κεκαλλιγραφημένοι.

[2] Hor. *Carm.* I. 15.
[3] Bacch. fr. 46. See note on fr. 6.

of Nereus in the ode of Horace may be compared, from
this standpoint, to the warning speech of Menelaus with
which the fourteenth ode of Bacchylides abruptly closes.
The integrity of that ode, and of the fifteenth, as the
papyrus has them, is indirectly confirmed by the imitative
ode of Horace, which ends with a like suddenness. We
can perceive also that Horace felt the curious felicity which
is sometimes seen in the Greek poet's phrases. The power
of wine in stimulating the fancy is described by Bacchylides
as γλυκεῖ ἀνάγκα (fr. 16). Horace says of Bacchus, *Tu
lene tormentum ingenio admoves Plerumque duro (C. III.
21. 13 f.)*[1]. His choice of *tormentum* was evidently prompted
by the special associations of the Greek word in such
expressions as ἀνάγκην προστιθέναι or προσάγειν τὰς
ἀνάγκας: though Bacchylides presumably meant nothing
more specific than 'a sweet compulsion.'

There are, indeed, several points of analogy between
the genius of Horace and that of Bacchylides. Both poets
could succeed in stately odes, but were perhaps more
thoroughly at home in poems of a lighter strain. Both
excelled in lyric cameo-work. Both were men of a modest
and genial temper, with a homely philosophy which in-
culcated the virtue of contentment. A notable resemblance
to the tone of Horace appears in those verses of Bacchylides
which proffer a hospitality not set off by 'gold or purple
carpets,' but commended by 'a kindly spirit, and good
wine in Boeotian cups[2].' Under the Empire, during those
centuries when the faculty of comprehending a Pindar
was becoming rarer, the last representative of the classical
Greek lyric may well have retained a quiet popularity by
qualities like those which have endeared Horace to the
modern world.

---

[1] Verses 16—20 of Horace's ode
suggest a general reminiscence of
Bacch. fr. 16. 5—8, and perhaps also
of Pindar fr. 218.

It is unnecessary to suppose that
Horace's *apis Matinae (C.* IV. 2. 28 f.)
was suggested by Bacch. IX. 10 (see

n. there). But the words *caliginosa
nocte* (referring to the hidden future,
in *C.* III. 29. 30) are curiously parallel
with the νυκτὸς δνόφοισιν of Bacchylides in a like context (VIII. 89 f.).

[2] Bacch. fr. 17. Compare Horace
Carm. I. 38 and II. 18.

IV. DIALECT AND GRAMMAR.

The dialect prescribed by tradition for choral lyric poetry was Doric in its general colouring. But the Doricism could be more or less strongly marked, and more or less tempered by an admixture of non-Doric forms, according to the taste of the poet. Indeed, as Pindar shows, the same poet might vary the complexion of his dialect from ode to ode. In the dialect of Bacchylides, the Doricism,—which for him, an Ionian, was purely conventional,—is of the mildest type. It is further distinctive of him that, in numerous instances, he modifies Doric forms by compromises which his own sense of euphony dictated, but which it is difficult to bring under any consistent rules.

He sometimes retains η, instead of the Doric α, in order *Doric α.* to avoid the occurrence of the *a*-sound in two successive syllables. Thus he writes ἀδμήτα (V. 167), but ἄδματοι (X. 84): λῃσταί (XVII. 8), but λαΐδος (XV. 17): φήμα (II. 1), but φαμὶ καὶ φάσω (I. 49). It is not easy to see why he should agree with Pindar in writing προφάτας (VIII. 3, IX. 28), and yet differ from him in writing κυβερνήτας (V. 47, XI. 11). Pindar has ζαλωτός: Bacchylides has ἐπίζηλος (V. 52), πολύζηλος (X. 63), πολυζήλωτος (VII. 10, etc.). His Ἀθάνα (XII. 195, etc.) and Ἀθᾶναι (XVII. 60) may be explained by supposing that, in these instances, the Doric convention of the choral lyric was too strong for him. A like explanation possibly applies to the case of σελάνα (VIII. 29); and of ἀλάθεια (once ἀλαθεία), which is so spelled in five places : in one place (V. 187) the MS. has ἀληθείας, but manifestly by an error. As to στραταγέ (V. 2), used in addressing Hieron, he had no choice ; it was an official title, and he was bound to use the Doric form. In XVI. 121 we find also στραταγέτας. Comparing σκᾶπτρον (III. 70) with ἐπισκήπτων (V. 42, VII. 41), we may perhaps infer that α after σκ displeased the poet's ear in the middle of a word, but not in the first syllable. There are some instances in which the preference of η to Doric α is not peculiar to Bacchylides, but was general in the less strict type of Doricism; such are εἰρήνα (V. 200, etc.), ἥβα (III. 90), μῆλον 'sheep' (V. 109): στῆθος (V. 15). To these, Ἀλκμήνιος (V. 71) may probably be added : several editors of Pindar, including Bergk and W. Christ, give Ἀλκμήνα, with some MS. authority, in his text, though Schröder now prefers Ἀλκμάνα.

The variations in the poet's practice with regard to the Doric α are warnings that, when the MS. has an exceptional η, it should not lightly be altered, unless the case is as clear as it is in V. 187 (ἀληθείας). There are two places in which Blass alters η to α, but in which it appears to me safer to retain η. Each of these must be considered in the light of the euphonic context. (1) X. 45 f. ...παραπλῆγι φρένας | καρτερᾷ ζεύξασ' ἀνάγκᾳ. Here Blass, writing παραπλᾶγι, can appeal to πλάξιππον (V. 97) and πλᾶξεν (X. 86). But, as is shown by the examples given above, we cannot assume that, with Bacchylides, the desire of consistency would have prevailed over considerations of euphony ; and it seems very probable that the number of α sounds in V. 46, καρτερᾷ ζεύξασ' ἀνάγκᾳ, may have led him to write παραπλῆγι. (2) Similarly in X. 92 f., τρισκαίδεκα μὲν τελέους | μῆνας κατὰ δάσκιον ἠλύκταζον ὕλαν, Blass writes ἀλύσκαζον : but the vicinity of -ας, -α, δασκ-, -αν would, in the case of this poet, explain the preference of ἠ- to ἀ.

Other Doricisms. He uses, as Pindar does, the Doric (and Aeolic) inflexion ὄρνιχες (V. 22). The Doric αἰ occurs twice (V. 5 αἴ τις, XVI. 64 αἴ κε), as against some fourteen instances of εἰ or εἴπερ. The Doric ὦτε, 'as,' used by Pindar, is found once (XVI. 105). The Doric ending of the 3rd pers. plur. in -οντι seems to be preferred by Bacchylides under two conditions : viz., (1) when ξ or σσ precedes, as in καρύξοντι (XII. 231) and πτάσσοντι (V. 22); though, for metrical convenience, he can write αὔξουσιν (IX. 45): (2) when the final ι is elided; as in βρίθοντ' (fr. 3. 12), and σεύοντ' (XVII. 10). Pindar uses either the Doric -οντ(ι), or the Aeolic ending (not used by Bacchylides) in -οισι(ν), preferring the latter, as a general rule, where the paragogic ν is required. But Bacchylides can also use -ουσι, as in ἴσχουσι (V. 24), or (for verbs in -έω) -εῦσι, as in οἰκεῦσι (VIII. 43). From verbs in -μι we find φασίν (V. 155), not Pindar's φαντί. Pindar uses both εἰσί(ν) and ἐντί: Bacchylides, only the former (VIII. 88, fr. 19. 2).

The Doric infinitive in -εν occurs four times; ἐρύκεν (XVI. 41), θύεν (XV. 18), ἴσχεν (XVI. 88), φυλάσσεν (XVIII. 25). On the other hand, we find ζώειν (I. 57), λαγχάνειν (IV. 20), λέγειν (III. 67 and V. 164): and, from verbs in -έω, εὐμαρεῖν (I. 65), ὑμνεῖν (VIII. 6). The infin. of φαμί is φάμεν (III. 65), as with Pindar (O. I. 36), not φάναι.

The sporadic Aeolicisms are not numerous. κλεεννός *Aeolic forms.* appears thrice (I. 6, V. 12, 182), as against six instances of κλεινός. Pindar, too, supplies only three examples of κλεεννός (one of these being the superl. κλεεννότατον, P. IV. 280), as against fourteen of κλεινός. Once only does Bacchylides use Μοῖσα (V. 4, the form always employed by Pindar), while in ten places he has Μοῦσα. The Aeolic ἄμμι (XVI. 25) is the only part of the pronoun of the 1st pers. plur. which occurs in his text.

The Aeolic ending of the first aorist in -ξα instead of -σα is used by Bacchylides for some verbs in -άζω or -ίζω; δοίαξε (X. 87): εὐκλέϊξας (VI. 16): παιάνιξαν (XVI. 129). But we find also ἀγκομίσσαι (III. 89), as in Pindar's usage κομίσαι alternates with κομίξαι. When κ precedes, euphony forbids -ξα: hence ᾤκισσεν (VIII. 22), a form used also by Pindar (*Isthm.* VII. 20). As to the Aeolic ἔλλαθι, see note on X. 8. The infin. ἔμμεναι (XVII. 14) is Aeolic and Homeric. Two Aeolic forms of the participle occur; ἐπαθρήσαις (XII. 227) and λαχοῖσαν (XVIII. 13).

The diction of epic poetry contributes another element. *Epic and Ionic forms.* Bacchylides (like Pindar) uses the epic genitive in -οιο, sometimes called Thessalian, as ἀριγνώτοιο (IX. 37). In XVI. 20 φερτάτου should perhaps be φερτάτοι': but in XVI. 42 the ἀμβρότοι' of the MS. should be ἀμβρότου. The genit. plur. of ἀνήρ is once ἀνέρων (XII. 196), though in six other places ἀνδρῶν: the dat. ἄνδρεσσι is used (V. 96, X. 114) as well as ἀνδράσι (fr. 16. 6). We find the epic form κλισίῃσιν

(XII. 135), and the genitive of the epic παιήονες (XV. 8).
The Ionic παρηΐς (whence παρηΐδων, XVI. 13) is not
Homeric, but was probably old in Ionian poetry, for its
use in tragedy dates from Phrynichus (fr. 13) and Aeschylus
(*Theb.* 534, etc.). The Homeric forms, found in the plural
only, are παρειαί (common to the *Iliad* and the *Odyssey*),
and παρήϊα (peculiar to the latter): the Doric is παράα.
The epic ending -σι for the 3rd pers. sing. of the subjunctive is used by Bacchylides in λάχῃσι (XVIII. 3 f.); and
probably in θάλπῃσι[1] (fr. 16. 3).

Digamma. The digamma, which is not written in the papyrus, is
indicated by hiatus or by metre before certain words. The
use of it by Bacchylides is, like Pindar's, inconstant; and
it is also far more limited than Pindar's.

1. ἄναξ takes ϝ in VIII. 45, πολυζήλωτε (ϝ)άναξ: but
not in III. 76 or V. 84 (δ᾽ ἄναξ).

2. ἕκατι takes ϝ in I. 6f.; but not in V. 33, VI. 11, or
X. 9 (δ᾽ ἕκατι).

3. The group of compounds with ἰον. ϝ is assumed
before ἰοβλεφάρων in VIII. 3, ἰοπλόκων in VIII. 72, and
ἰοστέφανον in III. 2: but not before ἰόπλοκοι in XVI. 37,
ἰοστεφάνου in XII. 122, or ἰοστεφάνων in V. 3.

In ode XV., where v. 26 ends with ταλαπενθέα, ϝ is
perhaps assumed before the name Ἰόλαν at the beginning
of the next verse. ϝιόλα occurs on an early vase from
Caere (*Mon. d. Inst.* 6, 33).

4. In V. 75 the ϝ assumed before ἰόν, acc. of ἰός 'arrow,'
is an error due to the analogies of ϝιός 'poison,' and ϝίον
'violet' (see note). In XVI. 131 ἰανθείς, preceded by
φρένα, is possibly a similar instance; though φρένας would
be an easy correction[2].

[1] It is doubtful whether, in such subjunctive forms, the ι adscript is correct: Blass prefers λάχῃσι, θάλπῃσι. See Kühner-Blass, *Gr. Gramm.* II. p. 46. θάλπῃσι in fr. 16. 3 has some-times been taken as an indicative.

[2] In Pind *O.* III. 12 f. we find Ἀλφεοῦ, | ἰανθεὶς ἀοιδαῖς. It is not necessary to suppose ϝ there. If Pindar assumed it in that passage, at any rate he did not do so in *O.* VII. 43 θυμὸν ἰάναιεν, nor in *P.* II. 90 νόον ἰαίνει.

5. ἰσθμός takes ϝ in II. 7, but not in VII. 40. (Pindar's use is similarly inconstant: see n. on II. 7.)

6. The pronoun οἱ (= αὐτῷ) always takes ϝ, except in the second of the two elegiac epigrams attributed to Bacchylides (fr. 34. 3 εὐξαμένῳ γάρ οἱ ἦλθε).

The following words, which sometimes have ϝ in Pindar, do not take it in Bacchylides:—εἶπον (see III. 48): ἐλπίς (III. 75): ἔργον (VIII. 82): ἔρδω (XVII. 43): εἴκοσι (X. 104): ἴδον (XVI. 16): οἶκος (fr. 16. 9).

Hiatus occurs in III. 64 ὦ μεγαίνητε Ἱέρων : *ib.* 92 τρέφει. *Hiatus.* Ἱέρων (where the pause helps): XV. 5 ἀνθεμόεντι Ἕβρῳ (see n.): *ib.* 20 ὀβριμοδερκεῖ ἄζυγα.

The final ο of the genitive-ending -οιο is elided in *Elision.* V. 62, ἀπλάτοι’, and X. 120, Πριάμοι’. Pindar has this elision (*P.* I. 39 Δάλοι’ ἀνάσσων), which is post-homeric. The elision of ι in the dative case is epic : XVII. 49 ἐν χέρεσσ’. The ι of -οντι in the Doric 3rd pers. plur. can also be elided: XVII. 10 σεύοντ’: fr. 3. 12 βρίθοντ’. (So Pindar, *P.* IV. 240, ἀγαπάζοντ’.)

Synizesis is frequent. 1. -εα or -έᾳ : VIII. 2 Νεμέᾳ. In *Synizesis.* XV. 26, ταλαπενθέα, synizesis is not certain. 2. -εο : V. 50 θεός (last word of the verse): *ib.* 95 θεῶν (first word): and so X. 60 θεοφιλές (first word). ἐόντα is scanned as – ◡ in XVIII. 23 f., though as ◡ – ◡ in IV. 19. 3. -εω. The participle of a verb in -έω suffers synizesis in VII. 46 ὑμνέων : but not in V. 152 ὀλιγοσθενέων, or XII. 118 κλονέων. In VII. 46 ἐών is scanned as a monosyllable. In VIII. 32 the ῥιπτῶν of the papyrus is perhaps an error for ῥίπτων rather than for ῥιπτέων. The absence of synizesis in XVII. 12 δοκέω (scanned ◡ ◡ –) is noteworthy as being rare in the 1st pers. sing.: another example is Aesch. *Ag.* 147 καλέω. 4. -ιω. XVII. 39 Κνωσίων (scanned – –). 5. Two doubtful cases should be noted. In XII. 103 βοαθόον, if right, must be scanned ◡ – – : the synizesis is a somewhat harsh one. In III. 22, where the papyrus has ἀγλαϊζέθω γὰρ ἄριστον ὄλβον, the least improbable reading is ἀγλαϊζέτω, ὁ γὰρ ἄριστος ὄλβων : but the synizesis is very harsh.

Contraction. The infinitive-ending of the -έω verbs is contracted: I. 65 εὐμαρεῖν: VIII. 6 ὑμνεῖν. But in I. 34 the -βολοῖ of the MS. is anomalous: we should expect -βολέοι.

Diaeresis. In XV. 7 it seems almost certain that we must read ἀδείᾳ: but the diaeresis in that word is unexampled.

Apocope. Apocope of the simple preposition occurs in XIII. 10 πὰρ χειρός, but elsewhere is confined to compounds; as III. 7 ἀμπαύσας: XII. 58 f. (probably) ἀνδεθεῖσιν: X. 100 ἀντείνων (cp. fr. 13. 4): X. 103 πάρφρονος.

Quantity. It may be useful to add some notes on the practice of Bacchylides with regard to the shortening or lengthening of certain vowels and diphthongs. 1. In XII. 206 καλῶς has ᾱ, which is epic and Ionic, but not Pindaric. 2. The diphthong αι is short in 'Αθαναίων (XVI. 92) and παιάνιξαν (*ib.* 128). 3. The poet has ἴσος in V. 54, but ἴσον in I. 172 and fr. 2. 2. 4. In V. 182 the ι of Πίσαν is short, as with Pindar (see note). 5. κυάνεον has ῡ in XII. 64, but all the poet's compounds with κυανο have ῠ (V. 33, VIII. 53, X. 83, XII. 124, 160, XVI. 1). 6. χρύσεος has the lyric (but non-epic) ῠ in V. 174 and XV. 2.

Vowels before mute and liquid. The frequency with which a naturally short syllable is lengthened before *muta cum liquida* varies considerably in different classes of poets. The Homeric tendency is strongly towards allowing the mute and liquid to make position, *i.e.* to lengthen the preceding vowel. The choral lyric poets lengthen the vowel in such cases more often than they shorten it, but less often than is the Homeric rule. In Attic tragedy the shortening of the vowel is, on the whole, far more frequent than the lengthening[1]. The subjoined table gives the statistics for Bacchylides. I do not claim for the figures that they are always exact; but in every case they are at least approximately correct, and will therefore suffice to indicate the general state of the facts. The column headed *S* shows the number of instances in which a naturally short vowel remains short before each combination of mute and liquid. The column headed *L*

---

[1] Kühner-Blass, *Gramm.* I. p. 303.

shows the number of instances in which such a vowel is lengthened.

	S	L		S	L		S	L		S	L
βλ	0	3	δρ	3	6	κν	0	2	τν	0	1
βρ	3	10	θλ	0	6	κρ	5	18	τρ	10	26
γλ	0	9	θμ	0	2	πλ	5	20	φλ	0	1
γν	0	5	θν	2	1	πν	1	2	φν	1	4
γρ	1	5	θρ	1	5	πρ	5	15	φρ	1	14
δμ	0	5	κλ	5	21	τλ	1	2	χν	1	1
δν	0	2	κμ	0	1	τμ	0	2	χρ	12	9

Thus Bacchylides lengthens the syllable in about 198 places, and leaves it short in about 57, a ratio of between 4 and 3 to 1. It is not surprising to find that an Ionian poet leans to the Homeric usage. So also, and in a still more marked degree, does Simonides[1]. Pindar, on the other hand, neglects 'position' more often than they do, coming nearer in this respect to the practice of Attic tragedy. It will be seen from the table that βλ, γλ, δμ, δν, θλ, θμ, κμ, φλ are among those combinations before which no instance of a short syllable occurs in Bacchylides. Before each of these a short syllable is occasionally found in Pindar[2]. It is worthy of remark that, despite the general Attic tendency towards neglecting position, the poets of the Old Comedy observe it more often than tragedy does: they do not admit a short syllable before βλ, γλ, γν, δμ, δν.

A few details of accidence may be noted.   *Accidence.*

Substantives. In IV. 17 ὀλυμπιονίκας is acc. plur. of the rare fem. form, meaning an 'Olympian victory'; and in X. 8 μουνοπάλαν also is fem., meaning 'the match in wrestling only,' as distinguished from the pancration. In II. 3 ἐπινικίοις is the earliest known example of the word used as a substantive.

---

[1] Schneidewin, preface to the fragments of Simonides, p. xlviii.

[2] Examples:—(1) βλ: Pindar *N.* VIII. 7 ἔβλαστε. (2) γλ: *N.* VII. 52 παντὶ γλυκεῖα. (3) δμ: *P.* VIII. 57 Κάδμου. (4) δν: *P.* X. 72 κεδναί. (5) θλ: *O.* II. 43 ἀέθλοις. (6) θμ: *O.* X. 45 σταθμᾶτο. (7) κμ: *O.* VI. 73 τεκμαίρει. (8) φλ: *P.* III. 12 ἀποφλαυρίξαισα.

Adjectives. The forms τανίσφυρος (III. 60, V. 59) and
τανίφυλλος (X. 55) are given in the papyrus. Euphony
may have been the poet's reason for preferring them to
the more correct τανύσφυρος and τανύφυλλος. The accusatives fem. ὑψικέραν (XV. 22) and καλλικέραν (XVIII. 24)
are formed as if from N. -κέρα. An epic freedom is shown
in forming patronymics: I. 14 Εὐρωπιάδας (= Εὐρωπίδας,
'son of Europa'): VIII. 19 Ταλαϊονίδαν ('son of Talaüs'),
where -ίων is combined with -ίδης, as in Ἰαπετιονίδης. With
regard to declension, it may be noted that πολέων (V. 100)
is gen. plur. *fem.*, as with Callimachus, whereas in Homeric
and Hesiodic usage it is always masc.: the Homeric fem. is
πολλέων or πολλάων, the Pindaric πολλᾶν. Some compound
adjectives are of three terminations: XII. 178 ἀκαμάτᾳ:
IX. 8 ἀπράκταν: XII. 181 πολυπλάγκταν.

Pronouns.   *Personal Pronouns* as used by Bacchylides. *1st pers.
plur.*: D. ἄμμι (XVI. 25), the only part which occurs. *2nd
pers. sing.*: N. σύ: Pindar has also the Doric τύ. G. σέο
and σέθεν (old Ionic and Homeric): Pindar has also σεῦ.
D. σοί, and once, before a vowel, τίν (XVII. 14), both
orthotone: the enclitic is always τοι. (Pindar uses these
three forms; but, with him, σοί can be either orthotone or
enclitic.) *2nd pers. plur.*: D. ὕμμιν is conjectured in VIII.
97; no other part occurs. *3rd pers. sing.* D. οἱ. A. νιν.
The only example of μιν occurs in X. 111, χραῖνόν τέ μιν
αἵματι μήλων, where, after χραῖνον, the poet may have
wished to avoid a third ν-sound. (μιν is traditional in
a few passages of Pindar, but the tendency of recent
criticism has been to correct it into νιν: see Rumpel,
Lex. Pind. s.v., and Schröder, *Proleg.* to Pindar, p. 37.)
The acc. of the 1st pers. sing. is once αὐτόν (XVII. 41).
3rd pers. plur. A. νιν (VIII. 15, where see n.).

      Possessive pronouns. 2nd pers. sing., σός or Doric τεός
(both used by Pindar). For the 3rd pers., σφέτερος is
either singular, 'his' (III. 36), or plural, 'their' (X. 50),
as with Pindar and Aeschylus. σφέτερος as = ἑός, 'his,'
occurs first in Hes. *Scut.* 90.

Verbs.   The infinitive of εἰμί appears in three forms. I. ἔμμεν,

V. 144, XVII. 31, 56, in all three places followed by a consonant. This form, which is Thessalian Aeolic, also old Ionic and epic, occurs in the *Iliad* once (18. 364), and a few times in the *Odyssey* (as 14. 332), but only before a vowel; whence some would write ἔμμεν', as it is now written in Sappho 2. 2. Pindar uses it both before a vowel and (like Bacchylides) before a consonant. 2. ἔμμεναι, XVII. 14, is Lesbian Aeolic, old Ionic and epic. 3. εἶμεν, VIII. 48. This is the 'milder' Doric form, the 'stricter' being ἦμεν. Pindar has only ἔμμεν, ἔμμεναι: for in the one place of his text where εἶναι is traditional, *Isthm.* V. [VI.] 20, ἔμμεν is now restored. The other Homeric forms, ἔμεν and ἔμεναι, are not used either by him or by Bacchylides. The participle is with both poets ἐών: but Bacchylides once (III. 78) has εὖντα, a Doric form used by Theocritus (II. 3). It seems possible that ἐόντα (- ◡) should be corrected to εὖντα in XVIII. 23 f.: but the synizesis in ἐών (VII. 46) shows that such a change is not necessary.

Notes on the following verbal forms will be found in the commentary on the passages where they severally occur:—ἀμαρτεῖν=ὀμαρτεῖν (VIII. 103 f. and XVII. 46). ἀνέπαλτο (X. 65). δίνασεν (XVI. 18). δίνηντο (XVI. 107). ἔλλαθι (X. 8). ἐρχθέντος and ἔργμενον (XII. 65 f., 207). ἷξον (XII. 149). ἵσταν (X. 122). ὄρνυο (XVI. 76). πέφαται (VIII. 52). προσήνεπεν (XIV. 9).

Examples of rare middle forms are κομπάσομαι (VII. 42): νωμᾶται (V. 26 f.): ὑφαιρεῖται (probable in VIII. 18): ὠρίνατο (XII. 112).

To the epic adverbs εἴσαντα and ἄντην, Bacchylides *Adverbs.* adds a new form, εἰσάνταν (V. 110). In XVI. 91 the unmetrical ἐξόπιθεν of the MS. should probably be corrected to the Aeschylean ἐξόπιν. The Homeric τῶ ('therefore') occurs in XVI. 39. It may be noticed that the enclitic νυν is found only in XVIII. 8. The epic and Aeschylean τώς, not used by Pindar, stands in V. 31.

εἰς occurs once (before a), XIV. 43 : elsewhere the form *Preposi-* is always ἐς. The poetical form ὑπαί appears in XII. 139 f., *tions.*

and παραί (MS. ΠΑΡΑ) must be restored in X. 103. In X. 21 we have the earliest example of ἦρα used, like χάριν, as a preposition with the genitive.

Syntax.

In the syntax of Bacchylides there is little which is distinctive; but a few points are deserving of remark.

Noun.

I. Noun. 1. *Number.* A dual substantive with a plural adjective occurs in XVII. 46 δύο φῶτε μόνους. 2. *Case.* βρύειν is construed, first with the dative, and then with the genitive, in two successive clauses, with no apparent difference of sense (III. 15 f.). After the passive θαυμάζομαι, the admirers are denoted (as in Thuc. I. 41 § 4) by the dative case (I. 42). An accusative of the person is combined, in epic fashion, with an accusative of 'the part affected': τὸν δ' εἷλεν ἄχος κραδίην (X. 85). 3. *Gender.* V. 77 ψυχὰ προφάνη Μελεάγρου | καί νιν εὖ εἰδὼς προσεῖπεν. This is in the style of the epic poets, who, when they describe a person by a periphrasis with βίη, ἴς, or ψυχή, use the masculine participle (see n.).

Verb.

II. Verb. 1. *Tense.* In X. 110—112 the imperfects τεῦχον, χραῖνον, ἵσταν denote the series of things which the persons 'proceeded' to do. This is worth noticing in connexion with two other passages where the aorist has been conjecturally substituted for the imperfect which stands in the MS. (1) In XIV. 38 Blass alters σάμαινεν to σάμανεν: but the former is parallel with ἆγον in verse 37, which means in strictness, 'they proceeded to lead.' (2) In XVI. 51, where the same editor changes ὕφαινε to ὕφανε, the imperfect (though preceded and followed by aorists) admits of a similar defence; especially as the reference is to a process of thought.—*Tenses of the Infinitive.* After μέλλω we find the present inf. in III. 31 and XV. 18, but the future inf. in XII. 165. In V. 164 τελεῖν is ambiguous, but probably the future. The aorist inf. is regularly used where a moment (as distinguished from a continuing action) is indicated: V. 30 (ἰδεῖν), 161 (προσιδεῖν): X. 88 (πᾶξαι): XII. 43 ἰδεῖν (where see note).

2. *Mood.* (i) In III. 57 f. we have an example of the indicative used in a relative clause expressing a general condition : ἄπιστον οὐδέν, ὅ τι θεῶν μέριμνα τεύχει (instead of ὅ τι ἂν...τεύχῃ). The alteration (made by Blass) of τεύχει into τεύχῃ is unnecessary : see the note *ad loc.* (ii) The subjunctive is used with εἰ: VIII. 86 εἴπερ καὶ θάνῃ τις. Also with αἴ κε, after a verb of knowing : XVI. 64 εἴσεαι...αἴ κε...κλύῃ. Both usages are Homeric. (iii) The optative with εἰ is used to express a general supposition in a dependent clause, after a present indicative in the principal clause : XV. 187 f. χρὴ δ'...αἰνεῖν..., εἴ τις εὖ πράσσοι (see n.).—The optative stands in a relative clause after a hypothetical optative with ἄν in the principal clause : XVI. 41—44, οὐ γὰρ ἂν θέλοιμ'...ἐπεὶ δαμάσειας.—The optative of indefinite frequency occurs in I. 33 f. ὁπότε... (συμ)βολοῖ. (iv) The infinitive, as a verbal noun, takes the definite article in I. 64 f. τὸ...εὐμαρεῖν (nominative case). The articular infinitive, which is post-homeric, occurs first in Pindar, and always as a subject nominative, unless an exception is to be recognised in *O.* II. 97 (τὸ λαλαγῆσαι θέλων).

III. The use of prepositions by Bacchylides is, on the whole, normal ; but several points are noteworthy. *Prepositions.*

1. ἀμφί (i) with the dative has either (a) the local sense, XVII. 52 f. στέρνοις...ἀμφί: or (b) the figurative, 'in respect to,' 'concerning'; I. 39 ἀμφί τ' ἱστορίᾳ: IX. 44 ἀμφὶ βοῶν ἀγέλαις. (ii) With the accusative it means either 'around,' X. 18f. ἀμφ' Ἀλεξίδαμον...ἔπεσον (where motion is implied), or merely describes position in a certain region, IX. 34 ἀμφί τ' Εὔβοιαν. Pindar joins ἀμφί with the genitive also (in the sense, 'concerning'): but this use does not occur in Bacchylides.

2. ἀνά with accusative occurs in V. 66 f., Ἴδας ἀνά... πρῶνας ('up along'). [In III. 50 ἀνὰ ματρὶ...ἔβαλλον = ἀνέβαλλον.]

3. διά (i) with genitive denotes that through which a passage is being made: VIII. 47 στείχει δι' εὐρείας κελεύθου: XII. 52 (of a sword) χωρεῖν διὰ σώματος. (ii) With

accusative, it denotes the range throughout which a motion extends: XIV. 40 f. δι᾿ εὐρεῖαν πόλιν ὀρνύμενοι: VIII. 30 f. δι᾿ ἀπείρονα κύκλον | φαῖνε θαυμαστὸν δέμας,—where the prep. may be rendered 'amidst,' but properly means that the sensation made by the sight went *right through* the vast crowd. (The athlete is not running, but throwing the quoit.) The causal διά also occurs: III. 61 δι᾿ εὐσέβειαν (cp. VI. 4 and XII. 156).

4. ἐπί (i) with genitive denotes position 'on': XVI. 84 f. ἐπ᾿ ἰκρίων σταθείς: fr. 3. 2 ἐπὶ βωμῶν. (ii) With dative: (*a*) VII. 9 ἐπ᾿ ἀνθρώποισιν, 'among men' (where see n.): (*b*) VIII. 12 ἄθλησαν ἐπ᾿ Ἀρχεμόρῳ, 'in memory of him': (*c*) V. 83 ψυχαῖσιν ἔπι φθιμένων, 'against them' (and so in 133). (iii) With acc., of movement 'to': VIII. 41 ἦλθεν καὶ ἐπ᾿ ἔσχατα Νείλου; XII. 88, 149, etc.

5. κατά (i) with genitive occurs once: XVI. 94 ff. κατὰ λειρίων ὀμμάτων δάκρυ χέον, 'down from.' (ii) With the accusative, this prep. is notably frequent in Bacchylides, as meaning (*a*) 'throughout,' X. 93 κατὰ δάσκιον...ὕλαν: (*b*) 'along down,' XVI. 87 f. κατ᾿ οὖρον: (*c*) 'according to,' IX. 32 κατ᾿ αἶσαν: (*d*) of time, 'during,' XVIII. 26 f. κατ᾿ εὐφεγγέας ἀμέρας.

6. μετά is found only twice: (i) with genitive, X. 123 μετ᾿ Ἀτρειδᾶν: (ii) with dative, V. 30 μετ᾿ ἀνθρώποις, 'among' them.

7. παρά (i) with genitive, of the giver: III. 11 παρὰ Ζηνός: so XV. 35; XVIII. 3, 13. Also in the phrase τὸ πὰρ χειρός (XIII. 10, where see n.). (ii) With dative, either of persons, VIII. 84 παρὰ δαίμοσι: or of river-banks, παρὰ ῥεέθροις, III. 20; cp. V. 64, XII. 150. So Pindar, O. I. 21 παρ᾿ Ἀλφεῷ, X. 85 παρὰ...Δίρκᾳ. (iii) With accusative, denoting (*a*) *motion to* a place, especially to the banks of a river, VIII. 39, XVIII. 39; but also fr. II. 3 f. παρὰ...ναὸν ἐλθόντας: cp. Pind. N. V. 10 πὰρ βωμὸν...στάντες. (*b*) *motion along*, III. 6, V. 38. (*c*) *extension* or *position along* (without motion), IX. 29 f., X. 119, XII. 58 παρὰ βωμόν, XV. 12 παρὰ...ναόν, XVI. 119 νᾶα παρὰ λεπτόπρυμνον φάνη (unless φάνη be taken as implying motion). (*d*) *of time*, 'in

the course of,' 'during': fr. 7. 4 τό τε παρ' ἆμαρ καὶ νύκτα.
(In Pind. *P.* XI. 68 παρ' ἆμαρ = ' on alternate days.')

8. **περί** (i) with genitive, (*a*) in a local sense, 'around,'
XVII. 51 κρατὸς πέρι (κρατὸς ὕπερ MS.): (*b*) denoting that
'for' which one strives, V. 124 f. περί...δορᾶς μαρνάμεθ'.
(ii) With dative, (*a*) in local sense, VII. 50 περὶ κρατί,
XVII. 47 περὶ...ὤμοις: (*b*) denoting the prize, just like
(i) (*b*), XII. 55 περὶ στεφάνοισι.

9. **πρός** (i) with dative, once, X. 23 πρὸς γαίᾳ πεσόντα
(like *Od.* 5. 415 βάλῃ ποτὶ πέτρῃ, etc.) (ii) With accusative, of *motion to* or *towards*, V. 45, 149: X. 100.—The
constr. with the genitive does not occur.

10. **σύν** is frequent, occurring about 31 times (cp. μετά).
The temporal sense may be noted: X. 23 κείνῳ γε σὺν
ἄματι (see note): *ib.* 125 σὺν ἅπαντι χρόνῳ.

11. **ὑπό** (i) with genitive, 'from under,' XII. 139 f.,
XVI. 17 : of the agent, V. 43 f., IX. 48, XII. 154. (ii) With
dative, (*a*) 'under,' IX. 4 (?): XII. 125 f. ὑπὸ κύμασιν, *ib.* 166
ὑπ' Αἰακίδαις: (*b*) to denote an attendant circumstance,
where it may be rendered 'with': III. 17 λάμπει δ' ὑπὸ
μαρμαρυγαῖς ὁ χρυσός (see note). (iii) With accusative,
once, XVI. 30: λέχει Διὸς ὑπὸ κρόταφον Ἴδας | μιγεῖσα.
This is noteworthy, since the sense is simply 'beneath'
(= ὑπὸ κροτάφῳ). Elsewhere, when ὑπό governs the acc.,
and motion is not implied, at least the idea of extension
('*along* under') is present, as it is (*e.g.*) in Pind. *P.* X. 15, referring to a victory in running gained ὑπὸ Κίρρας...πέτραν.
It would perhaps be difficult to find an exact parallel for
the use of ὑπό with acc. which Bacchylides admits here.

12. *Anastrophe.* In a few passages where the
preposition stands after the substantive, an attributive
genitive follows: IV. 6 ἀρετᾷ σὺν ἵππων : V. 83 ψυχαῖσιν
ἔπι φθιμένων: *ib.* 133 ψυχαῖς ἔπι δυσμενέων. The other
instance is XII. 150 ναυσὶ δ' εὐπρύμνοις παραί.

13. *Tmesis.* (*a*) The preposition precedes the verb, as
in III. 50 f. ἀνὰ ματρὶ χεῖρας | ἔβαλλον. (*b*) Or follows it ;
IV. 20 λαγχάνειν ἄπο μοῖραν (see note): XVIII. 7 βάλωσιν
ἀμφὶ τιμάν.

IV. Particles. 1. ἦ is affirmative in XII. 54, XVII. 41:
interrogative in XVII. 5, where three questions are asked by
ἦ...ἦ...ἤ...; The Homeric interrogative ἦ ῥα (*Il.* 5. 421)
stands in V. 165, where Blass writes ἦρα (ἦ + ἄρα): see
Kühner-Blass, *Gramm.* I. 217. 2. The intensive particles
γε μέν occur in III. 63 ὅσοι γε μέν (where μέν merely
emphasizes the limiting γε): and *ib.* 90 ἀρετᾶς γε μέν (where
the sense is that of the Attic γε μήν, 'however'). 3. μέν
is used, without a corresponding δέ, in III. 15 f. (see note),
IX. 47, XVI. 1. 4. The epic combination δέ τε is found in
XII. 129 (see note), and fr. 3. 1. 5. In XV. 5 f. the dis-
junctive εἴτε is followed by ἤ in the second clause. In
XVIII. 29—35 we have εἴτ᾽ οὖν...ἤ ῥα...ἦ.... 6. ὥστε
occurs only once, viz. in XII. 124, where it means 'as' (see
note). In this sense Pindar employs ὧτε (found also in
Bacchylides, XVI. 105), while he uses ὥστε only with the
infinitive.

V. METRES.

With the exception of Odes XV and XVI, the poems of
Bacchylides are seldom difficult from a metrical point of
view. The metres are well-known, and his treatment of
them is simple. Such difficulties as occur (outside of the
two odes named above) are confined, for the most part, to
verses in which the text seems to be corrupt, or at least
doubtful.

I. The metre most largely used by Bacchylides is that
which is generally known as 'dactylo-epitritic'[1]: *e.g.*,

$$\text{Εὔμοιρε Συρακοσίων}$$
$$\text{ἱπποδινάτων στραταγέ (V. 1 f.).}$$

One of its two elements is dactylic, as seen in the first of these
two verses. The other is the so-called *epitritus*, – ◡ – –, as

---

[1] The term 'dactylo-epitritic' is
modern. Prof. Blass prefers to describe
verses of this measure as being κατ᾽
ἐνόπλιον εἶδος, for reasons fully given
in the Preface to his Bacchylides,
pp. xxxv ff. (3rd ed.). He observes
that in the Pindaric scholia they are
called δίμετρα or τρίμετρα προσοδιακά.
Dr W. Headlam would call them
simply 'Dorian.'

seen in the second, a trochaic dipody, $- \cup - \cup$, with the second $- \cup$ slowed down to $- -$. The name 'epitritus' means that the time-value of $- \cup$ is to that of $- -$ as 3 to 4. It is possible that when epitriti were combined with dactyls, the first syllable of the epitritus had the time-value of $\llcorner$, so that the measure became ♩. ♪ ♩ ♩, and the first half of it was equal in time to a dactyl.

Stesichorus, the founder of the τριὰς ἐπῳδική in the Dorian choral lyric, is supposed to have been the first who composed dactylo-epitritic strophes. An epitritic trimeter, like Pindar's ἑσπέρας ὀφθαλμὸν ἀντέφλεξε Μήνα (*O*. III. 5), was called Στησιχόρειον. Such verses alternated, in the composition of Stesichorus, with long dactylic measures, of which the dominant rhythm was the ἐνόπλιος, $- \cup \cup - \cup \cup - -$. It was left for later poets, Simonides, Pindar, and Bacchylides, to effect a subtler and more artistic fusion of the two elements. The dactylo-epitritic metre was well-suited for choral odes on a large scale, and especially for such as had an epic character. It is used by Pindar in nineteen of his forty-four extant epinikia. His first Pythian might be instanced as an ode which exhibits all the capabilities of this metre in their most splendid form; and his fourth Pythian, as an unrivalled example of its adaptation to heroic narrative.

Among the nineteen odes of Bacchylides represented by the papyrus, no fewer than ten are dactylo-epitritic. That number includes all his odes of victory, except those three (II, IV, VI) which are merely short songs; also the poem (XIV) on the mission of Menelaus and Odysseus to Troy, which has a kinship in subject and in style with the epic hymns of Stesichorus. The same metre appears in the epode of Ode III; where the strophe, though logaoedic, prepares for the other measure by verses (1—3) containing rhythms common to logaoedics and dactylo-epitrites[1].

But the use of the dactylo-epitritic strophe was by no means confined to epinikia or to poems on epic themes.

[1] See Dr W. Headlam in *Journal of Hellenic Studies* XXII. p. 214, n. 10 (1902).

Pindar applies it to the dithyramb (fr. 57); Bacchylides, to the hymn (fr. 2), the paean (fr. 3), the hyporcheme (fr. 10), the prosodion (fr. 9). What was perhaps less to be expected, Pindar found it suitable also for choral skolia (fr. 99—101); and Bacchylides for some kindred songs of love or of festivity (fr. 14, 16). It may be noted that neither Pindar nor Bacchylides ever uses the combination $- \cup - \cup - \circ$ (the so-called 'ithyphallicum') in a dactylo-epitritic strophe, though it is frequent with Simonides, Aeschylus, and Euripides. This observation was made long ago by Westphal (who, for Bacchylides, had only the old fragments). and is now confirmed (as Blass remarks, *Praef.* p. XLV) by the new papyrus.

Pindar's mode of composition in his dactylo-epitritic strophes is, on the whole, very different from that of Bacchylides. Pindar writes in ample periods, which flow on without marked division into smaller 'members' or 'kola.' The tendency of Bacchylides, on the other hand, is to divide his periods rhythmically into short kola, usually of two or three *metra* each. His *technique* in this respect has been carefully analysed by Dr Paul Maas[1]. These kola are so regularly divided that they do not essentially differ from periods except in being shorter. They are so compact, and so sharply marked off, that they tend to obscure the unity of the period. In many cases there is room for difference of opinion as to the points at which, within a strophe of Bacchylides, the periods begin and end[2]. Briefly, in the dactylo-epitrites of Pindar, the most evident unit is the period: in those of Bacchylides, it is the kolon. This characteristic of the Cean's versification is sometimes, as Maas remarks, scarcely in accord with the dignity of his subject-matter. 'It almost seems,' he adds, 'that in one place the poet himself became conscious of this. Read

[1] *Kolometrie in den Daktyloepi-triten des Bakchylides:* In *Philologus*, vol. LXIII. pp. 297—309 (1904).

[2] A division of periods is indicated by Blass (3rd ed.) in respect to Ode I; III (epode); v (strophe, doubtfully as to epode); VIII; x (doubtfully). Paul Maas (p. 298, n. 1) differs from the division of periods by Blass in v (epode), and x (epode), agreeing as to these with O. Schröder, *Hermes*, 1903, pp. 240 ff.

the hexameter which announces the apparition of Meleager, the only one which Bacchylides allows to run on with rhythmical division into kola (v. 68—70), ταῖσιν δὲ μετέπρεπεν εἴδωλον θρασυμέμνονος ἐγχεσπάλου Πορθανίδα : it stands out among the short lines of the poem just as Meleager does among the other shades.'

It has often been held that the verses, mostly very short, into which the papyrus divides the poems of Bacchylides, do not represent the division intended by the poet himself. Certainly the Alexandrian κωλισταί treated Pindar's periods in a similar fashion, though, in his case, the division into short verses was, as a rule, inadmissible. But the result of Maas's investigation is to show that, in the case of Bacchylides, the manuscript division is largely confirmed by the internal evidence of the metrical text. It may be noted that, while the lines in the MS. are usually short, there are three instances of long verses (tetrameters); and two of them probably represent the metrical intention of the poet. These two are :—(1) The second verse of the epode in Ode VIII, as v. 46, ἐγγόνων γεύσαντο καὶ ὑψιπύλου Τροίας ἕδος. (2) The tenth verse of the strophe in Ode IX, as v. 48, ἄνδρα πολλῶν ὑπ' ἀνθρώπων πολυζήλωτον εἶμεν. Those verses did not admit of a rhythmical division into shorter kola. In the third instance, however, the papyrus gives one verse where (as Maas thinks) the poet made two. This is the sixth verse of the strophe in Ode XIV : Λαρτιάδᾳ Μενελάῳ | τ' Ἀτρεΐδᾳ βασιλεῖ, = v. 48 Πλεισθενίδας Μενέλαος | γάρυϊ θελξιεπεῖ. Here considerations of calligraphy may have come in ; since, if the verse had been divided, two short lines would have stood between two long ones. Conversely, the MS. in some places gives two verses, the second being a monometer, where Bacchylides probably made only one. Three instances occur in Ode XII. (1) Strophe, verses 1 and 2, as 46 f., οἵαν τινὰ δύσλοφον ὠ-| μηστᾷ λέοντι. (2) Strophe, vv. 7 and 8, as 52 f.: χωρεῖν διὰ σώματος, ἐ-|γνάμφθη δ' ὀπίσσω. (3) Epode, vv. 2 and 3, as 92 f.: ἀνθέων δόνακός τ' ἐπιχω-|ρίαν ἄθυρσιν. The same period occurs in nine other places, and in all

of them is given by the MS. as *one* verse: see v. 9 (ἦ σὺν
Χαρίτεσσι βαθυζώνοις ὑφάνας): *ib.* 31, 33: VIII. 3: IX. 1:
X. 9, 12, 30: XIV. 2.   Two other examples must be added:
XI. 1, 2, ὡσεὶ κυβερνήτας σοφός, ὑμνοάνασ|σ' εὔθυνε Κλειοῖ:
XIII. 2, 3, εὖ μὲν εἱμάρθαι παρὰ δαίμονος ἀν|θρώποις
ἄριστον.   In these two cases, the reason of the division is
more obvious.   Without it, the first verse would have
consisted of 17 syllables, and the second of 16; whereas
the normal limit of length for a verse in the papyrus is 15.
There are several instances in which, within the same
poem, the kolometry of the MS. is inconsistent with itself,
verses metrically identical being rightly divided in some
places, and wrongly in others.   These anomalies are
indicated in the notes appended to the metrical schemes
of the Odes.   See note 4 on I, n. 1 on V, n. 3 on IX, n. 1 on
XII, n. 5 on XVI.

The Alexandrian division of verses in the papyrus of
Bacchylides did not rest on metrical principles syste-
matically applied.   It was, no doubt, the aim to make
such a division as seemed to suit the rhythm; but formal
considerations, reasons of space and of calligraphy, also
came into account; and in particular there was a wish to
limit as far as possible the number of instances in which a
word was divided between two verses.   The result was a
division which, in fact, usually coincided with that which
Bacchylides seems to have intended; but the coincidence
was in some measure accidental.

One of Maas's remarks on the poet's versification is especially
deserving of attention in view of its bearing on the criticism of
the text.   It concerns a rule which had been regularly observed
by the lyric poets (with the exception of Pindar), as can be seen
in the verses of Alcman, Anacreon, Simonides, and Aeschylus.
This general rule may be stated as follows.   In a dactylo-epitritic
period, when a verse ends with $\perp \cup \underset{\smile}{}$, and the syllable *before* $\perp \cup \underset{\smile}{}$
is long, that syllable is normally not the last of a word.   The
rhythmical principle is the same as in Porson's law regarding the
final cretic in an iambic trimeter.   Thus in the verse, ἁ τρισευδαίμων ἀνήρ (III. 10), the syllable δαι- is long: were it the last of a

word, the rule would be broken. The same general rule applies to a long syllable *after* $\overset{\_}{} \cup -$ at the beginning of the verse: thus ὃς παρὰ Ζηνὸς λαχών (III. 11) is normal, but (*e.g.*) ὃς πάρεδρος Ζηνὸς ὤν would be abnormal. The exceptions to this rule in Bacchylides are comparatively rare. In Ode v, for example, there is only one (v. 12 -πει κλεεννὰν ἐς πόλιν). In Ode I alone are such exceptions frequent: there we have νείμας ἀποπλέων ᾤχετ᾽ ἐς (v. 12 = 122 Blass): ποσσίν τ᾽ ἐλαφρός, πατρίων (35): -ξος Ἀπόλλων ὤπασεν (38): αἰῶν᾽ ἔλυσεν, πέντε παῖ- (43): πρώτοις ἐρίζει· παντί τοι (58). Maas accounts for this peculiarity in Ode I by suggesting that Bacchylides was there imitating the *technique* of Pindar, the first poet, it seems, who broke through the old rule. Even when the syllable before the final $- \cup \overset{\vee}{}$ is *short*, it is not often the last of a word, as in v. 4 ἄγαλμα, τῶν γε νῦν: *ib.* 19 εὐρυάνακτος ἄγγελος: XI. 4 ἐς γὰρ ὀλβίαν: XII. 190 μεγάλαισιν ἐλπίσιν: XIV. 190 μέλπετ᾽, ὦ νέοι: XIV. 51 ἄπαντα δέρκεται.

As it can be shown that (except in Ode I) Bacchylides usually observed this rule, Maas holds that the following conjectures are inadmissible:—

(1) III. 26 Ζηνὸς τελε[ίου νεύμασιν.
(2) V. 8 δεῦρ᾽ ἄθρησον <σὺν> νόῳ.
(3) VIII. 20 ...Πολυνείκεϊ πλα[γκτῷ πρόξενον.
(4) VIII. 77 Αὐτόμηδες, νασι]ώταν.
(5) XII. 97 ἔτι[κτεν Πηλέα.
(6) XII. 124 θύων ναυβάτας.

With regard to (1), (2), (3), (4), and (6), I may add that the conjecture in each case introduces an exception to the rule such as does not occur in any corresponding verse of the same Ode: see III. 12, 40, 54, 68, 96: VIII. 46, 72, 98: XII. 58, 91, 157, 190, 222. As to (5), XII. 97, there is another exception in a corresponding verse of the same ode; for v. 64 ends with καλύψῃ, λείπεται (where ὅταν in v. 63 excludes κάλυψε).

II. Another class of metres used by Bacchylides is the 'logaoedic[1].' The origin of the name is disputed; but perhaps no account of it is more probable than the old one, given by Aristides Quintilianus (p. 51), that it originated with the Lesbian poets, and was applied to such a

---

[1] Prof. Blass prefers the term, κατὰ βακχεῖον εἶδος. See his Preface, pp. XLVIII ff.

verse as Sappho's ἠρά|μαν μὲν ἐγὼ σέθεν, Ἄτθι, πάλαι
πόκα. Here a trochee is prefixed to dactyls. The 'song,'
ἀοιδή, was regarded as beginning with the dactyls: the
trochee, leading up ·to the song but outside of it, was
considered as 'prose,' λόγος. At all events, the essence of
'logaoedic' metre lay in combining rhythms of two distinct
kinds, the dactylic, and the trochaic or iambic :—

> Βασιλεῦ τᾶν ἱερᾶν 'Αθανᾶν,
> τῶν ἀβροβίων ἄναξ 'Ιώνων (XVII. 1 f.).

Bacchylides uses logaoedics in his three minor epinikia
(II, IV, VI); in the strophe (though not in the epode) of
III; and in a dithyramb (XVII). Pindar's employment of
the metre was less restricted ; some of his larger odes are
logaoedic: and his verses of this kind are usually more
complex in structure than those of Bacchylides.

III.   Four of the odes are neither dactylo-epitritic nor
logaoedic: viz. XV, XVI, XVIII, XIX.   As to the metres used
in these, see the notes prefixed and appended to the
metrical schemes.

IV.   Viewed with regard to metre, the 32 lyric fragments of Bacchylides may be classed as follows.   The
numbering of the fragments is that used in this edition.

1.   *Dactylo-epitritic.*   Fragments 1, 2, 3, 6, 9, 10, 14, 16,
18, 19, 20, 21, 22, 24, 28.

2.   *Logaoedic.*   Fragments 4, 7, 8.

3.   *Other metres.*   (i) *Iambic.*   Fragments 15, 27, 30
(ii) *Trochaic.*   13, 17, 32.   (iii) *Paeonic or cretic.*   11, 12
23, 25.

4.   *Doubtful.*   Fragments 5, 26, 29, 31.

A. ΕΠΙΝΙΚΟΙ.

ODE I.

Dactylo-epitritic.

Strophe (8 verses).

```
ᵕᵕ − −, − ᵕ ᵕ −, ¯
    ᵕ ᵕ − ᵛ, − ᵕ − ∧ |
− ᵕ ᵕ −, ᵕ ᵕ − ¯
    −, − ᵕ ᵕ −, ᵕ ᵕ − − |
5  − ᵕ ᵕ −, ᵕ ᵕ − ¯
    −, − ᵕ − ᵛ, − ᵕ − ∧ |
− − ᵕ −, − − ᵕ −, ¯
    − ᵕ − −, − ᵕ − ∧
```

Epode (7 verses).

```
− ᵕᵕ −, ᵕ ᵕ −
    −, − ᵕᵕ −, ᵕ ᵕ − − |
− ᵕ − −, − ᵕ ᵕ −, ᵕ ᵕ − − ¯
    − ᵕ ᵕ −, ᵕ ᵕ − −
5  − ᵕ − −, − ᵕ − ᵛ
    − ᵕ ᵕ −, ᵕ ᵕ − −, ¯
    − ᵕ − −, − ᵕ − −, − ᵕ − ᵛ
```

Notes.

1. The ode, when entire, probably contained 8 'systems' (strophe, antistrophe, epode). The part preserved with approximate completeness includes the last three systems. In this part, the *first* and *second* verses of each strophe and antistrophe are wrongly divided in the MS. See in this edition vv. 6 f., Διὸς Εὐκλείου δὲ ƒέκα-|τι, where the MS. divides thus, ƒέ|κατι: similarly in vv. 29 f., 37 f., 52 f., 60 f. [The end of v. 14 is mutilated, but the position of ...δεκάτωι in 15 shows that the same thing happened there also.] But it would seem that the earlier part of the ode, fragments of which have been conjecturally pieced together by Blass, exhibited at least two instances in which this error was avoided: if, that is, the first verse of one antistrophe ended with ἀελίου (v. 55 Blass), and of another with . εντερομαι (μὲν στέρομαι, v. 78 Bl.). The point is worthy of notice, since, if this was the case, it is a somewhat curious example of that inconsistency which occasionally appears elsewhere also in the kolometry of the papyrus.

2. In the second verse of the strophe, the fourth syllable is everywhere long except in ant. 8 (v. 61), πενίας τ᾽ ἀμαχάνου. In the sixth verse of the strophe, the fifth syllable is everywhere long except in str. 7 (v. 34), χρεῖός τι συμ]βολοῖ μάχας.

3. In epode 7 the third verse (47) has the form, θῆκεν ἀντ᾽ εὐεργεσιᾶν, λιπαρῶν τ᾽ ἀλ-. But in epode 8,—the only other which has been preserved,—

the MS. gives (v. 70), ὅσσον ἂν ζώῃ χρόνον τόνδε λάχεν τι-. Blass retains this, holding that −◡−− could replace −◡◡−. But that seems, in this place, a metrical impossibility. It can scarcely be doubted, I think, that the poet wrote, ὅσσον ἂν ζώῃ, λάχε τόνδε χρόνον τι-. There are some certain instances in this papyrus of words erroneously transposed (see commentary). Here the transposition, if not merely inadvertent, may have been prompted by the wish to bring χρόνον into the relative clause.

4. The seventh verse of epode 5 becomes two in the MS.: ναυσὶ πεντή- κοντα σὺν | Κρητῶν ὁμίλῳ. But this error is not made in either of the two corresponding verses which remain (51, 70).

ODE II.

Logaoedic.

Strophe (5 verses).

◡−◡−, −◡◡−, ◡−− ∧ |
−◡◡≏, −◡◡−, ⁻
◡−◡−, −◡◡−⁻
◡◡◡, −◡, ◡−, ◡−⁻
5   −◡, −◡, ◡−, −∧

Epode (4 verses).

◡−◡−, −◡◡−,
◡−◡−, −◡◡−,
◡−, −◡, ◡−, ◡−,
−−, −◡, ◡−, −∧

The first three verses of the strophe, and the first two of the epode, consist of iambic dipodiae and choriambi. The fourth verse of the strophe is a glyconic (with ◡◡◡ as first foot): so also is the third verse of the epode (but with ◡− as first foot). The fifth verse of the strophe is a pherecratic (with −◡ as first foot): as is also the fourth verse of the epode (with −− in that place).

Notes.

1. In verse 2, ἐς Κέον ἱεράν, χαριτώ-, the resolution of the fourth syllable of the first choriamb (which does not recur in the antistrophe, v. 6) might suggest that we should read ἱράν. That form, however, is not elsewhere found in Bacchylides. In III. 15 βρύει μὲν ἱερά (where Ludwich suggests ἱρά), the trisyllabic form is confirmed by v. 85, φρονέοντι συνετὰ γαρύω κ.τ.λ.

2. In v. 4 the θρασύχειρ of the MS. (= ◡◡−◡ in v. 9) is a mere error for θρασύχειρος.

ODE III.

The strophe is logaoedic in general character, but in verses 1—3 makes a preparation for the rhythm of the epode which is dactylo-epitritic.

Strophe (4 verses).

$$\bar\cup - \cup \overset{\smile\smile}{} \bar\cup \overline{\cup\cup} \cup - \cup - \overset{\cup}{-} \mid$$
$$\bar\cup - \cup\cup - \cup\cup - \cup - \overset{\cup}{-} \mid$$
$$\overset{\cup}{-} - \cup\cup - \cup\cup - \cup - \cup ^-$$
$$- \cup - \bar\cup \overset{\cup}{-}\mid\cup\cup - \cup - \overset{\cup}{-}$$

Epode (6 verses).

$$\overset{\cup}{-} - \cup\cup, - \cup\cup -, - ^-$$
$$- \cup -, \overset{\cup}{-} - \cup - \mid$$
$$- \cup - \overset{\cup}{-}, - \cup - ^-$$
$$-, - \cup\overset{\smile\smile}{}-, - \cup - \wedge\mid$$
$$5 \quad \overset{\smile\smile}{}\cup - \overset{\cup}{-}, - \cup - \overset{\cup}{-}, - \cup - \wedge^-$$
$$- \cup - \overset{\cup}{-}, - \cup \overset{\cup}{-} \wedge$$

Verse 1 of the strophe is an iambic trimeter catalectic, ἀριστοκάρπου Σικελίας κρέουσαν. Verse 2 consists of a prosodiacus ($\bar\cup - \cup\cup - \cup\cup -$) and a bacchius ($\cup - \overset{\cup}{-}$), Δάματρα ϝιοστέφανόν τε κούραν. Verse 3 is the same, ὑμνεῖ, γλυκύδωρε Κλειοῖ, θοάς τ᾽ Ὀ-. Verse 4 is the Sapphic hendecasyllable, -λυμπιοδρόμους Ἱέρωνος ἵππους.

Notes.

1. The first verse of the strophe always contains a tribrach, except in the case of ant. 7 (v. 89), γῆρας, θάλειαν αὖτις ἀγκομίσσαι. The place of the tribrach in the verse is (i) the *second* in vv. 15 and 85: (ii) the *third*, in vv. 1, 5, 19, 29 (probably), 33, 47, 56, 61, 71, 75. Verse 43 is lost.

2. In the second verse of ant. 5 (v. 62), the επεμψε of the MS. must be corrected to ἀνέπεμψε (ἀν having been lost after ἀγαθέαν). The second v. of ant. 7 (v. 90) ends with μινύθει, *i.e.* $\cup\cup-$ instead of the $\cup--$ found in all the eleven other places where the end of the corresponding verse remains. See commentary.

3. The third verse of ant. 5 (v. 63) begins, in the MS., with ὅσοι μέν, $\cup-\cup$, instead of the $\overset{\cup}{-}-\cup\cup$ found elsewhere. γε must be inserted after ὅσοι. The last syllable of the third verse is everywhere short, and in str. 1 Ο|λυμπιοδρόμους is divided between v. 3 and v. 4.

4. The fourth verse of the strophe has the fourth syllable long in str. 2 (v. 18), ὑψιδαιδάλτων, and in ant. 5 (v. 64), ὦ μεγαίνητε, but elsewhere short.

5. Hiatus, with lengthening of a short syllable, occurs before Ἱέρων, after the fifth syllable of the fourth verse, in ant. 5 (v. 64), ὦ μεγαίνητε Ἱέρων: also in ant. 7 (v. 92) Μοῦσά νιν τρέφει. Ἱέρων κ.τ.λ.

6. The thesis is resolved in verse 4 of epode 3 (v. 40), in a proper name: πίτνουσιν Ἀλυάττα δόμοι. It is also resolved at the beginning of verse 5 in epode 6 (v. 83), ὅσια δρῶν.

ODE IV.

Logaoedic.—A pair of strophes, without epode.

Strophe (10 verses).

∪ ∪ ∪, − ∪, ∪ −, ∪ − ‾

  ∪ ∪ ∪, − ∪, ∪ −, ∪ −, − ⋀

− ∪ ∪ − ∪ ∪ − ∪ ∪ − −

  ∪ −, − ∪, − ∪, ∪ −, ∪ −, − ∪, − ⋀

5 − ∪ ∪ − ∪ ∪ − ∪ ∪

  ‾ ∪ ∪ − ∪ ∪ − ∪ − −

  ∪ ∪ ∪, − ∪, ∪ −, − ⋀

  ∪ −, − ∪, − ∪, ∪ −, ∪ −, − ⋀

  ∪ ∪ ∪, − ∪, − ∪, ∪ −

10 − ∪, − ∪, ∪ −, ∪ −, − ⋀

Notes.

1. The first verse of this strophe is identical in measure with the fourth verse of Ode II, ὅτι μάχας θρασύχειρος ᾿Αρ-.

2. In verse 4, where the MS. has τρίτον γαρ......λον, the faint traces of the letter which followed γαρ suit Π better than Α: hence Blass gives τρίτον γὰρ παρ᾿ ὀμφαλόν, κ.τ.λ., and in the ant. 14 (where the MS. has παρ᾿ ἑστίαν), πάρεστίν νιν. Otherwise we might read in v. 4 τρίτον γὰρ ἀμφ᾿ ὀμφαλόν, and in v. 14 πάρεστι νῦν.

ODE V

Dactylo-epitritic.

Strophe (15 verses).

− − ∪ ∪, − ∪ ∪ −,

  − ∪ − −, − ∪ − ⌣, |

− − ∪ ∪, − ∪ ∪ −, ‾

  − − ∪ ∪, − ∪ ∪ −, ⊡ − ∪ −

5 − ∪ ∪ −, ∪ ∪ − ‾

  −, − ∪ ∪ −, ∪ ∪ ⌣ ⋀̅ |

− ⌣ − −, − ∪ − −, ‾

  − ∪ − (⌣), − ∪ − ⋀ |

− − ∪ ∪, − ∪ ∪ −, − − ∪ −, − ‾

10 − ∪ ∪, − ∪ ∪ ⌣ |

  − − ∪ ∪, − ∪ ∪ −, (−) ‾

  − ∪ −, − − ∪ ⌣ |

  − − ∪ ∪, − ∪ ∪ −, ⌣ ‾

  − ∪ ∪, − ∪ ∪ −, (⌣) ‾

15 − ∪ −, − − ∪ ⌣

Epode (10 verses).

```
  – – ‿ ‿ ,  – – ‿ – ,  – – ‿ – ,  ⏒
  – ‿ ‿ ,  – ‿ ‿ –
  – – ‿ ‿ ,  – ‿ ‿ – ,  ⏒ – ‿ – ,  –
  – ‿ – ,  – – ‿ – ,  – ‾
5  – ‿ ‿ ,  – ‿ ‿ – ,  ‾
  – – ‿ – ,  – – ‿ – ,  ⏒ – ‿ ⏒ |
  – – ‿ ‿ ,  – ‿ ‿ – ,  ⏑
  – ‿ – ,  ⏒ – ‿ – ,  ⏑
  – ‿ ‿ ,  – ‿ ‿ –
10  – ‿ – – ,  – ‿ – ⏑ ,  – ‿ – –
```

Notes.

1. (i) In verses 13, 14 of str. 1 the MS. wrongly divides thus, Οὐρανίας | κλεινός, instead of Οὐρανίας κλει|νός, though in the corresponding verses of ant. 1 the division is correctly made, σὺν ζεφύρου πνο(ι)-|αῖσιν.

(ii) Verses 5 and 6 of the epode are wrongly divided in 35 f., ἀγέρωχοι | παῖδες, instead of ἀγέρω-|χοι παῖδες: in 75 f., ἀναπτύ-|ξας, instead of ἀνα-|πτύξας : and in 115 f., κατέπεφνε | σῦς, instead of κατέπε-|φνεν σῦς. But the division is correct in 155 f. and in 195 f.

2. Some apparent instances of exceptional shortening in arsis are easily removed: v. 28, for πνο|αῖσιν, read πνοι|αῖσιν : 49, for φιλοξένῳ, read φιλοξείνῳ : 115 f., for κατέπε|φνε, read κατέπε|φνεν : 137, for κόρα, read κούρα.

3. The MS. has lost a syllable in v. 184, where ἐς must be inserted after Φερένικος : and in 193, where ἂν must be inserted after ὄν.

4. The metre of the first strophe and antistrophe differs in two places from that of the four other pairs.

(i) Verses 11 f. of strophe 1 are :—νάσου ξένος ὑμετέραν πέμ-|πει κλεεννὰν ἐς πόλιν, = 26 f., δυσπαίπαλα κύματα· νωμᾶ-|ται δ᾽ ἐν ἀτρύτῳ χάει. Here v. 11 (= 26) is longer by a syllable than the corresponding verses elsewhere.

(ii) Verses 14 f. of strophe 1 are: -νὸς θεράπων· ἐθέλει δὲ | γᾶρυν ἐκ στηθέων χέων = 29 f. -αῖσιν ἔθειραν ἀρίγνω-|τος μετ᾽ ἀνθρώποις ἰδεῖν. Here, again, v. 14 (= 29) exceeds the normal length by a syllable. See commentary and Appendix.

5. Other instances of defective response are the following.

(i) In verse 8 of str. 1 the MS. gives δεῦρ᾽ ἄθρησον νόῳ, – ‿ – – ‿ –, instead of the – ‿ – – ‿ – found in the nine other places. Blass explains the exception as – ‿ ∟ – ‿ –. But it seems more probable that the text is corrupt in v. 8 (see commentary).

(ii) In epodes 1, 2, and 3 the first verse has this form : – – ‿ ‿ , – – ‿ ‿ , – – ‿ – , ⏒ : e.g. v. 31 τὼς νῦν καὶ ἐμοὶ μυρία παντᾷ κέλευθος. (Cp. 71 and 111.) But in epode 4 the MS. gives (151), Πλευρῶνα· μινυνθα [without accent] δε μοι ψυχα γλυκεια. Blass defends μίνυνθα, holding that – – ‿ – (·νυνθα δέ μοι) is here substituted for – – ‿ –: see his Preface, pp. XXXIX f. (3rd ed., 1904). I read μινύνθη (see commentary).

In epode 5, v. 1 (191), Βοιωτὸς ἀνὴρ τάδε φών[ησεν..., τᾷδε (Wilamowitz) is a probable correction.

(iii) In epode 3, v. 5 (115), the MS. has θάπτομεν τοὺς (κατέπε|φνεν σῦς), *i.e.* –◡– where the four corresponding verses (35, 75, 155, 195) have –◡◡. Yet Blass refrains from reading σῦς, thinking that the poet wrote τούς 'ne videretur esse θαπτομένους.'

(iv) The tenth verse of the epode begins with –◡– in 40, 80, 200, and presumably so in 120 (πατρὸ]ς 'Αλθ-). But in 160, where the first hand wrote ΤΟΙΔ'ΕΦΑ, a corrector (A³) changed τοιδ' to τόδ', or, as Blass thinks, to τάδ' ἔφα, which he gives. The true reading is probably τοῖ' ἔφα, or τοῖα φᾶ.

6. In 189 ἀπωσάμενον, followed in 190 by εἴ | τις, is noteworthy: see commentary. The *syllaba anceps* is perhaps justified by the slight pause; though the conjecture ἀπωσαμένους (Housman) is attractive.

ODE VI.

Logaoedic.—A pair of strophes, without epode, as in IV.

Strophe (8 verses).

```
     ◡ – ◡ –, ◡ – └,
     ◡◡ – ◡, – ◡ – ◡ |
   – ◡◡ –, – ◡◡ –, ◡ – └
     ◡ – ◡◡ – ◡
 5 – ◡ – ◡ – ◡ ◡ |
     ◡ –, – ◡, ◡ –, ◡ – ‾
   – ◡, – ◡◡ –, ◡ –, –
     ◡, ◡ –, ◡ –, —
```

Notes.

1. Verse 1, Λάχων Διὸς μεγίστου, is an iambic dimeter catalectic. Verse 2, λάχε φέρτατον πόδεσσι, is an 'anacreontic' verse, with anaclasis (–◡–◡ instead of ––◡◡). Sappho has the same sequence:

γλύκεια μᾶτερ, οὔτοι
δύναμαι κρέκην τὸν ἴστον.

2. The measures of vv. 4 and 5, δι' ὅσσα πάροιθεν | ἀμπελοτρόφον Κέον, recur in XVIII. 17, where they form a single verse, εὐρυσθενέος φραδαῖσι φερτάτου Διός.

ODE VII.

(1) In the first eleven verses (ὦ λιπαρὰ...στεφάνοισι Λάχωνα) the metre is dactylo-epitritic. After these, about 24 verses are lost. (2) Then come 16 verses (Πυθῶνά τε μηλοθύταν...κλεινοῖς ἀέθλοις), in which the metre is again dactylo-epitritic.

Kenyon held that (2), the group of sixteen verses, belonged to an ode (his VIII) distinct from the ode which began with (1) the group of eleven verses. Paul Maas also thinks that there were two odes, each consisting of one pair of strophes. Blass refers both groups to the same ode (VII). I incline to the latter opinion; partly because, if there were two odes, both must have been very short; and it seems improbable that the poet's first and second tribute to Lachon (VI, VII) should both have been on so small a scale. (See Introduction to Ode VII., p. 204, n. 1.)

There is a further question. Supposing that groups (1) and (2) both belonged to ode VII, was that ode composed in strophe, antistrophe, and epode? Blass formerly thought so, conjecturing that the epode began with the second group, Πυθῶνά τε μηλοθύταν. In his third edition, however (1904, p. LV, and p. 5), he holds that this ode, alone among the poet's extant pieces, was written in non-strophic verses (ἀπολελυμένα). That does not seem very probable. Maas observes that the division of κέκλη-|ται between verses 9 and 10 'would be singular, if it could not be explained by reference to an antistrophe'; and the point deserves consideration, whether we suppose (as he does) that there were two odes, or that there was only one. That part of the ode which would have contained the antistrophe has perished with the lost column XIII. No endings of antistrophic verses can be traced in the left margin of col. XIV: but this may be, as Maas suggests, because the scribe wrote more compactly in that place than he did in the strophe.

The metrical schemes of the two groups, (1) and (2), are subjoined; but, in view of the uncertainty, it is better to refrain from indicating 'strophe' or 'epode.'

(1) Group of 11 verses, ὦ λιπαρὰ...στεφάνοισι Λάχωνα.

$$-\cup\cup-, \cup\cup-\cup, -\cup[-$$
$$--\cup-, --\cup[- \ \cdot \ \cdot \ \cdot \ \cdot \ \cdot$$
$$--\cup\cup, -\cup\cup-, [\cup- \cdot \ \cdot \ \cdot$$
$$\cdot \ \cdot \ \cdot \ \cdot \ \cdot \ \cdot \qquad \cdot \ \cdot \ \cdot \ \cdot \ \cdot \ \cdot \ \cdot \ \cdot$$

5    $-]\cup- \cdot \ \cdot \ \cdot \ \cdot \ \cdot \ \cdot \ \cdot$
$$--\cup[\cup, -\cup\cup]-, --\cup-$$
$$--\cup-, -[-\cup]-, --\cup\overset{\smile}{} |$$
$$-\cup\cup-, \cup\cup--, -\cup-$$
$$--\cup-, --\cup-, --\cup-, \bar{}$$

10   $--\cup-, -[-\cup]\cup, [-\cup\cup-], -$
$$-]\cup--, [-\cup]\cup[-, \cup\cup-]\overset{\smile}{}$$

(2) Group of 16 verses, Πυθῶνά τε...κλεινοῖς ἀέθλοις.

```
      − − ∪ ∪ , − ∪ ∪ − ,
      − − ∪ ∪ , − ∪ ∪ − , −
      − ∪ − − , − ∪ ≚ ∧ |
      − ∪ ∪ − , ∪ ∪ − ¯
  5   − , − ∪ − − , − ∪ ≚ ∧ |
      − ∪ − − , − ∪ − − , ¯
      ∪ ∪ − ∪ , − ∪ ∟ ,
      − − ∪ − , − [ − ¯
      ∪ ∪ , − ∪ ∪ − , −
 10   − − ∪ − , − − ∪ [ ∪ , − ∪ ] ∪ − , − |
      − − ∪ − , − − ∪ ∪ , [ − ∪ ] ∪ − , −
      − ∪ − − , − ∪ ∪ [ − , ∪ ∪ ] − − ,
      − ∪ ∟ , − ∪ ≚ |
      − − ∪ − , −
 15   − ∪ ∪ , − ∪ ∪ −
      − − ∪ − , −
```

ODE VIII. [IX.]

Dactylo-epitritic.

Strophe (9 verses).

```
      − ∪ − − , − ∪ ∪ − , ∪ ∪ −
      − − ∪ − − − ∪ − |
      − − ∪ ∪ , − ∪ ∪ − , − − ∪ − , −
      − ∪ − − − ∪ ∪ − ∪ ∪ − −
  5   − ∪ − − − ∪ ≚ |
      − − ∪ ∪ , − ∪ ∪ − −
      − ∪ − ≚ − ∪ ≚ |
      − − ∪ − , − − ∪ − , −
      − ∪ − − − ∪ − − − ∪ − ∪
```

Epode (8 verses).

```
      (−) − ∪ − , − − ∪ ∪ , − ∪ ∪ − ,
      − ∪ − − , − ∪ ∪ − , ∪ ∪ − − , − ∪ − ∧
      − − ∪ − , − − ∪ − , −
      − ∪ − , − − ∪ −
  5   − ∪ ∪ − , ∪ ∪ − ¯
      − , − ∪ − − , − ∪ − ∧
      − ∪ − − , − ∪ − − , ¯
      − ∪ − − , − ∪ − −
```

Notes.

1. In v. 5, εὐθαλές is best taken as Doric for εὐθηλές, since in the 5th verse of the strophe the 4th syllable is elsewhere always long. In verse 7 of the strophe, the 4th syllable is once, at least, *anceps*, if εὐναεῖ be right in v. 42. In verse 9 of the strophe, the 4th syllable is normally long, and κόραι (MS.) in 44 should þe corrected to κοῦραι.

2. In verse 1 of epode 1 (v. 19) where the first hand wrote ΔΗΤΟΤʼ, A³ʼs correction ΑΚΑΙ ΤΟΤʼ is confirmed by σῶν ὦ in v. 1 of epode 2 (45). The beginning of v. 1 of ep. 3 (71) is lost; so also is that of ep. 4 (97), where ὔμμιν δέ seems probable.

ODE IX. [X.]

Dactylo-epitritic.

Strophe (10 verses).

$$\smile - \cup \cup - \cup \cup -, \; - - \cup -, \; -$$
$$- \cup - -, \; - \cup - \smile$$
$$- \cup \cup -, \; \cup \cup -$$
$$-, \; - \cup \cup -, \; \cup \cup - \triangledown$$
5
$$- \cup -(-), \; - \cup - \smile \mid$$
$$- \cup - -, \; - \cup \cup -, \; \cup \cup \sqcup, \; \cup \cup - \wedge$$
$$- \cup - -, \; - \cup - -,$$
$$- \cup - -, \; - \cup - \smile,$$
$$- \cup - -, \; - \cup - -, \; - \cup - -,$$
10
$$- \cup \sqcup, \; \smile \cup - -, \; - \cup - \smile, \; - \cup - -$$

Epode (8 verses).

$$- \cup - -, \; - \cup \cup -, \; \cup \cup - \overline{\wedge} \mid$$
$$- - \cup -, \; \smile - \cup -, \; \smile \mid$$
$$- - \cup - - - \cup -, \; - - \cup - -$$
$$- \cup \cup - \cup \cup - -, \; - \cup - -$$
5
$$- \cup \cup -, \; \cup \cup - \overline{\wedge} \mid$$
$$- [- \cup] \cup -, \; - \cup \cup -, \; -$$
$$- [\cup -] -, \; - \cup - -, \; -$$
$$- [\cup - -, \; -] \cup - -$$

Notes.

1. In verse 5 of ant. 1 (15), the MS. has ὅσσα where metre requires $- \cup -$. ὁσσάκις is a probable correction.

2. The MS. misplaces the division between verses 5 and 6 of the strophe. In ant. 1 (15 f.) it gives...ἔκατι ἄνθεσιν ξαν-|θάν, instead of ἔκατι | ἄνθεσιν ξανθάν: in str. 2 (33 f.)...νέμονται, ἀμφί τ' Εὔβοι-|αν, ihstead of νέμονται, | ἀμφί τ' Εὔβοιαν: in ant. 2 (43 f.), τιταίνει· οἱ δ' ἐπ' ἔργοι-|σιν, instead of τιταίνει, | οἱ δ' ἐπ' ἔργοισιν. In each of these three places, the hiatus bewrays the error. That the same mistake occurred in the mutilated first strophe, is certain from the fact that the lost word ending in -ῳ (χώρῳ?) stood at the end of verse 5. But, in that place, there was probably no hiatus; and having made the wrong division in the first strophe, the scribe repeated it in the other three.

3. Verses 9 and 10 of the strophe are wrongly divided by the MS. in 37 f. (τεύξεται being added to v. 37), though the division is correct in 9 f., 19 f., and 47 f.

4. In verse 10 of strophe 1, νασιῶτιν gives – ⌣ – ⌣ where we find – ⌣ – – in the other three places (20, 38, 48). This might suggest νασιώταν (see comment.), though the *arsis correpta* is, of course, possible.

5. In the 10th verse of ant. 1 (v. 20) the MS. has ταχεῖαν ὁρμάν. This should be ὁρμὰν ταχεῖαν (cp. 10, 38, 48).

ODE X. [XI.]

Dactylo-epitritic.

Strophe (14 verses).

$$- - \cup \cup, - \cup \cup -, - \bar{}$$
$$- \cup -, - - \cup -, \overset{\cup}{\smile}$$
$$- - \cup \cup, - \cup \cup -, \bar{}$$
$$- \cup - \overset{\cup}{\smile}, - \cup - -, |$$
5 $$- \cup \cup -, \cup \cup -$$
$$- - \cup \cup -, \cup \cup \sqcup -$$
$$- \cup - -, - \cup \cup -,$$
$$- - \cup \cup, - \cup \cup -,$$
$$- - \cup \cup, - \cup \cup -, \overset{\cup}{\smile} - \cup -, \overset{\cup}{\smile}$$
10 $$- - \cup \cup, - \cup \cup -, \bar{}$$
$$- - \cup \cup, - \cup \cup -,$$
$$- - \cup \cup, - \cup \cup -, \overset{\cup}{\smile} - \cup -, \overset{\cup}{\smile} |$$
$$- - \cup \cup, - \cup \cup -, - \bar{}$$
$$- \cup -, - - \cup -, -$$

Epode (14 verses).

$$- - \cup \cup, - \cup \cup -,$$
$$- - \cup \cup, - \cup \cup -, \cup - \cup -, -$$
$$- \cup \cup -, \cup \cup -$$
$$- - \cup \cup, - \cup \cup -,$$
5 $$- \cup - -, - \cup - \overset{\cup}{\smile},$$
$$- - \cup \cup, - \cup \cup -,$$
$$- - \cup -, - - \cup \overset{\cup}{\smile}, \bar{}$$
$$- - \cup \cup, - \cup \cup -, \overset{\cup}{\smile} - \cup -,$$
$$- - \cup \cup, - \cup \cup -,$$
10 $$- - \cup \cup, - \cup \cup \overset{\cup}{\smile}, |$$
$$- \cup - -, - \cup - -, - \cup - \overset{\cup}{\smile},$$
$$- \cup \cup -, \cup \cup - \bar{}$$
$$-, - \cup \cup -, \cup \cup \sqcup -$$
$$- \cup - \bar{}, - \cup - -$$

Notes.

1. It is of some interest to observe in this ode the poet's preferences with regard to a long or a short syllable in arsis, where either was admissible. (i) In v. 4 of str. 1, ἐν πολυχρύσῳ δ' Ὀλύμπῳ, the fourth syllable is long, as it is also in three of the other five places (vv. 46, 88, 102). It is short only in v. 18 (in a proper name) and v. 60. (ii) Similarly in v. 9, κούρα Στυγὸς ὀρθοδίκου· σέθεν δ' ἕκατι, the ninth syllable is short only there and in v. 107, while it is long in the other four places (18, 51, 65, 93). (iii) On the other hand, in v. 12, κῶμοί τε καὶ εὐφροσύναι θεότιμον ἄστυ, the ninth syllable is long only there (where εο is –, by synizesis) and in 110, while it is short in 26, 54, 68, 96. (iv) Verse 2 of the epode remains integral only in v. 72, κτίζειν, πρὶν ἐς ἀργαλέαν πεσεῖν ἀνάγκαν, where the ninth syllable is short; and so it must have been also in 114 (where the MS. has πόλιν Ἀχαιοῖς, instead of ‿ – ‿ – –), and presumably in the mutilated v. 30 (πάτραν θ' ἱκέσθαι?). (v) In verse 8 of epode 1 (v. 36), ἄμερσαν ὑπέρτατον ἐκ χειρῶν γέρας, the ninth syllable is long, as also in v. 78; while it is short in v. 120.

2. At the end of v. 1 of str. 2 (v. 43), ν must be added to the ἐφόβησε of the MS. (Cp. v. 115 f., where κατεπέ-|φνε should be κατεπέ-|φνεν.)

3. In verse 2 of epode 3 (v. 114) ἐς should be inserted before ἱπποτρόφον. With regard to πόλιν Ἀχαιοῖς, see commentary.

4. In verse 7 of epode 2 (v. 77) the second syllable of κάμον seems to be a *syllaba anceps*: see commentary. Of the two corresponding verses, one (35) ends with βροτῶν, and the other (119) with the corrupt πρόγο-|νοι.

ODE XI. [XII.]

Dactylo-epitritic.—Only eight verses remain, of which the last, τάν τ' ἐν Νεμέᾳ γυιαλκέα μουνοπάλαν, is metrically identical with the first, ὡσεὶ κυβερνήτας σοφός, ὑμνοάνασ-, and may possibly, therefore, mark the beginning of the antistrophe; but this, of course, is by no means certain.

Strophe.

```
        – – ∪ –, – – ∪ ∪, – ∪ ∪ –, ‾
        – – ∪ –, –
        – ∪ ∪, – ∪ ∪ –
        – – ∪ ∪, – ∪ ∪ –, ∪ – ∪ –,
  5     – – ∪ ∪, – ∪ ∪ –, –
        – ∪ – –, – ∪ – – |
        – – ∪ –, – – ∪ –, – – ∪ –,
(antistr.?)  – – ∪ –, – – ∪ ∪, – ∪ ∪ –,
```

＊　　＊　　＊

Ode XII. [XIII.]

Dactylo-epitritic.

Strophe (12 verses).

```
    − − ∪ ∪, − ∪ ∪ −,
      ⊻ − ∪ −, ⊻ |
    − − ⊻ ∪ ∪ − ⊽ |
    − ∪ − ⊻, − ∪ − ⊻, |
5   − − ∪ ∪, − ∪ ∪ −, ⊻
    − ∪ − −, − ∪ − ⁻
      −, − ∪ ∪ −, ∪ ∪ − ⁻
      ⊻, − ∪ − −, |
    − ∪ ∪ −, ∪ ∪ − ⊻,
10  − ∪ ∪ −, ∪ ∪ − ⊻,
    − ∪ ∪ −, ∪ ∪ −
      −, − ∪ − ⊻, − ∪ − ⊻
```

Epode (9 verses).

```
    − − ∪ ∪, − ∪ ∪ −, ⊻ − ∪ −,
    − − ∪ ∪, − ∪ ∪ −, ⁻
      ∪ − ∪ −, −
    − ∪ − −, − ∪ ∪ −, ∪ ∪ −
5   −, − ∪ − −, − ∪ − Λ |
    − − ∪ ∪, − ∪ ∪ −, ⊽
    − ∪ − ⊻, − ∪ − ⊻, − ∪ ⊻ Λ |
    − ∪ ∪ −, ∪ ∪ − ⊻, ⁻
    − ∪ − ⊻, − ∪ − −
```

Notes.

1. The seventh verse of ant. 3 (v. 85) is wanting in the MS. Some remains of it (now represented by the letters ραν) seem to have been pieced on to the sixth verse (84): see crit. n. there.—The third verse of epode 5 (v. 159) has also been lost. The fourth verse (160) seems to have been added to it in the same line.

2. The second verse of the strophe is a pherecratic, −−−∪∪−⊻, Περσείδας ἐφίησιν (48). As there, so also in 81, 102, 114, 135, 147, 168, 180, 201, the second syllable is long; and I cannot think that in 69 πανθαλέων presents, as Blass suggests, a solitary exception. πανθᾰλής occurs, no doubt, in 229: but πανθᾰλής (Doric for πανθηλής) would be parallel with εὐθᾰλής (see on VIII. 5).

3. In the fourth verse of the strophe the last syllable is short only once (115, ἄστυ), but long in all the other instances (49, 70, 136, 148, 181, 202).

4. In the third verse of the epode, the first syllable is everywhere short (93, 126, 192, 225). This fact supports the conjecture ἀν|δεθεῖσιν (Housman) in 59 f., as against ἀν|θρώποισιν (Blass).

5. At the beginning of verse 7 of epode 2 (v. 64) κυάνεον must be –◡–, though in compounds with κυανο- Bacchylides has ῠ. A resolution of the thesis would be against his rule in this place : see 97, 130, 163, 196, 229.

6. Verse 8 of the epode ends with a long syllable in 65, 164, 197, 230 ; yet once with a short (131).

7. In verse 9 of the epode, the fourth syllable is normally long (99, 165, 198, 231); yet once short (66, -χθέντος ἀσφαλεῖ σὺν αἴσᾳ). In 132 ἐξίκοντο might have either ῑ or ῐ (cp. XV. 16).

ODE XIII. [XIV.]

Dactylo-epitritic.

Strophe (7 verses).

$$-\,\cup\,-\,-,\;-\,\cup\,\cup\,-,\;\cup\,\cup\,-$$
$$-,\;-\,\cup\,-\,-$$
$$-\,\cup\,-\,-,\;-\,\cup\,-\,-,\;^{-}$$
$$-\,\cup\,-\,-,\;-\,\cup\,-\,\cup,$$
$$5\;\;-]\,-\,\cup\,\cup,\;-\,\cup\,\cup\,-,\;-\,^{-}$$
$$-]\,\cup\,-,\;-\,-\,\cup\,-,\;-$$
$$-]\,\cup\,-,\;-\,-\,\cup\,-$$

Epode (8 verses).

$$-]\,-\,\cup\,\cup,\;-\,\cup\,\cup\,-,$$
$$\mathrm{\sigma}]\,-\,\cup\,\cup,\;-\,\cup\,\cup\,-,\;-$$
$$-\,\cup]\,-\,-,\;-\,\cup\,\cup\,-,\;^{-}$$
$$-\,\cup\,-\,-,\;-\,\cup\,\cup\,-,\;\cup\,\cup\,-\,-,$$
$$5\;\;(\cup?)\,-\,\cup\,\cup\,-\,\cup\,\cup\,-$$
$$-\,-\,\cup\,-,\;-\,-\,\cup\,-,\;-\,^{-}$$
$$-\,\cup\,\cup,\;-\,\cup\,\cup\,-,\;-$$
$$-\,\cup\,-\,-,\;-\,\cup\,-\,\cup,\;[-\,\cup\,-\,-]$$

Note.

In verse 3 of strophe 1 the MS. seems to have lost τ' after ἐσθλόν : and in verse 5 a corruption has occurred. See commentary.

B. ΔΙΘΥΡΑΜΒΟΙ.

ODE XIV. [XV.]

Dactylo-epitritic.

Strophe (7 verses).

$$- - \cup \cup, - \cup \cup -,$$
$$- - \cup \cup, - \cup \cup -, \underset{\smile}{-} - \cup - \mid$$
$$\underset{\smile}{-} - \cup -, - - \cup \cup, - \cup \cup -,$$
$$- - \cup -, - - \cup -,$$
$$5 \quad - \cup - -, - \cup - -, - \cup - -,$$
$$- \cup \cup -, \cup \cup - -, - \cup \cup -, \cup \cup - \overline{\wedge},$$
$$- \cup - -, - \cup - -, - \cup - \underset{\smile}{-}$$

Epode (7 verses).

$$- - \cup -, - - \cup \cup, - \cup \cup -,$$
$$- - \cup -, - - \cup -, -$$
$$- \cup - -, - \cup \cup -, \cup \cup - \overline{\wedge}$$
$$- - \cup \cup, - \cup \cup -, -$$
$$5 \quad - \cup -, - - \cup -, \overline{-}$$
$$- - \cup \cup, - \cup \cup -,$$
$$- - \cup -, - - \cup -, \cup$$

Notes.

1. In verse 6 of ant. 1 (v. 13) the MS. has σὺν θεοῖς where –∪∪– stands in the corresponding verses (6, 48, 55) : a short syllable (γε, δέ, or τε) seems to be lost after σύν.

2. In verse 7 of epode 3 (v. 63) the MS. ὤλεσεν should be ὤλεσσεν, as v. 42 shows.

ODE XV. [XVI.]

The metres of this ode are complex, and the precise analysis is in many points doubtful. *Dactylic* measures of various lengths predominate, both in strophe and in epode. Mingled with these are *paeonic* rhythms. The *paeon primus*, –∪∪∪, appears certainly in verse 9 of the strophe; and almost certainly (I think) in verse 1, where it is followed by the kindred cretic; though the mutilation of that verse in the strophe, and the ambiguous quantity of γε before κλ in the antistrophe (v. 13), differentiate the case from that of verse 9. The *paeon quartus*, ∪∪∪–, may be recognised at the beginning of verses 4 and 11 in the strophe,

and probably in the second part of v. 5 of the epode (v. 29).
There are also some anapaests (or apparent anapaests). Dr W.
Headlam, who has given special study to the metres used in
this ode, describes the strophe as composed of three elements,
paeonic, dactylic, and *logaoedic*; the epode being constructed, as
usual, of the same material in a different arrangement. By this
complexity, and by somewhat abrupt transitions from one rhythm
to another, Bacchylides seems here to aim at expressing agitated
feelings, in unison with the tragic pathos of Deianeira's fate.
Such a metrical character was not ill-suited to a Dionysiac
dithyramb.

Strophe (12 verses).

```
    – ⏑ ⏑ ⏑ – ⏑ – |
    – ⏑ ⏑ – ⏑ ⏑ – ⏑ ⏑ –
    – ⏑ ⏑ – ⏑ ⏑ – ⏑ ⏑ – ⏑ ⏑ – ̄
    ⏑ ⏑ ⏑ – ⏑ – ⏑ – –
 5  – ⏑ ⏑ – ⏑ ⏑ – ⏑ ⏑ – ⏒ – –
    – ⏑ ⏑ – ⏑ ⏑ – ⏑ ⏑ – ⏑ ⏑ – –
    ⏑ ⏑ – ⏑ ⏑ – ⏑ ⏑ – ⏑ ⏑ –
    ⏑ ⏑ – – ⏑ ⏑ – ⏒ | – ⏑ ⏒ |
    – ⏑ ⏑ ⏑ – – |
10  – ⏑ ⏑ – –
    ⏑ ⏑ ⏑ – – –
    – ⏑ ⏑ – – ⏑ ⏑ – ⏑ ⏑ – –
```

Epode (11 verses).

```
    – ⏑ ⏑ – ⏑ ⏑ –
    ⏑ ⏑ – ⏑ ⏑ – ⏑ ⏑ – ⏑ –
    ⏑ ⏑ – ⏑ ⏑ – – ⏑ –
    ⏑ ⏑ – ⏑ ⏑ – ⏑ ⏑ –
 5  ⏑ ⏑ – ⏑ ⏑ – ⏑ ⏑ ⏑ – – – |
    – – ⏑ ⏑ – ⏑ – – ⏑ ⏑ – ⏑ –
    ⏑ ⏑ – ⏑ ⏑ – ⏑ ⏑ – ⏑ –
    ⏑ ⏑ – ⏑ ⏑ – ⏑ –
    – ⏑ ⏑ – ⏑ ⏑ –
10  ⏑ ⏑ – ⏑ ⏑ – ⏑ ⏑ – –
    – ⏑ ⏑ – – ⏑ ⏑ – ⏑ ⏑ – ⏑ –
```

Notes.

1. The question as to the metre of verse 1 is bound up with the palaeographical data: see crit. note *ad loc.* If the verse did not begin with – ⏑ ⏑ as
[Πυθί]ου, but with – – ⏑, then two long syllables were formed by 4 letters (for

which alone there is room before oὐ); and the fourth of these was either I, or a letter ending with a vertical stroke, such as N. In verse 1 of the antistr. (v. 13) γε before κλ might, according to B.'s practice, be either short or long: for the statistics, see above, p. 85.

2. Verse 3 of the strophe is a dactylic pentapody with catalexis, not a frequent verse, but one which occurs in Alcman, fr. 51, Pindar *P.* III. 4 (Οὐρανίδα γόνον εὐρυμέδοντα Κρόνον), etc.

3. Verse 5 of the strophe ends with ἀνθεμόεντι Ἔβρῳ, answering to εὐρυνεφεῖ Κηναίῳ in v. 17. The hiatus before Ἔβρῳ recalls that in III. 64, ὦ μεγαίνητε Ἱέρων, a passage which also suggests that the ι of ἀνθεμόεντι might be lengthened before the aspirate. But such a lengthening is easier to understand in thesis (III. 64) than, as here, in arsis; and moreover it is needless to assume it. Blass surely mars the metre by inserting που after ἀνθεμόεντι.— The double spondee of v. 17 occurs in Aesch. *Ag.* 121 αἴλινον αἴλινον εἰπέ, τὸ δ' εὖ νικάτω.

4. Verse 6 (=18), composed of four dactyls and a spondee, is the same as that in Aesch. *Eum.* 360, σπευδομένα δ' ἀφελεῖν τινα τάσδε μερίμνας.

5. Verse 7 (=19) might be read either as an anapaestic dimeter, or as a dactylic tetrapody catalectic with anacrusis (⏑⏑). The former view is the simpler.

6. The eighth verse, mutilated in the strophe, is preserved entire in the antistrophe, -λε κόρᾳ τ' ὀβριμοδερκεῖ ἄζυγα,—anapaest, dactyl, trochee, cretic. In verse 8 the last four syllables are formed by παιηόνων, where the first might be short, as in παιάνιξαν (XVI. 129). Blass, to avoid the hiatus and the shortening of -κει, inserts γε after ὀβριμοδερκεῖ.

7. Verse 9, ἄνθεα πεδοιχνεῖν (=21 παρθένῳ Ἀθάνᾳ), consists of a *paeon primus* and a spondee. In verse 11, τόσα χοροὶ Δελφῶν (=23, τότ' ἄμαχος δαίμων), we have a *paeon quartus* and a spondee. Thus the place where the paeonic element becomes prominent is also that which, in the antistrophe, marks the turning-point of tragic interest. Verse 23 introduces Deianeira's resolve.

8. Verse 12, the last of the strophe, is a choriambus followed by an enhoplius, σὸν κελάδησαν παρ' ἀγακλέα ναόν. It will be noticed that both here and in the antistrophic verse (24), Δαϊανείρᾳ πολύδακρυν ὕφανε, the fifth syllable coincides with the end of a word.

9. The first verse of the epode (25), a dactylic tripody catalectic, is metrically the same as the ninth (33).

10. In verse 2 of the epode (26), πύθετ' ἀγγελίαν ταλαπενθέα, it seems most probable that the final -έα of the last word is to be scanned ⏑-. The metre will then be the same as that of the 7th verse of the epode (31), φθόνος εὐρυβίας νιν ἀπώλεσεν. In 27 Ἰόλαν can take ϝ.

11. In verse 5 of the epode (29), ἄλοχον λιπαρὸν ποτὶ δόμον πέμποι, two anapaests are followed by the combination already found in the strophe (vv. 11 and 23), a *paeon quartus* and a spondee.

12. Verse 6 of the epode (30), ἆ δύσμορος, ἆ τάλαιν', οἷον ἐμήσατο is followed at the beginning of v. 7 by φθόνος, and the last syllable of ἐμήσατο is therefore long. The first ἆ is anacrusis: then we have a dactyl, and a trochaic dipody catalectic (twice). The movement is slow, with a slight pause after τάλαιν', and gives a wailing effect, which is continued in the next verse.

13. The 11th and last verse of the epode (35), δέξατο Νέσσου πάρα δαιμόνιον τέρας, has a general likeness to the last v. of the strophe, but ends with $-\smile-$ instead of $--$. As in the strophic verses (12 and 24), the fifth syllable coincides with the end of a word.

ODE XVI. [XVII.]

In the metre of this ode much is difficult and obscure. One element, which Wilamowitz regards as predominant (*Gött. Gelehr. Anz.* 1898, pp. 137 ff.), is formed by iambic dipodies or 'diiambi.' Some verses, such as the second of the epode (v. 48), τάφον δὲ ναυβάται, are simply iambic. There are also trochaic rhythms (as *e.g.* in v. 9). But there are other elements also. Bacchylides uses cretics in frag. 11 (= 15 Blass), οὐχ ἕδρας ἔργον οὐδ᾽ ἀμβολᾶς, | ἀλλὰ χρυσαίγιδος Ἰωνίας etc., where the second foot of the second verse is a *paeon primus*: and Blass asks (*Praef.* p. LIV, 3rd ed.) whether this ode is to be regarded as cretic or paeonic. 'It is clearly,' he says, 'a paean; it concerns the Cretan Minos, and the word Κρητικόν occurs in the fourth verse : but if cretics and paeons are to be recognised in it, at any rate they are strangely mingled with trochees, iambics, and even anapaests.' He further observes that the first three verses of the strophe, between which synaphea seems to exist, can be more easily reduced to trochaic dipodies (*ditrochaeos*), such as Aristoxenus is said to have called κρητικοὶ κατὰ τροχαῖον (Diomedes p. 481), than to 'cretics' in the ordinary sense of the word. A complete metrical analysis of the ode has been essayed by Housman in the *Classical Review*, vol. XII. pp. 134 ff. (March, 1898).

While the technical aspects of the metre present so much that divides the opinions of experts, a reader can feel that its general character is well adapted to the subject-matter. The verses suit a rapid and spirited narrative, fraught with excitement, startling incident, and reversals of fortune.

Strophe (23 verses).

10 $-\cup\cup-\cup-\cup^{-}$

   $-\cup-\cup\cup-\cup\cup-$

   $\varpi-\cup-\cup-\cup-$

   $\cup--\cup-\cup-^{-}$

   $\cup-\cup\underset{\smile}{\smile}-\cup-(\cup)^{-}$

15 $\varpi-\cup--\cup^{\vee}\mid$

   $-\cup\cup\cup-\cup--^{-}$

   $\varpi(\cup\cup)-\cup-\cup^{\vee}\mid$

   $\varpi-\cup-\cup-\cup-\cup-^{-}$

   $-\cup\cup\cup-\cup-^{\vee}\mid$

20 $\varpi-\cup\cup\cup\underset{\smile}{\smile}\cup-\cup-\mid$

   $\underset{\smile}{\smile}\cup-\cup\cup\cup-$

   $\cup-\cup--\cup-$

   $-\cup-\cup\cup\cup-\cup\underset{\smile}{\smile}-\cup-$

Epode (20 verses).

   $\cup-\cup\cup\cup, \llcorner\cup-, \llcorner$

   $\cup-, \cup-\cup-,$

   $\llcorner\cup\cup\cup, \llcorner\cup-,$

   $\llcorner\cup\underset{\smile}{\smile}, \cup-\cup-, \llcorner\cup-, \llcorner\cup-,$

5 $\cup-\cup\cup\cup, \llcorner\cup-,$

   $\llcorner\cup-, \llcorner\cup\cup\cup, \llcorner\cup-,$

   $\llcorner\cup\cup\cup, \llcorner\cup-, \llcorner\cup-, -\mid$

   $--\cup--\cup-\cup\cup$

   $-\cup-\cup-\cup-\cup-$

10 $\cup\cup\cup-\cup-\cup-$

   $-\cup--\cup-^{-}$

   $\cup-\cup--\cup---\cup\cup^{-}$

   $\cup-\cup--\cup-^{-}$

   $-\cup-\cup-\cup-\mid$

15 $-\cup-\cup\cup^{-}$

   $\cup-\cup-\cup-\cup--\cup-$

   $\cup-\cup-, \llcorner\cup\cup\cup, \llcorner\cup^{\vee}$

   $\llcorner\cup\underset{\smile}{\smile}\llcorner\cup-, \cup-$

   $\cup\cup\cup, \llcorner\llcorner$

20 $\cup-\cup-, \llcorner\cup-, \llcorner\cup-$

Notes.

The number of places where apparent breaches of metre suggest some disturbance of the text is larger in this Ode than in any other.

1. In several instances the metrical fault can be cured by some very slight correction; as in v. 4, by writing τάμνε for τάμνεν: 42, ἀμβρότου for ἀμβρότοι᾽: 80, ἠΰδενδρον for εὔδενδρον: 88, ἴσχεν for ἴσχειν: 91, ἐξόπιν, or ἐξόπιθε, for ἐξόπιθεν: 112, ἀμφέβαλεν for ἀμφέβαλλεν: 118, θέωσιν for θέλωσιν.

2. The *defect of a syllable* sometimes occurs in one of two verses which ought to correspond metrically. (i) In verse 4 of ant. 2 (v. 93) a long syllable has been lost after ἠϊθέων. (ii) In verse 8 of str. 1 the MS. has Μίνω where we expect – ⏑ –. (iii) The same v. of str. 2 (74) ends with Θησεῦ, τάδε, instead of – – ⏑ ⏑ –. (iv) In v. 14 of ant. 1 (37), τέ(ϝ)οι δόσαν ἰόπλοκοι, a short syllable is wanting at the end.

3. Conversely, *excess of a syllable* appears (i) in v. 8 of ant. 2 (97), φέρον δὲ δελφῖνες ἐναλι-|ναιέται, where metre requires ἁλι-|ναιέται: and (ii) in v. 19 of ant. 2 (108), -πον κέαρ ὑγροῖσιν ἐν ποσίν, where metre requires ὑγροῖσι ποσσίν.

4. There are other and more complex cases of defective responsion where the most probable remedy is afforded by *transposition.* (i) In verses 11 and 12 of ant. 2 (100 f.), where the MS. has ἔμολέν τε θεῶν | μέγαρον, two faults are removed by writing μέγαρόν τε θεῶν | μόλεν. (ii) In vv. 13 f. of ant. 2 (102 f.), the MS. has ἔδεισε Νηρέος ὀλ-|βίου, where we require ⏑ – – – ⏑ – ⏑ – | ⏑ –: this is obtained by writing ἔδεισ᾽ ὀλβίοιο Νη-|ρέος.

These two instances, in which the probability of the transposition approaches to certainty, should be carefully noted as tending to prove that a displacement of verses was possible in this papyrus; not necessarily through an error of the scribe, but perhaps because, in some earlier MS., a verse had been omitted, and then re-inserted in a wrong place. We should remember this in considering two other places. (iii) In vv. 20 f. of ant. 2 (109 f.) the MS. has εἶδέν (made from ἴδεν) τε πατρὸς ἄλοχον φίλαν | σεμνὰν βοῶπιν ἐρατοῖ-, where, instead of σεμνάν, metre requires either ⏑ ⏑ or –. Housman is surely right in making v. 20 begin with σεμνάν, and v. 21 with ἴδε. (iv) In vv. 16 f. of epode 1 (62 f.) the MS. has δικὼν θράσει σῶμα πατρὸς ἐς δόμους | ἔνεγκε κόσμον βαθείας ἁλός· where a short syllable is wanting after θράσει. I agree with Blass in transposing the verses, and adding ἐκ before βαθείας.

For a fuller discussion of all the passages indicated in notes 2—4, the reader is referred to the commentary.

5. Verses 6 and 7 of the strophe are wrongly divided by the MS. in ant. 2 (95 f., δάκρυ | χέον instead of δά-|κρυ χέον), though rightly in the other three places (6 f., 29 f., 72 f.).

6. In his third edition (1904) Blass, referring to *Hermes* XXXVI. 284 f., makes a new division of verses 5—6 of the strophe, thus:—(1) str. 1: τηλαυγέϊ γὰρ ἐν φάρεϊ βορῆϊαι | πίτνον αὖραι κλυτᾶς | ἕκατι κ.τ.λ. (2) ant. 1 (28—30): ἔλθῃ· σὺ δὲ βαρεῖαν κάτεχε μῆτιν, εἰ | καί σε κεδνὰ τέκεν | λέχει κ.τ.λ. Note here that the new division of εἰ καί between two verses is objectionable. This awkwardness becomes still more marked if (as is desirable) a colon or full stop, and not merely a comma, is placed after μῆτιν. (3) str. 2 (71—73): ἄστραψέ θ᾽· ὁ δὲ θυμάρμενον ἰδὼν τέρας | χέρας πέτασσε κλυτὰν | ἐς αἰθέρα κ.τ.λ. In the MS. v. 72 is ἰδὼν τέρας χεῖρας πέτασσε: where the simple correction, πέτασε χεῖρας (see comm.), restores the metre. The new division dispenses with the transposition (though requiring χέρας instead of χεῖρας): but it introduces a new discrepancy, viz. ⏑ – ⏑ – (χέρας πέτασσ-) instead of the – – ⏑ – found in all the corresponding places (6, 29, 95). (4) ant. 2 (94—96) ἥρως θόρεν πόντονδε, κατὰ λειρίων | τ᾽ ὀμμάτων δάκρυ χέον | βαρεῖαν κ.τ.λ.

It seems to me that the division of these verses in the MS. (with the exception of 95 f., on which see n. 5) is, on the whole, more probable than the new division now made by Blass. One fact especially should be observed.

As Maas has noted (see above, p. 96), the general tendency of the Alexandrian κωλιστής was to avoid, as far as possible, the division of a word between two verses. Where, therefore, the MS. so divides a word, there is a presumption that such division is authentic. But the effect of the new arrangement is to produce κάτεχε where the MS. (28 f.) has κάτε|χε : and κατά where the MS. (94 f.) has κα|τά.

Ode XVII.

Logaoedic.

Strophe (15 verses).

```
      ∪∪ − − ∪∪ − ∪ −, −
      ⌣, − ∪, ∪ −, ∪ −, ∪ −, ∟
      ∪∪∪, − ∪, ∪ −, ∪ −, − ‾
      −, − ∪, ∪ −, ∪ −, ∪ −, ⌐
  5   ⌣ ⊽, − ∪, ∪ −, ∪ − ‾
      − ⊽, − ∪, ∪ −, ∪ −, −
      ⊽, − ∪, − ∪, ∟
      ⌣ −, − ∪, ∪ −, ∪ ⌣ |
      − ∪, − ∪, ∪ −, ∪ −, −
 10   −, − ∪, ∪ −, ∪ ⌣ |
      − ⊽, − ∪, ∪ −, ∪ −, −
      ⌣, − ∪, ∪ −, ∪ −, ∪ −, ∪ − |
      − ⌣, − ∪, ∪ −, ∪ − ‾
      − ∪, − ∪, − ∪, ∟
 15   − −, − ∪, ∪ −, ∪ −, ∪ −, ∟
```

Notes.

1. The MS. text shows many corruptions of metre, but they are such as can easily be removed. In v. 9, δ' ἕκατι has been corrected to δέκατι : 16, ἦλθε to ἦλθεν : 24, Κρεμνῶνος to Κρεμμνῶνος : 28, ἐξέβαλλεν to ἐξέβαλεν : 35, ὅπλοισιν to ὁπάοσιν : 40, καρτερὸν to κρατερόν : 51, κρατὸς ὕπερ to κρατὸς πέρι.

2. In 52 f. the transposition στέρνοις τε...χιτῶνα (instead of the MS. χιτῶνα ...στέρνοις τ') is required, not by metre, but by the place of τε : see commentary.

Ode XVIII. [XIX.]

The metre does not conform to any well-known type, but blends certain rhythms as the poet's fancy prompts. In the first fourteen verses of the strophe, iambic dimeters alternate with short dactylic measures. In verses 15, 16 and 18 the rhythm becomes trochaic,—v. 18 being of a logaoedic character; while v. 17 is an iambic trimeter with an anapaest for the second foot.

In the epode the MS. has lost the ending of every verse except the first (37, ἐμοὶ μὲν οὖν). Blass, indeed, thinks that the words τίκτε Διόνυσον (50), where he writes Δῖον υἱόν, form a complete verse; but this seems improbable. The endings of at least four verses in the epode (46—49) can, however, be restored without much difficulty. The remains of the epode suffice to show that there, as in the strophe, iambic rhythms were combined with trochaic. The tenth verse of the epode (46) was clearly a prosodiacus, ὅθεν καὶ 'Αγανορίδας, like the sixth verse of the strophe, φερεστέφανοι Χάριτες.

In this ode the iambics are pure. The only spondee in an iambic verse is the proper name 'Ιώ in 41.

Strophe (18 verses).

∪−∪−, ∪−∪−, ∪
−∪∪, −∪∪−,
∪−∪∪, −∪∪−, ∪⁻
−∪−, ∪−L |
5 ∪−∪∪, −∪(∪?)−, ⁻
∪−∪∪, −∪∪−,
∪−∪−, ∪−⌐
−−∪∪, −∪∪−, ⁻
−∪∪−, ∪−∪−, ∪
10 −∪−, ∪−L |
−−∪∪, L∪−, ∪−L
∪−∪−, ∪−∪≚ |
∪−∪∪, −∪∪−, ∪⁻
−∪−, ∪−∪≚ |
15 ☐≚−∪∪−∪−∪−∪
−∪−∪−−
−−∪∪−∪−∪−∪−∪≚ |
−∪−∪∪−∪−∪−

Epode (15 verses).

∪−∪−
−∪−∪∪− · · · · ·
∪−∪−∪− · · · · · ·
−∪∪−∪ · · · · ·
5 −−∪−∪−[∪ · · · ·
∪∪∪−∪☐ · · · · ·
∪−∪−∪[∪− · ·
∪∪∪−∪− · · · ·
∪−−∪−[− · ·

10 ⌣ – ⌣ ⌣ – ⌣ ⌣ [–
⌣ – ⌣ ⌣ – . . . .
≍ – ⌣ ⌣ [– . . .
– ⌣ – ⌣ – –
– ⌣ – ⌣ – –
15 – ⌣ – ⌣ ⌣ . . . . . .

Notes.

1. In the fifth verse of the ant. (23), ἄκοιτον ἄϋπνον ἐόν-|τα (= 5 λοβλέφαροί τε καί), there is synizesis of εο, unless εὖν-|τα should be read.

2. In v. 15 of the strophe, ἦεν seems a probable correction of the MS. τί ἦν: the metre clearly indicates a trochee. Blass keeps τί ἦν, but suggests Ἄργος ἦν ποθ' ὅθ' ἵππιον λιποῦσα : with some sacrifice of euphony.

3. In v. 17 εὐρυσθενέος is scanned – – ⌣ ⌣ –, not – – ⌣ –, as is indicated by the antistrophic words ἤ Πιερίδες (v. 35).

ODE XIX. [XX.]

The first eleven verses are partly preserved. All begin with ≍ – ⌣ ⌣, and all are mutilated at the end. The rhythm is the προσοδιακός, ≍ – ⌣ ⌣ – ⌣ ⌣ –, or the ἐνόπλιος with anacrusis, ≍ – ⌣ ⌣ – ⌣ ⌣ – –. Verse 8, commencing with the words ἀναξίαλος Ποσει[δάν, differs from the rest in that the initial ≍ – ⌣ ⌣ is followed, not by – ⌣ ⌣ –, but by – ⌣ –. This is a form of prosodiacus used by Aristophanes (*Av.* 1371 ff.) in the nuptial strain, Ἥρᾳ ποτ' Ὀλυμπίᾳ (see Introd. to Ode XIX).

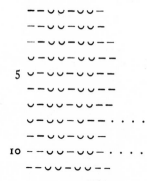

– – ⌣ ⌣ – ⌣ ⌣ –
– – ⌣ ⌣ – ⌣ ⌣ –
– – ⌣ ⌣ – ⌣ ⌣ – –
⌣ – ⌣ ⌣ – ⌣ ⌣ – –
5 ⌣ – ⌣ ⌣ – ⌣ ⌣ – –
– – ⌣ ⌣ – ⌣ ⌣ – –
⌣ – ⌣ ⌣ – ⌣ ⌣ – –
⌣ – ⌣ ⌣ – ⌣ – . . .
– – ⌣ ⌣ – ⌣ ⌣ –
10 – – ⌣ ⌣ – ⌣ ⌣ – . . . .
– – ⌣ ⌣ – ⌣ ⌣ – –

Notes.

1. Verse 1 may have ended either with – ⌣ ⌣ – (εὐρυχόρῳ), or with – ⌣ ⌣ – – (εὐρυαγυίᾳ); but the former is more probable. Verses 2 and 9 presumably ended with – ⌣ ⌣ –. In 3, 4, 5, 6, 7, 11, the ending seems to have been – ⌣ ⌣ – –.

2. In verse 8 the words ἀναξίαλος Ποσειδάν may have been followed by ⌣ ⌣ – ⌣ ⌣ – – (*e.g.* ὅτε δίφρον ὀπάσσας). In v. 10, Πλευρῶν' ἐς ἐϋκτιμέναν may have been followed by ⌣ ⌣ – ⌣ ⌣ – (*e.g.* ἐπόρευσε παραί). These, at least, are possibilities suggested by a consideration of the whole context.

VI. THE PAPYRUS.

The papyrus of Bacchylides (Brit. Mus. Pap. DCCXXXIII) was found in Egypt by natives; the place of discovery is uncertain. It was brought to the British Museum towards the end of 1896, in the condition which Dr F. G. Kenyon thus describes[1] :—

'When it reached England the manuscript consisted of about 200 torn fragments. The largest of these measured 20 inches in length, and contained four and a half columns of writing; there were fourteen pieces of some considerable size, containing one or more columns; while the rest were small fragments ranging from pieces measuring a few inches in either direction to scraps containing barely one or two letters. For the most part the fractures were recent, and were probably due to the Egyptian discoverers; but in a few places the completely different colours of adjoining fragments show that the fracture must be of old standing. If the manuscript was deposited in a tomb (as is *a priori* probable, though no authentic information on the point is forthcoming), this might be due to ancient plunderers in search of treasure; but the matter is not one of great importance, except as indicating that the modern discoverers are not solely to blame for the present condition of this precious manuscript.'

That the poems were those of Bacchylides, appeared from the occurrence in the papyrus of some verses known to be his[2]. The patient skill of Dr Kenyon accomplished the difficult task of arranging the larger part of the fragments in their proper order, and thus reconstructing the body of the manuscript from its mutilated members.

In this papyrus a column of writing never contains *The columns.* more than 36 lines, nor less than 32; the usual number is 35 or 34. The average length of a column, from the topmost line of writing to the lowest, is 7 inches, or a fraction more: the width of a column,—measured from the beginning of the text on the left to the beginning

---

[1] Introduction to Bacchylides, p. xv.   [2] See introduction to the Fragments in this volume.

of the text in the next column on the right,—varies from about 5 to 5½ inches. Only a very few verses reach (or slightly exceed) the length of 5 inches (see, *e.g.*, IX. 48 ἄνδρα...εἶμεν, col. 18, l. 6 from the foot): the average length ranges from about 3 to 4½ inches.

The three sections of the MS. The reconstructed papyrus is in three parts or sections.

I. **The first section** (9 feet in length) contains columns I—XXII. Column I begins in the latter portion of Ode I, with the mutilated first verse of a strophe (πόλιν...βαθυδει-), which was perhaps the seventh strophe of the poem. Column XXII breaks off after verse 8 of Ode XI (τάν τ' ἐν Νεμέᾳ γυιαλκέα μουνοπάλαν). Between the end of this first section and the beginning of the next, there has been a loss of at least one column, and probably of more.

II. **The second section** (2 feet 3 inches in length) contains columns XXIV—XXIX, preceded by a few minute traces of the lost column XXIII. Column XXIV begins with the eleventh verse of a strophe of Ode XII (ὕβριος ὑψινόου). If, as is probable, that strophe was the second, this verse was the 44th of the poem. Column XXIX breaks off after v. 23 of Ode XIII (ὃς φιλοξείνου τε καὶ ὀρθοδίκου). The scale of the exordium might suggest that Ode XIII was on a somewhat large plan; in that case, more than one other column would have been required to complete it. Nor is it at all certain that the thirteenth epinikion was the last poem of that class. It is therefore impossible to conjecture how much has been lost between the end of this section and the beginning of the next.

III. **The third section** (3 feet 6 inches in length) consists of columns XXX—XXXIX. Column XXX is represented only by a fragment of the upper portion, belonging to the exordium of Ode XIV, the first of the 'dithyrambs.' The title Ἀντηνορίδαι ἢ Ἑλένης ἀπαίτησις is written at the top of the column, and not (as usual) in the margin. This circumstance, with the fact that the initial of the title is A, suggests that a new division of the volume began here. Column XXXIX (of which the right-hand part is torn off) ends with v. 11 of Ode XIX, Ἴδας. It is fairly certain that, in the complete papyrus, other dithyrambs followed the *Idas*.

After the reconstruction of the MS. in these three principal sections, there remained about 40 fragments, nearly all minute, for which no place had been found. All these have now had places assigned to them, chiefly by Prof. Blass; but with varying degrees of probability.

Prof. Blass supposes that the column numbered by Kenyon as the first was originally the fifth. It was pre- *The lost part of Ode I.* ceded by four columns which contained the beginning and the middle part of Ode I. He has arranged a large number of small fragments in the places which he supposes them to have held in these four columns, and in many cases has added conjectural supplements. Even with the supplements, a continuous sense is seldom effected; but we obtain what might be called a hypothetical skeleton of the four lost columns. I give this reconstruction in an Appendix to Ode I. It reflects much credit on the eminent critic's ingenuity and industry. But the element of conjecture involved is so extremely large as to render it questionable whether the skeleton of these four columns should be printed as part of the ascertained text.

Column I of Kenyon is designated by Blass thus V (I); *Numbering of the columns.* and so on up to Kenyon's twenty-ninth column, designated as XXXIII (XXIX). At this point a further difference comes in. A small fragment, giving morsels of 4 verses (XIII. 40—43), is regarded by Blass as representing a lost column, XXXIV, which he inserts between XXXIII (Kenyon's XXIX) and XXXV (Kenyon's XXX). Hence, from that point to the end, the difference between the two numberings is no longer four, but five; the last column, Kenyon's XXXIX, being Blass's XLIV. In this edition I retain Kenyon's numbering of the columns, which is also that used in the autotype facsimile of the papyrus (1897).

The thirteen epinikia are not arranged, as those of *Arrangement of contents.* Simonides were, according to the class of the contest[1];

[1] See p. 37, n. 4.

I. Epini-kia. nor, like those of Pindar, according to the festivals. Nor do they stand in the alphabetical sequence of the victors' names, or of their cities. Finally, the order is not chronological: the few dates which can be fixed suffice to prove that. The first two Odes, for Argeius, may, indeed, have been among the poet's earliest compositions (see p. 60). But Ode III belongs to 468; IV, to 470; V, to 476; VI and VII, to 452; XII (probably) to 481 or 479. As to Ode XIII, its place is doubtless due to the fact that it pertains to a minor festival. It may have been followed by other poems relating to local games; but not (we may presume) by any which concerned Olympia or Delphi, Nemea or the Isthmus. Perhaps we now possess the greater part of the epinikia written by Bacchylides. Among the fragments of his epinikia quoted by ancient writers, there is only one (fr. 1) which does not occur in the papyrus:—ὡς δ' ἅπαξ εἰπεῖν, φρένα καὶ πυκινὰν | κέρδος ἀνθρώπων βιᾶται. That fragment is excluded by metre from every extant strophe and epode of the recovered epinikia: but it may possibly have stood (as Blass suggests) in one of the lost epodes of Ode XI. There is no reason to suppose that in antiquity this class of the poet's works formed more than one book. Stobaeus quotes simply from Βακχυλίδου Ἐπινίκων.

II. Dithy-rambs. The six 'dithyrambs,' contained in the third section of the MS., are arranged in the alphabetical order of initials (but not of second letters also):—Ἀντηνορίδαι ἢ Ἑλένης ἀπαίτησις, Ἡρακλῆς, Ἠίθεοι ἢ Θησεύς, Θησεύς, Ἰώ, Ἴδας. In the book of 'dithyrambs,' when entire, some other pieces must have followed the Ἴδας in alphabetical order. There was probably a Κασσάνδρα (fr. 46), and a Λαοκόων (fr. 51). The story of Philoctetes being brought from Lemnos to Troy was told in a dithyramb of which that hero's name was doubtless the title (fr. 39). If the poem which related Europa's story (fr. 47) was a dithyramb, Εὐρώπη, it should have come between Odes XIV and XV: unless, indeed, the original title of XIV was simply Ἑλένης ἀπαίτησις, in which case Εὐρώπη might have stood before it, as Ἰώ before Ἴδας. But the fact already noticed, that the title of XIV is written at the head of col. XXX, makes this improbable.

The character of the handwriting in the papyrus will be seen from the specimens reproduced in the plates given below. It is a fine uncial, firm, clear, regular, and of a fairly large size. The size is not, however, quite uniform throughout. In some places (as *e.g.* in col. XXXI) the writing becomes slightly smaller, as if the scribe was desirous of economizing his space. On the whole, the MS. is among the most beautiful examples of Greek writing on papyrus. As the calligraphy indicates, it was probably designed for sale, or for a public library. *Character of the hand-writing.*

The only evidence as to the age of the MS. is that afforded by the handwriting. The term 'Ptolemaic,' as applied to literary papyri written in a formal book-hand, denotes that the hand is such as prevailed in the Greek book-world at large during the period when the Ptolemies ruled in Egypt[1]; *i.e.* from the beginning of the third century to about the middle of the first century B.C. This style was modified in the course of the transition to the first century of our era, when the 'Roman' period in Greek literary handwriting begins. *Age of the MS. The Ptolemaic period. The Roman period.*

Now the Bacchylides papyrus has some forms of letters which are distinctly Ptolemaic: but it also exhibits some traits which indicate that a transition to the Roman style is at hand. The A is Ptolemaic; it is angular, without any trace of a curve, and is written with two strokes of the pen. The M is broad, with a shallow dip, and is, so far, Ptolemaic; but the dip is usually curved. The Ξ, the most characteristic letter of all, is thoroughly Ptolemaic, being formed with exceptionally long strokes at top and bottom, and a mere dot in the middle. These are the three most significant letters. But some others also are noteworthy. E is thin, the central stroke projecting slightly beyond the short strokes above and below it. Θ is thin. O is very small. Π is remarkably broad. The curve at the top of Υ is much shallower than in the Roman period. All these features occur in papyri of the Ptolemaic age. On the other hand, the form of Λ, in *Character-istic letters in the Bac-chylides MS.*

[1] Kenyon, *Palaeography of Greek Papyri*, pp. 72 f.

which the right-hand stroke runs up a little beyond the other, shows the incipient influence of Roman style. In the narrow C, the upper part is sometimes separated from the rest, a peculiarity found also in the Harris MS. of *Iliad* XVIII (Brit. Mus. Pap. CVII), a papyrus of the first century[1].

Probable date.

Guided chiefly by these or like indications, Dr Kenyon assigns the Bacchylides papyrus to the first century B.C., when the Ptolemaic style was beginning to pass into the

Other papyri of the same period.

Roman. In confirmation of this approximate date, he refers to some other literary papyri of the same period. (1) Some of the Herculaneum rolls (all of which must be earlier than 79 A.D.) contain writings of the Epicurean Philodemus, a contemporary of Cicero, and may probably be referred to the middle or latter part of the first century B.C. These papyri show the Ptolemaic style in some test-letters, such as A, M, Ξ. (2) Another papyrus contains Hypereides *In Philippidem*, and also (but in a different hand) the third Epistle of Demosthenes (Brit. Mus. Papp. CXXXIII, CXXXIV). In the work of both these hands, some letters, as A, M, and Ξ, have Ptolemaic forms, akin to those in the MS. of Bacchylides: and both the hands belong to the period of transition from the Ptolemaic style to the Roman[2].

Condition of the text.

If the approximate date thus obtained be correct, the papyrus of Bacchylides was written about four centuries after the poet's death. In order to estimate the character

---

[1] Kenyon, *op. cit.* p. 76: cp. p. 85.

[2] Messrs Grenfell and Hunt (*Oxyrhynchus Papyri* I. 53) would refer the Bacchylides papyrus to the first or second century of our era. (1) They compare a papyrus of Demosthenes, which they would place in the early part of the second century. Dr Kenyon, however, observes (*Palaeography of Greek Papyri*, p. 76, n. 1) that the forms of some characteristic letters in the Bacchylides, such as M, Ξ, Υ, Ω, differ from those in the Demosthenes. He would refer the Demosthenes not to the second, but to the first century. (2) They also compare the M and Υ of the Bacchylides with those found in papyrus fragments of Thucydides and Aristoxenus which belong to the Roman period. But Dr Kenyon observes that, in these fragments, M is less broad, and also more deeply indented, than in the Bacchylides; while in the case of Υ the resemblance is not close. 'On the whole,' he concludes, 'the Oxyrhynchus papyri, which are all of the Roman period, seem to me to confirm the date here assigned to the Bacchylides.'

of the manuscript, the following subjects must be considered. I. The manner in which the scribe performed his task of transcription, and the classes of error which his work exhibits. II. The nature and extent of the corrections made by later hands. III. The condition in which the text was left by the latest corrector. IV. The signs used in the papyrus.

I. The hand of the scribe, A.

The first fact to be noted is the number of the instances which prove that the scribe habitually worked in a mechanical manner, merely transcribing the letters which he seemed to see before him, without regard for the sense. Such *Errors destructive of the sense.* instances are frequent throughout, and fall under two classes: (*a*) those in which the right reading is replaced by a word, or words, plainly unsuitable to the context; and (*b*) those in which it is replaced by an unmeaning series of letters. Some of these errors also violate metre. Thus :—

(*a*) III. 78 **A** wrote ευταν for εὖντα. v. 23 φοιβωι for φόβῳ: 106 ἐς for ὅς: 117 ἄγγελον for 'Αγέλαον: 170 τονκε for τὸν δέ. VIII. 6 ὅτι for ὅθι: 36 τάλας for πάλας: 41 μάθε for ἦλθεν. IX. 27 Εὐβοι|.ων for εὐβού|λων. X. 54 ὄμμα for νόημα: 94 κατακαρδίαν for κατ' 'Αρκαδίαν: 120 ἐπὶ for ἐπεί. XVI. 119 λᾶα for νᾶα. XVII. 6 ορει for ὄρι'. One instance of this class is so characteristic that it deserves to be signalised. In XII. 87 (where a maiden is compared to 'a joyous fawn'), instead of νεβρός, **A** wrote νεκρός.

(*b*) III. 15 ερα for ἱερά: 48 ἀβροβαώταν for ἀβροβάταν. VIII. 12 παρμεμορωι συν for ἐπ' 'Αρχεμόρῳ τόν. IX. 14 μανοον for μανῦον: 47 βρισενομεν for βρίσει. τὸ μέν: *ib.* εσελων for ἐσθλὸν (or ἐσθλῶν). XII. 127 αντασανυμ- for ἀντάσ(ας) ἀνατ-. XIV. 54 δικαληθηαν for Δίκαν ἰθεῖαν. XVII. 2 αβροβικων ... ιερωνων for ἀβροβίων ... 'Ιώνων. XVIII. 12 ενθενι for ἔνθα νιν. XIX. 8 πασι- for ποσ(ε)ι- (Ποσειδάν).

Errors destructive of metre.

Next, **A** made a number of errors which, though they do not always mar the sense, prove that the scribe was either ignorant or regardless of metre. Thus: III. 47 πρόσθεν δ' for πρόσθε δ': 48 ἔπεμψε for ἀνέπεμψε (ἀν- lost after ἀγαθέαν). V. 15 τοὺς for οὕς: 31 μοι for ἐμοί: 78 προσέειπεν for προσεῖπεν: 121 ὤλεσεν for ὤλεσε: 154 προλιπὼν for προλείπων: 169 θέλων for ἐθέλων. VI. 3 Ἀλφειοῦ for Ἀλφεοῦ (– –). VIII. 45 πολυζήλωτ' ἄναξ for πολυζήλωτε (ϝ)άναξ. X. 24 καὶ ἐπὶ ζαθέοις for καὶ ἐν ζαθέοις: 54 στήθεσιν for στήθεσσι. XII. 62 παύροισι for παύροις: 110 ὁπότε for ὁππότε. XIV. 56 σύνδικον for σύνοικον. XVI. 91 βορεους ἐξόπιθεν for βορεὰς ἐξόπιν (or ἐξόπιθε): 118 θέλωσιν for θέωσιν (– –). XVII. 40 καρτερὸν for κρατερόν: 41 ἔχεν for ἔσχεν.

It appears, then, that the scribe was habitually regardless both of sense and of metre. The particular forms of error found in his work may be classed under the following heads.

1. (i) *Case-endings of nouns.* I. 48 ἐπιμοίρων by error for -ον. V. 23 μεγάλαις for -ας. VIII. 46 ἔγγονοι for -ων. XII. 118 πεδίον for -ῳ. XIII. 18 ἔρδοντι for -α. XIV. 12 τυχόντας for -ες. XVII. 13 ἀλκίμου for -ων.

(ii) *Dialectic or poetical forms.* I. 60 νούσων by error for νόσων. V. 49 φιλοξένῳ for φιλοξείνῳ: 137 κόρα for κούρα. XVI. 42 ἀμβρότοι' for ἀμβρότου: 80 εὔδενδρον for ἠΰδενδρον.

2. (i) *Moods and tenses of verbs.* I. 65 εὐμαρεῖ by error for εὐμαρεῖν. V. 16 αἰνεῖ for αἰνεῖν: 35 ὑμνεῖ for ὑμνεῖν. 154 προλιπὼν for προλείπων. XVI. 112 ἀμφέβαλλον for ἀμφέβαλον. XVII. 28 ἐξέβαλλεν for ἐξέβαλεν. 41 ἔχεν for ἔσχεν.

(ii) *Paragogic ν* wrongly added: V. 121 ὤλεσεν. XVI. 3 τάμνεν. 109 ἰδ·ν (ἴδεν).

3. *Errors in spelling*[1].

(i) ει instead of ι occurs in Αἰγείνας (XI. 6): δεινῆντο

---

[1] From the spelling in the papyrus Prof. Blass has drawn an inference as to its date. The iotacism of ει for ι, or ι for ει, is comparatively rare in it. Such iotacism became extremely common in the first century of our era;

(XVI. 107, διvῆvτo A²?): ἐκείνησεν (IX. 10): θεῖνα (XII. 149, in accordance with the view of Aristarchus, who derived θείς from θείνω): νειν (= νιν, XVI. 91): Φερένεικος (V. 184, though Φερένικος in 37): ὡρείνατο (XII. 112).

(ii) ι instead of ει occurs in ἐριψιπύλαν (V. 56, made by a corrector, from ἐρειψ-: though in XII. 167 we find ἐρειψ-): ἤριπον (= ἤρειπον, X. 68, unless this was an error of tense): στίχειν (XVII. 36). The ει of Ποσειδάν is preserved in XVI. 59 f. and 79; but becomes ι in IX. 19, XIII. 20, XVI. 36, XIX. 8.

(iii) Other errors in single letters. V. 164 κρη for χρή. VIII. 16 Οἴλλειδας for 'Οϊκλείδας. X. 93 ἠλύκταξον for ἠλύκταζον. XVI. 16 ἀναξιβρέντας. XVII. 59 χαλκενκτύπου for χαλκεοκτύπου.

(iv) Non-assimilation of consonants. ν instead of γ: V. 69 ἐνχεσπάλου, VIII. 2 πεισίνβροτον, 33 μελανφύλλου. -τ' instead of θ': VIII. 15 ὅτ' ἵππιον.

4. *Omission of letters.*

(i) Single letters omitted. (*a*) The first letter of a word. III. 68, the π of πιαίνεται: V. 22, the π of πτάσσοντι: IX. 39, the γ of γάρ: VIII. 25, the γ of γε. (*b*) A letter in the middle of a word. X. 66, the first ι of 'Ακρισίῳ: XVI. 116, the ι of δόλιος: XVI. 35, the ι of στρατίαν: XVII. 26, the first o in Κερκυόνος: XVII. 24, one μ in Κρεμμυῶνος: *ib.* 56 one μ in ἔμμεν: X. 35 the τ of πολύπλαγκτοι: XVI. 124, the first ι of γυίοις, and the second a of ἀγλαό-.

(ii) In some places, a syllable, or a small group of letters, has been omitted. I. 73 f.: the λει of λείπει. XII. 176 ἀλαμπέσι, written αλαεπι. XV. 12 ἀκλέα for ἀγακλέα.

but an improvement began towards the end of that century, and was carried still further, under the influence of Herodian, in the second half of the second century. Hence Prof. Blass, in the 1st edition of his Bacchylides (pp. VII f.), was disposed to place the papyrus in the latter part of the first century, *after* the improvement had begun. Now, however (3rd ed. pp. VIII f., as already in the 2nd), he is content to refer the papyrus to a period *before* the tendency to greater iotacism had set in; and so acquiesces in Dr Kenyon's approximate date, viz. the first century B.C. In the *Palaeography of Greek Papyri* (p. 77, note) Dr Kenyon observes that, in the absence of fuller manuscript evidence, orthography cannot safely be accepted as the main guide to the date of a MS.

5. *Words wrongly transposed.*

IX. 20 ταχεῖαν ὁρμὰν by error for ὁρμὰν ταχεῖαν : XIV. 47
ἆρχεν λόγων for λόγων ἆρχεν : XVI. 100f. ἔμολέν τε .. μέγαρον,
for μέγαρόν τε .. μόλεν : ib. 102 f. ἔδεισε Νηρέος ὀλβίου for
ἔδεισ᾽ ὀλβίοιο Νηρέος : XVII. 52 χιτῶνα .. στέρνοις τ᾽ for
στέρνοις τε .. χιτῶνα. (Other probable instances occur in
XVI. 62 f. and 109 f., where see commentary.)

6. *Omission of words.*

III. 63 γε after ὅσοι. V. 129 οὐ γάρ : 183 ἐς after
Φερένικος. XIV. 55 ἀκόλουθον. XVII. 39 (perhaps) τε
after ὅς.

7. *Errors due to confusion of similar letters.*

(i) Instances of an ordinary kind.—A confused with
Δ or Λ : ΕΙ with Η : Η with Μ (the Ptolemaic Μ having
a shallow curve, while the cross-stroke of Η is often placed
high, and slightly curved).

XVII. 35 ϲΥΝΟΠΛΟΙϲΙΝ for ϲΥΝΟΠΛΟϲΙΝ (Λ for Α : then Ι added
after Ο).

V. 117 ΑΓΓΕΛΟΝ for ΑΓΕΛΛΟΝ (Λ dropped after Α : then a
second Γ added).

VIII. 41 ΜΑΘΕ for ΗΛΘΕ (Μ for Η : Α for Λ).

X. 54 ΕΜΒΑΛΕΝ ΟΜΜΑ for ΕΜΒΑΛΕΝ ΝΟΗΜΑ (Η of ΝΟΗΜΑ changed
to Μ : then the second Ν dropped).

XIV. 54 ΔΙΚΑΛΗΘΗΑΝ for ΔΙΚΑΝ ΙΘΕΙΑΝ (ΝΙ became ΛΗ, and
ΕΙ became Η).

(ii) Instances of a rarer kind.

IX. 47 ΒΡΙϲΕΝΟΜΕΝ for ΒΡΙϲΕΙ ΤΟ ΜΕΝ. Here ΙΤ became Ν.

XIV. 56 ϲΥΝΔΙΚΟΝ for ϲΥΝΟΙΚΟΝ. Here Ο is replaced by Δ.
This was possible, owing to the irregular manner in which
the small Ptolemaic Ο was sometimes formed.

(iii) Instances which appear probable, but are not
certain.

In VIII. 13 ΑϲΑΓΕΥΟΝΤΑ seems to have come from
ΛΩΤΕΥΟΝΤΑ (Ω passed into ϹΑ, and Τ into Γ).

In XII. 95 ΠΛΙӸΕ (ΙΝΟΥ) may have come from ΠΑΓӸΕΙΝΟΥ : if
so, Γ became Ι.

[In IX. 23 ΛΙӸΕ may have been a corruption of ΛΥΤΕ.

With the Ptolemaic forms of ⲩ and ⲍ, this is conceivable: see p. 125.]

8. *Omission of verses or parts of verses.*

The instances fall into three classes.

(i) Those in which whole verses, omitted by the scribe, have been supplied by a later hand.

(*a*) X. 106 τοῦ δ' ἔκλυ' ἀριστοπάτρα. Added by the later corrector **A³** at the top of col. XXII.

(*b*) XVII. 55, 56, 57 στίλβειν .. ἀθυρμάτων. Added by **A³** at the top of col. XXXVIII. See Plate I below.

(*c*) XVII. 16 νέον ἦλθεν δολιχὰν ἀμείψας. This, the last line in col. XXXVI, has been added by a later hand (probably distinct from **A³**), but with the unmetrical ἦλθε instead of ἦλθεν.

(*d*) XVIII. 22 χρυσόπεπλος Ἥρα. Added by **A³** at the foot of col. XXXVIII.

(ii) In one instance the first words of a verse were written by the scribe, and the rest supplied by a later hand. This is X. 23, κείνῳ γε σὺν ἄματι πρὸς γαίᾳ πεσόντα. Only the words κείνῳ γε were written by **A**: the rest were added by the hand mentioned above as supplying XVII. 16.

(iii) Lastly there are instances in which a verse, or part of a verse omitted by the scribe, has not been supplied by any later hand.

(*a*) After v. 84 of XII (καί τις ὑψαυχὴς κόρα) a verse has been lost. The letters ρᾶν, which appear in the papyrus at the end of v. 84, being separated from κό[ρα by a space equivalent to some 7 letters, seem to have been the last letters of the lost verse.

(*b*) In XVII. 48 only the first two words, ξίφος ἔχειν, remain; the rest of the verse (◡ ◡ – ◡ – ◡) is wanting. Here there may have been a defect, not only in the archetype of the MS. from which our papyrus was copied, but also in that of the copy or copies used by the correctors.

(A verse, the last in col. 19, has been lost after v. 30 of Ode X.: but this is due to mutilation of the papyrus.)

9. *Incorrect division of verses.* See above, pp. 95 f. It is doubtful how far the scribe is responsible, if he is responsible at all, for the errors of this kind which occur in the papyrus. They may have been due to Alexandrian κωλισταί of an earlier date.

Corrections made by the scribe himself (A¹). The limits of such corrections are very narrow.   1. The most frequent case is that in which the scribe corrects an error of his own in the ending of a word.   Thus he deletes the incorrect final ι in II. 14 Πανθείδαι: V. 46 Βορέαι: X. 1 Νίκαι(?): 86 μέριμναι.   He corrects I. 51 ἀνθρώποις to -ων: X. 69 παῖδες to -ας, 83 κυανοπλόκαμος to -οι: III. 50 ἔβαλλεν to -ον: XVII. 10 σεύοντι to σεύοντ', 18 λέγειν to λέγει.

2.   He sometimes adds (either in the text or above the line) a letter which he had omitted: as I. 39 the initial ι of ἱστορίᾳ: XVI. 1 the ι adscript after ω in κυανόπρῳρα: XVII. 8 the σ of λῃσταί.   Or he deletes a letter which he had wrongly added, as V. 129 the second α in 'Αφαρητα.

3.   Here and there he amends some graver mistake: thus in I. 56 he corrects ΕΛΑΚΕΝ to ΕΛΑΧΕΝ: III. 12 ΓΕΝΟΣ to ΓΕΡΑΣ: *ib.* 13 f. ΜΕΛΛΗ to ΜΕΛΑΜ, and ΦΑΡΕΙΝ to ΦΑΡΕΙ: in V. 134 ΑΘΑΝΑΤΟΝ to ΘΑΝΑΤΟΝ.

The scribe's corrections of his own errors are merely sporadic and casual. They seem to have been made *inter scribendum*, at the moment when he happened to observe a mistake. On the other hand, the numerous errors of every kind, many of them gross, which he left uncorrected show that he did not attempt a systematic revision of his work by comparing it with the archetype. There are several cases in which it is doubtful whether a correction is to be attributed to the scribe or to a later hand. Two of these are cases of *false correction*: V. 56 where the correct ἐρειψιπύλαν was written at first, but the second ε was afterwards deleted: X. 20 where παγξένῳ was first written, and then altered (against metre) to παγξείνῳ.   In XVII. 53, where στέρνοις had been rightly written, it seems to have been the scribe himself who incorrectly changed it to στέρνοισι.

II. The correctors, A² and A³.

The hand of the earlier corrector, denoted by **A²**, seems to be contemporary with the papyrus, *i.e.* of the first century B.C. It might even be asked whether this hand is not that of the scribe himself: but it is probably distinct from his. A specimen of it may be seen in col. XXXVIII. (Plate I below), where this hand has written the title of Ode XVIII in the left-hand margin, 'Ιὼ 'Αθηναίοις. It will be noticed that the difference between this hand and the writing in the text is not merely that the former is smaller. The writing of the text suggests a professional scribe, whose calligraphy is of a formal and somewhat mechanical type. The finer hand of the marginal title is more suggestive of a scholar.

The hand of the later corrector, denoted by **A³**, is a Roman cursive, probably not earlier than the second century. It is by this hand that the three verses, στίλβειν ...ἀθυρμάτων, have been written at the top of col. XXXVIII (see Plate I).

The work of A².—I. He corrected some small errors of an obvious kind. Thus he sometimes supplied letters which the scribe had omitted, as in I. 55 the first ι of ὑγιείας, in 73 the λει of λείπει, in V. 22 the π of πτάσσοντι. He also corrected a few (but very few) of the scribe's grosser errors, as by changing εὐμαρεῖ in I. 65 to εὐμαρεῖν: ἐπὶ in X. 24 to ἐν: νεκρὸς in XII. 87 to νεβρός: πασι- in XIX. 8 to ποσι-.

In one instance, on the other hand, he seems to be responsible for a false correction,—Πορθαονίδα in V. 70, where A had correctly written Πορθανίδα. On the whole, his work as a corrector seems to have been very limited, and not of much moment.

2. He added, in the left-hand margin, the *titles* of Odes II, XVIII, and XIX.

The work of A³ was far more considerable than that of his predecessor. Even he, indeed, did not undertake a thorough or systematic revision. But he left the text, as a whole, in a much better condition than that in which he found it.

1. He corrected a large number of small and evident errors in spelling (as when one or more letters of a word had been omitted),—wrong case-endings, such corruptions as επι for ἐπεί (X. 120), etc.

2. A more distinctive merit was that he restored the right word or words in a number of places where the scribe had written nonsense. Thus he restored in VIII. 2 ἐπ' Ἀρχεμόρῳ, τόν : 36 πάλας : 41 ἦλθε[ν : IX. 27 εὐβού|λων : 38 ἐπίσταμαι : 47 βρίσει. τὸ μέν : XII. 127 ἀντάσας ἀνατ- : XIV. 54 Δίκαν ἰθεῖαν : 56 σύνοικον : XV. 12 ἀγακλέα : XVI. 91 βορεάς : XVII. 2 ἀβροβίων...Ἰώνων.

3. He added some words which had been omitted ; as V. 129 οὐ γάρ : XIV. 6 τ' after Μενελάῳ : 55 ἀκόλουθον.

4. He also supplied some missing verses (five in all) : see above, I. 8 (i).

5. But he was as ignorant or regardless of metre as the scribe himself, and made several *false corrections*, which metre refutes. Thus in III. 47, τὰ πρόσθε δ' ἐχθρὰ φίλα, he wished to insert νῦν after ἐχθρά. In V. 179 he altered the correct Ὀλύμπιον to Ὀλυμπίων : in XII. 53 ὀπίσσω to ὀπίσω : and *ib*. 152 ἔρευθε to ἐρεύθετο.

He wished to double the ν in σῦνεχέως (V. 113) : to alter the Doric θατήρων (IX. 23) to θεατήρων : and to insert μ after the first ο of ὀβριμοσπόρου (XVIII. 32).

6. The *titles* of many Odes were added in the left-hand margin by **A³**. To him are probably due the titles of III and IV : and certainly those of VI, VII, VIII, X, XI, XIII, XIV (this at the top of the column), XV, XVI, XVII. He neglected, however, to supply the title of Ode V. With regard to Odes I, IX, XII, and XV, the mutilations of the papyrus leave it uncertain whether the titles were given.—It may be noted that, in the title of XI, **A³** writes Τισίαι instead of the correct Τεισίαι.

The fact that **A³** could supply words and verses omitted by **A** proves that he had access to some copy or copies other than our papyrus. But there is nothing to show that he possessed a MS. of which the text was better than that of the archetype from which our papyrus was copied.

III. The text as left by the latest corrector.

We have now seen the characteristics of the work done by the original scribe, and also the limits to the subsequent work of correction. As left by the latest of the ancient correctors (perhaps in the second century), the MS. still contained (1) many mis-spelt words, (2) many errors destructive of the sense, and (3) many flagrant breaches of metre. The following are examples:

1. *Mis-spelt forms of words.* V. 71 Ἀλκμήϊος, 146 f. ἐξαναρίζων: X. 66 Ἀκρσίῳ, 93 ἠλύκταξον: XVI. 66 ἀναξιβρέντας, 91 νειν (= νιν), 124 γύοις (= γυίοις): XVII. 36 στίχειν: XVIII. 3 Πειερίδων.

2. *Errors destructive of the sense* (with or without violations of metre also). V. 35 ὑμνεῖ (for ὑμνεῖν), 106 ἐς (for ὅς), 117 ἄγγελον (for Ἀγέλαον): IX. 47 εσελων (for ἐσθλόν or ἐσθλῶν): X. 54 ἔμβαλεν ὄμμα (for ἔμβαλεν νόημα), 94 κατακαρδίαν (for κατ᾽ Ἀρκαδίαν), 119 f. πρόγο|νοι ἐσσάμενοι.

3. Where violations of metre did not evidently mar the sense, the correctors passed them over. In a few instances they happened to heal a breach of metre, as (*e.g.*) by restoring ἐπ᾽ Ἀρχεμόρῳ in VIII. 2: βρίσει τὸ μέν in IX. 47: ἐν (for ἐπί) in X. 24: σύνοικον in XIV. 56: ἀγακλέα in XV. 12. But, allowing for such exceptions, it may be said that nearly all the unmetrical readings contained in the text, as written by the scribe, remained in it after **A³** had done his work. Indeed, as we have seen, some new breaches of metre were introduced, or suggested, by the correctors.

IV. The signs used in the papyrus.

1. **Accents.**—The Bacchylides papyrus is the earliest extant in which accents are used; and there is no other papyrus in which the use made of them is so large[1]. That

---

[1] Kenyon, *Palaeography of Greek Papyri*, p. 28.

which comes next to the Bacchylides in this respect is a papyrus which may probably be referred to the latter part of the first century, the fragment of Alcman in the Louvre. On the other hand there are no accents in the Petrie papyri of the third century B.C., nor in the Louvre Hypereides of the second century B.C. During the period of Greek literary writing on papyrus (which goes down to about A.D. 300), accents, when used at all, were intended as aids to the reader, especially in those poetical texts which presented difficulties of dialect, vocabulary, or metre. Accents in Greek papyri of prose-writers[1] are very rare.

In the Bacchylides papyrus accents are given to a very large number of words, but by no means to all. The longer words, and especially compounds, are usually accented. A preposition is very seldom accented, unless for some special reason, as when it follows its case (XVII. 51 κράτος ὕπερ): and this is true also of articles, pronouns, and adverbs[2]. The following points should be noted.

1. In the Bacchylides papyrus an oxytone word never has the acute accent on the last syllable, but receives the grave accent on the preceding syllable or syllables: thus πὰντι (XII. 231), θὰητον (X. 14), κεραυνὲγχες (VII. 48), πολὺκρὰτες (VIII. 15). The theory was that every syllable has an accent, but that in each word only one syllable can have the acute accent; if the word is of more than one syllable, the other syllable or syllables have the grave accent. According to this theory, the strictly correct mode of accenting would be (*e.g.*) παντί, πολὺκρατές. The practice which ultimately prevailed was to write the acute accent, and to omit the grave[3].

[1] As in Oxyrhynch. pap. 25 and 231 (Demosthenes), and 229 (Plato).

[2] See the photographs facing pp. 144—146.

[3] Dr Kenyon (*Palaeography of Greek Papyri*, p. 30) notes that traces of the practice observed in the Bacchylides occur in the Harris papyrus of *Iliad* XVIII (Brit. Mus. Pap. CVII, probably of the first century), and in the Bankes papyrus of *Il.* XXIV (Brit. Mus. Pap. CXIV, prob. of the second century), *e.g.* ἐλὼν, φρὲσιν: also in a *proparoxytone* word, ἐπὲσσεύοντο. (The latter may be compared with the peculiar case of ἐνὰλιναιέται in Bacch. XVI. 97, where α further has the rough breathing.) In an oxytone word of more than three syllables, the Bacchylides papyrus usually has the grave accent only on the second and third syllables from the end.

2. In the case of a perispomenon word (*i.e.* one which takes the circumflex on the last syllable), the practice of the papyrus is inconstant. Sometimes such a word is treated like an oxytone: thus βλῆχρας (X. 65), ὀβριμοδέρκει (XV. 20): on the other hand, we find πεδοιχνεῖν (XV. 9). Even a properispomenon word can have grave accents on syllables preceding that which takes the circumflex ; as in τελευτὰθεῖσα (I. 72 = 182 Blass).

3. The papyrus sometimes adds the acute accent on the last syllable of a word when an enclitic follows, as ἀεισάν ποτ' (VI. 6).

4. An acute accent falling on a diphthong is always placed on the first vowel, and not (as in later usage) on the second: *e.g.* μάινοιτ' (XII. 119), ὀύλιον (XVII. 53), γένσαντο (VIII. 46). A circumflex on a diphthong is generally so written as to cover both vowels, instead of being placed (as now) on the second.

5. Noteworthy accents on particular words.—φοὶβαν (XII. 139), *i.e.* φοιβάν, instead of φοίβαν: πολεμαίγιδος (XVI. 7): τριέτει (VIII. 23). I follow the papyrus in the accentuation of these three words, though with some doubt as to φοιβάν. Blass follows it in regard to the first two words ; but writes τριετεῖ (with the Attic accent).

In VIII. 32 ριπτῶν should be either ρίπτων or ριπτέων, to judge by the practice of the papyrus itself (see above, p. 83).

6. There are some *false accents* in the papyrus: ἐπεῖ (III. 23): μολῶν (III. 30; see Appendix): παράπληγι (X. 45); δινῆντο (XVI. 107). To these διχομηνίδος (VIII. 29) must surely be added ; though Blass retains it in his text. Editors of Pindar are agreed in giving διχόμηνις (*O.* III. 19).

II. **Breathings.**—The signs ⊦ and ⊣ (the two halves of the letter Η, originally used as an aspirate) sometimes occur in the Bacchylides papyrus to denote the rough and the smooth breathing respectively; as they do sometimes in the British Museum papyrus of the *Odyssey* (Pap. CCLXXI, written early in the first century). But the more usual signs, both in these two papyri and in others, are ∟ or ⌐ ,

⌐ or ⌐. The rounded comma-like breathings are not found in papyri[1].

The breathings are not seldom omitted in our papyrus. But the rough breathing is added to ὁ, ἁ, etc.; ὅς, ὅν, etc.: οἱ (= αὐτῷ); ὅτε: ὅτι: ὧδε: ὡς: ἅμα: ἵνα. It is omitted in V. 110 θ' οστις, perhaps because θ' implies it, and (without that reason) in III. 87 δ' ο χρυσος. It is added to ἁμετέρας in XI. 3; but not in V. 144, V. 90, or XVII. 5. There is no breathing on the ambiguous η (probably ᾗ) in V. 9. Among words to which the smooth breathing is added are, ἤ in XV. 6, ἄμμι, ὄρουσε, ὄφρα. The use of breathings, like that of accents, is sporadic and inconstant.

III. **Diaeresis.**—The marks of diaeresis (two dots) are usually placed in the papyrus over initial ι or υ as ἴσχουσι (V. 24), ὕδωρ (III. 86): and on ι sometimes when it is not initial, as εσϊδοντες (XII. 139). The proper use of these marks is to show that the vowel above which they stand does not form a diphthong with the vowel before it: as in ταὔσιον (V. 81). Owing, however, to the practice with regard to ι, that distinction is sometimes effaced. Thus in XVI. 38 νηρηϊδες, the marks of diaeresis serve their proper purpose, the scansion being – – ◡ ≍ : but in XII. 123 the dots appear also over the ι of νηρῆϊδος, though (as the accent shows) the scansion there is – – ◡ (Νηρῆϊδος).

IV. **Apostrophe.**—The apostrophe ('), marking the place of an elided vowel, is generally added; but it is sometimes omitted, as in VIII. 47 διευρέιας (δι' εὐρείας).

The apostrophe is not used where crasis occurs, as in κᾶμε (XVI. 33), κἤυτυκτον (XVII. 50).

V. **Marks on long and short syllables.**—1. The mark –, indicating a long syllable, is placed in the papyrus: (i) on long α in the case-endings of nouns and pronouns: in the last syllable of an adverb such as παντᾶι, and in the ending of 2nd or 3rd pers. sing. of a verb (as κυβερνᾶι). (ii) On any long vowel where the grammarians deemed such guidance needful, however

---

[1] Kenyon, *Palaeography of Greek Papyri*, p. 30.

superfluous it may seem (as *e.g.* in V. 52 ἐπιζήλωι): so θωρᾶκα, κᾶρυξ, κῦδος, νᾶον, σάπεται, etc.

Yet there is no mark on the last syllable of ἀληθεία in XII. 204, nor on the first of καλῶς *ib.* 206, though in each case the ᾱ is specially noteworthy.

2. (i) The mark ◡, indicating a short syllable is placed on α in the ending -αι of a *nominative plural*, in order to distinguish it from the ending ᾱι of the dative singular. Thus: XVI. 6 βορηῑᾰι, 97 f. ἐναλιναιέτᾰι, 107 ταινῑᾰι: XIX. 2 ξανθᾰι (but V. 92 ξανθᾱι dative).

(ii) The same mark is very often placed on a short *a, ι,* or *v*, even where no doubt as to the quantity was possible; as *e.g.* on the ι of ἁλίου and μυρίας: on the *v* of the penultimate in ἰσχύϊ, Δαϊπύλου, εὐφροσύναι.

Conversely, this mark is absent in XVI. 92 from the penultimate syllable of Ἀθαναίων, and *ib.* 129 from the first of παιάνιξαν, though the αι is exceptional.

VI. **Hyphen.**—The ὑφέν, ‿, is placed in the papyrus under a compound adjective, at the point of juncture between its two elements, to show that these form a single word. This is not confined to cases where a doubt is possible, such as that of ἀρηϊφίλου (V. 166), which could be read as two words. The mark is applied to compound adjectives generally, as (*e.g.*) δαμασίππου (III. 23), εὐρυάνακτος (V. 19), λιγύφθογγοι (*ib.* 23), and *passim*. But the practice is inconstant: *e.g.*, the hyphen is added to πολύπλαγκτον (X. 35), but not to πολυζήλωτ᾽ (VI. 45): to ἀναξιμόλπου (VI. 10), but not to ἀναξιβρόντας (XVI. 66). Among several compounds which do not receive the hyphen are εὐρυβία (XV. 31), διωξίπποι (VIII. 44), θεόπομπον (XVI. 132), θεότιμον (X. 12), Πυθιόνικον (*ib.* 13), τοξόκλυτος (*ib.* 39).

A peculiar instance occurs in XII. 199 (εἰ μή τινα θερσιεπής). A mark resembling a very small circle has been placed after the letters ΤΙΝ, perhaps to indicate that the words should be read as τιν᾽ ἀθερσιεπής.

VII. **Diastole.**—The διαστολή, a comma, occurs once,

viz. in XVI. 102, ἔδεισε, .νηρεος (to guard against ν being joined to ἔδεισε).

VIII. **Punctuation.**—The only point used in the Bacchylides papyrus is a single dot, placed level with the tops of the letters, or slightly above them[1]. This point serves to mark pauses of various lengths, doing duty sometimes for a full stop, sometimes for a colon, a semicolon, or a comma. There is no distinctive note of interrogation (such as the later ;). The punctuation is, on the whole, fairly full and regular; but it is not complete. A necessary point is sometimes omitted: as (*e.g.*) in I. 48 (= 158 Bl.), 58, 61, 67 : V. 169, 172 : XVI. 129. At the end of an ode a point was not practically required; and in that place it is more often omitted. It stands, however, at the end of IV, and of X.

The authority of the punctuation in the papyrus cannot be deemed great. In I. 70 (= 180 Bl.), for instance, the point after λάχεν has little weight as an argument against reading τιμάν rather than τί μάν ;

IX. **Paragraphus and Coronis.**—In lyric texts the Alexandrian practice was to place (1) the *paragraphus*, a straight line, below the last verse of a strophe or antistrophe; and (2) the *coronis with paragraphus,*)——, below the last verse of an epode, to mark the end of a system. The same symbol could stand at the end of an ode; but the end of an ode composed in systems was more properly marked by an asterisk, ⁂, with or without the addition of)——.

The use of these signs in the Bacchylides papyrus will appear from the following statement; in which, for brevity, the word '*coronis*' denotes '*coronis with paragraphus.*'

I. (1) Excluding places where mutilation leaves it doubtful whether the sign stood there, there remain 64 places where the *paragraphus* ought to appear as marking

---

[1] In one place (XIV. 47, after δικαίαν) the point is placed on a level with the bottom of the letters.; perhaps by a slip of the pen (Kenyon, *Introd.* p. xxi). In VIII. 83 a point after τυχὸν is so placed, but that seems to be an error, as there is no break in the sense.

141

the end of a strophe or of an antistrophe. The *paragraphus*
(or its equivalent) is written in only 24 of these places,
while it is omitted in 40. (2) Similarly there are 31 places
in which the *coronis* ought to appear. It (or its equivalent)
is present in 30 of these, being absent only after v. 26 of
Ode VIII.

That is, the papyrus seldom fails to mark the end of a
system or of an ode. But, far more often than not, it
neglects to mark the end of a strophe or antistrophe.

II. *Errors in the use of the signs.* (i) Interchange of
paragraphus and *coronis.*—A *coronis* stands for a *paragraphus*
in V. 175: a *paragraphus* for a *coronis*, in IX. 28 and XII. 99
(but not, I think, in III. 14). (ii) Misplacement of either
sign.—The *paragraphus* which ought to follow v. 64 of
Ode III is wrongly placed after v. 63. In Ode I a *coronis*
is rightly placed after v. 51 (= 161 Bl.), but incorrectly
repeated after 52. In Ode IX the *coronis* is wrongly placed
after 55, but is repeated after 56.

III. *Notes on particular points.*—1. At the end of Odes
VI and VII. but of no other, the asterisk is added to the
coronis. Ode VI is 'monostrophic' (written in strophes
without epode), and therefore, according to Hephaestion
Περὶ ποιήματος c. X, should have been followed by a coronis
only[1].

2. The following facts will illustrate the curiously
inconstant practice of the papyrus with regard to the
paragraphus.

In Ode III the *paragraphus* follows vv. 8, 50, 60, 63
(instead of 64), 92: but not 18, 22, 32, 46, 78, 88. (Mutilated: the places after vv. 4, 36, 74.) In V it follows 30,
and (in the form of coronis) 175: but not 15, 70, 95, 110,
135, 150, 190. (Mutilated: the place after 55.) In VIII it
follows 44 and 87: but not 9, 18, 35. (Mutilated: the
places after 61, 70, 96.) In X it occurs nowhere: in XII,
only as a substitute for the coronis after 99. In XV, XVI[2],
XVII it is nowhere omitted.

[1] Blass, *Praef.* p. xiv.
[2] Kenyon (p. 171) and Blass[3] (p. 143) do not, indeed, indicate it after XVI. 112; but a trace of it remains there.

Three autotype plates are subjoined. Plate I gives the
first 29 verses of Col. XXXVIII of the papyrus (a column
which contains 34 verses in all), besides three verses which
have been added at the top. It is a good page for reproduction, as showing additions made both by the earlier
corrector (**A**ᵛ) and by the later (**A**³)[1]. Plates II and III give
a series of eight shorter passages. I have selected these
partly on palaeographical grounds, as illustrating characteristic traits of the papyrus, but chiefly in view of their
interest for the textual criticism.

[1] The choice of this column was suggested to me by Dr Kenyon, who has himself reproduced it in *Palaeography of Greek Papyri* (p. 76). His plate and mine were independently taken from the original papyrus in the British Museum. As the plate given here is slightly wider than his, it includes ΙΔΑϹΛΑΚΕΔΑΙΜ in its right margin, and in its left margin a few letters from the ends of the longer verses in Col. XXXVII.

PLATE I.

Col. XXXVIII.—Ode XVII. 50—60, and XVIII. 1—21.

55 ⌉ στιλβειναπολαμνιαν
    φοινισσανφλογαπαιδαδ᾿ εμεν
    πρωθηβον· αρηϊωνδ᾿ αθυρματων

50   κήυτυκτονκυνεανλακαι
    νανκρὰτοσύπερπυρσοχάιτου·
    χιτωναπορφυρεον
    στερνοισιτ᾿ αμφικαιόυλιον

ν   θεισσαλανχλαμυδ᾿· ομματωνδε
    μεμνασθαιπολεμουτεκαι
    χαλκεοκτυπουμαχασ

60   διζησθαιδεφιλαγλάουσαθανασ
   ⟩—

Ἰω   παρεστιμυρῖακελευθοσ
ΑΘΗΝΑΙΟΙϹ   αμβροσίͅωνμελεων
    ὁσανπαραπειερίͅδωνλά
    χηισιδωραμουσᾶν

5   ϊοβλέφαρόιτεκαι
    φερεστέφανοιχαριτεσ
    βάλωσιναμφιτιμαν
    υμνοισιν· υφαινεννυεν
    ταισπολυηράτοιστικαινον

10   ολβῖαισαθαναισ
    εὐάινετεκηῖͅαμέριμνα·
    πρεπεισεφερτατανίͅμεν
    οδονπαρακαλλιοπασλα
    χο͞ισανεξοχονγερασ·

15   τιηναργοσοθ᾿ ιππιονλιπουσα
    φευγεχρυσέᾱβουσ   Ἰδασ
    ευρυσθενεοσφραδ͞αισιφερτάτουδιοσ   λακεδαιμ
    ϊναχουροδοδάκτυλοσκορα·
    δτ᾿ αργονομμασιβλεποντα

20   πάντοθενακαμάτοισ
ϟ   μεγιστο͞ανασσακελευσεν

Notes.—1. The three verses at the top of the column are vv. 55—57 of Ode XVII, which had been omitted by the scribe, and were added there by the second corrector, **A³**, in a hand of the Roman period, perhaps of the second century.—2. Below v. 60 is seen the coronis with paragraphus,)—, marking the end of Ode XVII.—3. The title of Ode XVIII, Ἰὼ Ἀθηναίοις, in the left-hand margin, is in a hand (**A²**) which was probably contemporary with that of the scribe. So also is the title of XIX, Ἴδας Λακεδαιμ[ονίοις, written in the left-hand margin of the next column, and partly seen to the right of XVIII. 16.—4. In XVIII. 9 the scribe wrote καινόν: but ε has been added (by **A³**) above ι, indicating κλεινόν.—5. In v. 15 ὀτιππειον has been corrected (probably by **A³**) to ὅθ᾿ ἵππιον.—6. After v. 21, μεγιστόανασσα etc., the verse χρυσόπεπλος Ἥρα was omitted by the scribe, but added by **A³** in the lower margin, which does not come into the photograph. The marginal sign opposite v. 21 calls attention to this.

COLUMN XXXVIII.—ODE XVII. 50-60, AND XVIII. 1-21.

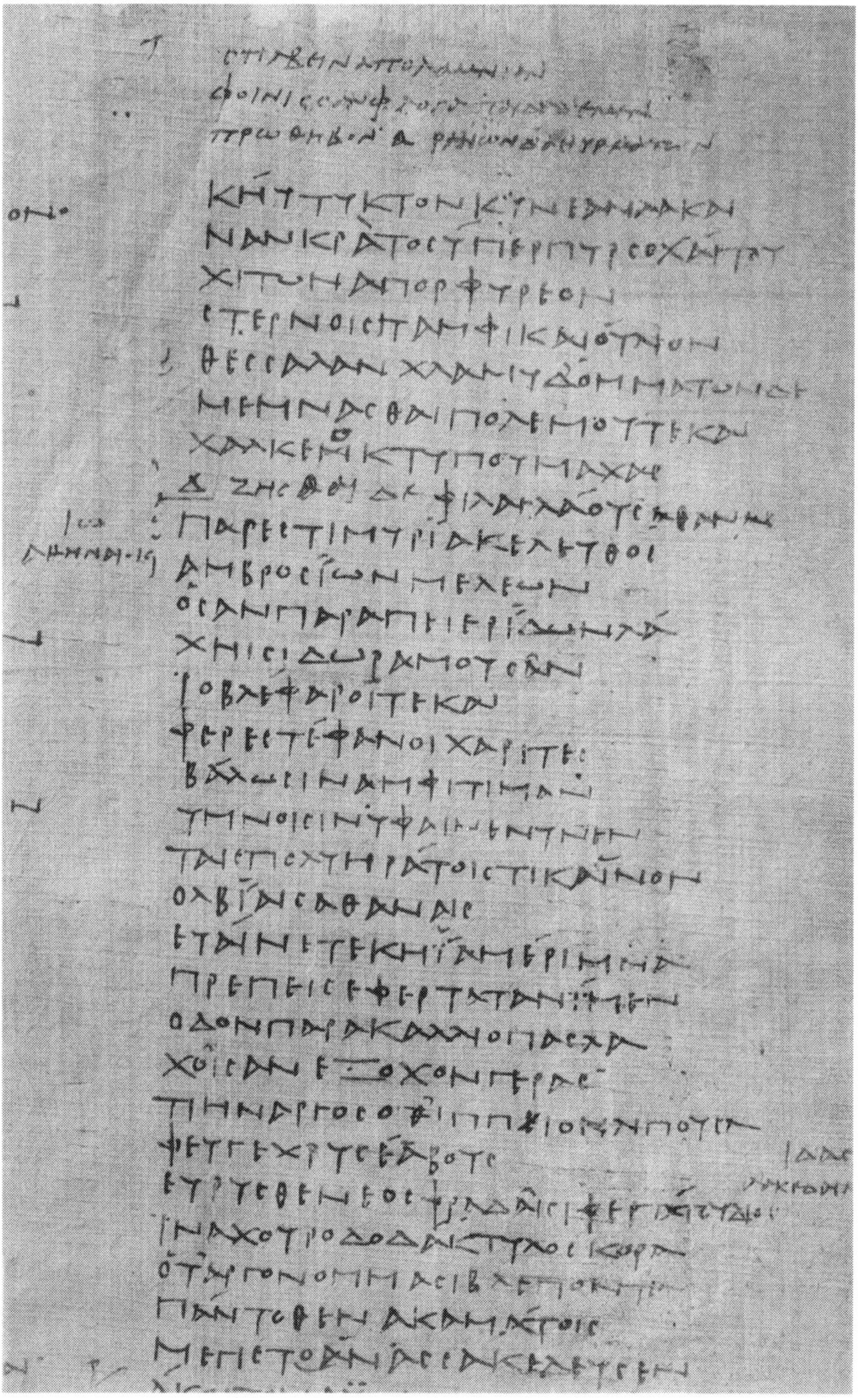

PLATE II

1 COL. I.—ODE I. 32-36.

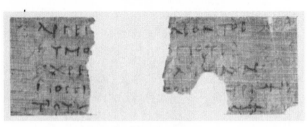

2 COL. IV.—ODE III. 71-77.

3. COL. XIV.—ODE VIII. 12-19

4. COL. XVII.—ODE IX. 6-11.

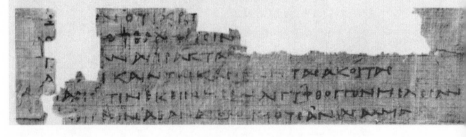

PLATE II.

1. Col. I.—Ode I. 32—36.

αργειο . . . . λεοντοσ
θυμο . . . . . οποτε
χρει . . . . βολοῖμαχασ·
ποσσι . . . . . φρο . . ατριων
τ᾽ ουκ . . . . ἀλων

2. Col. IV.—Ode III. 71—77.

. . . . . ΄κωντεμερο[. . . . . .
. . . . . μαλέαιποτ[. . . . . . .
. . . . γοσεφᾱμερονα[
. . . . . . σκοπεισβραχ[
. . . . ΄εσσαδ᾽ ελπισυπ[
. . . . εριων·οδ᾽ αναξ[
. . . . . . ΄λοσειπεφερη[

3. Col. XIV.—Ode VIII. 12—19.

αθλησαν· παρχεμορωι· τονξανθοδερκησ
πεφν᾽ ασαγένονταδρακωνυπέροπλοσ
σᾱμαμελλ· ντοσφονου·
ωμοιραπολὺκρᾱτεσ· ὁυνιν
πειθ᾽ οἴκλειδασπαλιν
στειχεινεσευάνδρουσαγ[
ελπισανθρωπωνυφαιρ[
ακαιτοτ᾽ αδραστονταλ[

4. Col. XVII.—Ode IX. 6—11.

ξ . . |ον·οτιχρυ[
ọ . . . . |οφθαλμοι̣|σιν[
π . . . αναπράκταν[
α . . α̣ ̑ ικαιννκασιγνητασακόιτασ
γασιω̑τινεκεινησενλιγύφθογγονμελισσαν
. . ειρεσὶν᾽ αθανατονμουσᾱναγαλμα

Notes.—**1.** Col. I.—Ode I. 32—36. In v. 34 the letter A has been deleted before X.—**2.** Col. IV.—Ode III. 71—77. Verse 71 was *ιοπλό]κων τε μέρο[s ἔχοντα Μουσᾶν*. (The letters α Μουσᾶν are supplied by two other fragments.) In v. 72 a corrector has wished to substitute κ for π (*κοτε* for *ποτε*). A separate fragment supplies the last letters of this v., which were ων, probably preceded by μ.—**3.** Col. XIV.—Ode VIII. 12—19. In v. 12 **A**³ has written X above M, and . TO above CT. In the transcript the point after *αθλησαν* means that a letter (E) is lost. In v. 16 **A**³ corrected the first λ of οἴλλειδασ to κ. In v. 19 **A**³ has written ἀ *και* above ΔΗ.—**4.** Col. XVII.—Ode IX. 6—11. In the MS. v. 6 began with ξυνόν, as words which ought to have stood before it (*παντὶ χώρῳ?*) had been wrongly added to the end of v. 5. See critical notes and commentary.

PLATE III.

5. Col. xviii.—Ode ix. 22—28.

θερμ . . . . . . πνεωνάελλαν
εστα . . . . . . δ᾽ αυτεθεατήρωνελαιωι
φάρε . . . . νεμπίτνωνομιλον
τετρ . . . . νεπει
καμ . . . . . . μονϊσθμιονικαν
δισν . . . . . ἁρυξανευβου
λων . . . . ωνπροφαται·

6. Col. xxv.—Ode xii. 84 f.

καιτισυφαυχησκο . . . . ρ̄αν
ποδεσσιταρφέω[

7. Col. xxvi.—Ode xii. 124—129.

ωστ᾽ ενκυανανθέϊθ[
ποντ|ωιβορ|έασυποκυ
μασι|νδ|αϊζει
νυκτ|ο|σαντασασανατε[
ληξενδεσυνφαεσιμ[
αοῖ· στορεσενδετεπο[

8. Col. xxxi.—Ode xv. 1—8.

. . . ιου . . . . . επει
. . . αδ᾽ επεμψενεμοιχρυσεαν
. . . . ἱᾱθε . . . . ρον . . . υρανία[
. . . . . ατωνγέμουσανυμνων
. . . . . νειτ . ρ . πανθεμοεντιεβρωι
. . . . γαλλεταιῃδολιχάυχενικυ[
. . . δεϊαφ . ενατερπομενοσ
. . . . . . δικηιπαιηονων

Notes.—**5.** Col. xviii.—Ode ix. 22—28. In v. 23 the scribe wrote AΪΞE. **A**³ has changed Ϊ to Υ, transfixed Ξ, and written Υ above it, thus making αὗτε. The ε above θα (indicating θεατήρων) is also from **A**³. At the end of v. 27 the scribe wrote (ε)υβοι : the I was corrected to Υ by **A**³, who also wrote Λ above the line at the beginning of v. 28.—**6.** Col. xxv.—Ode xii. 84 f. In v. 84 the I of KAI was added by a corrector (**A**²?). Above the second A of υψαυχας **A**³ wrote H. Between v. 84 and the verse beginning with ποδεσσι a verse has been lost. The letters ραν, seen to the right of 84, were probably the last of the missing verse, remains of which had been tacked on to v. 84.—**7.** Col. xxvi.—Ode xii. 124—129. In v. 127 the scribe wrote ANTACANΥΜ. **A**³ has added *as* above the line after AC, making ἀντάσας : has changed Υ into A (ἀνα-) : and has written TE above M.—**8.** Col. xxxi.—Ode xv. 1—8. In v. 1 the letter before OΥ was either Ϝ, N, or (though this is less probable) M. Note that the A of OΛKAΔ' (the first word of v. 2), comes beneath I, and extends a little to the right of it. The number of letters which preceded I in verse 1 was probably not more than three. (If the letter before OΥ was not I, but N or M, there would not have been room before it for more than two letters.)—For the rest of this passage, see critical notes and commentary.

PLATE III

5. COL. XVIII—ODE IX. 22-28

6. COL. XXV.—ODE XII. 84 f

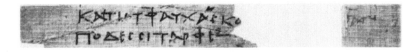

7. COL. XXVI.—ODE XII. 124-129.

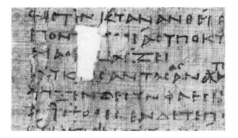

8. COL. XXXI.—ODE XV. 1-8

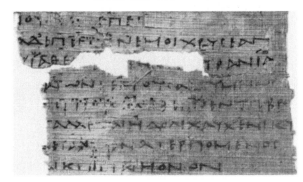

VII. THE TEXT OF THE PAPYRUS.

The following is the text as it stands when the smaller fragments, which had become detached from the continuous portions of the papyrus, have been fitted into their places. Hence this text contains, in many verses, some letters or words which appear only in the plates of fragments at the end of the Autotype Facsimile published in 1897, since, at that time, those fragments were still unplaced[1].

The object is to exhibit the text of the papyrus as it was left by the ancient correctors, before any modern hand had touched it.

1. A vertical line, | , denotes that the letters or words following it are supplied by a separate fragment. See, *e.g.*, vv. 3—5.

2. A dot on the line denotes a lost letter.

3. A letter which has a dot under it is doubtful.

4. The sign] denotes that a lacuna precedes, and the sign [that a lacuna follows.

5. The marks – – – –, in a verse of which some part remains, denote the loss of a considerable but uncertain number of letters (as in III. 41). When those marks occupy a whole line, they denote that a verse is lost (as after x. 30).

6. Asterisks, * * * *, denote a loss of several verses.

7. The metrical divisions (strophe, antistrophe, epode) are shown in the margin. These indications make it easy to verify the use or omission in the MS. of paragraphus and coronis.

---

[1] The only fragments which do not appear at all in the Facsimile are parts of III. 8—10 and of VIII. [IX.] 82—84, which were separately acquired in Egypt by Mr B. P. Grenfell, and were received just after the photographs had been taken (Kenyon, *Introd.* p. xvi).

8. Verses omitted by the scribe, and added by a corrector at the head or at the foot of a column, are printed in uncial type. See x. 106; xvii. 16, 55—57; xviii. 22. That type is used also in x. 23, where only the first two words were written by the scribe.

9. The title printed here at the head of an Ode (as Τωι αντωι at the head of Ode II) is that which is given in the papyrus. In the papyrus, however, such a title is written in the left-hand margin; except in the case of Ode XIV, where it is written at the head of the column.

I.

*   *   *   *

ἐπ. ε΄.   ..... ΑΦΘΕ
         .. ϹΤΡΙΤΑΤΑΙΜΕ[
         .. ΕΡΑΙΜΙΝΩϹΑΡ... |Ϲ
         .. ΥΘΕΝΑΙΟΛΟΠΡ... |ΝΟΙϹ[
     5   . ΑΥϹΙΠΕΝΤΗΚΟΝΤ. |ϹΥΝ
         . ΡΗΤΩΝΟΜΙΛΩΙ.

στρ. ϛ΄.   . ΙΟϹΕΥΚΛΕΙΟΥΔΕΕ
         . ΑΤΙΒΑΘΥΖΩΝΟΝΚΟΡ|ΑΝ
         . ΕΞΙΘΕΑΝΔΑΜΑϹΕΝ
         . ΑΙΟΙΛΙΠΕΝΗΜΙϹΥΛΑ|ΩΝ
     10   . ΝΔΡΑϹΑΡΗΙΦΙΛΟΥϹ
         .. ϹΙΝΠΟΛΥΚΡΗΜΝΟΝ|ΧΘΟΝΑ
         . ΕΙΜΑϹΑΠΟΠΛΕΩΝΩ.. |Τ΄ ΕϹ
         ΚΝΩϹϹΟΝΙΜΕΡΤΑΝ... ΛΙΝ

ἀντ. ϛ΄.   . ΑϹΙΛΕΥϹΕΥΡΩΠΙΑ[
     15   ... ΔΕΚΑΤΩΙΔ΄ ΕΥΞ... |ΟΝ
         .... Κ΄ ΕΥΠΛΟΚ[
         .... ΕΚΥΔΕ[
         .... ΠΡΥΤΑ[
     19   .... ΔΝ[
ἐπ. ϛ΄.   *   *   *   *
                 ]ΞΑΝ ΘΥΓΑΤΡΕϹ

στρ. ζ΄. **Col. 1** ΠΟΛ....... ΝΒΑΘΥ
     30   ΔΕΙΕΛΟΙ.... ϹΜΕΝΓΕΝΟϹ
         ΕΠΛΕ....... ΡΟΧΕΙΡ
         ΑΡΓΕΙΟ....... ΛΕΟΝΤΟϹ

ΘΥΜΟ......ΟΠΟΤΕ
ΧΡΕΙ.....ΒΟΛΟΙΜΑΧΑΣ·
35 ΠΟϹϹΙ.....ΦΡΟ...ΑΤΡΙΩΝ
Τ' ΟΥΚ.....Α.....ΑΛΩΝ

ἀντ. ζ'.   ΤΟϹΑΠΑ|Ν[
       ΤΟΞΟϹΑ|ΠΟ.........Ν
       ΑΜΦΙΤ' ΙΑΤ|Ο[
40 ΞΕΙΝΩΝΤΕ..ΛΑΝΟΡΙ...ΑΙ·
       .ΥΔΕΛΑΧΩΝ.ΑΡΙΤΩΝ
       ΠΟΛΛΟΙϹΤΕΘ..ΜΑϹΘΕΙϹΒΡΟΤΩΝ
       ΑΙΩΝ' ΕΛΥϹΕΝ.ΕΝΤΕΠΑΙ
       ΔΑϹΜΕΓΑΙΝΗ.ΟΥϹΛΙΠΩΝ·

ἐπ. ζ'. 45 .ΩΝΕΝΑΟΙΚ..ΝΙΔΑϹ
       ΥΨΙΖΥΓΟϹΙϹ..ΙΟΝΙΚΟΝ
       ΘΗΚΕΝΑΝΤ...ΡΓΕϹΙΑΝΛΙΠΑΡΩΝΤ' ΑΛ
       ΛΩΝϹΤΕΦΑΝ..ΕΠΙΜΟΙΡΟΝ
       ΦΑΜΙΚΑΙΦΑϹΩ..ΓΙϹΤΟΝ
50 ΚΥΔΟϹΕΧΕΙΝΑΡΕΤΑΝ·ΠΛΟΥ
       ΤΟϹΔΕΚΑΙΔΕΙΛΟΙϹΙΝΑΝΘΡΩΠΩΝΟΜΙΛΕΙ

στρ. η'.   ΕΘΕΛΕΙΔ' ΑΥΞΕΙΝΦΡΕΝΑϹ
       ΑΝΔΡΟϹ·ΟΔ' ΕΥΕΡΔΩΝΘΕΟΥϹ
       ΕΛΠΙΔΙΚΥΔΡΟΤΕΡΑΙ
55 ϹΑΙΝΕΙΚΕΑΡ·ΕΙΔ' ΥΓΙΕΙΑϹ
       ΘΝΑΤΟϹΕΩΝΕΛΑΧΕΝ
       ΖΩΕΙΝΤ' ΑΠΟΙΚΕΙΩΝΕΧΕΙ
       ΠΡΩΤΟΙϹΕΡΙΖΕΙΠΑΝΤΙΤΟΙ
       ΤΕΡΨΙϹΑΝΘΡΩΠΩΝΒΙΩΙ

ἀντ. η'. 60 ΕΠΕΤΑΙΝΟϹΦΙΝΓΕΝΟΥ
       ..ΝΠΕΝΙΑϹΤ' ΑΜΑΧΑΝΟΥ
       ΙϹΟΝΟΤ' ΑΦΝΕΟϹΙ
       ΜΕΙΡΕΙΜΕΓΑΛΩΝ·ΟΤΕΜΕΙΩ[
Col. 2   ΠΑΥΡΟΤΕΡΩΝΤΟΔΕΠΑΝ
65 ΤΩΝΕΥΜΑΡΕΙΝΟΥΔΕΝΓΛΥΚΥ
       ΘΝΑΤΟΙϹΙΝ·ΑΛΛ' ΑΙΕΙΤΑΦΕΥ
       ΓΟΝΤΑΔΙΖΗΝΤΑΙΚΙΧΕΙΝ

ἐπ. η'.   ΟΝΤΙΝΑΚΟΥΦΟΤΑΤΑΙ
       ΘΥΜΟΝΔΟΝΕΟΥϹΙΜΕΡΙΜΝΑΙ
70 ΟϹϹΟΝΑΝΖΩΗΙΧΡΟΝΟΝΤΟΝΔ'ΕΛΑΧΕΝ·ΤΙ

ΜΑΝ·ΑΡΕΤΑΔ' ΕΠΙΜΟΧΘΟC
..... ΛΕΥΤΑΘΕΙCΑΔ' ΟΡΘΩC
...... ΑΙΕΥΤΕΘΑΝΗΙΛΕΙ
,...... ΖΗΛΩΤΟΝΕΥΚΛΕΙΑCΑ ... ΜΑ
)‾‾‾

II.

Τωι αυτωι

στρ.
Α ..... ϹΕΜΝΟΔΟΤΕΙΡΑΦΗΜΑ[
ΕϹΚ ..... ΕΡΑΝΧΑΡΙΤΩ
ΝΥΜ .. ΦΕΡΟΥC' ΑΓΓΕΛΙΑΝ
ΟΤΙΜ .. ΑϹΘΡΑCΥΧΕΙΡΑΡ
5 ΓΕΙΟ .. ΡΑΤΟΝΙΚΑΝ

ἀντ.
ΚΑΛΩΝΔ' ΑΝΕΜΝΑCΕΝΟ͡C' ΕΝΚΛ ... ΝΩΙ
ΑΥΧΕΝΙΙϹΘΜΟΥΖΑΘΕΑΝ
ΛΙΠΟΝΤΕCΕΥΞΑΝΤΙΔΑΝΑ
CΟΝΕΠΕΔΕΙΞΑΜΕΝΕΒΔΟΜΗ
10 ΚΟΝΤΑ .. ΝϹΤΕΦΑΝΟΙϹ . Ν·

ἐπ.
ΚΑΛΕΙΔΕΜΟΥC' ΑΥΘΙΓΕΝΗC
ΓΛΥΚΕΙΑΝΑΥΛΩΝΚΑΝΑΧΑΝ
ΓΕΡΑΙΡΟΥC' ΕΠΙΝΙΚΙΟΙϹ
ΠΑΝΘΕΙΔΑΦΙΛΟΝΥΙΟΝ
)‾‾‾

III.

Ιερωνι συρακοσιωι ιπποις .... πια

στρ. α'.
ΑΡ|ΙϹ|ΤΟΚΑΡΠΟΥϹΙΚΕΛΙΑϹΚΡΕΟΥϹΑΝ
Δ . |ΜΑΤ|ΡΑΙΟϹΤΕΦΑΝΟΝΤΕΚΟΥΡΑΝ
Υ|ΜΝ|ΕΙΓΛΥΚΥΔΩΡΕΚΛΕΙΟΙΘΟΑϹΤΟ
... ΠΙΟΔΡΟΜΟΥϹΙΕΡΩΝΟϹΙΠΠ . ΥϹ·

ἀντ. α'. 5
.... ΤΟΓΑΡϹΥΝΥΠΕΡΟΧΩΙΤΕΝΙΚΑΙ
..... ΛΑΙΑΙΤΕΠΑΡΕΥΡΥΔΙΝΑΝ
.... ΕΙΝΟΜΕΝΕΟϹΕΘΗΚΑΝ
. ΛΒΙΟΝ .... ΝΚΥΡΗϹΑΙ·

ἐπ. α'.
ΘΡΟΗϹΕΔΕΛ[
10 ΑΤΡΙϹΕΥΔΑΙΜ[
Col. 3
Ο͡ϹΠΑΡΑΖΗΝΟϹΛΑΧΩΝ
ΠΛΕΙϹΤΑΡΧΟΝΕΛΛΑΝΩΝΓΕΡΑϹ

ΟΙΔΕΠΥΡΓΩΘΕΝΤΑΠΛ . ΥΤΟΝΜΗΜΕΛΑΜ
ΦΑΡΕΙΚΡΥΠΤΕΙΝCΚΟΤΩΙ·

στρ. β'. 15 ΒΡΥΕΙΜΕΝΙΕΡΑΒΟΥΘΥΤΟΙCΕΟΡΤΑΙC·
ΒΡΥΟΥCΙΦΙΛΟΞΕΝΙΑCΑΓΥΙΑΙ·
ΛΑΜΠΕΙΔ' ΥΠΟΜΑΡΜΑΡΥΓΑΙCΟΧΡΥCΟC
ΥΨΙΔΑΙΔΑΛΤΩΝΤΡΙΠΟΔΩΝCΤΑΘΕΝΤΩΝ

ἀντ. β'. ΠΑΡΟΙΘΕΝΑΟΥ·ΤΟΘΙΜΕΓΙ . . ΟΝΑΛCΟC
20 Φ . . ΒΟΥΠΑΡΑΚΑCΤΑΛΙΑ . . . ΕΘΡΟΙC
Δ . ΛΦΟΙΔΙΕΠΟΥCΙΘΕΟΝΘ . . ΝΤΙC
ΑΓΛΑΙΖΕΘΩΓΑΡΑΡΙCΤΟC . ΛΒΩΝ·

ἐπ. β'. ΕΠΕΙΠΟΤΕΚΑΙΔΑΜΑCΙΠ . ΟΥ
ΛΥΔΙΑCΑΡΧΑΓΕΤΑΝ
25 ΕΥΤΕΤΑΝΠΕΠ[. .
ΖΗΝΟCΤΕΛΕ . . . . CΙΝ
CΑΡΔΙΕCΠΕΡCΑ . . . . ΑΤΩΙ
ΚΡΟΙCΟΝΟΧΡΥCΑ[

στρ. γ'. ΦΥΛΑΞ' ΑΠΟΛΛΩΝ . . . . . . ΕΛΠΤΟΝΑΜΑΡ
30 Μ . ΛΩΝ·ΠΟΛΥΔ . . . . . . ΟΥΚΕΜΕΛΛΕ
ΜΙΜΝΕΙΝΕΤΙΔ . . . . . . ΝΑΝ·Π . . ΑΝΔΕ
ΧΑΛ . . ΤΕΙΧΕΟCΠ . . . . . . ΘΕΝΑΥ[

ἀντ. γ'. ΝΑΗ . ΑΤ' ΕΝΘΑCΥ . . . . . . ΤΕΚΕΔ[
CΥ . ΕΥΠΛΟΚΑΜΟΙ . ΕΠΕΒΑΙΝ' ΑΛΑ[
35 . Υ . . ΤΡΑCΙΔΥΡΟ . ΕΝΑΙC·ΧΕΡΑCΔ[
. . ΠΥΝΑΙΘΕΡΑC . ΕΤΕΡΑCΑΕΙΡΑ[

ἐπ. γ'. . . . . ΝΕΝ·ΥΠΕΡ . . ΕΔΑΙΜΟΝ
. . ΥΘΕΩΝΕCΤΙ . ΧΑΡΙC·
. . ΥΔΕΛΑΤΟΙΔ . . ΑΝΑΞ·
40 . . . . . ΙΝΑΛΥΑ . ΤΑΔΟΜΟΙ
— — — — — — ΜΥΡΙΩΝ
— — — — — — Ν·

στρ. δ'. — — — — — ΝΑCΤΥ
— — — — — ΔΙΝΑC
Col. 4 45 ΠΑΚΤΩΛΟC·Α . ΙΚΕΛΙΩCΓΥΝΑΙΚΕC
ΕΞΕΥΚΤΙΤ . ΝΜΕΓΑΡΩΝΑΓΟΝΤΑΙ·

ἀντ. δ'.   ΤΑΠΡΟΣΘΕΝΔ .. ΘΡΑΝΥΝΦΙΛΑΘΑΝΕΙΝΓΛΥΚΙΣΤΟΝ·
TΟΣ' ΕΙΠΕΚΑΙΑΒ .. ΒΑΤΑΝΚ ... ΥCΕΝ
ΑΠΤΕΙΝΞΥΛΙΝΟΝΔΟΜΟΝ·ΕΙ ... ΟΝΔΕ
50   ΠΑΡΘΕΝΟΙ·ΦΙΛΑΣΤΑΝΑΜΑΤΡΙΧΕΙΡΑC

ἐπ. δ'.   ΕΒΑΛΛΟΝ·ΟΓΑΡΠΡΟΦΑΝΗCΘΝΑ
ΤΟΙCΙΝΕΧΘΙCΤΟCΦΟΝΩΝ·
ΑΛΛ' ΕΠΕΙΔΕΙΝΟ .. ΥΡΟC
ΛΑΜΠΡΟΝΔΙΑΙ ...... ΝΟC
55   ΖΕΥCΕΠΙCΤΑCΑ .... ΘΕCΝΕΦΟC
CΒΕΝΝΥΕΝΞΑΝΘΑ[

στρ. ε'.   ΑΠΙCΤΟΝΟΥΔΕΝΟΤΙΘ ..... ΡΙΜΝΑ
ΤΕΥΧΕΙ·ΤΟΤΕΔΑΛΟΓΕΝΗ .... ΛΛΩΝ
ΦΕΡΩΝΕCΥΠΕΡΒΟΡΕΟ ... |ΕΡΟΝ|ΤΑ
60   CΥΝΤΑΝΙCΦΥΡΟΙCΚΑΤ .. |ΑCCΕ|ΚΟΥΡΑΙC

ἀντ. ε'.   ΔΙΕΥCΕΒΕΙΑΝ·ΟΤΙΜΕ ..... |ΝΑ|ΤΩΝ
ΕCΑ . ΑΘΕΑΝΕΠΕΜΨΕΠ .. |Ω·
ΟCΟ . ΜΕΝΕΛΛΑΔ' ΕΧΟΥC|ΙΝ| . ΥΤΙ[
ΩΜ . ΓΑΙΝΗΤΕΙΕΡΩ|ΝΘΕΛ|ΗCΕ|Ι

ἐπ. ε'.   65   ... ΕΝ . ΕΟΠΛΕΙΟΝΑ|ΧΡΥC|ΟΝ
.... ΑΙΠΕΜΨΑΙΒΡΟΤΩΝ
... ΓΕΙΝΠΑΡΕCΤΙΝΟC
.... ΗΦΘΟΝΩΙΠΙΑΙΝΕΤΑΙ
.... ΛΗΦΙΛΙΠΠΟΝΑΝΔΡΑ| . ΗΙΟ|Ν
70   .... ΙΟΥCΚΑΠΤΡ . ΝΔΙΟ·

στρ. ϛ'.   .... 'ΚΩΝΤΕΜΕΡΟ[......]|ΑΜΟΥ|CΑΝ·
..... ΜΑΛΕΑΙΠΟΤ[...... ']ΩΝ
.... ΝΟCΕΦΑΜΕΡΟΝΑ[
.... ΑCΚΟΠΕΙCΒΡΑΧ[

ἀντ. ϛ'.   75   .... 'ΕCCΑΔ' ΕΛΠΙCΥΠ[
.... ΕΡΙΩΝ·ΟΔ' ΑΝΑΞ[
...... 'ΛΟCΕΙΠΕΦΕΡΗ[
Col. 5   ΘΝΑΤΟΝΕΥΝΤΑΧΡΗΔΙΔΥΜΟΥCΑΕΞΕΙΝ

ἐπ. ϛ'.   ΓΝΩΜΑCΟΤΙΤ' ΑΥΡΙΟΝΟΨΕΑΙ
80   ΜΟΥΝΟΝΑΛΙΟΥΦΑΟC
ΧΩΤΙΠ·ΕΝΤΗΚΟΝΤ' ΕΤΕΑ

ΖΩΑΝΒΑΘΥΠΛΟΥΤΟΝΤΕΛΕΙC·
ŎCΙΑΔΡΩΝΕΥΦΡΑΙΝΕΘΥΜΟΝΤΟΥΤΟΓΑΡ
ΚΕΡΔΕΩΝΥΠΕΡΤΑΤΟΝ·
)⎯⎯⎯

στρ. ζ'. 85 ΦΡΟΝΕΟΝΤ . CΥΝΕΤΑΓΑΡΥΩ·ΒΑΘΥCΜΕΝ
ΑΙΘΗΡΑΜΙΑΝΤΟC·ΥΔΩΡΔΕΠΟΝΤΟΥ
ΟΥCΑΠΕΤΑ . ·ΕΥΦΡΟCΥΝΑΔ' ΟΧΡΥCΟC·
ΑΝΔΡΙΔ' Ο . . ΕΜΙCΠΟΛΙΟΝΠ . . ΕΝΤΑ

ἀντ. ζ'. ΓΗΡΑCΘΑΛ . . . ΝΑΥΤΙCΑΓΚΟΜΙCΑΙ
90 ΗΒΑΝ·ΑΡΕΤΑ . . . . ΕΝΟΥΜΙΝΥΘΕΙ
ΒΡΟΤΩΝΑΜΑC . . . ΤΙΦΕΓΓΟC·ΑΛΛΑ
ΜΟΥCΑΝΙΝΤΡ . . . . ΙΕΡΩΝCΥΔ' ΟΛΒΟΥ

ἐπ. ζ'. ΚΑΛΛΙCΤ' ΕΠΕΔ . . . ΑΟΘΝΑΤΟΙC
ΑΝΘΕΑ·ΠΡΑΞΑ . . . Δ' ΕΥ
95 ΟΥΦΕΡΕΙΚΟCΜ . . . . Ω
ΠΑ·CΥΝΔ' ΑΛΑΘ . . . . ΚΑΛΩΝ
ΚΑΙΜΕΛΙΓΛΩCCΟΥΤΙCΥΜΝΗCΕΙΧΑΡΙΝ
ΚΗΙΑCΑΗΔΟΝΟC
)⎯⎯⎯

IV.

Τωι αυτωι πυθια

στρ. α'. ΕΤΙCΥΡΑΚΟCΙΑΝΦΙΛΕΙ
ΠΟΛΙΝΟΧΡΥCΟΚΟ . ΑCΑΠΟΛΛΩΝ
ΑCΤΥΘΕΜΙΝΘ' ΙΕ . . ΝΑΓΕΡΑΙΡΕΙ·
ΤΡΙΤΟΝΓΑΡΠ . . . . . ΛΟΝΥΨΙΔΕΙΡΟΥΧΘΟΝΟC
5 ΠΥ . ΙΟΝΙΚ . . . . ΤΑΙ
Ω . . ΠΟΔ . . . . CΥΝΙΠΠΩΝ·

⎯ ⎯ ⎯ ⎯ ⎯ ⎯
⎯ ⎯ ⎯ ⎯ ⎯ ⎯· 'ΑCΑΛΕΚΤΩΡ
⎯ ⎯ ⎯ ⎯ ⎯ ⎯ ΤΙΝΟΩΙ
10 ⎯ ⎯ ⎯ ⎯ ⎯ ⎯ ΥΜΝΟΥC

στρ. β'. ⎯ ⎯ ⎯ ⎯ ⎯ ⎯ |ΙCΟΡ
⎯ ⎯ ⎯ ⎯ ⎯ ⎯ |ΑCΤΑΛΑΝ[
Col. 6 ΔΕΙΝΟΜΕΝΕΟCΚ' ΕΓΕΡΑ . . ΜΕΝΥΙΟΝ
ΠΑΡΕCΤΙΑΝΑΓΧΙΑΛΟΙCΙ . . . . ΑCΜΥΧΟΙC
15 ΜΟΥΝΟΝΕΠΙΧΘΟΝΙΩ . ΤΑΔΕ
ΜΗCΑΜΕΝΟΝCΤΕΦΑΝΟΙCΕΡΕΠΤΕΙΝ

ΔΥΟΤ' ΟΛΥΜΠΙΟΝΙΚΑϹ
   ΑΕΙΔΕΙΝ·ΤΙΦ . ΡΤΕΡΟΝΗ . ΕΟΙ . ΙΝ
   ΦΙΛΟΝΕΟΝΤΑΠΑΝΤΟ . . ΠΩΝ
20 ΛΑΓΧΑΝΕΙΝΑΠΟΜΟΙΡΑ . . . ΘΛΩΝ·

V.

στρ. α΄.   ΕΥΜΟΙΡΕ . ΥΡΑΚ . . . Ν
   ΙΠΠΟΔΙΝΗΤΩΝϹΤΡΑΤΑ . Ε·
   ΓΝΩΧΙΜΕΝ . ΟϹΤΕΦΑΝ . Ν
   ΜΟΙϹΑΝΓΛΥΚ . ΔΩΡΟΝΑΓΑΛΜΑΤΩΝΓΕΝΥΝ
5 ΑΙΤΙϹΕΠΙΧΘΟΝΙΩΝ
   ΟΡΘΩϹ·ΦΡΕΝΑΔ' ΕΥΘΥΔΙΚ . Ν
   ΑΤΡΕΜ' ΑΜΠΑΥϹΑϹΜΕΡΙΜΝΑΝ
   ΔΕΥΡ' ΑΘΡΗϹΟΝΝΟΩ[.]
   ΗϹΥΝΧΑΡΙΤΕϹϹΙΒΑΘΥΖΩΝΟΙϹΥΦΑΝΑϹ
10 ΥΜΝΟΝΑΠΟΖΑΘΕΑϹ
   ΝΑϹΟΥΞΕΝΟϹΥΜΕΤΕΡΑΝΠΕΜ
   ΠΕΙΚΛΕΕΝΝΑΝΕϹΠΟΛΙΝ
   ΧΡΥϹΑΜΠΥΚΟϹΟΥΡΑΝΙΑϹ
   ΚΛΕΙΝΟϹΘΕΡΑΠΩΝ·ΕΘΕΛΕΙΔΕ
15 ΓΑΡΥΝΕΚϹΤΗΘΕΩΝΧΕΩΝ

ἀντ. α΄.   ΑΙΝΕΙΝΙΕΡΩΝΑ·ΒΑΘΥΝ
   Δ' ΑΙΘΕΡΑΞΟΥΘΑΙϹΙΤΑΜΝΩΝ
   ΥΨΟΥΠΤΕΡΥΓΕϹϹΙΤΑΧΕΙ
   ΑΙϹΑΙΕΤΟϹΕΥΡΥΑΝΑΚΤΟϹΑΓΓΕΛΟϹ
20 ΖΗΝΟϹΕΡΙϹΦΑΡΑΓΟΥ
   ΘΑΡϹΕΙΚΡΑΤΕΡΑΙΠΙϹΥΝΟϹ
   ΙϹΧΥΙ·ΠΤΑϹϹΟΝΤΙΔ' ΟΡΝΙ
   ΧΕϹΛΙΓΥΦΘΟΓΓΟΙΦΟΙΒΩΙ·
   ΟΥΝΙΝΚΟΡΥΦΑΙΜΕΓΑΛΑϹΙϹΧΟΥϹΙΓΑΙΑϹ
25 . ΥΔ' ΑΛΟϹΑΚΑΜΑΤΑϹ
Col. 7 ΔΥϹΠΑΙΠΑΛΑΚΥΜΑΤΑ·ΝΩΜΑ
   ΤΑΙΔ' ΕΝΑΤΡΥΤΩΙΧΑΕΙ
   ΛΕΠΤΟΤΡΙΧΑϹΥΝΖΕΦΥΡΟΥΠΝΟ
   ΑΙϹΙΝΕΘΕΙΡΑΝΑΡΙΓΝΩ
30 ΤΟϹΜΕΤΑΝΘΡΩΠΟΙϹΙΔΕΙΝ·

ἐπ. α΄.   ΤΩϹΝΥΝΚΑΙΜΟΙΜΥΡΙΑΠΑΝΤΑΙΚΕΛΕΥΘΟϹ
   ΥΜΕΤΕΡΑΝΑΡΕΤΑΝ
   ΥΜΝΕΙΚΥΑΝΟΠΛΟΚΑΜΟΥΘ' ΕΚΑΤΙΝΙΚΑϹ
   ΧΑΛΚΕΟϹΤΕΡΝΟΥΤ' ΑΡΗΟϹ

35 ΔΕΙΝΟΜΕΝΕΥΣΑΓΕΡΩΧΟΙ
    ΠΑΙΔΕΣ·ΕΥΕΡΔΩΝΔΕΜΗΚΑΜΟΙΘΕΟC·
    ΞΑΝΘΟΤΡΙΧΑΜΕΝΦΕΡΕΝΙΚΟΝ

    ΑΛΦΕΟΝΠΑΡΕΥΡΥΔΙΝΑΝ
    ΠΩΛΟΝΑΕΛΛΟΔΡΟΜΑΝ
40 ΕΙΔΕΝΙΚΑCΑΝΤΑΧΡΥCΟΠΑΧΥCΑΩC
)⎯⎯⎯⎯

στρ. β'.   ΠΥΘΩΝΙΤ' ΕΝΑΓΑΘΕΑΙ·
    ΓΑΙΔ' ΕΠΙCΚΗΠΤΩΝΠΙΦΑΥCΚΩ
    ΟΥΠΩΝΙΝΥΠΟΠΡΟΤΕ.. Ν
    ΙΠΠΩΝΕΝΑΓΩΝΙΚΑΤΕΧΡΑΝΕΝΚΟΝΙC
45 ΠΡΟCΤΕΛΟCΟΡΝΥΜΕΝΟΝ·
    ΡΙΠΑΙΓΑΡΙCΟCΒΟΡΕΑ

    ΟΝΚΥΒΕΡΝΗΤΑΝΦΥΛΑCCΩΝ
    ΙΕΤΑΙΝΕΟΚΡΟΤΟΝ
    ΝΙΚΑΝΙΕΡΩΝΙΦΙΛΟΞΕΝΩΙΤΙΤΥCΚΩΝ·

50 ΟΛΒΙΟCΩΙΤΙΝΙΘΕΟC
    ΜΟΙΡΑΝΤΕΚΑΛΩΝΕΠΟΡΕΝ
    CΥΝΤ' ΕΠΙΖΗΛΩΙΤΥΧΑΙ
    ΑΦΝΕΙΟΝΒΙΟΤΑΝΔΙΑΓΕΙΝ·ΟΥ
    ΓΑ.... ΕΠΙΧΘΟΝΙΩΝ
55 Π... ΑΓ· ΕΥΔΑΙΜΩΝΕΦΥ·

ἀντ. β'.   ...... ΟΤ' ΕΡΙΨΙΠΥΛΑΝ
    .... ΑΤΟΝΛΕΓΟΥCΙΝ
    .... ΑΡΓΙΚΕΡΑΥ
Col. 8   ΝΟΥΔΩΜΑΤΑΦΕΡCΕΦΟΝΑCΤΑΝΙCΦΥΡΟΥ
60 ΚΑΡΧΑΡΟΔΟΝΤΑΚΥΝ' Α
    ΞΟΝΤ' ΕCΦΑΟCΕΞΑΙΔΑ
    ΥΙΟΝΑΠΛΑΤΟΙ' ΕΧΙΔΝΑC·
    ΕΝΘΑΔΥCΤΑΝΩΝΒΡΟΤΩΝ
    ΨΥΧΑCΕΔΑΗΠΑΡΑΚΩΚΥΤΟΥΡΕΕΘΡΟΙC

65 ΟΙΑΤΕΦΥΛΛ' ΑΝΕΜΟC
    ΙΔΑCΑΝΑΜΗΛΟΒΟΤΟΥC
    ΠΡΩΝΑCΑΡΓΗCΤΑCΔΟΝΕΙ·
    ΤΑΙCΙΝΔΕΜΕΤΕΠΡΕΠΕΝΕΙΔΩ
    ΛΟΝΘΡΑCΥΜΕΜΝΟΝΟCΕΓ
70 ΧΕCΠΑΛΟΥΠΟΡΘΑΟΝΙΔΑ·

ἐπ. β'.   ΤΟΝΔ' ΩCΙΔΕΝΑΛΚΜΗΙΟCΘΑΥΜΑCΤΟCΗΡΩC
    .. ΥΧΕCΙΛΑΜΠΟΜΕΝΟΝ
    ΝΕΥΡΑΝΕΠΕΒΑCΕΛΙΓΥΚΛΑΓΓΗΚΟΡΩΝΑC·
    ΧΑΛΚΕΟΚΡΑΝΟΝΔΕΠΕΙΤ' ΕΞ

75　ΕΙΛΕΤΟΙΟΝΑΝΑΠΤΥ
ΞΑΣΦΑΡΕΤΡΑΣΠΩΜΑ·ΤΩΙΔ᾽ ΕΝΑΝΤΙΑ
ΨΥΧΑΠΡ . ΦΑΝΗΜΕΛΕΑΓΡΟΥ·
ΚΑΙΝΙΝΕΥΕΙΔΩΣΠΡΟΣΕΕΙΠΕΝ·
ΥΙΕΔΙΟΣΜΕΓΑΛΟΥ
80　ΣΤΑΘΙΤ᾽ ΕΝΧΩΡΑΙΓΕΛΑΝΩΣΑΣΤΕΘΥΜΟΝ

στρ. γ΄.　ΜΗΤΑΥΣΙΟΝΠΡΟΙΕΙ
ΤΡΑΧΥΝΕΚΧΕΙΡΩΝΟΙΣΤΟΝ
ΨΥΧΑΙΣΙΝΕΠΙΦΘΙΜΕΝΩΝ·

ΟΥΤΟΙΔΕΟΣῶΣΦΑΤΟ·ΘΑΜΒΗΣΕΝΔ᾽ ΑΝΑΞ
85　ΑΜΦΙΤΡΥΩΝΙΑΔΑΣ·
ΕΙΠΕΝΤΕ·ΤΙΣΑΘΑΝΑΤῶΝ
ΗΒΡΟΤΩΝΤΟΙΟΥΤΟΝΕΡΝΟΣ
ΘΡΕΨΕΝΕΝΠΟΙΑΙΧΘΟΝΙ·
ΤΙΣΔ᾽ ΕΚΤΑΝΕΝ·ΗΤΑΧΑΚΑΛΛΙΖΩΝΟΣΗΡΑ
90　ΚΕΙΝΟΝΕΦΑΜΕΤΕΡΑΙ
ΠΕΜΨΕΙΚΕΦΑΛΑΙ·ΤΑΔΕΠΟΥ
Col. 9　ΠΑΛΛΑΔΙΞΑΝΘΑΙΜΕΛΕΙ·
ΤΟΝΔΕΠΡΟΣΕΦΑΜΕΛΕΑΓΡΟΣ
ΔΑΚΡΥΟΕΙΣ·ΧΑΛΕΠΟΝ
95　ΘΕΩΝΠΑΡΑΤΡΕΨΑΙΝΟΟΝ

ἀντ. γ΄.　ΑΝΔΡΕΣΣΙΝΕΠΙΧΘΟΝΙΟΙΣ·
ΚΑΙΓΑΡΑΝΠΛΑΞΙΠΠΟΣΟΙΝΕΥΣ
ΠΑΥΣΕΝΚΑΛΥΚΟΣΤΕΦΑΝΟΥ

ΣΕΜΝΑΣΧΟΛΟΝΑΡΤΕΜΙΔΟΣΛΕΥΚΩΛΕΝΟΥ
100　ΛΙΣΣΟΜΕΝΟΣΠΟΛΕΩΝ
Τ᾽ ΑΙΓΩΝΘΥΣΙΑΙΣΙΠΑΤΗΡ
ΚΑΙΒΟΩΝΦΟΙΝΙΚΟΝΩΤΩΝ·

ΑΛΛΑΝΙΚΑΤΟΝΘΕΑ
ΕΣΧΕΝΧΟΛΟΝ·ΕΥΡΥΒΙΑΝΔ᾽ ΕΣΣΕΥΕΚΟΥΡΑ
105　ΚΑΠΡΟΝΑΝΑΙΔΟΜΑΧΑΝ·

ὋΣΚΑΛΛΙΧΟΡΟΝΚΑΛΥΔΩ
Ν᾽ ΕΝΘΑΠΛΗΜΥΡΩΝΣΘΕΝΕΙ
ΟΡΧΟΥΣΕΠΕΚΕΙΡΕΝΟΔΟΝΤΙ
ΣΦΑΖΕΤΕΜΗΛΒΡΟΤΩΝ
110　Θ᾽ ΟΣΤΙΣΕΙΣΑΝΤΑΝΜΟΛΟΙ·

ἐπ. γ΄.　ΤΩΙΔΕΣΤΥΓΕΡΑΝΔΗΡΙΝΕΛΛΑΝΩΝΑΡΙΣΤΟΙ
ΣΤΑΣΑΜΕΘ᾽ ΕΝΔΥΚΕΩΣ
ΕΞΑΜΑΤΑΣΥΝΝΕΧΕΩΣ·ΕΠΕΙΔΕΔΑΙΜΩΝ
ΚΑΡΤΟΣΑΙΤΩΛΟΙΣΟΡΕΞΕΝ

ODE V. 157

115 ΘΑΠΤΟΜΕΝΤΟΥϹΚΑΤΕΠΕΦΝΕ
ϹΥϹΕΡΙΒΡΥΧΑϹΕΠΑΙϹϹΩΝΒΙΑΙ
Α . . ΑΙΟΝΕΜΩΝΤ' ΑΓΓΕΛΟΝ
Φ . . . ΑΤΟΝΚΕΔΝΩΝΑΔΕΛΦΕΩΝ
. . . . . ΚΕΝΕΝΜΕΓΑΡΟΙϹ
120 . . . . . . ϹΑΛΘΑΙΑΠΕΡΙΚΛΕΙΤΟΙϹΙΝΟΙΝΕΟϹ·

στρ. δ'. . . . . . . ΛΕϹΕΜΟΙΡ' ΟΛΟΑ
. . . . Ϲ·ΟΥΓΑΡΠΩΔΑΙΦΡΩΝ
. . . . ΧΟΛΟΝΑΓΡΟΤΕΡΑ
Col. 10 ΛΑΤΟΥϹΘΥΓΑΤΗΡ·ΠΕΡΙΔ' ΑΙΘΩΝΟϹΔΟΡΑϹ
125 ΜΑΡΝΑΜΕΘ' ΕΝΔΥΚΕΩϹ
ΚΟΥΡΗϹΙΜΕΝΕΠΤΟΛΕΜΟΙϹ·
ΕΝΘ' ΕΓΩΠΟΛΛΟΙϹϹΥΝΑΛΛΟΙϹ
ΙΦΙΚΛΟΝΚΑΤΕΚΤΑΝΟΝ
ΕϹΘΛΟΝΤ' ΑΦΑΡΗΤΑΘΟΟΥϹΜΑΤΡΩΑϹ·ΟΥΓΑΡ
130 ΚΑΡΤΕΡΟΘΥΜΟϹΑΡΗϹ
ΚΡΙΝΕΙΦΙΛΟΝΕΝΠΟΛΕΜΩΙ·
ΤΥΦΛΑΔ' ΕΚΧΕΙΡΩΝΒΕΛΗ
ΨΥΧΑΙϹΕΠ . ΔΥϹΜΕΝΕΩΝΦΟΙ
ΤΑΙΘΑΝΑΤΟΝΤΕΦΕΡΕΙ
135 ΤΟΙϹΙΝΑΝΔΑΙΜΩΝΘΕΛΗΙ·

ἀντ. δ'. ΤΑΥΤ' ΟΥΚΕΠΙΛΕΞΑΜΕΝΑ
ΘΕϹΤΙΟΥΚΟΡΑΔΑΙΦΡΩΝ
ΜΑΤΗΡΚΑΚΟΠΟΤΜΟϹΕΜΟΙ
ΒΟΥΛΕΥϹΕΝΟΛΕΘΡΟΝΑΤΑΡΒΑΚΤΟϹΓΥΝΑ·
140 ΚΑΙΕΤΕΔΑΙΔΑΛΕΑϹ
ΕΚΛΑΡΝΑΚΟϹΩΚΥΜΟΡΟΝ
ΦΙΤΡΟΝΕΓΚΛΑΥϹΑϹΑ·ΤΟΝΔΗ
ΜΟΙΡ' ΕΠΕΚΛΩϹΕΝΤΟΤΕ
ΖΩΑϹΟΡΟΝΑΜΕΤΕΡΑϹΕΜΜΕΝ·ΤΥΧΟΝΜΕΝ
145 ΔΑΙΠΥΛΟΥΚΛΥΜΕΝΟΝ
ΠΑΙΔ' ΑΛΚΙΜΟΝΕΞΑΝΑΡΙ
ΖΩΝΑΜΩΜΗΤΟΝΔΕΜΑϹ
ΠΥΡΓΩΝΠΡΟΠΑΡΟΙΘΕΚΙΧΗϹΑϹ·
ΤΟΙΔΕΠΡΟϹΕΥΚΤΙΜΕΝΑΝ
150 ΦΕΥΓΟΝΑΡΧΑΙΑΝΠΟΛΙΝ

ἐπ. δ'. ΠΛΕΥΡΩΝΑ·ΜΙΝΥΝΘΑΔΕΜΟΙΨΥΧΑΓΛΥΚΕΙΑ·
ΓΝΩΝΔ' ΟΛΙΓΟϹΘΕΝΕΩΝ·
ΑΙΑΙ·ΠΥΜΑΤΟΝΔΕΠΝΕΩΝΔΑΚΡΥϹΑΤΛ[
ΑΓΛΑΑΝΗΒΑΝΠΡΟΛΙΠΩΝ·
155 ΦΑϹΙΝΑΔΕΙϹΙΒΟΑΝ

Col. 11   ΑΜΦΙΤΡΥΩΝΟCΠΑΙΔΑΜΟΥΝΟΝΔΗΤΟΤΕ
              ΤΕΞΑΙΒΛΕΦΑΡΟΝΤΑΛΑΠΕΝΘΕΟC
              ΠΟΤΜΟΝΟΙΚΤΕΙΡΟΝΤΑΦΩΤΟC·
              ΚΑΙΝΙΝΑΜΕΙΒΟΜΕΝΟC
    160   ΤΟΔ' ΕΦΑ ΘΝΑΤΟΙCΙΜΗΦΥΝΑΙΦΕΡΙCΤΟΝ

στρ. ε'.   ΜΗΤ' ΑΕΛΙΟΥΠΡΟCΙΔΕΙΝ
              ΦΕΓΓΟC·ΑΛΛΟΥΓΑΡΤΙCΕCΤΙΝ
              ΠΡΑΞΙCΤΑΔΕΜΥΡΟΜΕΝΟΙC·
              ΧΡΗΚΕΙΝΟΛΕΓΕΙΝΟΤΙΚΑΙΜΕΛΛΕΙΤΕΛΕΙΝ·
    165   ΗΡΑΤΙCΕΝΜΕΓΑΡΟΙC
              ΟΙΝΗΟCΑΡΗΙΦΙΛΟΥ

              ΕCΤΙΝΑΔΜΗΤΑΘΥΓΑΤΡΩΝ
              CΟΙΦΥΑΝΑΛΙΓΚΙΑ·
              ΤΑΝΚΕΝΛΙΠΑΡΑΝΘΕΛΩΝΘΕΙΜΑΝΑΚΟΙΤΙΝ·
    170   ΤΟΝΔΕΜΕΝΕΠΤΟΛΕΜΟΥ
              ΨΥΧΑΠΡΟCΕΦΑΜΕΛΕΑ
              ΓΡΟΥΛΙΠΟΝΧΛΩΡΑΥΧΕΝΑ
              ΕΝΔΩΜΑCΙΔΑΙΑΝΕΙΡΑΝ
              ΝΗΙΝΕΤΙΧΡΥCΕΑC
    175   ΚΥΠΡΙΔΟCΘΕΛΞΙΜΒΡΟΤΟΥ·

ἀντ. ε'.   ΛΕΥΚΩΛΕΝΕΚΑΛΛΙΟΠΑ
              CΤΑCΟΝΕΥΠΟΙΗΤΟΝΑΡΜΑ
              ΑΥΤΟΥ·ΔΙΑΤΕΚΡΟΝΙΔΑΝ
              ΥΜΝΗCΟΝΟΛΥΜΠΙΩΝΑΡΧΑΓΟΝΘΕΩΝ·
    180   ΤΟΝΤ' ΑΚΑΜΑΝΤΟΡΟΑΝ
              ΑΛΦΕΟΝΠΕΛΟΠΟCΤΕΒΙΑΝ
              ΚΑΙΠΙCΑΝ·ΕΝΘ' ΟΚΛΕΕΝΝΟC
              .. CCΙΝΙΚΑCΑCΔΡΟΜΩΙ
              ... ΕΝΦΕΡΕΝΕΙΚΟCΕΥΠΥΡΓΟΥCCΥΡΑΚΟΥC
    185   CΑCΙΕΡΩΝΙΦΕΡΩΝ
              ... ΑΙΜΟΝΙΑCΠΕΤΑΛΟΝ·

              ... Δ' ΑΛΗΘΕΙΑCΧΑΡΙΝ
Col. 12   ΑΙΝΕΙΝΦΘΟΝΟΝΑΜΦ[
              ΧΕΡCΙΝΑΠΩCΑΜΕΝΟΝ
    190   ΕΙΤΙCΕΥΠΡΑCCΟΙΒΡΟΤΩ[

ἐπ. ε'.   ΒΟΙΩΤΟCΑΝΗΡΤΑΔΕΦΩΝ[
              ΗCΙΟΔΟCΠΡΟΠΟΛΟC
              ΜΟΥCΑΝΟΝΑΘΑΝΑΤΟΙΤΙ[
              ΚΑΙΒΡΟΤΩΝΦΗΜΑΝΕΠ[
    195   ΠΕΙΘΟΜΑΙΕΥΜΑΡΕΩC

ΕΥΚΛΕΑΚΕΛΕΥΘΟΥΓΛΩCCΑΝΟ[
ΠΕΜΠΕΙΝΙΕΡΩΝΙ·ΤΟΘΕΝΓΑ[
ΠΥΘΜΕΝΕCΘΑΛΛΟΥCΙΝΕCΘΛ[
ΤΟΥCΟΜΕΓΙCΤΟΠΑΤΩΡ
200 ΖΕΥCΑΚΙΝΗΤΟΥCΕΝΕΙΡΗΝ[
)

VI.

Λαχωνι κειωι σταδιει ολυμ^π

στρ. α΄.   ΛΑΧΩΝΔΙΟCΜΕΓΙCΤΟΥ
ΛΑΧΕΦΕΡΤΑΤΟΝΠΟΔΕCCΙ
ΚΥΔΟCΕΠΑΛΦΕΙΟΥΠΡΟΧΟΑΙC[
ΔΙΟCCΑΠΑΡΟΙΘΕΝ
5 ΑΜΠΕΛΟΤΡΟΦΟΝΚΕΟΝ

ΑΕΙCΑΝΠΟΤ' ΟΛΥΜΠΙΑΙ
ΠΥΞΤΕΚΑΙCΤΑΔΙΟΝΚΡΑΤΕΥ[
CΤΕΦΑΝΟΙCΕΘΕΙΡΑC

στρ. β΄.   ΝΕΑΝΙΑΙΒΡΥΟΝΤΕC·
10 CΕΔΕΝΥΝΑΝΑΞΙΜΟΛΠΟΥ

ΟΥΡΑΝΙΑCΥΜΝΟCΕΚΑΤΙΝΙΚ[
ΑΡΙCΤΟΜΕΝΕΙΟΝ
ΩΠΟΔΑΝΕΜΟΝΤΕΚΟC
ΓΕΡΑΙΡΕΙΠΡΟΔΟΜΟΙCΑΟΙ
15 ΔΑΙCΟΤΙCΤΑΔΙΟΝΚΡΑΤΗCΑC
ΚΕΟΝΕΥΚΛΕΙΞΑC
✥)

VII.

Τωι αυτωι

ΩΛΙΠΑΡΑΘΥΓΑΤΕΡΧΡΟΝΟΥΤΕΚ[
ΝΥΚΤΟCCΕΠΕΝΤΗΚΟΝΤΑΜ[
ΕΚΚΑΙΔΕΚΑΤΑΝΕΝΟΛΥΜΠ[
Col. 13   .... ΑΡ . Ι[
5 .. ΙΤΟCΑΙΙΜ[
ΚΡΙΝΕΙΝΙΤΑΙ...... ΛΑΙΨΗΡΩΝΠΟΔΙΩΝ
ΛΛΑCΙΚΙΑΙΓΥΙ.... ΡΙCΤΑΛΚΕCCΘΕΝΙΟC·
ΩΙΔΕCΥΠΙΡΕCΙΒΥΙ.... ΝΝΕΙΜΗΙCΓΕΡΙΑC
ΝΙΚΑCΕΙΠΑΝΙΘΡ.. ΟΙCΙΝΕΥΔΟΞΟCΚΙΕΚΛΗ
10 ΤΑΙΚΑΙΠΙΟΛΥΙΖΗ... ΟC·ΑΡΙ... ....ΟΝ

... ' EKO|ϹMH| ...... ΦAN| .... NA

. . . .

. . . .

. . . . · OMΩI

   *   *   *   *

Col. 14 ΠΥΘΩΝΑΤΕΜΗΛΟΘΥΤΑΝ
  40 ΥΜΝΕΩΝΝΕΜΕΑΝΤΕΚΑΙΙϹΘ . ON ·
    ΓΑΙΔΕΠΙϹΚΗΠΤΩΝΧΕΡΑ
    ΚΟΜΠΑϹΟΜΑΙ·ϹΥΝΑΛΑ
  (5) ΘΕΙΑΙΔΕΠΑΝΛΑΜΠΕΙΧΡΕΟ·
    ΟΥΤΙϹΑΝΘΡΩΠΩΝΚ[
  45 ΝΑϹΕΝΑΛΙΚΙΧΡΟΝΩ[
    ΠΑΙϹΕΩΝΑΝΗΡΤΕΠ[
    ΝΑϹΕΔΕΞΑΤΟΝΙΚΑϹ·
  (10) ΩΖΕΥΚ . ΡΑΥΝΕΓΧΕϹΚΑ[.... ..]|ΡΟΔΙΝΑ[
    ΟΧΘΑΙϹΙΝΑΛΦΕΙΟΥΤΕΛΕϹϹ[......]|ΑΛΟΚΛΕΑ|Ϲ
  50 ΘΕΟΔΟΤΟ . Ϲ|ΕΥΧΑϹ·ΠΕΡΙΚ[.......]|ΠΑ[...]|Ϲ
    ΓΛΑΥΚΟΝΑΙΤΩΛΙΔΟ[
    ΑΝΔΗΜ' ΕΛΑΙΑϹ
  (15) ΕΝΠΕΛΟΠΟϹΦΡΥΓΙΟΥ
    ΚΛΕΙΝΟΙϹΑΕΘΛΟΙϹ·

✠)————

VIII. [IX.]

Αυτομηδει φλιασιωι πενταθλωι νεμεα

στρ. α'. ΔΟΞΑΝΩΧΡΥϹΑΛΑΚΑΤΟΙΧΑΡΙ . ΕϹ
    ΠΕΙϹΙΜΒΡΟΤΟΝΔΟΙΗΤΕΠΕΙ
    ΜΟΥϹΑΝΤΕΙΟΒΛΕΦΑΡΩΝΘΕΙΟϹΠΡΟΦ .. ΑϹ
    ΕΥΤΥΚΟϹΦΛΕΙΟΥΝΤΑΤΕΚΑΙΝΕΜΕΑΙΟΥ
  5 ΖΗΝΟϹΕΥΘΑΛΕϹΠΕΔΟΝ
    ΥΜΝΕΙΝ·ΟΤΙΜΗΛΟΔΑΙΚΤΑΝ
    ΘΡΕΨΕΝΑΛΕΥΚΩΛΕ .. Ϲ
    ΗΡΑΠΕΡΙ .... ΤΩΝΑΕΘΛΩΝ
    ΠΡΩΤΟΝ ... ΚΛΕΙΒΑΡΥΦΘΟΓΓ . ΝΛΕΟΝΤΑ·

ἀντ. α'. 10 ΚΕ ...... ΝΙΚΑϹΠΙΔΕϹΗΜΙΘΕΟΙ
    ΠΡ ...... ΝΑΡΓΕΙΩΝΚΡΙΤΟΙ
    ΑΘΛΗϹΑΝ . ΠΑΡΧΕΜΟΡΩΙ·ΤΟΝΞΑΝΘΟΔΕΡΚΗϹ

ΠΕΦΝ' ΑCΑΓΕΥΟΝΤΑΔΡΑΚΩΝΥΠ|ΕΡΟΠΛΟC
CΑΜΑΜΕΛΛ . ΝΤΟCΦΟΝΟΥ·
15 ΩΜΟΙΡΑΠΟΛΥΚΡΑΤΕC· ΟΥΝΙΝ
ΠΕΙΘ' ΟΙΚΛΕΙΔΑCΠΑΛΙΝ
CΤΕΙΧΕΙΝΕCΕΥΑΝΔΡΟΥCΑΓ[
ΕΛΠΙCΑΝΘΡΩΠΩΝΥΦΑΙΡ[

ἐπ. α'.   ΑΚΑΙΤΟΤ' ΑΔΡΑCΤΟΝΤΑΛ[
Col. 15 20 ΠΕΜΠΕΝΕCΘΗΒΑCΠΟΛΥΝΕΙΚΕΙΠΛΑ[¹
ΚΕΙΝΩΝΑΠΕΥΔΟΞΩΝΑΓΩΝΩΝ
ΕΝΝΕΜΕΑΙΚΛΕΙΝΟ . . ΡΟΤΩΝ
ΟΙΤΡΙΕΤΕΙCΤΕΦΑΝΩΙ
ΞΑΝΘΑΝΕΡΕΨΩΝΤΑΙΚΟΜΑΝ
25 ΑΥΤΟΜΗΔΕΙΝΥΝΓΕΝΙΚΑ
CΑΝΤΙΝΙΝΔΑΙΜΩΝΕ . ΩΚΕΝ·

στρ. β'.   ΠΕΝΤΑΕΘΛΟΙCΙΝΓΑΡΕΝΕΠΡΕΠΕΝΩC
ΑCΤΡΩΝΔΙΑΚΡΙΝΕΙΦΑΗ
ΝΥΚΤΟCΔΙΧΟΜΗΝΙΔΟ . . ΥΦΕΓΓΗCCΕΛΑΝΑ·
30 ΤΟΙΟCΕΛΛΑΝΩΝΔΙΑ . . . ΡΟΝΑΚΥΚΛΟΝ
ΦΑΙΝ . ΘΑΥΜ . CΤΟΝΔΕ . ΑC
ΔΙCΚΟΝΤΡΟΧΟΕΙΔΕΑΡΙΠΤΩΝ
ΚΑΙΜΕΛΑΜΦΥΛΛΟΥΚΛΑΔΟΝ
ΑΚΤΕΑCΕCΑΙΠΕΙΝΑΝΠΡΟΠΕΜΠΩΝ
35 ΑΙΘΕΡ' ΕΚΧΕΙΡΟCΒΟΑΝΩΤΡΥΝΕΛΑΩΝ

ἀντ. β'.   ΗΤΕ . . ΥΤΑΙΑCΑΜΑΡΥΓΜΑΠΑΛΑC
ΤΟΙΩ . . . . . . ΥΜΩΙC . . . . Ι
ΓΥΙΑ . . . . ΜΑΤΑ . . . . . ΑΙΑΙΠΕΛΑCCΑ.
ΙΚΕΤ . . . . . . ΝΠΑΡΑΠΟΡΦΥΡΟΔΙΝΑ[
40 ΤΟΥΚ . . . . . ΑCΑΝΧΘΟΝΑ
ΗΛΘΕ . . . . . ΕΠΕCΧΑΤΑΝΕΙΛΟΥ·
ΤΑΙΤΕΠΕ . . ΑΕΙΠΟΡΩΙ
ΟΙΚΕΥCΙΘΕΡΜΩΔΟΝ . . . . ΓΧΕΩΝ
ΙCΤΟΡΕCΚΟΡΑΙΔΙΩΞΙΠΠ . . . ΡΗΟC

ἐπ. β'.   45 CΩΝΩΠΟΛΥΖΗΛΩΤ' ΑΝΑΞΠΟΤΑΜΩΝ
ΕΓΓΟΝΟΙΓΕΥCΑΝΤΟΚΑΙΥΨ . ΠΥΛΟΥΤΡΟΙΑCΕΔΟC·
CΤΕΙΧΕΙΔΙΕΥΡΕΙΑCΚΕΛΕ . ΘΟΥ
ΜΥΡΙΑΠΑΝΤΑΙΦΑΤΙC
CΑCΓΕΝΕΑCΛΙΠΑΡΟ

---

¹ At the end of v. 20 Blass places fragment 35 (Kenyon, p. 210) ΠΡΟΞΕΝ.

50 ΖΩΝΩΝΘΥΓΑΤΡΩΝ·ΑΣΘ..Ι
    ΟΥΝΤΥΧΑΙΟΩΚΙΟΟΑΝΑΡΧΑ
    ΓΟΥΟΑΠΟΡΘΗΤΩΝΑΓΥΙΑΝ·
)⸺

στρ. γ'. ΤΙΟΓΑΡΟΥΚΟΙ...ΚΥΑΝΟΠΛΟΚΑΜΟΥ
    ΘΗΒΑΟΕΥΔΜ........Ν
Col. 16 55 — — — — ΜΟΝΑΙΓΙΝΙΑΝ·ΜΕΓ[—]ΟΥ
    — — — — ΕΧΕΙΤΕΚΕ|ΝΗΡΩ
    —.ΔΕΟΩ| — — ΟΥ·
    — ΑΟΒΑΟΑ| — — ΑΙΩΝ
    — — Α| — —
60 Τ — — —
    Α| — — Ω|......ΥΠ.ΠΛΟΝ[

ἀντ. γ'. Η| — — — ΑΝΕΛΙΚΟΟΤΕΦΑ[
    Κ| — — — ΟΑΙΤ'ΑΛΛΑΙΘΕΩΝ[
    Ο| — — ΑΜ|ΗΟΑΝΑΡΙΓΝΩΤ.|ΙΟ|Π.ΛΑΙ[
65 — — — ΛΟ|Α|ΠΟΤΑΜΟΥΚΕ|.ΑΔΟ|ΝΤΟΟ·
    — —.— ΑΝΠΟΛΙΝ
    — — — ΟΙΤΕΝΙΚΑ[
    — — — ΛΩΝΒΟΑΙ[
    — — — ΥΟΑΙ·ΜΕ[
70 — — — — — |Ν·

ἐπ. γ'. — — — — — |ΝΕΟΟ[
    ..ΥΟΕΑ|—ΘΕΝΤΑΙΟΠΛΟΚΟΝ|ΕΥΕΙΠΕΙΝ[
    ..ΑΤ| — ΝΑΜ.ΤΩΝΕΡΩΤ|ΩΝ
    — — ΙΝΑΝΒΡΟΤΟ[
75 — — ΛΕΩΝ
    — — — —
    — — —ΩΤΑΝ
    — — — ΝΥΜΝΟΝ·

στρ. δ'. — — — ΚΑΙΑΠΟΦΘΙΜΕΝ|ΩΙ
80 — — — ΡΥΤΟΝΧΡΟΝΟ|Ν
    — — — ΙΝΟΜΕΝΟΙΟΑ|ΕΙ|ΠΙΦΑΥΟΚΟΙ
    ......|ΜΕΑΝΙ|ΚΑΝ·ΤΟ..ΤΟΙΚΑΛΟ|ΝΕΡΓΟΝ
    ΓΝΗΟΙΩ|ΝΥΜ|ΝΩΝΤΥΧΟΝ.
    ΥΨΟΥΠΑ|ΡΑΔΑ|ΙΜΟΟΙΚΕΙΤΑΙ·
85 ΟΥΝΔ'Α|.ΑΘΕΙΑΙ|ΒΡΟΤΩΝ
    ΚΑΛΛΙΟ|ΤΟΝΕΙ[
    Λ..ΠΕΤΑ|ΙΜΟΥΟ.......ΡΜΑ·

ἀντ. δ'. ΕΙΟΙΔ'ΑΝ|ΘΡ[

Col. 17 ΠΟΛΛΑΙ·ΔΙ| . ΚΡΙΝ . ||ΔΕΘΕΩΝ

90 . ΟΥΛΑ[— —|ΜΕΝΟΝΝΥ|ΚΤΟC[

— — — — ΓΕΚ|ΑΙΤΟΝΑΡΕΙΩ[

— — — — — |ΠΟΥ·

— — — — —| . . ΕΥCΩΝ

— — — —

95 — — — — — ΑΥΡΟΙC

. . ΔΡ| — — — ΤΟΜΕΛΛΟΝ·

ἐπ. δ'.   . . ΜΙΔ| — — — ΔΩΚΕΧΑΡΙΝ

. ΑΙΔΙΩΝ| — — ΘΕΟΤΙΜΑΤΟ . ΠΟΛΙΝ

. ΑΙΕΙΝΑΠΟ| — — ΕΥΝΤΑC

100 . ΡΥCΕΟCΚΑΠΤΡ[

. . ΤΙΚΑΛΟΝΦΕ[

ΑΙΝΕΟΙΤΙΜΟΞ[

ΠΑΙΔΙCΥΝΚΩ[

. . ΟΙΤΕΠΕΝΤ[

IX. [X.]

στρ. α'.   . . ΜΑ·CΥΓ . |ΡΑ| — — ΟΙΧΝΕΙC

. . ΛΑ·ΚΑ|ΙΠΑ — —

. . . . . ' . ΕΛΑΜΠ — —

. . . . . ΠΟΚΕΥ — —

5 . . . . ΝΩΝΤΑΙ|— — —'.ΩΙ

Ξ . . |ΟΝ·ΟΤΙΧΡΥ[

Ο . . . . |ΟΦΘΑΛΜΟΙ|CΙΝ[

Π . . . . ΑΝΑΠΡΑΚΤΑΝ[

Α . . Α:ΙΚΑΙΝΥΝΚΑCΙΓΝΗΤΑCΑΚΟΙΤΑC

10 ΝΑCΙ:ΤΙΝΕΚΕΙΗCΕΝΛΙΓΥΦΘΟΓΓΟΝΜΕΛΙCCΑΝ

ἀντ. α'.   . . ΕΙΡΕCΙΝ' ΑΘΑΝΑΤΟΝΜΟΥCΑΝΑΓΑΛΜΑ

ΞΥΝΟΝΑΝΘΡΩΠΟΙCΙΝΕΙΗΙ

ΧΑΡΜΑΤΕΑΝΑΡΕΤΑΝ

ΜΑΝΥΟΝΕΠΙΧΘΟΝΙΟΙCΙΝ

15 ΟCCΑΝΙΚΑCΕΚΑΤΙΑΝΘΕCΙΝΞΑΝ

Θ| . . ΑΝΑΔΗCΑΜΕΝΟCΚΕΦΑΛΑΝ

Κ|ΥΔΟCΕΥΡΕΙΑΙCΑΘΑΝΑΙC

Θ|ΗΚΑCΟΙΝΕΙΔΑΙCΤΕΔΟΞΑΝ

Ε|ΝΠΟCΙΔΑΝΟCΠΕΡΙΚΛΕΙΤΟΙCΑΕΘΛΟΙC

Col. 18 20 . . . . ΑCΕΛΛΑCΙΝΠΟΔΩΝΤΑΧΕΙΑΝΟΡΜΑΝ

ἐπ. α΄.   . . . . ΡΟΙϹΙΝΕΠΙϹΤΑΔΙΟΥ
ΘΕΡΜ . . . . . . ΠΝΕΩΝΑΕΛΛΑΝ
ΕϹΤΑ . . . . . . ΝΔ᾽ ΑΥΤΕΘΕΑΤΗΡΩΝΕΛΑΙΩΙ
ΦΑΡΕ . . . . ΝΕΜΠΙΤΝΩΝΟΜΙΛΟΝ
25 ΤΕΤΡ . . . . ΝΕΠΕΙ
ΚΑΜ . . . . . . ΜΟΝΙϹΘΜΙΟΝΙΚΑΝ
ΔΙϹΝ . . . . . . ΑΡΥΞΑΝΕΥΒΟΥ
ΛΩΝ . . . . . . ΩΝΠΡΟΦΑΤΑΙ·

στρ. β΄.   ΔΙϹΔ᾽ Ε . . . . . . ΑΙΚΡΟΝΙΔΑΖΗΝΟϹΠΑΡΑΓΝΟΝ
30 ΒΩΜΟ . . . . . . ΝΑΤΕΘΗΒΑ
ΔΕΚΤ . . . . . . ΥΡΥΧΟΡΟΝ
Τ᾽ ΑΡΓΟ . . . . . ΝΤΕΚΑΤΑΙϹΑΝ·
ΟΙΤΕΠ . . . . . . ΑΝΝΕΜΟΝΤΑΙ·ΑΜΦΙΤ᾽ ΕΥΒΟΙ
ΑΝΠΟ . . . . . Ν·ΟΙΘΙΕΡΑΝ
35 ΝΑϹΟ . . . . . . ΑΝ·ΜΑΤΕΥΕΙ
Δ᾽ ΑΛΛ . . . . . . ΑΝΚΕΛΕΥΘΟΝ
ΑΝΤΙ . . . . . . ΩΝΑΡΙΓΝΩΤΟΙΟΔΟΞΑϹΤΕΥΞΕΤΑΙ·
ΜΥΡΙΑΙΔ᾽ ΑΝΔΡΩΝΕΠΙϹΤΑΜΑΙΠΕΛΟΝΤΑΙ·:

ἀντ. β΄.   ΗΓΑΡϹ . ΦΟϹΧΑΡΙΤΩΝΤΙΜΑΝΛΕΛΟΓΧΩϹ
40 ΕΛΠΙΔΙΧΡΥϹΕΑΙΤΕΘΑΛΕΝ·
ΗΤΙΝΑΘΕΥΠΡΟΠΙΑΝ
ΕΙΔΩϹΕΤΕΡΟϹΔΕΠΙΠΑΙϹΙ
ΠΟΙΚΙΛΟΝΤΟΞΟΝΤΙΤΑΙΝΕΙ·ΟΙΔ᾽ ΕΠΕΡΓΟΙ
ϹΙΝΤΕΚΑΙΑΜΦΙΒΟΩΝΑ . ΕΛΑΙϹ
45 ΘΥΜΟΝΑΥΞΟΥϹΙΝ·ΤΟΜΕΛΛΟΝ
Δ᾽ ΑΚΡΙΤΟΥϹΤΙΚΤΕΙΤΕΛΕΥΤΑϹ
ΠΑΙΤΥΧΑΒΡΙϹΕΙ·ΤΟΜΕΝΚΑΛΛΙϹΤΟΝΕϹΕΛΩΝ
ΑΝΔΡΑΠΟΛΛΩΝΥΠΑΝΘΡΩΠΩΝΠΟΛΥΖΗΛΩΤΟΝ[1]
ΕΙΜΕΝ·

ἐπ. β΄.   ΟΙΔΑΚΑΙΠΛΟΥΤΟΥΜΕΓΑΛΑΝΔΥΝΑϹΙΝ·
50 ΑΚΑΙΤ . ΝΑΧΡΕΙΟΝΤΙ . . . Ι
ΧΡΗϹΤΟΝ·ΤΙΜΑΚΡΑΝΓ . Ω . ϹΑΝΙΘΥϹΑϹΕΛΑΥΝΩ[1]
Ε . ΤΟϹΟΔΟΥ·ΠΕΦΑΤΑΙΘΝΑΤΟΙϹΙΝΙΚΑϹ
. . . . ΡΟΝΕΥΦΡΟϹΥΝΑ
Col. 19   ΑΥΛΩΝ[
55 ΜΙΓ[
)———)
ΧΡΗΤΙΝ[
)———·

[1] So **A** wrote : for **A³**'s obscure correction, see crit. n., p. 320.

X. [XI.]

Ἀλεξιδαμωι μεταποντινωι παιδι παλαιστηι πυθια

στρ. α'.   ΝΙΚΑΓ[¹
ΚΟΙΠΑΤ[
ΥΨΙΖΥ[
ΕΝΠΟΛ............ΠΩΙ
5   ΖΗΝΙ[
ΚΡΙΝΕ....Λ.ϹΑΘΑΝΑΤΟΙ
ϹΙΝΤΕ....ΝΑΤΟΙϹΑΡΕΤΑϹ·
ΕΛΛΑΘΙ....ΠΛΟΚΑΜΟΥ
ΚΟΥΡΑ......ΘΟΔΙΚΟΥ·ϹΕΘΕΝΔ᾽ΕΚΑΤΙ
10   ΚΑΙΝΥ....ΑΠΟΝΤΙΟΝΕΥ
ΓΥΙΩΝ.....ΟΥϹΙΝΕΩΝ
ΚΩΜΟΙ|ΤΕΚΑΙ|.ΥΦΡΟϹΥΝΑΙΘΕΟΤΙΜΟΝΑϹΤΥ·
ΥΜΝΕ|ΥϹΙΔΕΠ|ΥΘΙΟΝΙΚΟΝ
ΠΑΙΔΑ|ΘΑΗΤ.|ΝΦΑΙϹΚΟΥ·

ἀντ. α'.   15   ΙΛΕΩΙ.|ΙΝΟΔ|..ΟΓΕΝΗϹΥΙ
ΟϹΒΑΘΥ|ΖΩΝ|...ΛΑΤΟΥϹ
ΔΕΚΤ.|ΒΛΕΦ|...Ι·ΠΟΛΕΕϹ
Δ᾽ΑΜΦΑΛΕΞ...ΜΟΝΑΝΘΕΩΝ
ΕΝΠΕΔΙΩΙϹΤΕΦΑΝΟΙ
20   ΚΙΡΡΑϹΕΠΕϹΟΝΚΡΑΤΕΡΑϹ
ΗΡΑΠΑΝΝΙΚΟΙΠΑΛΑϹ·
ΟΥΚ..ΔΕΝΙΝΑΕΛΙΟϹ
ΚΕ..ΩΙΓΕϲγΝΑΜΑτιπροϲγαιαιπεϲοντα·
ΦΑϹΩΔΕΚΑΙΕΝΖΑΘΕΟΙϹ
25   ΑΓΝΟΥΠΕΛΟΠΟϹΔΑΠΕΔΟΙϹ
ΑΛΦΕΟΝΠΑΡΑΚΑΛΛΙΡΟΑΝΔΙΚΑϹΚΕΛΕΥΘΟΝ
ΕΙΜΗΤΙϹΑΠΕΤΡΑΠΕΝΟΡΘΑϹ
ΠΑΓΞΕΙΝΩΙΧΑΙΤΑΝΕΛΑΙΑΙ

ἐπ. α'.   ΓΛΑΥΚΑΙϹΤΕΦΑΝΩϹΑΜΕΝΟΝ
30   ΠΟΡΤΙΤΡΟΦΟ..........ΡΑΝΘ᾽ΙΚΕϹΘΑΙ·

Col. 20   ΠΑΙΔ᾽ΕΝΧΘΟΝΙΚΑΛΛΙΧΟΡΩΙ
ΠΟΙΚΙΛΑΙϹΤΕΧΝΑΙϹΠΕΛΑϹϹΕΝ·
.ΛΛ᾽ΗΘΕΟϹΑΙΤΙΟϹΗ
35   .ΝΩΜΑΙΠΟΛΥΠΛΑΓΚΟΙΒΡΟΤΩΝ
.ΜΕΡϹΑΝΥΠΕΡΤΑΤΟΝΕΚΧΕΙΡΩΝΓΕΡΑϹ·
.ΥΝΔ᾽ΑΡΤΕΜΙϹΑΓΡΟΤΕΡΑ
.ΡΥϹΑΛΑΚΑΤΟϹΛΙ.ΑΡΑΝ
..:΄ΡΑΤΟΞΟΚΛΥΤΟϹΝΙΚΑΝΕΔΩΚΕ·

---

¹ As to the doubtful Γ, see crit. n. on p. 320.

40 .. ΙΠΟΤ' ΑΒΑΝΤΙΑΔΑC
. ΩΜΟΝΚΑΤΕΝΑCCΕΠΟΛΥΛ
.. CΤΟΝΕΥΠΕΠΛΟΙΤΕΚΟΥΡΑΙ·

στρ. β'.   ΤΑCΕΞΕΡΑΤΩΝΕΦΟΒΗCΕ

ΠΑΓΚΡΑΤΗCΗΡΑΜΕΛΑΘΡΩΝ
45 ΠΡΟΙΤΟΥΠΑΡΑΠΛΗΓΙΦΡΕΝΑC
ΚΑΡΤΕΡΑΙΖΕΥΞΑC' ΑΝΑΓΚΑΙ.
ΠΑΡΘΕΝΙΑΙΓΑΡΕΤΙ
ΨΥΧΑΙΚΙΟΝΕCΤΕΜΕΝΟC
ΠΟΡΦΥΡΟΖΩΝΟΙΟΘΕΑC·
50 ΦΑCΚΟΝΔΕΠΟΛΥCΦΕΤΕΡΟΝ
ΠΛΟΥΤΩΙΠΡΟΦΕΡΕΙΝΠΑΤΕΡΑΞΑΝΘΑCΠΑΡΕΔΡΟΥ
CΕΜΝΟΥΔΙΟCΕΥΡΥΒΙΑΙ·
ΤΑΙCΙΝΔΕΧΟΛΩCΑΜΕΝΑ
CΤΗΘΕCΙΝΠΑΛΙΝΤΡΟΠΟΝΕΜΒΑΛΕΝΟΜΜΑ·
55 ΦΕΥΓΟΝΔ' ΟΡΟCΕCΤΑΝΙΦΥΛΛΟΝ
CΜΕΡΔΑΛΕΑΝΦΩΝΑΝΙΕΙCΑΙ

ἀντ. β'.   ΤΙΡΥΝΘΙΟΝΑCΤΥΛΙΠΟΥCΑΙ
ΚΑΙΘΕΟΔΜΑΤΟΥCΑΓΥΙΑC·
ΗΔΗΓΑΡΕΤΟCΔΕΚΑΤΟΝ
60 ΘΕΟΦΙΛΕCΛΙΠΟΝΤΕCΑΡΓΟC
ΝΑΙΟΝΑΔΕΙCΙΒΟΑΙ
ΧΑΛΚΑCΠΙΔΕCΗΜΙΘΕΟΙ
CΥΝΠΟΛΥΖΗΛΩΙΒΑCΙΛΕΙ·
ΝΕΙΚΟCΓΑΡΑΜΑΙΜΑΚΕΤΟΝ
65 ΒΛΗΧΡΑCΑΝΕΠΑΛΤΟΚΑCΙΓΝΗΤΟΙCΑΠΑΡΧΑC
Col. 21   ΠΡΟΙΤΩΙΤΕΚΑΙΑΚΡCΙΩΙ·
ΛΑΟΥCΤΕΔΙΧΟCΤΑCΙΑΙC
ΗΡΙΠΟΝΑΜΕΤΡΟΔΙΚΟΙCΜΑΧΑΙCΤΕΛΥΓΡΑΙC·
ΛΙCCΟΝΤΟΔΕΠΑΙΔΑCΑΒΑΝΤΟC
70 ΓΑΝΠΟΛΥΚΡΙΘΟΝΛΑΧΟΝΤΑC

ἐπ. β'.   ΤΙΡΥΝΘΑΤΟΝΟΠΛΟΤΕΡΟΝ
ΚΤΙΖΕΙΝΠΡΙΝΕCΑΡΓΑΛΕΑΝΠΕCΕΙΝΑΝΑΓΚΑΝ·
ΖΕΥCΤ' ΕΘΕΛΕΝΚΡΟΝΙΔΑC
ΤΙΜΩΝΔΑΝΑΟΥΓΕΝΕΑΝ
75 ΚΑΙΔΙΩΞ .ΙΠΠΟΙΟΛΥΓΚΕΟC
ΠΑΥCΑΙCΤΥΓΕΡΩΝΑΧΕΩΝ·
ΤΕΙΧΟCΔΕΚΥΚΛΩΠΕCΚΑΜΟΝ
ΕΛΘΟΝΤΕCΥΠΕΡΦΙΑΛΟΙΚΛΕΙΝΑΙΠ . . . ΕΙ

ΚΑΛΛΙCΤΟΝΙΝ' ΑΝΤΙΘΕΟΙ
80 ΝΑΙΟΝΚΛΥΤΟΝΙΠΠΟΒΟΤΟΝ

ΑΡΓΟCΗΡΩΕCΠΕΡΙΚΛΕΙΤΟΙΛΙΠΟΝΤ[
ΕΝΘΕΝΑΠΕCCΥΜΕΝΑΙ
ΠΡΟΙΤΟΥΚΥΑΝΟΠΛΟΚΑΜΟΙ

ΦΕΥΓΟΝΑΔΜΑΤΟΙΘΥΓΑΤΡΕϹ·

στρ. γ'. 85 ΤΟΝΔ·ΕΙΛΕΝΑΧΟϹΚΡΑΔΙΑΝ·ΞΕΙ
ΝΑΤΕΝΙΝΠΛΑΞΕΝΜΕΡΙΜΝΑ·
ΔΟΙΑΞΕΔΕΦΑϹΓΑΝΟΝΑΜ
ΦΑΚΕϹΕΝϹΤΕΡΝΟΙϹΙΠΑΞΑΙ·
ΑΛΛΑΝΙΝΑΙΧΜΟΦΟΡΟΙ
90 ΜΥΘΟΙϹΙΤΕΜΕΙΛΙΧΙΟΙϹ
ΚΑΙΒΙΑΙΧΕΙΡΩΝΚΑΤΕΧΟΝ·
ΤΡΙϹΚΑΙΔ·ΚΑΜΕΝΤΕΛ|ΕΟΥϹ
ΜΗΝΑϹ..|ΤΑΔΑϹΚΙΟΝΗΛΥΚΤΑΞ¹ΟΝΥΛΑΝ
ΦΕΥΓΟΝΤΕ|ΚΑΤΑΚΑΡΔΙΑΝ
95 ΜΗΛΟΤΡΟ|ΦΟΝ·ΑΛΛ'ΟΤΕΔΗ
ΛΟΥϹΟΝΠΟ|ΤΙΚΑΛΛΙΡΟΑΝΠΑΤΗΡΙΚΑΝΕΝ
ΕΝΘΕΝΧΡΟΑ|ΝΙΨΑΜΕΝΟϹΦΟΙ
ΝΙΚΟΚ.......ΟΛΑΤΟΥϹ
ἀντ. γ'. ΚΙΚΛΗ..........ΒΟΩΠΙΝ
Col. 22 106 *τουδ' εκλγ' αριστοπατρα
100 ΧΕΙΡΑϹΑΝΤΕΙΝΩΝΠΡΟϹΑΥΓΑϹ
ΙΠΠΩΚΕΟϹΑΕΛΙΟΥ
ΤΕΚΝΑΔΥϹΤΑΝΟΙΟΛΥϹϹΑϹ
ΠΑΡΦΡΟΝΟϹΕΞΑΓΑΓΕΙΝ·
ΘΥϹΩΔΕΤΟΙΕΙΚΟϹΙΒΟΥϹ
105 ΑΖΥΓΑϹΦΟΙΝΙΚΟΤΡΙΧΑϹ·
*ΘΗΡΟϹΚΟΠΟϹΕΥΧΟΜΕΝΟΥ·ΠΙΘΟΥϹΑΔ'ΗΡΑΝ
ΠΑΥϹΕΝΚΑΛΥΚΟϹΤΕΦΑΝΟΥϹ
ΚΟΥΡΑϹΜΑΝΙΑΝΑΘΕΩΝ·
110 ΓΑΙΔ'ΑΥΤΙΚΑΟΙΤΕΜΕΝΟϹΒΩΜΟΝΤΕΤΕΥΧΟΝ
ΧΡΑΙΝΟΝΤΕΜΙΝΑΙΜΑΤΙΜΗΛΩΝ
ΚΑΙΧΟΡΟΥϹΙϹΤΑΝΓΥΝΑΙΚΩΝ·
ἐπ. γ'. ΕΝΘΕΝΚΑΙΑΡΗΙΦΙΛΟΙϹ
ΑΝΔΡΕϹϹΙΝΙΠΠΟΤΡΟΦΩΝΠΟΛΙΝΑΧΑΙΟΙϹ
115 ΕϹΠΕΟ·ϹΥΝΔΕΤΥΧΑΙ
ΝΑΙΕΙϹΜΕΤΑΠΟΝΤΙΟΝΩ
ΧΡΥϹΕΑΔΕϹΠΟΙΝΑΛΑΩΝ·
ΑΛϹΟϹΤΕΤΟΙΙΜΕΡΟΕΝ
ΚΑϹΑΝΠΑΡΕΥΥΔΡΟΝΠΡΟΓΟ
120 ΝΟΙΕϹϹΑΜΕΝΟΙΠΡΙΑΜΟΙ'ΕΠΕΙΧΡΟΝΩΙ
ΒΟΥΛΑΙϹΙΘΕΩΝΜΑΚΑΡΩΝ
ΠΕΡϹΑΝΠΟΛΙΝΕΥΚΤΙΜΕΝΑΝ
ΧΑΛΚΟΘΩΡΑΚΩΝΜΕΤΑΤΡΕΙΔΑΝ·ΔΙΚΑΙΑϹ
ΟϹΤΙϹΕΧΕΙΦΡΕΝΑϹΕΥ
125 ΡΗϹΕΙϹΥΝΑΠΑΝΤΙΧΡΟΝΩΙ
ΜΥΡΙΑϹΑΛΚΑϹΑΧΑΙΩΝ·

¹ Kenyon now thinks that the apparent Ξ is only an abraded Z.

XI. [XII.]

Τισιαι αιγινητηι παλαιστηι νεμεα

στρ.

ΩϹΕΙΚΥΒΕΡΝΗΤΑϹϹΟΦΟϹΥΜΝΟΑΝΑϹ
Ϲ' ΕΥΘΥΝΕΚΛΕΙΟΙ
ΝΥΝΦΡΕΝΑϹΑΜΕΤΕΡΑϹ
ΕΙΔΗΠΟΤΕΚΑΙΠΑΡΟϹ· ΕϹΓΑΡΟΛΒΙΑΝ
5 ΞΕΙΝΟΙϹΙΜΕΠΟΤΝΙΑΝΙΚΑ
ΝΑϹΟΝΑΙΓΕΙΝΑϹΑΠΑΡΧΕΙ
ΕΛΘΟΝΤΑΚΟϹΜΗϹΑΙΘΕΟΔΜΑΤΟΝΠΟΛΙΝ·
ΤΑΝΤ' ΕΝΝΕΜΕΑΙΓΥΑΛΚΕΑΜΟΥΝΟΠΑΛΑ[

Here there has been a loss of at least one column, and probably of more than one.

XII. [XIII.]

στρ. α'.   *   *   *   *
Col. 23   — — —
          — — — — ΛΕΙΩ
10   — — — — — ·' ΕΡ[
          — — —
          — — — — — — ΔΑΝ·

στρ. β'.   *A lacuna of thirty-one verses.*

Col. 24   ΥΒΡΙΟϹΥΨΙΝΟΟΥ
45   ΠΑΥϹΕΙΔΙΚΑϹΘΝΑΤΟΙϹΙΚΡΑΙΝΩΝ

ἀντ. β'.   ΟΙΑΝΤΙΝΑΔΥϹΛΟΦΟΝΩ
          ΜΗϹΤΑΙΛΕΟΝΤΙ
(15)   ΠΕΡϹΕΙΔΑϹΕΦΙΗϹΙ
          ΧΕΙΡΑΠΑΝΤΟΙΑΙϹΙΤΕΧΝΑΙϹ·
50   . . . . ΔΑΜΑϹΙΜΒΡΟΤΟϹΑΙΘΩΝ
          . . . ΚΟϹΑΠΛΑΤΟΥΘΕΛΕΙ
          . . . . ΙΝΔΙΑϹΩΜΑΤΟϹ· Ε
(20)   . . . . . ΦΘΗΔ' ΟΠΙϹΩ
          . . . . . ΝΟΝ· ΗΠΟΤΕΦΑΜΙ
55   . . . . . . ΠΕΡΙϹΤΕΦΑΝΟΙϹΙ
          . . . . . . ΑΤΙΟΥΠΟΝΟΝΕΛ
          . . . . . . ΝΙΔΡΩΕΝΤ' ΕϹΕϹΘΑΙ·

ἐπ. β'. (25)   . . . . ΑΒΩΜΟΝΑΡΙϹΤΑΡΧΟΥΔΙΟϹ
          . . . . . . Ρ. . . ΥΔΕΟϹΑΝ

60 .... ỊCINA . |ΘEA

..... ANΔOΞANΠOΛỴΦANTONENAI

.... TPEΦEIΠAYPOICIBPOTῶN

(30) . ỊEỊKAIOTANΘANATOIO

KYẢNEONNEΦOCKAΛYΨHIΛEIΠETAI

65 AΘANATONKΛEOCEYEP

XΘENT . CACΦAΛEICỵNAICAI ·

)̲—̲—̲

στρ. γ'. TῶNKẠ . . ỴTYXῶNNEMEAI

(35) ΛAMΠῶNOCYIE

ΠẠNΘAΛEῶNCTEΦANOICIN

70 . . ̣. . . XAITAN . . |EΦΘEIC

. . . . ΠOΛINY|ΨIAΓYIAN

. . . . PΨIM . . ỌTῶN

(40) . . . . Ạ . . . . OῶN

Kῶ . . . ΠATP . . N

75 NACO . ỴΠẺPBI . . ICXYN

ΠAMMẠXIANANAΦAINῶN ·

ῶΠOTAMOYΘYΓATEP

(45) ΔINANTOCAIΓIN' HΠIOΦPON

Col. 25 ἀντ. γ'. HTOIMEΓAΛAN[

80 EΔῶKETIMAN[

ENΠANTECCIN[

ΠYPCONῶ̣CEΛΛ[

(50) ΦAINῶN · TOΓECO[. . . . . . .]NEI

84 f. KAITICYΦAYXHCKO[. . . . . .]PAN

ΠOΔECCITAPΦEῶC[

HYTENEBPOCAΠEN[

(55) ANΘEMOENTACEΠ[

KOYΦACYNAΓXIΔO[

90 ΘPῶCKOYC' AΓẢKΛEITA[. . . . . .]IC ·

ἐπ. γ'. TAIΔECTEΦANῶCAME . . . .]EῶN

ANΘEῶNΔONAKOCT' E[

(60) PIANAΘYPCIN

ΠAPΘENOIMEΛΠOYCIT . . . . Ọῶ

95 Δ . CΠOINAΠAIΞẸ[

. . ΔAIΔATEPOΔO[

ATỌ . . . . . . ẠNETI[

(65) KA . TEΛA . . . A[

AIAKῶIMIX|ΘEIC' ENẸ[
̲—̲—̲

στρ. δ'. 100   ΤΩΝΥΙΕΑϹ|ΑΕΡϹΙΜΑΧ[
                ΤΑΧΥΝΤ' ΑΧ|ΙΛΛΕΑ
                ΕΥΕΙΔΕΟϹΤ'|ΕΡΙΒΟΙΑϹ
     (70)   ΠΑΙΔ' ΥΠΕΡΘ|ΥΜΟΝΒΟΑ[
                ΑΙΑΝΤΑϹΑΚ|ΕϹΦΟΡΟΝΗ[
     105   ΌϹΤ' ΕΠΙΠΡΥΜ|ΝΑΙϹΤΑΘ[
                ΕϹΧΕΝΘΡΑϹΥ|ΚΑΡΔΙΟΝ[
                ΜΑΙΝΟΝΤΑΝ[
     (75)   ΘΕϹΠΕϹΙΩΙΠΥ[
                ΕΚΤΟΡΑΧΑΛ[   ]|Ν·
     110   ΟΠΟΤΕΠ[
                ΤΡΑ . ΕΙΑΝ[   ]ΑΝΙΝ

ἀντ. δ'.   ΩΡΕΙΝΑΤ[
     (80)   Τ' ΕΛΥϹΕΝΑ[
                ΟΙΠΡΙΝΜΕΝ[   ]Ν
Col. 26   . . ΙΟΥΘΑΗΤΟΝΑϹΤΥ
     116   ΟΥΛΕΙΠΟΝ·ΑΤΥΖΟΜΕΝΟΙ[
                Π . ΑϹϹΟΝΟΞΕΙΑΝΜΑΧΑ[
     (85)   ΕΥΤ' ΕΝΠΕΔΙΩΙΚΛΟΝΕΩ[
                ΜΑΙΝΟΙΤ' ΑΧΙΛΛΕΥϹ
     120   ΛΑΟΦΟΝΟΝΔΟΡΥϹΕΙΩΝ
                ΑΛΛ' ΟΤΕΔΗΠΟΛΕΜΟΙ[
                ΛΗΞΕΝΙΟϹΤΕΦΑΝΟ[
     (90)   ΝΗΡΗΙΔΟϹΑΤΡΟΜΗΤΟ[

ἐπ. δ'.   ΩϹΤ' ΕΝΚΥΑΝΑΝΘΕΙΘ[
     125   ΠΟΝΤ|ΩΙΒΟΡ|ΕΑϹΥΠΟΚΥ
                ΜΑϹΙ|ΝΔ|ΑΙΖΕΙ
                ΝΥΚΤ|Ο|ϹΑΝΤΑϹΑϹΑΝΑΠ[
     (95)   ΛΗΞΕΝΔΕϹΥΝΦΑΕϹΙΜ[
                ΑΟΙ· ϹΤΟΡΕϹΕΝΔΕΤΕΠΟ[
     130   ΟΥΡΙΑΙΝΟΤΟΥΔΕΚΟΛΠ[
                ΙϹΤΙΟΝΑΡΠΑΛΕΩϹΑ[
                ΕΛΠΤΟΝΕΞ'. ΟΝΤΟΧΕ[

στρ. ε'. (100) ΩϹΤΡΩΕϹΕΠ . . ΚΛΥΟΝ[
                ΧΜΑΤΑΝΑΧΙΛΛΕΑ
     135   ΜΙΜΝΟ . . ΕΝΚΛΙϹΙΗΙϹΙΝ
                ΕΙ . ΕΚ . ΝΞΑΝΘΑϹΓΥΝΑΙΚΟϹ
                . Ρ . ϹΗΙΔΟϹΙΜΕΡΟΓΥΙΟΥ
     (105)   ΘΕΟΙϹΙΝΑΝΤΕΙΝΑΝΧΕΡΑϹ
                ΦΟΙΒΑΝΕϹΙΔΟΝΤΕϹΥΠΑΙ
     140   ΧΕΙΜΩΝΟϹΑΙΓΛΑΝ·

ΠΑССΥΔΙΑСΔΕΛΙΠΟΝΤΕС
ΤΕΙΧΕΑΛΑΟΜΕΔΟΝΤΟС
(110) ˙ СΠΕΔΙΟΝΚΡΑΤΕΡΑΝ
ΑΙΞΑΝΥ . ΜΙΝΑΝΦΕΡΟΝΤΕС˙

ἀντ. ε΄. 145　ΩΡСΑΝΤ . ΦΟΒΟΝΔΑΝΑΟΙС˙
ΩΤΡΥΝΕΔ᾽ ΑΡΗС
. ΥΕΓΧΗСΛΥΚΙΩΝΤΕ
(115) . ΟΞΙΑСΑΝΑΞΑΠΟΛΛΩΝ˙
ΙΞΟΝΤ᾽ Ε . ΙΘΕΙΝΑΘΑΛΑССΑС˙

Col. 27　. ΑΥСΙ|Δ᾽ ΕΥΠΡΥΜΝΟΙСΠΑΡ|Α
151　ΜΑΡΝ|ΑΝΤ᾽ · ΕΝΑΡΙΖ . . . . .| ΩΝ
. . . ΕΥ|ΘΕΤΟΦΩΤΩΝ
(120) . . . . ΤΙΓΑΙΑΜΕΛΑ[
. . . . . ΕΑСΥΠΟΧΕΙ[
155 . . . . . ΕΓ᾽ ΗΜΙΘΕΟΙС[
. . . . . . ΙС . ΘΕΩΝΔ᾽Ι══ΟΡΜΑΝ˙

ἐπ. ε΄.　. . . . . Ο|ΝΕС˙ ΗΜ|ΕΓ|ΑΛΑΙСΙΝΕΛΠΙСΙΝ
(125) . . . . |ΟΝΤΕСΥΠΕΡ|Φ| . . ΛΟΝ
160 — — — СΙΠΠΕΥΤΑΙΚΥΑΝΩΠΙΔΑСΕΚ
— — — ΝΕΑС
— — — ΠΙΝΑСΤ᾽ ΕΝ
(130) . . . . . |Ρ . ΙСΕΞΕΙΝΘ| . . . ΜΑΤΟΝΠΟΛΙΝ˙
. |ΕΛΛΟΝΑΡΑΠΡΟΤ| . . . ΝΔΙ
165 . |ΑΝΤΑΦΟΙΝΙΞΕΙ| . . . ΑΜΑΝΔΡ[

στρ. ς΄.　. |ΝΑСΚΟΝΤΕСΥΠ| . . . ΚΙΔΑΙС
| ΕΡΕΙΨ[| . . . —
(135) | ΤΩΝΕΙΚΑΙ[
| ΗΒΑΘΥΞΥΛ[
170 — — — —
— — — —
(140) — — — —
— — — —
175 ΟΥΓΑΡΑΛΑ . . Ε . ΙΝΥ[¹
ΠΑСΙΦΑΝΗСΑΡΕΤ[
ΚΡΥΦΘΕΙС᾽ ΑΜΑΥΡΟ[

ἀντ. ς΄. (145)　ΑΛΛΕΜΠΕΔΟΝΑΚ[
ΒΡΥΟΥСΑΔΟΞΑΙ
180 СΤΡΩΦΑΤΑΙΚΑΤΑΓΑΝ[
ΚΑΙΠΟΛΥΠΛΑΓΚΤΟΝΘ[
ΚΑΙΜΑΝΦΕΡΕΚΥΔΕΑΝ[
(150) ΑΙΑΚΟΥΤΙΜΑΙ·СΥΝΕΥ

¹ See crit. n., p. 350.

Col. 28

ΚΛΕΙΑΙΔΕΦΙΛΟΣΤΕΦ[
186   Π|ΟΛΙΝΚΥΒΕΡΝΑ|Ι
EΥΝΟΜΙΑΤΕCΑΟΦΡ|ΩΝ
ÁΘΑΛΙΑCΤΕΛΕΛΟΓΧ . |Ν
(155) ΆCΤΕΑΤ᾽ ΕΥCΕΒΕΩ|Ν
ΆΝΔΡΩΝΕΝΕΙ . ΗΝ|ΑΙΦΥΛΑCC . |Ι·

ἐπ. ϛ'. 190   ΝΙΚΑΝΤ᾽ ΕΡΙΚ. . . . |ΜΕΛΠΕΤ᾽ Ω|ΝΕΟΙ
. ΥΘΕΑΜΕΛΕΤΑ . . . ΒΡΟΤΩ
Φ . ΛΕΑΜΕΝΑΝΔΡ . |Υ·
(160) ΤΑΝΕΠΑΛΦΕΙΟΥΤΕΡΟ . . . ΘΑΜΑΔΗ
ΤΙΜΑCΕΝΑΧΡΥCΑΡΜΑΤΟC
195   CΕΜΝΑΜΕΓΑΘΥΜΟCΑΘΑΝΑ·
ΜΥΡΙΩΝΤ᾽ ΗΔΗΜΙΤΡΑΙCΙΝΑΝΕΡΩΝ
ΕCΤΕΦΑΝΩCΕΝΕΘΕΙΡΑC
(165) ΕΝΠΑΝΕΛΛΑΝΩΝΑΕΘΛ|ΟΙC·

στρ. ζ'.   . ΙΜΗΤΙΝΑΘΕΡCΙ .᾿ ΠΗ|C
200   . ΘΟΝΟCΒΙΑΤΑΙ
ΑΙΝΕΙΤΩCΟΦΟΝΑ|ΝΔΡΑ
. ΥΝΔΙΚΑΙ· ΒΡΟΤ|ΩΝΔΕΜΩΜΟC
(170) ΠΑΝΤΕCCΙΜΕΝΕ|CΤΙΝΕΠΕΡΓΟΙ[
. Δ᾽ ΑΛΑΘΕΙΑΦΙΛΕΙ
205   ΝΙΚΑΝΟΤΕΠΑΝΔ|. ΜΑΤΩ[
ΧΡΟΝΟCΤΟΚΑΛΩC
. ΡΓΜΕΝΟΝΑΙΕΝΑ[
(175) . Υ . ΜΕΝΕ . ΝΔΕΜΑ[
. . . . CΜΙΝ

A lacuna of ten verses.

Col. 29 ἀντ. ζ'.   ΕΛΠΙΔΙΘΥΜΟΝΙΑΙ|Ν[
221   ΤΑΙΚΑΙΕΓΩΠΙCΥΝ|Ο[
ΦΟΙΝΙΚΟΚΡΑΔΕΜΝΟ|ΙΟ[

ἐπ. ζ'. (190) ΥΜΝΩΝΤΙΝΑΤΑΝ|ΔΕΝ[
ΦΑΙΝΩΞΕΝΙΑΝ|ΤΕ[
225   ΓΛΑΟΝΓΕΡΑΙΡΩ·
ΤΑΝΕΜΟΙΛΑΜΠΩ|Ν[
ΒΛΗΧΡΑΝΕΠΑΘΡΗ|CΑΙC|Τ[
(195) ΤΑΝΕΙΚ᾽ ΕΤΥΜΩCΑ|ΡΑΚΛ|ΕΙΩ[
ΠΑΝΘΑΛΗCΕΜΑΙC|ΕΝΕC|ΤΑΞ[
230   ΤΕΡΨΙΕΠΕΙCΝΙΝ|. . ΙΔΑ|Ι
ΠΑΝΤΙΚΑΡΥΞ|ΟΝΤΙΛΑ[

XIII. [XIV.]

στρ. α′.   Κλεοπτολεμ[. .] θεσσαλωι ιπποις πετραι[.]

ΕΥΜΕΝΕΙΜΑΡΘ|ΑΙΠΑΡΑΔΑΙ[
ΘΡΩΠΟΙϹΑΡΙϹΤ|ΟΝ·
. ΥΜΦΟΡΑΔ᾽ ΕϹΘ|ΛΟΝΑΜΑΛΔΥ
. . . . ΑΡΥΤΛ . . |ΟϹΜΟΛΟΥϹΑ·
5 . . . . ΟΝΚΑΙ . . . |ΥΨΙΦΑΝΗΤΕ[
. . . ΑΤΟΡΘΩΘ|ΕΙϹΑ· ΤΙΜΑΝ
. . . ΛΟϹΑΛΛΟΙΑ|ΝΕΧΕΙ·

ἀντ. α′.   . . . . ΑΙΔ᾽ ΑΝΔΡΩΝΑΡΕ . . . |ΜΙΑΔ᾽ Ε[
. . . . ΝΠΡΟΚΕΙΤΑΙ
10 . . . . ΠΑΡΧΕΙΡΟϹΚΥΒΕΡΝ|Α
. . . . ΚΑΙΑΙϹΙΦΡΕΝΕϹϹΙ|Ν·
. . . . ΝΒΑΡΥΠΕΝΘΕϹΙΝ|ΑΡΜΟ
. . . . ΑΧΑΙϹΦΟΡΜΙΓΓΟϹΟ|ΜΦΑ
. . . . ΓΥΚΛΑΓΓΕΙϹΧΟΡΟΙ·

ἐπ. α′.   15 . . . . ΝΘΑΛΙΑΙϹΚΑΝΑΧΑ
. . . . ΟΚΤΥΠΟϹ· ΑΛΛΕΦΕΚΑϹΤΩΙ
. . . . . . ΝΔΡΩΝΕΡΓΜΑΤΙΚΑΛ
ΛΙϹΤΟϹ . ΥΕΡΔΟΝΤΑΔΕΚΑΙΘΕΟϹΟ[
ΚΛΕΟΠΤΟΛΕΜΩΙΔΕΧΑΡΙΝ
20 ΝΥΝΧΡΗΠΟϹΙΔΑΝΟϹΤΕΠΕΤΡ[
ΟΥΤΕΜΕΝΟϹΚΕΛΑΔΗϹΑΙ
ΠΥΡΡΙΧΟΥΤ᾽ ΕΥΔΟΞΟΝΙΠΠΟΝ[

στρ. β′.   ΟϹΦΙΛΟΞΕΙΝΟΥΤΕΚΑΙΟΡΘΟΔ[

A lacuna of sixteen verses.

ἐπ. β′.   40 — — ΥΩΔΕΑΘΕϹϹΑ[
— — ΕΝΓΥΑΛΟΙϹ·
— — ΝΤΕΛΗϹΚ[
— — ΕΛ . . ΔΩΝ

The rest of the ode is lost.

XIV. [XV.]

Col. 30   ]τηνοριδαι

                  ]ϛ απαιτησις

στρ. α′.   — — — ANTIΘEOY

          — — ΩΠΙϹΑΘΑΝΑϹΠΡΟϹΠΟΛΟϹ

          — — — ΠΑΛΛΑΔΟϹΟΡϹΙΜΑΧΟΥ

          — — — ΡΥϹΕΑϹ

    5   — — — ΝΑΡΓΕΙΩΝΟΔΥϹϹΕΙ

          — — — ΑΩΙΤ’ ΑΤΡΕΙΔΑΙΒΑϹΙΛΕΙ

          — — — ΖΩΝΟϹΘΕΑΝΩ

ἀντ. α′.   — — — ΟΝ

          — — — ΝΠΡΟϹΗΝΕΠΕΝ·

   10 — — — ΥΚΤΙΜΕΝΑΝ

          — — — —

          — — — — ΔΩΝΤΥΧΟΝΤΕϹ

          — — — — ϹΥΝΘΕΟΙϹ

          — — — — — ΔΟΥϹ

A lacuna of eight verses.

στρ. β′. 23 — — — — — | ΚΤΙΟϹΚΕΑΡ |

A lacuna of thirteen verses.

Col. 31 ἐπ. β′. ΑΓΟΝ·ΠΑΤΗΡΔ’ ΕΥΒΟΥΛΟϹΗΡΩϹ

        ΠΑΝΤΑϹΑΜΑΙΝΕΝΠΡΙΑΜΩΙΒΑϹΙΛΕΙ

        ΠΑΙΔΕϹϹΙΤΕΜΥΘΟΝΑΧΑΙΩΝ·

   40 ΕΝΘΑΚΑΡΥΚΕϹΔΙΕΥ

        ΡΕΙΑΝΠΟΛΙΝΟΡΝΥΜΕΝΟΙ

        ΤΡΩΩΝΑΟΛΛΙΖΟΝΦΑΛΑΓΓΑϹ

στρ. γ′.   ΔΕΞΙϹΤΡΑΤΟΝΕΙϹΑΓΟΡΑΝ·

        ΠΑΝΤΑΙΔΕΔΙΕΔΡΑΜΕΝΑΥΔΑΕΙϹΛΟΓΟϹ

   45 ΘΕΟΙϹΔ’ ΑΝΙϹΧΟΝΤΕϹΧΕΡΑϹΑΘΑΝΑΤΟΙϹ

        ΕΥΧΟΝΤΟΠΑΥϹΑϹΘΑΙΔΥΑΝ·

        ΜΟΥϹΑ·ΤΙϹΠΡΩΤΟϹΑΡΧΕΝΛΟΓΩΝΔΙΚΑΙΩΝ.

        ΠΛΕΙϹΘΕΝΙΔΑϹΜΕΝΕΛΑΟϹΓΑΡΥΙΘΕΛΞΙΕΠ|ΕΙ

        ΦΘΕΓΞΑΤ’ ΕΥΠΕΠΛΟΙϹΙΚΟΙΝΩϹΑϹΧΑΡΙϹϹΙ|Ν·

ἀντ. γ′. 50 ΩΤΡΩΕϹΑΡΗΙΦΙΛΟΙ·

        ΖΕΥϹΥΨ . . . . Ϲ . ΠΑΝ . ΑΔΕΡΚΕΤΑΙ

        ΟΥΚΑΙΤΙΟϹΘΝΑΤΟΙϹΜΕΓΑΛΩΝΑΧΕΩΝ

        ΑΛΛΕΝ . . . . . ΚΕΙΤΑΙΚΙΧΕΙΝ

ΠΑCΙΝΑΝΘΡΩΠΟΙCΔΙΚΑΝΙΘΕΙΑΝΑΓΝΑC
55 ΕΥΝΟΜΙΑCΑΚΟΛΟΥΘΟΝΚΑΙΠΙΝΥΤΑCΘΕΜΙΤΟC
ΟΛΒΙΩΝΠ‥Δ‥ΝΙΝΑΙΡΕΥΝΤΑΙCΥΝΟΙΚΟΝ

ἐπ. γ́. ἈΔΛ'ΑΙΟΛΟΙ‥ΚΕΡΔΕCCΙΚΑΙΑΦΡΟCΥΝΑΙC
ΕΞΑΙCΙΟΙCΘΑΛΛΟΥC'ΑΘΑΜΒΗC
ΥΒΡΙCἈΠΛΟΥΤ‥ΔΥΝΑΜΙΝΤΕΘΟΩC
60 ΑΛΛΟΤΡΙΟΝΩΠΑCΕΝΑΥΤΙC
Δ'ΕCΒΑΘΥΝΠΕΜΠΕΙΦΘΟΡΟΝ·
‥ΙΝΑΚΑΙΥΠΕΡΦΙΑΛΟΥC
‥‥ΠΑΙΔΑCΩΛΕCΕΝΓΙΓΑΝΤΑC

XV. [XVI.]

στρ. ‥‥ΙΟΥ‥‥‥ΕΠΕΙ
‥‥ΑΔ'ΕΠΕΜΨΕΝΕΜΟΙΧΡΥCΕΑΝ
‥‥ΙΑΘΕ‥‥‥ΡΟΝΟC‥ΥΡΑΝΙΑ[
‥‥‥‥‥ΑΤΩΝΓΕΜΟΥCΑΝΥΜΝΩΝ
5 ‥‥‥‥ΝΕΙΤΑΡΕΠΑΝΘΕΜΟΕΝΤΙΕΒΡΩΙ
‥‥‥‥‥ΓΑΛΛΕΤΑΙΗΔΟΛΙΧΑΥΧΕΝΙΚΥ[
‥‥‥‥‥ΔΕΙΑΝΦ‥ΕΝΑΤΕΡΠΟΜΕΝΟC
‥‥‥‥‥ΔΙΚΗΙΠΑΙΗΟΝΩΝ
Col. 32 ΑΝΘΕΑΠΕΔΟΙΧΝΕΙ‖Ν
10 ΠΥΘΙ'ΑΠΟΛΛΟΝ
ΤΟCCΑΧΟΡΟΙΔΕΛΦΩΝ
CΟΝΚΕΛΑΔΗCΑΝΠΑΡΑ‖ΓΑΚΛΕΑΝΑΟΝ

ἀντ. ΠΡΙΝΓΕΚΛΕΟΜΕΝΛΙΠ‖ΕΙ‖Ν
ΟΙΧΑΛΙΑΝΠΥΡΙΔΑΠΤΟΜ‖ΕΝΑΝ
15 ΑΜΦΙΤΡΥΩΝΙΑΔΑΝΘΡΑCΥΜ‖‥ΔΕΑΦΩ
Θ'‥ΙΚΕΤΟΔ'ΑΜΦΙΚΥΜΟΝ'ΑΚΤΙΑΝ·
ΕΝΘ'ΑΠΟΛΑΙΔΟCΕΥΡΥΝΕΦΕΙΚ‖ΗΝΑΙΩΙ
ΖΗΝΙΘΥΕΝΒΑΡΥΑΧΕΑCΕΝΝΕΑΤ‖ΑΥΡΟΥC
ΔΥΟΤ'ΟΡCΙΑΛΩΙΔΑΜΑCΙΧΘΟΝΙΜΕ[
20 ΛΕΚΟΡΑΙΤ'ΟΒΡΙΜΟΔΕΡΚΕΙΑΖΥΓΑ[
ΠΑΡΘΕΝΩΙΑΘΑΝΑΙ
ΥΨΙΚΕΡΑΝΒΟΥΝ·

ΤΟΤ' ΑΜΑΧΟΣΔΑΙΜΩΝ
ΔΑΙΑΝΕΙΡΑΙΠΟΛΥΔΑΚΡΥΝΥΦΑ[

ἐπ.   25   ΜΗΤΙΝΕΠΙΦΡΟΝ' ΕΠΕΙ
ΠΥΘΕΤ' ΑΓΓΕΛΙΑΝΤΑΛΑΠΕΝΘΕΑ[
ΙΟΛΑΝΟΤΙΛΕΥΚΩΛΕΝΟΝ
ΔΙΟΣΥΙΟΣΑΤΑΡΒΟΜΑΧΑΣ

ΑΛΟΧΟΝΛΙΠΑΡΟ . . ΙΟΤΙΔΟΜΟΝΠΕΙ . . |ΟΙ·

30   ΑΔΥΣΜΟΡΟΣΑΤΑΛ . . Ν' ΟΙΟΝΕΜΗΣΑΤ[
ΦΘΟΝΟΣΕΥΡΥΒΙΑ . . ΙΝΑΠΩΛΕΣΕΝ
ΔΝΟΦΕΟΝΤΕΚΑ|ΛΥ|ΜΜΑΤΩΝ
ΥΣΤΕΡΟΝΕΡΧΟΜ|ΕΝΩ|Ν·
ΟΤ' ΕΠΙΠΟΤΑΜΩ . |ΡΟΔ|ΟΕΝΤΙΛΥΚΟΡΜΑΙ[

35   ΔΕΞΑΤΟΝΕΣΣΟΥ|ΠΑ|ΡΑΔΑΙΜΟΝΙΟΝΤΕΡ[

)―――――

XVI. [XVII.]

]ἴθεοι

]θησευς

στρ. α΄.   ΚΥΑΝΟΠΡΩΙΡΑΜ . |Ν|ΝΑΥΣΜΕΝΕΚΤΥ[
ΘΗΣΕΑΔΙΣΕΠΤ . |Τ' |ΑΓΛΑΟΥΣΑΓΟΥΣΑ
ΚΟΥΡΟΥΣΙΑΟΝΩ[.]
ΚΡΗΤΙΚΟΝΤΑ|ΜΝ|ΕΝΠΕΛΑΓΟΣ·

5   ΤΗΛΑΥΓΕΙΓΑΡ . . |ΦΑΡΕΙ
ΒΟΡΗΙΑΙΠΙΤΝΟ . |Α|ΥΡΑΙ
ΚΛΥΤΑΣΕΚΑΤΙΠ . |ΛΕ|ΜΑΙΓΙΔΟΣΑΘΑΝ[

Col. 33   ΚΝΙΣΕΝΤΕΜΙΝΩΚ|ΕΑΡ
ΙΜΕΡΑΜΠ . ΚΟΣΘΕΑ[

10   ΚΥΠΡΙΔΟΣ . . ΝΑΔΩ . |Α·
ΧΕΙΡΑΔ' ΟΥ . . . . ΠΑΡΘ . |ΝΙΚΑΣ
ΑΤΕΡΘΕΡΑ . ΥΕΝ·ΘΙΓΕ|Ν
ΔΕΛΕΥΚΑΝΠΑΡΗΙ|ΔΩΝ·
ΒΟΑ . . |Τ' ΕΡ|ΒΟΙΑΧΑΛΚΟ

15   ΘΩΡΑ . . . . . ΝΔΙΟΝΟΣ
ΕΚΓ . ΝΟΝ·ΙΔΕΝΔΕΘ|ΗΣΕΥΣ·

ΜΕΛΑΝΔ' ΥΠΟΦΡΥΩ|Ν

ΔΙΝΑ . ΕΝΟΜΜΑΚΑ|ΡΔΙΑΝΤΕΟΙ
CΧΕΤΛΙΟΝΑΜΥΞΕΝ|ΑΛΓΟC·
20 ΕΙΡΕΝΤΕ·ΔΙΟCΥΙΕΦΕΡ|ΤΑΤΟΥ
ΟCΙΟΝΟΥΚΕΤΙΤΕΑΝ
ΕCΩΚΥΒΕΡΝΑΙCΦΡΕΝ|ΩΝ
Θ . . . . |·ΙCΧΕΜΕΓΑΛΟΥΧΟ|ΝΗΡΩCΒΙΑΝ

ἀντ. α΄.   ΟΤΙΜ| . ΝΕΚΘΕΩΝΜΟΙΡΑ|ΠΑΓΚΡΑΤΗC
25 ΑΜΜΙΚΑΤΕΝΕΥCΕΚΑΙΔΙ|ΚΑCΡΕΠΕΙΤΑ
ΛΑΝ|ΤΟΝΠΕΠΡΩΜΕΝ . |Ν

ΑΙCΑΝ| . ΚΠΛΗCΟΜΕΝΟΤ . |Ν
ΕΛΘΗ·| . . ΔΕΒΑΡΕΙΑΝΚΑΤΕ
ΧΕΜ . |ΤΙΝΕΙΚΑΙCΕΚΕΔΝΑ
30 ΤΕΚΕΝ|ΛΕΧΕΙΔΙΟCΥΠΟΚΡΟΤΑ|ΦΟΝΙΔΑC
ΜΙΓΕΙC|ΑΦΟΙΝΙΚΟCΕΡΑ
ΤΩΝΥ|ΜΟCΚΟΡΑΒΡΟΤΩΝ
ΦΕΡΤ| . . ΟΝ·ΑΛΛΑΚΑΜΕ
ΠΙΤΘ| . ΟCΘΥΓΑΤΗΡΑΦΝΕΟΥ
35 ΠΛΑΘ|ΕΙCΑΠΟΝΤΙΩΙΤΕΚΕΝ
ΠΟCΙΔ|ΑΝΙ·ΧΡΥCΕΟΝ

ΤΕΟΙΔ|ΟCΑΝΙΟΠΛΟΚΟΙ
ΚΑΛΥΜ|ΜΑΝΗΡΗΙΔΕC·
ΤΩCΕΠ|ΟΛΕΜΑΡΧΕΚΝΩCCΙΩΝ
40 ΚΕΛΟΜ|ΑΙΠΟΛΥCΤΟΝΟΝ
ΕΡΥΚΕ|ΝΥΒΡΙΝ·ΟΥΓΑΡΑΝΘΕΛΟΙ
Col. 34   Μ᾽ΑΜΒΡΟΤΟΙ᾽ΕΡΑΝΝΟΝΑΟ[
ΙΔΕΙΝΦΑΟCΕΠΕΙΤΙΝ᾽ΗΙΘΕ[
CΥΔΑΜΑCΕΙΑCΑΕΚΟΝ
45 ΤΑΠΡΟCΘΕΧΕΙΡΩΝΒΙΑΝ
ΔΕ . ΞΟΜΕΝ·ΤΑΔ᾽ΕΠΙΟΝΤΑΔΑ . . . |ΝΚΡΙΝ|ΕΙ·
. . . . . ΠΕΝΑΡΕΤΑΙΧΜΟCΗΡΩ[.]

ἐπ. α΄.   . . ΦΟΝΔΕΝΑΥΒΑΤΑΙ
. . Τ . . ΥΠΕΡΑΦΑΝΟΝ
50 ΘΑ . COC·ΑΛΙΟΥΤΕΓΑΜΒΡΩΙΧΟΛΩ[
ΥΦΑΙΝΕΤΕΠ . ΤΑΙΝΙΑΝ
ΜΗΤΙΝ·ΕΙΠΕΝΤΕΜΕΓΑΛΟCΘ[
ΖΕΥΠΑΤΕΡΑΚΟΥCΟΝ·ΕΙΠΕΡΜ . . . . . |Α
ΦΟΙΝΙCCΑΛΕΥΚΩΛΕΝΟCCΟΙΤΕΚ[
55 ΝΥΝΠΡΟΠΕΜΠ᾽ΑΠΟΥΡΑΝΟΥΘ[
ΠΥΡΙΕΘΕΙΡΑΝΑCΤΡΑΠΑΝ
CΑΜ᾽ΑΡΙΓΝΩΤΟΝ·ΕΙ

ΔΕΚΑΙϹΕΤΡΟΙΖΗΝΙΑϹΕΙϹ . . . |ΟΝΙ
ΦΥΤΕΥϹΕΝΑΙΘΡΑΠΟϹΕΙ
60 ΔΑΝΙΤΟΝΔΕΧΡΥϹΕΟΝ
ΧΕΙΡΟϹΑΓΛΑΟΝ
ΔΙΚΩΝΘΡΑϹΕΙϹΩΜΑΠΑΤΡΟϹ . |ϹΔΟΜΟΥϹ
ΕΝΕΓΚΕΚΟϹΜΟΝΒΑΘΕΙΑϹΑ|ΛΟϹ·
ΕΙϹΕΑΙΔ' ΑΙΚ' ΕΜΑϹΚΛΥΗΙ
65 ΚΡΟΝΙΟϹΕΥΧΑϹ

ΑΝΑΞΙΒΡΕΝΤΑϹΟͅΠΑΝΤΩ . . . .|΄. Ν·

στρ. β'.   ΚΛΥΕΔ' ΑΜΕΠΤΟΝΕΥΧΑΝΜΕΓΑϹΘΕΝΗ[.]
ΖΕΥϹ·ΥΠΕΡΟΧΟΝΤΕΜΙΝΩΙΦΥΤΕΥϹΕ
ΤΙΜΑΝΦΙΛΩΙΘΕΛΩΝ
70 ΠΑΙΔΙΠΑΝΔΕΡΚΕΑΘΕΜΕΝ·

ΑϹΤΡΑΨΕΘ'·ΟͅΔΕΘΥΜΑΡΜΕΝΟΝ
ΙΔΩΝΤΕΡΑϹΧΕΙΡΑϹΠΕΤΑϹϹΕ
ΚΛΥΤΑΝΕϹΑΙΘΕΡΑΜΕΝΕΠΤΟΛΕΜΟϹΗΡΩϹ
ΕΙΡΕΝΤΕ·ΘΗϹΕΥΤΑΔΕ
75 ΜΕΝΒΛΕΠΕΙϹϹΑΦΗΔΙΟϹ
ΔΩΡΑ ϹΥΔ' ΟΡΝΥ' ΕϹΒΑ
ΡΥΒΡΟΜΟΝΠ . ΛΑΓΟϹ·ΚΡΟΝΙ[

Col. 35   ΔΕΤΟΙΠΑΤΗΡΑΝΑΞΤΕΛΕΙ͡
ΠΟϹΕΙΔΑΝΥΠΕΡΤΑΤΟΝ
80 ΚΛΕΟϹΧΘΟΝΑΚΑΤΕΥΔΕΝΔΡΟΝ·
ΩϹΕΙΠΕ·ΤΩΙΔ' ΟΥΠΑΛΙΝ
ΘΥΜΟϹΑΝΕΚΑΜΠΤΕΤ' ΑΛΛΕΥ
ΠΑ̇ΚΤΩΝΕΠΙΚΡΙΩΝ

ϹΤΑΘΕΙϹΟ͡ΡΟΥϹΕ·ΠΟΝΤΙΟΝΤΕΝΙΝ
85 ΔΕΞΑΤΟΘΕΛΗΜΟΝΑΛϹΟϹ·
ΤΑΦ̇ΕΝΔΕΔΙΟϹΥΙΟϹΕΝΔΟΘΕΝ

ΚΕΑΡ·ΚΕΛΕΥϹΕΤΕΚΑΤΟΥ͡
ΡΟΝΙϹΧΕΙΝΕΥΔΑΙΔΑΛΟΝ
ΝΑΑ·ΜΟΙΡΑ ͗ ΕΤΕΡΑΝΠΟΡϹΥΝ' ΟΔΟΝ

ἀντ. β'. 90 ΙΕΤΟΔ' ΩΚΥΠΟΜΠΟΝΔΟΡΥ·ϹΟΕΙ
ΝΕΙΝΒΟΡΕΑϹΕΞΟΠΙΘΕΝΠΝΕΟΥϹ' ΑΗΤΑ·
ΤΡΕϹϹΑΝΔ' ΑΘΑΝΑΙΩΝ
ΗΙΘΕΩΝΓΕΝΟϹΕΠΕΙ
ΗΡΩϹΘΟΡΕΝΠΟΝΤΟΝΔΕ·ΚΑ
95 ΤΑΛΕΙΡΙΩΝΤ' ΟΜΜΑΤΩΝΔΑΚΡΥ
ΧΕΟΝΒΑΡΕΙΑΝΕΠΙΔΕΓΜΕΝΟΙΑΝΑΓΚΑΝ·

ΦΕΡΟΝΔΕΔΕΛΦΙΝΕϹΕΝΑ̇ΛΙ
ΝΑ̇Ι̇Ε̇ΤΑΙΜΕΓΑΝΘΟΟϹ

ΘΗ . ΕΑΠΑΤΡΟϹΙΠΠΙ
100 ΟΥΔΟΜΟΝ·ΕΜΟΛΕΝΤΕΘΕΩΝ
ΜΕ . . ΡΟΝ·ΤΟΘΙΚΛΥΤΑϹΙΔΩΝ
ΕΔΕΙϹΕ,ΝΗΡΕΟϹΟΛ
ΒΙΟΥΚΟΡΑϹ·ΑΠΟΓΑΡΑΓΛΑ
ΩΝΛΑΜΠΕΓΥΙΩΝϹΕΛΑϹ
105 ΩΙΤΕΠΥΡΟϹ·ΑΜΦΙΧΑΙΤΑΙϹ
ΔΕΧΡΥϹΕΟΠΛΟΚΟΙ
ΔΙΝΗΝΤΟΤΑΙΝΙΑΙ·ΧΟΡΩΙΔΕΤΕΡ
ΠΟΝΚΕΑΡΥΓΡΟΙϹΙΝΕΝΠΟϹΙΝ·
ΕΙΔΕΝΤΕΠΑΤΡΟϹΑΛΟΧΟΝΦΙΛΑΝ
110 ϹΕΜΝΑΝΒΟΩΠΙΝΕΡΑΤΟΙ
ϹΙΝΑΜΦΙΤΡΙΤΑΝΔΟΜΟΙϹ·
ᾹΝΙΝΑΜΦΕΒΑΛΛΕΝΑΙΟΝΑΠΟΡΦΥΡΕΑΝ·

ἐπ. β′. ΚΟΜΑΙϹΙΤ᾽ ΕΠΕΘΗΚΕΝΟΥΛΑΙϹ
Col. 36 ΑΜΕΜΦΕΑΠΛΟΚΟΝ·
115 ΤΟΝΠΟΤΕΟ͂ΙΕΝΓΑΜΩΙ
ΔΩΚΕΔΟΛΙΟϹΑΦΡΟΔΙΤΑΡΟΔΟΙϹΕΡΕΜΝΟΝ·
ΑΠΙϹΤΟΝΟΤΙΔΑΙΜΟΝΕϹ
ΘΕΛΩϹΙΝΟΥΔΕΝΦΡΕΝΟΑΡΑΙϹΒΡΟΤΟΙϹ·
ΝΑΑΠΑΡΑΛΕΠΤΟΠΡΥΜΝΟΝΦΑΝΗ·ΦΕΥ
120 Ο͂ΙΑΙϹΙΝΕΝΦΡΟΝΤΙϹΙΚΝΩϹΙΟΝ
ΕϹΧΑϹΕΝϹΤΡΑΤΑΓΕΤΑΝΕΠΕΙ
ΜΟΛ᾽ ΑΔΙΑΝΤΟϹΕΞᾹΛΟϹ
ΘΑΥΜΑΠΑΝΤΕϹϹΙ·ΛΑΜ
ΠΕΔ᾽ ΑΜΦΙΓΥΟΙϹΘΕΩΝΔΩΡ᾽ ΑΓΛΟ
125 ΘΡΟΝΟΙΤΕΚΟΥΡΑΙϹΥΝΕΥ
ΘΥΜΙΑΙΝΕΟΚΤΙΤΩΙ
ΩΛΟΛΥΞΑΝ·Ε
ΚΛΑΓΕΝΔΕΠΟΝΤΟϹ·ΗΙΘΕΟΙΔ᾽ ΕΓΓΥΘΕΝ
ΝΕΟΙΠΑΙΑΝΙΞΑΝΕΡΑΤΑΙΟΠΙ
130 ΔΑΛΙΕΧΟΡΟΙϹΙΚΗΙΩΝ
ΦΡΕΝΑΙΑΝΘΕΙϹ
ΟΠΑΖΕΘΕΟΠΟΜΠΟΝΕϹΘΛΩΝΤΥΧΑΝ

XVII. [XVIII.]

Θησευς

στρ. α΄.
BACIΛΕΥΤΑΝΙΕΡΑΝΑΘΑΝΑΝ
ΤΩΝΑΒΡΟΒΙΩΝΑΝΑΞΙΩΝΩΝ
ΤΙCΝΕΟΝΕΚΛΑΓΕΧΑΛΚΟΚΩΔΩΝ
CΑΛΠΙΓΞΠΟΛΕΜΗΙΑΝΑΟΙΔΑΝ·
5 ΗΤΙCΑΜΕΤΕΡΑCΧΘΟΝΟC
ΔΥCΜΕΝΗCΟΡΙ᾽ΑΜΦΙΒΑΛΛΕΙ
CΤΡΑΤΑΓΕΤΑCΑΝΗΡ·
ΗΛΗCΤΑΙΚΑΚΟΜΑΧΑΝΟΙ
ΠΟΙΜΕΝΩΝΔ᾽ΕΚΑΤΙΜΗΛΩΝ
10 CΕΥΟΝΤ᾽ΑΓΕΛΑCΒΙΑΙ
ΗΤΙΤΟΙΚΡΑΔΙΑΝΑΜΥCCΕΙ·
ΦΘΕΓΓΟΥΔΟΚΕΩΓΑΡΕΙΤΙΝΙΒΡΟΤΩΝ
ΑΛΚΙΜΩΝΕΠΙΚΟΥΡΙΑΝ
ΚΑΙΤΙΝΕΜΜΕΝΑΙΝΕΩΝ
15 ΩΠΑΝΔΙΟΝΟCΥΙΕΚΑΙΚΡΕΟΥCΑC

στρ. β΄.
Col. 37
. . ΟΝΗΛΘΕΔΟΛΙΧΑΝΑΜΕΙΨΑC
ΚΑΡΥΞΠΟCΙΝΙCΘΜΙΑΝΚΕΛΕΥΘΟΝ·
ΑΦΑΤΑΔ᾽ΕΡΓΑΛΕΓΕΙΚΡΑΤΑΙΟΥ
ΦΩΤΟC·ΤΟΝΥΠΕΡΒΙΟΝΤ᾽ΕΠΕΦΝΕΝ
20 CΙΝΙΝΟ̆CΙCΧΥΙΦΕΡΤΑΤΟC
ΘΝΑΤΩΝΗΝΚΡΟΝΙΔΑΛΥΤΑΙΟΥ
CΕΙCΙΧΘΟΝΟCΤΕΚΟC·
CΥΝΤ᾽ΑΝΔΡΟΚΤΟΝΟΝΕΝΝΑΠΑΙC
ΚΡΕΜΥΩΝΟCΑΤΑCΘΑΛΟΝΤΕ
25 CΚΙΡΩΝΑΚΑΤΕΚΤΑΝΕΝ·
ΤΑΝΤΕΚΕΡΚΥΟΝΟCΠΑΛΑΙCΤΡΑΝ
ΕCΧΕΝ·ΠΟΛΥΠΗΜΟΝΟCΤΕΚΑΡΤΕΡΑΝ
CΦΥΡΑΝΕΞΕΒΑΛΛΕΝΠΡΟΚΟ
ΠΤΑCΑΡΕΙΟΝΟCΤΥΧΩΝ
30 ΦΩΤΟC·ΤΑΥΤΑΔΕΔΟΙΧ᾽ΟΠΑΙΤΕΛΕΙΤΑΙ·

στρ. γ΄.
ΤΙΝΑΔ᾽ΕΜΜΕΝΠΟΘΕΝΑΝΔΡΑΤΟΥΤΟΝ
ΛΕΓΕΙ·ΤΙΝΑΤΕCΤΟΛΑΝΕΧΟΝΤΑ·
ΠΟΤΕΡΑCΥΝΠΟΛΕΜΗΙΟΙCΟ
ΠΛΟΙCΙCΤΡΑΤΙΑΝΑΓΟΝΤΑΠΟΛΛΑΝ·
35 ΗΜΟΥΝΟΝCΥΝΟΠΛΟΙCΙΝ
CΤΙΧΕΙΝΕΜΠΟΡΟΝΟ̆Ι᾽ΑΛΑΤΑΝ
ΕΠΑΛΛΟΔΑΜΙΑΝ

ICXYPONTEKAIAΛKIMON

ὮΔEKAIΘPACYNὸCTOYTΩN

40 ANΔPΩNKAPTEPONCΘENOC

ECXEN·HΘEOCAYTONOPMAI

ΔIKACAΔIKOICINὸΦPAMHCETAI

OYΓAPPAIΔIONAIENEP

ΔONTAMHNTYXEINKAKΩI·

45 ΠANT' ENTΩIΔOΛIXΩIXPONΩITEΛEITAI·

στρ. δ'. ΔYOOIΦΩTEMONOYCAMAPTEIN

ΛEΓEI·ΠEPIΦAIΔIMOICIΔ' ΩMOIC

ΞIΦOCEXEIN·

ΞECTOYCΔEΔY' ENXEPECC' AKONTAC

Col. 38   55 * cτιλΒειναπολαμνιαν

φοινιccανφλογαπαιδαδ' εμεν

πρωθ^нΒον·αρηιωνδ' αθυρματων

50 KHYTYKTONKYNEANΛAKAI

NANKPATOCYΠEPΠYPCOXAITOY·

XITΩNAΠOPΦYPEON

CTEPNOICIT' AMΦIKAIOYΛION

ΘECCAΛANXΛAMYΔ'·OMMATΩNΔE

*MEMNACΘAIΠOΛEMOYTEKAI

XAΛKEOKTYΠOYMAXAC

60 ΔIZHCΘAIΔEΦIΛAΓΛAOYCAΘANAC

)

XVIII. [XIX.]

Ιω αθηναιοις

στρ. ΠAPECTIMYPIAKEΛEYΘOC

AMBPOCIΩNMEΛEΩN

ὸCANΠAPAΠEIEPIΔΩNΛA

XHICIΔΩPAMOYCAN

5 IOBΛEΦAPOITEKAI

ΦEPECTEΦANOIXAPITEC

BAΛΩCINAMΦITIMAN

YMNOICIN·YΦAINENYNEN

TAICΠOΛYHPATOICTIKÁINON[1]

10 OΛBIAICAΘANAIC

EYAINETEKHIAMEPIMNA·

ΠPEΠEICEΦEPTATANIMEN

OΔONΠAPAKAΛΛIOΠACΛA

_____

[1] See crit. n. on p. 398.

XOĨCANEΞOXONΓEPAC·

15 TIHNAPΓOCOΘ᾽ IΠΠIONΛIΠOYCA

ΦEYΓEXPYCEABOYC

EYPYCΘENEOCΦPAΔAICIΦEPTATOYΔIOC

INAXOYPOΔOΔAKTYΛOCKOPA·

ἀντ.   ὌT᾽ APΓONOMMACIBΛEΠONTA

20 ΠANTOΘENAKAMATOIC

 *   MEΓICTOANACCAKEΛEYCEN

AKOITONAYΠNONEON

TAKAΛΛIKEPANΔAMAΛIN

25 ΦYΛACCEN· OYΔEMAIAC

YIOCΔYNAT᾽ OYTEKATEY

ΦEΓΓEACAMEPACΛAΘEINNIN

        22 * χργcoπεπλocHPa

Col. 39   OYTENYKTACAΓN[

EIT᾽ OYNΓENET᾽ E[

30 ΠOΔAPKE᾽ AΓΓEΛO[

KTANEINTOT[

OMBPIMOCΠOPOYΛ[

APΓON· HPAKAI[

ACΠETOIMEPIMN[

35 HΠEIEPIΔECΦYTEY[

KAΔEΩNANAΠAYC[

ἐπ.   EMOIMENOYN

ACΦAΛECTATONAΠP[

EΠEIΠAPANΘEMΩ[

40 NEIΛONAΦIKET᾽ O[

IΩΦEPOYCAΠAIΔ[

EΠAΦON· ENΘANI[

ΛINOCTOΛΩNΠPYT[

YΠEPOXΩIBPYONT[

45 MEΓICTANTEΘNA[

OΘENKAIAΓANOPI[

ENEΠTAΠYΛOIC[

KAΔMOCCEMEΛ[

ĀTONOPCIBAKXA[

50 TIKTEΔIONYCON[

KAIXOPΩNCTEΦA[

XIX. [XX.]

Ἰδας λακεδαιμονιοις

ϹΠΑΡΤΑΙΠΟΤ'ΕΝΕ̣[
ΞΑΝΘΑΙΛΑΚΕΔΑ[
ΤΟΙΟΝΔΕΜΕΛΟϹΚ[
ΟΤ' ΑΓΕΤΟΚΑΛΛΙΠΑ[
5　ΚΟΡΑΝΘΡΑϹΥΚΑΡ̆[
ΜΑΡΠΗϹϹΑΝΙΟΤ̣[
ΦΥΓΩΝΘΑΝΑΤΟΥΤ̣[
ΑΝΑΞΙΑΛΟϹΠΟϹΙ
ΙΠΠΟΥϹΤΕΌΙΙϹΑΝ[
10　ΠΛΕΥΡΩΝ' ΕϹΕΥΚΤ[
ΧΡΥϹΑϹΠΙΔΟϹΥΙΟ[

The rest of the ode is lost.

INTRODUCTIONS TO THE ODES.

A. EPINIKIA.

THE CYCLE OF THE FOUR GREAT FESTIVALS.

The Olympian games were held towards the end of summer, at the time of a full moon (Pind. *O.* III. 19), and lasted five days (*O.* v. 6). The incidence of the festival was regulated by a cycle of 99 lunar months, in such a manner that the interval between two celebrations was alternately one of 49 lunar months and one of 50. In the former case the festival seems to have coincided with the second full moon after the summer solstice, and in the latter with the third (Schröder, Prolegomena to Pindar, p. 48). According to scholia on Pind. *O.* III. 35, the celebration was alternately in the month Apollonius and in the month Parthenius (*ib.* p. 46); but it is not known to what Attic months these corresponded.

The Nemean games were held in summer, probably in July, at the beginning of the second and fourth years of each Olympiad.

The Isthmian games were held in spring, probably in April (cp. Thuc. VIII. 7—10), in the latter half of the second and fourth years of each Olympiad.

The Pythian games were held in August (the Delphian month Bucatius, the Attic Metageitnion), early in the third year of each Olympiad.

To exemplify this cycle, we will take the 74th and 75th Olympiads.

Olympiad.	B.C.			
74. 1.	484/3	484.	Late summer. *Olympia*	Pind. *O.* x, xi
74. 2.	483/2	{ 483.	Summer. *Nemea*	
		482.	Spring. *Isthmia*	
74. 3.	482/1	482.	August. *Pythia*	
74. 4.	481/0	{ 481.	Summer. *Nemea*	Pind. *N.* v, **Bacch. XII**?
		480.	Spring. *Isthmia*	Pind. *I.* v [vi]?
75. 1.	480/79	480.	Late summer. *Olympia*	
75. 2.	479/8	{ 479.	Summer. *Nemea*	
		478.	Spring. *Isthmia*	Pind. *I.* iv [v]? iii [iv]?
75. 3.	478/7	478.	August. *Pythia*	
75. 4.	477/6	{ 477.	Summer. *Nemea*	
		476.	Spring. *Isthmia*	

DATES OF SOME EPINIKIA.

Olympiad.	B.C.		Olympiad.	B.C.	
70. 3.	498	Pind. *P.* x	78. 1.	468	**Bacch. III**
72. 3.	490	Pind. *P.* vi, xii			
73. 3.	486	Pind. *P.* vii	78. 2.	467	Pind. *N.* vii ?
75. 2.	478	Pind. *I.* vii [viii]?	79. 1.	464	Pind. *O.* vii, ix, xiii
76. 1.	476	Pind. *O.* i, ii, iii, xiv.	79. 3.	462	Pind. *P.* iv, v
		Bacch. V	80. 1.	460	Pind. *O.* viii
76. 2.	475	Pind. [*P.*] ii	80. 4.	456	Pind. *I.* vi [vii]?
76. 3.	474	Pind. *P.* iii ? ix, xi	81. 1.	456	Pind. *O.* iv, v ? *N.* iv ?
76. 4.	473	Pind. *N.* i ?	82. 1.	452	**Bacch. VI, VII**
77. 1.	472	Pind. *O.* vi ?			
77. 3.	470	Pind. *P.* i, **Bacch. IV**	83. 3.	446	Pind. *P.* viii

ODE I.

For Argeius of Ceos, victor in the boys' boxing-match [or pancration?] at the Isthmia.—Date unknown.

§ 1. The title is lost, and the occasion of the ode is known only from internal evidence, which, however, happens to be confirmed by an inscription found in Ceos. The name of the victor was Ἀργεῖος (I. 32, II. 4 f.). His father was Πανθείδης (IV. 14: only the letters ΠΑΝ remain in I. 37), a man skilled in medicine, 'well-dowered by the Graces,' and famed for hospitality (I. 39—41), though, as may be inferred from vv. 49—67, of modest fortune. Argeius was one of five brothers, all of good repute (43 f.). The family belonged to Ceos (II. 2).

That the festival was the Isthmian appears from I. 46 and II. 6 f. The nature of the contest is indicated only by καρτερόχειρ, the epithet of Argeius in I. 31, and μ[άχ]ας θρασύχειρος in II. 4. These words suggest the boxing-match, though they would also suit the pancration (boxing and wrestling).

§ 2.   The inscription above-mentioned is on a marble slab which was found at Iulis in Ceos, and is now in the Museum at Athens[1].   It is of interest as a specimen of the form taken by a local record of victories at the national festivals.   The slab seems originally to have formed the lower left-hand portion of a large stele : in its present state, it measures about 19 inches in length and 11¼ in breadth.   It has been broken across, but the two pieces have been cemented together, so as practically to restore the unity of the stone, and no writing has been destroyed in the fracture.   The inscription is in 29 lines, 27 of which record victories[2].   Each entry of a victory occupies one line.   Each entry, when entire, gave (1) the victor's name, with his father's ; (2) the class, with respect to age, in which he competed,— ἀνδρῶν, ἀγενείων or παίδων: and (3) the nature of the contest: *e.g.* Σίνις Ἀξίλεω παίδων παγκράτιον.   But the left-hand edge of the stone has been injured, so that the initial letter of several names is lost.   And the right-hand edge has been cut away, to the extent of at least four inches, judging by the number of letters which are certainly missing at the end of some lines.   This was done, no doubt, by masons who adapted the slab

---

[1] I am indebted to Mr R. C. Bosanquet, Director of the British School at Athens, for kindly sending me an impression of the inscription, with some valuable notes.

[2] The names of four of the victors are illegible. The remaining twenty-three victories were won by thirteen persons, one of whom gained 4, another 3, and five (including Argeius) gained 2 apiece. Of the seven who gained more than one victory each, six were victorious both at the Isthmus and at Nemea ; the seventh, at the Isthmus only. The rule followed in the arrangement of the names was (I conceive) as follows. In each section (the Isthmian and the Nemean) the victories were entered in chronological order. When, in the same year, there had been Cean victors in more than one class of age, the order was 'men,' 'youths,'

'boys.' Where, then, the name of a youth *precedes* that of a man (as in lines 9 and 21), this means that the man's victory belongs to a later year. In one instance the record notes that a man and a youth whose name follows his were 'brothers who won on the same day' (line 10), but their relationship was not the only reason for so placing them. The same remark applies when the name of a boy precedes that of a youth (l. 13). The name of 'Leon son of Leomedon,' a victor in the κηρύκων ἀγών, stands last both in the Isthmian and in the Nemean section, in each case following the name of a boy. That order would be the natural one even if they won in the same year, as the herald's victory belonged to a different category, and was not declared until the end of the games.

to serve as a rude capital or impost in a Byzantine church[1]. Hence the last word, specifying the contest, is wholly lost in all the lines except three; viz., lines 13 and 24, where παγ and πα respectively remain from παγκράτιον, and line 29, where κῆρυξ remains. Above the last twelve entries is the heading or title (forming line 17), οἵδε Νέμεια ἐνίκων. The Nemean games ranked last among the four great festivals; hence it may safely be inferred that the immediately preceding section of the record contained the victories in the Isthmian games, though the heading of this section has been lost, along with the earlier entries under it. In the fifteenth extant line of the Isthmian section we read:—

ΑΡΓΕΙΟΣ ΠΑΝΘ[ ]ΔΕΩ ΠΑΙΔΩ[Ν

This entry presumably refers to the victory commemorated in the first and second odes of Bacchylides. The word lost after παίδων may have been either ΠΥΞ or ΠΑΓΚΡΑΤΙΟΝ.

The name of Argeius recurs in the Nemean section (l. 26):

ΑΡΓΕΙΟΣ ΠΑΝΘ[ ]ΔΕΩ ΑΓΕ[ΝΕΙΩΝ

where again the specification of the contest is lost. Nothing else is known as to the Nemean victory of Argeius. Nor do we know precisely at what point the limit of age between παῖδες and ἀγένειοι was drawn for the purposes of these games. The term ἀγένειος may have denoted the age from 17 to 19 inclusive, and παῖς that from 14 to 16[2]. In that case the interval separating the victory of a παῖς from one gained by the same person as an ἀγένειος might vary from one year to five. The name of Argeius stands last but one in the Isthmian section of the record, and last but three in the Nemean. Neither Argeius nor any one of five other persons named as victors among the 'boys' or the 'youths' recurs as a victor among 'men.' The record, as we have it, clearly breaks off at or soon after the date of the Nemean victory won by Argeius.

The inscription itself is of a date much later than the latest that could be assigned to any poem of Bacchylides. It has been referred to the period from *circa* 400 to 350 B.C.[3]. If that view

---

[1] Mr Bosanquet observes that the back and sides of the stone have been treated in a manner which suggests such a purpose.

[2] See Introd. to Ode XII, § 2.

[3] This was the opinion of Halbherr, by whom the inscription was first edited (in 1885): and it is shared, as Mr

be correct, the list must have been copied from some older record, such as certainly existed in the poet's day[1]. The register of Cean victors had doubtless been continued from the time of Argeius down to the date of the inscription, and the existing slab can be but a small fragment of a record which filled more than one stele.

§ 3.   The ode, so far as it is preserved in the MS., practically begins with the fragment which stands first in the text of this edition, describing the arrival of Minos in Crete (vv. 1—19). This is followed by a lacuna of nine verses; and then comes the last part of the poem, virtually complete, which is concerned with the victor Argeius and his father Pantheides (vv. 29—74). There are also, however, several smaller fragments, which belonged to the earlier portion of the ode. From these it appears that the poet commenced with a reference to the Isthmian festival, and proceeded to relate the heroic saga of his native island.   The myth was in outline as follows.   Dexithea ('she who entertains a god') was one of several sisters, daughters of Damon, chief of the Telchines.   Those volcanic daemons, connected with Poseidon and his realm, figured in legend as the earliest craftsmen in metal, but also as spiteful enchanters ($\tau\epsilon\lambda\chi\iota\nu = \theta\epsilon\lambda\gamma\iota\nu$, from $\theta\epsilon\lambda\gamma\omega$), who had blighted the fruits of the earth in Rhodes, their first home.   Their malignity provoked the wrath of Zeus, who slew them with his thunderbolts.   But

Bosanquet informs me, by Dr Wilhelm, who is now Keeper of the Inscriptions in the Museum at Athens.

Ω is used in the inscription, and sigma has the form Σ, not the older ς. In Attica Σ had supplanted ς in ordinary epigraphic use as early as Ol. 83. 3 =446 B.C. (E. S. Roberts, *Greek Epigraphy*, p. 102): the earliest appearance of Ω in an Attic inscription which can be dated seems to be in CIA 338, which Kirchhoff has fixed to Ol. 93. 1=408 B.C. (*ib.* p. 104). But, with regard to the usage of Ceos, there does not appear to be any definite evidence as to approximately the time at which those forms began to be used; and the presumption (at least as regards Ω) is probably in favour of a date later than *circa* 410 B.C.

One point may be noted.   If the

Cean stone is merely a copy made *c.* 400—350 B.C. from an older document, one of its characteristics is the more curious.   The size of the letters, and the spacing, vary much in different lines. *E.g.*, the first entry of $\Lambda E\Omega N$ $\Lambda E\Omega ME$-$\Delta ONTO\Sigma$ in l. 16 is so spaced out as to fill the whole width of the existing slab, and hence $KHPT\Xi$ has been lost after it. But the second entry of the same name in l. 29 is so much more compressed that $KHPT\Xi$ comes in.   Such variations would be more natural if the successive entries had been made from time to time, than if the stone-cutter was simply copying an older record which stood complete before him.

[1] See Appendix on Ode II. 9 f., $\dot{\epsilon}\beta\delta o\mu\dot{\eta}\kappa o\nu\tau a$ $\sigma\dot{\upsilon}\nu$ $\sigma\tau\epsilon\phi\dot{a}\nu o\iota\sigma\iota\nu$.

he spared Dexithea and her sisters, who had shown hospitality to him and Apollo. Minos, coming from Crete to Ceos, there wedded Dexithea. Their son was Euxantius, who became lord of Ceos, father of the hero Miletus, and ancestor of a Milesian clan, the Euxantidae.

It is impossible, with our data, to say exactly how much of the ode has been lost, or how the earlier part of the myth was told. A discussion of these questions will be found in the Appendix.

ODE II.

For the same.

The title in the MS. (attributable to the hand of the first corrector) attests that this short song is in honour of the same person ; and the Isthmian victory to which it refers is doubtless the same. The last four verses suggest that the ode may have been sung, to an accompaniment of flutes, as a welcome to Argeius when he landed in Ceos on his return. Ode I, the regular epinikion, was presumably written later, for the formal celebration of the victory at the young athlete's home.

ODES III, IV, V.

For Hieron.

Before dealing separately with each of these three poems, it will be useful to give a synopsis of the chief events in the history of Hieron and his dynasty, with the chronology of the odes written for him by Bacchylides and by Pindar.

Deinomenes was a citizen of Gela, hereditary ἱεροφάντης of Demeter and Persephone. The origin of his sacred office is related by Herodotus (VII. 153). One of the ancestors of Deinomenes was Τηλίνης, himself descended from one of the first settlers at Gela, who came with its founders, Antiphemus of Rhodes and Entimus of Crete [*circ.* 690 B.C. : Thuc. VI. 4 § 3]. This Telines possessed, says Herodotus, certain mysterious ἱρὰ τῶν χθονίων θεῶν : *i.e.* the secret of certain rites (probably associated with visible symbols) of the two goddesses. Some citizens of Gela, vanquished in a party struggle, had seceded to a place called Μακτώριον : Telines undertook to bring them back by means of his ἱρά, on condition that, if he did so, he and his descendants should be ἱροφάνται τῶν χθονίων θεῶν. He succeeded,—how, we are not told ; and the priesthood remained thenceforth in his house.

Deinomenes had four sons, Gelon, Hieron, Thrasybulus, and Polyzelus. Gelon, the eldest, had been commander of cavalry under Hippocrates, tyrant of Gela. On the death of Hippocrates, the city of Gela refused to acknowledge his sons. Gelon took up their cause, reduced Gela, and then seized the supreme power for himself.

OLYMP.	B.C.	
72. 2–73. 4	491–485	**Gelon,** eldest of the four sons of Deinomenes, succeeds Hippocrates as tyrant of **Gela,** where he reigns for about six years.
73. 1	488	Gelon dedicates a bronze chariot at Olympia as a thank-offering for victory in the chariot-race (Paus. 6. 9. § 4).
73. 4	485	The oligarchic land-owners ·(γαμόροι) of Syracuse, having been banished by the Syracusan democracy and retired to Casmenae, invoke Gelon's aid. He leads them against Syracuse. At his approach the democracy submits, and he becomes master of the city. **Syracuse** is thenceforth the seat of his rule.
		Hieron, the second son of Deinomenes, becomes ruler of Gela, as vice-gerent of Gelon.
		Gelon enlarges and strengthens Syracuse by carrying the wall of Achradina down to the Great Harbour, thus bringing Achradina and Ortygia within a single fortified enclosure. The greatness of Syracuse as a city, and its naval power, date from his reign.
74. 3	482	Hieron wins a victory in the horse-race (κέλητι) at Delphi, in the 26th Pythiad. This is the first of the three Pythian victories to which Bacchylides refers (IV. 4).
75. 1	480	The Carthaginians, under Hamilcar, are defeated at **Himera** by the Syracusans and other Siceliots, στρατηγοῦντος Γέλωνος αὐτοκράτορος (Diod. XIII. 94). As a thank-offering for this victory, Gelon dedicated at Delphi a golden tripod surmounted by a Nike. Hieron afterwards placed a like offering at the side of his brother's. (See Appendix on Ode III. 17 ff.)

OLYMP.	B.C.	
75. 3	478	**Death of Gelon. Hieron succeeds him as ruler of Syracuse.** Second Pythian victory of Hieron (cp. 482 B.C.). He wins the horse-race in the 27th Pythiad. The κέλης on this occasion was certainly Pherenicus (Pind. *P.* III. 73 f.), who possibly was the winner also in 482.
75–76	478–476	At this period there was war between Hieron and Theron, the tyrant of Acragas. According to one account, this war was connected with the protection afforded by Theron to Polyzelus, the youngest brother of Hieron, with whom he was at enmity. Theron had invaded Hieron's territories, and advanced as far as the river Gelas, when the poet **Simonides** 'fell in with them, and reconciled them to each other' (περιτυχόντα διαλῦσαι). Hieron then took Polyzelus into favour again. (Diod. XI. 48.) The words of Bacchylides (v. 35 f.) suggest that he then (in 476) supposed Hieron to be on good terms with both his surviving brothers, Thrasybulus and Polyzelus.
75. 4	477	Anaxilas, tyrant of Rhegium, aims at subjugating the Epizephyrian Locri. Hieron sends his brother-in-law Chromius as an envoy to Anaxilas, and secures the continued independence of the Locrians.
76. 1	476	Hieron's first victory at Olympia, gained with the κέλης Pherenicus. **First Olympian of Pindar:** who seems to have been at Syracuse when the ode was written, or at least when it was sung (v. 10). **Fifth ode of Bacchylides:** who sends the poem from Ceos, but may have already visited Syracuse, as he calls himself Hieron's ξένος (10 f.). Hieron transports the citizens of Catana and Naxos to Leontini. On the vacant site of

OLYMP.	B.C.	

Catana he founds a new city, with 5000 settlers from Syracuse and as many more from Peloponnesus, and calls it **Aetna**, placing it under the protection of Ζεὺς Αἰτναῖος.

76. 2 | **475**

A great eruption of Mount Aetna, which Pindar describes in *P.* I. 21 ff. (470 B.C.), and to which Aeschylus alludes (*P. V.* 367 ff.), is fixed to this year, if the words πεντηκοστῷ ἔτει in Thuc. III. 116 § 2 are to be taken strictly. But the Parian Chronicle (Müller I. 550, 68) puts the eruption in 479 B.C.: and it is possible that Thuc. gave merely a 'round number.' Or the volcano may have been active at intervals for several years.

Second 'Pythian' of Pindar. This ode, incorrectly classed as Pythian, celebrated a victory of Hieron in the chariot-race at some Theban festival (perhaps the Ἡράκλεια or Ἰόλαια). The poet alludes to Hieron's recent intervention on behalf of the Italian Locri (vv. 18—20).

76. 3 | **474**

The Etruscans, coming by sea, attack **Cumae**, the ancient Chalcidic settlement in Ὀπικία (Campania). Hieron sends a Syracusan fleet, which, with the Cumaean, utterly overthrows the Etruscan armada (Diod. XI. 51). [There is a trophy of this victory in the British Museum; viz., an Etruscan helmet which Hieron dedicated at Olympia, with the inscription HIA-PONOΔEINOMENEOΣKAITOIΣYPAKOΣIOI-TOIΔITYPAN[= Tυρρανὰ]AΠOKYMAΣ.]

The Third Pythian of Pindar may belong to this year: this is, at any rate, its approximate date. The poet calls Hieron Αἰτναῖον ξένον (v. 69), showing that the ode is later than 476: and there is no reference to Hieron's Pythian victory with the chariot (470). The poem is not an ἐπινίκιον of the ordinary kind: *i.e.*, it does not celebrate a victory which had

OLYMP.	B.C.	

just been gained. It refers to the former success of the horse Pherenicus at Delphi (in 478, perhaps also in 482): vv. 73 f. But it is largely an ode of comfort and exhortation: Hieron was suffering from a painful disease (λιθιῶν).

76. 4 — **473**

The probable date of **Pindar's first Nemean**, for Hieron's brother-in-law Chromius, who was now guardian (or 'Mayor of the Palace') to Hieron's son, Deinomenes, who had been appointed to rule the newly-founded Aetna (Αἴτνας βασιλεῖ, Pind. *P.* 1. 60). Chromius was proclaimed at Nemea as Αἰτναῖος. Pindar seems to have been in Sicily then (*N.* 1. 19 ff.).

[The ninth 'Nemean' ode, wrongly so classed, concerns a victory of Chromius in the Pythian games at Sicyon, and seems to be earlier than the first Nemean: it calls Aetna τὰν νεόκτισταν (v. 2), and may belong to 472 B.C.]

77. 1 — **472**

Hieron's second victory at Olympia, in the horse-race. [The fragment of the Olympic register contained among the Oxyrhynchus papyri proves that Hieron won with the κέλης at Olympia both in Ol. 76 and in Ol. 77.]

77. 3 — **470**

Hieron's third Pythian victory. He wins the four-horse chariot-race, in the 29th Pythiad.

First Pythian of Pindar, Ἱέρωνι Αἰτναίῳ: a title indicating that, at this Pythian festival, he was proclaimed as Αἰτναῖος. Pindar alludes to the victory at Himera in 480 (75 ff.), and to that at Cumae in 474 (71 f.).

Fourth ode of Bacchylides: which speaks of Hieron as having now won three victories at Delphi (*i.e.*, in 482, 478, 470), and two at Olympia (*i.e.*, in 476 and 472): vv. 4 and 17.

194 INTRODUCTIONS TO THE ODES.

OLYMP.	B.C.	
78. 1	468	Hieron's victory at Olympia with the four-horse chariot. **Third ode of Bacchylides:** who probably was at Syracuse when the ode was written, or when it was sung (vv. 15 ff.). The tone of vv. 85—92 indicates that Hieron was not expected to live long.
78. 2	467	**Hieron dies at Aetna** (Diod. XI. 66). He receives τιμαὶ ἡρωϊκαί, as κτίστης of that city. After his death, his son Deinomenes dedicates thank-offerings in his name at Olympia, viz. (1) a bronze chariot and charioteer, (2) two bronze κέλητες, with boy-riders; one being placed on each side of the chariot (Paus. 6. 12 § 1). The inscription (id. 8. 42 § 9) recorded that Hieron had won τεθρίππῳ μὲν ἅπαξ, μουνοκέλητι δὲ δίς. **Thrasybulus**, the younger brother of Hieron, succeeds him as ruler of Syracuse.
78. 3	466	Having reigned about eleven months, Thrasybulus, a cruel tyrant, is expelled by the Syracusans, and withdraws to the Epizephyrian Locri; after which nothing more is heard of him. The dynasty of the Deinomenidae then comes to an end, and the Syracusan democracy is restored.

ODE III.

For Hieron of Syracuse, victor in the chariot-race at Olympia.
Ol. 78, 468 B.C.

§ 1. This ode, the latest in date of the three, is placed first, because the victory which it concerns is the most important. It falls into three main sections, (*a*) an exordium, vv. 1—22; (*b*) the myth of Croesus, 23—62; (*c*) the conclusion, 63—97.

(*a*) The Muse is bidden to sing of Demeter and Persephone, whose priest Hieron is: then comes a reference to the chariot-race itself, and to the applause which greeted the victory.

From a notice of the festivities at Syracuse, where he may have been present (vv. 15 f.), the poet passes to a mention of the golden tripods dedicated at Delphi by Gelon and Hieron. The proem concludes with a sentiment which is the key-note of the ode: *Let a man bring choice gifts to the god; that is the surest pledge of prosperity.* To this sentiment he knits on, as an illustration, the story of Croesus. It is interesting to remember that in an ode, then recent, for Hieron, Pindar had pointed to the Lydian king as an example of generosity rewarded by lasting fame : οὐ φθίνει Κροίσου φιλόφρων ἀρετά (*Pyth* I. 94, 470 B.C.).

§ 2. (*b*) The story of Croesus is told in a form which occurs nowhere else in ancient literature. According to our other authorities, Cyrus dooms Croesus to the pyre[1]. Here it is Croesus who voluntarily resolves to burn himself and his family, in order to escape enslavement to the Persian conqueror. The Croesus of Herodotus appeals on the pyre to Apollo (I. c. 87), though he afterwards taunts the god with ingratitude (c. 90); the Croesus of Bacchylides seems rather to invoke Zeus (v. 37). The quenching of the pyre by rain is common to both versions; but here Zeus is expressly named as the agent (v. 55). The Croesus of Herodotus, after his deliverance from the pyre, figures as the friend and counsellor of Cyrus, and lives to admonish Cambyses (III. 36); when or how he died, we are not told. Here Apollo transports Croesus, with his wife and daughters, to the happy land of the Hyperboreans.

Ancient art comes to our aid where literature fails, and proves that the version of the Croesus-myth followed by Bacchylides was a current one before his time. An early red-figured amphora in the Louvre, dating from the close of the sixth century B.C. or the opening years of the fifth, shows Croesus enthroned on a great pyre, which is beginning to burn. He is clad in royal robes, and crowned with laurel ; his left hand bears a sceptre, while with his right he pours a

---

[1] Herod. I. 86 ff., and III. 16: Ctesias *ap.* Phot. *cod.* 72 : Nicolaus of Damascus (in the Augustan age), frag. 61 (Müller, *Frag. Hist.* III. p. 406). Nicolaus may have been indebted to the Λυδιακά of Xanthus, *circ.* 470 B.C. (Müller I. 36). Lucian, *Gallus* c. 23.

libation. An attendant, who has the significant name of ΕΤΘΤΜΟΣ, is bending in front of the pyre, and applying to it, with both hands, objects which some critics explain as the 'whisks' (περιρραντήρια, *aspergilla*) used in sprinkling lustral water, while others suppose them to be fans, or torches[1]. The act of Croesus is manifestly conceived as voluntary. A majestic serenity, or even gladness, is the sentiment indicated by the picture[2].

What were the sources of this version? It is one which dignifies Croesus by an intrepid resolve; and that resolve is of an oriental cast. These features point to a native Lydian origin. It is also honourable to Apollo, who promptly recompenses his faithful votary with a supreme reward. But it is improbable that this account of Apollo's action came from Delphi. The Delphian legend is rather to be recognised in the answer of the Pythia to the complaint of Croesus, as reported by Herodotus (I. 91). At the central shrine of Loxias it was the interest of the priests to keep up the tradition that a great Lydian king had been guided from Delphi, even though they had only a lame defence for the ambiguous responses which lured him to his ruin. But the Aegean seat of the god had no such responsibility for oracles given to Croesus. Another trait of the story should also be noted. Here, and here alone, the Hyperborean land appears as a place to which pious mortals are translated without dying; and the Hyperborean legends had a very special place in the Apollo-cult of Delos. It is '*Delos-born*' Apollo, says Bacchylides (v. 58), who carries Croesus to that elysium. The Ionian poet of Ceos would know the Delian temple-legend. He wrote for Delian festivals, and was no stranger to the sacred lore of the island[3]. I should conjecture, then, that the form of the Croesus-myth given in his ode (468 B.C.), and attested by the somewhat earlier vase, was one which originally came from Lydia, and was worked up at Delos.

[1] They are, however, quite unlike torches as usually represented : see (*e.g.*) the torches applied to Alcmena's pyre by the attendant in Python's vase-painting (*Journ. Hellen. Stud.* XI. pl. 6).

[2] The amphora (no. 194 in the Louvre) has been published in *Monumenti dell' Instituto*, I. pl. XLIV.: Baumeister, *Denkmäler*, p. 796. See also A. H. Smith in *Journ. Hellen. Stud.* XVIII. (1898) pp. 267 f.

[3] See Introd. to Ode XVI, *ad init.*

Later in the fifth century, this version gave way to that found in Herodotus, which represented the Asiatic Greek conception of the manner in which a Persian conqueror would act, while it also suited the interests of Delphi. Herodotus makes Croesus survive in Persia during many years after the capture of Sardis. For that account he presumably had some data furnished by traditions current in Asia Minor: but such evidence would at once dissolve the Delian myth, the free creation of Ionian fancy, as to Apollo's prompt removal of Croesus to the seats of the blest.

§ 3. (c) From the Croesus-myth the poet returns to the praises of Hieron—a benefactor of Delphi unsurpassed by any Greek; 'lover of horses,' warrior, just ruler, and disciple of the Muses. After some verses in a different strain, which suggest that Hieron's end was believed to be near (75—92), the ode closes with a forecast of renown for him,—and for 'the nightingale of Ceos.'

ODE IV.

For Hieron of Syracuse, victor in the chariot-race at Delphi.
Ol. 77. 3, 470 B.C.[1]

This short song, in two strophes of ten verses each, congratulates Hieron on the growing series of his victories. After winning the horse-race at Delphi in 482 and in 478 B.C., he has now won the chariot-race; a Pythian record which the poet declares to be unequalled. At Olympia he has also won two horse-races (viz. in 476 and 472). Hieron's brilliant fortunes show the favour of heaven (18 ff.).

Hieron's new victory (celebrated by Pindar in his first *Pythian*) was one of high importance. This song is exceedingly slight: it resembles the brief greeting to Argeius (Ode II), and to Lachon (Ode VI).

[1] According to the Pindaric scholia (*Argum. ad Pyth.*) the date of the first Pythiad was 582 B.C., and this victory was won in the 29th Pythiad, = 470 B.C. Pausanias (X. 7 § 3) places the first Pythiad in 586 B.C., so that the date of this victory would be 474; a view which Boeckh accepted. Bergk, on the other hand, prefers the authority of the Pindaric scholia, and recent criticism has confirmed his conclusion.

ODE V.

For Hieron of Syracuse, victor in the horse-race at Olympia.

Ol. 76, 476 B.C.

§ 1.   A fragment from a copy of the Olympic register, written in the second or third century, and found at Oxyrhynchus by Messrs Grenfell and Hunt, proves that Hieron won with the κέλης at Olympia both in Ol. 76 (476 B.C.) and in Ol. 77 (472); thus confirming the statement in the Pindaric scholia[1]. The victory celebrated in this ode is the same which Pindar commemorates in his first *Olympian.* As both odes clearly indicate, this was the first race won at Olympia by the horse Pherenicus. But Pherenicus had already won the Pythian race at least once[2], viz. in 478 B.C.   These facts make

---

[1] Schol. on *Olymp.* 1, where ογ´ (Ol. 73=488 B.C., obviously too early) was rightly corrected by Bergk to οϛ´ (76).

[2] Whether Pherenicus was the winner at Delphi in 482 B.C., as well as in 478, depends on the interpretation of Pind. *P.* III. 73 f., στεφάνοις | τοὺς ἀριστεύων Φερένικος ἕλ᾽ ἐν Κίρρᾳ ποτέ. Does the plural στεφάνοις denote more than one victory? If so, the victories are those of 482 and 478: if not, the reference is to 478 only. The plural of στέφανος could, apparently, be used with reference to a single victory; see *e.g.* Pind. *Isthm.* III. 11 ἐν βάσσαισιν Ἰσθμοῦ δεξαμένῳ στεφάνους, where the reference is to Melissus, who is not said to have won any Isthmian victory other than that (in the pancration) which the ode commemorates. But, in a general reference, such as we find in *Pyth.* III. 73 f., to the horse's record, στεφάνοις would more naturally denote a plurality of victories. On the other hand the allusion of Bacchylides to the success of Pherenicus at Delphi does not imply more than a single victory (III. 41).

Bacchylides in III. 39 calls Pherenicus πῶλον. But if he won his first race, let us say as a three-year-old, in 478, he would in 476 have been already five years

old, a ἵππος τέλειος, no longer properly πῶλος. The use of the latter word, which in poetry is sometimes a mere synonym for ἵππος, cannot be pressed, then, as an argument against supposing that Pherenicus won his first race in 482.

If he did so, he would have been nine years old (at least) in 476. But modern horses of that age, or even of an age considerably higher, have successfully borne the severest tests of endurance and speed. Mr Kenyon quotes the case of a celebrated steeple-chaser, the Lamb, who won the Grand National (over a course of 4½ miles) twice, viz. in 1868 and 1871, being six years old on the first occasion, and nine on the second. The same race in 1904 furnished some facts not less noteworthy from this point of view (see the *Times* of March 26). Twenty-six horses started: the age of four among these was 9; of one, 10; of one, 13; and of one (Manifesto), not less than 16. The last-named was one of nine who alone completed the arduous course.

Herodotus (VI. 103) mentions that Cimon, the father of Miltiades, won the four-horse chariot-race at Olympia with the same team of mares on three succes-

it probable that his Olympian victory belongs to 476 B.C., rather
than to 472 : for it is not likely that, while Pherenicus was still
in full vigour, another κέλης of Hieron's should have been the
winner in 476. The date 476 is confirmed by the circumstance
that neither in Pindar's first Olympian, nor in this ode of
Bacchylides, is there any reference to Hieron's foundation of
Aetna in 476, or to his victory at Cumae in 474. Pindar, at
least, would scarcely have omitted some allusion to one or
both of these events. His third *Pythian*, written for Hieron
in or about 473, refers to Aetna (v. 69), and his first *Pythian*
(470 B.C.) to Cumae.

Bacchylides sent this ode from Ceos to Syracuse. From
the tone of the opening verses, we may infer that it was the
first which he had written for Hieron; and πείθομαι in v. 195
seems to imply that it was written by invitation. In verse 11
the poet calls himself Hieron's ξένος. Simonides had been in
Sicily during some part at least of the years 478—476, and
Bacchylides may then have been introduced to the ruler of
Syracuse.

§ 2. Verses 1—55 form the first principal division of the
ode. Addressing Hieron as στραταγός of the Syracusans,
the poet declares that no one can better estimate a gift
of the Muses. The exploits of Hieron and his brothers offer
a wide range to the singer,—wide as the realms of air to
a soaring eagle (16—36). The running of Pherenicus at
Olympia is then described (17—49). Happy indeed is the man
to whom heaven has granted such a fortune as Hieron's [even
though, like Hieron, he suffers from disease] : *for no mortal is
blest in all things.*

This sentiment serves to introduce the beautiful myth which
occupies the largest part of the poem (56—175). Heracles,
going down to Hades for Cerberus, meets the shade of Meleager.

sive occasions (viz., in Ol. 62 = 532 B.C.,
Ol. 63 = 528, and Ol. 64 = 524, as appears
from the context). He adds that the
same feat had been accomplished by a
team belonging to a Spartan named
Evagoras, but that (as we can easily
believe) it had never been surpassed.

Pelagonius (*circ.* 410 A.D.) *veterin.* p. 32
(quoted by W. Christ and Blass) makes
the following statement:—'It is maintained (*adseverant*) that horses are generally fit for the circus and the contests at
festivals from their fifth to their twentieth
year.'

Both those heroes, so victorious, and so great, illustrate the truth that 'no mortal is blest in all things.' Just when the name of Deianeira has been uttered by the spirit of her brother, and the fatal resolve of Heracles to wed her is being taken, the poet leaves his myth with a Pindaric abruptness, and returns to his theme.

The concluding portion of the ode (176—200) touches once more on the victory, and claims praise for Hieron as a debt of candour (ἀλάθεια), which only envy could withhold. When a man's fortunes have once struck root, just praise is as the dew which brings leaf and flower. May Zeus grant that Hieron's fortunes shall be stedfast and untroubled.

§ 3. It is not without interest to compare the general attitude of Bacchylides towards Hieron, as seen in these three odes, with that of Pindar in the four poems which he wrote for the same ruler (*Ol.* I, *Pyth.* I, II, III). From other accounts it would seem that Hieron, in his government of Syracuse, presented many of the characteristics of the typical τύραννος,—guarded by foreign mercenaries[1]; suspicious of the citizens, to the point of setting spies[2] on their private conversation ; greedy of money, which he raised by laying heavy burdens on his people; and not incapable of cruel acts[3]. Gelon had been a τύραννος only in his way of seizing power, not in his way of using it : Hieron exemplified the usual tendency of the Greek τυραννίς to deteriorate in the hands of the inheritor[4].

Yet it would be unjust to the poets who praise him to regard them merely as professional flatterers. They saw in him, not merely the brilliant and munificent victor in the games, but a man who fostered the cult of the Muses, and made his home a centre of attraction to the foremost men of letters. A new age of Greek literature was dawning : and just then there was no one man in all Hellas who was doing so much as this ruler of Syracuse to encourage and to honour poets. This was the aspect of Hieron's reign which naturally appealed most forcibly to his laureates : he was to them, in some measure, what

---

[1] Diod. XI. 48 (cp. Xen. *Hier.* VI. 5).
[2] Arist. *Pol.* V. 9 § 3 mentions his ποταγωγίδες and ὠτακουσταί.
[3] Diod. XI. 67 φιλάργυρος καὶ βίαιος.
[4] See Freeman, *Sicily* II. 232 ff.

Augustus was to Virgil and Horace, what Lorenzo de' Medici was to the members of the Florentine Academy. As guests at his court, they would not necessarily see much of what was amiss with his system of government. Pindar and Bacchylides may reasonably be acquitted, then, of any gross or deliberate perversion of the truth about Hieron as they knew or felt it.

But let us now observe some points of difference between them. It may be noted that Pindar speaks more strongly than Bacchylides of Hieron's virtues, especially his gentler virtues : there is nothing in Bacchylides so explicit or so comprehensive as Pindar's πραῢς ἀστοῖς, οὐ φθονέων ἀγαθοῖς, ξείνοις δὲ θαυμαστὸς πατήρ (*P.* III. 71), or as his δρέπων...κορυφὰς ἀρετᾶν ἄπο πασᾶν (*Ol.* I. 13). Bacchylides is less emphatic ; though he describes Hieron as a just ruler, of fine gifts, who owes his high fortunes to the favour of heaven (III. 67—71 : IV. 1—3, 18—20 : V. 1—8, 191—193). But the main difference is of a broader kind. Pindar, whose range of view is Panhellenic, does ample justice to Hieron as the champion of Western Hellas against Phoenician and Etruscan (*Pyth.* I. 72—80). Alluding to his intervention (in 477) on behalf of the Epizephyrian Locrians, Pindar renders this tribute, honourable and beautiful above any that Hieron is known to have received :—' *Son of Deinomenes, the maiden of Locri in the West sings of thee before her door; because, after the bewildering troubles of war, thy power hath taken fear away from her eyes.*' (*Pyth.* II. 18—20.) Bacchylides once, indeed, alludes to the victory of Himera, but only in a vague and colourless phrase (v. 34, χαλκεοστέρνου τ' Ἄρηος). Hieron is, among his other qualities, a ' warrior' (III. 69) : but Bacchylides has no word of recognition for that aspect of his activity in which he appears as the defender of Hellene against barbarian. For Bacchylides he is only the ruler of Syracuse, upright and wise, bountiful to gods and men, a warrior who is no stranger to the Muses, a man fortunate in much, though there be one drop of bitterness in his cup. It is to Pindar alone that Hieron's memory is indebted for the larger and more splendid picture of his place in Hellas.

There is also a marked difference of tone between the two poets when they address Hieron. Pindar, the descendant of the

Aegeidae, the honoured guest of Delphi, is wont to speak in lofty accents. Splendid as are his praises of Hieron, they seldom have the note of deference, while occasionally they imply something like equality : as at the close of the first *Olympian,—* 'Be it *thine* to walk on high throughout thy mortal life, and *mine* to consort with victors all my days, pre-eminent for my art among Hellenes in every land.' Contrast with this haughty utterance the gentle fashion in which Bacchylides intimates his poetical claim at the close of his third ode,—in which, it may be noted, there is at least one distinct imitation of Pindar (vv. 85—87), so that Pindar's example may have prompted him here also :—'And along with (Hieron's) genuine glories, men will praise also the charm of the melodious nightingale of Ceos.'

But it is in the admonitory passages that this contrast of tone is most marked. Take, for instance, the last twenty verses of Pindar's first *Pythian.* Their character has been well described by Mr Freeman[1]. 'The whole latter part of the first Pythian ode is a sermon of advice to a ruler, which might have been professedly meant rather for the young Deinomenes than his father, but in which one cannot but feel throughout that the father is glanced at. Elementary precepts of truth and justice, warnings not to listen to deceivers, all winding up the famous exhortation to make Croesus and not Phalaris the model, certainly suggest that Pindar knew that there was something not as it should be in Hieron's rule.' Hieron, who unless he has been much belied, was far from admiring freedom of speech, can scarcely have found it agreeable to be the object of such a discourse. Even in the third *Pythian,* where Pindar wishes that he could bring Cheiron to heal his 'Aetnaean guest-friend,' the real solicitude which the poet evidently feels, and which finds such noble expression, lacks the sympathetic note of tenderness. But that is precisely the note which Bacchylides touches in the passage of veiled consolation to Hieron which closes the third ode (vv. 75—end). The tone is quiet, medita-tive, soothing. Again, the opening of the fifth ode, the first, probably, which Bacchylides addressed to Hieron, has a felicity of its own ; the homage is simply rendered, and the tone

[1] *Sicily,* II. p. 540.

(marked by the word ξένος) is that of one who trusts that his great critic will be friendly. An Ionian ease and grace belong to Bacchylides, as the pride and the fire of an Aeolic temperament can be recognised in Pindar. The poet of Thebes soars immeasurably above the poet of Ceos. But, when they are considered in their relations to the lord of Syracuse, it seems not inconceivable that there should have been some ground for the tradition preserved by the Pindaric scholiast[1], παρὰ Ἱέρωνι προκρίνεσθαι τὰ Βακχυλίδου ποιήματα.

ODE VI.

For Lachon of Ceos, victor in the foot-race for boys at Olympia.
Ol. 82, 452 B.C.

The Oxyrhynchus fragment of the Olympic register, already mentioned (p. 198), contains lists of victors from Ol. 75 (480 B.C.) to Ol. 83 (448 B.C.) inclusive. Under π͞β (Ol. 82) is the entry: Λακων Κε[ιος] παιδων σταδιον. There can be no doubt that it refers to the victory which is the subject of this Ode. In the agonistic inscription of Ceos (see Introd. to Ode I; § 2), Λ]αχων Αριστομενεος παιδω[ν occurs in two successive lines among the Nemean victors,—the mention of the contest in each case being lost in the fracture of the stone. The name Λάχων (further attested by the play on λάχε in verse 2) occurs nowhere else, whereas Λάκων as a proper name is frequent. Hence the mis-spelling in the fragment of the Olympic register is easily explained.

This short ode was sung before the house of Aristomenes, Lachon's father, in Ceos (v. 14). Like the little song to Argeius (Ode II),—a similar greeting to the victor on his return,—it alludes to previous Cean successes at the same festival. That trait would have a special point if we might suppose that, on each occasion, former victors in the games were among those who welcomed the young athlete.

---

[1] On *Pyth.* II. 166.

ODE VII.

For the same.

The ode begins with an invocation of 'Day, daughter of Time and Night': but the personified Hemera is identified with a particular date, viz. the prize-day at Olympia, which has set the wreath on the brows of Lachon. There is a mention of 'pre-eminence in speed of foot'; and clearly the victory is that which was more briefly announced in Ode VI. This is the regular epinikion, analogous to Ode I in the case of Argeius.

The first three verses are the last in column XII of the papyrus. Column XIII has perished; but the final syllables of some rather long verses in the upper third of it have run on into the left margin of column XIV. With the help of these, and of some small fragments, verses 4—11 of the ode have been partly restored.

Column XIV begins with 16 verses, which formed the end of Ode VII. The first verse is Πυθῶνά τε μηλοθύταν¹. The poet is enumerating the places where Lachon had been a winner before his success at Olympia,—viz. Delphi, Nemea, and the Isthmus. No one, 'boy or man,' had won so many victories in an equal space of time². The poem closes with a reference to his crowning triumph at Olympia.

The Cean inscription indicates (see Introd. to Ode VI) that Lachon's two Nemean victories were gained either at the same festival or at two successive festivals. 455 and 453 B.C. were Nemean years. His Pythian victory must have been in 454. For his Isthmian prize, the choice seems to be between 454 and

---

¹ In the *editio princeps* Dr Kenyon supposed that a new ode (his VIII) began in the lost column XIII. Both that ode and Ode VII must then have been extremely short. If the verse Πυθῶνά τε μηλοθύταν was preceded by (say) 10 verses —and that is a moderate estimate—in the poem to which it belonged, then only some 28 verses would be left for Ode VII. But it is very improbable that both the odes for Lachon's victory (VI and VII) should have been on such a diminutive scale. In v. 49 (=11 K.) ΤΕΛΕΣΣ can be supplied as τέλεσσας not less well than as τέλεσσον : and there is therefore no ground for assuming that the athlete to whom these verses refer had not yet been victorious at Olympia.

² See note on verses 46 f.

452 : 456 would probably be too early. Thus his five victories as a boy would have been gained in the years from 455 (or 454) to 452.

In respect to metrical composition, Ode VII must have formed a single system (strophe, antistrophe, and epode). If the lost column XIII contained 35 verses (the most frequent number), the ode consisted of 54 verses (3 + 35 + 16). If, then, there had been two systems, part of the second antistrophe must have come into column XIV; but no metrical correspondence is traceable between verses in that column and the first eleven verses of the poem.

As in the case of Ode IX, the scale of the poem was too small for the introduction of a myth. The analogy of passages in Ode VIII (27—39) and Ode IX (19—26) might suggest that the lost portion in column XIII was occupied, at least in part, with the circumstances of the victory at Olympia.

ODE VIII. [IX. ed. Kenyon.]

For Automedes of Phlius, victor in the pentathlon at Nemea.—
Date unknown.

§ 1. Phlius, a Dorian state, was situated in a hill-girt valley, some nine-hundred feet above sea-level. To the north of it was Sicyonia; to the south, Argolis: on the west, its territory touched the Arcadian highlands; to the east lay the vale of Nemea, and beyond that, the broader vale of Cleonae. Phliasia was a land of vineyards and cornfields; Dionysus and Demeter held the foremost place among its deities. At Phlius, as at Sicyon, a Dionysiac cult with satyr-choruses had existed from olden time. The poet Pratinas, who won Athenian applause by his satyr-plays in the earlier years of Aeschylus, was a native of Phlius; and his son Aristias, who excelled in the same kind of drama, had a monument in the agora.

The river Asopus (now the Hagios Georgios), rising in a mountain-range, the ancient Carneates, S. E. S. of the town, flows northwards through Phliasia and Sicyonia into the

Corinthian Gulf[1]. The lesser streams and springs of that whole region were regarded by folk-poetry as 'daughters of Asopus,' and were personified as nymphs who became the brides of heroes or gods. Some of these, as Nemea and Cleone, dwelt near their father. Others were the guardian heroines of cities far away; as Aegina, carried off from him by Zeus,—Thebe, Tanagra, Thespia (names transferred from the Boeotian to the Phliasian Asopus),—Salamis,—Peirene, the fountain-nymph of Corinth,—Corcyra, Sinope, and many more. The wide geographical range of the list is partly to be explained by the fact that Asopus is one of those general river-names, like Achelous and Alpheus, which occur in various parts of the Hellenic lands.

The people of Phlius, intent on the vintage and the harvest, and on the worship of the gods who gave them, found their chief link with the heroic age of Greece in the renown of the river whose upper course lay through their secluded valley. Bacchylides has made an artistic use of this motive. Indeed it is the charm of his ode that it takes us into the heart of these Peloponnesian uplands.

§ 2. Announcing that he will sing of Phlius and of Nemea (vv. 1—9), the poet tells the story of the Nemean games being founded by Argive warriors in memory of Archemorus (10—24). Simonides had already touched upon this theme (fr. 52). Three feats of Automedes in the pentathlon are next described (25—39). His return in triumph 'to the Asopus' gives the cue for an elaborate passage on the daughters of the river-god (40—65)[2]. This is the chief mythic embellishment of the ode.

---

[1] The character of the flute-music used at Dionysiac or other festivals in the valley of the Asopus gave rise to a quaint piece of folk-lore concerning the river itself. According to a local myth of Phlius and Sicyon, the Maeander, passing beneath the sea from Asia Minor to Peloponnesus, had 'generated' (ποιεῖν) the Asopus (Paus. II. 5 § 3). The flutes of Marsyas, floating down the Maeander, were transmitted to the Asopus, which carried them to Sicyon (id. II. 7 § 9).

[2] Special reference is made (vv. 42—46) to those 'descendants' of Asopus whose valour had been felt by the Amazons and by Troy. The mythical stemma was as follows:—

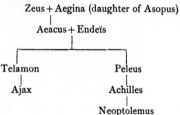

Zeus + Aegina (daughter of Asopus)
|
Aeacus + Endeïs
|
Telamon   Peleus
| |
Ajax   Achilles
                 |
                 Neoptolemus

The poet then turns to the rejoicings at Phlius (vv. 68 ff.), with some mention of the chief deities worshipped there; but the text is much mutilated. In the closing part, some general reflections are interwoven with a further reference to the athlete's victory.

ODE IX. [X.]

For [Aglaos ?] of Athens, victor in running at the Isthmus.

§ 1. The athlete's name must have stood at the beginning of verse 9 or of verse 11, and in both places, unfortunately, the MS. is defective. In v. 9 Blass supplies Ἀγλάῳ, and nothing more likely has been suggested. This Athenian belonged to the tribe Oeneis (v. 18): his father's name does not occur[1].

The ode begins with an invocation of Φήμα, who makes tidings known 'even in the depths of the nether world' (v. 4). The poet then says that he has been moved by the victor's brother-in-law to compose this tribute, a memorial of prowess for 'all men living' (ἐπιχθονίοισιν). These traits might suggest that the athlete was dead. But the words at the end (v. 52 f.), 'After victory, festal joy is appointed for mortals,' seem to cast some doubt on that view. Do they mean merely that the friends of the deceased victor held a banquet when this commemorative ode was sung? All that appears certain is that some interval of time had separated the athlete's victories from the date of the ode.

According to the most probable interpretation of a passage in which some words have been lost (vv. 12—26), the athlete had achieved a signal feat at the Isthmus by winning two

---

[1] The mention of the φυλή, without the father's name, is regarded by Wilamowitz as indicating that the athlete's family was an obscure one. (From vv. 49 ff. it may perhaps be inferred, at least, that he was not wealthy.) Blass further refers to the rule made by Cleisthenes, when he introduced many foreigners and resident aliens into the new Attic tribes, that the addition to a citizen's name, used in addressing him, should be the name of his deme, and not of his father (Arist. *Athen. Polit.* c. 21 § 4). This athlete, he suggests, may have been of foreign extraction. That is possible. But a simpler possibility also remains open,—viz. that the father's name did not suit the metre. It seems less likely that this name has been lost after μειγνύμεν in v. 55.

consecutive foot-races. The first may have been the simple stadion, or possibly the diaulos. The second was one in which he traversed the length of the stadion four times,—a race technically known as the ἵππιος δρόμος (v. 25, n.). He had also won two wreaths at Nemea, to say nothing of successes at six minor festivals (vv. 29—35).

§ 2. The moderate compass of this ode (56 verses) renders it instructive in regard to the manner of treatment adopted by Bacchylides for his minor epinikia,—*i.e.*, for those of which the scale was too small to allow the effective use of a myth. We find that, after a proem of 18 verses,—somewhat long in proportion to the rest,—he relies on two resources;—first, an account of the athlete's feats (vv. 19—35),—and secondly, a 'gnomic' element,—general reflections on life and conduct. Here, a part of the gnomic passage (vv. 39—45) is abridged from Solon. The ode ends somewhat abruptly, with an apology for digression, and a brief reference to the rejoicings which should follow a victory. It leaves with us a sense that he has executed his commission with sympathy and good taste, but without much spirit or zest.

ODE X. [XI.]

For Alexidamus of Metapontion, winner of the boys' wrestling match at Delphi.—Date unknown.

§ 1. With the exception of Pindar's two odes[1] for Agesidamus, the boy pugilist from the Epizephyrian Locri, this is the only extant epinikion for a native of Magna Graecia; though it is known that Simonides wrote for Anaxilas of Rhegium and for Astylus of Croton. Nowhere were the different branches of the Greek race more conscious of their difference than in the Italiote colonies; and it is perhaps more than a mere coincidence that, while the young victor from the Aeolic Locri was celebrated by Pindar, Ionian poets sang of feats belonging to Rhegium, a foundation of the Chalcidians, and to the Achaean settlements of Croton and Metapontion. The Ionian cities of the Aegean

---

[1] *Ol.* x, xi.

in many instances claimed Achaean heroes as their founders[1]; and we can feel that Bacchylides was proud of the legendary tie which connected his own folk with the home of Alexidamus.

Metapontion (the Latin Metapontum),—best known in Greek tradition as the place where Pythagoras ended his days,—was situated on the Tarentine gulf, at a distance (measured by the coast-line) of some twenty-eight miles south-west of Tarentum. The period from about 740 to 680 B.C. was roughly that during which most of the Greek cities in south-eastern Italy originated. Rhegium, Sybaris, and Croton had already been planted before Dorian colonists from Laconia, about 708 B.C., arrived at Tarentum. Not many years later, it would seem, Achaean settlers from the shores of the Corinthian gulf came to Metapontion. Coins of that city bear the image of the oekist, Leucippus, and, on the reverse, an ear of corn. For, while Tarentum was the chief commercial centre in those regions, Metapontion depended on agriculture, stock-raising, and horse-breeding. 'A golden harvest'—perhaps a sheaf of corn wrought in gold—was, according to Strabo[2], the thank-offering which its prosperous citizens sent to the Delphian Apollo. Metapontion was indeed most favourably placed for such pursuits. The country behind it, sloping up gently from the flat coast to the Lucanian highlands, is irrigated by two nearly parallel rivers. That which Bacchylides calls the Casas,—Pliny's Casuentus, now the Basiento,—flows into the gulf at a point which was near the south side of the ancient town. On the banks of this stream stood a famous temple and grove of Artemis. The other river, the Bradanus,—still called the Bradano,—enters the sea a few miles to the north of the site. Well-watered, fertile, and enjoying a good climate, these lands were suited alike for corn-growing and for pasturage.

In the true spirit of an Achaean colony, the Metapontines cherished a legend which carried back the first settlement on that spot to the heroic age of Greece. Achaeans from Pylos, it was said, had come thither after the fall of Troy, under the leadership of Nestor. Had not the citizens, from time

---

[1] See Appendix on Ode X. 119 f.   [2] Strabo 6, p. 264.

immemorial, offered sacrifice to the spirits of the Neleidae?[1]
Bacchylides does due honour to this venerable tradition, which
was in accord with all the feelings and beliefs of Magna Graecia.
There was no corner of Hellas where the memory of the
Homeric heroes was kept more fully alive. Achaeans, Chalcidians and Dorians alike had local cults and festivals of those
heroes. Stesichorus of Himera describes his epic hymns as
'gifts of the Graces to the people[2],' to be sung 'as spring comes
on'; and at such festivals he would have found zealous
audiences. Even alleged relics were not wanting. Near Metapontion, for instance, there was a temple of Athena Hellenia,
which boasted possession of the tools with which Epeius had
made the wooden horse[3].

§ 2. Our poet begins his ode with an invocation of Victory
(1—14), and then briefly describes the triumph of Alexidamus
in the wrestling-match at the Pythian games (15—23). If there
had not been a miscarriage of justice, he adds, the boy would
have been a victor also at Olympia. (As the Pythian festival
fell in the third year of each Olympiad, it would appear that
Alexidamus had visited Olympia two years before.) But now
his disappointment has been healed, and success has been given
to him, by Artemis, *the soothing goddess* (Ἡμέρα, v. 39). This is
the link between the immediate subject of the ode and the myth
with which the poet adorns it. He proceeds to relate how the
cult of Artemis Hemera was established at Lusi in Arcadia by
Proetus, king of Argos, when the goddess had cured the dis-
temper of his daughters (vv. 40—112). From Arcadia (ἔνθεν,
v. 113) Artemis came to Metapontion with the Achaean
warriors, who founded it after the capture of Troy (113—123).
The ode closes with a brief tribute to the old renown of the
Achaeans.

§ 3. The prominence of Artemis in the religion of Metapontion
would be sufficiently explained by her attributes as a goddess of
rural life, who blesses the produce of the earth and claims
the first-fruits, while she is also a protectress of flocks and

---

[1] Strabo 6, p. 264.
[2] Χαρίτων δαμώματα : Stesich. fr. 37.
[3] See the Aristotelian treatise περὶ
θαυμασίων ἀκουσμάτων, p. 840, § 108.

herds[1]. But it is the specific cult of Artemis Hemera at Lusi
that provides the poet with a cue for the myth. His words
(in vv. 113 ff.) might naturally imply that this particular cult had
been carried from Arcadia to Metapontion. Whether that was
the case or not, we do not know. If not, then the appro-
priateness of the myth is reduced to this,—that, by consoling
Alexidamus for his mischance at Olympia, Artemis has mani-
fested towards him the same quality which she had shown to
the Proetides at Lusi. The link, if it was only that, would be
rather slight and artificial; but some latitude might be allowed
to the author of an epinikion in search of such embellishment.

As to the treatment of the myth, we note, in the first place,
that it is an example of the leisurely epic manner. After relating
how the Proetides had angered the Argive Hera, and how she
drove them in madness from Tiryns, the poet pauses to explain
why Proetus was living there. Twenty-two verses are then
occupied with the feud between Proetus and Acrisius, and its
results, before the story returns to the frenzied maidens. Another
noteworthy feature is the absence of Melampus. In the best-
known form of the legend, Proetus, when his daughters become
insane, applies for aid to that priest and seer, son of Amythaon,
at Pylos. Melampus bargains for a portion of the king's realm,
and Proetus refuses: but things grow worse,—other Argive
women go mad,—and the monarch again turns to the priest.
This time Melampus demands a share for his brother Bias
as well as for himself; and Proetus yields. Melampus then
collects a band of youths, and chases the Proetides from the
hills to Lusi, where he propitiates Hera, and heals them by
mystic rites[2]. Whether Bacchylides had or had not mythological
warrant for ignoring Melampus, he certainly had a poetical

---

[1] See n. on verses 115 f. The epithet
ἀγροτέρα, which Bacchylides gives to
Artemis when he first mentions her in
this poem (v. 37), seems usually to denote
her as the huntress (as if it were taken
from ἄγρα). But it may well be that in
its original usage it had a larger sense, as
though taken from ἀγρός, denoting the
goddess of the fields and of rural life. (Cf.

Schreiber on Artemis in Roscher I. p. 566.)
[2] This story, which went back in substance to Hesiod, occurs with variations
of detail in Her. IX. 34, Apollod. I. 9. 12,
Diod. IV. 68, Aelian *V.H.* 3. 42, etc.
The mythographer Pherecydes, with whom
Bacchylides agrees in at least one detail
(see n. on vv. 50—52), brought in
Melampus (schol. *Od.* 15. 235).

motive. His aim is to magnify the beneficence of Artemis. No
priest is interposed between the goddess and the afflicted father.
It is directly to her that Proetus makes his prayer; and she
promptly grants it.

ODE XI. [XII.]

*For Teisias of Aegina, victor in the wrestling-match
at Nemea.*—Date unknown.

The eight verses which remain from the beginning of this
ode are the last in column XXII. After that, there is a break in
the papyrus. The rest of Ode XI and the beginning of Ode XII
were contained in that part which has been lost between
column XXII and the column numbered XXIV. It is scarcely
doubtful that the part so lost consisted of more than one column;
but there is no other clue to its extent. The original length of
Ode XI is therefore wholly uncertain.

As the poet indicates (Ode XII, vv. 75 f.), wrestling and
boxing were exercises in which Aegina was pre-eminent. Of
the ten Aeginetans, men or boys, for whom Pindar wrote, no
fewer than eight had won their wreaths either by wrestling alone,
or in the pancration.

ODE XII. [XIII.]

For Pytheas of Aegina, victor in the boys' pancration at Nemea.
Date, perhaps 481 B.C.: in any case, probably not later
than 479.

§ 1. This is the victory commemorated in the fifth Nemean of
Pindar, who has also celebrated, in his fourth and fifth Isthmian
odes, two victories in the pancration won by Phylacidas, a
younger brother of Pytheas. Both Pindar and Bacchylides
signalise the hospitality of Lampon, the father of these youths ;
a man who is described as encouraging his sons, by example and
by precept, to excel in athletics. To this purpose he applied
Hesiod's maxim, 'study prospers work[1]'; and he spared no cost

---

[1] Pind. *I.* v. 66 ff. Λάμπων δὲ μελέταν |
ἔργοις ὀπάζων Ἡσιόδου μάλα τιμᾷ τοῦτ'
ἔπος, | υἱοῖσί τε φράζων παραινεῖ. (Hes.
Op. 410 μελέτη δέ τοι ἔργον ὀφέλλει.)

in engaging the best trainers, such as Menander of Athens. From the three Pindaric poems we glean some further facts concerning 'the family of Cleonicus,'—for so Lampon's father was named. It belonged to the clan (πάτρα) of the Psalychidae, —not mentioned elsewhere, but evidently of local distinction. Lampon's brother-in-law, Euthymenes, had won the pancration at the Isthmus. And when Lampon's sons entered the Aiakeion in Aegina, they saw in the vestibule a statue of their maternal grandfather Themistius, still decked with the garlands woven of grass and flowers which recalled his victories, as boxer and pancratiast, in the games of Asclepius at Epidaurus[1].

§ 2. The chronology of the odes for Pytheas and his brother cannot be precisely determined; but there are some general data which assist conjecture. Pindar's fourth Isthmian refers to the later of the two victories gained by Phylacidas, and his fifth Isthmian to the earlier. Both the successes of Phylacidas were subsequent to that victory of Pytheas which is the theme of Pindar in his fifth Nemean, and of Bacchylides in this poem. Now the fourth Isthmian was certainly written not very long after the battle of Salamis. Having alluded to the ancient glories of Aegina, Pindar adds (*Nem.* v. 48 ff.):—

'*And now* Salamis, city of Ajax, could bear witness that she was saved from shipwreck in war by Aegina's seamen,—in that destroying storm of Zeus when death came thick as hail on hosts unnumbered.'

The words καὶ νῦν, with which the passage begins, could scarcely have been used, if this addition to the achievements of Aegina had not then been comparatively recent. The date of the battle being September, 480, the second victory of Phylacidas, to which the ode relates, may have been gained at the Isthmia of 478. In any case, the festival of 476 seems to be the latest that can be assumed, consistently with the tone of the reference just cited. The first Isthmian victory of Phylacidas might then be placed in 480; or, at latest, in 478.

Pytheas, whose victory preceded both those of his brother, is thus described in the fifth Nemean (vv. 4—6): Λάμπωνος υἱὸς... εὐρυσθενής...οὔπω γένυσι φαίνων τέρειναν ματέρ' οἰνάνθας ὀπώραν,

---

[1] Pind. *N.* v. 52 ff.

'as yet showing no sign on cheek or chin of the down that comes with the delicate bloom of ripening youth.' It is clear, then, that he did not compete among the adults,—a fact which is confirmed by the mention of his trainer, Menander. But Pindar's words, though not incompatible with the supposition that Pytheas was still a παῖς, distinctly suggest an ἀγένειος. There was an ἀγενείων as well as a παίδων παγκράτιον at Nemea and at the Isthmus[1]. Unfortunately we do not know where precisely the limits between the three ages, παῖς, ἀγένειος and ἀνήρ, were drawn for the purposes of those games. It would be natural to suppose that the age of the παῖς was from fourteen to sixteen,— as the sixteenth year marked the attainment of physical ἥβη (puberty). It seems improbable that, where these three classes of competitors were recognised, the ἀνήρ can have been less than twenty years old. The period from seventeen to nineteen years of age would then be left for the ἀγένειος. (It is possible that where, as at Olympia and at Delphi in the fifth century B.C., there was no separate class of ἀγένειοι, the limit for παῖδες may have been placed somewhat higher, and that for ἄνδρες somewhat lower.) The hypothesis that the limit for the ἀγένειος extended up to nineteen agrees well enough with the passage in Plato's *Laws* (p. 833 C), where he proposes that, in certain foot-races, the course for the ἀγένειος should be two-thirds of the course for the ἀνήρ, while that for the παῖς should be only one-third.

In view of all the data, the following chronology seems possible, though it cannot claim to be anything more:—

Ol. 74. 4. 481 B.C. Victory of Pytheas as an ἀγένειος at Nemea, at the age (say) of 18. (Pindar, *Nem.* v.: Bacchylides XII.) See the table on p. 185.

---

[1] This is shown by the agonistic inscription of Ceos, cited in the Introduction to Ode I; which Dr W. Christ seems to overlook, when he says (Pindar, p. lxxv, 1896) that there is no evidence for a παίδων (or ἀγενείων) παγκράτιον at Nemea or at the Isthmus.—The title of *Nem.* v., as usually printed by editors, is Πυθέᾳ Αἰγινήτῃ παιδὶ παγκρατιαστῇ. W. Christ (p. 270) cites *B* (Vaticanus) as having Πυθέᾳ παιδὶ Αἰγινήτῃ ᾠδὴ ε΄, where he suggests that Λάμπωνος may have dropped out before παιδί. *D* (Mediceus) has Πυθέᾳ υἱῷ Λάμπωνος παγκρατιαστῇ. But the word παιδὶ in the title may have been merely a grammarian's inference from vv. 4—6. W. Christ omits it, in conformity with his view stated on p. lxxv. Blass does so, because he supposes (rightly, as I think) that Pytheas was not a παῖς, but an ἀγένειος.

Ol. 74. 4. 480 B.C. First victory of Phylacidas, the younger
brother of Pytheas, at the Isthmus. (Pindar, *Isthm.* v. [vi].) If
he was then (say) 17, he would compete among the ἀγένειοι.
The traditional title of *Isthm.* v. is simply Φυλακίδᾳ Αἰγινήτῃ
παγκρατίῳ. But that is not inconsistent with his having been
ἀγένειος. And on the other hand, the words in v. 62, where
Phylacidas and his brother, in contradistinction to their uncle
Euthymenes, are called ἀγλαοὶ παῖδες, indicate that Phylacidas
was not yet ἀνήρ. (παῖδες, used in a general and not a technical
sense, would of course include ἀγένειοι.)

Ol. 75. 2. 478 B.C. Second victory of Phylacidas at the
Isthmus. (Pindar, *Isthm.* IV.) He would then be (say) 20,
and would compete among the ἄνδρες.

It remains to consider an objection raised by Professor Blass
to placing the victory of Pytheas as early as 481 B.C. There
had been hostilities between Athens and Aegina, which began
apparently about 488 or 487 B.C., and lasted for some time. It
was only in 481 B.C., on the eve of the Persian invasion, that
the two states were definitely and formally reconciled[1]. But
Menander, the trainer of Pytheas, was an Athenian. Would an
Aeginetan boy have been sent for training to Athens in 482 or
481? Would Pindar and Bacchylides in 481 have praised an
Athenian to Aeginetans? We may reply, in the first place,
that we do not know whether, in 482/1, Athens and Aegina
were still actually at war, though it is probable that a hostile
feeling still existed. But it is not necessary to suppose that the
boy Pytheas was sent to Athens. It is more likely that his
father Lampon, a wealthy man, would engage the Athenian
trainer to visit Aegina. That this indeed was the case would be
a legitimate inference from Pindar's phrase,—Χρὴ δ' ἀπ' 'Αθανᾶν
τέκτον' ἀεθληταῖσιν ἔμμεν (*Nem.* V. 49). Even if, in 482/1, the
relations between Athens and Aegina were still unfriendly, a
professional trainer, who had his livelihood to make, would
surely not be precluded from accepting such an engagement.
Nor would it be just to the Aeginetans,—so often extolled for
their hospitality and fair-dealing,—to suppose that they would
have felt resentment when the Athenian's services to the

[1] Her. VII. 145; Grote c. xxxix, vol. v. p. 65.

Aeginetan youth were commended by the poets of Thebes and Ceos[1].

§ 3. The ode is mutilated at the beginning. The verses with which column XXIV commences are the last two of a strophe. In this ode the strophe consists of 12 verses, and the epode of 9; the system, therefore, of 33. The question is: Was the strophe, of which the last two verses stand at the top of col. XXIV, the first strophe of the poem; or was it preceded by (at least) one whole system? The answer is clear from the nature of the subject-matter. At the words ὕβριος ὑψινόου, the first in col. XXIV, we are already in the middle of a mythical narrative. More than 10 verses must have preceded; and therefore not less than 43. It seems unnecessary to suppose the loss of more than one system before the strophe of which two verses remain; and the first of those verses may therefore be numbered 44.

In verses 44—57 a speaker, who is watching the struggle of Heracles with the Nemean lion, predicts his future, and prophesies that in days to come Greeks shall strive on that spot in the pancration. In a note on these verses I have given reasons for conjecturing that the prophecy is uttered by Athena, the guardian goddess of Heracles, in presence of the nymph Nemea.

The poet next describes (vv. 58—76) how Pytheas has returned in triumph from the Nemean games. He then addresses the nymph Aegina (77—99). Her praises are chanted by the maidens of the island, who link them with those of Endeïs, bride of Aeacus, mother of Peleus and of Telamon. They sing also of Achilles and of Ajax.—It is told how Ajax bore himself in 'the fight at the ships,—when Achilles had withdrawn from the field, and had fired the Trojans with vain hopes. The bodies of the Aeacidae have perished, but their fame lives evermore. (100—174.)

Arete, whose light cannot be hidden, honours Aegina, in company with Eucleia and Eunomia (175—189).—Let due praise be given to Pytheas and to his trainer Menander. Truth upholds genuine merit against envy. (190—209.)—The poet,

---

[1] Blass (*Praef.* LXIV) thinks that the victory of Pytheas at Nemea may have been gained in 479 or 477. The first Isthmian victory of Phylacidas would then fall in 478 or 476, and the second in 476 or 474.

trusting in the Muse, offers this song to Lampon, the victor's hospitable father. (220—231.)

§ 4. It is interesting to compare Bacchylides with Pindar in regard to his manner of rendering the indispensable tribute to the Aeacidae. In each of Pindar's eleven odes for Aegina such a reference occurs; and his variety of resource is notable. As a rule, he takes some one moment or incident in the story of an Aeacid hero, and, with a few touches, paints a vivid picture, often instinct with dramatic life: but he seldom insists or enlarges on the theme. The fifth Nemean, written for this same victory, supplies an example. Peleus and Telamon, with their half-brother Phocus,—whom they were destined to slay,—are standing in Aegina at the altar of their grandsire, Zeus Hellanios: with hands uplifted to him they pray that the island may be blest in her sons and famous on the sea[1]. It is all given in five verses. More than sixty are here devoted by Bacchylides to an episode, with Achilles and Ajax for its central figures, in which he is on familiar Homeric ground. It is an epic narrative, forming, indeed, a distinct section of the poem.

Ode XIII. [XIV.]

For Cleoptolemus of Thessaly, victor in the chariot-race at the Petraia.—Date unknown.

The position of this ode in the series is presumably due to the fact that it relates to a minor festival. The only other reference to the Petraia seems to be that of the scholiast on Apollonius Rhodius, who mentions 'the Thessalian Petra' as a place 'where a festival of Poseidon is held' (see n. on vv. 19—21). The scene of these games is unknown: it is merely a conjecture that it may have been somewhere in the region of Tempe.

The waters of eastern Thessaly, gathered into the Peneius (now the Salamvrias), flow to the sea through a narrow valley between lofty peaks of Mount Olympus and Mount Ossa. This outlet, called Τέμπη—'the cutting'—was said in local legend

---

[1] *N.* v. 9—13.

to have been made by the earth-shaking god. He was called Petraios as 'cleaving the rocks[1].' The title Λυταῖος, also given to him in Thessaly, was similarly explained as meaning that he had opened a way for the river out of its rocky prison[2]. Philostratus the Lemnian (*c.* 230 A.D.) describes a series of pictures which he professes to have seen in a portico at Naples. One of them, he says, showed Poseidon, with the trident in his uplifted right hand, preparing to strike the hills, and to make a passage for the Peneius, represented by the reclining figure of a river-god ; while Thessalia, crowned with a wreath of olive-leaves and corn-ears, was seen rising from the flood under which her lower valleys had hitherto been submerged[3].

The extant portion of the ode consists only of the first system (23 verses), with a few words from the second strophe and epode. After 18 verses of gnomic strain, the poet comes to Cleoptolemus, victor in the chariot-race, who was probably a rich Thessalian landowner. The large scale of the exordium might suggest an ode of some length ; but the break in the papyrus after column XXIX leaves that point in doubt.

B. DITHYRAMBS.

Ode XIV. [XV.]

The Sons of Antenor: or the Demand for the restitution of Helen.

§ 1. The subject is an embassy of Menelaus and Odysseus from the Greek camp at Tenedos to Troy, for the purpose of demanding that Helen should be restored. This mission is supposed to take place shortly before the commencement of the Trojan war.

The primary source used by Bacchylides was presumably the 'Cyprian epic' (Κύπρια), so called because its reputed author,

---

[1] Schol. Pind. *P.* IV. 138. See note in commentary on XIII. 19—21.

[2] See note on ode XVII. 21.

[3] Philostr. *Imag.* II. 14.

Stasīnus, was a native of Cyprus; but the ancients knew nothing definite concerning him, and the authorship must be regarded as uncertain. The date of the *Cypria* cannot well be placed later than the eighth century B.C. Its contents are known in outline through the summary given in the *Chrestomatheia* of Proclus. From this abstract, and from the fragments of the epic itself (about fifty verses in all), it is clear that the author of the *Cypria* knew the *Iliad*, and composed his work as a kind of introduction to it,—starting from the first cause of the war, and going down to that moment in the tenth year at which the *Iliad* opens. It was told in the *Cypria* how, after sailing from Aulis, the Greek fleet first put in at Tenedos. On landing from their camp in that island, the Greeks were resisted by the Trojans, and in the first battle Protesilaus was slain by Hector. In a second battle, Achilles routed the enemy, slaying Cycnus son of Poseidon. Then (says Proclus in his summary) 'the Greeks sent an embassy to the Trojans, demanding the restitution of Helen and of her possessions. The Trojans refused to comply; and thereupon the siege of Troy began[1].'

The Greek envoys, Menelaus and Odysseus, were hospitably received at Troy by Antenor[2], whose wife, Theano, was priestess of the city's guardian goddess, Pallas Athena. He stood their friend throughout; and was said to have saved their lives, when they were endangered by the hostility of certain Trojans[3].

§ 2. Bacchylides does not relate the arrival of the envoys, or their reception by Antenor: that is presupposed. The first verses describe how Theano, on the acropolis of Troy, opens the temple of Athena to her guests; perhaps in order that they may bespeak

---

[1] καὶ διαπρεσβεύονται πρὸς τοὺς Τρῶας, Ἑλένην καὶ τὰ κτήματα ἀπαιτοῦντες· ὡς δὲ οὐχ ὑπήκουσαν ἐκεῖνοι, ἐνταῦθα δὴ τειχομαχοῦσιν.

[2] In *Iliad* 3. 205—224 Antenor himself refers to this. He goes on to compare Menelaus and Odysseus as orators in the Trojan agora.

[3] Proclus: ὅτε γὰρ ἐκ Τενέδου ἐπρεσβεύοντο οἱ περὶ Μενέλαον, τότε 'Αντήνωρ ὁ 'Ελικάονος ὑπεδέξατο αὐτούς, καὶ δολοφονεῖσθαι μέλλοντας ἔσωσεν.—From the

words of Agamemnon in *Iliad* 11. 138—142 it appears that the Trojan Antimachus had urged in the assembly that the two Greek envoys should be put to death. The Ulysses of Ovid (*Met.* 13. 196—204) briefly relates how narrowly he and Menelaus escaped being murdered by Paris and his supporters. His appeal had moved Priam, *Priamoque Antenora iunctum*. Tzetzes (*Ante-homerica* 158) also relates how Antenor befriended the envoys.

15—2

the favour of the goddess before making their appeal. Here occurs a lacuna in the papyrus, which contained at least one speech; possibly both Theano and Odysseus spoke (vv. 8—36). Next, we find the sons of Antenor conducting the envoys to the marketplace of Troy, while Antenor himself proceeds to inform Priam of their errand. Presently heralds summon the Trojans to the assembly. 'Everywhere the loud rumour ran abroad; and men lifted up their hands to the gods, praying for rest from their woes':—an allusion to those hostilities, noticed above, which had preceded the embassy. The agora is now filled, and the debate is about to begin. (37—46.)

The poet proceeds in epic style:—'Say, Muse, who was the first to plead the righteous cause?' Then comes the speech by Menelaus. It occupies only 13 verses,—breaking off with a warning to the Trojans against insolence, which ruined the Giants. So abrupt is the ending, that it would be natural to regard the poem as incomplete. That inference does not, however, appear certain. It should be observed that the beginning of the piece is also abrupt. The little poem is, in fact, a sort of epic vignette, finished in detail, but intended to suggest a situation rather than to relate a story. In the next piece (*Heracles*) this intention is still more evident.

§ 3. The double title, written by the second corrector at the top of column XXX, but now mutilated, was Ἀντηνορίδαι ἢ Ἑλένης ἀπαίτησις[1]. In the text, as we have it, the part of the Antenoridae is limited to conducting the envoys from the

---

[1] Among the titles of lost plays of Sophocles are Ἀντηνορίδαι (Nauck[2], *Trag. Frag.* p. 160) and Ἑλένης ἀπαίτησις (*ib.* p. 171). The subject of the latter was undoubtedly this embassy of Menelaus and Odysseus. As to the Ἀντηνορίδαι, Welcker (*Gr. Trag.* I. 466 ff.), with whom Nauck agrees, recognises its subject in a passage of Strabo 13. p. 608. After the capture of Troy, when Antenor's house was spared, he and his sons migrated, with their allies the Paphlagonian Ἐνετοί (*Il.* 2. 852), to the land afterwards known as Venetia. On the other hand, Blass and Wilamowitz regard the double title of the Bacchylidean poem as making it probable that the Ἀντηνορίδαι of Sophocles was only another name for his Ἑλένης ἀπαίτησις. Such a second title for the tragedy is intelligible, however, only if the sons of Antenor formed the chorus; but, in the case of such a drama, is that probable? Welcker held that the chorus must have been composed of Phrygians, who could mediate between the views of Antenor, the friend of the envoys, and those of their foes, such as Paris (*Gr. Trag.* I. 121). But the question is one which we must be content to leave doubtful.

acropolis of Troy to the agora. It is known that Bacchylides spoke of Theano as having borne fifty sons to Antenor (schol. *Il.* 24. 496), a mention which doubtless occurred in the lost verses of this poem (32—36). Fifty was the number of a dithyrambic chorus; and if, when this dithyramb was produced, the Antenoridae formed such a chorus, that fact would help to account for the prominence given to them in the title. It would also explain the number itself, which the Homeric scholiast notes as prodigious. The *Iliad* recognises only ten sons of Antenor[1].

In verse 6 Menelaus is Atreides, but in verse 48 Pleisthenides. The genealogy which made him and his brother sons of Pleisthenes, and only grandsons of Atreus, appears first with Stesichorus (fr. 42), whose influence on Bacchylides is suggested by this trait. The lyric treatment of epic themes, with occasional speeches in epic style, is indeed a species of composition in which Stesichorus was the earliest master.

ODE XV. [XVI.]

Heracles.

§ 1. The first eleven verses, which are much mutilated, form a prelude to the theme of Heracles and Deianeira. The poet says that he will betake him to the temple of Apollo at Delphi, as Urania has provided him with songs fitted for the season. Apollo is away in the north, taking his pleasure on the banks of the Hebrus, until it shall be time for him to revisit his Pythian home, and to rejoice once more in the paeans of the Delphian choruses.

During the winter months, Dionysus was prominent at Delphi. The paean was mute, since the Healer was absent, and its place was taken by the dithyramb[2]. A tragic theme of

---

[1] Acamas (*Il.* 2. 822), Agenor (11. 59), Archelochus (2. 822), Coön (the eldest, 11. 248), Demoleon (20. 295), Helicaon (3. 123), Iphidamas (11. 221), Laodocus (4. 87), Pedaeus (νόθος, 5. 69), Polybus (11. 49).

[2] Plutarch περὶ τοῦ Εἰ τοῦ ἐν Δελφοῖς, c. 9 : τὸν μὲν ἄλλον ἐνιαυτὸν παιᾶνι χρῶνται περὶ τὰς θυσίας, ἀρχομένου δὲ χειμῶνος ἐπεγείραντες τὸν διθύραμβον, τὸν δὲ παιᾶνα καταπαύσαντες, τρεῖς μῆνας ἀντ᾽ ἐκείνου τοῦτον κατακαλοῦνται τὸν θεόν.

passion and anguish, such as that which Bacchylides touches here, was congenial to the Dionysiac cult, but would have been wholly alien from a festival of Apollo.

The treatment of the subject is very brief, occupying only twenty-two verses. Heracles has sacked Oechalia in Euboea, and has arrived at Cenaeum, the north-western cape of the island, where he is preparing a sacrifice in thanksgiving to Zeus. Then it is that destiny impels Deianeira to send him the robe anointed with the gift of Nessus, on learning that Iole is coming to her home.

So ends the song,—much as its predecessor broke off with the hint that impenitent ὕβρις would prove the bane of Troy. Here, however, the somewhat abrupt close has a clearer warrant in poetical art, since Deianeira's resolve is a fateful turning-point; and the artist's aim in work on this scale can be more distinctly seen. It is to mark a moment on the eve of a catastrophe,—a moment which will be the more impressive because the sequel is left untold.

§ 2. It is a feature of some interest in this poem that it suggests certain older poetical sources to which Bacchylides may have been indebted. The reference to Apollo disporting himself in the north recalls a hymn of Alcaeus concerning the god's visit to the Hyperboreans, some traits of which are preserved in the prose of Himerius[1]. The Lesbian poet designated the Hebrus as 'fairest of rivers[2]'; and his influence may probably be traced in those exquisite lyrics of Aristophanes which describe how the swans on the Hebrus chant their songs to Apollo[3]. A detail of language seems to confirm the surmise that the thoughts of Bacchylides may have been running on Alcaeus. Nowhere else does he employ πεδά instead of μετά, but here we find πεδοιχνεῖν.

The passage relating to Heracles at Cenaeum presents a general parallelism with some verses in the *Trachiniae* of Sophocles[4]. But it affords no ground for supposing that the

---

[1] Or. XIV. 10 = Alcae. frgg. 2, 3, 4, Bergk⁴ III. p. 147.
[2] Schol. Theocr. VII. 112 (= Alcae. fr. 109, Bergk⁴); Ἀλκαῖος φησιν ὅτι Ἕβρος

κάλλιστος ποταμῶν.
[3] *Aves* 772 ff.: see n. on v. 5.
[4] *Trach.* 750—762. See n. on Bacch. XV. 15 f.

dramatist imitated Bacchylides. Such resemblance as exists is rather to be explained by a common source; That source was probably the old epic, entitled the *Capture of Oechalia*, popularly ascribed to the Ionian Creophylus of Samos, a poem of which the repute is attested by an epigram of Callimachus[1].

ODE XVI. [XVII.]

Theseus, or the Athenian youths and maidens.

§ 1. Servius (*circ.* 400 A.D.) found this poem, as we find it, classed among the 'dithyrambs' of Bacchylides, in the later and larger sense of that term[2]. But it is, in fact, a paean to Apollo, for a chorus of Ceans at Delos[3]. It seems probable that Bacchylides wrote for Delian festivals on other occasions also[4].

Minos, king of Crete, after reducing Athens, had imposed upon it a periodical tribute[5] of seven youths and seven maidens, to be the prey of his wife Pasiphae's monstrous offspring, the Minotaur, whom he had immured in the labyrinth built by Daedalus at Cnosus. On the third occasion when the tribute fell due, Minos came in person to Athens and selected the victims[6].

[1] See the editor's Introduction to the *Trachiniae*, p. xviii.

[2] Servius on Verg. *Aen.* VI. 21 (*septena quotannis Corpora natorum*). Quidam septem pueros et septem puellas accipi volunt, quod et Plato dicit in Phaedone et Sappho in Lyricis et Bacchylides in Dithyrambis et Euripides in Hercule, quos liberavit secum Theseus.

[3] Cp. 128 ff.: ἤίθεοι δ' ἐγγύθεν | νέοι παιάνιξαν ἐρατᾷ ὀπί. | Δάλιε, χοροῖσι Κηΐων κ.τ.λ. The subject itself, so closely connected with the Theseus-legend of the Delian cult, might well suggest that the poem was for Delos.

[4] See frag. 42 (=57 Bergk); and fr. 12 (=31 Bergk).—Pindar intimates in *Isthm.* I. 6 ff. that he is under a promise to write an ode for the Ceans, Φοῖβον χορεύων | ἐν Κέῳ ἀμφιρύτᾳ σὺν ποντίοις | ἀνδράσιν. The scholiasts there say that the Ceans had asked him to write a Δηλιακὸν παιᾶνα or a προσοδιακὸν παιᾶνα.

At any rate Pindar thought of the poem as one which was to be sung *in Ceos*. In the splendid fr. 87, Χαῖρ' ὦ θεοδμάτα κ.τ.λ., he addresses Delos ; and it can hardly be doubted that the poem which opened with those verses was to be sung at a Delian festival. It seems therefore very questionable whether fr. 87 can be referred to the poem indicated in *Isthm.* I. 6 ff.

[5] The period for the tribute was variously represented as one year, three, seven, or nine years: Plutarch *Theseus* 15 adopts the last. Preller (II. 295) thinks that the nine-year cycle points to expiatory rites, and that the young Athenians, mythical food for the Minotaur, were made hieroduli of a Cretan cult.

[6] In the ordinary form of the story, the victims are chosen by lot. Hellanicus alone is mentioned by Plutarch (*Thes.* 17) as saying that Minos came to Athens himself and chose them.

When our poem begins, he is on board ship with them, sailing before a north wind to Crete. Besides the seven youths and seven maidens, there is the young Theseus[1], commonly reputed the son of Aegeus, king of Athens. Minos makes advances to one of the maidens, Eriboea[2], and is rebuked by Theseus, who threatens to oppose him by force, should he persist. If Minos is the son of Zeus and Europa, the father to whom Aethra bore Theseus is Poseidon. Minos, incensed by the reproof, and still more by the implied doubt of his divine parentage, prays to Zeus for the sign of the lightning,—which is granted; and then challenges Theseus, if he be indeed Poseidon's son, to bring back a gold ring which he throws into the sea. Theseus springs overboard: dolphins carry him to Poseidon's palace beneath the waves, where the sea-god's wife, Amphitrite, gives him a mantle and a wreath. Presently, wearing these gifts, he reappears, to the dismay of Minos, at the stern of the ship; and the young Athenians raise a paean.

There the poem ends. But those who heard it sung by the Cean chorus in Delos would think of the sequel which linked this story with the local cult. After slaying the Minotaur in Crete, Theseus sailed with his companions for Athens. On their way, they landed in Delos,—a scene depicted on the François amphora (now at Florence) by the vase-painters Clitias and Ergotimus[3]; the ship which the Athenians have left is by the shore; Theseus, as a citharist, leads the way, while the youths and maidens (among whom Eriboea[4] is prominent) follow him in couples. It was then that they performed, in honour of Apollo, a dance known in Delian tradition as the geranos ('crane-dance'), with movements symbolical of Theseus threading the mazes of the Cretan labyrinth[5]. That dance was said to

[1] The fact that there are fourteen persons besides Theseus might suggest that Bacchylides followed the tradition according to which the young hero volunteered for Crete, while the others went perforce (Plut. *Thes.* 17). Theseus is usually counted as one of the fourteen. Hellanicus said that he was the first choice of Minos.

[2] Daughter of Alcathous, king of Megara. (Cp. C. Robert in *Hermes*, vol. XX. p. 355, 1885.)

[3] Given from *Mon. dell' Inst.* by A. H. Smith in *Journ. Hellen. Stud.* vol. XVIII. p. 280. Cp. C. Robert in *Hermes*, vol. XXXIII. p. 144 (1898).

[4] The name on the vase is either EPIBOIA or ΕΠΙΒΟΙΑ.

[5] Plut. *Thes.* 21.

have been held at the ancient altar of the Delian god, the 'horn altar,' near to the palm-tree where Latona gave him birth, and to the oval basin on which floated his sacred swans[1]. The geranos was still in Plutarch's time a regular feature of the Delian festivals.

§ 2. In the episode which Bacchylides relates with so much beauty and spirit, two mythical elements can be distinguished. One of these, and doubtless the older, is the welcome which Amphitrite, the wife of Poseidon, gives to the young Theseus, her husband's son by a mortal bride, Aethra. There is an Ionian graciousness in this conception; it might be contrasted with the Dorian legend of Hera's relentless enmity to the son of Alcmena. This part of the myth was current at least as early as the beginning of the fifth century B.C. It is the subject of a painting by Euphronius on a cup (kylix) in the Louvre, a very fine red-figured vase found at Caere, of which the date is about 500—490 B.C.[2] This is the earliest known document for any portion of the story contained in the poem. Amphitrite, seated in her home beneath the sea,—as is indicated by three swimming dolphins,—extends her right hand in greeting to the young Theseus, whose feet are borne up by a Triton. Athena stands in the centre, a little in the background, wearing helmet and aegis, holding an owl in her right hand, and a spear in her left;— her face is turned with a benign expression towards the smiling sea-goddess. In this picture, however, Amphitrite bestows no wreath on Theseus. Another and perhaps earlier story made the wreath a gift to him from Ariadne, daughter of Minos[3]: the substitution of Amphitrite as the giver may have been an Attic touch, presumably somewhat later than the date of the Euphronius cup.

---

[1] Apollo's Delian altar, and the palm-tree beside it, are known to the *Odyssey* (6. 162). The altar was called κερατών (Plut. *Thes.* 21), or κεράτινος, because Apollo in building it was said to have used the horns of she-goats slain by Artemis on Mount Cynthus. The famous τροχοειδὴς λίμνη was in its neighbourhood. See my article on 'Delos,' with reference to M. Homolle's explorations, in *Journ.*

Hellen. Stud. vol. I. p. 39 (1880).

[2] See the article 'Illustrations to Bacchylides' by A. H. Smith in *Journ. Hellen. Stud.* vol. XVIII. p. 278; with Plate XIV.

[3] C. Robert in *Hermes*, vol. XXXIII. (1898), p. 132. He has also traced the development of the myth in *Archaeol. Anzeiger*, 1889, p. 142.

The other element of the myth is the quarrel between
Theseus and Minos on board ship, and the challenge given
by Minos when he throws his ring into the sea. This looks
like a free invention of poetical fancy, linked on to the older
legend of the welcome ; it is of stirring interest in itself, and also
serves to bring Theseus into the presence of Amphitrite. The
poetical combination had been made, at any rate, before
c. 474—470 B.C.; for the substance of that story was represented
by the painter Micon on a wall of the Theseion at Athens[1].
The earliest extant representation in art is supplied by a
red-figured crater of the fifth century B.C., now in the Museo
Civico at Bologna[2]. There we see Theseus, supported by a
Triton, clasping the knees of Amphitrite in suppliant fashion :
she holds out in both hands the wreath which she is about
to place upon his head. Four Nereids stand or sit behind their
queen,—not dancing, as in the poem of Bacchylides ; but one of
them plays a tambourine. In the lower part of the picture
Poseidon reclines on a couch, watching the scene, while a
winged Eros pours out wine for him[3]. On the left is seen the
stern of the ship from which Theseus has sprung into the deep ;
also the Sun-god's chariot rising from the waves,—for the
painter's idea was to show in section both the sea-depths and
the upper world. Robert[4] holds that this painting on the Bologna
vase reproduces a part of Micon's work in the Theseion,—
namely the central and the right-hand portion. In Micon's

[1] Paus. I. 17. 3.

[2] Ghirardini, *Museo Italiano di Ant.
Class.* III. p. 1, Plate I. A. H. Smith in
J. H. S. XVIII. p. 277 (fig. 7), where
other references are given on p. 278 (n. 1).

[3] This detachment of Poseidon from
the reception of Theseus is in agreement
with the poem, which does not mention
the sea-god as greeting his son (vv. 100ff.).
Amphitrite's welcome of him is the central
incident. There are, however, two vases
on which Poseidon is the chief figure.
(1) A red-figured crater, of the early fifth
century, found at Girgenti, and now in the
Bibliothèque Nationale at Paris : see *J.
H. S.* XVIII. p. 278, fig. 8. Poseidon, on

a throne, takes the hand of Theseus, who
stands before him. Behind Poseidon
stands Amphitrite (or a Nereid?), holding up the wreath. (2) A vase of *c.* 450
B.C., found at Ruvo, and now in the
possession of the Princess di Tricase :
J. H. S. XVIII. p. 279, fig. 9. There are
five persons, all standing. Poseidon, in
the centre, clasps the hand of Theseus,
who is on his left. Behind Theseus is a
figure holding up the wreath. On the
right of Poseidon is Nereus, and next to
Nereus a figure who is about to pour a
libation.

[4] *Hermes*, vol. XXXIII. pp. 234 ff.

picture, he supposes, the whole of the ship, with the company on board, was shown on the left, but the vase-painter's limits precluded him from bringing in more than the stern. This hypothesis is at least quite consistent with the account given by Pausanias of Micon's work. He observes that the story—which he relates—is not quite clear from the painting, partly through the ravages of time, and partly because Micon has not painted the whole[1]. The meaning of that expression is at once intelligible, if Micon's general scheme was the same as that of the vase-painter: there is the ship,—here is Theseus received by Amphitrite; but Micon could not also show Minos throwing the ring, or Theseus in the act of diving.

§ 3. The incident of the ring, as treated by Bacchylides, raises a curious question. Pausanias is careful to let us know that Theseus fulfilled the demand of Minos, and returned to the surface with the ring as well as the wreath. Hyginus says the same, adding the pretty touch that the ring was restored to Theseus by the Nereids. Bacchylides, however, is silent as to Theseus bringing back the ring. This omission has been regarded as deliberate. The poet, it is suggested, felt that it was beneath the dignity of Theseus to give the proof of his birth in precisely the form prescribed by the Cretan king[2]. Be that as it may, the omission renders it unlikely that Bacchylides was himself the inventor of the ring-motive. Had he been so, he would presumably have treated it with more care, instead of simply ignoring it after it had served the purpose of bringing Theseus to the sea-god's abode. There must have been some older source for the story of the challenge given to Theseus by Minos,—a source common to Bacchylides and Micon. Whether that source was (as seems most probable) a poet, or a compiler

---

[1] Paus. I. 17. 2 τοῦ δὲ τρίτου τῶν τοίχων (of the Theseion) ἡ γραφὴ μὴ πυθομένοις ἃ λέγουσιν οὐ σαφής ἐστι, τὰ μέν που διὰ τὸν χρόνον, τὰ δὲ Μίκων οὐ τὸν πάντα ἔγραψε λόγον.

[2] Thus Gomperz observes that Theseus, by bringing back the θεῶν δῶρα, 'die einleuchtendsten Beweise seiner göttlichen Abstammung erbracht hatte : sie gerade in der Weise zu liefern, wie sein Gegner

es heischt, würde als des Heroen unwürdig gelten.' And Weil: 'Il légitime sa naissance divine sans se faire le serviteur du roi de Crète.' This may be the true explanation. At the same time it is difficult to feel quite sure that Bacchylides, preoccupied with the mantle and the wreath, may not simply have forgotten the ring.

of myths in prose, or merely floating folk-lore, it is impossible now to say.   There is no trace of the ring-motive on the vases, except in one very doubtful instance[1].   In two other particulars also the vases differ from the poem.   According to the poem, Amphitrite's gifts are a mantle and a wreath : the vases know only the wreath.   Dolphins, according to the poem, convey Theseus to his father's home.   This may have been the invention of Bacchylides himself, suggested by the legends of Arion, Enalus, and Phalanthus[2].   On the Euphronius cup and the vase at Bologna it is a Triton who renders this office to his mortal step-brother.

§ 4.   It would seem that after the fifth century B.C. the story told in this poem dropped out of sight.   There are only two traces of it in subsequent literature.   One is the account, already noticed, given by Pausanias of Micon's painting.   The other is a passage in the *Poetica Astronomica* (II. 5) ascribed to C. Julius Hyginus, a freedman of Augustus, and director of the Palatine library[3] (founded in 28 B.C.).   Hyginus agrees closely with Bacchylides, down to the point at which Theseus reaches the depths : thus he names Eriboea ; he mentions the dolphins ; and he notes that Theseus springs into the sea '*sine ulla precatione aut religione parentis*' (*i.e.* without any prayer, or observance, addressed to Poseidon)[4].   As to the wreath, however,—which he describes as 'brilliant with precious stones,'—Hyginus says that it was given to Theseus by Thetis.   'Others,' he adds, say that it was a gift from Amphitrite[5].   It has been suggested[6] that the principal source of Hyginus was an astronomical epic by Hegesianax of Alexandria Troas (*c.* 200 B.C.), and that

---

[1] On the Tricase vase, mentioned above (p. 226, n. 3), Theseus seems to hold in his left hand a small object, which some take to be a box containing the ring : others, however, explain it as merely a fold of drapery brought over the girdle.

[2] Arion, Her. I. 24 : Enalus, Plut. *Mor.* p. 163 A : Phalanthus (the legendary founder of Tarentum), Paus. 10. 13. 10.

[3] Suet. *De illust. gramm.* 20 : *Praefuit Palatinae bibliothecae.* Cp. Suet. *Aug.* 29.

[4] See verses 81—84.   It has not been noticed (I think) how strongly this detail suggests an acquaintance with the text of Bacchylides,—whether Hyginus knew it at first hand, or only through some older source.

[5] *Alii autem a Neptuni uxore accepisse dicunt coronam.*

[6] By Carl Robert, *Eratosthenis Catasterismorum relliquiae*, pp. 221 ff. (1878): *Arch. Anzeiger*, 1889, p. 142.

Hegesianax had used the poem of Bacchylides. But Hyginus had also some secondary source, in which Thetis was substituted for Amphitrite. After the fashion of the later mythographers, he wove the variant into his story, and mentioned the version given by his chief source as a variant. There is no doubt that the *Poetica Astronomica* was mainly derived from Alexandrian sources[1]. If, however, Hyginus had no first-hand knowledge of Bacchylides, we must infer that, in this story, the adherence of Hegesianax to Bacchylides had been close.

§ 5. In this poem Theseus is the son of Poseidon. In that which follows it, he is on his journey to the seat of his putative father, Aegeus, king of Athens. The mythological. significance of Theseus, as the embodiment of Ionian adventure and achievement on the sea, is illustrated by the double legend of his paternity. Poseidon and Aegeus were originally identical, Aegeus, 'lord of the waves' (αἴγες)[2], from being a title of Poseidon, became an independent hero, with an Athenian shrine. Aethra, daughter of Pittheus, king of Troezen,—an ancient home of Poseidon's worship,—was the acknowledged mother of Theseus. But while Athens maintained that his father was Aegeus, Troezen asserted the claim of Poseidon. In the first half of 'the fifth century, under the patriotic impulse given by the victory at Marathon, followed by the development of Athenian sea-power, the cult of Theseus became prominent at Athens. His temple, the Theseion, was built *circ.* 474—470 B.C. His reputed relics were brought from Scyros by Cimon, and deposited there, in 467. It is not surprising that Theseus should hold a prominent place in the work of an Ionian poet who lived at this period[3].

---

[1] Cp. Teuffel, *Hist. of Roman Lit.* I. § 257.

[2] See n. on v. 36.

[3] Simonides, too, wrote on the voyage of Theseus to Crete. His narrative must have been circumstantial, to judge from the fact that he knew the name of the Athenian κυβερνήτης (Phereclus), and varied from the usual story by saying that the sail given to him by Aegeus, to be hoisted in the event of success, was not white, but red. (Plut. *Thes.* 17 = Bergk[4] fr. 54.)

ODE XVII. [XVIII.]

Theseus.

§ 1. The youth, already victorious over foes of superhuman strength, is journeying as a stranger to Athens, the home of the father whom he has never seen, the city which is hereafter to know him as the most glorious of her kings. This situation, so suggestive for an Ionian poet, is the true subject of Bacchylides. The brief recital of the young hero's deeds is merely incidental.

A few words will suffice to recall that earlier part of the story which is here presupposed. Pandion, son of Cecrops, had been driven out of Attica by his cousins, the sons of Metion, brother of Cecrops and son of Erechtheus. He went to Megara, where he was made king ; and there Aegeus and three other sons were born to him. After Pandion's death, Aegeus, aided by his three brothers, reconquered Attica, which the four shared among them ; he himself became king of Athens. But he lived in fear of the Pallantidae, the fifty giant sons of his brother Pallas, who had designs on his throne. He was childless ; and on consulting Apollo at Delphi as to his hope of issue, received an obscure response, on which he resolved to seek light from the wise Pittheus, king of Troezen[1]. Pittheus, who divined the meaning of the oracle, was led by it to desire that Theseus should be united with his daughter Aethra ; and he laid his plans accordingly[2]. But Aethra had already been visited by the sea-god Poseidon, whom Troezen worshipped ; and he (as the Troezenians deemed) was the true father of the son whom she afterwards bore. Before leaving Troezen, Aegeus left with Aethra his

---

[1] Apollod. 3. 15. 5: Plut. *Thes.* 3. Cp. Eur. *Med.* 674—686.

[2] Apollod. *l.c.* μεθύσας αὐτὸν τῇ θυγατρὶ συγκατέκλινεν : Plut. *l.c.* ἔπεισεν αὐτὸν ἢ διηπάτησε τῇ Αἴθρᾳ συγγενέσθαι. The purport of the oracle (ἀσκοῦ τὸν προὔχοντα πόδα .. μὴ λύσῃς κ.τ.λ.) was to

enjoin continence on Aegeus until he should have returned to Athens. Pittheus, inferring that his guest was not doomed to be childless, wished that his own house should furnish the heir to the Athenian throne.

sandals, and an ivory-hilted sword[1], charging her to hide these under a hollow rock[2] on a mountain between Troezen and Hermione. When their son should have grown to such strength that he could move the rock, she was to give him these tokens of his birth, and send him to Athens. The day came at last when Aethra brought Theseus, now sixteen years old, to that place in the hills : he moved the great stone with ease ; she gave him the sandals and the sword, and told him that he must now seek his father Aegeus at Athens. She and Pittheus wished him to take ship across the Saronic gulf. But the youth was bent on going by land, though the road was beset with perils. The legend of his journey from Troezen to Athens goes back to a time when Ionians were dominant on those coasts. Theseus was the hero who had purged the seaboard of malefactors and monsters, as the security of the route from eastern Thessaly to Delphi was associated with like deeds of Heracles.

§ 2. The dithyramb of Bacchylides is in four strophes, each of fifteen verses. In the first an unnamed person, who must be conceived as the leader of a chorus of Athenians[3], asks Aegeus, king of Athens, why a call to arms has just been sounded. The speaker's anxious surmises reflect a time of unrest in Attica, when danger from the Pallantidae was impending. Aegeus replies, in the second strophe, that a messenger[4] from the Isthmus has brought news of wondrous deeds done by an

---

[1] It seems almost certain that in v. 48 ἐλεφαντόκωπον is rightly supplied by Desrousseaux as an epithet for the sword carried by Theseus. Ovid (*Met.* 7. 421 ff.) speaks of the sword's 'ivory hilt' bearing some device which Aegeus recognised. Here, then, we should have a slight but sufficient proof that Bacchylides knew the story of the πατρῷα σύμβολα given by Aethra to her son. A pointed reference to the youth's πέδιλα was hardly to be expected.

[2] The πέτρα Θησέως, which, according to Pausanias (2. 32. 7), was formerly called the Βωμὸς Σθενίου Διός. Near it was the source of the river Taurius (afterwards known as the Hyllicus), and a shrine of Aphrodite Nympha or Nymphia,

which claimed Theseus as founder.

[3] Neither of the persons is indicated in the margin of the ms. The ἀόριστον πρόσωπον is an Athenian (v. 5 ἀμετέρας χθονός), and his tone is much like that of the elders in a tragic chorus (vv. 12 ff., 41 ff.). He represents the folk whom in time of perplexity have recourse to their king, as the afflicted Thebans turn to Oedipus.

[4] This messenger is designated as κᾶρυξ (v. 17). It does not appear from the text whether he is so called merely as being the proclaimer of the tidings, or whether he is supposed to be a professional 'herald' who had been sent by Aegeus on some mission to the Isthmus.

unknown youth, who is now approaching Athens; and hints that these tidings make him uneasy. In a third strophe, the Chorus-leader asks for some further particulars. The fourth strophe is a short description by Aegeus of the youth's equipment and aspect.

Though the ending might seem somewhat abrupt, the poem is unquestionably complete. Just as in the *Antenoridae* and in the *Heracles*, the poet has presented a situation, and his purpose is fulfilled.

§ 3. Certain points in the mythology are noteworthy. (1) The wife of Pandion and mother of Aegeus, elsewhere called Pylia[1], is here Creusa, who, in the Attic legend as given by Euripides, is wife of Xuthus and mother of Ion. Bacchylides, whose poem was undoubtedly destined for Athens, would scarcely have made this use of Creusa's name, if he had been aware of any positive Attic tradition which was against it: and we may infer that in his time the tradition had not yet become fixed.

(2) Diodorus and Plutarch name six victims of Theseus on this journey,—Periphetes, Sinis, Phaia, Sciron, Cercyon, Procrustes[2]. The 'club-bearing' Periphetes, slain at Epidaurus, is ignored by Bacchylides, who mentions the five others. This omission might be explained by the fact that the poet's narrative starts only from the Isthmus of Corinth. But it is more probable that, when he wrote, the Epidaurian deed had not yet been included in the cycle. Periphetes is absent, as Carl Robert points out, from the earlier illustrations of the journey in works of art, and first occurs on a vase of which the date is *c.* 450—440 B.C.[3]. He may have been added in order to bring the number of feats up to six, *i.e.* half a dodecathlos[4].

(3) Theseus is described as having two comrades (verse 46). It seems probable that the allusion is to Peirithous and Phorbas, whom some vase-paintings associate with Theseus in

---

[1] See note on v. 15.

[2] Diod. IV. 59: Plut. *Thes.* 8—11.

[3] *Hermes* vol. XXXIII. pp. 149 f. The vase, now at Munich, is given by Gerhard, *Auserl. gr. Vas.*, 232, 233 nr. 2: Jahn, nr. 372, p. 119: etc. In his careful article on Periphetes in Roscher's *Lexikon*,

Höfer accepts Robert's view: see esp. pp. 1276 f.

[4] Epidaurus would be a natural choice for the scene of the additional feat, as no other adventure occurs in the comparatively long interval between Troezen and the Isthmus.

the act of carrying off the Amazon Antiope. There is also a vase which gives him two companions in his encounter with Sinis and with Procrustes[1]. Now the presence of such supporters is distinctly alien from the spirit of the original legend. The very essence of that legend is that the youth is alone on his perilous journey, as he appears in the sculptures of the Theseion[2]. A vase-painter might introduce other figures for the sake of balance or symmetry in his scheme, and would naturally select heroes associated with Theseus in his later deeds : but such an addition betrays the instinct of a painter rather than that of a poet. The agreement of Bacchylides with the vases in this detail is all the more significant. He was influenced by those versions of current myths which the vase-painters popularized, and which, within certain limits, they could modify by introducing traits suited to the peculiar requirements of their own art.

§ 4. A special interest belongs to this poem as the only extant example of a dithyramb in the form of a dialogue. Aristotle traces the origin of tragedy to the leader of the dithyramb (ὁ ἐξάρχων τὸν διθύραμβον). It cannot be doubted that in the early dithyramb there was some element of dialogue between leader and chorus, the subject being the fortunes of Dionysus, or of a hero. Thespis is said to have introduced an actor,— distinct from the chorus-leader,—who could give a distinctly dramatic character to the part formerly taken by the leader. The word for 'actor,' ὑποκριτής, is usually explained as the 'answerer,' because his recitals were elicited by the inquiries of the chorus,—just as, in mature tragedy, a question by the chorus often gives the cue for a narrative. In this poem of Bacchylides, the chorus interrogates Aegeus, and he is the 'answerer.' But the tradition of dialogue is presumably the only link between the early dithyramb, from which tragedy originated, and this dithyramb written by Bacchylides in days when Attic tragedy was mature. The coryphaeus and Aegeus have alternate strophes of equal length. A result is that, while the questions of the coryphaeus are somewhat diffuse, the replies

---

[1] Robert in *Hermes* XXXIII. p. 150: Weizsäcker on Peirithous in Roscher's *Lex.* p. 1783: *Arch. Zeit.* 23 (1865), fig. 195   (Jahn).

[2] Baumeister, *Denkm.* vol. III. pp. 1779 ff.

of Aegeus are closely packed. It is not to be supposed that the older type of dithyramb was on such a model. This artificial structure has the stamp of developed lyric art, and, in the case of dialogue, is suited only to a poem on a small scale. Bacchylides is seen here, not as the inheritor of the old dithyramb, but rather as a precursor of the new. He illustrates a tendency in form which was carried much further by dithyrambic poets in the latter part of the fifth century. The most prominent of these was Philoxenus (c. 435—380 B.C.), in whose hands the dithyramb, with florid music and scenic accessories, approximated to the character of opera. One of his pieces, the *Cyclops*, is parodied by Aristophanes in a passage of the *Plutus*[1].

§ 5. The subject, and the reference to Athens at the close, make it probable that this dithyramb of Bacchylides was performed by an Athenian chorus at an Athenian festival. Two of the principal occasions on which dithyrambic contests took place were the Great Dionysia, towards the end of March, and the Thargelia, towards the end of May[2]. At the Great Dionysia, there was a competition between five cyclic choruses of boys, and another between five such choruses of men. Each of these ten choruses represented one of the ten Attic tribes, which furnished the choregus, and all the fifty choreutae.

The Thargelia was a festival in honour of Apollo and Artemis, especially as deities who bless the fruits of the earth (θαργήλια). The first day was devoted to certain expiatory rites: on the second, there was a contest of cyclic choruses. Now the expiatory rites of the Thargelia were said to have been founded by Theseus, when he visited the temple of Apollo Delphinius

---

[1] Ar. *Plut.* 290—315. Carion personates Polyphemus, while the Chorus are his sheep (a parody, as the scholia attest, on the *Cyclops* of Philoxenus, from which some of the words are taken): then he is Circe, and the chorus are swine. Carion and the Chorus sing alternate strophes of equal length, as do the persons in the dithyramb of Bacchylides. But we cannot be sure that this feature of the parody was taken from the dithyramb of Philoxenus.

[2] The Great Dionysia, Thargelia, Prometheia, and Hephaisteia are mentioned in *Corp. Inscr. Gr.* no. 213 as festivals at which dithyrambic contests took place. From Dem. *In Mid.* § 10 it appears that there was then no dithyrambic contest at the Lenaea.—At the Oschophoria in Pyanepsion (October) the memory of Theseus, the reputed founder, was honoured: but there seems to be no evidence for a contest of cyclic choruses on that occasion.

at Athens before his departure for Crete[1]. A dithyramb relating to Theseus would therefore have been especially appropriate at the Thargelia. But, whatever the occasion of performance may have been, this vivid little poem would doubtless have been welcome to an Athenian audience.

ODE XVIII. [XIX.]

Io. For the Athenians.

§ 1. The reference at the close to Dionysus and his cyclic choruses clearly indicates a dithyramb; and the place of performance was Athens (v. 10). Io was the mythical ancestress of Dionysus, the stemma being as follows :—

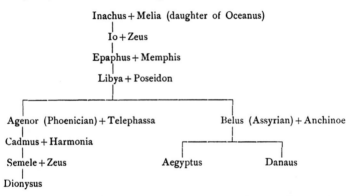

Aeschylus, in his *Supplices* (*c.* 491—490 B.C. ?) and *Prometheus Vinctus* (probably later than 468), is the oldest authority for the Io-myth. The maiden Io, daughter of the Argive king Inachus, and priestess of the Argive Hera (*Suppl.* 291), was urged in repeated dreams to visit the meadow by the marsh of Lerna, where she was destined to receive the embraces of Zeus. Her troubled father consulted the oracles at Delphi and Dodona. At first the responses were dark : but in the end Apollo clearly commanded him, on pain of destruction, to turn her out of house and home. He obeyed ; for Zeus was driving him (*Prom. V.* 671). Then the god's wrathful wife, Hera, whom Io had

---

[1] A. Mommsen, *Heortol.* p. 421 : Preller, *Gr. Myth.* p. 209. Plut. *Thes.* 18.

once served, transformed her into a cow (*Suppl.* 299)[1], and sent the hundred-eyed Argus to watch her.   But Zeus sent Hermes ; and by some sudden doom—the Io of Aeschylus does not define it (*Prom. V.* 698 f.)—Argus perished.   Even then Io was not free : Hera's malice still pursued her.   Vexed by a gad-fly (οἶστρος), she roamed from land to land.   At last Zeus guided her steps to the Nile.   There, by his touch (ἐπαφή), she was restored to the human form, and bore Epaphus, destined to be lord of Egypt and founder of a mighty race.

The conception of the transformed Io in mythology and art exhibits three phases.   (1) In the earliest, she is a white cow or heifer.   (2) In the second,—which dates from the early part of the fifth century,—she is a maiden with the horns of a cow, the βούκερως παρθένος of Aeschylus (*Prom. V.* 588).   The dramatist himself may have been responsible, at least in part, for this compromise ; which was, indeed, inevitable, if Io was to be brought on the scene as a speaking person.   The language of Bacchylides (verses 16—18) rather suggests that such an image was in his mind.   (3) In the third and latest phase, Io is once more depicted as a white cow[2].

§ 2.   Nothing could be slighter than the treatment of Io's story by our poet, who scarcely fulfils the promise of his exordium.   It will be noticed that his hesitation between the different traditions as to the death of Argus (vv. 29—36) is illustrated by the mysterious vagueness of Aeschylus on that subject (*Pr. V.* 698 f.).   Evidently Io interests Bacchylides chiefly as the ancestress of Dionysus ; the god's birth is the climax towards which he hastens.

Is the poem, as we have it, complete ?   It ends with the 15th line of an epode, and with a completed sense.   That epode cannot have been much longer, or its length would be disproportionate to that of the strophe (18 lines).   If, then, any considerable part of the poem has been lost, that part must have contained not less than 51 verses ; and, since we have now taken leave of Io, they must have been occupied with Dionysus.

---

[1] According to another version it was Zeus who transformed Io ; then Hera obtained the cow as a gift from him (Apollod. 2. 1. 3).

[2] See Appendix on v. 16.

That is possible; but it seems hardly probable. Having regard to the author's manner of breaking off other poems of this class (as XV and XVII), we might well suppose that the *Io* is complete as it stands.

ODE XIX. [XX.]
Idas. For the Lacedaemonians.

§ 1. Only the first eleven verses remain. 'The maidens of Lacedaemon sang such a song as this, when Idas was bringing home Marpessa, after escaping death by the help of Poseidon'; such is their purport.

Idas, son of the Messenian Aphareus and Arene, was a suitor for Marpessa, daughter of Evenus, king of Pleuron in Aetolia. Evenus compelled every suitor to contend with him, and slew those whom he vanquished. Already he had covered the roof of Poseidon's temple with the skulls of his victims[1]. But Poseidon furnished Idas with a chariot drawn by winged steeds[2]; and in this, after defeating Evenus, he carried off Marpessa. Evenus pursued the fugitives as far as the Aetolian river Lycormas; but, finding that he could not overtake them, slew his horses, and drowned himself in the torrent, which thenceforth bore his name[3]. Idas brought Marpessa to his home; which the older form of the legend placed in Messenia[4]. Apollo, enamoured of Marpessa, carried her off[5] from her husband; but the undaunted Idas bent his bow against the

[1] Bacchylides mentioned that detail, no doubt in this poem: see n. on v. 7, and fr. 49 (= 61 Bergk).
[2] He gave like aid to Pelops, in carrying off Hippodameia from Oenomaus (Pind. *O.* 1. 86 f.).
[3] See n. on XV. 34.
[4] At Arene, mentioned along with Pylos in *Il.* 2. 591. Aphareus came Ἀρήνηθεν (Ap. Rhod. 1. 152). In Apollod. 1. 7. 8 Idas brings Marpessa εἰς Μεσσήνην. Theocr. XXII. 208 Μεσσάνιος Ἴδας.
[5] Folk-lore connected the name Μάρπησσα with the words μ' ἄρπασε, 'he has carried me off!' Hence the

legend of the rape by Apollo, and of her agonized cry,—in memory of which her daughter Cleopatra had been called Ἀλκυόνη. (There was a belief that the female halcyon, when separated from the male, continually utters a plaintive cry.) Cp. *Il.* 9. 564 κλαῖ', ὅτε μιν ἑκάεργος ἀνήρπασε etc.: Paus. 5. 18. 3 (inscription on Cypselus-chest) Ἴδας Μάρπησσαν καλλίσφυρον, ἄν οἱ Ἀπόλλων | ἅρπασε, τὰν ἐκ ναοῦ ἄγει πάλιν οὐκ ἀέκουσαν. (Apollo is there supposed to have placed her for safety in his temple, pending the issue of his strife with Idas.)

archer-god. Zeus interfered, and gave Marpessa her choice
between her two lovers. She chose the mortal, fearing lest the
god might forsake her when she grew old[1].

§ 2. The nature of this poem, when it was entire, can only
be conjectured from the opening words:—

$$\Sigma\pi\acute{a}\rho\tau\alpha\ \pi o\tau'\ \acute{\epsilon}\nu\ \epsilon[\mathring{v}\rho\upsilon\chi\acute{o}\rho\psi$$
$$\xi\alpha\nu\theta\alpha\grave{\iota}\ \Lambda\alpha\kappa\epsilon\delta\alpha\iota\mu o\nu[\acute{\iota}\omega\nu$$
$$\tau o\iota\acute{o}\nu\delta\epsilon\ \mu\acute{\epsilon}\lambda o\varsigma\ \kappa[\acute{o}\rho\alpha\iota\ \mathring{v}\mu\nu\epsilon\upsilon\nu:$$

the maidens sang '*such a song as this.*' We are reminded of the
hymenaeus with which, in the *Birds* of Aristophanes (1731 ff.),
the Chorus welcome the newly-married Peithetaerus and Basileia,
where the rhythm is somewhat similar:—

$$\H{}\rho\alpha\ \pi o\tau'\ \text{'}\text{O}\lambda\upsilon\mu\pi\acute{\iota}\alpha$$
$$\tau\hat{\omega}\nu\ \mathring{\eta}\lambda\iota\beta\acute{a}\tau\omega\nu\ \theta\rho\acute{o}\nu\omega\nu$$
$$\acute{a}\rho\chi o\nu\tau\alpha\ \theta\epsilon o\hat{\iota}\varsigma\ \mu\acute{\epsilon}\gamma\alpha\nu$$
$$\text{M}o\hat{\iota}\rho\alpha\iota\ \xi\upsilon\nu\epsilon\kappa o\acute{\iota}\mu\iota\sigma\alpha\nu$$
$$\tau o\iota\hat{\omega}\delta'\ \mathring{v}\mu\epsilon\nu\alpha\acute{\iota}\psi.$$
$$\text{'}\Upsilon\mu\grave{\eta}\nu\ \mathring{\omega}\ \text{'}\Upsilon\mu\acute{\epsilon}\nu\alpha\iota'\ \mathring{\omega}.$$

There, the words $\tau o\iota\hat{\omega}\delta'\ \mathring{v}\mu\epsilon\nu\alpha\acute{\iota}\psi$ are immediately followed by
the refrain itself. But here Bacchylides proceeds to explain the
occasion of the maidens' song,—

$$\H{o}\tau'\ \acute{a}\gamma\epsilon\tau o\ \kappa\alpha\lambda\lambda\iota\pi\acute{a}[\rho\alpha o\nu$$
$$\kappa\acute{o}\rho\alpha\nu\ \theta\rho\alpha\sigma\upsilon\kappa\acute{a}\rho[\delta\iota o\varsigma\ \text{'}\text{'}\text{I}\delta\alpha\varsigma—$$

when Idas was bringing Marpessa home, after escaping death at
the hands of Evenus. The poet's prefatory outline of the story
has not yet been finished when, at the eleventh verse, our
fragment breaks off: how much more space was given to it, we
cannot tell. But, at any rate, when this introductory passage
was complete, the poet much have returned to the theme
announced at the outset,—$\tau o\iota\acute{o}\nu\delta\epsilon\ \mu\acute{\epsilon}\lambda o\varsigma\ \kappa\acute{o}\rho\alpha\iota\ \mathring{v}\mu\nu\epsilon\upsilon\nu$. If those
words could mean merely that the *subject* of the maidens' song
was the exploit of Idas, then, indeed, we might suppose that the
rest of the poem consisted in the poet's own narrative of the
deed. But manifestly the phrase $\tau o\iota\acute{o}\nu\delta\epsilon\ \mu\acute{\epsilon}\lambda o\varsigma$ promises that the
poem is to give us some idea of the *manner* in which they sang.

_____

[1] Simonides *ap.* schol. *Il.* 9. 556 = fr. 216 Bergk: Apollod. 1. 7. § 9.

A chant of welcome by maidens to a newly-married couple on their home-coming would necessarily have the character of a hymeneal strain. The eighteenth Idyll of Theocritus is an epithalamium for Helen and Menelaus, sung by twelve Spartan maidens at the doors of the bridal chamber. Its themes are, praise of the peerless bride, congratulations to the bridegroom, and good wishes for their future. The song of the maidens for Idas and Marpessa need not be conceived as an epithalamium sung outside the thalamos. But at least it must have been somewhat in the style and tone of a hymenaeus : it must have had some reference to the nuptials. This would by no means preclude interwoven allusions to the details of the adventure by which the bridegroom had won the bride. We might conjecture, then, that the framework of the piece was of the following kind. (1) Bacchylides began with a short sketch of the story, sufficient to orientate his hearers. (2) Then he returned to the song of the maidens. They greeted Idas and Marpessa with a joyous nuptial strain, interspersed with references to the hero's contest with Evenus, to his escape with his bride in the winged chariot, and to the fate of the baffled pursuer at the Lycormas. The poem of Bacchylides could not, of course, be classed as a ὑμέναιος. It was a free effort of lyric fancy in the treatment of the myth, so planned as to form a setting for the hymeneal song of the maidens.

§ 3. One point, which is of some mythological and even historical interest, comes out clearly. The home to which Lace-daemonian maidens welcome Idas must be in Lacedaemon. Now Idas and his brother Lynceus, the Apharetidae, were originally Messenian heroes. As is indicated by the name Λυγκεύς, they were primarily Messenian gods of light, as the Dioscuri were at Sparta[1]. The best known episode in the story of the Apharetidae is their deadly feud with the Dioscuri. Pindar is our oldest source for it (*Nem.* x. 60—72). The Dioscuri carry off the cattle of the Apharetidae. Idas slays Castor. Both the Messenian brothers are then pursued by Polydeuces, who overtakes them at the tomb of their father Aphareus. He there slays Lynceus, while

[1] See the article ' Idas ' by Weizsäcker in Roscher's *Lexikon* II. 98.

Idas perishes by the thunderbolt of Zeus[1]. Whether that legend was shaped on the west or on the east of Mount Taÿgetus, the sentiment which animates it reflects the history of Spartan conquest. The cause of the Messenian brethren is overthrown 'at the paternal tomb,'—on the sacred soil of their fatherland; and the Spartan heroes, who have been the aggressors, gain a victory which Zeus confirms. Yet, before the beginning of the fifth century, the Apharetidae had been annexed by the mythology of Lacedaemon. Simonides is said to have described Idas as a Lacedaemonian; though he mentioned Arene in Messenia as the place where Apollo sought to deprive him of Marpessa[2]. Pausanias saw a tomb of Idas and Lynceus at Sparta, near the rotunda called the Skias[3]. He observes that, according to a more probable account, they were buried in Messenia; and adds a pertinent remark. The overthrow and exile of the Messenians had, he says, left their local traditions at the mercy of any neighbours who wished to appropriate them. Indeed, during the interval between the Spartan capture of Eira, about 668 B.C., and the rebuilding of Messene in 369, the name of Messenia, as a distinct country, was virtually blotted out. That is the historical significance of the fact that Simonides and Bacchylides could make Idas a Lacedaemonian.

[1] Theocritus (XXII. 137—213) varies the details. The cause of the quarrel is that the Dioscuri have carried off the daughters of Leucippus, to whom the Apharetidae were betrothed. At the tomb of Aphareus, Castor slays Lynceus, while Polydeuces merely looks on. Idas (as with Pindar) is smitten by Zeus. Theocritus had to provide an ἀριστεία for Castor, as the first part of this Idyll had told how Polydeuces vanquished Amycus. He makes the Apharetidae first cousins of the Dioscuri (Aphareus having been a brother of Tyndareus): v. 170.

[2] Simonides fr. 216. The Homeric scholiast's summary of that poet's story begins thus:—Ἴδας, ὁ Ἀφαρέως μὲν παῖς κατ' ἐπίκλησιν, γόνος δὲ Ποσειδῶνος, Λακεδαιμόνιος δὲ τὸ γένος. It is remarkable that, according to the scholiast, Simonides named Ὀρτυγίαν τὴν ἐν Χαλκίδι, instead of Pleuron, as the place from which Idas carried off Marpessa.

[3] Paus. 3. 13. 1: cp. E. Curtius, Pelop. II. 220.—Lycophron (559) places the tomb of the Apharetidae at Amyclae, some three miles S. of Sparta. Ovid (Fasti 5. 708) mentions the Laconian Aphidna as the scene of the strife between the Apharetidae and the Dioscuri. He follows Theocritus in representing the Leucippides as the cause of the quarrel; and Aphidna was their home. Cp. Steph. Byz. s.v.: Ἀφιδνα δῆμος Ἀττικῆς· ἔστι καὶ Λακωνικῆς, ὅθεν ἦσαν αἱ Λευκίππιδες κ.τ.λ. Hyginus (Poet. Astron. II. 22) also says, in oppido Aphidnis (so Lemaire, for Ariadnis).

ΒΑΚΧΥΛΙΔΟΥ

ΛΕΙΨΑΝΑ

ΕΠΙΝΙΚΟΙ.

I.

< ΑΡΓΕΙΩΙ ΚΕΙΩΙ

ΠΑΙΔΙ ΠΥΚΤΗΙ ΙΣΘΜΙΑ >

* * * * * *

ἐπ. έ. 3   – ⌣]αφθε[– ⌣ ⎺ – ⌣ ⌣ – –

4   .. σ· τριτάτᾳ με[⌣ – –

5 ἀμέρᾳ Μίνως ἀρ[ῇο]ς

6 ἤλυθεν αἰολοπρύμνοις

5 7 ναυσὶ πεντήκοντα σὺν Κρητῶν ὁμίλῳ·

στρ. ϛ΄. 1 Διὸς Εὐκλείου δὲ (F)έκα-

2 τι βαθύζωνον κόραν

3 Δεξιθέαν δάμασεν·

4 καί (F)οι λίπεν ἤμισυ λαῶν,

10 5 ἄνδρας ἀρηϊφίλους,

I. 1—19 This fragment, representing 19 verses, is fr. 1 in Kenyon's *ed. princeps* (p. 194). The column of the papyrus to which it belonged immediately preceded that with which the continuous text now begins. Verse 1 was the 3rd of an epode, and, according to Blass, the 111th of the Ode: see Appendix. Verse 19 was the 6th of an antistrophe. After it, 9 verses have been lost from the bottom of the

---

I. 2 τριτάτᾳ. The passage which immediately preceded these verses probably described how Zeus and Apollo, coming to Ceos in human guise, were hospitably received by Dexithea and her sisters. (See Appendix.) One of the two gods may have predicted the high destiny which was in store for the maiden. τριτάτᾳ...ἀμέρᾳ is presumably the third day after the divine visit. What letter followed με, is wholly uncertain. If it was τ, μετὰ κείναν would be possible: if ν, μενεχάρμας.

3 ἀρ..ς. If the second letter was ρ, the word was probably ἀρήϊος, scanned as ἀρῆος. Such a scansion of ἀρήϊος does not occur elsewhere; but Theognis (552) has δηίων (δῄων). Dialect forbids ἄρειος. The other possibilities are ἄριστος and ἀρωγός, but neither is so fitting.

4 αἰολοπρύμνοις (only here), 'with glittering sterns' (cp. the Homeric αἰολομίτρης),—referring to the gilding or painting of the ornamental ἄφλαστον, the high curved stern of the ship (*Il.* 15. 717, = ἄκρα κόρυμβα of *Il.* 9. 241). Cp.

ODES OF VICTORY.

I.

*For Argeius of Ceos, victor in the boys' boxing-match
at the Isthmus.*

*　　*　　*　　*　　*　　*

On the third day thereafter came warlike Minos, bringing epode 5.
a Cretan host, in fifty ships with gleaming sterns:

and by the favour of Zeus who gives glory, he wedded the str. 6.
deep-girdled maiden Dexithea; and left with her the half of
his folk, warriors

same column; viz., vv. 7 and 8 of that antistrophe, and the whole of an epode.
The continuous text then begins in a new column with πολ.......ν βαθυ-, the first verse
of a strophe.
  1 αφθε. Doubtful: only traces of the lower portions of the letters remain.
2 The faint traces of a letter before τριτάτᾳ suit σ. It can hardly have been ν.—The
letter after με may have been τ or ν. **3** AP...C. The traces of the letter after A
suit P best, but would also be consistent with Γ or Π (ἀρήιος Blass: ἀγανός Platt).
8 . EΞIΘEAN. The N was at first Δ.

Soph. *Ph.* 343 νηὶ ποικιλοστόλῳ, a ship
'with gaily decked prow.'
  5 ναυσὶ...ὁμίλῳ. The MS. wrongly
divides this verse into two, the first ending
with σύν. It does not, however, so divide
the corresponding verses, 51 and 70.
  6 f. Διὸς Εὐκλείου. Zeus Εὔκλειος is
here the god by whose grace the union of
Minos with Dexithea is effected. The
epithet suggests the renown which might
commend the warrior to the maiden, and
also the glory which was in store for their
offspring. But some further associations
were probably blended with this thought.
Among the Boeotians and Locrians Artemis Εὔκλεια, the virgin goddess of fair
fame, received offerings from brides and
bridegrooms before marriage (Plutarch
Aristid. 20, βωμὸς γὰρ αὐτῇ καὶ ἄγαλμα
κατὰ πᾶσαν ἀγορὰν ἵδρυται, καὶ προθύουσιν

αὐτῇ αἱ γαμούμεναι καὶ οἱ γαμοῦντες).
Again, Εὔκλεια is found associated with
Πειθώ (*C. I. Gr.* 8364). There was a
Corinthian festival called Εὔκλεια (Xen.
H. IV. 4 § 2), though we do not know to
what deity it pertained.—Εὔκλειος is not
elsewhere found as a title of Zeus. It
occurs as the name of a month in the
Corcyraean calendar (cp. Boeckh *C. I.* II.
p. 93).
  (F)έκατι, by grace of: cp. v. 33 f.
The MS. divides the verses wrongly,
giving -κατι to v. 7. It has the same
metrical error in the corresponding places,
vv. 23 f., 37 f., 52 f., 60 f.: see also n. on
16.
  9 Foι, lit. 'for her,' *i.e.*, to protect her.
This form occurs eight times in the odes,
and always with F.

17—2

244 ΒΑΚΧΥΛΙΔΟΥ [I

6 τοῖσιν πολύκρημνον χθόνα
7 νείμας ἀποπλέων ᾤχετ᾽ ἐς
8 Κνωσὸν ἱμερτὰν πόλιν

ἀντ. ς΄. 1 βασιλεὺς Εὐρωπιάδας·
15 2 δεκάτῳ δ᾽ Εὐξάντιον
3 μηνὶ τέ]κ᾽ εὐπλόκ[αμος
4 νύμφα φερ]εκυδέ[ϊ νάσῳ
5 – ∪ ∪ –]πρύτα[νιν
6 δν

ἐπ. ς΄. * * * * * *
7 ἄλλα]ξαν θύγατρες

Col. 1 στρ. ζ΄. 1 πόλ[ιν – – –]ν βαθυδεί-
30 2 ελον· [ἐκ τᾶ]ς μὲν γένος
3 ἔπλε[το καρτε]ρόχειρ
4 Ἀργεῖος [∪ – ∪] λέοντος
5 θυμὸ[ν ἔχων], ὁπότε

14 Εὐρωπιάδας Blass². **17** The ms. has εκυδέ: Blass² ascribes to it εκυδέϊ: but there is no trace which warrants the assumption of ϊ. **20** ΔΝ] The ν alone is certain. (αν K.: εδν Bl.², who suggests κ]εδν[·).

* * * * * *

28 ξαν θύγατρες = fr. 34 K., placed here by Blass, the colour and shape of

11 πολύκρημνον χθόνα. Ceos is a mountainous island, the highest summit (now Hagios Elias) being near the site of Iulis, the birthplace of Bacchylides. The ridges which traverse it, like those in some adjacent islands, are a prolongation, in a s.e.s. direction, of the range in which the Attic peninsula terminates at Sunium. **13 Κνωσόν,** with a single σ, is the more correct form. The ms. has κνωσσον here, but κνωσιον in XVI. 120. In Soph. *Ai.* 699 the Laurentian gives κνώσια, while most of the other mss. have κνώσσια.—**ἱμερτὰν πόλιν.** Greek legend associated the embellishment of Cnosus with works wrought by Daedalus for Minos and his family. The recent excavations have shown that Minoan Cnosus was a seat of rulers, whose palaces were adorned with works of an advanced art, at a period which Mr Arthur Evans would place c. 2500—1500 B.C. **14** The ms. has ΕΤΡΩΠΙΙΑ, the final Α

having been made from Δ. We must therefore read **Εὐρωπιάδας.** The normal patronymic would be Εὐρωπίδης: but the irregular formation, prompted by metrical convenience, is analogous to that of Χαλκωδοντιάδης (*Il.* 2. 541) for Χαλκωδοντίδης, and Τελαμωνιάδης (*ib.* 9. 623) for Τελαμωνίδης: see n. on Soph. *Ph.* 1333. **15 δεκάτῳ.** Before this word, two or three letters are lost in the ms. These may have been the -as or -δας of Εὐρωπιάδας, carried over from v. 15. Another possibility is that τῷ, ἐν, or σὺν had been interpolated before δεκάτῳ. The division between the first and second verses of the strophe and of the antistrophe is wrong throughout in the ms.: see on ϝέκατι in v. 6. **Εὐξάντιον**: see Appendix. **17** Kenyon supplies κούρα: Blass, **νύμφα.** The fact that κόραν has occurred in 7 is of no weight; Bacchylides, like other Greek poets of his age, is not

to whom he gave the rocky land, ere he sailed away to Cnosus,
lovely city,

that king born of Europa. And in the tenth month the maiden ant. 6.
with beautiful locks bore Euxantius, to be lord of the glorious
isle.

* * * * * *

......the daughters (of Damon) had changed (their old abode) str. 7.
for the city steeped in sunshine. From that city sprang Argeius,
strong of hand, with the dauntless heart of a lion, whenever

the fragment being suitable. **29 f.** The second word of v. 29 ended in Ν,
and must have been an epithet of πόλιν (such as ἱμερτάν).—ΔΕΙΕΛΟ] The first ε has
been added by a corrector.—Before ΜΕΝ there is a slight trace which would suit
either C or Υ. **32** The letter after ΑΡΓΕΙ is lost in the rent of the MS., but a
faint trace points to Ο.

---

careful to avoid repetition of a word.
κόρα or κούρα (usually 'a maiden,' Soph.
Tr. 536 n.) is applicable to a young wife
and mother,—though, in such a case, her
father is usually named: *e.g.* v. 137
Θεστίου κούρα (Althaea), XVI. 31 f. Φοίνικος...κόρα (Europa): *Il.* 6. 247 κουρδων,
Priam's married daughters (Πριάμοιο
standing in v. 246). Bacchylides uses
κόρα or κούρα some 18 times, but νύμφα
(as it happens) nowhere. And once, at
least, he uses κόρα where νύμφα would be
more fitting, viz. in XIX. 4 f., ὅτ' ἄγετο
καλλιπάρᾳον | κόραν θρασυκάρδιος Ἴδας.
Yet there is, I think, one reason for
preferring νύμφα here. A measurement
of the space in the papyrus between
εκυδέ and the point where the verse
began shows that νυμφα φερ- suits this
space (Ν and Μ being broad letters), while
κουρα φερ- would be somewhat too short.

φερεκυδέϊ νάσῳ (Blass) : as in XII. 183
the poet calls Aegina φερεκυδέα νᾶσον.
The adj. is not found elsewhere. Each
of the corresponding verses (9, 32, 40, 55,
63) ends with a long syllable.

18 πρύτανιν : a term applied in XVIII.
43 to Epaphus, 'lord' of the Egyptians.
The lost word may have been an epithet
(as μοιρίδιον).

28 ff. ἄλλαξαν θύγατρες. This is the
point at which the poet linked on his
myth—the story of Dexithea—to his
immediate theme, the victory of Argeius.
The family of Argeius evidently belonged
to the Cean town called Κορησσός or
Κορησία, which was on the coast, near

the port of Iulis (Strabo x. 486: A.
Pridik *De Cei rebus* p. 7). In a fragment
belonging to an earlier part of this ode
(13 K.), one of Dexithea's sisters proposes
that they shall leave their ἀρχαίαν πόλιν
for a new abode by the sea, open to
the αὐγαῖς ἀελίου (see Appendix). A
local legend doubtless connected the
name Κορησσός with the migration of
the κόραι. It seems almost certain that
in the verses lost between 19 and 28 the
poet mentioned or indicated Κορησσός,
adding that it was so called, 'because (or
after) the daughters (of Damon) had
migrated to that sunny town. Thence
sprang Argeius,' etc.

βαθυδείελον (found only here) probably
means 'steeped in sunshine.' εὐδείελος,
of which the Homeric sense is 'far-seen,'
appears to mean 'sunny' in Pind. *P.* IV.
76 (as an epithet of Iolcus), and may have
that meaning in *O.* I. 111 (as an epithet
of the Κρόνιον at Olympia). So the author
of the Hymn to Apollo (438) speaks of
Κρίσην εὐδείελον ἀμπελόεσσαν.

31 καρτερόχειρ, like θρασύχειρος in
II. 4, indicates that the victory of Argeius
was gained in boxing, or perhaps in the
pancration (boxing and wrestling).

32 Ἀργεῖος ⏑–⏑ λέοντος. We might
supply ἐύν τε or ἀεί τε, the τε answering
to that after ποσσίν in 35. Or ἀκμᾶτα,
'stubborn': Soph. *Ant.* 352 οὔρειόν τ'
ἀκμῆτα ταῦρον (with initial ἄ).—L. Barnett
suggests ὀλοῖο: but ὀλὸς rests only on the
doubtful ὦ ὀλὲ δαῖμον in Alcman fr. 55 (ὦ
'λὲ Bergk. οὖλε ?).

6 χρεῖ[ός τι συμ]βολοῖ μάχας,
35 7 ποσσί[ν τ' ἐλα]φρό[ς, π]ατρίων
8 τ' οὐκ [ἀπόκλαρος κ]αλῶν,

ἀντ. ζ'. 1 τόσα Παν[θείδᾳ κλυτό]το-
2 ξος Ἀπό[λλων ὤπασε]ν,
3 ἀμφί τ' ἰατορίᾳ
40 4 ξείνων τε φιλάνορι τιμᾷ·
5 εὖ δὲ λαχὼν Χαρίτων
6 πολλοῖς τε θαυμασθεὶς βροτῶν
7 αἰῶν' ἔλυσεν, πέντε παῖ-
8 δας μεγαινήτους λιπών.

45 ἐπ. ζ'. 1 τῶν ἔνα (F)οι Κρονίδας
2 ὑψίζυγος Ἰσθμιόνικον
3 θῆκεν ἀντ' εὐεργεσιᾶν, λιπαρῶν τ' ἄλ-
4 λων στεφάνων ἐπίμοιρον.

34 The letter A has been deleted before ΧΡΕ. After E there is a trace of an accent, consistent with either ἐι (=εί, p. 137), or εῖ.—The letters ΒΟΛΟΙ are certain.

---

34 χρεῖός τι...μάχας, some *need* of, occasion for, fight; some call to it. Ar. *Ach.* 454 ΕΤ. τί δ', ὦ τάλας, σε τοῦδ' ἔχει πλέκους χρέος; Bion fr. 13. 2 μηδ' ἐπὶ πάντ' ἄλλω χρέος ἰσχέμεν. συμβολοῖ (Aesch. *Theb.* 352 ξυμβολεῖ φέρων φέροντι, 'encountered him' (Argeius). Cp. Eur. *I. T.* 874 τίς τύχα μοι συγκυρήσει; Soph. *Ai.* 313 πᾶν τὸ συντυχὸν πάθος. Plut. *Sull.* 2 συνήντησεν αὐτῷ τὸ τοιοῦτον.—The optative of indefinite frequency in past time is correct, since the principal verb ἔπλετο is in a past tense, and θυμὸν ἔχων = ὃς θυμὸν εἶχε (not ἔχει). These verses (30—36) contain a *retrospect* of the qualities shown by Argeius from early boyhood, before his success at the Isthmus. Next comes the eulogy of his deceased father (37—44), and then the reference to the Isthmian victory (45—48). The MS. has -βολοῖ: but we should expect -βολέοι. The contraction may be due to a transcriber.

Since χρεῖ- is no less possible than χρεῖ-, we might also suggest χρείαισι συμβολοῖ μάχας: 'when he (Argeius) encountered the stress of fight' (Arist. *Pol.* VI. 8. 14 τὰς πολεμικὰς χρείας: Soph. *Ai.* 963 ἐν χρείᾳ δορός).—See Appendix.

35—38 ἐλαφρός is better than ἐλαφροῖς here. —πατρίων ... καλῶν, 'his father's noble qualities' (πατρίων = πατρῴων),—'all those which Apollo gave to Pantheides.' The meaning is that Argeius, as a boy, showed the promise of such mental gifts as made his father an eminent physician (v. 39), while he also manifested that kindly and generous disposition which marked his father's hospitality (v. 40). For ἀπόκλαρος (Housman), cp. Pind. *P.* v. 54. (Blass² reads καταισχυντάς, a form which does not seem to occur, though Aesch. *Ag.* 1363 has καταισχυντήρ.) Note the following points. (1) The reference to the *origin* of Argeius in v. 30 (ἐκ τᾶς μὲν γένος etc.) is clearly the first which occurred in the ode; and the mention of Pantheides in v. 37 is also probably the first. Hence there is a presumption that πατρίων announced his relationship to Argeius. (2) τόσα as relative pron. in v. 37 is illustrated by XV. 11, where τόσα must be the relative to which ἄνθεα in v. 9 is antecedent. Cp. τόθι in III. 19 as = 'where.' [This use of τόσος is, however, rare, except where another τόσος precedes, as in Pind. *N.* IV. 4 f. οὐδὲ θερμὸν ὕδωρ τόσον γε μαλθακὰ τεύχει | γυῖα, τόσσον εὔλογα: Callim. *Apoll.* 93 οὐδὲ πόλει τόσ' ἔνειμεν ὀφέλσιμα,

a call to fight came upon him,—swift of foot, and not without a
portion in his father's noble gifts,—

those which Apollo, glorious archer, bestowed on Pantheides, ant. 7.
in respect to the healer's art and the kindly honouring of
strangers. Favoured by the Graces, and much admired among
men, he passed from life, leaving five sons of high repute.

In requital of his good deeds, the offspring of Cronus throned epode 7.
on high has made one of those sons a victor at the Isthmus,
and has given him other bright wreaths for his portion.

39 ΑΜΦΙ Τ' ΙΑΤ] The second Ι has been added above the line by the first hand.
48 ΕΠΙΜΟΙΡΩΝ **Α**, corr. **Α³**.

τόσσα Κυρήνῃ.] (3) If a full stop followed
καλῶν, and τόσα meant 'So many,' verses
37 ff. would not cohere in sense with
what precedes; since the reference of
τόσα is limited by vv. 39 f. (4) The MS.
does not punctuate after ΑΛΩΝ in 36.
This fact is not, in itself, cogent; but it
comes into account. — These are the
reasons which decide me against inter-
preting πατρίων...καλῶν as 'the exercises
which Ceos holds in honour,' such as
boxing and wrestling: cp. II. 6 ff. καλῶν
...ὅσ'...ἐπεδείξαμεν, and VI. 5 ff. Κέον...
πύξ τε καὶ στάδιον κρατεῦσαν : when a
word in the sense of ἀπαίδευτος or ἀγύ-
μναστος would be required.
  The genitive Πανθείδα is preserved in
II. 14. In the Cean inscription (Introd.
§ 3), the vowels between θ and δ are
lost. For the form Πανθείδης see Fick-
Bechtel, Griech. Personennamen, 229.
39 ἀμφί, with dat., 'in respect to':
so IX. 44 ἀμφὶ βοῶν ἀγέλαις. Apollo, as
Παιών, can confer the gift of ἰατορία.
40 φιλάνορι, 'kindly.' Pindar (fr. 256)
spoke of the φιλάνορα...βιοτάν of dolphins
('friendly to man'). In Aesch. Ag. 411
the word refers to a wife ('loving her
husband'). Cp. Il. 6. 15 πάντας γὰρ
φιλέεσκεν, ὁδῷ ἔπι οἰκία ναίων (' was hospitable to all'). φιλοξενία is a gift of
Apollo, in so far as he bestows the graces
of character which lend charm to it: while
Zeus ξένιος or ἐφέστιος is the protector of
the guest.
41 εὖ δὲ λαχὼν Χαρίτων : the sense is
strictly, 'having obtained a good portion
in (or of) the Charites,'—those goddesses
being identified with their gifts: cp.
Bergk fr. adesp. 53 ἐγώ φαμι ἰοπλοκάμων
Μοισᾶν εὖ λαχεῖν. If the literal sense
had been, 'having received a good

portion from the Charites,' an acc.
would have been added. Cp. VI. 1 f.
  Pindar (O. XIV. 1 ff.), invoking the
Χάριτες, says, 'By your help come all
things glad and sweet to mortals, whether
wisdom is given to any man, or come-
liness, or fame.' In particular, the
Charites give those qualities which win,
and adorn, victory in the games (Pind. O.
II. 55, VI. 76 : N. v. 54, x. 38). With
Bacchylides (as with Pindar) they are the
goddesses who lend charm to poetry (v.
9, VIII. 1, XVIII. 6), or to eloquence
(XIV. 49). If Pantheides had been a
successful athlete, that may be implied
here ; but the meaning seems at any rate
to include other things. He had received
'the gifts of the Charites' in a large
sense. There is a like generality in
IX. 39, Χαρίτων τιμὰν λελογχώς : where,
however, there is more reason than here
to suppose a reference to the games.
42 πολλοῖς : for the dat., cp. Thuc. II.
41 § 4 τοῖς τε νῦν καὶ τοῖς ἔπειτα θαυ-
μασθησόμεθα.
44 μεγαινήτους, as in III. 64 μεγαίνητε:
but in XVIII. 11 εὐαίνετε.
45 Ϝοι, 'for him,' 'for his joy.' (Cp.
ϝοι above, in v. 9.) The spirit of the
deceased Pantheides will · rejoice. So
Pindar more than once speaks of the joy
which a departed kinsman will feel in
the victor's success : O. XIV. 20 f. με-
λαντειχέα νῦν δόμον | Φερσεφόνας ἐλθέ,
ϝαχοῖ, πατρὶ κλυτὰν φέροισ᾽ ἀγγελίαν : see
also O. VIII. 81 ff.
47 f. εὐεργεσιᾶν : cp. 53 εὖ ἔρδων θεούς:
III. 21 f. θεόν, θεόν τις ἀγλαϊζέτω.
  ἄλλων στεφάνων. The Cean inscription (Introd. § 3) attests that Argeius
won an Isthmian victory among the
παῖδες, and a Nemean victory among the

ΒΑΚΧΥΛΙΔΟΥ [I

5 φαμὶ καὶ φάσω μέγιστον
50 6 κῦδος ἔχειν ἀρετάν, πλοῦ-
7 τος δὲ καὶ δειλοῖσιν ἀνθρώπων ὁμιλεῖ,

στρ. η'. 1 ἐθέλει δ' αὔξειν φρένας ἀν-
2 δρός· ὁ δ' εὖ ἔρδων θεοὺς
3 ἐλπίδι κυδροτέρᾳ
55 4 σαίνει κέαρ· εἰ δ' ὑγιείας
5 θνατὸς ἐὼν ἔλαχεν,
6 ζώειν τ' ἀπ' οἰκείων ἔχει,
7 πρώτοις ἐρίζει· παντί τοι
8 τέρψις ἀνθρώπων βίῳ

60 ἀντ. η'. 1 ἔπεται νόσφιν γε νόσων
2 πενίας τ' ἀμαχάνου.
3 ἶσον ὅ τ' ἀφνεὸς ἱ-
4 μείρει μεγάλων ὅ τε μείων
Col. 2 5 παυροτέρων· τὸ δὲ πάν-
65 6 των εὐμαρεῖν οὐδὲν γλυκὺ
7 θνατοῖσιν, ἀλλ' αἰεὶ τὰ φεύ-
8 γοντα δίζηνται κιχεῖν.

49—51 The words from φάσω to ὁμιλεῖ are quoted by Plut. *de aud. poet.* c. 14 (*Mor.* 36 c), who, instead of φάσω μέγιστον κῦδος, has φάσωμεν πιστὸν κῦδος (the Γ of ΜΕΓΙΣΤΟΝ having become Π, when Ν was added to ΜΕ). **51** ἀνθρώπων, corr. by the first hand from ἀνθρώποις. Most MSS. of Plut. *l.c.* have the genitive,

ἀγένειοι. If that Isthmian victory was the same with which this ode is concerned, the Nemean victory was still to come. These 'other wreaths' may have been won in local games of lesser note. Had Argeius already been a victor at Olympia or Delphi, it is improbable that the poet would have omitted to mention it.

ἐπίμοιρον. The only other place where the word occurs is in an extract (Stobaeus *Flor.* 103. 27) from the treatise Περὶ Βίου by the Pythagorean Euryphamus: Βίος ἀνθρώπω...ἀλόγων...ζῴων καθυπερέχει τῷ ἀρετᾶς καὶ εὐδαιμοσύνας ἐπίμοιρος ἦμεν. Cp. ἐπήβολος, ἐπίκληρος.

49—74. The merits and circumstances of the deceased Pantheides suggest reflections which occupy the rest of the ode. Ἀρετή alone gives lasting fame; any man should be content who has health and a competence. The Ionian poet flows on in his quiet moralizing

strain,—a contrast to Pindar's abrupt and pointed γνῶμαι. He has a somewhat similar passage in IX. 35—51 (ματεύει δ'...χρηστόν). There, however, he finally returns to his festal theme, with an apology for the digression. Here we have a singular instance of an ἐπινίκιον ending with twenty-five verses which are wholly 'gnomic.' Pindar would have brought in, before the close, some touch of allusion to the victory.

51 f. καὶ δειλοῖσιν: and not with the ἐσθλοί alone.—The best punctuation here seems to be a comma after ὁμιλεῖ, and a colon (as in the MS.) after ἀνδρός.

ἐθέλει does not necessarily imply a personification of πλοῦτος, but merely denotes (as often) what happens in accordance with a natural tendency or law: cp. Arist. περὶ αἰσθήσεως c. 5 (p. 445 a 21), ἔτι δ' οὐδὲ τὸ ὕδωρ ἐθέλει αὐτὸ μόνον ἄμικτον ὂν τρέφειν.—The form ἐθέλω occurs also in V. 14, 169; X. 73: and θέλω in five

The best glory is that of Virtue, so deem I now and ever:
wealth may dwell with men of little worth,

and will exalt the spirit; but he who is bountiful to the gods str. 8.
can cheer his heart with a loftier hope. If a mortal is blessed
with health, and can live on his own substance, he vies with
the most fortunate. Joy attends on every state of life,

if only disease and helpless poverty be not there. The rich ant. 8.
man yearns for great things, as the poorer for less; mortals find
no sweetness in opulence, but are ever pursuing visions that flee
before them.

---

but some the dative.	**55** ὑγιείας. The first ι has been added by **A**².
56 ἔλαχεν **A**¹, ἔλακεν **A**.	**57** ἔχει] ἔχειν **A**: but a corrector has transfixed ν,
and added a comma after ι.	**58** ΠΡΩΤΟϹ **A**: corr. **A**¹? **60 f.** ΝΟΤΙ..Ν
(νούσων) MS.: νόσων Housman, Blass, etc.	**65** ΕΤΜΑΡΕΙ **A**: **A**² has added Ν
above the line.	

---

other places. Pindar always uses ἐθέλω,
except in *O.* II. 107 (θέλων) and *P.* II. 5
(θέλοντες).

αὔξειν φρένας, to 'exalt' or 'elate'
the mind, making the rich man ambitious,
proud, self-confident. So Pindar (fr. 218)
says of the power of wine, ἀέξονται
φρένας ('men are exalted in spirit') ἀμπελίνοις τόξοις δαμέντες. Cp. IX. 44 f.
ἀμφὶ βοῶν ἀγέλαις θυμὸν αὔξουσιν (they
'enlarge their spirit,'—*i.e.* 'take their
delight,'—in herds of oxen).

53 ff. εὖ ἔρδων: cp. v. 47.—**κυδροτέρᾳ**:
because imperishable fame (vv. 73 f.) is a
more splendid prospect than the honour
which ends with life.

σαίνει κέαρ, 'cheers his heart': a
strange and scarcely felicitous use of the
verb, since the image involved in σαίνει
('fawning on,' 'caressing') so distinctly
implies an agency external to the person
soothed. The poet has used σαίνει, in
fact, much as he might have used θέλγει
or εὐφραίνει.

ὑγιείας: cp. scolia fr. 8 (Bergk), ὑγιαίνειν μὲν ἄριστον ἀνδρὶ θνατῷ. Arist. *Rh.*
II. 21 § 5 ἀνδρὶ δ᾽ ὑγιαίνειν ἄριστόν ἐστιν,
ὥς γ᾽ ἡμῖν δοκεῖ.

57 ζώειν τ᾽ ἀπ᾽ οἰκείων. We might
compare what Solon, in Her. I. 31, says
of Cleobis and Biton: τούτοισι...βίος τε
ἀρκέων ὑπῆν καὶ πρὸς τούτῳ ῥώμη σώματος
τοιήδε κ.τ.λ.

58 f. πρώτοις, the foremost in respect
to (real) happiness, the most truly fortunate.—**παντὶ...βίῳ**, not 'every life,' but
rather 'all human life,' *i.e.* life in every
grade and phase.

60 f. νόσφιν, 'apart' from them, *i.e.*
provided they are absent.—The MS. had
νούσων: but the first syllable answers to
one which is short in the corresponding
verses (6, 14, 29, 37, 52), showing that
we must read **νόσων**. The corruption
may have been due to the incorrect division of these two verses in the MS. (see
n. on 6 f.), leading a transcriber to prefer
νού|σων, because it gave a long syllable
for the end of the verse.

πενίας τ᾽ ἀμαχάνου, helpless, desperate,
poverty. Alcaeus fr. 92 πενία...ἀμαχανία
σὺν ἀδελφέᾳ: Her. VIII. 111 πενίην τε καὶ
ἀμηχανίην.—The short initial ἀ of ἀμαχάνου answers to a syllable which is long
in vv. 7, 15, 30, 38, 53.

62 ἴσον, as in fr. 2 ἀφθέγκτοισιν ἴσον.
Elsewhere the poet has only ἴσος.

63 f. ὅ τε μείων, the lesser in respect
to wealth; as in Soph. *Ai.* 161 μικροτέρων
are the men of humbler station.—**παυροτέρων**, though opposed to μεγάλων, means
strictly 'fewer' (not 'smaller') things.
παῦρος (sing.) can mean 'small,' but the
plural seems always to denote 'few.' (It
is otherwise with ὀλίζων : *Il.* 18. 519 λαοὶ
δ᾽ ὑπ᾽ ὀλίζονες ἦσαν, 'of smaller size.')

65 εὐμαρεῖ, 'to have ease, abundance'
in all things: cp. Soph. *Ph.* 284 τούτου
δὲ πολλὴν εὐμάρειαν, 'plenteous store' of
that. The verb, which occurs only here,
takes a genitive, like πλουτεῖν, etc.—
οὐδὲν (adverb) γλυκύ, is a thing nowise
sweet: opulence, however great, fails to
satisfy human desires.

66 f. τὰ φεύγοντα: objects which for
ever elude them; *i.e.* as one prize after

ἐπ. η΄. 1 ὅντινα κουφόταται
2 θυμὸν δονέουσι μέριμναι,
70 3 ὅσσον ἂν ζώῃ λάχε τόνδε χρόνον τι-
4 μάν· ἀρετὰ δ᾽ ἐπίμοχθος
5 μέν, τε]λευταθεῖσα δ᾽ ὀρθῶς
6 ἀνδρὶ κ]αὶ εὖτε θάνῃ λεί-
7 πει πο]λυζήλωτον εὐκλείας ἄγαλμα.

II.

ΤΩΙ ΑΥΤΩΙ

στρ.   Ἄ[ϊξεν ἁ] σεμνοδότειρα Φήμα
ἐς Κέον ἱεράν, χαριτώ-
νυμον φέρουσ᾽ ἀγγελίαν,
ὅτι μ[άχ]ας θρασύχειρος Ἀρ-
5   γεῖος ἄρατο νίκαν·

73 The traces before ΕΤΤΕ seem to be those of ΑΙ: Blass supplies ἀνδρὶ κ]αί. K. referred them to Ν.—ΛΕΙ (of λεί|πει) om. **A**, add. **A²**.

---

another is gained, and proves unsatisfying, the vision of happiness continually recedes.

68 f. κουφόταται...μέριμναι, vain, empty ambitions, in contrast with the cultivation of ἀοετή. Cp. Soph. *O. C.* 1230 κούφας ἀφροσύνας. For μέριμναι, thoughts intent on certain objects or pursuits, cp. fr. 16. 6 ἀνδράσι δ᾽ ὑψοράτω πέμπει μερίμνας.—**δονέουσι**, as winds shake the branches of a tree: *Il.* 17. 55 τὸ δέ τε πνοιαὶ δονέουσι. So stormy waves are said δονεῖν θυμόν, to shake the mariner's soul, Pind. *N.* IV. 58.

70 f. λάχε τόνδε χρόνον. The normal metre of the verse is ‒◡‒‒, ‒◡◡‒, ◡◡‒‒, as seen in the corresponding v., 47 (the only one available for comparison), θῆκεν ἀντ᾽ εὐεργεσιᾶν, λιπαρῶν τ᾽ ἀλ-. But the MS. has χρόνον τόνδε λάχεν, so that an epitritus (-η χρόνον τόν-) is here substituted for the choriambus in v. 47 (-εργεσιᾶν). Blass holds this substitution to be legitimate. In any case, the metrical effect is intolerable. It is far more probable that the poet wrote λάχε·τόνδε χρόνον, and that the words were wrongly transposed by a scribe, either through an

oversight, or to obtain what he regarded as a clearer and better order. Similarly in IX. 20 ταχεῖαν ὁρμὰν (MS.), in XIV. 47 ἆρχεν λόγων δικαίων (MS.), and in XVI. 72 χείρας πέτασσε (MS.), a transposition is required.

τιμάν. The MS. has a point after λάχεν, and another after μάν. If we read τί μάν; (*quid vero?*) the meaning is, ‘How could it be otherwise?’ ‘How else?’ Soph. *Ai.* 668 ἀρχοντές εἰσιν, ὥσθ᾽ ὑπεικτέον· τί μήν; ‘of course’ (we must yield). Aesch. *Ag.* 672 λέγουσιν ἡμᾶς ὡς ὀλωλότας· τί μήν; ‘of course’ (they do). The sense of the whole passage then is:—The man of frivolous ambitions has only his life-time *for his portion.* τί μάν; How could it be otherwise? How could he expect a lasting renown? But τί μάν, in such a context, is weak: and the sense given to λάχεν is also somewhat forced; since it implies that the man who leaves an enduring name could be said λαγχάνειν the space of time during which his posthumous renown lasts.

The true reading is clearly (I think) **τιμάν**: the man of light ambitions ‘*wins*

He whose mind is blown about by ambitions light as air, epode 8.
wins honour only for his life-time.   The task of Virtue is
toilsome ; but, when it has been duly wrought to the end, it
leaves the enviable meed of bright renown, outlasting death.

II.

For the same.

Fame, giver of glorious gifts, has sped to sacred Ceos str.
with a message of gracious import, that Argeius has conquered
in the strife of boxers;

II. τωι αυτωι] added (by **A**²?) in the left margin, opposite v. 1.   **1** ἅ[ἴξεν ἁ]
L. Levi, N. Festa, Blass, etc.: ἅ[ἴξον ὤ] K.   **2** ἱρὰν conj. Headlam, Blass.
4 μάχας Blass, Festa: πάλας Wil. (but μ is certain).

---

honour only for his life-time' (τόνδε χρόνον,
acc. of duration of time),—as opposed to
the man who wins a fame that survives
his death (73 f.).   τι|μάν gives, too, the
normal long syllable at the end of v. 70
(cp. ἅλ|λων in v. 47), so that there is a
metrical reason also for preferring it.
The erroneous punctuation after λάχεν in
the MS. may have arisen from the division
of τιμάν between the two verses, leading
a scribe to read it as τί μάν;
71 ἀρετὰ δ' ἐπίμοχθος. Hes. *Op.* 287
τῆς δ' ἀρετῆς ἱδρῶτα θεοὶ προπάροιθεν
ἔθηκαν | ἀθάνατοι.
72 τελευταθείσα.   τελευτᾶν ἀρετὰν is
a phrase like τελευτᾶν ἔργον,—to 'accomplish' ἀρετή, considered as a course
of life-long effort.   The epithet ἐπίμοχθος
serves to mark this.
74 πολυζήλωτον : for the η, cp. v. 52
(ἐπιζήλῳ), x. 63 πολυζήλῳ.   Pindar has
ζαλωτόν (*O.*VIII. 6).—**ἄγαλμα** is something
which confers splendour or delight, as a
gift of honour, or an ornament : in v. 4
the ode is Μοισᾶν γλυκύδωρον ἄγαλμα, as in
IX. 11 ἀθάνατον Μουσᾶν ἄγαλμα.
II. 1 ἅ[ἴξεν ἁ] seems the most probable
supplement.   The good news has just
come, and this short song welcomes it;
the formal ἐπινίκιον (Ode I.) was written
afterwards.   If **ἅ[ἴξον, ὤ]** were read, it
would imply that the poet himself was at
the Isthmus.   O. Schroeder (Blass² p. LV)
prefers this, arguing, '*de proficiscendo apte
dici ἀΐσσειν, non de veniendo.*'   But, if
one who sees a person *start* could say

ᾔξεν ἐκεῖσε, one who sees him *arrive*
could surely say ᾖξε δεῦρο.   The words in
11 f. καλεῖ δὲ Μοῦσ' αὐθιγενὴς κ.τ.λ. imply
that the poet is in Ceos.
σεμνοδότειρα, 'giver of stately gifts';
she announces victory, and so gives
renown.   Cp. Aesch. *Th.* 975 Μοῖρα
βαρυδότειρα: Eur. *Bacch.* 419 ὀλβοδό-
τειρα: Orphic Argon. 354 'Ερινύες
αἰνοδότειραι. — **Φήμα** : the Doric form
(always φάμα in Pindar) is modified to
avoid twofold **a** : so v. 47 κυβερνήταν,
167 ἀδμήτα, 200 εἰρήνᾳ.
2 f. χαριτώνυμον..ἀγγελίαν, a message
'*of gracious import*'; lit., 'fraught with a
gracious name,' *i.e.* speaking of 'victory'
(v. 5).   A thought of personified Νίκη is
implied.   [Not, 'containing the welcome
name of Argeius.']—Another possible
explanation would be, 'a message *in
terms* of gracious omen' (χαρίεντα ὀνό-
ματα), so that the phrase would resemble
ἀδυεπὴς φάτις in Soph. *O. T.* 151.   But
against this is the analogy of εὐώνυμος,
δυσώνυμος, μεγαλώνυμος, etc., which always
refer to a name.
4 μάχας..θρασύχειρος, probably the
contest in boxing: cp. I. 31 καρτερόχειρ.
Pind. *P.* VIII. 37 νίκαν Ἰσθμοῖ θρασύγυιον.
—The letters μ and -ας being certain, the
other possibilities are μέλας ('sunburnt,'
like μελαγχροιής in *Od.* 16. 175), or
μέγας.   Then θρασύχειρος would be a
nominative, like ἑκατόγχειρος in *Il.* 1.
402.   But μάχας seems better.

ἀντ. καλῶν δ᾽ ἀνέμνασεν, ὅσ᾽ ἐν κλεεννῷ
αὐχένι (Ϝ)ισθμοῦ ζαθέαν
λιπόντες Εὐξαντίδα νᾶ-
σον ἐπεδείξαμεν ἑβδομή-
10 κοντα σὺν στεφάνοισιν.

ἐπ. καλεῖ δὲ Μοῦσ᾽ αὐθιγενὴς
γλυκεῖαν αὐλῶν καναχάν,
γεραίρουσ᾽ ἐπινικίοις
Πανθείδα φίλον υἱόν.

III.

ΙΕΡΩΝΙ ΣΥΡΑΚΟΣΙΩΙ

ΙΠΠΟΙΣ ΟΛΥΜΠΙΑ.

στρ. α΄. Ἀριστοκάρπου Σικελίας κρέουσαν
Δάματρα (Ϝ)ιοστέφανόν τε κούραν
ὕμνει, γλυκύδωρε Κλειοῖ, θοάς τ᾽ Ὀ-
λυμπιοδρόμους Ἱέρωνος ἵππους.

14 ΠΑΝΘΕΙΔΑΙ **A**, corr. **A**¹.

III. The title, written in minuscule (probably by **A**³), is in the left margin, opposite to vv. 1—3.

---

6 ff. καλῶν.. ὅσ᾽.. ἐπεδείξαμεν, 'the goodly feats which we have displayed': cp. III. 96 n.—**κλεεννῷ**, Aeolic, as in v. 12, 182, while κλεινός is used in six other places.—**αὐχένι Ϝισθμοῦ,** a pleonasm; like Pindar's in *I.* I. 9 τὰν ἁλιερκέα **Ϝισθμοῦ δειράδ᾽,** where δειράς = 'neck.' Cp. *O.* VIII. 52 Κορίνθου δειράδ᾽, where the schol. rightly explains the word by τράχηλος. The Isthmus itself is a narrow plain, with hills N. and S. of it. In Her. VI. 37 τὸν αὐχένα τῆς Χερσονήσου = τὸν ἰσθμὸν τῆς X. in VI. 36. But the pleonasm is not felt, Isthmus having become a proper name. — Pindar prefixes Ϝ to ἰσθμὸς not only in *I.* I. 9 (just cited, where ἁλιερκέος is unlikely), but also probably in *I.* v. 5 νῦν αὖτε Ἰσθμοῦ δεσπότᾳ, a reading which one of the scholia supports, though the MSS. have αὖτ᾽ ἐν. Elsewhere, however, he uses ἰσθμός without Ϝ, as in *O.* VIII. 48 ἐπ᾽ Ἰσθμῷ ποντίᾳ.
λιπόντες κ.τ.λ.: 'we,' the subject to

the verb, may include friends of the competitors who went with them from Ceos to the Isthmus.—**Εὐξαντίδα νᾶσον**: cp. I. 15, and Appendix II. (Euxantius). In a fragment belonging to the exordium of Ode I., νάσοιό τ᾽ Εὐ[ξαντιαδ]ᾶν is conjecturally read: see Appendix.
ἑβδομήκοντα σὺν στεφάνοισιν, with the result of winning seventy wreaths. This can only mean that, before the victory of Argeius, seventy others had already been won at the Isthmus by natives of Ceos. See Appendix.
11 ff. καλεῖ δὲ κ.τ.λ. The Muse summons the flutes to accompany her strains; much as in Pind. *I.* VII. 10 f. the poet himself is said χρυσέαν καλέσαι Μοῖσαν. These verses, written when the news first came, may have been sung to the flutes as a welcome to Argeius on his return; his presence is rather suggested by vv. 13 f. — **αὐθιγενής**: cp. Her. IV. 49 τῷ αὐθιγενεῖ θεῷ.—**ἐπινικίοις,** sc. μέλεσι. Note the substantival use of the plural in this

and has renewed the memory of all those goodly feats which ant.
have been shown forth at the famous Isthmus by us who came
from the beautiful isle of Euxantius, winners of seventy wreaths.

The native Muse summons the sweet clear sound of flutes, epode.
honouring with strains of victory the beloved son of Pantheides.

III.

For Hieron of Syracuse, victor in the four-horse chariot-race at Olympia. (468 B.C.)

Cleio, giver of sweet gifts, praise Demeter, queen of fertile str. 1.
Sicily, with her daughter of the violet crown; and sing of
Hieron's swift steeds that ran at Olympia.

---

poetical phrase. (Pindar *N.* IV. 78 has
ἐπινικίοισιν ἀοιδαῖς.) A substantival use
of the singular, as a name for the ode of
victory, occurs first in scholia of the
Alexandrian age.
14 Πανθείδα: cp. I. 37.
III. 1—4 The names of Demeter
and Persephone, the guardian deities
of Sicily, lend majesty to this proem;
though, considering the peculiar awe
which surrounded them, there is a certain
crudeness in their close conjunction with
the 'swift mares.' Hieron was the hereditary priest of these goddesses (ἱεροφάντης
τῶν χθονίων θεῶν, Her. VII. 153): indeed,
it has been held that he took his name
from those rites of which the supreme
charge belonged to his house: cp. Pindar's address to him, fr. 105 ζαθέων
ἱερῶν | ὁμώνυμε πάτερ. So the poet says,
in effect:—'Sing the dread goddesses,
and the latest victory of their great
Priest.' Cp. Pind. *O.* VI. 93 ff.
His brother and predecessor Gelon,
who also was their hierophant, had built
for them at Syracuse twin temples (ναούς,
Diod. XI. 26), in the precinct called by
Plutarch (*Dion* c. 56) τὸ τῶν Θεσμοφόρων
τέμενος. This was the most famous of
all their Sicilian shrines, next to that at
Enna, the place from which Aïdoneus
was said to have carried off the Korê.
It is curious to find that Bacchylides had
somewhere made Crete the scene of that
rape (schol. Hes. *Theog.* 914),—a 'heresy,'
as Freeman remarks (*Sicily* II. 266),

'against all Sikel and Sikeliot belief.'
1 ἀριστοκάρπου: so Pind. *N.* I. 14
describes Sicily as ἀριστεύουσαν εὐκάρπου
χθονός, and in his fr. 106 it is ἀγλαόκαρπος,
as in Aesch. *P. V.* 369 καλλίκαρπος. It
is still, as in ancient times, a rich grana-
ry, about three-fourths of the cultivated
surface being given to cereals (chiefly
wheat); the yield of fruit (especially
of oranges) is also large.—κρέουσαν, the
fem. (not elsewhere found, except as a
proper name) of κρέων (Pind., etc.),=the
Homeric κρείων: κρείουσα occurs only in
Il. 22. 48.
2 Ϝιοστέφανον, as in VIII. 3 ϝιοβλέ-
φαρον and 72 ϝιόπλοκον. But ἰοστεφάνων
(-ον) has no ϝ in V. 3 or XII. 89, nor
ἰόπλοκος in XVI. 37. So Pindar assumes
ϝ in ἰόπλοκον *O.* VI. 30, but not in ἰοπλοκάμων, *P.* I. 1.
3 f. Κλειοῖ, with εἰ. The only other
example of this scansion is Pind. *N.* III.
83 Κλεοῦς, as most edd. now write it,
with good MS. authority, though Κλειοῦς
is a *v.l.* It is tempting to write Κλεοῖ
here. But there is no reason to doubt
that Κλειοῖ could be ⏑‒ (*i.e.* Κλεγοῖ):
cp. XVI. 92 n.
θοάς..ἵππους: mares were most generally used in racing: see, *e.g.*, Pind. *I.* IV.
4 f., *N.* IX. 52: Soph. *El.* 705. In the
Homeric chariot-race, however (*Il.* 23),
there are three teams of horses, and two
of mares, and the horses win the first and
second places.—Ὀλυμπιοδρόμους only
here.

5 ἀντ. α΄.　σεύον]το γὰρ σὺν ὑπερόχῳ τε Νίκᾳ
　　　　　σὺν ᾿Αγ]λαΐᾳ τε παρ᾽ εὐρυδίναν
　　　　　᾿Αλφεόν, τόθι Δ]εινομένεος ἔθηκαν
　　　　　ὄλβιον [γόνον　στεφάνω]ν κυρῆσαι.

ἐπ. α΄.　θρόησε δὲ λ[αὸς ἀπείρων·
10　　　ᾶ τρισευδαίμ[ων ἀνήρ,
Col. 3　ὃς παρὰ Ζηνὸς λαχὼν
　　　　　πλείσταρχον ῾Ελλάνων γέρας
　　　　　οἶδε πυργωθέντα πλοῦτον μὴ μελαμ-
　　　　　φαρέϊ κρύπτειν σκότῳ.

15 στρ. β΄.　βρύει μὲν ἱερὰ βουθύτοις ἑορταῖς,
　　　　　βρύουσι φιλοξενίας ἀγυιαί·
　　　　　λάμπει δ᾽ ὑπὸ μαρμαρυγαῖς ὁ χρυσὸς
　　　　　ὑψιδαιδάλτων τριπόδων σταθέντων

5 f. [σεύον]το K.—Νίκᾳ..᾿Αγλαΐᾳ Weil : νίκᾳ..ἀγλαΐᾳ K.—σὺν (in v. 6) Palmer. **7** τόθι Palmer.　　**9** ἀπείρων Blass.　　**12** γέρας] ΓΕΝΟC **A**, corr. **A**[1].

5 ff. σεύοντο. *Il.* 22. 22 σευάμενος ὥς
θ᾽ ἵππος ἀεθλοφόρος σὺν ὄχεσφιν: Pind. *O.*
I. 20 (of the horse Pherenicus) παρ᾽
᾿Αλφεῷ σύτο.
Νίκᾳ..᾿Αγλαΐᾳ: personified attendants
on the rushing steeds. The epithet
ὑπερόχῳ might seem slightly in favour of
writing νίκᾳ etc.: yet it is not unsuitable
to the goddess. ᾿Αγλαΐα is with Pindar
esp. the glory of victory: *Ol.* XIII. 14 f.
ὕμμιν δέ, παῖδες ᾿Αλάτα, πολλὰ μὲν νικα-
φόρον ἀγλαΐαν ὤπασαν | ἄκραις ἀρεταῖς
ὑπερελθόντων ἱεροῖς ἐν ἀέθλοις. *I.* II. 18
ἐν Κρίσᾳ δ᾽ εὐρυσθενὴς εἶδ᾽ ᾿Απόλλων μιν
πόρε τ᾽ ἀγλαΐαν.
εὐρυδίναν ᾿Αλφεόν: the Alpheus has
this epithet again in v. 38: in v. 181 it
is ἀκαμαντορόας, in VII. 49 ἀργυροδίνας,
in X. 26 καλλιρόας. Pindar in *O.* v. 18
has ᾿Αλφεὸν εὐρὺ ῥέοντα, but elsewhere
dispenses with an epithet for the famous
river.—E. Curtius (*Pelop.* II. 49) describes
the Alpheus, at its entrance into Pisatis,
as being about 180 feet wide. Leake
writes (*Morea* I. 23): 'It is now [Feb. 25]
full and rapid, but turbid : in summer the
stream, though much clearer, is scanty,
and divided into several torrents, running
over a wide gravelly bed.'
7 f. Δεινομένεος. Before a vowel one
would prefer Δεινομένευς, the form which
the MS. gives in v. 35 (where ἀγέρωχοι

follows): though the synizesis is natural
before a consonant, as in Pind. *P.* 1. 179
Δεινομένεος τελέσαις. In Simonides fr.
141. 4 Δεινομένευς is read, where τὸν (or
τοὺς) follows.
ἔθηκαν..κυρῆσαι: the acc. and inf.
with τίθημι is not rare in poetry: Pind.
fr. 177 πεπρωμέναν θῆκε μοῖραν μετατρα-
πεῖν: Eur. *Her.* 990 ῞Ηρα με κάμνειν τήνδ᾽
ἔθηκε τὴν νόσον.
9 ἀπείρων: *Il.* 24. 776 ἐπὶ δ᾽ ἔστενε
δῆμος ἀπείρων. Cp. VIII. 30 ῾Ελλάνων
δι᾽ ἀπείρονα κύκλον. (Another possibility
would be ἀγασθείς.)
10 The exclamation ᾶ is regularly
found in expressions of *pity* or *reproof*, as
in the Homeric ᾶ δειλ᾽ (*Il.* II. 441 etc.):
Soph. *O. T.* 1147 ᾶ, μὴ κόλαζε: cp. *Ph.*
1300 (n.). This seems to be the only
classical example of it in an utterance
of admiration. We should expect ὦ.
12 πλείσταρχον ῾Ελλάνων γέρας, 'the
privilege of ruling over the largest number
of Greeks': *i.e.*, over more than are
subject to any other ruler. πλείσταρχον = consisting in πλείστη ἀρχή (cp.
αὔχημα..εὔιππον, Soph. *O. C.* 710 f.):
then ῾Ελλάνων further defines the ἀρχή.
Kenyon cp. Her. VII. 157 μοῖρά τοι
(Gelon) τῆς ῾Ελλάδος οὐκ ἐλαχίστη, ἄρχοντί
γε τῆς Σικελίας.
13 f. οἶδε..μὴ..κρύπτειν, knows how

Pre-eminent Victory and Glory were with them as they sped ant. 1.
by the broad tide of the Alpheus, where they won wreaths for
the blest son of Deinomenes ;

and a cry went up from the vast multitude: 'O thrice-happy epode 1.
man, honoured by Zeus with the widest rule in Hellas, who
knows how to keep the lofty fabric of his fortunes from being
wrapt in a mantle of darkness.'

The temples are rife with festal sacrifice of oxen, the streets str. 2.
with hospitable feasting ; and the gold shines with flashing rays
from high tripods, richly wrought,

13 f. ΜΕΛΛΗ **A**, ΜΕΛΑΜ **A**¹.—ΦΑΡ̣ΕΙΝ **A**, corr. **A**¹ : μελαμφαρέϊ Palmer.
15 ἱερά] ΕΡΑ **A** : ῐ̈ has been added above the line (by **A³**?). **18** ὑψιδαιδάλων
conj. Blass.

---

not to hide it, =knows how to manifest
it : his instincts tell him what befits a
prince. πυργωθέντα..πλοῦτον: the image
is that of a lofty and stately edifice (cp.
Ar. *Ran.* 1004 πυργῶσαι ῥήματα σεμνά),
made strong against assault: Weir Smyth
cp. Solon fr. 13. 9 f. πλοῦτον δ' ὃν μὲν δῶσι
θεοί, παραγίγνεται ἀνδρὶ | ἔμπεδος ἐκ νεάτου
πυθμένος εἰς κορυφήν.—μελαμφαρέϊ..σκό-
τῳ: cp. Eur. *Ion* 1150 μελάμπεπλος Νύξ.
Here, however, σκότος is scarcely personified ; the phrase rather means,
'enshrouding darkness'; *i.e.* the σκότος
is itself the μέλαν φάρος.
Pindar's precepts against πλοῦτος κρυ-
φαῖος (*I.* 1. 67, cp. *N.* 1. 31) occur
especially in odes which, like this,
concern the chariot-race,—one of the
most popular forms in which wealth
could be shown. πλοῦτος ἀρεταῖς δεδαι-
δαλμένος should be an ἀστὴρ ἀρίζηλος (*O.*
II. 58 ff.).
15 f. These two verses describe the
rejoicings at Syracuse, where Bacchylides
was perhaps Hieron's guest.—βρύει..
ἑορταῖς: here βρύω takes the dat.,—its
more frequent construction, the primary
sense being to swell or burgeon (ἔρνος
βρύει ἄνθεϊ, *Il.* 17. 56): in v. 16 it takes
the gen., as a verb of 'fulness' (cp.
Soph. *O. C.* 16 f.), with no difference in
sense, unless it be that the dative is more
animated and picturesque. I would not
change φιλοξενίας to -ίαις, though Plato
has that plur. (*Legg.* 953 A), and Pindar
ξενίαις (*O.* 1. 15).—βρύει μὲν..βρύουσι.
Note the absence of δέ. In such 'epana-
phora,' where μέν..δέ is normal, the
omission of μέν is frequent (Soph. *Ant.*
606 n.), but that of δέ very rare: Plut.

Mor. 965 C πολλοῖς μὲν ἐνάλου, ὀρείου
πολλοῖς ἄγρας ἀκροθινίοις [where the
chiasmus is against inserting δέ, as edd.
do]. Platt cites Orphic hymn 22. 7
μῆτερ μὲν Κυπρίδος, μῆτερ νεφέων ἐρε-
βεννῶν.—ἀγυιαί: cp. fr. 3. 12.
17 ff. λάμπει δ' κ.τ.λ. While Syracuse
rejoices in Hieron's Olympic victory, his
munificence has a witness at Delphi also;
golden tripods, given by him and his
brother Gelon, shine before the temple of
Apollo. ὑπὸ μαρμαρυγαῖς, 'with flashing rays' (*Od.* 8. 265 μαρμαρυγὰς θηεῖτο
ποδῶν): for ὑπό, cp. Pind. fr. 48 αἰθομένα
δᾷς ὑπὸ ξανθαῖσι πεύκαις: but the gen. is
more frequent in this sense.—It seems
better to join ὁ χρυσὸς with τριπόδων
than to suppose a genitive absolute.
ὑψιδαιδάλων. This compound adj.
signifies, 'curiously wrought *to a* (certain)
height' from the ground. The only
peculiarity is in the shade of meaning
thus given to ὑψι-, rendering the compound equivalent in sense to ὑψηλῶν καὶ
δαιδάλων. In the few other verbal
compounds where it occurs, ὑψι- means
'on high,' as in ὑψίβατος, ὑψιτέλεστος,
ὑψιφόρητος. [Weir Smyth renders ὑψιδαιδάλων 'deep-chased,' as though ὑψι-
referred to 'high relief.' I cannot think
this possible.]—The fourth syllable of
ὑψιδαιδάλων answers to one which is
short in the corresponding verses, except
64 (ὦ μεγαλήνητε—): hence Blass conjectures ὑψιδαιδάλων. As, however, the
fourth syllable is *anceps* when this verse
is used in the Sapphic stanza, so it
doubtless may be here also.
τριπόδων σταθέντων. The French explorers of Delphi have found the in-

ἀντ. β'. πάροιθε ναοῦ, τόθι μέγιστον ἄλσος
20   Φοίβου παρὰ Κασταλίας ῥεέθροις
        Δελφοὶ διέπουσι. θεόν, θεόν τις
        ἀγλαϊζέτω, ὁ γὰρ ἄριστος ὄλβων.

ἐπ. β'. ἐπεί ποτε καὶ δαμασίππου
         Λυδίας ἀρχαγέταν,
25   εὖτε τὰν πεπ[ρωμέναν
        Ζηνὸς τελε[ιοῦσαι κρίσιν
        Σάρδιες Περσᾶ[ν ἐπορθεῦντο στρ]ατῷ,
        Κροῖσον ὁ χρυσά[ορος

στρ. γ'. φύλαξ' Ἀπόλλων. [ὁ δ' ἐς ἄ]ελπτον ἆμαρ
30   μολὼν πολυδ[άκρυον] οὐκ ἔμελλε

22 APICTON OΛBON **A** : corrected to ἄριστος ὄλβων by **A³**, who has written σ and
ω above, also transfixing Ω and the first N.   **23** The MS. seems to have a circumflex on ἐπεί.—A later hand has sought to make the Π of ποτε into K : so also in v. 72.
25 f. πεπρωμέναν . . τελειοῦσαι K. (τελέσσαντος Wackernagel) : κρίσιν Weil and others
(κτίσιν Kenyon, τίσιν Sandys).—Ζηνὸς τελείου νεύμασιν Blass.   **27** ἐπορθεῦντο

---

scribed bases which supported the tripods
of Gelon and Hieron. These offerings
stood side by side, under the open sky,
before the E. front of the temple, a little
N.N.E. of the Great Altar. To a visitor
ascending by the Sacred Way, they were
most conspicuous objects.

Gelon's golden tripod, surmounted by
a golden Victory, was the work, as an
inscription on the base records, of an
Ionian artist, Bion of Miletus. It was
dedicated, doubtless in 479, to commemo-
rate his victory over the Carthaginians
at Himera in September, 480. Hieron's
offering was similar. From certain indications afforded by the bases, M. Homolle
infers that the two dedications were not
separated by any great interval of time.
On the other hand it seems probable that
Hieron's gift was made after his accession,
on Gelon's death in 478, to the rule of
Syracuse.—See Appendix.

The key-note of the ode is θεόν τις
ἀγλαϊζέτω. This links Hieron's victory
by the Alpheus with his gifts at Pytho.
His piety towards Apollo illustrates the
grace shown him by Olympian Zeus.
Our poet, aiming at the Croesus-myth,
thus brings in Delphi; not, indeed, with
perfect art, yet by a coherent thought.

ἄλσος, a poetical word for the whole
sacred enclosure (ἱερόν, τέμενος), containing the various buildings of the sanctuary.
So in Soph. *Ant.* 844 the city of Thebes
is called ἄλσος, as ground sacred to its
gods.—**Κασταλίας** : fitly named in this
context, since its water was used by the
priests for sacred purposes. Rising in
the high cliffs above Delphi, the stream
descends to the site of the temple, below
which it joins the Pleistus.

21 f. θεόν, θεόν : cp. Diagoras fr. 1
(Bergk) θεὸς, θεὸς πρὸ παντὸς ἔργου
βροτείου | νωμᾷ φρέν' ὑπερτάταν.
The scribe of the MS. read **ἀγλαϊζέθω
γὰρ ἄριστον ὄλβον**. The accus. must
have been taken as being in apposition
either with θεόν or with the sentence.
But the correction by a later hand,
ἄριστος ὄλβων, is doubtless right. And
this confirms the view (first propounded
by Otto Crusius in *Philolog.* LVII. *N. F.*
XI. p. 153) that **θω** in **ἀγλαϊζέθω** is a
crasis of -τω with **ὁ**. For such a crasis
there is, indeed, no proper parallel; and
here the slight pause in the sense after
ἀγλαϊζέτω is a further objection to it:
but Alexandrian grammarians were sometimes bold in such matters. Crusius
proposed to read, **ἀγλαϊζέτω, ὁ[s] γὰρ
ἄριστος ὄλβων**, supposing the ω to be
shortened, and ‒ ◡ ◡ ◡ to be substituted

set in front of the temple, where Delphians minister in the great ant. 2.
sanctuary of Phoebus by Castalia's stream. To the god let
men bring their choicest gifts; that is the best pledge of
welfare.

For Croesus, lord of horse-taming Lydia, was preserved of epode 2.
yore by Apollo of the golden sword, when, in fulfilment of the
doom decreed by Zeus, Sardis was being sacked by the Persian
host.

When he had come to that unlooked-for day, Croesus was str. 3.
not minded

Housman: ἐάλωσαν Palmer, ἁλίσκοντο Wackernagel. **28** χρυσάορος Palmer:
χρυσάρματος conj. K. **30** The MS. has μολῶν. This mis-accenting of μολών
(as of some other 2nd aor. participles) is very common in MSS.: see Appendix.
There is no point after the N. Blass² says, 'post quintam nunc punctum agnovi':
but the trace to which he probably refers seems to belong to the partly effaced right-
hand stroke of N.

---

for the – ‿ – ‿ found in the corresponding
verses. It seems better to suppose a
synizesis of -τω and ο (Blass compares Ar.
Th. 269 'Απόλλω̲ οὐκ). But it must be
allowed that such a synizesis, harsh at
the best, is made much harsher by the
slight pause before ὁ γάρ. It is, indeed,
difficult to understand how so graceful
and facile a poet could have written such
a verse. For other conjectures see Appendix.
ἀγλαϊζέτω, honour, glorify (the god)
with gifts: a rare use; but cp. Plut.
Mor. 965 C πολλοῖς..ἀκροθινίοις ἀγλαΐσας
τὴν 'Αγροτέραν (Artemis).
ὁ γὰρ ἄριστος ὄλβων: for that (ὄλβος),
—viz. τὸ θεὸν ἀγλαΐζειν,—is the best. [ὁ
should not be taken as=θεός.] The
plural of ὄλβος occurs elsewhere only in
Soph. fr. 297.
23 f. ἐπεί. The story of Croesus is
introduced as an illustration of the general
truth just stated. As to the form of the
myth adopted here, see Introduction to
this Ode, § 3.—δαμασίππου Λυδίας:
Her. (1. 79) speaks of the Lydian cavalry
in the time of Croesus as unsurpassed in
Asia. Cp. Mimnermus fr. 14. 3 Λυδῶν
ἱππομάχων.
25 f. τὰν πεπρωμέναν..κρίσιν. The
genitive Ζηνὸς makes it likely that the
last word in v. 26 was a noun agreeing
with τὰν πεπρωμέναν, though the latter
could stand alone. κρίσιν seems slightly

preferable to κτίσιν (=a deed ordained
by the god, as in Pind. *O.* 13. 83), or
τίσιν.
28 χρυσάορος, with golden sword.
The epithet suits Apollo as defender and
rescuer: cp. *Il.* 15. 254 ff., τοῖόν τοι
ἀοσσητῆρα Κρονίων | ἐξ 'Ίδης προέηκε
παρεστάμεναι καὶ ἀμύνειν, | Φοῖβον 'Απόλ-
λωνα χρυσάορον, ὅς σε πάρος περ | ῥύομ̓.
In the only other Homeric passage where
Apollo receives this epithet, it is again in
his warlike character (*Il.* 5. 509). [On
the other hand in Pind. *P.* v. 104,
χρυσάορα Φοῖβον, Gildersleeve explains,
'hung with the golden φόρμιγξ': and acc.
to schol. *Il.* 15. 256 Pindar called Orpheus
χρυσάορα.] Some vase-paintings arm
Apollo with the sword in the Giganto-
machia, and in his fight with Tityos
(Preller I. 232).—χρυσάρματος would
also be suitable, since he bears Croesus
away (vv. 59 f.). In Pind. *P.* IX. 6 Apollo
bears Cyrene to Libya in a golden chariot.
But a regular epithet of the god is more
probable.
29—31 ὁ δ'...δουλοσύναν. The restoration of this passage given above is
mine, and was adopted in the *editio
princeps.* A different restoration, by
Blass, is discussed in the Appendix. I
read ὁ δ', rather than τὸ δ', because the
subject to ἔμελλε and ναῆσατ̓ is Croesus,
and, after φύλαξ̓ 'Απόλλων, some indication of this is needed. Then ὁ δ' ἐς

μίμνειν ἔτι δ[ουλοσύ]ναν· πυρὰν δὲ
χαλκοτειχέος π[ροπάροι]θεν αὐ[λᾶς

ἀντ. γ΄.   ναῆσατ᾽, ἔνθα σὺ[ν ἀλόχῳ] τε κεδνᾷ
σὺν εὐπλοκάμοις τ᾽ ἐπέβαιν᾽ ἄλα[στον
35   θυγατράσι δυρομέναις· χέρας δ᾽ ἐς
αἰπὺν αἰθέρα σφετέρας ἀείρας

ἐπ. γ΄.   γέγω]νεν· ὑπέρβιε δαῖμον,
ποῦ θεῶν ἐστιν χάρις;
ποῦ δὲ Λατοίδας ἄναξ;
40   πίτνουσ]ιν Ἀλυάττα δόμοι,
τίς δὲ νῦν δώρων ἀμοιβὰ] μυρίων
φαίνεται Πυθωνόθε]ν;

στρ. δ΄.   πέρθουσι Μῆδοι δοριάλωτο]ν ἄστυ,
φοινίσσεται αἵματι χρυσο]δίνας
Col. 4   45   Πακτωλός· ἀεικελίως γυναῖκες
ἐξ ἐϋκτίτων μεγάρων ἄγονται·

ἀντ. δ΄.   τὰ πρόσθε δ᾽ ἐχθρὰ φίλα· θανεῖν γλύκιστον.
τόσ᾽ εἶπε, καὶ ἀβροβάταν κέλευσεν

31 δουλοσύναν J.   33 ναῆσατ᾽ Blass.   34 σὺν εὐποκλάμοις τ᾽ (cp. v. 6) Platt :
σύν τ᾽ εὐπλοκάμοις K.   37 ὑπέρβιε Blass.   (There is not room for ὑπέρτατε.)
40 πίτνουσι]ν Herwerden.   The letter before N is uncertain : it may have been I.

is preferable to ὁ γάρ, because μολεῖν is seldom followed by an acc. without a preposition, except when the acc. denotes a place (or a folk) ; e.g. γῆν, λαόν (Pind. N. x. 36). In Eur. Med. 920 f., ἥβης τέλος μολόντες, the τέλος is conceived as a goal.

μίμνειν : the pres. inf. θύειν follows μέλλω in XV. 18 : the fut. φοινίξειν in XII. 165 : in V. 164 τελεῖν is ambiguous.

32 χαλκοτειχέος : plates of bronze which are affixed to the walls ; a mode of ornament which came into Hellas from Asia. Cp. Od. 7. 86 (in the palace of Alcinous), χάλκεοι μὲν γὰρ τοῖχοι ἐληλάδατ᾽ ἔνθα καὶ ἔνθα. The pyre was built in front of the αὐλή, the courtyard of the king's palace.—Bacchylides, following epic precedent, forms compounds either with χαλκεο-, χρυσεο-, or with χαλκο-, χρυσο-: Pindar, with χαλκο-, χρυσο- only.

33 ναῆσατ᾽, rogum exstruendum curavit : Doric for νήσατο, from νήω, 'to heap up.' This midd. aor. occurs in Il. 9. 137, 279 : also in Ap. Rhod. 1. 364, and later poets.

34 f. σὺν εὐπλοκάμοις τε : Platt seems right in thus placing τε, on the ground that there is not room for NT between Υ and ΕΥ.—ἄλαστον, 'inconsolably' : Od. 14. 174 νῦν αὖ παιδὸς ἄλαστον ὀδύρομαι.

36 σφετέρας, = ἑάς, 'his,' as often in posthomeric poetry. In Homer, and in classical prose, σφέτερος is always a plural possessive.—ἀείρας : cp. the Homeric χεῖρας ἀνέσχον (Il. 3. 318, etc.). It is an epic trait in Bacchylides that he loves to mention this gesture, in connexion with prayer (XI. 100, XIII. 35, XV. 9), or with appeal to a heavenly sign (XVII. 72).

37 ff. γέγωνεν, = ἐγέγωνεν, imperf. from γεγώνω, as in Il. 14. 469 Αἴας δ᾽ αὖτ᾽ ἐγέγωνεν. (Not from perf. γέγωνα, as a vivid present.)

δαῖμον : the Sky-father ; it is Zeus who sends the rain (v. 55).—ποῦ θεῶν ......χάρις ; In Her. I. 90 Croesus, after his fall, sends a message to Delphi, asking

to await the further woe of grievous slavery. He caused a pyre
to be built in front of his courtyard with walls of bronze ;
he mounted thereon with his true wife and his daughters with ant. 3.
beauteous locks, who wailed inconsolably ; and, lifting up his
hands to the high heaven,

he cried aloud :—' O thou Spirit of surpassing might, where is epode 3.
the gratitude of the gods? where is the divine son of Leto?
The house of Alyattes is falling ; [and what recompense for
countless gifts is shown from Delphi? The Persians are sacking
the city taken by the spear ;]

the gold-fraught tide of Pactolus runs red with blood ; women str. 4.
are ruthlessly led captive from the well-built halls :

what once was hateful is welcome ; 'tis sweetest to die.' So ant. 4.
spake he, and bade a softly-stepping attendant

41 μυρίων] Before the M was C, but a line has been drawn through it.   **44** φοινίσσεται Blass : αἵματι χρυσο]δίνας K.   **47** ΠΡΟCΘΕΝ Δ **A**: πρόσθεν (without δ')
Fraccaroli: πρόσθε δ' K.—ἐχθρὰ Palmer.—νυν was inserted above ΦΙΛΑ by **A**³; a
notable instance of inattention to metre.   **48** AB.. BΑΩΤΑΝ **A**, but Ω has
been transfixed (by **A**³?).—'Αβροβάταν (as a proper name) Palmer, Jurenka.

εἰ ἀχαρίστοισι νόμος εἶναι τοῖσι Ἑλληνικοῖσι
θεοῖσι.—Cp. Eur. *Tro.* 428 ποῦ δ' 'Απόλλωνος λόγοι;
40 ff. 'Αλυάττα δόμοι, the palace of
the Lydian kings at Sardis,—τὰ βασιλήϊα
of Her. i. 30, comprising the treasure-
houses (θησαυροί) there mentioned. The
prominence given here to the father of
Croesus is historically correct. Gyges,
of whom Croesus was the fourth successor,
established the dynasty of the Mermnadae;
but Alyattes, in his long reign (*circ.*
617—560 B.C.), became the real founder
of the Lydian empire.
41 f. The word μυρίων clearly points
to some such context as that which I
restore (*exempli gratia*) above. The C
cancelled before ΜΤΡΙΩΝ in the ms.
suggests an acc. plural (as ἀμοιβὰς)
written by error instead of a nom.
singular.
44 f. φοινίσσεται: XII. 164 f. μέλλον
ἄρα πρότερον δι|ῃᾶντα φοινίξειν Σκάμαν-
δρον.—χρυσοδίνας: the Pactolus (now
Sarabat) was said to carry gold-dust
down from Mt Tmolus: Aen. 10. 141
(Lydia) *ubi pinguia culta | exercentque
uiri, Pactolusque irrigat auro.* Pliny
H. N. 33. 21 § 1 (gold is found)
fluminum ramentis (in the rubbish
brought down by rivers), *ut in Tago
Hispaniae, Pado Italiae, Hebro Thraciae,*

Pactolo Asiae, Gange Indiae. He might
have added the *auro turbidus Hermus*
(Virg. *Geo.* 2. 137), into which the Pactolus
flows.
45 f. γυναῖκες...ἄγονται. Cp. *Il.* 9.
591—4 : καί οἱ κατέλεξεν ἅπαντα | κήδε'
ὅσ' ἀνθρώποισι πέλει τῶν ἄστυ ἀλῴη· |
ἄνδρας μὲν κτείνουσι, πόλιν δέ τε πῦρ
ἀμαθύνει, | τέκνα δέ τ' ἄλλοι ἄγουσι βαθυ-
ζώνους τε γυναῖκας.
47 τὰ πρόσθε δ' ἐχθρὰ φίλα, i.e.,
the pains of death; θανεῖν γλύκιστον.—
The ms. has τὰ πρόσθεν δ', against
metre. It is rather more likely that the
poet wrote πρόσθε (as in XVI. 45, the
only other place where he has the word),
than that δ' was interpolated. πρόσθεν
being much commoner than πρόσθε, the ν
might easily have been added.
Fraccaroli supposes that v. 43 began
with νῦν δ' εὖτε, that ἄγονται should have
only a comma after it, and that τὰ πρόσθε
δ' (etc.) is the last clause of the protasis, θανεῖν γλύκιστον being apodosis: or
else that τὰ πρόσθεν (without δ') ἐχθρὰ
φίλα is the apodosis. Rather, I think,
we have a series of abrupt utterances,
enumerating the calamities, down to
ἄγονται. Then, at τὰ πρόσθε δ' ἐχθρὰ
φίλα, he turns (as δέ marks) to his
conclusion.
48 ἀβροβάταν, 'a softly-stepping

ἄπτειν ξύλινον δόμον. ἔ[κλαγ]ον δὲ
50   παρθένοι, φίλας τ᾽ ἀνὰ ματρὶ χεῖρας

ἐπ. δ΄.   ἔβαλλον· ὁ γὰρ προφανὴς θνατοῖσιν ἔχθιστος φόνων·
ἀλλ᾽ ἐπεὶ δεινοῦ πυρὸς
λαμπρὸν διάι[σσεν μέ]νος,
55   Ζεὺς ἐπιστάσα[ς μελαγκευ]θὲς νέφος
σβέννυεν ξανθὰ[ν φλόγα.

στρ. ε΄.   ἄπιστον οὐδέν, ὅ τι θ[εῶν μέ]ριμνα
τεύχει· τότε Δαλογενὴς Ἀπόλλων
φέρων ἐς Ὑπερβορέους γέροντα
60   σὺν τανισφύροις κατένασσε κούραις

ἀντ. ε΄.   δι᾽ εὐσέβειαν, ὅτι μέγιστα θνατῶν
ἐς ἀγαθέαν ἀνέπεμψε Πυθώ.

49 ἔκλαγ]ον. The letter before ΟΝ was Γ or Τ.   **51** ΕΒΑΛΛΕΝ **A**, corr. **A**¹.
51 f. θνα-] **A** wrote ΘΙΑ, but then transfixed Ι, and wrote Ν above.   **53** πυρὸς]
The lower parts of the letters υρος are on fragment 26 K.   **54** διάι[σσεν.

attendant.' So in Eur. *Tro.* 820 Gany-
mede, the young cupbearer of Zeus,
is described as χρυσέαις ἐν οἰνοχοαῖς
ἁβρὰ βαίνων, 'softly moving' while he
ministers. (ἁβροβάτης occurs elsewhere
only in Aesch. *Pers.* 1072, where Xerxes
says to the Chorus of Persian elders,
γοᾶσθ᾽ ἁβροβάται,—*i.e.* 'treading softly,'
as in a procession of mourners.) The
use of the word here is significant. It
shows that Greeks had noted a *dainty
or mincing gait* as characterizing the
effeminate palace-slaves of Asiatic princes.
That trait would strike a Greek by its
strong contrast with the manly bearing
and the freedom in movement which
Hellenic youth acquired in gymnasium
and palaestra. Hence it is easy to
understand how ἁβροβάτης could denote,
—with only such aid as the context gives
here,—an Asiatic attendant. See Appendix.
49 δόμον, 'structure'; Nairn cp.
Pind. *P.* III. 67 ἀλλ᾽ ἐπεὶ τείχει θέσαν ἐν
ξυλίνῳ | σύγγονοι κούραν (when they
placed Coronis on the pyre).
50 ff. ἀνά..ἔβαλλον (tmesis), a stronger
ἀνεῖχον, lifted in supplication. Cp. 36 n.

—προφανής: a violent death is bitterest
when seen beforehand (instead of being
sudden and instantaneous). Cp. Soph.
O. C. 1440 προῦπτον Ἅιδην: Her. IX. 17
προόπτῳ θανάτῳ.—φόνων, forms of violent
death (like θανάτων). The plur. φόνοι
usu. = 'slaughters' (*O. C.* 1235, etc.).
55 Ζεύς, the cloud-gatherer, the giver
of rain or drought (Soph. fr. 481. 4), is a
fitter agent than Apollo here. On a red-
figured crater by Python (late 4th cent.
B.C.) Zeus appears as quencher of a pyre
on which Alcmena is about to be burned:
he has cast his thunderbolts, and the
Hyades are pouring rain on the pile
(*Journ. Hellen. Studies*, vol. XI. pl. 6 ;
see A. S. Murray *ib.* p. 226).—In fr. 25
Bacchylides has μελαγκευθὲς εἴδωλον (the
shade of Odysseus), where the word seems
to mean, '*shrouded in gloom*'; the spec-
tral form is dimly seen. If μελαγκευθὲς
was the word here, the verbal element
was active rather than passive: 'a cloud
carrying rain in its dark bosom.' Our
choice is limited by the virtual certainty
that the penult. was long (which excludes
e.g. μελαμβαθές). κελαινανθές, which
Herwerden suggests, had occurred to me

kindle the wooden pile. The maidens shrieked, and threw up their hands to their mother;

for the violent death which is foreseen is to mortals the most *epode* 4. bitter. But when the bright strength of the dread fire began to rush abroad, Zeus brought a dark rain-cloud above it, and began to quench the yellow flame.

Nothing is past belief that is wrought by the care of the *str.* 5. gods. Then Delos-born Apollo carried the old man to the Hyperboreans, with his daughters of slender ankle, and there gave him rest,

in requital of his piety; because of all mortals he had sent up *ant.* 5. the largest gifts to divine Pytho.

The scribe erroneously placed marks of diaeresis on the first I as well as on the second. **55** μελαγκευθὲς K. **56** φλόγα Palmer. **58** τεύχει] τεύχῃ Herwerden, Blass². **60** τανισφύροις MS.: τανυσφύροις Weir Smyth. **62** ἀνέπεμψε Housman and others (ἀν- lost after -αν): ἔπεμψε MS.

also: but it is not extant, though μελανθής is analogous.

57 ἄπιστον κ.τ.λ. : the γνώμη prefaces the incident, just as in XVI. 117 ff.: cp. Pind. *P. X.* 48 ff.

58 τεύχει need not be changed to τεύχῃ, though a subjunct. stands in the similar passage, XVII. 118. ὅστις often takes the indicative (instead of subjunct. with ἄν) in a relative sentence expressing a general condition: Soph. *Ant.* 178 f. ὅστις.. | μὴ τῶν ἀρίστων ἅπτεται βουλευμάτων : Thuc. II. 64 § 6 οἵτινες..ἥκιστα λυποῦνται.

Δαλογενής: the Ionian island-poet might naturally associate Apollo with his chief Ionian shrine. (In fr. 12 he says, ὦ περικλειτὲ Δᾶλ᾽, ἀγνοήσειν μὲν οὔ σ᾽ ἔλπομαι.) But the epithet has a special fitness here. Delian legend connected Delos with the earliest offerings of the Ὑπερβόρεοι to Apollo (Her. IV. 32—35).

59 φέρων ἐς Ὑπερβορέους. A passage of some mythological interest. The Hyperborean land is here (as nowhere else) a paradise to which a pious mortal is translated, without dying, by Apollo. It takes the place of the Homeric Ἠλύσιον πεδίον (*Od.* 4. 563), and of the posthomeric μακάρων νῆσοι (Hes. *Op.* 171, Pind. *O.* II. 78), in the Far West. Pindar describes the Hyperboreans as δᾶμον Ἀπόλλωνος θεράποντα (*O.* III.

13—16), who worship him with sacrifice, feast, and praise (*P.* X. 29 ff.). He clearly thinks of them as dwelling 'beyond Boreas' (cp. *I.* v. 23). Among them, Apollo passes his ἀποδημίαι from his southern shrines. Argive legend sent Heracles, Perseus, and Io thither,—but only as visitors.—As to the origin of the 'Hyperborean' legend, see Appendix.

60 τανισφύροις, with slender ankles.— The MS. has the wrong spelling ταυι- (instead of the correct τανυ-) again in v. 59 (τανισφύρου) and X. 55 (τανίφυλλον). The poet may have preferred that spelling in order to avoid the occurrence of υ in two successive syllables, as he avoids such a recurrence of α (see II. 1, n. on Φήμα). In *Od.* 13. 102 (etc.) the MSS. have τανύφυλλος, and in *Hom. hymn. Cer.* 2 τανύσφυρον.

62 ἀγαθέαν, 'divine': an epithet applied only to *places* connected with gods, —as to Pytho in Hes. *Theog.* 499, Pind. *P.* IX. 77. It probably comes from ἄγα (ἄγα-ν, cp. ἀγήνωρ) and θεο. ἀνέπεμψε, as to a sacred metropolis (cp. Polyb. I. 7 ἀναπεμφθέντων εἰς τὴν Ῥώμην). Herodotus (1. 51 f.), in speaking of the gifts sent to Delphi by Croesus, says ἀπέπεμψε (thrice) or ἀπέπεμπε,—the fitting word from a Lydian point of view, as ἀνέπεμψε is from that of a Greek.

ὅσοι γε μὲν Ἑλλάδ' ἔχουσιν, οὔτι[ς,
ὦ μεγαίνητε Ἱέρων, θελήσει

65 ἐπ. ε'. φάμ]εν σέο πλείονα χρυσὸν
Λοξίᾳ πέμψαι βροτῶν.
εὖ λέγ]ειν πάρεστιν, ὅσ-
τις μὴ φθόνῳ πιαίνεται,
θεοφι]λῆ φίλιππον ἄνδρ' ἀρήϊον,
70   τεθμ]ίου σκᾶπτρον Διὸς

στρ. ς'. ἰοπλό]κων τε μέρο[ς ἔχοντ]α Μουσᾶν·
ὡς δ' ἐν] Μαλέᾳ ποτέ, [χεῖμα δαί]μων
ἐπ' ἔθ]νος ἐφάμερον α[ἰψ' ἴησι.
καίρι]α σκοπεῖς· βραχ[ὺς ἄμμιν αἰών·

75 ἀντ. ς'. δολό]εσσα δ' ἐλπὶς ὑπ[ὸ κέαρ δέδυκεν
ἐφαμ]ερίων· ὁ δ' ἄναξ [Ἀπόλλων
ὁ βουκό]λος εἶπε Φέρη[τος υἷι·

63 ὅσοι γε μὲν] γε added by Wilamowitz, Blass and others.—The paragraphus, which should follow 64, is wrongly placed in the MS. after 63.   **65** φάμεν Thomas. There is a faint trace of E before N.—[σ]έο Palmer.   **66** βροτῶν Nairn : βροτῷ K. The faint trace after ω might belong either to I or to N.   **67 f.** εὖ | λέγειν Blass, Platt, a.o.: the trace before EIN suits either Γ or T. (εὐλογεῖν Jurenka.)—ὃς | τις μὴ Palmer.—ἰαίνεται A : π added above by **A³**.   **69** θεοφιλῆ Herwerden : so Jurenka, and Blass². (εὐθαλῆ Bl.¹)—ἀρήϊον Blass : an apostrophe is traceable after ἄνδρ' : one fragment supplies ρηιο and another (21 b) the final ν.   **70** ....ΙΟΥ τεθμ]ίου Blass (or δαμίου): ὀλβ]ίου Jurenka, which is too little for the space.   **71** The letters -α Μον,

63 ὅσοι γε μὲν Ἑλλάδ' ἔχουσιν,—as distinguished from non-Hellenes; the poet is not prepared to say that Hieron had surpassed Croesus: hence γε is right. Remark that μέν, added to γε here, merely emphasizes the limitation (as in ἐγὼ μέν, etc.). This is not the Ionic γε μέν in the sense of γε μήν ('however,' *Il.* 2. 703 etc., Her. VII. 152), which occurs below in v. 90.
64 ὦ μεγαίνητε Ἱέρων. The hiatus before Ἱέρων, with lengthening of ε, is remarkable. A strong aspiration of ἱ would help to explain it; and there may be also a metrical reason, viz., a slight pause after the fifth foot. In 92 (Μοῦσά νιν τρέφει. Ἱέρων, σὺ δ' ὄλβου) the hiatus occurs at the same place; but there the full stop after τρέφει makes a difference. That verse may, however, make us more cautious in assuming that v. 64 is corrupt. (Wilamowitz suggests ὦ μεγαίνητ' ὦ: A. Ludwich, ὦ μεγ' αἰνηθείς.)—Ἱέρων (like

ἱερός) never had Ϝ.
65 f. φάμεν (Aeolic)=φάναι, Pind. *O.* I. 35, III. 38, *N.* VIII. 19.—Λοξίᾳ: a title given to Apollo especially in his oracular character, owing to the popular derivation from λοξός ('oblique,' in ref. to indirect, ambiguous responses): Soph. *O. T.* 853 (n.).
67 f. εὖ λέγειν πάρεστιν..ὅστις μὴ κ.τ.λ. The antecedent to ὅστις is τούτῳ understood (cp. Soph. *Ant.* 35 f. ὃς ἂν τούτων τι δρᾷ, | φόνον πρόκεισθαι): 'any man who is not envious may well praise,' etc.—πιαίνεται, battens on envy, feeds his heart on it: Pind. *P.* II. 55 ψογερὸν Ἀρχίλοχον, βαρυλόγοις ἔχθεσιν | πιαινόμενον.
69 θεοφιλῆ suits the space, and is appropriate: cp. IV. 1—3, and v. 1 (εὔμοιρε). Pind. *I.* v. 65 f. πόλιν | θεοφιλῆ: Plat. *Phileb.* 39 E δίκαιος ἀνὴρ καὶ εὐσεβὴς..ἆρ' οὐ θεοφιλής ἐστιν;
70 τεθμίου, Doric for θεσμίου (Pind.

But of all who now live in Hellas there is not one, illustrious Hieron,

who will say that he has sent more gold to Loxias than thou epode 5. hast. Well may any man, who does not batten on envious thoughts, praise the favourite of the gods, the lover of horses, the warrior, who bears the sceptre of justice-guarding Zeus,

and has fellowship with the Muses of violet locks. [? But, as oft str. 6. at Malea, the god sends sudden stress of trouble on the children of a day. Thou lookest to the needs of the time : our life is short ;]

but deceitful Hope has crept into the hearts of men, children ant. 6. of a day. Yet the lord Apollo [, the shepherd,] said to the son of Pheres :—

with ων (the last of v. 72) below, are on fr. 21 a : -σᾶν on fr. 21 b (placed by Blass). **72** ποτ(ε) is certain : as in v. 23 a later hand has indicated a correction of Π into Κ (κοτε).—Before ΩΝ (fr. 21 a) there are distinct traces of an upright stroke, with a slight trace of a stroke joining this from the left ; Μ is possible, but doubtful. **73** The trace before ΟС is merely an upright stroke, | , but such as to suggest Ν.— On fr. 21 a, below the final ΩΝ of 72, there is a very faint trace (little more than a dot) of the bottom of a letter which was the last of v. 73. Blass thinks that it was Ι : but Ν is equally possible. **74** After σκοπεῖς something has been deleted (σ?). **75** δολόεσσα...ὑπὸ κέαρ δέδυκεν J.: δολόεσσα...ὑποφέρει μερίμνας Wilamowitz. **77** .....ΛΟC] The Λ is not quite certain, but the traces point to it. ὁ βουκόλος conj. Κ.: ἐὼν φίλος Blass: ἑκαβόλος J.—(τοιόνδ' ἔπος Wilamowitz: τοιοῦτ' ἔπος Jurenka : but even if Π could be assumed, the space is too small for this.) —υἶι Platt, Wackernagel (υἱί Wilam.).

N. XI. 27 ἑορτὰν Ἡρακλέος τέθμιον) : the Zeus of law and justice, under whom Hieron is the guardian of civic order : cp. IV. 3 ἀστύθεμίν θ' Ἱέρωνα : Pind. O. I. 12 (Hieron) θεμιστεῖον ὃς ἀμφέπει σκᾶπτον. But θέσμιος does not elsewhere occur as an epithet of Zeus (nor does δάμιος, the other word suggested by Blass). ξεινίου (Nairn) seems too special for the context. **71** μέρος ἔχοντα Μουσᾶν : cp. n. on I. 41. Hieron was said to have been, like Gelon, utterly indifferent to μουσική and literature, until the enforced leisure of an illness gave him a love for them, which thenceforth was ardent. (Aelian *V. H.* 4. 15 : ἐπεὶ δὲ αὐτῷ συνηνέχθη νοσῆσαι, μουσικώτατος ἀνθρώπων ἐγένετο.) **72—74** All that is certain as to the sense of these mutilated verses is that they formed a transition from the theme of Hieron's achievements (69—71) to that of the *brevity and insecurity of life* (75—92). It would seem that the letters ΜΑΛΕΑΙ must be either (1) Μαλέᾳ, or (2) part of δειμαλέᾳ or ρωμαλέᾳ. (1) Malea was a proverbial terror to sailors (Strabo VIII. p. 378). This ode was written after

the Olympian festival of 468 : Hieron died of his disease in 467. At this time (as verses 85—92 hint) it must have been known that he could not live long. Verses 72 f., as I tentatively restore them above, would express a general γνώμη ('trouble oft comes suddenly on mortals'), veiling a reference to the fact that Hieron's malady had lately become worse. καίρια σκοπεῖς would be a tribute to his fortitude and resignation : he is calmly taking such measures as his state requires. Such a context would certainly agree well with the tone of 75—92.—(2) If the word in 72 was (δει)μαλέᾳ (with χειρί), the sense may have been : 'formerly thy hand was terrible in battle ; but now thou lookest for solace from the Muses.' See Appendix, where both alternatives are more fully examined. **75** δολόεσσα δ' ἐλπὶς κ.τ.λ. In the immediately preceding words the poet had said, in effect, 'life is short and uncertain.' *But* hope beguiles men into looking for an indefinite term of prosperity. **77** Apollo served as βουφορβός to Admetus, son of Pheres, and king of

Col. 5   θνατὸν ἐῦντα χρὴ διδύμους ἀέξειν

ἐπ. ς΄. γνώμας, ὅτι τ᾽ αὔριον ὄψεαι
80   μοῦνον ἀλίου φάος,
χὤτι πεντήκοντ᾽ ἔτεα
ζωὰν βαθύπλουτον τελεῖς.
ὅσια δρῶν εὔφραινε θυμόν· τοῦτο γὰρ
κερδέων ὑπέρτατον.

85 στρ. ζ΄. φρονέοντι συνετὰ γαρύω· βαθὺς μὲν
αἰθὴρ ἀμίαντος· ὕδωρ δὲ πόντου
οὐ σάπεται· εὐφροσύνα δ᾽ ὁ χρυσός·
ἀνδρὶ δ᾽ οὐ θέμις, πολιὸν π[αρ]έντα

ἀντ. ζ΄. γῆρας, θάλειαν αὖτις ἀγκομίσσαι
90   ἥβαν. ἀρετᾶ[ς] γε μ[ὲ]ν οὐ μινύθει
βροτῶν ἅμα σ[ώμα]τι φέγγος, ἀλλὰ
Μοῦσά νιν τρ[έφει]. Ἱέρων, σὺ δ᾽ ὄλβου

ἐπ. ζ΄. κάλλιστ᾽ ἐπεδ[είξ]αο θνατοῖς
ἄνθεα· πράξα[ντι] δ᾽ εὖ

78 ΕΤΤΑΝ Α—a corrector (Α²?) added Ν above the line between Υ and Τ, and transfixed the final Ν.   88 παρέντα J.   89 ΑΓΚΟΜΙCΑΙ ms.: corr. K.
91 σώματι J. K. Ingram.

Pherae in Thessaly; having been doomed by Zeus to become a mortal's thrall, because he had slain the Cyclopes (Eur. *Alc.* 1—8). Kenyon's supplement, ὁ βουκόλος, is very attractive.—υἱι: the last syllable of this verse must be short. Cp. XII. 100 υἷας.

78 εὖντα = ἐόντα: rare, but found in Theocr. II. 3. Cp. XVIII. 23 n. ἀέξειν, make to grow, 'nourish': *Od.* 17. 489 ἐν μὲν κραδίῃ μέγα πένθος ἄεξε.

79—82 ὅτι τ᾽ αὔριον κ.τ.λ. This is a general precept from a friendly god. (It was he who, when the time approached for Admetus to die, persuaded the Moirae to accept another life in exchange: Eur. *Alc.* 9—14.) '*Be prepared to die to-morrow*:—use your time as if you had none to spare. *But reflect also that you may live for many years,*—and exercise forethought accordingly.' πεντήκοντ᾽ ἔτεα, acc. of duration, 'for fifty (*i.e.* an indefinite number of) years': there is no allusion to Hieron's actual age.

βαθύπλουτον (used by Aesch. and

Eur.) like βαθύδοξος (Pind. *P.* 1. 66), etc. Cp. Soph. *Ai.* 130 μακροῦ πλούτου βάθει. —τελεῖς, accomplish, carry on to its goal.

83 ὅσια δρῶν εὔφραινε θυμόν: *i.e.* so long as you are doing your duty to gods and men, keep a cheerful spirit, and enjoy the present aright, without counting on the future. This is in a higher strain than *carpe diem.*

85—87 φρονέοντι συνετὰ γαρύω. Veiled counsels of resignation and of comfort to the moribund Hieron.

These three verses are remarkable for the open imitation of Pindar. With φρονέοντι κ.τ.λ. cp. φωνάεντα συνετοῖσιν (*O.* II. 93, 476 B.C.). The short clauses (from βαθὺς to χρυσὸς) copy Pindar's abruptness, and his splendour: cp. *O.* I. 1 ff. (also of 476 B.C.), ἄριστον μὲν ὕδωρ· ὁ δὲ χρυσὸς αἰθόμενον πῦρ ἅτε διαπρέπει κ.τ.λ. But the strain hardly suits Bacchylides: a lapse comes at the tame word εὐφροσύνα (which has to mean, 'a joy *for ever*'). Blass, indeed, in his

' As a mortal, thou must nourish each of two forebodings ;—

that to-morrow's sunlight will be the last that thou shalt see ; epode 6.
or that for fifty years thou wilt live out thy life in ample wealth.
Act righteously, and be of a cheerful spirit : that is the supreme
gain.'

I speak words of meaning for the wise : the depths of air str. 7.
receive no taint; the waters of the sea are incorrupt; gold is
a joy : but for a man it is not lawful to pass by hoary eld,

and to recover the bloom of youth.   Yet the radiance of manly ant. 7.
worth wanes not with the mortal body ; it is cherished by the
Muse.   O Hieron,

thou hast shown to mankind the fairest flowers of good fortune. epode 7.
Toward one who has so prospered,

2nd ed., changes it to a word which is
not extant, εὐχροσύνα (as = 'a glory of
colour'); citing Theognis 451 f. τοῦ (gold)
χροιῆς καθύπερθε μέλας οὐχ ἅπτεται ἰός, |
οὐδ' εὑρώς, αἰεὶ δ' ἄνθος ἔχει καθαρόν.

88 παρέντα: a mortal cannot *pass by*
old age, and enter (after middle life) on
a second youth. Cp. Plat. *Rep.* 460 E
ἐπειδὰν τὴν ὀξυτάτην δρόμου ἀκμὴν παρῇ,
' when a man has passed that moment
in life's course when the passions are
keenest.' Soph. *O. C.* 1229 εὖτ' ἂν τὸ
νέον παρῇ, when he has seen youth go
by.—The initial π being certain, the
only alternative is **προέντα**: which would
be required to mean, 'having let go,'
'having given up,' old age; a sense
which, even if it were satisfactory, would
rather demand προέμενον. Further, the
space in the papyrus seems too large for
προέντα: in this MS. the letter Ο takes up
less room than A.

90 ἀρετᾶς γε μέν. Here γε μὲν is
equivalent to the Attic γε μήν, 'however':
cp. 63 n.
The MS. has μινύθει, ‿ ‿ ‿ where we
expect ‿ – –. The ode contains seven
strophes and seven antistrophes. There
are therefore thirteen verses which answer
metrically to this. In two of them (72
and 76) the ending is lost. In all the
other eleven, a bacchius (‿ – –) and not
an anapaest, answers to μινύθει. And to
these eleven, verse 76 may be added,
since 'Απόλλων is practically certain there.
The probabilities, then, are very strongly
against a solitary exception here ; even if
such a variation was admissible. Crusius

and Blass hold that the substitution of
– ‿ ‿ – for – ‿ – – in this place of the
verse was legitimate. They refer to
Alcman's partheneion (Bergk, vol. III.
30 ff.). There we have remains of seven
strophes. Of these, strophes 1, 3, and
7 end with – ‿ ‿ –, while 4, 5, and 6 end
with – ‿ – –. (The close of strophe 2 is
lost.) Bergk suggests, however, that in
Alcman's poem these *clausulae* were not
freely interchangeable; but that he varied
the measure in the last verse of his strophe
by rule, on some plan connected with the
nature of the subject-matter. In any
case, it seems rash to take the Alcman
fragment (in which much is obscure) as a
sufficient warrant for the isolated anomaly
here.
I have little doubt that **μινύθει** is
corrupt. The poet may have written
μινύνθη or μινύθη (a gnomic aor.). ἐμινύθη
is the vulg. reading, though a doubtful
one, in Hippocr. 3. 63 and 3. 219. Cp.
v. 151. No pres. μινύω or μινύνθω is
extant.

92 ff. τρέφει. 'Ιέρων. On the hiatus,
see v. 64 n.—**ὄλβου..ἄνθεα**: cp. Pind. *P.*
X. 17 f. ἔποιτο μοῖρα.. | ..πλοῦτον ἀνθεῖν
σφίσιν : *P.* 4. 131 εὐζώας ἀώτον.

94 πράξαντι δ' εὖ κ.τ.λ. Silence is
not meet in the case of (in regard to) one
who has prospered. Cp. v. 187—190,
χρὴ δ' ἀλαθείας χάριν | αἰνεῖν... | εἴ τις εὖ
πράσσοι βροτῶν.—The dative would more
naturally denote the person who ought
not to be silent (Soph. *Ai.* 293 γυναιξὶ
κόσμον ἡ σιγὴ φέρει): but εὖ πράξαντι
cannot here refer to the poet.

95 οὐ φέρει κόσμον σιω-
πά· σὺν δ' ἀλαθείᾳ καλῶν
καὶ μελιγλώσσου τις ὑμνήσει χάριν
Κηΐας ἀηδόνος.

IV.

ΤΩΙ ΑΥΤΩΙ

<ΙΠΠΟΙΣ> ΠΥΘΙΑ.

στρ. α´. 1 Ἔτι Συρακοσίαν φιλεῖ
2 πόλιν ὁ χρυσοκόμας Ἀπόλλων,
3 ἀστύθεμίν θ' Ἱέρωνα γεραίρει·
4 τρίτον γὰρ παρ' ὀμφα]λὸν ὑψιδείρου χθονὸς
5 Πυθιόνικ[ος ἀείδε]ται
6 ὠκυπόδ[ων ἀρετᾷ] σὺν ἵππων.
7 παρὰ δ' εὔρροον Ἀλφεὸν
8 δὶς Ἥρας (ϝ)οι εὐρυβί]ας ἀλέκτωρ
9 γέρας ἔνειμ' ἑκόν]τι νόῳ,
10 πρευμενὴς δ' ἐπάκουεν] ὕμνους

στρ. β´. 1 κελαδέοντας, οἷς ἰσόρ-
2 ροπον ἔχοντα Δίκ]ας τάλαν[τον
Col. 6 3 Δεινομένεός κ' ἐγερα[ίρο]μεν υἱόν.

96 καλέων Jurenka. **98** In ἀηδόνος the scribe had written O for Δ, but corrected it. **IV.** The title, in minuscule letters, has been added (by **A**³?) in the left margin. ΙΠΠΟΙC is inserted by K. **4** The faint traces after ΓΑΡ indicate Π rather than Λ, *i.e.* παρ' (Blass) rather than ἀμφ'. **6** ἀρετᾷ Crusius, καμάτῳ K.: στεφάνοις W. Christ. **8** AC ΑΛΕΚΤΩΡ] Blass², who writes ἇς, finds an

---

96 σὺν δ' ἀλαθείᾳ καλῶν: 'and along with his (Hieron's) genuine glories' (lit. 'reality of glories') 'men will praise also the charm of the melodious nightingale of Ceos.' For this sense of καλά, cp. II. 6: for ἀλαθείᾳ, Thuc. VI. 33 § 1 τοῦ ἐπίπλου τῆς ἀληθείας, the 'reality' of it. We have already found in this poem a trace of Pindar's first *Olympian* (85 ff., n.). In the last words of that ode, Pindar links his own fame with Hieron's: εἴη σέ τε τοῦτον ὑψοῦ χρόνον πατεῖν, ἐμέ τε τοσσάδε νικαφόροις | ὁμιλεῖν, πρόφαντον σοφίᾳ καθ' Ἕλληνας ἐόντα παντᾷ. Bacchylides does the like here, only in his gentler Ionian fashion.

If καλῶν were the participle, the sense would be: 'and calling (the poet) so with truth, men will praise the charm of the .. nightingale of Ceos.' But then we should expect καλέων: cp. VII. 40 ὑμνέων, and (without synizesis) V. 152 ὀλιγοσθενέων, XII. 118 κλονέων. In I. 34, certainly, we find βολοῖ (=βολέοι). The presumption, however, is in favour of καλῶν being the noun.

IV. 3 ἀστύθεμιν, 'just ruler of cities.' ἀστυ- here defines the relation of θέμις: the compound means, 'concerned with (upholding) themis in the city': cp. *Hymn. Hom.* 5. 103 θεμιστοπόλων βασιλήων.—See on III. 70.

silence is not meet. And along with thy genuine glories men shall praise also the charm of the sweet singer, the nightingale of Ceos.

IV.

For Hieron, victor in the four-horse chariot-race at Delphi.

Still is Syracuse dear to Apollo of the golden locks; still str. 1.
does he honour Hieron, just ruler of cities, who now for the third time, at earth's central shrine beneath the lofty cliffs, is hymned as a Pythian victor, through the prowess of his swift steeds. [Twice, too, by the fair stream of Alpheus, was the prize given to him with good will by Hera's wide-ruling lord; and graciously did Zeus hearken to those resounding songs

wherewith] we used to honour the son of Deinomenes, who str. 2.
holds the scales of Justice in even poise.

apostrophe before it: but Kenyon does not think that the faint trace suits an apostrophe. **11 f.** Blass inserts frag. 19 K., which gives parts of the endings of two verses, viz. ICOP, and below that ACTAΛAN. *ἰσόρροπον* Headlam: Blass³. **13** Δεινομένεος κ'] The κ̓ is clear and certain.—ἐγεραίρομεν] The letters E.EPA...MEN are certain. After the first E, the top of Γ is also traceable.

4 τρίτον. This victory with the τέθριππον was gained by Hieron at the Pythia of 470 B.C. He had twice been victorious there with the κέλης, viz. in 482 and 478. He had also won with the κέλης at Olympia in 476 and 472. **ὀμφαλόν:** Pind. *P.* XI. 9 Πυθῶνά τε καὶ..γᾶς ὀμφαλόν: Soph. *O. T.* 398 τὸν ἄθικτον γᾶς ἐπ' ὀμφαλόν. The omphalos in the Delphian temple (Aesch. *Eum.* 40) was a large white stone, supposed to mark the centre of the earth (Pind. *P.* IV. 74: Livy 38. 48 *Delphos, umbilicum orbis terrarum*). **ὑψιδείρου,** with high ridges or cliffs (δειρή = δειράς, Pind. *O.* IX. 63 Μαιναλίαισιν ἐν δειραῖς). Above Delphi rise the cliffs which were called Φαιδριάδες, with two peaks (the δίλοφος πέτρα of Soph. *Ant.* 1126). **6 ἀρετᾷ** suits the space. It is slightly prosaic here; yet cp. Pind. X. 23 ποδῶν ἀρετᾷ κρατήσας. Another possible word is ἀέθλοις: cp. Pind. *P.* IX. 125 σὺν δ' ἀέθλοις (‿ ‿ -)..ποδῶν, and *N.* IX. 9 ἱππίων ἄθλων. We might prefer στεφάνοις, but it is too long for the lacuna. καμάτῳ would be too suggestive of *painful* toil.

For σὺν following its case, cp. *Od.* 9. 332 ἐμοὶ σὺν μοχλὸν ἀείρας: Pind. *N.* x. 48 δρόμῳ σὺν ποδῶν. **7—13** Here there was doubtless a mention of Hieron's two victories at Olympia, parallel with the notice of them in the seventh verse of the second strophe (v. 17). In v. 8 ἀλέκτωρ was, I conjecture, Hera's spouse; as Apollo (v. 2) gives the crown at Delphi, so Zeus at Olympia. Cp. X. 51 f. ξανθᾶς παρέδρου | σεμνοῦ Διὸς εὐρυβία, n. What Blass takes for a mark of elision before as may be a trace of the accent on εὐρυβίας. (For ἀλέκτωρ = *maritus* cp. Soph. fr. 767 οὑμὸς δ' ἀλέκτωρ αὐτὸν ἦγε πρὸς μύλην: Lycophron 1094, where Tzetzes explains ἀλεκτόρων by ὁμολέκτρων, συζύγων.) I show above, *exempli gratia*, how vv. 7—9 might be restored.

In vv. 11, 12 Blass places fr. 19 K., containing the letters I(?)COP, and below them ACTAΛAN, which he completes thus:—ἰσόρ-|ροπον ἔχοντα Δίκας τάλαν-τον. This collocation of the fragment can scarcely be deemed certain; but it is possible. In v. 13 Blass deletes the κ' of the MS. after Δεινομένεος. But, even if,

4 πάρεστίν νιν ἀγχιάλοισ[ι Κρίσ]ας μυχοῖς
15 5 μοῦνον ἐπιχθονίων τάδε
6   μησάμενον στεφάνοις ἐρέπτειν
7 δύο τ᾽ ὀλυμπιονίκας
8 ἀείδειν. τί φέρτερον ἢ θεοῖσιν
9 φίλον ἐόντα παντο[δα]πῶν
20 10 λαγχάνειν ἄπο μοῖρα[ν ἐσ]θλῶν;

V.

< ΤΩΙ ΑΥΤΩΙ

ΚΕΛΗΤΙ ΟΛΎΜΠΙΑ. >

στρ. α΄.   1 Εὔμοιρε Συρακοσίων
2   ἱπποδινήτων στραταγέ,
3 γνώσει μὲν ἰοστεφάνων
4   Μοισᾶν γλυκύδωρον ἄγαλμα, τῶν γε νῦν
5 αἴ τις ἐπιχθονίων,

14 ΠΑΡΕCΤΙΑΝ] πάρεστίν νιν (with τρίτον γὰρ παρ᾽ in 4) Blass: or πάρεστι νῦν
(with...ἀμφ᾽ in 4): πάρεστι μὰν Wilam.—ΑΓΧΙΑΛΟΙC. Between this word and
ΑCΜΤΧΟΙC there is room for at least five letters; probably for six (assuming one or

as Blass thinks, κ᾽ was made from another
letter (ε?),—which is doubtful,—we are
not warranted in deleting it; least of all
in a mutilated passage. κ᾽ ἐγεραίρομεν
may mean, 'we used to honour'; implying that, on each of the two occasions
when Hieron won at Olympia, there were
several songs in his praise. The alternative explanation of κε would be to
understand it in the ordinary conditional
sense :—'(If we had not been unavoidably
prevented,) we should have been honouring Hieron.' The poet would then be
excusing himself for absence from the
celebration of Hieron's Pythian victory;
or, perhaps, for not having sent some
worthier tribute than this short song.
In view of the whole context, however,
this interpretation seems less probable. In
v. 10 ὕμνους are presumably songs sung
at Olympia. With these data, vv. 10
and 11 might be tentatively completed
somewhat in the manner suggested above.
For ἰσόρροπον..Δίκας τάλαντον cp.
XVI. 25 f. Δίκας ῥέπει τάλαντον (with n.
there). Praise for even-handed justice
was naturally acceptable to a τύραννος,

more especially, perhaps, if his claim to
it was disputable; and in Hieron's case
that praise is frequently given or implied.
See above, v. 3 : III. 70: v. 6 (εὐθύδικον):
Pind. O. I. 12; VI. 93 ff.: P. III. 70 ff.—
See Appendix.

14—18 πάρεστίν νιν seems a true
correction of the MS. παρ᾽ ἑστίαν. (The
form of A in the MS. would help a change
of N into A.) This assumes τρίτον γὰρ
παρ᾽ in v. 4. If, instead of παρ᾽, ἀμφ᾽
stood there, πάρεστι νῦν could stand here.
But we note that the eighth v. of the strophe
also begins with ⏑ – – (v. 18, ἀείδειν). The
sense is :—'We can crown him with
wreaths as one who, alone of men, has
compassed these triumphs in the recesses
of Crisa near the sea (=at Delphi); and
also sing of two Olympian victories.'
τάδε, —three equestrian victories at
Delphi,—a record which the poet avers
to be unique. The point of νῦν is
exultation in the total of Hieron's victories at the two greatest festivals.
παρ᾽ ἑστίαν, if sound, would mean
either 'to' or 'at' (cp. IX. 29 f.) Hieron's
hearth. Intrinsically this is quite possible.

We can crown him with wreaths as one who, alone of
mortals, has compassed such deeds in the hill-girt vale of Crisa
by the sea, while we can sing also of two Olympian victories
What is better than to find favour with the gods, and to receive
a full portion of blessings in every kind?

V.

To Hieron, victor in the horse-race at Olympia. (476 B.C.)

Blest war-lord of Syracuse, city of whirling chariots, thou, str. 1.
if any mortal, wilt rightly estimate the sweet gift brought in thy
honour by the Muses of violet crown.

more to be thin). The letter next before AC may have been either P or C : all that
remains of it is a short curving stroke from the top.—ἀγχιάλοισιν Αἴτνας K. : ἀγχιάλοισι
Κούρας Wilam.: Κρίσας J.: Κίρρας Blass² (Γαίας, = Delphi, Bl.¹): γαίας Jurenka.
20 ἐσθλῶν Wilam., Blass: ἀέθλων K.

V. The MS. omits the title, which is supplied by K. In the other cases (odes I,
IX, XII, XV) where the title is wanting the MS. is mutilated.

But ἐρέπτειν and ἀείδειν cannot tolerably
be made infinitives of purpose (' *in order
to* crown,' etc.). Given παρ' ἑστίαν, they
must be governed by some verb or
participle of 'wishing' or 'purposing.'
But that must have preceded v. 13. And
on such a hypothesis, the sentence as a
whole becomes extremely complex and
cumbrous, in a manner foreign to this
poet. With πάρεστι, on the other hand,
the construction is clear and simple.
The diction is also characteristic: see
III. 65 εὖ λέγειν πάρεστιν (n.).
Κρίσας μυχοῖς, with μνησάμενον. Crisa
was about two miles w.s.w. of Delphi.
Cp. Pind. *P.* VI. 17 f. εὔδοξον ἅρματι
νίκαν | Κρισαίαις ἐνὶ πτυχαῖς. Soph. *El.*
180 (of Orestes at Delphi) ὁ τὰν Κρῖσαν |
βούνομον ἔχων ἀκτάν,—which illustrates
ἀγχιάλοισι.—See Appendix.
17 ὀλυμπιονίκας from ὀλυμπιονίκη, a
word used by Antiphon, fr. 131 ὀλυμπιο-
νῖκαι καὶ πυθιονῖκαι καὶ οἱ τοιοῦτοι ἀγῶνες.
18 ff. θεοῖσιν φίλον ἐόντα : such
prosperity is indeed enviable when it is
conferred *by the favour of the gods*, and
not gained by unworthy means.—παντοδαπῶν.. ἐσθλῶν, 'good things of every
kind.' To power, wealth, warlike fame,
Hieron added success in the games.—If
we read ἀέθλων, the range of the thought
would be too narrow, and παντοδαπῶν
(bearing its local sense) too wide. Cp.
v. 50 (of Hieron) ὄλβιος ᾧτινι θεὸς | μοῖράν
τε καλῶν ἔπορεν κ.τ.λ.—λαγχάνειν ἄπο =
ἀπολαγχάνειν (to receive a *full* portion).
The preposition *after* the verb in tmesis

is very rare. *Il.* 2. 699 τότε δ' ἤδη ἔχεν
κάτα γαῖα μέλαινα. Aesch. *Pers.* 871
(πόλεις) εἰληλαμέναι πέρι πύργον (compassed with embattled walls): Eur.
Bacch. 554 τινάσσων ἄνα θύρσον (where
ἄνα should not be taken as vocative).
Cp. XVIII. 7.

V. 2 ἱπποδινήτων, whirled in chariots.
(In Aesch. *Theb.* 460 f. ἵππους.. δινεῖ is
said of the driver.) The reference is to
the distinction of Syracuse in chariot-
races: it seems improbable that there is
any allusion to the Syracusan cavalry
(though in Pind. *P.* II. 2, Syracuse is
ἀνδρῶν ἵππων τε σιδαροχαρμᾶν...τροφοί).
Syracusan coins of the time of Gelon
bear a *quadriga*, with a winged Νίκη
above (Gelon was victorious at Olympia).
On those of an earlier date a quadriga
appears without the Νίκη. (P. Gardner,
Types of Greek coins, Pl. II., and p. 107.)
στραταγέ. This may be merely a
poetical title, 'war-lord': as στραταγέτας
is said of Minos (XVI. 121), or as Creon,
βασιλεὺς of Thebes (Soph. *Ant.* 155), is
called στραταγός (*ib.* 8). It is also possible, however, that Hieron held the office
of στραταγὸς αὐτοκράτωρ, as Gelon seems
to have done at one time. Whether Gelon
or Hieron was ever formally styled βασιλεύς, is uncertain. Pindar calls Hieron
so (*O.* I. 23, *P.* III. 70): Bacchylides does
not; but the silence proves nothing.
See Appendix.
3—6 γνώσει...ὀρθῶς, wilt rightly re-
cognize it for what it is,—rightly *iudge*

6 ὀρθῶς· φρένα δ' εὐθύδικον
7 ἀτρέμ' ἀμπαύσας μεριμνᾶν
8 δεῦρ' ἐπάθρησον νόῳ,
9 ᾗ σὺν Χαρίτεσσι βαθυζώνοις ὑφάνας
10 ὕμνον ἀπὸ ζαθέας
11 νάσου ξένος ὑμετέραν πέμ-
12 πει κλεεννὰν ἐς πόλιν,
13 χρυσάμπυκος Οὐρανίας κλει-
14 νὸς θεράπων· ἐθέλει δὲ
15 γᾶρυν ἐκ στηθέων χέων

ἀντ. α'. 1 αἰνεῖν Ἱέρωνα. βαθὺν
2 δ' αἰθέρα ξουθαῖσι τάμνων
3 ὑψοῦ πτερύγεσσι ταχεί-

8 ἐπάθρησον H. Richards: ἄθρησον MS.   9 H MS.: ᾗ K. : ἤ Platt: ἦ Blass:
εἰ conj. Palmer.   13 f. κλει-νὸς] ΚΛΙΝΟC A, corr. A³.—The MS. wrongly

it: cp. Aesch. *Ag.* 795 προβατογνώ-
μων: *ib.* 1099 θεσφάτων γνώμων ἄκρος.
—ἰοστεφάνων: epithet of Persephone in
III. 2; of Thetis in XII. 122.—Μοισᾶν.
This Aeolic form, always used by Pindar,
occurs only here in Bacchylides, who has
the Ionic and Attic Μοῦσα nine times.
The Doric was Μῶσα (Alcman fr. 3, etc.).
—γλυκύδωρον ἄγαλμα, *i.e.* the ode: 'a
sweet gift brought in thy honour': for
ἄγαλμα, see on I. 74.—τῶν γε νῦν κ.τ.λ.:
cp. Pind. *O.* I. 103 ff. (written for this
same victory), πέποιθα δὲ ξένον | μή τιν'
ἀμφότερα καλῶν τε ϝίδριν ἅμμε καὶ
δύναμιν κυριώτερον | τῶν γε νῦν κλυταῖσι
δαιδαλωσέμεν ὕμνων πτυχαῖς. Thus both
poets say that Hieron has no living superior as a judge of poetry. The scholiast
on Pind. *P.* II. 166 is the authority for
the statement that Hieron preferred the
odes of Bacchylides to those of Pindar
(παρὰ Ἱέρωνι τὰ Βακχυλίδου ποιήματα
προκρίνεσθαι).
6 f. εὐθύδικον: cp. III. 70, and IV. 3.
εὐθυδίκαν would be possible, but is not
required by metre. A vowel at the beginning of the seventh verse follows
πίσυνος in 21, βορέα in 46, Ἀίδα in 61,
and ἀρηϊφίλου in 166.
ἀτρέμ' ἀμπαύσας: the adv. is proleptic,
the phrase being a compressed mode of
saying, ἀμπ. ὥστε ἀτρέμα ἔχειν.
8 The MS. reading, δεῦρ' ἄθρησον νόῳ,

gives –‿–‿–, instead of –‿––‿–,
which we find in all the corresponding
verses. Blass defends the text by supposing that the second syllable of ἄθρησον
is prolonged. (He assumes the same
licence in IX. 15, where see n.) It is
far more probable that a syllable has
dropped out. Kenyon supplies σὺν (easily
lost after -σον). The phrase σὺν νόῳ is
usually found in negative sentences, as=
'without intelligence' (Her. VIII. 86 οὔτε
σὺν νόῳ ποιεόντων οὐδέν: Plat. *Crito* 48 C
τῶν ῥαδίως ἀποκτεινύντων...οὐδενὶ ξὺν νῷ).
Here the sense would be, 'with earnest
attention.' But there is a metrical objection, viz. the caesura after ἄθρησον:
see p. 97. I now prefer to read, with
Richards, ἐπάθρησον: cp. XII. 227 ἐπαθρήσαις. The sense of νόῳ will then be
adverbial, 'attentively.' Another possible
emendation would be δεῦρ' ἄθρησον εὐ-
νοέων. But we should then have to suppose that, after the loss of ΕΥ, ΝΟΕΩΝ
(written ΝΟΩΝ) became ΝΟΩΙ.—Cp.
Pind. *P.* II. 69 f. τὸ Καστόρειον δ' ἐν
Αἰολίδεσσι χορδαῖς θέλων | ἄθρησον.
9 f. The MS. has H. Should we read
(1) ᾗ, (2) ἤ, or (3) ἦ?
(1) ᾗ is best. We must then suppose,
indeed, that in the MS. the letter Ι has
been lost after H: but such a loss would
be very easy. δεῦρο distinctly suggests ᾗ.
'Look hither, with good heed,—to the

Suffer thy mind, ever upright in judgment, to have repose from
cares; bend thy thoughts hither, and see where a song woven
with the aid of the deep-girdled Graces is sent from a lovely
isle to your famous city by a guest-friend, a servant not in-
glorious of Urania whose locks are bound with gold. Fain is he
to pour forth his voice

in praise of Hieron. The eagle, cleaving the deep ether on ant. 1.
high with his swift tawny wings,

places κλεινὸς wholly in v. 14, though in the antistr. it rightly divides πνο-|αῖσιν
between v. 28 and v. 29: corr. K.   **16** αἰνεῖν] ΑΙΝΕΙ **A**: but the final N
has been added above the line (by **A²**?).

---

quarter in which (ᾗ) a poet is sending
his song.' The present πέμπει also supports the picturesque ᾗ: Hieron is invited
to note the advent of the poem, as if he
could see in imagination the ζαθέα νᾶσος
afar, and the ship on its way.
(2) ἢ (proposed by Platt) is also
possible. Then there is a full stop (or a
colon at least) after νόῳ. Pindar sometimes begins a sentence with ἢ (O. I. 28:
P. I. 47: N. VIII. 24). The objections to
ᾗ are (1) that after verse 8, δεῦρ' ἄθρησον
κ.τ.λ., a stop seems hardly fitting; and
(2) that ᾗ itself is here somewhat weak.
(3) ᾗ is read by Blass, who explains it as = 'whether.' But I can find
no example of ᾗ as 'whether' (=εἰ) in a
single indirect question. In Homer we
find, indeed, (1) ἠέ...ᾗ, 'whether'...'or':
Od. I. 174 ὄφρ' εὖ εἰδῶ | ἠὲ νέον μεθέπεις,
ἦ καὶ πατρώϊός ἐσσι | ξεῖνος.—Palmer pro-
posed to read εἰ.
σὺν Χαρίτεσσι βαθυζώνοις: for the
Charites as inspiring song, cp. VIII. 1,
XVIII. 5 f. Pindar has the same phrase
in a like context, P. IX. 1 ff. ἐθέλω... | σὺν
βαθυζώνοισιν ἀγγέλλων | Τελεσικράτη Χα-
ρίτεσσι γεγωνεῖν,—written probably in
474 (see Schröder's ed., p. 67), i.e.
about two years after the date of this
ode.—ὑφάνας: cp. XVIII. 8: Pind. fr.
179 ὑφαίνω δ' Ἀμαθονίδαις ποικίλον |
ἄνδημα ('a wreath of song').—ζαθέας:
cp. II. 7, X. 24: and see n. on ἀγαθέαν,
III. 62.
11 ξένος, 'guest-friend.' We do not
know when Bacchylides first visited
Syracuse. The date of this ode is 476.
It was in that year, or in 477, that his
uncle Simonides, according to Timaeus
(fr. 90, Müller vol. I. p. 214), effected
a reconciliation between Hieron and
Theron of Acragas. It seems probable

that, before this ode was written, Bacchylides had been the guest of Hieron, and
had thus become privileged to claim the
tie of ξενία. Pindar alludes to Hieron as
ξένον in O. I. 103.
This verse, and the corresponding v.
of the antistrophe (26), are longer by a
syllable than those which hold the same
places in the other four systems. But
the text is probably sound. See Appendix.
13 f. χρυσάμπυκος: Pind. P. III. 89
χρυσαμπύκων | ...Μοισᾶν. The ἄμπυξ, a
head-band, worn to confine the hair, was
often plated with gold or silver, and
sometimes set with gems. Artemis in
Eur. Hec. 465 has a χρυσέαν ἄμπυκα.
—κλεινός, though we have just had
κλεεννάν: a strong example of verbal
repetition, which the change of dialectic
form scarcely palliates. For similar instances in Sophocles, see n. on O. C.
554.—ἐθέλει: see on I. 52.
Verse 14, and the antistrophic v., 29,
are longer by a syllable than the corresponding verses of the other systems.
Here again, as in the similar case of
verses 11 and 26, the text appears sound.
See Appendix.
16 f. βαθὺν δ' αἰθέρα κ.τ.λ. Wide as
air is the path opened by Hieron's deeds:
strong as an eagle's is the poet's soaring
flight. The simile evidently involves
both points. But it is quite unnecessary
to suppose that this is a retort to Pindar,
who in O. II. 95—97 (written in this same
year, 476) implies that he is an eagle, and
that two other poets unnamed are crows.
The eagle, as an image for the poet,
occurs also in Pind. N. v. 20 f. (481 B.C.?),
and N. III. 80 ff. (circ. 469—459).
ξουθαῖσι...πτερύγεσσι: 'tawny.' The
golden or mountain eagle (aquila chrys-

4 αἷς αἰετὸς εὐρυάνακτος ἄγγελος
20 5 Ζηνὸς ἐρισφαράγου
6 θαρσεῖ κρατερᾷ πίσυνος
7 ἰσχύϊ, πτάσσοντι δ᾽ ὄρνι-
8 χες λιγύφθογγοι φόβῳ·
9 οὔ νιν κορυφαὶ μεγάλας ἴσχουσι γαίας,
25 10 οὐδ᾽ ἁλὸς ἀκαμάτας

Col. 7 11 δυσπαίπαλα κύματα· νωμᾶ-
12 ται δ᾽ ἐν ἀτρύτῳ χάει
13 λεπτότριχα σὺν ζεφύρου πνοι-
14 αἷσιν ἔθειραν ἀρίγνω-
30 15 τος μετ᾽ ἀνθρώποις ἰδεῖν·

ἐπ. α'. 1 τὼς νῦν καὶ ἐμοὶ μυρία πάντᾳ κέλευθος
2 ὑμετέραν ἀρετὰν
3 ὑμνεῖν, κυανοπλοκάμου θ᾽ ἕκατι Νίκας
4 χαλκεοστέρνου τ᾽ Ἄρηος,
35 5 Δεινομένευς ἀγέρω-
6 χοι παῖδες· εὖ ἔρδων δὲ μὴ κάμοι θεός.

22 TACCONTI **A**: the first T corrected to Π, and T added above the line (by **A²**?).
23 φόβῳ] ΦΟΙΒΩΙ MS. 24 ΜΕΓΑΛΑΙC **A**: I transfixed (by **A²**?). 26 ΝΩ-
ΜΑΙ **A**: the I has been transfixed, either by the scribe himself (as seems probable), or

aetus) 'is of a rich dark brown, with the elongated feathers of the neck, especially on the nape, light tawny, in which imagination sees a golden hue.' (Prof. Alfred Newton in *Enc. Brit.* VII. p. 590.)
20 ἐρισφαράγου: epithet of Poseidon (Γαιηόχου) in *Hom. hymn.* 3. 187. Pindar also used the word (Eustath. on *Od.* ι p. 1636. 7).
22 ὄρνιχες. The forms from the stem ὀρνιχ-, always used by Pindar, occur also in Alcman (fr. 54), and Theocritus (5. 48, 7. 47). The Alexandrians called this inflexion Aeolic (cp. Meister *Gr. Dialekte*, p. 152): it was also Doric.
26 f. δυσπαίπαλα κύματα, waves which offer *a rough and difficult path* to the mariner. (Compare Marlowe's phrase in *Dido* III. 3, 'Neptune's hideous hills.') δυσπαίπαλος (formed from παιπάλλω, Hesych., = σείω) occurs in Archil. fr. 115 βήσσας ὀρέων δυσπαιπάλους: Nicander *Ther.* 145 δυσπαίπαλος Ὄθρυς. The Homeric παιπαλόεις is similarly applied to hills, rocky islands, and steep or rugged paths.

νωμᾶται...λεπτότριχα...ἔθειραν, he plies his wing of delicate plumage. The place of the words σὺν ζεφύρου πνοιαῖσιν shows that ἔθειραν depends on the verb, and must not be taken as acc. of respect with ἀρίγνωτος. The middle of νωμᾶν occurs elsewhere only in Quint. Smyrn. 3. 439 οὐ γάρ τις πίσυνός γε σάκος μέγα νωμήσασθαι: but there is no reason for suspecting it here. It was read by the schol. on Hes. *Theog.* 116 (see cr. n.). In Soph. fr. 855. 11 I would read νωμᾷ τ᾽ ἐν οἰωνοῖσί που κείνη πτερόν (vulg. τούκείνης, but one MS. of Stobaeus has τοῦ κείνη: and Κύπρις is the subject of the preceding sentences in the frag.). Cp. also *Anth.* 9. 339 ἔν ποτε παμφαίνοντι μέλαν πτερὸν αἰθέρι νωμῶν.
ἀτρύτῳ, 'illimitable'; a sense derived from that of 'inexhaustible.' Cp. VIII. 80 ἄτρυτον χρόνον ('unending'). Arist. *De Caelo* 2, p. 284 a 35 Ἰξίονός τινα μοῖραν ...ἀΐδιον καὶ ἄτρυτον. Theocr. XV. 7 ἁ δ᾽ ὁδὸς ἄτρυτος. In the citation by schol. Hes. *Theog.* 116 ἀτρυγέτῳ is evidently an error, due probably to the second T of

messenger of wide-ruling Zeus the lord of thunder, trusts boldly
to his mighty strength; the shrill-voiced birds crouch in fear
of him; the heights of the wide earth stay him not, nor the
rough, steep waves of the unwearied sea; he plies his wing of
delicate plumage in the illimitable void, sped by the breath
of the west wind, conspicuous in the sight of men.

And so for me a boundless course is open on every side epode 1.
to hymn your prowess, ye lordly sons of Deinomenes, by grace
of Victory, dark-haired queen, and of Ares with bronze-clad
breast. May Heaven weary not of blessing you!

by **A**². **27** ἀτρύτῳ] Schol. Hes. *Theog.* 116 Βακχυλίδης δὲ χάος τὸν ἀέρα ὠνόμασε,
λέγων περὶ τοῦ ἀετοῦ· νωμᾶται δ᾿ ἐν ἀτρυγέτῳ χάει. **28 f.** ΠΝΟ|ΑΙϹΙΝ MS. :
πνοι|αῖσιν Weil, a. o. **31** MOI MS.: ἐμοὶ Blass. **33** ΥΜΝΕΙ̂ MS. : corr.
Palmer. **35 f.** The MS. places ἀγέρωχοι wholly in 35: corr. K. Cp. 75 f. : 115 f.

ἀτρύτῳ having become Γ : ἀτρύγῳ would
lead to ἀτρυγέτῳ.

χάει, the 'void,' as a poetical term for
'space,' or 'the air': a usage which
occurs first in Ibycus (flor. *circ.* 550 B.C.),
fr. 28 ποτᾶται δ᾿ ἐν ἀλλοτρίῳ χάει. It is
possible, indeed, (though we can scarcely
assume this,) that the schol. on Ar. *Av.*
192, who quotes the words, confused
Ibycus with Bacchylides, and intended this
passage. Bergk suggests that ἀλλοτρίῳ
may have been a slip of the scholiast's,
due to the verse on which he comments,
διὰ τῆς πόλεως τῆς ἀλλοτρίας καὶ τοῦ χάους.
It might also be a corruption of ἀμέτρῳ
(ΛΛ for M).

29 f. ἀρίγνωτος μετ᾿ ἀνθρώποις. In
v. 14 the δέ after ἐθέλει seems clearly indispensable, and is therefore presumably
genuine. An asyndeton there would be
unendurable. That is the reason against
deleting μετ᾿ here. (μέγ᾿ would be weak,
and οἰωνοῖς for ἀνθρώποις is improbable.)
But the phrase ἀρίγνωτος μετ᾿ ἀνθρώποις,
as applied to the soaring bird, can be
explained only as a bit of rather careless
writing. The thought in the writer's mind
is that the eagle's *flight* is '*much noted
among men*'; *i.e.* a number of men follow
his course with their eyes.—ἰδεῖν, not ὁρᾶν,
because the poet thinks of the moment at
which the eagle sails into view.

31 τώς is used by the epic poets and
by Aesch. (cp. *Suppl.* 61 τὼς καὶ ἐγώ),
but not by Pindar. μυρία πάντᾳ
κέλευθος: cp. VIII. 47 f. : XVIII. 1
πάρεστι μυρία κέλευθος | ἀμβροσίων μελέων.
In one of his Isthmian odes (III. 19 = IV.
1), composed perhaps in 478, and in any

case before this ode of Bacchylides, Pindar
writes: ἔστι μοι θεῶν ἕκατι μυρία παντᾷ
κέλευθος, | ὦ Μέλισσ᾿, εὐμαχανίαν γὰρ
ἔφανας Ἰσθμίοις | ὑμετέρας ἀρετὰς ὕμνῳ
διώκειν. This is the only instance in which
a verbal parallelism between a passage of
Bacchylides and an earlier passage of
Pindar suffices to prove imitation on the
part of the younger poet (cp. p. 65).

33—36 κυανοπλοκάμου, merely a
general epithet for goddesses or heroines;
as for Thebe in VIII. 53, and the Proetides in X. 83.—ἕκατι, 'by grace of':
cp. I. 6 f.—Νίκας : here, more especially
victory in the games.—χαλκεοστέρνου =
χαλκοθώρακος. As to the form, see on
III. 32.—Ἄρηος, alluding chiefly to the
victory over the Carthaginians at Himera
(480 B.C.), in which Gelon's glory was
shared by his brothers. Simonides fr. 141
φημὶ Γέλων᾿ Ἱέρωνα Πολύζηλον Θρασύ-
βουλον | παῖδας Δεινομένευς τὸν τρίποδ᾿
ἀνθέμεναι (τοὺς τρίποδας θέμεναι, schol.
Pind. *P.* I. 155). Cp. Pind. *P.* I.
79 (470 B.C.), where he speaks of himself as having sung of Salamis and
Plataea, παρὰ δ᾿ εὔυδρον ἀκτὰν Ἱμέρα
(the river Himeras) παίδεσσιν ὕμνον Δει-
νομένεος τελέσαις | τὸν ἐδέξαντ᾿ ἀμφ᾿ ἀρετᾷ.
Hieron succeeded Gelon in 478. We do
not hear of any signal military exploits as
having marked the interval between that
year and the date of this ode (476). But
Hieron had intervened as the protector of
Sybaris against Croton (Diod. XI. 48),
and of the Italian Locri against Anaxilas
of Rhegium (477 B.C.: schol. Pind. *P.*
II. 34). See Freeman, *Sicily* II. 237—241.

Δεινομένευς...παῖδες. The collective

J. B.   19

7 ξανθότριχα μὲν Φερένικον
8 Ἀλφεὸν παρ᾽ εὐρυδίναν
9 πῶλον ἀελλοδρόμαν
40 10 εἶδε νικάσαντα χρυσόπαχυς Ἀώς,

στρ. β΄. 1 Πυθῶνί τ᾽ ἐν ἀγαθέᾳ·
        2 γᾷ δ᾽ ἐπισκήπτων πιφαύσκω·
        3 οὔπω νιν ὑπὸ προτέρων
        4 ἵππων ἐν ἀγῶνι κατέχρανεν κόνις
45   5 πρὸς τέλος ὀρνύμενον·
        6 ῥιπᾷ γὰρ ἴσος Βορέα
        7 ὃν κυβερνήταν φυλάσσων
        8 ἵεται νεόκροτον
        9 νίκαν Ἱέρωνι φιλοξείνῳ τιτύσκων.
50 10   ὄλβιος ᾧτινι θεὸς

39 ἀελλοδρόμαν] ἀελλοδρόμον schol. Pind. *O.* 1 argum. (fr. 6 Bergk).   **46** ΒΟ-
ΡΕΑΙ **Α**, corr. **Α**¹.   **49** ΦΙΛΟΞΕΝΩΙ ms.: corr. K.   **50—55** ὄλβιος...ἔφυ.

address is interesting, because it shows
that, so far as the poet knew,—and he
was doubtless well-informed, — Hieron
was now (in 476) on good terms with
both his surviving brothers, Polyzelus
and Thrasybulus. But shortly before
this date (in 478—477) he appears to
have been at enmity with Polyzelus.
The latter, according to Diodorus (XI. 48),
had sought refuge with Theron of Agrigas,
who, on being reconciled to Hieron (in
477—6), τὸν Πολύζηλον εἰς τὴν προϋπάρ-
χουσαν εὔνοιαν ἀποκατέστησε. Thus Bacchylides indirectly confirms Diodorus.—
For the form of the genit. Δεινομένευς,
cp. III. 7.

ἀγέρωχοι: 'lordly.' The word has a
good sense in Homer (where it is an
epithet of the Trojans and other nations,
but only once of a single hero, Pericly-
menus, in *Od.* 11. 286); also in Pindar
(who applies it to victory, high deeds,
wealth, but not to persons). Archilochus
(fr. 154) and Alcaeus (fr. 120) are said to
have used it in a bad sense ('overbearing').
The derivation is uncertain: for the theo-
ries, see Leaf on *Il.* 2. 654.

37 ξανθότριχα, 'chestnut.' In Soph.
El. 705 an Aetolian enters for the chariot
race ξανθαῖσι πώλοις. Nestor speaks of
having carried off 150 ἵππους ξανθάς from
Elis (*Il.* 11. 680).

38 Ἀλφεὸν...εὐρυδίναν: cp. III. 6 f.

39 πῶλον, not properly 'colt,' but

merely =ἵππον: cp. Soph. *El.* 705 (n.)—
748, where the word has this general
sense throughout. At Olympia no special
contest for πῶλοι existed before 384 B.C.
—ἀελλοδρόμαν, paraphrased in v. 46.
ἀελλόπος is the Homeric epithet of Iris
(*Il.* 8. 409, etc.): then Simonides (fr. 7)
and Pindar (*N.* I. 6) spoke of ἀελλοπόδων
ἵππων: cp. *Il.* 10. 437 θείειν δ᾽ ἀνέμοισιν
ὁμοῖοι.

40 χρυσόπαχυς Ἀώς, who touches
the earth with gold. (Cp. ῥοδοδάκτυλος.)
Soph. *Ant.* 103 f. ὦ χρυσέας | ἀμέρας
βλέφαρον.—In XII. 96 ῥοδό[παχυν is certain.—The horse-races, like the chariot-
races (Soph. *El.* 699 n.), were held early
in the morning.

41 Πυθῶνί τ᾽ ἐν ἀγαθέᾳ. Hieron had
won with a κέλης at Delphi in 482 and
478 B.C. Pherenicus was certainly the
κέλης in 478; perhaps also in 482; but
the only ground for thinking that this
horse had won twice at Delphi is the
plural στεφάνοις in Pind. *P.* III. 73 f.,
στεφάνοις | οὓς ἀριστεύων Φερένικος ἕλ᾽ ἐν
Κίρρᾳ ποτέ: which could, however, refer
to a single victory. See Introd. to the
ode, § 1. For ἀγαθέᾳ, cp. III. 62.

42 γᾷ δ᾽ ἐπισκήπτων, 'laying (my
hand) on the earth,' calling it to witness:
the full phrase occurs in VII. 41, γᾷ δ᾽
ἐπισκήπτων χέρα κομπάσομαι. The act of
touching the sacred Earth meant that the
person who did so invoked the χθόνιοι to

Morning with her golden ray saw Pherenicus, that chestnut
steed swift as the wind, victorious by the wide-eddying Alpheus,
as also at divine Pytho. And I call Earth to witness: never str. 2.
yet in a race has he been soiled by dust from horses in front of
him, as he sped to his goal. Like the rush of Boreas, he darts
onward, heedful of his pilot, winning for hospitable Hieron a
victory greeted by fresh plaudits.
Happy is he to whom the god

Quoted by Stobaeus *Flor.* 103. 2 (fr. 1, Bergk): who cites 53 (from οὐ)—55 also in
Flor. 98. 26. Verses 50—53 (to διάγειν) are quoted by Apostolius XII. 65 e.

---

punish him if he swore falsely. Similarly
persons who invoke the *help* of the χθόνιοι
strike the earth: *Il.* 9. 568 f. (Althaea)
πολλὰ δὲ καὶ γαῖαν πολυφόρβην χερσὶν
ἀλοία, | κικλήσκουσ᾽ Ἀΐδην καὶ ἐπαινὴν
Περσεφόνειαν: *Hom. hymn. Apoll.* 2. 162
(Hera, invoking Γαῖα and the Τιτῆνες),
ὣς ἄρα φωνήσασ᾽ ἵμασε χθόνα χειρὶ παχείῃ·
| κινήθη δ᾽ ἄρα Γαῖα φερέσβιος. Pindar,
too, often emphasizes praise by solemn
asseveration: *O.* II. 101 αὐδάσομαι ἐνόρκιον
λόγον: VI. 20 καὶ μέγαν ὅρκον ὀμόσσαις
τοῦτό γέ Fοι σαφέως | μαρτυρήσω: *N.* XI.
24 ναὶ μὰ τὸν ὅρκον.
The poet keeps the η in ἐπισκήπτων,
though he has σκᾶπτρον in III. 70. Cp.
I. 74 n.
43 προτέρων, in front of him. This
local sense of πρότερος is very rare, except
when it is figurative (denoting precedence
in rank, etc., as in Dem. or. 3 § 15 τὸ...
πράττειν τοῦ λέγειν...πρότερον τῇ δυνάμει
καὶ κρεῖττόν ἐστι). But cp. Plat. *Rep.*
516 C τῷ ὀξύτατα καθορῶντι τὰ παριόντα,
καὶ μνημονεύοντι μάλιστα ὅσα τε πρότερα
αὐτῶν καὶ ὕστερα εἰώθει καὶ ἅμα πο-
ρεύεσθαι. [In *Od.* 19. 228 προτέροισι
πόδεσσι = προσθίοις. In *Il.* 15. 569 (= 17.
274) πρότεροι is temporal.]
46 ῥιπᾷ...Βορέα: *Il.* 15. 171 ὑπὸ ῥιπῆς
αἰθρηγενέος Βορέαο. Soph. *Ant.* 137 ῥιπαῖς
ἐχθίστων ἀνέμων.
47 ὃν κυβερνήταν φυλάσσων, 'heedful
of his pilot.' He rivals the wind in
speed; but his *course* obeys the hand that
steers him. φυλάσσων means not merely
'bearing his rider safe,' but 'attending to
his guidance': the word κυβερνήταν brings
this out.—The Ionic η is retained in
κυβερνήταν (cp. XI. 1), as in φήμα (II. 1)
and ἀδμήτα (v. 167). Pindar has κυβερ-
νάτας (*P.* I. 91).
48 ἵεται. The historic present here is
unusual, but intelligible. Verses 37—45
deal with the horse's record as a whole.

Now the poet comes to his latest victory.
The historic present, combined with
νεόκροτον, gives a touch of animation
which marks the transition.—Cp. Pind.
O. I. 20 ff. (of Pherenicus) ὅτε παρ᾽
Ἀλφεῷ σύτο δέμας | ἀκέντητον ἐν δρόμοισι
παρέχων, | κράτει δὲ προσέμιξε δεσπό-
ταν.
νεόκροτον, 'greeted with fresh plaudits.'
κρότος is the regular word for 'applause'
(Xen. *An.* VI. 1. 13 ἐνταῦθα κρότος ἦν
πολύς). In III. 9 the poet similarly refers
to the shouts which greet Hieron's victory
(θρόησε δὲ λαὸς ἀπείρων). The only other
extant compounds with κρότος refer to
sound, viz. (1) εὔκροτος: Alciphron *Epist.*
3. 43 ἀνάπαιστα εὔκροτα: (2) πολύκροτος:
Hom. hymn. 19. 37, epithet of Pan, as
'making loud music' on his pipe: Athen.
p. 527 F epithet of the lyre χελωνίς (from
the comic poet Poseidonius). On this
view νεόκροτον is not merely a poetical
equivalent for 'new,' but means 'new
and popular.'
Others take νεόκροτον to mean '*newly-
welded*,' *i.e.* 'newly wrought,' νεότευκτον,
comparing Pind. fr. 194 κεκρότηται χρυσέα
κρηπίς. The only extant derivative of
κροτεῖν in the sense of 'hammering or
welding together' seems to be εὐκρότητος
(though συγκρότητος may also have been
in use). νεόκροτον in this sense would be
a clumsy epithet,—made still more so by
the neighbourhood of τιτύσκων, which
would serve to emphasize the metaphor
of 'welding.' No emendation is probable.
The easiest, νεόκριτον, would be unsuitable
to this context: the race is being run.
49 φιλοξείνῳ. Cp. III. 16: Pind. *P.*
III. 71 (of Hieron) ξείνοις δὲ θαυμαστὸς
πατήρ.
50—55 The γνώμη which leads from
the proem to the myth. A man is happy
if he has (1) **μοῖραν..καλῶν,** 'a portion
of honours,'—such as those gained at

11 μοῖράν τε καλῶν ἔπορεν
12 σύν τ᾽ ἐπιζήλῳ τύχᾳ
13 ἀφνεὸν βιοτὰν διάγειν· οὐ
14 γάρ τις ἐπιχθονίων
55 15 πάντα γ᾽ εὐδαίμων ἔφυ.

ἀντ. β'. 1 καὶ μάν π]οτ᾽ ἐρειψιπύλαν
2 παῖδ᾽ ἀνίκ]ατον λέγουσιν
3 δῦναι Διὸς] ἀργικεραύ-
Col. 8 4 νου δώματα Φερσεφόνας τανισφύρου,
60 5 καρχαρόδοντα κύν᾽ ἄ-
6 ξοντ᾽ ἐς φάος ἐξ Ἀΐδα,
7 υἱὸν ἀπλάτοι᾽ Ἐχίδνας·
8 ἔνθα δυστάνων βροτῶν
9 ψυχὰς ἐδάη παρὰ Κωκυτοῦ ῥεέθροις,
65 10 οἷά τε φύλλ᾽ ἄνεμος
11 Ἴδας ἀνὰ μηλοβότους
12 πρῶνας ἀργηστὰς δονεῖ.
13 ταῖσιν δὲ μετέπρεπεν εἴδω-
14 λον θρασυμέμνονος ἐγ-
70 15 χεσπάλου Πορθανίδα·

53 ἀφνεὸν MS., Stobaeus, Apostolius: corr. K.   55 πάντα γ] Stob. omits γ in
Flor. 103. 2, but not in 98. 26.   56 καὶ μάν add. K.: καὶ γάρ Jurenka: δῦναι
Weil, Wilam. (cp. n. on 58).—ἐρειψιπύλαν] In the MS. the second E has been trans-
fixed, perhaps by the first hand.   58 δῦναι Palmer: πατρὸς Weil: φῆμαι Wilam.

Olympia and Delphi; (2) wealth, ἀφνεὸν
βιοτάν, combined with prosperous fortune.
Hieron had now (in 476) been ruler of
Syracuse since 478; his position was a
splendid one, and he had met with no
reverse: this is ἐπίζαλος τύχα. But no
mortal is πάντα γ᾽ εὐδαίμων: and Hieron
had weak health. The illness mentioned
by Aelian (see n. on III. 71) seems to
have occurred early in his life. He
suffered from an internal disease (λιθιῶν,
Plut. Mor. 403 C: cp. schol. Pind. O.
I. I, P. I. 89, III. I). A strain of allusion
to his malady appears in Pindar's third
Pythian (circ. 476—5 B.C.?), vv. I—8,
and especially 80—92, where the Theban
poet, like the Cean here, dwells on the
blending of glory with suffering in Hieron's
lot. In Pyth. I. 52—55 (474 B.C.) a
parallel is implied between Hieron and
Philoctetes, the warrior ἀσθενεῖ σὺν χρωτὶ
βαίνων. See also above, III. 85 (n.).

The general sentiment of this passage
has a close parallel in Pind. I. IV. 12 ff.:
δύο δέ τοι ζωᾶς ἄωτον μοῦνα ποιμαίνοντι
τὸν ἄλπνιστον εὐανθεῖ σὺν ὄλβῳ, | εἴ τις εὖ
πάσχων λόγον ἐσλὸν ἀκούσῃ· | μὴ μάτευε
Ζεὺς γενέσθαι· πάντ᾽ ἔχεις, | εἴ σε τούτων
μοῖρ᾽ ἐφίκοιτο καλῶν.

56 καὶ μάν, 'and verily': as in XII.
182. This formula implies that the myth
illustrates and confirms the general truth
just stated. καὶ μήν often introduces
some new consideration, in support of a
view which has already been urged (e.g.
Dem. or. 21 § 56 καὶ μὴν ἴστε γε τοῦτ᾽
ἔτι: cp. Isocr. or. 4 § 185). So, in drama,
καὶ μήν announces a new comer on the
scene (e.g., Soph. Ai. 1168). Pindar has
καὶ μάν in P. IV. 289, N. II. 13, etc.
It is, however, difficult to choose here
between καὶ μάν and καὶ γάρ. In favour
of the latter, it may be noted that Pindar
has καὶ γάρ ποτε in O. VII. 27, and N. VI.

has granted a portion of honours, and a life of opulence, with enviable fortune : for no mortal man is blest in all things.

And verily they tell how he who broke down the gates ant. 2. of cities, the unconquered son of Zeus, lord of the bright thunderbolt, descended of old to the house of Persephone with slender ankles, that he might bring up from Hades to the sunlight the hound with jagged teeth, offspring of unapproachable Echidna.

There, by the waters of Cocytus, he perceived the souls of hapless mortals, countless as leaves quivering in the wind, where flocks graze on the gleaming headlands of Ida. And well seen among them was the shade of the bold-hearted warrior, the spear-shaker, sprung from Porthaon.

---

69 ἐγ-] ΕΝ **Α**: γ written above Ν by **Α**³. **70** ΠΟΡΘΑΝΙ´ΔΑ **Α**: o has been added above, between the first A and N (by **Α**²?).—The short mark above I, which at first sight seems to denote a long syllable, is like that on the ι of εὐκτίτων in III. 46 and on the second ι of ἐπιχθονίοις in v. 96. In all three places it may have been meant for ˘: in v. 96, indeed, it shows a slight curve.

35, as a preface to mythical allusions. The fact that here **οὐ γάρ τις** comes just before, is a slight objection, but by no means decisive: iteration of γάρ is common. **καὶ γάρ**, as distinguished from **καὶ μάν**, would assert *more directly* the logical connexion between the maxim and the myth. On the whole, I prefer καὶ μάν, because (1) it rather implies than asserts such connexion ; and (2) is, partly on that account, more impressive.

The γνώμη links proem to myth by the thought, 'even the most famous and prosperous mortal is not happy in all things.' Heracles had won great glory, but also endured great trials. Meleager is an example of fame and valour prematurely struck down by fate. **ἐρειψιπύλαν**: Heracles took the Troy of Laomedon; also Oechalia, and Pylus (*Il.* 11. 689 f.). Cp. Aesch. *Th.* 880 f. δωμάτων ἐρειψίτοιχοι.

59 τανισφύρου: cp. III. 60 n.

60—62 καρχαρόδοντα : a general epithet for dogs in Homer (*Il.* 13. 198). Heracles speaks of his descent to Hades as the crowning ἆθλος laid on him by Eurystheus (*Od.* 11. 623—6). *Il.* 8. 368 ἐξ ἐρέβευς ἄξοντα κύνα στυγεροῦ ᾿Αΐδαο.—**υἱὸν**..᾿Εχίδνας, as in Hes. *Th.* 310 (the father being Typhaon), Soph. *Tr.* 1099: but in *O. C.* 1574 he is the son of Tartarus and Earth.

64 ἐδάη here=ἔμαθε in the sense of 'perceived.' Similar, though not identical,

is the use of the word in Pind. fr. 166, ἀνδροδάμαντα δ᾽ ἐπεὶ Φῆρες δάεν ῥιπὰν μελιαδέος οἴνου, 'perceived' (*i.e.* 'felt') the impulse.

65 οἷά τε : *i.e.* ψυχὰς ἐδάη, (τοιαύτας) οἷά τε φύλλ᾽ ἄνεμος δονεῖ, = οἷά τε φύλλα ἐστὶν ἃ ἄνεμος δονεῖ. The use of οἷά τε for the simple οἷα suits the epic manner. *Il.* 2. 468 μυρίοι, ὅσσα τε φύλλα καὶ ἄνθεα γίγνεται ὥρῃ. For the simile, cp. also Ap. Rhod. IV. 216: Virg. *Aen.* VI. 309 f. (of the departed spirits), *Quam multa in silvis autumni frigore primo Lapsa cadunt folia.* Seneca *Oed.* 600. Milton *P. L.* I. 301 ff.

67 πρῶνας ἀργηστάς, headlands 'gleaming' in the sunlight. ἀργηστής (from ἀργής, ἀργήεις, 'shining,' esp. 'white') occurs as an epithet of foam (Aesch. *Th.* 60), of a serpent (*ib.* 181), and of swans (Theocr. XXV. 131). The use of it here may have been suggested by *Il.* 16. 297 (when 'Zeus removes a thick cloud from the summit of a great mountain '), ἔκ τ᾽ ἔφανεν πᾶσαι σκοπιαὶ καὶ πρώονες ἄκροι | καὶ νάπαι.

Marlowe, speaking of a great host, says,— ' *In number more than are the quivering leaves Of Ida's forest* ' (*Tamburlaine* pt 2, III. 5. 3, quoted by Headlam).

69 f. θρασυμέμνονος, of a brave spirit: epithet of Heracles in *Il.* 5. 639, *Od.* 11. 267. The -μέμνων is usu. referred to μένω ('bravely *steadfast*'), but may better

ἐπ. β'.　 1 τὸν δ' ὡς ἴδεν Ἀλκμήνιος θαυμαστὸς ἥρως
　　　 2 τεύχεσι λαμπόμενον,
　　　 3 νευρὰν ἐπέβασε λιγυκλαγγῆ κορώνας,
　　　 4 χαλκεόκρανον δ' ἔπειτ' ἐξ-
　 75 5 είλετο (F)ιὸν ἀνα-
　　　 6 πτύξας φαρέτρας πῶμα· τῷ δ' ἐναντία
　　　 7 ψυχὰ προφάνη Μελεάγρου
　　　 8 καί νιν εὖ εἰδὼς προσεῖπεν·
　　　 9 υἱὲ Διὸς μεγάλου,
　 80 10 στᾶθί τ' ἐν χώρᾳ, γελανώσας τε θυμόν

στρ. γ'.　 1 μὴ ταύσιον προΐει
　　　 2 τραχὺν ἐκ χειρῶν ὀϊστὸν
　　　 3 ψυχαῖσιν ἔπι φθιμένων·
　　　 4 οὗτοι δέος. ὡς φάτο· θάμβησεν δ' ἄναξ
　 85 5 Ἀμφιτρυωνιάδας,
　　　 6 εἶπέν τε· τίς ἀθανάτων
　　　 7 ἢ βροτῶν τοιοῦτον ἔρνος
　　　 8 θρέψεν ἐν ποίᾳ χθονί;
　　　 9 τίς δ' ἔκτανεν; ἦ τάχα καλλίζωνος Ἥρα
　 90 10 κεῖνον ἐφ' ἀμετέρᾳ

71 ΑΛΚΜΗΪΟC ms. : corr. K.　　**75 f.** The ms. divides the verses wrongly, as in

be connected with μέμαα, μένος (cp.
Ἀγαμέμνων).—ἐγχεσπάλου : epithet of
warriors in the *Iliad* (2. 131 etc.).
Πορθανίδα. Meleager was the son of
Oeneus, and grandson of Porthaon, king
of Pleuron and Calydon. See the stemma
of the mythical genealogy in the Appendix. Πορθανίδης is from Πορθάν, a
compressed form of Πορθάων, as Ἀλκμάν
(Pind. *P.* VIII. 46) of Ἀλκμάων. The corrector of the ms. wished to read **Πορθαονίδα,** which would be possible, with a
synizesis of αο : but Πορθανίδα is confirmed
by the analogy of Ἀλκμανίδᾶν in Pind.
P. VII. 2.
71 Ἀλκμήνιος, son of Alcmena: cp.
VI. 12 f. Ἀριστομένειον..τέκος : *Il.* 11.
562 Τελαμώνιον υἱόν : Aesch. *P. V.* 705
Ἰνάχειον σπέρμα : Soph. *O. T.* 267 τῷ
Λαβδακείῳ παιδί.
73 νευρὰν..λιγυκλαγγῆ. He drew
the bow-string taut, so that it gave a
ringing sound at the touch. Cp. *Od.* 21.
410 f. (Odysseus proving his bow-string,
after stringing his bow) : δεξιτερῇ δ' ἄρα

χειρὶ λαβὼν πειρήσατο νευρῆς · | ἡ δ' ὑπὸ
καλὸν ἄεισε, χελιδόνι ϝεικέλη αὐδήν.
κορώνας, the tip of the bow. A notch
or hook in this received the loop of the
string when the bow was strung. At the
other end the string must have been
fastened, either in a like way, or by
being passed through a hole in the κέρας.
Only the tip at the upper end of a bow
seems to have been called κορώνη : that
on the bow of Pandarus was gilt (*Il.*
4. 111).
75 f. ἐξείλετο ἰόν. The hiatus indicates
that the poet attributed ϝ to ἰός, *arrow.*
This ἰός (the Sanskrit *ishas*, Curt. *Etym.*
§ 616) occurs in *Iliad, Odyssey,* and
Homeric hymns, but never takes ϝ. See
(*e.g.*) *Il.* 4. 116, the source of this
passage : αὐτὰρ ὁ σύλα πῶμα φαρέτρης,
ἐκ δ' ἕλετ' ἰόν. But ἰός, *poison* (Skt
visham, Lat. *virus,* Curt. § 591), had ϝ.
So also had ἴον, *viola.* The similarity of
form between these words might easily
lead to the false digamma which we find
here ; though the mistake shows that the

But when the wondrous hero, Alcmena's son, beheld him epode 2.
shining in armour, he drew the shrill bow-string to the horn
of his bow; then he raised the lid of his quiver, and took
out a bronze-tipped arrow. But the spirit of Meleager came
and stood before his face, and spake unto him, for he knew
him well: 'Son of great Zeus, stay where thou art, and calm
thy soul,

and speed not vainly from thy hand a fierce shaft against the str. 3.
souls of the dead. There is no cause to fear.'
So spake he; but the princely son of Amphitryon marvelled,
and said: 'Who among immortals or among men, and in what
land, was the parent of an offspring so glorious? And who
was his slayer? Soon will fair-girdled Hera send that man

epode a′ (35 f.) and epode γ′ (115 f.): corr. K.   **78** ΠΡΟCΕΕΙΠΕΝ ms. : corr. K.
80 τε] The first hand wrote A instead of T, but corrected it.

---

poet had not very closely observed his
epic model.—Cp. XVI. 131 n.
78 εἰδώς after ψυχά, constr. κατὰ
σύνεσιν: *Od.* 11. 90 ἦλθε δ᾽ ἐπὶ ψυχὴ
Θηβαίου Τειρεσίαο, | χρύσεον σκῆπτρον
ἔχων: 16. 476 ἱερὴ ἲς Τηλεμάχοιο | ἐς
πατέρ᾽ ὀφθαλμοῖσιν ἰδών: *Il.* 11. 690
ἐλθὼν γὰρ ἐκάκωσε βίη Ἡρακληείη.
80 ἐν χώρᾳ, = where thou art. Xen.
H. IV. 2 § 20 ἐν χώρᾳ ἔπιπτον (at their
post). Thuc. IV. 26 § 1 τὸ στρατόπεδον..
κατὰ χώραν ἔμενεν.
γελανώσας. γελανός occurs nowhere
else: but Pind. *O.* V. 2 has καρδίᾳ
γελανεῖ (and *P.* IV. 121 θυμῷ γ.), 'cheerful.'
γελάω and γαλήνη show respectively the
stronger and the weaker form (γελ-, γαλ-)
of a common root, expressing the idea of
'bright' or 'clear': cp. γάλα, and Lat. gelu.
The primary sense of γελᾶν was
'smiling,' not 'laughing,' as appears in
the figurative uses (e.g. κυμάτων | ἀνήριθ-
μον γέλασμα, Aesch. *P. V.* 90). Thus
γελανόω, to make γελανής, might well
mean, 'to tranquillize'; and it is needless
to conjecture γαλανώσας. [The extant
verbs from γαλην- are γαληνίζω (trans. in
Hippocr. and Eur., intrans. in Arist.),
γαληνιάω, and γαληνιάζω (intrans.)]
81 ταῦσιον, 'vain.' This Doric form
occurs also in a corrupt fr. of Alcman,
no. 92. Cp. *Od.* 3. 316 τηϋσίην ὁδὸν
ἔλθῃς; Theocr. XXV. 230 τηϋσίως. The
deriv. is unknown : but the theory which
connects it with ταῦς, 'big' (through the
notion, 'too big to be practicable'), takes
some colour from *Hom. hymn. Apoll.*
2. 36 εἰ δέ τι τηΰσιον ἔπος ἔσσεται, ἠέ τι

ἔργον, where the sense is 'rash' (as
ὕβρις in the next v. indicates): cp. μέγ᾽..
ἔπος (Soph. *Ai.* 128).
82 τραχύν, 'fierce'; properly, 'rough,'
'harsh,' like war and the warrior's spirit;
cp. Pind. *P.* I. 10 f. Ἄρης, τραχεῖαν
ἄνευθε λιπὼν | ἐγχέων ἀκμάν.
83 ψυχαῖσιν ἔπι φθιμένων. For this
sense of ἐπί with dat., denoting hostile
movement, cp. 90, 133 : it is frequent in
poetry, from the Homeric ἐπ᾽ ἀλλήλοισιν
ἰόντες (*Il.* 3. 15 etc.) onwards.
84 οὔτοι δέος, as we say, 'there is no
fear' (*i.e.* cause for it). The phrase is
Homeric, *Il.* 1. 515, ἐπεὶ οὔ τοι ἔπι δέος :
only that there τοι = σοι (Zeus). Cp. *Il.*
12. 246 σοὶ δ᾽ οὐ δέος ἔστ᾽ ἀπολέσθαι.—
Here it seems better to write οὔτοι than
to take οὔ τοι as = οὔ σοι.
86—88 τίς...ἐν ποίᾳ χθονί; Cp.
XVII. 31: *Od.* 1. 170 τίς πόθεν εἰς ἀνδρῶν;
—ἔρνος, like θάλος and ὄζος: Pind. *N.*
VI. 64 ἔρνεσι Λατοῦς (Apollo and Ar-
temis): *I.* III. 62 f. Μελίσσῳ.. | ἔρνεϊ
Τελεσιάδᾳ: and so in Tragedy. In
Homer a youth or maiden is sometimes
compared to an ἔρνος (*Il.* 18. 56 etc.), but
is not called so.
89 f. τίς δ᾽ ἔκτανεν; Heracles assumes
that the slayer of Meleager was some
great warrior (κεῖνον, v. 90), whom Hera
will next send against himself. He is
presently to learn (136 ff.) that the death
of Meleager was the work of Althaea.
The touch of poetical art given by κεῖνον
is like that of Sophocles in the *Antigone*
(v. 248), when Creon, never dreaming
that the breaker of his edict is a woman,

11 πέμψει κεφαλᾷ· τὰ δέ που
Col. 9   12 Παλλάδι ξανθᾷ μέλει.
         13 τὸν δὲ προσέφα Μελέαγρος
         14   δακρυόεις· χαλεπὸν
95 15   θεῶν παρατρέψαι νόον

ἀντ. γ'.   1 ἄνδρεσσιν ἐπιχθονίοις.
           2 καὶ γὰρ ἂν πλάξιππος Οἰνεὺς
           3 παῦσεν καλυκοστεφάνου
           4   σεμνᾶς χόλον Ἀρτέμιδος λευκωλένου
100 5 λισσόμενος πολέων
     6   τ' αἰγῶν θυσίαισι πατὴρ
     7 καὶ βοῶν φοινικονώτων·
     8 ἀλλ' ἀνίκατον θεὰ
     9 ἔσχεν χόλον· εὐρυβίαν δ' ἔσσευε κούρα
105 10 κάπρον ἀναιδομάχαν
      11 ἐς καλλίχορον Καλυδῶ-
      12 ν', ἔνθα πλημύρων σθένει
      13 ὄρχους ἐπέκειρεν ὀδόντι,
      14 σφάζε τε μῆλα, βροτῶν

106 ἐς Palmer: ὄC MS. The rough breathing may be due to **A³**.   107 ΠΛΗ-
ΜΥΡΩΝ MS.

---

asks, τί φῄς; τίς ἀνδρῶν ἦν ὁ τολμήσας τάδε;
91 κεφαλᾷ, 'my life': cp. *Il.* 17. 242 ἐμῇ κεφαλῇ περιδείδια: *Od.* 2. 237 παρθέμενοι κεφαλάς (=ψυχὰς παρθέμενοι, 3. 74): Soph. *O. C.* 564 ἤθλησα κινδυνεύματ' ἐν τῷμῷ κάρᾳ (at the risk of my life). In other places, where the thought of danger is not present, κεφαλή is merely an emphatic 'self,' as in *Il.* 18. 82 τὸν ἐγὼ περὶ πάντων τῖον ἐταίρων, ἴσον ἐμῇ κεφαλῇ. So Pind. *O.* VI. 60 αἰτέων..τιμάν τιν' ἑᾷ κεφαλᾷ ('to crown him'): *O.* VII. 67 f. ἑᾷ κεφαλᾷ | .. γέρας ἔσσεσθαι.
92 Παλλάδι, the hero's guardian-goddess, who in *Il.* 8. 363 says of him, τειρόμενον σώεσκον ὑπ' Εὐρυσθῆος ἀέθλων. Speaking in *Od.* 11. 626 of his descent to Hades, Heracles says, Ἑρμείας δέ μ' ἐπεμψεν ἰδὲ γλαυκῶπις Ἀθήνη. She often appears as his protrectress on Attic black-figured vases, and in other works of ancient art. Cp. Soph. *Tr.* 1031, where he invokes her in his agony.

94 f. χαλεπὸν κ.τ.λ. The inflexibility of fate is illustrated by that purpose of Heracles which is declared at the end of the myth (v. 169),—to wed Deianeira. Cp. XV. 23 τότ' ἄμαχος δαίμων | Δαϊανείρᾳ πολύδακρυν ὕφανε | μῆτιν.—**θεῶν**: for the synizesis cp. 50.
97 πλάξιππος: Homeric epithet of Pelops (*Il.* 2. 104), and other heroes. Cp. *Il.* 9. 581 ἱππηλάτα Οἰνεύς.
98 f. καλυκοστεφάνου, 'crowned with flower-buds' (epithet in x. 108 of the Proetides). Plutarch *Mor.* 993 E quotes an unnamed poet, who spoke of Ἥλιος as ἐπιστέψας κάλυκος στεφάνοισιν Ὥρας. Artemis was a goddess of vegetation and fertility (Callim. *hymn. Dian.* 125 ff.: *Anthol. Pal.* 6. 157, 267: Catullus 34. 17).
Of the three epithets here given to Artemis, **καλυκοστεφάνου** denotes a conventional attribute; **σεμνᾶς**, divine rank; and **λευκωλένου**, a personal quality. A parallel series is that in XII. 194 f.,

to take my life; but golden-haired Pallas, I ween, is watchful against that.'

And to him spake Meleager with tears: 'It is hard for mortal men to turn aside the purpose of the gods:

else would my father, horse-smiting Oeneus, have appeased the ant. 3. wrath of Artemis crowned with flower-buds, the majestic, the white-armed, when he entreated her with sacrifices of many goats and red-backed oxen.

'But the maiden goddess had conceived anger that could not be overcome; and she sped a wild boar, of vast might, a ruthless foe, into the fair lawns of Calydon; where, in the flood-tide of his strength, he ravaged the vine-rows with his tusks, and slew the sheep, and every mortal

---

χρυσάρματος | σεμνὰ μεγάθυμος Ἀθάνα. (Cp. also XVI. 109 f. σεμνὰν..βοῶπιν.. Ἀμφιτρίταν.)
100 πολέων, fem. The epic πολέες, πολέων, πολέσι, πολέας are always masc. in Homer and Hesiod (though πουλὺν ἐφ' ὑγρὴν occurs in Il. 10. 27, etc.). But Callimachus has πολέας δ' ἐπελέξατο νύμφας (Hymn. Dian. 42), and πολέες σε περιτροχόωσιν ἀοιδαί (Hymn. Del. 28).
102 φοινικονώτων. Cp. X. 105 (βοῦς) φοινικότριχας: Pind. P. IV. 265 φοίνισσα δὲ Θρηϊκίων ἀγέλα ταύρων (a 'red' herd). In Il. 23. 454 φοῖνιξ (ἵππος) is chestnut, or perhaps light bay.
104 ἔσχεν, 'had conceived' (aor.). It is only the context which shows the sense, as the word could also mean 'restrained' (Od. 5. 451 ἔσχε δὲ κῦμα).— Oeneus had failed to offer harvest first-fruits (θαλύσια) to Artemis (Il. 9. 534).
105 ἀναιδομάχαν (only here), ruthless in fight. Several of B.'s new words have this scansion, as ἀδεισιβόας (V. 155), ἀερσίμαχος (XII. 100), ἀταρβομάχας (XV. 28).
106 f. καλλίχορον, 'with its fair lawns,' or dancing-grounds. It is applied to Olympia (X. 32); to the Phocian Panopeus (Od. 11. 581), Athens (Eur. Her. 359), Thebes (Hom. hymn. 15. 2). It is not merely a topographical epithet, but one which suggests the civic life and festivals. Thus Simonides (fr. 164, 2) calls Apollo Λητοΐδην ἀγορῆς καλλιχόρου πρύτανιν. Here it depicts a city at peace, with fair lawns around it. There is no reason to suppose that it is (incorrectly) used in the sense of καλλίχωρος: see Appendix.
Καλυδῶν'. The site of Calydon was

identified by Leake, doubtless rightly, with a place called Kurt-agâ, a little to the west of the river Evenus (the Fidhari). The town stood on the lowest slopes of Mt Aracynthus (now Zygos), the range from which the coast plain of Aetolia stretches to the sea. This accounts for the Homeric epithets of Calydon (Il. 2. 640 πετρήεσσαν, 13. 217 αἰπεινῇ), though its actual position was not lofty. The territory of Calydon, in the plain between Aracynthus and the marshy seaboard, was fertile (Strabo p. 450 τῆς μεσογαίας... εὐκάρπου τε καὶ πεδιάδος). Cp. Il. 9. 577 πίοτατον πεδίον Καλυδῶνος ἐραννῆς.
107 πλημύρων. I retain the spelling of the papyrus: good MSS. have the form with a single μ in Hippocr. De sacro morb. vol. I. p. 604 (ed. Kühn) πλημυρεῖν, and De Diaet. Acut. II. p. 60 πλημυρίδα. The same spelling appears in Archilochus fr. 97 (as quoted by Eustath. Od. 1597, 28) ἐπλήμυρον. In Od. 9. 486 πλημυρίς too has the best MS. authority. If the word was formed directly, as Buttmann held, from the root πλε (πίμπλημι), the single μ would be right: while the old deriv. from πλήν and μύρω would account for the doubling of μ.
108 ὄρχους, rows (of vines). Od. 7. 127 παρὰ νείατον ὄρχον (the furthest row of vines). Xen. Oecon. 20 § 3 οὐκ ὀρθῶς τοὺς ὄρχους ἐφύτευσαν.
109 σφάζε τε μῆλα. Wilamowitz assumes that our poet's 'sheep' were suggested by a confused reminiscence of Homer's 'apples': Il. 9. 541 f. (the boar) χαμαὶ βάλε δένδρεα μακρὰ | αὐτῇσιν ῥίζῃσι καὶ αὐτοῖς ἄνθεσι μήλων. A wild boar (he says) would not attack sheep. Apollodorus (I. 8. 2, § 2) agrees with Bacchylides:

110 15 θ' ὅστις εἰσάνταν μόλοι.

ἐπ. γ'. 1 τῷ δὲ στυγερὰν δῆριν Ἑλλάνων ἄριστοι
         2 στασάμεθ' ἐνδυκέως·
         3 ἐξ ἄματα συνεχέως· ἐπεὶ δὲ δαίμων
         4 κάρτος Αἰτωλοῖς ὄρεξεν,
   115   5 θάπτομεν οὓς κατέπε-
         6 φνεν σῦς ἐριβρύχας ἐπαΐσσων βίᾳ,
         7 Ἀγκαῖον ἐμῶν τ' Ἀγέλαον
         8 φ[έρτ]ατον κεδνῶν ἀδελφεῶν,
         9 οὓς τέ]κεν ἐν μεγάροις
   120 10 πατρὸ]ς Ἀλθαία περικ'λειτοῖσιν Οἰνέος·

στρ. δ'. 1 τῶν δ' ὤ]λεσε μοῖρ' ὀλοά
         2 πλεῦνα]ς· οὐ γάρ πω δαΐφρων

113 ΣΥΝΕΧΕΩΣ] A second N has been added above the line by **A³**.   **115 f.** τοὺς
MS., Blass²: οὓς K., Blass¹.—The MS. divides these two verses wrongly (cp. 35 n.):

μηνίσασα ἡ θεὸς κάπρον ἐφῆκεν ἔξοχον
μεγέθει τε καὶ ῥώμῃ, ὃς τὴν τε γῆν
ἄσπορον ἐτίθει καὶ τὰ βοσκήματα καὶ
τοὺς ἐντυγχάνοντας διέφθειρεν. This boar
was a δαιμόνιον τέρας, which destroyed
all living things that came in its way.
110 εἰσάνταν. While εἴσαντα is
Homeric (*Il.* 17. 334 etc.), εἰσάντην is
not found. But ἄντην is epic no less
than ἄντα, and εἰσάνταν is certainly the
true reading here.—εἴσαντ' ἄν μόλοι could
be explained only as an archaizing imitation of the Homeric δς κε with optative
in such places as *Od.* 4. 600, δῶρον δ'
ὅττι κέ μοι δοίης, κειμήλιον ἔστω ('whatever
gift you might give me'); *Od.* 4. 222
ἐπὴν κρητῆρι μιγείη, 'whenever it was
mingled.' In Attic the simple ὅστις μόλοι
would be normal: while ὅστις ἄν μόλοι
would be admissible only if ἄν were joined
with μόλοι as a potential optative.
111 f. δῆριν..στασάμεθ', *Il.* 18. 533
στησάμενοι δ' ἐμάχοντο μάχην ('set their
battle *in array*, and fought'). Her.
VII. 175 τῇ τε στήσονται τὸν πόλεμον. So
too the active, *Od.* 11. 314 φυλόπιδα
στήσειν. Cp. also *Il.* 17. 158 ἀνδράσι
δυσμενέεσσι πόνον καὶ δῆριν ἔθεντο. The
phrase marks the gravity of the task.
ἐνδυκέως (as again in v. 125), 'strenuously.' Hes. *Scut.* 427 (of a lion rending a
carcase), ὅς τε μάλ' ἐνδυκέως ῥινὸν κρατεροῖς
ὀνύχεσσι | σχίσσας κ.τ.λ. The sense is
similar in *Od.* 14. 109, ἐνδυκέως κρέα τ'

ἤσθιε πῖνέ τε οἶνον ('eagerly'). But in
Od. 7. 256 ἐνδυκέως ἐφίλει τε καὶ ἔτρεφεν,
the meaning is softened into 'carefully,'
'sedulously.' (The deriv. is uncertain:
one theory connects the word with δοκ-,
so that the primary sense would be
'reputably.')
113 συνεχέως, with ῠ. So *Il.* 12. 26
συνεχές, ὄφρα κε θᾶσσον κ.τ.λ. : *Od.* 9. 74
δύο τ' ἤματα συνεχὲς αἰεί : Hes. *Theog.* 636
συνεχέως ἐμάχοντο. The ῠ has been explained by the root σεχ- (*quasi* συσσεχές):
and this is confirmed by the remarkable
scansion in *Od.* 19. 113, θάλασσα δὲ
παρέχῃ ἰχθῦς (*quasi* παρσέχῃ). Cp. also
Il. 1. 51 βέλος ἐχεπευκές ἐφείη.—The
alternative would be to suppose that the
ῠ is merely a licence excused by the
metrical ictus in arsis: cp. θύγατέρα
(*Il.* 5. 37), δυναμένοιο (*Od.* 1. 276),
Πέλοπίδης (Her. VII. 159, in a parody of
Il. 7. 125), etc.
114 Αἰτωλοῖς, instead of a simple
ἡμῖν, is in keeping with the diction of
vv. 111 f.; this was the struggle of a
whole people against a supernatural pest.
115 θάπτομεν οὓς κ.τ.λ. In his
second edition Blass reads τοὺς (with the
MS.), assuming that - ⏑ - is here substituted for the - ⏑ ⏑ which stands in all
the corresponding verses (35, 75, 155,
195). This seems metrically impossible.
The MS. has many small errors like that
of τοὺς for οὓς.

that crossed his path.

'Against him we, the flower of the Greeks, strenuously waged epode 3. grim fight for six days together. And when the god gave the mastery to us Aetolians, we buried those whom the squealing boar had slain in his violent onset, even Ancaeus, and Agelaus, that bravest of my trusty brethren, whom Althaea bare in the far-famed house of my father Oeneus.

'But deadly fate destroyed more than these; for the fierce str. 4.

corr. K.   **117** Ἀγέλαον K.: ΑΓΓΕΛΟΝ ms.   **121** τῶν δ' J.: νῦν δ' Blass².—
ὤλεσε]..ΔΕCΕΝ ms.; the N transfixed (by **A**³?).   **122** πλεῦνας Housman, and
others; (πλέονας Smyth): πάντας Ludwich, Blass².

---

116 σῦς ἐριβρύχας, 'the squealing boar.' βρυχᾶσθαι usually means to 'roar,' 'bellow'; it is said (*e.g.*) of a lion, a bull, or a man in agony. Plutarch applies it to the 'trumpeting' of an elephant (*Pyrrh.* 33).

117 Ἀγκαῖον, son of Lycurgus, a hero of Tegea; named in the *Iliad* (2. 609) as father of Agapenor, leader of the Arcadians. He was an Argonaut, and, in right of his great strength, sat with Heracles on the middle bench of the Argo (Apoll. Rh. I. 531). The temple of Athena Ἀλέα at Tegea displayed on its pediment the Calydonian boar-hunt, by Scopas; who had represented Ἀγκαῖον, ἔχοντα ἤδη τραύματα καὶ ἀφέντα τὸν πέλεκυν (his characteristic weapon), supported in the arms of his brother, the hero Epochus. (Paus. 8. 45 § 6.)

Ἀγέλαον: mentioned (as Ἀγέλεως) by Antoninus Liberalis (*c.* 150 A.D.) in his Μεταμορφώσεων συναγωγή, c. 2: who, however, describes him as slain in the later fight with the Curetes (125 f.), and not by the boar. Apollodorus (I. 8 § 1) does not name him.

118 ἀδελφεῶν: the other sons of Oeneus and Althaea, acc. to Antoninus Liberalis (*l. c.*), were Toxeus, Clymenus, Phereus, Periphas; while Apollodorus (*l. c.*) omits Periphas, and substitutes Thyreus for Phereus: the last name may, indeed, have been merely an error or a variant.

119 f. οὓς τέκεν...Ἀλθαία. Wilamowitz would read ὅν (*Gött. gel. Anz.* 1898 Nr. 2, p. 130). But οὓς seems right. The brothers of Meleager who took part in the boar-hunt were all, like himself, sons of Oeneus and Althaea. After her death, Oeneus married Periboea, daughter

of Hipponoos, who bore Tydeus (Apollod. I. 8 § 5: Diod. IV. 35: Hygin. *fab.* 69). Thus the plural pronoun has a point.

121 f. τῶν δ'...πλεῦνας: Fate slew others besides Ancaeus and Agelaus; for the wrath of Artemis was not yet appeased. (πλεῦνας is probably to be read in VII. 46. For ευ from εο, cp. εὖντα in III. 78.)—This suits the context better than νῦν δ'...πάντας (cr. n.), *i.e.* 'but, as it was, Fate slew them all' (referring to ἀδελφεῶν).

ὤλεσε...ὀλοά: the tautology, so inelegant in a modern view, was perhaps hardly felt, since the familiar phrase μοῖρ' ὀλοά was almost equivalent to a single word. (μοῖρ' ὀλοή *Il.* 16. 849, 21. 83, 22. 5: *Od.* 2. 100, 3. 238, 19. 145, 24. 135.) A similar phenomenon occurs where the stress is on the first element of a compound adj., while the second is identical with the verb; *e.g.* Aesch. *Th.* 552 πανώλεις...ὀλοίατο: and in epithets of proper names, when the etymology of the name is not present to the poet's mind; *e.g. Il.* 2. 758 Πρόθοος θοός: Soph. *Ai.* 607 ἀΐδηλον Ἅιδαν.

122 δαΐφρων, bent on strife, 'fierce,' as in 137. In this sense the word is usually referred to δαΐς, 'strife' (ἐν δαΐ λυγρῇ, *Il.* 13. 286). In the *Iliad*, where it is an epithet of heroes, 'warlike' is everywhere a suitable meaning, except in *Il.* 24. 325, where, as applied to the charioteer Idaeus, 'prudent' would be fitter. As used in the *Odyssey*, where it seems always to mean 'prudent' or 'skilful,' it is commonly referred to δαῆναι. Nitzsch would harmonize the divergent senses by supposing that the word always means 'skilled' or 'wise' (δαῆναι),— whether the 'skill' be that of the proved

3 παῦσεν] χόλον ἀγροτέρα

Col. 10 4 Λατοῦς θυγάτηρ· περὶ δ᾽ αἴθωνος δορᾶς
125 5 μαρνάμεθ᾽ ἐνδυκέως
6 Κουρῆσι μενεπτολέμοις·
7 ἔνθ᾽ ἐγὼ πολλοῖς σὺν ἄλλοις
8 Ἴφικλον κατέκτανον
9 ἐσθλόν τ᾽ Ἀφάρητα, θοοὺς μάτρωας· οὐ γὰρ
130 10 καρτερόθυμος Ἄρης
11 κρίνει φίλον ἐν πολέμῳ·
12 τυφλὰ δ᾽ ἐκ χειρῶν βέλη
13 ψυχαῖς ἔπι δυσμενέων φοι-
14 τᾷ θάνατόν τε φέρει
135 15 τοῖσιν ἂν δαίμων θέλῃ·

ἀντ. δ΄. 1 ταῦτ᾽ οὐκ ἐπιλεξαμένα
2 Θεστίου κούρα δαΐφρων
3 μάτηρ κακόποτμος ἐμοὶ
4 βούλευσεν ὄλεθρον ἀτάρβακτος γυνά·
140 5 καῖέ τε δαιδαλέας

---

126 ΚΟΥΡΗΙCΙ **A**: the first I transfixed (by **A**¹?).   **129** ΑΦΑΡΗΑΤΑ ms.: the third A transfixed by the first hand.   This points to a *v.l.* Ἀφαρῆα (Herwerden).—

---

warrior, or another. F. W. Allen (*Amer. Journ. of Phil.* I. 133 ff.) would refer it in all cases to δαΐς, 'torch' (δαίω, to kindle); the warrior is 'fiery'; Penelope is 'high-spirited.' This last sense, however, does not suit the 'skilled' maker of the σφαῖρα in *Od.* 8. 373.

123 ἀγροτέρα (ἄγρα), the huntress: *Il.* 21. 470 f. πότνια θηρῶν, | Ἄρτεμις ἀγροτέρη. Under this name she had a temple at Athens in the suburb Ἄγραι, on high ground near the Ilissus. She is also ἐλαφηβόλος, ἐλλοφόνος, θηροκτόνος, ἰοχέαιρα.

Cp. Paus. 4. 31 § 7 Καλυδωνίοις ἡ Ἄρτεμις, ταύτην γὰρ θεῶν μάλιστα ἔσεβον, ἐπίκλησιν εἶχε Λαφρία. This title (connected with λαβ-, λάφυρα) probably designated her as the goddess who gives the spoils of the chase.

124 αἴθωνος δορᾶς, *fulvae pellis.* αἴθων seems to denote colour (rather than 'fiery spirit') in *Il.* 2. 838 f. ἵπποι | αἴθωνες μεγάλοι: 15. 690 αἰετὸς αἴθων: 16. 487 ταῦρον | αἴθωνα μεγάθυμον (a more

doubtful case): Pind. *O.* XI. 20 αἴθων ἀλώπηξ.—Cp. *Il.* 9. 548 (they fought) ἀμφὶ συὸς κεφαλῇ καὶ δέρματι λαχνήεντι.

125 ἐνδυκέως: 112 n.

126 Κουρῆσι: schol. *Il.* 9. 529, Κουρῆτες τὸ ἐθνικόν, κούρητες δὲ οἱ νεανίαι [*Il.* 19. 123 κούρητας ἀριστῆας Παναχαιῶν]. But the ethnic was often written Κούρητες: the mss. and edd. vary; see Roscher *Myth.* II. 1587. These Curetes (distinct from the hieratic Curetes of the Cretan Zeus-myth) appear in legend as a tribe living in Aetolia at Pleuron. That is what Bacchylides supposes here; for in 149 τοί refers to them, and Pleuron is their city (151). A scholiast on *Il.* 9. 529, Κουρῆτές τ᾽ ἐμάχοντο καὶ Αἰτωλοὶ μενεχάρμαι, explains that Αἰτωλοί is there a more general term for Καλυδώνιοι: Aetolia, he says, was divided into two regions,—the Calydonian, ruled by Oeneus, and the Pleuronian (the seat of the Curetes), ruled by Thestius. The Curetes were afterwards driven westward into Acarnania (Strabo p. 464).

goddess of the chase, Leto's daughter, had not yet stayed her wrath; and we fought strenuously for the beast's tawny hide with the Curetes steadfast in battle.

'There slew I, among many others, Iphiclus and doughty Aphares, gallant brethren of my mother : for the vehement spirit of War discerns no kinsman in fight, but missiles go blindly from our hands against the lives of foemen, fraught with death for whom the god will.

'Reflecting not on this, the fierce daughter of Thestius, my *ant.* 4. ill-starred mother, a woman without fear, planned my destruction. She lifted up a voice of wailing, and set about burning

οὐ γὰρ] Omitted by **A**, added by **A³**.   **134** θάνατον] ΑΘΑΝΑΤΟΝ **A**, corr. **A¹**.
137 κούρα] ΚΟΡΑ ms., corr. K.

---

127 πολλοῖς σὺν ἄλλοις : whom he slew. The words, by picturing a *mêlée*, add point to vv. 129 ff., οὐ γάρ...κρίνει κ.τ.λ.
Ἴφικλον: for ἶ before κλ, cp. VII. 9 f. κέ|κληται : XVI. 127 f. ἔκλαγεν with initial ἔ. Iphiclus was said to have been the first to hit the boar. On this ground he and his brothers, the Thestiadae, claimed the carcase. Hence the war between the Curetes, to whom the Thestiadae belonged, and the Calydonians (Apollod. 1. 8. 2, § 2): cp. v. 124 ff.
129 Ἀφάρητα, from Ἀφάρης. Plut. *Mor.* 315 F (*Parallela* 40) Ἴδας ὁ Ἀφάρητος. Cp. Ἀφαρητίδαι (Pind. *N.* x. 65). Ἀφαρεύς was the more usual form. No son of Thestius is elsewhere so called. The best-known Aphareus is a Messenian hero, son of Περιήρης and Γοργοφόνη (daughter of Perseus); Apollod. 1. 9. 5. Pindar's Apharetidae are his sons, Idas and Lynceus; whom Ovid (*Met.* 8. 304) calls *duo Thestiadae, proles Aphareïa*: showing that he, at least, supposed their father to be this son of Thestius. The sons of Thestius, acc. to Apollod. 1. 7. 10, were Iphiclus, Euippus, Plexippus, Eurypylus.
Homer (*Il.* 9. 567) says of Althaea, πόλλ' ἀχέουσ' ἠρᾶτο κασιγνήτοιο φόνοιο, as if only one of her brothers had been slain. Since this contradicted the legend, Aristarchus and others wished to write κασιγνητοῖο (adj., 'fraternal'). Apollodorus (1. 8. 2) says merely, ἐξελθόντος δὲ Μελεάγρου, καί τινας τῶν Θεστίου παίδων φονεύσαντος, Ἀλθαίαν ἀράσασθαι κατ' αὐτοῦ.
θοούς denotes 'dash,' the impetuous

valour of the warrior, rather than the mere rush of war-chariot or horseman: *Il.* 5. 536, θοὸς ἔσκε μετὰ πρώτοισι μάχεσθαι : *ib.* 571 θοός περ ἐὼν πολεμιστής : 13. 477 βοῇ θοόν.
131 φίλον, a 'friend,' meaning here a kinsman. Meleager's uncles were now fighting against him, on the side of the Curetes (cp. 127 n.), as δυσμενέων (133) indicates. But τυφλά (132) implies that, even so, he would not wittingly have slain a Thestiad.
133 ψυχαῖς ἔπι: for the prep. cf. 83 n.
136 ἐπιλεξαμένα = λογισαμένη, an Ionic phrase; Her. 1. 78, etc.
137 δαΐφρων, 'fierce,' as in 122 (n.). Phrynichus called her αἰνᾶς, κακομηχάνου (n. on 142).
139 ἀτάρβακτος : Pind. *P.* IV. 84 γνώμας ἀταρβάκτοιο=ἀταρβάτου : where Hermann proposed ἀταρμύκτοιο (Hesych. ταρμύξασθαι, φοβηθῆναι).
140—142 The construction καῖε φιτρὸν ἐκ λάρνακος is harshly compressed, but not impossible. I should not retain ἀγκλαύσασα (my correction of the ms. ἐγκλαύσασα), if any satisfactory emendation could be found which would supply a participle in the sense of 'having taken out.' The least unsatisfactory would be ἐκλύσασα (ἐγλύσασα, Wilamowitz): 'having *released*' the brand from the chest, by undoing the fastenings of the latter. But this is not likely to have become ἐγκλαύσασα. The same may be said of ἑλκύσασα (Housman), which is also metrically dubious, since the ἐ answers to a syllable which is long in 7, 22, 47, 62, 102, 127, 167, 182, and *anceps* only in 87 (the τοι- of τοιοῦτον).

6 ἐκ λάρνακος ὠκύμορον
7 φιτρὸν ἀγκλαύσασα, τὸν δὴ
8 μοῖρ᾽ ἐπέκλωσεν τότε
9 ζωᾶς ὅρον ἀμετέρας ἔμμεν. τύχον μὲν
145 10 Δαϊπύλου Κλύμενον
11 παῖδ᾽ ἄλκιμον ἐξεναρί-
12 ζων ἀμώμητον δέμας,
13 πύργων προπάροιθε κιχήσας·
14 τοὶ δὲ πρὸς εὐκτιμέναν
150 15 φεῦγον ἀρχαίαν πόλιν

ἐπ. δ´.   1 Πλευρῶνα· μινύνθη δέ μοι ψυχὰ γλυκεῖα,
2 γνῶν δ᾽ ὀλιγοσθενέων·
3 αἰαῖ· πύματον δὲ πνέων δάκρυσα τλ[άμων
4 ἀγλαὰν ἥβαν προλείπων.

142 ΕΓΚΛΑΤϹΑϹΑ ms.: ἀγκλαύσασα J.: ἐκκλάσασα or ἐγλύσασα (=ἐκλύσασα)
Wilamowitz: ἐγκλάσασα or ἐγκλάξασα Tyrrell: ἐλκύσασα Housman: ἐγκαύσασα Festa

Tyrrell's **ἐγκλάσασα** is excellent as an explanation of the MS. reading, and gives a possible, though somewhat involved, sense (she burned the brand... 'which she had formerly locked up'; cp. λύει πεδήσας in Soph. *Ai.* 676): but it leaves the construction καῖε ἐκ λάρνακος unmitigated. **ἐκκλάσασα** (Wilamowitz) would mean 'having shut out' (not 'having unlocked').

Weir Smyth defends **ἐγκλαύσασα** (though ἐγκλαίω is otherwise unknown), as meaning that 'she shed tears *over* the brand' when she drew it from the chest. In this sense, however, we should rather expect ἐπικλαίω (used with a dative by Nonnus 30. 114). ἐγκλαίειν, were it used, would be rather to weep *at* something, *e.g.* κακοῖς. (In Aesch. *Ag.* 541 ἐνδακρύειν ὄμμασιν is strictly 'to have tears in the eyes'.)

δαιδαλέας, curiously carved: Simon. fr. 37. 1 λάρνακι...ἐν δαιδαλέᾳ.

φιτρόν: Homer does not mention Althaea's brand, but only the curse which she invoked on Meleager (*Il.* 9. 567). But the brand was probably a very old element in the story,—older, it may be, than the epic sources used by the Homeric poet of the Πρεσβεία. Phrynichus, says Pausanias (10. 31, § 4), was the first to mention it ἐν δράματι: the drama was his Πλευρώνιαι (fr. 6, Nauck², p. 721):

κρυερὸν γὰρ οὐκ | ἤλυξεν μόρον, ὠκεῖα δέ
νιν φλὸξ κατεδαίσατο | δαλοῦ περθομένου
ματρὸς ὑπ᾽ αἰνᾶς κακομαχάνου. That play was probably earlier than the date of this ode (476 B.C.). Cp. Aesch. *Ch.* 604 ff.—See Appendix.

143 f. ἐπέκλωσεν, 'ordained'; here with acc. and inf., as in Aesch. *Eum.* 335 τοῦτο γὰρ λάχος διαντίαια | μοῖρ᾽ ἐπέκλωσεν ἐμπέδως ἔχειν.—**τότε**, of yore. Apollod. I. 8. 1 τούτου δὲ (Meleager) ὄντος ἡμερῶν ἑπτὰ παραγενομένας τὰς Μοίρας φασὶν ἐπεῖν· τότε τελευτήσει Μελέαγρος, ὅταν ὁ καιόμενος ἐπὶ τῆς ἐσχάρας δαλὸς κατακαῇ. τοῦτο ἀκούσασα τὸν δαλὸν ἀνείλετο Ἀλθαία καὶ κατέθετο εἰς λάρνακα.

ζωᾶς ὅρον ἀμετέρας: the limit or canon, the 'measure' of his life. Cp. Dion Chrysost. or. 67 § 7 (Μελεάγρῳ) δαλόν τινα λέγουσι ταμιεύειν τὸν τῆς ζωῆς χρόνον. Aesch. *Ch.* 607 ff. (Althaea) παιδὸς δαφοινὸν | δαλὸν ἥλικ᾽ ἐπεὶ μολὼν | ματρόθεν κελάδησεν, | ξύμμετρόν τε διαὶ βίου | μοιρόκραντον ἐς ἆμαρ.

145 Δαϊπύλου Κλύμενον, one of the Curetes, otherwise unknown. The name Κλύμενος, a frequent one, was also borne by one of Meleager's brothers (117 n.).

146 f. ἐξεναρίζων. The ἐξαναρίζων of the MS. is a mere error: in no dialect would the εν- become αν-.

148 πύργων προπάροιθε, before the battlemented walls of Pleuron, to which the brand of speedy doom, taken from the carven chest,—the brand which fate had ordained of yore to be the measure of my life.

'It so befell that I was in the act of slaying Clymenus, the valiant son of Daïpylus, a warrior of noble mien, whom I had overtaken in front of the walls,—for our foes were in flight to their ancient city of Pleuron;—

when the sweet life grew faint within me, and I knew that epode 4. my strength was ebbing away. Ah me! and as I drew my latest breath, I wept, hapless one, at passing from my glorious youth.'

(with δαῖε in 140), Desrousseaux (with εἷλε). **146 f.** ἐξεναρίζων] ΕΞΑΝΑΡΙΖΩΝ MS. **151** ΜΙΝΥΝΘΑ MS.: μυνύνθα (=μινύνθη) L. C. Purser: μίνυνθεν or μινύνθει Housman: μίνυθεν Wilamowitz. **154** προλείπων K.: ΠΡΟΛΙΠΩΝ MS.

---

the Curetes were being driven in flight from Calydon.

149 ff. τοὶ δὲ...Πλευρῶνα: a parenthesis, explanatory of v. 148. Ancient Pleuron (ἡ παλαιά, Strabo p. 451) stood in the fertile μεσογαία of Aetolia, some seven or eight miles N.W.N. of Calydon. About 230 B.C. that site was deserted, and a new Pleuron (ἡ νεωτέρα) was founded more to the S. W., not far from the modern Mesolonghi. A schol. on *Il.* 9. 529 describes the Κουρῆτες as οἱ τὴν Πλευρῶνα οἰκοῦντες (p. 451) speaks of ἡ Κουρητική as ἡ αὐτὴ τῇ Πλευρωνίᾳ. He also mentions a mountain named Κούριον as πλησίον τῆς παλαιᾶς Πλευρῶνος.

151 If μίνυνθα δέ μοι, the reading of the MS., be sound, we have here - ᴗ ᴗ - where, in three of the other four epodes, we find --ᴗ- (vv. 31, 71, 111). But the fifth epode has the same metrical peculiarity, if in v. 191 the MS. τάδε be sound. Hence the case of μίνυνθα is different from that of an isolated metrical anomaly like μινύθει in III. 90, or δεῦρ' ἄθρησον νόῳ in v. 8. It is more like the case of v. 11 and 14, where the metrical peculiarity occurs also in the antistrophe (11=26, 14=29). That is, we have to ask:—Did the poet, in these last two epodes, deliberately modify the metre of the first verse? In order to judge of this question, the *sense* yielded by μίνυνθα must be considered. In *Il.* 1. 416 f. Thetis says to Achilles: αἴθ' ὄφελες παρὰ νηυσὶν ἀδάκρυτος καὶ ἀπήμων | ἦσθαι, ἐπεὶ νύ τοι αἶσα μίνυνθά περ, οὔ τι μάλα δήν :—'seeing that thy lot [is] very brief'

(literally 'is only *for a little while*': cp. *Il.* 4. 466 μίνυνθα δέ οἱ γένεθ' ὁρμή, 'his effort lasted only a little while'). In the Homeric ἐπεί νύ τοι αἶσα μίνυνθα, the use of the adverb with ἐστί understood is most unusual, if not unique: but the sense, at any rate, is clear. Now, if μίνυνθα be genuine in this verse of Bacchylides, there is the same singularity, but in a far harsher form, since we have to supply, not ἐστί, but ἦν. And when ἦν has been supplied, what is the sense? 'My life *was but for a short while*.' The meaning required, however, is: '*grew feeble*,'—'began to ebb away.' The true reading may be **μινύνθη**. A scribe may have changed this to μινύνθα, wrongly supposing the latter to be the Doric form; as in Theocr. 1. 7 the MSS. have ποιμάν. A reminiscence of the adv. μίνυνθα in *Il.* 1. 417 may have helped. In v. 191 τάδε is easily corrected to τᾷδε. —Cp. III. 90 n.

152 ὀλιγοσθενέων: the verb is not found elsewhere (though the adj. occurs in schol. Oppian *Hal.* 1. 623). The poet may have felt that, in relation to the sufferer's consciousness (γνῶν), this word was fitter than the Homeric ὀλιγοδρανέων or ὀλιγηπελέων (*Il.* 15. 24, 246 etc.), which are more objective.—γνῶν without augment: *Il.* 4. 357, Hes. *Th.* 551.

Cp. Swinburne, *Atalanta in Calydon*, p. 88 (the dying Meleager speaks):—'My heart is within me As an ash in the fire'... And the Semichorus, *ib.* p. 83: 'He wastes as the embers quicken; With the brand he fades as a brand.'

154 ἀγλαὰν ἥβαν. Simon. fr. 105

155　5 φασὶν ἀδεισιβόαν

Col. 11　6 Ἀμφιτρύωνος παῖδα μοῦνον δὴ τότε
　　　7 τέγξαι βλέφαρον, ταλαπενθέος
　　　8 πότμον οἰκτίροντα φωτός·
　　　9 καί νιν ἀμειβόμενος
160　10 τοῖ᾽ ἔφα· θνατοῖσι μὴ φῦναι φέριστον,

στρ. ε᾽.　1 μηδ᾽ ἀελίου προσιδεῖν
　　　2 φέγγος· ἀλλ᾽ οὐ γάρ τίς ἐστιν
　　　3 πρᾶξις τάδε μυρομένοις,
　　　4 χρὴ κεῖνο λέγειν ὅ,τι καὶ μέλλει τελεῖν.
165　5 ἦ ῥα τις ἐν μεγάροις
　　　6 Οἰνῆος ἀρηϊφίλου
　　　7 ἔστιν ἀδμήτα θυγάτρων,
　　　8 σοὶ φυὰν ἀλιγκία;
　　　9 τάν κεν λιπαρὰν ἐθέλων θείμαν ἄκοιτιν.

170　10 τὸν δὲ μενεπτολέμου
　　　11 ψυχὰ προσέφα Μελεά-
　　　12 γρου· λίπον χλωραύχενα
　　　13 ἐν δώμασι Δαϊάνειραν,

160 τοῖ᾽ Housman, A. Ludwich : ΤΟΙΔ **A** : but a corrector (**A³**?) has altered this to ΤΑΔ᾽ by transfixing I with a sloping line which at the same time converts O into Α.— τάδ᾽ ἔφα Blass : τόδ᾽ ἔφα K.　**160—162** The words θνατοῖσι...φέγγος are quoted by Stobaeus *Flor.* 98. 27, who, placing a comma after φέγγος, adds in the same line

οἵδε παρ᾽ Εὐρυμέδοντά ποτ᾽ ἀγλαὸν ὤλεσαν ἥβην : Theognis 985 αἶψα γὰρ ὥστε νόημα παρέρχεται ἀγλαὸς ἥβη.
155 f. ἀδεισιβόαν, only here and in X. 61 : cp. ἀδεισιδαίμων (Clem. Alex. p. 302) ἀδεισίθεος orac. *ap.* Iulian. p. 297 D.—
Ἀμφιτρύωνος. This lengthening of the *i* in Amphitryo is very exceptional : it is short above in v. 85, and in XV. 15. Pindar, who uses the name in six places (*P.* IX. 81 ; *N.* I. 52, IV. 20, X. 13 : *I.* I. 55, VI. 6) always has ῐ. In the *Amphitruo* of Plautus the *i* is regularly short, and no-where appears to be necessarily long. The name does not seem to be extant in Greek iambic verse ; possibly we might have found examples of this scansion in the Ἀμφιτρύων of Sophocles, of Aeschylus Alexandrinus (Nauck² p. 824), or of the comic poet Archippus. Cp. Ἀμφῑτρίτη (*Od.* 3. 91, etc.).
157 βλέφαρον: the sing., as in XI. 17 ; twice in Sophocles (*Ant.* 104, fr. 645), and often in Euripides. Homer and Aeschylus

have only the plur. βλέφαρα, Pindar only γλέφαρα. — **ταλαπενθέος**, lit. ' bearing grief' (*Od.* 5. 222) : in XV. 26 it means ' grievous.'
160 τοῖ᾽ ἔφα. The first syllable is long in three at least of the corresponding verses (40, 80, 200) : and presumably long, though *anceps*, in the fourth (120, πατρός). And the first hand wrote ΤΟΙΔ, which a corrector has changed into ΤΑΔ᾽. Blass (*praef.* p. XLII) defends τάδ᾽, holding that ˘ ˘ — could be substituted for — ˘ — — at the beginning of the verse. To the ear at least, such a change in the rhythm is very unpleasing. It seems much more probable that the author wrote τοῖ᾽ ἔφα. It is true, as the same critic ob-serves, that we do not elsewhere find τοῖα as = τοιάδε, before a speech : but it is not doubtful that a poet could have so used it. The objection would be met by reading τᾷδ᾽ (cp. 191 n.): but the MS. reading points rather to τοῖ᾽.
θνατοῖσι μὴ φῦναι φέριστον: the first

'Tis said that then, and then alone, tears came to the eyes of
Amphitryon's intrepid son, in pity for the ill-fated hero's doom ;
and he answered him with such words as these : ' It were best
for mortals that they had never been born,

and never looked upon the sunlight. But, seeing that these str. 5.
laments avail not, a man should speak of that which he can
hope to accomplish. In the halls of the warrior Oeneus is there
a maiden among his daughters like in form to thee? Fain were
I to make her my queenly bride.'
And to him spake the spirit of Meleager steadfast in war :
' I left Deïaneira at home, in the fresh bloom of youth,

ὄλβιος δ' οὐδεὶς βροτῶν πάντα χρόνον, a fragment otherwise unknown (Bergk fr. 2).
161 μηδ' Stobaeus : ΜΗΤ ms. **164** χρή] ΚΡΗ ms., but with Χ written above
(by **A²**?). **169** ΘΕΛΩΝ ms., corr. Κ.—AKOITAN **A** : corr. **A¹**? **170** τὸν δὲ]
TONKE ms., with Δ written above (by **A²**?). **172** χλωραύχενα] The grave accent
was at first placed on the letter υ, but two lines have been drawn through it.

---

half of the familiar maxim; Theognis
425 ff. πάντων μὲν μὴ φῦναι ἐπιχθονίοισιν
ἄριστον, | μηδ' ἐσιδεῖν αὐγὰς ὀξέος ἠελίου. |
φύντα δ' ὅπως ὤκιστα πύλας Ἀΐδαο περῆσαι
κ.τ.λ. : Soph. O. C. 1225 ff., etc. This
passage illustrates the pathetic power of
Bacchylides. It is impressive, indeed,
that this should be said by Heracles,
'the unconquered' (v. 57). Yet a subtler
poet would scarcely have made him say
it here, within the gates of Hades, to
Meleager, whose fate he pities. For
the first part of the adage,—'It is best
not to be born,'—inevitably suggests
that other which is not spoken,—'and
next best, to die soon.' Contrast the
manner in which the whole γνώμη is introduced by Sophocles (l. c.). As uttered
by the men of Colonus, it is not only a
comment on the trials of Oedipus, but
also a thought which turns the mind
towards his approaching release.
161 προσιδεῖν, aorist, like ἐσιδεῖν
αὐγὰς in Theognis 426 (see last n.), because the moment of birth is meant : cp.
Il. 16. 187 f. αὐτὰρ ἐπεὶ δὴ τόν γε μογο-
στόκος Εἰλείθυια | ἐξάγαγε πρὸ φόωσδε καὶ
ἠελίου ἴδεν αὐγάς.
162 f. ἀλλ' οὐ γὰρ πρᾶξις κ.τ.λ. :
Od. 10. 202 ἀλλ' οὐ γάρ τις πρῆξις ἐγίγνετο
μυρομένοισιν ('no effect,' no good). Il. 24.
524 οὐ γάρ τις πρῆξις πέλεται κρυεροῖο
γόοιο. Bacchyl. fr. 12 τί γὰρ ἐλαφρὸν ἔτ'
ἐστὶν ἄπρακτ' ὀδυρόμενον δονεῖν | καρδίαν ;
164 μέλλει, sc. τις, easily supplied
from the indefinite plural partic. in 163.
(Not: 'a word which is likely to have

effect.')—τελεῖν is here probably the fut.,
though it might be the pres.: cp. III.
30 n.
165 ἦ ῥα, interrogative, as in Il. 5.
421; Pind. P. IX. 40, I. VII. 3; Soph. Ai.
172 (lyric). Some edd. prefer to write
ἦρα (i.e. ἦ + ἄρα) in this sense.
167 ἀδμήτα: Hom. hymn. Ven. 82
παρθένῳ ἀδμήτῃ : Aesch. Suppl. 149 (the
prayer of the Danaïdes to Artemis),
ἀδμάτας ἀδμάτα | ῥύσιος γενέσθω. In Il.
and Od. this form of the word is applied
only to cattle; but παρθένος ἀδμής occurs
in Od. 6. 109, etc.—The Ionic η is kept
here to avoid a double α sound; but cp.
x. 84 ἄδματοι.—θυγάτρων, partitive gen.
with τις in 165.
169 λιπαράν. The notion of the
epithet is that of rich adornment,
splendid surroundings. It may perhaps
be rendered by 'queenly.' Cp. Hes.
Th. 901 δεύτερον ἠγάγετο λιπαρὴν Θέμιν.
Except in Od. 15. 332, where λιπαροὶ
κεφαλάς is said of youths whose heads
are anointed with oil, λιπαρός is never in
Homer the epithet of a person, nor is it
ever so used by Pindar.
θείμαν ἄκοιτιν. Od. 21. 72 ἱέμενοι
γῆμαι θέσθαι τε γυναῖκα. Aesch. Th. 930
πόσιν αὐτᾷ θεμένα.
Pindar represented Meleager as pro-
posing the marriage with Deianeira to
Heracles, in order that he might defend
her from her dread suitor, Achelous
(schol. Il. 21. 194). See Appendix.
172 f. χλωραύχενα, with the freshness
(the fresh bloom) of youth upon her neck.

J. B.

14 νῆϊν ἔτι χρυσέας
175 15 Κύπριδος θελξιμβρότου.

ἀντ. ε'. 1 λευκώλενε Καλλιόπα,
2 στᾶσον εὐποίητον ἅρμα
3 αὐτοῦ· Δία τε Κρονίδαν
4 ὕμνησον Ὀλύμπιον ἀρχαγὸν θεῶν,
180 5 τόν τ' ἀκαμαντορόαν
6 Ἀλφεόν, Πέλοπός τε βίαν,
7 καὶ Πίσαν, ἔνθ' ὁ κλεεννὸς
8 ποσσὶ νικάσας δρόμῳ
9 ἦλθ]εν Φερένικος < ἐς > εὐπύργους Συρακόσ-
185 10 σας Ἱέρωνι φέρων
11 εὐδ]αιμονίας πέταλον.

179 ΟΛΥΜΠΙΟΝ] ω has been written by Α³ above the second Ο : a notable instance of a true reading depraved by this corrector, though metre clearly forbade.

Nightingales, when they begin their song in the early Greek spring, are called χλωραύχενες by Simonides (fr. 73), who meant (I think) 'with *fresh* throat,' *i.e.* with throat of fresh, youthful vigour,—in Keats's phrase, 'full-throated.' Thus for both poets χλωραύχην implies χλωρός as an epithet, not of *colour*, but of *young life*; though with diverse applications. See Appendix.

Δαϊάνειραν, see XV. 23 ff. The bare mention of her name suffices here : enough has been said to enforce the truth, χαλεπὸν | θεῶν παρατρέψαι νόον (94 f.). 174 f. χρυσέας, with ῠ, as in XV. 2, Pind. P. IV. 4 etc. This ῠ was borrowed from the lyrists by the dramatists, but only in lyrics (Soph. O. T. 157, etc.). In Homer the υ is always long, and such forms as χρυσέης are to be scanned as two syllables (with synizesis) ; cp. Il. I. 15 χρυσέῳ ἀνὰ σκήπτρῳ.—θελξιμβρότου, the enchantress, who bewitches mortals. In Il. 14. 214 ff. is described the embroidered cestus (κεστὸν ἱμάντα) of Aphrodite, wherein are 'all her enchantments' (θελκτήρια),—'love, desire, and sweet converse, that steals the wits even of the wise.'

176 ff. Καλλιόπα is now bidden to turn from the heroic myth to the immediate theme of the epinikion. In XVIII. 13 she is the Muse who inspires a dithyramb concerning Io. Above, in 13 f., the poet is Οὐρανίας...θεράπων, as in VI.

11 Urania again prompts his strain ; while in XV. 3 she moves him to sing of Heracles. In III. 3, XI. 2, and XII. 228 it is Κλειώ who presides over the ode of victory. Bacchylides uses the names of these Muses interchangeably, without assigning a special function to each. Pindar names Καλλιόπα only once (O. X. 16), Κλειώ once (N. III. 83), and Οὐρανία nowhere : he usually speaks of Μοῖσα or Μοῖσαι. In later mythology Calliope was the Muse of heroic song, Cleio of history, and Urania of astronomy.

177 στᾶσον κ.τ.λ. : cease to pursue the story of Heracles, and revert to Hieron's victory. The example of an abrupt return from myth to theme was set by Pindar in the earliest of his extant odes, written in 498 B.C., when he was only twenty ; P. X. 51 κώπαν σχάσον κ.τ.λ.: cp. N. V. 15 f. στάσομαι : P. IV. (462 B.C.) 247 f. μακρά μοι νεῖσθαι κατ' ἀμαξιτόν· ὥρα γὰρ συνάπτει· καί τινα | οἶμον ἴσαμι βραχύν· where he adds, πολλοῖσι δ' ἄγημαι σοφίας ἑτέροις, words which imply that other lyric poets (like Bacchylides here) had imitated this trait. εὐποίητον : Hom. Hymn. Apoll. 265 ἅρματά τ' εὐποίητα.—ἅρμα : the 'chariot' is Pindaric, but Pindar always gives it to 'the Muses' collectively, and never materializes it by such an epithet as 'well-wrought': he conceives the poet as borne along in it (O. IX. 81 ἐν Μοισᾶν δίφρῳ) : the singers of old are they οἱ

a stranger still to golden Aphrodite the enchantress.'
White-armed Calliope, stay thy well-wrought chariot there ; ant. 5.
and now sing Zeus, son of Cronus, Olympian ruler of the gods,—
and Alpheus, of untiring stream, with mighty Pelops, and Pisa,
where the famed Pherenicus prevailed by his speed in the race,
ere he returned to the embattled walls of Syracuse, bringing
Hieron the leaf of good fortune.

184 f. ἦλθ]εν and ἐς are supplied by Housman (κῦρεν..ἐς Ludwich).—Συρακούσσας
MS., K., Herwerden: Συρακόσσας Blass.

χρυσαμπύκων | ἐς δίφρον Μοισᾶν ἔβαινον
(*I.* II. 2) : the patron τόδ' ἔζευξεν ἅρμα
Πιερίδων (*P.* X. 65) : in a poetic effort,
ἔσσυται... | Μοισαῖον ἅρμα (*I.* VII. 61). As
the chariot is an image for the poet's ὁρμή,
and belongs to the Muses only in their
relation to the poet, it is not attributed
to the Muses, or to any of them, in
ancient art.
180 ἀκαμαντορόαν : cp. III. 6 n.
181 Πέλοπός τε βίαν : cp. VII. *ad fin.*
ἐν Πέλοπος Φρυγίου | κλεινοῖς ἀέθλοις : X.
24 f. ἐν ζαθέοις | ἁγνοῦ Πέλοπος δαπέδοις.
Hero and god are similarly linked in
Pind. *O.* X. 26 ff. : ' The ordinances of
Zeus have moved me to sing of the
peerless festival which Heracles founded
by the ancient tomb of *Pelops*, with altars
six in number ' (the βωμοὺς ἓξ διδύμους
of *O.* v. 5, which Heracles dedicated to
six pairs of deities). In the altis at
Olympia, west of the great altar of Zeus at
which the Iamidae divined by ἔμπυρα, was
the precinct called the Πελόπιον, enclosing
the hero's traditional grave,—a low tumu-
lus of elliptic form. A Doric propylaion,
with three doors, gave access from the
s.w. side. Here sacrifices, the αἱμακουρίαι
of Pind. *O.* I. 91, had been offered to the
spirit of Pelops from early times : Pausanias (5. 13 § 2) mentions the yearly
offering of a black ram.
182 Πίσαν, with ῐ : so Pindar (*O.*
II. 3, etc.). But Simonides fr. 158 has
Πίσῃ : cp. Theocr. IV. 29 ποτὶ Πίσαν.
Euripides (*I. T.* I and *Helen.* 393) has
Πίσαν (so edd.), but in the fifth foot: cp.
I. T. 824 παρθένον Πισάτιδα, where the
quantity of the ι is doubtful. The name
is probably connected with πῖσος (πίνω),
' water-meadow.'—Pisa, the old Achaean
capital of Pisatis, the mythical seat of
Oenomaus and Pelops, seems to have
stood about three-quarters of a mile east
of the temple of the Olympian Zeus.

The site has been conjecturally identified
with a hill near the stream Miráka, an
affluent of the Alpheus. (Cp. E. Curtius,
Pelop. II. 51.) Pisa was destroyed in
572 B.C. by the Eleans, who then
succeeded to the presidency of the games.
Pindar uses Πίσα as a poetical synonym
for Olympia: *O.* I. 18 Πίσας τε καὶ
Φερενίκου χάρις : VIII. 9 ὦ Πίσας εὔδενδρον
ἐπ' Ἀλφεῷ ἄλσος. So Herodotus (II. 7)
measures the distance from Athens ἔς τε
Πίσαν καὶ ἐπὶ τὸν νηὸν τοῦ Διὸς τοῦ
Ὀλυμπίου.
184 f. ἦλθεν..ἐς εὐπύργους κ.τ.λ. We
must insert ἐς, lost after -ος through the
recurrence of σε (-ΟCΕCΕΤΙΠΤΡΓΟΥC).
εὐπύργους is inadmissible, because the ὔ of
εὐ- is always short before a single consonant. There is, indeed, one apparent
exception, *Od.* 14. 63 κλῆρόν τε εὔμορφόν
τε γυναῖκα, but there the v.l. πολυμνηστήν
is doubtless right. The ὔ is long only
when the consonant is doubled, as in
εὔμμελίης, εὔρροος, εὔσσελμος.—Συρακόσσας. The MS. has CΤΡΑΚΟΥCCAC, but
the double σσ indicates that the Doric
form should be restored by deleting v.
The forms were (1) Doric Συράκοσαι
(Pind. *P.* II. 1), or *metri gratia* Συράκοσσαι: (2) Attic Συράκουσαι: (3) Ionic
Συρήκουσαι.
186 εὐδαιμονίας πέταλον : alluding to
the garland of wild olive (κότινος) which
was the prize at Olympia. The singular
πέταλον is poetically substituted for the
plural, as in Soph. *O. C.* 701 φύλλον
ἐλαίας. It is a phrase resembling that in
III. 92 ff. ὄλβου .. ἄνθεα. Victory is the
leaf which εὐδαιμονία puts forth. There
is a like metaphor in 198, πυθμένες
θάλλουσιν ἀρετᾶν. The use of πέταλον,
instead of ἄνθος, is fitting, since the word
is intended to suggest the olive-wreath :
cp. Pind. *N.* I. 17 Ὀλυμπιάδων φύλλοις
ἐλαιᾶν χρυσέοις : *O.* VIII. 76 στέφανος

20—2

¹² χρὴ δ' ἀλαθείας χάριν

Col. 12 ¹³ αἰνεῖν, φθόνον ἀμφοτέραισιν

¹⁴ χερσὶν ἀπωσάμενον,

190 ¹⁵ εἴ τις εὖ πράσσοι βροτῶν.

ἐπ. ε΄. ¹ Βοιωτὸς ἀνὴρ τᾷδε φών[ησεν, γλυκειᾶν

² Ἡσίοδος πρόπολος

³ Μουσᾶν, ὃν < ἂν > ἀθάνατοι τι[μῶσι, τούτῳ

⁴ καὶ βροτῶν φήμαν ἔπ[εσθαι.

195 ⁵ πείθομαι εὐμαρέως

187 ἀλαθείας Blass; ΑΛΗΘΕΙΑC MS. **191** τᾷδε Wilamowitz, for τάδε : see comment.—After φώνησεν K. supplies παλαιός : Wilam., λιγειᾶν : Bruhn, γλυκειᾶν (so Blass) : Pingel, βαθύφρων.—Housman conj. τάνδε φώνησέν ποτ' ὀμφάν. **193 f.** ὃν

φυλλοφόρων ἀπ' ἀγώνων : *N.* VI. 65 ἄνθε' Ὀλυμπιάδος. Some take πέταλον as '*a voting-leaf*,' Pind. *I.* VII. 43 μηδὲ Νηρέος θυγάτηρ νεικέων πέταλα δὶς ἐγγυαλιζέτω | ἄμμιν, 'place leaves of strife in our hands' (force us to vote on opposite sides) : a passage which shows that the use of leaves in voting was known long before the Syracusans employed the πέταλον ἐλαίας (Diod. XI. 86) in the form of ostracism called πεταλισμός. ('Petalism' was instituted probably *c.* 454 B.C., and abolished after no long interval : Diod. XI. 87 : Freeman *Sicily* II. 332.) Leaves were used in the Athenian Βουλή when the senators voted on the question of expelling one of their own number : Aeschin. or. I § 111 ἡ βουλὴ καταγνοῦσα τουτονὶ ἀδικεῖν καὶ ἐκφυλλοφορήσασα. What, then, would be the exact sense of εὐδαιμονίας πέταλον? It has been rendered, 'a *token* of heaven's favour.' But that meaning can be reached only through the literal one, 'a *suffrage for* (Hieron's) happiness,'—given by the god who decreed the victory. That, however, is too artificial : it seems also too obscure, without help from the context. There is a further objection ; viz. that, on the analogy of φέρειν ψῆφον (*suffragium ferre*), φέρων πέταλον should refer to the voter.

187 ἀλαθείας : the MS. has ἀλη- here, but the Doric α is found in all the five other places where the poet uses the word (III. 96; VII. 42 f.; IX. 85; XII. 204; fr. 10). Bacchylides refers more than once to the φθόνος which may put constraint on

a man's inward sense of merit in others, and keep him silent, while 'truth,' candour, makes the poet speak out : see III. 67 ff. ; VIII. 85 ff. σὺν δ' ἀλαθείᾳ βροτῶν κ.τ.λ. : XII. 199 ff. εἰ μή τινα θερσιεπὴς | φθόνος βιᾶται, | αἰνείτω σοφὸν ἄνδρα | σὺν δίκᾳ... | ἁ δ' ἀλαθεία φιλεῖ | νικᾶν κ.τ.λ. His tone is that of one who praises because it is the plain duty of a fair mind.

188 f. ἀμφοτέραισιν χερσίν, 'with might and main.' Cp. the proverbial phrase, οὐ τῇ ἑτέρᾳ ληπτέον (Plat. *Soph.* 226 A).—ἀπωσάμενον. Housman would write ἀπωσαμένους, as εἰ follows. The last syllable of the verse is, indeed, long in all the strictly corresponding verses (54, 69, 94, 109, 134, 149, 174). Verses 14 and 29, though holding the same place, are, as we saw, metrically peculiar in having an additional syllable : still, ἐθέλει δέ in v. 14 suggests that here also the final syllable could be *anceps*. As a matter of idiom, the singular seems here more natural than the plural.

190 εἴ τις εὖ πράσσοι, after χρὴ (187). In general statements or maxims the present indicative is sometimes thus followed by εἰ with the optative, where we should rather expect a general supposition expressed by εἰ with pres. indic., or ἐάν with pres. subjunctive. *Od.* 14. 56 ξεῖν', οὔ μοι θέμις ἔστ', οὐδ' εἰ κακίων σέθεν ἔλθοι, | ξεῖνον ἀτιμῆσαι. Pind. *P.* VIII. 13 κέρδος δὲ φίλτατον, | ἑκόντος εἴ τις ἐκ δόμων φέροι. Similarly when the condition is contained in a relative clause : Soph. *Ant.* 666 ἀλλ' ὃν πόλις στήσειε, τοῦδε χρὴ κλύειν.

191—194 Hieron's success and glory

We must give praise, for truth's sake, and thrust envy away
from us with might and main, if any man should prosper.

Thus spake the Boeotian, Hesiod, servant of the sweet epode 5.
Muses: 'Whomsoever the immortals honour, the good report
of men goes with him also.' Readily am I won

< ἂν >..τιμῶσι τούτῳ...ἔπ[εσθαι Housman: and Wilamowitz (but with κείνῳ instead
of τούτῳ). So also Blass², but with χρῆμεν after τιμῶσι (Pingel having conjectured
χρῆναι). **195** πείθομαι] πειθόμεθ' Blass².

---

are so manifestly given *by the gods*,
that envy is put to silence, and men's
applause cannot be withheld. The poet
constantly refers Hieron's victories to the
favour of heaven: cp. above, 36: IV.
1—3, and more especially 18—20, τί
φέρτερον ἢ θεοῖσιν | φίλον ἐόντα κ.τ.λ.
Βοιωτὸς ἀνήρ. Virgil's *Ascraeus senex*
(*Eel.* 6. 70); so Homer is Χῖος ἀνήρ
(Simonid. fr. 85. 2); Simonides, ἀοιδὸς ὁ
Κήϊος (Theocr. XVI. 44); Pindar, *Dircaeus
cygnus* (Hor. *C.* IV. 2. 25); Alcaeus,
Lesbius civis (id. *C.* I. 32. 5); Anacreon,
ὁ Τήϊος κύκνος (Antipater Sidon. in *Anth.*
7. 30).
τᾷδε, 'on this wise': cp. Soph. *El.*
643 τῇδε γὰρ κἀγὼ φράσω (where, however, 'on this wise' means 'darkly,'—
not, 'in these terms'): *O. C.* 1300 κἀπὸ
μαντέων ταύτῃ κλύω ('and *so* I hear'...).
The MS. τάδε cannot be sound, if in 151
μίνυνθα is (as it seems to be) corrupt:
see n. there.
φώνησεν. All Dorian dialects have
-ήσω, -ησα in fut. and 1st aor. of verbs in
-έω. In Pindar *N.* v. 44 Boeckh read
φίλασ' (as also in other places of Pindar);
but recent editors agree in giving φίλησ'.
In *O.* XIII. 67 W. Christ and others give
φώνασε, though φώνησε in *N.* X. 76, and
φωνήσαις in *I.* v. 51. The form φωνάω,
of which ἐφώνασα would be the Doric
aorist, does not seem to occur, though
it would be the natural form for the verb
from φωνά.
The word lost after φώνησεν may have
been an epithet of Μουσᾶν (such as
γλυκειᾶν or λιγειᾶν). Both the poet's
style and the rhythm of the passage
suggest this as probable.
ὃν ἂν ἀθάνατοι κ.τ.λ. The supplement given in the text seems the best
(see cr. n.). **τούτῳ** is not grammatically
indispensable, since a dat. could be
understood (cp. Soph. *Ant.* 35 f., ὃς ἂν
τούτων τι δρᾷ, | φόνον πρόκεισθαι): but it
makes the sentence clearer; and the
emphasis is fitting here.—In Hesiod's

extant poems and fragments there is
nothing nearer to this sentiment than the
passage in *Theog.* 81 ff., ὅντινα τιμήσωσι
Διὸς κοῦραι μεγάλοιο |,... | τοῦ μὲν ἐπὶ
γλώσσῃ γλυκερὴν χείουσιν ἐέρσην, |...οἱ
δέ νυ λαοὶ | πάντες ἐς αὐτὸν ὁρῶσι κ.τ.λ. :
where he says that the *Muses* give
winning eloquence to kings, and fame to
poets. But Theognis v. 169 is exactly
apposite: ὃν δὲ θεοὶ τιμῶσ', ὃν καὶ
μωμεύμενος αἰνεῖ, i.e., a man, though
inclined to blame, is constrained to praise.
I cannot think that Bacchylides was
alluding to Hes. *Theog.* 81 ff. References of this kind to other poets are, as
a rule, verbally close: see, *e.g.*, Pind. *I.*
v. 67 Λάμπων δὲ μελέταν | ἔργοις
ὀπάζων Ἡσιόδου μάλα τιμᾷ τοῦτ' ἔπος
(alluding to Hes. *Op.* 410 μελέτη δέ τε
ἔργον ὀφέλλει). The saying may have
occurred in some lost passage of Hesiod,
—possibly the source of Theognis 169:
or our poet may have meant the verse
of Theognis, and named Hesiod by mistake.

195 f. πείθομαι κ.τ.λ. 'Readily do
I consent to send'... This is a phrase,
like many in Pindar, intimating that the
epinikion was written by invitation. Cp.
O. XIII. 96 Μοίσαις γὰρ ἀγλαοθρόνοις ἐκ ὼν |
Ὀλιγαιθίδαισίν τ' ἔβαν ἐπίκουρος : *P.* v.
43 f. ἐκ ὄντι τοίνυν πρέπει | νόῳ τὸν εὐερ-
γέταν ὑπαντιάσαι.—**εὐκλέα,** scanned – – :
Soph. *O. T.* 161 has (θρόνον) εὐκλέα
(– ‿ ‿). In Pind. *P.* XII. 24 εὐκλεᾶ (acc.
sing., for εὐκλεέα) is – – ‿ -. εὐκλέα γλώσ-
σαν means 'an utterance fraught with
glory' (for Hieron): cp. Pind. *N.* VI. 29
ἐπέων...οὖρον | εὐκλέα (=εὐκλεέα): *O.* II.
90 εὐκλέας ὀϊστούς ('shafts of song, winged
by fame').—For **γλῶσσαν,** cp. Pind. *O.*
IX. φέροις δὲ Πρωτογενείας | ἄστεϊ
γλῶσσαν ('lend thy voice' to Opus): *N.*
IV. 86 κεῖνος...ἐμὰν | γλῶσσαν εὑρέτω
κελαδῆτιν, 'Let him (in the shades) become aware that my song is resounding.'
So here the γλῶσσα is a song sent from
Ceos.

6 εὐκλέᾳ κελεύθου γλῶσσαν οὐ[κ ἐκτὸς δίκας
7 πέμπειν Ἱέρωνι· τόθεν γὰρ
8 πυθμένες θάλλουσιν ἐσθλ[ῶν,
9 τοὺς ὁ μεγιστοπάτωρ
200 10 Ζεὺς ἀκινήτους ἐν εἰρήν[ᾳ φυλάσσοι.

VI.

ΛΑΧΩΝΙ ΚΕΙΩΙ

<ΠΑΙΔΙ> ΣΤΑΔΙΕΙ ΟΛΥΜΠΙΑ

στρ. α'. Λάχων Διὸς μεγίστου
          λάχε φέρτατον πόδεσσι
          κῦδος ἐπ' Ἀλφεοῦ προχοαῖς, [κάλ' αὔξων
          δι' ὅσσα πάροιθεν
      5   ἀμπελοτρόφον Κέον
          ἄεισάν ποτ' Ὀλυμπίᾳ

196 After γλῶσσαν only the letter o remains, the rest of the verse having been torn off.—οὐκ ἐκτὸς δίκας J. (1898), and (independently) A. Drachmann : οὐκ ἐκτὸς θεῶν Blass: οὐκ ἐκτὸς προεὶς Jurenka : οἰακοστρόφον K. : οἰωνὸν καλᾶς Platt. **198** ἐσθλῶν Jurenka, Blass : ἐσθλοί K. **200** φυλάσσοι Wilamowitz, Platt. φυλάσσει was supplied by Palmer.

οὐκ ἐκτὸς (κελεύθου) δίκας: the poet's strain of praise *has not wandered from the path of justice.* Cp. X. 26 δίκας κέλευθον : and for ἐκτός, IX. 51 f. τί μακρὰν γλῶσσαν ἰθύσας ἐλαύνω | ἐκτὸς ὁδοῦ; Both Bacchylides and Pindar frequently claim that their praise is in accord with δίκα : XII. 201 f. αἰνείτω σοφὸν ἄνδρα | σὺν δίκᾳ : X. 123 f. δικαίας ὅστις ἔχει φρένας εὑρήσει κ.τ.λ. : Pind. *P.* VIII. 70 f. κώμῳ μὲν ἀδυμελεῖ | Δίκα παρέστακε : *N.* III. 29 ἔπεται δὲ λόγῳ δίκας ἄωτος, ἐσλὸς (acc. pl.) αἰνεῖν.

197 f. τόθεν, 'thence,' referring to εὐκλέα γλῶσσαν : by means of the just praise of the poet. As θάλλουσιν indicates, πυθμένες ἐσθλῶν are (literally) the *stocks* or *stems* of happy fortunes' (ἐσθλά), here compared to plants or trees. The just praise of the poet is as the dew which makes them flourish. The poet confers a glory which is the flower and crown of established prosperity. (For the diction, cp. Aesch. *Suppl.* 104 f. νεάζει πυθμὴν | .. τεθαλώς, the old stock puts forth new buds and blossoms.) Pindar has a like thought in *N.* VIII. 40 ff., αὔξεται δ' ἀρετά,

χλωραῖς ἐέρσαις ὡς ὅτε δένδρεον ἄσσει, | ἐν σοφοῖς ἀνδρῶν ἀερθεῖσ' ἐν δικαίοις τε πρὸς ὑγρὸν | αἰθέρα : 'As, watered by fresh dews, a tree shoots upward, so grows the fame of manly worth, when it is lifted towards the liquid air of heaven by masters of song who give just praise.' For ἐσθλῶν, cp. IV. 20 μοῖραν ἐσθλῶν : XVI. 132 ἐσθλῶν τύχαν : Hom. *hymn. Cer.* 225 θεοὶ δέ τοι ἐσθλὰ πόροιεν.

199 f. μεγιστοπάτωρ = μέγιστος πατήρ : so XVIII. 21 μεγιστοάνασσα : Soph. *Ph.* 1338 Ἕλενος ἀριστόμαντις.—ἀκινήτους : the πυθμένες of Hieron's ἐσθλά are already well-set ; the prayer is that they may never be uprooted.—εἰρήνᾳ : for the form, see on II. 1. There is an allusion to the security gained for Sicily by the victory at Himera four years earlier (480 B.C.). Cp. XII. 188 f. (of Εὐνομία) ἄστεά τ'... | ἐν εἰρήνᾳ φυλάσσει. Here φυλάσσοι is preferable. Pind. *O.* VIII. ends with a like wish,...ἀπήμαντον ἄγων βίοτον | αὐτοῖς τ' ἀέξοι καὶ πόλιν (sc. Ζεύς) : while *O.* XIII. and *N.* IX. end with a direct prayer to Zeus.

to send Hieron the song that tells forth his fame, without swerving from the path of justice; for by such praise it is that happy fortunes, once firmly planted, flourish: and may Zeus, the supreme father, guard them steadfast in peace.

VI.

For Lachon of Ceos, victor in the foot-race for boys at Olympia. (452 B.C.)

Lachon has won from great Zeus surpassing glory by his speed, where the waters of Alpheus seek the sea; enhancing those goodly deeds for which ere now vine-nurturing Ceos has been sung at Olympia, str. ι.

VI. The title has been added by **A**³ in the left margin. ΠΑΙΔΙ is inserted by Blass, as the Oxyrhynchus fragment of the Olympic register shows that Lachon's victory was in the παίδων στάδιον. **3** ΑΛΦΕΙΟΥ **A**: corr. K.—After προχοαισ K. supplies -ι σεμναῖς (and so Jurenka), Housman ἀέθλων, Blass -ι νικῶν (with a full stop): J., κάλ' αὔξων.

VI. 1 f. Λάχων. In the Oxyrhynchus fragment of the Olympic register the entry referring to this victory gives the name as Λάκων. But Λάχων is confirmed by the agonistic inscription of Ceos (see Introduction to Ode I. § 3), where [Λ]άχων Ἀριστομένεος παίδων occurs (twice) among the Nemean victors. The origin of such short names as Λάχων and Λάχης is illustrated by the Attic Λαχέμοιρος (*C. I. A.* II. No. 1512 *b* 2 add.): cp. Fick-Benseler, *Griech. Personennamen,* p. 184.—The play on words in **Λάχων...λάχε** is not sportive; it brings out the omen of the name, in this case a happy one. So Pindar fr. 105 (of Hieron), ϝαθέων ἱερῶν ὁμώνυμε πάτερ. Cp. Soph. *Ai.* 430 f., n. —**Διὸς...λάχε,** *i.e.* παρὰ Διός: cp. Soph. *O. T.* 580 πάντ' ἐμοῦ κομίζεται: *ib.* 1163 ἐδεξάμην δέ του. **3 f. Ἀλφεοῦ.** The distance of Olympia from the mouth of the Alpheus was in ancient times about eight miles, and is now about ten. But the poet's phrase, ἐπὶ προχοαῖς, is correct in a broad sense. Olympia is near the point where the Alpheus, descending from the Arcadian highlands, enters on the last stage of its course amidst the sandy levels near the coast, and then passes between lagoons to the sea. After ΠΡΟΧΟΑΙC the MS. has lost three syllables, ⌣---. Compare II. 6 ff., referring to the Cean victor Argeios:— καλῶν δ' ἀνέμνασεν, ὅσ' ἐν κλεεννῷ | αὐχένι

(ϝ)ισθμοῦ...ἐπεδείξαμεν: 'he has renewed the memory of *all those goodly feats* which we (Ceans) have displayed' at the Isthmus. So, here also, **ὅσσα** clearly refers to the whole series of victories won by Ceans in the national games. Lachon had now gained a signal success at the chief festival. (1) The poet may conceivably have said that this victory was the most brilliant of all which had brought fame to Ceos: if so, we might read προχοαῖς, **ἀέθλων** (Housman), or προχοαῖσι, **πάντων** (the genitive, with either word, depending on φέρτατον). (2) Or, as is perhaps more probable, Lachon may have been described as enhancing the previous glories of Ceos. That sense would be given by **κάλ' αὔξων,** where καλά would have the same meaning as in II. 6.—See Appendix. **5 ἀμπελοτρόφον.** The word πολυάμπελος, traceable in frag. 7 (K.), was also doubtless applied to Ceos. Coins of that island sometimes bore a grape (Bröndsted, *Voyages* I. pl. XXVII., quoted by Jurenka here). **6 ff.** Join Ὀλυμπίᾳ with ἄεισαν, not with κρατεῦσαι. These tributes of song were paid by young men of Ceos at Olympia; the occasion would be a festal procession, escorting the Cean victor to the temple of the Olympian Zeus, where he would give thanks; or it might be a banquet. The formal ἐπινίκιον was more usually sung after the victor's return to his home.

πύξ τε καὶ στάδιον κρατεῦ-
σαν] στεφάνοις ἐθείρας

στρ. β'.   νεανίαι βρύοντες.
10   σὲ δὲ νῦν ἀναξιμόλπου
Οὐρανίας ὕμνος ἔκατι νίκ[ας
Ἀριστομένειον
ὦ ποδάνεμον τέκος,
γεραίρει προδόμοις ἀοι-
15   δαῖς, ὅτι στάδιον κρατήσας Κέον εὐκλέϊξας.

VII.

ΤΩΙ ΑΥΤΩΙ

Ὦ λιπαρὰ θύγατερ Χρόνου τε κ[αὶ
Νυκτός, σὲ πεντήκοντα μ[ῆνες ἄγαγον
ἐκκαιδεκάταν ἐν Ὀλυμπ[ίᾳ φανεῖσαν,
Col. 13 ᾷ π]αρ[' Ἀλφειῷ Πέλοπός τε τάφῳ χαίρ-
5   ον]τος αἱμ[ακουρίαις πέπρωται
κρίνειν τα[χυτᾶτά τε] λαιψηρῶν ποδῶν
Ἕλλασι καὶ γυίων ἀρισταλκὲς σθένος·
ᾧ δὲ σὺ πρεσβύτατον νείμῃς γέρας
νίκας ἐπ' ἀνθρώποισιν εὔδοξος κέκλη-
10   ται καὶ πολυζήλωτος. Ἀρ[ιστομένει]ον

13 ΠΟΔΑΝΕΜΟΝ] O has been deleted after A.
VII. The title has been written over an erasure of three lines, by A³, in the left margin.   1 ΛΙΠΑΡΑ corrected from ΛΙΠΑΡΟ.   2 μ[ῆνες ἄγαγον J. (ἀμέραν Blass): μ[ηνῶν φθιμένων Jurenka.   4—11 Column XII. ends with verse 3.

βρύοντες denotes the luxuriance of leaves or flowers in the wreaths. Cp. XII. 69 f. πανθαλέων στεφάνοισιν | ἀνθέων χαίταν ἐρεφθείς. Eubulus (a poet of the middle comedy), in his Κυβευταί fr. I. 6, describes a wreathed drinking-cup as κισσῷ κάρα βρύουσαν.
10 f. ἀναξιμόλπου: cp. XVI. 66 ἀναξι-βρόντας : XIX. 8 ἀναξίαλος. So Pindar O. II. 1 ἀναξιφόρμιγγες ὕμνοι.—Οὐρανίας : see n. on v. 176.
12 f. Ἀριστομένειον...τέκος : see n. on v. 71.
14 προδόμοις. Aesch. fr. 388 Ἑκάτη | τῶν βασιλείων πρόδομος μελάθρων. The ode in honour of a victor was sometimes

sung before the doors of his house: Pind. I. VII. 1—4 Κλεάνδρῳ τις...παρὰ πρόθυρον ἰὼν | ἀνεγειρέτω κῶμον : Nem. I. 19 ἔσταν δ' ἐπ' αὐλείαις θύραις.
16 εὐκλέϊξας. The Doric aor.: so x. 87 δοίαξε : XVI. 129 παιάνιξάν. Cp. Tyrtaeus 12. 24 ἄστυ εὐκλεῖσας : Simonides 125. 2 πατρίδ' ἐπευκλεῖσας.

VII. 1—3 λιπαρά, 'resplendent' (cp. v. 169 n.). The 'daughter of Time and Night' is Day: Hes. Theog. 124 Νυκτὸς δ' αὖτ' Αἰθήρ τε καὶ Ἡμέρη ἐξεγένοντο.
πεντήκοντα (μῆνες) are the fifty lunar months which have elapsed since the last preceding festival at Olympia. There

as foremost in boxing or in foot-race, by youths crowned with luxuriant wreaths.

And to thee now, son of Aristomenes, thou whose feet are str. 2. swift as the wind, the hymn of Urania queen of song renders honour for thy victory, in strains chanted before thy house; because by thy triumph in the foot-race thou hast brought renown to Ceos.

VII.

For the same.

Radiant daughter of Time and Night, the fifty months have brought thee, sixteenth day of the month at Olympia; [thee, to whom by the Alpheus, near the tomb of Pelops who rejoices in blood-offerings, it has been allotted] to give judgment for the Greeks on pre-eminence in speed of foot and strength of limb. To whomsoever thou awardest the foremost prize of victory, his name is thenceforth famous and admired among men.

Column XIII. is lost; but a few syllables, belonging to the ends of verses in the upper third of it, remain in the left margin of col. XIV. Verses 4–11 have been put together by Blass from several small fragments; and, of these, verses 6–11 have been combined with the endings of verses left from col. XIII.   **6** τα[χυτᾶτά τε] Platt, Wackernagel.

was an Olympic cycle of 99 lunar months, making up eight years. The interval between two Olympic festivals was alternately one of 49 lunar months and one of 50 such months. See schol. Pind. *O.* III. 5 γίνεται δὲ ὁ ἀγὼν ποτὲ μὲν διὰ τεσσαράκοντα ἐννέα μηνῶν, ποτὲ δὲ διὰ πεντήκοντα. Hence the festival fell sometimes in the Olympian (or Elean) month Ἀπολλώνιος, sometimes in the month Παρθένιος.

In an old legend of Elis, the 50 lunar months of this cycle appear as fifty daughters borne by Selene to Endymion (Paus. 5. 1 § 3).

ἐκκαιδεκάταν. The Olympian festival began on the 11th day of the month, and ended on the 16th: schol. Pind. *O.* IV. 14 ἐπὶ πέντε ἡμέρας ἐγένετο τὰ Ὀλύμπια, ἀπὸ ἑνδεκάτης μέχρις ἐκκαιδεκάτης. On the 16th, the last day, the prizes were given to the victors; processions, sacrifices and banquets took place. This exordium suggests that the ode may (like Pindar's eighth *Olympian*) have been sung at Olympia.

4 f. The letters ΤΟCΑΙΜ in v. 5

recall Pind. *O.* I. 90 f. νῦν δ' ἐν αἱμακουρίαις ἀγλααῖσι μέμικται | Ἀλφεοῦ πόρῳ κλιθείς, 'and now (Pelops) hath part in the honour of blood-offerings at his grave by Alpheus' stream.' Hence the supplement which I suggest above.

6—10 κρίνειν κ.τ.λ. There is a general parallelism between this passage and Pindar *O.* I. 95 ff., ἵνα ταχυτὰς ποδῶν ἐρίζεται | ἀκμαί τ' ἰσχύος θρασύπονοι· ὁ νικῶν δὲ λοιπὸν ἀμφὶ βίοτον | ἔχει μελιτόεσσαν εὐδίαν ib. 248).

ἀρισταλκὲς σθένος: note the adj. compounded with a noun (ἀλκή) akin in sense to σθένος: cp. Soph. *O.T.* 518 βίου...τοῦ μακραίωνος: *Tr.* 791 δυσπάρευνον λέκτρον.

ἐπ' ἀνθρώποισιν, 'among men': cp. Soph. *Tr.* 356 τἀπὶ Λυδοῖς (λατρεύματα), his servitude in Lydia (nearly the same as ἐν Λυδοῖς *ib.* 248). This use of ἐπί with dat., though rare, seems tenable. Blass joins **νίκας ἐπ'**, *i.e.*, 'on the occasion of victory'; a phrase which seems somewhat weak here. νίκας would naturally go with γέρας.

Ἀριστομένειον: VI. 12 n.

νῦν γ]' ἐκόσμη[σας στε]φάν[οισι Λάχω]να
παῖδα]

. . . .

. . . . ομῳ

                 *   *   *   *

          Πυθῶνά τε μηλοθύταν

Col. 14 40 ὑμνέων Νεμέαν τε καὶ Ἰσθμόν·
          γᾷ δ' ἐπισκήπτων χέρα
          κομπάσομαι· σὺν ἀλα-
   (5)   θείᾳ δὲ πᾶν λάμπει χρέος·
          οὔτις ἀνθρώπων κ[αθ' Ἕλλα-
   45   νας ἐν ἅλικι χρόνῳ
          παῖς ἐὼν ἀνήρ τε π[λεῦ-
          νας ἐδέξατο νίκας.
   (10)   ὦ Ζεῦ κεραυνεγχές, κα[ὶ ἐπ' ἀργυ]ροδίνα
          ὄχθαισιν Ἀλφειοῦ τέλεσσ[ας μεγ]αλοκλέας
   50   θεοδότους εὐχάς, περὶ κ[ρατί τ' ὅ]πα[σσα]ς
          γλαυκὸν Αἰτωλίδος
          ἄνδημ' ἐλαίας
   (15)   ἐν Πέλοπος Φρυγίου
          κλεινοῖς ἀέθλοις.

---

11 νῦν γ'] Blass.—ἐκόσμη[σας στε]φάν[οισι Ewald, Bruhn, Housman, Wilamowitz. **14** ΟΜΩΙ] These letters were the last of the 11th verse in the lost col. XIII. After that v., about 24 more were needed to complete col. XIII. Blass finds vestiges of 14 of these in some minute fragments which he prints here,—mostly single words, or parts of two words. I give them in the Appendix. **44 f.** καθ' Ἕλλανας Blass. **46** π[λεῦνας Blass: ποσσὶ πλεῦνας Sandys, Jurenka. **48** κα[ὶ

---

11 νῦν γ', though only conjectural, derives support from VIII. 25 Αὐτομήδει νῦν γε νικά|σαντί νιν δαίμων ἔδωκεν. **39 f.** Πυθῶνά τε. After the verse (no. 14 of the ode, and no. 11 in the lost column XIII of the papyrus) which ended with the letters ομωι, 24 verses (15–38) have been lost: see cr. n. The poet is now singing (ὑμνέων) of Delphi, Nemea, and Isthmus. The reference is doubtless to successes gained by Lachon before his victory at Olympia.—μηλοθύταν: an epithet of altars in Eur. *I. T.* 1116. At Delphi those who wished to consult the oracle offered sacrifice before entering the adyton: id. *Ion* 229 πάριτ' ἐς θυμέλας· ἐπὶ δ' ἀσφάκτοις | μήλοισι δόμων μὴ πάριτ' ἐς μυχόν. So Pind. *P.* III. 27 μηλοδόκῳ Πυθῶνι.

41 ff. γᾷ δ' ἐπισκήπτων: see v. 42 n. —κομπάσομαι. The passive of this verb occurs in classical poetry; but is there any other instance of the middle? For the fut., cp. x. 24 φάσω: Soph. *Ai.* 422 f. ἔπος | ἐξερῶ μέγα: Pind. *O.* IV. 17 οὐ ψεύδεϊ τέγξω λόγον.—σὺν ἀλαθείᾳ (a phrase which recurs in VIII. 85): it is only 'with the aid of truth,'—*i.e.* by speaking out frankly,—that any matter (χρέος) can be set in a clear, full light (λάμπει). He means that anything short of the strong statement which follows would be less than just to this victor's merits. Cp. n. on v. 187 f. **44 f.** It is doubtful how the gap in the MS. between K at the end of v. 44 and NAC at the beginning of v. 45 should be filled. There is no clue to the exact

And now thou hast given the honours of the wreath to Lachon,
son of Aristomenes...

*   *   *   *   *   *

...singing of Pytho, where sheep are sacrificed, and of Nemea,
and of the Isthmus.   And laying my hand on the earth as a
witness, I will make this vaunt ;—for only by the voice of truth
can anything be set in a full light,—no one among the Greeks,
as boy or as man, has gained more victories in an equal time.
O Zeus, whose spear is the thunder-bolt, on the banks of
silver-eddying Alpheus also hast thou fulfilled his prayers, for
his great fame, by gift divine ; and hast set upon his brow the
gray wreath of the Aetolian olive, in the glorious games of
Phrygian Pelops.

ἐπ' ἀργυ]ροδίνα Blass, taking ροδινα from frag. 17 (K.).   **49** After ΤΕΛΕϹϹ
in the MS. there is a lacuna equal to about 11 or 12 letters, and then C, the
final letter of the last word in the verse. τέλεσσον K.: so Jurenka, adding <ἐς
μέγιστόν οἱ γέρα>s, which is too long for the space.   τέλεσας Blass, adding μεγ]α-
λοκλέας (which fits the gap) from frag. 17 K.   **50** περὶ κ[ρατί τ' δ]πα[σσα]s
Blass, taking πα from frag. 17 K.—περὶ κ[ρατά τέ οἱ τίθει] K.: so Jurenka, but with
θές instead of τίθει.   **52** ἀνδημ'] ΑΝΔΗ **A**: μ' added above the line by **A²**.

number of letters lost after K, nor to
the quantity of NAC. To the obvious
κ[λεεν]νὰs it might be objected that its
position in the sentence is awkward. I
prefer Blass's κ[αθ' "Ελλα]ναs, though
without regarding it as certain. The
sense ('among the Greeks') might be
illustrated from Pind. O. I. 120 πρόφαντον
σοφίᾳ καθ' "Ελλανας.

ἐν ἄλικι χρόνῳ.   ἦλιξ = 'of the same
age': ἦλιξ χρόνος here is 'a time of the
same duration,' 'an equal space of time.'
46 f. παῖς ἐὼν ἀνήρ τε, 'whether as
boy or as man.'   Following οὔτις ἀνθρώπων, this is a short equivalent for οὔτε
παῖς ἐὼν οὔτ' ἀνήρ. The phrase in Aesch.
Eum. 521 ff. τίς...ἢ πόλις βροτός τε ('who
—be it city or be it man—?') is so far
similar that τε there marks the second of
two alternative cases included under τίς
(an interrogative implying a negative),
and must therefore, in our idiom, be
rendered by 'or.' But the irregular co-
ordination of ἤ and τε is special to that
passage.—Note that the words here
could also mean, 'as boy and man.'
This would imply that the subject of
ἐδέξατο was no longer a boy. (See Introduction to the Ode.)
48–50 κεραυνεγχές: a word found
only here : but cp. Pind. P. IV. 194
ἐγχεικέραυνον Ζῆνα.—καὶ ἐπ' ἀργυροδίνα.
The fragment (17 K.) which gives the
endings of 48 and 49, and the letters πα

of ὅπασσας in 50, has been rightly
pieced on here by Blass. It cannot be
an accident that it helps three consecutive
verses.   And the word μεγ]αλοκλέας,
while suiting the sense, also fits the gap
in 49.
ΤΕΛΕϹϹ in the MS. was probably
τέλεσσας.   Blass writes τέλεσας : but
there is at least a presumption in favour
of the σσ, and there is nothing to show
that it is metrically inadmissible. (We
have no strophic test here.)—The alternative τέλεσσον would imply that the
athlete concerned had not yet been victorious at Olympia, and therefore that
the ode to which these verses belong was
distinct from Ode VII. (See Introduction.)
τέλεσσας...εὐχάς: 'thou hast fulfilled
his prayers, for his great glory (μεγαλοκλέας), by gift divine (θεοδότους).'
εὐχάς here are the things prayed for, viz.,
victorious feats in the games. Cp. Pind.
I. IV. 23 θεοδότων ἔργων.
51 γλαυκόν: Pind. O. III. 13 ἀμφὶ
κόμαισι βάλῃ γλαυκόχροα κόσμον ἐλαίας.
—Αἰτωλίδος. The Aetolian Oxylus was
one of the leaders of the Heracleidae at
their return, and received Elis. Hence
the Eleans are poetically called Aetolians.
Her. VIII. 73 Δωριέων μὲν πολλαί τε καὶ
δόκιμοι πόλεες, Αἰτωλῶν δὲ "Ηλις μούνη.
Cp. Pind. O. III. 12 ἀτρεκὴς Ἑλλανοδίκας
...Αἰτωλὸς ἀνήρ.

VIII. [IX.]

ΑΥΤΟΜΗΔΕΙ ΦΛΕΙΑΣΙΩΙ

ΠΕΝΤΑΘΛΩΙ ΝΕΜΕΑ

στρ. α'.　ι Δόξαν, ὧ χρυσαλάκατοι Χάριτες,
　　　　2 πεισίμβροτον δοίητ', ἐπεὶ
　　　　3 Μουσᾶν γε (F)ιοβλεφάρων θεῖος προφάτας
　　　　4 εὔτυκος Φλειοῦντά τε καὶ Νεμεαίου
　　　5 Ζηνὸς εὐθαλὲς πέδον
　　　6 ὑμνεῖν, ὅθι μηλοδαΐκταν
　　　7 θρέψεν ἁ λευκώλενος
　　　8 Ἥρα περικλειτῶν ἀέθλων
　　　9 πρῶτον Ἡρακλεῖ βαρύφθογγον λέοντα.

ἀντ. α'.　ιο κεῖ[θι φοι]νικάσπιδες ἡμίθεοι

VIII. The title written by **A³** in the left margin.　**2** The first hand wrote N instead of M in πεισίμβροτον: but the N has been retouched as if to correct it (by **A³**)? Cp. v. 33.—ἐπεὶ Blass and others: ἔπει K.　**3** Μουσᾶν τε MS., K.: Μουσᾶν γε Blass¹, -τοι Bl.³　**6** ὅθι K.: ὅτι MS.　**10** κε[ῖθι φοι]νικάσπιδες

VIII. 1—3 δόξαν...πεισίμβροτον, the 'repute' that is gained by a poet who 'persuades' his hearers, *i.e.*, carries them with him, wins their favour. In Aesch. *Cho.* 362 the Laurentian MS. has πισίμβροτον, where the editors rightly give πεισιβρότῳ (epithet of βάκτρῳ, the sceptre that wins reverence). If that was our poet's source for the rare word, this ode would be later than 458 B.C.: but we cannot assume it. For the form with euphonic μ inserted, cp. ἀλεξίμβροτος, μελησίμβροτος, ὄμβριμος, etc.
χρυσαλάκατοι. The ἠλακάτη, 'distaff,' is the attribute of a woman; in the case of a goddess, it is of gold. The epithet is general, not distinctive of the Charites as such. Pindar gives it to Amphitrite (*O.* vi. 104 f.), the Nereids (*N.* v. 36), Latona (*N.* vi. 37 f.), etc. In the particular case of *Artemis*, however, the sense is different (cp. x. 38 n.).
EΙΙEΙ in *v.* 2 is probably ἐπεί. If so, the τε after Μουσᾶν in 3 must be corrected. (1) ἐπεί γε, a strengthened ἐπεί, is not uncommon : in ἐπεί..γε, however, γε normally emphasizes the word next before it, as in *Il.* 1. 352, μῆτερ, ἐπεί μ' ἔτεκές γε μινυνθάδιόν περ ἐόντα : Hes.

Theog. 171 ἐπεὶ πατρός γε δυσωνύμου οὐκ ἀλεγίζω. Here, a stress could scarcely fall on Μουσᾶν. (2) ἐπεί..τοι is also frequent (Soph. *Tr.* 320 f., etc.), and τοι might become τε through loss of ι before ιο-: but the sententious τοι (little used by this poet) is less suitable here than in 1. 58 or VIII. 82.
The alternative for ἐπεί is to write ἔπει (depending on δοίητ'), the poet's 'word' or utterance. Cp. Pind. *P.* II. 66 βουλαὶ δὲ πρεσβύτεραι | ἀκίνδυνον ἐμοὶ ἔπος σὲ ποτὶ πάντα λόγον | ἐπαινεῖν παρέχοντι. Then the τε after Μουσᾶν in 3 must be changed to τὸ (as Housman proposed, assuming ῥιοβλεφάρων) : or to ὅτ' (as I formerly suggested, assuming ιοβλεφάρων). For ὅτ' it may be said that, if it had been written as ὅτε without elision (on an assumption of F), that would help to account for the actual τε. (As to the poet's inconstant use of F before ιο-, see p. 82.)
θεῖος, 'inspired' ; cp. θεῖος ἀοιδός (*Od.* 4. 17, etc.).—**προφάτας**, *i.e.* the poet. Cp. Plato *Phaedr.* p. 262 D (speaking of the birds) οἱ τῶν Μουσῶν προφῆται οἱ ὑπὲρ κεφαλῆς ᾠδοί. Pindar fr. 90 calls himself ἀοίδιμον Πιερίδων προφάταν.

VIII. [IX.]

For Automedes of Phlius, victor in the pentathlon at Nemea.

Graces of the golden distaff, may ye grant the charm that   str. 1.
wins mortal ears; for the inspired prophet of the violet-eyed
Muses is ready to sing Phlius and the verdure-clad domain of
Nemean Zeus; where white-armed Hera nourished the deep-
voiced lion, slayer of sheep, first of the foes on whom Heracles
was to win renown.

There the heroes with red shields,   ant. 1

Housman, Wilamowitz, Blass: κεῖθι γὰρ νικάσπιδες Κ. (κινάσπιδες Richards). κεῖθι
γὰρ χαλκάσπιδες Nairn: κεῖθι καὶ λευκάσπιδες Jurenka and others: but the letters
ΝΙ are certain.

4 f. εὔτυκος (supply ἐστί), *i.e.* εὐτρεπής,
ἕτοιμος: with infin., as in Aesch. *Suppl.*
973 f. πᾶς τις ἐπειπεῖν ψόγον ἀλλοθρόοις |
εὔτυκος.
Φλειοῦντά τε κ.τ.λ. The spelling in
the MS. here (with ει) is confirmed by
Φλειάσιος in *Corp. Inscr. Att.* I. 45. 15
(421 B.C.), and II. add. 57 *b* 2. 15 (362
B.C.): Meisterhans, *Gramm. der Att.
Inschr.* p. 26. As to Phlius, see Introd.
to this Ode.
Νεμεαίου Ζηνός. The vale of Nemea
is next on the east to that of Phlius, from
which it is divided by the ridge of
Trikaranon. Hence Pindar says of a
Nemean victor (*N.* VI. 47 ff.), βοτάνα τέ
νίν ποθ' ἁ λέοντος | νικῶνθ' ἤρεφε δα-
σκίοις | Φλιοῦντος ὑπ' ὠγυγίοις ὄρεσιν, 'the
lion's herb (the σέλινον or wreath of
parsley) shadowed his victorious brow
beneath the forest-clad primeval hills of
Phlius.' The temple of the Nemean Zeus
stood on moist ground in the lower part
of the vale, surrounded by a grove of
cypresses. In the time of Pausanias (2.
15 § 2), *c.* 170 A.D., the roof had fallen
in; though games and sacrifices were
still held in winter, the immemorial Zeus-
cult being maintained, doubtless, at βω-
μοὶ ὑπαίθριοι. Three columns are still
standing in the lonely valley.
εὐθαλές, Doric for εὐθηλές (θηλέω): the
syllable answering to θα is long in the
corresponding verses. So Pind. *P.* IX.
79 εὐθαλεῖ τύχᾳ: Ar. *Av.* 1062 εὐθαλεῖς
καρπούς. Aesch. frag. 300. 5 has εὐθαλής
(θάλλω). Cp. XII. 69 πανθαλέων: but in
XII. 229 πανθαλής.—Nemea was well-

watered (εὔυδρος, Theocr. XXV. 182);
wood throve there (εὐφύλλου Νεμέης,
Pind. *I.* V. 61), and the vale afforded cool
pastures. (Cp. E. Curtius *Pelop.* II. 506.)
6—9 μηλοδαΐκταν. Cp. Aesch. *Pers.*
104 πολέμους πυργοδαΐκτους ('destroying
walled cities,' where we should perhaps
read πυργοδαΐκτας): αὐτοδάϊκτος (*Theb.*
735) and λουτροδάϊκτος (*Cho.* 1071) are
passive in sense.
The Nemean lion was a ζῷον ἄτρωτον,
ἐκ Τυφῶνος γεγεννημένον (Apollod. II. 5.
1): a legend which symbolized the destructive force of the winter-torrent
rushing down from the hills. In Zenobius VI. 39 the monster is χαραδραῖος
λέων, from the Νεμεὰς χαράδρα: cp.
Aeschin. or. 2 § 168. He is described
by Hesiod (*Theog.* 331) as κοιρανέων
Τρητοῖο Νεμείης ἠδ' 'Απέσαντος. *Treton*
('the cavernous') was a hill E. of Nemea,
in which the lion's cave was shown
(Paus. 2. 15. 2, Diod. Sic. IV. 11):
Apesas, a rocky height on the N.E. of
the vale. Pindar denotes Nemea by the
phrase χόρτοις ἐν λέοντος ('pastures of the
lion'), *O.* XIII. 44.
ἀέθλων πρῶτον. The order of the
twelve ἄθλοι of Heracles was probably
first established in legend by the Dorians
of Argolis. Peisander of Rhodes in his
'Ηράκλεια (6th cent. B.C.?) may have
helped to popularize it. The Nemean
lion always comes first (see, *e.g.*, Eur.
H.F. 359 ff.: Soph. *Tr.* 1092 f.).
10 φοινικάσπιδες is the only conjecture which satisfies the data in the papyrus, if νικάσπιδες be rejected. In Tragedy

2 πρώτιστον Ἀργείων κριτοὶ
3 ἄθλησαν ἐπ᾽ Ἀρχεμόρῳ, τὸν ξανθοδερκὴς
4 πέφν᾽ ἀωτεύοντα δράκων ὑπέροπλος,
5 σᾶμα μέλλοντος φόνου.
15 6 ὦ μοῖρα πολυκρατές· οὔ νιν
7 πεῖθ᾽ Ὀϊκλείδας πάλιν
8 στείχειν ἐς εὐάνδρους ἀγυιάς.
9 ἐλπὶς ἀνθρώπων ὑφαιρ[εῖται προνοίας·

ἐπ. α'.   1 ἃ καὶ τότ᾽ Ἄδραστον Ταλ[αϊονίδαν

---

12 ἄθλησαν ἐπ᾽ Ἀρχεμόρῳ, τὸν] The scribe omitted E before Π, wrote Μ instead of Χ, and CΤΝ instead of ΤΟΝ. **Α³** has corrected the last two errors above the line,

---

the Argive warriors have white shields (Aesch. *Th.* 90, Soph. *Ant.* 106, Eur. *Phoe.* 1099). Red shields are nowhere mentioned in classical Greek literature. Pindar (*P.* VIII. 46) describes the Argive Alcmaeon, son of Amphiaraus, as δράκοντα ποικίλον αἰθᾶς νωμῶντ᾽ ἐπ᾽ ἀσπίδος: and Bacchylides (fr. 3. 6 f.) has the αἰθᾶν ἀραχνᾶν, where the sense seems to be 'reddish-brown.' In the Pindaric verse, however, αἰθᾶς, as epithet of the shield, would naturally mean 'bright,' 'glittering' (like αἴθων and αἶθοψ, said of burnished metal), rather than 'of a bright *colour*.' (Quintus Smyrnaeus V. 27, imagining a scene of slaughter depicted on the shield of Achilles, says, πέδον δ᾽ ἄπαν αἵματι πολλῷ | δευομένῳ ἤϊκτο,—as if the ground were painted red; but that scarcely helps us.) On the other hand it should be noted that Bacchylides has φοινικόθριξ (X. 105), φοινικοκράδεμνος (X. 97, XII. 222), and φοινικόνωτος (V. 102).

As to **νικάσπιδες**, it would clearly be infelicitous: the heroes were not 'victorious' at this moment, nor would that epithet be suitable to 'shields': the only question is whether it is possible. Our poet has some strange compounds, such as πολεμαιγίς (XVI. 7), 'with warlike aegis'; ἀρέταιχμος (XV. 47), 'valiant with the spear.' But νίκασπις would be stranger than these. There are such forms as νικόβουλος and νικομάχας, but no example in which νίκη is compounded with a word denoting the instrument of victory. ἡμίθεοι, = ἥρωες, as in X. 62, XII. 155, Pindar *P.* IV. 12: the seven Peloponnesian chiefs (including Adrastus king of Argos, the leader) who marched against Thebes to restore Polyneices (Aesch.

Theb. 377 ff., Soph. *O.C.* 1313 ff.).

11 f. πρώτιστον...ἄθλησαν: these, according to the legend, were the first contests ever held at Nemea, and gave origin to the festival.
ἐπ᾽ Ἀρχεμόρῳ, in his memory. Apollod. III. 6. 4 οἱ δὲ ἔθεσαν ἐπ᾽ αὐτῷ τὸν τῶν Νεμέων ἀγῶνα. Marching from Argos towards the Isthmus of Corinth, Adrastus and his comrades made their first halt in the vale of Nemea. Opheltes, the infant son of Lycurgus king of Nemea by Eurydice, was there in charge of his nurse Hypsipyle (formerly queen of Lemnos). She guided the thirsty warriors to a spring; and meanwhile the child was killed by a huge dragon. The heroes came back in time to slay the monster; then they buried the child, and changed his name from Opheltes to *Archemorus*, because his death was a beginning of doom. And in his memory they instituted the Nemean games. (Apollod. *l.c.*: Statius *Thebais* V. 624 ff.: Hyginus *Fab.* 74, cp. *Fab.* 273.)—Simonides alludes to the grief of the warriors, fr. 52 : (Εὐρυδίκας) ἰοστεφάνου | γλυκεῖαν ἐδάκρυσαν | ψυχὰν ἀποπνέοντα γαλαθηνὸν τέκος.—The grave of Opheltes was shown at Nemea; also a mound commemorating his father Lycurgus; and a πηγὴ Ἀδραστεία (Paus. 2. 15. § 3).—Pindar [*N.*] X. 28 speaks of the Nemean festival as held ἐν Ἀδραστείῳ νόμῳ, 'according to the institution of Adrastus.'

ξανθοδερκής, with fiery eyes. Cp. III. 56 ξανθὰν φλόγα. Arist. *De Color.* p. 791 a 4, τὸ δὲ πῦρ καὶ ὁ ἥλιος ξανθά. Statius V. 508 (with reference to this dragon), *Livida fax oculis.*

13 ἀωτεύοντα, 'sleeping' (R. A. Neil's

the flower of the Argives, held the earliest games, in memory
of Archemorus, who was slain in his sleep by the huge dragon
with fiery eyes, an omen of slaughter to come. Ah, Fate of
mighty power! The son of Oicles could not persuade them to
return to the streets of the good city. Hope robs men of
prudent thoughts,—

she who then sent Adrastus son of Talaüs   epode 1.

---

and may have written ε above π, where the papyrus is mutilated.   **18** ἀωτεύοντα
R. A. Neil. ACAΓΕΤΟΝΤΑ ms.   The letter Ῑ is a correction (from P?) by **A³**.
16 'Οϊκλείδας] κλ from λλ by **A³**.   **19** ἆ καὶ **A³**: δὴ (without ἆ) **A**.

---

excellent correction), could have been
corrupted into the ACAΓΕΤΟΝΤΑ of the
papyrus through ω being read as σα.
Such a form of σα, from a papyrus of
162 B.C., may be seen in Gardthausen's
Griech. Palaeographie, table 3 (at the end
of the book). The change of Τ to Γ
would do the rest. Hesychius has
ἀωτεύειν· ἀπανθίζεσθαι. This suggests
that the word here might mean, 'while
gathering flowers': Eur. fr. 754 (from
the 'Ὑψιπύλη, ap. Plut. *Mor.* p. 93 D)
described the child as thus engaged:
ἕτερον ἐφ' ἑτέρῳ αἰρόμενος | ἄγρευμ' ἀνθέων
κ.τ.λ.: though we do not know how
Euripides told the story of the death.
According to Statius (v. 502—504),
Opheltes was killed while *sleeping* on the
grass (cp. Paus. 2. 15. 2 τεθέντα ἐς τὴν
πόαν). Now Simonides has ἀωτεῖν (without the Homeric addition of ὕπνον) as
meaning 'to sleep': fr. 37. 6 σὺ δ' ἀωτεῖς
γαλαθηνῷ τ' ἦτορι κνώσσεις. It seems
very probable, then, that his nephew
used ἀωτεύοντα in the sense of ἀωτέοντα.
Cp. ζατεύω (Alcman fr. 33. 8), ἀχεύω,
οἰνοχοεύω, at the side of the forms in
-έω.
ὑπέροπλος, of huge size and strength;
cp. Hes. *Theog.* 670 βίην ὑπέροπλον
ἔχοντες.
14 σᾶμα, 'omen' (as in Pind. fr. 107):
φόνου, their overthrow at Thebes.
15 f. οὔ νιν πείθ': 'could not persuade
them' (impf.). νιν is plural (referring to
the heroes), as in fr. 5 (K.), προσεφώνει
τέ νιν (placed by Blass as v. 76 of Ode 1.,
2nd ed. p. 25), where Apollonius *De
pronom.* p. 368 A noticed the use. The
plural νιν occurs also in Pindar (fr. 7. 2),
Sophocles (*O.T.* 868 etc.), and Euripides
Suppl. 1140).
16 'Οϊκλείδας. Amphiaraus, the great

warrior and seer (Soph. *O.C.* 1313), was
the son of Οἰκλῆς (an Argive hero who
had gone with Heracles against Laomedon, Apollod. II. 6. 4).
17 εὐάνδρους, in contrast with the
lonely vale of Nemea.—ἀγυιάς, of Argos.
It is noteworthy that Pindar *P.* VIII.
52 ff. (where Amphiaraus predicts the
return of Adrastus) denotes Argos by the
phrase Ἄβαντος εὐρυχόρους ἀγυιάς.
18 ὑφαιρεῖται: this rare middle occurs
in Eur. *El.* 271 σιγῇ τοῦθ' ὑφαιρούμεσθά
νιν. The middle of ἀφαιρεῖν is used by
Pind. *P.* IV. 218, and *I.* 1. 62.—The lost
object of the verb ought to express the
idea of 'prudence,' 'caution,' or 'fore-
sight.' W. Christ reads πρόνοιαν (and so
Weir Smyth, *Greek Melic Poets* p. 104).
A long final would be preferable: for
that reason, and also on poetical grounds,
I suggest the plur. προνοίας, as used by
Aesch. *Ag.* 684 ('Helen' was so named
by some one) προνοίαισι τοῦ πεπρωμένου,
'with forebodings of her doom.' This
ode shows distinct traces of Aeschylean
diction (see on v. 2 πεισίμβροτον, and
v. 6 μηλοδαΐκταν).—Blass gives νόημα
(referring to x. 54): but its normal sense,
as there, is 'a thought,' rather than
'thought' or 'forethought.' μερίμνας
(Wilamowitz) also seems less suitable (cp.
n. on XVIII. 34).—Jurenka supplies φρέν'
ὀρθάν, which is possible, if somewhat
too general.—Kenyon, reading ὑφαιρεῖ,
suggests μῆτιν ἐσθλάν. It is perhaps
worth noting that such a caesura as that
made by ὑφαιρεῖ does not occur in any of
the corresponding verses.
19 Ταλαϊονίδαν, son of Talaos (a
name ominous of suffering). The double
patronymic (-ίων combined with -ίδης) is
sometimes used by poets *metri causa*:
cp. Ἰαπετιονίδη in Hes. *Op.* 54.

Col. 15 2 πέμπεν ἐς Θήβας Πολυνείκεϊ πλα[γκτῷ] πρόξεν[ον.
3 κείνων ἀπ᾽ εὐδόξων ἀγώνων
4 ἐν Νεμέᾳ κλεινοὶ βροτῶν
5 οἳ τριέτει στεφάνῳ
6 ξανθὰν ἐρέψωνται κόμαν.
25 7 Αὐτομήδει νῦν γε νικά-
8 σαντί νιν δαίμων ἔδωκεν.

στρ. β΄. 1 πενταέθλοισιν γὰρ ἐνέπρεπεν ὡς
2 ἄστρων διακρίνει φάη
3 νυκτὸς διχομήνιδος εὐφεγγὴς σελάνα·
30 4 τοῖος Ἑλλάνων δι᾽ ἀπείρονα κύκλον
5 φαῖνε θαυμαστὸν δέμας,
6 δισκὸν τροχοειδέα ῥίπτων,
7 καὶ μελαμφύλλου κλάδον
8 ἀκτέας ἐς αἰπεινὰν προπέμπων
35 9 αἰθέρ᾽ ἐκ χειρὸς βοὰν ὤτρυνε λαῶν,

25 The final ι of Αὐτομήδει and the γ of γε have been added by **A³** above the line. **26** ἔδωκεν] The first hand wrote Ε. ΗΚΕΝ: **A³** wrote ω over Η.   **29** διχομήνιδος]

---

20. After Πολυνείκεϊ the letters πλα alone are certain. πλαγκτῷ πρόξενον Blass, 'a *patron*' (or 'protector') for the *wandering* (*i.e.* exiled) Polyneices. Cp. Eur. *Suppl.* 961 where the chorus of Argive matrons, who have come from Thebes to Eleusis, say, πλαγκτὰ δ᾽ ὡσεί τις νεφέλα | πνευμάτων ὑπὸ δυσχίμων ἀίσσω. For πρόξενον, cp. Aesch. *Suppl.* 418 f., γενοῦ | πανδίκως εὐσεβὴς | πρόξενος ('protector'). Blass takes the word from fr. 35 (K.), πρόξεν: it is only a conjecture, however, that it belongs here. There is a metrical objection to this reading, viz. the caesura after πλαγκτῷ, which is against the poet's usual practice (see p. 97). No such caesura at that point occurs in any one of the corresponding verses (46, 72, 98). Nevertheless πλαγκτῷ πρόξενον appears more probable than anything else. The number of other possible supplements is narrowly limited by πλα: they are such as πλαθέντα ξένῳ, πλαξίππῳ πέλας (or παραί), πλάξοντα πτόλιν, πλαγχθέντι ξένον: and not one is satisfactory. In this context, σύμμαχον might seem a fitter word than πρόξενον: but the ally of an exile, who supports him with armed

forces, could be called his 'patron.'
22 f. Νεμέᾳ, ‿– by synizesis, as in xi. 8 (probably), and Pind. *N.* iv. 75.— τριέτει : the fact that the ms. gives the older Attic accent here seems a reason for keeping it: the later τριετεῖ is preferred by Blass.—The Nemean games were held in the second and fourth years of each Olympiad. The older view, supported by Scaliger, that the season of the festival was alternately summer and winter, has been abandoned, since it has been shown by G. Unger (*Philol.* xxxiv. 50 ff., xxxvii. 1 ff.) that in the fifth century the Nemea always took place at midsummer, in the Argive month Πάναμος (Πάνημος). The στέφανος was of parsley, a symbol of mourning for the death of Archemorus.
24 ἐρέψωνται: for the midd., cp. Eur. *Bacch.* 323 κισσῷ τ᾽ ἐρεψόμεσθα καὶ χορεύσομεν.
27 πενταέθλοισιν, the competitors in the pentathlon: Her. ix. 75 ἄνδρα πεντάεθλον.
28 διακρίνει. Only two interpretations are possible. (1) 'The moon *distinguishes* the lights of the stars' (from

to Thebes, as patron of the exile Polyneices.
Illustrious are the mortals who, from those famous contests
at Nemea, crown golden hair with the triennial wreath. To
Automedes the god has now given it for his victory.

For he shone among his rivals in the pentathlon as the str. 2.
brilliant moon of the mid-month night makes the rays of the
stars seem pale beside her own. Even thus, amidst the vast
concourse of the Greeks, showed he his wondrous form, as he
threw the round quoit, and roused the shouts of the people
when he sped the branch of the dark-leaved elder-tree from his
hand to the high heaven,

διχομηνίδος MS.; a wrong accent, it would seem.   **32** ρίπτων Blass. : ριπτῶν MS.
33 μελαμφύλλου] The second M made by **A**³ from N: cp. v. 2.   **35 f.** Housman
conj. βοάν τ' ὤρινε λαῶν | οἱ τελευταίας κ.τ.λ.

---

her own): *i.e.* 'makes them seem different
from her own,' and inferior to it. This
is forced; to me it seems barely possible;
yet, if διακρίνει be sound, it is the view
in which I should acquiesce. (2) 'The
moon *parts* the stars,'—*i.e.*, 'moves a-
mong them.' For this sense of the verb
cp. Plat. *Crat.* 388 B κερκίζοντες δὲ τί
δρῶμεν; οὐ τὴν κρόκην καὶ τοὺς στήμονας
συγκεχυμένους διακρίνομεν; But, as there
a movement of the things 'parted' is involved, so here the phrase would imply
that the stars yield place to the moon
as she cleaves her path among them.—
Blass writes **διακρινεῖ** (adjective), a form
not extant, but analogous to εὐκρινής, and
alters **φάη** to **φάει**. This would mean
(I suppose), 'as the moon is conspicuous
(ἐμπρέπει, supplied from ἐνέπρεπεν) amidst
the *different* light of the stars': or, 'is
conspicuous with a light different from
(that of) the stars.' The syllable answering
to the second of διακρινεῖ is, however,
long in the corresponding vv.; and διακρίνει is so accented in the papyrus. It
must be added that there is no reason to
suspect **φάη**. The plural **φάεα** (as 'eyes')
was familiar from the *Odyssey* (16. 15
etc.), and is not rare in later poetry
(Callimachus *Hymn. Dian.* 71, *Anthol.*
8. 77, etc.). Aratus uses it in exactly
the sense which it has here, *Phaenom.* 90
ἀλλ' αἱ μὲν (the constellation called Χηλαί)
φαέων ἐπιδευέες, οὐδὲν ἀγαναί.
I would suggest **διωχραίνει**: 'the moon
spreads paleness over the radiance of the
stars.' Cp. the Orphic Argonautica 1315
δέος δ' ὤχραινε παρειάς. If διωχραίνει had
been partly mutilated or obscured in the
archetype, a copyist might have written

διακρίνει, which occurs in v. 89 of this
ode.—Tyrrell proposed **διαχραίνει**, in the
sense 'blurs.'
     29 νυκτός, gen. of time, rather than
depending on σελάνα. — **διχομήνιδος** :
Pind. *O.* III. 19 διχόμηνις Μήνα : *I.* VIII.
47 διχομηνίδεσσιν ἐσπέραις.—**σελάνα** : the
Doric **α** in two consecutive syllables is
against the poet's general rule (see n. on
Φήμα in II. 1): but cp. XII. 195 Ἀθάνα.
     30 κύκλον: so Pind. *O.* IX. 93 διήρ-
χετο κύκλον ὅσσα βοᾷ.
     32 δίσκον. The order of the contests
in the pentathlon was probably (1) jumping, (2) quoit, (3) javelin-throwing,
(4) foot-race, (5) wrestling. So Eustathius p. 1320 (*Il.* 23. 621), quoting
ἄλμα ποδῶν δίσκου τε βολὴ καὶ ἄκοντος
ἐρωὴ | καὶ δρόμος ἠδὲ πάλη, μία δ' ἔπλετο
πᾶσι τελευτή (*i.e.* 'one result,' decided by
a majority of feats). Simonides fr. 153,
for metre's sake, puts no. 4 between 1
and 2 : ἄλμα ποδωκείην δίσκον ἄκοντα
πάλην. Here the poet mentions *quoit*,
javelin, *wrestling*: probably Automedes
lost the jump and the foot-race. Three
feats gave the prize: Aristeides *Pana-
then.* III. 339 (ed. Dind.) ἀρκεῖ τοῖς
πεντάθλοις τρία τῶν πέντε πρὸς νίκην.
ρίπτων. The papyrus gives ριπτῶν
with the circumflex: but, on its own
evidence, B. regularly has -έων in the
participle: see III. 96 n. (Cp. Soph.
Ai. 239, s.n. ριπτεῖ.)
     34 f. ἀκτέας, the elder-tree. Theo-
phrastus *Hist. Plant.* II. v. 4 remarks
that its wood has few knots or branches
(ἄοζα...τὰ τῆς ἀκτῆς),—one of the qualities
which fitted it to furnish ἀκόντια.
     35 f. βοάν...πάλας. The MS. has

ἀντ. β΄. 1 ἢ τελευταίας ἀμάρυγμα πάλας·
2 τοιῷ[δ᾽ ὑπερθύ]μῳ σ[θένε]ι
3 γυια[λκέα σώ]ματα [πρὸς γ]αίᾳ πελάσσας
4 ἵκετ᾽ ['Ασωπὸ]ν παρὰ πορφυροδίναν,
40 5 τοῦ κ[λέος π]ᾶσαν χθόνα
6 ἦλθε[ν καὶ] ἐπ᾽ ἔσχατα Νείλου·
7 ταί τ᾽ ἐπ᾽ ε[ὐν]αεῖ πόρῳ
8 οἰκεῦσι Θερμώδοντος, ἐγχέων
9 ἴστορες κοῦραι διωξίπποι ῎Αρηος,

ἐπ. β΄. 45 1 σῶν, ὦ πολυζήλωτε (F)άναξ ποταμῶν,
2 ἐγγόνων γεύσαντο, καὶ ὑψιπύλου Τροίας ἕδος.
3 στείχει δι᾽ εὐρείας κελεύθου
4 μυρία παντᾷ φάτις
5 σᾶς γενεᾶς λιπαρο-
50 6 ζώνων θυγάτρων, ἃς θεοὶ

πάλας] ΙΙ made from Τ by **A**³.   **37** Restored by Κ.   **38** [πρὸς γ]αίᾳ Κ.: πέντ᾽ αἴᾳ
Jurenka.   πελάσσας] ΠΕΛΑΣΣΩ[Ν **A**: **A**³ drew a stroke through ω (also transfixing
the second σ), and seems to have written ασ above; but the papyrus is mutilated.

no point either after λαῶν or after πάλας.
(1) With the text as it stands, I should
place only a comma after **λαῶν**, and
suppose that from **προπέμπων** we are to
supply some participle of a more general
sense (such as φαίνων or προδεικνύς) to
govern the acc. **ἀμάρυγμα**. ' He roused
the shout of the people as he sped (προπέμπων) the javelin from his hand..., or
as he *put forth* (sc. φαίνων or the like) his
flashing swiftness in the final wrestling-
match.' It is then a kind of 'zeugma,'
like that in Soph. *Ai.* 1035 ἄρ᾽ οὐκ Ἐρινὺς
τοῦτ᾽ ἐχάλκευσε ξίφος | κάκεῖνον῍Αιδης...;
where for κάκεῖνον (the girdle) we supply
εἰργάσατο or the like. This view seems
to me, on the whole, the best.
(2) The construction would be clearer,
if we placed a comma after χειρός, and
read βοάν [τ᾽] ὤτρυνε λαῶν | οἳ τελευταίας
ἀμάρυγμα πάλας· as Prof. Housman proposed (who also changed ὤτρυνε to ὤρινε).
But οἳ as a correction of the MS. η is not
quite satisfactory: still less so is δή (which
I formerly suggested); though δή can
commence a verse, and even a sentence
(*Od.* 13. 92 : Pind. *O.* III. 25).
(3) Blass puts a full stop after λαῶν.
He does not, however, explain how he
takes ἢ...πάλας. With that punctuation,
only two resources seem open. (*a*) To

regard v. 36 as a sort of exclamation: ' or
think of his flashing movement in the
wrestling-match!' (*b*) to read **ἦν** for η,
with a stress on ἀμάρυγμα: '*Flashing
movement* was there in the wrestling-
match ...; with such might did he bear
his men to earth.'
ὤτρυνε, as in *Il.* 5. 470 ὤτρυνε μένος
καὶ θυμὸν ἑκάστου, or 12. 277 μάχην
ὤτρυνον: 'stirred up,' 'roused.'
ἀμάρυγμα, the 'flash' of quick motion:
Hes. fr. 225 Χαρίτων ἀμαρύγματ᾽ ἔχουσα
(in dancing): Ar. *Av.* 925 οἶάπερ ἵππων
ἀμαρυγά (with epic ῠ, as in *Hom. hymn.*
III. 45).
38 πρὸς γαίᾳ. The redundant preposition, though only a conjecture, is
partly supported by x. 23 πρὸς γαίᾳ
πεσόντα. As Jurenka observes, there is
no other example of a prep. being added
to the dative after πελάζω. The only
objection to his ingenious **πέντ᾽ αἴᾳ** is
that αἶα is not elsewhere found in Bacchylides.
39 'Ασωπόν. See Introduction to the
Ode.—The long **α** in this name (*Il.* 4. 383,
Pind. *N.* IX. 9, Ovid *Amor.* III. 6. 33,
etc.) is against connecting it with ἄσις,
' mud,' ' silt ' (*Etym. M.*), which has ἄ
(*Il.* 21. 321).
41 καὶ ἐπ᾽ ἔσχατα Νείλου, *i.e.* to the

or put forth his flashing swiftness of movement in the wrestling- ant. 2.
match at the end. Such was the mighty spirit and strength
with which he brought stalwart forms to earth, ere he returned
to the Asopus with dark-eddying tide ; that river whose fame
has gone out into all lands, even to the uttermost regions of the
Nile.

Yea, the maidens who dwell by the fair-flowing stream of
Thermodon, the skilled spear-women, daughters of horse-urging
Ares,

have tasted the valour of thy descendants, O thrice-glorious lord epode 2.
of streams: Troy also has known it, city of lofty gates.

The vast fame of thy children goes forth on a wide path in
every land,—those bright-girdled daughters whom the gods

39 ['Ασωπὸ]ν Blass, Housman, Richards, Wilamowitz. **41** ἦλθε[ν]. ΜΑΘΕ **A**:
corr. **A³**. **42** ε[ὐν]αεῖ J. **43** κοῦραι K.: κόραι MS. **45** πολυζήλωτε (ϝ)άναξ
Housman and others: πολυζήλωτ' ἄναξ MS. **46** ἐγγόνων Jurenka, Weil,
Wilamowitz (σοῖν...ἐγγόνοιν or ἐκγόνοιν Housman): ἔγγονοι MS.

remotest regions ; an image like Pindar's
in *I.* v. [VI.] 22 f. ('countless roads...are
cleft for the onward course of noble
deeds') καὶ πέραν Νείλοιο παγᾶν καὶ δι'
Ὑπερβορέους.—I scarcely think that there
is an allusion to Memnon and his Aethio-
pians at Troy, as having carried the fame
of the Aeacidae home with them.

42 ff. εὐναεῖ. εὐναής occurs nowhere
else, nor is εὔναος found : but cp. ἀειναής
in a quotation by Athenaeus (p. 61 A)
from Nicander.

Θερμώδοντος, a river of Pontus, now
the *Termeh.* Near its mouth on the coast
of the Euxine was the town of Θεμίσκυρα,
with a fertile plain which fed great herds
of oxen and horses. This was the legendary seat of the Amazons. (Aesch. *P. V.*
723 ff.: Verg. *Aen.* XI. 659: Apoll.
Rhod. II. 995 Θεμισκύρειαι Ἀμαζόνες.)
The Amazon-myth first came into Greek
poetry with the Cyclic epic Αἰθιοπίς (*c.*
775—700 B.C.?), ascribed to Arctinus.—
ἐγχέων ἵστορες, skilled with the spear.
Poetry armed the Amazons, however, not
only with the spear and sword of the
Greek hero, but also with the bow (Pind.
O. XIII. 89 τοξόταν στρατόν), and with
the axe, either single-edged (σάγαρις,
Xen. *An.* IV. 4. 16), or double (πέλεκυς,
bipennis, Quint. Smyrn. I. 597). Their
shield was πέλτα or γέρρον (like that of
Thracians or Persians).—κοῦραι...Ἄρηος.
Penthesileia, their queen, is called Ἄρηος
θυγάτηρ in the verse which linked the
Aethiopis to the *Iliad* (schol. *Il.* 24. 804).

The Amazons figure in legend as worshippers of the war-god, sacrificing to him
at an island-shrine near Themiscyra (Ap.
Rhod. II. 385 f.), as on the Ἄρειος πάγος
at Athens (Aesch. *Eum.* 689 ; cp. schol.
Ar. *Lys.* 191).

45 f. ϝ is assumed before ἄναξ here,
but not in III. 76 (ὁ δ' ἄναξ) or v. 84
(θάμβησεν δ' ἄναξ). Cp. III. 2 n.—σῶν...
ἐγγόνων γεύσαντο : 'the Amazons tasted
the valour of thy offspring,—and só did
Troy.' Cp. *Il.* 20. 258 γευσόμεθ' ἀλλήλων
χαλκήρεσιν ἐγχείῃσιν. The 'descendants'
meant are Telamon, Ajax, and Achilles ;
perhaps also Peleus and Neoptolemus.
Telamon (and according to one account,
Peleus) went with Iolaus on an expedition
against the Amazons, and slew Melanippe,
the sister of their queen (schol. Pind. *N.*
III. 64=38). Telamon took part with
Heracles in his war on Laomedon. When
the Amazons came to Troy as allies of
the Trojans, Achilles slew Penthesileia
(as told in the *Aethiopis*). Ajax fought
against Troy ; and Neoptolemus was its
captor. (See Introd. to this Ode, § 2,
note 2.)—The MS. corruption of ἐγγόνων
into ἔγγονοι may have been prompted by
the desire of a subject for γεύσαντο (κοῦραι
being so far back).—ἐκγόνων (XVI. 16)
might seem preferable, but is not necessary.

47 f. στείχει κ.τ.λ. : 'Everywhere on
a broad path goes forth the vast renown...'
Cp. v. 31 μυρία πάντα κέλευθος, n.
49 f. σᾶς γενεᾶς...θυγάτρων. Dio-

7 σὺν τύχαις ᾤκισσαν ἀρχα-
8 γοὺς ἀπορθήτων ἀγυιᾶν.

στρ. γ′. 1 τίς γὰρ οὐκ οἶδεν κυανοπλοκάμου
2 Θήβας εὔδμ[ατον πόλι]ν,
Col. 16 3 ἢ τὰν μεγαλώνυ]μον Αἴγιναν, μεγίστου
56 4 Ζηνὸς ἃ πλαθεῖσα λέ]χει τέκεν ἥρω
5 - δεσω - - ου·
6 ὃς γ]ᾶς βασά[νοισιν Ἀχ]αιῶν
7 - ᴗ - ᴗ - ᴗ -
60 8 - - ᴗ - - - ᴗ - -
9 ἁ[ᴗ - - - ᴗ ε]ὖπ[ε]πλον [Κλεώναν

ἀντ. γ′. 1 ἡ[δὲ Πειράν]αν ἑλικοστέφα[νον
2 κ[ούραν, ὅ]σαι τ′ ἄλλαι θεῶν
3 ε[ὑναῖς ἐδ]άμησαν ἀριγνώτοις π[α]λαι[οῦ
65 4 παῖδες αἰ]δοῖαι ποταμοῦ κελάδοντος·
5 τοῦ νῦν ἀρχαί]αν πόλιν
6 κῶμοι κατέχου]σί τε νίκα[ς
7 καὶ λύραις αὐ]λῶν βοαὶ
8 σύμφωνα πνείο]υσαι· με[γίστου
70 9 χρὴ Διὸς πρῶτον σέβας θ′ Ἥραν τ′ ἀείδει]ν·

51 ἀρχα-] ΑΡΧΑΙ **A**: corr. **A³**. 55—88 These 34 verses were contained in column XVI., of which only mutilated fragments remain. The fragments have been combined by Kenyon and Blass, on the evidence of metre, contents, colour of the papyrus, etc.: but the combination is necessarily in some measure conjectural. 55 f. -MNON **A**, corrected to -μον by **A³**: this (as K. saw) was from an adj. ending in -υμον, taken by the scribe for ὕμνον. Blass supplies ἢ τὰν μεγαλώνυμον

dorus (IV. 72) says that Asopus, 'having made his home (κατοικήσας) in Phlius,' married Μετώπη (Pind. *O.* VI. 84), daughter of Ladon (the river of Elis), by whom he had two sons, Pelasgus and Ismenus, and *twelve daughters*,—Corcyra, Salamis, Aegina, Peirene, Cleone, Thebe, Tanagra, Thespia, Asopis, Sinope, Oinia, and Chalcis. (In c. 73 Diodorus mentions a thirteenth, Harpīna.) Apollodorus (III. 12. 6) raises the number of daughters to twenty (but does not enumerate them). At Olympia the Phliasians dedicated a group representing Asopus and five of his daughters, viz. Nemea (not mentioned by Diodorus), Aegina (with Zeus beside her), Harpina (the mother of Oenomaus by Ares), Corcyra, and Thebe (Paus. V. 22. 5).—The wide geographical range of

these names (from Corcyra to Sinope) illustrates the μυρία φάτις of v. 48.

In the mutilated text of this ode the names of only two daughters remain,— *Thebe* and *Aegina*, who, according to Pindar, were the youngest,—'Ασωπίδων ὁπλόταται (*I.* VII. 17 f.): see, however, n. on 61—65.

51 f. σὺν τύχαις. Cp. X. 115 σὺν... τύχᾳ. Here the plur. is used because several persons and cities are concerned: it is, in fact, a distributive σὺν τύχᾳ.— **ἀρχαγούς.** This term is applied to the founder of a city, or the eponymous ancestor of a family. Plat. *Tim.* 21 E τῆς πόλεως θεὸς ἀρχηγός τίς ἐστιν. Cp. Soph. *O. C.* 60 n.—**ἀπορθήτων** is proleptic in sense: the gods decreed that the places founded by the Asopides should ever be

established, with happy fortunes, as ancestral heroines of cities
which should defy the spoiler.

Who does not know the well-built town of dark-haired Thebe? str. 3.
Or Aegina of glorious name, who in wedlock with mighty Zeus
bore the hero (Aeacus)?   . . . .
. . . .
fair-robed Cleone,

and Peirene with diadem on her brows, and all those other ant. 3.
gracious daughters of the ancient river-god, lord of sounding
waters, who became the illustrious brides of gods.

[*Verses* 66—81, *as partially restored*. Now is the ancient city of
Asopus filled with revelry for victory, and with the blended strains of
flutes and lyres....It is meet to hymn first the majesty of great Zeus
and Hera;

(ἐρατώνυμον Wilamowitz): Piccolomini and others, καὶ τὰν (τίς δ' οὐ Housman)
χαριτώνυμον: Ellis, τίς δ' οὐ δολιχήρετμον (Pind. *O.* VIII. 20).—μεγίστου (μέγιστον
Housman) ἃ Διὸς πλαθεῖσα λέχει Blass, Housman: μεγίστῳ Ζηνὸς ἃ πλαθεῖσα λέχει
Wilam.   **57 f.** Blass supplies τοῦ]δε σω[τῆρα πέδ]ον, | ὃς γ]ᾶς βασά[νοισιν
'Αχ]αιῶν.   **61** If the letters υπ are rightly read, εὔπεπλον (or ἐύπεπλον) is certain.
63 Blass prints κ[– –˘]s, αἴτ' ἄλλαι: but the σ belonged (I think) to ὅσαι. Read
κούραν, ὅσαι τ' ἄλλαι.   **65** παῖδες αἰ]δοῖαι J.: παρθένοι] δοιαί Blass: but see comm.

virgin cities, unravaged by foes. Cp.
Lysias or. 33 § 7 (of Sparta) μόνοι...
οἰκοῦντες ἀπόρθητοι καὶ ἀτείχιστοι. Eur.
Hec. 906 (of Troy) τῶν ἀπορθήτων πόλις
οὐκέτι λέξει. Below, in v. 99, the word
was probably applied to Phlius.
55 f. These verses refer to Aegina,
bride of Zeus, and her son Aeacus (ἥρω).
Verse 55 may have begun with καὶ τὰν
(Jurenka),—τίς δ' οὐ (which is rather too
rhetorical),—or ἢ καί (Blass, who compares Pind. *O.* XIII. 20 ff.).
57 f. As to the conjecture τοῦ]δε
σω[τῆρα πέδ]ου (Blass), all the four letters
δεσω (fr. 37 K.) are uncertain. The
syllable answering to the ă of σωτῆρα
is long in all the corresponding verses
(5, 14, 31, 40, 66, 83). That might be
cured by changing πέδ]ου to στρατ]οῦ
(as = δήμου). But the restoration seems
doubtful.—In v. 58 βασά(νοισιν?) probably referred to some tests of valour or
wisdom which Aeacus had successfully
borne. He must have been the subject
of v. 59, if not also of 60.
61—65. In these five verses the
mention of the Asopides was continued
and ended. Verses 61 and 62 evidently
contained two proper names. I conjecture with some confidence that v. 61

ended with Κλεώναν, and v. 62 began
with ἠδὲ Πειράναν. For the place in
v. 61, Ταναγραν or Σινώπαν is also possible. But the poet would probably
prefer Peloponnesian names, appealing to
Cleonae and to Corinth. In 62 metre
would not admit Κέρκυραν or (ἢ καὶ)
Ἄρπιναν (Lycophron 167 Ἄρπινναν Ἀρ-
πύιαις ἴσην).
63 f. ὅσαι τ'...κελάδοντος: *i.e.* and
all the other daughters of the ancient
river-god Asopus who became the brides
of gods. The conjectures κούραν, ὅσαι
τ', and παῖδες αἰ]δοῖαι, are (I venture to
think) hardly doubtful. Blass's παρθένοι]
δοιαί cannot be right, since, as the context shows, more than two maidens are
in question.
66 ff. Here the poet turned from the
Asopides to speak of the rejoicings at
Phlius for the victory of Automedes.
Sounds of revelry fill the 'ancient city.'
Praises are due to the gods.
69, 70 These and the next five or six
verses doubtless referred to the principal
deities worshipped at Phlius. I suggest
a partial restoration (*exempli gratia*) a-
bove.—Ἥραν τ' ἀείδειν. There was
a temple of Hera at Phlius (Paus. 2.
13. 4).

ἐπ. γ́. 1 "Ηβαν τ᾽ ἔπειτα Ζηνὸς ἐρισθε]νέος
  2 χρ]υσέα[ν προσ]θέντα (F)ιόπλοκον εὖ εἰπεῖν [κόραν,
  3 καὶ μ]ατ[έρ᾽ ἀγ]νάμπτων ἐρώτων
  4 – ‿ – κλε]ινὰν βροτο[ῖς
75 5 – ‿‿ – ‿]λέων
  6 – – ‿ – – – ‿ –
  7 – ‿ – νασι]ώταν
  8 – ‿ – – – ‿]ν ὕμνον,

στρ. δ́. 1 – ‿ – – –] καὶ ἀποφθιμένῳ
80 2 τὸν πάντ᾽ ἐς ἄτ]ρυτον χρόνον,
  3 καὶ τοῖς ἐπιγ]ιγνομένοις αἰεὶ πιφαύσκοι
  4 σὰν Νε]μέᾳ νίκαν· τό [γέ] τοι καλὸν ἔργον
  5 γνησίων ὕμνων τυχὸν
  6 ὑψοῦ παρὰ δαίμοσι κεῖται·
85 7 σὺν δ᾽ ἀλαθείᾳ βροτῶν
  8 κάλλιστον, εἴπ[ερ καὶ θάνῃ τις,
  9 λείπεται Μουσᾶν [ἀγακλειτᾶν ἄθυ]ρμα.

ἀντ. δ́. 1 εἰσὶ δ᾽ ἀνθρ[ώπων ἀρεταῖσιν ὁδοὶ
Col. 17 2 πολλαί· διακρίνει δὲ θεῶν
90 3 βουλὰ [τὸ καλυπτό]μενον νυκτὸς [δνόφοισιν·
  4 τὸν δὲ χείρω τ᾽ ἄγα]γε καὶ τὸν ἀρείω
  5 Ζηνὸς αἶσ᾽ ὀρσικτύ]που.
  6 κρυπτὸς γὰρ ὅ τ᾽ ἐσθλὰ φυτ]εύσων
  7 ἔργα χὠ μὴ πρὶν μολεῖν
95 8 ἐς πεῖραν· ὤπασσαν δὲ π]αύροις
  9 ἀν]δρ[άσιν Μοῖραι τεκμαίρεσθαι] τὸ μέλλον·

77 νασι]ώταν Herwerden: Αὐτόμηδες, νασιώταν Blass: but see p. 97.   **81** [καὶ τοῖς ἐπιγ]ιγνομένοις Headlam.   **82** τό [γέ τοι] Headlam.   **83** After ΤΥΧΟΝ the ms. has a point, level with the bottom of the letter; cp. XIV. 47 cr. n.   **87** ἀγακλειτᾶν K.: βαθυζώνων Blass: μελιφθόγγων Piccolomini and Jurenka.   **89—94** Column XVII. began with v. 89, but the upper part (containing 89-104 and IX. 1-5) was torn

71 f. Hebe, worshipped at Phlius and Sicyon under the name of Δία (Strabo 8, p. 382), had an ancient shrine of peculiar sanctity (ἁγιώτατον Paus. II. 13. 3) on the acropolis of Phlius. Dia-Hebe, then, would fitly be named here, after her parents (Hes. *Theog.* 922) Zeus and Hera. Her spouse Heracles was also commemorated at Phlius, along with Cyathus, the cup-bearer whom he accidentally killed (Paus. *l. c.*). The epithet χρυσέα is elsewhere

given by B. not only to Aphrodite (v. 174), but also to Artemis (X. 117) and to Io (XVIII. 16).
If, on the other hand, *Aphrodite* was the subject of these two verses, we could read in 71 κἄπειτα κούραν Ζηνὸς ἐρισθ., and at the end of 72, εὖ εἰπεῖν Κύπριν. I incline to think, however, that the first mention of her came in v. 73.
73 καὶ ματέρ᾽ ἀγνάμπτων ἐρώτων, Aphrodite: Pindar fr. 122. 4 calls her ματέρ᾽ ἐρώτων. The καί, for which there

then also to praise Hebe, daughter of mighty Zeus, maiden divinely epode 3.
fair, with violet locks,—and the Mother of the pitiless Loves.......
Automedes, we have brought thee the song of the island Muse,

which shall remain for thee, in thy life and after thy death, for endless str. 4.
years, to tell all generations of thy victory at Nemea.]

A goodly deed that has won the strains of a true poet is laid
up on high with the gods. When mortal lips give honest praise,
there is a glory that survives death in song, the joy of the
[glorious] Muses.

[*In verses 88—104 the general sense is fairly clear: the details* ant. 4.
are partly conjectural.] There are many paths for the excellences
of men: but it is the counsel of the gods that decides what is
veiled in the gloom of night. [The weaker man and the stronger are
alike led on their way by the doom of Zeus the thunderer. Who is to
put forth high deeds, and who is to fail, is a secret, till they come to the
trial;] and to few mortals have the Fates granted the gift of conjecturing
the future.

away. The remains of 89–94 have been put together by Blass from small fragments,
metre giving the clue.   **95—99** The endings of these verses are on a fragment
which K. placed here because the metre suits this poem and no other.   **96—99** The
earlier parts of these verses, also the remains of 100—104 and of IX. 1, 2, are on a

is not room in 73 before .ατ, may have
been added to v. 72 : something similar
has happened in vv. 101 f., and there are
other instances of wrong division (as in
IX. 15 f., 33 f., 43 f.).—ἀγνάμπτων,
inflexible, not to be resisted or subdued.
The older Greek poets are apt to speak
of Eros, not in his gentler aspects, but
rather as a stern and terrible power : see
e.g. Sappho fr. 40 Ἔρος...μ' ὁ λυσιμέλης
δόνει : Ibycus fr. 1 Ἔρος...ἐγκρατέως...
τινάσσει : Soph. *Tr.* 441 f. : id. fr. 855.
13 (of Κύπρις) τίν' οὐ παλαίουσ' ἐς τρὶς
ἐκβάλλει θεῶν;
74 f. In these two verses there may
have been a mention of Demeter and of
Dionysus. Cp. 97 f.
76—87 The fame of the victor will
endure in song. νασιώταν...ὕμνον, the
Cean poet's ode : so IX. 10 νασιῶτιν...
μέλισσαν.
79—81 πιφαύσκοι in 81 cannot
have expressed a wish ('may it declare!'). We need, then, κε, κεν, or ἄν.
This probably stood in 79 (*e.g.*, κῦδος ὅς κ'
αὔξων καὶ ἀποφθιμένῳ): or possibly in 80
(*e.g.*, τὸν πάντα κ' ἄτρυτον χρόνον).—
ἄτρυτον, 'unending' : see n. on v. 27.
82—84 τό γέ τοι καλὸν ἔργον: cp.
XII. 83 τό γε σὸν κλέος αἰνεῖ.—γνησίων,

'of genuine strain,' *i.e.* genuinely inspired.—ὑψοῦ...κεῖται : 'is laid up on
high with the gods'; is consigned to
immortality.
85—87 σὺν δ' ἀλαθείᾳ βροτῶν
κ.τ.λ.: lit., 'and, with the help of truth
on the part of men, most glorious (for
the dead man) is that joy of the Muse
(the ode) which is left, even after his
death.' For σὺν ἀλαθείᾳ, see VII. 41 ff.
n.—εἴπερ .. θάνῃ : the epic εἰ with
subjunct., found also in tragic lyrics
(Soph. *O. T.* 198 n.).—ἄθυρμα : cp. the
poet's first *epigramma*, v. 3, ἐν ἀθύρμασι
Μουσᾶν. In Pindar *P.* v. 21 the κῶμος
is Ἀπολλώνιον ἄθυρμα, his favourite
'pastime,' or 'delight.' So ἀθύρειν, of
the poet's efforts, *I.* III. 57 : Lat. *lusus*,
ludere.
As regards the lost epithet of **Μουσᾶν**
here, ἀγακλειτᾶν or πολυκλειτᾶν would
perhaps best suit the context.
88—96 εἰσὶ δ' ... τὸ μέλλον. A
'gnomic' passage, consisting of general
reflections suggested by the athlete's
success in his special line of effort.
The hints in the mutilated text plainly
indicate the general tenor : the supplements which I suggest may serve to
illustrate it. For the Doric ᾱ of ἄγαγε in

ἐπ. δ´.   1 ὑμ]μι[ν δὲ καὶ Δάματρος ἔδ]ωκε χάριν
          2 κ]αὶ Διων[ύσου Κρονίδας] θεοτίματον πόλιν
          3 ναίειν ἀπο[ρθήτους θαλ]εῦντας·
    100   4 χρυσεοσκάπτρ[ου Διὸς
          5 ὅς] τι καλὸν φέ[ρεται,
          6 πᾶς αἰ]νέοι· Τιμοξ[ένου
          7 πα]ιδὶ σὺν κώ[μοις ἀμαρ-
          8 τέ]οιτε πεντ[άθλου (Ϝ)έκατι.

                        IX. [X.]

               <ΑΓΛΑΩΙ (?) ΑΘΗΝΑΙΩΙ

                    ΔΡΟΜΕΙ ΙϹΘΜΙΑ>

στρ. α´.   1 Φή]μα, σὺ γ[ὰ]ρ ἀ[γγελίαις θνατῶν ἐπ]οιχνεῖς
          2 φῦ]λα, καὶ πᾶ[σιν πιφαύσκεις
          3 τηλόσ]ε λαμπ[ομένα

separate fragment, placed here by Blass (in K.'s edition).   **97** The verse began with
.. MI.   The letter before MI was M or I.   The letter after MI had a base like that
of Δ or Ptolemaic ω.   These traces suit ΥΜΜΙ(Ν)Δ.   For omission of N in the MS.,
see p. 128, 2. (i).—Blass (1st ed.) wrote ὕμμιν (Jurenka, ὕμμι[ν δὲ καὶ ταύταν παρέ]δωκε
χάριν).   In 2nd and 3rd ed. Blass writes τιμίῳ [δ᾽ Ἡρακλέϊ δ]ῶκε χάριν.   As the verse
then begins with - ‿ -, he proposes in v. 19 to read δὴ τότ᾽ for ἁ καὶ τότ᾽, and in 45
to omit ὤ.   **99** ευντες **A**: **A³** wrote α over the second ε.   **102** The traces
before νεοι indicate either N or ΑΙ.   Blass (1st ed.) read them as ὤ, and wrote νῦν]

---

v. 91, cp. ἄγετο (ᾱ) in XIX. 4.   In
v. 90 δνόφοισιν is hardly doubtful : cp.
XV. 32 f.   Perhaps Horace, a student
of Bacchylides, had that phrase in mind
when he wrote, *Prudens futuri temporis
exitum* Caliginosa nocte *premit deus* (III.
xxix. 29 f.).   Theognis, indeed, has ὀρφνη
γὰρ τέταται (1077) in a like context, but
that is not so verbally near.—There is
a close parallelism here with the train of
thought in IX. 35 ff., ματεύει | δ᾽ ἄλλος
ἀλλοίαν κέλευθον... 45 ff. τὸ μέλλον | δ᾽
ἀκρίτους τίκτει τελευτάς, | πᾷ τύχα βρίσει.
97—102 The conclusion.   Here the
poet seems to address the people of
Phlius.   The general sense may have
been somewhat as follows :—'To you,
for the sake of (Demeter and) Dionysus,
Zeus has given to dwell in a city honoured
of gods and unravaged.'   Then the ode
ends with another reference to the victory
of Automedes.
97 ff.   The καὶ Διων- in 98 makes it
strongly probable that *Demeter* was named

in 97.   These two were prominent among
the divinities of Phlius, which depended
on vines and agriculture.   On the acropolis there was a sacred περίβολος of
Demeter, and within it a ναός containing
images of her and Persephone.   A festival
in her honour, with a mystic ritual, was
held every fourth year at Κελεαί, near
Phlius.   In the lower town was an
ancient ἱερόν of Dionysus.   Cp. Paus. II.
13. 5—7, and E. Curtius, *Pelop.* II.
471 ff.
   Verse 97 must have begun with - ‿ -,
like vv. 19 and 45, where there is no
reason to doubt the text : and ὕμ[μι]ν
δὲ is most probable.   A tentative restoration is shown (*exempli gratia*) above.
99 ἀπορθήτους: cp. 52.   The absence
of an accent on o in the MS. affords a
presumption in favour of acc. plur. rather
than acc. sing.—**θαλεῦντας.**   θαλέω was
an alternative form for θάλλω: Pindar
has θάλησε (*N.* IV. 88, cp. X. 42):
Hippocr. 6. 654 (Littré) θαλέοντα (*v. l.*

To you (of Phlius), for the sake of Demeter and of Dionysus, the son epode 4.
of Cronus has granted to dwell in a god-honoured city, unravaged and
prosperous.   When a man wins a meed of honour from golden-sceptred
Zeus, let all give praise:—attend ye with festal songs on the son of
Timoxenus, for his victory in the pentathlon.

IX. [X.]

For an Athenian [Aglaos?], winner of foot-races at the Isthmus.

Fame! thou roamest with tidings o'er the tribes of men, and str. 1.
declarest them to all, shining afar,

ὦ νέοι, supposing that, as there is not room for νῦν in 102, it had adhered to 101.
He now accepts K.'s αι (instead of ω), and reads τοῦτ' αἰνέοι.   **103 f.** Restored
by Blass.
   IX.   The title has perished with the lost part of column XVII. (see cr. n. on VIII.
89—94).   **1 f.** Cp. cr. n. on VIII. 96. Small parts of 1—4 are supplied by a
fragment (23 K.) which Blass has placed here.—ἀμερίων νήριθμ' ἐποιχνεῖς | φῦλα
Wilamowitz: ἀθανάτων θνατῶν τ' ἐποιχνεῖς | φῦλα Headlam: ἀγγελέουσ' ἐπὶ χθόν'
οἰχνεῖς | καλὰ καὶ πᾶσαν θάλασσαν Jurenka: αἰὲν ἐπ' ἀνθρώπους (or ἐν ἀνθρώποις)
πεδοιχνεῖς | ἆθλα Nairn.

θαλέθοντα): Quint. Smyrn. 11. 96 θαλέ-
ουσι: Nonnus 16. 78 θαλέει. (In Mosch.
11. 67 θαλέεσκε is a v. l. for θαλέθεσκε.)
   100—102 Διὸς and φέρεται seem
fairly certain. Before αἰνέοι I supply
πᾶς (=πᾶς τις, as in Soph. O. T. 596,
O. C. 597, El. 972, and often), because
these words introduce the exhortation,
σὺν κώμοις ἀμαρτέοιτε. The genitive χρ.
Διὸς recalls VI. 1 ff., Λάχων Διὸς μεγί-
στου | λάχε φέρτατον πόδεσσι | κῦδος: it
denotes the source from which the honour
comes. καλόν (τι) is the Nemean victory:
cp. 11. 6, Pind. P. VIII. 88 ὁ δὲ νέον τι
καλὸν λαχών ('a fresh honour'). If ὃς
be read, φέρεται (midd.) is 'wins.' I
slightly prefer this to ᾧ (Blass), with
which φέρεται (pass.) = 'is borne': though
that is tenable. Blass supplies τοῦτ'
before αἰνέοι, i.e. 'to whomsoever an
honour is borne (from the gods), let him
be thankful for it.' ᾧ would naturally
mean the victor, who, on this view, is
the subject of αἰνέοι. In this context,
however, the subject of αἰνέοι should be,
not the victor, but one who praises
him.—The long syllable before αἰνέοι,
whatever it was, must have been added
in the MS. to v. 101: cp. 73 n.
   104 f. ἀμαρτέοιτε: a probable supplement. It is in favour of ἀ- rather
than ὀ-, that the MS. has ἀμαρτεῖν (=ἀκο-

λουθεῖν) in XVII. 46. That form is found
also in Herodas IV. 95 and V. 43 : and
is attested by Eustathius (Il. p. 592, 21)
as coexisting with ὁμαρτεῖν. The adv.
ἁμαρτῇ occurs in Il. 5. 656, etc.—Cp.
Aesch. fr. 355. 2 μιξοβόαν πρέπει | διθύ-
ραμβον ὁμαρτεῖν | σύγκωμον Διονύσῳ.—
έκατι (supplied by Blass) as in 1. 6 f.
Cp. V. 33 ὑμνεῖν...ἕκατι νίκας (also VI. 11,
IX. 15).

   IX.   **1—3** Φήμα bears far and wide,
even to the nether world, the tidings of
an athlete's victory: cp. III. 1 ff. Φήμα
...φέρουσ' ἀγγελίαν. The supplements
suggested above are mine. For the dat.
ἀγγελίαις, cp. Theocr. XXV. 32 (ἁλωαὶ)
ἃς ἡμεῖς ἔργοισιν ἐποιχόμεθα : for πιφαύ-
σκεις, VIII. 81. Note that the last
syllable of the second verse of the strophe
is long in 12 and 30, though anceps in
40.—πᾶσιν: the papyrus has πᾶ..., as it
has πᾶσιν (πᾶσιν) in XIV. 54.
   Blass writes: ἀμφ' ἀρετᾷ ('in the cause
of prowess') θνατῶν ἐποιχνεῖς | φῦλα, καὶ
πᾶσιν τίθησθα | γῆλόσε λαμπομέναν. He
conceives Φήμα as being here, 'non...
nuntius victoriae alicuius,...sed gloria.'
The two notions are closely akin : but
the personified Φήμα is surely, like Fama,
a bearer of tidings.

4 καὶ γᾶς ὑ]πὸ κεύ[θεσι· κλεινοὶ
5 5 δ' οἳ γέ]νωνται [χάρμ' ἔχουσιν
6 παντὶ χώρ]ῳ ξ[υν]όν, ὅ,τι χρυ[σέαν ἴδον εὔ-
7 ο[λβον] ὀφθαλμοῖσι Ν[ίκαν
8 π[αῦλ]αν ἀπράκταν [τε μόχθων.
9 Ἀ[γλ]αῷ καὶ νῦν κασιγνήτας ἀκοίτας
10 νασιῶτιν ἐκίνησεν λιγύφθογγον μέλισσαν,

ἀντ. α'.   1 ἀχ]ειρὲς ἵν' ἀθάνατον Μουσᾶν ἄγαλμα
2 ξυνὸν ἀνθρώποισιν εἴη
3 χάρμα, τεὰν ἀρετὰν
4 μανῦον ἐπιχθονίοισιν,
15 5 ὁσσάκις Νίκας ἕκατι
6 ἄνθεσι ξανθὰν ἀναδησάμενος κεφαλὰν
7 κῦδος εὐρείαις Ἀθάναις
8 θῆκας Οἰνείδαις τε δόξαν.

5 The v. ended with 'ωι (from χώρῳ ?). The word belonged metrically to v. 6.
7 The first letter of the verse was certainly Ο. **9** Between Α and Ι there is
space for about four letters, of which the third may have been Α; but this is not

4—8 I give above (*exempli gratia*)
a tentative restoration.— καὶ γᾶς ὑπὸ
κεύθεσι : cp. Soph. *El.* 1066 f. ὦ χθονία
βροτοῖσι φάμα : and Pind. *O.* VIII. 81,
where Ἀγγελία, daughter of Hermes,
brings news of an athlete's victory to his
father in the shades.—For κλεινοὶ δ' | οἳ
γένωνται, cp. VIII. 22 ff., κλεινοί...οἳ...
ἐρέψωνται κόμαν.—χάρμ'...ξυνόν. ξυνὸν...
χάρμα occurs in 12 f., where the general
sentiment expressed here is applied to
the particular case of Aglaos (if that was
his name). It seems not unlikely that
the phrase in 12 f. was an echo from
5 f.—χώρῳ. The letters ωι alone remain.
There is no trace whatever of the letter
before them, but only an acute accent,
showing that the word was paroxytone.
δάμῳ (the victor's people) is possible;
but the context here and in 12 f. rather
favours χώρῳ. Fame creates a wide-
spread sympathy with the victor's triumph:
the tidings come even to the shades.
As to the rest of vv. 6—8, note these
points. (1) Verse 7 began with Ο. The
Ν of ΟΦΘΑΛΜΟΙΣΙΝ, in connexion with
ΧΡΤ in v. 6, suggests Nike. (2) In v. 8
the first word began with Π or Γ, and
ended with ΑΝ. (3) After ἀπράκταν
the first letter was Τ, Γ, Π, or Ι. The
next letter was almost certainly Ε.—

ἴδον εὔολβον. I had thought also of
ἴδεν εὔχονται. Another resource would
be ποτιλεύσσ]ουσιν : but we rather require
an aorist.—παῦλαν ἀπράκταν, 'a restful
pause' from the toils of the athlete.
Plut. *Mor.* 270 A (ἡμέρας) ἀποφράδας
καὶ ἀπράκτους (*dies nefastos et otiosos*).
Walz *Rhet.* vol. IV. p. 15 ἑορτὴν ἄπρακτον,
'a holiday on which no work is done.'
For the place of τε cp. Soph. *O. T.* 528
ἐξ ὀμμάτων δ' ὀρθῶν τε κἀξ ὀρθῆς φρενός.
For the sentiment, Pind. *O.* I. 97 ff. ὁ
νικῶν δὲ λοιπὸν ἀμφὶ βίοτον | ἔχει μελι-
τόεσσαν εὐδίαν | ἀέθλων γ' ἕνεκεν : *O.*
VIII. 5 ff. μαιομένων μεγάλαν | ἀρετὰν
θυμῷ λαβεῖν, | τῶν δὲ μόχθων ἀμπνοάν,
'(athletes) whose spirit is eager to attain
great glory, and a respite from their
toils.'—Jurenka gives παῦσαν ἀπράκταν
μέριμναν, 'have made an end of ineffectual anxiety' (for victory) : but the initial
of the third word cannot have been Μ.

9—14 For Aglaos, his brother-in-
law has commissioned the poet of Ceos
to write an ode, that his prowess (ἀρετή)
may have a lasting record. On the
problem presented by the lacunas in
verses 9 and 11, see the Appendix. In
v. 9 Ἀγλαῷ, supplied by Blass, is very
probable. In v. 11 his ἀχειρὲς seems less
so. The word occurs in *Batrachomyo-*

even in the depths of the nether world : and those who win
renown have a joy that is shared in every place, because their
eyes have seen golden, blessed Victory, and they have found a
restful pause from their toils.

'Tis on behalf of Aglaos now that his sister's husband has
moved the clear-voiced singer, the island bee,

in order that the immortal tribute of the Muses, a monument ant. 1.
not made with hands, might be a common joy for mankind,—
that it might tell all men, Aglaos, of thy prowess, seen as oft as,
by grace of Victory, thou hast caused thy golden hair to be
crowned with flowers, and hast brought glory to spacious
Athens, with honour for the Oeneidae.

certain. Ἀγλαῶι Blass.   10 νασιῶτιν MS. K. doubted whether the first
letter was not Π: hence Πασία, τὶν (τὶν δ' Pearson) Wilam. and Platt.   11 The
letters ειρες are certain. The letter before them may have been X or Λ.   14 μανῦον
made from μανοον by A³.   15 f. The MS. adds ἄνθεσιν ξαν- to v. 15.   The final
ν of ἄνθεσιν, so ill-sounding here, is doubtless due to error.

machia 300 as = 'without hands': here
it is to mean 'not made with hands.'
To justify it, we must suppose that it
was meant to distinguish the poet's
ἄγαλμα from the sculptor's: that would
be Pindaric (N. v. 1), but is less like
Bacchylides.

9 καὶ νῦν, 'e'en now,' marking the
transition from the proem to the immediate theme, just as in X. 9 f., σέθεν
δ' ἕκατι | καὶ νῦν.

10 The νασιῶτιν of the MS. shortens
a syllable (-ιν) which is long in vv. 20,
38, and 48. The poet perhaps wrote
νασιώταν: cp. Aesch. Ag. 111 χερὶ
πράκτορι, 664 τύχη...σωτήρ, Eum. 186
δίκαι καρανιστῆρες, etc. The correction
is such as a grammarian might have
made.—μέλισσαν: cp. Pind. P. X. 748 f.
ἐγκωμίων γὰρ ἄωτος ὕμνων | ἐπ' ἄλλοτ'
ἄλλον ὥτε μέλισσα θύνει λόγον, 'the glory
of songs of praise flits like a bee from
theme to theme.' The comparison of the
poet to a bee is frequent: Plat. Ion 534 A
λέγουσι γὰρ...οἱ ποιηταὶ ὅτι...ἐκ Μουσῶν
κήπων τινῶν ...τὰ μέλη ἡμῖν φέρουσιν
ὥσπερ αἱ μέλιτται: Ar. Av. 748 f.
ὡσπερεὶ μέλιττα | Φρύνιχος κ.τ.λ.: Leoni-
das of Tarentum (Anthol. I. 1) describes
Erinna as μέλισσαν...Μουσῶν ἄνθεα δρεπ-
τομέναν: Hor. C. IV. ii. 28 f. ego apis
Matinae | more modoque, etc.

11 Μουσᾶν ἄγαλμα, the ode: see
n. on I. 74.

13 τεὰν ἀρετὰν is better here than
τεᾶν ἀρετᾶν (to go with χάρμα). Our

poet uses the plur. ἀρεταί only in XIII. 8
(and probably VIII. 88), and then with
reference to several men.—If Ἀγλαῷ be
right in v. 9, there is a transition here
to the second person; cp. XV. 6—10.

15 f. The ὅσσα of the MS. should
probably be ὁσσάκις, as several critics
have suggested. The syllable -κις may
have been missed by the scribe through
its likeness to -κας. ὅσσαπερ or ὅσσα δή
would also serve. (Blass defends ὅσσα
by supposing that the first syllable of νίκας
to be metrically ∟: see n. on v. 8.)—
Νίκας ἕκατι: cp. I. 6 n.
The MS. wrongly joins ἄνθεσιν ξαν- to
v. 15; there is a like error in vv. 33 and
43. Here the hiatus after ἕκατι gives
a clue. (I indicated this in Kenyon's
editio princeps, p. 87.)

16 ἀναδησάμενος κεφαλάν: Her. I.
195 τὰς κεφαλὰς μίτρῃσι ἀναδέονται. The
midd. is normal in this sense; cp. Pind.
N. XI. 28, I. I. 28, etc. In P. X. 40, however, ἀναδήσαντες has the same meaning.

18 Οἰνείδαις. Oeneus, son of Pandion,
was one of the ten ἐπώνυμοι of the Attic
tribes. Οἰνεῖδαι are the members of the
tribe Οἰνηίς. Cp. [Dem.] or. 60 § 30
οὐκ ἔλαθεν Οἰνείδας κ.τ.λ. In mythology
Οἰνείδης is a designation of Meleager,
Tydeus, or Diomedes.—The fact that the
victor's tribe, but not his father, is named,
has been thought to indicate that his
family was an obscure one; but this can
hardly be inferred: though vv. 47—51
suggest that he was not rich. The reason

9 ἐν Ποσειδᾶνος περικλειτοῖς ἀέθλοις

Col. 18 20 10 εὐθὺς ἔνδειξ]ας Ἕλλασιν ποδῶν ὁρμὰν ταχεῖαν·

ἐπ. α'. 1 δεύτερον δ' οὔ]ροισιν ἔπι σταδίου,
2 θερμ[ὰν ἔτι] πνέων ἄελλαν,
3 ἔστα[· βρέχω]ν δ' ᾆξ αὖτε θατήρων ἐλαίῳ
4 φάρε[· ἐς εὔθροο]ν ἐμπίτνων ὅμιλον,
25 5 τετρ[αέλικτο]ν ἐπεὶ
6 κάμ[ψεν δρό]μον. Ἰσθμιονίκαν
7 δίς ν[ιν ἀγκ]άρυξαν εὐβού-
8 λων [ἀεθλάρχ]ων προφᾶται·

στρ. β'. 1 δὶς δ' ἐ[ν Νεμέ]ᾳ Κρονίδα Ζηνὸς παρ' ἀγνὸν
30 2 βωμό[ν· ἁ κλει]νά τε Θήβα
3 δέκτ[ό νιν ε]ὐρύχορόν
4 τ' Ἄργο[ς Σικυώ]ν τε κατ' αἶσαν·

19 ποσιδανος MS., as XIII. 20 ποσιδανος, XVI. 36 ποσιδανι, XIX. 8 ποσι-: but XVI. 59 f. ποσειδανι, 79 ποσειδᾶν. 20 εὐθὺς ἔνδειξ]ας Blass: ὁρμὰν ταχεῖαν A. Ludwich, Th. Reinach: ταχεῖαν ὁρμὰν MS. 21 οὔροισιν Blass. 23 βρέχων] δ' ἄιξε Blass. The letter before δ' was probably N, and cannot have been C.—δ' αὖτε] Δ' ΑΪΞΕ A.

for the absence of the father's name may be simply metrical. Cp. n. on 54 ff.

There should probably be a full stop (or at least a colon) after **δόξαν**. For verses 15—18 refer, as ὅσσα indicates, to all the athlete's victories, and not to those won at the Isthmus alone. He had been successful at seven other places (vv. 29—35).

19 Ποσειδᾶνος...ἀέθλοις. Cp. Pind. *O*. XIII. 40 ἐν δ' ἀμφιάλοισι Ποτειδᾶνος τεθμοῖσιν.

Metre requires **ὁρμὰν ταχεῖαν** (not ταχ. ὁρμ.): see vv. 10, 38, 47. Similarly in XIV. 47 the MS. has ἄρχεν λόγων instead of λόγων ἄρχεν: and in XVI. 72 χεῖρας πέτασσε instead of πέτασε χεῖρας. Cp. also I. 70 n.

19—26 The restoration of this passage given above is tentative in some details, but hardly doubtful as to the general sense. See the discussion in the Appendix. Here I note the following points. (1) An inscription from Thera, of the first cent. B.C., quoted by Blass (= Kaibel *Epigr. Gr.* 942), concerns a boy who won a boxing match, and then forthwith engaged in the pancration, which he also won:—ἔτι θερμὸν | πνεῦμα φέρων σκληρᾶς παῖς ἀπὸ πυγμαχίας | ἔστα παγκρατίου βαρὺν ἐς πόνον· ἁ

μία δ' ἀὼς | δὶς Δωροκλείδαν εἶδεν ἀεθλοφόρον. This suggests that εστα in 23 is **ἔστα.** The signal exploit of this athlete was that he ran in two *consecutive* races, and won them both. Paus. VI. 13. 3 mentions an athlete who at Olympia won the δόλιχος, and then *forthwith* (παραυτίκα) the stadion, and after that the δίαυλος. **οὔροισιν ἔπι σταδίου,** 'at the bounds of the course,' means, 'at the starting-line' (γραμμή), from which the runners were despatched. **βρέχων δ'..αὖτε**: that is, again he came in first,—the sweat and olive-oil from his naked body sprinkling the clothes of the spectators who pressed near to him at the finish. δεύτερον δ' (21), ᾆξ' αὖτε (23), and ἐς εὔθροον (24) are my conjectures: for the last, cp. III. 9 θρόησε δὲ λαὸς ἀπείρων. (2) The use of the second person is made certain by -ᾰς in 20. A transition to the third person is certainly made in v. 23. The pronoun of the 3rd person occurs in v. 27, **δίς νιν ἀγκάρυξαν**, when the poet turns from the vivid picture of the race to a list of the victor's successes. (3) My tentative explanation of the fact that the scribe's ἄιξε was corrected by A³ into αὖτε would be that the original reading, βρέχων δ' ᾆξ' αὖτε, generated two others, (a) βρέ-

In Poseidon's renowned games thou didst show thy rushing
speed to the Greeks at the outset:—

then a second time did he take his stand at the bounds of the epode 1.
course,—still breathing a storm of hot breath,—and again he
darted forward, the olive-oil from his body sprinkling the
garments of the spectators as he rushed into the cheering
crowd, after finishing the fourth round of the course.
Twice have the spokesmen of the prudent judges declared
him a victor at the Isthmus, and twice at Nemea by the holy
altar of Zeus son of Cronus:

illustrious Thebes too has duly welcomed him, and spacious str. 2.
Argos, and Sicyon;

A³ has changed Ϊ to Υ, transfixed Ξ, and written T above it (αὖτε).—ΘΑΤΗΡΩΝ **A**:
A³ has added E above the line between Θ and A. **27** ἀγκάρυξαν J.—εὐβού-]
ΕΤΒΟΙ **A** (cp. 34): corr. **A³**. **28** λων] Λ superscript by **A³**: the letter written
by **A** is lost. **30** ἁ κλεινά J.

χων δ' ἄϊξε, and (b) βρέχων δ' αὖτε. See
Appendix, p. 478.—**θατήρων**. θατήρ
(from Doric θαέομαι) is attested by
Hesychius.
25 τετραέλικτον (Jurenka and Platt):
Anthol. VII. 210. 4 τετραέλικτος ὄφις (with
four-fold coils). The foot-race equal in
length to a double δίαυλος was technically
called ἵππιος. It was in use at the
Isthmian and the Nemean games (perhaps
at others also): in the case of Nemea, at
least, there was a ἵππιος for boys. In
later times it dropped out of both festivals; but Hadrian restored it to the
winter Nemea (Paus. VI. 16. 4). The
δόλιχος was longer still, but always consisted of an even number of rounds.
27 f. εὐβούλων...προφᾶται. There is
no metrical test, as only the words χρή τιν'
remain in v. 56.
(1) If the metre of v. 28 was –⏑⏑–⏑⏑–,
then the lost word was an anapaest.
W. Christ suggests συνέδρων: H. Richards,
βραβέων. Kenyon and Jurenka read
Χαρίτων. The Charites give victory in
the games: Pind. O. II. 50 Χάριτες...
ἄνθεα τεθρίππων ἄγαγον: cp. N. VII. 54.
They are εὔβουλοι as 'judging aright,'—
giving the prize to the most deserving.
The προφᾶται would then be the judges
of the games.
(2) If the verse was –⏑⏑––⏑–, then we
need such a word as ἀεθλάρχων, proposed
by Platt. It is not extant, but is a
possible word. A careful estimate has
now led me to think that there is just
room for it in the lacuna, as ε, θ and ρ are

thin letters in the papyrus. ἀγωναρχᾶν
(Soph. Ai. 572) would be slightly too
large. It may fairly be urged that
εὐβούλων is in favour of a word denoting
the actual judges. Then προφᾶται would
be the heralds.
30—37 The following were some of
the festivals connected with the places
mentioned. 1. Thebes: Ἡράκλεια, Ἰόλαια.
(Pindar's so-called 'second Pythian' relates to a Theban festival.) 2. Argos:
Ἥραια, for which (according to a probable
view) Ἑκατόμβαια was another name.
A bronze shield (χαλκός in Pind. O. VII.
83) was the prize. 3. Sicyon: Πύθια.
4. Pellene in Achaia, west of Sicyon:
Θεοξένια (to Apollo). The prize was a
cloak, χλαῖνα (cp. Pind. O. IX. 97).
5. Euboea: Γεραίστια (to Poseidon),
Ἀμαρύνθια (to Artemis). 6. Aegina:
Ἥραια, Αἰάκεια.—All these places are in
Pindar's list (O. XIII. 107—112), which
includes also Megara, Eleusis, Marathon,
the Arcadian Λύκαια (noticed also in O.
IX. 104), and Aetna. In Boeotia there
were other ἀγῶνες besides the Theban
(cp. O. VII. 84 ff.). These local games
must have done more for the physical
training of Greeks at large than even the
four greater festivals.
31 f. δέκτο, from ἐδέγμην, 2nd aor. of
δέχομαι (Il. 2. 420: Pind. O. 2. 49
ἔδεκτο). Cp. the Homeric aorists ἆλτο,
λέκτο ('counted'), ὦρτο, etc. Take δέκτο
with κατ' αἶσαν (Il. 10. 445), 'gave him
welcome due': i.e. his prowess won its
reward.—εὐρύχορον: see n. on VIII. 17.—

5 οἵ τε Π[ελλάν]αν νέμονται,
6 ἀμφί τ' Εὔβοιαν πολ[υλάϊο]ν, οἵ θ' ἱερὰν
35 7 νᾶσο[ν Αἴγιν]αν. ματεύει
8 δ' ἄλλ[ος ἀλλοί]αν κέλευθον,
9 ἄντι[να στείχ]ων ἀριγνώτοιο δόξας
10 τεύξεται. μυρίαι δ' ἀνδρῶν ἐπίσταμαι πέλονται·

ἀντ. β'.   1 ἢ γὰρ σοφὸς ἢ Χαρίτων τιμᾶν λελογχὼς
40   2 ἐλπίδι χρυσέᾳ τέθαλεν·
3 ἤ τινα θευπροπίαν
4 εἰδώς· ἕτερος δ' ἐπὶ πάσι
5 ποικίλον τόξον τιταίνει·
6 οἱ δ' ἐπ' ἔργοισίν τε καὶ ἀμφὶ βοῶν ἀγέλαις
45   7 θυμὸν αὔξουσιν· τὸ μέλλον
8 δ' ἀκρίτους τίκτει τελευτάς,
9 πᾷ τύχα βρίσει. τὸ μὲν κάλλιστον, ἐσθλὸν
10 ἄνδρα πολλῶν ὑπ' ἀνθρώπων πολυζήλωτον εἶμεν·

33 f. The ms. adds the syllables ἀμφί τ' Εὔβοι- to v. 33.   **37 f.** The ms. adds τεύξεται to v. 37.   **38** ΕΠΙCΤΑΤΑΙ **A**: corr. **A³.**   **39** ἢ γὰρ] Γ added above the line by **A³.**—τιμᾶν ms.: τιμὰν K.   **42** πάσι Blass: ΠΑΙCΙ ms.   **43 f.** The

---

Σικυών : Σεκυών in Bekker *Anecd.* p. 555, and on coins : as O. Rossbach would read here.
34 πολυλάϊον (λήϊον, a crop, or a corn-field): *Il.* 5. 613 ναῖε πολυκτήμων, πολυλήϊος.
36 f. κέλευθον: cp. VIII. 88 f.: Pind. *O.* IX. 104 ff.: ἐντὶ γὰρ ἄλλαι | ὁδῶν ὁδοὶ περαίτεραι, | μία δ' οὐχ ἄπαντας ἄμμε θρέψει | μελέτα.—After ἄντι-, various supplements are possible: ἄντινα στείχων, Blass, Jurenka: ἄν τις εὖ τάμνων Kenyon : ἄν τις ἐμβαίνων Tyrrell, Richards. More spirit would be given to the phrase by ἄντιν' ὁρμαίνων (intrans.), 'pressing along' his chosen path.
39—45 ἢ γὰρ σοφὸς...αὔξουσιν. If in 42 we read πάσι (Blass, 1st and 3rd ed.) instead of the ms. παισί, the enumeration is as follows.
1. σοφός is the man of intellectual pursuits, and especially the poet: cp. Pind. *O.* I. 9, II. 94, *P.* IV. 295, *I.* I. 45, etc.
2. Χαρίτων τιμᾶν λελογχώς (the gen. with λαγχάνω as in I. 55 f.). Here, probably, it is the successful athlete of whom the author is chiefly thinking: εὐάγων τιμά (Pind. *N.* X. 38) is the gift of the Charites. But they also give skill in

song, in music (*P.* IX. 89), and in other arts. More generally, it is due to them εἰ σοφός, εἰ καλός, εἴ τις ἀγλαὸς ἀνήρ (*O.* XIV. 7).
3. ἤ τινα θευπροπίαν εἰδώς: alluding to the μάντις, who divines by augury or by sacrifice (ἔμπυρα), and to the χρησμολόγος, learned in old prophecies.—The Homeric θεοπροπίη is concrete, 'a prophecy,' or 'oracle' (*Il.* 11. 793 etc.): the neut. sing. θεοπρόπιον, used by Herodotus, occurs only in *Il.* 1. 85: but here the abstract sense is fitter.
4. πάσι, the acquisition of wealth : Hesych. πᾶσις· κτῆσις. The reference is to the various forms of ἐμπορία and χρηματισμός.—ποικίλον, 'wily' (in pursuit of κέρδος). [Or, 'of varied aim,'—the modes of πᾶσις being diverse: but this is perhaps too artificial.]
With the ms. παισὶ the sense would be : 'Another aims at youths the cunningly-wrought shaft of song.' Cp. Pind. *I.* 11. 1—3 οἱ μὲν πάλαι... | ῥίμφα παιδείους ἐτό-ξευον μελιγάρυας ὕμνους, 'the men of old lightly bent at youths their shafts of honey-voiced song.' Pindar was thinking, as Bacchylides would be here, of such poets as Ibycus and Anacreon ; perhaps also of Alcaeus. Examples of

also the dwellers in Pellene, and in the region of Euboea with many cornfields, and in the sacred isle of Aegina.

Men seek various paths which they shall tread to the winning of bright renown. And countless are the kinds of human knowledge. A man is rich in golden hope

because he has wisdom ; or has been honoured with the gifts of ant. 2. the Graces, or has skill in some manner of soothsaying ; another aims his wily shaft at wealth ; while some there be who take delight in the works of husbandry, and in herds of oxen.

The future brings forth issues which cannot be judged beforehand, so as to tell how Fortune will incline the scale. The noblest lot for a man is that his own worth should make him widely admired among his fellows.

MS. adds the syllables οἱ δ᾽ ἐπ᾽ ἔργοι- to v. 43. **47** ΠΑΙ. The I seems to have been added by **A³**.—βρίσει. τὸ μὲν] BPICENOMEN **A** (*i.e.* he read IT as N): corr. **A³**.—ECEΛΩΝ **A** (ε for θ). ἐσθλὸν Wilamowitz, Blass.

such songs would be the ode of Ibycus to Gorgias (fr. 30 Bergk) and those of Anacreon to Cleobulus and Smerdias (fr. 3, 5, 47). Cp. also Alcaeus, fr. 46. This species of lyric poetry had become very popular (largely through Anacreon) before our poet's time. Bacchylides himself, in describing the joys of peace, says (fr. 3. 12), παιδικοί θ᾽ ὕμνοι φλέγονται. The epithet ποικίλον would denote poetic art: Pind. fr. 179 ὑφαίνω δ᾽ Ἀμυθαονίδαις ποικίλον | ἄνδημα : fr. 194 τειχίζωμεν ἤδη ποικίλον | κόσμον αὐδάεντα λόγων. But there are strong objections to παισί. (1) Poetry should clearly be included under the phrase in 39, ἢ σοφὸς κ.τ.λ. (2) It seems almost grotesque that poetry, as a pursuit, should be represented by this one species of lyric. (3) The order of enumeration is perverse ; since poetry, if not included under the pursuits indicated in v. 39, should at least be mentioned in close connexion with them.

5. ἔργοισίν τε καὶ...βοῶν ἀγέλαις. The conjunction shows that ἔργα are the works of husbandry. These are the farmers and the herdsmen. (Otherwise, the ἔργα might have been those of the craftsman or artist : cp. Pind. *O.* VII. 52 ἔργα δὲ ζωοῖσιν ἑρπόντεσσί θ᾽ ὁμοῖα κέλευθοι φέρον.)—θυμὸν αὔξουσιν, 'enlarge their spirit,' 'take delight,' therein: see n. on l. 52.

Headlam has well observed that in vv. 39—45 B. concisely paraphrases Solon fr. 13. 43—54, where we have

(1) *the pursuit of wealth*, 43—46: (2) *agriculture*, 47 f.: (3) *artistic handicrafts*, 49 f.,—which would come under the gifts of the Χάριτες here : (4) *poetry*, 51 f., and (5) *soothsaying*, 53 f. This further confirms πάσι in 42.—See Appendix.

46 f. ἀκρίτους is explained by πᾷ τύχᾳ βρίσει : the future brings forth issues which cannot be judged (beforehand), (so as to decide) in what way fortune will incline. That is, the future is to bring forth success or failure ; but no one can tell *now* which it will be.— βρίσει is a metaphor from the scales of a balance. Cp. Arist. *Problem.* 16. 11 (p. 915 *b* 3) ὅταν βρίσῃ ὁ κύκλος ἐπὶ θάτερον μέρος.

47—49 τὸ μὲν κάλλιστον κ.τ.λ. The MS. supports ἐσθλῶν : but I think that ἐσθλὸν must be right. 'The fairest lot is that one should be admired as a *man of worth* by many of his fellows.' The antithesis is between personal ἀρετή and wealth. 'I know *also*'—the poet continues—'the great power of wealth,' etc. The train of thought is parallel with that in I. 49—53 φαμὶ καὶ φάσω μέγιστον | κῦδος ἔχειν ἀρετάν, πλοῦ|τος δὲ καὶ δειλοῖσιν ἀνθρώπων ὁμιλεῖ. For μέν, cp. XVI. 1.

If ἐσθλῶν were read, it would be neuter (as the plural is in IV. 19 f., v. 198, and XVI. 132), and might best be joined with πολλῶν : 'the fairest lot is that a man should be admired by his fellows for many excellent things.' But these ἐσθλά would be too vague for the

ἐπ. β'.   1 οἶδα καὶ πλούτου μεγάλαν δύνασιν,
50   2 ἃ καὶ τὸν ἀχρεῖον τί[θησ]ι
   3 χρηστόν. τί μακρὰν γλῶσσαν ἰθύσας ἐλαύνω
   4 ἐκτὸς ὁδοῦ; πέφαται θνατοῖσι νίκας
   5 ὕστε]ρον εὐφροσύνα·
Col. 19   6 αὐλῶν [καναχαῖσι γλυκεῖαν
55   7 μειγν[ύμεν φόρμιγγος ὀμφὰν
   8 χρή τιν' [εὐμούσους τ' ἀοιδάς.

X. [XI.]

ΑΛΕΞΙΔΑΜΩΙ ΜΕΤΑΠΟΝΤΙΝΩΙ

ΠΑΙΔΙ ΠΑΛΑΙΣΤΗΙ ΠΥΘΙΑ

στρ. α'.   1 Νίκα [γλυκύδωρε, μεγίσταν
   2 σοὶ πατ[ὴρ ὤπασσε τιμὰν
   3 ὑψίζυγ[ος Οὐρανιδᾶν
   4 ἐν πολυχρύσῳ δ' Ὀλύμπῳ
5 Ζηνὶ παρισταμένα
   6 κρίνεις τέλος ἀθανάτοι-
   7 σίν τε καὶ θνατοῖς ἀρετᾶς.
   8 ἔλλαθι, [βαθυ]πλοκάμου

49 δύνασιν] ΔΥΝΑΜΙΝ **A**: corr. **A³**.   51 ἰθύσας] ΙΘΥΓΑC (Θ made from Ο) **A**.

A³ has written Υ over Ϊ, but what he meant is doubtful. K. thinks that a line was drawn through -ΑC. This does not seem quite certain: there is a small blot between A and C, but C is intact.

X. The title has been added by **A³** in the left margin.   **1—7** The letter after ΝΙΚΑ is read by K. as Γ: by Blass, as I with a stroke drawn through it.

context: they would not be specifically 'worthy *qualities* or *deeds*,'—marks of ἀρετή.

εἶμεν is a Doric form (also Boeotian Aeolic, Meister I. 279), not found in Homer: Bacchylides uses it only here, but ἔμμεν in v. 144, XVII. 31, 56.

51 f. μακράν, adv.—**γλῶσσαν ἰθύσας.** 'Why have I turned my strain to far-off things? Why am I driving out of my course?' Cp. Pind. *N.* VII. 71 f. ἄκονθ' ὥτε χαλκοπάρᾳον ὄρσαι | θοὰν γλῶσσαν: see also above, v. 196 n.—**ἰθύσας.** ἰθύω is elsewhere intrans. ; hence Robinson Ellis conj. ἰθύνας. (ἰθείας, Housman.)—**ἐκτὸς ὁδοῦ.** So Pindar (*P.* XI. 38) says, after a digression, ἦ ῥ', ὦ φίλοι, κατ' ἀμευσίπορον τρίοδον ἐδινήθην, | ὀρθὰν κέ-

λευθον ἰὼν τὸ πρίν.—The poet apologizes for the irrelevance of the gnomic passage beginning with ματεύει in v. 35. The metaphor in γλῶσσαν ἰθύσας, if it is to harmonize with ἐλαύνω, should be from guiding the course of a chariot (cp. *Il.* 11. 528 κεῖσ' ἵππους τε καὶ ἄρμ' ἰθύνομεν),—not from launching a missile.

πέφαται = πέφανται (*Il.* 2. 122 etc.), 'has been set forth,' 'appointed.' This form occurs elsewhere only in an Ionic excerpt from Περικτιόνη (Plato's mother) in Stobaeus *Flor.* 85. 17.

54—57 The reference in the closing verses to festal music and song resembles that in VIII. 102 ff. and XII. 230 f. The context may have been somewhat of the kind suggested above. For αὐλῶν κανα-

I know also the mighty power of riches, which can clothe even epode 2. the useless man with merit.—But wherefore have I turned my strain so far out of its due course? After victory, festal joy is appointed for mortals: blend ye the shrill sounds of flutes with the clear voice of the lyre, and with tuneful songs.

X. [XI.]

For Alexidamus of Metapontion, winner of the boys' wrestling-match at Delphi.

Victory, giver of sweet gifts, great is the honour assigned to str. 1. thee by the Father of the Heaven-born, throned on high: standing at the side of Zeus in golden Olympus thou judgest the issue of prowess for immortals and for men. Be gracious to us, O daughter of Styx with the flowing tresses,

Fulvius Ursinus (*Carmina novem illustrium feminarum et lyricorum*, Antwerp 1568, p. 206) quotes from Stobaeus *Flor.* III. (Περὶ φρονήσεως) the following words, which are not now extant in any MS. or edition of Stobaeus: Βακχυλίδης δὲ τὴν Νίκην γλυκύδωρόν φησι καὶ ἐν πολυχρύσῳ Ὀλύμπῳ Ζηνὶ παρισταμένην κρίνειν τέλος ἀθανάτοισί τε καὶ θνητοῖς ἀρετῆς. Hence Neue (*Bacchyl. Fragm.* p. 18, 1832) and Bergk (fr. 9) gave Νίκα γλυκύδωρος...ἐν πολυχρύσῳ κ.τ.λ....κρίνει τέλος ἀθανάτοισί τε κ.τ.λ.—μεγίσταν Jurenka: ὤπασσε τιμὰν J. (τιμὰν ὄπασσεν Jurenka): Οὐρανιδᾶν J.   8 βαθυπλοκάμου J.

χαῖσι cp. II. 12 : and for φόρμιγγος ὀμφὰν XIII. 13.—Blass thinks that the name of the victor's father may have stood in 55 (*e.g.*, Δάμωνος υἱῷ) : cp. 18 n.

X. 1—3 The first three verses probably spoke generally of the high honour given to Nike by Zeus; then vv. 5—8 define her function. Cp. *Il.* 4. 166 Κρονίδης ὑψίζυγος.
4 f. πολυχρύσῳ, the epithet of rich cities (Mycenae etc.), fitly applied by Pindar (*P.* VI. 8) and Sophocles (*O. T.* 151) to Delphi, is too material to Olympus: very different is the Homeric ἀπ᾽ αἰγλήεντος Ὀλύμπου (*Il.* I. 532).—Ζηνὶ παριστταμένα (of Νίκη and the other children of Styx), τῶν οὐκ ἔστ᾽ ἀπάνευθε Διὸς δόμος οὐδέ τις ἕδρη, | ἀλλ᾽ αἰεὶ πὰρ Ζηνὶ βαρυκτύπῳ ἐδριόωνται.
6 f. κρίνεις τέλος...ἀρετᾶς, 'decidest the *issue* of prowess' (rather than 'adjudgest the prize' for it). Pindar indeed sometimes uses τέλος in a sense equivalent to 'prize': the clearest case is *O.* XI. 67 Δόρυκλος δ᾽ ἔφερε πυγμᾶς τέλος, which may fairly be rendered, he 'won the prize for boxing' (lit., 'secured the *result*'). Cp. *I.* I. 26 f. οὐ γὰρ ἦν

πενταέθλιον, ἀλλ᾽ ἐφ᾽ ἑκάστῳ | ἔργματι κεῖτο τέλος, 'a (separate) result was appointed for each feat' (where it is usually rendered 'prize'; and that is implied). In *P.* IX. 118 the maiden is placed at the end of the course, τέλος ἔμμεν ἄκρον: where, as the adj. shows, it means 'goal' (rather than 'prize';—though she was that also).
8 ἕλλαθι, 'be propitious.' On this form see H. Weir Smyth, *Greek Melic Poets* p. 418; and Meister, *Gr. Dial.* I. 413. It is the imperat. of an Aeolic perfect (cited by Herodian II. 499. 19 and 605. 8). Two points should be noted. (1) λλ is from σλ: the primary form of the present (not extant) would be σίσλημι: and of the perf. stem, σέσλᾱ. Cp. Aeolic χέλλιοι (χίλιοι), from χέσλιοι. (2) The perfect ought to have ᾱ: cp. Callim. fr. 121 ἕλλᾶτε : Theocr. XV. 143 ἵλᾶθι. The ᾱ here may be due to the preceding long syllable (by levelling of quantity): in *Il.* I. 583 we have ἵλᾱος, though in 9. 639 (etc.) ἵλαος. Or it may be a simple imitation of the epic η in ἵληθι (*Od.* 3. 380). In Simonides fr. 49 (vulg. ἵλᾱθι) ἕλλαθι should perhaps be read: the quantity is there uncertain.

9 κούρα [Στυγὸς ὀρ]θοδίκου· σέθεν δ' ἕκατι
10 καὶ νῦν Μεταπόντιον εὐ-
11 γυίων [κατέχ]ουσι νέων
12 κῶμοί τε καὶ εὐφροσύναι θεότιμον ἄστυ·
13 ὑμνεῦσι δὲ Πυθιόνικον
14 παῖδα θαητὸν Φαΐσκου.

ἀντ. α'. 15 1 ἵλεῴ νιν ὁ Δαλογενὴς υἱ-
2 ὃς βαθυζώνοιο Λατοῦς
3 δέκτο βλεφάρῳ· πολέες
4 δ' ἀμφ' Ἀλεξίδαμον ἀνθέων
5 ἐν πεδίῳ στέφανοι
20 6 Κίρρας ἔπεσον κρατερᾶς
7 ἧρα παννίκοιο πάλας·
8 οὐκ εἶδέ νιν ἀέλιος
9 κείνῳ γε σὺν ἄματι πρὸς γαίᾳ πεσόντα.
10 φάσω δὲ καὶ ἐν ζαθέοις
25 11 ἁγνοῦ Πέλοπος δαπέδοις
12 Ἀλφεὸν παρὰ καλλιρόαν, δίκας κέλευθον
13 εἰ μή τις ἀπέτραπεν ὀρθᾶς,
14 παγξένῳ χαίταν ἐλαίᾳ

ἐπ. α'. 1 γλαυκᾷ στεφανωσάμενον

9 Στυγὸς Fennell, Blass.   10 ΕΥ corrected from ΕΙ by Α¹?   11 κατέχουσι
Nairn, Bruhn, Blass, κελαδοῦσι Κ. (cp. however 13 ὑμνεῦσι).   15 ΙΛΕΩᵢ is
due to correction (probably by Α¹) : Λ seems to be written over C : and ι is added
above the line.   Had the scribe inadvertently repeated -ισκου from the end of 14?
17 βλεφάρῳ] The ending has been corrected (from -ων or -οιν?).   21 ΠΑΝΝΙΚΟΙ

9 κούρα Στυγός. Nike is the daughter
of Styx by the Titan Pallas : Bacchylides
epigr. I. 1 κούρα Πάλλαντος πολυώνυμε,
πότνια Νίκα. Hes. Theog. 383 ff. Στὺξ
δ' ἔτεκ' Ὠκεανοῦ θυγάτηρ Πάλλαντι μιγεῖσα
Ζῆλον καὶ Νίκην καλλίσφυρον ἐν μεγάροισι,
καὶ Κράτος ἠδὲ Βίην. Styx and these her
children helped Zeus in his war with
their Titan kinsfolk, and were received
by him into Olympus. The mother had
a further reward ; αὐτὴν μὲν γὰρ ἔθηκε
θεῶν μέγαν ἔμμεναι ὅρκον (Theog. 400).
ὀρθοδίκου: Styx is such because the
ὅρκος is a fence against wrong-doing. As
ὅρκος in its primary sense denoted the
witness or sanction of the oath, rather
than the act of taking it, Styx is herself
the ὅρκος θεῶν.

10 Μεταπόντιον is here the name of
the town, not the neut. of Μεταπόντιος
(Thuc. VII. 33 §4): the later form of
the adj. was Μεταποντῖνος (Paus., etc.).
Metapontion (Lat. Metapontum) was on
the west coast of the Gulf of Tarentum,
about 28 miles s.w. of that city. (See
Introduction.)
12 εὐφροσύναι, 'festivities' (like θα-
λίαι, XII. 187): cp. Solon 4. 10 εὐφροσύνας
κοσμεῖν δαιτὸς ἐν ἡσυχίᾳ, and Aesch. P.V.
540. The sing. (III. 87, IX. 53), alone
used by Pindar, is more frequent.—θεότιμον: so he calls Phlius θεοτίματον πόλιν
(VIII. 98).
14 θαητόν: said in XII. 115 of Troy.
Pindar often uses the word, in the sense
of 'conspicuous' (P. X. 58 θαητὸν ἐν

who guards the right. 'Tis due to thee even now that Metapontion, city honoured by gods, is full of rejoicings, while festal
bands of stalwart youths hymn the Pythian victor, the brilliant
son of Phaiscus.

The Delos-born son of Latona the deep-girdled gave him ant. 1.
welcome with kindly eyes ; and many were the wreaths of flowers
that fell around Alexidamus in Cirrha's plain, for his triumph in
the strenuous wrestling. Never in the course of that day did
the sun behold him brought to earth.

And I will avouch that in the glorious domain of holy Pelops
also, by the fair stream of Alpheus, if some one had not warped
the course of righteous sentence, he would have crowned his hair

with the gray olive for which all comers strive, epode 1.

MS.: παννίκοιο Κ.—ΠΑΛΛΑC **A**, but a line has been drawn through the second Λ.
23 ΓΕ made from ΤΕ (by **A**¹?).—The words σὺν...πεσόντα have been added by
another hand, the same which supplied XVII. 16. **24** ΕΠΙ **A**: ΕΝ **A**².—κ' ἐπὶ
Housman. **26** δίκαν κελεύθου conj. Herwerden. **28** ΠΑΓΞΕΝΩΙ **A**:
ΠΑΓΞΕΙΝΩΙ **A**¹?—ΕΛΑΙΑΙ] The final Ι has been written by a corrector (over C?).

ἄλιξι), or 'comely' (γυῖα, P. IV. 80 ;
δέμας, N. XI. 12).
17—20 δέκτο: cp. VIII. 31 n.—
ἀνθέων...στέφανοι. Pindar P. IX. 123
describes a victor in olden days as thus
greeted by the spectators,—πολλὰ μὲν
κεῖνοι δίκον | φύλλ' ἐπὶ καὶ στεφάνους: and
doubtless he took this from the usage of
his own time. So in P. VIII. 57 he says
(figuratively) Ἀλκμᾶνα στεφάνοισι βάλλω.
This custom was called φυλλοβολία.—
Κίρρας. Cirrha, the harbour-town of
Crisa on the Corinthian Gulf, was destroyed by the Delphians (with aid from
Cleisthenes of Sicyon) about 585 B.C.:
but the name, like that of Crisa, was still
used by the fifth-century poets in connexion with Delphi: Pind. P. XI. 12
ἀγῶνί τε Κίρρας: VIII. 19 Κίρραθεν
ἐστεφανωμένον.
21 ἦρα...πάλας. ἦρα as=χάριν, 'on
account of,' occurs in Callimachus fr. 41,
ἦρα φιλοξενίης: and in Anthol. Planud.
4. 299 οὐκ ἐρέω.—τίνος ἦρα; ('why not?').
In Il. 1. 572 μητρὶ φίλῃ ἐπὶ ἦρα φέρων,
'doing kind service' to her (= φέρων
χάριν in Il. 9. 613): 'a very ancient
phrase, appearing in the Vedic vâra bhar,
lit. to bring the wishes' (Leaf ad loc.).
Cp. also Il. 14. 132 θυμῷ ἦρα φέροντες,
'indulging their resentment'; which (as
Smyth remarks) illustrates the origin of
the prepositional use.
23 κείνῳ γε σὺν ἅματι: 'in the course
of that day': σύν denoting concurrent

duration. So XI. 125 σὺν ἅπαντι χρόνῳ,
'through all the years' ('in the whole
course of history'): Pind. fr. 123 σὺν
ἁλικίᾳ, 'while we are in our prime.'
Slightly different is the temporal use in
which σύν marks the arrival of a moment:
Pind. P. IV. 10 σὺν δεκάτᾳ γενεᾷ: P. XI.
10 ἄκρα σὺν ἑσπέρᾳ.—πρὸς γαίᾳ: cp.
VIII. 38.—πεσόντα: part. after εἶδε. (instead
of pres.) part. after εἶδε, cp. V. 40 εἶδε
νικάσαντα: Her. IX. 22 πεσόντα εἶδε.
24 φάσω, i.e. 'I will make bold to
say': cp. VII. 42 κομπάσομαι.—In pro-
posing κ' ἐπὶ here, Housman meant κε
to go with ἱκέσθαι in 30 (where see n.):
but the interval would be a long one.
The scribe's ἐπὶ seems to have been a
mere error: ἐν is the more natural word
here.
25 Πέλοπος: see n. on v. 181.
—δαπέδοις: cp. Pind. N. VIII. 24 ἐν
Πυθίοισί τε δαπέδοις. δάπεδον (ζάπεδον=
διάπεδον) is a level surface or ground: in
the plur., 'grounds,' 'domain.'
26 f. δίκας κέλευθον ... ὀρθᾶς, 'the
course of righteous judgment.' As against
reading δίκαν κελεύθου (= 'path') it may
be noted that hiatus does not occur at
the end of the corresponding verses,
except in v. 12, where it is excused by
the point after ἄστυ.—εἰ μή τις: 'some
one' (god or man).
28 f. παγξένῳ...ἐλαίᾳ, as a prize open
to all competitors: cp. Soph. fr. 348
πολὺν δ' ἀγῶνα πάγξενον κηρύσσεται:

30 2 πορτιτρόφ[ον ἀν πεδίον πάτ]ραν θ' ἱκέσθαι.

3 [οὔ τι δόλος κακόφρων]

Col. 20 4 παῖδ' ἐν χθονὶ καλλιχόρῳ

5 ποικίλαις τέχναις πέλασσεν·

6 ἀλλ' ἢ θεὸς αἴτιος, ἢ

35 7 γνῶμαι πολύπλαγκτοι βροτῶν

8 ἄ]μερσαν ὑπέρτατον ἐκ χειρῶν γέρας.

9 νῦν δ' Ἄρτεμις ἀγροτέρα

10 χρυσαλάκατος λιπαρὰν

11 ἡμέ]ρα τοξόκλυτος νίκαν ἔδωκε.

40 12 τᾷ ποτ' Ἀβαντιάδας

13 βωμὸν κατένασσε πολύλ-

14 λιστον εὔπεπλοί τε κοῦραι·

30 ΝΘ' ΪΚΕCΘΑΙ is certain: before Ν is seen the top of a letter which may have been Α: and before this, again, a trace which is consistent with Ρ.

Pind. *O.* VI. 63 πάγκοινον ἐς χώραν (Olympia): *O.* III. 18 (the Olympian olive) φύτευμα ξυνὸν ἀνθρώποις στέφανόν τ' ἀρετᾶν.—γλαυκᾷ: VII. 51.—στεφανω-σάμενον: Pindar has the same use of this midd. aorist (*O.* VII. 81, XII. 17).

30 πορτιτρόφον...ἱκέσθαι. The letters νθ' preceded ἱκέσθαι. In considering possible supplements, we have to provide for the κε, κεν, or ἀν which ἱκέσθαι requires. In the whole passage (24—30) there are only three possible places for it, one of which is very improbable as being too remote (viz. 24, if κ' ἐπὶ replaced καὶ ἐν): the other two are v. 28 (if χαίταν κ' were read), and v. 30. The last is the most probable. πορτιτρόφον may have been followed by ἀν: the other possibility is κ' in one of two places (*e.g.*, ἐς χθόνα κ' εὖ πράσσονθ', or Ἰταλίαν κ' ἕδραν θ'). ἀν seems the more likely. We might have, then, either πεδίον πάτραν θ' (Blass), or (*e.g.*) πατρίδ' εὔκαρπόν θ' (Jurenka): I prefer the former, as yielding the fitter sense. '*The heifer-nourishing plain*' denotes the pasture-lands of Messapia (=Calabria) about Metapontion; πάτραν is that city itself. Cp. the Homeric hymn to the Delian Apollo, v. 21, ἠμὲν ἀν' ἤπειρον πορτιτρόφον ἠδ' ἀνὰ νήσους. In writing πορτιτρόφον, was Bacchylides thinking of the etymology which derived Ἰταλία from ϝιταλός, *vitulus*, a calf? That etymology was adopted by

the Sicilian historian Timaeus, and was therefore older at any rate than *c.* 300 B.C. See Gellius XI. 1. Timaeus (and Varro), he says, *terram Italiam de Graeco vocabulo appellatam scripserunt, quoniam boves Graeca vetere lingua* ιταλοὶ *vocitati sint, quorum in Italia magna copia fuerit, buceraque* ['horned cattle,' vulg. *buceta,* 'pastures'] *in ea terra gigni pascique solita sint complurima.*

31—36 The general sense of the lost verse would probably be represented by οὔ τι δόλος κακόφρων or the like. Verses 26 f. might seem to suggest corrupt conduct on the part of the judges: so the poet hastens to guard against such an inference. Some god may have warped the minds of the judges; as Athena did (according to one legend) when the Greek chiefs preferred Odysseus to Ajax in awarding the arms of Achilles. Or it may have been purely an error of human judgment.

Alexidamus, whose forte was wrestling, may have gone in for the pentathlon, and lost the odd event through being just beaten in the foot-race, according to the verdict of the judges (or a majority of them), while he and his friends held that he had won. Or there may have been a question as to the fairness of a throw in the wrestling-match. Pausanias (VI. 3. 7) tells a story which is in point. Eupolemus, an Elean, ran in the men's *stadion* at

ere he returned to the horse-feeding plain of his own land. Not that a malignant fraud made the boy a prey to crafty arts in the fair precincts of Olympia: no, a god was the cause, or else the oft-erring judgments of mortals snatched the supreme prize from his grasp. But now bright victory has been given to him by the Huntress with golden shaft and bow of fame, Artemis, the Soother. To her an altar, goal of many a prayer, was set up of old by the son of Abas and his well-robed daughters.

—ἂν πεδίον πάτραν θ' Blass: ἂν πατρίδ' εὔκαρπόν θ' Jurenka: ἐς χθόνα κ' εὐτυχέονθ' K.: Ἰταλίαν νικῶνθ' Platt (with κ' ἐπὶ in 24). **31** The verse is lost.—οὔ τι δολοφροσύνα conj. Festa: ἀλλὰ τύχα φθονερὰ Palmer: ἀντιπάλῳ δύ' ἐπεὶ Blass, taking παῖδ' (32) as παῖδε. **35** πολύπλαγκοι MS.: corr. K. **36** ἄμερσαν Palmer. **39** ἡμέρα Blass: ἀμέρα Palmer.

Olympia. Three Ἑλλανοδίκαι were the judges. Two of them awarded the victory to Eupolemus; but the third, to Leon, an Ambraciot: and 'it was said' that Leon, going before the Olympic Council (βουλή), had got a fine inflicted (χρημάτων καταδικάσαιτο) on each of the two judges who had voted against him. The Eleans, as presidents at Olympia, were sometimes charged with favouring their countrymen: Plut. Quaest. Platon. 2 Ἠλείους τῶν σοφῶν εἰπέ τις βελτίους ἂν εἶναι τῶν Ὀλυμπίων ἀγωνοθέτας εἰ μηδὲ εἰς Ἠλείων ἦν ἀγωνιστής. (Cp. also Diodorus I. 95.) It is easy, then, to understand why our poet may have wished to make it clear that he did not impute fraud.

32 καλλιχόρῳ: v. 106 n. Here the idea of enclosure contained in χορός serves to suggest the scenes of the contests at Olympia.

33 ποικίλαις, in a bad sense; cp. Pind. O. I. 29, N. v. 28.—πέλασσεν: cp. Il. 5. 766 ὀδύνῃσι πελάζειν: Aesch. P. V. 155 δεσμοῖς...πελάσας.

35 πολύπλαγκτοι, usu. 'much wandering'; here 'often erring,' as in Epigr. Gr. 594. 4 (4th cent. A.D.?) βροτῶν πολυπλάγκτοισιν πραπίδεσσιν. Cp. Eur. Hipp. 240 παρεπλάγχθην γνώμας ἀγαθᾶς.

36 ἄμερσαν, Doric for ἤμερσαν, like ἄγετο for ἤγετο in XIX. 4: the first syll. of the verse should be long (cp. 78).—ἀμέρδω takes a double acc. in Hom. hymn. v. 312 τιμὴν | ...ἤμερσεν Ὀλύμπια δώματ' ἔχοντας: but not elsewhere a simple acc. (instead of gen.) denoting that which is taken away.

37—39 νῦν δ' Ἄρτεμις. So far as appears, it is simply as the goddess of

Metapontion (116) that she favours him. —ἀγροτέρα: v. 123 n.—χρυσαλάκατος, 'with golden shaft' (Hesych. καλλίτοξος· ἠλακάτη γὰρ ὁ τοξικὸς κάλαμος): epithet of Artemis in Il. 16. 183, Soph. Tr. 636. This sense is not incompatible with the addition of τοξόκλυτος, which is more general; 'renowned with the bow,' 'famed for archery.'

ἡμέρα, the 'gentle,' the 'assuager of pain.' This (or Ἡμερασία, Paus. VIII. 18. 8) was the name under which Artemis was worshipped at Λουσοί in the north of Arcadia. She was so called because she had healed the madness of the Proetides: ἡμέρῃ, οὕνεκα θυμὸν ἀπ' ἄγριον εἵλετο παίδων (Callim. Dian. 237). See Introd. —Though ἄμερος is found in the MSS. of Pindar and the bucolic poets, the ἡ of ἥμερος seems to have been Panhellenic (cp. Smyth, Melic Poets p. 420).—The fem. form is used by Pind. N. IX. 44 and Her. v. 82.

40—42 Ἀβαντιάδας: Proetus. Abas, son of Lynceus and Hypermnestra, figured in legend as the twelfth king of Argos. He was the father, by Aglaïa, of Acrisius and Proetus; also of Κάνηθος (eponymus of a mountain near Chalcis in Euboea), and of Eidomene. (Apollod. 2. 2. 1: cp. Roscher s.v.)

βωμόν, at Lusi: cp. 110. — κατένασσε: aor., with caus. sense (here = ἱδρύσατο), on the analogy of ἔνασσα (ναίω). Only the aor. (active and middle) of κατανναίω occurs. Elsewhere it always denotes 'settling' persons in a place.— πολύλλιστον, 'of many prayers,' 'sought by many worshippers'; Hom. hymn. Pyth. Apoll. 169 ἐν νηοῖσι πολυλλίστοισι.

στρ. β'.　1 τὰς ἐξ ἐρατῶν ἐφόβησεν
　　　　2 παγκρατὴς Ἥρα μελάθρων
　45　3 Προίτου, παραπλῆγι φρένας
　　　　4 καρτερᾷ ζεύξασ' ἀνάγκᾳ·
　　　　5 παρθενίᾳ γὰρ ἔτι
　　　　6 ψυχᾷ κίον ἐς τέμενος
　　　　7 πορφυροζώνοιο θεᾶς·
　50　8 φάσκον δὲ πολὺ σφέτερον
　　　　9 πλούτῳ προφέρειν πατέρα ξανθᾶς παρέδρου
　　　10 σεμνοῦ Διὸς εὐρυβία.
　　　11 ταῖσιν δὲ χολωσαμένα
　　　12 στήθεσσι παλίντροπον ἔμβαλεν νόημα·
　55　13 φεῦγον δ' ὄρος ἐς τανίφυλλον,
　　　14 σμερδαλέαν φωνὰν ἱεῖσαι,

ἀντ. β'.　1 Τιρύνθιον ἄστυ λιποῦσαι
　　　　2 καὶ θεοδμάτους ἀγυιάς,
　　　　3 ἤδη γὰρ ἔτος δέκατον
　60　4 θεοφιλὲς λιπόντες Ἄργος
　　　　5 ναῖον ἀδεισιβόαι
　　　　6 χαλκάσπιδες ἡμίθεοι
　　　　7 σὺν πολυζήλῳ βασιλεῖ.

52 εὐρυβία K. : ΕΤΡΥΒΙΑΙ ms. : but the final ι, which is very small, and slightly above the line, may have been added by another hand. εὐρυβίᾳ Nairn, Blass,

---

45 f. παραπλῆγι…καρτερᾷ…ἀνάγκᾳ, 'a strong overmastering frenzy': ἀνάγκα is the resistless power of the divine plague.—Note the ῐ before φρένας : elsewhere in this poet (as Smyth observes) φρ makes position.—I hesitate to forsake the ms. and write παραπλᾶγι with Blass, because the ᾶ may be one of the poet's euphonic compromises, like φήμα, ἀδμήτα, etc. : πλάξιππος (V. 97) is different.— ζεύξασ' : Pind. N. VII. 6 πότμῳ ζυγένθ' : Eur. Helen. 255 τίνι πότμῳ συνεζύγην ;
47—49 παρθενίᾳ…ἔτι ψυχᾷ, 'while still in virginal life,' while still young maidens: cp. Soph. Ai. 558 f. νέαν | ψυχὴν ἀτάλλων. The addition of ἔτι emphasizes their youth as aggravating their presumption. — κίον ἐς τέμενος … θεᾶς: their offence was not the fact of entering Hera's precinct, but the spirit which they showed. There were occasions when maidens took a prominent part in the worship at the Argive Heraion. The chorus in Eur. El. 173 invite Electra

to attend a θυσία in honour of that goddess (πᾶσαι δὲ παρ' Ἥ|ραν μέλλουσι παρθενικαὶ στείχειν). At one such festival Hera was decked as a bride, her priestess enacting the νυμφεύτρια (bridesmaid) : the maidens of Argos attended in their best apparel, wearing wreaths of flowers.
50—52 φάσκον δὲ κ.τ.λ. The mythographer Pherecydes (c. 450 B.C.) agreed with our poet in assigning such a boast as the cause of Hera's anger against the Proetides: παραγενόμεναι γὰρ εἰς τὸν τῆς θεοῦ νεὼν ἐσκωπτον αὐτόν [αὐτήν ?], λέγουσαι πλουσιώτερον μᾶλλον εἶναι τὸν τοῦ πατρὸς οἶκον (Schol. Od. 15. 225 = fr. 24 Müller I. p. 74). They disparaged her *temple* as compared with their father's *house*. (Remark that this definition of the boast is, so far as it goes, against reading the dative εὐρυβίᾳ here. 'Wealth of wide dominion' suggests a more general vaunt.) The logographer Acusilaus (c. 500 B.C.) said that the Proetides had '*slighted the ancient image*

All-powerful Hera had driven those maidens from the fair str. 2.
halls of Proetus, their spirits in bondage to a strong overmastering
frenzy. For while yet in girlhood, they had entered the holy
place of the purple-girdled goddess, and boasted that their sire
far surpassed in wealth the golden-haired consort of Zeus, dread
lord of wide dominion. But she, in anger, smote their hearts
with a thought that turned them to flight; and with fearful
shrieks they fled to a forest in the hills,

far from the Tirynthian city and its god-built streets. ant. 2.
It was now the tenth year since the dauntless heroes with
shields of bronze had left Argos, dear to the gods, and were
dwelling at Tiryns with their much-envied king.

Jurenka, Herwerden, Festa. **54** στήθεσσι K. CTHΘECIN ms.—ἔμβαλεν νόημα K.
(ΕΜΒΑΛΕΝΟΜΜΑ ms.) **55** τανίφυλλον] τανύφυλλον Jurenka.

---

of Hera,' τὸ τῆς Ἥρας ξόανον ἐξηυτέλισαν
(Apollod. 2. 2. 2 = fr. Acus. 19, Müller I.
p. 102). Hesiod (ib.) said that they had
'refused to accept the rites of Dionysus.'
Rather the myth suggests votaries of some
new cult who show scorn for the older
deities of the land.

πλούτῳ προφέρειν: Her. VI. 127 πλούτῳ
καὶ εἴδεϊ προφέρων Ἀθηναίων.—παρέδρον,
'consort,' intended to be statelier than
συνεύνου.—I would read (as K. does)
εὐρυβία, gen., not εὐρυβίᾳ: the ms. has
the latter, but the ι may have been added
by a later hand. εὐρυβία, following σεμνοῦ
Διός, and referring back to πλούτῳ, is (to
my feeling) intolerable: let any one read
the verses, thinking of the sense, and
judge. Further, a second epithet for
Διός is thoroughly in B.'s manner: see
(e. g.) V. 99 σεμνᾶς χόλον Ἀρτέμιδος
λευκωλένου: ib. 174 χρυσέας Κύπριδος
θελξιμβρότου.—Of course εὐρυβίας is, in
itself, a perfectly suitable epithet for πλοῦτος
(cp. Pind. P. V. 1 ὁ πλοῦτος εὐρυσθενής):
but that is not the point.—εὐρυβίας is said
of Poseidon in Pind. P. VI. 58, and often of
heroes. B. has φθόνος εὐρυβίας in XV. 31.

54 παλίντροπον νόημα, 'an impulse
that turned them to flight,'—from the
τέμενος. Elsewhere παλίντροπος is found
(1) with ὄμματα, etc., as in Aesch. Ag.
778: or (2) with verbs of moving, as ἕρπειν
(Soph. El. 1222). The accent here might
be παλιντρόπον, but that is not required:
νόημα παλίντροπον is (strictly) the νόημα
of a παλίντροπος.—Note the error in the
ms., ΕΜΒΑΛΕΝΟΜΜΑ (through change
of H into M, and loss of the second N).

55 ὄρος. Callimachus (Dian. 236)
describes the Proetides as οὔρεα πλαζομέ-

vas Ἀζήνια, the hills of the region in
N.W. Arcadia called Ἀζανία (from the
Ἀζᾶνες, descendants of Ἀζάν, son of
Arcas): it was the hill-district about
Cleitor (some 12 miles S. of Lusi) and
Psophis.—τανύφυλλον (Theocr. XXV.
221) is the correct form, but B. may have
written τανίφυλλον to avoid υ in two
consecutive syllables: see n. on III. 60.

56 φωνὰν ἱεῖσαι: Verg. Ecl. 6. 48
Proetides implerunt falsis mugitibus agros
(they imagined themselves to be cows).

59—81 The Proetides having fled
from Tiryns, the poet pauses to explain
how it had come about that they were
living there.
Nearly the same story is told by Pausanias (II. 25. 7 f.). He describes the
brothers as fighting a drawn battle, after
which they were reconciled, ὡς οὐδέτεροι
βεβαίως κρατεῖν ἐδύναντο. Apollodorus
(2. 2. 1), on the other hand, says that
Acrisius drove Proetus out of Argolis.
Proetus took refuge with Iobates (or
Amphianax) king of Lycia; married his
daughter (the Anteia of the Iliad, the
Sthenoboea of Tragedy); and was restored
to Argolis by a Lycian army. Then he
and Acrisius divided the realm. The
dualism of royal seats is hinted in the
Iliad (2. 559); οἳ δ' Ἄργος τ' εἶχον
Τίρυνθά τε τειχιόεσσαν.

61 f. ἀδεισιβόαι, not quailing at the
βοὴ ἄσβεστος of battle: a new compound,
suggested by such words as δεισήνωρ,
δεισιδαίμων.—ἡμίθεοι (cp. VIII. 10), the
heroes who had fought under Proetus
against Acrisius, the ἀντίθεοι...ἥρωες of
vv. 79 ff.

63 πολυζήλῳ here seems best taken

8 νεῖκος γὰρ ἀμαιμάκετον
65 9 βληχρᾶς ἀνέπαλτο κασιγνητοῖς ἀπ' ἀρχᾶς
Col. 21 10 Προίτῳ τε καὶ 'Ακρισίῳ·
11 λαούς τε διχοστασίαις
12 ἤρειπον ἀμετροδίκοις μάχαις τε λυγραῖς.
13 λίσσοντο δὲ παῖδας 'Άβαντος
70 14 γᾶν πολύκριθον λαχόντας

ἐπ. β'. 1 Τίρυνθα τὸν ὁπλότερον
2 κτίζειν, πρὶν ἐς ἀργαλέαν πεσεῖν ἀνάγκαν·
3 Ζεύς τ' ἔθελεν Κρονίδας,
4 τιμῶν Δαναοῦ γενεὰν
75 5 καὶ διωξίπποιο Λυγκέος,
6 παῦσαι στυγερῶν ἀχέων.
7 τεῖχος δὲ Κύκλωπες κάμον
8 ἐλθόντες ὑπερφίαλοι κλεινᾷ πόλει

65 βληχᾶς...ἄκρας (*a primo vagitu*) conj. Tyrrell. **66** 'Ακρισίῳ] The MS. omits the first ι. **68** ἤριπον MS.: corr. K.—ἤρεικον conj. Housman. **69** ΠΑΙΔΕC

as 'much-envied,' or 'all-admired'; as in Soph. *Tr.* 185 πολύζηλος is said of the victorious Heracles. But it could also mean 'greatly prosperous': as ζῆλος sometimes='enviable happiness': Soph. *Ai.* 503 οἵας λατρείας ἀνθ' ὅσου ζήλου τρέφει.

64 f. νεῖκος...ἀμαιμάκετον: a *stubborn* feud. As an epithet of fire (Soph. *O. T.* 177) or of the sea (Hes. *Scut.* 207) the word expresses the notion of irresistible force, while as applied in *Od.* 11. 311 to a *mast* it is taken by some to mean 'of vast length' (from root μακ-), rather than, 'proof against any strain': that passage, however, stands alone.

βληχρᾶς...ἀπ' ἀρχᾶς, 'from a slight cause' (which the poet does not name). See however Apollod. 2. 4. 1 (speaking of Danae, daughter of Acrisius): ταύτην μέν, ὡς ἔνιοι λέγουσιν, ἔφθειρε Προῖτος· ὅθεν αὐτοῖς καὶ ἡ στάσις. It is not likely that B. had this story in his mind.—For βληχρός, cp. XII. 227. Alcaeus fr. 16 applies the word to faint breezes (βλήχρων ἀνέμων ἀχείμαντοι πνόαι), and Pindar (fr. 129) to sluggish streams.—Some take the phrase here as='from a feeble beginning,' *i.e.* 'from childhood.' (Apollod. 2. 1. 1 κατὰ γαστρὸς ἔτι ὄντες ἐστασίαζον πρὸς ἀλλήλους.) That seems forced.

ἀνέπαλτο, 'had sprung up,' 2nd aor. midd. of ἀναπάλλω: see *Il.* 23. 694 where

ἀνέπαλτο corresponds with ἀναπάλλεται in 692.—Not from ἀνεφάλλομαι, of which the only part found is ἀνεπάλμενος in Ap. Rhod. 2. 825.

67 f. διχοστασίαις: used in the sing. by Solon fr. 4. 37, and Theognis 78, of civil faction. ἀμετροδίκοις, not observing the μέτρα δίκης: 'feuds that broke the bounds of law.' The peculiarity consists in the fact that compounds with ἀμετρο- usually mean 'unmeasured' in respect to that which is denoted by the subst.; as ἀμετροεπής (*Il.* 2. 212), ἀμετροβαθής (Oppian *Hal.* 1. 85, 'of immense depth'). —ἤρειπον, 'they were ruining' the people: cp. Soph. *Ant.* 596 (of the Labdacidae) ἐρείπει | θεῶν τις, some god is ever bringing them to ruin.

70—72 After λαχόντας, τὸν ὁπλότερον is in partitive apposition: 'that (the two brothers) should share the land between them, and that the younger should make a new seat at Tiryns': cp. Soph. *Ant.* 21 τὼ κασιγνήτω Κρέων | τὸν μὲν προτίσας τὸν δ' ἀτιμάσας ἔχει (n.).— ἀργαλέαν ... ἀνάγκαν, 'grievous straits,' the last extremities of famine and misery.

74 f. Δαναοῦ...Λυγκέος. Abas, the father of Acrisius and Proetus, was son of Lynceus, and maternal grandson of Danaus. Lynceus succeeded Danaus as king of Argos; Herodotus (II. 91) names them together as ancestors of Perseus

For a stubborn strife had sprung up from a slight cause between
the brothers Proetus and Acrisius; and they had been ruining
their people with feuds that broke the bounds of law, and with
dire battles. But the folk besought the sons of Abas that they
would share the fertile land between them,

and that the younger should make a new seat at Tiryns, before epode 2.
they all fell into grievous straits. Then Zeus the son of Cronus,
honouring the race of Danaus and of Lynceus, urger of steeds,
was willing to give them rest from their cruel woes. So the
mighty Cyclopes came and wrought a goodly wall for the
famous city;

A, corr. **A**¹.   **70** λαχόντας MS.: λαχόντα Wilamowitz, Herwerden, Blass.
77 κάμοντ' conj. Platt.

(grandson of Acrisius). Lynceus was
reckoned also among the ancestors of
Heracles and of Iolaus, who are meant
by Λυγκῆος γενεή in Hes. *Scut.* 327.
A statue of him was dedicated by the
Argives at Delphi along with those of
his wife Hypermnestra and her father
Danaus (Paus. x. 10. 5). His grave
was shown at Argos (*id.* II. 21. 2).—
διωξίπποιο: epithet of Ares in VIII. 44:
Pind. *P.* IX. 4 διωξίππου...Κυράνας: cp.
the epic ἱππηλάτα.
77 f. **τεῖχος.** Tiryns was the most
impressive example of that prehistoric
wall-building which Greeks of a later
age ascribed to giants of superhuman
strength. The walls, which had a maxi-
mum thickness of 25 feet, were built of
limestone blocks, mostly polygonal, and
either unhewn or only roughly shaped,
piled on one another and bonded with
small stones and clay: the larger blocks
were from seven to ten feet long. Similar
remains exist at Mycenae (mixed with
later masonry), and at Argos (north of
the theatre).
Κύκλωπες ... **ὑπερφίαλοι**, 'the mighty
Cyclopes.' The adj. clearly has no bad
sense here: cp. *Od.* δ ἔκηλος ὑπερφιάλοισι μεθ' ἡμῖν | δαίνυσαι ;
('in our high company,' as Butcher and
Lang render). The derivation is still
doubtful: that from βία involves an abnormal change: while the old explanation, 'overflowing the φιάλη,' seems too
artificial. Curtius, with Buttmann, refers
it to root φυ ('overgrown,' 'luxuriant').
The *Iliad* (2. 559) knows the walls of
Tiryns; but the legend of the Cyclopes
as *builders* is post-Homeric, though older

than the fifth century. It is found in
Hellanicus (fr. 179) and Pherecydes
(fr. 26 b); in Pindar (fr. 169); Sophocles
(fr. 207); Euripides (*H. F.* 15 Κυκλωπία
πόλις, of Mycenae; *I. A.* 534 τείχη
Κυκλώπια, of Argos; and often else-
where); and in some later writers. For
Tiryns in particular, see Paus. II. 25. 8:
Statius *Theb.* 4. 150 *Cyclopum ductas
sudoribus arces.*
The poet leaves **ἐλθόντες** (78) vague.
But the story which made Proetus go to
Lycia for help said that he summoned
the Cyclopes thence after his return to
Argolis (Strabo p. 372 ἥκειν...μεταπέμπ-
τους ἐκ Λυκίας). Another account brought
them from Thrace (schol. Eur. *Or.* 965).
Here myth was blended with a tradition
of foreign builders.—The home of the
Homeric Cyclopes was popularly identified with Sicily (Thuc. VI. 2 § 1 : Eur.
Cycl. 297).
κάμον. Objection has been taken to
the *syllaba anceps* here: v. 35 ends with
βροτῶν, and in 119 f. πρόγο|νοι is
corrupt. But **κάμοντ'** seems impossible.
The aor. midd. ἐκαμόμην occurs only
twice in pre-Alexandrian Greek: (1) *Il.*
18. 341, τὰς αὐτοὶ καμόμεσθα, (the cap-
tives) whom we *won* by our toil: (2) *Od.*
9. 130 οἵ κέ σφιν καὶ νῆσον ἐϋκτιμένην
ἐκάμοντο, 'who *by toil* would have *gained*
for them a goodly island home.' In both
these cases the middle aor. has its
distinctive sense; it is not a mere substitute for the active aor. [In post-classical
Greek it may be otherwise: Ap. Rhod.
2. 718 ἱρὸν...ὅ ῥ' ἐκάμοντο | αὐτοί: 4. 1321
ὑπέρβια ἔργ' ἐκάμεσθε.]—It may be added
that a corruption of κάμοντ' into κάμον is

9 κάλλιστον, ἵν' ἀντίθεοι
80 10 ναῖον κλυτὸν ἱππόβοτον
11 Ἄργος ἥρωες περικλειτοὶ λιπόντες.
12 ἔνθεν ἀπεσσύμεναι
13 Προίτου κυανοπλόκαμοι
14 φεῦγον ἄδματοι θύγατρες,

στρ. γ'. 85 1 τὸν δ' εἷλεν ἄχος κραδίαν, ξεί-
2 να τέ νιν πλᾶξεν μέριμνα·
3 δοίαξε δὲ φάσγανον ἄμ-
4 φακες ἐν στέρνοισι πᾶξαι.
5 ἀλλά νιν αἰχμοφόροι
90 6 μύθοισί τε μειλιχίοις
7 καὶ βίᾳ χειρῶν κάτεχον.
8 τρισκαίδεκα μὲν τελέους
9 μῆνας κατὰ δάσκιον ἡλύκταζον ὕλαν
10 φεῦγόν τε κατ' Ἀρκαδίαν
95 11 μηλοτρόφον· ἀλλ' ὅτε δὴ
12 Λοῦσον ποτὶ καλλιρόαν πατὴρ ἵκανεν,
13 ἔνθεν χρόα νιψάμενος φοι-
14 νικο[κραδέμνοι]ο Λατοῦς

83 κυανοπλοκαμος **A**, corr. **A¹**.   **86** ΜΕΡΙΜΝΑΙ **A**, corr. **A¹**.   **93** ἡλύκταζον
K. (ἡλύκταξον ms.): ἀλύκταζον Blass (2nd ed.), ἀλύσκαζον (3rd ed.).   **94** κατ'
Ἀρκαδίαν Palmer: κατακαρδίαν ms.

---

improbable from a palaeographical point
of view. It could hardly have been
prompted by πρόγο|νοι in 119 f., since
v. 35 would have shown that a long
syllable might stand at the end of the
verse.
80 ἱππόβοτον, as in XVIII. 15 ἵππιον (n.).
82 ff. The story of the Proetides is
resumed from v. 58.—ἄδματοι: cp. n.
on v. 167.
85 f. τὸν δ' εἷλεν ἄχος κραδίαν: for
the second acc. cp. Il. 1. 362 τί δέ σε
φρένας ἵκετο πένθος; Ar. Lys. 542 οὐδὲ
γόνατ' ἂν κόπος ἕλοι με.—ξείνα, foreign to
his saner moods. Cp. Soph. Ai. 639
οὐκέτι συντρόφοις | ὀργαῖς ἔμπεδος, ἀλλ'
ἐκτὸς ὁμιλεῖ ('he is true no more to the
promptings of his inbred nature, but
dwells with alien thoughts'). Cp.
Aesch. P. V. 689 ξένους...λόγους (where
fear or horror of them is implied):
Timaeus Locrus p. 104 D τιμωρίαι ξέναι.

87 f. δοίαξε...πᾶξαι, 'he was minded'
to do so. For the infin., cp. Ap. Rhod.
4. 575 τὰ δ' ἠεροειδέα λεύσσειν | οὔρεα
δοιάζοντο Κεραύνια ('half thought that
they saw').—The aor. denotes the moment
at which the impulse seized him, as the
Homeric διάνδιχα μερμήριξεν (Il. 1. 189)
shows the thought flashing on Achilles,—
Shall he draw his sword, or still curb his
anger? It is thus more dramatic than the
imperfect would be.—Remark the designed series of harsh sounds here, ξείνα—
πλᾶξεν—δοίαξε: and contrast v. 90.
89 αἰχμοφόροι, his body-guard (δορυ-
φόροι): the sense of the word in Her. I. 8
and VII. 40.
92 f. τρισκαίδεκα: this indeclinable
form is read in Il. 5. 387, Ar. Ran. 50,
Xen. H. v. 1 § 5, etc. In Thuc. III. 69 § 1
and VIII. 88 § 1 Hude reads τρεῖς καὶ
δέκα, and in VIII. 22 § 1 τρισὶ καὶ δέκα: in
those places all or most of the good mss.
have τρισκαίδεκα (except that in VIII. 88 § 1

where the renowned heroes were dwelling, after leaving glorious Argos, nurse of steeds.

Thence it was that the dark-haired maidens, the daughters of Proetus, had rushed in flight.

Grief took hold of their father's heart; a strange thought smote str. 3. him, and he was minded to plunge a two-edged sword in his breast; but his spearmen restrained him with words of comfort, and by force of hand.

For thirteen whole months the maidens roamed wildly through the dense forest, and went in flight through the pastures of Arcadia. But when at length their father came to Lusus with its fair stream, he washed himself with water taken thence,

the Vaticanus B has τρεῖς καὶ δέκα). In Ar. *Plut.* 194 and 846 and *Pax* 990 and Andoc. or. 3. 4 τριακαίδεκα is read: in Isaeus or. 8 § 35 τριῶν καὶ δέκα: in Dem. or. 9 § 25 τρισὶ καὶ δέκα. The result seems to be as follows. The indeclinable form was current from the earliest times, at least in poetry, and was probably prevalent in post-classical Greek generally: but classical Attic writers (of prose at least) preferred the form in which τρεῖς was inflected.—The number *thirteen* probably had some mystic or symbolic meaning here in relation to Artemis as a lunar goddess. In Soph. *Tr.* 164 f. the last period in the ordeals of Heracles is τρίμηνος κἀνιαύσιος (χρόνος).

ἡλύκταζον: I follow the MS. in keeping the ἡ: the poet may have wished to break the series of α sounds.—ἀλύσκαζον Blass[3]: see Appendix.—ὕλαν: see n. on 55.

94 κατ' Ἀρκαδίαν. The wanderings of the Proetides over the hills of north-western Arcadia (Ἀζανία 55 n.) were more especially associated by legend with the Ἀροάνια ὄρη, now *Chelmos*. At the southern foot of this range rises the Aroanios, the chief tributary of the Ladon: and in the upper plain of its valley, in the N.E. corner, is *Sudena*, which probably marks the site of Lusi. In the Aroanian hills, above Nonacris,—which lay on their N.E. side,—was shown a cave to which the frenzied Proetides had fled (Paus. VIII. 18. 7). J. G. Frazer (*ad loc.*) mentions two caves, very near each other, 'on the brow of the mountain, overlooking the profound glen of the Styx.'

96 Λοῦσον: this accent, given in the papyrus, is that which has the older and better authority: Theophr. *Hist. Plant.*

9. 15. 8 Λοῦσα: Callim. *Dian.* 235 Λούσοις (implying Λοῦσσοι or -α): Polyb. IV. 18 Λούσσων. But later writers make the word oxytone: Λουσοί Paus., Λουσός Arcadius 75. 16, Λουσσοί Steph. Byz.

Λοῦσος is here the name of the famous κρήνη near the town of Λοῦσοι, at which the Proetides were said to have been healed (τὴν ἐν Λούσοις κρήνην, Theopompus fr. 287, Müller I. p. 327). Those who tasted it were said thenceforth to dislike wine: hence πηγὴ μισάμπελος, epigr. in Vitruvius 8. 3. 21; and Ovid *Met.* XV. 322, where it is called *Clitorius fons*, as Lusi was in the territory of Cleitor, being some twelve miles N. of it. So Phylarchus (Athen. p. 43 F) spoke of it as κρήνην ἐν Κλείτορι.

A narrow valley opens southward just to the west of Lusi. Three springs issue from the western edge of it; and at the middle one there are traces of ancient foundations. In winter these springs form a large pool or small lake: this is the *Clitorius lacus* of Pliny *H. N.* 31. 13. (Leake, *Morea* II. 110: Curtius, *Pelop.* I. 375.)

97 f. χρόα νιψάμενος. Folk-lore of course connected Λοῦσοι with λούεσθαι. So Paus. VIII. 28. 2 mentions an Arcadian stream ὀνομαζόμενος Λούσιος, ἐπὶ λουτροῖς δὴ τοῖς Διὸς τεχθέντος: and an Arcadian epithet of Demeter was Λουσία, ἐπὶ τῷ λούσασθαι τῷ Λάδωνι (id. VIII. 25. 6).—φοινικοκραδέμνοιο, 'with red kerchief.' The κρήδεμνον (worn by Hera in *Il.* 14. 184) was a kerchief worn over the back of the head, and hanging down to the shoulders, but not veiling the face. (So Hera's 'purple girdle' is mentioned in 49.)

ἀντ. γ'. 1 κίκλ[ησκε θύγατρα] βοῶπιν,
Col.22 100 2 χεῖρας ἀντείνων πρὸς αὐγὰς
        3 ἱππώκεος ἀελίου,
        4 τέκνα δυστάνοιο λύσσας
        5 πάρφρονος ἐξαγαγεῖν·
        6 θύσω δέ τοι εἴκοσι βοῦς
105   7 ἄζυγας φοινικότριχας.
        8 τοῦ δ' ἔκλυ' ἀριστοπάτρα
        9 θηροσκόπος εὐχομένου· πιθοῦσα δ' ᾽Ηραν
        10 παῦσεν καλυκοστεφάνους
        11 κούρας μανιᾶν ἀθέων·
110 12 ταὶ δ' αὐτίκα (F)οι τέμενος βωμόν τε τεῦχον,
        13 χραῖνόν τέ μιν αἵματι μήλων
        14 καὶ χοροὺς ἵσταν γυναικῶν.

ἐπ. γ'. 1 ἔνθεν καὶ ἀρηϊφίλοις
        2 ἄνδρεσσιν < ἐς > ἱπποτρόφον πόλιν < τ' > ᾽Αχαιοῖς

---

99 Before ΒΟΩΙΙΝ there is a faint trace of A.   106 This v. was omitted by **A**:
A³ wrote του δ' εκλυ' αριστοπατρα at the top of col. XXII.   110 ΓΑΙ MS. : ταὶ

---

99 **βοῶπιν** : the Homeric epithet of
Hera is nowhere else given to Artemis.
100 **ἀντείνων** : for the apocope, cp.
fr. 17. 4 ἀντείνασα : III. 7 ἀμπαύσας.
103 **πάρφρονος** : apocope as in παρ-
φάμεν (Pind. *O.* 7. 66), πάρφασις (*N.* VIII.
32), πάρφυκτος (*P.* XII. 30). Cp. XIII.
10 πὰρ χειρός.
ἐξαγαγεῖν depends on κίκλησκε (99). It
is not infin. for imper. in *oratio recta*.
When, *in a prayer*, the infin. stands as
imperative, a (1) a vocative, addressed to
the god, normally precedes ; *e.g.*, *Il.* 7.
179 Ζεῦ πάτερ, ἢ Αἴαντα λαχεῖν ἢ Τυδέος
υἱόν : Aesch. *Th.* 253 θεοὶ πολῖται, μή με
δουλείας τυχεῖν. (2) The subject to the
infin. is *not* usually the god: *e.g.*, here
we should expect an infin. in the sense
of ἀπαλλαγῆναι, to which the subject
would be τέκνα.
105 **φοινικότριχας** : cp. V. 102 n.
106 **ἀριστοπάτρα**. The mother of
Craterus was ᾽Αριστόπατρα (Strabo 15.
p. 702) : cp. the name Κλεινόπατρος
(Paus. VI. 2. 6).
108 **καλυκοστεφάνους**, crowned with
young flowers, in honour of Artemis ;
who herself, in v. 98, has this epithet.
109 **μανιᾶν ἀθέων**. Pindar uses only
the plural of μανία (*O.* IX. 39 ; *N.* 48 ;
fr. 208 μανίαις τ' ἀλαλαῖς τ' ὀρινόμενοι).

It suggests the 'throes' or 'outbreaks'
of madness.—**ἀθέων**, god-forsaken, *i.e.*
due to the wrath of Hera : Soph. *O. T.*
661 f. ἄθεος, ἄφιλος...ὀλοίμαν.—Not, ' inflicted on account of impiety.'
110 **ταὶ** δ' seems right. For the MS.
γᾶ it might be said that Proetus could
then be included among the subjects of
τεῦχον : but γᾶ would be weak ; and it
is natural that the foundation should be
described as a thank-offering on the part
of the maidens.
τέμενος βωμόν τε. The temple of
Artemis ᾽Ημέρα or ᾽Ημερασία at Lusi is
mentioned by Polybius as being N. of
Cleitor and s. of Cynaetha: IV. 18
προῆγον ὡς ἐπὶ Λούσων· καὶ παραγενόμενοι
πρὸς τὸ τῆς ᾽Αρτέμιδος ἱερόν, ὃ κεῖται μὲν
μεταξὺ Κλείτορος καὶ Κυναίθων κ.τ.λ. He
notes its inviolable sanctity (ἄσυλον...
νενόμισται παρὰ τοῖς ῞Ελλησιν). Leake
(*Morea* II. 110) conjectured that the
remains at the spring (mentioned in n. on
96) marked the site of the temple ; and
Kiepert accepted this view, which has
been the prevalent one. Curtius, however (*Pelop.* I. 397), would identify the
shrine with a temple-cella found by Dod-
well (II. 447) nearer Sudena (the probable
site of Lusi), at the upper end of the plain.
111 **μιν** (*i.e.* βωμόν) was here preferred

and invoked the ox-eyed daughter of Latona with purple ant. 3.
kerchief, stretching hands aloft to the rays of the Sun-god in
swift chariot, to deliver his children from the curse of raging
madness : 'and I will offer to thee,' he cried, 'twenty red oxen,
strangers to the yoke.'

His prayer was heard by the Huntress, daughter of a peerless
sire ; she prevailed with Hera, and healed the maidens, crowned
with young flowers, of the madness sent by angry heaven. But
they straightway made for her a precinct and an altar, and shed
the blood of sheep thereon, and set choruses of women around it.

From that place didst thou pass with Achaean warriors to epode 3.
their city, nurse of steeds,—

Blass and others.—TETETETXON **A** : corr. **A**¹? **114** ἐς add. J. : ἐν (=ἐς)
Jurenka: -σσι πρὸς Housman.—πόλιν MS. : πόλιν τ᾿ Blass³ : πόλινδ᾿ Ludwich : ποίαν
Housman, Hense : χώραν Wilamowitz.—I had conjectured πόλισμ᾿, but now prefer
πόλιν τ᾿.

by the poet, who elsewhere always uses
νιν, on account of the preceding χραῖνον.

112 ἴσταν: cp. Pind. *P.* III. 65
τίθεν: *I.* I. 25 ἵεν. The imperfects
(τεῦχον — χραῖνον —ἴσταν) express the
series of acts.

113 ἔνθεν...ἀρηϊφίλοις. The ἀρηΐφιλοι ἄνδρες are the Achaean warriors
who founded Metapontion (Strabo 6.
p. 264). They brought the cult of
Artemis with them from the old home.
She figures on a Metapontine coin
(British Museum, Italy no. 263 : noticed
by Smyth). See also Hyginus *Fab.*
186.—The Metapontines dedicated an
ivory Endymion in their θησαυρός at
Olympia (Paus. VI. 19. 11) ; which shows
that the lunar attributes were among
those of their Artemis (cp. 92 f. n.).—
The Achaean settlement of the country
about the Tarentine Gulf is traceable in
the Arcadian name of the river Λουσίας
near Thurii (Aelian *N. A.* X. 38); also
in the Κρᾶθις a little further s., a namesake of the river near Aegae in Achaia.—
Arist. *Mir. auscult.* 106—110 (p. 840)
notices a cult of the Homeric heroes at
Tarentum and Sybaris, and a temple of
'Αθηνᾶ 'Αχαιΐα in s. E. Italy.

114 ἄνδρεσσιν...'Αχαιοῖς. The metre
is shown by 72. The -ιν of πόλιν could
not be lengthened before 'Αχαιοῖς.
Housman supports his conjecture ποίαν
by Eur. *Andr.* 1229 ἱπποβότων πεδίων :
but that surely is very different. A
corruption of χώραν into πόλιν is im-

probable ; and in 72 we find πεσεῖν.
    (1) The simplest remedy is πόλιν < τ᾿ >,
the τ᾿ answering to τε after ἄλσος in
v. 118:—ἔσπεό τ᾿ ἐς πόλιν .., ἄλσος τέ
τοί (ἐστιν). The sub-clause, σὺν δὲ τύχᾳ
ναίεις .. λαῶν (115—117), then supplements the first principal clause, ἔσπεό τ᾿
ἐς πόλιν. Or ἔσπεό τ᾿ might be co-ordinate
with σὺν δὲ τύχᾳ ναίεις: for the irregular
sequence, τε .. δέ, is not rare, esp. when
the chief stress is on the second clause:
cp. *e.g.* Thuc. I. 25 § 10, Soph. *Ant.*
1096 f. (with my n.), Kühner-Gerth
Gramm. ii. vol. II. p. 244. (2) πόλινδ᾿,
which Blass read in his 2nd ed., would
be satisfactory, if it could stand along
with ἐς: for, except ἐς (ἐν or πρός), the
only supplements possible seem to be
ἄμ᾿ or ποθ᾿, either of which would be
weak. The only parallel is *Od.* 10. 351,
ποταμῶν οἵ τ᾿ εἰς ἅλαδε προρέουσι: so
Aristarchus read ; but Zenodotus had
wished to eliminate εἰς by reading οἵ τε
ἅλαδε (Ludwich, *Aristarch. hom. Text-
kritik,* I. 583). The redundant phrase
might be compared with ἀπὸ Τροίηθεν
(*Od.* 9. 38). (3) Another resource is
πόλισμ᾿, freely used in poetry as an
equivalent for πόλις. Aesch. *Th.* 120
πόλισμα Κάδμου : Euripides applies it
to Athens (*Med.* 771, *I. T.* 1014,
H. F. 1323); Troy (*I. A.* 777);
Mycenae (*ib.* 1500); Thebes (*Bacch.*
919). Those places where the word
precedes a vowel are suggestive in connexion with the present passage, as
illustrating the metrical convenience of

115 3 ἕσπεο, σὺν δὲ τύχᾳ
4 ναίεις Μεταπόντιον, ὦ
5 χρυσέα δέσποινα λαῶν·
6 ἄλσος τέ τοι ἱμερόεν
7 Κάσαν παρ᾽ εὔυδρον πρὸ να-
120 8 οῖ᾽ ἐσσαμένων, Πριάμοι᾽ ἐπεὶ χρόνῳ
9 βουλαῖσι θεῶν μακάρων
10 πέρσαν πόλιν εὐκτιμέναν
11 χαλκοθωράκων μετ᾽ Ἀτρειδᾶν. δικαίας
12 ὅστις ἔχει φρένας, εὐ-
125 13 ρήσει σὺν ἅπαντι χρόνῳ
14 μυρίας ἀλκὰς Ἀχαιῶν.

XI. [XII.]

ΤΕΙCΙΑΙ ΑΙΓΙΝΗΤΗΙ

ΠΑΛΑΙCΤΗΙ ΝΕΜΕΑ

στρ.   Ὡσεὶ κυβερνήτας σοφός, ὑμνοάνασ-
σ᾽ εὔθυνε Κλειοῖ
νῦν φρένας ἁμετέρας,

118 τε MS.: γε Herwerden.   **119 f.** ΠΡΟΓΟ|ΝΟΙ ΕCCΑΜΕΝΟΙ MS.:
προγό|νων ἐσσαμένων Wilamowitz, Blass: πρόγο|νοι ἔσσαν ἐμοὶ Palmer, K.: πρὸ
γου|νοῖ᾽ Platt: ἔσσαν ἐμέν Housman.—ἐπεὶ] EIII **A**: corr. **A³**.

---

this substitute for πόλις:—*Bacch.* 919
πόλισμ᾽ ἑπτάστομον : *Heracl.* 193 f. Ἀχαϊ-
κὸν | πόλισμ᾽, ὅθεν κ.τ.λ.: *ib.* 957 πόλισμ᾽
ἐλεύθερον. On the whole, I prefer πόλιν τ᾽.
ἱπποτρόφον hints the traditions of
Achaean chivalry, as πορτιτρόφον (30)
suggests the prosperous Metapontine
stock-breeders.
115 ff. σὺν...τύχᾳ : cp. VIII. 51 n.—
χρυσέα: VIII. 72 n.—δέσποινα λαῶν.
Metapontion throve by agriculture (Strabo p. 264), cattle, and horse-breeding.
Artemis was concerned with all these
(cp. V. 98 and 104 nn.). As to horses,
at Pheneos in Arcadia she was worshipped
as Εὐρίππα (Paus. VIII. 14. 4) : in Pind.
O. III. 26 she is ἱπποσόα. Artemis was
also in a general sense σώτειρα (as at
Pellene in Achaia, Paus. II. 31. 1), σωσί-
πολις, etc. In Arcadia she was closely
associated with the cult of the Δέσποινα
(Persephone) and Demeter (Paus. VIII.
37. 1 etc.). Cp. Soph. *El.* 626 τὴν
δέσποιναν Ἄρτεμιν. [Preller II. 243 held

that Δέσποινα was an Arcadian title of
Artemis herself.]
119 f. Κάσαν. The Κάσας is not
mentioned elsewhere (unless it is to be
recognized in Suidas, Κῆσος· ὄνομα
ποταμοῦ). But Pliny (*H. N.* III. 15. 3)
mentions the river *Casuentus* near Metapontion, and this is doubtless the Κάσας,
the modern *Basiento*. Its course is
nearly parallel with that of the Bradanus
(*Bradano*): both flow into the Tarentine
Gulf near the site of Metapontion.—
εὔυδρον. 'Though here the coast is
everywhere perfectly flat, yet the land
rises gently from the sea, and, being
well-watered, is pre-eminently adapted
for pasture and wheat.' (Curtius, *Hist.
Gr.* I. p. 445 Eng. ed.)
πρὸ ναοῖ᾽ ἐσσαμένων is the remedy
which I would suggest for the corrupt
πρόγονοι ἐσσάμενοι of the papyrus.
(The metre is shown by vv. 35 and 77.)
I suppose that in ΠΡΟΝΑΟΙ the letters
ΝΑ had been mutilated or partly ob-

and with happy fortune dost thou dwell in Metapontion, O
glorious mistress of her people—and a lovely grove is thine,
which they dedicated to thee by the fair stream of the Casas,
[in front of thy temple,] when at last, in the counsels of the
blessed gods, they sacked Priam's stately town with the mail-clad
Atreidae. Whoso has a just spirit will find, through all the course
of time, countless deeds of valour wrought by the Achaeans.

XI. [XII.]

For Teisias of Aegina, victor in the wrestling-match at Nemea.

Like a skilful pilot, guide thou my thoughts, Cleio, queen str.
of song,

XI. Title added by A³ in left margin, opposite to vv. 1–4.   TEICIAI Blass :
TICIAI ms.

---

literated, so as to leave ΠΡΟΝ ΟΙ or
ΠΡΟ ΟΙ. This was taken to be some
nominative plural, and was conjecturally
restored as ΠΡΟΓΟΝΟΙ, causing ἐσσαμένων to become ἐσσάμενοι. On my
view, ἐσσαμένων is a genit. absolute,
referring to the Achaean warriors who
are mentioned in 113 f. (ἀρηϊφίλοις
ἄνδρεσσιν), and who are the subject of
πέρσαν in 122. ἄλσος is nomin., ἐστί
being understood;—'And a lovely grove is
thine, (the Achaeans) having founded it by
the fair stream of the Casas in front of thy
temple.' For πρὸ ναοῖ', compare Alcaeus
fr. 9 (from a hymn to the Athena of
Coroneia): ἅ ποι Κορωνείας ἐπὶ πισέων (so
Bergk) | ναύω πάροιθεν ἀμφιβαίνεις |
Κωραλίω ποτάμω παρ' ὄχθαις : where, as
here, there is a sacred temenos (πίσεα)
on the banks of a river, in front of the
temple. Speaking of the same Athena,
Callimachus says (*Hymn* v. 63 f.), ἵνα
οἱ τεθνωμένον ἄλσος | καὶ βωμοὶ ποταμῷ
κεῖντ' ἐπὶ Κουραλίῳ. Cp. also III. 19 f.
πάροιθε ναοῦ, τόθι μέγιστον ἄλσος | Φοίβου
παρὰ Κασταλίας ῥεέθροις κ.τ.λ.—ἐσσαμέ-
νον (ἵζω): the midd. is normal in this
sense: Pind. P. IV. 204 Ποσειδάωνος ἔσ-
σαντ' εἰναλίου τέμενος: Her. I. 66 ἱρὸν
εἰσάμενοι: Thuc. III. 58 § 5 (θυσίας) τῶν
ἐσσαμένων καὶ κτισάντων: Eur. *Hipp.* 31
ναὸν . . ἐγκαθείσατο.
    Whatever the original reading may
have been, πρόγονοι is impossible : προγόνων also seems impossible. A short
syllable in the middle of a word divided
between two verses could not stand as
a *syllaba anceps* (representing a long
syllable) at the end of the first verse.—

See Appendix.
120 f. Πριάμοι' ἐπεὶ πέρσαν πόλιν :
Strabo says of Metaponton (p. 264),
Πυλίων δὲ λέγεται κτίσμα τῶν ἐξ Ἰλίου
πλευσάντων μετὰ Νέστορος. The safe
return of Nestor to Pylus is mentioned in
the *Odyssey* (3. 182), and was told in the
Cyclic *Nosti*. Among the heroes from
Pylos (Πύλιοι) who afterwards founded
Metapontion, the legend doubtless included some of his sons; possibly even
Nestor himself. Sacrifices (ἐναγισμός)
to the spirits of the Neleidae (so called
from Nestor's father Νηλεύς) were offered
at Metapontion down to Strabo's time.—
χρόνῳ, after ten years' war : Aesch. *Ag.*
126 χρόνῳ μὲν αἱρεῖ Πριάμου πόλιν ἄδε
κέλευθος.
123 δικαίας : see n. on V. 196.
125 σὺν ἄπαντι χρόνῳ : X. 23 n.
Some of the Achaean legends (such as
those of the Aeacidae) embraced many
successive generations of a family.
126 ἀλκάς, *virtutes* : Pind. *N.* VII.
12 ταὶ μεγάλαι γὰρ ἀλκαὶ | σκότον πολὺν
ὕμνων ἔχοντι δεόμεναι.—Ἀχαιῶν. The
Ionian communities of the Aegean islands
and coasts were very proud of their
legendary Achaean founders, especially
of the Neleidae (or Nestoridae). Timotheus of Miletus, in the newly-found fragment of his nome, the *Persae*, vv. 246 ff.,
speaks of the Ionian folk of the dodecapolis as λαοῦ πρωτεῖς ἐξ Ἀχαιῶν, 'a
foremost scion of the Achaeans'; Miletus
having been founded, according to tradition, by Neleus son of Codrus.

XI. 1—3 κυβερνήτας with η, as in

336 ΒΑΚΧΥΛΙΔΟΥ [XI, XII

εἰ δή ποτε καὶ πάρος· ἐς γὰρ ὀλβίαν
5 ξείνοισί με πότνια Νίκα
νᾶσον Αἰγίνας ἀπάρχει
ἐλθόντα κοσμῆσαι θεόδματον πόλιν·

ἀντ. ? τάν τ᾽ ἐν Νεμέᾳ γυιαλκέα μουνοπάλαν

[The rest is lost.]

XII. [XIII.]

<ΠΥΘΕΑΙ ΑΙΓΙΝΗΤΗΙ
ΠΑΓΚΡΑΤΙΑΣΤΗΙ ΝΕΜΕΑ>

στρ. α΄. [Eight verses lost.]

Col. 23 _ ∪ ∪ _ ∪ ∪ _ _
  _ ∪ ∪ _ ∪ ∪ λειω
10 _ ∪ ∪ _ ∪ ∪ _ _ ΄ερ[
  _ ∪ ∪ _ ∪ ∪ _
  _ _ ∪ _ _ _ ∪ _ δαν·

στρ. β΄. [ἀντ. α΄, ἐπ. α΄, and the first ten verses of στρ. β΄, are lost.]

Col. 24 11 ὕβριος ὑψινόου
45 12 παύσει, δίκας θνατοῖσι κραίνων·

6 ἀπάρχει] ἀπαίρει conj. Crusius, J. (ἀπαιτεῖ also J.) : ἐπάρκει (= ἐπήρκει, plpf. of ἐπαίρω)
Tyrrell. 8 τάν] τόν conj. Desrousseaux, W. Christ.—After this verse, the last in
col. XXII, the papyrus breaks off. There is no clue to the extent of the lacuna, nor,
therefore, to the original length of the ode.

XII. In column XXIII, the second verse ended with λειω, and the
fifth with δαν : the third, with ρ . . or β . . (Blass traces ΄ερ). The rest of col.

v. 47 (n.)—**σοφός**, a frequent epithet of
this subst. : Archilochus fr. 45 κυβερνήτην
σοφόν: Aesch. *Suppl.* 770 κυβερνήτῃ
σοφῷ: Phaedrus 4. 17. 8 *gubernator
sophus.* Cp. Pind. *P.* IV. 274 εἰ μὴ θεὸς
ἀγεμόνεσσι κυβερνάτηρ γένηται.

ὑμνοάνασσα, like μεγιστοάνασσα(XVIII.
21), implying ϝάνασσα (see VIII. 45).
Cp. VI. 10 f. ἀναξιμόλπου | Οὐρανίας.—
Κλειοῖ: see n. on v. 176 ff. In III. 3 the
name scans as ∪ _: here it is _ _, as in
XII. 228.

5 ξείνοισι, dat. of interest after κοσμῆσαι, 'for hospitable friends.' The
poet doubtless had formed ties of ξενία
in Aegina. Cp. n. on ξένος in III. 11.

6 ἀπάρχει, if sound, must mean 'leads
off,' 'shows the way'; this use being
borrowed from that in which the verb is
applied to one who leads a dance or

song: *Anthol.* 9. 189. 3 ἔνθα καλὸν
στήσεσθε θεῇ χορόν· ὕμμι δ᾽ ἀπάρξει |
Σαπφώ, χρυσείην χερσὶν ἔχουσα λύρην.
As ὕμμι there shows, we should expect
here the dative μοι...ἐλθόντι, which, however, is excluded by metre. It seems
scarcely possible that ἀπάρχει should
govern the accus. (as = ἀπάγει). Blass
compares ἀφηγεῖσθαι: which, when it
governs a case, takes the genitive. The
construction with the accus. can only be,
'leads the way, (so that) I should go to
Aegina.' This is awkward : but the
only alternative is to suppose that ἀπάρχει
governs the acc. κατὰ σύνεσιν, because
felt as equivalent to ἀπάγει or the like.
ἀπαίρει, 'causes to set forth,' 'despatches,'
is possible : cp. Eur. *Helen.* 1519 τίς δέ
νιν ναυκληρία | ἐκ τῆσδ᾽ ἀπῆρε χθονός; If
the first ι of ἀπαίρει had been lost, leaving

now if ever before; for divine Victory leads the way, bidding
me go to Aegina's happy isle, in honour of hospitable friends,
and do grace to that god-built city,

and to the sinewy strife of the wrestler at Nemea....　　　　ant.?

XII. [XIII.]

For Pytheas of Aegina, victor in the pancration at Nemea.

*　　　*　　　*　　　*　　　*　　　*

...'He shall stay them from their arrogant violence, con- str. 2.
firming the reign of law for mortals.

XXIII is lost. If, as Blass thinks, these verses belonged to the first strophe of ode XII,
then at least one whole column (containing the end of XI and the first 7 verses of XII)
has been lost between columns XXII and XXIII. (See Introd. to Ode, § 3.)—The title
is supplied by Kenyon from the internal evidence: ΠΤΘΕΑΙ ΑΙΓΙΝΗΤΗΙ παιδὶ
παγκρατιαστῇ Νέμεα. Blass omits παιδὶ, inferring from Pind. *N.* v. 6 f. that Pytheas
competed, not among the παῖδες, but among the ἀγένειοι: see Introd.

ἀπάρει, this might have been altered by
conjecture to ἀπάρχει. Another possibility is ἀπαιτεῖ, 'bids,' 'requires me.'

7 θεόδματον : epithets in θεο- are
especially given by B. to cities: VIII. 98 :
X. 12, 58 : XII. 163.

8 μουνοπάλαν : the only certain instance of the feminine form; it is, however, possible in an epigramma found at
Delphi (*Bull. de Corr. Hellén.* 1898, 593.
3), νικῶν μουνοπάλη(ν), which would be
in harmony, as Blass observes, with
companion inscriptions giving παγκράτιον
νικᾷς and νικῶ δὲ στάδιον. The masc.
occurs in Paus. 6. 4. 4 (an inscription at
Olympia), μουνοπάλης νικῶ δὶς Ὀλύμπια
Πύθιά τ' ἄνδρας. The epithet γυιαλκέα
tells neither way; and it seems best to
keep the MS. τάν.—μουνοπάλη is the
simple wrestling-match as distinguished
from the παγκράτιον, in which wrestling
was combined with boxing. For the
form cp. Paus. 8. 4 § 9 (inscr. recording
Hieron's victories) τεθρίππῳ μὲν ἅπαξ,
μουνοκέλητι δὲ δίς.

XII. 44—57 After a large lacuna
(see Introd.), in which the first part of
the ode has been lost, column XXIV of
the papyrus begins in the midst of a
prophecy concerning Heracles...'*He shall
put down violence, and establish the reign
of law. Behold how he grapples with the
Nemean lion! In this place, some day,
Greeks shall strive for the prize of the
pancration.*'

J. B.

Who is the speaker, before whose eyes
the struggle is going on? Many vases,
both red- and black-figured, show Heracles subduing the Nemean lion, in the
presence of the hero's half-sister and
guardian-goddess *Athena*, who stands on
the right; over against her on the left,
behind Heracles, is another female form,
who (in many instances at least) presumably represents the nymph *Nemea.*
(See Roscher, *Lex. Myth. s.v.* : Baumeister, *Denkmäler* p. 655, fig. 722.) It
is Athena, I conjecture, who speaks here,
addressing Nemea. At this, the first
labour of Heracles (VIII. 8 f.), she who is
to protect him through all (*Il.* 8. 363 ff.)
predicts his great destiny,—to be the
purger of Hellas from pests and wickedness. (Prophecy by Athena was not
strange to Greek poetry: cp. Aesch.
Eum. 685 ff.)—Blass and Wilamowitz
think that Nemea speaks: but the tone
seems too lofty and authoritative for the
nymph. Further, it can scarcely be
doubted that the poet would have followed the tradition attested by art, in
conceiving Athena as present; but, in
her presence, Nemea could not take such
a part.

44 f. ὕβριος...παύσει : so Teiresias
predicted of Heracles (Pind. *N.* I. 64 f.),
καί τινα σὺν πλαγίῳ | ἀνδρῶν κόρῳ στεί-
χοντα τὸν ἐχθρότατον | φᾶσέ νιν δώσειν
μόρῳ ('he should give to death those
hatefullest of men who walk in guile and
insolence').

23

ἀντ. β΄. 1 οἵαν τινὰ δύσλοφον ὠ-
2 μηστᾷ λέοντι
(15) 3 Περσείδας ἐφίησι<ν>
4 χεῖρα παντοίαισι τέχναις·
50 5 οὐ γὰρ] δαμασίμβροτος αἴθων
6 χαλ]κὸς ἀπλάτου θέλει
7 χωρε]ῖν διὰ σώματος, ἐ-
(20) 8 γνάμ]φθη δ᾽ ὀπίσσω
9 φάσγα]νον· ἦ ποτέ φαμι
55 10 τᾷδε] περὶ στεφάνοισι
11 παγκ]ρατίου πόνον Ἑλ-
12 λάνεσσι]ν ἱδρώεντ᾽ ἔσεσθαι.

ἐπ. β΄.(25) 1 ὃς νῦν παρ]ὰ βωμὸν ἀριστάρχου Διὸς
2 Νίκας ἐ]ρ[ικ]υδέος ἀν-
60 3 δεθε]ῖσιν ἄνθεα,
4 χρυσέ]αν δόξαν πολύφαντον ἐν αἰ-
5 ῶνι] τρέφει παύροις βροτῶν
(30) 6 αἰ]εί, καὶ ὅταν θανάτοιο
7 κυάνεον νέφος καλύψῃ, λείπεται
65 8 ἀθάνατον κλέος εὖ ἐρ-
9 χθέντος ἀσφαλεῖ σὺν αἴσᾳ.

---

52 f. χωρεῖν Blass, Herwerden.—ἐγνάμφθη Tyrrell, Blass.—ΟΠΙΣΣΩ **A** : the second C deleted (by **A³**?). **55** τᾷδε] So Blass. **56 f.** Ἑλλάνεσσιν Blass,

---

δίκας... κραίνων, 'confirming judgments'; *i.e.* securing that justice shall not be overridden by violence. Cp. Solon fr. 4. 37 (of Eunomia), εὐθύνει δὲ δίκας σκολιὰς ὑπερήφανά τ᾽ ἔργα | πραΰνει: Pind. *P.* IV. 153 εὔθυνε λαοῖς δίκας.

46—49 οἵαν. This eager exclamation is illustrated by the vases (*e.g.* fig. 722 in Baumeister, p. 655), on which Athena and the other female figure are holding up their hands in wonder and delight.—δύσλοφον, 'pressing heavily' (lit. 'heavy on the neck'); Aesch. *P.V.* 931 δυσλοφωτέρους πόνους. The vase just noticed shows Heracles grappling with the lion, who is erect on his hind feet; the hero has his left arm round the monster's neck; his right hand is on the throat.—Περσείδας. Perseus was grandfather of Amphitryon, Alcmena's husband, and great-grandfather of Heracles.—τέχναις, 'devices' in grappling with the monster, since the sword is useless.

51 ἀπλάτου: Soph. *Tr.* 1092 Νεμέας ἔνοικον, βουκόλων ἀλάστορα, | λέοντ᾽, ἄπλατον θρέμμα κάπροσήγορον ('that no man might approach or confront'). The lion was invulnerable : n. on VIII. 6 ff.

52—54 χωρεῖν: Blass cp. Xen. *An.* IV. 2. 28 τὸ τόξευμα ἐχώρει διὰ τῶν θωράκων. (πείρειν is also possible, but is usually said of the man, not of his weapon; as *Il.* 16. 405 διὰ δ᾽ αὐτοῦ πεῖρεν ὀδόντων | ἐγχεϊ.)—ἐγνάμφθη: *Il.* 3. 348 ἀνεγνάμφθη δέ οἱ αἰχμή. This is said by the spectator of the struggle, which is still in progress; it is a parenthesis : 'see, his *hands* are on the monster (for his *sword* is useless,—it *was bent back*'). Heracles had thrown his sword aside before closing with the lion. The aorist is another indication that the poet had in his mind some picture of the type found on the vases. Heracles is there represented as using his hands alone. In one example (fig. 733 in Baumeister, p. 666) his sword

'See how that scion of Perseus, skilled in every resource, lays ant. 2.
a crushing hand on the savage lion ; for the gleaming bronze,
slayer of men, refuses to pierce the dread monster's body ; the
sword was bent back.
'Verily I prophesy that here the Greeks shall strive for
wreaths in the strenuous toil of the pancration.'

And now, for those who have been crowned with the flowers epode 2.
of glorious Victory at the altar of Zeus the peerless king, that
toil nourishes a golden renown, conspicuous in their life-time
evermore ; few are they among men. And when the dark cloud
of death enfolds them, there remains the undying fame of a deed
bravely done, with a fortune that can fail no more.

Ἔλλασίν τιν' K.   **58—63** For the supplements here see Appendix.   **62** παύροις
Platt and others : παύροισι MS.   **63** ΟΤΑΘΑΝΑΤΟΙΟ **A**, corr. **A³**.   **64** καλυψη
A, corr. **A¹**.

is hanging on the branch of a tree in the
background ; his bow and club have also
been discarded.
  55—57 τᾷδε is right : ' Here '—in the
vale of Nemea. The strenuous *wrestling*
of Heracles with the lion foreshadows
the conflicts of wrestlers (and boxers) in
the pancration.
  The traces Ἐλ......ν in the MS. seem
to leave only three choices : (1) Ἑλλάνεσσιν (Blass), which is the simplest.
Cp. Pind. *I.* III. 47 Πανελλάνεσσι. (2)
Ἔλλασίν τιν' (Kenyon). The MS. has
no apostrophe after the ν before ἱδρώεντ',
and that must be considered : it is not,
however, decisive. τιν' might seem
slightly weak ; but, in a prophecy, might
be intended to add a touch of mystery.
(3) πόνον Ἔλλασιν τὸν ἱδρώεντ' ('*that
arduous toil*') seems improbable here.
On the whole, I incline to (1).
  58—63 In the lacuna before παρὰ
(v. 58) I insert ὃς νῦν. ὃς refers to
παγκρατίου πόνον in 56, and is subject
to τρέφει in 62. The whole passage is
then clear. From Athena's prophecy
concerning the pancration the poet
passes to the victory of Pytheas, effecting
the transition by means of a relative
word, as Pindar often does (*e.g.* in *O.* I.
25 the relat. τοῦ links proem to myth ; in
95 ἵνα links myth to conclusion). '*And
now that toil* (of the pancration), *for men
who have been crowned with the flowers of
victory at the altar of* (*Nemean*) *Zeus,
nourishes a golden glory,*' etc.—ἀνδεθεῖσιν
(Housman) seems certain : the first syllable of v. 60 must be short, as it is

in all the five corresponding verses, 93,
126, 159, 192, 225. (Blass's ἀνθρώποισιν
is therefore very improbable.) ἄνθεα,
acc. denoting the ἀνάδημα : cp. *C. I. G.*
στέμμ' ἀναδησάμενος : Athen. p. 676 D
στέψονται...ρόδα. The dat. ἄνθεσι (IX.
16) would be more usual.—ἐν αἰῶνι, ' in
their life-time'; as opposed to καὶ ὅταν
θανάτοιο κ.τ.λ. This reading is confirmed
by the fact that the syllable answering to
the second of αἰῶνι is long in all the
corresponding verses where it remains,
viz. 95, 129, 194, 227; and presumably
was so also in 162.—παύροις βροτῶν,
a sort of afterthought, serves to explain
πολύφαντον : few there be that win such
glory.—For other views of the passage,
see Appendix.
  64 κυάνεον : the only example in B.
of κυαν- with ῠ.
  65 f. ἐρχθέντος, from ἔρδω : so in 207
ἐργμένον (perf. pass. part.). Both forms
are unique. Of the passive the only other
part extant is the pres. part. ἐρδόμενος
(Pind. *O.* VIII. 78, Her. IV. 60). In
Il. 21. 282 ἐρχθέντ' ἐν μεγάλῳ ποταμῷ
('pent'), the word is from ἔργω. Hippocr.
5. 384 has ῥεχθείη : *Il.* 9. 250 ῥεχθέντος,
and 20. 198 ῥεχθέν : from ῥέζω. It may
be noticed, as Headlam remarks, that
some writers of Ionic prefer -ἐρκτης to
-ρέκτης : as Herodas V. 42 παντοερκτέω
(but Anacreontea X. 11 παντορέκτᾳ);
Antipater of Thessalonica in *Anth.* IX.
92. 4 εὐέρκταις.
  ἀσφαλεῖ σὺν αἴσᾳ. Thenceforth their
fame is beyond the reach of φθόνος
εὐρυβίας.

στρ. γ′. 1 τῶν καὶ σὺ τυχὼν Νεμέᾳ,
(35) 2 Λάμπωνος υἱέ,
    3 πανθαλέων στεφάνοισιν
70 4 ἀνθέων] χαίταν ἐρεφθείς,
    5 αὔξων] πόλιν ὑψιάγυιαν
    6 ἦλυθες τερψιμβρότων
(40) 7 αὐλῶν ὑπό θ᾽ ἁ[δυπν]όων
    8 κώμων πατρῴαν
75 9 νᾶσον, ὑπέρβιον ἰσχὺν
    10 παμμαχιᾶν ἀναφαίνων.
    11 ὦ ποταμοῦ θύγατερ
(45) 12 δινᾶντος Αἴγιν᾽ ἠπιόφρον,

Col. 25 ἀντ. γ′. 1 ἦ τοι μεγάλαν [Κρονίδας
80 2 ἔδωκε τιμὰν
    3 ἐν πάντεσσιν [ἀέθλοις,
    4 πυρσὸν ὡς Ἑλλ[ασι παντᾷ
(50) 5 φαίνων· τό γε σὸ[ν κλέος αἰ]νεῖ
    6 καί τις ὑψαυχὴς κό[ρα,
85 7 [λευκοῖς ἀνὰ γᾶν ἱερὰν]
    8 πόδεσσι ταρφέω[ς,

71—74 For the conjectural supplements see Appendix. **73** ἁ[δυπν]όων. The letter after Α was, Blass thinks, Β, Ρ, C, or Ε. But Δ is also possible. Kenyon remarks that the top of Δ in this ms. often resembles that of the letter following Α here; see *e.g.* the Δ of δύσλοφον in v. 46. ἁδυπνόων will then serve. Blass formerly conj. ἁβροπνόων : now, ἀερσινόων. See Appendix. **76** παμμαχιάν ms. : παμμαχιᾶν Κ. **78** δινᾶντος] Τ made from Ε by Α¹. **79** Κρονίδας Blass : ὅδε παῖς Κ. **81** ἀέθλοις Κ. : ἀγῶσιν Blass, Jurenka. **82** πάντᾳ J.:

---

69 πανθαλέων, – – –, being Doric for πανθηλ- (*Anth.* 9. 182. 6 ὕλη πανθηλής) : see n. on εὐθαλές in VIII. 5.

71—76 In the restoration tentatively given above, these points may be noted. (1) The vestiges in 73 f. suggest (*e.g.*) αὐλῶν ὑπό θ᾽ ἁδυπνόων | κώμων. But, if such words stood there, a verb of *coming* or *returning* stood in 71 or in 72. (2) In v. 75 NACO(N) is more probable than NACO(T), as the space between O and the Τ of ὑπέρβιον requires a very broad letter, and in this ms. N can be broader than Τ. In any case, πατρῴαν νάσον...ἰσχὺν παμμαχιᾶν would be awkward. νᾶσον probably depended on a verb such as ἦλυθες (cp. I. 4 ἦλυθεν) in 72. If it depended on ἀναφαίνων, ἰσχὺν must be acc. of respect; and the sense

would be, 'illustrating thy native isle as of great might in the feats of the pancration': but this is improbable; ὑπέρβιον should be the epithet of ἰσχύν. (3) The acc. πόλιν ὑψιάγυιαν in 71 can hardly have been in apposition with νᾶσον : the interval is too long. It may have been governed by a participle such as αὔξων : cp. Pind. *O.* v. 4 τὰν σὰν πόλιν αὔξων, *P.* VIII. 38 αὔξων .. πάτραν (said of victors).—παμμαχιᾶν. παμμαχία occurs elsewhere only in Eusebius *De laud. Constantini* 7 *init.*: but Photius and Suidas give παμμάχιον· παγκράτιον. For πάμμαχος as = παγκρατιαστής, cp. Plat. *Euthyd.* p. 271 C : Theocr. XXIV. 111 ff., where the πάμμαχοι are those who have learned all the σοφίσματα of wrestling and of boxing.

Such honours thou also, son of Lampon, hast won at Nemea ; str. 3.
wreaths of luxuriant flowers have crowned thy head ; for the
glory of the stately city, amidst the gladdening sound of flutes
and the choice strains of festal companies, thou hast returned
to thy native isle, illustrating her pre-eminent strength in the
feats of the pancration.

O daughter of the eddying river, Aegina of gentle soul,

verily the son of Cronus has given thee honour in all contests, ant. 3.
making it to shine everywhere as a beacon-light for the Greeks.

Yea, and thy glory is a theme for the high vaunt of some maiden,
as oft with her white feet she moves o'er thy sacred soil,

ἀλκάν K., Jurenka: τῆλε Blass. **84 f.** καί τις] The I of ΚΑΙ added by **A²**?—
ΤΨΑΤΧΑC **A** : η written above the second A by **A³**.—At the extreme right of v. 84
are the letters ρᾶν. (The ρ seems certain : though Jurenka finds ιᾶν.) They are
separated from κο by the space of some seven letters only. But a whole verse (85)
has been lost. That verse probably ended in -ραν, and the mutilated remains of it
were pieced on to v. 84. **86** ταρφέω[ν] K. : but Blass thinks that the final letter
was s, and writes ταρφέως (with Headlam and Platt).

ἀναφαίνων: *Il.* 20. 411 ποδῶν ἀρετὴν
ἀναφαίνων.—Blass (3rd ed.) reads παμμαχίαν ἄνα φαίνων: but this does not seem
good.
77 f. ποταμοῦ, the Asopus (VIII.
47 ff.). Zeus, transformed into an eagle
(or according to Ovid *Met.* VI. 113 into a
fiery shape, *igneus*), carried off Aegina
from her father to the island formerly
called Οἰνώνη, which thenceforth bore
her name.—ἠπιόφρον : Aegina's isle
was a place ἔνθα Σώτειρα Διὸς Ξενίου |
πάρεδρος ἀσκεῖται Θέμις | ἔξοχ᾽ ἀνθρώπων
(Pind. *O.* VIII. 27): *I.* IV. 22 εὔνομον
πόλιν : cp. also Pind. fr. 1. It was
a centre of commerce at which visitors
from all parts of Hellas found hospitality
and upright dealing.
The passage on the glories of Aegina
which begins here fills the greater part
of the ode. Only at v. 190 does the
poet return to the victory of Pytheas.
81 ἀέθλοις is more euphonious than
ἀγῶσιν here. Blass prefers the latter
because it will include sea-fights as well
as athletic games : but the poetical sense
of ἀέθλοις covers both.
82 πυρσὸν ὡς κ.τ.λ. The fourth verse
of the strophe ends with a long syllable
in 49, 70, 136, 148, 181 (where θάλασσαν
is certain), 202 ; *i.e.* in every place where
it can be ascertained, except v. 115
(ἄστυ). There is therefore a strong
presumption against τῆλε, which Blass

supplies. The word may have been
παντᾷ : cp. v. 31 μυρία παντᾷ κέλευθος.
As τιμὰν has just preceded, this seems
slightly preferable to ἀλκάν : but the
latter is quite possible.
84—86 καί τις ὑψαυχὴς κόρα :
some daughter of the island, who exults
in its legendary glories ; one, perhaps,
whose family claims descent from the
Aeacidae. So Pindar imagines Hieron's
praises as sung in Magna Graecia by
Locrian maidens: *P.* II. 18 σὲ δ᾽, ὦ
Δεινομένεις παῖ, Ζεφυρία πρὸ δόμων | Λο-
κρὶς παρθένος ἀπύει.—ὑψαυχὴς occurs only
here : but Pindar and Aeschylus use
μεγαυχής.
ταρφέως, 'frequently'; the Homeric
form of the adverb is ταρφέα (*Il.* 12. 47,
etc.). **πόδεσσι** may have had an epithet
in the lost verse (85), such as λευκοῖς
(cp. Eur. *Bacch.* 863, *Ion* 221); it could
then go with θρώσκουσ᾽ (90). The rest
of v. 85 may have been something like
ἀνὰ γᾶν ἱεράν, or πλάκ᾽ ἀνὰ χλοεράν.
[I formerly thought of πολλὰν προφέρουσα
κορᾶν | πόδεσσι ταρφέων, *pedibus frequen-
tium* (ταρφὺς is fem. in Aesch. *Th.* 535) :
cp. Soph. *O.C.* 718 f. τῶν ἑκατομπόδων |
Νηρήδων. But it seems more likely that
the *companions* were first mentioned in
89 f.]—Blass would point after **κόρα** ·
(taking her to be *Athena*;) and then
read, στείχεις δ᾽ ἀνὰ γᾶν ἱεράν, referring
to the nymph *Aegina*, with ἀγακλειταῖσι

9 ἠΰτε νεβρὸς ἀπενθής,
(55) 10 ἀνθεμόεντας ἐπ᾽ [ὄχθους
11 κοῦφα σὺν ἀγχιδό[μοις
90 12 θρῴσκουσ᾽ ἀγακλειτα[ῖς ἑταίραις·

ἐπ. γ'.   1 ταὶ δὲ στεφανωσάμε[ναι πλόκοις ν]έων
2 ἀνθέων δόνακός τ᾽ ἐ[πιχω-
(60) 3 ρίαν ἄθυρσιν
4 παρθένοι μέλπουσι τ[εὸν κράτος], ὦ
95 5 δέσποινα παγξε[ίνου χθονός,
6 Ἐνδαΐδα τε ῥοδό[παχυν,
7 ἃ τ[ὸν ἱππευτὰ]ν ἔτ[ικτε Πηλέα
(65) 8 καὶ Τελαμῶνα [κορυστάν,
9 Αἰακῷ μειχθεῖσ᾽ ἐν ε[ὐναῖς·

στρ. δ. 100 1 τῶν <θ᾽> υἷας ἀερσιμάχους,
2 ταχύν τ᾽ Ἀχιλλέα
3 εὐειδέος τ᾽ Ἐριβοίας
(70) 4 παῖδ᾽ ὑπέρθυμον βοα[θόον
5 Αἴαντα σακεσφόρον ἦ[ρω,

87 νεβρὸς] ΝΕΚΡΟC **A**, corr. **A²**: noteworthy as showing how mechanically **A** sometimes worked.   **89** ἀγχιδόμοις J.   **90** ἀγακλειταῖς ἑταίραις K.: ἀγακλειταῖσι Νύμφαις Blass.   **91** After στεφανωσάμε[ναι there is room for about seven letters before -εων. The traces of σν, which Blass supposes before εων, seem altogether doubtful.   **92 f.** ἐπιχωρίαν J.   **94** In K.'s editio princeps (p. 118) I suggested τεὸν κλέος ὦ. For κλέος Blass substitutes κράτος: and this is preferable, as the space between τ and ω admits about nine letters.—τεὸν γόνον (so also Thomas), or γάμον,

Νύμφαις (the other nymphs of the island) in 90. But the comparison to 'a joyous fawn' suggests a mortal rather than a semi-divine maiden.
87 For νεβρὸς cp. Eur. Bacch. 862 ff.; ἆρ᾽ ἐν παννυχίοις χοροῖς | θήσω ποτὲ λευκὸν | πόδ᾽ ἀναβακχεύουσα, δέραν | εἰς αἰθέρα δροσερὸν | ῥίπτουσ᾽, ὡς νεβρὸς χλοεραῖς | ἐμπαίζουσα λείμακος ἡδοναῖς κ.τ.λ.—ἀπενθής: fr. 7. 2 θυμὸν...ἀπενθῆ.
88 ὄχθους, 'hills': Eur. Heracl. 781 ἀνθεμόεντι γᾶς ἐπ᾽ ὄχθῳ. The word could also mean 'river-banks' (=ὄχθας), as in Aesch. Ag. 1161, Ἀχερουσίους ὄχθους. B. often associates flowers with rivers (XV. 5, 34; XVIII. 39): δόνακος also (92) might suggest this. But then we should expect some distinct mention of a river, to define ὄχθους.
89 f. ἀγχιδόμοις occurs only here: but cp. Theognis 302 γείτοσί τ᾽ ἀγχιθύροις.—ἀγακλειταῖς: the epithet might

mean merely, 'famed for beauty': Pindar P. IX. 105 calls the daughter of Antaeus ἀγακλέα κούραν. But the word also suggests the idea of 'high-born,' 'illustrious' (cp. Od. 17. 370 ἀγακλειτῆς βασιλείης).
91—93 πλόκοις νέων (or the like) is a safer supplement than χρυσαυγέων or φοινικέων. If either of the latter words were read, the construction of στεφανωσάμεναι must be either (1) with acc. ἄθυρσιν,—'crowned with festal wreaths of flowers and reeds,' the genitives depending on that noun: or (2) with gen. ἀνθέων, ἄθυρσιν being the acc. in apposition. A genitive with the simple στεφανοῦσθαι or στέφεσθαι is not unexampled (cp. Nonnus Dionys. 5. 282); but the dative is normal. [We cannot properly compare Il. 1. 470 κρητῆρας ἐπεστέψαντο ποτοῖο = ἔπλησαν, nor Alcman fr. 61 ἐπιστέφοισαι ἄρτων.] The fourth syllable from

bounding lightly as a joyous fawn towards the flowery hills,
with her glorious neighbours and companions.

And when they have crowned themselves with wreaths of epode 3.
young flowers and of reeds, in the festive fashion of their isle,
they hymn thy power, O queen of a thrice-hospitable land. They
sing also of Endeïs with rosy arms, who in wedlock with Aeacus
bare chariot-driving Peleus, and the warrior Telamon ;

and also of their sons, the kindlers of battle, swift Achilles, and str. 4.
fair Eriboea's offspring, the great-hearted helper at need, Ajax,
shield-bearing hero ;

conj. Housman. 95 ΠΑΙΞΕ MS. : but the I may have been made from Γ.—
παγξείνου χθονός (πέδου Blass) Housman. 96 'Ενδαΐδα τε ροδόπαχυν Palmer and J.
97 τὸν ἱππευτὰν Headlam.—ἔτικτε Πηλέα J. 98 κορυστάν J. (κραταιόν conj. K.)
99 After ΕΝ Kenyon read A (hence ἐν αἴσᾳ Blass[1]): but the letter seems rather to
have been Ε.—ἐν εὐναῖς J.: ἐνηεῖ Blass[2]. 100 θ᾿ add J.—υἷας W. Christ, Blass :
υἱέας MS. 103 βοαθόον K. : βοατὰν Blass.—βοάσω (reading τῶν in 100 as relat.,
without θ᾿) Wilamowitz, Housman.

the end of the verse is long in 58 and
124, but short in 157 and 190.—ἐπιχωρίαν
ἄθυρσιν, acc. in appos. with sentence,
'a local sport,' i.e. 'in the festal fashion
of the isle': ἄθυρσις (only here) from
ἀθύρειν, which was said of dancing,
singing, or other pastime: cp. Plat.
Legg. 746 B ἡ...παρ᾿ ἡμῖν Κόρη καὶ Δέσποινα, εὐφρανθεῖσα τῇ τῆς χορείας παι-
διᾷ, κεναῖς χερσὶν οὐκ ᾤήθη δεῖν ἀθύρειν.—
The local trait was the blending of reeds
with flowers in the wreath.
94 f. κράτος, 'majesty': Aesch. Ag.
258 ἥκω σεβίζων σόν, Κλυταιμνήστρα,
κράτος.—παγξείνου: see n. on παγξένῳ
in x. 28. Pindar says of Aegina (O. VIII.
25 ff.) τεθμὸς δέ τις ἀθανάτων καὶ τάνδ᾿
ἁλιερκέα χώραν | παντοδαποῖσιν ὑπέστασε
ξένοις | κίονα δαιμονίαν. [I formerly pro-
posed παῖ ξείνου πατρός, supposing B. to
refer to the Phliasian legend that Asopus
was of Phrygian origin, Paus. 2. 5 § 3,
'Ασωποῦ τὸ ὕδωρ ἔπηλυ καὶ οὐκ ἐγχώριον.
But, as it seems that the first hand may
have written ΠΑΓ, I now prefer παγξείνου.]
96 'Ενδαΐδα, the daughter of Σκίρων
(a Megarian hero, XVII. 25 n.) and wife
of Aeacus, to whom she bore Peleus and
Telamon. (Apollod. III. 12. 6: Pindar
N. v. 12 'Ενδαΐδος ἀρίγνωτες υἱοί.) See
stemma in Introd.—ροδόπαχυν: Hes.
Theog. 247 Εὐνείκη ροδόπηχυς (cp. ib. 251):
Hom. hymn. XXXI. 6 'Ηῶ τε ροδόπηχυν:
Sappho fr. 69 βροδοπάχεες ἄγναι Χάριτες.—
For τέ before ροδο-, cp. XV. 34 ἐπὶ ροδό-
εντι.

97 ἱππευτάν, the Homeric ἱππότα
Πηλεύς (Il. 16. 33 etc.). Thessalians
were breeders and riders of horses.
Pind. P. IV. 152 f. Κρηθεΐδας (Aeson,
Jason's father)...ἱππόταις εὔθυνε λαοῖς
δίκας.
98 κορυστάν, helmed warrior (Il. 4.
457 etc.). I propose this, rather than
a word like κραταιόν, because the last
syllable of this verse is always long
(see 44, 56, 77, 110, 122, 143, 155, 188,
221).
99 ἐν εὐναῖς (or εὐνᾷ) must, I think,
be right here. For the statelier plural
cp. Pind. P. II. 27, IX. 12.
100 τῶν θ᾿. In adding θ᾿ (which
Kenyon, Blass and Jurenka accept) I was
guided by the fact that υἷας ought to
be governed by μέλπουσι (94): it is still
the maidens that sing of Achilles and
Ajax. If θ᾿ is absent, then βοα- in 103
must be read βοάσω (cp. Eur. Helen.
1108 f. σὲ... | ...ἀναβοάσω, 'loudly hymn
thee'): but this is much less fitting or
probable.—ἀερσιμάχους: cp. Hes. Op.
775 ἀερσιπότητος ἀράχνης: Scut. 316
ἀερσιπόται: Ap. Rhod. 2. 1061 ἀερσιλό-
φους. On the other hand ἀρσίποδας in
Hom. hymn. IV. 211 is exceptional. We
might suppose synizesis in υἱέας: but
υἷας is more likely. Cp. III. 77 where
υἷι is not impossible.
102—104 'Εριβοίας, daughter of
Alcathous, king of Megara; wife of
Telamon (Pind. I. v. 45 : Soph. Ai.
569).
103 f. βοαθόον (βοή and rt θεϝ), hast-

105 6 ὅς τ᾽ ἐπὶ πρύμνᾳ σταθεὶς
7 ἔσχεν θρασυκάρδιον [ὁρ-
8 μαίνοντα ν[ᾶας
(75) 9 θεσπεσίῳ πυ[ρὶ καῦσαι
10 Ἕκτορα χαλ[κεομίτρα]ν,
110 11 ὁππότε Π[ηλείδας
12 τραχεῖαν ['Αργείοισι μ]ᾶνιν

ἀντ. δ´. 1 ὥρίνατ[ο, Δαρδανίδας
(80) 2 τ᾽ ἔλυσεν ἄ[τας·
3 οἳ πρὶν μὲν [πολύπυργο]ν
Col.26 115 4 Ἰλίου θαητὸν ἄστυ
5 οὐ λεῖπον, ἀτυζόμενοι [δὲ
6 πτ]ᾶσσον ὀξεῖαν μάχαν,
(85) 7 εὖτ᾽ ἐν πεδίῳ κλονέων
8 μαίνοιτ᾽ Ἀχιλλεύς,
120 9 λαοφόνον δόρυ σείων·
10 ἀλλ᾽ ὅτε δὴ πολέμοιο
11 λῆξεν ἰοστεφάνου
(90) 12 Νηρῆδος ἀτρόμητος υἱός·

ἐπ. δ´. 1 ὥστ᾽ ἐν κυανανθέϊ Θ[ρᾳκὶ ναυβάτας
125 2 πόντῳ Βορέας ὑπὸ κύ-
3 μασιν δαΐζει

106 ἔσχεν] ἴσχεν Ludwich.—καῦσαι Blass (καίειν K.).   109 The final N of this v., the ANIN in 111, and the final N of 114, are found in a fragment (18 K.) which was placed here by Blass.—χαλκεομίτραν K. (suggesting also χαλκεοχάρμαν): χαλκοκορυστάν Smyth (conj. Blass).   110 ὁππότε K.: ὁπότε MS.   111 τραχεῖαν Desrousseaux, Blass: the letters Α...Α alone are certain.—'Αργείοισι Blass¹ ('Ατρείδαισι Bl.²).—μᾶνιν] ΗΝΙΝ **Α**: but Η has been changed to Α by a corrector.   112 f. Δαρδανίδας |

ing at the war-cry, prompt to aid (*Il.* 13. 477, 17. 481). The synizesis is harsh: but I hesitate to adopt βοατάν, which would be a strange substitute for βοὴν ἀγαθόν.—σακεσφόρον, as in Soph. *Ai.* 19. Cp. *Il.* 7. 219 (of Ajax), φέρων σάκος ἠΰτε πύργον, | χάλκεον, ἑπταβόειον.
105 The Homeric relative ὅς τε (*Il.* 1. 279 etc.) is freely used by lyric poets (as Alcman fr. 26. 3, and Pindar *passim*).—ἐπὶ πρύμνᾳ σταθεὶς, at the stern of his own ship. These services of Ajax are related in *Il.* 15. 415—745. The stubborn conflict between Ajax and Hector is pithily described there in 417 f.: οὔθ᾽ ὁ τὸν ἐξελάσαι καὶ ἐνιπρῆσαι πυρὶ

νῆα | οὔθ᾽ ὁ τὸν ἂψ ὤσασθαι, ἐπεὶ ῥ᾽ ἐπέλασσέ γε δαίμων. Cp. Soph. *Ai.* 1273 —1279.
108 θεσπεσίῳ, 'terrible,' cp. *Od.* 9. 68 λαίλαπι θεσπεσίῃ: *Il.* 12. 440 f. (Hector's cry to the Trojans) ῥήγνυσθε δὲ τεῖχος | 'Αργείων καὶ νηυσὶν ἐνίετε θεσπιδαὲς πῦρ ('fiercely blazing').
109 χαλκεομίτραν: Pindar *N.* x. 90 has χαλκομίτρα (gen.). The very fact that χαλκοκορυστής is a stock Homeric epithet of Hector seems rather against supplying it here: B. might naturally wish to vary. χαλκεοχάρμαν (Pind. *P.* v. 82 χαλκοχάρμαι) would also serve.— Cp. *Il.* 4. 187 ζῶμά τε καὶ μίτρη τὴν

who stood at his vessel's stern, and stopped bold Hector, the
bronze-girdled, when he was rushing on to burn the ships with
dread fire ; what time the son of Peleus had set up his fierce
wrath against the Greeks,

and had given the children of Dardanus a respite from doom.　　ant. 4.
Hitherto they had forborne to leave the goodly town of
many-towered Ilion, and had shrunk in dismay from the keen
fight, so oft as furious Achilles, brandishing his deadly spear,
made turmoil in the plain. But when at last the intrepid son
of the violet-crowned Nereid had ceased from war,—

as Boreas, on the dark Thracian sea, falls in with mariners by epode 4.
night and buffets them with billows,

τ᾽ ἔλυσεν ἄτας Desrousseaux (which had occurred to me also): Δαρδανιδᾶν | τ᾽ ἔλυσεν
ἄταν is also possible.—Τρωσὶ δὲ πάν|τ᾽ ἔλυσεν αἰνά Blass.　　114 πολύπυργον Blass :
θεότιμον Jurenka, Smyth.　　116 [οὐ] λεῖπον Blass.　　117 πτᾶσσον Blass,
Platt, Thomas.　　118 ΠΕΔΙΟΝ Α : corr. Α³.　　120 λαοφόνον] There has been
some correction between Α and Φ: perhaps of ΙΟ to Ο.　　124 Θ[ρᾳκὶ ναυβάτας
Herwerden : θύων ναῦν θοὰν Blass : Θρῇξ ναυβάτας Crusius. θύων ναυβάτας Smyth.

χαλκῆες κάμον ἄνδρες. The μίτρα was
a metal girdle, protecting a part of the
body to which the θώραξ did not reach
(Helbig, Hom. Epos p. 200).

111—113 Ἀργείοισι seems fitter
here than Ἀτρείδαισι: the antithesis is
between Greeks and Trojans.—ὠρίνατο:
the aor. midd. is found nowhere else.
The impf. pass. occurs in Il. 9. 595 τοῦ
δ᾽ ὠρίνετο θυμός, and the aor. act. in
11. 792 ὀρίναις.—ἄτας, the 'destruction'
which was impending over them : cp.
Pind. O. XI. 37 ὑπὸ στερεῷ πυρὶ | πλαγαῖς
τε σιδάρου βαθὺν εἰς ὀχετὸν | ἄτας ἴζοισαν
ἐὰν πόλιν. (ἄλγους is unsuitable here.)—
Another possible supplement is that of
Blass, Τρωσὶ δὲ πάν|τ᾽ ἔλυσεν αἰνά: but
such a use of αἰνά seems questionable.

114 f. The lost word, ending in ν, was
doubtless an epithet of Ilium. πολύ-
πυργον suits the context, as suggesting
the security of the Trojans within their
walls. The word occurs only in Hom.
hymn. II. (Apoll. Pyth.) 64. θεότιμον,
however, is also possible : see n. on XI. 7.
—ἄστυ. This is the only instance of
hiatus between verses 4 and 5 in the
strophe (cp. 70, 82, 136, 148, 181, 202):
but ἄστυ <τ᾽>...ἀτυζόμενοί <τε> is
improbable.

115 οὐ λεῖπον is certainly right. Cp.
141 f., where their sally in force is de-
scribed by πασσυδίᾳ δὲ λιπόντες | τείχεα.

117 πτᾶσσον...μάχαν: cp. Aesch.
P. V. 174 οὔποτ᾽ ἀπειλὰς πτήξας: Ly-

cophron 280 πτήσσων δόρυ. So in Il. 20.
426 f. οὐδ᾽ ἂν ἔτι δὴν | ἀλλήλους πτώσσοι-
μεν.

118 κλονέων, absolute, 'making tur-
moil': Il. 21. 532 f. ἦ γὰρ Ἀχιλλεὺς |
ἐγγὺς ὅδε κλονέων.

122 ἰοστεφάνου, here the epithet of
Thetis, is that of Persephone in III. 2.
It might seem to have a special fitness
for these dwellers in dark depths: but
such a theory fails when we find the
word applied also to the Muses (v. 3),
to Aphrodite (Hom. hymn. VI. 18), and,
in a late epigram, to the Charites (Anth.
VIII. 127).

124—126 ὥστ᾽=ὡς, 'as,' an epic
use admitted by Aeschylus and Sophocles
not only in lyrics but also in trimeters:
Pindar, however, uses ὥστε only with
infin., and in this sense employs ὥτε.

κυανανθέϊ (only here), 'of dark hue'
(cp. μελανθής), under a stormy wind;
little more than κυανέῳ: for ·ανθής in this
compound could not refer to the white
crests of waves. Cp. Eur. I. T. 7 (the
Euripus) πυκναῖς | αὔραις ἑλίσσων κυανέαν
ἅλα στρέφει. (In Helen. 179, κυανοειδὲς
...ὕδωρ, the epithet is a general one.)
Dionysius Periegetes (c. 130 A.D.) 169
has κυαναυγής of the sea.

Θρακί: Il. 23. 230 Θρηΐκιον.. πόντον:
Boreas blows Θρήκηθεν (ib. 9. 5). For
Θρᾷξ=Θράκιος, cp. Simon. 31 Κρῆτα . .
τρόπον: Eur. Alc. 346 f. Λίβυν . . αὐλόν.
(θύων Blass: but see p. 97.)—ναυβάτας

4 νυκτὸς ἀντάσας, ἀνατ[ελλομένᾳ
(95) 5 λῆξεν δὲ σὺν φαεσιμβρότῳ
6 Ἀοῖ, στόρεσεν δέ τε πόντον
130 7 οὐρία· νότου δὲ κόλπ[ωσαν πνοᾷ
8 ἱστίον, ἁρπαλέως τ᾽ ἄ-
9 ελπτον ἐξίκοντο χέρσον·

στρ. ε΄. 1 ὣς Τρῶες, ἐπεὶ κλύον αἰ-
(101) 2 χματὰν Ἀχιλλέα
135 3 μίμνοντ᾽ ἐν κλισίῃσιν
4 εἴνεκεν ξανθᾶς γυναικός,
5 Βρισηΐδος ἱμερογυίου,
(105) 6 θεοῖσιν ἄντειναν χέρας,
7 φοιβὰν ἐσιδόντες ὑπαὶ
140 8 χειμῶνος αἴγλαν·
9 πασσυδίᾳ δὲ λιπόντες
10 τείχεα Λαομέδοντος

127 ἀντάσας ἀνα-] ANTACANTM **A.** The corrector (**A**³) added ασ above the line after AC, and altered Υ into A. Over M he wrote what has hitherto been read as Π. But this (as Blass was the first to observe, and as Kenyon recognizes) looks more like T followed by E or O (the rest of the second letter having been torn off). 128 δὲ] TE **A**: corr. **A**³?—φαυσιμβρότῳ Blass. 130 οὐρία K.: ΟΥΡΙΑΙ MS., made from ΟΥΡΑΝΙΑ (by **A**¹?).—κόλπωσαν Blass (ἐκόλπωσαν πνοαῖς E. Bruhn, -εν πνοά Ludwich): πνοᾷ J. (Class. R. XII. p. 152, but with -ῇ), Housman: so Blass² (πνοαῖς

(XVI. 48) is better than **ναῦν θοάν.** The reason is not **ἐξίκοντο** in 132, for the 'ship' would imply the crew (cp. Soph. O. C. 942 where αὑτούς refers to πόλιν in 939); it is rather the sense of **δαΐζει.** If **ναῦν** were read, that verb must have its literal meaning, 'cleaves,' 'shatters'; but the ship comes safe to land. With ναυβάτας, it is figurative, 'afflicts': cp. Od. 13. 320 ἔχων δεδαϊγμένον ἦτορ. The notion of rough treatment is combined with that of harassing anxiety. —**ὑπὸ κύμασιν**: the waves rise above the ship: cp. Soph. Ant. 335 ff. (man) καὶ πολιοῦ πέραν πόντου χειμερίῳ νότῳ | χωρεῖ, περιβρυχίοισιν | περῶν ὑπ᾽ οἴδμασιν. **127 νυκτός,** gen. of time: **ἀντάσας,** sc. αὑτοῖς.—The correction in the MS. points to **ανατε-** rather than to **αναπ-**: see cr. note. I therefore conjecture **ἀνατελλομένᾳ** (cp. Pind. I. III. 83 φλὸξ ἀνατελλομένα). No exception can be taken to the place of **δὲ** as third word. It often holds a place later than the second: Aesch. Eum. 530 ἄλλ᾽ ἄλλᾳ δ᾽

ἐφορεύει: Soph. O. T. 485 ὅ τι λέξω δ᾽ ἀπορῶ: Ph. 959 φόνον φόνου δὲ ῥύσιον: Ai. 116 τοῦτο σοὶ δ᾽ ἐφίεμαι: Eur. fr. 776 δεινόν γε, τοῖς πλουτοῦσι τοῦτο δ᾽ ἔμφυτον. [In I. 6 we find Διὸς Εὐκλείου δέ, and in XVII. 47 περὶ φαιδίμοισι δ᾽: these instances, however, are of the still commoner kind in which the words before δέ are instar unius; as Aesch. Ag. 606 γυναῖκα πιστὴν δ᾽, P. V. 384 ἐν τῷ προθυμεῖσθαι δέ.]—For the conjectures which have assumed αναπ-, see Appendix. **128 λῆξεν,** like the aorists which follow, is gnomic.—**φαεσιμβρότῳ** (with synizesis) appears more probable in an Ionic poet than the Pindaric φαυσιμβρότῳ (O. VII. 39). **129—132 στόρεσεν ... οὐρία**: the gentle, favouring breeze 'lays' the sea after the storm, i.e. allows it to subside: Verg. Aen. 6. 763 placidi straverunt aequora venti. The MS. has οὐρίᾳ, probably an error due to πνοᾷ: though Βορέας could be the subject to στόρεσεν, in the sense that, by ceasing to blow, he

but ceases with the rise of light-bringing dawn, when a gentle breeze smooths the deep, and the breath of the south-wind swells their sail, till they joyfully reach the land for which they had ceased to hope,—

even so, when the Trojans heard that the warrior Achilles was str. 5. tarrying in his tent on account of Briseïs, the golden-haired, the lovely, they lifted up their hands to the gods ; for now they saw a bright gleam of sunshine from under the shadow of the storm. Leaving the walls of Laomedon with all their forces,

Bl.¹). **131** ΑΡΠΑΛΕΩΤΑ **A** : but T has been altered to C (by **A³**?). **133** ἐπεὶ κλύον was K.'s first reading, but in his ed. he gave ἐπέκλυον, with θεοῖσι δ' in 138. **138** θεοῖσιν] OIC is written above an erasure : it is impossible to say what first stood there. **139** φοιβὰν] φοίβαν K. **141** δὲ λιπόντες] **A** wrote ΜΕΛΠΟΝΤΕΣ : Δ has been written above M, and I has been added above the line between Λ and Π (by **A¹**?).

---

makes a calm (cp. Soph. *Ai.* 674 f. δεινῶν τ' ἄημα πνευμάτων ἐκοίμισε | στένοντα πόντον). The epic δέ τε occurs also in fr. 3. 1 τίκτει δέ τε, but (as Smyth notes) not elsewhere in lyric poetry, except in Sappho fr. 94. 2. In this formula, τε marks the statement as general ; hence it sometimes stands (as here) after a gnomic past tense (*Od.* 6. 185 μάλιστα δέ τ' ἔκλυον αὐτοί). It was more especially used to introduce an additional touch in a simile : *Il.* 2. 455 f. ἠΰτε πῦρ ἀΐδηλον ἐπιφλέγει ἄσπετον ὕλην | οὔρεος ἐν κορυφῆς, ἕκαθεν δέ τε φαίνεται αὐγή, | ὥς κ.τ.λ.: where the clause with δέ τε comes next before the apodosis, just as it does in v. 463 (*ib.*), σμαραγεῖ δέ τε λειμών. In Sappho fr. 94. 2 also it brings in the second clause of a simile (οἴαν τὰν ὑάκινθον... | πόσσι καταστείβουσι, χάμαι δέ τε πόρφυρον ἄνθος — but there the fragment breaks off).

κόλπωσαν: so Meleager (*c.* 80 B.C.) in *Anthol.* IX. 10 (ναῦται) πνοιῇ ἀπημάντῳ Ζεφύρου λίνα κολπώσαντες. Lucian *Ver. Hist.* 2. 9 ἄνεμος ἐμπεσὼν τοῖς ἱστίοις ἔφερε, κολπώσας τὴν ὀθόνην. Apart from our verse, the word is extant in no writer earlier than Polybius.

ἁρπαλέως properly means 'eagerly' (*Od.* 6. 250 etc.), here 'joyfully.' In Mimnermus 12. 5—8, where the Sun's voyage in his cup is described,—(εὐνὴ) φέρει—εὕδονθ' ἁρπαλέως,—Bergk would take the adv. with φέρει as = 'rapidly'; but the context rather indicates that Mimnermus meant, 'in *welcome* sleep,'— after toil.

133—138 ἐπεὶ κλύον is confirmed, as against ἐπέκλυον, by the size of the space in the papyrus between Π and K. —κλισίησιν. B. has the epic -ησιν of dat. plur. only here; but the Homeric colouring of the passage sufficiently accounts for it.—θεοῖσιν: cp. θεῶν as first word of the verse in v. 95 (v. 50 ends with θεός.)

139 f. I leave φοιβὰν oxytone, since the papyrus indicates it (φοιβαν); but we should expect φοίβαν (φοῖβος).

ὑπαὶ χειμῶνος, lit. '*from under*' the storm': the bright sunshine flashes out from beneath the rim of the storm-cloud that passes away. Cp. *Il.* 17. 645 Ζεῦ πάτερ, ἀλλὰ σὺ ῥῦσαι ὑπ' ἠέρος υἷας Ἀχαιῶν, | ποίησον δ' αἴθρην, δὸς δ' ὀφθαλμοῖσιν ἰδέσθαι.

141 πασσυδίᾳ = πανστρατιᾷ, sallying forth (σευόμενοι) with all their forces. This is the regular sense of the word in Attic writers: Xen. *H.* IV. 4. 9 πασσυδίᾳ βοηθοῦντες: Eur. *Tro.* 792 πανσυδίᾳ | χωρεῖν ὀλέθρου διὰ παντός: Thuc. VIII. 1 πανσυδὶ διεφθάρθαι (where Hude gives that form, with the acc. Vaticanus: πασσυδὶ and πασσυδεὶ are variants). In *Il.* 2. 11 f., however, θωρῆξαί σ' ἐκέλευσε κάρη κομόωντας Ἀχαιοὺς | πασσυδίῃ, the word is usually rendered, 'with all speed.' On the other hand in *Il.* 11. 725 the sense 'with all our forces' is fitter (as vv. 723 f. show).

142 τείχεα Λαομέδοντος: *Il.* 7. 452 f. (Poseidon speaking of the τεῖχος of Troy), τὸ ἐγὼ καὶ Φοῖβος Ἀπόλλων | ἥρῳ Λαομέδοντι πολίσσαμεν ἀθλήσαντε. (In *Il.* 21.

(110) 11   ἐς πεδίον κρατερὰν
   12   ἀΐξαν ὑσμίναν φέροντες·

ἀντ. ε΄. 145 1 ὦρσάν τε φόβον Δαναοῖς·
   2   ὤτρυνε δ' Ἄρης
   3   εὐεγχής, Λυκίων τε
(115) 4 Λοξίας ἄναξ Ἀπόλλων·
   5   ἷξόν τ' ἐπὶ θῖνα θαλάσσας·
Col. 27 150 6 ναυσὶ δ' εὐπρύμνοις παραὶ
   7   μάρναντ', ἐναριζομένων
   8   δ' ἔρ]ευθε φώτων
(120) 9 αἷμα]τι γαῖα μέλαινα
   10   Ἑκτορ]έας ὑπὸ χειρός,
  155 11 πῆμα μ]έγ' ἡμιθέοις
   12   ὀξεῖαν] ἰσοθέων δι' ὁρμάν.

ἐπ. ε΄. 1 ἃ τλάμ]ονες, ἦ μεγάλαισιν ἐλπίσιν
(125) 2 πνεί]οντες ὑπερφίαλον
   3   [φρόνημ' ἐθάρσευν]
  160 4 Τρῶε]ς ἱππευταὶ κυανώπιδας ἐκ-
   5   πέρσασιν Ἀργείων] νέας
   6   παύραις χορὸν εἰλα]πίνας τ' ἐν
(130) 7 ἀμέ]ρ[α]ις ἕξειν θεόδματον πόλιν.

149 θῖνα K. : θεῖνα MS. (the spelling of Aristarchus, who derived it from θείνω): cp. however IX. 10 ἐκείνησεν, XVI. 91 νειν (=νιν), etc.   **150** παραὶ Blass, with Platt and Housman: cp. 139 ὑπαί.   **152** ἔρευθε Palmer : ...ΕΤΘΕ **A** : το added above the line by **A³** (ἐρεύθετο).   **155** πῆμα μέγ' J. : δεῖμα μέγ' Jurenka.   **156** ὀξεῖαν J.: τεύχοντος Desrousseaux : βαρεῖαν Blass.—ἰσοθέων] The Ο is written above an erasure.— δι' ὁρμάν] ΔΙ ΟΡΜΑΝ **A** : Δ'==ΟΡΜΑΝ a corrector (the horizontal lines being

446—457, where the king's fraud is told, Poseidon alone builds, while Apollo is serving as herdsman.) A pious gloss associated Aeacus with Poseidon and Apollo : the vulnerable point in the stronghold was the work of man, and not of gods (Pind. *O.* VIII. 42). Heracles Ἰλίου ἐξαλάπαξε πόλιν (*Il.* 5. 642); *bis periura capit superatae moenia Troiae* (Ovid *Met.* 11. 215): but here, as in *Il.* 7 *l.c.*, it is assumed that 'Laomedon's walls' survived that capture.

146 Ἄρης. This is not Homeric; nay, it is in marked contradiction to the *Iliad*. The Homeric Ares takes no part in the fight at the ships, being under the general interdict which Zeus had laid on the gods (*Il.* 8. 10 ff.). But that is not all. At one moment, stirred by the fall of his son Ascalaphus, he arms himself for battle, in defiance of Zeus; but is detained in Olympus by the remonstrance of Athena (*Il.* 15. 113—142).

147 f. Λυκίων ... ἄναξ. No other Greek poet places Apollo in a personal relation with the Lycians quite so definite as is denoted by this phrase. His titles Λύκιος (Pind. *P.* 1. 39, Eur. fr. 700) and λυκηγενής (*Il.* 4. 101) were popularly explained as 'Lycia-born' (Hor. *C.* 3. 4. 62 *qui Lyciae tenet Dumeta natalemque silvam*). Both epithets, like Λύκειος, originally denoted a god of light (λυκ): the name Λυκία itself may have come from the cult.—The Lycians are prominent in the Homeric fighting at the

they rushed into the plain, intent on stubborn strife,
and roused terror in the Danai; while Ares of the mighty spear ant. 5.
urged them on, and the lord of the Lycians, the soothsayer,
Apollo.

So they came to the seashore, and fought at the sterns of the
good ships; and the black earth grew red with the blood of men
slain by Hector's hand; a grievous woe for the heroes, through
the keen onset of their godlike foes.

Hapless ones! Uplifted in spirit by great hopes, the chariot- epode 5.
borne warriors of Troy were sure that they would sack the dark-
prowed ships of the Greeks, and that in a few days dancing and
feasting would be the portion of their god-built city.

meant simply to fill the space: cp. XVIII. 48). **157—163** For other conjectural
supplements see Appendix. **157 f.** The letters NEC · HM in 157 and
ΟΝΤΕϹΤΠΕΡ in 158 are supplied by a fragment placed here by Blass; who in
163—166 also fitted in a fragment giving the earlier portions of those verses; and in
167—169 a third fragment (τῶν εἰ καὶ...ἢ βαθυξύλ)ῳ.

---

ships (*Il.* 15. 424 f.).—**Λοξίας**, the title of
the oracle-god, is out of place here:
indeed it is seldom joined with Ἀπόλλων.
(In Aesch. *Cho.* 549 f., ἢ καὶ Λοξίας
ἐθέσπισεν, | ἄναξ Ἀπόλλων, the second
title is in apposition with the first.)
149 ἴξον (*Il.* 5. 773 etc.), a weak (or
'sigmatic') aorist, formed with ο (and ε in
2nd pers.) instead of ᾰ. Cp. the epic
ἐ-βήσε-το (*Il.* 14. 229), ἐ-δύσε-το (*ib.* 2.
578), imper. ὄρσε-ο (*ib.* 3. 250), infin.
ἀξέ-μεναι (*ib.* 23. 50), ἔ-πεσο-ν, etc.
152 ἔρευθε: a solitary but certain
instance of the active used intransitively.
For the normal use, see *Il.* 11. 394 f. ὁ δέ
θ' αἵματι γαῖαν ἐρεύθων | πύθεται.
155 πῆμα μέγ', acc. in apposition
with the preceding sentence. ἡμιθέοις,
the Greek heroes (VIII. 10, X. 62).
156 It is possible that there has been
some corruption here. If, however, **ἰσοθέων** is sound, the sense seems to be,
'*owing to the fierce onset of the Trojan
heroes.*' The first syllable of the verse
is long in all the corresponding places
where it is preserved (45, 57; 78, 90;
111, 123; 144; 177, 189). We might
supply **ὀξεῖαν** (epithet of μάχαν in 117),
or **ἄτλατον**.—**τεύχοντος**, referring κατὰ
σύνεσιν to Ἑκτορέας...χειρός (cp. *Od.* 11.
90 f.), is also possible; but a *recurrence*
to him seems less apt here: these two
verses speak of heroes pitted against
heroes. — **ἰσοθέων** after **ἡμιθέοις** (both

having the same sense) illustrates the
use of a synonym to avoid repeating a
word: so Soph. *O. T.* 54 ἄρξεις...κρατεῖς,
O. C. 1501 σαφὴς...ἐμφανὴς (n.), etc.—
Blass supplies **βαρεῖαν** (in which, however, the first ᾰ is a drawback), and
understands, 'through the resentful impulse of Achilles' (ἰσοθέων), in refusing to
help the Greeks.
157—163 In the restoration of this
passage given above, the following points
may be noted. (1) 157 **ἃ δυσφρονες**
(Blass) is quite possible (Aesch. *Theb.*
174 ἰὼ δύσφρονες, 'alas, misguided ones':
Soph. *Ant.* 261 φρενῶν δυσφρόνων ἁμαρ-
τήματα): but δύσφρων more often means
either 'melancholy' or 'malevolent'; so
that **ἃ τλάμονες** (Kenyon) seems slightly
more probable. (2) 158 f. Before **οντες**
there is room for 4 letters, or for 5
if one of them was thin (like I). **πνείοντες** (Jurenka, Ludwich) is more likely
than **πνέοντες** (Blass), because in all the
corresponding verses (59, 92, 125, 191,
224) the first syllable is long.—**ὑπερφίαλον** might be adv., but I rather prefer
ὑπερφίαλον **φρόνημ'**. (3) 160 f. **ἱππευται**,
if it stood alone, would be too vague:
the insertion of **Τρῶες** before it is a gain.
—**ἐκπέρσασιν**: the participle (whatever
it was) should be in the dative, if (as
seems almost certain) **πόλιν** was the
subject of **ἕξειν**. A nomin., ἐκπέρσαντες,
would, in that case, imply that they

8 μέλλον ἄρα πρότερον δι-
165 9 νᾶντα φοινίξειν Σκάμανδρον,

στρ. ς΄. 1 θνᾴσκοντες ὑπ' Αἰακίδαις
2 ἐρειψ[ιλάοις·
(135) 3 τῶν εἰ καὶ [διόλωλεν
4 ἢ βαθυξύλ[ῳ πυρᾷ -
170 5 − − ∪∪ − ∪∪ − −
6 − ∪ − − − ∪ −
7 − − ∪∪ − ∪∪ −
(140) 8 − − ∪ − −
9 − ∪∪ − ∪ − −]
175 10 οὐ γὰρ ἀλα[μπέσ]ι νυ[κτὸς
11 πασιφανὴς Ἀρετὰ
12 κρυφθεῖσ' ἀμαυρο[ῦται δνόφοισιν,

ἀντ. ς΄. 1 ἀλλ' ἔμπεδον ἀκ[αμάτᾳ
(146) 2 βρύουσα δόξᾳ
180 3 στρωφᾶται κατὰ γᾶν [τε
4 καὶ πολυπλάγκταν θ[άλασσαν.
5 καὶ μὰν φερεκυδέα ν[ᾶσον
(150) 6 Αἰακοῦ τιμᾷ, σὺν Εὐ-
7 κλείᾳ δὲ φιλοστεφ[άνῳ
Col. 28 185 8 πόλιν κυβερνᾷ,

---

175 ἀλαμπέσι] ΑΛΑΕΠΙ **A**: but a corrector has cancelled Π, and written letters (μπ?)

actually destroyed the ships. (4) 162 f. παύραις...ἐν ἁμέραις (Nairn) seems probable. Blass (whose own restorations are given in the Appendix) objects that the space in 163 before P suggests more than three letters (AME). But in this handwriting A and M are sometimes very broad. I had thought, indeed, of ἐσθλαῖς ...ἐν συμφοραῖς (Eur. *Alc.* 1155 χορούς ἐπ' ἐσθλαῖς συμφοραῖσιν ἱστάναι), but rather prefer ἁμέραις.
166 f. ὑπ' Αἰακίδαις, under their hands : *Il.* 10. 452 ἐμῆς ὑπὸ χερσὶ δαμείς : 13. 98 ὑπὸ Τρώεσσι δαμῆναι.—For ἐρειψιλάοις cp. X. 67 f. λαούς τε διχοστασίαις | ἤρειπον : v. 56 ἐρειψιπύλαν.—In Aesch. *Th.* 880 f. the brothers are δωμάτων ἐρειψίτοιχοι (they destroy the τοῖχοι of their house): but I doubt whether that word could mean 'destroying τείχη,'

πτολίπορθοι, as an epithet of heroes generally.
168—174 τῶν εἰ καί. The pronoun refers to the Aeacidae. *Though their bodies have perished, their names live evermore.* βαθύξυλος is elsewhere said of deep forest shades : Eur. *Bacch.* 1138 ὕλης ἐν βαθυξύλῳ φόβῃ. Here (πυρὰ) βαθύξυλος is a pyre built high with wood (III. 49 ξύλινον δόμον) ; as in Pind. IX. 40 βαθύκρημνοι ἀκταί are shores with high, steep cliffs. For the sentiment, cp. III. 90 f. ἀρετᾶς γε μὲν οὐ μινύθει | βροτῶν ἅμα σώματι φέγγος (where γε μὲν = the Attic γε μήν, 'however'). The ἢ before βαθυξύλῳ shows that a second clause with ἢ followed. The tenor of the passage may have been somewhat as follows:—
τῶν εἰ καὶ διόλωλεν
ἢ βαθυξύλῳ πυρᾷ καυ-

Ah, they were doomed, or ever that should be, to redden the
eddying Scamander with their blood,

as they fell under the hands of the death-dealing Aeacidae. str. 6.

And if [the bodies] of the Aeacidae [have perished, burnt] on
high-built pyre [or buried in the tomb, yet their names live for
ever...].

For shining Virtue can never be hid from view in the murky
shades of night;

hers is the unfading flower of a steadfast fame; she goes abroad ant. 6.
over the earth, and with the wanderers on the sea.

And verily she honours the renowned isle of Aeacus; with
Eucleia, to whom wreaths are dear, she rules that city;

above, from which only a few dots remain. **177** δνόφοισιν Tyrrell. **178** ἀκαμάτᾳ Blass, Platt : ἀκάματος Κ. **181** ΠΟΛΥΠΛΑΓΚΤΑΝ **A** : -ΟΝ **A**³.

θέντ' ἢ κεκαλυμμένα τύμβοις
σώματ', ἄφθαρτόν γε μὲν
ζώει κλέος ἀθάνατον
Μουσᾶν λιγειᾶν
εὐκελάδοις ἐν ἀοιδαῖς.
175—177 ἀλαμπέσι ... ἀμαυροῦται.
Cp. Plut. *Phocion* 1 (quoted by Kenyon),
τὴν δὲ Φωκίωνος ἀρετὴν ...αἱ τύχαι τῆς
'Ελλάδος ἀμαυρὰν καὶ ἀλαμπῆ πρὸς δόξαν
ἐποίησαν, where the verbal coincidences
with this passage are noteworthy.—
'Aρετά is here personified, as by Simonides (fr. 58) and by Aristotle in his hymn
in memory of Hermeias, 'Aρετὰ πολύμοχθε
γένει βροτείῳ (Bergk⁴ II. 360). An epigram ascribed to Asclepiades of Samos
(c. 300 B.C., *Anth.* VII. 145) refers to
a work of art in which she was represented as mourning by the tomb of Ajax:
ἅδ' ἐγὼ ἁ τλάμων 'Aρετὰ παρὰ τῷδε
κάθημαι | Αἴαντος τύμβῳ κειρομένα πλοκά-
μους.—πασιφανὴς is not found elsewhere
in classical poetry.—δνόφοισιν : for the
plur., cp. Aesch. *Cho.* 52.
178 ἀκαμάτᾳ, not to be exhausted,
'unfailing.' Though ἀκαμάτα might
naturally be the epithet of 'Aρετά here,
the dative is more probable, as an
epithet for δόξᾳ seems needful. The
fem. form occurs in Soph. *Ant.* 339,
which also illustrates the sense; (Γᾶν)
ἄφθιτον, ἀκαμάταν : and in Hes. *Th.* 747
ἀκαμάτῃσι χέρεσσιν.
181 Poetical use justifies πολυπλάγκταν, the form given by the first hand,
as against the correction πολύπλαγκτον.
Cp. n. on 178: IX. 8 ἀπράκταν : Aesch.
Ag. πολυκλαύτην (Porson on *Med.* 822),

Ar. *Pax* 978 πολυτιμήτη, *Lys.* 217
ἀταυρώτη.—The sense of the adj. here is
passive, 'much-traversed'; in X. 35 it is
active. 'Aρετά, the Virtue that survives
death and is never hid in dark oblivion,
'roams over land and sea'; *i.e.* the fame of
great deeds is spread throughout the world.
182—189 καὶ μάν : v. 56 n.—φερεκυδέα : cp. I. 17.
'Aρετά 'honours' Aegina as a home of
Themis : see n. on 77 f.: she 'governs'
the land in company with Εὔκλεια 'who
delights in wreaths' (won by Aeginetan
athletes in the national games). Εὐνομία
also bears sway there, she who keeps
cities ἐν εἰρήνᾳ.
Two points should be noted here.
(1) The association of Εὔκλεια with
Εὐνομία. In the theatre at Athens there
was in later times a seat for the ἱερεὺς
Εὐκλείας καὶ Εὐνομίας (*C. I. A.* III. 277).
(2) Eunomia was one of three 'Ωραι
(daughters of Zeus and Themis, and
sisters of the Moirae),—the other two
being Δίκη and Εἰρήνη : Hes. *Th.* 901 f.:
Pind. *O.* XIII. 6 f. : Bergk⁴ *adespota* 140
(perhaps by Simonides) Εὐνομίαν λιπαρο-
θρόνους τ' ἀδελφάς, Δίκαν | καὶ στεφανο-
φόρον Εἰράναν. As in the natural sphere
the Horae represent a fixed order, so as
ethical powers they are Loyalty, Justice
and Peace. Cp. Diod. v. 73 'Ωρῶν
ἑκάστῃ δοθῆναι τὴν ἐπώνυμον τάξιν τε καὶ
βίου διακόσμησιν.
The same group of ideas is expressed
here, though εἰρήνα, instead of being
personified, appears as a gift bestowed by
Εὐνομία. Cp. XIV. 54 f.

9 Εὐνομία τε σαόφρων,
10 ἃ θαλίας τε λέλογχεν
(155) 11 ἄστεά τ᾽ εὐσεβέων
12 ἀνδρῶν ἐν εἰρήνᾳ φυλάσσει·

ἐπ. ϛ´. 190 1 νίκαν τ᾽ ἐρικυδέα μέλπετ᾽, ὦ νέοι,
2 Πυθέα, μελέταν τε βροτω-
3 φελέα Μενάνδρου,
(160) 4 τὰν ἐπ᾽ Ἀλφειοῦ τε ῥοαῖς θαμὰ δὴ
5 τίμασεν ἁ χρυσάρματος
195 6 σεμνὰ μεγάθυμος Ἀθάνα,
7 μυρίων τ᾽ ἤδη μίτραισιν ἀνέρων
8 ἐστεφάνωσεν ἐθείρας
(165) 9 ἐν Πανελλάνων ἀέθλοις.

στρ. ζ´. 1 εἰ μή τινα θερσιεπὴς
200 2 φθόνος βιᾶται,
3 αἰνείτω σοφὸν ἄνδρα
4 σὺν δίκᾳ. βροτῶν δὲ μῶμος
(170) 5 πάντεσσι μέν ἐστιν ἐπ᾽ ἔργοις·

186 Εὐνομία σαοσίφρων conj. Housman. **193** θαμὰ J., Nairn. **199** εἰ] E is lost : the short stroke above I is part of the paragraphus with coronis,)——, written between 198 and 199 to mark the end of a system—εἰ μή τινα θερσιεπής. Between the N and the A of τινα there is a mark like a very small and partly broken ο, perhaps intended to indicate that the words should be read as τιν᾽ ἀθερσιεπής.

186 Εὐνομία τε σαόφρων, *sc.* κυβερνᾷ. The construction is harsh : but I follow the MS., rather than read Εὐνομίᾳ (to depend on σύν). With the dative, the position of σαόφρων (referring to Ἀρετά) would be awkward ; though it might be regarded as practically adverbial (=σω-φρόνως). Housman's Εὐνομία σαοσίφρων would meet the difficulty ; but that form of the adj. is not found, and can scarcely be assumed from σαοσίμβροτος in Hesychius.

187 θαλίας, acc. plur., 'festivities'; Her. III. 27 ἦσαν ἐν θαλίῃσι. Eunomia has these for her portion, because they belong to the peace which she maintains. Cp. fr. 3 (on the blessings of εἰρήνα), 12 συμποσίων δ᾽ ἐρατῶν βρίθοντ᾽ ἀγυιαί.

190 From the praises of Aegina and the Aeacidae, which began at v. 77, the poet now returns to his immediate theme.

ὦ νέοι : the youths, wearing wreaths (VI. 8 f.), who form the κῶμος. So Pindar *I.* VII. 2 Κλεάνδρῳ τις...ὦ νέοι... ἀνεγειρέτω κῶμον : cp. *N.* III. 4 f. μελιγαρύων τέκτονες | κώμων νεανίαι : *ib.* 65 f. ὕμνος...ὀπὶ νέων ἐπιχώριον χάρμα κελαδέων : *P.* V. 103 ἐν ἀοιδᾷ νέων. See also VIII. 102 ff.

191 f. μελέταν is the 'care' used by the trainer, who, in preparing a competitor for the great contests, not only supervised his exercises, but prescribed his diet (Arist. *Eth.* II. 5), and regulated his whole life. The scientific trainer of athletes was, so far, a physician. He is called γυμναστής (Xen. *Mem.* II. 1. 20), or ἀλείπτης (Arist. *l.c.*) : while παιδοτρίβης is properly the ordinary teacher of boys in a palaestra.—βροτωφελέα : not found elsewhere ; cp. δημωφελής.—Μενάνδρου, an Athenian, mentioned by Pindar also in

as doth also temperate Eunomia, to whom festivities belong,
and who keeps the towns of pious men in peace.

Sing, O youths, the glorious victory of Pytheas, and the helpful epode 6.
care of the trainer Menander: oft has that care been honoured
on the banks of Alpheus by Athena of the golden chariot,
majestic queen of lofty soul, when ere now she has set garlands
on the heads of countless men at the great games of Hellas.

Let those who are not thralls of bold-tongued Envy give just str. 7.
praise to a master of his art. Disparagement waits on every
work of man:

ΘΕΡC ∴ ΠΗC : the letter after the first C seems to have been I, but is not certain.
Nairn conj. ἀθερσοεπής, 'disparaging in speech' (ἀθερίζειν): Housman, ἀμερσιεπής (envy
' bereaves of speech,' when praise is due). Jurenka reads ἀθερσιεπής (θερ-μός, ' chill
of speech '), comparing Ov. *Met.* II. 763 (the *domus Invidiae*) *ignavi plenissima
frigoris*. 202 ΒΡΤΩΤΩΝ A: corr. A¹.

his ode on this same victory, *N.* v. 48:
ἴσθι, γλυκεῖάν τοι Μενάνδρου σὺν τύχᾳ
('by Menander's happy aid') μόχθων
ἀμοιβὰν | ἐπαύρεο· χρὴ δ' ἀπ' Ἀθανᾶν
τέκτον' ἀθληταῖσιν ἔμμεν. Lampon, the
victor's father, is described by Pindar
(*I.* v. 66 f.) as μελέταν | ἔργοις ὀπάζων,
'bestowing care on feats of prowess'
(*i.e.* on athletics), and recommending it
to his sons,—thus observing Hesiod's
maxim (*Op.* 382 μελέτη δέ τοι ἔργον
ὀφέλλει). Pindar's meaning (or a part of
it) must be that Lampon, a rich man
(cp. 224 f.), procured the best training
for his sons. It was natural, then, that
both poets should pay a tribute to
Menander.
193—198 Athena has 'honoured'
the skill of the Athenian trainer by
giving several Olympian victories to his
pupils, whose successes in the four 'Panhellenic' festivals, taken all together,
have been 'countless.'—θαμά (the accent
given by Apollonius *De adverb.* p. 563. 3)
is emphasized by δή, as in Pind. *I.* 1. 17.
—Of Athena's three epithets, χρυσάρματος denotes a conventional attribute;
σεμνά, divine rank; and μεγάθυμος a
personal quality: cp. v. 98 f.—'Ἀθάνα:
cp. σελάνα VIII. 29.
196 μίτραισιν. This μίτρα was a
woollen headband to which the sprays
or leaves of the wreath were attached:
Pind. *I.* IV. 62 λάμβανέ Fοι στέφανον,
φέρε δ' εὔμαλλον μίτραν. Hence the
word is used as an equivalent for στέ-

φανος: *O.* IX. 84 Ἰσθμίαισι Λαμπρομάχου
μίτραις.—ἀνέρων: this inflexion of ἀνήρ
is not elsewhere extant in B.: Pindar
uses it freely.
198 Πανελλάνων: Pind. *I.* III. 47
Πανελλάνεσσι δ' ἐριζόμενοι δαπάνᾳ χαῖρον
ἵππων. *I.* II. 38 ἐν Πανελλάνων νόμῳ.
The four great πανηγύρεις are 'Panhellenic' as distinguished from minor local
festivals, such as those mentioned in
IX. 30—35 (n.).
199 f. φθόνος can bluster as well as
whisper: θερσιεπής denotes loud, im-
pudent detraction. The Aeolic θέρσος
(θάρσος) is found only in proper names,
such as Θέρσανδρος, Θέρσης, Θέρσιππος,
Θερσίτης. For the connecting vowel ι in
θερσιεπής cp. Θερσίλοχος. (Θερσολόχειος
occurs, however, as the patronymic in an
inscription: see Pape-Benseler *s.v.*) The
sense of the word is illustrated by the
name Θερσαγόρας (Dem. or. 23 § 142),
'bold in debate.'—βιᾶται: B. pictures
φθόνος as a malignant force within the
man, against which candour has to
wrestle: v. 187 f. χρὴ δ' ἀλαθείας χάριν
αἰνεῖν, φθόνον ἀμφοτέραισιν | χερσὶν ἀπω-
σάμενον. Cp. XV. 31 φθόνος εὐρυβίας.
Frag. trag. adesp. 547. 12 f. πρὸς γὰρ τὸ
λαμπρὸν ὁ φθόνος βιάζεται, | σφάλλει δ'
ἐκείνους οὓς ἂν ὑψώσῃ τύχη.
202 f. σὺν δίκᾳ: cp. v. 196 (n.):
x. 123 f.—μῶμος: Smyth refers to Anth.
Planud. 84 παντὶ δ' ἐπ' ἔργῳ | μῶμος:
and Theogn. 1184 (there is no man) ᾧ μὴ
μῶμος ἐπικρέμαται.

J. B.   24

354 ΒΑΚΧΥΛΙΔΟΥ [XII

6 ἁ δ' ἀλαθεία φιλεῖ
205 7 νικᾶν, ὅ τε πανδαμάτωρ
8 χρόνος τὸ καλῶς
9 ἐ]ργμένον αἰὲν ἀ[έξει·
(175) 10 δυσμενέων δὲ μα[ταία
11 γλῶσσ' ἀϊδ]ὴς μιν[ύθει

[The last v. of στρ. ζ', and the first nine of ἀντ. ζ', are lost.]

Col. 29 ἀντ.ζ'.220 10 ἐλπίδι θυμὸν ἰαίνει·
11 τᾷ καὶ ἐγὼ πίσυνο[ς
12 φοινικοκραδέμνοισ[ι Μούσαις

ἐπ. ζ. 1 ὕμνων τινὰ τάνδε ν[εόπλοκον δόσιν
(191) 2 φαίνω, ξενίαν τε [φιλά-
225 3 γλαον γεραίρω,
4 τὰν ἐμοὶ Λάμπων [παρέχων χάριν οὐ
5 βληχρὰν ἐπαθρήσαις τ[ίει,
(195) 6 τὰν εἴ γ' ἐτύμως ἄρα Κλειὼ

207 ἐργμένον] Wackernagel conj. ἀργμένον (cp. ὑπαργμένον Her. VII. 11). **208** The faint traces after M would suit either A or I. **209** An upright can be traced before CMIN. Blass² supplies γλῶσσ' ἀϊδὴς μινύθει from Cramer *Anecd. Oxon.* I. 65. 22 (=fr. 46 Bergk⁴, 36 Bl.²), Βαρυτόνως δὲ τὸ 'Αΐδης· τὸ γὰρ ἐπιθετικὸν ὀξύνεται· δυσμενέων δ' ἀϊδὴς λέγει Βακχυλίδης. **220 f.** ἰαίν[ει]. τᾷ Κ.: ἰαίν[ε|ται· καὶ Blass. **222** φοινικοκραδέμνοισι Μούσαις Blass (-οις τε Μούσαις Nairn): -οιο Μούσας Housman: -οιο Κλειοῦς Jurenka. **223** νεοπλόκων δόσιν Blass: who after ΤΑΝΔΕ finds a small trace of N written above I (or P), as if ἰ(οπλόκων) had

204 ἀλαθεία. This may be merely the Ionic poet's conventional Doricizing of ἀληθείη. See however Choeroboscus (Bekk. *Anecd.* p. 1314), ἀλήθεια κοινῶς καὶ ἀλήθεια 'Αττικῶς. This was the older Attic accent (Chandler § 103, 2nd ed.). Cp. Ar. fr. 29 ὦ παρανοία καὶ ἀναιδεία (instead of παράνοια etc.). **205 ff.** πανδαμάτωρ: epithet of χρόνος in Simonides fr. 4, 5.—καλῶς with the epic (and Ionic) ἅ, which is not found in Pindar.—ἐργμένον: see on ἐρχθέντος in 65 f.—ἀέξει, 'exalts,' strengthens in repute. In *Od.* 15. 372 ἔργον ἀέξουσιν μάκαρες θεοί, ᾧ ἐπιμίμνω, the sense is 'prospers.' **209** ἀϊδής. In Hes. *Scut.* 477, σῆμ' ἀϊδὲς ποίησεν, the word is passive in sense, as it must be here. **220 ff.** ἐλπίδι, as in IX. 40, the 'hope' or ambition of a man who aspires to win

fame by the exercise of some gift. The ten verses lost before v. 220 may have spoken of various pursuits, ending with a reference to the poet's. In 221 the MS. has no point after ται: and ἰαίνει· τᾷ καὶ gives a far better rhythm than ἰαίν|εται· καὶ etc., though the latter is otherwise unobjectionable (cp. Archil. fr. 36 ἄλλος ἄλλῳ καρδίην ἰαίνεται). In 222 a dat. plur. is more probable than a genit. sing. (which would go with ὕμνων). The dat. will depend on πίσυνος: 'In (or with) which hope, trusting to the Muses,' etc. (We might read -οις τε Μούσαις: but it seems less fitting that the Muses should be thus subjoined to the ἐλπίς.) —φοινικοκραδέμνοισι: a merely ornamental epithet, given to Latona in X. 97 (n.). **223** The letter after τάνδε may have been N: but it is very uncertain. As a conjectural supplement, νεόπλοκον δόσιν

but truth is wont to prevail; and all-subduing time ever strengthens the repute of fine achievement. The vain speech of foes covertly detracts [from worth; but fails in the end…]

* * * * * *

[Every one who works aright at his appointed task] has ant. 7. a hope to cheer his heart. With such hope I also, trusting in the Muses of purple kerchief,

now present a gift of newly-woven song; thus honouring the epode 7. splendid hospitality shown to me by Lampon, his tribute to the Muse's charm, not slight, which has found favour in his eyes. And if it be indeed radiant Cleio

been corrected to ν(εοπλόκων). **226 f.** οὐ at the end of 226 was first proposed by Housman : ἐπαθρήσαις (as part.) by Platt (who after it placed τέχναν) : παρέχων and χάριν by J.: τίει by Blass. **228 f.** ΕΙΚ' MS.: εἰ γ' J. (in 1897), Blass, Platt: εἰκ as = εἰ W. Schulze (cp. οὐκ = οὐ), on analogy of Arcadian εἰκαν: Wilamowitz cp. Ar. *Lys.* 1099 αἰκ εἰδον, and the Cnidian verse in Her. I. 174, where he reads αἰκ (vulg. εἴ κ') ἐβούλετο. —Κλειώ | —ἐνέσταξ[εν φρασίν] : so I had conjectured (but with φρεσίν) from ΚΛ- and ΕΝΕΩ, before ΕΙΩ and ΤΑΞ were furnished by a small fragment, containing the ends of vv. 227—230, which Blass identified as belonging here.—φρασίν Housman and Blass.

is suitable: Blass gives νεοπλόκων. I rather prefer the acc. sing., on account of τινά, which serves to soften the figurative sense. ὕμνων ἥδε νεόπλοκός τις δόσις seems better than the same phrase with νεοπλόκων. Another possibility would be νεόδροπον. (Or, if the letter after τάνδε was Μ, μελίφθογγον or μελί-γλωσσον.)—For δόσιν cp. Pind. *O.* VII. 7 Μοισᾶν δόσιν, and *I.* I. 45 κούφα δόσις ἀνδρὶ σοφῷ κ.τ.λ. **226 f.** In the restoration of these verses two points may, I think, be taken as certain. (1) χάριν must have stood in 226, meaning the poet's 'charm,' as in III. 97 καὶ μελιγλώσσου τις ὑμνήσει χάριν | Κηΐας ἀηδόνος. There is no other word to which the τὰν in 228 could so fitly refer. (2) ἐπαθρήσαις, aor. partic., must be read in 227. The Aeolic form in -αις is not elsewhere used by B.: but his λαχοῖσαν in XVIII. 13 f., and Μοῖσα in v. 4, are also exceptional Aeolisms. ἐπαθρῆσαι, with or without κε in 226, would require after it a word beginning with στ: but the possible words (στέφων, στίχων, στόμα) are all inadmissible. The remaining question seems to be between (i) παρέχων…τίει (Blass), and (ii) e.g. μελέων (XVIII. 2) …τελεῖ or τίνει. I prefer (1), because, (a) after ξενίαν, παρέχων is fitter than τελεῖ or τίνει: and

(b) τίει, governing χάριν, is better *in that place* than a verb governing ξενίαν would be, since τὰν in 228 refers to χάριν. For the ἴ in τίει, cp. Aesch. *Ag.* 942, Eur. *Heracl.* 1013. The meaning is, then, that Lampon, in affording (παρέχων) hospitality to the poet, 'honours the poetic charm, not slight, on which he has looked with favour.' οὐ βληχρὰν (cp. X. 65), as being the Muse's gift. The compound ἐπαθρεῖν recurs only in later verse (Ap. Rhod. 4. 497 ἐπαθρήσαντας, where ἐσ- is a *v. l.*, and Quint. Smyrn. I. 111, where Heyne reads ἐσάθρησα). Here the word denotes favourable regard; as ἐπιβλέπειν (τινί) does in Lucian *Astrol.* 20. Cp. v. 8 δεῦρ' ἀθρησον. **228 f.** εἰ γ', siquidem: Plat. *Phaedr.* 242 D εἰ γε σὺ ἀληθῆ λέγεις.—πανθαλής, as giving bloom to the flowers of song; Pind. *O.* VI. 105 ὕμνων…εὐτερπὲς ἄνθος. One of the Muses was Θάλεια (Hes. *Th.* 77). Distinguish this form, with ᾰ, from that with ᾱ (69 n.).—ἐνέσταξεν: *Od.* 2. 271 εἰ δή τοι σοῦ πατρὸς ἐνέστακται μένος ἠΰ: Her. IX. 3 ἀλλά οἱ δεινὸς ἐνέστακτο ἵμερος κ.τ.λ.—φρασίν, Doric. This form occurs in Pindar, either without a variant (*N.* III. 62), or, as is far more often the case, with the *v. l.* φρεσίν (*O.* VII. 24, *P.* II. 56, III. 108, IV. 109, 219). In

24—2

7 πανθαλὴς ἐμαῖς ἐνέσταξ[εν φρασίν,
230 8 τερψιεπεῖς νιν ἀοιδαὶ
9 παντὶ καρύξοντι λαῷ.

XIII. [XIV.]

ΚΛΕΟΠΤΟΛΕΜΩΙ ΘΕΣΣΑΛΩΙ

ΙΠΠΟΙC ΠΕΤΡΑΙΑ

στρ. α'.   1 Εὖ μὲν εἰμάρθαι παρὰ δαί[μονος ἀν-
2 θρώποις ἄριστον·
3 συμφορὰ δ' ἐσθλόν τ' ἀμαλδύ-
4 νει βαρύτλατος μολοῦσα·
5 κἀγατ]ὸν ἰδ' ὑψιφανῆ τε[ύ-
6 χει κ]ατορθωθεῖσα· τιμὰν
7 δ' ἄλ]λος ἀλλοίαν ἔχει·

ἀντ. α'.   1 μυρί]αι δ' ἀνδρῶν ἀρεταί, μία δ' ἐ[κ
2 πασᾶ]ν πρόκειται,

XIII. The title added in the left margin by **A³**. **1** δαίμονος Platt and others (δαίμοσιν K.).   **3** ἐσθλόν τ' or ἐσθλοὺς conj. J. (ἐσθλοὺς K.): ἐσθλὸν MS. **5**.....ΟΝΗΔΗΤΨΙΦΑΝΗΤΕ **A**: **A³** cancelled ΗΔΗ and wrote ΚΑΙ above.—κἀγατὸν ἰδ' ὑψιφανῆ conj. J.: ἢ κυδρὸν ἠδ' Blass: see comment.—τεύχει Blass and others.

P. III. 59, where the MSS. agree in φρεσίν, Boeckh restored φρασίν. Pindar also uses φρένεσσιν (*I.* III. 5), as B. does (XIII. 11). If the Ionian's conventional Doricism was consistent, he would have written φρασίν here; and we are not justified in assuming the reverse.
230 The stress is on τερψιεπεῖς. If Cleio has really inspired the poet, this ode, which honours Lampon (νιν), will please.—For the compound with ἔπος as epithet of ἀοιδαί cp. VII. 7 n.

XIII. 1 εἰμάρθαι, impersonal. παρὰ δαίμονος: the best thing for men is that a good destiny should have been assigned (to them) by the gift of heaven: cp. XVI. 24 ἐκ θεῶν μοῖρα: Aesch. *Ag.* 1026 μοῖραν ἐκ θεῶν: *Pers.* 101 θεόθεν μοῖρα: Xen. *H.* VI. 3. 6 ἐκ θεῶν πεπρωμένον ἐστί: Pind. *N.* IV. 61 τὸ μόρσιμον Διόθεν πεπρωμένον. *P.* III. 59 χρὴ τὰ ϝεοικότα πὰρ δαιμόνων μαστευέμεν.—παρὰ δαίμοσιν is also possible (mortal destiny is *laid up with* the gods, is in their keeping): but here the god is rather the *dispenser* of fate.

2—6 The MS. has a point after μολοῦσα. Fortune, when it comes in a grievous shape, crushes (ἀμαλδύνει, weakens, brings low) even a brave spirit: but, when it has a prosperous course (κατορθωθεῖσα), makes a man admired and eminent (ὑψιφανῆ).
After ἐσθλόν in 3 τ' has dropped out: unless, indeed, the poet wrote ἐσθλούς, but the transition from that plural to the singular in v. 5 would be very harsh. It can hardly be doubted that the metre here was the same as in the antistrophic verse (10), – ᴗ – – – ᴗ – –. [Blass, accepting ἐσθλὸν without τε, supposes that – ᴗ ᴗ – here is substituted for the – ᴗ – – in verse 10. But this seems very improbable, even if it be metrically possible.]
5 f. The first hand wrote ...ον ἤδη ὑψιφανῆ: where ἤδη was doubtless a corruption of ἠδ', this, in turn, having replaced the less common form, ἰδ'. The metre is shown by v. 12, – – ᴗ ᴗ – ᴗ ᴗ –. [Blass however reads ἢ κυδρὸν ἠδ' ὑψιφανῆ τεύ-, assuming that – – ᴗ – could be sub-

who has imbued my spirit with that charm, sweet will be the
strains that tell forth his name to all the folk.

XIII. [XIV.]

For Cleoptolemus of Thessaly, victor in the chariot-race at the Petraia.

A happy destiny is heaven's best gift to mortals. Fortune str. 1.
can crush worth, if she comes fraught with suffering; she can
make a man admired and eminent, if her course be prosperous.
The honour won by men takes various shapes :

the forms of human excellence are countless; but one merit has ant. 1.
the foremost place among all,—

8 f. The end of v. 8 (ΜΙΑΔΕ) is contained in a small fragment placed here by K., which
gives also the last letters or syllables of v. 10 (Α), 11 (Ν), 12 (ΑΡΜΟ), and 13 (ΜΦΑ).
—ἐκ πασέων conj. Richards (ἐκ πασᾶν Jurenka): ἐξ ἀλλᾶν Housman: ἐς τιμὰν R. Ellis.

stituted for the – – ‿ ‿ in v. 12: but here
again it seems more than doubtful whether
such a substitution is possible. The metrical effect is almost intolerably harsh.]
I regard ἰδ' as well-nigh certain. ἰδέ is
Homeric, but is not used by Pindar: it
is probable in Soph. *Ant.* 969, but does
not elsewhere occur in Tragedy. (For
an instance of elided ἰδ', see *Od.* 3. 10.)
We might, indeed, read (κλεινὸν) δὲ καὶ
ὑψιφανῆ (δέ sometimes follows τε : Soph.
O. C. 367 ff.) : or κλεινόν τε κ.τ.λ. Then,
however, the scribe's ἤδη would remain
without satisfactory explanation, since it
is unlikely that it could have arisen from
so familiar a word as δέ.
There is room before ον for four or five
letters. Five is the number required by
Blass's ἢ κυδρ]όν : but his ἤ cannot (in
my opinion) be right. We need καί, δέ,
or τέ. I would suggest κἀγατ]ὸν (ἀγητός)
or κἀγανόν : for crasis of καί at the beginning of a verse, see III. 81 χὤτι, and
XVII. 50 κηΰτυκτον. In *Class. R.* XII.
p. 131 (Mar. 1898) I proposed καὶ κλεινόν, which still seems to me improbable.
In ΚΑΙΚΛΕΙΝΟΝ the re-
semblance of ΚΑ to ΚΛ might have led
to the loss of ΚΑΙ, leaving in our MS.
only ΚΛΕΙΝΟΝ. The number of letters
before ον for which this conjecture requires space is, therefore, only the same
as that demanded by the emendations
noticed above,—five. In objecting to it

as requiring too much room ('nimia pro
spatio,' 2nd ed. p. 121) Blass evidently
overlooked the fact that, on my hypothesis, καί had dropped out.
τεύχει=τίθησι: *Od.* 13. 397 ἀλλ' ἄγε
σ' ἄγνωστον τεύξω : so Pind. *N.* IV. 83 ff.
ὕμνος...ἰσοδαίμονα τεύχει | φῶτα : Aesch.
Eum. 668 τὸ σὸν πόλισμα καὶ στρατὸν
τεύξω μέγαν.
8 f. μυρίαι δ'...ἀρεταί. From the
importance of *happy fortune* for the
attainment of honour, the poet passes
to the *various kinds of honour* that men
may win, and the variety of *excellences* in
different aspirants. Cp. VIII. 88 f., and
IX. 38 ff.
μία...πρόκειται. It seems possible, and
even probable, that πρόκειται here means,
' *is set in front*' (of all others), ' *holds the
first place*') as προτιθέναι τί τινος can
mean 'to prefer' (Her. III. 53, etc.).
Cp. Arist. *Top.* VI. 5 (p. 142 b 24) ἐν οἷς
οὐ πρόκειται τοῦ λόγου τὸ τί ἐστιν ('where
the nature of the thing is not *put first* in
the account of it'). We might then read :
(1) ἐκ πασᾶν, 'ranks first among them
all,' as suggested by H. Richards (writing
ἐκ πασέων) in *Class. R.* XII. 76 (ἐξ ἀλλᾶν
Housman, *ib.* 73). Or : (2) εἰς ὄλβον,
'in respect to happiness.' (ἐς τιμὰν
Robinson Ellis, *ib.* 65: but cp. 6.) I
slightly prefer (1), as better fitted to interpret the sense of πρόκειται. [Blass writes
ἐς ξυνὸν πρόκειται, *i.e.* 'is set before men

10 3 ὃς τὸ] πὰρ χειρὸς κυβερνᾶ-
4 ται δι]καίαισι φρένεσσιν.
5 οὔτ᾽ ἐ]ν βαρυπενθέσιν ἁρμό-
6 ζει μ]άχαις φόρμιγγος ὀμφὰ
7 καὶ λι]γυκλαγγεῖς χοροί,

ἐπ. α΄. 15 1 οὔτ᾽ ἐ]ν θαλίαις καναχὰ
2 χαλκ]όκτυπος· ἀλλ᾽ ἐφ᾽ ἑκάστῳ
3 καιρὸς] ἀνδρῶν ἔργματι κάλ-
4 λιστος· εὖ ἔρδοντα δὲ καὶ θεὸς ὀ[ρθοῖ.
5 Κλεοπτολέμῳ δὲ χάριν
20 6 νῦν χρὴ Ποσειδᾶνός τε Πετραί-
7 ου τέμενος κελαδῆσαι,
8 Πυρρίχου τ᾽ εὔδοξον ἱππόν[ικον υἱόν,

10 f. ὃς τὸ Headlam, Pearson : ὃς τὰ Wilamowitz : ἇ τὰ Blass : εἰ τὸ Richards :
ὅς γε K.—ΚΤΒΕΡΝΑΙ **A** : corr. **A¹**.—κυβερνᾶται K. : κυβέρνασεν Wilamowitz.
12 οὔτ᾽ ἐν] οὐκ ἐν K. : οὗτοι Ellis : οὐκ ἂν (with ἁρμόζοι) Platt. **13** μάχαις J.

---

for their common good,'—whatever the
special ἀρετή of each may be.—My former
conjecture, accepted by Kenyon and
Smyth, was εὐδαίμων πρόκειται, 'is set
before men,'—' is proposed to their
efforts,'—' as truly happy,' *i.e.* ' with a
sure promise of happiness.']
10 f. ὃς...κυβερνᾶται, a relative clause
serving to define the ἀρετή meant in 8 f. ;
equivalent in sense to εἴ (or ὅτε) τις
κυβερνᾶται. Thuc. II. 44 § 1 τὸ δ᾽
εὐτυχές, οἶ ἂν τῆς εὐπρεπεστάτης (ξυμφορᾶς)
λάχωσι : VI. 14 τὸ καλῶς ἄρξαι τοῦτ᾽ εἶναι,
ὃς ἂν τὴν πατρίδα ὠφελήσῃ ὡς πλεῖστα.
Cp. also VII. 68 § 1 : *Od.* 24. 286.
τὸ πὰρ χειρός, 'his immediate task' ;
the act which is next to come from his
hand. The phrase resembles τὸ πὰρ
ποδός : Pind. *P.* III. 60 (a man should
pray for things which befit men), γνόντα τὸ
πὰρ ποδός, οἵας εἰμὲν αἴσας, 'aware of *what
lies in front of him,* and of our mortal
destiny.' There, τὸ πὰρ ποδός is the
thing to which one will come at the next
step *from where his foot now is* : *i.e.,*
what lies directly in front of him,—
decay and death. Cp. also *P.* x. 62 f.
τυχών κεν ἁρπαλέαν σχέθοι φροντίδα τὰν
πὰρ ποδός· | τὰ δ᾽ εἰς ἐνιαυτὸν ἀτέκμαρτον
προνοῆσαι : ' if he succeeds, he will seize
with rapture on his *immediate* desire;
but what a year may bring forth, no sign
can foreshow.' As τὸ πὰρ ποδός suits

Pindar's thought of men moving on their
appointed paths, so τὸ πὰρ χειρός suits
our poet's thought here. Happy is he
who is guided by a just mind in *that
which his hand finds to do* at each
successive moment.
12—16 μάχαις is on the whole much
more probable in v. 13 than λαχαῖς, the
conjecture of Blass (2nd ed.). Hesychius
gives λάχη (*sic*)· λῆξις, ἀποκλήρωσις.
(In Aesch. *Th.* 914 τάφων πατρώων λαχαί
are their ' portions ' in those graves.) It
may be granted that B. could have used
λαχή as = λάχος. And at first sight
λαχαῖς is distinctly commended by βαρυπενθέσιν. Compare, however, x. 68
μάχαις...λυγραῖς. The reasons which
weigh with me in favour of μάχαις are
chiefly these. (1) The antithesis between joyous music and καναχὰ...ὀκτυπος
(15 f.). With λαχαῖς, we must there read,
as Blass does, στερνόκτυπος. But καναχά
denotes some sharp sound, esp. the
clanging of metal : *Il.* 16. 105 πήληξ
βαλλομένη καναχὴν ἔχε : Soph. *Ant.* 130
χρυσοῦ καναχῆς. In II. 12 B. uses
γλυκεῖαν αὐλῶν καναχάν to describe the
brisk, high-pitched notes of flutes. καναχὰ
στερνόκτυπος could not well denote the
sound made by *beating the breast* (cp.
Soph. *Ai.* 631 ff. χερόπλακτοι δ᾽ | ἐν
στέρνοισι πεσοῦνται | δοῦποι). It would
have to mean, ' a *shrill sound* (of γόοι)

his, who is guided by just thoughts in each thing that his
hand finds to do.

The voice of the lyre, the clear strains of choral song, accord
not with the grievous stress of battle,

as the clash of arms has no place amidst festivity. To every epode 1.
work of man the fitting season lends the fairest grace; and
heaven prospers him who works aright.

Now, in tribute to Cleoptolemus, 'tis meet to celebrate the
sacred domain of Poseidon Petraios, and the glorious son of
Pyrrhichus, victor in the chariot-race...

(so K., and Blass[1]) : λαχαῖς Blass[2].—ὀμφὰ J. (a conjecture afterwards confirmed by
the letters ΜΦΑ in the fragment mentioned above in n. on 8 f.).   **16** χαλκόκτυπος K.:
στερνόκτυπος Blass[2].   **17** καιρὸς J.   **18** ΕΡΔΟΝΤΙ **A**: corr. **A**[3]?—ὀρθοῖ J.

---

accompanied by beating of the breast ' :
this, however, would be a forced sense.
On the other hand **καναχὰ χαλκόκτυπος**
(the clash of arms) is a natural phrase :
and it is strongly confirmed by XVII. 59
χαλκεοκτύπου μάχας. (2) In 16 f. the
poet adds that καιρός should be observed
in every *deed* or *work* of man, ἐφ' ἑκάστῳ...
ἔργματι. This is suitable if the antithesis to festivity is *fighting*; but less so,
if it is *mourning*. (3) Music and choral
song are prominently named by B. himself (fr. 4. 2) among the gifts of Εἰρήνα.
Cp. *Il.* 18. 490 ff.,—the city at peace,
with its festal music of αὐλοί and φόρμιγ-
γες, contrasted with the city at war.
λιγυκλαγγεῖς (only here) : cp. IX. 10
λιγύφθογγον. λιγύς is notably frequent
as an epithet of the Muse, the lyre, or
song (*e.g. Od.* 24. 62, Terpander fr. 6,
Alcman fr. 1, Stesichorus fr. 44, Pind.
O. IX. 47, etc.).

17 καιρός: from Theognis 401 μηδὲν
ἄγαν σπεύδειν· καιρὸς δ' ἐπὶ πᾶσιν ἄριστος |
ἔργμασιν ἀνθρώπων : cp. also Hes. *Op.*
694 καιρὸς δ' ἐπὶ πᾶσιν ἄριστος : Pind. *O.*
XIII. 47 f. ἕπεται δ' ἐν ἑκάστῳ | μέτρον·
νοῆσαι δὲ καιρὸς ἄριστος ('a just measure
goes with every deed ; and to discern it
is the highest opportuneness').

18 εὖ ἔρδοντα: suggested by ἔργματι.
Each deed should be done in season ;
and if a man does it aright, the god, too,
prospers him. Cp. Eur. fr. 432. 2 τῷ
γὰρ πονοῦντι καὶ θεὸς συλλαμβάνει. There
is an allusion to success in the games (cp.
III. 94 πράξαντι δ' εὖ), which smooths
the transition from the prefatory moralizing to the proper subject of the ode.

19—21 χάριν: the poetical tribute.

The acc. is in apposition with the sentence (**χρὴ...τέμενος κελαδῆσαι**). An
exact parallel is afforded by Pind. *O.* XI.
78 ff. (484 B.C.) καὶ νυν ἐπωνυμίαν χάριν |
νίκας ἀγερώχου κελαδησόμεθα | βροντὰν
καὶ πυρπάλαμον βέλος etc. : where χάριν
has a like sense, and is similarly in apposition with the sentence.—νῦν, as so
often, when B. passes from proem to
theme : IX. 9 n.

Πετραίου: schol. Pind. *P.* IV. 138
(where Pelias, king of Iolcus, is addressed
by Jason as παῖ Ποσειδᾶνος Πετραίου),
Πετραῖος τιμᾶται Ποσειδῶν παρὰ Θετταλοῖς,
ὅτι διατεμὼν τὰ ὄρη τὰ Θετταλικά, λέγω
δὴ τὰ Τέμπη, πεποίηκε δι' αὐτῶν ἐπιτρέχειν
τὸν ποταμὸν Πηνειόν, πρότερον διὰ μέσης
τῆς πόλεως (*sic*) ῥέοντα καὶ πολλὰ τῶν
χωρίων διαφθείροντα. Her. VII. 129 gives
the legend, without mentioning the cult.
Cp. schol. Ap. Rhod. 3. 1244 (on πέτρην
θ' Αἱμονίην)· τὴν Θεσσαλίαν Πέτραν·
χωρίον δέ ἐστιν ἐν ᾧ Ποσειδῶνος ἄγεται
ἀγών. It is only a conjecture that the
scene of the Πετραῖα was somewhere
near Tempe.

22 f. Πυρρίχου, probably the victor's
father. Cleoptolemus has been named
in 19 as the recipient of the poetical
offering. But there is no unfitness in
this second reference to him as victor.
Blass's supplement **ἱππόνικον υἱόν** may
therefore be accepted. In v. 23 ὃς refers
to υἱόν, *i.e.* Cleoptolemus, and the two
epithets refer to his father Pyrrhichus.
Verse 24 may have been, as Herwerden
suggests, πατρὸς πεφυκώς.—Jurenka, supposing Pyrrhichus to be the charioteer,
supplies ἱππόν[ωμον ὁρμάν] : but see on
v. 43.

στρ. β'. ¹ ὃς φιλοξείνου τε καὶ ὀρθοδ[ίκου

[The last six verses of στρ. β', the whole of ἀντ. β', and the first three verses of ἐπ. β', are lost.]

ἐπ. β'. 40 ₄ — ∪ — ε]ὐώδεα Θεσσα[λ ∪ — —
         ₅ ∪ — ∪ ∪] ἐν γυάλοις·
         ₆ — — ∪ Πα]ντέλης κ[∪ — —
         ₇ — ∪ ∪ — ∪ ∪ —]δων

[The rest of the ode is lost.]

23 This verse, the first of the second strophe, is the last in column XXIX. After this at least one whole column has been lost, as ode XIV begins at the top of the next column which has been preserved. **40—43** These words belonged, as metre indicates, to verses 4—7 of an epode (probably the second). They are supplied by a small fragment (no. 11) which K. placed here.

40—43 Metre indicates that these vestiges belonged to verses 4—7 of an epode. εὐώδεα was probably the epithet of Poseidon's temple or altar (cp. Pind. *O*. VII. 32 εὐώδεος ἐξ ἀδύτοιο : Eur. *Tro*. 1061 f. θυόεντα βωμόν). γυάλοις must denote the valley in which the chariot-race was held. Thus (*e.g.*): βωμὸν ἀμφ'] εὐώδεα Θεσσαλ[ίας εὐδαίμονος] ἐν γυάλοις, if in v. 19 there was synizesis in Κλεοπτο-λέμῳ : if there was not, the epithet of Θεσσαλίας might be ἱπποκυδέος, or ἱπ-πομήτιδος (Pind. *I*. VI. 9).—The letters ντέλης belonged, as the accent in the MS. shows, to a proper name, doubtless Παν-τέλης. (The names Παντέλειος and Παντέλεος are extant.) This was presumably the charioteer. The κ might suggest κυβέρνα|σεν or κυβερνή|τας : see v. 47.—We might conjecture that the poet, having no myth available which would suit his Thessalian theme, had recourse to description of the chariot-race itself, such as Simonides is known to have used in some epinikia.

ΔΙΘΥΡΑΜΒΟΙ

XIV. [XV.]

ΑΝ]ΤΗΝΟΡΙΔΑΙ

Η ΕΛΕΝΗ]C ΑΠΑΙΤΗCΙC

Col. 30 στρ. α'.   1 Ἀντήνορος] ἀντιθέου
2 σύζυξ θεμερῶ]πις, Ἀθάνας πρόσπολος,
3 ὤιξεν ἁγνὸν Π]αλλάδος ὀρσιμάχου
4 ναὸν θύρας τε χ]ρυσέας
5 ἀγγέλοις δισσοῖσι]ν Ἀργείων Ὀδυσσεῖ
6 Λαρτιάδᾳ Μενελ]άῳ τ᾽ Ἀτρεΐδᾳ βασιλεῖ
7 – ◡ – – – – βαθύ]ζωνος Θεανὼ

ἀντ. α'.   1 – – – ◡ ◡ – ◡ ◡]ον
2 ◡̱ – ◡ ◡ – ◡ ◡ –] προσήνεπεν
10 3 ◡̱ – ◡ – – – – ◡ ἐ]ϋκτιμέναν
4 – – ◡ – – – ◡ –
5 – ◡ – – – ◡ – –]δων τυχόντες
6 – ◡ ◡ – ◡ ◡ – – – ◡ ◡ –] σὺν θεοῖς
7 – ◡ – – – ◡ – – – ◡ –]ους

[ἐπ. α', and the first v. of στρ. β', are lost.]

XIV.   Ἀν]τηνορίδαι [ἢ Ἑλένη]ς ἀπαίτησις.   The title was written by **A³**, not, as usual, in the left margin, but at the top of the column, since this ode, the first of the extant Διθύραμβοι, began a new volume or a new section.   See Introduction to the Ode.   **1** Ἀντήνορος is certain, agreeing with such vestiges as remain before ἀντιθέου.   **2** The letters before C ΑΘΑΝΑC were almost certainly ΠΙ : the epithet must then have ended in -ῶπις.   Blass further thinks that ΕΝΩΙ (or ΕΡΩΙ ?) preceded Π : but this is wholly uncertain : he supplies δάμαρ τερενῶπις.   The first syll. of the v., however,

XIV. 1—9   With regard to the embassy of Odysseus and Menelaus to Troy, and the treatment of the subject by Bacchylides, see the Introduction to this Ode.   The poem begins somewhat abruptly.   Theano, wife of the Trojan Antenor and priestess of Athena, is with the two envoys at the temple of the goddess on the acropolis of Troy.   So much is clear from the remains of

vv. 1—5.   Probably she has taken them thither in order that they may supplicate Athena to prosper their mission.   Their hospitable reception at the house of Antenor is presupposed.   The traces in verses 2—4 favour some such conjecture as that of Crusius (see cr. n.): she opened the temple of Pallas, with its golden doors, to the Greek envoys.   No point occurs in the MS. before that

DITHYRAMBS.

XIV. [XV.]

THE SONS OF ANTENOR

OR THE DEMAND FOR THE RESTITUTION OF HELEN.

God-like Antenor's [wife of grave mien], priestess of Athena, str. 1.
deep-girdled Theano, [opened the holy temple] of battle-rousing
Pallas with its golden doors [to the two envoys] of the Greeks,
Odysseus, son of Laertes, and Menelaus, the prince sprung from
Atreus...

*   *   *   *   *   *

is long in 44 and 51. I suggest σύζυξ θεμερῶπις.   **3 f.** Crusius supplies ὥϊξεν ἁγνὸν]
Παλλάδος ὁρσιμάχου [ναὸν πύλας τε χ]ρυσέας: perhaps θύρας would be better; *Il.* 6. 297 f.
αἱ δ᾿ ὅτε νηὸν ἵκανον Ἀθήνης ἐν πόλει ἄκρῃ, | τῆσι θύρας ὥϊξε Θεανὼ καλλιπάρηος κ.τ.λ.
5 ἀγγέλοις ἵκουσιν Crusius : – ⏑ – πρέσβεσσιν Blass.   **6** Λαρτιάδᾳ Μενελ]άῳ Crusius,
Nairn, Wilamowitz.—τ᾿ added above line by **A³.**   **7** βαθύζωνος K.   **12** The
letter before ΩΝ seems to have been Λ or Δ.   [παρ᾿ ἀλλή]λων τυχόντες?—ΤΥΧΟΝΤΑC
A : corr. **A³.**   **13** σὺν θεοῖς] These words answer to -ᾳ βασιλεῖ in 6, θελξιεπεῖ
in 48, and -ᾶς Θέμιτος in 55. Probably γε, τε, or δέ has dropped out after σύν.
14 After this verse all the rest of column XXX is lost. Column XXXI begins with
v. 37 (ἄγον κ. τ. λ.), the second v. of epode β΄. The number of verses lost is
therefore 22 (15—36).

---

which follows προσήνεπεν in v. 9.
There was certainly no break in the first
sentence before βασιλεῖ in v. 6, and
perhaps none before Θεανώ in v. 7.
But, whether she or Odysseus was subject
to προσήνεπεν, a new sentence or clause
must have begun in the lost part of v. 8
or of v. 9.

2 Ἀθάνας πρόσπολος: *Il.* 6. 297 ff.
αἱ δ᾿ ὅτε νηὸν ἵκανον Ἀθήνης ἐν πόλει
ἄκρῃ, | τῆσι θύρας ὥϊξε Θεανὼ καλλιπά-
ρηος, | Κισσηΐς, ἄλοχος Ἀντήνορος ἱπποδά-
μοιο· | τὴν γὰρ Τρῶες ἔθηκαν Ἀθηναίης
ἱέρειαν. Her father Κισσῆς, a Thracian
prince,—to be distinguished from He-
cuba's father Κισσεύς (Eur. *Hec.* 3),—is
mentioned in *Il.* 11. 223.—The epithet
ended in -ῶπις (see cr. n.). θεμερῶπις,
'of grave mien' (epithet of αἰδώς in
Aesch. *P.V.* 134), would be not unfitting
for the priestess.—Blass (2nd ed.) gives
τερενῶπις (not extant).

5 Possibly ἀγγέλοις δισσοῖσιν: cp. *Il.*
11. 140 ἀγγελίην (of this embassy).—

[πρέσβεσσιν Blass: there is, however, no
instance in classical poetry of πρέσβεις
as = 'ambassadors.' In Aesch. *Suppl.*
727, where πρέσβη is commonly read,
πρέσβυς could mean only *senex.*]

9 προσήνεπεν, impf., a form given by
MSS. in Pind. *P.* IV. 97 and IX. 29, where
some edd. read προσέννεπε.—Was the
subject to this verb Theano or Odysseus?
It might seem fitting that she, as priestess
of the temple, should speak here. In any
case, a speech by Odysseus presumably
occurred before v. 37. A fragment, not
unsuitable to a speech by him, is conjecturally placed in vv. 30 and 31 (n.).
If that conjecture be right, several lines
before v. 30 must also have been spoken
by him. Supposing, then, that a speech
by Theano began at v. 10, it cannot
have been long. τυχόντες in 12 may have
referred (whoever was the speaker) to
the 'obtaining' of satisfactory terms by
the Greek envoys.

στρ. β′.　　－ － ᴗᴗ － ᴗᴗ －

23　2 － － ᴗᴗ － μεσονύ]κτιος κέαρ

[The last five vv. of στρ. β′, and the first v. of ἀντ. β′, arè lost.]

ἀντ. β′.　　－ － ᴗᴗ － ᴗᴗ －

30　2 ᴗ‿ － ᴗ ᴗ < οὐ γὰρ ὑπόκλοπον φορεῖ

3 βροτοῖσι φωνάεντα λόγον σοφία.>

[The last four vv. of ἀντ. β′, and the first v. of ἐπ. β′, are lost.]

ἐπ. β′. 36　　－ － ᴗ － － － ᴗᴗ － ᴗᴗ －

Col. 31　2 ἆγον, πατὴρ δ᾽ εὔβουλος ἥρως

3 πάντα σάμαινεν Πριάμῳ βασιλεῖ

4 παίδεσσί τε μῦθον Ἀχαιῶν.

40　5 ἔνθα κάρυκες δι᾽ εὐ-

6 ρεῖαν πόλιν ὀρνύμενοι

7 Τρώων ἀόλλιζον φάλαγγας

στρ. γ′.　1 δεξίστρατον εἰς ἀγοράν.

2 παντᾷ δὲ διέδραμεν αὐδάεις λόγος·

45　3 θεοῖς δ᾽ ἀνίσχοντες χέρας ἀθανάτοις

4 εὔχοντο παύσασθαι δυᾶν.

5 Μοῦσα, τίς πρῶτος λόγων ἆρχεν δικαίων;

6 Πλεισθενίδας Μενέλαος γάρυϊ θελξιεπεῖ

23 μεσονύ]κτιος κέαρ is fr. 9 K., conjecturally placed here by Blass; though (as he says) the colour is darker than that seen in the extant part of col. xxx. A similar tint is found, however, in parts of col. xxxi. These two words ended v. 2 of a *strophe*, as is shown by the large vacant space above them (the last three verses of an epode, as well as the first of a strophe, being short). **30 f.** On the suggestion of G. F. Hill, Blass places here fr. 35 (Bergk), preserved by Clem. Alex. *Paedag.* iii.

---

23 μεσονύκτιος κέαρ. If (which is doubtful) the words belonged to this place, Odysseus may have been contrasting the bliss of peace with 'the midnight fear' which torments the heart in war-time. Cp. what the poet says of peace in fr. 3. 10: οὐδὲ συλᾶται μελί-φρων | ὕπνος ἀπὸ βλεφάρων. **30 f.** οὐ γὰρ ὑπόκλοπον. Metre is the only definite ground for placing these words here. Clement quotes them in his *Paedagogus*, as in his *Stromateis* he quotes vv. 50—56 (cr. n.). The fact that this ode was familiar to him may be viewed as slightly strengthening the conjecture based on the metre. On the other hand, verses of this measure may have occurred in more than one of the

poet's odes. It seemed best, on the whole, to print the words here, with a due indication of the doubt. If they were spoken by Odysseus, what was the context? Possibly he was deprecating the suspicion that his plea for a peaceful settlement veiled some insidious design: σοφία would then be the art of the orator. That word might, however, suggest rather the art of the poet, as though B. were saying that there is nothing 'furtive' in the 'clear utterance' of poetry. (Contrast Pind. *O.* ii. 91 ff. φωνάεντα συνετοῖσιν· ἐς δὲ τὸ πᾶν ἑρμηνέων χατίζει.)

37 ff. ἆγον: (the sons of Antenor) proceeded to conduct Odysseus and Menelaus to the Trojan agora. Mean-

[*Verses* 30 f. ?...for no guile lurks in the clear utterance that
wisdom brings to mortals.]

* * * * * *

[The sons of Antenor] then led [the envoys to the market-
place of Troy]; while their father, the sage hero, went to declare
all the word of the Achaeans to king Priam and his sons.
Thereupon heralds, hastening through the wide city, began
to gather the array of Trojans

into the marketplace where warriors muster. Everywhere the
loud rumour ran abroad; and men lifted up their hands to the
immortal gods, praying for rest from their woes.
Say, Muse, who was the first to plead the righteous cause?
Menelaus son of Pleisthenes spake with winning voice,

310, οὐ γὰρ ὑπόκλοπον φορεῖ | βροτοῖσι φωνάεντα λόγον σοφία : but he writes βροτοῖς δὲ
instead of βροτοῖσι. As metre shows (cp. 44 f.), these words formed v. 2 (latter part)
and v. 3 of a strophe or antistr.; so, if fr. 9 is rightly referred to str. β', they belonged
to antistr. β'.   38 σάμαινεν] σάμανεν Blass. Cp. XVI. 51.   47 λόγων ἆρχεν
K., with Purser: ΑΡΧΕΝ ΛΟΓΩΝ MS.—The ὑποστιγμή after ΔΙΚΑΙΩΝ is abnormally
placed on a level with the bottom of the letters. (Cp. VIII. 83 cr. n.)

---

while their father (**εὔβουλος ἥρως**, as
in *Il.* 3. 148 πεπνυμένος) 'went to lay'
(imperf.) 'all the word of the Achaeans
before Priam,' and to obtain his sanction
for the calling of the assembly. Thereupon (**ἔνθα**, v. 40) the heralds went
forth to convoke it. (I can see no need
for changing the **σάμαινεν** of the MS.
to σάμανεν, with Blass.)

Somewhere, then, in the course of the
lost verses the sons of Antenor came
on the scene. Antenor himself (we may
suppose) had previously learned the wishes
of the envoys : there is nothing to show
that he is imagined as present here.
According to the schol. on *Il.* 24.
496, B. represented Theano as having
borne fifty sons to Antenor (only ten are
named in the *Iliad*). This mention may
have occurred in the verses lost between
31 and 37. Was his choice of that
surprising number connected with the
requirements of a κύκλιος χορός, which
consisted of fifty members (Simon. fr.
147, 476 B.C.)? The Antenoridae, as
such a chorus, may have formed a
spectacular element in the production
of this dithyramb.

42 f. **φάλαγγας**: a term applied in
the *Iliad* only to the 'ranks' of men
drawn up in battle array, or engaged
in fighting. But the poet may have had
in mind the phrase describing how the

Achaeans 'marched forth by companies
to the place of assembly,' ἐστιχόωντο |
ἰλαδὸν εἰς ἀγορήν (*Il.* 2. 92).—**δεξίστρατον**
only here : cp. δεξίδωρος, δεξίθεος, δεξί-
μηλος, δεξίπυρος.—**εἰς** (instead of ἐς) is
extant in B. only here and in εἰσάνταν
(v. 110).

44 f. **αὐδάεις**, 'loud': Aesch. *Eum.*
380 αὐδᾶται φάτις.—**ἀνίσχοντες χέρας** :
III. 36 n.

46 **παύσασθαι δυᾶν.** Weil observes
that B. seems here to conceive the
embassy as occurring in the middle
of the war, and not before its commencement. Rather, I think, he is
following the Κύπρια, which must have
been his chief authority. According to
the summary of that epic given by Proclus
in his Χρηστομάθεια, two battles between
Greeks and Trojans occurred soon after
the landing of the invaders, and *before*
the embassy. In the first encounter the
Trojans were victorious; in the second,
they were defeated.

47 **Μοῦσα, τίς πρῶτος...**; in the
epic style (*Il.* 1. 8 etc.). Pind. *P.* IV. 70
τίς γὰρ ἀρχὰ δέξατο ναυτιλίας;—**λόγων**...
δικαίων, 'righteous pleas' for the restoration of Helen.—The MS. places ἆρχεν
before λόγων: cp. IX. 19 n.
48 **Πλεισθενίδας.** According to a
post-Homeric genealogy of the Pelopidae,
the father of Agamemnon and Menelaus

7 φθέγξατ᾽, εὐπέπλοισι κοινώσας Χάρισσιν·

ἀντ. γ. 50 1 ὦ Τρῶες ἀρηΐφιλοι,
2 Ζεὺς ὑψιμέδων, ὃς ἅπαντα δέρκεται,
3 οὐκ αἴτιος θνατοῖς μεγάλων ἀχέων,
4 ἀλλ᾽ ἐν μέσῳ κεῖται κιχεῖν
5 πᾶσιν ἀνθρώποις Δίκαν ἰθεῖαν, ἁγνᾶς
55 6 Εὐνομίας ἀκόλουθον καὶ πινυτᾶς Θέμιτος·
7 ὀλβίων παῖδές νιν αἱρεῦνται σύνοικον.

ἐπ. γ. 1 ἁ δ᾽ αἰόλοις κέρδεσσι καὶ ἀφροσύναις
2 ἐξαισίοις θάλλουσ᾽ ἀθαμβὴς
3 Ὕβρις, ἁ πλ[οῦτον] δύναμίν τε θοῶς
60 4 ἀλλότριον ὤπασεν, αὖτις
5 δ᾽ ἐς βαθὺν πέμπει φθόρον,
6 κεῖνα καὶ ὑπερφιάλους
7 Γᾶς παῖδας ὤλεσσεν Γίγαντας.

50—56 These seven verses are quoted by Clem. Alex. *Strom.* v. 731, without the poet's name (ὁ λυρικός φησι). Sylburg and Boeckh rightly gave them to B., though for a wrong reason, viz. because B. had made Cassandra predict the fall of Troy (Porphyrion on Hor. *C.* I. 15, and schol. Statius *Th.* VII. 330): Bergk⁴ fr. 29. Clement supplies the defects of our MS. in 51—53. **54** Δίκαν ἰθεῖαν] ΔΙΚΑΛΗΘΗΑΝ (ΛΗ instead of ΝΙ) **A**: **A**³ wrote ΝΪ above, and altered the second

---

was not Atreus, but his son Pleisthenes. This occurs first in Stesichorus fr. 42, where Agamemnon is βασιλεὺς Πλεισθενίδας. Aesch. *Agam.* 1602 πᾶν τὸ Πλεισθένους γένος: *id.* 1569 δαίμονι τῷ Πλεισθενιδᾶν.

In **θελξιεπεῖ** the second part of the compound denotes the θέλκτρον (and not, as in θελξίνοος, the object): cp. *Epigr. Gr.* 1053 θελξιμελὴς...φόρμιγξ.

49 κοινώσας Χάρισσιν, having taken counsel of the Graces, *i.e.* happily inspired by them. The object of κοινώσας is left to be understood from the context: it is φθέγματα, λόγον, or the like, suggested by φθέγξατο. (Jurenka, less well, supplies γᾶρυν.) In Pind. *P.* IV. 115 the object is expressed, νυκτὶ κοινάσαντες ὁδόν ('when Night alone knew the secret of their way'). The use of the middle voice, however, illustrates the ellipse here. The full phrase is κοινοῦσθαί τινί τι, 'to consult one about a thing' (Xen. *H.* VII. 1. 27 τῷ μὲν θεῷ οὐδὲν ἐκοινώσαντο,...αὐτοὶ δὲ ἐβουλεύοντο): but κοινοῦσθαί τινι (without an acc.) also occurs (Xen. *An.* V. 6. 27). —The Charites gave eloquence no less

than song; thus an epigram (*Anth.* VII. 416) describes a poet who was also an orator as τὸν σὺν Ἔρωτι | καὶ Μούσαις κεράσαντ᾽ ἡδυλόγους Χάριτας.

50—56 Clement's citation of these verses (cr. n.) is introduced by the words, κακῶν γὰρ ὁ θεὸς οὔποτε αἴτιος.

52 οὐκ αἴτιος: cp. the words of Zeus to the gods (*Od.* I. 32), ὦ πόποι, οἷον δή νυ θεοὺς βροτοὶ αἰτιόωνται· | ἐξ ἡμέων γάρ φασι κάκ᾽ ἔμμεναι· οἱ δὲ καὶ αὐτοὶ | σφῇσιν ἀτασθαλίῃσιν ὑπὲρ μόρον ἄλγε᾽ ἔχουσιν. Eur. fr. 254 πόλλ᾽, ὦ τέκνον, σφάλλουσιν ἀνθρώπους θεοί.—τὸ ῥᾷστον εἶπας, αἰτιάσασθαι θεούς.

53—55 ἐν μέσῳ κεῖται, it is 'open to all men,'—like a prize proposed in a competition for which all may enter. Dem. or. 4 § 5 ἄθλα τοῦ πολέμου κείμενα ἐν μέσῳ. Cp. the fragment in Clem. Alex. *Strom.* 5. 654 (Bergk⁴ *adesp.* 86 B), οὐ γὰρ ἐν μέσοισι κεῖται | δῶρα δυσμάχητα Μοισᾶν | τὠπιτυχόντι φέρειν. — κιχεῖν, 'reach,' 'attain to,' as to a goal. Hesiod (*Op.* 289 ff.) and Simonides (fr. 58) place Ἀρετή on a height which men must climb with toil.—Δίκαν ἰθεῖαν 'straightforward'

counselled of the fair-robed Graces:

'Warriors of Troy, Zeus, who rules on high and beholds all ant. 3.
things, is not the author of grievous woes for mortals. No,
open before all men is the path that leads to unswerving Justice,
attendant of holy Eunomia and prudent Themis: happy the
land whose sons take her to dwell with them.

'But Insolence,—the spirit, void of reverence, who luxuriates epode 3.
in shifty wiles and illicit follies,—who swiftly gives a man his
neighbour's wealth and power, but anon plunges him into a
gulf of ruin,—she it was who destroyed the Giants, overweening
sons of Earth...'

Η to ΕΙ.—Δίκαν ὁσίαν Clem.—ἀγνᾶς] ἀγνὰν Clem. : corrected conjecturally by Bergk.
55 ἀκόλουθον omitted by A: added above line by A³.—Θέμιτος] Θέμιδος Clem. : corr.
Bergk.   56 νιν] ὦ νιν Clem. : ὦ deleted by Neue.—αἱρεῦνται] εὑρόντες Clem.—
σύνοικον] CΥΝΔΙΚΟΝ A: corr. A³.   57 κέρδεσσι Blass : ψεύδεσσι K. (Palmer):
the traces before ΔΕCCI seem to suit the former best.   59 ἃ J.: ἁ K.—πλοῦτον
Palmer.   61 δ'] The slight traces before ΕC suit Δ', as I noted in Class. Rev.
XII. 131 (Mar. 1898).—σφ' conj. Platt.   63 ὤλεσσεν K.: ΩΛΕCΕΝ MS.

Justice (v. 6 εὐθύδικος): contrast Hes.
Op. 219 σκολιῇσι δίκῃσι. Justice is 'attendant on holy Eunomia and prudent
Themis': i.e. justice as between men is
secured by good laws administered in
a righteous spirit. Δίκη guards the relative rights derived from a principle of
Right, Θέμις. Hence Themis was called
the mother of Eunomia and Dike: see
n. on XII. 182—186.
56 ὀλβίων παῖδες: Il. 6. 127 δυστή-
νων δέ τε παῖδες ἐμῷ μένει ἀντιόωσιν.—
σύνοικον: Soph. Ant. 451 οὐδ' ἡ σύνοικος
τῶν κάτω θεῶν Δίκη. Smyth refers to
Ariphron (of Sicyon, c. 410 B.C.?), fr.
of a paean to Ὑγίεια (Bergk⁴ III. p. 596),
σὺ δέ μοι πρόφρων σύνοικος εἴης.
57—63 In v. 59 we should read ἁ
πλοῦτον, not ἅ. Two views of the construction are possible: I prefer the first.
(1) Place a comma only after φθόρον,
when κείνα will serve merely to resume
the subject Ὕβρις: 'Insolence,...who
enriches and then ruins men,—she too
it was who destroyed the Giants. (2) A
colon or full stop might stand after
φθόρον. The δ' after αὗτις would then
bring in the apodosis. 'Insolence,...
who enriches men,...then presently (αὗτις
δὲ) ruins them. She too is was,' etc.
For this use of δέ, cp. Il. 5. 438 ἀλλ'
ὅτε δὴ τὸ τέταρτον ἐπέσσυτο δαίμονι ἶσος, |
δεινὰ δ' ὁμοκλήσας προσέφη ἑκάεργος
Ἀπόλλων: and Thuc. I. 11 § 1 ἐπειδὴ
δὲ...ἐκράτησαν, φαίνονται δ' κ.τ.λ.

57 f. αἰόλοις, 'shifty': Pind. N. VIII.
25 αἰόλῳ ψεύδει.—κέρδεσσι, 'wiles': Il.
23. 709 κέρδεα εἰδώς: Pind. P. I. 92
εὐτραπέλοις κέρδεσι.—ἐξαισίοις, exceeding αἶσα, breaking the bounds set for
mortals: 'illicit,' 'lawless': Od. 4. 690
ῥέξας ἐξαίσιον. In ἀφροσύναις ἐξαισίοις
there is a reference to Paris, led by his
mad passion to sin against Zeus Xenios.
—ἀθαμβής, devoid of awe, reverencing
nothing: cp. ἀναιδής. Ibycus fr. 1 (Ἔρως)
ἄσσων παρὰ Κύπριδος ἀζαλέαις μανίαισιν
ἐρεμνὸς ἀθαμβής. Phrynichus fr. 2 σῶμα
δ' ἀθαμβὲς γυιοδόνηται. Plut. Lyc. 16
βρέφη . . ἀθαμβῆ σκότου ('unawed by').
61 δ' ἐς: for δέ as first word of
the verse, cp. XVI. 13, Pind. P. IV.
180.
62 f. ὑπερφιάλους: here in the bad
sense, 'overweening': see on X. 78. Γᾶς
παῖδας...Γίγαντας. The Γίγαντες, who
are unknown to the Iliad, appear in the
Odyssey as a 'haughty' race (ὑπερθύμοισι),
ruled by Eurymedon (an ancestor of the
Phaeacian king Alcinous): 'he destroyed
his infatuate folk (λαὸν ἀτάσθαλον), and
was himself destroyed' (Od. 7. 60),—
how, we are not told. The Odyssey
says nothing of a Giants' War with gods.
Neither does the Theogony, though it
describes the Giants as the fierce sons of
Gaia, τεύχεσι λαμπομένους, δολίχ' ἔγχεα
χερσὶν ἔχοντας (185 f.). Here, however,
B. must be alluding to their war against
the Olympians. Xenophanes refers to

XV. [XVI.]

[ΗΡΑΚΛΗC]

στρ.

1 Πυθ]ίου [ἔπ᾿ εἶμ᾿], ἐπεὶ
2 ὁλκ]άδ᾿ ἔπεμψεν ἐμοὶ χρυσέαν
3 Πιερ]ίαθε[ν ἐΰθ]ρονος Οὐρανία,
4 πολυφ]άτων γέμουσαν ὕμνων
5 ἐς θεόν,] εἴτ᾿ ἄρ᾿ ἐπ᾿ ἀνθεμόεντι Ἕβρῳ

XV. The title [ΗΡΑΚΛΗC] is conjecturally supplied by K. The left margin of the papyrus, in which it may have stood, has been torn off. The rent begins at XIV. 61, and extends to the bottom of the column (XV. 8), being widest in XV. 4—8. **1** The letter before ΟΥ is either I, or a letter ending with an upright stroke, such as Ν. The space before ΟΥ would not suffice for more than 4 letters, even if one of them was thin. The space between ου and ἐπεὶ corresponds to 4 letters (ΔΑϹΩ) in the line above (XIV. 63), and again to 4 (ΕΠΕΜ) in v. 2: but there would be room for 5, if one or more were thin (as Ε, Ι). The first letter after ΟΥ is torn out: the second may have been Π or Γ: the third, which Blass makes Ο, might (as Kenyon agrees) equally well be Ε. Hence Πυθίου ἄγ᾿ οἶμ᾿ (Blass), or ἔπ᾿ εἶμ᾿ (J.), is possible. But Λαός μου ἄκου᾿ (Crusius) requires too much space before ου: while πᾶς

this, fr. 1. 21 μάχας διέπειν Τιτήνων οὐδὲ Γιγάντων : but the earliest source for a definite myth is in Pindar *N.* I. 67 f. ὅτάν θεοὶ ἐν πεδίῳ Φλέγρας Γιγάντεσσιν μάχαν | ἀντιάζωσιν : Heracles fought on the gods' side. This Phlegra was identified with the isthmus of Pallene (Her. VII. 123). The Γιγαντομαχία was a sequel to the Τιτανομαχία : Earth brought forth the Giants to avenge the Titans (Claudian *Gigantom.* 2 *Titanum...crebros miserata dolores*). Zeus was Γιγαντολέτωρ (Lucian *Timon* 4), and Athena Γιγαντολέτειρα (Suidas *s.v.*). The Giant-saga was a product of local folk-lore rather than a poetic creation, being associated with places where volcanic forces were or had been active : eruptions and earthquakes were ascribed to δαίμονες imprisoned under ground. The Γιγαντομαχία often supplied motives to vase-painting and to sculpture, as on the pediment of the Megarian thesaurus at Olympia (Paus. 6. 19. 3), the metopes of Selinus, and the metopes of the Parthenon.

The ancients took γίγας as = 'earth-born' (*Etym. M.*, Eustath. on *Il.* 4. 159, p. 1490. 19) ; a derivation which Lobeck sought to support by assuming γίς as =γῆ. G. Curtius (I. p. 204) refers the word to rt γα (γε-γα-ώς), γι-γα(ντ)-s : and Schwenck (*ap.* Roscher p. 1653) regards γι as a re-

duplication. The primary sense might then be merely, 'of mighty growth' ; as Hesych. explains γίγας by μέγας, ἰσχυρός, ὑπερφυής. At any rate no awkward tautology was felt in such a phrase as Γᾶς παῖδες Γίγαντες, or γηγενὴς | στρατὸς Γιγάντων (Soph. *Tr.* 1058 f.).

XV. 1—12 On the text of this passage see Appendix.

1—4 Πυθίου ἔπ᾿ εἶμ᾿. At Delphi during the three winter months, when Apollo was supposed to be absent, the cult of Dionysus was in the foreground, and *dithyrambs* took the place of *paeans* (Plut. περὶ τοῦ Ε τοῦ ἐν Δελφοῖς, c. 9). This ode seems to be a dithyramb written for performance at Delphi, probably towards the end of winter. The πολύφατοι ὕμνοι which Urania has sent to the poet must be such as suited the Pythian cult. There is perhaps a special reference to hymns of the kind called κλητικοί, by which Apollo would be invited to return from the north to Delphi. Menander of Laodicea (*c.* 200 A.D.?), in his Περὶ ἐπιδεικτικῶν c. 2 (Walz *Rhet.* IX. p. 132), mentions Bacchylides as a writer of the kindred class called ἀποπεμπτικοί, hymns by which a god was sped on his journey. Thus the poet says, in effect :—'I will repair to Apollo's temple, for the Muse

XV. [XVI.]

HERACLES.

I will go towards the temple of Pytho's lord, since fair- str.
throned Urania has sent me from Pieria a golden argosy
freighted with songs of fame [concerning the god],—whether,
on the flowery banks of Hebrus,

μου τις ἄκου' (Jurenka) inserts too much between ου and ἐπεί.   **2** ὀλκάδ' Sandys.
3 Πιερίαθεν Blass: εὔθρονος J. (*Class. R.* XII. 132), and now Blass (who first proposed
ἐπὶ φρένας).   **4** The space before -άτων suffices for 5 letters.   πολυφάτων K.: see
comment.   **5—8** For the conjectural supplements see Appendix.   **5** At
a distance of about six letters from the beginning of the verse, E is clear. The letter
before it was probably N. The right-hand vertical stroke is traceable; also a spot of
ink in a position which would correspond with the middle of the cross-stroke. A space
of about 6 letters separates this E from ἀνθεμόεντι "Εβρω[ι. The letters after E seem
to have been ΙΤ (or ΙΓ). The next (4?) letters are uncertain. Blass gives εἴτ' ἄρ'
ἐπ', and there is nothing in the traces which excludes this.—Between ἀνθεμόεντι and
"Εβρωι Blass inserts που.

---

has given me themes meet for this season
at Delphi.' Cp. fr. 11 (οὐχ ἕδρας κ.τ.λ.),
the beginning of a ὑπόρχημα: ''Tis no
time for sitting still or tarrying; we must
go to the rich temple of Itonia with
golden aegis, and show forth some choice
strain.'—Πυθίου, neut.: ἐπί with gen.,
'towards' (Her. IV. 14 ἰόντι ἐπὶ Κυζί-
κου).
2 ὀλκάδ'. Poets not seldom compare
themselves to voyagers (Pind. *P.* II. 62,
Verg. *G.* IV. 116 ff., etc.); and Pindar says
of an ode, τόδε μὲν κατὰ Φοίνισσαν ἐμπο-
λὰν | μέλος ὑπὲρ πολιᾶς ἁλὸς πέμπεται (*P.*
II. 67). But the image used here,—that
of an argosy sent by the Muse,—is novel.
The word ὀλκάς is used by Pindar with
reference to his song, but in a wholly
different context: his work is not fixed
in one place, like a statue, but is to
go forth from Aegina ἐπὶ πάσας ὀλκάδος
ἔν τ' ἀκάτῳ, 'on every ship of burden
and in every boat.' ὀλκάς there is not
figurative but literal.—χρυσέαν with ῠ,
as in IX. 6.
3 Πιερίαθεν] Pieria, a narrow district
in the s.w. corner of Macedonia on the
w. coast of the Thermaic Gulf, between
the Peneius and the Haliacmon. It was
the cradle of a primitive poetry linked
with a cult of the Muses ('Pierides'),
and was the legendary birthplace of
Orpheus.—Οὐρανία: see v. 176 n.
4 πολυφάτων seems probable (Pind.
O. I. 8 ὁ πολύφατος ὕμνος: *N.* VII. 81

πολύφατον θρόον ὕμνων). After Οὐρανία,
a word beginning with a consonant is
wanted, since in the corresponding vv.,
15 and 16, the division of φῶθ' between
the two verses shows synaphea.
5 About six letters, of which the last
was probably N, formed the dactyl lost
before εἴτ'. I suggest ἐς θεόν, to go with
ὕμνων, hymns 'relating to the god.' Such
would be (e.g.) ὕμνοι κλητικοί, praying
him to return (see on 1—4). A reference
to Apollo is not indispensable here, since
the subject to ἀγάλλεται in v. 6 might be
Πύθιος, supplied from Πυθίου (v. 1); but
it is desirable.
εἴτ', followed by ἤ, as in Eur. *I. T.*
272 f. εἴτ' οὖν ἐπ' ἀκταῖς θάσσετον Διοσ-
κόρω, | ἢ Νηρέως ἀγάλμαθ': conversely
ἤ...εἴτε in Soph. *Ai.* 177 f., Eur. *Alc.* 114.
—"Εβρῳ: now the *Maritza*. It rises in
the N.W. of Thrace, s. of the Haemus
range, and flows into the Aegean: the
broad mountain wilds of Rhodope (*Despot
Planina*) lie s.w. of its upper course.
ἀνθεμόεντι: a purely conventional epithet
(cp. 34 βαθυέντι and XVIII. 39 f.). Classical
poets more often associate the Hebrus
with wintry cold (Theocr. VII. 110, Verg.
Aen. XII. 331, Hor. *Epist.* I. xvi. 13).
Alcaeus was our poet's authority for
naming the Hebrus in connexion with
Apollo's northern ἀποδημία. Schol.Theocr.
l.c., 'Αλκαῖός φησιν ὅτι "Εβρος κάλλιστος
ποταμῶν: this occurred no doubt in his
hymn (of which Himerius or. XIV. 10

6 θηρσὶν ἀ]γάλλεται ἢ δολιχαύχενι κύκνῳ,
7 ὀπὶ ἀ]δεῖα φρένα τερπόμενος,
8 μέχρι Πυθῶνά]δ᾽ ἵκῃ παιηόνων
Col. 32   9 ἄνθεα πεδοιχνεῖν,
10 Πύθι᾽ Ἄπολλον,
11 τόσα χοροὶ Δελφῶν
12 σὸν κελάδησαν παρ᾽ ἀγακλέα ναόν.

ἀντ.   1 πρίν γε κλέομεν λιπεῖν
2 Οἰχαλίαν πυρὶ δαπτομέναν
15   3 Ἀμφιτρυωνιάδαν θρασυμηδέα φῶ-
4 θ᾽, ἵκετο δ᾽ ἀμφικύμον᾽ ἀκτάν·
5 ἔνθ᾽ ἀπὸ λαΐδος εὐρυνεφεῖ Κηναίῳ
6 Ζηνὶ θύεν βαρυαχέας ἐννέα ταύρους

6 Before Α]ΓΑΛΛΕΤΑΙ there is room for 6 letters, if at least two of them were thin (as Β, Ε, Θ, Ι, or C).—The letter after ἀγάλλεται is Ĥ (ἤ), not Ĥ (ᾗ Κ.).   **7** After ΔΕΪΑ there has been an erasure. Blass thinks that the scribe wrote Ι, that a corrector cancelled it, and that finally it was made into Ν.—What now stands there looks like Ν with a line drawn through it.   Before [Α]ΔΕΪΑ(Ι) there cannot have been room for more than four letters, of which one at least must have been thin.   **8** παιηόνων

---

gives a brief abstract in prose) describing Apollo's visit to the Hyperboreans. Aristophanes, too, may have had Alcaeus in mind, *Av.* 772 ff.: τοιάδε κύκνοι... | ξυμμιγῆ βοὰν ὁμοῦ | πτεροῖς κρέκοντες ἴαχον Ἀπόλλω,... | ὄχθῳ ἐφεζόμενοι παρ᾽ Ἔβρον ποταμόν.   In ἀνθεμόεντι Ἔβρῳ (⏑–⏑–⏑–) the hiatus is excused by the aspirate.   In εὐρυνεφεῖ Κηναίῳ (v. 17) ⏒–– is substituted for ⏒⏑–.   **6** I suggest θηρσὶν as a possible supplement. In the passage of the *Aves* just quoted, the φῦλα...ποικίλα θηρῶν are mentioned (777). As to Apollo *the hunter*, often associated with Artemis Agrotera, see Aesch. fr. 200 ἀγρεὺς δ᾽ Ἀπόλλων ὀρθὸν ἰθύνοι βέλος: Soph. *O. C.* 1091 τὸν ἀγρευτὰν Ἀπόλλω: the Xenophontic *Cynegeticus* 1, § 1 τὸ μὲν εὕρημα θεῶν, Ἀπόλλωνος καὶ Ἀρτέμιδος, ἄγραι καὶ κύνες: *ib.* 6. 13 (the hunter should pray) τῷ Ἀπόλλωνι καὶ Ἀρτέμιδι τῇ Ἀγροτέρᾳ μεταδοῦναι τῆς θήρας. At Megara there was a temple dedicated to Ἄρτεμις Ἀγροτέρα and Ἀπόλλων Ἀγραῖος (Paus. 1. 41. 3).   —κύκνῳ: the swan was sacred to Apollo, being probably a symbol of the spring-god. A chariot drawn by swans was the gift of Zeus to him (Alcaeus fr. 2).   **7** ἀδείᾳ: there is no other example of

diaeresis in this word; but it is certain here.   **8 f.** The lacuna in the MS. before δ᾽ ἵκῃ could not hold more than six letters. But the scansion required for the lost syllables is ⏑⏑–⏑ (cp. v. 20). To find six letters which shall give that metre, and also fit the sense, seems impossible. The corresponding syllables in v. 20 contain thirteen letters. The hypothesis that syllables belonging to v. 8 had been wrongly attached to v. 7 is excluded by the space in the MS. after τερπόμενος. It seems, then, almost certain that the text of the papyrus was defective here. A defect may have existed in the MS. which the scribe copied; or, as is perhaps more likely, he did not infrequently; thus in v. 12 he left out the letters γα of ἀγακλέα, and in XIV. 55 the word ἀκόλουθον. I suggest μέχρι Πυθῶνάδ᾽ ἵκῃ. The last syllable (-νος) of v. 7 must be long, and therefore, as there is synaphea (cp. 19 f.), v. 8 must begin with a consonant. For μέχρι with a simple subjunctive, cp. Her. IV. 119, Thuc. I. 137 § 2: for the ἔ, Ar. *Vesp.* 700.   —See Appendix.   Πυθῶνάδ᾽ (Πυθῶαδ Blass, see Appendix): cp. Pind. *O.* VI. 37 Πυθῶνάδ᾽... ᾤχετ᾽ ἰών: IX. 12 ἵει γλυκὺν Πυθῶνάδ᾽

he is taking his joy [in the chase], or in swan with slender
neck, charmed in soul by its sweet voice ;—[until,] O Pythian
Apollo, thou returnest [to Pytho], to seek those flowers of
song, those many paeans, which choruses of Delphians are
wont to uplift at thy glorious shrine.

Meanwhile, we sing how Amphitryon's son, the adventurous ant.
hero, left Oechalia a prey to fire : then came he to the sea-
washed cape, where he was to offer from his spoil nine bellowing
bulls to Cenaean Zeus, lord of far-spread clouds,

(Wilamowitz, Desrousseaux) is certain : in the MS. the top of the II has been effaced.
The letters before παιηόνων are ΙΚΗΙ (of Η only ΙΙ remains). The letter before
ΙΚΗΙ must have been Δ or Λ. The space between Δ and the beginning of the verse
may just have held 6 letters (if one at least was thin), but not more.   11 τόσα K.:
ΤΟCCΑ MS.   12 ἀγακλέα] ΑΚΛΕΑ Α : γα added above line by Α³.   13 κλέομεν]
κλεέμεν (inf.) Blass.

ὀϊστόν.—παιηόνων ἄνθεα : Pind. O. IX. 48
ἄνθεα δ' ὕμνων νεωτέρων. — πεδοιχνεῖν,
infin. of purpose after ἵκη (cp. Thuc. VI.
50 § 4 δέκα τῶν νεῶν προὔπεμψαν...κατα-
σκέψασθαι). The Aeolic πεδ- does not
occur elsewhere in B. : was he influenced
here by a reminiscence of Alcaeus? (See
on v. 5.)
    11 f. τόσα, relative ; a rare use (I.
37 n.), admitted here, perhaps, to avoid
a syllaba anceps at the end of v. 10 (cp.
v. 22, ending with βοῦν).—κελάδησαν,
gnomic aor.
    13 πρίν γε κλέομεν. The meaning of
πρίν is shown by the preceding verses
(8—12), which speak of Apollo's return
(in spring) to Delphi. πρίν is the adverb.
'Before (that moment)'—i.e. 'Ere thou
comest,'—while Delphi yet awaits thee,
and it is still the season of dithyrambs,—
'we sing how Heracles left Oechalia,'
etc. The emphasis given by γε is thus
appropriate.—For ἔ before κλ, cp. III. 3,
VII. 9 f., XVI. 127 f.
    14 Οἰχαλίαν, the city of Eurytus,
father of Iole. The Euboean Oechalia
was placed by legend in the territory
of Eretria (Hecataeus ap. Paus. 4. 2. 3:
Strabo 10, p. 448). After sacking
Oechalia, Heracles marched some fifty
miles N.W. to Κήναιον, the ἀμφικύμων
ἀκτά of v. 16. This promontory (now
Cape Litháda) forms the end of a
peninsula which runs out westward, at
the N.W. extremity of Euboea, towards
the mouth of the Malian Gulf. Zeus
Κήναιος was worshipped on the hill-tops
near it: Aesch. fr. 29 Εὐβοῖδα κάμπτων
ἀμφὶ Κηναίου Διὸς | ἀκτήν : Soph. Tr.

238. At Cenaeum Heracles prepared sacrifices to Zeus from the spoils of Oechalia.
But meanwhile he had sent Iole, in
charge of his herald Lichas, to his home
at Trachis. Deianeira, seeing that she
had a rival, then resolved to use the
'philtre' given her by Nessus. The
fatal χιτών, steeped in it, was brought
by Lichas to Heracles at the moment
when he was about to begin the sacrifice;
and he put it on. As soon as the flames
blazed up at the altar at which he stood,
the tunic became glued to his flesh, and
'the venom began to devour him' (Soph.
Tr. 771): he was carried across the strait
to Mount Oeta, and there, by his own
command, burned on a pyre.
    15 f. Ἀμφιτρυωνιάδαν : v. 156 n.—
ἵκετο with ἵ (cp. v. 4), as in Il. 13. 837,
19. 115.—ἀμφικύμον' ἀκτάν : Soph. Tr.
752 ἀκτή τις ἀμφίκλυστος : the only point
which distinctly suggests that these verses
were in the mind of Sophocles when he
wrote Tr. 750—762. The epithets were,
however, obvious. The epic Οἰχαλίας
ἅλωσις, attributed to Creophylus of Samos,
must have been one of the sources from
which Sophocles derived his material,
and may have been also used by B. This
would suffice to account for a general
resemblance between our passage and
that in the Trachiniae. As to the details
of the sacrifice, those given in vv. 18—20
differ from Tr. 760—762. It would be
gratuitous to assume that μέλλοντι...
τεύχειν in Tr. 756 was imitated from
θύεν...μέλλε here, or λείας ἀπαρχὴν ib.
761 from ἀπὸ λαΐδος.
    17 f. Κηναίῳ : n. on 14. — θύεν,

25—2

7 δύο τ' ὀρσιάλῳ δαμασίχθονι μέλ-
20 8 λε κόρᾳ τ' ὀβριμοδερκεῖ ἄζυγα
9 παρθένῳ Ἀθάνᾳ
10 ὑψικέραν βοῦν.
11 τότ' ἄμαχος δαίμων
12 Δαϊανείρᾳ πολύδακρυν ὕφανε

ἐπ. 25 1 μῆτιν ἐπίφρον', ἐπεὶ
2 πύθετ' ἀγγελίαν ταλαπενθέα,
3 Ἰόλαν ὅτι λευκώλενον
4 Διὸς υἱὸς ἀταρβομάχας
5 ἄλοχον λιπαρὸ[ν π]οτὶ δόμον πέμποι.
30 6 ἆ δύσμορος, ἆ τάλαιν', οἷον ἐμήσατο·
7 φθόνος εὐρυβίας νιν ἀπώλεσεν,
8 δνόφεόν τε κάλυμμα τῶν
9 ὕστερον ἐρχομένων,
10 ὅτ' ἐπὶ ῥοδόεντι Λυκόρμᾳ
35 11 δέξατο Νέσσου πάρα δαιμόνιον τέρ[ας.

---

20 ΚΟΡΑΙΔ **A**: T written above Δ (by **A²**?).　　**22** ὑψικέρᾱν sic MS.
24 ΔΑΪΑΝΕΙΡᾹ **A**: I added by **A¹**.　　**29** λιπαρὸν] λιπαρὰν Platt (cp. v. 169).

Doric inf.; cp. ἐρύκεν XVI. 41, ἴσχεν 88: φυλάσσεν XVIII. 25.—μέλλε with pres.: III. 30 n.

19 Neither epithet for Poseidon occurs elsewhere. **δαμασίχθονι**, 'earth-subduing,' having earth in his power; as he is able to upheave it with his τρίαινα: the notion is the same, then, as in σεισίχθων, ἐννοσίγαιος. From another point of view he is γαιήοχος, 'earth-encircling' (or perhaps 'earth-upholding,' as though it rested on his waters).

20 ὀβριμοδερκεῖ (only here), 'of fierce aspect' (cp. ὀβριμοεργός, the notion of 'strong' passing into that of 'violent'). So it is said of her in Il. 1. 199, δεινὼ δέ οἱ ὄσσε φάανθεν: Soph. Ai. 450 ἡ Διὸς γοργῶπις ἀδάματος θεά (γοργ. also in fr. 760. 2). The attribute of flashing eyes suits her as a war-goddess (περσέπολις etc.), but really points to her older meaning as a weather-daimon, the Athena who springs armed from the head of Zeus

(the lightning that splits the storm-cloud). —The hiatus is unobjectionable, since the syllable before ἄζυγα, though corresponding with one which is long in v. 8, might equally well be short. (The γ' which Blass adds after ὀβριμοδερκεῖ is undesirable.)

ἄζυγα: so, in the sacrifice to Athena prescribed by Helenus (Il. 6. 94), the oxen are to be ἠκέστας, such as 'have not felt the goad.'

22 ὑψικέραν (like καλλικέραν in XVIII. 24), as if from a fem. nomin. ὑψικέρα. If it were contracted from -κεράν, the accent should be -κερᾶν. Pindar fr. 325 has ὑψικερᾶτα πέτραν, as if from a nomin. ὑψίκερας.

23 τότ' refers to the time denoted by θύεν ... μέλλε, when Heracles, having reached Cenaeum, 'was intending to sacrifice.' It was from Cenaeum that he sent Lichas with Iole to Trachis, and then Deianeira made her plan. Thus τότε, though not clear, is correct. In

and twain to the god who rouses the sea and shakes the earth:
also a high-horned ox, untouched by the yoke, to the maiden
with the flashing eyes, the virgin Athena.

Then it was that the God with whom none may strive wove
for Deïaneira

a shrewd device, fraught with sorrow; when she learned the *epode.*
bitter tidings that the dauntless son of Zeus was sending to
his goodly house the white-armed Iole, his bride.
Ill-fated, hapless one, what a plan did she conceive! Potent
jealousy was her bane, and that dark veil which hid the future
when, on the rose-clad banks of Lycormas, she received from
Nessus his fateful gift of wondrous power.

32 ΔΝΟΦΕΟΝ ms.: δνοφερόν K. **34** ΕΠΙ ΠΟΤΑΜΩ. ΡΟΔΟΕΝΤΙ ms.:
corr. Ludwich and Wilamowitz. **35** ΠΑΡ **A**: α added above line by **A³**.

Tr. 756 μέλλοντι (unlike μέλλε here)
refers to the *moment just before* the
sacrifice — when Lichas returned with
Deianeira's gift.
ἄμαχος δαίμων, irresistible Destiny.
(Jurenka, less well, I think, understands
the φθόνος εὐρυβίας of v. 31, where he
prints Φθόνος.)
25 μῆτιν ἐπίφρον', the 'shrewd device' that was to work woe. ἐπίφρων =
'in possession of φρήν' (cp. ἐπίτιμος):
in *Od.* 19. 325 f. Penelope says, εἴ τι
γυναικῶν | ἀλλάων περίειμι νόον καὶ ἐπί-
φρονα μῆτιν. Cp. 23. 12 (the gods have
power) ἄφρονα ποιῆσαι καὶ ἐπίφρονά περ
μάλ' ἐόντα. In Soph. *Tr.* 554 Deianeira
speaks of her plan as λυτήριον, and the
Chorus say (589) δοκεῖς παρ' ἡμῖν οὐ
βεβουλεῦσθαι κακῶς.
26 ταλαπενθέα, here merely = 'grievous,' 'cruel': but cp. v. 157.
28 f. ἀταρβομάχας, a word peculiar
to B., like ἀδεισιβόας (v. 155 etc.). —
ἄλοχον...πέμποι, was sending her (to be)
his bride. In Soph. *Tr.* 365, where
Lichas speaks with Deianeira, Heracles
is described as sending Iole 'in no careless fashion,'—δόμους ὡς τούσδε πέμπων
οὐκ ἀφρόντιστως, γύναι, | οὐδ' ὥστε δού-
λην.—It is safer to keep the λιπαρὸν of
the ms. as a conventional epithet of
δόμον ('opulent' or 'stately'). It may
serve to suggest a contrast with Iole's

own home, a prey to sword and fire
(v. 14). λιπαρὰν (cp. v. 169) would be
unsuitable here.
30 τάλαιν' gives the more probable
metre, and is confirmed by the space
in the ms. between Λ and Ν. (So far
as the form is concerned, τάλαν could
stand: it is fem. in Ar. *Eccl.* 124, etc.)
32 δνόφεον is supported by Hesych.
δνοφέη· σκοτεινῇ. Nicander *Alex.* 501
ζοφέη νύξ.
34 ὅτ'] ὅτε is relative to the moment
implied in κάλυμμα: 'the veil which
rested on the future' at the time when
she received the gift: τὰ ἐρχόμενα ἐκαλύπ-
τετο ὅτε ἐδέξατο κ.τ.λ.—Before ῥοδόεντι
the papyrus has ποταμῷ, which mars
the metre, and was evidently a gloss
on Λυκόρμᾳ. For the epithet cp. v. 5
ἀνθεμόεντι.
Λυκόρμᾳ, the older name of the Evenus
(*Fidhári*), which rises in the Oeta-range,
and flows through Aetolia to the Corinthian
Gulf. Strabo 7. 327: ὁ Εὔηνος, ὁ Λυκόρμας
πρότερον καλούμενος. Tozer (*Geo. of Greece,*
p. 96) describes it as 'one of the fiercest
and most treacherous torrents in Greece.'
Λυκόρμας expressed the 'wolf-like rush'
of its waters.
35 τέρας: a term applied in *Il.* 5. 742
to the Γοργείη κεφαλή of Athena's aegis,
and in Pind. *O.* XIII. 73 to the golden
χαλινός given by Athena to Bellerophon.

XVI. [XVII.]

ΗΙΘΕΟΙ

Η] ΘΗCΕΥC

στρ. α΄.　1 Κυανόπρωρα μὲν ναῦς μενέκτυπον
　　　2 Θησέα δὶς ἑπτά τ᾽ ἀγλαοὺς ἄγουσα
　　　3 κούρους Ἰαόνων
　　　4 Κρητικὸν τάμνε πέλαγος·
　　5 τηλαυγέϊ γὰρ [ἐν] φάρεϊ
　　6 βορήϊαι πίτνον αὖραι
　　7 κλυτᾶς ἕκατι π[ο]λεμαίγιδος Ἀθάνας·
Col. 33　8 κνίσεν τε Μίνωϊ κέαρ
　　9 ἱμεράμπυκος θεᾶς
　10 Κύπριδος αἰνὰ δῶρα·
　11 χεῖρα δ᾽ οὐκέτι παρθενικᾶς
　12 ἄτερθ᾽ ἐράτυεν, θίγεν
　13 δὲ λευκᾶν παρηΐδων·
　14 βόασέ τ᾽ Ἐρίβοια χαλκο-

XVI. The title was added in the left margin, opposite v. 1, by **A³**: ΪΘΕΟΙ remains, with ΘΗCΕΤC below it : the rest has been torn off. Before Θησεύς, ἤ is supplied by Blass : καὶ by K. **1** ΚΤΑΝΟΠΡΩΡΑ **A**: ΚΤΑΝΟΠΡΩΙΡΑ **A¹**. **4** τάμνε K.: ΤΑΜΝΕΝ MS. **6** βορήϊαι] The ⏑ placed over A in the MS. meant that the word was nom. plur., not dat. sing. **7** πολεμαίγιδος]

XVI. 1 κυανόπρωρα, contracted from κυανοπρώειρα (spelt -πρώϊρα in *Etym. M. s. v.* πρῷρα, where the word is ascribed to Simonides). A different form is read in *Od.* 3. 299, νέας κυανοπρῳρείους.—μὲν without a following δέ: cp. IX. 47, and n. on III. 15 f.—μενέκτυπον (only here), steadfast in the din of battle: cp. Orph. Argon. 541 μενέδουπος Ἀθήνη. So μενεδήϊος, μενεπτόλεμος, μενεχάρμας. **2 f.** ἀγλαούς, of youthful beauty: cp. 103 f. ἀγλαῶν ... γυίων: v. 154 ἀγλαὰν ἥβαν.—κούρους, the seven youths and seven maidens : ἤθεοι is similarly collective in 43, 93, 128.—Ἰαόνων, Athenians, as in XVII. 2. **4** Κρητικὸν...πέλαγος, the part of the Aegean south of the Cyclades and north of Crete, often a stormy sea; Soph. *Tr.* 117 πολύπονον ὥσπερ πέλαγος Κρήσιον: Hor. *C.* 1. 26. 2 f.—The ship is sailing from Athens to Crete, and has left the

Cyclades behind. It has the north wind astern, the course being now due south. **5** τηλαυγέϊ. According to Attic legend, the ship had a black sail; but Aegeus, confident that his son would triumph, gave a white one also to the κυβερνήτης, telling him to hoist it on his return, if all had gone well. Simonides varied the story by describing the sail of good omen as *red* (φοινίκεον Plut. *Thes.* 17): τηλαυγέϊ here rather suggests a white sail.—φάρεϊ with ᾱ, as in Homer and Aesch. *Ch.* 11 (but ᾰ in Soph. *Tr.* 916: cp. *ib.* 662). **7** πολεμαίγιδος, 'with warlike aegis.' A cup (now in the Louvre) by Euphronius, a painter of red-figured vases, shows Theseus received by Amphitrite beneath the sea (vv. 109 ff.): Athena, who stands in the background, has aegis, helmet and spear: see Introd., p. 225. For the compound with πόλεμος, cp.

XVI. [XVII.]

THESEUS

OR THE ATHENIAN YOUTHS AND MAIDENS.

A dark-prowed ship was cleaving the Cretan sea, bearing str. 1.
Theseus, steadfast in the battle din, with seven goodly youths
and seven maidens of Athens; for northern breezes fell on
the far-gleaming sail, by grace of glorious Athena with warlike
aegis.
And the heart of Minos was stung by the baneful gifts of
the Cyprian goddess with lovely diadem; he could no longer
restrain his hand from a maiden, but touched her fair cheeks.
Then Eriboea cried aloud

πελεμαίγιδος conj. Housman, Headlam, Wackernagel: and so Jurenka.   **8** Μίνωϊ
J. (K.): ΜΙΝΩ ms.   **10** αἰνὰ K. (Jurenka, Smyth): ἀγνὰ Blass² (ἀβρὰ Bl.¹).
The faint traces before ΝΑ are indecisive: but the letter was either I or a thin Γ.
14 f. βόασέ τ' Blass (who found the letters Τ' ΕΡ on a small fragment): βόασε δ' K.—
λινο|θώρακα conj. Wilamowitz.

(1) *Batrachm.* 475 Παλλάδα πέμψωμεν
πολεμόκλονον: (2) Dionys. *De comp. verb.*
17 Βρόμιε...πολεμοκέλαδε: (3) schol. *Od.*
1. 48 πολεμόφρων. For the accent, cp.
μελάναιγις in *Etym. Magn.* 518, 54
(cited by Headlam). In fr. 23 (Bergk),
where the mss. give χρυσαιγίδος ('Ιτωνίας),
χρυσαίγιδος should be written.—The ingenious conjecture πελεμαίγιδος would
mean 'aegis-shaking' (πελεμίζω as =
πάλλω). The aegis of Athena, however,
is usually depicted as a short cape or
mantle, with Gorgon's head and snaky
fringes: she can spread it to the breezes
as a sail (Aesch. *Eum.* 404), but is
never described as shaking it like a
shield.
8 f. κνίσεν (ῑ), 'stung': Her. VI. 62
τὸν δὲ 'Αρίστωνα ἔκνιζε ἄρα τῆς γυναικὸς
ταύτης ὁ ἔρως: Pind. *P.* X. 60 ἔρως
ὑπέκνιξε φρένας.—Μίνωϊ (‒‒‒) is required
by metre (cp. 31, 74, 97). That form
of the dative occurs in Diod. 5. 79,
Aelian *Nat. An.* 5. 2, Nonnus 7. 361,
etc.: but Μίνῳ in [Plat.] *Minos* 319 c.—
B. follows the same account as Hellanicus
(Plut. *Thes.* 17): Minos came to Athens
and himself chose the fourteen victims,
whom he is now taking to Crete in an
Athenian ship.—ἱμεράμπυκος: cp. v.
13 n.: Pind. *N.* VII. 15 Μναμοσύνας...
λιπαράμπυκος.
10 αἰνὰ δῶρα: she gives desires that

work woe. *Il.* 24. 30 (Paris) τὴν δ'
ἤνησ' (Aphrodite) ἥ οἱ πόρε μαχλοσύνην
ἀλεγεινήν. Soph. *Ant.* 791 (of Ἔρως),
σὺ καὶ δικαίων ἀδίκους φρένας παρασπᾷς
ἐπὶ λώβᾳ.—For αἰνὰ the only alternative
seems to be ἀγνὰ, which is unsuitable
here. (The traces in the ms. exclude
ἀβρὰ, which would otherwise be possible.) In v. 40 the ὕβρις of Minos is
πολύστονος.
11 f. παρθενικᾶς = παρθένος: as Hes.
Op. 699 παρθενικήν. These are rare
instances of the sing. used as a subst.
(though πάρθενική...νεήνιδι occurs in *Od.*
7. 20): but the plural παρθενικαί is
frequent (*Il.* 18. 567, *Od.* 11. 39, Alcman
fr. 21, Theocr. XVIII. 2).—ἐράτυεν, epic
(*Il.* 2. 97 ἐρήτυον, but 8. 345 ἐρητύοντο
with ῡ).
13 For δὲ as first word of the verse,
cp. XIV. 61 n.—λευκᾶν, 'fair,' as probably
in Eur. *Med.* 923 λευκὴν......παρηΐδα:
though there it might be 'pale,' as it
certainly is in Soph. *Ant.* 1239 λευκῇ
παρειᾷ (of the dead Antigone). The
pallor of *fear* is expressed by χλωρός.
14 f. Ἐρίβοια: so Hyginus, *Astron.*
II. 5: the François amphora (see p. 224)
has Ἐρίβοια or Ἐπίβοια. The wife
of Telamon and mother of Ajax is
called Eriboea by Pindar (*I.* v. 45) and
Sophocles (*Ai.* 569); but Periboea by
Apollod. 3. 12. 7 and Paus. I. 42. 1.

15 θώρακα Πανδίονος
16 ἔκγονον· ἴδεν δὲ Θησεύς,
17 μέλαν δ' ὑπ' ὀφρύων
18 δίνασεν ὄμμα, καρδίαν τέ (F)οι
19 σχέτλιον ἄμυξεν ἄλγος,
20 εἰρέν τε· Διὸς υἱὲ φερτάτου,
21 ὅσιον οὐκέτι τεᾶν
22 ἔσω κυβερνᾶς φρενῶν
23 θυμόν· ἴσχε μεγαλοῦχον ἤρως βίαν.

ἀντ. α'. 1 ὅ τι μὲν ἐκ θεῶν μοῖρα παγκρατὴς
25 2 ἄμμι κατένευσε καὶ Δίκας ῥέπει τά-
3 λαντον, πεπρωμέναν
4 αἶσαν ἐκπλήσομεν, ὅταν
5 ἔλθῃ· σὺ δὲ βαρεῖαν κάτε-
6 χε μῆτιν. εἰ καί σε κεδνὰ
30 7 τέκεν λέχει Διὸς ὑπὸ κρόταφον Ἴδας
8 μιγεῖσα Φοίνικος ἐρα-
9 τώνυμος κόρα βροτῶν

20 εἰρεν] εἶπεν conj. Wilamowitz.—φερτάτοι' Wilamowitz, Platt. 22 ΚΥΒΕΡ-
ΝᾶC **A** : ι added after Â (by **A²**?). 25 f. τά|λαντον. The letters ΤΑ were repeated

χαλκοθώρακα : B. thinks of the youth-ful Theseus as hero and warrior, wearing the usual armour. (Acc. to Hellanicus, Plut. *Thes.* 17, Minos stipulated at Athens that the ἤθεοι should go on board *unarmed*; but this detail, if it was known to B., is ignored.)—**Πανδίονος**. Pandion, son of Cecrops, was father of Aegeus, the reputed father of Theseus. See on v. 36.
17—19 μέλαν probably refers simply to colour. Smyth renders it 'sombre,' 'indignant,' remarking that μέλας is seldom (as in Anacreont. 16. 12) an epithet of the eye. See, however, Arist. *Anim. Gener.* 5 a 34 τὰ δὲ τῶν ἀνθρώπων ὄμματα πολύχροα συμβέβηκεν εἶναι· καὶ γὰρ γλαυκοὶ καὶ χαροποὶ καὶ μελανό-φθαλμοί τινές εἰσι.—ὑπ' ὀφρύων, lit., 'from under...'; cp. XII. 139 f. ὑπαὶ | χει-μῶνος.—**δίνασεν**, if sound, must be from δινάω (cp. v. 191 n. on φώνησεν): we should have expected δίνησεν, from δινέω: cp. 107 δίνηντο, and v. 2 ἱππο-δινήτων.—Eur. *Or.* 837 δινεύων βλεφάροις, 'wildly rolling his eyes' (in madness), —**σχέτλιον**, 'cruel'; the only instance of the word in B.

20 εἰρεν, imperf. of εἴρω, as again in 74. This part of εἴρω occurs nowhere else. B. sought variety, having εἶπε(ν) in 47, 52, 81.—**φερτάτου**. As v. 21 begins with a vowel, it is tempting to read φερτάτοι': cp. 43 f., 86 f., 109 f. But if there was no synaphea, φερτάτου could stand.
21 f. ὅσιον ... κυβερνᾶς, keepest it within the moral law.—Cp. Aesch. *Pers.* 767 φρένες γὰρ αὐτοῦ θυμὸν ᾠακοστρόφουν.
23 μεγαλοῦχον (only here), if sound, means lit. 'possessing great things' (μεγαλο + οχος), as a king of wide dominion might be so called; hence 'lordly,' and then, in a bad sense, 'arrogant,' 'over-weening.'—Kenyon suggested **μεγάλ-αυχον**, which Blass and Jurenka adopt : cp. Pind. *P.* VIII. 15 βία δὲ καὶ μεγάλαυχον ἔσφαλεν ἐν χρόνῳ. That word would be fitter if a vaunt had accompanied the act; but Minos has not yet spoken. Further, Hesych. has μεγαλουχία· μεγαλαυχία· ὑψηλοφροσύνη. Headlam, indeed, suggests that the true reading there may be μεγαλογκία (a word used by Democritus, Stob. *Flor.* 103. 25): here, he would read μεγάλαυχον or

to Pandion's grandson with breastplate of bronze; Theseus saw, and wildly rolled his dark eyes beneath his brows, and cruel pain pricked his heart as he spake:—
'O son of peerless Zeus, the spirit in thy breast no longer obeys righteous control; withhold, hero, thy presumptuous force.

'Whatever the resistless doom given by the gods has decreed ant. i. for us, and the scale of Justice inclines to ordain, that appointed fate we will fulfil when it comes. But do thou forbear thy grievous purpose. If the noble daughter of Phoenix, the maiden of gracious fame, taken to the bed of Zeus beneath the brow of Ida, bare thee, peerless among men;

by mistake in 26 *init.*: corr. **A¹**? Cp. 58.   **29** After μῆτιν a full stop is placed by K., Jurenka, Smyth; a comma by Blass.   **31** Housman would transpose μιγεῖσα and πλαθεῖσα (35).

μεγάλογκον. But the MS. reading here and the traditional reading in Hesych. must be considered together. On the whole, I think it safer to retain μεγαλοῦχον. **24—27** ὅ τι is governed by ῥέπει as well as by κατένευσε. Δίκας τάλαντον ῥέπει τι when one of the two scales, by sinking, shows that the doom which it carries is preponderant, and so decides that it shall be operative. This transitive sense of ῥέπω is implied in the use of the passive by Aesch. *Suppl.* 405 τῶνδ' ἐξ ἴσου ῥεπομένων, 'these alternatives being evenly balanced.' Otherwise it occurs only in compounds; as Aesch. *Eum.* 888 οὖ τἂν δικαίως τῆδ' ἐπιρρέποις πόλει | μῆνίν τιν' (*cause* wrath to *descend* on the city'): *Ag.* 250 f. Δίκα δὲ τοῖς μὲν παθοῦ|σιν μαθεῖν ἐπιρρέπει: Soph. *Ant.* 1158 f. τύχη καταρρέπει | τὸν εὐτυχοῦντα ('depresses,' 'humbles').—If ῥέπει were taken here as intransitive, it would be necessary (1) to supply ὅποι from ὅ τι: or (2) to take καὶ Δίκας ῥέπει τάλαντον as a parenthesis (the so-called διὰ μέσου construction): 'whatever fate has decreed (the scales of justice inclining thereto'). But either of these two would be harsh. —For the image, cp. *Il.* 22. 210 ff.: Zeus puts δύο κῆρε...θανάτοιο in the scales, one for Achilles, and one for Hector; the latter proves the heavier (ῥέπε δ' Ἔκτορος αἴσιμον ἦμαρ), and so Hector is doomed to die.—In *Anth.* 6. 267. 4 it is said of a just man, ἰθείης οἶδε τάλαντα δίκης.—ἐκ θεῶν μοῖρα: XIII. 1 n.—ἐκπλήσομεν, a frequent phrase, as with μοῖραν (Her. III. 142), μοχθήματα (Eur. *Helen.* 741), κίνδυνον (*I.T.* 90). **29 f.** βαρεῖαν...μῆτιν, 'thy grievous

purpose' (in regard to Eriboea: vv. 8 ff.). A full stop (or at least a colon) should be placed after μῆτιν, and only a comma after φέρτατον in 33. By placing only a comma after μῆτιν, and a colon after φέρτατον (as Blass does), the spirit of the sentence beginning with εἰ καί σε is much impaired. **30** ὑπὸ κρόταφον, 'beneath the brow' of Ida. ὑπό with acc. normally means, 'along under': *Il.* 5. 27 ὅσσοι ἔασιν ὑπ' ἠῶ τ' ἠέλιόν τε: Her. v. 10 τὰ ὑπὸ τὴν ἀρκτόν: id. VI. 137 τὴν χώρην... ὑπὸ Ὑμησσὸν ἐοῦσαν (but presently κατοικημένους...ὑπὸ τῷ Ὑμησσῷ, with ref. to the fixed abode). Here the accus. (not elsewhere used by B. with ὑπό) seems to have been prompted by metrical convenience, and hardly differs in sense from the dative.—κρόταφος is the side of the forehead, in plur. the temples: said of a hill, it denotes the cliffs just below the summit (cp. ὀφρύς). Aesch. *P.V.* 721 (ὄρους) κροτάφων ἀπ' αὐτῶν: *Anthol.* append. 94 ἔναιον ὑπὸ κροτάφοις Ἑλικῶνος. **31 f.** Φοίνικος. The father of Europa was Phoenix, acc. to *Il.* 14. 321 (Zeus speaks); Φοίνικος κούρης τηλεκλειτοῖο, | ἣ τέκε μοι Μίνω τε καὶ ἀντίθεον 'Ραδά- μανθυν: and Hesiod gave the same account (schol. *Il.* 12. 292). Apollo- dorus (3. 1. 3) makes Agenor the father of Europa, Phoenix, and Cadmus; but recognizes the other version. Sidon or Tyre was named as the place from which Europa was carried off by Zeus. The legend points to the blending of Phoenician with Hellenic elements in Crete.

10 φέρτατον, ἀλλὰ κἀμὲ
11 Πιτθέος θυγάτηρ ἀφνεοῦ
35 12 πλαθεῖσα ποντίῳ τέκεν
13 Ποσειδᾶνι, χρύσεον
14 τέ (F)οι δόσαν ἰόπλοκοι
15 κάλυμμα Νηρηΐδες.
16 τῶ σε, πολέμαρχε Κνωσίων,
40 17 κέλομαι πολύστονον
18 ἐρύκεν ὕβριν· οὐ γὰρ ἂν θελοι-
Col. 34 19 μ' ἀμβρότου ἐραννὸν Ἀοῦς
20 ἰδεῖν φάος, ἐπεί τιν' ἠϊθέων
21 σὺ δαμάσειας ἀέκον-
45 22 τα· πρόσθε χειρῶν βίαν
23 δείξομεν· τὰ δ' ἐπιόντα δαίμων κρινεῖ.

---

39 τῶ Platt: τῷ K.—Κνώσιε Blass.
42 ἀμβρότου Wilamowitz: ΑΜΒΡΟΤΟΙ' MS.
40 πολύστονον κέλομαι Wilamowitz.
43 ἐπεί] ἔτ', εἰ conj. Herwerden.

ἐρατώνυμος, 'of gracious fame': cp. Hes. *Theog.* 409 Ἀστερίην εὐώνυμον. This is the sense of the adj. in Stesich. fr. 44 (in his proem to the love-story of Rhadina and Leontichos) ἄρξον ἀοιδᾶς ἐρατωνύμου | Σαμίων περὶ παίδων. (Cp. II. 2 f. χαριτώνυμον, n.)
33 φέρτατον, 'peerless' (epithet of Zeus himself in v. 20),—here emphasized by its place.—**ἀλλὰ** introduces the apodosis after εἰ καί (29): Sappho fr. 1. 22 αἱ δὲ δῶρα μὴ δέκετ', ἀλλὰ δώσει: Soph. fr. 854 εἰ σῶμα δοῦλον, ἀλλ' ὁ νοῦς ἐλεύθερος. This use of ἀλλά after εἰ μή occurs in the *Iliad* (1. 181 f.), where αὐτὰρ also is so used (22. 389).
34 Πιτθέος. Pittheus, son of Pelops, king of Troezen, was the father of Aethra (v. 59), the mother of Theseus. He was said to have founded Troezen by a συνοικισμός: hence his name has been explained as the 'Persuader' (rt πιθ-: Schneidewin *De Pittheo Troezenio*). A monument, near the Troezenian temple of Artemis Soteira, showed him sitting in judgment, with two assessors. At the Μουσεῖον there he 'taught the art of words' (Paus. 2. 30. 9, 31. 3: Plut. *Thes.* 3).—**ἀφνεοῦ,** ∪∪–: the same scansion is found in Pind. fr. 218. 4 ὃς μὲν ἀχρήμων, ἀφνεὸς τότε: Aesch. fr. 96. 3 λιπεῖν ἀφνεοῖσι δόμοισιν. Cp. ἀράχνᾶν in fr. 3. 7.
35 πλαθεῖσα: the first syllable is short

in all the corresponding places, 12, 78, 101; but as it might be *anceps*, there is no reason to suspect the reading. It is very improbable that this word should have changed places with μιγεῖσα in v. 31. (The syllable answering to the first of μιγεῖσα is long in 74, but short in 8 and 97.)
36 Ποσειδᾶνι. Isocr. or. 10 § 18 Θησεύς, ὁ λεγόμενος μὲν Αἰγέως (15 f. n.), γενόμενος δ' ἐκ Ποσειδῶνος. The story was that Poseidon had been the lover of Aethra either before or just after her union with Aegeus (Paus. 2. 33. 1: Apollod. 4. 15. 7, Hyginus *Fab.* 37). The key to the confused legend is that Aegeus and Poseidon were originally identical. Αἰγ-εύς is connected with αἶγ-ες, 'waves' (Artemidorus 2. 12 τὰ μεγάλα κύματα αἶγας ἐν τῇ συνηθείᾳ λέγομεν), αἰγ-ίς 'storm-wind,' αἰγι-αλό-ς 'shore': Curt. *Etym.* § 140. Poseidon has his deep-sea palace at the Euboean Αἰγαί (*Il.* 13. 21 ff.): he is Αἰγαῖος, Αἰγαίων. Then Αἰγεύς, from being a name for the Sea-god, became an independent hero, with a ἡρῷον at Athens (Paus. 1. 22. 5), where he was the eponymus of the Αἰγηΐς φυλή. The legends of Aegeus embody the oldest traditions of an Attic and Ionic Poseidon-cult. Troezen, where Poseidon was peculiarly honoured (Plut. *Thes.* 6), claimed Theseus as the son of her own Sea-god; and Athens did likewise.

yet I, too, was borne by the daughter of wealthy Pittheus, in wedlock with the sea-god Poseidon, and the violet-crowned Nereids gave her a golden veil.

'Therefore, O war-lord of Cnosus, I bid thee restrain thy wantonness, fraught with woe; for I should not care to look on the fair light of divine Eos, after thou hadst done violence to one of this youthful company: before that, we will come to a trial of strength, and Destiny shall decide the sequel.'

—ἠϊθέων (with the MS.) Crusius, Blass, Jurenka, assuming synizesis of έω: cp. 93, 128. ἠθέων K.

Hence the double paternity in the myth.

37 f. Verse 37, τέ (F)οί δόσαν ιόπλο-κοι, lacks a short syllable at the end, as compared with each of the three corresponding verses, 14, 80, and 103. Verse 38 begins with a short syll. (καλ), where a long is found in 15, 81, 104. (1) These two facts might suggest ιόπλοκοι κά|λυμμ' -◡. (2) If κάλυμμα belonged wholly to 38, one short syllable might be supplied after ιόπλοκοι. But no satisfactory emendation, on either plan, has yet been made. See Appendix.

38 Νηρητδες here are the same as the Νηρέος κόραι of 102 f. In his commentary on our poet's ἐπίνικοι, Didymus mentioned a distinction drawn by some grammarians:—εἰσὶ τοίνυν οἵ φασι διαφέρειν τὰς Νηρεΐδας τῶν τοῦ Νηρέως θυγατέρων, καὶ τὰς μὲν ἐκ Δωρίδος [the wife of Nereus] γνησίας αὐτοῦ θυγατέρας νομίζεσθαι, τὰς δὲ ἐξ ἄλλων ἤδη κοινότερον (as a more general term) Νηρεΐδας καλεῖσθαι. These words are quoted in the treatise περὶ ὁμοίων καὶ διαφόρων λέξεων, p. 79, which bears the name of the Alexandrian Ammonius (c. 390 A.D.); Bergk, Bacchyl. fr. 10. Nairn pointed out the neglect of the distinction here (Class. R. XI. 453).

39 τῶ (Il. 1. 418 etc.) is the spelling given by the codex Venetus (10th cent.) in all Homeric passages where the sense is 'therefore.' This was the Alexandrian tradition (cp. Lenz on Herodian I. 492, 10). Leaf regards this epic τῶ as 'a genuine relic of the old instrumental.' The Attic poets probably wrote τῷ (Soph. O. T. 511 n.).—πολέμαρχε : Aesch. Ch. 1071 f. 'Αχαιῶν | πολέμαρχος ἀνήρ.—Κνωσίων, scanned – – (see vv. 16, 82, 105): for the synizesis, cp. Od. 14. 263 Αἰγυπτίων (also Il. 9. 382 -ίας, Od. 4. 83 -ίους, etc.): Il. 2. 537 Ἱστίαιαν: Pind. P. IV. 225 γενύων (◡–).—For the spelling of Κνωσός, see I. 13 n.

41 f. ἐρύκεν: XV. 18 θύεν n.—ἀμβρότου. Keeping the MS. ἀμβρότοι', Blass supposes the last syllable to be short; he compares 92 and 129 (-αΐ in 'Αθαναίων and παιδνιξαν). But a shortening of οι in the genitive-ending -οιο is unexampled. Others defend ἀμβρότοι', holding that – ◡ – could replace the – ◡ ◡ found in 19, 85, and 108.—ἐραννὸν (an epic epithet of places) is used by Simonides fr. 45 (ἐραννὸν ὕδωρ): Pindar has only ἐρατός and ἐρατεινός.

43—45 ιδεῖν. As the sense is, 'I should not wish to live longer,' we should have expected the present inf. ὁρᾶν. But the aor. infin. may perhaps be explained in connexion with the clause ἐπεί... δαμάσειας. 'After any such deed of thine, I should not care to look again on the sunlight,'—or 'to live one moment longer.' Cp. the Homeric θαῦμα ἰδέσθαι, expressing the way in which the object strikes the beholder; as contrasted (e.g.) with ἐπεὶ οὔπω τλήσομ' ὁρᾶσθαι | μαρνάμενον φίλον υἱόν (Il. 3. 306).

ἐπεὶ...δαμάσειας: the optative in the relative clause corresponds to the hypothetical optative with ἄν in the principal clause: cp. Soph. O. C. 560 δεινὴν γάρ τιν' ἂν πρᾶξιν τύχοις | λέξας, ὁποίας ἐξαφισταίμην ἐγώ: Il. 13. 343 μάλα κεν θρασυκάρδιος εἴη | ὃς τότε γηθήσειεν.—ἠϊθέων here, as in 93 and 128, includes both youths and maidens. The word usually denotes unmarried youths only : Il. 18. 593 ἠΐθεοι καὶ παρθένοι: Plut. Thes. 15 ἠϊθέους ἑπτὰ καὶ παρθένους τοσαύτας.—ἀέκοντα : the masc. is used in the general statement, though the special reference is to Eriboea and the other maidens : Soph. El. 771 δεινὸν τὸ τίκτειν ἐστίν· οὐδὲ γὰρ κακῶς | πάσχοντι μῖσος ὧν τέκῃ προσγίγνεται.—δαμάσειας: Il. 3. 301 ἄλοχοι δ' ἄλλοισι δαμεῖεν: Od. 6. 109 παρθένος ἀδμής.

45 f. χειρῶν βίαν (X. 91) δεῖξομεν,

ἐπ. α'. 1 τόσ' εἶ]πεν ἀρέταιχμος ἥρως·
2 τάφον δὲ ναυβάται
3 φωτός] ὑπεράφανον
50 4 θάρσος· Ἀλίου τε γαμβρῷ χολώ[σατ' ἦτορ,
5 ὕφαινέ τε ποταινίαν
6 μῆτιν, εἶπέν τε· μεγαλοσθενὲς
7 Ζεῦ πάτερ, ἄκουσον· εἴπερ μ[ε κούρ]α
8 Φοίνισσα λευκώλενος σοὶ τέκε,
55 9 νῦν πρόπεμπ' ἀπ' οὐρανοῦ θ[οὰν
10 πυριέθειραν ἀστραπὰν
11 σᾶμ' ἀρίγνωτον· εἰ
12 δὲ καὶ σὲ Τροιζηνία σεισίχθονι
13 φύτευσεν Αἴθρα Ποσει-
60 14 δᾶνι, τόνδε χρύσεον
15 χειρὸς ἀγλαὸν
16 ἔνεγκε κόσμον <ἐκ> βαθείας ἁλός,
17 δικὼν θράσει σῶμα πατρὸς ἐς δόμους.
18 εἴσεαι δ' αἴ κ' ἐμᾶς κλύῃ

---

49 φωτὸς Blass : ἀνδρὸς K. The only trace of the word in the MS. is a long stroke which goes below the line, decidedly suggesting P rather than T : on the other hand the space before it seems scarcely large enough for ΑΝΔ.—ΤΠΕΡΑΦΝΟΝ **A** : after Φ the letter α has been written above the line by **A³**. **50** χολώ[σατ' ἦτορ K. : χόλῳ [ζέσ' ἦτορ Jurenka : χολώ[θη κέαρ Blass : cp. 116. **51** ὕφαινέ] ὕφανε Blass.

---

i.e. we two will come to a trial of strength. *Od.* 20. 180 f. πάντως οὐκέτι νῶϊ διακρινέεσθαι ὅτω | πρὶν χειρῶν γεύσασθαι.

47 ἀρέταιχμος : probably a compound of the same class as πολέμαιγις : *i.e.* the notions of ἀρετή and αἰχμή were present to the poet's mind, and he simply conjoined them, meaning, 'valiant with the spear.' [The Homeric verb ἀρετᾶν, 'to prosper' (*Od.* 8. 329, 19. 114), might suggest the sense, 'successful with the spear'; but this seems too artificial.]—According to Wackernagel (cited by Blass) ἀρέταιχμος is = ἀρέσαιχμος, *i.e.*, ἀρεσκόμενος τῇ αἰχμῇ, 'delighting in the spear.' He compares Ἀρέσανδρος. [Add Ἀρέ[η]σαιχμος, a proper name given by Pape-Benseler from an inscr. in Keil *Analecta Epigraphica* p. 108 : also Ἀρέσιππος, 'delighting in horses.'] For the τ, Wackernagel compares βωτιάνειρα (Alcman fr. 40); but σ would there be

impossible (cp. βότης, βούτης) : and it is not likely that ἀρέταιχμος was B.'s attempt to Doricize ἀρέσαιχμος.

49 f. φωτὸς is more probable than ἀνδρὸς, in view of the space (cr. n.) : and a consonant is preferable after ναυβάται (cp. 114 f.). φώς is a favourite word with B., who often uses it of heroes (v. 158, Meleager : XV. 15, Heracles : XVII. 19 and 30, Theseus).—ὑπεράφανον, 'lofty': Plat. *Symp.* 217 E Σωκράτους ἔργον ὑπερήφανον : *Phaedo* 96 A (αὕτη ἡ σοφία) ὑπερήφανος...ἐδόκει εἶναι, γνῶναι τὰς αἰτίας ἑκάστου. This good sense is much rarer than the bad; but the primary meaning of the word was merely = ὑπερφανής. Curtius *Etym.* § 392 explains the form by supposing that ὑπέρη contains the adj. stem ὑπερο with epic lengthening (cp. νεηγενής, ἐλαφηβόλος).

Ἀλίου γαμβρῷ : the wife of Minos was Πασιφάη, daughter of Helios : Apoll. Rh. 3. 999 : Paus. V. 25. 9. (The name

Thus far the hero valiant with the spear: but the seafarers epode I.
were amazed at the youth's lofty boldness ; and he whose bride
was daughter of the Sun-god felt anger at his heart; he wove
a new device in his mind, and said :—
' O Zeus, my sire of great might, hear me ! If the white-armed
daughter of Phoenix indeed bare me to thee, now send forth from
heaven a swift flash of streaming fire, a sign for all to know.
And thou, if Troezenian Aethra was thy mother by earth-shaking
Poseidon,—cast thyself boldly down to the abode of thy sire,
and bring from the deep this ring of gold that glitters on my
hand.—But thou shalt see whether my prayer is heard

Cp. XIV. 38.　**53** εἴπερ [με κούρα] Festa, Blass : [με νύμφα] conj. Jurenka : [μ'
ἀλαθέως] Palmer, K. A vestige of the last letter remains in the left margin of
col. XXXV : it cannot have been C, but may have been A. **55** θοὰν Palmer.
58 EI was wrongly repeated *ad init.*: corr. **A**¹? Cp. n. on 25 f.—Τροζηνία Blass.
62 f. θράσει] θ written (by **A**³?) over another letter, perhaps I. After θράσει K. inserts
τό, Jurenka σὸν (σὺ conj. J., Headlam, R. Ellis).—δικὼν θράσει σῶμα πατρὸς ἐς δόμους |
ἔνεγκε κόσμον βαθείας ἁλός MS. : Blass transposes 62 and 63, adding ἐκ before βαθείας.

originally denoted a moon-goddess: Paus.
III. 26. 1 Σελήνης ἐπίκλησις...ἐστὶν ἡ
Πασιφάη.)—χολώσατ᾽ ἦτορ is the most
probable supplement, if in 116 ἐρεμνόν is
sound : see n. there. (Blass, reading
εἱρμένον there, writes χολώθη κέαρ.) *Il.*
15. 155 ἐχολώσατο θυμῷ: *Od.* 9. 480
χολώσατο κηρόθι μᾶλλον· Hes. *Th.* 568
ἐχόλωσε δέ μιν φίλον ἦτορ (' he angered
him at his heart ').
　51 f. ποταινίαν, 'of a new kind,'
'new and strange,' as in Soph. *Ant.* 849
τάφου ποταινίου (' a strange tomb '):
id. fr. 153. 4 ἡδονὰς ποταινίους.—μῆτιν :
he would invite Theseus to show his
trust in Poseidon (v. 36) by jumping
overboard. If Theseus should decline
the challenge, he would be humiliated ;
if he should accept it, he would be lost.
Cp. 86.
　55 f. πυριέθειραν: the ἔθειρα is the
shimmer of the lightning.
　58 Τροιζηνία. I follow the MS. in
keeping the usual spelling. Blass writes
Τροζηνία (referring to Kühner-Blass,
Gramm. I. 13, 137). Τροζήνιοι occurs in
C. I. G. I. 106, II. 5. 10. (Pape-Benseler
s. v. cites no other evidence for that
form.) In *Il.* 2. 561 Τροιζῆν᾽, and 847
Τροιζήνοιο, are traditional.
　62 f. There are several reasons for
transposing vv. 62 and 63, as Blass does,
and adding ἐκ before βαθείας. (1) If
the order of these two verses is correct
in the MS., then v. 62, δικὼν κ.τ.λ., is

shorter by a syllable than v. 128. It has
been proposed to insert σὺ, τό, or σὸν
before σῶμα. Some critics, however,
hold that no such remedy is needed, and
that – ‿ – (-κὼν θράσει) here answers to
– ‿ ‿ – (-εν δὲ πόντος) in 128. (2) A
graver objection to the MS. order is the
well-nigh intolerable awkwardness of
τόνδε χρύσεον | χειρὸς ἀγλαὸν separ-
ated by a whole verse (δικὼν...δόμους)
from **κόσμον**: and this is made still worse
by the fact that **ἀγλαὸν** (v. 2, n.) might
equally well be the epithet of **σῶμα**.
(3) **ἔνεγκε...βαθείας ἁλός** is in itself
admissible : cp. Soph. *El.* 324 ff. δόμων...
ἐντάφια...φέρουσαν : *Ph.* 613 ἄγοιντο νή-
σου. But the addition of **ἐκ** is here a
decided gain in clearness. (4) With
the MS. order, -είας ἁλός in 63 answers
to ἐρατᾷ (ϝ)οπί in 129 : while, if v. 63
ends with **πάτρος ἐς δόμους,** the correspondence is exact. (5) Minos hints a
doubt as to whether Theseus is Poseidon's
son ; that is the sting. The ironical
πατρὸς ἐς δόμους comes most forcibly at
the end.—The MS. order may have arisen
from the verse δικὼν...δόμους (which is
not necessary to the sense) having been
accidentally omitted, and then inserted
in the wrong place.
　64 εἴσεαι...αἴ κε...κλύῃ: *Il.* 4. 249
ὄφρα ἴδητ᾽ αἴ κ᾽ ὔμμιν ὑπερσχῇ χεῖρα
Κρονίων : *ib.* 15. 32 ὄφρα ἴδῃς ἤν τοι
χραίσμῃ φιλότης τε καὶ εὐνή.

65 19 Κρόνιος εὐχὰς
20 ἀναξιβρόντας ὁ πάντων μεδέων.

στρ. β'. 1 κλύε δ' ἄμετρον· εὐχὰν μεγασθενὴς
2 Ζεύς, ὑπέροχόν τε Μίνωϊ φύτευσε
3 τιμὰν φίλῳ θέλων
70 4 παιδὶ πανδερκέα θέμεν,
5 ἄστραψέ θ'· ὁ δὲ θυμάρμενον
6 ἰδὼν τέρας πέτασε χεῖρας
7 κλυτὰν ἐς αἰθέρα μενεπτόλεμος ἥρως,
8 εἶρέν τε· Θησεῦ, <σὺ> τάδε
75 9 μὲν βλέπεις σαφῆ Διὸς
10 δῶρα· σὺ δ' ὄρνυ' ἐς βα-
11 ρύβρομον πέλαγος· Κρονίδας
Col. 35 12 δέ τοι πατὴρ ἄναξ τελεῖ
13 Ποσειδὰν ὑπέρτατον
80 14 κλέος χθόνα κατ' ἠΰδενδρον.
15 ὣς εἶπε· τῷ δ' οὐ πάλιν
16 θυμὸς ἀνεκάμπτετ', ἀλλ' εὐ-

66 ἀναξιβρέντας MS.: corr. K. **67** The papyrus has AMEITPON, but a short stroke has been drawn through the middle of I. (The sixth letter is clearly P, not T.) So νειν for νιν in 91, ἐκείνησεν for ἐκίνησεν in IX. 10.—ἄμετρον K.—Blass, who thinks that the MS. has ἄμεπτον, writes ἄμεμπτον, with Herwerden; so also Jurenka. **68** Μίνωϊ K., Wilamowitz, Jurenka: Μίνωι (= Μίνῳ) Blass, Housman.

---

66 ἀναξιβρόντας (only here): cp. VI. 10 ἀναξίμολπος, XX. 8 ἀναξίαλος. B. has ῐ before βρ only here and in V. 109 μῆλᾰ βροτῶν.

67 ἄμετρον εὐχάν. To ask Zeus for the sign of the lightning was to pray for a very extraordinary mark of favour; the εὐχή was ἄμετρος as exceeding the ordinary limit of a mortal's prayer. There is a similar phrase in Il. 15. 598, where the prayer of Thetis, that the Greeks might suffer defeat until they had made amends to Achilles (1. 508 ff.), is called ἐξαίσιον ἀρήν, an 'exorbitant' or 'immoderate' prayer. The τιμή which Zeus gave to Minos was, as the poet says, a 'surpassing' one: thus ὑπέροχον confirms ἄμετρον.—The conjecture ἄμεμπτον is against the MS., and gives a weak sense; Zeus heard the 'blameless' prayer; i.e. heard it without disapproval.

68—70 The Μίνωι of the MS. has been scanned in three different ways.

(1) As - ‿ ‿, which corresponds with vv. 2 (ἀγλαοὺς), 25 (καὶ δίκας), and 91 (-ιν πνέουσ'). This is supported by Wilamowitz, who remarks that the lengthening of ι may be partly compensatory for the shortening of ω. For the ῑ cp. Il. 1. 283 λίσσομ' Ἀχιλλῆϊ μεθέμεν χόλον (in thesis): for ῶ before another vowel, Od. 6. 303 ἥρῶος. (2) As - - (= Μίνῳ): so Housman, and (in his 2nd ed.) Blass. The syllables -όν τε Μιν-, - ‿ ‿, then answer to - ‿ - ‿ in the other places. (3) As - - ‿: so Blass (1st ed.), assuming that - - - ‿ (Μίνωϊ φυτ-) could answer to - ‿ - ‿ elsewhere. The first of these three views seems to me the most probable, though the ῑ can be justified only by a metrical stress on that syllable (assisted, perhaps, by the shortening of ω).—A transposition, φύτευσε Μίνῳ, is unsatisfactory, because the last syllable is short in 2 and 25, and probably in 91 also (see n. there). It is possible that Μίνωι is a gloss; but it

by the son of Cronus, the all-ruling lord of thunder.'

Mighty Zeus heard the unmeasured prayer, and ordained a str. 2.
surpassing honour for Minos, willing to make it seen of all men,
for the sake of his well-loved son. He sent the lightning. But
the steadfast warrior, when he saw that welcome portent, stretched
his hands towards the glorious ether, and said :—
'Theseus, there thou beholdest the clear sign given by Zeus.
And now do thou spring into the deep-sounding sea; and the
son of Cronus, king Poseidon, thy sire, will assure thee supreme
renown throughout the well-wooded earth.'
So spake he: and the spirit of Theseus recoiled not;

69 f. φίλῳ...παιδὶ] φίλον...παῖδα Housman, Blass². **72** πέτασε χεῖρας Wilamowitz,
Christ, Richards (who suggests also χέρα πέτασσε), Ludwich: πέτασσε χεῖρας Blass²:
χεῖρας πέτασσε MS. (χεῖρε πέτασε K.). **74 f.** <σὺ> τάδε | μὲν βλέπεις J. (K.),
and so Jurenka, Smyth: τάδ' <ἐμὰ> | μὲν βλέπεις conj. Platt: τάδε μὲν | ἔβλεπες
Richards, Blass². **80** ΕΤΑΕΝΔΡΟΝ MS.: ἠΰδενδρον K., Blass² (εὐρύεδρον
Herwerden formerly, but he now accepts ἠΰδενδρον).

does not seem likely. The obvious ϝῷ
γόνῳ would be too near φίλῳ...παιδί:
ϝοι κλέος would be scarcely compatible
with τιμάν. Verses 39 and 120 might
suggest Κνωσίῳ: but this also is improbable.

φύτευσε τιμάν: remark the early recurrence of the verb used in 59. Pind.
P. IV. 69 θεόπομποί σφισιν τιμαὶ φύτευθεν :
I. v. 12 σύν τέ οἱ δαίμων φυτεύει δόξαν.—
φίλῳ...παιδί, 'for (the sake of) his dear
son,' to be taken with θέλων...θέμεν.—
πανδερκέα, 'seen by all.' Elsewhere,
'all-seeing' (*Anth.* 9. 525. 17, Quint.
Smyrn. 2. 443).

72 f. τέρας: the lightning had come
from a clear sky (αἰθέρα, 73). So in
Od. 20. 114, Zeus having thundered, at
the prayer of Odysseus, from a cloudless
sky, the hero says, οὐδέ ποθι νέφος ἐστί·
τέρας νύ τεῳ τόδε φαίνεις.—πέτασε χεῖρας
answers metrically to πίτνον αὔραι in v. 6,
καί σε κεδνά in 29, and ὀμμάτων δα- in 95.
The MS. has χεῖρας πέτασσε: cp. IX. 19 n.
74 f. A short syllable is wanting after
Θησεῦ: cp. 8, 31, 97. The best remedy
would be to read **τάδ' <ἐμά>**, and that
may be what the poet wrote. In our MS.,
however, nothing has been lost after
ΤΑΔΕ, with which this v. ends. If
ΤΑΔΕΜΑ was the original reading, the
letters ΜΑ must have dropped out at
some earlier stage in the transmission of
the text. (2) Another resource is to
insert σὺ after Θησεῦ, where it might so
easily have dropped out. The σὺ δ'

ὄρνυ' in 76 is not a decisive objection.
When σὺ δὲ precedes an imperative, the
stress on the verb is much stronger than
that on the pronoun, as is seen when it
follows a protasis with the same person
as subject: *e.g.* Her. VII. 159 εἰ δ' ἄρα
μὴ δικαιοῖς ἀρχεσθαι, σὺ δὲ μηδὲ βοήθεε
(where σὺ δὲ is merely '*then*'): cp. Her.
III. 68, *Il.* 9. 301 f., Aesch. *Ag.* 1061,
Xen. *Cyr.* 5. 5. 21. (3) Others read
τάδε μὲν | ἔβλεπες (see cr. n.). An
aorist, referring to the moment just past,
might be substituted for the present: thus
εἶσιδες would be analogous to ἐπήνεσα
(Soph. *Ai.* 536), ἔφριξα (*ib.* 693), etc.
But the imperfect ἔβλεπες is surely impossible.

76 f. ὄρνυ', ὄρνυο,=ὄρνυσο, pres. imperat. midd. of ὄρνυμι. Neither the act.
nor the midd. present imperat. of that
verb seems to occur elsewhere, though
the aor. imperat. is not rare (ὄρσο, ὄρσεο,
ὄρσευ). For the dropping of σ in 2nd
pers. sing. pres. imperat. middle, cp.
Il. 10. 291 παρίστασο, 16. 497 μάρναο,
Od. 18. 171 φάο ('speak').—βαρύβρομον :
Eur. *Helen.* 1305 βαρύβρομον...κῦμ' ἅλιον.
—When **Κρονίδας** or Κρόνιος is said of
Poseidon, he is always named (as here
and in Corinna fr. 1, Pind. *O.* VI. 29),
or indicated, as in XVII. 21 by Λυταίου |
σεισίχθονος.
80 ἠΰδενδρον: Pind. *P.* IV. 74 εὐ-
δένδροιο (Earth).
82 ἀνεκάμπτετ', like a bending sword
(XII. 52 ff. ἐγνάμφθη δ' ὀπίσσω φάσγανον).

17 πάκτων ἐπ' ἰκρίων
18 σταθεὶς ὄρουσε, πόντιόν τέ νιν
85 19 δέξατο θελημὸν ἄλσος.
20 τά[φ]εν δὲ Διὸς υἱὸς ἔνδοθεν
21 κέαρ, κέλευσέ τε κατ' οὖ-
22 ρον ἴσχεν εὐδαίδαλον
23 νᾶα· μοῖρα δ' ἑτέραν ἐπόρσυν' ὁδόν.

ἀντ. β'. 90 1 ἵετο δ' ὠκύπομπον δόρυ· σόει
2 νιν βορεὰς ἐξόπιν πνέουσ' ἀήτα·
3 τρέσσαν δ' Ἀθαναίων
4 ἠϊθέων <πᾶν> γένος, ἐπεὶ
5 ἥρως θόρεν πόντονδε, κα-
95 6 τὰ λειρίων τ' ὀμμάτων δά-
7 κρυ χέον, βαρεῖαν ἐπιδέγμενοι ἀνάγκαν·

86 τάφεν Pearson, Weil, Blass[2] (υἱὸς δὲ Διὸς ἔνδοθεν κέαρ τάφε conj. Richards): τάξεν K.: τᾶκεν Bl.[1] 87 f. κατοῦ[ρ]ον MS.: κατ' οὖρον K., Jurenka, Smyth: κάτουρον Housman.—ἴσχεν K.: ἴσχειν MS.—ἐκατοντόρον (Pollux 1. 82) σχὲν Blass[2] ('Remis navis cohibenda erat; hinc epitheton'). 91 f. νιν Housman and others:

83—85 ἰκρίων, a raised half-deck at the stern, on which, in the Homeric ship, the chiefs have their place (*Od.* 13. 72; 15. 282, 557): beneath it there was room for storage (*ib.* 15. 206). An equivalent term was ἐδώλια (Soph. *Ai.* 1277 n.): Her. I. 21 describes Arion as στάντα ἐν τοῖσι ἐδωλίοισι when he sang, before springing into the sea.—σταθεὶς is here a poetical substitute for στάς, as in Pind. IV. 84 ἐστάθη = ἔστη. [In *Od.* 17. 463 ὁ δ' ἐστάθη ἠΰτε πέτρη | ἔμπεδον, the pass. perhaps emphasizes the idea of fixity.]—θελημὸν (the accent prescribed by the MS.), from θελημός: Hes. *Op.* 118 ἐθελημοί: Callim. *Dian.* 31 ἐθελημός. Arcadius 61. 3 τὸ δὲ θελεμὸς ἀπὸ τοῦ θελημὸς ὀξύνεται. [Aesch. *Suppl.* 1027 θελεμὸν πῶμα (of the Nile) is usually explained with Hesych. as = ἥσυχον.]—πόντιον...ἄλσος: the phrase of Aesch. *Pers.* 111, suggesting the sacredness of the sea as the domain of Poseidon (*Neptunia prata*): it is thus peculiarly fitting here.
86 f. τάφεν (cp. v. 48)...ἔνδοθεν κέαρ, 'felt a secret awe in his heart.' Minos had expected that Theseus would decline his challenge. The prompt and dauntless manner in which Theseus had accepted it filled him with amazement; though he

seemed to have got rid of his foe, he felt an inward misgiving. But he did not allow his feeling to appear.—[τᾶκεν (or τᾶξεν) ...κέαρ would mean, 'he wasted his heart within him'; *i.e.* 'he felt his soul melt within him,'—the emotion being one of surprise and fear. Cp. *Od.* XIX. 263 μηδ' ἔτι θυμὸν | τῆκε πόσιν γοάουσα. But the word is more suitable there than it would be here.]
87—89 κατ' οὖρον ἴσχεν...νᾶα, 'to keep the ship before the wind.' When Theseus sprang overboard, the impulse of the κυβερνήτης (an Athenian, cp. Plut. *Thes.* 17) would naturally be to bring up the ship, which was running before the north wind (v. 6): but Minos ordered him to keep on his course. Secretly disquieted by the confidence of Theseus, Minos did not care to wait at that spot. If he went on, at any rate—so he thought (v. 121 n.)—he should see Theseus no more. 'Fate,' however, 'was preparing a different issue.' The ship sped on its way; but Theseus reappeared at a later moment (119).—For ἴσχεν (Dor. inf., 41 n.) = ἔχειν, said of steering a ship on a certain course, cp. *Od.* 10. 91 ἔνθ' οἵγ' εἴσω πάντες ἔχον νέας: Her. VI. 95 οὐ παρὰ τὴν ἤπειρον εἶχον τὰς νέας.
Reading κάτουρον, Housman under-

he took his place on the well-built stern, and sprang thence, and the domain of the deep received him in kindness.

The son of Zeus felt a secret awe in his heart, and gave command to keep the cunningly-wrought ship before the wind; but Fate was preparing a different issue.

So the bark sped fast on its journey, and the northern breeze, ant. 2. blowing astern, urged it forward. But all the Athenian youths and maidens shuddered when the hero sprang into the deep; and tears fell from their bright young eyes, in prospect of their grievous doom.

νειν MS.—ΒΟΡΈΟΤC **A**: a written above ΟΤ by **A**³.— ἐξόπιν K. : ἐξόπιθε Wilamowitz, Blass; εξοπιθεν MS.—ἀῆτα] ἄητα Housman, Smyth (ἆῆτα Wilamowitz). **93** ἠθέων <πᾶν> K.: <γᾶς> Weil. **94 f.** θόρεν] ἔθορε Purser, Christ.—Richards conj. πόντονδε θόρεν ἥρως, κατά | τε λειρίων ὀμμάτων. **95 f.** δά|κρυ χέον J., and so Blass, Jurenka, Smyth: δάκρυ | χέον MS.—ἐπιδέγμενοι Jurenka, Smyth: ἐπιδεγμένοι Blass.

---

stands, 'he ordered them to *stop* the ship *which was running before the wind*.' But, even with κάτουρον, the sense would be, 'to keep the ship before the wind': κάτουρον could not stand for τὴν κατ' οὖρον πλέουσαν. Blass, also, supposes that ἴσχεν means 'stop'; but of κάτουρον he says, '*non sufficit*,' and has recourse to a much bolder emendation;—κέλευσέ θ' ἑκατόντορον σχὲν...νᾶα, 'to stop the hundred-oared ship.'

90 ὠκύπομπον: Eur. *I. T.* 1136 ναὸς ὠκυπόμπου. — δόρυ, 'ship' (like *trabs*, Hor. *C.* I. i. 13 etc.): Aesch. *Pers.* 411 ἐπ' ἄλλην (*sc.* ναῦν) δ' ἄλλος ηὔθυνεν δόρυ (cp. *Ag.* 1618). Pind. *P.* IV. 27 εἰνάλιον δόρυ, and 38 ἐκ δούρατος.—The υ is lengthened before σόει as υ before σσ in δορυσσόος. Cp. also *Il.* 17. 463 ὅτε σεύαιτο διώκειν (and 23. 198). σόει is imperf. of σοέω: with the augment it would be ἐσσόει (cp. ἔσσενα, ἔσσυμαι, ἐσσύθην). The only other part of σοέω extant is preserved in Hesych., ἐσσοημένον· τεθορυβημένον, ὡρμημένον.

91 ἐξόπιν occurs only in Aesch. *Ag.* 115 (though κατόπιν = κατόπισθεν is frequent): and its rarity would account for the ἐξόπιθεν of the MS. It is decidedly preferable on metrical grounds to ἐξόπιθε, which would weaken the rhythm; nor is the long syllable answering to ·ιθε resolved in 2, 25, or 68.—ἀῆτα is the accent in the MS., indicating the Doric form of ἀήτη (Hes. *Op.* 643, etc.). ἄητα (with Aeolic accent) would be preferable, since in all the corresponding verses (2, 25, 68) the last syllable is short. The Aeolic form is probable (if not certain)

in Simonides fr. 41, οὐδὲ γὰρ ἐννοσίφυλλος ἄητα τότ' ὦρτ' ἀνέμων (ἄητα Bergk⁴, though formerly ἄητα). But ἄητα (or ἀῆτα) would be *masc.* (= ἀήτης): and the fem. βορεάς (attested by the accents in the MS.) is certain. No such form as βόρεος (for βόρειος) was in use. Cp. Aesch. frag. 195. 2 βορεάδας ἥξεις πρὸς πνοάς. For this reason alone I refrain from altering the MS. accent on ἀῆτα.

92 'Αθαναίων with αἴ: so 128 παίδνιξαν : Ar. *Vesp.* 282 φιλαθήναιος, *Eq.* 139 δείλαιος: Eur. *H. F.* 115 γεραιέ: Anth. 9. 281. 3 παλαιός: Orph. fr. 2. 2 δικαίων.

93 The corresponding verses (4, 27, 70) begin with - ⏑ ⏑ -. A long syllable is therefore wanting between ἠΰθέων and γένος. Kenyon inserts πᾶν, and nothing better has been proposed.

94—96 The iambus θόρεν answers to ⏑ ⏑ ⏑ in 5, 28, 71. This discrepancy would be removed by the transposition which Richards suggests, πόντονδε θόρεν ἥρως, κατά | τε λειρίων : and the emphatic place given to πόντονδε would also be fitting. I hesitate to adopt it only because it presupposes that τε had either (1) been shifted to its place after λειρίων, which seems improbable: or (2) lost, and then wrongly inserted there; which we are not entitled to assume, since the MS. text is metrically possible, ⏑ - (θόρεν) being an admissible substitute for ⏑ ⏑ ⏑.

λειρίων...ὀμμάτων, eyes of delicate beauty,—the bright eyes of *youth*. Cp. Shakespeare's 'young-eyed cherubins' (*Merchant of Venice*, v. i. 62). In *Il.* 13. 830 χρόα λειριόεντα is 'delicate' skin: and in *Il.* 3. 152 the chirping sound

8 φέρον δὲ δελφῖνες ἁλι-
9 ναίεται μέγαν θοῶς
10 Θησέα πατρὸς ἱππί-
100 11 ου δόμον, μέγαρόν τε θεῶν
12 μόλεν· τόθι κλυτὰς ἰδὼν
13 ἔδεισ' ὀλβίοιο Νη-
14 ρέος κόρας· ἀπὸ γὰρ ἀγλα-
15 ῶν λάμπε γυίων σέλας
105 16 ὧτε πυρός, ἀμφὶ χαίταις
17 δὲ χρυσεόπλοκοι
18 δίνηντο ταινίαι· χορῷ δ' ἔτερ-
19 πον κέαρ ὑγροῖσι ποσσίν·
20 σεμνάν τε πατρὸς ἄλοχον φίλαν
110 21 ἴδε βοῶπιν ἐρατοῖ-
22 σιν Ἀμφιτρίταν δόμοις·

97 f. ἁλιναιέται K. (deleting ἐν before ἁλι-), Jurenka, Smyth ; ἐναλι|ναιέται MS., Blass. **100 f.** δόμον, μέγαρόν τε...μόλεν Housman, Wilamowitz, Blass, Richards, Smyth, and others : δομὸνδ' ἔμολέν τε...μέγαρον Jurenka : δόμον· ἔμολέν τε...μέγαρον MS. **102 f.** ἔδεισ' ὀλβίοιο Νη|ρέος Richards, Ludwich, Blass[2] : ἔδεισεν Νηρῆος ὀλ|βίου K. (ἔδεισε Νηρῆος ὀλ|βίου Bl.[1], Smyth) : ἔδεισε, Νηρέος ὀλ|βίου MS., the diastole marking the division of the words. **105** ὧτε] The MS. seems to have had ΩΙΤΕ.—ὧστε K. **107** δίνηντο Blass : δινεῦντο K. : ΔΕΙΝΗΝΤΟ **A**, but the E has been cancelled (by

made by the cicada is called ὄπα λειριόεσσαν, a 'delicate' voice. Pind. *N.* VII. 79 calls the white coral λείριον ἄνθεμον ποντίας...ἔρσας (where the notion of delicate beauty is joined to that of the colour). —Suidas gives λειρόφθαλμος [λειρ(ι)όφθαλμος?], ὁ προσηνεῖς ἔχων τοὺς ὀφθαλμούς, 'with *gentle* eyes.' The idea of 'gentle' may have been first associated with λειριόεις, λείριος as an epithet of the *voice*: thus Ap. Rh. 4. 903 calls the chant of the Seirens ὄπα λείριον. Here, in reference to the youths and maidens collectively, λειρίων can hardly mean 'gentle'; a more general sense is needed.

δάκρυ χέον. The division of the verses given above (and suggested by me in Kenyon's edition, p. 169) is required by the metre : see 6, 29, 72.—ἐπιδέγμενοι, 'expecting.' In *Il.* 9. 191 δέγμενος Αἰακίδην, where the sense is 'awaiting' (as in 18. 524), the word is accented as the partic. of 2nd aor. ἐδέγμην, while its meaning indicates the perfect partic. (*Il.* 4. 107 δεδεγμένος ἐν προδοκῇσιν). B. would probably have kept the irregular Homeric accent of δέγμενος, and it is therefore better not to write ἐπιδεγμένοι.—

ἀνάγκαν, the 'doom' of becoming victims to the Minotaur.

97 f. δελφῖνες, the usual agents in the miraculous conveyance of mortals through or beneath the sea : pseudo-Arion (Bergk[4] III. p. 80) 11 f. οἵ μ' εἰς Πέλοπος γᾶν...ἐπορεύσατε : Plut. *Mor.* p. 163 A (Enalos of Lesbos and the maiden whom he rescued from drowning) ἐπὶ δελφίνων φορητοὶ διὰ θαλάττης. Some of the vase-painters, however, depicted Theseus as borne up in the arms of a Triton. (See Introd.)—ἁλιναιέται (only here): pseudo-Arion 9 f. δελφῖνες, ἔναλα θρέμματα | κουρᾶν Νηρεΐδων θεᾶν.—The MS. has ἐναλιναιέται, which Blass retains, comparing ἐμπυριβήτης (*Il.* 23. 702) and ἐγχειρίθετος (Her. v. 108). But it seems scarcely doubtful that, as metre indicates (cp. 8 f. and 31 f.), εν was written by error.

99—101 ἱππίου, Poseidon, as creator of the horse, and as horse-tamer (δαμαῖος, ἵμψιος); Soph. *O. C.* 711 ff. He is ἵππων πρύτανις (Stesich. fr. 49), ἵππαρχος (Pind. *P.* IV. 45). Poseidon ἵππιος had an altar at Colonus Hippius near Athens (*O. C.* 55). Greek poets use constant epithets without regard to their fitness in

Meanwhile dolphins, dwellers in the sea, were swiftly bearing mighty Theseus to the abode of his sire, lord of steeds; and he came unto the hall of the gods. There beheld he the glorious daughters of blest Nereus, and was awe-struck; for a splendour as of fire shone from their radiant forms; fillets inwoven with gold encircled their hair; and they were delighting their hearts by dancing with lissom feet. And in that beautiful abode he saw his father's well-loved wife, the stately, ox-eyed Amphitrite;

A²?).—Wilamowitz conj. δονεῦντο. ὑγροῖσιν ἐν ποσίν MS., Blass. ν written above I (by **A³**?).—σεμνάν τε πατρὸς ἄλοχον φίλαν | ἴδε conj. Housman: σεμνὰν τότ᾽ ἄλοχον πατρὸς φίλαν | ἴδε Richards. εἰδέν τε πατρὸς ἄλοχον φίλαν | σεμνὰν MS.

108 ὑγροῖσι ποσσίν K., Jurenka, Smyth: **109 f.** ΙΔ. Ν **A**: εἶδεν **A³**.—ΒΟΩΠΙ **A**:

---

the particular context; sleeping birds are called ταννπτέρνγες by Alcman (fr. 60. 7), and ships drawn up on shore can still have the epithet θοαί (Soph. *Ai.* 710).—**δόμον**, the palace of Poseidon in the depths of the sea: *Il.* 13. 21 f. ἔνθα δέ (near Aegae) οἱ κλντὰ δώματα βένθεσι λίμνης | χρύσεα μαρμαίροντα τετεύχαται, ἄφθιτα αἰεί. The second syllable of **δόμον** should be long (see 11, 34, 77). Two remedies are possible. (1) To write **δομόνδ᾽** with Jurenka, keeping the MS. ἐμολεν...μέγαρον. (2) Keeping **δόμον**, to write μέγαρον...μόλεν. This seems best. Of the three verses corresponding to 101, two (12 and 78) begin with ⏑⏑–, and the third (35) with – – : hence μόλεν is more probable than μέγαρον as the first word of 101.—**μέγαρον** is the great hall in Poseidon's δόμος. The plur. **θεῶν** refers to Poseidon and Amphitrite: perhaps it is meant to include the 'bright-throned Nereids' also. On the cup of Euphronius Athena too is present (see p. 225). **102 f.** ὀλβίοιο Νηρέος. The transposition (see cr. n.) brings the metre into agreement with that of 13, 36, and 79. It may be regarded as certain.—**κόρας**: cp. n. on 38 Νηρηΐδες. **105** ὥτε: Δωρικῶς ἀντὶ τοῦ ὥστε, schol. Pind. *N.* VI. 47. Pindar has it frequently (*P.* IV. 64, X. 54, etc.): cp. XII. 124 n. —**πυρός**: *Il.* 19. 366 (the eyes of Achilles) λαμπέσθην ὡς εἴ τε πυρὸς σέλας.— **ἀμφὶ χαίταις**: for the dat., cp. 124, XVII. 53 : Pind. *O.* XIII. 39 ἀμφὶ κόμαις. **106 f.** χρυσ. ταινίαι, 'fillets inwoven with gold,' *i.e.* with gold thread. The ταινία was a ribband worn by maidens (and matrons) round the head, to confine

the hair (*crinales vittas* Verg. *Aen.* 7. 352).—**δίνηντο.** (1) This must be (I think) for ἐδεδίνηντο, pluperf. of δινέω, 'had been twirled' round the hair, 'encircled' it : cp. *Il.* 23. 562 (a θώρηξ) ᾧ περὶ χεῦμα φαεινοῦ κασσιτέροιο | ἀμφιδεδίνηται, around which a casting of bright tin has been carried (*i.e.* which has been overlaid with tin-plate). (2) If δίνηντο were taken (with Blass) as imperf. of an Aeolic δίνημι (= δινέω), the sense must have been, 'were being twirled.' But the close-fitting head-band, ταινία, would not be shaken by the movements of the dance. Cp. 18 δίνασεν, n. **108** ὑγροῖσι, supple, 'lissom.' ὑγρός here is opposed to σκληρός ('stiff'), Plat. *Theaet.* p. 162 B. So of horses, ὑγρὰ ἔχειν τὰ σκέλη (Xen. *Eq.* 1. 6). Arist. *A nim.* 6. 35 (ὁ θὼς) ταχυτῆτι διαφέρει...διὰ τὸ ὑγρὸς εἶναι. Pollux 4. 96 ὑγρὸς ὀρχηστής.—The use of the word in reference to Nymphs of the *sea* is not very felicitous. **109 f.** The scansion of the syllables before βοῶπιν in 110 ought to be either ⏑⏑ (as in 21, 44), or else – (as in 87, κέαρ with synizesis). The – – given by σεμνὰν seems metrically impossible. Sitzler (quoted by Jurenka p. 128) regards σεμνὰν as a gloss on βοῶπιν, and would substitute τάν. But then the words ἐρατοῖσιν...δόμοις, which go with the verb, would be locked into the clause τὰν... Ἀμφιτρίταν. In 109 the first hand wrote ΙΔ. Ν, not εἶδεν. The transposition σεμνάν...ἴδε (Housman) is the only satisfactory remedy. Verse 109 still differs from 20, 43, and 86 in so far as – – – ⏑⏑ (πατρὸς ἄλοχ-) here replaces ⏑⏑ – ⏑ in these verses. This difference would be

²³ ἅ νιν ἀμφέβαλεν αἰόλαν πορφύραν,

ἐπ. β'. ¹ κόμαισί τ' ἐπέθηκεν οὔλαις
Col. 36 ² ἀμεμφέα πλόκον,
  ³ τόν ποτέ (F)οι ἐν γάμῳ
116 ⁴ δῶκε δόλιος Ἀφροδίτα ῥόδοις ἐρεμνόν.
  ⁵ ἄπιστον ὅ τι δαίμονες
  ⁶ θέωσιν οὐδὲν φρενοάραις βροτοῖς·
  ⁷ ναα παρὰ λεπτόπρυμνον φάνη· φεῦ,
120 ⁸ οἵαισιν ἐν φροντίσι Κνώσιον
  ⁹ ἔσχασεν στραταγέταν, ἐπεὶ
  ¹⁰ μόλ' ἀδίαντος ἐξ ἁλὸς
  ¹¹ θαῦμα πάντεσσι, λάμ-
  ¹² πε δ' ἀμφὶ γυίοις θεῶν δῶρ', ἀγλαό-
125 ¹³ θρονοί τε κοῦραι σὺν εὐ-
  ¹⁴ θυμίᾳ νεοκτίτῳ
  ¹⁵ ὠλόλυξαν, ἔ-

112 ἀμφέβαλεν K.: ἀμφέβαλλεν MS.—αϊόνα πορφυρέαν MS. For conjectures see
Appendix. 116 δόλιος] ΔΟΛΙΣ A : o written above I (by A²?).—ἐρεμνόν] ἐερμένον
Weil : εἱρμένον Blass : ἐραννόν Piccolomini. 118 θέωσιν Crusius, Richards,

removed by reading, with Richards, σεμνὰν τότ' ἄλοχον πατρὸς φίλαν (πᾶτρὸς as in v. 63). τότε is fitting, since the approach of Theseus to Amphitrite is the crowning moment of the scene. And the placing of πατρὸς before ἄλοχον might easily have caused the shrinkage of τότε into τε.
βοῶπιν. This epithet of Hera is given to mortal women in Il. 3. 144, 7. 10, 18. 40.
111 Ἀμφιτρίταν. The wife of Poseidon (Pind. O. VI. 105) is the Sea that 'moans around the shores of earth' (τρίζω, τρύζω) : cp. Od. 12. 97 ἀγάστονος Ἀμφιτρίτη. She is unknown to the Iliad, and in the Odyssey is scarcely more than a symbol for the sea (as in the phrase μετὰ κύμασιν Ἀμφιτρίτης, 3. 91). Hes. Th. 243 makes her a daughter of Nereus, and her connexion with the Nereids was always close. In art Poseidon and Amphitrite were often associated with Hestia, the goddess of terra firma (cp. Paus. v. 26. 2).
112 αϊόνα in the MS., if sound, is an otherwise unknown name for some kind of garment. It is possible that ἠϊών, ἠών, 'sea-bank,' 'margin,' may have been used to mean the 'border' of a robe, and that 'purple border' here may have

meant a robe with such a border. But there is no evidence for this; and it seems very improbable. Far the best emendation is that which Tyrrell was the first to propose, αἰόλαν πορφύραν, 'gleaming purple.' The corruption of αἰόλαν into αϊόνα can be explained in either of two ways. (1) In ΑΙΟΛΑΝ the ΛΑ may have become ΝΑ, when the final Ν would be deleted. Or (2) the similarity of Λ to Α may have led to the loss of Λ, leaving ΑΙΟΑΝ : then Ν would be transposed, so as to make ΑΙΟΝΑ. Housman illustrates this process from v. 117, where Ἀγέλαον became ἄγγελον : i.e. Α was lost after Λ, leaving ΑΓΕΛΟΝ, and then this was made into a Greek word by adding a second Γ.—The change of πορφύραν into πορφυρέαν would follow the change of αἰόλαν into αϊόνα.—For other conjectures see Appendix.
113 οὔλαις : Od. 6. 230 (Athena changing the aspect of Odysseus) κὰδ δὲ κάρητος | οὔλας ἧκε κόμας ('thick, curly locks').
114—116 ἀμεμφέα πλόκον, 'a choice wreath.' Pausanias (I. 17. 3) describes it as στέφανον χρυσοῦν: Hyginus (Astron. II. 5) as coronam...compluribus lucentem gemmis. B., too, doubtless conceived it as a wreath of gold; the word λάμπε in

who clad him in gleaming purple,
and set on his thick hair a choice wreath, dark with roses, given epode 2.
to her of yore at her marriage by wily Aphrodite.
Nothing that the gods may ordain is past belief to men of a
sound mind.   Theseus appeared by the ship with slender stern.
Ah, in what thoughts did he check the war-lord of Cnosus,
when he came unwetted from the sea, a wonder to all, his form
resplendent with the gifts of the gods! The bright-throned
Nereids cried aloud with new-born gladness;

Weil : θέλωσιν MS.: λῶσιν Palmer, K.   119 νᾶα] ΛΑΑ A : ν written above Λ
(by A²?).   120 φροντίσι] φόντισσι A : corr. A¹?   124 γυίοις...ἀγλαό- K. :
ΓΥΟΙΣ...ΑΓΛΟ MS.

123 refers to wreath as well as robe.
ῥόδοις ἐρεμνόν, the reading of the MS., is
right : the golden wreath was '*dark* with
roses,' *i.e.* thickly entwined with dark-
red roses,—the flowers of Aphrodite,—
when she gave it to Poseidon's bride as a
wedding-gift. When Amphitrite gave it
to Theseus, the roses may still have been
there ; but the words do not require us to
assume that.—Modifying Weil's emenda-
tion **ἑρμένον**, Blass reads **εἱρμένον**, 'strung
with roses.' (Cp. *Od.* 18. 296 (ὅρμον)
χρύσεον, ἠλέκτροισιν ἐερμένον, 'strung
with amber beads.') The phrase πλόκον...
ῥόδοις εἱρμένον, however, would suggest,
not a golden wreath 'twined' with roses,
but simply a chaplet formed by 'stringing' roses together; and the gift can
scarcely have been such. [ἑρμένον, it
may be added, would be closer to the
MS. than εἱρμένον. In Her. IV. 190,
ἐνερμένων has good warrant (ἐνειρμένων
Stein) : cp. id. I. 154 ἀπεργμένος, II. 121
ἔργασται.]
δόλιος, fem., as in Eur. *Alc.* 35, *Tro.*
530, *Cycl.* 449, *Helen.* 20, 242, 1605.
Sappho addresses Aphrodite as δολόπλοκε
(fr. 1. 2): Simonides fr. 43 δολόμητις
Ἀφροδίτα : Eur. *I. A.* 1301 δολιόφρων
Κύπρις.
117 f. ἄπιστον κ.τ.λ. : in III. 57 a
like phrase comes between two miracles.
After relating the deeds of Perseus,
Pindar's comment is,—ἐμοὶ δὲ θαυμάσαι |
θεῶν τελεσάντων οὐδέν ποτε φαίνεται |
ἔμμεν ἄπιστον (*P.* X. 48 ff.).—**θέωσιν**,
'ordain' : *Od.* 8. 465 οὕτω νῦν Ζεὺς θείη.
This is a certain correction of the MS.
θέλωσιν. With regard to Palmer's λῶσιν,
the verb λῆν was in common use in
Laconian (Ar. *Lys.* 1162 f.) as in other
Doric dialects ; and, in the Alexandrian

age at least, it was not confined to Doric
poetry (thus Callim. *Dian.* 19 has λῇs).
But it is not likely to have been used
by an Ionian of the classical period.—
φρενοδραις, 'of sound mind': so φρενήρης
is opposed to ἐμμανής (Her. III. 25). For
the form cp. Pind. *I.* IV. 41 Μέμνονα
χαλκοάραν : *P.* V. 35 χεριαρᾶν τεκτόνων.
119 λεπτόπρυμνον : the conjecture
λεπτόπρῳρον is improbable. The *stern*
is mentioned, because Minos would be
there. (Cp. n. on ἱκρίων in 83.)
120 f. οἵαισιν...ἔσχασεν κ.τ.λ. : 'In
what (exultant) thoughts did he check'
Minos. σχάζω, 'to let loose,' means
(1) 'to split open,' (2) 'to let drop,'
(3) then 'to stop' by relaxing a tension :
Pind. *P.* X. 51 κώπαν σχάσον, '*ease* the
oar,' 'stop rowing': Eur. *Ph.* 454 σχάσον
δὲ δεινὸν ὄμμα καὶ θυμοῦ πνοάς, 'remit
thy frown and thy blustering wrath.' In
Pind. *N.* IV. 64 the victory of Heracles
over monsters is described by σχάσαις :
he 'stayed' their violence. So here the
apparition of Theseus 'gave pause' to
Minos in his secret exultation.
122 ἀδίαντος, 'unwetted.' Simonides
fr. 37. 3 οὐκ ἀδιάντοισιν παρειαῖς : Pind.
N. VII. 73 σθένος ἀδίαντον (schol. ἄνευ
ἱδρῶτος).
124 f. θεῶν δῶρα : the mantle and
wreath bestowed by Amphitrite are regarded as coming also from Poseidon.—
According to Pausanias and Hyginus
(n. on 114), Theseus brought back also
the ring of Minos : it was given to him,
says Hyginus, by the Nereids. B. ignores
the ring. The 'gifts of the gods' suffice
to prove the origin of Theseus. 'Il
légitime sa naissance divine sans se faire
le serviteur du roi de Crète' (Weil).
ἀγλαόθρονοι...κοῦραι : 'the bright-

16 κλαγεν δὲ πόντος· ἠίθεοι δ' ἐγγύθεν
17 νέοι παιάνιξαν ἐρατᾷ (F)οπί.
130 18 Δάλιε, χοροῖσι Κηίων
19   φρένα ἰανθεὶς
20 ὅπαζε θεόπομπον ἐσθλῶν τύχαν.

XVII. [XVIII.]

ΘΗΣΕΥΣ

στρ. α΄. ΧΟ. 1 Βασιλεῦ τᾶν ἱερᾶν Ἀθανᾶν,
2 τῶν ἀβροβίων ἄναξ Ἰώνων,
3 τί νέον ἔκλαγε χαλκοκώδων
4 σάλπιγξ πολεμηίαν ἀοιδάν;

131 φρένα MS. : φρένας conj. J.
XVII. The title added in the left margin by A³.   **2** ΑΒΡΟΒΙΚΩΝ
...ΙΕΡΩΝΩΝ **A** : corr. **A³**?—The words τῶν ἀβροβίων Ἰώνων ἄναξ are quoted from
Bacchylides in that order (which Wilamowitz had already corrected, *Isyllos* p. 143) by
(1) Maximus Planudes (14th cent.) in his scholia to Hermogenes περὶ ἰδεῶν α΄, Walz

---

throned maidens' are the Nereids : Pind.
N. IV. 65 (Peleus) ἔγαμεν ὑψιθρόνων μίαν
Νηρεΐδων. The epithet ἀγλαόθρονος is
given by Pindar to the Muses (*O.* XIII.
96), and to the Danaides (*N.* X. 1). The
Horae, and the semi-divine daughters of
Cadmus, are εὔθρονοι (*P.* IX. 60, *O.* II. 22).
126—129 νεοκτίτῳ, the form used
by Nonnus 18. 294, while Pindar and
classical prose have νεόκτιστος. Cp. the
Homeric ἐΰκτιτος (III. 46). The glorifi-
cation of Theseus gave the Nereids a
sudden emotion of delight.—ὠλόλυξαν:
the word usually denoted a cry of women,
and especially a joyous cry (*Od.* 22. 408,
Eur. *El.* 691).—ἔκλαγεν...πόντος. The
sympathy of the sea with Poseidon is
more than once marked in the *Iliad*:
as when it joyously makes way for his
chariot (13. 29 γηθοσύνῃ δὲ θάλασσα
διίστατο), or is stirred by his champion-
ship of the Greeks (14. 392 ἐκλύσθη δὲ
θάλασσα κ.τ.λ.). For ἔ before κλ, cp.
XV. 13 n.
ἠίθεοι, both youths and maidens, as
in 43, 93. Here νέοι is probably adj.,
not subst.; cp. κοῦροι νέοι (*Il.* 13. 95).
But we find other phrases in which ἤθεος
is clearly adj., as Eupolis fr. incert.

40 κόρη...ἤθεος, Plut. *Thes.* 17 ἤθεοι
παῖδες.—ἐγγύθεν, 'hard by,' *i.e.* near
Theseus, who was now beside the ship;
while the cry of the Nereids was heard
from the depths.
129 παιάνιξαν: for the αἴ, see n. on
92.—ἐρατᾷ (F)οπί : XV. 7. The hiatus
is excused by the tradition of F (*Il.* 3.
221 ἀλλ' ὅτε δὴ ὅπα τε μεγάλην, *Od.* 14.
492 ὀλιγῇ ὀπί, etc.).
130 Δάλιε: this paean to the Delian
Apollo may have been sung in Delos.
χοροῖσι: the reference is peculiarly fitting
here. Theseus, returning with his companions from Crete to Athens, touched
at Delos, and there ἐχόρευσε μετὰ τῶν
ἠθέων χορείαν (Plut. *Thes.* 21), — the
dance called γέρανος. (See Introd.)
131 φρένα ἰανθείς. There is a strong
case for writing φρένας, since the similar
Homeric phrases are so frequent that
it is difficult to understand how B. could
have assumed F before the verb:—*Il.* 19.
174 φρεσὶ σῇσιν ἰανθῇς, 23. 600 θυμὸς
ἰάνθη, *Od.* 4. 840 ἦτορ ἰάνθη, 23. 47
θυμὸν ἰάνθης, etc. [In 24. 382, φρένας
ἔνδον ἐγήθεις, Eustath. read ἰάνθης.] But
on the other hand B. could write εἴλετο
Fιόν (v. 75), in face of *Il.* 4. 116 ἐκ

the deep resounded; while the youths and maidens hard by
raised a paean with their lovely voices.

God of Delos, may the choruses of the Ceans be pleasing to
thy soul; and mayest thou give us blessings for our portion,
wafted by thy power divine!

XVII. [XVIII.]

THESEUS.

CHORUS. King of sacred Athens, lord of the delicately- str. 1.
living Ionians, why has the trumpet lately sounded a war-note
from its bell of bronze?

Rhet. Graeci v. 493; and (2) by an anonymous scholiast on the same work, *ib.* VII.
982. (3) A third commentator, Joannes Siceliota (9th cent.), *ib.* VI. 241, quotes from
B. ἀβρότητι ξυνέασιν Ἴωνες βασιλῆες. Bergk (fr. 42) took this last to be the original
source of the citation τῶν ἀβροβίων Ἰώνων ἄναξ, but used the latter in changing Ἴωνες
into Ἰώνων. **3** τί **A**: σ added above by **A³**.—ΧΑΛΚΟΔΩΔΩΝ **A**: κ written
above the first Δ (by **A³**?).

δ᾽ ἔλετ᾽ ἰόν, the very passage which was
his model. [In III. 68, where A wrote
φθόνῳ ἰαίνεται, A³'s πιαίνεται is clearly
right.] This warning instance is my
sole reason for leaving φρένα in the
text.
132 ὄπαζε: so the Homeric hymn
to Demeter ends (v. 494) with the prayer
βίον θυμήρε᾽ ὀπάζειν: as does also Hymn
XXX.—θεόπομπον, 'sent to us by divine
power.' Pindar's θεόπομποί σφισιν τιμαὶ
φύτευθεν (*P.* IV. 69), which perhaps
suggested φύτευσε τιμάν in 68 f., may have
prompted this word also.—ἐσθλῶν τύχαν: cp. IV. 20 μοῖραν ἐσθλῶν. The
genitive with τύχα in Pindar usually
denotes the giver (as in *N.* IV. 7 σὺν
Χαρίτων τύχᾳ), but can also denote the
gift, *O.* XIII. 115 τύχαν τερπνῶν γλυκεῖαν.
Invocation of a god at the close of the
ode occurs in Pind. *O.* VI. 176 (Poseidon),
XIII. 115 (Zeus), *I.* VI. 49 (Apollo).
Sometimes, again, there is a prayer
without invocation (*O.* VIII. 84: *P.* V.
114).

XVII. 1—15 A Chorus of Athenians, addressing Aegeus, ask why a call
to arms has just been sounded. (See
Introd.)
1 ἱεράν, a frequent epithet of Athens:
Soph. *Ai.* 1221 (n.), Ar. *Eq.* 1319, Pind.
fr. 75. 4, etc.

2 τῶν ἀβροβίων. The epithet means
that from early days the Athenians had
prided themselves on their union of
refinement with valour (cp. v. 13).
Thucydides (I. 6, § 3) speaks of τὸ
ἀβροδίαιτον as a trait of the wealthier
Athenians down to a time not long
before his own; instancing the long
linen tunic, from which Ionians were
called ἑλκεχίτωνες (*Il.* 13. 685 etc.), and
the use by men of golden τέττυγες as
brooches to fasten up the hair. Cratinus
(Χείρωνες fr. 239) adds some touches,
such as the wearing of a flower 'at the
ear,' and the carrying of an apple in
the hand. Heracleides Ponticus (in
Athenaeus p. 512 B) insists that Athens
had been greatest when most luxurious:—
Καὶ ἡ Ἀθηναίων πόλις, ἕως ἐτρύφα, μεγίστη τε ἦν καὶ μεγαλοψυχοτάτους ἔτρεφεν
ἄνδρας.—Ἰώνων, Athenians: cp. XVI. 3.
3 f. νέον, 'lately,' as in 16. (Not
'afresh.')—χαλκοκώδων: Soph. *Ai.* 17
χαλκοστόμου κώδωνος ὡς Τυρσηνικῆς.—
ἀοιδάν: an unexampled use of the
term in reference to such a sound as
that of the trumpet. The meaning of
the verb is wider than that of the
subst., so that ἄεισε σάλπιγξ would seem
less strange. It was perhaps some reason
of euphony that restrained B. from using
the fitter word employed by Aesch., *Pers.*
395 σάλπιγξ δ᾽ ἀϋτῇ πάντ᾽ ἐκεῖν᾽ ἐπέ-
φλεγεν.

5 ἢ τις ἀμετέρας χθονὸς
6 δυσμενὴς ὅρι᾽ ἀμφιβάλλει
7 στραταγέτας ἀνήρ;
8 ἢ λῃσταὶ κακομάχανοι
9 ποιμένων ἀέκατι μήλων
10 σεύοντ᾽ ἀγέλας βίᾳ;
11 ἢ τί τοι κραδίαν ἀμύσσει;
12 φθέγγευ· δοκέω γὰρ εἴ τινι βροτῶν
13 ἀλκίμων ἐπικουρίαν
14 καὶ τὶν ἔμμεναι νέων,
15 ὦ Πανδίονος υἱὲ καὶ Κρεούσας.

στρ. β'. ΑΙΓ. 1 Νέ]ον ἦλθεν δολιχὰν ἀμείψας
Col. 37 2 κᾶρυξ ποσὶν Ἰσθμίαν κέλευθον·
3 ἄφατα δ᾽ ἔργα λέγει κραταιοῦ
4 φωτός· τὸν ὑπέρβιόν τ᾽ ἔπεφνεν
20 5 Σίνιν, ὃς ἰσχύϊ φέρτατος
6 θνατῶν ἦν, Κρονίδα Λυταίου
7 σεισίχθονος τέκος·
8 σὺν τ᾽ ἀνδροκτόνον ἐν νάπαις
9 Κρεμμυῶνος, ἀτάσθαλόν τε
25 10 Σκίρωνα κατέκτανεν·

6 ὅρι'] OPEI **A**: corr. **A³**? 8 λῃσταὶ] ΛΗΤΑΙ **A**, ΛΗCΤΑΙ **A¹**? 9 ἀέκατι] Δ' ΕΚΑΤΙ MS.: corr. Palmer, van Branteghem. 10 CETONTI **A**: corr. **A¹**. 12 φθέγγευ Blass, Wackernagel: φθέγγου MS. 13 ἀλκίμων] ΑΛΚΙΜΟΥ **A**:

5 The interrogative ἢ is followed by ἢ (8)...ἤ (11), as in Pind. *I.* VII. 3—12, Soph. *Ai.* 172—182.
6 ἀμφιβάλλει, 'besets,' with the στρατός implied by στραταγέτας. Eur. *Andr.* 706 f. Ἰλιάδα τε πόλιν...ὁ Διὸς ἶνις ἀμφέβαλε φόνῳ ('encompassed').
8 λῃσταί, not the Doric λᾳσταί, to avoid double αι; yet in XV. 17 λαΐδος: so V. 194 φήμα, but VIII. 3 προφάτας: v. 167 ἀδμήτα, but X. 84 ἄδματοι.
10 σεύοντ᾽, 'drive off.' For the elision of ι in Doric 3rd plur., cp. fr. 3. 12: Pind. *O.* VII. 10 κατέχοντ᾽: *P.* IV. 241 ἀγαπάζοντ᾽.—ἀγέλας, distinguished from ποίμνας in Hes. *Th.* 445 f. as 'herds' from 'flocks,' but here a substitute for it.
11 ἀμύσσει, 'gnaws': *Il.* 1. 243 σὺ δ᾽ ἔνδοθι θυμὸν ἀμύξεις: Aesch. *Pers.* 161 καί με καρδίαν ἀμύσσει φροντίς.
12 δοκέω, ‿‿- (cp. 27), as καλέω is scanned in Aesch. *Ag.* 147. Smyth

observes that disyllabic εω in the 1st pers. sing. of contracted verbs is nowhere else proved by metre in Ionic verse (*Ionic Dialect*, § 638. 2).
13 f. ἐπικουρίαν, 'aid': Aesch. *Pers.* 731 ὦ πόποι κεδνῆς ἀρωγῆς κἀπικουρίας στρατοῦ.—In καὶ τίν, after εἴ τινι, the καί is normal according to Greek idiom, though redundant for ours: 'if any man has, thou *also* hast.' Antiphon or. 5 § 23 ἐζητεῖτο οὐδέν τι μᾶλλον ὑπὸ τῶν ἄλλων ἢ καὶ ὑπ᾽ ἐμοῦ. (Cp. Soph. *O.C.* 53 n.)
—ἔμμεναι is used by B. only here: ἔμμεν in 31, 56, and v. 144: εἶμεν only in IX. 48.
15 Κρεούσας. It is only here that Creusa figures as wife of Pandion and mother of Aegeus. In the ordinary Attic legend (as old at least as Euripides) she is daughter of Erechtheus, wife of Xuthus, and mother by Apollo of Ion. The mother of Aegeus is elsewhere Πυλία,

Is the leader of a hostile army besetting the borders of our land? Or are robbers, devisers of evil, driving off our flocks of sheep perforce, in despite of the shepherds? Or what is the care that gnaws thy heart? Speak; for thou, methinks, if any mortal, hast the aid of valiant youth at hand, O son of Pandion and Creusa.

AEGEUS. A herald has lately come, whose feet have traversed str. 2. the long road from the Isthmus; and he tells of prodigious deeds by a man of might.

That man has slain the tremendous Sinis, who was foremost of mortals in strength, offspring of the Earth-shaker, the Lytaean son of Cronus. He has laid low the man-killing sow in Cremmyon's woods, and the wicked Sciron.

corr. **A³**.   **16** This verse, the last in col. XXXVI, has been added by another hand, the same which supplied the latter part of x. 23.—νέον Palmer: ..ΟΝ MS.— ἦλθεν K.: ΗΛΘΕ MS.   **18** ΛΕΓΕΙΝ **A**: corr. **A¹**.   **24** ΚΡΕΜΤῦΝΟΣ MS.: corr. K.

daughter of Πύλας, king of Megara, Apollod. 3. 15. 5 (where Πελία was a false reading): Paus. 1. 5. 3, where she is described as 'daughter of Pylas,' but not named. The mention of Creusa by B. suggests that there was as yet no fixed tradition.

16 f. ἀμείψας, 'having traversed'; Aesch. *Pers.* 69 πορθμὸν ἀμείψας (having 'crossed' the Hellespont): so Eur. *Or.* 1295 ἀμείβω κέλευθον.—'Ισθμίαν κέλευθον: the road along the coast from the Isthmus of Corinth to Athens, a distance of about 45 miles.

18 ἔργα. The five feats here ascribed to Theseus on his journey from the Isthmus to Athens are given in the same order by Diodorus IV. 59 and Plutarch *Thes.* 8—11. Those writers, however, relate another ἆθλος, which was the first,—the slaying of the robber Περιφήτης, called Κορυνήτης from his club, at Epidaurus. This feat may have been a later addition (C. Robert, *Hermes* 1898, p. 149). At any rate it is only the journey from the Isthmus (v. 17) that falls within the scope of the poem.—In enumerating the feats, τε is five times repeated (19, 23, 24, 26, 27).

20—22 Σίνιν: he dwelt at the Isthmus, and was called πιτυοκάμπτης from the manner in which he rent his victims, Diod. *l. c.*:—δύο πίτυς κάμπτων, καὶ πρὸς ἑκατέραν τὸν ἕνα βραχίονα προσδεσμεύων, ἄφνω τὰς πίτυς ἠφίει. Ovid *Met.* VII. 441 f. *qui poterat curvare trabes, et agebat ab alto | ad terram late sparsuras corpora*

pinus.—**Κρονίδα**, of Poseidon: XVI. 77 n. —**Λυταίου**, a Thessalian title of Poseidon, popularly explained as the 'looser' or 'opener,' because he had cleft a passage for the Peneius through the vale of Tempe: Steph. Byz. *s.v.* Λυταί (the name of a place in Thessaly), διὰ τὸ λῦσαι τὰ Τέμπη Ποσειδῶνα. See XIII. 20, n. on Πετραίου. Λυταίη is cited as a name of Thessaly by Hesychius. —**σεισίχθονος τέκος.** Höfer observes in Roscher's Lexicon (p. 1973) that all the robbers slain by Theseus on his way to Athens are somewhere connected with Poseidon as father.

23—25 σῦν τ' ἀνδροκτόνον: Plut. *Thes.* 9 ἡ Κρομμυωνία σῦς, ἣν Φαιὰν προσωνόμαζον. In some vase-paintings which depict this feat, a woman is seen, horror-stricken at the creature's fate: this is explained by a passage in the Vatican epitome of Apollod. 11. 54 (published by R. Wagner, and cited by Höfer *s.v.* Krommyon in Roscher II. p. 1450) σῦν τὴν καλουμένην Φαιὰν ὑπὸ τῆς θρεψάσης γραὸς αὐτήν.—**Κρεμμυῶνος**: Crommyon, on the Saronic gulf, about 12 miles E. of Corinth, and about 14 W.S.W. of Megara. Strabo (p. 380) reckons it to the Corinthian territory (as Paus. does, 3. 1. 3), but says that it formerly belonged to the Megarid. The form is Κρομμυών in Thuc., Κρομυών in Paus.; but Steph. Byz. attests Κρεμμυών: *Cremmyon* in Plin. *N. H.* 4. 7. 11, Hyginus *Fab.* 38. **ἀτάσθαλον** denotes reckless evil-doing; in *Il.* 22. 418 it is joined with ὀβριμοεργόν,

11 τάν τε Κερκυόνος παλαίστραν
12 ἔσχεν, Πολυπήμονός τε καρτερὰν
13 σφῦραν ἐξέβαλεν Προκό-
14 πτας, ἀρείονος τυχὼν
30 15 φωτός. ταῦτα δέδοιχ' ὅπᾳ τελεῖται.

στρ. γ'. ΧΟ. 1 Τίνα δ' ἔμμεν πόθεν ἄνδρα τοῦτον
2 λέγει, τίνα τε στολὰν ἔχοντα;
3 πότερα σὺν πολεμηΐοις ὅ-
4 πλοισι στρατιὰν ἄγοντα πολλάν;
35 5 ἢ μοῦνον σὺν ὀπάοσιν
6 στείχειν ἔμπορον οἷ' ἀλάταν
7 ἐπ' ἀλλοδαμίαν,
8 ἰσχυρόν τε καὶ ἄλκιμον
9 ὧδε καὶ θρασύν, ὅς τε τούτων
40 10 ἀνδρῶν κρατερὸν σθένος
11 ἔσχεν; ἦ θεὸς αὐτὸν ὁρμᾷ,
12 δίκας ἀδίκοισιν ὄφρα μήσεται·
13 οὐ γὰρ ῥᾴδιον αἰὲν ἐρ-
14 δοντα μὴ 'ντυχεῖν κακῷ.

26 Κερκυόνος] ΚΕΡΚΤΝΟC **A** : corr. **A**³.   **28** ΕΞΕΒΑΛΛΕΝ ms.: corr. K.
34 CTPATAN **A** : corr. **A**³.   **35** σὺν ὀπάοσιν Weil, Festa, Goligher: so Blass,
Smyth.   CΤΝΟΠΛΟΙCΙΝ ms.: συνόπλοιό νιν Ludwich: μόνον τ' ἀνοπλόν τέ νιν K. (So

and in Her. VIII. 109 with ἀνόσιον.—Σκίρωνα, a robber who used to throw travellers
from the 'Scironian rocks' into the sea.
The coast-road from Megara to Corinth
was called ἡ Σκιρωνικὴ ὁδός (Her. VIII. 71),
because, according to a Megarian legend,
Sciron had first made it practicable (Paus.
I. 44. 6). A few miles w. of Megara,
this road passed along the cliffs known as
Σκιρωνίδες (or Σκιράδες) πέτραι, formed
by the end of a rocky spur which runs
down from Mount Geraneia to the coast.
While in Ionic legend Sciron was a
malefactor, in the Megarian he was a
warlike hero, father of Endeïs the wife
of Aeacus (Plut. Thes. 10): cp. XII. 96 n.
26 Κερκυόνος : Diod. IV. 59 τὸν δια-
παλαίοντα τοῖς παριοῦσι, καὶ τὸν ἡττηθέντα
διαφθείροντα. He dwelt near Eleusis.
Theseus 'closed his wrestling-school'
(**παλαίστραν**). Ov. Met. VII. 439 Cer-
cyonis letum vidit Cerealis Eleusis. Pausanias (I. 39. 3), speaking of a place on
the road from Megara to Eleusis, says,

ὁ τόπος οὗτος παλαίστρα καὶ ἐς ἐμὲ
ἐκαλεῖτο Κερκυόνος.
27—30 Πολυπήμονος. Procoptes
(or Procrustes) is here his successor,
perhaps his son. Ovid Ibis 409 Ut
Sinis et Sciron et cum Polypemone natus :
where the 'son' is almost certainly
Procrustes, whom Ovid associates with
the others in Met. VII. 436 ff. and Heroid.
II. 69 ff. According to Paus. I. 38. 5
Procrustes was merely a surname of
Polypemon. But there may have been
different versions. B. supposes that Procrustes had received the σφῦρα, and
learned the use of it, from Polypemon.
For other views of the passage, see
Appendix.
ἐξέβαλεν : Il. 14. 419 (Hector falling)
χειρὸς δ' ἔκβαλεν ἔγχος : Eur. Andr. 629
ἐκβαλὼν ξίφος.—**Προκόπτας** (only here)
is 'he who cuts short' (though προ-
κόπτειν regularly means 'to make progress'), while Προκρούστης is 'he who
beats out' (as on an anvil). This brigand

He has closed the wrestling-school of Cercyon. The mighty
hammer of Polypemon has dropped from the hand of the
Maimer, who has met with a stronger than himself. I fear how
these things are to end.

CH. And who and whence is this man said to be, and how str. 3.
equipped? Is he leading a great host in warlike array? Or
travelling with his servants only, like a wayfarer who wanders
forth to a strange folk,—this man so vigorous, so valiant, and so
bold, who has quelled the stubborn strength of such foes? Verily
a god is speeding him, so that he shall bring a rightful doom on
the unrighteous; for it is not easy to achieve deed after deed
without chancing upon evil.

Jurenka, but with μοῦνον.)   **36** CTIXEIN MS. : corr. K.   **39** ὅς τε τούτων
Palmer, K. (ὃς τὸ τούτων Blass[1]): ὃς τοσούτων Platt, Blass[2] (ὃς τοιούτων conj. K.).
OC TOTTΩN MS.   **40** κρατερὸν] KAPTEPON MS.: corr. K.   **41** ἔσχεν]
EXEN **A**: corr. **A**[3]?

adjusted the length of his victims to his
κλίνη: Diod. IV. 59 τῶν μὲν μακροτέρων
τὰ προέχοντα μέρη τοῦ σώματος ἀπέ-
κοπτε, τῶν δ᾽ ἐλαττόνων τοὺς πόδας
προέκρουεν. B. may have used the new
word because he did not wish to shorten
the first ο of Προκρούστης.

The scene of this feat, the last on the
hero's journey, was always placed in
Attica; either at Hermos, an Attic deme
in the part of Aegaleos called Ποικίλον,
now the pass of Daphne (ἐν Ἕρμει Plut.
Thes. 11); or in Corydallos, the region
of Aegaleos nearest the sea (Diod. IV.
59); or close to Athens, on the banks
of the Cephisus (Ovid Met. VII. 438, Paus.
I. 38. 5).

30 ὅπᾳ τελεῖται, 'how all this will
end' ('where' would be ὅποι). Aegeus
fears that this hero may reach Athens,
and prove no less invincible there.—For
the fut. midd. of τελέω used as passive,
see Il. 2. 36, Od. 23. 254. In Aesch.
Ag. 68 τελεῖται is better taken as a
present; cp. 45 n.

31 τίνα...πόθεν: see on v. 86 ff. τίς...
ἐν ποίᾳ χθονί;

33 f. πότερα κ.τ.λ.: a question like
that asked in Soph. O. T. 750 f. concerning Laius: πότερον ἐχώρει βαιός ('in
small force'), ἢ πολλοὺς ἔχων | ἄνδρας
λοχίτας, οἶ᾽ ἀνὴρ ἀρχηγέτης;—ὅπλοισι,
the arms borne by the στρατιά, not merely
by the leader.

35 μοῦνον σὺν ὁπάοσιν, 'alone with
his attendants'; i.e. not leading a host,
but merely followed by one or two
servants, such as even a private traveller

might have with him. The relative sense
of μοῦνον is illustrated by Aesch. Pers.
734 μονάδα δὲ Ξέρξην ἔρημόν φασιν οὐ
πολλῶν μέτα.—The emendation σὺν ὁπάοσιν (σὺν ὅπλοισιν MS.) is palaeogra-
phically easy: for others, see Appendix.

36 ἔμπορον, viatorem (as in Soph.
O. C. 25, 303, 901): not 'merchant.'—
ἀλάταν=ἀλώμενον: in tragedy often said
of a roaming exile (Aesch. Ag. 1282 φυγὰς
δ᾽ ἀλήτης, τῆσδε γῆς ἀπόξενος).

37 ἀλλοδαμίαν, properly 'residence
abroad': Plat. Legg. 954 E ἐν ἀλλοδημίᾳ,
as opposed to living in Attica. Here the
word denotes the foreign place: cp. Il.
24. 480 f. ἐνὶ πάτρῃ | φῶτα κατακτείνας
ἄλλων ἐξίκετο δῆμον. For ἐπί, cp. Od. 11.
183 πλέων ἐπὶ οἴνοπα πόντον ἐπ᾽ ἀλλο-
θρόους ἀνθρώπους.

39 ὅς τε, as in XII. 105.—τούτων=
τοιούτων: Pind. O. IV. 26 οὗτος ἐγὼ
ταχυτᾶτι: talis ego pernicitate. The
conjecture ὃς τοιούτων (which would be
slightly preferable here to τοσούτων)
deserves to be weighed; but it seems
rather more likely that τε dropped out
between ὃς and τούτων.

42 ὄφρα μήσεται: for the fut. indic.
in the final clause, cp. Il. 16. 242 f.
θάρσυνον δέ οἱ ἦτορ ἐνὶ φρεσίν, ὄφρα καὶ
Ἕκτωρ | εἴσεται. Od. 1. 57 θέλγει, ὅπως
Ἰθάκην ἐπιλήσεται.

43 f. αἰὲν ἔρδοντα: the unbroken
series of his victories argues that Theseus
is under divine protection.—This is better
than to refer ἔρδοντα (as = 'doing evil')
to each of the vanquished.

45 15 πάντ᾽ ἐν τῷ δολιχῷ χρόνῳ τελεῖται.

στρ. δ΄. ΑΙΓ. 1 Δύο (F)οι φῶτε μόνους ἁμαρτεῖν
2 λέγει, περὶ φαιδίμοισι δ᾽ ὤμοις
3 ξίφος ἔχειν <ἐλεφαντόκωπον>·
4 ξεστοὺς δὲ δύ᾽ ἐν χέρεσσ᾽ ἄκοντας
Col. 38 50 5 κηΰτυκτον κυνέαν Λάκαι-
6 ναν κρατὸς πέρι πυρσοχαίτου·
7 στέρνοις τε πορφύρεον
8 χιτῶν᾽ ἄμφι, καὶ οὔλιον
9 Θεσσαλὰν χλαμύδ᾽· ὀμμάτων δὲ
55 10 στίλβειν ἄπο Λαμνίαν
11 φοίνισσαν φλόγα· παῖδα δ᾽ ἔμμεν

46 ἁμαρτεῖν] ὁμαρτεῖν K.   **48** ξίφος ἔχειν] Nothing has been lost in the MS.: the
rest of the verse was probably wanting in the archetype.   ἐλεφαντόκωπον, supplied by
Desrousseaux, is read by Blass, Jurenka, Smyth.—K. conj. κορύναν τε πυκνάν.
50 f. κηΰτυκτον] κηΰτυκον K.—πέρι J. (*Class. R.* XII. 155, Apr. 1898), Blass, Sitzler:

45 τῷ δολιχῷ χρόνῳ: for the art.,
cp. Her. v. 9 γένοιτο δ᾽ ἂν πᾶν ἐν τῷ
μακρῷ χρόνῳ: Soph. *Ai.* 646 ὁ μακρὸς...
χρόνος.—**τελεῖται** (pres.): an inten-
tional echo of τελεῖται (fut.) at the close
of the preceding strophe (30).
46 δύο...φῶτε. Are these merely
attendants of Theseus; or does the poet
indicate two heroes as his comrades?
The latter is the view of C. Robert
(*Hermes*, 1898, p. 150), who thinks that
Peirithous and Phorbas are meant. As
to Phorbas, son of Triopas, a famous
boxer, see *Hom. hymn. Ap. Pyth.* 33:
Paus. VII. 26. 12: schol. *Il.* 23. 660.
These two heroes are sometimes associated with Theseus, as in the carrying off
of the Amazon Antiope (Weizsäcker, art.
Peirithoos in Roscher's *Lex.*, p. 1783).
According to the usual legend, Theseus
journeyed alone from Troezen to Athens:
and in the sculptures of the Theseion,
depicting his feats on the way, he has
no companion (see Baumeister, *Denkm.*
vol. III. pp. 1779 ff.). But on a vase at
Munich (*Arch. Zeit.* 23, fig. 195) Theseus
has two comrades with him in his slaying
of Sinis and of Procrustes. Such an
addition is foreign to the spirit of the
original legend, the very point of which
is that Theseus braves the perils of the
road without support. It seems probable that the innovation may have
been due in the first instance to vase-

painters (p. 233).—As to the word
φῶτε, cp. n. on XVI. 49. **μόνους**, plur.
adj. with dual subst.: Plat. *Euthyd.*
p. 273 D ἐγελασάτην...ἄμφω βλέψαντες
εἰς ἀλλήλους.—**ἁμαρτεῖν** = ὁμαρτεῖν: n. on
VIII. 103 f.
48 ἐλεφαντόκωπον is aptly supplied
by Desrousseaux. According to Ovid
(*Met.* VII. 421 ff.) Theseus, after reaching
Athens, was about to drink the poisoned
chalice prepared for him by Medea, when
the *ivory hilt* of his sword revealed him
to Aegeus, who dashed the cup from his
lips:—*Cum pater in capulo gladii cognovit
eburno Signa sui generis, facinusque ex-
cussit ab ore.*
49 δύ᾽ ἄκοντας: the δύο δοῦρε of the
Homeric warrior (*Il.* 3. 18 etc.), the
αἰχμαὶ δίδυμαι of Pindar's Jason (*P.* IV.
79).—**χέρεσσ᾽**: epic elision of ι in the
dative: *Il.* 5. 5 ἀστέρ᾽ ὀπωρινῷ.
50 f. κηΰτυκτον: for the crasis cp. III.
81 χῶτι: also XVI. 33. The syllable
answering to the second of εὔτυκτον is
long in 35 (μοῦνον), though short in 5
and 20. It is unnecessary to write κηΰτυκον.—**κυνέαν Λάκαιναν.** The word
κυνέη, κυνῆ ('dog-skin') denoted (1) a
helmet, made either wholly of skin
(which might be ox-hide, marten-skin,
goat-skin, etc.), or of skin strengthened
with metal; hence χαλκήρης (*Il.* 3. 316).
In *Od.* 18. 378 κυνέη πάγχαλκος is one of
which leather forms merely the lining.

In the long course of time all things find their end.

AEG. Only two men attend him, says the herald. He str. 4.
has a sword, with ivory hilt, slung from his bright shoulders : he
carries in his hands a couple of polished javelins; a well-wrought
Laconian bonnet covers his ruddy locks ; around his breast he
wears a purple tunic and a thick Thessalian mantle. A fiery
light, as of the Lemnian flame, flashes from his eyes : a youth
he is

so Jurenka, Smyth. ΫΠΕΡ MS.   52 f. στέρνοις τε...χιτῶνα transposed by Wilamowitz and Platt: so also Smyth.—στέρνοις (rightly) **A**: στέρνοισι **A**¹.   55—57 omitted
by **A**, and added by **A**³ in the upper margin of col. XXXVIII.   56 ἔμμεν] ΕΜΕΝ MS.:
corr. K.

(2) But κυνῆ meant also a broad-brimmed
travelling hat (ἡλιοστερής, Soph. O. C.
313), such as was called 'Thessalian' or
'Arcadian' (id. fr. 251). Here the epithet
Λάκαινα probably denotes some kind of
κυνῆ worn by warriors.
κρατὸς πέρι. The MS. κρατὸς ὕπερ
gives ⌣ ⌣ - (-ὸς ὕπερ) where in 6, 21 and
36 we find - ⌣⌣. Crusius (Philol. LVII.
N. F. XI. p. 175) defends the variation
as a case of anaclasis, permissible in
Ionics: but it seems far more probable,
if not certain, that ὕπερ should be corrected to πέρι. When περί denotes
'position around,' the case is usually the
dative ; but the genitive also occurs:
Od. 5. 130 περὶ τρόπιος βεβαῶτα, 'be-
striding the keel' (cp. ib. 371 ἀμφ' ἑνὶ
δούρατι βαῖνε): also 5. 68 τετάνυστο περὶ
σπείους γλαφυροῖο | ἡμερίς ('about the
cave trailed a garden-vine'). — Smyth
suggests that κρατὸς πέρι here = 'above
the head.' For this old use of περί
as = ὑπέρ, cp. Alcaeus fr. 93 κεῖσθαι περ
κεφάλας...λίθος, Sappho fr. 1. 10 f. περὶ
γᾶς μελαίνας | πύκνα δίννεντες πτέρ' ἀπ'
ὠράνω αἴθε|ρος διὰ μέσσω, and fr. 92
πέρροχος = ὑπέροχος: also περίειμι, περι-
γίγνομαι as = 'to excel.' But, in reference to a helmet, the sense 'around'
is fitter.—πυρσοχαίτου: of a golden red
tint, which the Greeks admired: the
Daphnis and Menalcas of Theocritus (Id.
VIII. 3) are πυρροτρίχω.
52 f. In the reading of the MS., χιτῶνα
πορφύρεον | στέρνοις τ' ἀμφι, the place of
τε, as 4th instead of 2nd word, is impossible. [Jurenka defends it by referring
to Pind. O. III. 18 (φύτευμα) ξυνὸν ἀνθρώποις στέφανόν τ' ἀρετᾶν: but ξυνὸν there
belongs to φύτευμα, which he omits to
quote, and not to στέφανον.] The trans-

position στέρνοις τε...χιτών' is certain.
The error in the MS. was due, I suspect,
to some one who had noticed that two of
the three verses corresponding with 52,
viz. 7 and 37, begin with an iambus,
which he wished to obtain here by
shifting χιτῶν' from 53 to 52: though
the third, verse 22, might have shown
him that a spondee was equally admissible. All the three verses (8, 23, 38)
answering to 53 begin with a spondee;
but there, as at the beginning of v. 52,
an iambus was also correct.
53 f. οὔλιον here = οὔλάν, 'woolly,'
'thick.' Everywhere else in classical
Greek οὔλιος means 'destructive.'—Θεσσαλὰν χλαμύδ'. The χλαμύς, a short
mantle, was especially Thessalian (Pollux
VII. 46, X. 124),—a fact connected with
its fitness for riders on horseback. It
was often worn by soldiers: thus, in a
story told by Aelian (V. H. XIV. 10),
Demades asks Phocion for the chlamys
which he was wont to wear παρὰ τὴν
στρατηγίαν. The mention of it is the
more suitable here, in connexion with
πρώθηβον, as it was worn by the
Athenian ἔφηβοι: cp. Antidotus (of the
Middle Comedy) Πρωτόχορος fr. 1. 2
πρὶν ἐγγραφῆναι καὶ λαβεῖν τὸ χλαμύδιον,
—where the 'enrolment' is that of the
ephebus in the register of his deme
(ληξιαρχικὸν γραμματεῖον).
55 f. Λαμνίαν, i.e. fierce. The
volcano Μόσυχλος in Lemnos (Soph.
Phil. 800) gave rise to the proverbial
Λήμνιον πῦρ (Ar. Lys. 299): cp. Hesych.
Λήμνιον βλέπειν. — φοίνισσαν, fulvam,
the tawny-red hue of fire: Pind. P. I. 24
(of Aetna) φοίνισσα κυλινδομένα φλόξ:
Eur. Tro. 815 πυρὸς φοίνικι πνοᾷ. —
ἔμμεν: cp. 14 n.

12   πρώθηβον, ἀρηΐων δ' ἀθυρμάτων
13   μεμνᾶσθαι πολέμου τε καὶ
14   χαλκεοκτύπου μάχας·
60 15   δίζησθαι δὲ φιλαγλάους Ἀθάνας.

XVIII. [XIX.]

ΙΩ

ΑΘΗΝΑΙΟΙC

στρ.

1   Πάρεστι μυρία κέλευθος
2   ἀμβροσίων μελέων,
3   ὃς ἂν παρὰ Πιερίδων λά-
4   χῃσι δῶρα Μουσᾶν,
5   ἰοβλέφαροί τε καὶ
6   φερεστέφανοι Χάριτες
7   βάλωσιν ἄμφι τιμὰν
8   ὕμνοισιν· ὕφαινέ νυν ἐν
9   ταῖς πολυηράτοις τι κλεινὸν
10   ὀλβίαις Ἀθάναις,
11   εὐαίνετε Κηΐα μέριμνα.
12   πρέπει σε φερτάταν ἴμεν
13   ὁδὸν παρὰ Καλλιόπας λα-
14   χοῖσαν ἔξοχον γέρας.
15   ἦεν Ἄργος ὅθ' ἵππιον λιποῦσα

59 χαλκεοκτύπου] ΧΑΛΚΕΝΤΤΠΟΥ **A**: corr. **A³**.   **60** δίζησθαι δὲ] Blass thinks that all the letters after Δ were written by **A³** in a space left vacant by **A**. Θ has been made from A.
XVIII. The title added in the left margin by **A²**.—ΑΘΗΝΑΙΟΙC] Ἀθηναίοισι K.: but his final I may (as Ludwich and Blass think) have been part of a coronis

---

57 πρώθηβον: the Homeric form is πρωθήβης (*Il.* 8. 518 etc.): but a fem. πρωθήβη occurs once (*Od.* 1. 431). — ἀρηΐων ἀθυρμάτων: cp. Hor. *C.* I. 2. 37 f. (of Mars) *Heu nimis longo satiate ludo, Quem iuvat clamor galeaeque leves.* See n. on VIII. 87 Μουσᾶν...ἄθυρμα.
58 μεμνᾶσθαι, 'gives heed to,' 'is intent upon': Pind. fr. 94 μεμναίατ' ἀοιδᾶς, '(that they might) be mindful of song.' — The use of the perfect μέμνημαι in such phrases is distinct from that of the aorist in the Homeric μνήσασθε δὲ θούριδος ἀλκῆς (*Il.* 6. 112, '*bethink you...*').

59 χαλκεοκτύπου: n. on XIII. 15 f.
60 φιλαγλάους, 'splendour-loving,' 'brilliant.' Pindar, who perhaps invented the word, applies it (*P.* XII. 1) to the tutelary nymph of Acragas,—καλλίστα βροτεᾶν πολίων.

XVIII. 1 f. μυρία κέλευθος: v. 31 n. —ἀμβροσίων: Pind. *P.* IV. 299 παγὰν ἀμβροσίων ἐπέων.
3 f. ὃς ἂν: the antecedent to be supplied is τούτῳ, as in Soph. *Ant.* 35 f. ὃς ἂν τούτων τι δρᾷ, | φόνον προκεῖσθαι.— Πιερίδων: cp. 35: XV. 3 Πιερίαθεν.

in earliest manhood, intent on the pastimes of Ares,—on warfare
and the clangour of battle ; and he seeks brilliant Athens.

XVIII. [XIX.]

Io.

(FOR THE ATHENIANS.)

A thousand paths of poesy divine are open to him who has str.
received gifts from the Muses of Pieria, and whose songs have
been clothed with worship by the dark-eyed Graces who bring
the wreath.

Weave, then, some glorious lay in Athens, the lovely and the
blest, thou Cean fantasy of fair renown. A choice strain should
be thine, since Calliope has given thee a meed of signal honour.

There was a time when, by the counsels of wide-ruling Zeus

marking the end of ode XVII.　　　**3** ΠΕΙΕΡΙΔΩΝ MS.　　　**9** κλεινὸν K.,
Blass, Jurenka.—KAINON **A**: but **A**³ has written ε above AI, though without
changing A into Λ.　　　**15** TIHN MS.: see Appendix.—δθ'] OT **A**: corr. **A**³.—
ἵππιον] ΙΠΠΕΙΟΝ **A**: corr. **A**³?

—λάχῃσι, epic for λάχῃ: so fr. 16. 3
θάλπῃσι.

5—8 From ὃς ἄν we supply ᾧ ἄν for
this second clause ('and *for whom*').—
ἰοβλέφαροι, epithet of the Muses in
VIII. 3.—φερεστέφανοι, here with reference to victory in poetical contests:
epigr. 1. 2 f. πολέας δ' ἐν ἀθύρμασι
Μουσᾶν | Κηΐῳ ἀμφιτίθει Βακχυλίδῃ στε-
φάνους.—Χάριτες inspire song; v. 9 n.—
βάλωσιν ἄμφι = ἀμφιβάλωσιν : cp. IV.
20 n.—νυν with ὕ (cp. 21), the only
instance of the enclitic in B.

9 It is not easy to decide between
καινὸν, the scribe's reading, and κλεινὸν,
the corrector's. (1) καινόν is illustrated
by Pindar's frequent claim of 'newness'
for his song (O. III. 4, IX. 48: I. IV. 63,
etc.). But the ear of Bacchylides, peculiarly sensitive to recurrent vowel-
sounds, might have disliked καινόν so
soon after ὕφαινε. (2) For κλεινόν it
may be said that it is in good keeping
with the lofty tone of this proem; cp.
ἀμβροσίων μελέων—τιμάν—φερτάταν ὁδόν
—ἔξοχον γέρας. In v. 13 f. the poet is
Οὐρανίας κλεινὸς θεράπων. On the whole,
I accept κλεινόν, though without feeling
certain that it is right.

11 εὐαίνετε: cp. III. 64 μεγαλύνητε:

Pind. *P.* IV. 177 εὐαίνητος 'Ορφεύς. But
αἰνετός was used by Alcaeus and Antimachus (Steph. *Thesaur.*); as also by
Arist. *Rhet.* II. 25. 7. Pindar has αἰ-
νητός.—Κηΐα: cp. III. 98.—μέριμνα is
the *musing*, the fantasy, of the poet,—
here half-personified. (This is somewhat
different from Pindar's use of the word to
denote a 'pursuit,' *studium*,—*e.g.* in O.
VIII. 92 κρέσσονα πλούτου μέριμναν, 'an
ambition above wealth.')

13 f. ὁδόν, the course, or flight, of
poetry; cp. 1: IX. 51 f. ἐλαύνω | ἐκτὸς
ὁδοῦ. — Καλλιόπας: v. 176 n. — γέρας,
the 'meed of honour,' is the glorious
theme (Io) which the Muse has assigned
to the poet.

15 The MS. TIHN, if sound, must be
τί ἦν...; 'How was it?'—'What befell?'
—when Io was fleeing from Argos;—and
must be explained as an old formula for
beginning a story. There is, however,
no other trace of such a formula, though
a question to the Muse is, of course, a
common exordium, as in XIV. 47 Μοῦσα,
τίς πρῶτος λόγων ἄρχεν δικαίων; Neither
the hiatus nor the metre (‿‿ instead of
the ‿◡ found in 33) need in itself cause
doubt. Yet I find it very difficult to
believe that τί ἦν is right. The easiest

16 φεῦγε χρυσέα βοῦς,
17 εὐρυσθενέος φραδαῖσι φερτάτου Διός,
18 Ἰνάχου ῥοδοδάκτυλος κόρα·

ἀντ. 1 ὅτ᾽ Ἄργον ὄμμασιν βλέποντα
20 2 πάντοθεν ἀκαμάτοις
3 μεγιστοάνασσα κέλευσε
4 χρυσόπεπλος Ἥρα
5 ἄκοιτον ἄϋπνον ἐόν-
6 τα καλλικέραν δάμαλιν
25 7 φυλάσσεν· οὐδὲ Μαίας
8 υἱὸς δύνατ᾽ οὔτε κατ᾽ εὐ-
9 φεγγέας ἁμέρας λαθεῖν νιν
Col. 39 10 οὔτε νύκτας ἀγν[άς.
11 εἴτ᾽ οὖν γένετ᾽ ἐ[ν μάχας ἀγῶνι

21 κέλευσε Platt : κέλευσεν MS. **22** Omitted by **A**, but added in the lower margin by **A³**. **28** οὔτε] ΟΥΔΕ **A** : corr. **A³**?—ἀγνάς J., Sandys. **29** εἴτ᾽ οὖν J.

correction τίεν (G. E. Marindin), Doric inf., would go with γέρας, 'a choice theme for thee to celebrate'; but there is a point after γέρας in the MS. The most probable emendation (I think) is ἦεν (W. Headlam), 'There was a time when,' 'Once upon a time.' As Kenyon observes (p. 187), TI is very like H in the MS. A mis-reading of H as TI (τί) would naturally have led to EN being changed to HN (ἦν). See Appendix. ἵππιον: the epic ἱππόβοτον (Il. 2. 287 etc.): cp. x. 80 f. κλυτὸν ἱππόβοτον Ἄργος. The 'hill-girt' plain (τὸ κοῖλον Ἄργος, Soph. O.C.378) afforded excellent pasture. Strabo 8, p. 388 ἔστι δὲ καὶ τὸ γένος τῶν ἵππων ἄριστον τὸ Ἀρκαδικόν, καθάπερ καὶ τὸ Ἀργολικὸν καὶ τὸ Ἐπιδαύριον.
16 φεῦγε refers to the moment after the slaying of Argus by Hermes, when the gad-fly (οἶστρος) sent by Hera was driving Io forth from Argolis on her wanderings. Aesch. Suppl. 540 ff. λειμῶνα βούχιλον (the meadow where the cow was pastured), ἔνθεν Ἰὼ | οἴστρῳ ἐρεσσομένα | φεύγει ἁμαρτίνοος.
χρυσέα, 'precious' or 'peerless' (in the sight of Zeus); as the word so often denotes the beauty and charm of a goddess (v. 174 Aphrodite ; x. 117 Artemis ; Pindar I. VII. 5 f. the Muse). It seems probable that, like Aeschylus, Bacchylides imagined Io as a maiden with cow's horns (βούκερως παρθένος, Aesch. P.V. 588), and

not as completely transformed into a heifer. The word δάμαλις (24), like βοῦς, could be applied to the horned maiden. Such a conception gives greater fitness to χρυσέα. See Appendix.
17 εὐρυσθενέος: his power protects her in her wanderings far and wide.— φραδαῖσι, 'counsels,' a sense derived from the active φράζω: the god indicated the path of her wanderings. Cp. Aesch. 941 (of Orestes) θέσθεν εὖ φραδαῖσιν ὡρμημένος (as in Eum. 245 φραδαῖς are the 'hints' given to hounds by the scent): Eur. Phoen. 667 φραδαῖσι Παλλάδος. On the other hand in Pind. O. XII. 9 τῶν... μελλόντων... φραδαί ('perceptions,' γνώσεις schol.), the sense comes from the midd. φράζομαι. — φερτάτου, though φερτάταν occurs in v. 12: cp. XVI. 59 and 68, φύτευσε(ν).
18 Ἰνάχου. The Inachus (now the Bonitza), rising in the highlands on the Arcadian border, flows through the Argive plain into the Gulf. This river-god, son of Oceanus, figured as the earliest king of the land,—μέγα πρεσβεύων | Ἄργους τε γύαις Ἥρας τε πάγοις (Soph. Inachus, fr. 248).
19 f. Ἄργον, son of Earth; Aesch. P.V. 678 ff. βουκόλος δὲ γηγενὴς | ἄκρατος ὀργὴν Ἄργος ὡμάρτει, πυκνοῖς | ὄσσοις δεδορκώς: ib. 567 f. φοβοῦμαι | τὸν μυριωπὸν εἰσορῶσα βούταν. The poets and vase-painters of the fifth century imagined

most high, the heifer precious in his sight,—the rosy-fingered
maid born to Inachus,—was flying from Argos nurse of steeds :

when Argus, looking every way with tireless eyes, had been ant
charged by the great queen, Hera of golden robe, to keep
unresting, sleepless ward o'er that creature with the goodly horns.
Nor could Maia's son elude him in the sun-lit days or in the holy
nights.
Did it befall then that the

(*Class. R.* XII. 156), Blass, Jurenka : εἶτ' οὖν K.—The letter of which a vestige remains
after γένετ' is taken by Blass for E, by K. for A. It might be either ; but the former
seems slightly more probable. (Bl. supplies εἴτε μῦθος ἄλλως.)

him as having eyes all over his body :
Eur. *Phoen.* 1115 στικτοῖς πανόπτην
ὄμμασιν δεδορκότα (schol. κύκλῳ τὸ σῶμα
ὅλον ὠμματῶσθαι) : Ovid *Met.* I. 664
stellatus...Argus. It has generally been
assumed that Argus is the starry sky,
as Io is the moon. Cp. Plato *epigr.* 14
(Bergk II. p. 303) εἴθε γενοίμην | οὐρα-
νός, ὡς πολλοῖς ὄμμασιν ἐς σὲ βλέπω.
21 f. μεγιστοάνασσα (like ὑμνοάνασσα XI. 1, n.),=μεγίστη ἄνασσα : V.
199 μεγιστοπάτωρ, n. — χρυσόπεπλος :
here, a general epithet for a goddess.
In Pind. *I.* V. 75, χρυσοπέπλου Μναμοσύνας, it has a special fitness : Memory is
robed in golden hues.
23 ἄυπνον. In the older and simpler
myth all the eyes of Argus were sleepless :
the notion that they watched by relays
appears first in Euripides (*Phoen.* 1116 f.),
who is followed by Ovid (*Met.* 1. 686 f.),
and by Quintus Smyrnaeus 10. 191 :
Ἀργον, ὃς ὀφθαλμοῖσιν ἀμοιβαδὸν ὑπνώ-
εσκεν.—The first two syllables of ἐόν|τα
must have been scanned as one (cp. v. 5):
unless, indeed, B. wrote εὖν|τα, as in
III. 78.
24 καλλικέραν : see n. on XV. 22
ὑψικέραν.
25 φυλάσσεν : cp. XV. 18 θύεν (n.).
Aeschylus imagines Argus as closely
following Io's steps, wherever she moves
(*P.V.* 678 ff.). This is the conception
seen in some vase-paintings of Io, Argus,
and Hermes : Roscher's *Lexicon* II. p. 271 :
Baumeister, *Denkm.* I. p. 752. The story
that Argus tied her to an olive-tree in a
grove (Apollod. II. 1. 3, Plin. *N. H.* 16.
239) was suited to Io the complete heifer,
but not to the horned maiden.
Μαίας : Hes. *Theog.* 938 Ζηνὶ δ' ἄρ
Ἀτλαντὶς Μαίη τέκε κύδιμον Ἑρμῆν.
Ovid *Fast.* v. 663 *Clare nepos Atlantis,*

*ades, quem montibus olim Edidit Arcadiis
Pleïas una Iovi.* Cp. Hor. *C.* I. 10. 1.
28 ἁγνάς, 'holy'; the word expresses
a religious feeling for the beauty and
majesty of night, like the Homeric κνέφας
ἱερόν (*Il.* 11. 194), νὺξ ἀμβροσίη (2. 57
etc.). The epithet ἁγνός is applied by
Aesch. *P. V.* 28 to αἰθήρ: by Pindar to
the sun (*O.* VII. 60), to water (*I.* v. 74),
and to fire (*P.* I. 21).
29—36 εἶτ' οὖν—ἤ ῥα (33)—ἤ (35).
For εἶτε followed by ἤ (instead of a
second εἶτε), see Eur. *El.* 896 f., Plato
Phaedr. 277 D. Conversely ἤ ῥα...εἶτε,
Soph. *Ai.* 177 f.
Argus was slain by Hermes : about
that there was no doubt. But accounts
varied as to the manner of the slaying.
Some said that Hermes attacked him
openly : others, that Argus was first sent
to sleep, and then slain. Our poet sub-
divides this second alternative ; Argus
may have been sent to sleep (1) by sheer
exhaustion, or (2) by the lulling sounds
of music. The sense of the whole passage
is, in effect, as follows :—' Now (οὖν)
whether Hermes slew Argus [in open
fight];—or whether Argus was exhausted
by his anxieties, or lulled to sleep by
music,—for *me*, at any rate (37 ἐμοὶ μὲν
οὖν), it is safest [to pass on to the end
of the story,]—Io's arrival in Egypt.'
The hesitation of B. between different
forms of the story makes it likely that he
knew some authority, poetical or artistic,
for each. It is noteworthy that Aeschylus
also, while recognizing that Argus was
slain by Hermes (*Suppl.* 305), avoids
committing himself as to the manner of
the deed. Io says mysteriously (of Argus),
ἀπροσδόκητος δ' αὐτὸν αἰφνίδιος μόρος | τοῦ
ζῆν ἀπεστέρησεν (*P. V.* 680 f.).
29 γένετ', impers. (like συνέβη), with

J. B.   27

30 12 ποδαρκέ' ἄγγελο[ν Διὸς
13 κτανεῖν τότε [Γᾶς ὑπέροπλον
14 ὀβριμοσπόρου λ[όχον
15 Ἄργον· ἤ ῥα καὶ [ὄμματ' αἰνὰ λῦσαν
16 ἄσπετοι μέριμν[αι·
35 17 ἤ Πιερίδες φύτευ[σαν ἀδύμῳ μέλει
18 καδέων ἀνάπαυσ[ιν ἐμπέδων·

ἐπ.   ἐμοὶ μὲν οὖν
ἀσφαλέστατον ἁ πρ[ὸς ἔσχατ' οἶμα,
ἐπεὶ παρ' ἀνθεμώ[δεα
40 Νεῖλον ἀφίκετ' ο[ἰστροπλὰξ

31 Γᾶς ὑπέροπλον J.: Γᾶς ἀναφύντ' ἐξ Jurenka.   **32** ὀβριμοσπόρου] μ has been written above, between ὁ and β, by **A³**.—Jurenka finds after this word a trace of Λ, and supplies λέχευς : λόχον Blass. (γόνον conj. K. : τέκος formerly J.)   **33—51** For the conjectural supplements in these vv., see Appendix.   **33** ἤ ῥα J., Herwerden,

---

inf. **κτανεῖν**, 'it came to pass that...': a constr. used by Xen. *H.* v. 3. 10, who, however, adds ὥστε before the inf. (οὐδ' ἂν γενέσθαι ὥστε ἅμα ἀμφοτέρους...ἔξω Σπάρτης εἶναι). The Homeric epithet of Hermes, ἀργεϊφόντης, was traditionally explained as 'Argus-slayer,' though its real sense may have been 'swiftly appearing' (φαν).—The words lost after **γένετ'** probably expressed the idea, '*by an open attack,*'—as distinguished from an assault on the sleeping Argus. The first letter after **γένετ'** seems to have been E rather than A. Perhaps, then, ἐν μάχας ἀγῶνι (or ἐς χέρας μολόντα). If the first letter were Α, ἀμφαδὸν βαλόντα would be possible.—The *open* attack is shown on a vase figured in Roscher II. 279: Argus is prostrate; Hermes slays him with a sword. According to Apollod. II. 1, § 4, Hermes killed him λίθῳ βαλών.

31 Γᾶς: Argus is called 'the son of Earth' by Aesch. *P. V.* 678 (n. on 19 f.); *Suppl.* 305; also by Acusilaus (*c.* 500 B.C.), fr. 17 (Müller I. p. 102), whose source may have been Hesiod. Others made him a son of Agenor, of Arestor (Ov. *Met.* I. 624), or even of Inachus: Apollod. II. 1. §§ 2, 3.—**ὑπέροπλον**: cp. VIII. 13 : Argus is described by Apollodorus *l.c.* as ὑπερβάλλων...δυνάμει, and by Quintus Smyrn. 10. 190 as μέγας.

32 The letter after ὀβριμοσπόρου seems to have been Λ; hence Blass supplies **λόχον.** That word occurs only in the sense of 'parturition' (Aesch. *Suppl.* 676

λόχοι γυναικῶν, *Ag.* 137 πρὸ λόχοῦ), but doubtless might be used (like Lat. *partus*) in the sense of 'offspring,' as λοχεία is in Anth. Planud. 132. 3, δυοκαιδεκάπαιδα λοχείην (Niobe's children). If synaphea could be assumed, **λόχευμ'** would also be possible.

33 f. ἤ ῥα: as to the accent of ἤ, see Appendix.—**ἄσπετοι μέριμναι** are 'the immense *cares,*' '*anxieties,*' of Argus. This is the normal sense of the plural μέριμναι: cp. v. 7 : Theognis 343 : Pind. *I.* VII. 13, fr. 218, fr. 248: Aesch. *Theb.* 270, 831; *Eum.* 340: Eur. *Heracl.* 594, *Bacch.* 380: Diphilus *incert.* 5 λύπας, μερίμνας. (In another, but rarer, use μέριμναι refers to objects of pursuit or study: see I. 69: Emped. 113 δολιχόφρονες...μερίμναι, 'penetrating thoughts'; Ar. *Nub.* 1404.) It seems improbable, then, that μέριμναι here can mean either (1) 'the unceasing efforts,' or 'devices,' used by Hermes against Argus—as Kenyon takes it : or (2) 'the ineffable counsels' of Zeus, as Wilamowitz suggests. The general sense of the words which followed ἤ ῥα καὶ in 33 must have been, 'exhausted him,' 'made him succumb to sleep.' We might conjecture (*e.g.*) ἄνδρ' ὕπνῳ δάμασσαν, or ὄμματ' αἰνὰ λῦσαν ('relaxed,' 'caused to close,' Soph. *Ant.* 1302 λύει κελαινὰ βλέφαρα).

35 f. ἤ Πιερίδες κ.τ.λ. It seems hardly doubtful that **καδέων** are the troubles of Argus, not those of Io. The death of Argus brought no ἀνάπαυσις to

swift messenger of Zeus slew huge Argus, Earth's fierce offspring, [in combat]? Or did the watcher's unending cares [close his dread eyes;] or was he lulled to rest from weary troubles by the sweet melody of the Pierian sisters?

For me, at least, the surest path of song [is that which leads epode. me to the end]; when Io, driven by the gadfly, reached the flowery banks of Nile,

Jurenka: ἦ ῥα K., Blass: Ĥ PA ms.   **34** μέριμναι J., and so K., Jurenka, Blass[2]. [In his 1st ed., Bl., with K., read an accent on the I of MEPIM, which would be against the nomin.; but he now recognizes that there is no such accent.]   **38** The letters ÅΠ are certain. A faint trace after Π points, I think, to P. So Blass also holds; and Kenyon (who formerly suggested E) now inclines to this.

her: then came the οἶστρος.—**ἀδύμῳ**: a word used by the poet's uncle Simonides (Eustath. *Il.* p. 163. 28).—**ἐμπέδων**: cp. *Il.* 8. 521 φυλακή...ἔμπεδος: Soph. *O. C.* 1674 πόνον ἔμπεδον. I had thought also of · ὑστάταν (since he was to wake no more); but a simple epithet for καδέων is perhaps more in this poet's manner.

The story was that Hermes disguised himself as a shepherd, and lulled Argus to sleep by playing on the σῦριγξ. According to Ovid *Met.* 1. 673—719, while some of the watcher's eyes were closed by the music, others remained open; but these finally yielded to a discourse by Hermes on the invention of the instrument:—*Talia dicturus vidit Cyllenius omnes Succubuisse oculos, adopertaque lumina somno.* Hermes then deepens the slumber by waving his charmed wand above the sleeper's face. *Nec mora, falcato nutantem vulnerat ense Qua collo confine caput,* i.e. he decapitates Argus with a sickle (ἅρπη). Valerius Flaccus *Arg.* IV. 384—390 tells the tale more briefly, but with a similar ending;— *languentia somno Lumina cuncta videt, dulcesque sequentia somnos, Et celerem mediis in cantibus exigit harpen.* Lucan also arms Hermes with the *harpe* (*Phars.* 9. 663). Until this ode was recovered, the story was known only from the Latin sources. It is the subject of a wall-painting at Herculaneum (Baumeister I. p. 752, fig. 802), suggested by Ovid *Met.* 1. 687 f.: Hermes, who has just been playing the syrinx, is holding it out to Argus, who looks at it in wonder.

37 ἐμοὶ μὲν οὖν, 'for *me*, at any rate' (i.e. whatever may be the truth as to the slaying of Argus). μέν emphasizes ἐμοί: οὖν marks the return to the main

thread of the discourse (after vv. 29—36); a sense which it often has in the formula δ' οὖν (Aesch. *P. V.* 226, *Ag.* 224, etc.). —These three words always formed a complete verse in the ms.

38 ἀσφαλέστατον. The general sense is clear from the context. 'For me, at any rate, it is safest to pass (from disputed points) to the end of the story, which is certain.' The first two letters after ἀσφαλέστατον were ἀπ. The third letter, of which only a slight trace remains, was, according to Blass, ρ: Kenyon read it as ε. If it was ρ, then ἀ was certainly the definite article: and this affords the easiest line of restoration. As to metre, verses 15 and 33 might lead us to suppose that the measure of the lost words was $- \smile \smile - \smile - \stackrel{\smile}{\scriptstyle-}$; and this would at least be metrically fitting. (It cannot, however, be deemed certain: $- \smile - \stackrel{\smile}{\scriptstyle-} - \smile -$ is another possibility.) Such being the data, we might conjecture (e.g.), ἀ πρὸς ἔσχατ' οὖμα, '*the strain that brings me to the close.*' Or ἀ πρόσω κέλευθος '*the onward course*' (of song, v. 1), (telling of the time) when,' etc.—For other suggestions, see Appendix.

39 ἀνθεμώδεα: cp. XV. 5 (Hebrus), 34 (Lycormas).

40 The letter after ἀφίκετ' was ο: οἰστροπλάξ (Blass) is fairly certain. Aesch. *P. V.* 681 οἰστροπλὴξ δ' ἐγὼ | μάστιγι θεία γῆν πρὸ γῆς ἐλαύνομαι: cp. Soph. *El.* 5.—A Pompeian wall-painting (figured in Roscher's *Lexicon*, II. 275) depicts Io's arrival in Egypt. She has been carried by Nilus to the bank of his stream. The goddess of the country (Aegyptus) greets Io with outstretched right hand, while the left holds the

Ἰὼ φέρουσα παῖδ[α γαστρὶ τὸν Διός,
Ἔπαφον· ἔνθα νί[ν τέκ' εὐκλέα
λινοστόλων πρύ[τανιν πολιτᾶν,
ὑπερόχῳ βρύοντ[α τιμᾷ,
45 μεγίσταν τε θνα[τῶν ἔφανεν γενέθλαν,
ὅθεν καὶ Ἀγανορί[δας
ἐν ἑπταπύλοισ[ι Θήβαις
Κάδμος Σεμέλ[αν φύτευσεν,
ἃ τὸν ὀρσιβάκχαν
50 τίκτεν Διόνυσον, [εὐφρόνων τε κώμων
καὶ χορῶν στεφα[νοφόρων ἄνακτα.

---

42 ἔνθα νιν] ΕΝΘΕΝΙ **Α**: corr. **Α³**? **46** Ἀγανορίδας Crusius, Wilamowitz. **47** Κάδμος] ΚΑΔΟC **Α**: corr. **Α³**.—Σεμέλαν] Between CE and ΜΕΛ there is a space

---

Uraeus snake; beside her is the child Harpocrates, giving the sign of silence with finger on lip. In the background stand two women with rattles (σεῖστρα), symbolizing the association of Io with Isis. Io is described by Valerius Flaccus 4. 418 as *Aspide cincta comas et ovanti persona sistro*.

41 Ἰὼ φέρουσα παῖδα. To complete the verse I suggest γαστρὶ τὸν Διός, because: (1) φέρουσα alone could not well mean 'carrying in the womb'; on the other hand cp. *Il*. 6. 58 f. μηδ' ὄντινα γαστέρι μήτηρ...φέροι: Plat. *Legg*. 792 Ε τὰς φερούσας ἐν γαστρί. (2) A mention of Zeus as the father is here indispensable.

42 Ἔπαφον. Aeschylus derives the name from ἐπαφή. When Io reached the Canopic mouth of the Nile (*P.V.* 846), Zeus by the *touch* of his hand restored her natural form and her reason: ἐνταῦθα δή σε Ζεὺς τίθησιν ἔμφρονα, | ἐπαφῶν ἀταρβεῖ χειρὶ καὶ θιγὼν μόνον (*ib.* 848 f.). Hence Epaphus is ῥυσίων ἐπώνυμος (*Suppl*. 314) because the ἐπαφή was Io's 'deliverance.' Aeschylus further

conceived that the child was engendered by this touch: *Suppl*. 312 καὶ Ζεύς γ' ἐφάπτωρ χειρὶ φιτεύει γόνον, and *P.V.* 850 f. ἐπώνυμον δὲ τῶν Διὸς γεννημάτων (the fatherhood of Zeus) | τέξεις κελαινὸν Ἔπαφον. Bacchylides, on the other hand, imagines Io as already great with child when she reaches Egypt.— Herodotus (II. 153) says, ὁ δὲ Ἆπις κατὰ τὴν Ἑλλήνων γλῶσσαν ἐστὶ Ἔπαφος (cp. II. 27, 28). But the Greeks who thus connected the *names* would never have identified the Epaphus of their myth with the sacred calf of Egypt.

ἔνθα νιν τέκ': Apollod. II. I. 4 (Io) τελευταῖον ἧκεν εἰς Αἴγυπτον· ὅπου τὴν ἀρχαίαν μορφὴν ἀπολαβοῦσα γεννᾷ παρὰ τῷ Νείλῳ ποταμῷ Ἔπαφον παῖδα. For τέκ'...πρύτανιν, cp. I. 15 ff. δεκάτῳ δ' Εὐξάντιον | μηνὶ τέκ' εὐπλόκαμος | νύμφα φερεκυδέϊ νάσῳ | ...πρύτανιν.—εὐκλέα would be scanned --, as in v. 196.

43 λινοστόλων, epithet of the Egyptians: Her. II. 37 εἵματα δὲ λίνεα φορέουσι αἰεὶ νεόπλυτα. Kaibel *Epigr. Gr*. 1028 (an Egyptian hymn to Isis, of *c*. 350 A.D.), Αἰγύπτου βασίλεια λινό-

bearing in her womb Epaphus, child of Zeus.
There she brought him forth, to be glorious lord of the linen-
robed folk, a prince flourishing in transcendent honour; and
there she founded the mightiest race among men. From that
race sprang Cadmus, son of Agenor, who in Thebes of the seven
gates became father of Semele. And her son was Dionysus,
inspirer of Bacchants, [king of joyous revels] and of choruses
that wear the wreath...

of about half an inch, through which a horizontal line was drawn: cp. XII. 156.
50 f. See Appendix.

στολε.—**πολιτᾶν** seems a fitting supplement, since Epaphos was the legendary
founder of Memphis: Apollod. II. 1. 4
Ἔπαφος δὲ βασιλεύων Αἰγυπτίων γαμεῖ
Μέμφιν τὴν Νείλου θυγατέρα, καὶ ἀπὸ
ταύτης κτίζει Μέμφιν πόλιν. (Note that
Aeschylus, though he deemed Canopus
to be the scene of Io's healing, is careful
to bring in Memphis also: καὶ μὴν Κά-
νωβον κἀπὶ Μέμφιν ἵκετο : Suppl. 311.)
44 τιμᾷ is better here than πλούτῳ.—
Aesch. Suppl. 581 f. describes Epaphus
as παῖδ' ἀμεμφῆ, | δι' αἰῶνος μακροῦ πάν-
ολβον.
45 μεγίσταν τε θνατῶν, 'the mightiest
(race) among men' (cp. III. 61 μέγιστα
θνατῶν). These two bacchii suggest that
the form of the complete verse may
have been ‿ – –, ‿ – – | ‿ – –, ‿ – ≍, like
τίς ἀχώ, τίς ὀδμὰ προσέπτα μ' ἀφεγγής;
(Aesch. P. V. 115): see W. Christ,
Metrik p. 415. If so, we might supply
ἔφανεν (or **κτίσ' αὐτοῦ) γενέθλαν.**—
Epaphus was the father of Λιβύη (Aesch.
Suppl. 317), from whose union with
Poseidon sprang Agenor (father of
Cadmus), and Belus (father of Aegyptus
and Danaus): see the stemma in Introd.
to this Ode.
46 Ἀγανορίδας: Agenor was king
of Phoenicia. Eur. Phrixus (fr. 819)
Σιδώνιόν ποτ' ἄστυ Κάδμος ἐκλιπών, | Ἀγή-
νορος παῖς, ἦλθε Θηβαίων χθόνα | Φοῖνιξ
πεφυκώς, ἐκ δ' ἀμείβεται γένος | Ἑλληνικόν,

Διρκαῖον οἰκήσας πέδον. Cp. Roscher
Lex. II. p. 833. Hence to the Euripidean
chorus of Phoenician women Io is προμά-
τωρ (Phoen. 676), as she is also to the
Argive Danaidae (ἁ πρόγονος βοῦς, Aesch.
Suppl. 43 f., παλαιομάτωρ Eur. Suppl.
628).
48 f. Σεμέλαν, daughter of Cadmus
and Harmonia (Hes. Theog. 975 f.).—
τὸν ὀρσιβάκχαν (only here): cp. the poet
cited by Plut. De exsilio p. 607 C, Εὔϊον
ὀρσιγύναικα Διόνυσον μαινομέναις θύοντα
τιμαῖς: Soph. O. T. 211 ff. οἰνῶπα Βάκχον
εὔϊον, | Μαινάδων ὁμόστολον.
50 f. Διόνυσον in the MS. is presumably sound: Blass changes it to Δῖον
υἱόν, but this seems unwarrantable. The
MS. τίκτε should probably be **τίκτεν**: no
verse in this ode begins with – ‿ ‿ ‿.
After τίκτεν Διόνυσον Jurenka supplies
ἀγλαῶν τε κώμων. A possible substitute
for ἀγλαῶν would be εὐφρόνων: cp. X. 12
κῶμοί τε καὶ εὐφροσύναι. In 51 στεφανά-
φόρων ἄνακτα (Wilamowitz) gives a fitting
sense. As this is a dithyramb for Athens,
χορῶν probably refers to the contests of
dithyrambic choruses at the Dionysia.
Wreaths of ivy were worn by the members of a κύκλιος χορός: cp. Simonides
fr. 148 (which some ascribed to Bacchylides, Bergk[4] III. 496), πολλάκι δὴ φυλῆς
Ἀκαμαντίδος ἐν χοροῖσιν Ὧραι | ἀνωλόλυξαν
κισσοφόροις ἐπὶ διθυράμβοις.

XIX. [XX.]

ΙΔΑC

ΛΑΚΕΔΑΙΜΟΝΙΟΙC

Σπάρτᾳ ποτ᾽ ἐν ε[ὐρυχόρῳ
ξανθαὶ Λακεδαιμον[ίων
τοιόνδε μέλος κ[όραι ὕμνευν,
ὅτ᾽ ἄγετο καλλιπά[ρᾳον
5 κόραν θρασυκάρ[διος Ἴδας
Μάρπησσαν ἰότ[ριχ᾽ ἐς οἴκους,
φυγὼν θανάτου τ[αχὺν οἶτον,
ἀναξίαλος Ποσει[δὰν ὅτε δίφρον ὀπάσσας
ἵππους τέ (ϝ)οι ἰσαν[έμους
10 Πλευρῶν᾽ ἐς ἐϋκτ[ιμέναν ἐπόρευσε παραὶ
χρυσάσπιδος υἱὸ[ν Ἄρηος

[The rest is lost.]

XIX. The title added in the left margin by **A²**.   **1—11** For the conjectural supplements see Appendix.   **6** After ϊ are seen the remains of Ο. The third letter must have been Τ: there are slight traces of the left part of the cross-stroke.—

XIX. 1 Idas. son of Aphareus, carried off Marpessa, daughter of Evenus, from Pleuron in Aetolia, Poseidon having given him a chariot with winged horses. See Introduction to this Ode.—**εὐρυχόρῳ**, epithet of Argos in IX. 31. See Appendix. εὐρυαγυίᾳ is also possible.—Cp. the beginning of the ὑμέναιος for Peithetaerus and Basileia in Ar. *Αν.* 1731, Ἥρᾳ ποτ᾽ Ὀλυμπίᾳ, κ.τ.λ.: also that of Theocr. XVIII. (the Epithalamion of Helen), ἔν ποκ᾽ ἄρα Σπάρτᾳ ξανθότριχι πὰρ Μενελάῳ, κ.τ.λ. **2 f. Λακεδαιμονίων...κόραι ὕμνευν.** I prefer ὕμνευν to the ᾆδον of Wilamowitz:

B. would have written ἄειδον. The fact that κόραν occurs in v. 5 is scarcely an objection to κόραι. But a possible alternative is **Λακεδαιμόνιαι...κελάδησαν**: in XV. 12 that verb refers to choral singing. **4** ἄγετο: cp. Her. I. 59 γυναῖκα...ἄγεσθαι...ἐς τὰ οἰκία. The home to which Idas brought Marpessa was, according to Simonides (schol. *Il.* 9. 556), Ἀρήνη in Messenia (*Il.* 2. 591, 11. 723: Ap. Rhod. I. 152); Apollodorus also (I. 7. 8) says εἰς Μεσσήνην. But B., as these verses indicate, must have placed that home at Sparta. **6** ἰότριχ᾽. The letter after ιο was certainly τ. ἰόθριξ, though not extant, is

XIX. [XX.]

IDAS.

(FOR THE LACEDAEMONIANS.)

In spacious Sparta of yore the golden-haired maidens of
Lacedaemon chanted such a song as this, when bold-hearted
Idas was bringing home the fair maiden, Marpessa of the violet
locks, after escaping the swift doom of death; when Poseidon,
lord of the sea, had given him a chariot, with steeds swift as
the wind, and had sped him on his way to well-built Pleuron, to
the son of Ares with golden shield...

ἰότριχ' ἐς οἴκους J.   **7** The letter after θανάτου seems to have been Τ.—ταχὺν
οἶτον Jurenka.   **8** Ποσειδὰν] ΠΑΟΙ **Α** : Ο written above Α (by **Α²**?).—ὅτε δίφρον
ὁπάσσας conj. J.   **10** ἐπόρευσε παραὶ conj. J.

fully warranted by εὔθριξ, λεπτόθριξ (v. 28),
λευκόθριξ, μελανόθριξ, ξανθόθριξ (v. 37),
τανύθριξ, χρυσόθριξ.
7 φυγὼν θανάτου...οἶτον. As we learn
from the schol. on Pind. *I*. III. 72 (=ιν.
54), Bacchylides said, doubtless in this
poem, that Evenus roofed a temple of
Poseidon with the skulls of competitors
for the hand of Marpessa whom he had
defeated in a contest. (The skulls of
Hippodameia's vanquished suitors were
put to the same use by her father, according to Sophocles in his *Oenomaus*.)
φυγών refers, then, to the escape of Idas
from this doom at Pleuron; not (as Blass
takes it) to his escape from pursuit after
crossing the river Lycormas. Having once
started from Pleuron with Marpessa in
his magic chariot, Idas had nothing more
to fear.
8 ἀναξίαλος (only here): cp. vi. 10 n.—
The ποσι- of the MS. was doubtless
Ποσ(ε)ιδᾶν : as to the inconstant spelling
of that name, see crit. n. on ix. 19.—The
metre of ἀναξίαλος Ποσειδᾶν, (⏑)-⏑⏑-⏑--,
was a permissible variation on (⏑)-⏑⏑-
⏑⏑-(≚) in the prosodiacus (p. 120). No

supplement is metrically necessary. But, in
view of the whole context, it seems probable that some words followed, with the
rhythm, perhaps, of ⏑⏑-⏑⏑-(-): *e.g.*
ὅτε δίφρον ὁπάσσας, or ἐπεὶ ἄρμα πορών.
—Apollod. i. 7. 8 Μάρπησσαν...Ἴδας...
ἥρπασε, λαβὼν παρὰ Ποσειδῶνος ἄρμα
ὑπόπτερον. Poseidon gave aid to
Pelops, in view of his contest with
Oenomaus, Pind. *O*. i. 86 f. τὸν μὲν
ἀγάλλων θεὸς | ἔδωκεν δίφρον τε χρύσεον
πτεροῖσίν τ' ἀκάμαντας ἵππους. B. may
similarly have imagined the ἵππους ἰσανέμους (9) as winged.
10 Πλευρών' : see v. 151 n.—The
context indicates that a verb meaning
'sent,' to which Poseidon was subject,
stood in this verse (or in 9). ἐπόρευσε
παραὶ would serve. Cp. Pind. *O*. i. 77
(Pelops to Poseidon) ἐμὲ δ' ἐπὶ ταχυ-
τάτων πόρευσον ἁρμάτων | ἐς Ἆλιν. Or
πέμψεν παραὶ, which would give a verse
like that in Ar. *Ran*. 220. For παραί,
cp. xii. 150.
11 υἱὸν Ἄρηος : Evenus, son of Ares
by Demonice, daughter of Agenor of
Pleuron (Apollod. i. 7. 7).

FRAGMENTS OF BACCHYLIDES,

AND NOTICES OF HIS POEMS,

FOUND IN ANCIENT WRITERS.

In Bergk's *Poetae Lyrici Graeci*, vol. III. pp. 569—588 (4th ed. 1882), 69 passages are collected, which contain either fragments of Bacchylides or references to his works. Of the fragments, the following occur in the lately-recovered poems :—

Bergk's fr. 1 = v. 50—55, ὄλβιος .. ἔφυ.
2 (verses 1 and 2) = v. 160—162, θνατοῖσι .. φέγγος.
6 = v. 37—40, ξανθότριχα .. νικάσαντα.
8 = Kenyon's fr. 5, l. 5, προσφώνει τέ νιν, and certainly belonged to Ode I. (See Blass, 3rd ed., p. 25, v. 76.)
9 = X. 1 and 4—7, Νίκα .. ἀρετᾶς.
29 = XIV. 50—56, ὦ Τρῶες .. σύνοικον.
30 = I. 49—51, φάσω τε .. ὁμιλεῖ.
47 = v. 26 f. νωμᾶ|ται .. χάει.

Further, fr. 41, Ποσειδάνιον .. φορεῦντες, is *partly* preserved on a small piece of the papyrus, fr. 2 (Kenyon). See below, fr. 6 in my edition.

Fr. 17 (Servius on *Aen.* VI. 21) refers to XVI. 2 : see Introd. to that ode.

Fr. 52 (Apollon. *De Synt.* 186) refers to ἀριστάρχου Διός in XII. 58.

Fr. 59 (Schol. *Il.* 24. 496) refers to a statement probably contained in the lost part of XIV (see n. on XIV. vv. 37 ff.): and the same may be said of fr. 61 (Schol. Pind. *I.* IV. 92) relatively to XIX (see n. on XIX. v. 7).

There are also three of the old fragments which are conjecturally connected by Blass with the newly-found odes.

These are : (1) fr. 7 (Bergk), ὦ Πέλοπος .. πύλαι, which may well have belonged to the lost exordium of Ode I : Blass (2nd ed., p. 21 f.) places it there as vv. 13 f.

(2) Fr. 35, οὐ γὰρ ὑπόκλοπον .. σοφία, which, on the suggestion of G. F. Hill, Blass (p. 127) refers to XIV, as vv. 30 f.

(3) Fr. 46, δυσμενέων δ' ἀϊδής, used by Blass (p. 119), with the support of some slight traces in the papyrus, in supplying XII. 208 f. Lastly, with regard to Bergk's fr. 5, Blass (p. 160 n.) seems right in rejecting it*. On the other hand, no. 86 of Bergk's *fragmenta adespota* is assigned by Blass to Bacchylides : see below, no. 32.

The principle adopted in my edition has been that of distinguishing 'Fragments' in the proper sense,—*i.e.* citations giving the actual words of the poet,—from notices which do not give his words, but merely report the substance of what he said. There may be instances in which it is hard to say whether, or how far, a notice embodies a fragment. But in the case of Bacchylides there is, I think, only one such instance, viz. Bergk's no. 15 (my no. 5) ; and that should probably be reckoned among the fragments proper. Again, notices (as distinguished from fragments proper) may conveniently be brought under two distinct heads, according as they do, or do not, specify the class of the composition (such as dithyramb, paean, etc.) to which they severally refer.

I have therefore arranged these relics of Bacchylides as follows :— A. Fragments : B. Notices which specify a class of poem : C. Notices which do not specify a class. Under C it has been possible to facilitate reference by recognising two chief groups of subject-matter, the mythological and the geographical.

The subjoined table shows the correspondence between the numbering of the fragments and notices in (1) Bergk's *Poetae Lyrici*, 4th ed. : (2) Blass's 3rd ed. of Bacchylides : and (3) the present edition, denoted by 'J.' For reasons which will appear from what has been said above, the following fragments of Bergk are omitted ;—1, 2·(verses 1 and 2), 5, 6, 7, 8, 9, 17, 29, 30, 35, 46, 47, 52 : but 41, 59 and 61 are included †.

---

* It is Schol. Aristid. III. p. 317, referring to the origin of the chariot (ἄρμα) :— ἄλλοι δὲ λέγουσιν ὅτι ἐκ Σικελίας ἐφάνη τὴν ἀρχήν. Βακχυλίδης γὰρ καὶ Πίνδαρος Ἱέρωνα καὶ Γέλωνα τοὺς Σικελίας ἄρχοντας ὑμνήσαντες καὶ πλεῖστα θαυμάσαντες ἐν ἱππη- λασίᾳ πρὸς χάριν αὐτῶν εἶπον ὡς Σικελιῶται πρῶτοι ἄρμα ἐξεῦρον. So C. But the *Iliad* alone would have forbidden such a statement. Pindar, in fr. 106, merely praises the Theban ἄρμα and the Sicilian ὄχημα. And in the text of the schol. given by BD this passage runs thus :—οἱ γὰρ περὶ Βακχυλίδην καὶ Πίνδαρον ὑμνήσαντες τοὺς περὶ Ἱέρωνα καὶ Γέλωνα ἐν ἱππικῇ παρέσχον ὑπόνοιαν Σικελιώτας τὴν ἱππικὴν ἐξευρεῖν.

† Five of the items in my list of 61 are absent from this table, as they have no numbered counterparts in Bergk. These are :—(1) No. 32 = Blass 37 A. This is reckoned by Bergk, not among the fragments of Bacchylides, but among the *adespota*. (2) No. 37 ; cited by Bergk in a n. on his fr. 11, p. 572, and by Blass in a n. on his fr. 2, p. 160. (3) No. 40, which I do not find in Bergk : Blass has it on p. 165, but without a number. (4) No. 46 ; cited by Bergk in a n. on his fr. 29, p. 580, and noticed by Blass on p. 159. (5) No. 50, the passage of Natalis Comes, which Bergk gives at the end (p. 588), but without numbering it : so also Blass, p. 176.

Bergk.	Blass.	J.	Bergk.	Blass.	J.
2, verse 3	37	28	39	30	22
3	25	21	40	31	23
4	1	1	41	(p. 159)	6
10	(p. 137)	35	42	32	26
11	2	2	43	33	27
12	3	36	44	34	24
13	4	3	45	35	30
14	5	4	48	Ep. 1, p. 176	33
15	6	5	49	Ep. 2, ,,	34
16	7	39	50	38	41
18	8	38	51	39	31
19	11	7	53	40	60
20	12	8	54	41	45
21	13	9	55	42	54
22	14	10	56	10	49
23	15	11	57	(p. 166 n.)	42
24	17	13	58	43	59
25	18	14	59	(p. lxvii)	56
26	19	15	60	44	47
27	20	16	61	(p. 158)	48
28	21	17	62	45	44
31	16	12	63	46	52
32	9	51	64	47	53
33	22	18	65	48	58
34	23	19	66	49	57
36	24	20	67	50	61
37	27	29	68	51	43
38	29	25	69	52	55

A. FRAGMENTS.

ΕΠΙΝΙΚΟΙ.

1. [Bergk 4 : Blass 1.]

Ὡς δ' ἅπαξ εἰπεῖν, φρένα καὶ πυκινὰν
κέρδος ἀνθρώπων βιᾶται.

Stobaeus, *Flor.* 10. 14 : Βακχυλίδου Ἐπινικῶν (*sic* A : Βακχυλίδου simply, Trin-cavellus, ed. 1536).—'Be it said once for all, even wise minds are overmastered by love of gain.' **ὡς δ' ἅπαξ εἰπεῖν**, to sum up the matter in a single broad statement (without taking account of exceptions) : a phrase practically equivalent to ὡς ἁπλῶς (or καθόλου) εἰπεῖν, but more sententious and emphatic.—Cp. XII. 199 f., εἰ μή τινα θερσιεπὴς | φθόνος βιᾶται.

ΥΜΝΟΙ.

2. [B. 11 : Bl. 2.]

Αἰαῖ τέκος ἀμέτερον,
μεῖζον ἢ πενθεῖν ἐφάνη κακόν, ἀφθέγκτοισιν ἶσον.

Stob. *Flor.* 122. 1 : Βακχυλίδου Ὑμνων.—'Alas, my child, a sorrow has come, too great for tears, one of those that can find no voice.' Cp. Her. III. 14 τὰ μὲν οἰκήϊα ἦν μέζω κακὰ ἢ ὥστε ἀνακλαίειν : Thuc. VII. 75 §4 μείζω ἢ κατὰ δάκρυα...πεπονθότας.— For ἀφθέγκτοισιν cp. Pind. *P.* IV. 237 ἀφωνήτῳ..ἄχει.—Metre : dactylo-epitrite.

FRAGMENTS. 411

ΠΑΙΑΝΕΣ.

3. [B. 13 : Bl. 4.]

Τίκτει δέ τε θνατοῖσιν εἰρήνα μεγάλα
πλοῦτον μελιγλώσσων τ' ἀοιδᾶν ἄνθεα,
δαιδαλέων τ' ἐπὶ βωμῶν θεοῖσιν αἴθεσθαι βοῶν
ξανθᾷ φλογὶ μῆρα τανυτρίχων τε μήλων,
5 γυμνασίων τε νέοις αὐλῶν τε καὶ κώμων μέλειν.
ἐν δὲ σιδαροδέτοις πόρπαξιν αἰθᾶν
ἀραχνᾶν ἱστοὶ πέλονται·
ἔγχεά τε λογχωτὰ ξίφεα τ' ἀμφάκεα δάμναται εὐρώς.
χαλκεᾶν δ' οὐκ ἔστι σαλπίγγων κτύπος,
10 οὐδὲ συλᾶται μελίφρων ὕπνος ἀπὸ βλεφάρων,
ἀῷος ὃς θάλπει κέαρ.
συμποσίων δ' ἐρατῶν βρίθοντ' ἀγυιαί, παιδικοί θ' ὕμνοι
φλέγονται.

Stob. *Flor.* 55. 3 : Βακχυλίδου Παιάνων.—The paean to which our fragment belonged was presumably composed in strophe, antistrophe, and epode : but critics differ as to the place which the extant verses held in the scheme of the triad. (1) M. Schmidt (Pind. *Ol.* p. LXXII) thinks that vv. 1—5 form a complete antistrophe, the epode beginning at v. 6. (2) Hartung finds the epode in 1—5, and the strophe in 6—11. (3) Bergk, *Poet. Lyr. Gr.*⁴ III. 573, regards vv. 1—5 as the last part of the antistrophe, and 6—12 as a complete epode. (4) Blass, in *Rhein. Mus.* XXXII. 460, gives an ingenious reconstruction, according to which v. 1 is the last of an epode ; vv. 2—9 (as numbered by him, *i.e.* from πλοῦτον down to πέλονται) constitute the strophe ; and the remaining lines complete the antistrophe. To obtain this correspondence, however, it is necessary to make two assumptions. (i) That in v. 8 (=11 Blass) a dactyl beginning with a vowel has been lost between δάμναται and εὐρώς. (*E.g.* ἔμπεδον would serve.) (ii) That in v. 11 (=15 Bl.) the MS. ἆμος or ἆμος is corrupted from a word of which the scansion was – – ⏑. Blass writes ἀῷος, comparing Pind. *P.* IX. 23 ff., τὸν δὲ σύγκοιτον γλυκὺν | παῦρον ἐπὶ γλεφάροις | ὕπνον ἀναλίσκοισα ῥέποντα πρὸς ἀῶ: and [Eur.] *Rhes.* 554 f. θέλγει δ' ὄμματος ἕδραν | ὕπνος· ἄδιστος γὰρ ἔβα βλεφάροις πρὸς ἀοῦς. This may be accepted. The s of the corrupt ἆμος (or ἆμος) is a strong point in its favour. We have to suppose a form of ωι which could be mistaken for M. (iii) That ἀραχνᾶν (⏑ ⏑ –) in v. 9 (Bl.) answers to παιδικοί in the last verse : Blass holds this to be legitimate (*Praef.* p. XL).
On the whole, I incline to think (with Weir Smyth, *Melic Poets* p. 448) that Blass's arrangement, though worthy of careful consideration, is somewhat too hazardous. Our data, in fact, do not suffice to determine the question of structure here. I therefore print the verses without any attempt at indicating divisions.—The metre is dactylo-epitrite.
'Yea, and Peace, mighty goddess, brings forth wealth for mortals, and the flowers of honied song ; her gift it is that thigh-flesh of oxen and of fleecy sheep is burnt to the gods in the yellow flame on carven altars ; and that youths disport themselves with bodily feats, and with flutes and revels.
'The webs of red-brown spiders are on the iron-bound handles of shields ; sharp-pointed spears and two-edged swords are a prey to rust. No blast of bronze trumpet is heard ; sleep of gentle spirit, that comforts the heart at dawn, is not stolen from the eyelids. Joyous feasting abounds in the streets, and songs in praise of youths flame forth.'

1. δέ τε : cp. XII. 129 n.—Stephanus and Ursinus omit τε. Bergk would prefer

τοι.—**μεγάλα** is, as Smyth remarks, a somewhat rare epithet for a goddess (though it is given to Demeter and Persephone, to Moira, and to the Erinys) : but it seems not unsuitable here, where the poet insists on the beneficent *power* of Eirene over human life. In any case it is not endurable to take it as acc. neut. plur., in apposition with the following accusatives. Bergk would prefer μέγαν : Hartung, μέγαν τε.— **2. πλοῦτον μελιγλώσσων τ'** Boeckh, Neue, Blass : πλοῦτον καὶ μελιγλώσσων MSS. of Stobaeus: so Bergk, Smyth.—Cp. Philemon, Πύρρος 7 ff. (of Εἰρήνη), ὦ Ζεῦ φίλτατε, | τῆς ἐπαφροδίτου καὶ φιλανθρώπου θεοῦ· | γάμους, ἑορτάς, συγγενεῖς, παῖδας, φίλους, | πλοῦτον, ὑγίειαν, σῖτον, οἶνον, ἡδονὴν | αὕτη δίδωσι. In the marketplace at Athens (Paus. I. 8 § 2, 9. 16 § 2) there was a statue by Cephisodotus (*c.* 370 B.C.) of Peace nursing the infant Wealth, whom she supports on her left arm,—the original, as Brunn recognised, of a statue now at Munich (Ernest Gardner, *Greek Sculpture*, II. 352 f.).—**3. αἴθεσθαι** L. Dindorf and Schneidewin : ἔθεσθε the better MSS. of Stobaeus, whence Gesner τίθενται (correcting it, however, in the margin to τίθεσθαι) : αἴθεται P. Leopardus *Emend.* IV. 21.—The inf. αἴθεσθαι, like μέλειν in 5, depends on τίκτει as=ποιεῖ, τίθησι.—**4. ξανθᾷ φλογί**, as in Ode III. 56.—**μῆρα τανυτρίχων**. The MSS. of Stobaeus agree in εὐτρίχων, but before it have μεριταν, μηρίταν, or μηρύταν. These traces clearly point to μηρία (μῆρα) τανυτρίχων. It is possible that μηρί' εὐτρίχων was another old reading ; and Blass prefers this on the metrical ground ('soluta autem thesis parum cum Bacch. convenit'). But it should be remembered that, when ταν had once been absorbed into μεριταν (etc.), -υτρίχων would have generated εὐτρίχων. That is, while the existence of τανυτρίχων prior to the corruption in the MSS. is reasonably certain, that of εὐτρίχων is not so. Gesner and Grotius wrote μερίδες εὐτρίχων : Leopardus (and Stephanus), μηρία τῶν εὐτρίχων : Buttmann, μῆρα δασυτρίχων, which was received by Boeckh, and (in preference to his own μηρί' εὔτριχων) by Neue.—**5. γυμνασίων**, athletic exercises : Pind. fr. 129. 4 καὶ τοὶ μὲν ἵπποις γυμνασίοις τε, τοὶ δὲ πεσσοῖς, | τοὶ δὲ φορμίγγεσσι τέρπονται. Cp. Ar. *Nub.* 1002, where the Δίκαιος Λόγος describes the healthy pleasures in store for the Athenian youth, if he be well advised ;—ἀλλ' οὖν λιπαρός γε καὶ εὐανθὴς ἐν γυμνασίοις διατρίψεις.—**αὐλῶν** : associated with a κῶμος in II. 12 and in VIII. 68.

6—10 Plut. *Numa* 20 quotes these verses, without the poet's name. The blessings of Numa's reign were such, ὥστε καὶ τὰς ποιητικὰς ὑπερβολὰς ἐνδεῖν πρὸς τὴν τότε κατάστασιν λέγουσιν, ἐν δὲ σιδαροδέτοις πόρπαξιν αἰθᾶν ἀραχνᾶν ἔργα, καὶ εὐρὼς δάμναται ἔγχεά τε λογχωτά (and the rest, down to βλεφάρων). This inexact quotation, evidently made from memory, suggests how well-known the poem was in Plutarch's time. **6 πόρπαξιν.** ˙The πόρπαξ was a leathern thong, carried round the inner edge of the shield, and fixed at intervals by the πόρπαι or pins from which it took its name, so as to form a succession of loops : hence σιδαρόδετος. A figure from a Greek vase (Smith, *Dict. Ant.* I. 459, *clipeus*) shows a warrior whose left arm is passed through a band (ὄχανον or ὀχάνη) traversing the diameter of the shield, while his hand grasps the πόρπαξ. Cp. my ed. of Soph. *Ai.*, App. on 575 f. The context here implies that the shield is hung up with the πόρπαξ attached ; but the latter could be removed (cp. Ar. *Eq.* 849). In Ar. *Pax* 662 Eirene is addressed as ἃ γυναικῶν μισοπορπακιστάτη.—**αἰθᾶν**, of a reddish-brown colour : cp. n. on VIII. 10. **7 ἀραχνᾶν**, an unusual scansion, possible also (though not certain) in Eur. fr. 369 κεῖσθω δόρυ μοι μίτον ἀμφιπλέκειν ἀράχναις. Cp. the ἄ in ἄχνη (Eur. *Or.* 115). Smyth compares (*inter alia*) Theocr. XVI. 96 ἀράχνια δ' εἰς ὅπλ' ἀράχναι | λεπτὰ διαστήσαιτο : Nonnus *Dionys.* XXXVIII. 13 ἔκειτο δὲ τηλόθι χάρμης | Βακχιὰς ἑξαέτηρος ἀραχνιόωσα βοείη.—**πέλονται**, a word used in IX. 38 ; here somewhat weak, but not doubtful. (Ursinus conjectured πλέκονται.) **8 ἔγχεα**, like ξίφεα, is scanned as ‿‿. **λογχωτά**: Eur. *Bacch.* 761 λογχωτὸν βέλος (the sharp-pointed ἀκόντιον). λόγχη is the spear-head (= αἰχμή), ἔγχος here the shaft (δόρυ). **9 οὐκ ἔστι** Plut. *Num.* 20, Bergk : οὐκέτι MSS. of Stob., vulg. **11** Most MSS. have ἆμος (ἆμος Vindob.): ἀμὸν Heyne, Bergk : ἀμὸν (= ἡμέτερον) Smyth. **ἆφος** Blass (see p. 411). **12 βρίθοντ'.** When the ι of the 3rd plur. is to be elided, B. uses the form in -οντι : cp. XVII. 10 σεύοντ'.—**ἀγυιαί** : cp. III. 16.—**παιδικοί θ' ὕμνοι** : probably songs addressed to youths, the παίδειοι ὕμνοι of Pind. *I.* II. 3 ; see n. on IX. 42. The words could, however, mean 'songs sung by youths ' : cp. παιδικῷ χορῷ in Lys. or. 21 § 4.—**φλέγονται** : Aesch. *Ag.* 91 βωμοὶ δώροισι φλέγονται. (Bergk conj. φλέγοντι : but B. would probably have written φλέγουσι, as in V. 24 he has ἴσχουσι.) Cp. Pind. *O.* IX. 21 f. πόλιν | μαλεραῖς ἐπιφλέγων ἀοιδαῖς.

4. [B. 14 : Bl. 5.]

Ἕτερος ἐξ ἑτέρου σοφὸς τό τε πάλαι τό τε νῦν.
οὐδὲ γὰρ ῥᾷστον ἀρρήτων ἐπέων πύλας
ἐξευρεῖν.

Clem. Alex. *Strom.* v. 687 : Ἕτερος δὲ...τό τε νῦν, φησὶ Βακχυλίδης ἐν τοῖς
Παιᾶσιν, οὐδὲ γὰρ κ.τ.λ.—The metre is logaoedic.
'Poet is heir to poet, now as of yore; for in sooth 'tis no light task to find the
gates of virgin song.'—**ἀρρήτων ἐπέων,** verses, poetry, 'unuttered' before,—original :
cp. Soph. *Ant.* 556 ἀλλ' οὐκ ἐπ' ἀρρήτοις γε τοῖς ἐμοῖς λόγοις.—**πύλας,** Pindaric: *O.* VI.
27 πύλας ὕμνων ἀναπιτνάμεν. Contrast Pind. *O.* II. 86 σοφὸς ὁ πολλὰ ϝειδὼς φυᾷ·
μαθόντες δὲ λάβροι | παγγλωσσίᾳ, κόρακες ὥς, ἄκραντα γαρύετον | Διὸς πρὸς ὄρνιχα θεῖον.
On this and the similar passages in *O.* IX. 100 ff. and *N.* III. 40 ff., see pp. 15—17.
It seems not improbable that, in writing the words quoted by Clement, Bacchylides
was thinking of such Pindaric utterances, which express scorn for the man who has
learned from others, as distinguished from the man of original genius. If, however,
that be so, the tone of the reply is gentle and modest. See pp. 23 f.

5. [B. 15 : Bl. 5.]

Ἄρκτου παρούσης ἴχνη μὴ ζήτει.

Zenobius III. 36 : Ἐπὶ τῶν δειλῶν κυνηγῶν εἴρηται ἡ παροιμία· μέμνηται δὲ αὐτῆς
Βακχυλίδης ἐν Παιᾶσιν.—'Do not look for the bear's tracks when he is close by.'—
As μέμνηται does not necessarily imply more than an *allusion* to the proverb, it seems
doubtful whether, or how far, the words quoted can be assumed to be those used by
the poet : but ἄρκτου παρούσης, at least, might well be his.

ΔΙΘΥΡΑΜΒΟΙ.

6. [B. 41 : Bl. p. 159.]

Ποσει]δάνιον ὤ[ς
Μαντ]ινέες τριό[δοντα χαλκοδαιδάλοισιν ἐν
ἀσπίσι]ν φορεῦν[τες...
ἀφ' ἱπποτρ]όφου πό[λιος...

Schol. Pind. *O.* XI. 83 : Ὁ Δίδυμος δὲ οὕτω καθίστησι τὸν λόγον· τὴν Μαντινέαν
φησὶν ἱερὰν τοῦ Ποσειδῶνος καὶ παρατίθεται τὸν Βακχυλίδην λέγοντα οὕτω · Ποσειδάνιον
(Gott. Vrat. D., vulg. -ώνιον) ὡς Μαντινεῖς τριόδοντα χαλκοδαιδάλοισιν ἐν
ἀσπίσι φορεῦντες.—The citation is now supplemented by a fragment of the papyrus,
which gives the letters printed above between] and [in each verse. The occurrence
of the words in our MS. makes it certain that they come from a dithyramb,—as
Neue (p. 24) had conjectured, comparing Servius on *Aen.* XI. 93. (See below, no. 36.)
Blass supposes that the dithyramb was Κασσάνδρα, containing her prophecy of the
Trojan War, from which Horace (according to Porphyrion) imitated that of Nereus in
C. I. 15. These words occurred (Blass suggests) in an enumeration of the Greek
forces.—'(Seest thou)..how the Mantineans, bearing the trident of Poseidon on their
finely-wrought shields of bronze,..(come)..from their horse-nurturing city?'—Metre,
dactylo-epitrite.

ΠΡΟΣΟΔΙΑ.

7. [B. 19 : Bl. 11.]

Εἷς ὅρος, μία βροτοῖσίν ἐστιν εὐτυχίας ὁδός,
θυμὸν εἴ τις ἔχων ἀπενθῆ διατελεῖν δύναται βίον·
ὃς δὲ μυρία μὲν ἀμφιπολεῖ φρενί,
τὸ δὲ παρ᾽ ἆμάρ τε καὶ νύκτα μελλόντων χάριν
ἑὸν ἰάπτεται κέαρ, ἄκαρπον ἔχει πόνον.

Stob. *Flor.* 108. 26 : Βακχυλίδου Προσωδιῶν (*sic* A), *i.e.* Προσοδίων.—The metre is logaoedic.
'One canon is there, one sure way, of happiness for mortals—if one can keep a cheerful spirit throughout life. But he whose thoughts are busy with countless cares, and who afflicts his soul day and night about the future, has barren toil.'
1 ὅρος is the canon, the rule or standard, by which true εὐτυχία is to be measured : **ὁδός**, the course to be followed. **2 διατελεῖν δύναται** Bergk, Smyth : δύναται διατελεῖν MSS. **3 μυρία μὲν** MSS. : μυρίαν μενοινὰν Bergk. **4 τὸ δὲ παρ᾽ ἆμάρ τε**] παρόμαρτε MSS. : corrected by Grotius (who, however, wrote τόδε παρ᾽ ἦμάρ τε): τὸ δὲ πᾶν ἦμάρ τε Stephanus. **5 ἑὸν ἰάπτεται** Grotius: αἰὲν ἰάπτ., Boeckh, Blass[2] : ἀόνι (αονι Vindob.) ἄπτεται MSS. For ἄπτεται Stephanus conjectured δάπτεται, and so Ursinus, Brunck, Ilgen, Jacobs, the two latter changing ἀόνι to ἀνία.—ἰάπτεται lit. 'is hurt' : cp. *Od.* 2. 376 ὡς ἂν μὴ κλαίουσα κατὰ χρόα καλὸν ἰάπτῃ ('mar'). Moschus 4. 39 ἰάπτομαι ἄλγεσιν ἦτορ.—**ἄκαρπον** MSS. : ἀκάρπωτον Bergk.

8. [B. 20 : Bl. 12.]

τί γὰρ ἐλαφρὸν ἔτ᾽ ἐστὶν ἄπρακτ᾽ ὀδυρόμενον δονεῖν
καρδίαν ;

Stob. *Flor.* 108. 49 : Βακχυλίδου Προσωδιῶν (*sic* A). Metre, logaoedic. These words belong to the same poem as fr. 7, and may, as Neue thought, have immediately followed it.
'What ease is left to him who agitates his heart with vain laments?'—**ἐλαφρὸν** here is strictly 'ease-giving' :—'what alleviation (κούφισμα) is there any more (ἔτι) in lamenting?' etc. : *i.e.*, no comfort remains to him who indulges in it. Bergk says, '**ἔτ᾽** *displicet, fort.* ἔμ᾽ *legendum*' : I cannot agree.—ἐστὶν Blass : ἔστ᾽ MSS.—Bergk, keeping ἔστ᾽, inserts ὧδ᾽ before ὀδυρόμενον.—**δονεῖν** : cp. Ode 1. 69.

9. [B. 21 : Bl. 13.]

Πάντεσσι θνατοῖσι δαίμων ἐπέταξε πόνους ἄλλοισιν ἄλλους.

Stob. *Flor.* 118. 25 : Βακχυλίδου Προσωδιῶν (*sic* A).—Metre, dactylo-epitrite.—'On all mortals hath the god laid toils; each man bears his own.'

ΥΠΟΡΧΗΜΑΤΑ.

10. [B. 22 : Bl. 14.]

Λυδία μὲν γὰρ λίθος μανύει
χρυσόν, ἀνδρῶν δ᾽ ἀρετὰν σοφία τε παγκρατής τ᾽ ἐλέγχει
ἀλάθεια.....

FRAGMENTS. 415

Stob. *Flor.* 11. 7 : Βακχυλίδου Ὑπορχημάτων. The verses are found also on a gem in Caylus' *Rec. d'Antiq.* vol. v. pl. 50, 4.—Metre, logaoedic.

'The Lydian stone reveals gold ; the worth of men is evinced by the poet's art and by all-powerful truth.' **1 Λυδία..λίθος** (*lapis Lydius*), the βάσανος or *touchstone* (a flinty slate, black, grey, or white), on which pure gold is tested by rubbing : Theognis 449 εὑρήσεις δέ με πᾶσιν ἐπ' ἔργμασιν ὥσπερ ἄπεφθον | χρυσόν, ἐρυθρὸν ἰδεῖν τριβόμενον βασάνῳ. Pind. *P.* x. 67 πειρῶντι δὲ καὶ χρυσὸς ἐν βασάνῳ πρέπει | καὶ νόος ὀρθός. In Soph. fr. 732 Λυδία λίθος = Μαγνῆτις λίθος (Eur. fr. 567. 2).—**μανύει** with ὔ, as in Pind. *P.* i. 93 etc. (in Attic always ῡ). **2 σοφία τε παγκρατής τ'...** **ἀλάθεια.** This reading is found in several MSS. of Stobaeus (see Bergk⁴ III. p. 576), and on the gem of Caylus. It seems to me clearly the right one. The poet's faculty (σοφία) evinces, brings out (ἐλέγχει) the ἀρετή of men (as in the case of victors in the games), and the poet's just tribute is confirmed by ἀλάθεια. That is, candid men recognise that the poet has spoken truly ; and, even if there be some detraction at the moment, the true estimate prevails in the end. The strongest corroboration of this reading is (to my thinking) afforded by the poet's own words in Ode VIII. 82 ff. : τό γέ τοι καλὸν ἔργον | γνησίων ὕμνων τυχὸν | ὑψοῦ παρὰ δαίμοσι κεῖται· | σὺν δ' ἀλαθείᾳ βροτῶν | κάλλιστον, εἴπερ καὶ θάνῃ τις, | λείπεται Μουσᾶν ἀγακλειτᾶν ἄθυρμα. There, as here, σοφία renders the due praise, and ἀλάθεια ratifies it. See also XII. 202 ff. : βροτῶν δὲ μῶμος | πάντεσσι μέν ἐστιν ἐπ' ἔργοις· | ἀ δ' ἀλαθεία φιλεῖ | νικᾶν, ὅ τε πανδαμάτωρ | χρόνος τὸ καλῶς | ἐργμένον αἰὲν ἀέξει. Compare, too, Pind. *O.* x. 4 ff., where the agencies of Poetry and of Truth are invoked together : ὦ Μοῖσ', ἀλλὰ σὺ καὶ θυγάτηρ | Ἀλάθεια Διός, ὀρθᾷ χερὶ | ἐρύκετον ψευδέων | ἐνιπὰν ἀλιτόξενον. It is to the credit of Neue (*Bacchyl. Cei Fragmenta*, 1822, p. 32) that he supported this reading at a time when most critics,—indeed he says, ' *recentiores critici...omnes*,'—were against it. '*Sicut aurum probatur lapide Lydio admoto, ita virorum virtutem arguit poetica facultas cum veritate.*'—Weir Smyth also adopts this view.—The alternative reading is **σοφίαν τε παγκρατὴς ἐλέγχει ἀλάθεια.** The acc. σοφίαν is in some MSS. of Stobaeus (see Bergk *l.c.*). So Salmasius read, followed by Grotius, as now by Bergk and Blass. The sense given by this reading is, in itself, satisfactory enough ; whether σοφίαν be taken as 'wisdom' generally, or (as seems better) with reference to the poet's art. On the latter view, Bacchylides will say that the man of worth, and the genuine poet, are ultimately recognised by the voice of truth. There is, however, much less point in such a sentiment than in that afforded by the other reading. The alliance of poetry with truth in securing recognition, even though tardy, for ἀρετή is a thought specially characteristic of Bacchylides.—Cp. frag. 27.

[In Stob. *Flor.* 11. 2 (=20 Hense) we read : Ὀλυμπιάδος. Ἀλάθεια θεῶν ὁμόπολις, μόνα (-η MSS.) θεοῖς (βροτῶν conj. Bergk) συνδιαιτωμένα (-η MSS.). Bergk conjectures that this fragment belongs to Bacchylides, observing that Damascius places it immediately after the verses Λυδία μὲν γὰρ λίθος κ.τ.λ. The lemma Ὀλυμπιάδος may, he thinks, be due (as Meineke surmised) to the fact that Stobaeus here cited Pind. *O.* x. 65, which occurs in Damascius ; he would change θεῶν to βροτῶν.]

11. [B. 23 : Bl. 15.]

Οὐχ ἕδρας ἔργον οὐδ᾽ ἀμβολᾶς,
ἀλλὰ χρυσαίγιδος Ἰτωνίας
χρὴ παρ᾽ εὐδαίδαλον ναὸν ἐλθόντας ἁβρόν τι δεῖξαι < μέλος >.

Dionys. *De Compos. Verb.* c. 25 : παρὰ Βακχυλίδῃ. That the poem was a hypor-cheme is shown by a grammarian in Keil *Anal. Gramm.* 7. 21 : φιλεῖ δὲ τὰ ὑπορχήματα τούτῳ τῷ ποδὶ καταμετρεῖσθαι, οἷον Οὐχ ἕδρας ἔργον οὐδ᾽ ἀμβολᾶς; also by Athen. p. 631 C ἡ δ᾽ ὑπορχηματική (sc. ὄρχησις) ἐστιν ἐν ᾗ ᾄδων ὁ χορὸς ὀρχεῖται· φησὶ γοῦν ὁ Βακχυλίδης Οὐχ ἕδρας...ἀμβολᾶς. The first verse, which had become quasi-prover-bial, occurs also in Aelian *Nat. Anim.* VI. 1, Lucian *Scyth.* 11 οὐχ ἕδρας τοίνυν οὐδ ἀμβολᾶς ἔργον, ὡς ὁ Κεῖός φησιν, Achilles Tatius V. 12 οὐχ ἕδρας < ἔργον > οὐδ ἀναβολῆς.—The rhythm is paeonic, the verses consisting of a series of cretics.

'This is no time for sitting still or tarrying : we must go to the richly-wrought temple of Itonia with golden aegis, and show forth some choice strain of song.'— **2 Ἰτωνίας.** The cult of Athena Itonia seems to have had its earliest seat in Thessaly, where there was a temple of the goddess between Pherae and Larissa, and another at a town called Ἴτων or Ἴτωνος (Strabo 9. p. 436). Her festival, Ἰτώνια, at Crannon is noticed by Polyaenus (2. 34). But the cult was ancient in Boeotia also ; and perhaps the most famous shrine of the Itonia was that in the neighbourhood of Coroneia. This is the temple to which Alcaeus refers (fr. 9) in a hymn to Athena where she is called πολεμαδόκος. The Itonia was a war-goddess, the presiding deity of the Pamboeotic league, whose meetings were held at her sanctuary (Strabo 9. p. 411 : Paus. 9. 34. 1). Hence the epithet χρύσαιγις is appropriate (cp. Ode XVI. 7 n.). Her cult was also connected with that of Hades (Strabo *l. c.*). The title Ἰτωνία was derived by some from Itonus son of Amphictyon ; by others from the town Iton. Its meaning is uncertain. Can it have been popularly associated with ἰέναι (the onset)? According to Paus. 10. 1. 10 Ἀθηνᾶ Ἰτωνία was a watchword of the Thessalians in battle. The head of the goddess is found on silver coins of Coroneia (Brit. Museum, *Catal. of Coins, Central Greece*, p. 47, n. 12). **4** The iambus lost after **δεῖξαι** may have been **μέλος** : though the simple **ἁβρόν** τι would be parallel with ὕφαινέ...τι κλεινόν in XVIII. 8 f. With the exordium of this hyporcheme, cp. that of Ode XV (n. on vv. 1—4).

12. [B. 31 : Bl. 16.]

Ὦ περικλειτὲ Δᾶλ', ἀγνοήσειν μὲν οὔ σ' ἔλπομαι.

Hephaestion p. 76 : δεδηλώσθω δὲ ὅτι καὶ ὅλα ᾄσματα κρητικὰ συντίθεται, ὥσπερ καὶ παρὰ Βακχυλίδῃ, ὦ περικλειτὲ δ' ἄλλ' κ.τ.λ.—Neue (p. 35) inferred from the cretic metre that the verse probably belonged to a hyporcheme. Blass, who shares that view, has corrected the corrupt δ' ἄλλ' to Δᾶλ'. (Bergk follows Turnebus in reading τἄλλ', placing the fragment among those ἐξ ἀδήλων εἰδῶν.) The intrinsic probability of Δᾶλ' is strengthened by the presumption that the poem was a hyporcheme, a fitting tribute to Apollo. We know at least one other instance (Ode XVI) of a poem written by Bacchylides for the Delian god. The poet expresses a hope that Delos 'will not regard him as a stranger' (or, perhaps, 'will not fail to judge kindly of his tribute'). Cp. γνώσει in the exordium of Ode V, v. 3.—See no. 42.

The fragments of ὑπορχήματα quoted in Plut. *Quaest. Conv.* IX. 15. 2, and commonly ascribed to Simonides (fr. 29, 30, 31, Bergk III. p. 400), are claimed for Bacchylides by M. Théodore Reinach in *Mélanges Weil* p. 420 ff. The discussion is acute and interesting ; but the style of these verses seems hardly such as to suggest Bacchylides.

ΕΡΩΤΙΚΑ.

13. [B. 24 : Bl. 17.]

...εὖτε
τὴν ἀπ' ἀγκύλης ἵησι
τοῖσδε τοῖς νεανίαις
λευκὸν ἀντείνασα πῆχυν.

Athen. 15. p. 667 C : Βακχυλίδης ἐν Ἐρωτικοῖς· εὖτε κ.τ.λ. (Also XI. 782 E, where τοῖσδε is omitted in v. 2, and ἐντείνουσα stands in v. 3.)—Metre, trochaic.
...'when, lifting her white arm, with bent elbow she makes the cast, at the bidding of these youths.'—In the game of cottabos the player sought to throw a little wine (λάταξ) from a cup into a bronze saucer (πλάστιγξ) : if this was done with skill, the wine

struck the saucer smartly, making it descend (in some forms of the game) and ring on the head of a small bronze figure (μάνης) placed beneath it.

An omen of love, prosperous or the reverse, was often drawn from the throw, according as the sound of the λάταξ on the saucer was clear or dull.—**τὴν ἀπ' ἀγκύλης** (*sc.* βολήν), the throw made with the arm bent ; Athen. 15. p. 667 B, ἐκάλουν δ' ἀπ' ἀγκύλης τὴν τοῦ κοττάβου πρόεσιν, διὰ τὸ ἀπαγκυλοῦν τὴν δεξιὰν χεῖρα ('arm') ἐν τοῖς ἀποκοτταβισμοῖς. To bend the arm gracefully was a mark of the accomplished player : Hesych. *s.v.* ἀγκύλη·...ἡ καμπὴ τοῦ ἀγκῶνος...οἱ γὰρ τοὺς κοττάβους προϊέμενοι τὴν δεξιὰν χεῖρα ἠγκύλουν, κυκλοῦντες αὐτὴν ὡς ἐνῆν πρεπωδέστατα, καὶ σεμνυνόμενοι ὡς ἐφ' ἑνὶ τῶν καλῶν.—The dat. **τοῖσδε τοῖς ν.**, 'for' them, goes with ἵησι, not with ἀντείνασα : *i.e.* the girl (perhaps an αὐλήτρια) makes the throw at their request.

14. [B. 25 : Bl. 18.]

Ἦ καλὸς Θεόκριτος· οὐ μόνος ἀνθρώπων ὁρᾷς.

Hephaestion p. 130 (as corrected by Westphal) : Ἔστι δέ τινα καὶ τὰ καλούμενα ἐπιφθεγματικά, ἃ διαφέρει ταύτῃ τῶν ἐφυμνίων, ὅτι τὰ μὲν ἐφύμνια ἐκ περιττοῦ ὡς πρὸς τὸ λεγόμενον τῇ στροφῇ πρόσκειται, τὰ δὲ ἐπιφθεγματικὰ καὶ πρὸς τὸν νοῦν συντελεῖ· οἷον τὸ Βακχυλίδου, Ἦ καλὸς...ὁρᾷς· καὶ πάλιν παρὰ τῷ αὐτῷ Βακχυλίδῃ· Σὺ δ' ἐν χιτῶνι...φεύγεις [fr. 15]. Both the ἐπιφθεγματικόν, then, and the ἐφύμνιον are kinds of *refrain*, repeated at the end of successive strophes. But the ἐπιφθεγματικόν 'contributes to the sense' ; it is a sentence, as in the two examples cited from our poet. The ἐφύμνιον, on the other hand, is 'a superfluous addition, so far as the meaning of the passage is concerned' ; *i.e.* it may be a mere exclamation, like αἴλινον αἴλινον εἰπέ, or ἰήϊε Παιάν.—**ὁρᾷς** Hephaestion : ἐρᾷς Ursinus (p. 342, also suggesting ἐρᾷ), Bergk.—Metre, dactylo-epitrite.

15. [B. 26 : Bl. 19.]

Σὺ δ' ἐν χιτῶνι μούνῳ
παρὰ τὴν φίλην γυναῖκα φεύγεις.

Hephaestion p. 130 (see on fr. 14).—Metre, iambic.

[ΠΑΡΟΙΝΙΑ.]

16. [B. 27 : Bl. 20.]

....

...γλυκεῖ' ἀνάγκα   στρ. α'
σευομενᾶν κυλίκων θάλπῃσι θυμόν,
Κυπρίδος δ' ἐλπὶς διαιθύσσῃ φρένας,

5 ἀμμειγνυμένα Διονυσίοισι δώροις·   στρ. β'
ἀνδράσι δ' ὑψοτάτω πέμπει μερίμνας·
αὐτίκα μὲν πολίων κράδεμνα λύει,
πᾶσι δ' ἀνθρώποις μοναρχήσειν δοκεῖ·

χρυσῷ δ' ἐλέφαντί τε μαρμαίρουσιν οἶκοι·   στρ. γ'
10 πυροφόροι δὲ κατ' αἰγλάεντα < πόντον >
νᾶες ἄγουσιν ἀπ' Αἰγύπτου μέγιστον
πλοῦτον· ὣς πίνοντος ὁρμαίνει κέαρ.

J. B. 28

418   BACCHYLIDES.

Athen. 2. p. 39 E: Διὸ Βακχυλίδης φησί· Γλυκεῖ̓ κ.τ.λ. There is no extant
mention of Παροίνια or Σκόλια as forming a separate class among the writings of
Bacchylides: but that may well be an accident. Another possibility is that his
convivial pieces may have been subjoined, without a distinct heading, to the Ἐρωτικά.
—Metre : dactylo-epitrite.

'...[when], as the cups go swiftly round, a sweet subduing power warms the heart,
and, blending with the gifts of Dionysus, a presage of the Cyprian goddess flutters
the mind. That power sends a man's thoughts soaring ;—straightway he is stripping
cities of their diadem of towers,—he dreams that he shall be monarch of the world ;—
his halls gleam with gold and ivory ;—over the sunlit sea his wheat-ships bring wealth
untold from Egypt :—such are the raptures of the reveller's soul.'

2 The missing first verse, or the lost part of the second, probably contained a
temporal conjunction, such as ὅταν, on which θάλπῃσι and διαιθύσσῃ depended.—
γλυκεῖ̓ ἀνάγκα : Hor. C. III. 21. 13 *Tu lene tormentum ingenio admoves Plerumque
duro.* 3 σευομενᾶν Blass : σευομένα (v.l. γευομένα) MSS., vulg. : σευομένα <'κ>
κυλίκων Herwerden : ἐσσυμενᾶν Bergk. The choice seems to lie between (1) σευομενᾶν
κυλίκων as gen. abs., and (2) σευομένα κυλίκων as='rushing *from* the cups,' which,
though possible, would be harsh : we cannot join ἀνάγκα κυλίκων. I prefer (1). Cp.
Phocyl. 11 χρὴ δ' ἐν συμποσίῳ κυλίκων περινισσομενάων | ἡδέα κωτίλλοντα καθήμενον
οἰνοποτάζειν.—θάλπῃσι Weir Smyth : θάλπῃσι MSS. 4 Κυπρίδος δ' ἐλπὶς διαιθύσσει
Erfurdt (-ῃ Blass): Κυπρίδος· ἐλπὶς δ' αἰθύσσει MSS.: Κύπρις ὥς· ἐλπὶς γὰρ
αἰθύσσει Bergk.—Smyth takes the δέ after Κυπρίδος as introducing the apodosis
('*then*...': see my n. on Ode XIV. 61). It may be, however, that the apodosis was
contained in the lost part before γλυκεῖ̓ ἀνάγκα, and that a new sentence begins with
ἀνδράσι δ' in v. 6. 6 ἀνδράσι δ' MSS.: ἀνδράσι θ' Bergk.—ὑψοτάτω πέμπει μερίμνας,
exalts their thoughts or ambitions [not 'dissipates their cares'] : cp. Pind. fr. 218. 5
ἀέξονται φρένας ἀμπελίνοις τόξοις δαμέντες. For μερίμνας cp. Ode I. 69 n. 7 αὐτίκα
μὲν : αὐτίχ̓ ὁ μὲν Bergk (αὐτόθι μὲν formerly Meineke) : αὐτὸς μὲν or αὐτὴ μὲν MSS.—
Blass writes εὐκτιμενᾶν.—πολίων conj. Bergk (who, however, keeps the vulg.
πόλεων).—κράδεμνα λύει. Il. 16. 100 Τροίης ἱερὰ κρήδεμνα λύωμεν (cp. Od. 13. 388).—
The υ of the pres. λύω is regularly short in Homer, as it is in Pind. I. VII. 45 (λύοι)
and probably in fr. 248 (λύοντι, where the text is doubtful). But the Attic ῡ of λύω
(taken from the fut. λύσω) occurs in Od. 7. 74, νείκεα λύει: and it may be supposed
that B. could have used it here. I should not, then, alter λύει to λύσειν, with Blass:
the vivid λύει is intrinsically much better. 8 πᾶσι δ'. The dat. with ἄρχω (*rego*) is
poetical, and comparatively rare. In the Homeric use it is limited to the sense of
leading in war (Il. 2. 805 ; Od. 14. 230, 471) : cp. ἡγεῖσθαί τινι. But later poetry
ignores this limit : Aesch. P.V. 940 δαρὸν γὰρ οὐκ ἄρξει θεοῖς. [In Pind. P. III. 4
βάσσαισί τ' ἄρχειν the dat. may be local.] 10 Between αἰγλάεντα and ἄγουσιν the
text of Athenaeus has lost a spondee. Erfurdt supplies πόντον, which seems clearly
right. Cp. Il. 14. 273 ἅλα μαρμαρέην. For this votary of Bacchus, everything is
radiant,—his house with gold, the sea with sunshine.—Bergk and Blass supply
καρπόν. But is αἰγλάεντα an intelligible epithet for a cargo of wheat?—The fragment
of a skolion by Pindar (fr. 218) should be compared :—

Ἀνίκ̓ ἀνθρώπων καματώδεες οἴχονται μέριμναι
στηθέων ἔξω, πελάγει δ' ἐν πολυχρύσοιο πλούτου
πάντες ἴσᾳ νέομεν ψευδῆ πρὸς ἀκτάν·
ὃς μὲν ἀχρήμων, ἀφνεὸς τότε, τοὶ δ' αὖ πλουτέοντες...
...ἀέξονται φρένας ἀμπελίνοις τόξοις δαμέντες.

'When the weary cares of men have passed from their bosoms, and on a wide sea
of golden wealth we voyage, all alike, to a visionary shore,—then is the poor man
wealthy, and the rich [dream that they are great]....Men are exalted in spirit by the
piercing power of the grape.'—Pindar excels in splendour of imaginative diction ;
Bacchylides, in vivid detail and playful fancy.—Cp. also Ar. Eq. 90 ff.

17. [B. 28 : Bl. 21.]

Οὐ βοῶν πάρεστι σώματ', οὔτε χρυσός,
οὔτε πορφύρεοι τάπητες,
ἀλλὰ θυμὸς εὐμενής,
Μοῦσά τε γλυκεῖα, καὶ Βοιωτίοισιν
ἐν σκύφοισιν οἶνος ἡδύς.

Athen. 11. p. 500 B : Μνημονεύει δὲ τῶν Βοιωτικῶν σκύφων Βακχυλίδης ἐν τούτοις, ποιούμενος τὸν λόγον πρὸς τοὺς Διοσκούρους, καλῶν αὐτοὺς ἐπὶ ξένια. Was the entertainment (θεοξένια) to which B. thus invited the Dioscuri a public one, on the occasion of some festival in their honour? That seems the more natural supposition. On the other hand, the language (recalling Horace's in *C*. I. 20. 1, *Vile potabis modicis Sabinum Cantharis*) would perfectly suit a private invitation to a modest home. From another passage of Athenaeus (4. p. 137 E) we learn a fact which illustrates this fragment. At Athens, where the Dioscuri were styled Ἄνακες, their festival was the Ἀνάκεια : and the meal then set forth for them in the Prytaneion was of a frugal and old-fashioned kind. The authority of Athenaeus for this statement goes back to the time of Bacchylides. It is a play entitled the Πτωχοί, ascribed to Chionides, one of the earliest poets of the Old Comedy :—τοὺς Ἀθηναίους φησίν, ὅταν τοῖς Διοσκούροις ἐν Πρυτανείῳ ἄριστον προτιθῶνται, ἐπὶ τῶν τραπεζῶν τιθέναι τυρὸν καὶ φυστὴν (barley-cake) δρυπετεῖς τ' ἐλάας καὶ πράσα (leeks), ὑπόμνησιν ποιουμένους τῆς ἀρχαίας ἀγωγῆς.—Metre : trochaic.
' No flesh of oxen is here, nor gold, nor purple carpets ; but a kindly spirit, and the sweet strains of the Muse, and good wine in Boeotian cups.'—**1 f. οὐ..οὔτε.. οὔτε** : see my n. on Soph. *Tr.* 1058 f.—**οὔτε χρυσός κ.τ.λ.** Hor. *C.* II. 18. 1 *Non ebur neque aureum Mea renidet in domo lacunar.* **3 θυμὸς εὐμενής** : cp. Minucius Felix 32 *Est litabilis hostia bonus animus et sincera sententia.* **4 Βοιωτίοισιν** : the first οι is short, as with Corinna fr. 2 (ed. Hiller-Crusius, *Anth. Lyr.* p. 270) τὺ δέ, μάκαρ Κρονίδα, τὺ Ποτειδάωνος, ἄναξ Βοιωτέ : in the *Iliad* it is always long. **5 σκύφοισιν.** The σκύφος—of which there were Boeotian, Rhodian, Syracusan, Attic, and other varieties—was a large drinking-cup, generally with two handles projecting just beneath the brim. It appears in poetry as especially a rustic cup, such as was used by shepherds and peasants : Alcman fr. 34 μέγαν σκύφον, | οἶά τε ποιμένες ἄνδρες ἔχουσιν : it is used by Eumaeus (*Od.* 14. 112) : cp. Theocr. I. 143. Owing to its large capacity, it was specially the cup of Heracles (Stesich. fr. 7).

ΕΞ ΑΔΗΛΩΝ ΕΙΔΩΝ.

18. [B. 33 : Bl. 22.]

Ἔστα δ' ἐπὶ λάϊνον οὐδόν,
τοὶ δὲ θοίνας ἔντυον, ὧδε δ' ἔφα·
Αὐτόματοι δ' ἀγαθῶν
δαῖτας εὐόχθους ἐπέρχονται δίκαιοι
5 φῶτες.

Athen. 5. p. 178 B : Βακχυλίδης δὲ περὶ Ἡρακλέους λέγων ὡς ἦλθεν ἐπὶ τὸν τοῦ Κήϋκος οἶκον, φησίν· Ἔστη [ἔστα Neue] κ.τ.λ.—Κήϋξ, the powerful and gentle king of the Malians, dwelt at Trachis : δυνάμει δὲ καὶ αἰδοῖ | Τρηχῖνος προβέβηκε, Hes. *Scut.* 354 f. He was a kinsman of Heracles, being the son of a brother of Amphitryon (schol. Soph. *Tr.* 40). Once, when Ceÿx was celebrating the marriage of one of his children by a feast (γάμος), Heracles, being in those parts, presented himself, an

28—2

uninvited guest. This was told in Hesiod's Κήϋκος γάμος, from which only a few words remain (Rzach, frgg. Hes. **179** f., p. 199). That poem was doubtless the original source of the verse, αὐτόματοι δ' ἀγαθοὶ ἀγαθῶν ἐπὶ δαῖτας ἴασιν, quoted in that form, as a παροιμία, by Athen. 5. p. 178 B. Zenobius II. 19 quotes it with ἴενται in place of ἴασιν. But see Cratinus Πυλαία fr. 1 : οἶδ' αὖθ' ἡμεῖς, ὡς ὁ παλαιὸς | λόγος, αὐτομάτους ἀγαθοὺς ἰέναι | κομψῶν ἐπὶ δαῖτα θεατῶν. (Cratinus alludes to it again in fr. incert. 6 : ἦκον ἐστιώμενος | ἀγαθὸς πρὸς ἀγαθούς.) Athenaeus (*l.c.*) says that there was another form of the proverb,—αὐτόματοι δ' ἀγαθοὶ δειλῶν ἐπὶ δαῖτας ἴασιν. Bergk thinks that this parody was due to Eupolis. The schol. on Plat. *Symp.* p. 174 B, at any rate, cannot be right in supposing it to have been the original form of the verse.— Metre : dactylo-epitrite.

'He came and stood on the threshold of stone, while they were preparing their feast, and spake thus:—'Just men come unbidden to the plenteous banquets of the good.''

3 αὐτόματοι : paraphrased by ἄκλητος in Plat. *Symp.* p. 174 B, C.—**4 εὐόχθους** : Eur. *Ion* 1169 εὐόχθου βορᾶς. Cp. Hes. *Op.* 475 εὐοχθέων δ' ἵξεαι πολιὸν ἔαρ ('with good store').—The use of **δίκαιοι** by B. as a substitute for the original ἀγαθοί indicates that he took the latter as referring to character, and not (as epic usage would permit) to birth.

19. [B. 34 : Bl. 23.]

Οἱ μὲν ἀδμᾶτες ἀεικελιᾶν
νούσων εἰσὶν καὶ ἄνατοι,
οὐδὲν ἀνθρώποις ἴκελοι.

Clem. Alex. *Strom.* v. 715 : Ἀκούσωμεν οὖν πάλιν Βακχυλίδου τοῦ μελοποιοῦ περὶ τοῦ θείου λέγοντος· Οἱ μὲν ἀδμῆτες ἀεὶ καὶ λίαν νούσων εἰσὶ καὶ ἀναίτιοι κ.τ.λ. For the corrupt ἀεὶ καὶ λίαν Euseb. *Praep. Ev.* XIII. 679 gives ἀεικελίων (whence Neue ἀεικελιᾶν). ἄνατοι Neue.—Bergk reads εἰσὶ νόσων.—Metre : dactylo-epitrite.

'Cruel maladies subdue them not, nor harm them; they are in no way like to men.'

20. [B. 36 : Bl. 24.]

θνατοῖσι δ' οὐκ αὐθαίρετοι
οὔτ' ὄλβος οὔτ' ἄγναμπτος Ἄρης οὔτε πάμφθερσις στάσις,
ἀλλ' ἐπιχρίμπτει νέφος ἄλλοτ' ἐπ' ἄλλαν
γαῖαν ἁ πάνδωρος αἶσα.

Stob. *Ecl. Phys.* I. 5, 3 : Βακχυλίδου.—Metre : dactylo-epitrite.

'Not by their own choice comes prosperity to mortals, nor civil strife, the all-destroying ; but Destiny, who gives all things, brings down a cloud now on this land, now on that.'

1 θνατοῖσι Neue, for θνατοῖς.—**οὐκ αὐθαίρετοι**. This is the popular view, which in Ode XIV. 51 f. Menelaus controverts. (Cp. Plat. *Rep.* 617 E αἰτία ἑλομένου· θεὸς ἀναίτιος.) **2 ἄγναμπτος** Bergk (formerly; but now ἄκαμπτος with the MSS.): cp. VIII. 73 ἀγνάμπτων ἐρώτων.—Ἄρης has ᾱ here, as in XII. 146: but ᾰ in V. 34, 130, VIII. 44.—**πάμφθερσις** : cp. Aesch. *Eum.* 976 τὰν δ' ἄπληστον κακῶν | μήποτ' ἐν πόλει στάσιν | τᾷδ' ἐπεύχομαι βρέμειν.—**4 πάνδωρος**, giver of good, as of evil. But, since the mention of troubles came next before ἀλλά, the varying incidence of trouble alone is noticed.

21. [B. 3 : Bl. 25.]

Παύροισι δὲ θνατῶν τὸν ἅπαντα χρόνον δαίμων ἔδωκεν
πράσσοντας ἐν καιρῷ πολιοκρόταφον
γῆρας ἱκνεῖσθαι, πρὶν ἐγκύρσαι δύᾳ.

Clem. Alex. *Strom.* VI. 745 : Βακχυλίδου τε εἰρηκότος· Παύροισι κ.τ.λ.—Metre : dactylo-epitrite.

'To few mortals is Fate wont to grant that they should have happy fortunes through all their years, or come to the first grey hairs of age without encountering woe.'—**1 δαίμων ἔδωκεν** Neue (ὁ δ. ἔδ. Ursinus): τῷ δαίμονι δῶκεν MSS. **2 πράσσοντας ἐν καιρῷ**, lit. 'faring *opportunely*,' *i.e.* as they would wish at each successive step in life. For ἐν καιρῷ cp. Aesch. *P. V.* 379, Plat. *Crito* 44 A (with τινι added), etc.—**πολιοκρόταφον**, with gray hair on the *temples*, where it usually appears first : Theocr. XIV. 68 ἀπὸ κροτάφων πελόμεσθα | πάντες γηραλέοι.

22. [B. 39 : Bl. 30.]

Τὰν ἀχείμαντόν τε Μέμφιν
καὶ δονακώδεα Νεῖλον.

Athen. I. p. 20 D : Μέμφιν...περὶ ἧς Βακχυλίδης φησί· τὴν (τὰν Neue) κ. τ. λ.—
'Memphis, unvexed by wintry storms, and the reedy Nile.' Blass observes that, with τὸν inserted before δονακώδεα, these verses might be the 4th and 5th of a strophe or antistrophe in Ode XII, where there are several *lacunae* in the papyrus. The possible places are (1) str. α′ 4 f. : (2) ant. α′ 16 f. : (3) str. β′, 37 f. : (4) ant. ζ′ 214 f. But no one of these collocations seems really probable.—In XVIII. 39 Nile has the epithet ἀνθεμώδεα.—Metre : dactylo-epitrite.

23. [B. 40 : Bl. 31.]

Ἑκάτα δᾳδοφόρε, Νυκτὸς
μελανοκόλπου θύγατερ.

Schol. Ap. Rhod. III. 467 (where Hecate is addressed as πότνα θεὰ Περσηΐ), Βακ-χυλίδης δὲ Νυκτός φησιν αὐτὴν θυγατέρα· Ἑκάτα κ.τ.λ.—The metre seems to be paeonic. Weil, however, who inserts ὦ before μελανοκόλπου, regards it as cretic.

'Torch-bearing Hecate, daughter of dark-bosomed Night.'—**δᾳδοφόρε.** As a moon-goddess (akin to Ἕκατος, Apollo the sun-god) Hecate carries a torch,—her regular symbol. δᾳδοφόρος is actually the title under which she was worshipped, along with Zeus Πανημέριος, at Stratoniceia in Caria, *C. I. G.* 2715, 2. 2720 (see Spending's art. in Roscher's *Lex.*, p. 1885). So also she is φωσφόρος, λάμπτειρα, λαμπαδοῦχος, etc. : and in the Homeric hymn to Demeter (v. 52) she appears σέλας ἐν χείρεσσιν ἔχουσα. As the moon was supposed to rise from and descend into the underworld, Hecate is also the προθυραία or κλειδοῦχος (*Orphic hymn* 2. 5) of Hades : cp. Verg. *Aen.* VI. 255. She is a goddess of darkness (νυκτιπόλος, Ap. Rhod. IV. 1020 : μουνυχία *Orph. Argon.* 938). Bacchylides seems, however, to be the only extant authority for making her the *daughter* of Night. In the older mythology (followed by Apollonius Rhodius) she is the daughter of the Titan Perses (or Persaeus) and Asteria (herself the daughter of the Titan Koios) : Hes. *Theog.* 409 ff. In a later genealogy her parents are Zeus and Hera (or Zeus and Demeter).—**μελανοκόλπου** Ursinus, Bergk, Smyth. The text of the scholiast has μεγαλοκόλπου, a decidedly inferior reading, due probably to mere error.

422   BACCHYLIDES.

24. [B. 44: Bl. 34.]

Ὀργαὶ μὲν ἀνθρώπων διακεκριμέναι
μυρίαι.

Zenob. III. 25: Δίχολοι γνῶμαι· παρὰ τὸ διχῇ ἰδιότροποι, κατὰ μετάληψιν. Χόλος γὰρ ἡ ὀργή, ὀργὴ δὲ τρόπος. Βακχυλίδης· Ὀργαὶ κ.τ.λ. The fragment is also in Hesych. s.v. δίχολοι.—Metre: dactylo-epitrite.
'There are varied tempers, past numbering, in mankind.'—Nearly the same words are ascribed to *Alcman* by schol. Hippocr. v. 484 (ed. Littré): Ὀργὰς γὰρ τοὺς τρόπους ἐκάλουν οἱ ἀρχαῖοι, ὡς καὶ Ἀλκμάν φησιν· ἐν μὲν ἀνθρώπῳ ὀργαὶ κεκριμέναι μυρίαι. Bergk (III. p. 193) supposes that a grammarian had quoted both Bacchylides and Alcman. After the words of Alcman had dropped out of the text, his name was erroneously connected with the words of Bacchylides.

25. [B. 38: Bl. 29.]

Μελαγκευθὲς εἴδωλον ἀνδρὸς Ἰθακησίου.

Etym. M. 296. 1: Bachmann *Anecd.* I. 208. 13: Cramer *Anecd. Par.* IV. 168. 30: Schol. *Il.* 5. 449: Apostolius III. 37: Suidas *s.v.* εἴδωλον.—Metre: cretic or paeonic.
'The phantom of the man of Ithaca, shrouded in gloom.'—μελαγκευθὲς Neue: μελαγκεθὲς *Etym. M.*, etc. But μελαμβαφὲς is read by schol. *Il.*, Apostol., and Suid., whence Bernhardy conj. μελαμφαρὲς [cp. III. 13 f.], or μελαμφαές. In Ode III. 55 μελαγκευθὲς is probable.

26. [B. 42: Bl. 32.]

Ἀβρότητι ξυνέασιν Ἴωνες βασιλῆες.

Joannes Siceliota in Walz *Rhet. Gr.* VI. 241: Ἀβροὶ τὸ παλαιὸν οἱ Ἴωνες, ὥς που καὶ Βακχυλίδης φησί, τὸν σφῶν αὐτῶν ῥυθμὸν δηλῶν· Ἀβρότητι κ.τ.λ. Comparing the other citation, τῶν ἀβροβίων Ἰώνων ἄναξ (Walz v. 493 and VII. 982), now identified with XVII. 2, Bergk read Ἰώνων here. Wilamowitz (*Isyll.* 143) supposes Ἀβρότητι κ.τ.λ. to be a mere figment of Joannes Siceliota.—'The Ionian princes dwell with luxury.' See n. on XVII. 2.

27. [B. 43: Bl. 33.]

Χρυσὸν βροτῶν γνώμαισι μανύει καθαρόν.

Priscian *Metr. Terent.* (Keil, *Grammatici Latini* III. 428. 21): *Similiter Bacchylides*: Χρυσὸν κ.τ.λ. *Hic quoque iambus in fine tribrachium habet.*—Bergk formerly conjectured that this fragment should be used to complete fr. 10 (his fr. 22), thus: Λυδία μὲν γὰρ λίθος | χρυσὸν βροτῶν γνώμαισι μανύει καθαρόν | ἀνδρῶν δ' ἀρετάν κ.τ.λ. The sense would then be: 'The Lydian stone reveals pure gold *to the judgments* of men.' In his 4th ed., however, he keeps the fragments distinct. The context being unknown, it must remain doubtful whether the meaning of this fragment was such as that just noticed (which seems the more probable), or the following:—('Truth' or 'Time') 'reveals the pure gold *in* the minds (or dispositions) of men,'—χρυσόν being metaphorical.

28. [B. 2, v. 3: Bl. 37.]

Ὄλβιος δ' οὐδεὶς βροτῶν πάντα χρόνον.

Stob. *Flor.* 98. 27, where the words are added to a citation of Ode v. 160 ff. (θνατοῖσι...φέγγος). The lemma prefixed is Ἐν τῷ αὐτῷ, referring to that of the citation (Ode v. 53 ff.) which immediately precedes, Τοῦ αὐτοῦ 'Επινίκων. If the lemma meant, 'in the same *book*,' it would appear that the words ὄλβιος δ' κ.τ.λ., though wrongly attached to Ode v. 160 ff., occurred in another of the poet's epinikia. But this cannot be deemed certain.

29. [B. 37 : Bl. 27.]

Εἰ δὲ λέγει τις ἄλλως, πλατεῖα κέλευθος.

Plut. *Num.* 4: Εἰ δὲ λέγει (λέγοι C) τις ἄλλως, κατὰ Βακχυλίδην, πλατεῖα κέλευθος.—'If any man saith otherwise,—the path is broad.' Sintenis may well be right in thinking that the words εἰ δὲ...ἄλλως are Plutarch's own, and that the quotation is confined to πλατεῖα κέλευθος.

30. [B. 45 : Bl. 35.]

πλήμμυριν πόντου φυγών.

Etym. M. 676. 25 : Πλημμυρὶς...εἰ μέντοι ὄνομά ἐστιν, εὔλογον βαρύνεσθαι αὐτὸ διὰ τὴν παρὰ Βακχυλίδῃ αἰτιατικήν, οἶον · Πλήμμυριν κ.τ.λ.—Cp. *Od.* 9. 485 τὴν δ' ἄψ ἤπειρόνδε παλιρρόθιον φέρε κῦμα, | πλημμυρὶς ἐκ πόντοιο : the backward rush of the wave, 'as a *flood-tide from the deep*,' bore the ship to land.—For the spelling with μμ, or μ, see Ode v. 107 n.

31. [B. 51 : Bl. 39.]

πυργοκέρατα.

Apollonius *De Adverb.* (in Bekker *Anecd.* II. 596. 12—14) : ὃν τρόπον καὶ ἐπ' ὀνομάτων μεταπλασμοὶ γίνονται, καθάπερ...τὸ πυργοκέρατα παρὰ Βακχυλίδῃ. The sense may have been, 'with towering horns' : cp. the figurative πυργωθέντα (πλοῦτον) in Ode III. 13. Bergk suggests that B.'s phrase was πύργον ὑψικέρατα (comparing Pind. fr. 325, ὑψικ. πέτραν), but this seems very improbable.

32 (?). [B. adesp. 86 : Bl. 37 A.]

Οὐ γὰρ ἐν μέσοισι κεῖται
δῶρα δυσμάχητα Μοισᾶν
τὠπιτυχόντι φέρειν.

Clem. Alex. *Strom.* v. 654 quotes these verses without the poet's name. Blass conjectures that they belong to Bacchylides. There is at least one certain instance in which Clement quotes B. without naming him, viz. in *Strom.* v. 731, where the words ὁ λυρικός φησι introduce vv. 50—56 of Ode XIV. Blass also compares XIV. 53 f. ἐν μέσῳ κεῖται κιχεῖν | πᾶσιν ἀνθρώποις Δίκαν κ.τ.λ., and δῶρα Μουσᾶν in XVIII. 4. These points are perhaps not very cogent. But the general style of the verses resembles that of Bacchylides : and we know that his poetry was one of Clement's favourite sources of quotation.—δῶρα Μουσᾶν are the gifts of poetical faculty which the Muses bestow : these are δυσμάχητα, because poets vie keenly with each other, as in competing at the festivals. (δυσμάχητα should not be taken with οὐ . . κεῖται, as though the sense were, 'are not proposed as prizes to be keenly fought for.')— 'The keenly-contested gifts of the Muses are not prizes open to all, which the first comer may win.'

ΕΠΙΓΡΑΜΜΑΤΑ.

1. **33.** [B. 48 : Bl. p. 176.]

Κούρα Πάλλαντος πολυώνυμε, πότνια Νίκα,
　πρόφρων Καρθαίων ἱμερόεντα χορὸν
αἰὲν ἐποπτεύοις, πολέας δ' ἐν ἀθύρμασι Μουσᾶν
　Κηΐῳ ἀμφιτίθει Βακχυλίδῃ στεφάνους.

Anthol. Pal. VI. 313 : Βακχυλίδου A.

'Renowned daughter of Pallas, queenly Victory, mayest thou ever look with good will on the beauteous chorus of the Carthaeans, and crown Bacchylides of Ceos with many a wreath in the contests of the Muses.'—**1 Πάλλαντος**, a Titan : the mother of Nike was Styx : see x. 9 n.—**πολυώνυμε**, of wide fame : cp. Hes. *Th.* 785 πολυώνυμον ὕδωρ (Styx); Pind. *P.* I. 17 Κιλίκιον..πολυώνυμον ἄντρον. So Soph. *Ant.* 148 μεγαλώνυμος..Νίκα.—Not, 'of many names' (as *e.g.* Dionysus is πολυώνυμος, *ib.* 1115, being variously styled Bakchos, Iacchos, Zagreus, etc.): there was no variety of cult-names in the case of Νίκη, and the epithets given to her are usually of a general kind. **2 Καρθαίων**, a conjecture of Bergk (received by Blass in his 2nd ed.). The town of Κάρθαια or Καρθαία, on the S.E. coast of Ceos, had a temple of the Pythian Apollo, and near it a χορηγεῖον in which Simonides, when living in Ceos, used to teach choruses (Athen. 10. p. 456 F). His nephew, then, might feel some special interest in the place. Ode XVI was a paean written by Bacchylides to be performed by a Cean chorus at Delos. Similarly he may have composed a dithyramb with which a chorus from Carthaea competed successfully at a Delian festival. The addition of Κηΐῳ indicates that the contest did not take place in Ceos. This epigramma would have been placed on the ἀνάθημα dedicated as a thank-offering for the victory. [Bergk and Blass accent thus, Καρθαιῶν (as from Καρθαιεύς?). See, however, Pape-Benseler *s.v.* Κάρθαια, where ἡ Καρθαίων πόλις is cited from an inscr.]—The traditional reading here, **Κρανναίων**, is corrupt. The other emendations which have been proposed are :—(1) προφρονέως Κραναῶν, Schneidewin. (2) πρόφρων ἐν Κραναῶν, Hartung. (3) Κραναιδῶν Meineke (so Bergk⁴), a form not found,= the Athenians (παῖδες Κραναοῦ, Aesch. *Eum.* 1011). But could the first syllable be long? Further, if the chorus was Athenian, we should expect the name of a tribe, such as (4) Κεκροπιδῶν, suggested by Bergk. (5) Καρνείων, Stadtmüller. **3 ἐν ἀθύρμασι Μουσᾶν**, *i.e. ἐν μουσικοῖς ἀγῶσιν* : cp. XVII. 57 ἀρηΐων..ἀθυρμάτων.

2. **34.** [B. 49: Bl. p. 176.]

Εὔδημος τὸν νηὸν ἐπ' ἀγροῦ τόνδ' ἀνέθηκεν
　τῷ πάντων ἀνέμων πιστοτάτῳ Ζεφύρῳ.
εὐξαμένῳ γάρ οἱ ἦλθε βοηθόος, ὄφρα τάχιστα
　λικμήσῃ πεπόνων καρπὸν ἀπ' ἀσταχύων.

Anthol. Pal. VI. 5 : Βακχυλίδου. ἀνάθημα τῷ ζεφύρῳ ἀνέμῳ παρὰ Εὐδήμου γεωργοῦ A and corrector. Blass observes: 'Non habet fidem inscriptio, nisi alius est Bacchylides.' But at least there is nothing in the verses themselves which could warrant us in rejecting the traditional ascription.—Suidas *s.v.* πιότατος quotes the words from τόνδ' in v. 1 to Ζεφύρῳ without the author's name (ἐν ἐπιγράμματι).

'Eudemus has dedicated this shrine on his land to Zephyrus, trustiest of winds, who hastened to help him at his prayer, so that he might winnow his grain from the ripe ears of corn.'—**2** The MS. reading **πιοτάτῳ** is defended by Stadtmüller, who quotes Theocr. x. 46 f., ἐς βορέην ἄνεμον τᾶς κόρθυος ἀ τομὰ ὔμμιν | ἢ ζέφυρον βλεπέτω·

πιαίνεται ὁ στάχυς οὕτως: *i.e.*, 'let the cut end of the stalks in your sheaf be turned towards the north or west wind; for thus the corn-ear is filled out.' But is this relevant? (1) In the first place, it is hard to conceive how πιότατος could be said of a *wind*, in the sense of 'fattening' or 'nourishing': at any rate there is no example of it. (2) But, granting that πιότατος could be so used, it would be wholly out of place here. The maturing of the grain is not in question. The matter in hand is simply the winnowing (see on v. 4). What Eudemus wanted was fine weather, with a wind which should not bring rain (as the south often did), nor yet be too violent. Unger and Schneidewin long ago suggested what I hold to be the true reading, viz. πι(στ)οτάτῳ, which might so easily have been corrupted. There is a touch of playful fancy in it, alluding to βοηθόος in the next verse: Zephyrus was the trusty ally who came at need when he was called.—Other conjectures are πρηϋτάτῳ ('Schneider Saxo' *ap.* Bergk, also Headlam): λειοτάτῳ (Meineke). 3 In his Dorian lyrics, with their epic colouring, Bacch. always assumes ϝ before οἱ: but it does not follow that he would do so in writing Ionic elegiacs. I prefer γάρ οἱ here to Meineke's γὰρ ὅ γ', which Bergk (though retaining οἱ) thinks right.—βοηθόος Planudes: βοαθόος vulg. (but cp. Εὔδημος and νηόν). 4 λικμήσῃ, the more vivid subjunct., instead of the optative, after ἦλθε: cp. Xen. *An.* I. I. 18 (πλοῖα) κατέκαυσεν, ἵνα μὴ Κῦρος διαβῇ.— After threshing, the corn was put into a broad basket (λίκνον, *vannus*): it was then thrown up into the wind, so that the chaff (ἄχυρα, *paleae*) might be blown away from the grain. Verg. *G.* III. 123 f., *Cum graviter tunsis gemit area frugibus, et cum Surgentem ad Zephyrum paleae iactantur inanes.* Columella also (2. 21) says that a west wind is best for the operation of winnowing.

B. NOTICES WHICH SPECIFY A CLASS OF POEMS.

ΕΠΙΝΙΚΟΙ.

35. [B. 10: Bl. p. 137.]

The commentary of Didymus.—Ammonius p. 79: Νηρεΐδες τῶν τοῦ Νηρέως θυγατέρων διαφέρει. Δίδυμος ὁμοίως ἐν ὑπομνήματι Βακχυλίδου ἐπινίκων· φησὶ γὰρ κατὰ λέξιν· Εἰσὶ τοίνυν οἵ φασι διαφέρειν τὰς Νηρεΐδας τῶν τοῦ Νηρέως θυγατέρων, καὶ τὰς μὲν ἐκ Δωρίδος γνησίας αὐτῶν θυγατέρας νομίζεσθαι, τὰς δὲ ἐξ ἄλλων ἤδη κοινότερον Νηρεΐδας καλεῖσθαι κ.τ.λ.— See n. on XVI. 38.

ΥΜΝΟΙ.

36. [B. 12: Bl. 3.]

Schol. Ar. *Ach.* 47: τοῦ δὲ Κελεοῦ μέμνηται Βακχυλίδης διὰ τῶν Ὕμνων.—Celeus, the king of Eleusis; whose wife Metaneira received the disguised Demeter into her house, as a nurse for her son Demophon: *Hom. Hymn to Demeter*, vv. 96 ff. Celeus built the first temple of the goddess at Eleusis (*ib.* 296 ff.), and was one of a small group,—including Triptolemus and Eumolpus,—whom she taught to celebrate her rites (*ib.* 473 ff.).

37. [B. III. p. 572, n. on fr. 11 : Bl. p. 160, n. on fr. 2.]

The rhetor Menander in Walz *Rhet. Gr.* IX. 140 : Εἰσὶ τοίνυν καὶ τῷ Βακχυλίδῃ ὕμνοι ἀποπεμπτικοί.—These were hymns addressed to a god who was supposed to be leaving his temple on an excursion (ἀποδημία) to some other haunt ; as the κλητικοί were hymns which besought him to return. See n. on Ode XV. 1—4.

ΔΙΘΥΡΑΜΒΟΙ.

38. [B. 18: Bl. 8.]

Servius on Verg. *Aen.* XI. 93 : *Versis Arcades armis.*] Lugentum more mucronem hastae, non cuspidem contra terram tenentes, quoniam antiqui nostri omnia contraria in funere faciebant, scuta etiam invertentes propter numina illic depicta, ne eorum simulacra cadaveris polluerentur aspectu, sicut habuisse Arcades Bacchylides in *dithyrambis* dicit.—Servius may be referring to the dithyramb from which fragment 6 comes, and which Blass supposes to have been entitled Κασσάνδρα.

39. [B. 16: Bl. 7.]

Schol. Pind. *P.* I. 100 : Ταύτῃ τῇ ἱστορίᾳ καὶ Βακχυλίδης συμφωνεῖ ἐν τοῖς διθυράμβοις, ὅτι δὴ οἱ Ἕλληνες ἐκ Λήμνου μετεστείλαντο τὸν Φιλοκτήτην Ἑλένου μαντευσαμένου· εἵμαρτο γὰρ ἄνευ τῶν Ἡρακλείων τόξων μὴ πορθηθῆναι τὸ Ἴλιον.—The story of Philoctetes being brought from Lemnos to Troy, at the bidding of Helenus, was told in two of the Cyclic epics, the Ἰλιὰς Μικρά and the Ἰλίου Πέρσις. Bacchylides may have known also the *Philoctetes* of Aeschylus. The Pindaric scholiast does not enable us to decide whether (as seems most probable) Bacchylides had written a dithyramb called Φιλοκτήτης, or had merely referred to the story in a dithyramb on some other subject.

ΠΑΡΘΕΝΕΙΑ.

40. [Bl. p. 165.]

Plutarch, *De Musica* c. 17, after saying that Plato's preference for the Dorian ἁρμονία was due to its fitness for martial or stately strains, adds that, as Plato knew, it could also be used for compositions of a lighter kind :—οὐκ ἠγνόει δὲ ὅτι πολλὰ Δώρια Παρθένεια ἅμα Ἀλκμᾶνι καὶ Πινδάρῳ καὶ Σιμωνίδῃ καὶ Βακχυλίδῃ πεποίηται κ.τ.λ.

C. NOTICES WHICH DO NOT SPECIFY A CLASS.

41. [B. 50 : Bl. 38.]

Ammianus Marcellinus XXV. 4. 3. The Emperor Julian used to quote with approval the saying of Sophocles in old age (Plat. *Rep.* I. p. 329 C), that he was glad to have escaped from the tyranny of amorous passion:—Item ut hoc propositum validius firmaret, recolebat saepe dictum lyrici Bacchylidis, quem legebat iucunde id adserentem, quod *ut egregius pictor vultum speciosum effingit, ita pudicitia celsius consurgentem vitam exornat.*—The context here makes it probable that *pudicitia* was a rendering of σωφροσύνη.

42. [B. 57 : Bl. p. 166.]

Schol. Callim. *Hymn. in Del.* 28 εἰ δὲ λίην πολέες σε περιτροχόωσιν ἀοιδαί] Αἱ Πινδάρου καὶ Βακχυλίδου. In Pindar's case the reference must include the προσόδιον (called Δηλιακὸν παιᾶνα by schol. Pind. *I.* I. init.), fr. 87, 88 (Εἰς Δῆλον), Χαῖρ' ὦ θεοδμάτα κ.τ.λ. Had Bacchylides written some similar poem in praise of Delos?—Cp. no. 12.

43. [B. 68 : Bl. 51.]

Schol. Apoll. Rhod. IV. 973 : ὀρείχαλκος εἶδος χαλκοῦ· μνημονεύει καὶ Στησίχορος καὶ Βακχυλίδης.—The metal or alloy called ὀρείχαλκος ('mountain-copper') is first mentioned in Greek poems dating probably from about 600 B.C. The Aphrodite of the Homeric hymn (VI. 9) wears as ear-rings ἄνθεμ' ὀρειχάλκου χρυσοῖό τε τιμήεντος. Heracles, in the Hesiodic 'Shield' (122), has greaves ὀρειχάλκοιο φαεινοῦ: and the same words are applied by Apollonius Rhodius (IV. 973) to the shepherd's crook carried by Lampetia, daughter of the Sun-god. For Callimachus (*Lav. Pallad.* 19), orichalcum is a metal which can serve as a mirror. Plato frankly speaks of it as something which, in his time, was 'merely a legend,'—τὸ νῦν ὀνομαζόμενον μόνον (*Critias* p. 114 E). It flashed with fiery rays (μαρμαρυγὰς... πυρώδεις) from the innermost of the walls surrounding the citadel in the Island of Atlantis (*ib.* p. 116 c). Spenser is at once classical and medieval in the vagueness of his reference to 'costly orichalch from strange Phoenice' (*Muiopotmos* 81), where it figures in company with the steel of Bilbo and the brass of Corinth. But in the orichalc of the Greek classics the most distinctive quality is brilliant lustre. The mentions of it by Stesichorus and Bacchylides were probably connected with the

equipment or adornment of some hero or heroine. [Strabo
(13. p. 610) mentions a blend of ψευδάργυρος (zinc?) with copper,
'which some call orichalcum'; but the interpretation and the
authority of that passage are doubtful.]

The following notices, relating to points of mythology as
treated by Bacchylides, are arranged in the alphabetical order of
the mythological names.

44. [B. 62 : Bl. 45.]

Aristaeus.—Schol. Apoll. Rhod. II. 498: Τινὲς τέσσαρας
Ἀρισταίους γενεαλογοῦσιν, ὡς καὶ Βακχυλίδης· τὸν μὲν Καρύστου,
τὸν δὲ Χείρωνος [Χέρωνος Laur.], ἄλλον δὲ Γῆς καὶ Οὐρανοῦ, καὶ
τὸν <τέταρτον Bergk> Κυρήνης.

Ἀρισταῖος is the name, very ancient in Greece, of a god who
prospers agriculture, cattle-breeding, and hunting : it expresses
the pious faith that he is ἄριστος (cp. Ἄρτεμις ἀρίστη, Ζεὺς ὁ
λῷστος, etc.). Among the earliest seats of his cult were the
Thessalian plains about Iolcus and Pelion ; Arcadia ; and
Cyrene. In the Cyrenaic legend (Pind. *P.* IX. 5 ff., following
the Hesiodic Ἠοῖαι) he is the son of Cyrene, a great-grand-
daughter of Poseidon and Gaia, by Apollo, who carried her off
to Libya.

The worship of Aristaeus existed in Ceos, the island of
Bacchylides. He was said to have come to the help of the
islanders, bringing with him Parrhasians from Arcadia, at a
time when Ceos was afflicted by the parching summer heat of
Seirius, which had caused a plague in the Cyclades : he taught
the Ceans to erect an altar to Ζεὺς Ἰκμαῖος, and was himself
afterwards worshipped there as Ζεὺς Ἀρισταῖος. Two of the
three namesakes whom, according to the scholiast, Bacchylides
distinguished from Aristaeus son of Cyrene, were probably
identical with him. (1) The 'son of Carystus' may be this
rural god in his relation to the nymphs of Carystus in Euboea.
(2) The 'son of Cheiron' is a designation easily explained by the
fact that Aristaeus, who was a healing god, was said to have
been taken as a child by Apollo to Cheiron, in whose cave he
was brought up. With regard to the third namesake, the son
of Gaia and Uranos,' this may have been an allegorical description of the god who blesses the fruits of the earth ; that,
however, is more doubtful. Suidas has Ἀρισταῖος· εἷς τῶν
Γιγάντων. The bearded head of Aristaeus appears on coins
of Ceos and of the Cean town Carthaia. (See Schirmer's
article in Roscher's *Lexikon*, esp. p. 550.)

Blass suggests that the Bacchylides cited by the scholiast

on Apollonius may be a writer distinct from the poet (3rd ed.,
p. 174, fr. 45 : *Nisi alius hic est Bacchylides*).

In the Cean poet,
however, we are prepared to find the current popular mythology
of his day faithfully reflected, without any attempts at criticism
or reconciliation. If, then, there were different local cults which
assigned different genealogies to the rural god Aristaeus, it
is quite conceivable that these discrepant accounts should have
appeared in different passages of the poet's writings.

45. [B. 54 : Bl. 41.]

Athena as a giver of immortality.—Schol. Ar. *Av.* 1536:
Εὐφρόνιος [? the Alexandrian writer of tragedy mentioned by
schol. Hephaest. c. 9, see W. Christ, *Gesch. d. Gr. Litt.*, p. 539
n. 2], ὅτι Διὸς θυγάτηρ ἡ Βασιλεία, καὶ δοκεῖ τὰ κατὰ τὴν
ἀθανασίαν αὕτη οἰκονομεῖν, ἣν ἔχει καὶ παρὰ Βακχυλίδῃ ἡ
Ἀθηνᾶ, τῷ Τυδεῖ δώσουσα τὴν ἀθανασίαν.—δώσουσα,
because she did not fulfil her intention. Tydeus, son of Oeneus,
was wounded in the war of the Seven against Thebes. Athena
was going to heal him and make him immortal with a φάρμακον
which she had obtained from Zeus. But Amphiaraus, who
hated Tydeus for having persuaded the Argives into the war,
cut off the head of Melanippus, whom Tydeus had slain, and
brought it to him. Tydeus cut it in two, and ate the brains;
when Athena, in disgust, left him to die. (Apollod. 3. 6. 8.)

46. [B. p. 580 n. : Bl. p. 159 n.]

Cassandra.—Porphyrion on Hor. *C.* I. 15: Hac ode Bac-
chylidem imitatur; nam ut ille *Cassandram facit vaticinari
futura belli Troiani*, ita hic Proteum [written by error for
Nereum]. The same error occurs in the schol. on Stat. *Theb.* 7.
330: Hic Bacchylides Graecus poeta est, quem imitatus est
Horatius in illa oda in qua Proteus Troiae futurum narrat
excidium.—Cp. fr. 6.

47. [B. 56 : Bl. 10.]

Europa.—Schol. *Il.* 12. 292: Εὐρώπην τὴν Φοίνικος Ζεὺς
θεασάμενος ἔν τινι λειμῶνι μετὰ Νυμφῶν ἄνθη ἀναλέγουσαν
ἠράσθη, καὶ κατελθὼν ἤλλαξεν ἑαυτὸν εἰς ταῦρον καὶ ἀπὸ τοῦ
στόματος κρόκον ἔπνει. οὕτω δὲ τὴν Εὐρώπην ἀπατήσας ἐβάστασε
καὶ διαπορθμεύσας εἰς Κρήτην ἐμίγη αὐτῇ· εἶθ' οὕτω συνῴκισεν
αὐτὴν Ἀστερίωνι τῷ Κρητῶν βασιλεῖ. γενομένη δὲ ἔγκυος
ἐκείνη τρεῖς παῖδας ἐγέννησε, Μίνωα, Σαρπηδόνα καὶ Ῥαδάμανθυν.
ἡ ἱστορία παρὰ Ἡσιόδῳ καὶ Βακχυλίδῃ.—Bacchylides may have
written a dithyramb Εὐρώπη: though the story is one which
might also have occurred in a hymn.

430   BACCHYLIDES.

48. [B. 60: Bl. 44.]

Eurytion.—Schol. *Od.* 21. 295: Βακχυλίδης δὲ διάφορον (distinct from the Eurytion in v. 295) οἴεται τὸν Εὐρυτίωνα· φησὶ γὰρ ἐπιξενωθέντα Δεξαμενῷ ἐν Ἤλιδι ὑβριστικῶς ἐπιχειρῆσαι τῇ τοῦ ξενοδοχοῦντος θυγατρί, καὶ διὰ τοῦτο ὑπὸ Ἡρακλέους ἀναιρεθῆναι καιρίως τοῖς οἴκοις [τοῖς ἐκεῖ Eustath. 1909. 61] ἐπιστάντος.

Eurytion figures as an unruly Centaur in two stories. (1) At the wedding of Peirithous and Hippodameia on Mount Pelion he tries to carry off the bride, thus provoking the fight between the Lapithae and the Centaurs : *Od.* 21. 295 ff. (2) As a guest at the house of Dexamenus in Elis [or, acc. to Apollod. 2. 5. 5, at Olenus in Achaia] he insults his host's daughter ; Heracles appears opportunely, and slays him. This story is found, with some variations, in Apollodorus *l.c.*, Diod. IV. 33, and Hyginus *Fab.* 31. 33. The name of *Eurytus* is substituted for that of Eurytion in the first story by Ovid (*M.* 12. 219), and in the second story by Diodorus (IV. 33).—The timely appearance of Heracles at the house of Dexamenus followed his visit to the Centaur Pholus on mount Pholoe (between Arcadia and Elis). That visit was told by Stesichorus in his Γηρυονηΐς (fr. 7), which related the adventures of Heracles on his way back from the far West. That poem may have been the source, or one of the sources, from which Bacchylides derived his material for the story of Eurytion.

49. [B. 61: Bl. p. 158.]

Evenus.—Schol. Pind. *I.* III. 72 (=IV. 54): ἰδίως τὸν Ἀνταῖόν φησι (Πίνδαρος) τῶν ξένων τῶν ἡττωμένων τοῖς κρανίοις ἐρέφειν τὸν τοῦ Ποσειδῶνος ναόν· τοῦτο γὰρ ἱστοροῦσι τὸν Θρᾷκα Διομήδην ποιεῖν, Βακχυλίδης δὲ Εὔηνον ἐπὶ τῶν τῆς Μαρπήσσης [Μαρπίσσης Heyne, for Μαρσίππης] μνηστήρων· οἱ δὲ Οἰνόμαον, ὡς Σοφοκλῆς.—See note on XIX. 7.

50. [B. p. 588: Bl. p. 176.]

Galateia.—Natalis Comes *Mythol.* IX. 8, p. 987: Dicitur Polyphemus non modo amasse Galateam, sed etiam Galatum ex illa suscepisse, ut testatus est Bacchylides.—Bergk, with whom Blass concurs, justly remarks that the worth of this statement is doubtful. Later mythology, however, knew a son Γάλας (Appian *Illyr.* 2) or Γαλάτης borne by Galateia to Polyphemus (see Roscher's *Lex.* s. vv. Galas and Galateia); and it is possible that such a son may have been mentioned in some poem of Bacchylides.

51. [B. 32 : Bl. 9.]

Laocoon.—Servius on Verg. *Aen.* II. 201: Sane Bacchylides
de Laocoonte et uxore eius vel de serpentibus a Calydnis insulis
venientibus atque in homines conversis dicit.—Laocoon, priest
of Apollo at Troy, had incurred the god's wrath by marrying
[hence the words 'et uxore eius']. Two serpents, sent by Apollo,
swam over from the neighbouring islets of Calydnae,—then changed
into men, and killed the two sons of Laocoon, but not the
father. This was probably the outline of the story as told
by Bacchylides, perhaps in a dithyramb: and Sophocles in his
Λαοκόων seems to have followed him (so far at least as these
particulars are concerned). See Robert, *Bild und Lied*, pp. 192 ff.;
who, however, thinks that the two destroyers came over as
men from the islets, and afterwards changed into serpents.
Engelmann, art. *Laokoon* in Roscher (p. 1840), justly lays
stress on the words in the Apollodorus fragment, *Epit. Vat.* 21.
15, Ἀπόλλων δὲ αὐτοῖς σημεῖον ἐπιπέμπει· δύο γὰρ δράκοντες
διανηξάμενοι διὰ τῆς θαλάσσης ἐκ τῶν πλησίον νήσων τοὺς
Λαοκόωντος υἱοὺς κατεσθίουσιν.

52. [B. 63 : Bl. 46.]

Niobe's children.—Gellius *N.A.* XX. 7 : Nam Homerus pueros
puellasque eius (Niobae) bis senos dicit fuisse, Euripides bis
septenos, Sappho bis novenos, *Bacchylides* et Pindarus *bis denos.*

In giving the number of the Niobidae as 20, Bacchylides and
Pindar followed Hesiod (Apollod. 3. 5. 6); as Mimnermus also
did (Aelian, *Var. Hist.* 12. 36). The number 14, given by Eur.,
had been given before him by Lasus of Hermione (*ib.*). Alcman
went below Homer's 12, naming only 10 (*ib.*). The earliest
known authority for the tradition that two of Niobe's children
escaped is Telesilla (*c.* 510 B.C.), fr. 5 (Bergk III. p. 380). Enmann
(art. *Niobe u. Niobiden* in Roscher, p. 373) connects this legend
with the fact that Hesiod's 20 and Homer's 12 are numbers
from which the others (18, 14, 10) differ respectively by two.

53. [B. 64 : Bl. 47.]

Persephone.—Schol. Hes. *Theog.* 914: Ἡρπάσθαι δὲ τὴν
Περσεφόνην φασὶν οἱ μὲν ἐκ Σικελίας, Βακχυλίδης δὲ ἐκ
Κρήτης, Ὀρφεὺς ἐκ τῶν περὶ τὸν Ὠκεανὸν τόπων, Φανόδημος δὲ
ἀπὸ τῆς Ἀττικῆς, κ.τ.λ.—See n. on Ode III. 1—4. Bacchylides
seems to be the only known author of the classical period who
placed the rape of Persephone in Crete. That view is noticed,
but corrected, by the pseudo-Eudocia p. 109 (ed. Villoisin): ἐκ

Κρήτης ἢ μᾶλλον ἐκ Σικελίας. ; Writers of the Alexandrian and of the Roman age usually localise the story at Enna in Sicily. The Sicilian tradition must have been, in our poet's time, already old, but not yet so dominant as to exclude other versions. In the Homeric hymn to Demeter, the scene is ideal,—the Νύσιον πεδίον. In the 4th century B.C. it was possible for Phanodemus (Atthis, fr. 20, Müller I. 369) to say that Persephone had been carried off from Attica. Even in the Roman age Propertius (IV. 22. 4) can connect the legend with Cyzicus ; and Appian (*De Bell. Civ.* IV. 105), with Crenides, the later Philippi.

54. [B. 55 : Bl. 42.]

Rhea.—Schol. Pind. *O.* I. 37 : Ὁ δὲ Βακχυλίδης τὸν Πέλοπα τὴν Ῥέαν λέγει ὑγιάσαι καθεῖσαν διὰ τοῦ λέβητος (ἐγκαθεῖσαν πάλιν τῷ λέβητι coni. Bergk), ἀφ᾽ οὗ καὶ ὑγιὴς ἀνεδόθη.— Tantalus cut his son Pelops to pieces, and served up the flesh to the gods ; they, however, were not deceived, and shrank from tasting it,—all of them except Demeter, who consumed a shoulder. The remains were then boiled in a cauldron, from which Pelops came forth restored, with an ivory shoulder in place of the lost one. Pindar (*O.* I. 26 f.) makes Clotho the agent in this restoration ; Bacchylides assigned the part to Rhea, the wife of Cronus (and so schol. Aristid. p. 216); a third version named Hermes (schol. Pind.).

55. [B. 69 : Bl. 52.]

Telchines.—Tzetzes *Theogon.* 81 (Matranga *An.* 580): ἐκ δὲ τοῦ καταρρέοντος αἵματος τῶν μορίων ἐν μὲν τῇ γῇ γεγόνασι τρεῖς Ἐρινύες πρῶτον, ἡ Τεισιφόνη, Μέγαιρα, καὶ Ἀληκτὼ σὺν ταύταις, καὶ σὺν αὐταῖς οἱ τέσσαρες ὀνομαστοὶ Τελχῖνες, Ἀκταῖος, Μεγαλήσιος, Ὁρμενός τε καὶ Λύκος, οὓς Βακχυλίδης μέν φησι Νεμέσεως Ταρτάρου, ἄλλοι τινὲς δὲ λέγουσι τῆς Γῆς τε καὶ τοῦ Πόντου.—As to the Telchines, see Introd. to Ode I, p. 188. It is possible that this reference to them occurred in the lost part of that Ode (cp. p. 446).

56. [B. 59 : Bl. p. lxvii.]

Theano's sons.—Schol. *Il.* 24. 496 : Πιθανὸν μίαν τεκεῖν ἐννεακαίδεκα, οὐχ ὡς Βακχυλίδης πεντήκοντα τῆς Θεανοῦς ὑπογράφει παῖδας.—See n. on XIV. 37 ff.

The following notices, relating to geographical names, are arranged in the alphabetical order of those names.

57. [B. 66: Bl. 49.]

The river *Caicus.*—Strabo 13. 616: ὁ δὲ Κάϊκος οὐκ ἀπὸ τῆς
Ἴδης ῥεῖ, καθάπερ εἴρηκε Βακχυλίδης.—The sources of the
Caicus, Strabo says, are in a plain, west of the range of Temnus
(Τῆμνον ὄρος). The general line of the river's course is from
N.E. to S.W., through the plain of Mysia, to the Gulf of Elaea.
The cause of the Cean poet's error was that the non-
Asiatic Greeks of his time had no clear notions as to the
extent of the Ida range in· a S.E. direction. They probably
regarded the mountain system which later geographers called
Temnus as an offshoot or continuation of Ida. A much more
striking illustration of the vagueness with which the name Ἴδη
was used is the fact, also noticed by Strabo (*l.c.*), that Euripides
actually described the town of Κελαιναί in Phrygia, near the
sources of the Maeander, as being situated ἐσχάτοις Ἴδης
τόποις (Eur. fr. 1085 Nauck²).

58. [B. 65: Bl. 48.]

Ios.—*Vit. Homer.* v. p. 28 f. Westermann (Cramer, *Anecd.
Par.* III. 98. 15): Ὅμηρος...κατὰ δὲ Βακχυλίδην καὶ Ἀριστο-
τέλην τὸν φιλόσοφον Ἰήτης.
According to the pseudo-Plut. *De Vita Hom.* I. 3 (p. 101
Dübner), Aristotle said, in the third book of his Περὶ Ποιητικῆς,
that the mother of Homer was a native of Ios (the small island
S. of Naxos and N. of Thera); but that the poet himself was
born at Smyrna.—Gellius *N.A.* 3. 11 says of Homer: *Aristo-
teles tradit ex insula Io natum.* This may be only an inaccurate
version of the other statement. It cannot well be reconciled
with it by supposing that 'ex' refers merely to the mother's
origin.—The claim of Ios to be Homer's birthplace was never
prominent. More credence was given to the tradition that it
was the scene of his death and burial. Indeed, no rival of Ios
seems to have succeeded in establishing a claim to the possession
of his grave. (See the pseudo-Herodotean Βίος Ὁμήρου.)

59. [B. 58: Bl. 43.]

The town *Iulis.*—Himerius, *Orat.* XXIX.(speaking of Ἰουλίς):
Καὶ Σιμωνίδη καὶ Βακχυλίδῃ ἐσπούδασται ἡ πόλις: both poets
'have made much of the city,'—*i.e.* have paid tributes to it in
their verse. It was the native place of both. The town (now
Τζιά) is still the chief place in Ceos. It stands on the slopes of
Mt. Hagios Elias; as Strabo (10. p. 486) says of the ancient

J. B. 29

town, κεῖται δ᾽ ἐν ὄρει. It was distant about 3 or 4 miles from the
N.W. coast, where its port was near the town called Κορησσός
or Κορησία. Besides the two poets, Iulis produced Erasistratus
the physician, Ariston the Peripatetic, and Prodicus the sophist.
Plutarch *Dem.* 1 associates Iulis with Aegina in the repute of
'producing good actors and poets.' (Cp. Pridik, *De Cei Insulae
rebus*, pp. 6 f.)

60. [B. 53 : Bl. 40.]

Phoenice.—Athen. 4. p. 174 F : Γιγγραίνοισι (*sic* A) γὰρ οἱ
Φοίνικες, ὥς φησιν ὁ Ξενοφῶν [Ξενοφάνης coni. Bergk] ἐχρῶντο
αὐλοῖς, σπιθαμιαίοις τὸ μέγεθος (about 7½ inches long), ὀξὺ καὶ
γοερὸν φθεγγομένοις· τούτοις δὲ καὶ οἱ Κᾶρες χρῶνται ἐν τοῖς
θρήνοις, εἰ μὴ ἄρα καὶ ἡ Καρία Φοινίκη ἐκαλεῖτο, ὡς παρὰ
Κορίννῃ καὶ Βακχυλίδῃ ἔστιν εὑρεῖν.—The suggestion here is
that this small flute or fife (the γίγγρας or γιγγράϊνος αὐλός) may
have been altogether Carian,—being called 'Phoenician' merely
because the name 'Phoenice' was sometimes applied to Caria.
Apart from this passage, there seems to be no extant evidence
for such a use of Φοινίκη, though the Carians had much intercourse with Phoenician traders, and seem to have taken part in
Phoenician colonies.

61. [B. 67 : Bl. 50.]

The river *Rhyndacus.*—Schol. Apoll. Rhod. 1. 1165 : Ῥύνδακος
ποταμός ἐστι Φρυγίας, οὗ μέμνηται Βακχυλίδης.—This river of
northern Phrygia, rising in the district called Azanitis (from the
town of Azani, Strabo 10. p. 576), flows in a generally N.W.
direction to the Lake of Apollonia, and thence into the Propontis.
Schneidewin conjectures that the words quoted by schol. *Il.* 5.
335, Ῥύνδακον ἀμφὶ βαθύσχοινον, may be those of Bacchylides :
Hecker ascribes them to Callimachus (fr. anon. 335).

APPENDIX.

ON THE PROBABLE COMPASS AND CONTENTS OF ODE I, WHEN ENTIRE.

That portion of the Ode which has been preserved in a coherent form begins with the arrival of Minos in Ceos, his union with Dexithea, and the birth of Euxantius. It is evidently the last part of a mythical narrative. The probable nature of the part which preceded it will be discussed presently. One thing is certain,—that it was of considerable length.

The verse with which my text of Ode I begins is numbered as verse 111 of that Ode in the edition of Professor Blass. He supposes that, of the 110 verses which originally came before it, 64 are wholly lost, while 46 (not all consecutive) can be partly reconstructed from small separate fragments, with the aid of conjectural supplements.

This reconstruction is given below. The element of conjecture involved in it is so very large that (in my opinion) it is inexpedient to print it as if it formed part of the ascertained text. But it is interesting and suggestive. I will endeavour to state clearly the scope of the reconstruction, and the nature of the evidence on which it rests.

A metrical 'system' in this Ode consists of 23 verses (a strophe of 8, an antistrophe of 8, and an epode of 7). The number of lines in a column of the MS. varies from 32 to 36, 35 being the commonest total, while 34 is also frequent. Thus three systems $(23 \times 3 = 69)$ answer roughly to two average columns $(34 + 35)$. And the first column of the continuous MS., as we have it, begins with a strophe (the second strophe from the end of the Ode, $\pi\delta\lambda\iota(\nu)$......$\beta\alpha\theta\upsilon$-). These are the data from which Professor

Blass sets out in estimating the extent of the lost portion. But his estimate further assumes that the first strophe of the Ode began at the top of a column, as would have been the case if this Ode stood first in the papyrus. This being granted, it follows that the number of systems which preceded column I (of Kenyon's edition) must be either three (= 69 verses), or a multiple of three. And, from an examination of the fragments which he refers to this Ode, Prof. Blass infers that the number of such systems is six (23 × 6 = 138 verses), equivalent to four columns of the papyrus.

By combining and supplementing small fragments, he has conjecturally restored parts of the first four of these systems, as follows :—

              ]ΕΛΕΩΝ
              ]ΤΩΝ
       ]ΕΡΙΔΕΣ[
       ]ΕΝΥΦΑΙ[
5   ]ΟΥΣ·ΙΝΑΚ[
       ]ΓΑΙΑΣΙΣΘΜΙ[
       ]ΛΜΟ|ΝΕΥΒΟΥΛΟΥΝ[
       ]ΑΜ|ΒΡΟΝΝΗΡΕ[
       ]ΛΙΝΕΙ|ΝΑΣΟΙΟΤ' ΕΥ[
10   ]ΑΝ·ΕΝΘ[

            *   *   *

19   ]ΑΣΙΝΙΠΠΟΥΣ
20?   ]ΤΟΝΤΟΔ[
       ]ΕΣΣΙΝΑΝ[
       ]ΤΟΝΑΥΤ[
       ]ΑΛΛΑΙΣΙΝ[
       ]ΝΔ' ΕΤΕ[
25   ]ΓΟΝΩΤ[
          ]ΠΛ[

            *   *   *

στρ. α'.　∪ ∪ – – – μ]ελέων

　　　　∪ ∪ – – ἀμβρό ?]των

　　　　– ∪ ∪ Πι]ερίδες

　　　　– –]ἐννφαί[νετε δ' ὕμνους?

5　　　– ∪ ∪]ους, ἵνα κ[υ-

　　　　δαίνητε] γαίας Ἰσθμίας

　　　　ὀφθα]λμόν, εὐβούλου ν[έμου-

　　　　σάν τε γ]αμβρὸν Νηρέ[ος

ἀντ. α'.　πό]λιν, εἰ νάσοιό τ' Εὐ[ξαν-

10　　　τιαδ]ᾶν, ἔνθ[εν μολὼν

　　　　– ∪ ∪ – ∪ ∪ –

　　　　['Αργεῖος, ἐμεῦ τε μέλεσθε.]*

　　　　<ὦ Πέλοπος λιπαρᾶς

　　　　νάσου θεόδματοι πύλαι>

ἐπ. α'.　　*Lost, the last two vv. of ant. 1, and the first two of ep. 1.*

19　　　– ∪ – ἔζευξεν ὑφ' ἄρμ]ασιν ἵππους·

20　　　οἱ δὲ πε]τοντο δ[ι' – –

　　　　– ∪ – –]εσσιν ἀν[δρῶν?

　　　　– ∪ ∪ – ∪]τον αὐτ[–

　　　　– ∪ –] ἄλλαισιν [– – – ∪ – –

στρ. β'.　∪ ∪ – – – –]ν δ' ετε[–

25　　　∪ ∪ –]γονώτ[∪ –

　　　　　　　]πλ[

ἀντ. β'.　　*Lost, the rest of str. 2, and the first three of ant. 2.*

* Verse 12 ('Αργεῖος κ.τ.λ.) is conjecturally supplied by Blass : verses 13, 14 = frag. 7 (Bergk).

35 ΤΟΙΟ̣Ν̣[|ΤΑΙ
   ΚΑΛ[|vac.
        |ΕΜ|Ε|ΝΟ̈ΤΑ[
        |ΤΕΙΣ|Υ|ΝΕΥ
          |ΑΣ̲|vac.

        *   *   *

46   ]ΕΟΣ[
           ]Ν̣ΠΥΚ[
           ]ΓΟΙΚΟ̣Ρ[
           ]ΑΓΟΡΑ
50   ]ΜΕΛΙΦΡΟΝΟΣΥ[
           ]ΕΡΑΝ
           ]Χ̣ΑΙΑΝΠΟΛΙΝ
           ]ΓΟΙΜΕΝΟΙ
           ]Α̣ΝΔΗΡΟΙΣΑΛΟΣ[
55   ]Υ̣ΓΑΙΣΑΕΛ . . Υ
               ]Ι̣Δ̣[

        *   *   *

           ]ΣΑΓΟΡΑΙ[
           ] . ΕΛΩΔΕΤ[
           ]ΑΛΑΚΑΤΟΣ[
75   Δ' ΕΠΕΥΝΑΗ[
           ]Α·ΠΡΟΣΦΩΝΕ| . |ΤΕΝ
           ]ΣΑΙΝΟΥΣ' ΟΠ|Ι
           ] . ΕΝΤΕΡΟΜ|ΑΙ
           ]ΦΑΚΕΙΔΥ|ΑΙ
80   ]ΕΝΙΑΙ
           ]ΥΓΕΤ| . |ΠΑΜΠΑ[
               ]Α̣Σ
               ]ΟΜΟΙ

35 τοῖον [◡◡ – ◡◡ –]ται
κᾱλ[◡◡ – ◡◡ –
– – ◡ – –]εμεν, ὄτα[ν
– – ◡ – χή]τει συνεύ-
νων ◡ – – – ◡]ας

Lost, ep. 2.

46   ]εος[
στρ. γ′.   ◡◡ – – –]ν πυκ[ιν –
◡◡ ἰστουρ?]γοὶ κόρ[αι
– ◡◡ – σ]αγόρα
50   – – ◡] μελίφρονος ὕ[πνου
– ◡◡ ἀμετ]έραν
– – ◡ ἀρ]χαίαν πόλιν
– – ◡ – –]γοιμεν οἴ-
κους ἐπ′] ἀνδήροις ἁλὸς
55 ἀντ. γ′.   ὑπό τ′ α]ὐγαῖς ἀελίου
]ιδ[

(στρ. δ′.)   Lost, the last seven vv. of ant. 3, the whole of ep. 3, and the
first two vv. of str. 4.

72   – ◡◡ –]σαγόρᾳ
– – Μακ]ελὼ δὲ τ[◡ – –
– ◡ φιλ]ᾱλάκατος,
75   – –] δ′ ἐπ′ εὐναῇ [πόρον
– –]α· προσφώνει τέ ν[ιν
μαλθακᾷ] σαίνουσ′ ὀπί·
(ἀντ. δ′.)   ◡◡ – – μ]ὲν στέρομαι
◡◡ ἀμ]φάκει δύᾳ,
80   – ◡◡ – π]ενίᾳ·
– – – ◡◡ φε]ύγετε πάμπα[ν
– ◡◡ – ◡◡]ας
– – ◡ – – –]ομοι

Verse 83 was followed (as Prof. Blass supposes) by 27 verses of which nothing remains (*vv.* 84—110). Then comes the fragment which supplies *vv.* 111—129 (= 1—19 in my text); after which 8 verses, and part of a ninth, are lost. (129 + 9 = 138, or six systems.) Verse 139 is the first in col. I (Kenyon's ed.), and the first of the seventh system.

It may now be convenient to the reader if I show in a tabular synopsis the whole scheme of the Ode, as conjecturally completed by the reconstruction given above; indicating (*a*) the correspondence of the verses with the fragments which have been combined, and with the several parts of each metrical system; (*b*) the position and extent of the supposed lacunas; (*c*) the more salient points in the subject-matter, so far as they can be made out.

No. of verse in Ode I (acc. to Blass[3]).	No. of fragment (ed. Kenyon).	Place in metrical system.	Subject-matter, so far as it can be traced or surmised.
Column I.			Verse 3. Πι]ερίδες. Exordium: invocation of Muses.
1, 2	16 *a*	} strophe I;	
3–10	6	} antistr. I. 1, 2	6 ff. γαίας 'Ισθμίας | ὀφθαλμόν κ.τ.λ. Corinth : Isthmian festival.
			9 f. νάσοιό τ' Εὐ[ξαντιαδ]ᾶν. Ceos.
11–18	Lost.	antistr. I. 3–8 epode I. 1, 2	
19	24	epode I. 3	19 f. ἔξευξεν ὑφ' ἅρμ]ασιν ἵππους· |
20–26	15	ep. I. 4–7 str. II. 1–3	οἱ δὲ πέ]τοντο. Some one starts in a chariot; perhaps Zeus?
27–34	Lost.	str. II. 4–8 ant. II. 1–3	
Column II.			38 f. χή]τει συνεύ|νων. Does this refer to the forlorn state of the maidens, Dexithea and her sisters, after their father Damon and the other Telchines had been slain by Zeus?
35	16 *b* and 28	ant. II. 4	
36	16 *b*	,, ,, 5	
37	39, 40, 28	,, ,, 6	
38	39, 40, 28	,, ,, 7	
39	40	,, ,, 8	
40–45	Lost.	ep. II. 1–6	

46–56	13	ep. II. 7 str. III. ant. III. 1, 2	49–55. One of the maidens, on awaking from sleep, speaks to another about quitting their ἀρχαίαν πόλιν, and seeking a new abode 'on the verge of the sea' (ἀνδήροις ἁλός), in the full 'rays of the sun.'
57–71 Column III began about v. 70.	Lost.	ant. III. 3–8 ep. III. str. IV. 1, 2	In the next strophe, one of the maidens accosts certain visitors,—probably Zeus and Apollo (Nonnus 18. 35). Their arrival in Ceos may have been related in the course of these 16 lost verses.
72–83	5	str. IV. 3–8 ant. IV. 1–6	73. From -ἐλω in the MS., Bl. conj. Μακ]ελώ. 76. Macelo (or some other maiden) 'addressed them,' μαλθακᾷ σαίνουσ' ὀπί. The pron. νιν here meant αὐτούς (Apollon. de pron. 368 A);—probably (the disguised) Zeus and Apollo. In 79 f. she spoke of ἀμφάκει δύᾳ and πενίᾳ,—presumably in excuse for inability to provide better entertainment.
84–110 Column IV began about v. 105.	Lost.	ant. IV. 7, 8 ep. IV. str. V. ant. V. ep. V. 1, 2	This large lacuna of 27 verses must have comprised some further account of the interview between the maidens and their visitors. Zeus or Apollo may have foretold the high destiny in store for Dexithea.
111–129	1 (With which I begin my text.)	ep. V. 3–7 str. VI. ant. VI. 1–6	112 ff. 'On the third day' (after the visit of the gods to the maidens?) Minos arrives. He weds Dexithea. 'In the tenth month' is born Euxantius, the future lord of Ceos.
130–137	Lost.	ant. VI. 7, 8 ep. VI. 1–6	
138	34	ep. VI. 7	ἄλλα]ξαν θύγατρες. Bl. connects this with the maidens' change of abode (see above, 49–55).—If Dexithea and her sisters are the 'daughters,' this implies a reference to their father Damon.
Column V 139–174 Col. VI 175–184	= Col. I (Kenyon) = Col. II (K.)	str. VII. ant. VII. ep. VII. str. VIII. ant. VIII. ep. VIII.	139–146. The boy Argeius—his spirit and athletic skill. 147–154. His father Pantheides. 155–158. The Isthmian victory of Argeius. 159–184. Praise of ἀρετή.

For the purpose of piecing together the small separate fragments in vv. 1—83, three tests have been available; viz. (1) *metre;* (2) *sense;* (3) the *colour* of the papyrus.

As to metre, when *a single fragment* contains even very slight remains of *a series* of verses, such traces may suffice to make it certain that those verses belonged to a strophe, an antistrophe, or an epode, as the case may be. A good example is afforded by verses 47—55 (as now numbered by Prof. Blass), all contained in fragment 13. We may be certain that there we have the traces of a whole strophe, and of the first verse of an antistrophe. Even then, however, we have still to determine where that strophe (etc.) came in the Ode. In many other cases the metrical test is ambiguous: *e.g.* fr. 34 (= v. 138 Blass), -ξαν θύγατρες, might belong either to the 7th verse of an epode, or to the 5th.

As to the *sense*, there is at least one instance in Prof. Blass's reconstruction where he has justly deemed this second test to be conclusive. There can be no doubt that fragment 6, containing Πι]ερίδες, γαίας Ἰσθμίας | ὀφθα]λμόν, etc., belonged to the exordium of the Ode, and presumably to its first strophe. But, on the whole, there is very little coherent sense to be extracted from the mutilated words or phrases in these fragments; as an inspection will show. And where such sense is traceable (as in verses 19 f., 50—55, and 75—80), it does not suffice to exclude doubts as to the order in which the several groups of verses stood when the Ode was entire.

The third test is that afforded by the *colour* of the fragment of papyrus. Colour alone is a very uncertain guide, though it may be useful in suggesting a juxtaposition, or in confirming other evidence. There are, however, some instances in which colour is the principal or only test on which we have to rely for the position assigned to fragments. It is on this ground that fragments 24 and 15 (= vv. 19—26) are now referred to the first of the lost columns. Again, Prof. Blass and Dr Kenyon are agreed (and are doubtless right in thinking) that fragments 39, 40, and 28 cohere. But colour is the reason for assigning them to the second of the lost columns. Then as to fragment 13. In his first edition, Prof. Blass placed this (= verses 46—55 as now numbered) *after* fragment 5 (= vv. 72—83 as now numbered). But in subsequent editions he gives fragments 13 and 5 their present respective places, because the colour and condition (*color habitusque* p. 22, n.) of fragment 13 indicates that it belonged to one of the first two (lost) columns. And after all three tests, metre, sense, and colour, have been used, so far as the data permit, with the utmost sagacity and patience, large room for doubt remains, as the editor frankly recognises. Take, for example, three groups of verses, as numbered in his later editions,—(1) vv. 19—25 : (2) 47—56 : (3) 35—38. He observes (p. 23, note on v. 19) that it may be questioned whether, after all, the order of these groups should not be (3), (2), (1).

What has now been said will serve to make it clear why I have not printed Prof. Blass's ingenious reconstruction as part of the text. It must be regarded as very largely hypothetical : that follows from the nature of the case. But his acuteness and industry have not therefore been expended in vain. Several fragments have been rightly combined ; the context of some passages has been elucidated. And these fragments afford interesting glimpses of the matter which they contained, justifying the belief that the Ode, when entire, contained a large and highly-wrought mythical story.

The legend of Minos and Dexithea, which Bacchylides treated in this Ode, is epitomized in the scholia on the *Ibis* of Ovid[1]. It is there said that Macelo and her sisters, the daughters of Damon, had once been hospitable to Jupiter. On this account he spared them, when he slew the Telchines, of whom Damon was chief, for blighting the fruits of the earth by evil arts. Minos came to the sisters, wedded 'Dexione' or 'Desithone' (Dexithea), and begat Euxantius, ancestor of the Euxantidae. The longer of the two scholia which give this story cites the poet Nicander (*c.* 150 B.C.) as the source[2]. A verse in the

---

[1] Robinson Ellis in *Class. Rev.* XII. p. 66 (Feb., 1898): v. Wilamowitz in *Gött. gel. Anz.* 1898, 126 f.

[2] See Robinson Ellis's edition of the *Ibis* (Oxon. 1881), p. 83. (1) The shorter scholium on v. 475 runs thus :—*Macedo*

filia Damonis dicitur cum [here, I may observe, E. Rohde would insert II or III, which could easily have dropped out after m] *sororibus fuisse :* harum hospitio usus Iupiter, cum *Telchinas quorum hic princeps erat corrumpentes inuidia successus*

Dionysiaca of Nonnus, which unfortunately is followed by a lacuna, says that '*Macello entertained Zeus and Apollo*' at the same time[1]. The scholia, and this verse of Nonnus, are our only authorities (other than Bacchylides) for the myth. It has

omnium fructuum fulmine interficeret, seruauit. ad quas cum uenisset Minos cum Dexione concubuit: ex qua creauit Euxantium unde Euxantidae fuerunt. (2) The longer scholium is as follows :—*Nicander dicit Macelon filiam Damonis cum sororibus fuisse. harum hospitio Iupiter susceptus cum Thelonios* [Thelginas = Telchinas?] *quorum hic Damo princeps erat corrumpentes uenenis successus omnium fructuum fulmine interficeret* seruauit *eos* [sic: leg. *eas*]. *sed Macelo cum uiro propter uiri nequitiam periit. ad alias vero seruatas cum uenisset Minos cum Desithonè* [*Desitone* ed. Paris.] *concubuit, ex qua creauit Eusantium unde Eusantiae fuerunt.*—Cp. Otto Schneider, *Nicander*, p. 133 f., frag. 116. Nothing is known about Nicander's treatment of the subject beyond what is stated here.

This scholium says that, while the other sisters were spared, *Macelo* was killed, along with her husband, on account of the latter's wickedness. The verse of the *Ibis* (475), to which these scholia belong, is—*Ut Macelo* (v. 1. *Macedo*) *rapidis icta est cum coniuge flammis.* Two other scholia on that verse say merely that Macelo and her husband were struck with lightning by Jupiter at their marriage-feast *because he* (or *they*) *had invited all the gods except Jupiter.* It is surprising to learn that Macelo, one of the sisters whose hospitality to the god saved their lives, perishes for an act of the opposite kind, albeit the guilt was her husband's. The hospitality to Zeus (and Apollo) is ascribed by Nonnus (XVIII. 35), not to several sisters, but expressly to Μακελλώ. There may have been a contamination of myths here. In one (probably the older) form of the story, Macelo was simply the foremost of the sisters in offering hospitality to the god (or gods). Then, perhaps by some confusion with a similar

name, she became the bride who was involved in the punishment of the bridegroom for a sin of that type so common in mythology,—omission to ask a particular god to a feast. Thus a foreign and discordant element was interwoven with the original myth.

[1] Nonnus XVIII. 35 ff. :

Ζῆνα καὶ Ἀπόλλωνα μιῇ ξείνισσε Μακέλλω [leg. Μακελλώ]
*   *   *   *   *   *   *
καὶ Φλεγύας ὅτε πάντας ἀνερρίζωσε θαλάσσῃ,
νῆσον ὅλην τριόδοντι διαρρήξας Ἐνοσίχθων,
ἀμφοτέρας ἐφύλαξε καὶ οὐ πρήνιξε τριαίνῃ.

The substantive which went with μιῇ is lost in the lacuna. A. Köchly, in his edition (Teubner, 1857–8), has altered Μακέλλων (very unwarrantably) into τραπέζῃ,—the conjecture of G. Falkenburg (ed. princeps, Antwerp, 1569) ; and has also changed the ἀμφοτέρας of the MSS. into ἀμφοτέρους. The subject to ξείνισσε was, he supposes, one of the Phlegyes, who, with a companion, was spared by Poseidon, when he destroyed those savage islanders. E. Rohde (*Der griech. Roman und seine Vorläufer*, p. 506 2nd ed.) has judged more soundly of this passage. The traditional reading Μακέλλων (i.e. Μακελλώ) is corroborated by the *Ibis*-scholia. Nicander had told her story, which was connected with the destruction of the Telchines by Zeus. Euphorion of Chalcis (*c.* 220 B.C.) had related the destruction of the Phlegyes by Poseidon (Servius on *Aen.* VI. 618: Euphor. fr. CLV. p. 154 Meineke). Nonnus alluded in this passage to both legends: the verses lost after *v.* 35 contained the end of the first, and the beginning of the second.

three principal features: (1) the hospitality of the sisters to Zeus (and Apollo); (2) the slaying of the Telchines by Zeus; (3) the visit of Minos to the sisters, his union with Dexithea, and the birth of Euxantius.

This last part of the story,—the vital one for the Cean poet, —is contained in the first large fragment of the Ode. But how had Bacchylides conducted the mythical narrative up to that point? The fragments, though too scanty to help us far, afford some gleams of light which are suggestive. One of the sisters, *on awaking from sleep*, proposes (it would seem) that they shall quit their ἀρχαίαν πόλιν, and seek a new abode—'on the verge of the sea' (<ἐπ'> ἀνδήροις ἁλός), and open to the rays of the sun (<ὑπ'> αὐγαῖς ἀελίου). The words (λήξασα?) μελίφρονος ὕπνου suggest that the maiden's projects like Nausicaa's, had been prompted by a dream, sent to her in order that she and her sisters should meet visitants who were on their way to Ceos. (That all this happens in Ceos, may safely be inferred from the fact that Ceos is plainly the πολύκρημνος χθών of verse 11, in which Minos finds Dexithea.) Then in fragment 5 one of the sisters is found addressing certain persons 'in a soothing voice' (...σαίνουσ' ὀπί), near some stream which has the epithet εὐναῆ. This meeting occurred, no doubt, after the migration of the maidens from their 'old city' to the abode near the sea; and may have been placed by the poet near the mouth of a river. Are the persons whom this maiden accosts the disguised Zeus and Apollo? It is possible, or even probable: we can say no more. But it is interesting to note that the speaker touches on '*anguish sharp as a two-edged sword*' (ἀμφάκει δύᾳ), and on 'poverty.' Probably she is apologizing (as Prof. Blass suggests) for being unable to provide better entertainment for the strangers, and φεύγετε (in v. 81) was preceded by a negative: 'yet do not altogether decline what we can offer.' No stronger proof of φιλοξενία could be given than to offer hospitality in a season of private sorrow (cp. Eur. *Alc.* 512—567). But what was the cause of this ἀμφάκης δύα to which the speaker refers? The sisters are, it is apparent, in affliction and distress. This might be due to the knowledge that their father Damon, with the other Telchines, had incurred the wrath of Zeus, and that the divine chastisement was about to descend upon him. A warning of such peril, by dream or oracle, may have been the motive of their removal from their ἀρχαίαν πόλιν—which must have been also their father's seat—to the new abode by the sea. The scholia on the *Ibis*, at any rate, imply that the hospitality of the sisters to Zeus *preceded* the slaying of the Telchines. If the ἀμφάκης δύα is grief for Damon's death, then Bacchylides has followed a version according to which the danger of destruction menaced the sisters, not at the moment of their father's fall, but soon after it: their hospitality to Zeus and Apollo averted the peril, and brought, instead of it, a great reward.

With regard to the Telchines, we know that Bacchylides somewhere named four of them,—Ἀκταῖος, Μεγαλήσιος, Ὅρμενος, Λύκος,—and described them as the offspring of Nemesis[1]. If this Ode was the place where the mention occurred, we might conjecture that a good deal was said about the Telchines. That must remain wholly uncertain: the fragments tell us nothing. One thing, however, may be said. Rhodes was the primary seat of the Telchines; but it was not there (according to legend) that they perished. They quitted Rhodes (driven out by the Heliadae[2], or, according to another account, foreboding a deluge[3]): and then, as legend told, *they were scattered* (διασπαρῆναι)[4]. There was nothing, therefore, to prevent a poet from supposing that the Telchin Damon had established himself in Ceos, and was there slain by the bolt of Zeus.

A small town on the coast of Ceos was called Κορησία (Strabo 10, p. 486), Κόρησος, or Κορησσός[5]. Near it was the

---

[1] Tzetzes, *Theogon.* 81: see p. 432 (fr. 55). The words as to the origin of the Telchines are,—οὒς Βακχυλίδης μέν φησι Νεμέσεως Ταρτάρου, ἄλλοι τινὲς δὲ λέγουσι τῆς Γῆς τε καὶ τοῦ Πόντου. The singularity of the version which Bacchylides followed is that it does not connect the Telchines with the sea. These volcanic daemons were essentially, as Nonnus calls them (XIV. 42), δαίμονες ὑγρονόμοι: he makes them children of Poseidon, whose trident they wrought (Callim. *Del.* 31). According to Diodorus (v. 55) they were υἱοί...Θαλάσσης (no father is named), and were reared by

Poseidon. Are the words Νεμέσεως Ταρτάρου sound, or should a καὶ come between them? Nemesis is usually called a daughter of Night (Hes. *Theog.* 223: of Erebus, in Hygin. *Fab. praef.*): in Attic mythology the Rhamnusian Nemesis was a daughter of Oceanus (Paus. 7. 1 § 3).

[2] Nonnus XIV. 42 ff.

[3] Diod. v. 56 *ad init.* προαισθομένους ...τὸν μέλλοντα γίνεσθαι κατακλυσμόν.

[4] *Ib.*

[5] The little that has been ascertained or conjectured about this place is brought together by A. Pridik, *De Cei Insulae rebus* (Berlin, 1892), p. 7 f.

port of Iulis,—the latter town itself being about three miles
further inland. It has been ingeniously suggested by N.
Festa¹ that a local legend, deriving Κορησία from Κόραι, may have
connected it with the migration of Dexithea and her sisters
from their former home (the ἀρχαίαν πόλιν) to the coast; and
that Κορησία is the πόλις βαθυδείελος of vv. 29 f., of which
Argeius was a native. Some allusion to the foundation of that
town may have occurred in the lacuna which now exists
between v. 18 and v. 23.

To sum up:—the fragments, supplemented by conjecture on
the lines indicated above, might suggest that the argument of
the Ode was somewhat as follows. It began,—so much is
reasonably certain,—with an invocation of the Pierides,—a
reference to Corinth, 'eye of the Isthmian land,' 'the city which
worships Poseidon, wedded to the daughter of wise Nereus'
(Amphitrite),—and then a mention of Ceos, 'isle of the
Euxantidae.' This last served to link the prelude with the myth
of Minos and Dexithea, which occupied the larger part of the
poem. In Ceos was dwelling, with his daughters (Macelo,
Dexithea, and others), the Telchin Damon,—guilty, in the sight
of Zeus, along with his brethren now scattered in many lands, of
practising the malign arts by which they had once blighted the
fruits of the earth in Rhodes². A dream comes to one of the
daughters, warning them of a disaster impending on their house,
and counselling them to leave the city of their father for a place
on the sea-coast. They do so; and there meet two strangers of
noble mien, who have just reached the island. Though in deep
sorrow and distress, Macelo, on behalf of the sisters, offers them
such hospitality as they can give. One of the visitors speaks
words of comfort; and predicts that, though the maiden's father,
Damon, must presently be smitten by the wrath of Zeus, a great
hero shall come anon to Ceos, who shall wed one of the sisters,
and that the offspring of this union shall in future days be lord
of that land, and founder of a famous line. The strangers

---

¹ *Le ode e i frammenti di B.* (Florence, 1898).
² They drenched the crops with the sulphurous waters of the Styx. Nonnus

xIV. 46 f. :
χερσὶ βαρυζήλοισιν ἀρυόμενοι Στυγὸς ὕδωρ
ἄσπορον εὐκάρποιο ῾Ρόδου ποίησαν ἀλωήν.

vanish. Storm-clouds gather in the sky; and from their dwelling by the sea the sisters behold the lightnings which show where the doom of Zeus has fallen. But, on the third day thereafter, Minos arrives with his Cretan warriors; he weds Dexithea; and, when he departs for Crete, leaves the half of his host to protect her. In the tenth month her son Euxantius is born. And in after days he, or a descendant, founds a goodly city in the place by the sea where of yore Macelo and her sisters entertained Zeus and Apollo unawares; and calls it, in memory thereof, *Coresus*, 'the city of the maidens.' There was born the young victor at the Isthmian games, Argeius, son of the hospitable physician, Pantheides.

Thus, or somewhat in this fashion,—following the hints in the fragments, and the other evidence,—might we conceive the outline of the form which Bacchylides gave to the legend of his island. At any rate, we may be sure that those passages of which the fragments afford glimpses,—the scenes in which Dexithea and her sisters bore part,—exhibited to advantage the poet's most attractive gifts,—his graceful ease in narrative, his skill in bright and picturesque detail, his simple pathos. Few mutilations in the papyrus are more to be regretted than those which have rent away the earlier portion of this first ode.

Ode I. 15. EUXANTIUS.

I. 15   According to the scholiast on Apollonius Rhodius (I. 186), Euxantius was the father of Miletus. The source used by the scholiast may have been Aristocritus, the author of a work on Miletus, who mentioned the Εὐξαντίδαι (Müller, *Frag. Histor.* IV. p. 331). The renown of the *Milesia vellera* points to a connexion between Εὐξαντίδαι and ξάντης, *carminator*, 'woolcarder.' Such patronymics were often borne by hereditary guilds, in which the exercise of some art or craft descended from father to son. But it is easy to conceive that, when the Euxantidae of Miletus had become a clan of wealth and distinction, they should have aspired to the honours of heroic ancestry. It has been remarked by Prof. v. Wilamowitz-Moellendorff (*Gött. gel. Anz.*, 1898, no. 2, p. 128) that Εὐξάντιος is 'a strange formation.' He suggests that it means, ὁ κατ᾽ εὐχὴν ἀντίος ἐλθών. He thinks that, in the original form of the legend, Δεξιθέα ('she who receives a god') became a mother, not by Minos, but by a god (Zeus or Apollo), whose welcome epiphany was commemorated by the name Euxantius, given to the offspring of that union. Forced interpretations of traditional proper names were frequent enough in popular Greek mythology. It is not inconceivable that Εὐξάντιος should, at some time or other, have been *explained* as meaning, ὁ κατ᾽ εὐχὴν ἀντίος ἐλθών: but is it at all probable that it should have been *invented* to express that idea? I cannot think so. Surely it is far more likely that Εὐξάντιος was a name suggested by the patronymic Εὐξαντίδαι, and invented in order to provide the 'sons of the good wool-carders' with a heroic ancestor. This hypothesis is confirmed by the comparative obscurity in which the Euxantius-myth remained. That legend, so far as we know, had only what may be called a domestic currency,—viz., at Miletus and in Ceos. The learned Alexandrians, of course, knew it. Herodian has preserved part of a verse of Callimachus, αἷμα τὸ μὲν γενεῆς Εὐξαντίδος. But there is no reason to suppose that the Alexandrian knowledge of the myth was derived from any sources other than those which Ceos and Miletus themselves had furnished,—the poem of Bacchylides, and the prose-work of Aristocritus (with possibly other writers of local mythography). It is significant that pseudo-Apollodorus, usually so full and precise in regard to every mythological person of any importance, simply mentions Euxantius as a son whom Dexithea bore to Minos, and has not a word more to say about him (3. 1 § 2).

To sum up, the conclusion to which I am led is as follows. The Euxantidae were a clan at Miletus in whom the craft of wool-carding was hereditary. Ceos had an ancient local legend which made that island the place where Dexithea became the bride of Minos. Minos was associated in legend with Miletus also. It was an easy combination to call the son of Minos and Dexithea 'Euxantius,' and to represent him as the ancestor of the Milesian Euxantidae. The myth would be welcome to the Euxantidae themselves, whom it furnished with a lineage so illustrious; it would also be gratifying to the Ceans. A further embellishment of the legend was to make Euxantius the father of Miletus.

Ode I. 32—34. Ἀργεῖος...μάχας.

I. 32—34 It is certain that verse 34 began with the letters ΧΡΕ. The scribe had written the letter Α before these, but this has been deleted. As verse 33 ends with ὁπότε, and its final syllable must be long, verse 34 must have begun with χρ, before which ε could be lengthened. There is no room for ΖΑ before ΧΡΕ. The letter after Ε must have been Ι, and the only question is whether this Ι had the circumflex or the acute accent (the trace admits of either): *i.e.*, whether the word was (1) χρεῖος or χρεῖον: or (2) χρείη, or some part of χρεία. The fact that Α was written by error before ΧΡΕ is decidedly in favour of (1); since a transcriber, who had χρεῖος (or -ον) before him, might easily, by inadvertence, have written the much commoner word ἀχρεῖος (or -ον): whereas such a slip would have been less likely, if χρείη or some part of χρεία had stood in the text.

-βολοῖ is certain. This must be pres. optat. from a verb in -έω: for no verb ending in -βολόω is discoverable. Dialect would lead us to expect -έοι in the optat., not the contraction -οῖ. It is, of course, possible that the poet wrote -βολέοι, and that -βολοῖ is due to transcription.

What was the verb of which -βολοῖ formed the latter part? Blass reads κερβολοῖ ('irritate, provoke'). 'Κερβολεῖν *idem est atque κερτομεῖν*' (praef. p. xiii). He cites Hom. *Il.* 16. 261 where αἰεὶ κερτομέοντες is said of children who are teasing wasps. The form κερβολεῖν occurs in Hesych. s.v. κερβολοῦσα· λοιδοροῦσα, βλασφημοῦσα. Cp. Ar. *Eq.* 822 μὴ σκέρβολλε πονηρά (= λοιδόρει). Prof. Blass further supposes that, as the contraction in -βολοῖ is strange, and as the syllable βολ answers to one which is long in the corresponding place, the word in the text was originally κερβόλλοι. In his first edition, he read χρεῖόν τι κερβολοῖ μάχας, '(whenever) any creature ('*sive canis sive homo*'), desirous of fight, provoked (the lion).' In his later eds., he reads χρεῖός ἐ [= Ϝε] κερβολοῖ μάχας, '(whenever) any need of fight provoked him': adding; '*si litt. Ϝ positionem non facit, habemus* – ‿ ‿ – [χρεῖός ἐ κερ-] *pro* – – ‿ –.' In any case, I should prefer χρεῖός τι to χρεῖός Ϝε. But I cannot think that κερβολοῖ has any probability. Neither Hesychius nor Aristophanes warrants the supposition that κερβολεῖν or σκερβόλλειν was used in any sense except that of 'taunting' or 'reviling.' Prof. Blass assumes that κερβολεῖν = κερτομεῖν, and relies on *Il.* 16. 261 to prove that κερτομεῖν could mean to 'provoke' or 'worry' *otherwise than by words*. Now, that verse was suspected by Alexandrian critics precisely because κερτομεῖν seemed to be used in an unexampled sense. See the scholium of Aristonicus upon it : ἀθετεῖται, ὅτι τὸ κερτομεῖν οὐ τίθησιν ἐπὶ τοῦ δι' ἔργου ἐρεθίζειν, ἀλλὰ διὰ λόγων. If indeed, that verse be genuine, κερτομέοντες may best be referred to the *jeering cries* of the children, since noise would contribute to the irritation of the wasps. In -βολοῖ, I can find nothing but συμβολοῖ (see commentary).

Ode II. 9 f. ἑβδομήκοντα σὺν στεφάνοισιν.

The context makes it clear that these 'seventy victories' had been **II. 9 f.** won by Ceans at the Isthmus alone. The Isthmiads were reckoned from 580 B.C. This Ode is of unknown date, but was probably among the poet's earlier works. Suppose, for the sake of illustration, that Argeius won in 470 B.C. The Isthmiad of that year was only the 56th. If we assumed a date as low as 440 B.C. (the 71st Isthmiad), the record would still be a distinctly good one for so small an island as Ceos, competing with all Hellas. Still there is nothing marvellous about it. In the first place, it would not seldom happen that a victor at one Isthmian festival would repeat his success at one or more subsequent festivals. The fragmentary Cean inscription (noticed in the Introduction to Ode 1) records two men, each of whom had won three Isthmian victories. Again (though this case would be much rarer) the same competitor might win more than one wreath at the same festival. Pausanias (6. 15 § 3) mentions a Theban who, on the same day of the Isthmia, was victorious in three contests,—boxing, wrestling, and the pancration. The greater number of the 'seventy wreaths' must have been gained in boxing and running, for which Ceos was especially noted (VI. 7). Two inferences, at least, may safely be drawn from this passage. First, that Ceos was exceptionally prolific in athletes of these classes : secondly, that the Isthmian festival was that which Cean competitors more especially frequented. It was the most readily accessible from their island, and traditional associations had doubtless confirmed the preference.

Pind. *O.* XIII. 98—100, speaking of the clan of the Ὀλιγαιθίδαι at Corinth, to whom Xenophon (winner of stadion and pentathlon at Olympia in 464 B.C.) belonged, mentions that they had won thirty victories at the Isthmus, and thirty at Nemea (ἑξηκοντάκι δὴ ἀμφοτέρωθεν).

Ode III. 18 f.   ὑψιδαιδάλτων τριπόδων σταθέντων
                  πάροιθε ναοῦ.

III. 18 f. The French exploration of Delphi has shown that a tripod dedicated
by Gelon, and another dedicated by Hieron, stood side by side before
the east front of the temple. No votive offering in the entire sanctuary
of Apollo held a more conspicuous position. (See the *Bulletin de
Correspondance Hellénique*, vol. XXI. 1897, plate XVII, the spot marked
Ex-voto de Gélon.) This fact alone suffices to explain the reference of
Bacchylides.

I. The monumental evidence has been set forth with great
clearness and precision by M. Théophile Homolle (*Bulletin de Correspondance Hellénique*, vol. XXI. pp. 588 ff., 1898: *Mélanges Weil*,
pp. 207—224, Paris, 1898.) Here I can but briefly indicate the more
essential facts. The explorers found a large quadrangular base of
limestone, on which was superimposed a high limestone step, carefully
wrought. This in turn carried two stands or pedestals (*socles*), resembling bell-shaped capitals inverted, and placed a meter apart from
each other. Each of these pedestals once supported a metal tripod, as
is shown by the cavities in which the three feet were once secured.
One of the pedestals bears the following inscription :—

> ΓΕΛΟΝΟΔΕΙΝΟΜΕΝ
> ΑΝΕΘΕΚΕΤΟΠΟΛΛΟΝΙ
> ΣΥΡΑϘΟΣΙΟΣ
> ΤΟΝΤΡΙΠΟΔΑΚΑΙΤΕΝΝΙΚΕΝΕΡΓΑΣΑΤΟ
> ΒΙΟΝΔΙΟΔΟΡΟΥΙΟΣΜΙΛΕΣΙΟΣ

So Gelon dedicated a golden Νίκη along with his tripod,—both
being the work of the same artist, Bion, son of Diodorus, of Miletus [as
to whom see *Bull. Corr. Hellén.* 1896, pp. 654—6].

The inscription on the other pedestal is mutilated : all that remains
of it is the following :—

> ΝΕΟΣΑΝΕΘΕΚΕ ΕΛ
> ΘΕΠΤΑΜΝΑΙ

The dedicator was, then, a son of Deinomenes ; certainly not Gelon,
who, if both the tripods had been his, would not have placed two
separate inscriptions on offerings supported by the same base, but
rather one inscription on the base itself. Further, we know (from
Athenaeus) that Hieron dedicated a golden tripod at Delphi : and there
is no record of such a gift by Polyzelus or Thrasybulus. It may be

regarded as certain, then, that this second tripod was Hieron's. The inscription is thus restored by M. Homolle:—

[Ἱάρων *ho* Δεινομέ]νεος ἀνέθεκε· [*h*]ἔλ
[κε δὲ τάλαντα δέκα]*h*επτὰ μναῖ.

(The nominative μναῖ, instead of the accus. μνᾶς, is strange, as M. Homolle says, in so *short* a statement of the weight; though the Delian inscriptions afford instances of nominatives mixed with accusatives in longer statements of the same nature.)

The base on which both the tripod-pedestals stood was probably designed at first for one pedestal only,—that of Gelon's tripod; and was afterwards enlarged to receive Hieron's (*Mélanges Weil*, p. 220).

II. The literary evidence may be summed up as follows.

1. Diodorus (XI. 26), following Timaeus, mentions only one tripod, —that dedicated by Gelon after the victory at Himera:—χρυσοῦν δὲ τρίποδα ποιήσας ἀπὸ ταλάντων ἑκκαίδεκα ἐνέθηκεν εἰς τὸ τέμενος τὸ ἐν Δελφοῖς, ᾿Απόλλωνι χαριστήριον.

2. Athenaeus (6. pp. 231 E—232 C) makes certain statements concerning the votive offerings generally at Delphi. For these statements he quotes two authorities, viz. (1) Phanias of Eresus, a pupil of Aristotle, who wrote Περὶ τῶν ἐν Σικελίᾳ τυράννων (see Müller, *Frag. Hist.* III. p. 297): (2) Theopompus, Φιλιππικά, book 40 (written in the second half of the fourth century B.C.).

Phanias and Theopompus, says Athenaeus, state that, after Gyges and Croesus, Gelon and Hieron were the next donors of silver or gold ἀναθήματα at Delphi:—τοῦ μὲν (Gelon) τρίποδα καὶ νίκην χρυσοῦ πεποιημένα ἀναθέντος, καθ᾿ οὓς χρόνους Ξέρξης ἐπεστράτευε τῇ ῾Ελλάδι, τοῦ δὲ ῾Ιέρωνος τὰ ὅμοια. [Observe that the date is here appended to the notice of *Gelon's* gift, and separates it from the mention of Hieron's: whereas, if both gifts had been of the same date, the clause καθ᾿ οὓς.. ῾Ελλάδι should have followed ὅμοια.]

Then Athenaeus goes on to quote *verbatim* a passage of Theopompus. After relating that the Lacedaemonians, when they wished to gild (χρυσῶσαι) the face of the Amyclaean Apollo, were directed by the Delphic oracle to buy gold of Croesus, the historian proceeds :—῾Ιέρων δ᾿ ὁ Συρακόσιος, βουλόμενος ἀναθεῖναι τῷ θεῷ τὸν τρίποδα καὶ τὴν Νίκην ἐξ ἀπέφθου χρυσοῦ, ἐπὶ πολὺν χρόνον ἀπορῶν χρυσίου, ὕστερον ἔπεμψε τοὺς ἀναζητήσοντας εἰς τὴν ῾Ελλάδα. Hieron's emissaries (Theopompus goes on to say) finally discovered a man at Corinth, one Architeles, who had large stores of gold, and who allowed them to buy as much as they desired,—adding a *bonus* on the purchase,—a large handful of the precious metal: ἀνθ᾽ ὧν Ἱέρων πλοῖον σίτου καὶ ἄλλα πολλὰ δῶρα ἔπεμψεν ἐκ Σικελίας.

This extract from Theopompus is instructive in three respects. (1) Hieron, like Gelon, dedicated both a tripod and a Victory,—and Hieron's were of refined gold. (2) 'A long time' elapsed before he could procure a sufficient quantity of such gold. After search (presumably) in Sicily and Magna Graecia, he 'afterwards' (ὕστερον) sent messengers to Greece. (3) Hieron rewarded the Corinthian gold-merchant with princely munificence, sending him 'a ship-load of corn,' and 'many other gifts.'

All this clearly suggests that, when he dedicated his offerings at Delphi, Hieron was already ruler of Syracuse. The details of the story indicate a prince who wields large resources, whose commands are executed without stint of cost or trouble, and who royally repays those who serve him. Hieron became ruler of Syracuse in 478.

According, however, to an ingenious theory propounded by M. Homolle, Hieron's offering was placed beside Gelon's in the latter's life-time. The scholiast on Pind. *Pyth.* I. 155 records the tradition that Gelon, from affection towards his brothers (Hieron, Thrasybulus and Polyzelus), dedicated his thank-offering at Delphi in their names as well as in his own :—φασὶ δὲ τὸν Γέλωνα τοὺς ἀδελφοὺς φιλοφρονούμενον ἀναθεῖναι τῷ θεῷ χρυσοῦς τρίποδας, ἐπιγράψαντα ταῦτα·

> Φημὶ Γέλων᾽, Ἱέρωνα, Πολύζηλον, Θρασύβουλον,
> παῖδας Δεινομένευς, τοὺς τρίποδας θέμεναι,
> βάρβαρα νικήσαντας ἔθνη· πολλὴν δὲ παρασχεῖν
> σύμμαχον Ἕλλησιν χεῖρ᾽ ἐς ἐλευθερίην.

This inscription is ascribed to Simonides in the Palatine Anthology (VI. 214), where in verse 2 the reading is τὸν τρίποδ᾽ ἀνθέμεναι, as it is also in Suidas s.v. Δαρετίου. [The *Anthology* and Suidas further insert the following couplet after verse 2 : ἐξ ἑκατὸν λιτρῶν καὶ πεντήκοντα ταλάντων | Δαρετίου (Δαμαρέτου Bergk) χρυσοῦ, τᾶς δεκάτας δεκάταν.]

M. Homolle holds that the reading of the scholiast, τοὺς τρίποδας θέμεναι, is the true one. At Delphi, besides the two pedestals, standing on a common base, which supported the tripods of Gelon and Hieron, the French explorer found also two smaller pedestals, which bear no inscriptions. These smaller pedestals (*C* and *D*) have the same form (that of a bell-shaped capital inverted) as the two larger (*A* and *B*); a form which is exceptional at Delphi, and does not seem to occur elsewhere. One of them (*D*) shows the three cavities intended to receive the feet of a tripod; in the case of the other (*C*), the upper surface, where such cavities, if they existed, would have appeared, has been broken away.

The history of the relation between the four tripod-pedestals (*A, B, C, D*) is conceived by M. Homolle as follows. (1) Gelon dedicated *A* after the battle of Himera. (2) Hieron, ambitious and self-assertive, afterwards contrived that his offering, *B*, also dedicated on account of Himera, should be set up beside that of his elder brother; and the base which supported the pedestal of *A* was enlarged for that purpose. (3) Then the kindly Gelon caused the two smaller tripods, *C* and *D*, to be erected on the same spot, in order to associate the younger brothers (Thrasybulus and Polyzelus) with his renown, while at the same time he thus administered a mild reproof to Hieron. *C* is somewhat larger than *D*; and M. Homolle suggests that Gelon intended this gradation of size to correspond with the gradation of age in his younger brethren. The pedestals of *C* and *D* may have stood on a common base, and this base may have borne the inscription by Simonides, Φημὶ Γέλων', Ἱέρωνα κ.τ.λ. It could have been set, facing westward, at right angles to the larger base which carried the offerings of Gelon and Hieron.

This theory—that *C* and *D* were set up by Gelon in order to give Thrasybulus and Polyzelus a share in the glory of Himera—presupposes, as we have seen, that Hieron's tripod, *B*, was set up by him, beside Gelon's, in Gelon's life-time. But the latter hypothesis appears very improbable. In 480 Hieron was regent of Gela under his elder brother, then ruler of Syracuse. (Herod. VII. 155: Freeman, *Sicily* II. p. 129.) At Himera Gelon commanded in chief against the Carthaginians. Alike in a military and in a political sense, Gelon was paramount; Hieron's position was a secondary and a dependent one. Now, the position of Hieron's Delphian tripod, at the side of Gelon's, and the similarity of scale, imply (as M. Homolle has recognised) a claim of equality. Such a claim would be perfectly intelligible if Hieron's gift to Delphi was made after Gelon's death, when Hieron had succeeded him as ruler of Syracuse. But in 480/79, and with reference to the victory at Himera, the regent of Gela would have been strangely ill-advised, if, at the central sanctuary of Hellas, he had ostentatiously asserted such equality with his elder brother and overlord.

Prof. Blass has quite a different way of explaining the two smaller pedestals (Preface to the 3rd ed. of his Bacchylides, pp. lix. f.). He supposes that Hieron dedicated three tripods at Delphi. The two smaller ones, *C* and *D*, commemorated his Pythian victories with the κέλης in 482 and 478 ; the largest, *B*, his victory at Delphi with the four-horse chariot in 470. But, as we have seen, the authorities quoted by Athenaeus speak of Hieron as having dedicated only one tripod (with a Νίκη). On the view of Prof. Blass, we should have to assume that his other two tripods were ignored because they were smaller.

There are, however, certain considerations which seem to render it very improbable that Hieron's tripod, which stood beside Gelon's, can have been a thank-offering for Hieron's success in the Pythian games. (1) The conspicuous spot where these two tripods stood, before the east front of the temple, was peculiarly associated with the great national victories, those of Salamis, Plataea, and Himera. The bronze mast with gold stars, which the Aeginetans set up after Salamis, stood close to the gold crater of Croesus (Her. VIII. 122), which itself was on the right hand of one entering the temple (id. I. 51), *i.e.* near the N.E. angle. The Panhellenic thank-offering for Plataea,—the golden tripod on a three-headed serpent of bronze (Her. IX. 80),—was in the same neighbourhood, close to the Great Altar. Gelon's tripod and Nike, as we know, commemorated Himera. The memorial of a mere personal success in the games would have seemed strangely intrusive amidst such surroundings. (2) Further, the base on which Gelon's tripod stood was enlarged to receive Hieron's. Community of base suggests community of purpose. Hieron had fought at Himera. When his tripod and Nike were placed at the side of his brother's, and on the same plinth, can we doubt that the meaning was to assert his equality with Gelon as a champion of western Hellas? That significance would be enhanced, if we could suppose that the date was subsequent to Hieron's naval victory over the Etruscans at Cumae in 474.

Another question remains. If the epigram of Simonides (or at least the first couplet of it) was really used at Delphi, where was it placed ?

1. We now know that it was *not* placed on the pedestal of Gelon's tripod. The inscription there names Gelon only. That inscription also speaks of τὸν τρίποδα καὶ τὴν Νίκην : which clearly suggests that this pedestal supported both, the tripod being surmounted by the Victory. This seems almost conclusive against the hypothesis that Gelon's Nike stood on a separate pedestal, which bore the epigram of Simonides, the speaker (φημί) being the Nike herself (as suggested by v. Wilamowitz, *Götting. Nachr.*, pp. 313 ff.). Further, it would be strange that an inscription speaking of the tripod (or tripods) should be placed on a pedestal which supported only the Nike.

2. M. Homolle supposes that the epigram of Simonides was engraved on a lost base which once supported the two smaller tripod-pedestals (C and D), those for Thrasybulus and Polyzelus. In that case, the epigram referred to four tripods. But, as I have sought to show, it is not probable that Hieron's tripod was placed beside Gelon's till after the latter's death. We should have to suppose, then, that Hieron was originally represented by a tripod which stood on a separate pedestal, a tripod presumably of smaller size than that which he afterwards caused to be set up.

It seems to me that, with the existing data for the problem, we must be content to remain in doubt with regard to (1) to the history of pedestals C and D; and (2) to the place of the Simonidean epigram, if it was really used at all. But two things appear strongly probable : viz. (1) that the tripod and Nike of Hieron, which stood beside Gelon's, commemorated the victory at Himera; and (2) that they were placed there after he succeeded Gelon at Syracuse in 478.

Ode III. 21 f.   θεόν, θεόν τις
ἀγλαϊζέτω, ὁ γὰρ ἄριστος ὄλβων.

In verse 22 Kenyon reads, ἀγλαϊζέτω γάρ, ἄριστον ὄλβον. (For the III. 21 f. position of γάρ, cp. Soph. *Ph.* 1450.) Housman and Richards, ἀγλαϊζέτω παρ' ἄριστον ὄλβον ('in the time of greatest properity'). But the change of τ into θ in the MS. reading ἀγλαϊζέθω is then unexplained.

Others read ἀγλάϊζε. Marindin, ἀγλάϊζε, θεῷ γὰρ ἄριστος ὄλβων (*i.e.*, the god has the best happiness in his gift). Tyrrell, ἀγλάϊζ' ἔθ', ᾧ πάρ' ἄριστος ὄλβων. Butcher, ἀγλάϊζε, δῶτορ' ἄριστον ὄλβων. The use of τις here with the second person of the imper. is, however, difficult to justify. πᾶς, indeed, is often so used (*e.g.* Ar. *Pax* 555 πᾶς χώρει πρὸς ἔργον). In Ar. *Av.* 1187 τόξευε, παῖε, a *v.l.* for παῖε is πᾶς τις : and in [Eur.] *Rhes.* 687, where Dind. gives ἴσχε πᾶς ἴσχ', some MSS. have ἴσχε πᾶς τις. But, even if the use of τις with the second pers. imper. could be proved authentic in some passages of this special kind, where a hurried command is addressed to several persons, it would not follow that τις could be so used in a case like the present,—*i.e.* in a general moral precept.

Ode III. 25—31. Blass gives this passage as follows: I print in III. 25—31 black type the parts of the restoration which are his own :—

25   εὖτε τὰν πεπ[ρωμέναν
        Ζηνὸς τελε[ίου νεύμασιν

458   APPENDIX.

Σάρδιες Περσᾶ[ν ὑπ' ἐκπίμπλαν στρ]ατῶι,
Κροῖσον ὁ χρυσάορος
φύλαξ' Ἀπόλλων. [τὸ γὰρ ἄ]ελπτον ἆμαρ
30 μόλ' ὢν· πολυδ[άκρυον] οὐκ ἔμελλε
μίμνειν ἔτι δ[υσφροσύναν], πυρὰν δὲ (κ.τ.λ.)

(a) The sense of the first three verses then is :—'When, by decree
of Zeus who brings the end, Sardis was fulfilling its doom ὑπὸ στρατῷ
Περσᾶν, under the hands of the Persian host.' He compares XVI. 26 f.,
πεπρωμέναν αἶσαν ἐκπλήσομεν: and for ὑπό, XII. 166 θνᾴσκοντες ὑπ'
Αἰακίδαις. But verse 27 is not a good one; the position of ὑπό is
awkward. And in verse 26 the plural νεύμασιν (used once by Aesch.,
Suppl. 373 μονοψήφοισι νεύμασιν σέθεν) seems neither quite fitting nor
very probable. The caesura after τελείου is also against the rule usually
observed by Bacchylides: see p. 97. It is surely much more likely
that the government of πεπρωμέναν was provided in v. 26 by τελειοῦσαι
(or τελέσσαντος).

(b) From τὸ γὰρ κ.τ.λ. in v. 29 onwards, the sense is:—'For the
unexpected day had come indeed (ὢν): he (Croesus) was not minded
to await a further doom of tears and anguish,' etc. This suggests some
remarks. (1) Blass's reading μόλ' ὢν is prompted by the indication in
the MS. of ὤ. But μολῶν for μολών was one of the commonest errors in
accentuation. Headlam has collected the following (among other)
passages where μολῶν is so accented in one or more of the MSS.: Eur. *Alc.*
1153, *Hipp.* 656, *Med.* 246, *Phoen.* 480, 663: Lycophron, 824, 1312,
1370, 1376 (μολῶντες 925, 956). Cp. ἐπεῖ for ἐπεί in v. 23 of this Ode.
In his 2nd and 3rd editions (p. 36) Prof. Blass further observes that, after
the letter N, he has found a point in the MS. Of this I can perceive no
trace. The right-hand stroke of N has been partly effaced, and one of
the vestiges of that stroke might, indeed, be taken for a point; but it is
in the line of the upward stroke, and not to the right of it. (2) The
form ὢν occurs nowhere else in Bacchylides; whereas in XVIII. 29 and 37
he uses οὖν. Did he here prefer ὢν as Pindaric? It seems unlikely.
The *sense* given to it is such as it would bear if (*e.g.*) the sentence had
been, τὸ ἆμαρ ἄελπτον μὲν ἦν, μόλε δ' ὢν. This is (to my apprehension)
a little forced. (3) The *asyndeton* after μόλ' ὢν is somewhat harsh, and
certainly is not in this poet's narrative style. (In his note Prof. Blass
suggests, as an alternative, πολὺ δὲ στύγος .. δυσφροσυνᾶν.) (4) The
subject to ἔμελλε is Croesus: but, after two clauses with other subjects
(Ἀπόλλων and ἆμαρ), this needs to be indicated. (5) δυσφροσύναν,
'trouble of mind,' seems too weak a word here; the epithet πολυδάκρυον

prepares us for some word expressing a dire calamity, such as δουλοσύναν.

Ode III. 48 **ἀβροβάταν.**—There is perhaps only one instance in **III. 48**
which a classical Greek writer applies the term ἁβρός to the movement of
men without implying the reproach of effeminacy : viz. Eur. *Med.* 829 f.
(the Athenians) αἰεὶ διὰ λαμπροτάτου | βαίνοντες ἁβρῶς αἰθέρος, where, as
Verrall says, 'it denotes the soft motion of the body, luxuriating...in the
genial air.' The normal sense of ἁβρὸν βαίνειν is illustrated by verse
1134 of the same play, where the young bride Glauce, conscious of her
radiant beauty and splendid attire, is described as ἁβρὸν βαίνουσα
παλλευκῷ ποδί. Cp. *Helena* 1528, σοφώταθ᾽ ἁβρὸν πόδα τιθεῖσ᾽ ἀνέστενε
(where Helen is moving with the gentle tread of a mourner): and *I. A.*
614 (Iphigeneia) ἁβρὸν τιθεῖσα κῶλον. Jurenka compares Clem. Alex.
Paedag. III. 294 τὸ ἀβροδίαιτον τῆς περὶ τὸν περίπατον κινήσεως καὶ τὸ
σαῦλα βαίνειν, ὥς φησιν Ἀνακρέων, κομιδῇ ἑταιρικά. This is relevant in so
far as it illustrates the display of ἁβρότης in movement. But Clement
there has in view something much coarser than Euripides (*e.g.*) meant
by ἁβρὸν βαίνουσα : this is shown by τὸ σαῦλα βαίνειν ('a swaying gait'),
as also by ἑταιρικά, and, indeed, by τὸ ἀβροδίαιτον, which might be
rendered 'voluptuousness.' The idea which ἁβρὸν βαίνειν expresses,
and the antithesis which it implies, might be illustrated by the words of
Shakespeare's Portia, when she is about to enact the part of a man, and
says that she will 'turn two mincing steps into a manly stride' (*Merchant
of Venice* III. 4. 67 :—which might be rendered in Greek, ἁβρὸν μὲν οὐ
βαίνουσα, βῆμα δ᾽ ἄρσενος | τρόποις ἐπεκτείνουσα). Prof. J. B. Bury explains
ἀβροβάταν as 'a slippered eunuch.' But, as I understand the word, it
refers to *a delicate gait*, rather than to soft coverings for the feet (as
though ἀβροβάτης meant 'walking on ἁβρά'). It may be added that
the phrase of the oracle given to Croesus (Her. I. 55),—Λυδὲ ποδαβρέ,—
though verbally similar, is not really relevant. The oracle,—very
unjustly,—chose to assume that the Lydians were already what they
became after their subjection, an effeminate race. The 'Lydian with
delicate feet' is merely the 'effeminate' Lydian,—the epithet being
ironically adapted to the counsel given,—viz., φεύγειν. It was only after
his fall that Croesus advised Cyrus to enervate the Lydians by requiring
them κιθῶνάς τε ὑποδύνειν τοῖς εἵμασι καὶ κοθόρνους ὑποδέεσθαι (Her.
I. 155).

Some critics write Ἀβροβάταν, and take it as a proper name, like
Ἀβροκόμας in Her. VII. 224. This is surely improbable.

460 APPENDIX.

III. 59 Ode III. 59 ἐς 'Υπερβορέους.—Otto Crusius, in Roscher's *Lexikon der gr. und röm. Mythologie* (pp. 2805—2835), exhaustively discusses the Hyperborean legends. He adopts and enforces the view of H. L. Ahrens as to the original meaning of the name. That view may be summed up as follows. (1) In the Apollo-cult of Delos, it was said that the Hyperboreans had sent two maidens with offerings of first-fruits to Delos. (2) These maidens were escorted by five men, πομποί, whom the Hyperboreans sent with them. The Delians called these men Περφερέες: high honours were paid to them. (See Her. IV. 32—35.) (3) 'Υπερβέρετος was the name of a month (=July) in the Cretan Calendar: and 'Υπερβερεταῖος (= September) in the Macedonian Calendar. In these months there were harvest-festivals of Apollo. (4) In some North-Greek dialects, as in those of Macedonia and of Delphi, φ became β. Thus ὑπερβέρετος leads back to ὑπερφερέτης; and ὑπερβερεταῖος to ὑπερφερεταῖος. So ὑπέρφορος would in those dialects become ὑπέρβορος. Thus would come in a popular (or hieratic) derivation from βορέας. (5) The *bringers of offerings over* (*land and sea*) would originally have been a designation applicable to pious votaries of Apollo anywhere who sent offerings to his shrine. These votaries were transformed by the etymologizing legend into a people *dwelling beyond the north wind,*—a separate and blessed folk, devoted to the god's worship. (6) This explains how it happens that *e.g.* the Argive Perseus-saga places the 'Hyperboreans,' not in the far *North*, but in the far *West*, near the dwelling of the Gorgons. (See Crusius in Roscher, p. 2816, § 22.)

Bacchylides, who was in touch with Delos (cp. Ode XVI) and its Apollo-cult, treats the land of the 'Υπερβόρεοι as a paradise to which Apollo can transport pious mortals; a place like the 'Ηλύσιον πεδίον or the μακάρων νῆσοι in the far West. Doubtless he, like Pindar, thought of the 'Hyperboreans' simply as 'dwellers beyond the North Wind.' But unconsciously he has introduced a touch which is in perfect harmony with the derivation from ὑπερφέρω, and with the view that the name originally denoted pious votaries of Apollo in whatever region they might dwell. It is very possible that here he may have been influenced by Delian traditions which he knew. The Hyperborean legend was a temple-myth, developed at the sanctuaries of Apollo, and doubtless first of all at Delphi, whence it passed to Delos, and to other Aegean seats of the cult.

Ode III.   72   . . . . . μαλέαι ποτ . . . .'ων

73   . . . . νοϛεφᾱμεροναِ[

74   . . . . . ασκοπεισβραχ[

What was probably the general sense of the three mutilated verses, 72—74? This question must be viewed in the light of the whole context.

Verses 67—71 are an epitome of Hieron's glories, as victor in the games, warrior, just ruler, and votary of the Muses. In verses 73—74 there was clearly some reference to the shortness of life: and that strain was continued in verses 75—84. The general purport of the whole passage, from v. 74 to 84, was to this effect:—' Life is short and uncertain; a man must be prepared either to die to-morrow, or to live for many years: do your duty day by day, and be cheerful' (83). What we do not know is the nature of the transition by which, in verses 72—74, the poet passed from the theme of *Hieron's glories* to reflections on the *brevity and insecurity of human life*.

This ode was written after the Olympic festival of 468 B.C.; and Hieron died, in 467, of the disease from which he had long suffered. Pindar's third *Pythian* (written in or about 474 B.C.) shows that even then Hieron was a sufferer. The whole strain of Pindar's ode is, indeed, strikingly similar to that of Bacchylides here: it dwells on the shortness of life; and consoles the invalid with the thought that the Muse can give lasting fame. Compare especially verses 90 f. here, ἀρετᾶς γε μὲν οὐ μινύθει | βροτῶν ἅμα σώματι φέγγος, with Pind. *P.* III. 114 f., ἁ δ' ἀρετὰ κλειναῖς ἀοιδαῖς | χρονία τελέθει. When Bacchylides wrote his verses, it was perhaps known to him that Hieron had not long to live.

Two lines of restoration are possible, according to the view taken of ΜΑΛΕΑΙ in v. 72.

I. If δειμαλέᾳ (or ῥωμαλέᾳ) be assumed, the subst. agreeing with it must certainly have stood in the same verse; and nothing seems possible except χειρί. This suggests that the passage contained a contrast between Hieron's former activity in war (cp. v. 34) and his present state. The word σκοπεῖς in 74 is clearly addressed to him: it could mean either '*lookest for*' solace from the Muses, or '*contemplatest*' the approach of the end. Compare IX. 13, where τεὰν ἀρετάν, addressed to the victor, rather abruptly follows the mention of him in v. 9. Similarly in xv. 6 Apollo is the subject of ἀγάλλεται, and then is suddenly apostrophised in v. 10.

Prof. Blass restores thus :—

> 72 ὃς δειμαλέᾳ ποτὲ χειρὶ θύνων
> 73 γαλανὸς ἐφάμερον ἀδονὰν φι-
> 74 λάνορα σκοπεῖς. βραχύς ἐστιν αἰών,

i.e. 'who of yore didst rage with terrible hand, (but now) in tranquillity, lookest for some kindly enjoyment, sufficient unto the day' (*i.e.* for the pleasure afforded by the kindly Muses).—The following remarks suggest themselves. (1) **ἐφάμερον** is here used as by Pindar in *I.* VI. 39 ff., ὁ δ᾽ ἀθανάτων μὴ θρασσέτω φθόνος | ὅ τι τερπνὸν ἐφάμερον διώκων | ἕκαλος ἔπειμι γῆρας. That sense of ἐφάμερον is suitable to Pindar's prayer for himself. It is also suitable to Hieron's probable condition in 468 B.C. : but it may be doubted whether Bacchylides would have so openly referred to that condition. His allusions to Hieron's illness are elsewhere veiled. **βραχ-** in v. 74, and **ἐφαμερίων** in 76, might incline us to surmise that ἐφάμερον in 73 meant 'short-lived,' rather than 'sufficing for the day.' (2) I greatly doubt whether there is room for the letters ΓΑΛΑΝ before OC in 73. A careful measurement of the letters ΓΕΛΑΝ (of γελανώσας) in Ode v. 80 will show that they exceed the space available before OC here ; *a fortiori*, then, ΓΑΛΑΝ is too large, for A in this MS. is much broader than E. (3) **ἀδονὰν φιλάνορα** would more naturally mean 'the pleasure of being hospitable.' (cp. I. 40 ξείνων τε φιλάνορι τιμᾷ) than 'the kindly pleasure' given by the Muses.

The following modifications of Prof. Blass's reading have occurred to me as possible :—

> (1) ὃς δειμαλέᾳ ποτὲ χειρὶ θύνων
> γεραιὸς ἐφάμερον αὖτε τέρψιν
> ἄσυχα σκοπεῖς. βραχὺς ἄμμιν αἰών·

With regard to γεραιός, it may be remarked that the word connotes the *reverence* due to years ; and also that in verses 88—91 the poet clearly refers to Hieron's physical decay. This conjecture implies, like that of Blass, that ἐφάμερον = 'sufficing for the day.'

(2) If, on the other hand, ἐφάμερον meant 'short-lived,' we might conjecture :—

> γεραιὸς ἐφάμερον ἀνδρὸς αἶσαν
> ἄσυχα σκοπεῖς.

(For the sing. ἀνδρός cp. 88.)

II. Let us now turn to the other line of restoration,—that which presupposes **Μαλέᾳ**. If that was the word, the reference was to the dangers of that stormy cape for sea-farers, owing to the conflict of currents and winds. Cp. Strabo (8. 378): the sea off Malea is dreaded by sailors, διὰ τὰς ἀντιπνοίας· ἀφ' οὗ καὶ παροιμιάζονται,

Μαλέας δὲ κάμψας ἐπιλάθου τῶν οἴκαδε.

That proverb was doubtless made by Greeks living in the islands or on the coasts of the Aegean. If you have once got safely round Malea, be thankful, and do not tempt the gods by returning that way. (Cp. Curt. *Pelop.* ii. p. 298 and p. 330.)

Od. 9. 80 (Odysseus speaks) :—ἀλλά με κῦμα ῥόος τε περιγνάμπτοντα Μάλειαν | καὶ Βορέης ἀπέωσε, παρέπλαγξέν τε Κυθήρων. Her. iv. 179 (Jason and the Argonauts) : καί μιν ὡς πλώοντα γενέσθαι κατὰ Μαλέην, ὑπολαβεῖν ἄνεμον Βορέην καὶ ἀποφέρειν πρὸς τὴν Λιβύην. Statius *Theb.* 2. 33 : *Qua formidatum Maleae spumantis in auras It caput.* Virgil (*Aen.* v. 191) and Ovid (*Am.* ii. 16. 24) also allude to Malea's terrors. The name of Malea was thus proverbial, and might easily have furnished a poet with a simile. A simile from the perils of the sea is used by Bacchylides in Ode xii (124—132).

There is something to be said, then, in favour of such a restoration as that which is given, *exempli gratia*, in my text. 'But, as erenow at Malea, the god suddenly brings stress of storm on the children of a day. Thou lookest to the needs of the time : our life is short.' The reference to Malea would be a veiled, not an open, allusion to Hieron's state. It would be a general sentiment concerning unforeseen vicissitudes in human fortunes. The special application of it would be left to the hearer. This would be quite in the manner of Bacchylides (as of Pindar), when he glances at the element of adversity in Hieron's otherwise brilliant lot (see *e.g.* Ode v. 50—55).

In v. 74 a possible variant for καίρια σκοπεῖς· βραχὺς ἄμμιν αἰών· would be :—ἄσυχα σκοπεῖς βραχὺ μέτρον αἴσας. No point after σκοπεῖς now appears in the ms. : it may, however, have been obliterated in the correction made after that word (see cr. n., p. 263); or it may have been omitted by error.

It is not easy to choose between the two lines of restoration,—that which assumes δειμαλέᾳ and that which assumes Μαλέᾳ. If any one contends that the former is the more probable, I shall not gainsay him. My object has been to state the data of the problem as clearly as I could, and to indicate such tentative solutions as I have been able to find.

Ode IV. 7—13. In his third edition Blass prints this passage as
follows:—

ᵕᵕᵕ−ᵕᵕ−ᵕ
ᵕ−−ᵕ−ᵕᵕ], ᾶς ἀλέκτωρ
ᵕᵕᵕ− ἑκόν]τι νόωι
10 −ᵕ−ᵕᵕ−ᵕ] ὕμνους,
ᵕᵕᵕ ἐκ|λυεν, οἷς] ἰσόρ-
ροπον ἔχοντα Δίκ]ας τάλαν[τον
Δεινομένεος ἐγερα[ίρο]μεν υἱόν.

IV. 7—13 The supplements in verses 9, 11, 12, to the left of the bracket], are
his own; except that, in 11 f., where in his 2nd ed. he read δὶς ὀρ|θὸν
ἀνέχοντα, he now receives Headlam's ἰσόρ|ροπον ἔχοντα. The letters
ICOP . . and ΑΣΤΑΛΛΑΝ in v. 11 and in v. 12 are found on a small
fragment (no. 19 Kenyon) which Blass refers to this place. He
thinks that the same fragment shows the lower part of the first Υ in
ὕμνους (v. 10). This collocation of the fragment is possible, but it
cannot be regarded as certain. Then in verse 8 Prof. Blass finds traces
of an apostrophe in the MS. before ΑC (I fail to do so), and reads ᾶς.
He thinks that the sense of the whole passage was to the following effect.
Verse 6 contained some reference to Arethusa;—ᾶς ἀλέκτωρ, "whose
husband (the Alpheus) with willing soul (ἑκόντι νόῳ) was wont to hear
the songs with which we honoured the son of Deinomenes, who holds
the balance of Justice in even poise."

Now, I agree with Prof. Blass in thinking that the earlier part of
this passage referred to Hieron's two victories at Olympia. It seems
improbable, however, that the ἀλέκτωρ was the Alpheus. I should
rather surmise that he was the ἐρίγδουπος πόσις Ἥρας. Such a designation would be the more appropriate, since at Olympia the temple of
Hera was next in importance to the temple of Zeus.

In verse 13 Prof. Blass now deletes the κ' which the MS. exhibits
after Δεινομένεος. In his first edition he retained it, explaining it as
iterative (p. 41 'κ' repetitionis est'); i.e., he took κ' ἐγεραίρομεν as
meaning, 'we used to honour.' But in his second edition (p. 44) he
writes: 'Non est iustum κ: sed si omnino est, putandum ex alia littera
(ε?) corrigendo factum.' By the words, 'non est iustum κ,' Prof. Blass
means that it differs from the regular form of κ in this papyrus. That is
true. The κ is somewhat narrower, more compressed, than usual; as if
at this point the scribe was doubting whether he would have space
enough in the column for the words ἐγεραίρομεν υἱόν which he had still
to write. There are, however, many similar instances in the MS. of a

slight difference between the forms of the same letter in different places. And on the other hand the κ' here is perfectly distinct. I cannot perceive any ground for the suggestion that it has been made by correction out of some other letter. To delete it seems a wholly unwarrantable proceeding. It remains to speak of verse 14. In his first edition (1898) Prof. Blass wrote Γαίας μυχοῖς, meaning Delphi, the seat of τὴν πρωτόμαντιν Γαῖαν (Aesch. *Eum.* 2). In his second edition he gives Κίρρας μυχοῖς. My own conjecture, Κρίσας μυχοῖς, was made independently (in 1898), and before the appearance of his second edition. Cirrha was the ancient port of Crisa : if ἀγχιάλοισι better suits Cirrha, μυχοῖς is more suggestive of Crisa : cp. Pind. *P.* VI. 18 Κρισαίαις ἐνὶ πτυχαῖς. Wilamowitz proposed Κούρας μυχοῖς,—*i.e.* Syracuse, as the city of Persephone. But here we clearly need a mention of Delphi, to balance that of Olympia (ὀλυμπιονίκας) in v. 17. An indication of the Pythian victories merely by the word τάδε would be too obscure.

Ode V. 2 στραταγέ.—See Freeman, *Sicily*, vol. II. Appendix III. V. 2 pp. 499—502, on 'Gelôn as General and King': also pp. 135—137: and as to the title of βασιλεύς given to Hieron by Pindar, pp. 540—542. In *Class. Rev.* XIII. p. 98 (March, 1899) Prof. J. B. Bury holds that στραταγέ is 'a definite reference to the formal title στραταγὸς αὐτοκράτωρ.'

It is well to keep the following points clearly in view.

1. Gelon reigned at Gela from 491 to 485 B.C. In 485 the Gamoroi (oligarchic land-owners), who had been driven out of Syracuse by the democrats, and had established themselves at Casmenae, asked help from Gelon, who undertook to restore them. 'When he drew near to the city, the new democracy at once submitted, and Gelôn became lord of Syracuse' (Freeman, *Sic.* II. 127). He reigned at Syracuse from 485 to his death in 478.

2. That Gelon *at some time* held the office of στρατηγὸς αὐτοκράτωρ is a belief which rests on the following authorities. (i) Diodorus XIII. 94 says that, in 405 B.C., the elder Dionysius was made στρατηγὸς αὐτοκράτωρ against the Carthaginians. One motive for this measure was that in 480 the Carthaginians had been defeated at Himera, στρατηγοῦντος Γέλωνος αὐτοκράτορος. (ii) Polyaenus I. 27 § 1 says that, for the war against the Carthaginians in 480, Gelon was elected 'general with full powers' (στρατηγὸς αὐτοκράτωρ χειροτονηθείς). He 'rendered his account' of that office to the people (εὐθύνας δοὺς τῆς αὐτοκράτορος

ἀρχῆς), and, having thus laid it down, appeared unarmed before the armed people in the agora. They re-elected him general; and 'so' he became τύραννος. (οὕτω δὴ παρακληθεὶς δεύτερον στρατηγῆσαι τύραννος ἐγένετο Συρακουσίων.) This, as Freeman observes, is 'evidently the same scene as that which Diodorus (XI. 26) describes on Gelon's return from Himera, which ends with the people saluting Gelôn as *king.*' Polyaenus has misconceived the circumstances, but must have had some definite authority for the title στρατηγὸς αὐτοκράτωρ. (iii) The Schol. on Pind. *O.* II. 29 cites Timaeus of Tauromenium (d. *circ.* 256 B.C.?), who wrote a history of Sicily (Σικελικά) down to 264 B.C.: τοῦ δὲ Γέλωνος τελευτᾶν τὸν βίον μέλλοντος, Πολύζηλος ἀδελφὸς τὴν στρατηγίαν καὶ τὴν γαμετὴν τοῦ ἀδελφοῦ διαδέχεται. (Frag. 90, Müller, *Frag. Hist.* L. p. 214.)

3. It is probable, though it cannot be proved, that Gelon was made στραταγὸς αὐτοκράτωρ, not for the first time in 480, with a view to a war against the Carthaginians, but in 485, when he became master of Syracuse. It may have been the official title under which his virtual kingship was veiled. (See Freeman, *Sic.* II. p. 137.)

4. After his great victory at Himera in 480, Gelon was saluted by the Syracusans as 'benefactor, saviour, and king' (βασιλέα: Diod. XI. 26). Freeman doubts whether Gelon was ever 'clothed with any formal kingship' (*Sic.* II. p. 203). Diodorus, however, in XI. 38 styles him ὁ βασιλεὺς Γέλων. In Her. VII. 61 the Athenian envoy addresses him as ὦ βασιλεῦ Συρηκοσίων. (Freeman regards this address as 'more or less sarcastic'; which seems to me improbable: though it may readily be granted that no stress can safely be laid on the use of the word βασιλεῦ there.)

5. In regard to Hieron, there is no direct evidence that he was ever styled στραταγὸς αὐτοκράτωρ. The interpretation of στραταγέ in that sense here rests entirely on the hypothesis that the title was transmitted from Gelon to Hieron; as Timaeus states that it passed from Gelon to Polyzelus. Prof. Bury ingeniously observes that Pindar in *P.* II. 58 'addresses Hieron as πρύτανι κύριε...στρατοῦ, an accurate paraphrase of στραταγὲ αὐτοκράτωρ.' It is well, however, to consider the whole of Pindar's phrase:—πρύτανι κύριε πολλᾶν μὲν εὐστεφάνων ἀγυιᾶν καὶ στρατοῦ, 'sovereign prince of many streets encircled with goodly walls, and of a great host.' στρατοῦ is used as in verse 87 of the same ode,—ὁ λάβρος στρατός, = δᾶμος: cp. Aesch. *Eum.* 566. Hieron, in this passage of Pindar, is not specially the '*general with full powers,*' but the lord of a strong and fair city, of Syracuse and its people.

6. On the whole, I should be disposed to think that στραταγέ is

merely a general designation, 'war-lord,' and does not refer to a special office. But I do not regard the latter view as inadmissible. My object has been to define the amount and the limits of the evidence for that view.

7. I would only add that the fact of Pindar styling Hieron βασιλεύς, in Odes designed for performance at Syracuse (*O.* I. 23, *P.* III. 70), proves much more than the poet's belief that the title was one which Hieron would like. It shows that Hieron felt no danger in being publicly so styled. That being so, the motive for *veiling* royal power under the title of στραταγὸς αὐτοκράτωρ cannot, in Hieron's case, have been very strong, whatever it may have been in Gelon's earlier years of rule at Syracuse. Whether Hieron ever formally became βασιλεύς, we cannot say. But, if he was styled στραταγὸς αὐτοκράτωρ, it would not follow that he was not also styled βασιλεύς. The former title came down from Gelon : if the latter was also taken by Gelon, or by Hieron, the military title might well remain associated with it.

Ode V. 11 f.   νάσου ξένος ὑμετέραν πέμπει κλεεννὰν ἐς πόλιν

= 26 f.   δυσπαίπαλα κύματα νωμᾶται δ' ἐν ἀτρύτῳ χάει.

Verses 11 and 26 are longer by a syllable than the corresponding verses in the other strophes. It is easy to correct verse 26 by reading νωμᾷ instead of νωμᾶται. (The first hand had originally written ΝΩΜΑΙ, though the I has been deleted.) And νωμᾷ would be intrinsically preferable to νωμᾶται. But verse 11 resists emendation. The following conjectures may be mentioned. (1) R. J. Walker, πλεῖ for πέμπει. (2) A. Platt, πλέων for πέμπει (deleting, in 14, δὲ after ἐθέλει). H. Richards, πέμπει ἐς θείαν πόλιν. The easiest correction would be πέμψε κλεινὰν ἐς πόλιν, but πέμπει is clearly right. ὔμμι προπέμπει would depart too far from the MS. The conclusion must be, I think, that verse 11 is sound. If a corruption exists there, it is deeper than can now be traced. But if v. 11 is sound, verse 26 is so also. The same phenomenon recurs in verse 14, = v. 29 :

13   χρυσάμπυκος Οὐρανίας κλεινὸς θεράπων· ἐθέλει δέ

28   λεπτότριχα σὺν ζεφύρου πνοιαῖσιν ἔθειραν ἀρίγνω-

30   τος μετ' ἀνθρώποις ἰδεῖν.

V. 11 f.,
26 f.

31—2

Now in v. 30 μετ' is certainly awkward (though, as I have tried to show in the commentary, quite intelligible); Weil suggested μέγ', or (keeping μετ') οἰωνοῖς instead of ἀνθρώποις. R. J. Walker would delete μετ' (a remedy which Blass approves, p. xiii, and p. 49, 3rd ed.). This would doubtless be preferable to altering ἀρίγνωτος into ἀριγνώς (Pind. *N*. v. 12). But here, just as in the former case, it is the verse in the strophe which resists emendation. There is only one way of shortening verse 14, viz., by deleting δέ after ἐθέλει. But an asyndeton there would be intolerable. If δέ is to be removed, a participle must (as Platt saw) replace πέμπει in 11 f.; but this, again, is an improbable change.

Thus the first strophe and antistrophe present two instances (v. 11 = 26, and v. 14 = 29) in which the metre varies from that of the subsequent strophes and antistrophes. In neither case does it seem possible to find any really probable emendation. And it would be a very singular coincidence if corruption of the text had produced precisely this peculiarity in two passages of the first strophe and antistrophe, but nowhere else in the other 170 verses of the ode. Again, it is evident that the anomalies cannot be explained by supposing that, in all the pairs of strophes after the first, the final long syllable of the verses corresponding with 11 and 14 was protracted, so that *e.g.* in v. 51 μοῖράν τε καλῶν ἔπορεν the last syllable was equivalent in time to − ◡. I incline, then, to believe that in v. 11 (= 26) and 14 (= 29) the text is sound; and that for some reason or other the poet varied from this model in the corresponding verses of the later strophes. It seems possible that the slight variation was due to mere inadvertence.

Ode V. 56—175. The Meleager-myth.

V. 56—175 The mythical genealogy, so far as it appears in Bacchylides, is as follows :—

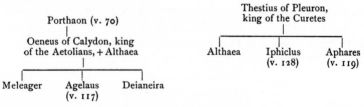

Porthaon (v. 70)
|
Oeneus of Calydon, king of the Aetolians, + Althaea
|
Meleager   Agelaus   Deianeira
             (v. 117)

Thestius of Pleuron, king of the Curetes
|
Althaea   Iphiclus   Aphares
          (v. 128)   (v. 119)

After the narrative in the Homeric Πρεσβεία (*Il.* 9. 529—599), that of Bacchylides is the oldest complete recital of the story which we possess. Certain points are deserving of notice.

The Homeric version is in outline as follows. Oeneus, king of Calydon, had angered Artemis by withholding the harvest first-fruits (θαλύσια) due to her; and she sent the wild boar to ravage his land. His Aetolian subjects were aided by their neighbours, the Curetes, in the boar-hunt. Meleager slew the boar. Then the Aetolians fell to fighting with the Curetes for the boar's head and hide. In the fight, Meleager slew some of Althaea's brethren, his uncles. Thereupon his mother cursed him (567 πόλλ' ἀχέουσ' ἠρᾶτο κασιγνήτοιο φόνοιο), calling on Hades and Persephone to avenge her brothers. Meleager, in wrath at her curse, withdrew to his house. Meanwhile the Curetes were at the gates of Calydon, pressing the town hard. The Aetolian elders sent priests to Meleager, beseeching him to come forth and help them; his father Oeneus, his sisters, even Althaea herself, implored his aid; but in vain. The Curetes were already climbing the walls and firing the city, when Cleopatra, Meleager's wife, prevailed with him. He donned his armour, and repelled the foe. But, so tardy had he been, he won no thanks. That is the point which Phoenix, in telling the story, wishes to urge :—If Achilles delays too long, then, even if at last he saves the Greeks, the service will have no grace. The Homeric poet was not concerned to tell *how* Meleager eventually died. He merely says that Althaea's curse was heard by 'the Erinys who walks in darkness' (571). And there is no allusion to the story of Althaea's brand.

But we know from Pausanias (10. 31 § 3) that, in two other epics, the Μινυάς and the Ἠοῖαι, Meleager was *slain by Apollo.* The Homeric poet was probably conscious of that version. Ernst Kuhnert, in his excellent article 'Meleagros' in Roscher's *Lexikon,* supposes, indeed, that the Homeric poet conceived Meleager as slain by the arrow of Apollo just when he had repelled the Curetes (597),—so that 'he bought the victory of the Aetolians by his death' (p. 2592). That, however, would destroy the force of τῷ δ' οὐκέτι δῶρα τέλεσσαν (598). The point is that he had to yield at last, and then missed the reward which a timely compliance would have won. But if he died before the reward could in any case have been given, the moral which Phoenix wishes to draw is lost. The poet of the Πρεσβεία must have imagined his death as occurring later.

The version of Meleager's death which made him fall by the shaft of Apollo was evidently well-suited to any epic poem which aimed at exalting the Aetolian hero. That was a glorious end for him. To perish with the wasting of Althaea's brand was a tragic, but not a glorious, death. Such a doom was fitted, by its pathos, for lyric treatment; while, as illustrating the power of destiny, it was a suitable motive for drama. And it is in Attic drama that the earliest extant notice of Althaea's brand is found. The verses of Phrynichus have been quoted in the commentary (on φιτρόν in v. 142): they occurred in his Πλευρώνιαι. Pausanias (10. 31 § 4) prefaces his citation of the verses with these words :—τοῦτον τὸν λόγον (the story of the brand) Φρύνιχος ὁ Πολυφράδμονος πρῶτος ἐν δράματι ἔδειξε Πλευρωνίαις. And he adds this comment :—οὐ μὴν φαίνεταί γε ὁ Φρύνιχος προαγαγὼν τὸν λόγον ἐς πλέον, ὡς εὕρημα ἄν τις οἰκεῖον, προσαψάμενος δὲ αὐτοῦ μόνον, ἅτε ἐς ἅπαν ἤδη διαβεβοημένου τὸ Ἑλληνικόν. 'It does not appear, however, that Phrynichus developed the story at greater length, as a man would naturally do if the invention was his own ; *he has merely touched upon it,* as if it were already notorious throughout Hellas.' So, according to Pausanias, the reference to Althaea's brand in the lyric passage of the *Pleuroniae* was merely a passing allusion,—just like that of Aeschylus to the same story in the lyrics of the *Choephori* (604 ff.). Kekulé, indeed (*Fabula Meleagrea*, p. 13, 1862), holds that the word ἔδειξε, used by Pausanias in reference to Phrynichus, implies that the story of the brand was a principal incident of the play. But I do not see how that view can be reconciled with the comment just quoted.

What was the subject of the *Pleuroniae*? It has been conjectured that the play dealt with the Calydonian boar-hunt ; that the scene was laid at Calydon ; and that the chorus was composed of handmaids whom Althaea had brought from her paternal home at Pleuron. Carl Robert[1], however, has lately re-affirmed the view of Welcker[2], that the scene of the play was laid at Pleuron, and that its theme was the siege of that town by the Aetolians.

Bacchylides relates how the Aetolians, among whom Meleager was foremost, drove the Curetes in flight to Pleuron. It was under the walls of Pleuron that Meleager expired (IV. 149—154). The rout of the Curetes was followed by the siege of their city. In the *Pleuroniae* of Phrynichus, Carl Robert suggests, the persons may have been Thestius, one or two of his sons, and two messengers, who narrated the boar-hunt, the fight for the trophies, the slaying of the Thestiadae by Meleager, and Althaea's vengeance on her son. At any rate, Robert thinks it certain that the outline of the story, so far as Bacchylides gives it, follows substantially the same version which was used by Phrynichus in the *Pleuroniae*. That

---

[1] *Hermes*, vol. XXXIII. (1898), pp. 151 ff.
[2] *Die griech. Tragödien*, I. 21 ff.

seems probable enough: though, in the absence of more data, it seems difficult to speak with any confidence on the subject. One remark, however, at once suggests itself. Pausanias says that the lyric reference in the *Pleuroniae* to Althaea's brand was merely a passing allusion. And he may be right, even though, in his day, that play was known only through fragments or notices. But, if he is right, then the death of Meleager through the burning of the brand cannot have been narrated in a messenger's speech. In any case, it is clear that the story of Althaea's brand is older than Phrynichus,—*i.e.* goes back to at least the sixth century B.C. The common source of Phrynichus and Bacchylides may have been some epic poem of which no trace remains.

With regard to the significance of the brand, Kuhnert has collected (*Rhein. Mus.* 49. pp. 40 ff.) a number of illustrations and analogies. The essential idea,—that of a link between the *light of life* within the man, and some external light on whose existence the other depends,—is frequent in mythology. A writer on modern Greece notices a belief existing among the peasants of Zacynthus, that in the other world there are countless little lights or tapers, each of which controls a human life; when the taper goes out, the life is quenched (B. Schmidt, *Volksleben d. Neugr.* p. 246). The legend that Meleager perished by the wasting of the brand may, indeed, be regarded as the element which connects the Meleager-myth with Aetolian folk-lore.

One thing must be added. The *Iliad* knows Althaea's curse only, not her brand. The curse is, in fact, a delegation of vengeance to the divine powers invoked. The burning of the brand is a mode of vengeance which the mortal could wreak without aid. But the curse and the brand cannot properly be regarded as alternatives, characteristic respectively of two versions in which the story was current. For the burning of the brand might naturally be conceived as preceded or accompanied by some form of imprecation. The chanting of a spell is a normal adjunct of evil magic. Bacchylides says,

> καῖέ τε δαιδαλέας
> ἐκ λάρνακος ὠκύμορον
> φιτρὸν ἀγκλαύσασα.

If ἀγκλαύσασα be the right reading (see n. on v. 140 ff.), this consideration may help to explain it. In her passionate anguish for the deaths of her brothers, she invoked a curse on her son. So the Antigone of Sophocles (vv. 427 ff.), when she saw the corpse of her brother denuded of the dust which she had sprinkled on it, γόοισιν ἐξώμωξεν, ἐκ δ' ἀρὰς κακὰς ἠρᾶτο κ.τ.λ.

Bacchylides, like the Homeric poet, is silent concerning Atalanta. It is certain that Atalanta had a place in old forms of the Meleager-myth. Her absence from the *Iliad* (which merely refers generally to hunters 'from many cities,' 9. 544) is certainly not significant in a contrary sense. She appears on some black-figured vases in the Calydonian hunt: where, however, she is not especially associated with Meleager, but with another hero, Melanion. Euripides, in his *Meleager*, was the first who made Meleager the lover of Atalanta. That love was the leading motive of the play. He gave her the trophies of the boar. His uncles, the Thestiadae, took them away from her; and he then slew them. The siege of Pleuron did not come in. (Cp. Ovid, *Met.* VIII. 428—461.)

The scholiast on *Iliad* 21. 194 quotes Pindar for a ἱστορία to the following effect. Heracles, when he visited Hades to bring up Cerberus, was besought by the shade of Meleager to wed Deianeira. Heracles afterwards obtained the consent of her father Oeneus, and delivered his bride from the pursuit of Achelous. In the version given by Bacchylides, Heracles first expresses the wish to marry a sister of Meleager: it is only then that the latter mentions Deianeira. At first sight a modern reader might be disposed to think that, in telling the story thus, Bacchylides has the advantage of Pindar. Surely it is fitting that Heracles should make the proposal, rather than that it should proceed from Meleager? But further consideration will show that the version followed by Pindar is in a truer and finer harmony with the spirit of the myth. The significance of the scene in Hades depends on the antithesis of the two great heroes,—the living and the departed. There is no longer a Meleager on the earth; but a Heracles has succeeded to his renown. Deianeira is beset by a suitor whom she abhors. Meleager, in the shades, asks protection for his helpless sister from the only living champion who can worthily fill her brother's place. In this conception there is a higher poetry, a deeper pathos, than in that which Bacchylides adopts. The Heracles of his ode seeks Deianeira's hand partly through admiration for Meleager, partly through pity for him. There is, however, no ground for assuming that Bacchylides was the first to tell the story in this way. And, given this form of the story, his manner of telling it has a great charm of its own. It is also impressive that the fateful marriage should spring from an impulse originating in the mind of Heracles himself.

There are some traces of Bacchylides in the later literature of the myth. Apollodorus I. 8. 2. § 2 follows him in the description of the boar (cp. verses 107—110). As the sisters of Meleager, who bewailed

him, were changed into μελεαγρίδες (guinea-fowls), compilers of meta-
morphoses treated his story. Nicander told it in the third book of his
Ἑτεροιούμενα. That source was one of those used by Antoninus
Liberalis (c. A.D. 150) in his μεταμορφώσεων συναγωγή, c. 2; but he drew
also on Homer, Bacchylides, and Euripides (see Carl Robert, *l.c.* p.
158).

Ode V. 106 f. καλλίχορον Καλυδῶνα.

εὐρύχορος is sometimes so used in poetry as to confirm the view of **V. 106 f.**
Aristarchus that the old poets made it serve, *metro cogente*, for εὐρύχωρος:
the strongest instance is *Il.* 9. 478 δι᾽ Ἑλλάδος εὐρυχόροιο. Cp. Pind. *P.*
VIII. 55 and Eur. *Bacch.* 77 εὐρυχόρους ἀγυιάς. This was an illegitimate
use : χορός is 'an enclosed place' (akin to χόρτος, 'courtyard,' and
hortus, but unconnected with χῶρος). But is there any good reason for
supposing that καλλίχορος was ever used in the sense of καλλίχωρος?
This verse is more favourable to such a supposition than perhaps any
other extant passage; yet even here it is quite unnecessary to assume
that sense.

Ode V. 172 f. χλωραύχενα...Δαϊάνειραν.

The sense of χλωρός, as a word of colour, is that which it derives **v. 172 f.**
from χλόη, young vegetation. It means properly pale green. Then it
is applied to verdure or foliage generally (χλωρὰν ἀν᾽ ὕλην, Eur. *Hipp.* 17).
But pale green may have a yellowish tinge; and χλωρός came to be
used (in poetry at least) to mean simply 'yellow': χλωρὰν ψάμαθον in
Soph. *Ai.* 1064 is the clearest instance: χλωρὸν μέλι (*Il.* 11. 631) is
probably another, though 'fresh' is a possible sense there. As an
epithet of the human complexion, the word means 'pale,' especially
with the greenish tint of sickness or fear: χλωρὸς ὑπαὶ δείους (*Il.* 10. 376).
Evidently, then, χλωραύχην, as an epithet of Deianeira, cannot mean
'with *fair* neck.'

Nor can χλωραύχην, as an epithet of the nightingale (Simonides,
fr. 73), refer to colour: that bird's neck is not pale green or yellow.
The phrase χλωρηῒς ἀηδών in the *Odyssey* (19. 518) has, indeed, been
understood by Buchholz (*Hom. Real.* I. 2. 123) as denoting plumage of
that tint; then, however, he is obliged to suppose that ἀηδών is not the
nightingale,—whose hue is a reddish-brown,—but a bird of some other
species,—perhaps the serin finch, akin to the canary. A more refined
and poetical interpretation of χλωρηῒς is that propounded by Mr W.
Warde Fowler, writing in the *Classical Review* (vol. IV. p. 50) on Verg.

Geo. IV. 511 f. ; viz., that it means 'green-tinted,' by the shadows of the thick foliage falling on the bird. Mr Marindin again (*Class. Rev.* vol. IV. p. 231) takes χλωρηΐς as = 'fresh, living, gushing': 'liquid' nightingale in the sense of 'liquid-voiced.' Yet I cannot help thinking that there is more probability in the simple explanation of χλωρηΐς given by the scholiast,—ἡ ἐν χλωροῖς φαινομένη (or διατρίβουσα), '*haunting the green covert.*' The bird is described just afterwards as

δενδρέων ἐν πετάλοισι καθιζομένη πυκινοῖσιν.

The interpretation of χλωραύχην must be sought through the other sense which χλωρός takes from χλόη,—that of 'fresh,' without any direct reference to colour. That sense appears in such phrases as χλωραῖς ἐέρσαις (Pind. *N.* VIII. 40), χλωρὸν...δάκρυ (Eur. *Med.* 906, 'the welling tear'): sometimes connoting vigour, as in Theocr. 14. 70, ἃς γόνυ χλωρόν, 'while the knee is nimble' (*dum . . virent genua*, Hor. *Ep.* 13. 4). When Simonides spoke of the vernal nightingale as χλωραύχην, he meant, I think, 'with *fresh* throat'; *i.e.* with a throat of fresh, youthful, elastic vigour. Thus the sense which I attach to χλωρός in the compound is less special and definite than that which Mr Marindin gives to it, when he suggests, as one rendering of χλωραύχην, 'with *supple* or *flexible* neck' (*Class. Rev.* XII. 37): but it is equally expressive of that quality which the Homeric poet describes;—θάμα τρωπῶσα χέει πολυηχέα φωνήν, 'with many a trill she pours her full-toned song' (*Od.* 19. 521). An alternative version, which Mr Marindin proposes, is, 'with *liquid* throat'; but this gives to the throat an epithet which belongs rather to the voice. The idea of χλωραύχην, as I conceive it, is contained in the phrase of Keats, when he speaks of the nightingale as singing 'in full-throated ease.' It is in favour of this explanation that, if it be right, the primary sense of χλωραύχην, as applied to the nightingale by Simonides, is the same which it bears when applied to Deianeira by Bacchylides. In both cases it means 'with fresh young throat (or neck)'; the reference in the case of the bird, being to the fresh life with which the throat pours forth song; and, in the case of the maiden, to the fresh bloom of youth on the neck.

VI. 3 f.   Ode VI. 3 f.—Blass supplies the syllables ◡ – –, lost after ΠΡΟΧΟΑΙC, by reading προχοαῖσ[ι νικῶν], with a full stop. He then takes δι' ὅσσα in v. 4 as exclamatory: 'For how many victories' has the praise of Ceos been sung! That seems too jerky for our poet's style; his sentences are wont to flow on smoothly. I cannot doubt that ὅσσα is here the relative. Dr Kenyon writes προχοαῖσ[ι σεμναῖς], and takes ὅσσα as referring to Lachon's feats: *i.e.*, 'L. has won glory, on account of all which deeds (of his) young men lately sang his praises at Olympia.' But πάροιθεν, followed by ποτέ, could scarcely denote so recent a moment. ὅσσα must (I think) refer to the whole series of victories gained by Ceans.

Ode VII. 14. Verse 14 (which was the eleventh verse of the lost **VII. 14** 13th column) ended with the letters ομῳ. After that verse, from 21 to 24 verses were needed to complete column 13. Two fragments, *a* (= Kenyon's frag. 7, pp. 199 f. of his ed.), and *b* (= Kenyon's frag. 12, p. 202), are placed by Blass after v. 14. The appearance of the papyrus makes it probable that these two fragments belonged to column 13. They supply minute fragments of 14 verses. (See above, p. 298.) Blass edits them, with a few small supplements, thus (3rd ed., p. 69):—

(*a*)   φιλάγλ]αε(?) Χαιρόλαν[
　　　　 — μ]ενον εὐσεβ[
　　　　]τωι θαν[άτω]ι? δ[
　　　　]ι πατρίδος·[
(5)　　　]νεοκρίτου[
　　　　]ἄτεκνον[
　　　　 *　 *　 *　 *

(*b*)   ]ιου αγων[
　　　　]ταν λιπα[ραν
　　　　]ναισεπα[
　　　　 πα]ῖδας Ἑλλά[νων?
(5)　　　 πο]λυάμπελ[ο.
　　　　]ατον ὕμν[ον
　　　　 Ζ]ηνὸς? ἐν κ[
　　　　]περ ἄνιπ[πος?
　　　　 *　 *　 *　 *

The Χαιρόλας of the first verse was (Blass conjectures) some kinsman of Lachon, after whose death (v. 2) Lachon has brought fresh honour to the family. At any rate πολυάμπελο- (*b* 5) was the epithet of Ceos: cp. VI. 5.

Ode VIII. 99—102.—Given αἰνέοι in v. 102, two views of the context **VIII. 99—** are possible. (1) A point may be placed after -ευντας in v. 99, so that **102** a new clause shall begin with χρυσεοσκάπτρου. That seems the more probable construction. (2) Or a point may be placed after Διός in v. 100, when the word ending in ευντας must be construed with Διός.

Thus Blass writes, ἅτ᾽ εὖντας | χρυσεοσκάπτρου Διός. | ᾧ τι καλὸν φέ]ρεται, | τοῦτ᾽] αἰνέοι.

Seeing that ἁμαρτέοιτε follows (103 f.), the most natural reading in v. 102 would be νῦν ὦ νέοι. (Cp. XII. 190 νίκαν...μέλπετ᾽, ὦ νέοι: and Pind. *I.* VII. 2 ὦ νέοι, addressed to the youths of the comus.) But the traces in the MS. seem to prove that the letters NEOI were preceded either by AI or by N. It is possible, indeed, that the poet wrote νῦν ὦ νέοι, and that ὦ afterwards dropped out, leaving NYNNEOI. If that could be assumed, it would follow that there was a stop after φέρεται. Verses 99—101 might then have run somewhat as follows : φιλεῦντας | χρυσεοσκάπτρου Διὸς | εἴ τι καλὸν φέρεται ('welcoming, cherishing, any good gift that is borne to them from Zeus').

Ode IX. 9—14.

9 α..α᾽ι καὶ νῦν κασιγνήτας ἀκοίτας
10 νασιῶτιν ἐκίνησεν λιγύφθογγον μέλισσαν
11 ..ειρες ἵν᾽ ἀθάνατον Μουσᾶν ἄγαλμα
12 ξυνὸν ἀνθρώποισιν εἴη
13 χάρμα, τεὰν ἀρετὰν
14 μανῦον ἐπιχθονίοισιν etc.

IX. 9—14   From τεὰν in v. 13 it is certain that a mention of the victor's name had preceded. That mention must have occurred either in v. 9 or in v. 10.

(1) If it occurred in v. 9, ʼΑγλαῷ (Blass) seems to be the only name which agrees with all the traces in the MS. ʼΑγλαός occurs as a mythological name (a son of Thyestes, schol. Eur. *Or.* 5, 812 : a son of Hermione, schol. Eur. *Andr.* 32), though not otherwise. There are, of course, several other names, beginning with A, which would scan here ; as Αἰσίῳ, ʼΑκτίῳ, ʼΑλκίᾳ, ʼΑντίᾳ, ʼΑρχίᾳ, Αὐγέᾳ, all of which occur as Athenian proper names ; but none of them satisfy the indications of a perispomenon vowel (ῶ or ᾶ) before the final ι, and of Α (or Λ, or Δ) as the letter before it. If the name stood here, I think that ʼΑγλαῷ is most probable.

Assuming ʼΑγλαῷ in 9, we must infer that the letters -ειρες in 11 belonged to an epithet of ἄγαλμα. The first letter of the verse is quite uncertain, but the slight trace would suit Α, Δ, or Λ. The second letter was (as Kenyon thinks) Χ or Λ; and so Blass (who had thought of Κ) now holds : all that remains is a trace (little more than a dot) of the top. The space between ειρες and the beginning of the verse is about the same as that which is usually filled by the letters ΑΧ (*e.g.* in ʼΑχαιῶν,

x. 126). But there would be room for three letters, if two of them were thin.

Blass's ἀχειρὶς therefore suits the data in the MS. The word occurs only in *Batrachomyomachia* 300 as an epithet of crabs (ἀχειρέες): here Blass takes it as = ἀχειροποίητον.

(2) The other possibility is that the proper name stood in v. 11, -ειρες being the end of a vocative. Εὔχειρες is Jurenka's conjecture; and I can find nothing better. Εὔχειρ and Εὔχειρος occur as names; Εὐχείρης does not: in view of ἀχειρής, however, that may be waived. A stronger objection is that the trace of the first letter in the MS. does not suit E. If the name stood in v. 11, then the word or words before καὶ νῦν in v. 9 must have marked the transition from the poem concerning Φήμα to the immediate theme.

Ode IX. 19—26.

19 ἐν Ποσειδᾶνος περικλειτοῖς ἀέθλοις
20 εὐθὺς ἔνδειξ]ας Ἕλλασιν ποδῶν ὁρμὰν ταχεῖαν
21 δεύτερον δ᾽ οὔ]ροισιν ἔπι σταδίου,
22 θερμ[ὰν ἔτι] πνέων ἄελλαν,
23 ἔστα[. βρέχω]ν δ᾽ ἂξ᾽ αὖτε θατήρων ἐλαίῳ
24 φάρε[᾽ ἐς εὔθροο]ν ἐμπίτνων ὅμιλον,
25 τετρ[αέλικτον ἐπεὶ
26 κάμψεν δρόμον. Ἰσθμιονίκαν etc.

With regard to this passage, the following points seem fairly certain. **IX. 19—26** (1) A sentence begins with v. 19. (2) A sentence ends with δρόμον in 26. Verses 25 and 26 complete the description of the athlete's running; they stand in close connexion with vv. 23 and 24. (3) In 21 οὔροισιν.. σταδίου denotes the end of the course from which the runners started. (4) In v. 24 ὅμιλον is *the crowd of spectators*, and not (as Blass takes it) *the throng of competitors.* ἐμπίτνων expresses how the victor rushed into the crowd of spectators who pressed around the goal, as he completed the fourth round of the course. (5) In v. 22 the supplement θερμ[ὰν ἔτι] is scarcely doubtful. That being so, the word ἔτι, and a comparison with the epigram quoted in the commentary, render it certain that this athlete ran with success in two *consecutive* foot-races. In v. 20 the -ας before Ἕλλασιν indicates the second person singular of an aorist. Blass well supplies εὐθὺς ἔνδειξ]ας. By εὐθύς I understand ' *at the outset,*'—*i.e.* in the *first* foot-race in which the athlete was engaged. Accordingly in verse 21, before οὔ]ροισιν, I supply δεύτερον δ᾽, which exactly fits the gap in the papyrus.

478   *APPENDIX.*

The most difficult question is that raised by verse 23. The first
hand wrote ΕΓΤΑ.....ΝΔ'ΑΪΞΕ ΘΑΤΗΡΩΝ ΕΛΑΙΩΙ. Of the Α in ΕΓΤΑ
only a small trace remains. The space between that Α and Ν would
admit not more than about five letters. The second corrector (A³)
changed ΑΪΞΕ to ΑΥΤΕ. We may be fairly sure that αὖτε was not a
mere guess by A³. The first hand made several gross errors in this
ode, as Εὔβοι.ων for εὐβούλων in 27 f., ἐπίσταται for ἐπιστᾶμαι in 38,
βρισενομεν for βρίσει.τὸ μὲν in 47 : the true reading is in each case due
to A³. (In 51, indeed, A³ seems to have tampered with a sound reading;
but what he meant there is doubtful.) (1) Now suppose that the
original reading was βρέχων δ' ᾇξ' αὖτε : our poet has elsewhere, of
ἀΐσσω, only ἄϊξον (II. 1) and ἄϊξαν (XII. 144): but Pindar *N.* VIII. 40
uses ᾆσσει : and Bacchylides could certainly have written ᾇξ' (ᾇξ').
The word suits a runner *darting forward* from the starting-point : cp.
Soph. *El.* 711 (of chariots), ὑπαὶ σάλπιγγος ᾖξαν. From βρέχων δ' ᾇξ'
αὖτε may have come two readings, (*a*) βρέχων δ' ᾇξε, and (*b*) βρέχων δ'
αὖτε. The latter violates metre ; but A³ regarded metre as little as the
scribe did (p. 134). It also mars the sense, a finite verb being wanted ;
but βρέχων may have become βρέχεν. If, then, A³ found αὖτε in his
copy, we can understand his substituting it, as he did, for ᾇξε.
(2) There is another possibility. Suppose that the original reading
was διανε]ν δ' αὖτε. For movable ν before a consonant, cp. v. 10, and
XII. 128 λῆξεν δέ. The scribe, heedless as he was of sense (p. 127),
may have misread αὖτε as ᾇξε, owing to the Ptolemaic forms of Υ and
Ξ (p. 125), especially if the letters ντ had been slightly damaged. But
in this obscure matter I incline at present to the former hypothesis.

It remains to notice the transition, in the course of verses 19—26,
from the second to the third person. The second person is proved by
the ending -ας in v. 20, whether the word was ἔνδειξ]ας or another. But
in v. 23 the verb of the clause introduced by δέ cannot have been in
the 2nd pers., since the traces of the letter before Δ' suit only Ν. Hence
it appears that, in v. 20, the poet continued to apostrophise the victor, as
he had been doing in the immediately preceding verses (13 τεάν,
18 θῆκας): but, when he came to narrate the victor's exploits, glided
into the third person (23 ἔστα κ.τ.λ., 26 κάμψεν).
Prof. Blass gives vv. 19—28 as follows :—

19 ἐν Ποσειδᾶνος περικλειτοῖς ἀέθλοις
20 εὐθὺς ἔνδειξ]ας Ἕλλασιν ποδῶν ὁρμὰν ταχεῖαν,
21 ἐκφανὴς οὔ]ροισιν ἔπι σταδίου·
22 θερ[μὰν δ' ἔτι] πνέων ἄελλαν

23 ἔστα[, βρέχων] δ᾽ ἄϊξε θατήρων ἐλαίωι
24 φάρε [᾽ ἐς ἵππιο]ν ἐμπίτνων ὅμιλον.
25 τετρ[αέλικτον ἐπεὶ
26 κάμψεν δρόμον, Ἰσθμιονίκαν
27 δίς ν[ιν ἀγκ]άρυξαν εὐβού-
28 λων[◡ – –]ων προφᾶται.

The words printed in thick type are those which he supplies. As to punctuation, he has a point after σταδίου in 21, and a full stop after ὅμιλον in 24. The sense (if I understand it aright) is as follows:—

'In Poseidon's renowned games thou didst show thy rushing speed to the Greeks at the outset, *when thou camest to the front (ἐκφανείς) at the bounds of the course* (at the goal). Then, still breathing a storm of hot breath, he took his place [at the starting-line], and darted forward, sprinkling the garments of the spectators with olive-oil, as he dashed into *the throng of runners in the fourfold stadion (ἵππιον ὅμιλον).*'

ἵππιος δρόμος was the technical name for a foot-race in which the course was four times that of the stadion: Paus. 6. 16. 4: δρόμου δέ εἰσι τοῦ ἱππίου μῆκος δίαυλοι δύο. But the technical term is scarcely felicitous here: and ὅμιλον is surely the crowd of spectators.

Then it seems far better to place the full stop after δρόμον than after ὅμιλον. The mention of the athlete's two victories at the Isthmus (26 ff.) is linked with that of his two victories at Nemea (29). The word Ἰσθμιονίκαν ought therefore to begin a new sentence.

Ode IX. 39—45. ἦ γὰρ σοφὸς...θυμὸν αὔξουσιν.

The parallel passage of Solon (fr. 13. 43—54)' is as follows:—   IX. 39—45

43 σπεύδει δ᾽ ἄλλοθεν ἄλλος· ὁ μὲν κατὰ πόντον ἀλᾶται
ἐν νηυσὶν χρῄζων οἴκαδε κέρδος ἄγειν
45 ἰχθυόεντ᾽, ἀνέμοισι φορεύμενος ἀργαλέοισιν,
φειδωλὴν ψυχῆς οὐδεμίαν θέμενος·
ἄλλος γῆν τέμνων πολυδένδρεον εἰς ἐνιαυτὸν
λατρεύει, τοῖσιν καμπύλ᾽ ἄροτρα μέλει·
ἄλλος Ἀθηναίης τε καὶ Ἡφαίστου πολυτέχνεω
50 ἔργα δαεὶς χειροῖν ξυλλέγεται βίοτον·
ἄλλος Ὀλυμπιάδων Μουσέων πάρα δῶρα διδαχθείς,
ἱμερτῆς σοφίης μέτρον ἐπιστάμενος·

480 APPENDIX.

ἄλλον μάντιν ἔθηκεν ἄναξ ἑκάεργος Ἀπόλλων,
ἔγνω δ᾽ ἀνδρὶ κακὸν τηλόθεν ἐρχόμενον...

(1) Verses 43—46, on *the pursuit of wealth*, correspond with verses 42 f. of Bacchylides, ἕτερος δ᾽ ἐπὶ πᾶσι κ.τ.λ. (2) Verses 47 f., on *agriculture*, = Bacch. v. 44. (3) The *artistic handicrafts* in verses 49 f., are included under Χαρίτων τιμᾶν in Bacch. v. 39. (4) The gift of *poetry* (σοφίης) in verses 51 f. is represented by σοφός in Bacch. v. 39. (5) Verses 53 f., on *soothsaying*, answer to Bacch. v. 41 f.

Ode X. 93. κατὰ δάσκιον ἠλύκταζον ὕλαν.

X. 93 The only other passage in which the verb ἀλυκτάζω occurs is Her. IX. 70 : οἱ δὲ βάρβαροι οὐδὲν ἔτι στῖφος ἐποιήσαντο πεσόντος τοῦ τείχεος, οὐδέ τις αὐτῶν ἀλκῆς ἐμέμνητο, ἀλύκταζόν τε οἷα ἐν ὀλίγῳ χώρῳ πεφοβημένοι τε καὶ πολλαὶ μυριάδες κατειλημέναι ἀνθρώπων. The sense there is, '*they were distracted.*' ἀλύω, ἀλυκτάζω, ἀλύσσω (*Il.* 22. 70), ἀλυκτέω, ἀλυκταίνω (Hesych.), are verbs in which the root ἀλ (ἀλάομαι) takes the special sense of *mental* wandering, unrest, distress. This notion is very easily associated with that of bodily unrest; as *e.g.* in *Il.* 24. 12 δινεύεσκ᾽ ἀλύων παρὰ θῖν᾽ ἁλός. In Lucian, *Dial. Mar.* 13, περὶ τὰς ὄχθας ἀλύουσα (said of the lovesick Tyro) means 'wandering forlorn.' Here Bacchylides has used ἠλύκταζον in a way which blends the notions of mental and physical unrest: 'roamed wildly.'

Blass in his 1st and 2nd editions read ἀλύκταζον, but now, in the 3rd, he changes it to ἀλύσκαζον. The use of ἀλυσκάζω in the *Iliad* may be seen from *Il.* 5. 253 f., οὐ γάρ μοι γενναῖον ἀλυσκάζοντι μάχεσθαι | οὐδὲ καταπτώσσειν, 'Not in my blood is it to fight a *skulking* fight, or cower down' (so Leaf). Similarly in *Il.* 6. 443, αἴ κε κακὸς ὣς νόσφιν ἀλυσκάζω πολέμοιο. In the *Odyssey* the verb takes an accus., 17. 581 ὕβριν ἀλυσκάζων ἀνδρῶν ὑπερηνορεόντων, 'avoiding,' 'shunning.' If, then, we read here, κατὰ δάσκιον ἀλύσκαζον ὕλαν, the meaning will be, 'they *went stealthily*' through the forest,—seeking to shun observation. But that is much less suitable to the case of the frenzied maidens than the sense given by ἠλύκταζον.

It is not probable that ἀλυσκάζω could mean merely 'to wander'; though Apollonius Rhodius once so uses the form ἀλύσκω (4. 57): οὔτ᾽ ἄρ᾽ ἐγὼ μούνη κατὰ Λάτμιον ἄντρον ἀλύσκω. Elsewhere ἀλύσκω is used like ἀλυσκάζω.

Ode X. 118—120. ἄλσος...ἐσσαμένων.

In the three epodes of this ode the MS. gives the 7th and 8th verses as follows :—

(1) Epode 1, vv. 35 f.

γνῶμαι πολύπλαγκτοι βροτῶν
ἄμερσαν ὑπέρτατον ἐκ χειρῶν γέρας.

(2) Epode 2, vv. 77 f.

τεῖχος δὲ Κύκλωπες κάμον
ἐλθόντες ὑπερφίαλοι κλεινᾷ πόλει.

(3) Epode 3, vv. 119 f.

Κάσαν παρ' εὔυδρον πρόγο-
νοι ἐσσάμενοι, Πριάμοι' ἐπεὶ χρόνῳ...

It is admitted on all hands that πρόγονοι ἐσσάμενοι is corrupt: this is X. 118— proved (a) by the construction, since there is no verb for the nominative; 120 and (b) by the hiatus.

Prof. v. Wilamowitz writes προγόνων ἐσσαμένων, which Prof. Blass adopts. There can be no doubt that ἐσσαμένων is right. The only question is whether προγόνων also is right.

In support of προγόνων, it has been pointed out by Prof. v. Wilamowitz that, if we assume synaphea between the 7th and 8th verses of the epode, we have – ᴗ – ᴗ in 35 f. (-οι βροτῶν ἄ-) answering to – ᴗᴗ – in 77 f. (-ες κάμον ἐλθ-) and in 119 f. (-ον προγόνων). The 'apparent choriambus' in 77 f. and 119 f. can be regarded, Wilamowitz observes, as a δίμετρον δακτυλικὸν καταλῆγον εἰς συλλαβήν, or as anaclasis of the trochaic metre – ᴗ – ᴗ (i.e. of the so-called epitritus). We have before us, he says, a kind of metrical correspondence which must in any case be allowed for ionics and dochmiacs, though no exact parallel to this example in Bacchylides can be produced.

Such an opinion is entitled to careful consideration. It is, however, difficult to believe that προγόνων is metrically tenable. Ingenious as is the theory just stated, there is an objection which it does not meet. The whole metrical structure and rhythm of the epode in this poem render it natural to think that verse 35, γνῶμαι πολύπλαγκτοι βροτῶν, is to be read as a verse complete in itself; and that in v. 77, τεῖχος δὲ Κύκλωπες κάμον (where κάμοντ' is most improbable), the second syllable of κάμον is to be regarded as a syllaba anceps. Now the defence of προγόνων rests essentially on the view that, given synaphea, – ᴗᴗ – is a permissible substitute for – ᴗ – ᴗ. But this, in turn, implies that the two verses, between which synaphea exists, *form, to the ear, a single verse*; since a division of 'the apparent choriambus' – ∪∪ – which placed – ∪∪ (-ον προγό-) at the end of the first verse, and – (-νων) at the beginning of the second, would evidently be intolerable. But verses 35 f. certainly (and, to my feeling, verses 77 f. also) are strongly against the hypothesis of such absolute rhythmical continuity in vv. 119 f. It is the teaching of the ear which demurs to acquiescence in the technical apology for προγόνων.

As to my πρὸ ναοῖ', it is a tentative suggestion for which, in a difficult case, one may venture to ask a hearing. It may be observed that it has, at least, one slight recommendation: that of serving to explain how ἐσσαμένων came to be corrupted into ἐσσάμενοι. If the true reading was προγόνων ἐσσαμένων, such a corruption becomes very difficult to understand. The case is wholly different from that in VIII. 46, where ἐγγόνων, *immediately preceding* γεύσαντο, was changed into ἔγγονοι. Here the nearest verb is πέρσαν in 122; and that verb stands in a new clause introduced by ἐπεί.

Professor A. Platt (*Class. Rev.* XII. 61, Feb. 1898) proposed πρὸ γουνοῖ'. This would be excellent if only it yielded a satisfactory sense. γουνός is usually explained as 'fruitful land' (from st. γεν): but Her. IV. 99 has τὸν γουνὸν τὸν Σουνιακόν, where it clearly means 'the hill-region of Sunium' (*Etym. M.* λέγεται δὲ γουνὸς ὁ ὑψηλὸς τόπος). So πρὸ γουνοῖ' might mean that the ἄλσος by the river had rising ground behind it. But, while the mention of the river is natural, the other detail seems rather lacking in point; there is nothing distinctive about it. As to the ναός, a mention of it was not, of course, necessary; but it would certainly be natural. (See the passages quoted in the commentary.)

Can προγόνων have been a gloss on some other word, scanned ∪ – –, meaning 'ancestors'? Dr W. Headlam thought of πατρώων, referring to Stesich. fr. 17, πάτρω' ἐμὸν ἀντίθεον Μελάμποδα, on which Eustathius says (316. 16) πάτρωα τὸν κατὰ πατέρα πρόγονον εἶπεν. But that seems hardly probable. Still less so is προπάππων, though πάπποι can mean 'ancestors' (Arist. *Pol.*, III. 2, 1): and παλαιῶν would (of course) be too vague.

[The late Prof. Arthur Palmer's emendation, πρόγο-|νοι ἔσσαν ἐμοί, was adopted by Dr Kenyon in the *editio princeps*. It was supported by Dr Otto Crusius in *Philol.* LVII. *N.F.* XI. p. 179. In the *Class. Rev.* XII. p. 126 (March, 1898) I endeavoured to show what could be said in favour of it. Two objections (the hiatus, and ἔσσαν instead of ἔσσαντο) could be removed by reading θέσσαν. Even with θέσσαν, however, I now regard the emendation as metrically untenable. But, in justice to the memory of a brilliant scholar, I still desire, in one respect, βοηθεῖν τῷ λόγῳ ὀρφανῷ ὄντι. Some scorn has been cast on the idea that Bacchylides could have alluded to the Achaean founders of Metapontion as πρόγονοι..ἐμοί. I still hold that it was perfectly possible and natural for him to do so. As Crusius said (quoting Mimnermus fr. 9), 'Neleus und Nestor sind die wichtigsten κτίσται der ionischen Inselwelt.' We have lately acquired a fresh illustration. Timotheus (*Persae* 246 ff.) thus speaks of his native city :—

> Μίλητος δὲ πόλις νιν ἁ
> θρέψασ' ἁ δυωδεκατει-
> χέος λαοῦ, πρωτέος ἐξ Ἀχαιῶν.

The people of the Ionian dodecapolis is 'a noble scion of the Achaean race.']

Ode XII. 58—63.

I. Prof. Blass restores this passage as follows :—

58 θάλλει παρ]ὰ βωμὸν ἀριστάρχου Διὸς
59 Νίκας ἐ]ρ[ικ]υδέος ἀν-
60 θρώποισιν ἄνθεα,
61 ἁ κλυτ]ὰν δόξαν πολύφαντον ἐν αἰ-
62 θέρι] τρέφει παύροις βροτῶν
63 αἰ]εί· καὶ ὅταν θανάτοιο κ.τ.λ.

1. With regard to ἀν|θρώποισιν, it should be observed that the **XII. 58—** second syllable of the word represents a syllable which is short in all **63** the corresponding verses, 93, 126, 159, 192, 225. This is not a decisive objection ; a long syllable may have been allowed there : but, so far as it goes, it is a reason for preferring a word which would give – ⌣ – ⌣.

2. In v. 61, ἁ, after ἄνθεα at the end of 60, is questionable, seeing that hiatus does not occur at the end of any one of the verses which correspond with v. 60 :—93, 126, 159, 192. This objection would be removed by reading τὰ (cp. VIII. 42 where ταί serves as relative pron., v. 41 ending with Νείλου). There is room for τὰ κλυτ in the lacuna before -άν.

3. In 61 f. αἰθέρι seems very improbable. The sense intended is :— 'The flowers of victory cherish renown for those few mortals *in heaven* evermore'; *i.e.* their fame, exalted by poetry, dwells on high with the immortals : cp. VIII. 82 ff. τό γέ τοι καλὸν ἔργον...ὑψοῦ παρὰ δαίμοσι κεῖται. Blass compares also Pind. fr. 227 λάμπει δὲ χρόνῳ | ἔργα μετ' αἰθέρ' ἀερθέντα. Now this sense is intrinsically good enough : but it does not suit this context. The poet is evidently saying, in effect :—'The

32—2

victors are famous *for the rest of their days*; and then, ὅταν θανάτοιο
νέφος καλύψῃ, they have κλέος ἀθάνατον.' Clearly we need, instead of
αἰθέρι, some word which denotes *the mortal life*. Further, the second
syllable of αἰθέρι answers to one which is long in all the corresponding
places, 95, 128, 161, 194, 227. It cannot be doubted, I think, that
we should read ἐν αἰῶνι, as I proposed in Kenyon's edition (p. 115,
note).

II. Prof. v. Wilamowitz would read as follows :—

> 58 ἐκ τοῦ] παρὰ βωμὸν ἀριστάρχου Διὸς
> 59 νίκας ἐρικυδέος ἀν-
> 60 δίδωσιν ἄνθεα,
> 61 καὶ κλυτ]ὰν δόξαν πολύφαντον ἐν αἰ-
> 62 ῶνι] τρέφει παύροις βροτῶν...

'Thence' [from the pancration?—or 'From that time onwards'?],
'by the altar of Zeus, flowers of victory *spring up, and* nourish fame,' etc.
The intransitive use of ἀναδιδόναι seems to be somewhat rare in Greek
of the classical age. In both places where Pindar uses it, it is transitive :
fr. 133 (Persephone ἀνδιδοῖ ψυχάς), and *I.* v. 39. But Herod. VII. 26
has ἵνα πηγαὶ ἀναδιδοῦσι Μαιάνδρου. In v. 61 καὶ κλυτ]ὰν is slightly too
large for the space : καὶ καλ]ὰν would suit it better.

III. Prof. Housman proposes :—

> 58 τᾷ δὴ παρ]ὰ βωμὸν ἀριστάρχου Διὸς
> 59 νίκας ἐρικυδέος ἀν-
> 60 δεθεῖσιν ἄνθεα
> 61 ἀγλαὰν δόξαν πολύφαντον ἐν αἰ-
> 62 ῶνι τρέφει παύροις βροτῶν...

'There,...for men who have been crowned with the flowers of
victory, [that wreath, or Zeus] cherishes,' &c. The drawback here
is that there is no evident subject for τρέφει. (It is hard to supply Ζεύς
from Διός, or the nom. ἄνθεα from the accus.) In 60 f. the hiatus
between ἄνθεα and ἀγλαάν is undesirable (see above).
Adopting Housman's ἀνδεθεῖσιν, I read ὃς νῦν in 58, and χρυσέαν in
61 (see commentary).

ODE XII. 485

Ode XII. 71—76.

Prof. Blass now restores the passage as follows (3rd ed., 1904):—

71 γενέις] πόλιν ὑψιάγυιαν
72 Αἰακοῦ] τερψιμβρότων
73 αὐλῶν καὶ] ἀε[ρσινόων
74 κώμ[ων], πατρ[ῴια]ν
75 νᾶσο[ν] ὑπέρβιον ἰσχὺν
76 παμμαχίαν ἄνα φαίνων.

'Through thee, the stately city of Aeacus tastes the delight of flutes **XII. 71—** and exhilarating revels, as thou showest thy paternal isle to be of **76** exceeding might in the feats of boxer and wrestler' (ἀνὰ παμμαχίαν). [I suppose Prof. Blass to intend that ὑπέρβιον should be the predicate of νᾶσον, and ἰσχύν an acc. of respect: since, if ὑπέρβιον were taken with παμμαχίαν, φαίνων νᾶσον could not mean 'glorifying' it.]

In v. 73, where the MS. has only.........A....OΩN, he thinks that the traces after A point to B, or P, or C, or E. He supplies ἀερσινόων, citing οἶνον ἀερσίνοον in Ion fr. 9 (= Athen. 2. 35 E), where, however, it is only Casaubon's conjecture: most MSS. have ἀερσίπνουν, one has ἀερσίπνοον. The word ἀερσίνοος is used by Nonnus: (1) in his paraphrase of the Gospel of St John, ch. viii. v. 44, where, in rendering ὑμεῖς ἐκ τοῦ πατρὸς τοῦ διαβόλου ἐστέ, he has the phrase πατρὸς ἀερσινόου. The word was there translated by *superbi*; but might also mean, 'inciting' to evil. (2) In *Dionysiaca* XXXIII. 68 f., ἀερσινόου...Οὐρανίης, the Muse who inspires and elevates the mind. Here, then, ἀερσινόων, as an epithet of κώμων, could mean 'exhilarating'; but I cannot think that the word is at all probable.

I rather hold, with Kenyon, that the letter which followed A here may have been Δ (only a trace of the top remains): and I would read αὐλῶν ὑπό θ' ἀδυπνόων. (Blass, in his first ed., suggested ἀβροπνόων.)

In his second ed. (1899) he read αὔξεις in v. 71,—a far better word (in my opinion) than γενέις. But,—having decided to read ἀερσινόων in 73, and having also reverted in 74 to κώμων (which in his second ed. he had changed to κώργάν),—he desired to find a verb which could govern a genitive as well as an accusative; since, with ἀερσινόων, αὐλῶν ὑπό τ' was impossible. For my part, if that adjective was to be used at all, I should have preferred αὔξεις...αὐλῶν ὑπό τ' ἀρσινόων.

With regard to 76, παμμαχίαν ἄνα φαίνων, the anastrophe of the

prep. does not seem quite happy, since, in this context, the hearer
would rather expect ἀναφαίνων ('illustrating': see commentary).

Dr Jurenka, in his edition (1898), restores thus :—

> αὖξες πόλιν ὑψιάγυιαν·
> νῦν δ' ὁρᾷς τερψιμβρότων
> μολπᾶν ὑπό θ' ἀδυπνόων κώμων πατρῴαν
> νᾶσον, ὑπέρβιον ἰσχὺν
> παμμαχὶ σὰν ἀναφαίνων.

Ode XII. 127.   νυκτὸς ἀντάσας κ.τ.λ.

XII. 127   It seems certain that the letters after ἀντάσας are to be read as ἀνατε-,
and not as ἀναπ-. But it may be of interest to record one or two of
the conjectures made on the latter hypothesis. Crusius proposed
ἀναπεπταμένας (to go with νυκτός as gen. abs.), 'when night is spread
abroad.' The phrase is, however, more suitable to the diffusion of light
than to that of darkness : and, in fact, the strictly similar phrases always
refer to light : e.g. Il. 17. 371 πέπτατο δ' αὐγὴ | ἠελίου ὀξεῖα : Od. 6. 44
αἴθρη | πέπταται ἀνέφελος : Il. 23. 227 ὑπεὶρ ἅλα κίδναται ἠώς : Her. VIII.
23 ἅμα ἠλίῳ σκιδναμένῳ.

I was more disposed to read ἀναπεπταμένῳ (with πόντῳ), 'the open
sea,' which gives just the needful sense. Cp. Her. VIII. 60 ἐν πελάγεϊ
ἀναπεπταμένῳ ναυμαχήσεις : Aratus, Phaen. 287 f. μὴ κείνῳ ἐνὶ μηνὶ
περικλύζοιο θαλάσσῃ, | πεπταμένῳ πελάγει κεχρημένος ('at the mercy of the
open sea'). The whole phrase from ἐν κυανθέϊ to ἀναπεπταμένῳ would
be one, without a pause. Blass formerly read νυκτὸς ἀντάσασαν ἀπεχθο-
μένας (with ναῦν θοὰν in 124), 'having fallen in with hateful night.'
(Pind. N. x. 83 γῆρας ἀπεχθόμενον.) [My earliest suggestion was
ἀναπαυομένων : they were resting, on a calm sea, in fancied security,
when the storm burst upon them.]

Ode XII. 158—163.   ἁ τλάμονες...πόλιν.

XII. 158—
163   158.   Before ὑπέρφιαλον Jurenka and Ludwich propose πνείοντες
(Blass πνέοντες). Kenyon, χαίροντες or κλάζοντες (so also Nairn, Tyrrell).
Platt, θάλλοντες.

159.   Nairn supplies μέγιστ' ἐθάρσεον (Jurenka, μάλιστ'—).   Blass,
δόκεον Ἀχαιῶν.   Tyrrell, ἔθρεψαν εὐχάν.   Platt, φρόνημ' ἔθρεψαν.

160 f.   Nairn, Jurenka, and Tyrrell supply Τρῶες.   Blass, νᾶας.
Nairn and Jurenka, ἐκ|φλέξασιν εὐσέλμους νέας.   Tyrrell, ἐκφλέξαντας
(or -ασαν) Ἑλλάνων νέας.   (Desrousseaux, ἐκκαύσαντες...)   Herwerden,
ἐκπέρσασιν εὐπρύμνους νέας.   Blass, ἐκπέρσαντες ἐξ ἀρχᾶς νέας (from νέος).

162 f. Nairn, παύραις χορὸν εἰλαπίνας τ' ἐν | ἀμέραις (and so
Jurenka). Herwerden, λεύκαις χάριν ('joy')—. Tyrrell, λοιπαῖς χάριν—.
Desrousseaux, δαῖτάς τε παρ' εἰλαπίνας τ' ἐν | εὐπόροις ἔξειν (i.e. παρέξειν).
Blass², ἐν νυξὶ μετ' εἰλαπίνας τ' ἐν | θ' ἀμέραις ἔξειν (i.e. μεθέξειν). Blass³,
– – ᴗ μετ' εἰλαπίνας τ' ἐν | καὶ χοροῖς ἔξειν. (χοροῖς Headlam : ἐν καὶ =
καὶ ἐν.)

Ode XV. 1—12.

I. *Verse* 1. Blass writes Πυθίου ἄγ' οἶμ', referring to Pind. *O.* ix. **XV. 1—12**
47, ἔγειρ' ἐπέων σφιν οἶμον λιγύν. He does not, however, define the
sense which he intends. (1) If Πυθίου (masc.) is construed with οἶμε,
the meaning will be, 'Lead me onward, thou Pythian strain' (lit., 'strain
concerning the Pythian god'). But the construction seems somewhat
harsh. (2) On the other hand, the words could not well mean, 'Lead
me, my strain, (to the temple) of the Pythian god.' For that, we should
expect ἐς Πυθίου.

The only letter between -ου and ἐπεὶ which is (approximately) certain
is the third letter after -ου, which must have been either E or O. The
first letter after -ου is torn out. The faint traces of the second letter
after -ου seem to suit Π at least as well as Γ. At present I can find
nothing more probable than Πυθίου ἐπ' εἶμ'.

II. *Verse* 5. The traces in the papyrus (see crit. n.) exclude such
supplements as οἶσιν ὁ Δάλιος (Crusius), and καὶ γὰρ ὁ Δάλιος (Jurenka).
Blass leaves a lacuna, writing – ᴗ ᴗ], εἶτ' etc. The only supplement
which he mentions is θεοῦ χάριν (Desrousseaux): but this is of nine
letters, whereas, before E, there is room only for about six.

III. *Verse* 7. ἀδείᾳ may be regarded as certain. The space before
it might have sufficed, at the most, for a word of four letters (if one of
them was thin), but a word of three letters is more probable. Crusius
and Jurenka supply ὀπί,—rightly, as I think.

IV. *Verse* 8 ended with δ' ἵκῃ παιηόνων. Before these words there
was just room for six letters (if one at least of them was thin). In the
antistrophe (v. 20) the syllables which answer metrically to those lost in
v. 8 are -λε κόραι τ' ὀβριμ-, ᴗ ᴗ – – ᴗ, and consist of 13 letters,—i.e. of
more than twice the number for which there was space in v. 8. Now to
obtain ᴗ ᴗ – – ᴗ with only six letters is extremely difficult, even when
the only condition imposed is that these six letters should form *some*
Greek word or words,—as, for example, ἀίω δῖα. But in verse 8, besides
the requirements of the sense, this further condition is present, that the
first of the six letters must be either a consonant or a digammated vowel.

For there is synaphea between verses 7 and 8 of the strophe (as verses 19, 20 prove); and therefore the last syllable of τερπόμενος in v. 7 must be long. To find six letters giving ◡ ◡ – – ◡, which shall satisfy all these conditions, is (so far as I can see) impossible. The space after τερπό-μενος at the end of v. 7 excludes the possibility that syllables metrically belonging to v. 8 had been tacked on to v. 7. There is therefore the strongest probability (to my mind it is a certainty) that verse 8, as originally written in our papyrus, was defective. The defect may have existed in the archetype, or the scribe of our papyrus may have inadvertently omitted something. In verse 12 of this same ode, he omitted the letters γα of ἀγακλέα: in Ode v. 129, οὐ γάρ: in XII. 55, ἀκόλουθον. Verse 8, as written by the scribe, may have been Πυθῶνά]δ' ἵκῃ παιηόνων. But in the verse as written by the poet, about 5 letters, forming two short syllables, came before Πυθῶνάδ'. All the conditions of sense of metre are fulfilled, if we suppose that the lost letters formed the word μέχρι.

That is not, however, the only possible restoration on the lines which have been indicated. We might also suggest in verse 8 ἐς ὃ χ' ἀδείᾳ (cp. *Il.* 16. 455 εἰς ὅ κε δὴ Λυκίης εὐρείης δῆμον ἵκωνται, 'until'): and in v. 8 (ϝ)οπὶ Πυθωνάδ' κ.τ.λ. But I prefer ὀπὶ ἀδείᾳ...μέχρι Πυθῶνάδ', because, in view of the synaphea, a consonant is preferable to (ϝ)ο after τερπόμενος at the end of v. 7.

A minor question remains. Is ἵκῃ to be taken as 2nd pers. sing. of ἵκωμαι, or as 3rd pers. sing. of ἵκω (subjunct.)?

(1) If it is the 3rd pers., then there should be a stop after πεδοιχνεῖν in v. 9; for, *immediately* after the 3rd pers. ἵκῃ (to which Apollo is subject), the vocative Πύθι' Ἄπολλον in v. 10 would be intolerable. A new sentence will now begin with Πύθι' Ἄπολλον. And therefore τόσα in v. 11 would mean,—'*Thus much*, Apollo, the Delphian choruses are wont to sing,' etc. The reference would be to the passing notice of Apollo's ἀποδημία in verses 5, 6. But such an interpretation of τόσα would be forced and unsatisfactory.

(2) It seems far more probable that, after v. 6, where the absent god is spoken of in the 3rd pers. (ἀγάλλεται), there is a transition to the 2nd person (ἵκῃ), as the thought of his return to Delphi rises in the poet's mind. On this view, only a comma will stand after πεδοιχνεῖν, and τόσα will be the relative, with ἄνθεα for its antecedent. See n. on Ode I. 37.

I subjoin the text of verses 5—12 as given by Blass (3rd ed., 1904, pp. 129 f.) :—

5 – ◡ ◡], εἴτ᾿ ἄρ᾿ ἐπ᾿ ἀνθεμόεντι <που> Ἕβρωι
δάφναι ἀ]γάλλεται ἦ δολιχαύχενι κύκνωι,
ὄφρ᾿ ἂν ἀ]δείαι φρένα τερπόμενος
ὀπὶ Πυθόα]δ᾿ ἴκηι παιηόνων
ἄνθεα πεδοιχνεῖν,
10 Πύθι᾿ Ἄπολλον,
τόσα χοροὶ Δελφῶν
σὸν κελάδησαν παρ᾿ ἀγακ|λέα ναόν.

A few observations may be offered. (1) The insertion of που in
v. 5 seems undesirable : see above, p. 114. (2) In v. 6 there is
scarcely room in the papyrus for ΔΑΦΝΑΙ, as I is the only thin letter.
In ΘΗΡCΙΝ [my conjecture], H and N are the only broad letters. (3) In
v. 7 the papyrus certainly has not space for ὄφρ᾿ ἂν before ἀδείᾳ : see
above, under III. (4) In v. 8, as Blass himself justly remarks (p. 131),
'pro spatio etiam οπιπνθοα (sive -θω fuit) paene nimia sunt.' In fact those
words require eight letters, where there is room only for six. Nor does
Πυθόαδ᾿ furnish – – ◡, which Blass's own scheme of the metre (p. 13)
requires. Again, as he notes (p. 131), 'ὀπὶ (Ϝοπὶ) eo laborat, quod
producenda est -νος syll., quam vim Ϝ ap. hos poetas [i.e. the lyric] habere
non solet.'

Ode XVI. 36—38.   χρύσεον
τέ Ϝοι δόσαν ἰόπλοκοι
κάλυμμα Νηρηΐδες.

(1) On the hypothesis that verses 37 f. were divided thus, ἰόπλοκοι XVI. 36—
κά-|λυμμ᾿ – ◡ Νηρηΐδες, the difficulty is to fill the gap. Neither ἀδύ[38]
(A. Ludwich) nor εἷμα (A. Platt) will serve. Slightly better, perhaps,
would be ἔνθα ('on that occasion'; cp. ποτέ in the similar mention of a
wedding-gift, v. 115 f.). But this, too, is unsatisfactory.

(2) The other mode of emendation would be to supply a short
syllable after ἰόπλοκοι. As Theseus is vaunting, ἰόπλοκοί γε is not
impossible :—'she was the bride of Poseidon, aye, and the Nereids gave
her a golden veil.' The only alternative which I can think of is ἰόπλοκοί
σφι (= αὐτῇ), with τοι instead of Ϝοι after τε. But σφι is not elsewhere
found in Bacchylides, while Ϝοι is frequent.

Others hold that it is unnecessary to suppose the loss of a short
syllable after ἰόπλοκοι, and that – ◡ – can stand here as a substitute for
the – ◡ – ◡ found in verses 14, 80, and 103. This is the view of Prof.
Housman (Class. Rev. XII. p. 138). But he suspects κάλυμμα (since
– – ◡ stands in 15, 81, 104), and suggests κάλλυσμα in the sense, not

490   APPENDIX.

found elsewhere, of *an ornament*. [Hesychius has σάρματα· καλλύσματα (*sweepings*).]

Ode XVI. 112.

XVI. 112   The emendations of ἀϊόνα fall into two classes; (A) those which substitute for it a word denoting *some article of apparel*; and (B) the rest.

(A) 1. ὤϊαν is suggested by Robinson Ellis (*Class. Rev.* XII. 66), 'a purple hem,' *i.e.* 'a robe with a purple border.' [*C. I. G.* 2554. 126, τὴν ἐπάνω ὤϊαν τᾶς πέτρας, its 'upper edge.' In Attic ὄα or ὀά meant the 'fringe' of a garment: Ar. frag. 27, etc.] 2. πορφυρέαν σινδόνα, H. Richards (*C. R.*, XII. p. 134). 3. Ἰαονίδα πορφυρᾶν, O. Crusius (*Philol.* LVII. *N. F.* XI. p. 182. 'A purple Ionian cloak'?) 4. W. Headlam (*C. R.* XII. 67) suggests 'some feminine substantive meaning "raiment," formed like ἀμπεχόνη, and from the same root as εἷμα, ἱμάτιον: *e.g.* εἱμόνᾳ, ἱμόνᾳ, εἰόνᾳ, εἰάνᾳ.' 5. ταινίαν, A. Ludwich and J. A. Nairn.

(B) 1. ἀγλαΐαν, Sitzler (quoted by Jurenka, p. 129). 2. ἀδονὰν (in the sense of χάριν, 'grace,' or 'charm') L. Barnett. 3. Ἀιόνα R. Walker (*C. R.* XII. p. 436), *i.e.* Ἀόνα, Doric for Ἠϊόνη, one of the Nereids (Hes. *Theog.* 255). 'We thus arrive at the reading, ἃ νιν ἀμφέβαλεν Ἀιόνα πορφυρέαν,' 'where Eione threw a purple cloak about him.' But the ἀνιν of the papyrus may have been (Walker suggests) a corruption of ἀλλικ', acc. of ἀλλιξ, a word used by Callimachus and Euphorion, one sense of which (acc. to *Etym. Magn.*) was πορφύρα.

Ode XVII. 27—30. Πολυπήμονος...Προκόπτας κ.τ.λ.

XVII. 27—30   I. '*Procoptes dropped the hammer of Polypemon.*' This, the most natural interpretation of the words, has been generally accepted. But is Polypemon here the father of Procoptes? On the strength of Ovid, *Ibis* 409, *ut Sinis et Sciron et cum Polypemone natus*, that view is adopted by Robinson Ellis (*C. R.* XII. p. 66), Housman (*ib.* p. 74), Jurenka (p. 135), and H. Weir Smyth (*Greek Melic Poets*, p. 443). C. Robert, however (*Hermes* XXXIII. p. 149), does not think that such a paternal relation is implied. Polypemon, he suggests, may be either (1) the *maker* of the hammer, a smith-daimon like Hephaestus and Palamaon; or (2) the *former possessor* of the hammer, which Procoptes has somehow inherited. Robert does not refer to the passage of the *Ibis*. In Apollodorus 3. 16. 2 the son of Polypemon is Sinis; but as Sinis is mentioned in the verse of the *Ibis*, the *natus* there can scarcely be other than Procrustes (= Procoptes): cp. *Met.* VII. 436 ff., and *Heroid.* II. 69 ff.

This is, however, a detail. C. Robert agrees with the other scholars above-mentioned as to the meaning of the words. 'Procoptes dropped the hammer of Polypemon.'

II. Other explanations have been proposed. (1) Blass places a point after σφῦραν, making it depend on ἔσχεν, and not on ἐξέβαλεν:— 'Theseus stayed...Polypemon's hammer; Procoptes let it fall.' Polypemon is thus identical with Procoptes (Procrustes). But it is awkward to denote the same person by different names in two successive clauses. Festa's view is similar; only he would read ἐξέβαλ' ἄν. He ingeniously suggests that a corrector had written E over the second A in ΕΞΕΒΑΛΑΝ (= ἐξέβαλ' ἄν), and that this second A became Λ, thus generating the ΕΞΕΒΑΛΛΕΝ of the MS. (2) Herwerden would make Theseus, not Procoptes, the subject of ἐξέβαλεν, and would change τυχὼν to τύχεν. 'Theseus struck the hammer from the hand of Polypemon; Procoptes met a stronger than himself.'

Ode XVII. 35.

Emendations of the MS. ἢ μοῦνον σὺν ὅπλοισιν.

In the *editio princeps* Dr Kenyon read ἢ μόνον τ' ἀνοπλόν | τέ | νιν. The other conjectures may be classed as follows.

I. Those which retain the letters συνοπλοι-. 1. A. Platt: σὺν ὅπλοισί νιν. 2. Sitzler: σὺν ὅπλοισιν οἷς ('with his own weapons' merely, as distinguished from those of an army). 3. Stahl: σὺν ὅπλοις νιν οἷς. 4. A. Ludwich: ἢ μοῦνον συνόπλοιό νιν, 'without a comrade in arms.' A very ingenious emendation. Eur. *H. F.* 127, has ξύνοπλα δόρατα, 'allied spears': but the adj. is very rare in classical Greek, and, so far, improbable here.

II. Emendations which suppose that the Λ came from Α. 1. Weil, Festa, Goligher: σὺν ὀπάοσιν (accepted by Blass and H. W. Smyth). The change of A into Λ led to the insertion of I after the second O, producing σὺν ὅπλοισιν. 2. Housman: ἢ μοῦνον συνοπαόνων ('without companions'). This also gives good sense, but does not so well account for σὺν ὅπλοισιν.

Ode XVIII. 15.

XVIII. 15 The MS. has ΤΙΗΝ (Ἄργος ὅθ' ἵππιον λιποῦσα). I. Can τί ἦν be
retained? (i) The hiatus is, of course, quite defensible. (Cp. Aesch.
Theb. 704 τί οὖν: Ar. *Nub.* 82 τί ἔστιν: *Av.* 149 τί οὐ: *Nub.* 80 τί, ὦ,
etc.) (ii) As to metre, a trochee stands in the corresponding place of the
antistrophe (33): but there is no reason to doubt that an iambus was
admissible here (cp. the verse of Catullus in the same metre, *meas esse
aliquid putare nugas*). (iii) The real question is as to the phrase itself.
(*a*) It is assumed that τί ἦν...ὅτε was an old formula in beginning a
story; and that is possible. '*How was it*, when the heifer fled from
Argos...?' But there is no other trace of that formula. (*b*) Jurenka
(p. 142) takes τί as a predicate: '*what* (= how pitiable) was Io, when,
as a heifer, she fled,' etc. (*wie elend war*). He compares Plat. *Charm.*
p. 154 D τί σοι φαίνεται ὁ νεανίσκος; and Plut. *Oth.* 3 τί γεγόνασιν οἱ
Καίσαρος πολέμιοι; I doubt that interpretation. (*c*) W. Christ would
write, τί; ἦν ὅτ' Ἄργος κ.τ.λ. 'How then? There was a time,' etc.
That would be intolerably jerky.

II. Emendations. (1) τίεν (G. E. Marindin, cp. Nairn in *C. R.*
XI. p. 453) is attractively simple. The construction would then be,
λαχοῖσαν ἔξοχον γέρας τίεν, *quae rem eximiam celebrandam acceperis.*
The point after γέρας in the MS. is not a grave objection; it would have
been added when ΤΙΕΝ became ΤΙΗΝ (τί ἦν). The difficulty which
I feel as to τίεν arises rather from its relation to the words which follow.
The sentence, ὅτ' Ἄργος...φεῦγε...βοῦς, has now to be taken as defining
either ὁδόν (*the strain of song*), or (better) γέρας, *the choice theme,*—
(namely, that) time *when Io was fleeing.* This is not impossible; but it
seems slightly harsh. (2) On the whole, I prefer ἦεν (W. Headlam,
C. R. XII. p. 68). The form ἦεν (from ἦα, epic form of Ionic ἔα) occurs
in *Il.* 12. 9, Hes. *Scut.* 15. Our poet might certainly have used it.
Kenyon's remark (p. 187, n. on this passage) must be borne in mind:
'ΤΙ is very like Η in the MS.' If ΗΕΝ had once been mis-read as ΤΙΕΝ,
ΤΙΗΝ (τί ἦν) would follow.

The formula ἦν ὅτ' is most often used in contrasting the past with
the present: *Anthol.* 8. 178 ἦν ὅτε ἦν ἀτίνακτος...νῦν δέ με θὴρ ἐτίναξεν
(cp. *ib.* 12. 44; 14. 52; 9. 344 (ἦν ὁπότε): Pind. fr. 83.) But that
formula could also be used, of course, simply to introduce a story,
when no such contrast was involved, as in *Anth.* 1. 92 ἦν ὅτε Χριστὸς
ἴανεν.

Ode XVIII. 15—18.

...Ἄργος ὅθ' ἵππιον λιποῦσα
φεῦγε χρυσέα βοῦς,
εὐρυσθενέος φραδαῖσι φερτάτου Διός,
Ἰνάχου ῥοδοδάκτυλος κόρα.

(1) According to the oldest version of the story, Io was changed **XVIII.** into a *cow*, usually described as white (Apollod. 2. 1. 3; Ovid, *Met.* **15—18** 1. 652, etc.). (2) In the fifth century, she was commonly depicted as *a maiden with the horns of a cow.* (3) At a later period, she was once more represented as a cow. R. Engelmann illustrates this third phase by a gem from *Mon. d. Inst.* 2. 59. 9 (Roscher's *Lexikon*, II. p. 275). He had previously discussed the whole subject in his essay, *De Ione dissertatio archaeologica* (Halle, 1868).

It seems probable that Bacchylides was here thinking of Io as the horned maiden. The epithet χρυσέα is one which he elsewhere gives to Aphrodite (v. 174), to Artemis (x. 117), and to an uncertain goddess (Hebe or Aphrodite?) in VIII. 72. In such cases the word denotes a divine beauty or glory,—or the preciousness of the deity in the eyes of her votaries. Here, whatever image of Io was in the poet's mind, χρυσέα means 'precious' to Zeus. But, if the poet imagined Io as *transformed into a cow*, the word would not be happily used; we should have expected rather some epithet, such as λευκή, which should be distinctive of her new form. Further, χρυσέα βοῦς is in apposition with Ἰνάχου ῥοδοδάκτυλος κόρα,—a fact which seems to strengthen the probability that Bacchylides was thinking of *the horned maiden.*

That compromise was inevitable for a dramatist who wished to bring Io on the stage as a speaking person. Aeschylus adopted it in the *Prometheus Vinctus*: 588 κλύεις φθέγμα τᾶς βούκερω παρθένου; the date of that play is uncertain,—perhaps between 467 and 458,—but indubitably later than the *Supplices*, which may be as early as *c.* 491/90.

Engelmann (in Roscher p. 271) assumes that the Aeschylean conception of Io in the *Supplices* (where she is only mentioned, not exhibited) is the same as in the *Prometheus*,—viz., the horned maiden. He infers that, if the *Supplices* was earlier than the *Prometheus*, some dramatist must have preceded Aeschylus in bringing Io on the scene in that shape. But it can (I think) be shown that the Io imagined in the *Supplices* is not the horned maiden of the *Prometheus*. The decisive passage on that point is *Suppl.* 299—301 :—

XO.   βοῦν τὴν γυναῖκ᾽ ἔθηκεν Ἀργεία θεός.
BA.   οὔκουν πελάζει Ζεὺς ἐπ᾽ εὐκραίρῳ βοΐ;
XO.   φασίν, πρέποντα βουθόρῳ ταύρῳ δέμας.

When he wrote the *Supplices*, Aeschylus thought of the transformed Io as a monstrous form, half cow, half woman; see verses 567—570 :—

...ὄψιν ἀήθη
βοτὸν ἐσορῶντες δυσχερὲς μιξόμβροτον,
τὰν μὲν [*v. l.* τὰ μὲν] βοός,
τὰν δ᾽ [τὰ δ᾽] αὖ γυναικός· τέρας δ᾽ ἐθάμβουν.

With μιξόμβροτον we may compare the description of the Sphinx in Eur. *Phoen.* 1023 f., μιξοπάρθενον | δάϊον τέρας. The words in the *Supplices* manifestly would not apply to a being whose form was wholly human, save for horns springing from the head. On the other hand, the βούκερως παρθένος of the *Prometheus* cannot have been also βουκέφαλος: that would have been too grotesque for a speaking person in tragedy.

It is probable, as Engelmann says (*l.c.* p. 271), that the extension of Io's wanderings to Egypt dates from the time when the Greeks recognised her in Isis. See Herodotus II. 41 : τὸ γὰρ τῆς Ἴσιος ἄγαλμα ἐὸν γυναικήϊον βούκερών ἐστι, κατάπερ Ἕλληνες τὴν Ἰοῦν γράφουσι. At the time, then, when Herodotus visited Egypt (probably between 449 and 445 B.C.), the horned maiden was already the form under which Greek artists commonly depicted Io. On the older Greek vases, the black-figured and the earliest red-figured, Io is still the cow. (Engelmann *l.c.*; cp. Preller, *Gr. Myth.* II.² p. 40, n. 5.)

Engelmann further remarks that, before the Greeks could have associated Io with Isis, they must already have been familiar with the representation of Io as the horned maiden. But can we be sure of that? Might not the horns of Isis have suggested such an association, even at a time when Greeks were still wont to think of Io as changed into a cow? Egypt was open to Greeks from about 550 B.C.; and they must have known the Isis of the monuments long before any dramatist (whether it was Aeschylus or a predecessor) had brought Io into a play. Painters of red-figured vases in the early part of the fifth century might have derived the new type of Io directly from Isis. On this hypothesis, that type need not have *originated* in the exigencies of drama. The *Prometheus* may have been the first play in which the βούκερως παρθένος figured; and Aeschylus may have been using a type which had already appeared in Greek art.

Ode XVIII. 33. ἤ ῥα.

The ms. has ῟ΗΡΑ. The cause of this is that some Alexandrian critics **XVIII. 33** wrote ἤ or ἤε, instead of ἦ or ἠέ, when that word introduced the second (or any later) question of a series; as in *Il.* 16. 12 f.:—

> ἠέ τι Μυρμιδόνεσσι πιφαύσκεαι, ἤ ἐμοὶ αὐτῷ,
> ἦε τιν᾽ ἀγγελίην Φθίης ἐξ ἔκλυες οἶος;

Cp. *Il.* 6. 378 f. And so also where the question is indirect; *Od.* 1. 174 ff.:—

> ὄφρ᾽ εὖ εἰδῶ
> ἠὲ νέον μεθέπεις ἤ καὶ πατρώϊός ἐσσι
> ξεῖνος.

Thus ἤ or ἤε, after ἦ or ἠέ in direct or indirect interrogation, was distinguished from the simply disjunctive ἤ (ἠέ)...ἤ (ἠέ), *either...or* (as in *Il.* 1. 503 f., εἴ ποτε δή σε μετ᾽ ἀθανάτοισιν ὄνησα | ἤ ἔπει ἤ ἔργῳ). But the refinement was an arbitrary one; and it is discarded in some modern texts of Homer.

Blass writes ἤ ῥα here, and ἤ in 35 (where the ms. has simply H). I prefer ἤ ῥα...ἤ.

Ode XVIII. 33—51.

The following are some of the supplements which have been **XVIII.** suggested in these verses. **33—51**

33. Jurenka: αἰνὰ γυῖ᾽ ἔλυσαν. (Blass thinks that the general sense was, *quamvis fortem delassaverunt.* But he makes no suggestion.)

35 f. Wilamowitz: ἤ Πιερίδες φύτευ[σαν Ἰνάχου κόρᾳ | καδέων ἀνάπαυσ[ιν ἀμέραν. Jurenka adopts ἀμέραν in 36, and my ἀδύμῳ μέλει in 35.

38. Wilamowitz: ἀσφαλέστατον ᾇπ[ερ ἐκράνθη λέγειν ('to tell how the matter was finally ordained'). This assumes that the ms. has lost the letter I between A and Π. Blass: ἀσφαλέστατον ἅ πρ[ίν ἐστ᾽ ἀοιδά. '*Acquiescit poeta in eo quod extremum proposuerat* [*i.e.* in vv. 35 f.]; *ea enim fuit vetus traditio.*' Jurenka, ἀσφαλέστατον ἀπ[λῶς (with ἐμοὶ μὲν οὖν [λέγειν in 37; but the first three words stood alone in that verse).

40 f. Jurenka: οἰστροδίνατος ἐντέροις | Ἰὼ φέρουσα παῖδα μεγαλοκλέα.

42 f. Blass suggests ἔνθα νι[ν τέκ᾽ ἀνδρῶν. Jurenka: ἔνθα νιν πατὴρ Κρονίδας | λινοστόλων πρύτανίν τ᾽ ἔθηκε λαῶν.

44. Blass and Jurenka: βρύοντ[α τιμᾷ.

45. Jurenka: μεγίσταν τε θνατῶν κτίσαι γενεάν (where κτίσαι depends on ἔθηκε in 43, 'caused him to found...').

50. Jurenka: τίκτεν Διόνυσον, [ἀγλαῶν τε κώμων. Blass writes τίκτε Δῖον υἱὸν (instead of the MS. Διόνυσον) as the complete verse.

51. Wilamowitz: στεφα[ναφόρων ἄνακτα (adopted by Jurenka; and approved by Blass, who, however, does not place it in his text).

Ode XIX. 1—11.

XIX. 1—11   1. In support of εὐρυχόρῳ, Headlam refers to Anaxandrides, Πρωτεσίλαος 19 ff. :—

> μέλπειν δ' ᾠδὰς
> τοτὲ μὲν Σπάρτην τὴν εὐρύχορον,
> τοτὲ δ' αὖ Θήβας τὰς ἑπταπύλους...

Gomperz and Jurenka conj. εὐρυαγνίᾳ.

2. Λακεδαιμονίων Wilamowitz : Λακεδαιμόνιαι Headlam : Λακεδαιμονίδες Jurenka.

3. κελάδησαν Gomperz, and so Jurenka.—κατᾶρχον (or κατᾶρξαν) Headlam.

4. καλλιπάρᾳον Kenyon : so Platt and Blass.—καλλίπαχυν also conj. Kenyon, and so Jurenka : καλλίπαχυν ἐς δόμους Headlam.

6. ἱοτρόφου πὰρ ποταμοῦ Blass (referring to the river Evenus : but see commentary).—ἰοπλόκαμον Rossbach : ἰόπλοκον, αἶσαν Sandys : ἰοστέφανον Platt, Jurenka. But it seems certain that the letter after IO was T.

7. ταχὺν οἶτον Jurenka : τέλος αἰπύ Pingel (quoted by Blass).—τελευτάν, ἐπεὶ conj. Blass.

8. (after Ποσειδᾶν) ἐπεὶ ἅρμα Jurenka : ἄρηγεν conj. Blass.

9. (after ἰσανέμους) πόρεν Jurenka : πόρεν, ταί νιν conj. Blass.

10. ἐΰκτιμέναν Kenyon, Wilamowitz, Jurenka.—ἐΰκτιμέναν πόρευσαν. ἢ μὰν—conj. Blass.—ἐς ἐΰκτιτον ὦρσεν Sandys.

11. υἱὸ[ν Ἄργος Reinach and others.—υἱὸ[s Ἄργος Jurenka :—υἱ' Ἀφάρηος Tyrrell.

VOCABULARY.

denotes a word found only in Bacchylides; †, a word which seems corrupt.

A

ᾶ, III. 10, XV. 30 (bis)
Ἀβαντιάδας, X. 40
Ἄβας: -ντος, X. 69
ἀβροβάτας: ἀβροβάταν, III. 48
ἀβρόβιος: -ίων, XVII. 2
ἀβρός: -ον, fr. 11. 4
ἀβρότης: -ῆτι, fr. 26
ἀγάθεος: -έαν, III. 62: -έᾳ, V. 41
ἀγαθός: -ῶν (masc.), fr. 18. 3
ἀγακλεής: -έα, XV. 12
ἀγακλειτός: -αῖς, XII. 90
ἀγάλλω: ἀγάλλεται, XV. 7
ἄγαλμα, I. 74, V. 4, IX. 11
Ἀγανορίδας, XVIII. 46
ἀγγελία: -αν, II. 3, XV. 26
ἄγγελος, V. 19: -ον, XVIII. 30
ἀγέλα: -ας (acc.), XVII. 10: -αις, IX. 44
Ἀγέλαος: -ον, V. 117
ἀγέρωχος: -οι, V. 35
Ἀγκαῖος: -ον, V. 117
ἀγκύλη: -ης, fr. 13. 13
Ἀγλαΐα: -ᾳ, III. 6
ἀγλαΐζω: -έτω, III. 22
ἀγλαόθρονος: -οι, XVI. 124
ἀγλαός: -όν, XVI. 61: -άν, V. 154: -ούς, XVI. 2: -ῶν, 103
Ἀγλαός (proper name): -ῷ, IX. 9 (?)
ἄγναμπτος, fr. 20. 2 (ἄκαμπτος MSS.): -ων, VIII. 73
ἀγνοέω: -ήσειν, fr. 12
ἀγνός: -όν, IX. 29: -οῦ, X. 25: -ᾶς, XIV. 54: -άς, XVIII. 28
ἀγορά: -άν, XIV. 43
ἀγρός: -οῦ Epigr. 2. 1 (fr. 34)
ἀγροτέρα, V. 123, X. 37
ἀγυιά: -αί, III. 16, fr. 3. 12: -άς, X. 58, VIII. 17: -ᾶν, 52
ἀγχίαλος: -ιάλοισι, IV. 14
ἀγχίδομος: -δόμοις, XII. 89
ἄγω: -ουσιν, fr. 16. 11: -ουσα, XVI. 2: -οντα, XVII. 34: ᾶγον (3rd pl.), XIV.

37: ἄξοντα, V. 60: ἄγονται, III. 46: ἄγετο, XIX. 4
ἀγών: -ῶνι, V. 44: -ώνων, VIII. 21
*ἀδεισιβόας: -αν, V. 155: -αι, X. 61
ἀδελφεός: -ῶν, V. 118
ἀδίαντος, XVI. 122
ἄδικος: -οισιν (masc.), XVII. 42
ἀδμάς: -ᾶτες, fr. 19. 1
ἄδματος: -ατοι, X. 84: ἀδμῆτα, V. 167
Ἄδραστος: -ον, VIII. 19
ἀδύπνοος: -ων, XII. 73 (?)
ἀδύς: ἀδεῖᾳ, XV. 7
ἄεθλος: -ων, VIII. 8: -οις, VII. 54, IX. 19, XII. 198
ἀείδω: -ειν, IV. 18: ἄεισαν, VI. 6: ἀείδεται, IV. 5
ἀεικέλιος: -ᾶν, fr. 19. 1
ἀεικελίως, III. 46
ἀείρω: -ρας, III. 36: ἄρατο, II. 5
ἄεκατι, XVII. 9
ἄεκων: -οντα, XVI. 44
ἀέλιος, X. 22: -ίου, V. 161, X. 101, p. 439 (I. 55 Blass).—See ἄλιος
ἄελλα: -αν, IX. 22
ἀελλοδρόμας: -αν, V. 39
ἄελπτος: -ον, III. 29, XII. 131
ἀέξω: ἀέξει, XII. 207: -ειν, III. 78. See αὔξειν
*ἀερσίμαχος: -μάχους, XII. 100
ἄξυξ: -γα, XV. 20: -γας, X. 105
ἀηδών: -όνος, III. 98
ἀήτα, XVI. 91
ἀθαμβής, XIV. 58
Ἀθάνα, XII. 195: -ας, XIV. 2, XVI. 7: -ᾳ, XV. 21
Ἀθᾶναι: -ας, XVII. 60: -ᾶν, XVII. 1: -άναις, IX. 17, XVIII. 10
Ἀθαναῖος: -αίων, XVI. 92
ἀθάνατος: -ον, IX. 11, XII. 65: -οι, V. 193: ἄτων, 86: οἰσ(ιν), X. 6, XIV. 45
ἄθεος: -έων, X. 109
ἀθλέω: ἄθλησαν, VIII. 12
ἀθρέω: ἄθρησον, V. 8 (MS.: but cp. ἐπαθρέω)

J. B.

ἄθυρμα, VIII. 87: -άτων, XVII. 57: -ασι
   Epigr. 1. 3 (fr. 33)
*ἄθυρσις: -ιν, XII. 93
αἰ (= εἰ): αἴ τις, V. 5: αἴ κε, XVI. 64
αἰαῖ, V. 153, fr. 2. 1
Αἰακίδας: Αἰακίδαις, XII. 166
Αἰακός: -οῦ, XII. 183: -ῷ, 99
Αἴας: -ντα, XII. 104
Αἴγινα, XII. 78: -αν, VIII. 55, IX. 35:
   -ίνας, XI. 6
αἴγλα: -αν, XII. 140
αἰγλάεις: -εντα, fr. 16. 10
Αἴγυπτος: -ύπτου, fr. 16. 11
'Αΐδας: -α, V. 61
ἀϊδής, XII. 209
αἰδοῖος: -αι, VIII. 65 (?)
αἰεί, I. 66, VIII. 81, XII. 63
αἰέν, XII. 207, XVII. 43, Epigr. 1. 3 (fr. 33)
αἰετός, V. 19
αἰθήρ, III. 86: -έρα, 36, V. 17, VIII. 35,
   XVI. 73: αἰθέρι, XII. 61
αἰθός: -θᾶν, fr. 3. 6
Αἴθρα, XVI. 59
αἴθω: -εσθαι, fr. 3. 3
αἴθων, XII. 50: -νος, V. 124
αἷμα: -ατι, X. 111, XII. 153
αἰνέω: αἰνεῖ, XII. 83: -έοι, VIII. 102 (?):
   -είτω, XII. 201: -εῖν, V. 16, 188
αἰνός: -νά (neut.), XVI. 10?
αἴξ: αἰγῶν, V. 101
αἰολόπρυμνος: -οις, I. 104
αἰόλος: -οις, XIV. 57
αἰπεινός: -άν, VIII. 34
αἰπύς: -ύν, III. 36
αἱρέω: -εῦνται, XIV. 56: εἷλεν, X. 85
αἴρω: see ἀείρω
αἶσα, fr. 20. 4: -αν, IX. 32, XVI. 27: -ᾳ,
   XII. 66, 99
ἀΐσσω: ἄϊξεν, II. 1: ἄϊξαν, XII. 144. See
   also IX. 23 n.
αἴτιος, X. 34, XIV. 52
Αἰτωλίς: -ίδος, VII. 51
Αἰτωλός: -οῖς, V. 114
αἰχματάς: αἰχματάν, XII. 133
αἰχμοφόρος: -οι, X. 89
†αἰών: αἰῶνα, XVI. 112
αἰών: -ῶνι, XII. 61 f. (?): -ῶνα, I. 43
*ἀκαμαντορόας: -αν, V. 180
ἀκάματος: -άτοις, XVIII. 20: -άτας, V. 25:
   -ατᾳ, XII. 178
ἄκαρπος: -ον, fr. 7. 5
ἀκίνητος: -ήτους, V. 200
ἀκοίτας, IX. 9
ἄκοιτις: -ιν, V. 169
ἄκοιτος: -ον, XVIII. 23
ἀκόλουθος: -ον, XIV. 55
ἀκούω: ἄκουσον, XVI. 53
'Ακρίσιος: -ίῳ, X. 66
ἄκριτος: -ίτους, IX. 46
ἀκτά: -άν, XV. 16

ἀκτέα: -έας, VIII. 34
ἄκων: -οντας, XVII. 49
ἀλαθεία, XII. 204: ἀλάθεια, fr. 10. 2:
   -είας, V. 187 (where see n.): -είᾳ, III.
   96, VII. 42, VIII. 85
ἀλαμπής: ἀλαμπέσι, XII. 175
ἄλαστος: -στον, III. 34
ἀλάτας: -ταν, XVII. 36
ἄλγος, XVI. 19
ἀλέκτωρ, IV. 8
'Αλεξίδαμος: -ον, X. 18
'Αλθαία, V. 120
ἀλίγκιος: -ία, V. 168
*ἀλιναιέτας: -αι, XVI. 97 f.
ἄλιξ: -ικι, VII. 45
ἄλιος: -ίου, III. 80: 'Αλίου, XVI. 50
ἀλκά: -άς, X. 126
ἄλκιμος: -ον, V. 146, XVII. 38: -ίμων,
   XVII. 13
'Αλκμήνιος, V. 71
ἀλλά, I. 66, etc.: after εἰ καί, XVI. 33:
   ἀλλ' οὐ γάρ, V. 162
ἀλλοδαμία: -ίαν, XVII. 37
ἀλλοῖος: -οίαν, IX. 36, XIII. 7
ἄλλος, IX. 36, XIII. 7: -αν, fr. 20. 3: -αι,
   VIII. 63: -ους, fr. 9: -ων, I. 47 f.: -οισ(ιν),
   V. 127, fr. 9: -αισιν, p. 437 (I. 23
   Blass)
ἄλλοτε, fr. 20. 3
ἀλλότριος: -ον, XIV. 60
ἄλλως, fr. 29
ἄλοχος: -ον, XV. 29, XVI. 109
ἅλς: ἁλός, V. 25, XVI. 62, 122, p. 439
   (I. 54 Blass)
ἄλσος, III. 19, X. 118, XVI. 85
'Αλυάττας: -ττα, III. 40
ἀλυκτάζω: ἠλύκταζον, X. 93
'Αλφεός or 'Αλφειός: -εοῦ, VI. 3: -εόν, III.
   7 (?), V. 38, 181, X. 26: -ειοῦ, VII. 49,
   XII. 193
ἅμα, III. 91
ἀμαιμάκετος: -ον, X. 64
ἀμαλδύνω: -ύνει, XIII. 3
ἆμαρ, III. 29, fr. 7. 4: -τι, X. 33: -τα, V.
   113
ἁμαρτέω (= ὁμ.): ἁμαρτέοιτε, VIII. 103 f.
   (?): -εῖν, XVII. 46
ἀμάρυγμα, VIII. 36
ἀμαυρόω: -οῦται, XII. 177
ἀμάχανος: -άνου, I. 171
ἄμαχος, XV. 23
ἀμβολά: -ᾶς, fr. 11. 1
ἀμβρόσιος: -ίων, XVII. 2
ἄμβροτος: -ότου, XVI. 42
ἀμείβω: -είψας, XVII. 16: -ειβόμενος, V.
   159
ἀμεμφής: -έα, XVI. 114
ἀμέρα: -ας, XVIII. 27: -ᾳ, I. 3
ἀμέρδω: ἄμερσαν, X. 36
ἀμέτερος: -ον, fr. 2. 1: -ας (gen.), V. 144,
   XVII. 5: -ᾳ, V. 90: -ας (acc.), XI. 3

VOCABULARY. 499

*ἀμετρόδικος: -οις, X. 68
ἄμετρος: -ον, XVI. 67 (?)
ἀμίαντος, III. 86
ἀμπελοτρόφος: -ον, VI. 5
ἀμύσσω: -ει, XVII. 11: ἄμυξεν, XVI. 19
ἀμφάκης: -ες, X. 87: -εα, fr. 3. 8: ἀμφάκει,
  p. 439 (I. 79 Blass)
ἀμφί, with acc., IX. 34, X. 18: with dat.,
  I. 39, IX. 44, XVI. 105, 124, XVII. 53:
  in tmesis, XVIII. 7
ἀμφιβάλλω: -βάλλει, XVII. 6: -έβαλεν,
  XVI. 112: βάλωσιν ἄμφι, XVIII. 7
ἀμφικύμων: -ονα, XV. 16
ἀμφιπολέω: -λεῖ, fr. 7. 3
ἀμφιτίθημι: -τίθει, Epigr. 1. 4 (fr. 33)
Ἀμφιτρίτα: -αν, XVI. 111
Ἀμφιτρύων: -ύωνος, V. 156
Ἀμφιτρυωνιάδας, V. 85: -αν, XV. 15
ἀμφότερος: -αισιν, V. 188
ἀμώμητος: -ον, V. 147
ἄν, I. 70, V. 97, 135, 193 (?), X. 30 (?),
  XVI. 41, XVIII. 3
ἀνά, with acc., V. 66: with dat., III. 50:
  in tmesis, III. 50 f.
ἀναβάλλω: ἀνὰ.. ἔβαλλον (tmesis), III.
  50 f.
ἀναβολά: see ἀμβολά
ἀνάγκα, fr. 16. 2: -αν, X. 72: -ᾳ, X. 46
ἀναδέω: -δησάμενος, IX. 16
ἀνάδημα: see ἄνδημα
*ἀναιδομάχας: -αν, V. 105
ἀνακάμπτω: ἀνεκάμπτετο, XVI. 82
ἀνακαρύσσω: ἀγκάρυξαν, IX. 27
ἀνακλαίω: ἀγκλαύσασα, V. 142 (?)
ἀνακομίζω: ἀγκομίσσαι, III. 89
ἀναμείγνυμι: ἀμμειγμένα, fr. 16. 5
ἀναμιμνᾴσκω: ἀνέμνασεν, II. 6
ἄναξ, III. 39, 76, V. 84, VIII. 45, XII. 148,
  XVI. 78, XVII. 2
*ἀναξίαλος, XIX. 8
*ἀναξιβρόντας, XVI. 66
*ἀναξίμολπος: -ου, VI. 10
ἀναπάλλω: ἀνέπαλτο, X. 65
ἀνάπαυσις: -ιν, XVIII. 36
ἀναπαύω: ἀμπαύσας, V. 7
ἀναπέμπω: ἀνέπεμψε, III. 62
ἀναπτύσσω: -ύξας, V. 75
ἀνατείνω: ἀντείνων, X. 100: ἄντειναν, XII.
  138: ἀντείνασα, fr. 13. 4
ἀνατέλλω: -τελλομένᾳ, XII. 127 (?)
ἀνατίθημι: ἀνέθηκε, Epigr. 2. 1 (fr. 34)
ἄνατος: -οι, fr. 19. 2
ἀναφαίνω: -ων, XII. 76
ἄνδημα, VII. 52
ἄνδηρον: -ήροις, p. 439 (I. 54 Blass)
ἀνδροκτόνος: -ον, XVII. 23
ἄνεμος, V. 65: -μων, Epigr. 2. 2 (fr. 34)
ἀνήρ, V. 191, VII. 46, XVII. 7: ἄνδρα, III.
  69, IX. 48, XII. 201, XVII. 31: -ός, I.
  52 f., fr. 25: -ί, III. 88: -ας, I. 10: -ῶν,
  IX. 38, XII. 189, XIII. 8, 17, XVII. 40,

fr. 10. 2: ἀνέρων, XII. 196: ἄνδρεσσι(ν),
  V. 96, X. 114: -άσι, fr. 16. 6
ἀνθεμόεις: -εντι, XV. 5: -εντας, XII. 88
ἀνθεμώδης: -δεα, XVIII. 39
ἄνθος: -εα, III. 94, XII. 59, XV. 9, fr. 3.
  2: -έων, X. 18, XII. 92: ἄνθεσιν, IX. 16
ἄνθρωπος: -ων, I. 51, 59, VII. 44, VIII. 18,
  88, IX. 48, fr. 1. 2, 14. 24: -οισ(ιν), V. 30,
  VII. 9, IX. 12, XII. 59, XIII. 1, XIV. 54,
  fr. 16. 8, 19. 3
ἀνίκατος: -ατον, V. 57
ἄνιππος (?), p. 475
ἀνίσχω: -οντες, XIV. 45
ἀντάω: -άσας, XII. 127
ἀντί, I. 147
ἀντίθεος: -ου, XIV. 1: -οι, X. 79
ἀοιδά: -άν, XVII. 4: -αί, XII. 230: -ᾶν,
  fr. 3. 2: -αῖς, VI. 14
ἀολλίζω: ἀόλλιζον, XIV. 42
ἅπαξ, fr. 1. 1
ἅπας: -ντι, X. 125: -τα, XIV. 51, fr. 21. 1
ἀπείρων: -ονα, VIII. 20
ἀπενθής, XII. 87: -θῇ, fr. 7. 2
ἄπιστος: -ον, III. 57, XVI. 117
ἄπλατος: -ον, XVII. 51: -οιο, V. 62
ἀπό, I. 57, V. 10, VIII. 21, X. 65, XV. 17,
  XVI. 55, 103, fr. 3. 10, 13. 2, 16. 11:
  ἄπο, XVII. 55: in tmesis, IV. 20, Epigr.
  2. 4
ἀπολαγχάνειν: λαγχάνειν ἄπο, IV. 20
ἀπόλλυμι: ἀπώλεσεν, XV. 31
Ἀπόλλων, I. 18, III. 29, 58, IV. 2, XII.
  148: Ἄπολλον, XV. 10
ἀποπλέω: -ων, I. 12
ἀπόρθητος: -ων, VIII. 52: -ους, 99
ἀποσεύω: ἀπεσσύμεναι, X. 82
ἀποτρέπω: ἀπέτραπεν, X. 27
ἀποφθίνω: -φθιμένῳ, VIII. 79
ἄπρακτος: -αν, IX. 8: -ακτα, fr. 8. 1
ἅπτω: -ειν, III. 49
ἀπωθέω: -ωσάμενον, V. 189
ἄρα, XII. 164, 228, XV. 5
ἀράχνα: -ᾶν, fr. 3. 7
ἀργαλέος: -αν, X. 72
Ἀργεῖος (Argive): -είων, VIII. 11, XIV. 5
Ἀργεῖος (proper name), I. 32, II. 4 f.
ἀργηστής: -άς, V. 67
ἀργικέραυνος: -ου, V. 58
Ἄργος, τό, IX. 32, X. 60, 81, XVIII. 15
ἀργυροδίνας: ἀργυροδίνα, VII. 48
ἀρείων: -ον, VIII. 91: -ονος, XVII. 29
ἀρετά, I. 71: -άν, 22, V. 32, IX. 13, fr.
  10. 2: -ᾶς, III. 90, X. 7: -αί, XIII. 8:
  Ἀρετά, XII. 176
*ἀρέταιχμος, XVI. 1 (?)
ἀρήϊος: ἀρῆος, I. 3 (?): -ήϊον, III. 69: -ηΐων,
  XVII. 57
ἀρηΐφιλος: -ου, V. 166: -οι, XIV. 50: -ους,
  I. 10: -οις, X. 113

33—2

Ἄρης, V. 130, XII. 146, fr. 20. 2: -ηος, V. 34, VIII. 44
ἀρίγνωτος, V. 29: -ον, XVI. 57: -οιο, IX. 37: -οις, VIII. 64
*ἀρισταλκής: ἀρισταλκές, VII. 7
ἀρίσταρχος: -ου, XII. 58
*ἀριστόκαρπος: -ου, III. 1
Ἀριστομένειον (τέκος), VII. 10
*ἀριστοπάτρα, X. 106
ἄριστος, III. 22: -ον, XIII. 2: -οι, V. 111
Ἀρκαδία: -αν, X. 94
ἅρμα, V. 177: -ασιν, p. 437 (I. 19 Blass?)
ἁρμόζω: -ζει, XIII. 12
ἀρπαλέως, XII. 98
ἄρρητος: -ων, fr. 4. 2
Ἄρτεμις, X. 37: -ιδος, V. 99
ἀρχά: -ᾶς, X. 65
ἀρχαγέτας: -αν, III. 24
ἀρχαγός: -όν, V. 179: -ούς, VIII. 51
ἀρχαῖος: -αν, V. 150, p. 439 (I. 52 Blass)
Ἀρχέμορος: -ῳ, VIII. 12
ἄρχω: ἄρχεν, XIV. 47
†ἀσαγεύοντα, VIII. 13
ἄσπετος: -οι, XVIII. 34
ἀσπίς: -ίσιν, XX. 3
ἄσταχυς: -ύων, Epigr. 2. 4 (fr. 34)
ἀστραπά: -άν, XVI. 56
ἀστράπτω: ἄστραψε, XVI. 71
ἄστρον: -ων, VIII. 28
ἄστυ, III. 43, X. 12, 57, XII. 115: -εα, 188
*ἀστύθεμις: -ιν, IV. 3
ἀσφαλής: -εῖ, XII. 66: -έστατον, XVIII. 38
Ἀσωπός: -όν, VIII. 39
ἀτάρβακτος, V. 139
*ἀταρβομάχας, XV. 28
ἀτάσθαλος: -ον, XVII. 24
ἄτεκνος: -ον, p. 475 (?)
ἄτερθε, XVI. 12
Ἀτρείδας: -εἴδᾳ, XIV. 6: -ᾶν, X. 123
ἀτρέμα, V. 7
ἀτρόμητος, XII. 123
ἄτρυτος: -ον, VIII. 80: -ῳ, V. 27
ἀτύζω: -όμενοι, XII. 116
αὐγά: -άς, X. 110: -αῖς, p. 439 (I. 55 Blass)
αὐδάεις, XIV. 44
αὐθαίρετος: -οι, fr. 20. 1
αὐθιγενής, II. 11
αὐλά: αὐλᾶς, III. 32
αὐλός: -ῶν, II. 12, VIII. 68, IX. 54, fr. 3. 5
αὔξω: -ουσιν, IX. 45: -ειν, I. 52
ἄϋπνος: -ον, XVIII. 23
αὔρα: -αι, XVI. 6
αὔριον, III. 79
αὖτε, IX. 23
αὐτίκα, X. 110
αὖτις, III. 89, XIV. 60
αὐτόματος: -οι, fr. 18. 3
Αὐτομήδης: -ει, VIII. 25
αὐτός: -όν, XVII. 41: αὐτ-, p. 437 (I. 22 Blass)

αὐτοῦ (adverb), V. 178
αὐχήν: -ένι, II. 7
Ἀφάρης: -ητα, V. 129
ἄφατος: -α, XVII. 18
ἄφθεγκτος: -οισιν, fr. 2. 2
ἀφικνέομαι: ἀφίκετο, XVIII. 40
ἀφνεός, I. 62: -όν, V. 53: -οῦ, XVI. 34
Ἀφροδίτα, XVI. 116
ἀφροσύνα: -αις, XIV. 57
Ἀχαιός: -ῶν, VIII. 58 (?), X. 126, XIV. 39: -οῖς, X. 114
ἀχείμαντος: -ον, fr. 22. 1
ἀχειρής: -ές, XI. 11 (?)
Ἀχιλλεύς, XII. 119: -έα, 101, 134
ἄχος, X. 85: -έων, 76, XIV. 52
ἀχρεῖος: -ον, IX. 50
ἀῷος, fr. 3. 11 (?)
ἀώς: δούς, XVI. 42: Ἀώς, V. 40: Ἀοῖ, XII. 129
ἀωτεύω: -οντα, VIII. 13 (?)

B

*βαθυδείελος: -ον, I. 29
βαθύζωνος, XIV. 7 (?): -ον, I. 7: -οιο, X. 16: -οις, V. 9
βαθύξυλος: -ῳ, XII. 169
βαθυπλοκάμου, X. 8
βαθύπλουτος: -ον, III. 82
βαθύς, III. 85: -ύν, V. 16, XIV. 61: -είας, XVI. 62
Βακχυλίδης: -η, Epigr. 1. 4 (fr. 33)
βάλλω: see under ἀναβάλλω and ἀμφι- βάλλω
βαρυαχής: -έας, XV. 18
βαρύβρομος: -ον, XVI. 76
βαρυπενθής: -έσιν, XIII. 72
βαρύς: -εῖαν, V. 18, 96
βαρύτλατος, XIII. 4
βαρύφθογγος: -ον, VIII. 9
βάσανος: βασάνοισιν, VIII. 58 (?)
βασιλεύς, I. 14: -εῦ, XVII. 1: -εῖ, X. 63, XIV. 6, 38: -ῆες, fr. 26
βέλος: -η, V. 132
βία: -αν, V. 181, XVI. 23, 45: -ᾳ, V. 116, X. 91, XVII. 10
βιάω: -άται, XII. 200, fr. 1. 2
βίος: -ον, fr. 7. 2: -ῳ, I. 59
βιοτά: -άν, V. 53
βλέπω: -εις, XVI. 75
βλέφαρον, V. 157: -ῳ, X. 17: -άρων, fr. 3. 10
βληχρός: -άν, XII. 227: -ᾶς, X. 65
βλώσκω: see μολ-
βοά: βοᾷ, VIII. 68: -άν, 35
βοαθόος Epigr. 2. 3 (fr. 34)
βοαθόος: -ον, XII. 103 (?)
βοάω: βόασε, XVI. 14
Βοιώτιος: -οισιν, fr. 17. 4
Βοιωτός, V. 191
Βορέας, XII. 125: -α, V. 46
βορεάς, XVI. 91

βορήϊος: -αι, XVI. 6
βούθυτος: -οις, III. 15
βουλά, VIII. 90 (?): -αῖσι, X. 121
βουλεύω: βούλευσεν, V. 139
βοῦς, XVIII. 16: βοῦν, XV. 22: βοῦς (acc.),
    X. 104: βοῶν, V. 102, IX. 44, fr. 3. 3,
    17. 1
βοῶπις: -ιν, X. 99, XVI. 110
βραχύς, III. 74
βρίθω: -θοντι (3rd plur.), fr. 3. 12: βρίσει,
    IX. 47
Βρισηΐς: Βρισηΐδος, XII. 137
βροτός: -ῳ, III. 66: -ῶν, I. 42, III. 66, 91,
    V. 63, 87, 109, 190, 194, VIII. 22, 85,
    X. 35, XII. 62, 202, XVI. 32, XVII. 2,
    fr. 26. 28: -οῖσ(ι), VIII. 74 (?), XIV. 31,
    XVI. 118, fr. 11. 1
*βροτωφελής: βροτωφελέα, XII. 191
βρύω: -ει, III. 15: -ουσι, 16: -ουσα, XII.
    179: -οντα, XVIII. 44: -οντες, VI. 9
βωμός: -όν, IX. 30, X. 41, 110, XII. 58:
    -ῶν, fr. 3. 3

Γ

γᾶ: γᾶν, X. 70, XII. 180: γᾶς, XIV. 63:
    γᾷ, V. 42, VII. 41
γαῖα, XII. 153: -αν, fr. 20. 4: -ας, V. 24,
    p. 437 (I. 6 Blass): -ᾳ, VIII. 38
γαμβρός: -ῷ, XVI. 50: -όν, p. 437 (I. 8
    Blass)
γάμος: -ῳ, XVI. 115
γάρ, III. 5, etc.: placed between a prep.
    and noun, XI. 4, XVI. 103 f.
γᾶρυς: -υν, V. 15: -υϊ, XIV. 48
γαρύω, III. 85
γε, with μέν, III. 63 (?), 90 (?): after εἰ,
    XII. 228 (εἴ κε MS.): νῦν, VIII. 25:
    πρίν, XV. 13
γέγωνεν, III. 37
*γελανόω: -ώσας, V. 80
γέμω: -ουσαν, XV. 4
γενεά: -άν, X. 74: -ᾶς, VIII. 49
γένος, I. 30, XVI. 93
γεραίρω, XII. 225: -ει, IV. 3, VI. 14:
    -ουσα, II. 13: ἐγεραίρομεν, IV. 13
γέρας, III. 12, VII. 8, X. 36, XVIII. 14
γέρων: -οντα, III. 59
γεύω: -σαντο, VIII. 46
γῆρας, III. 89, fr. 21. 3
Γίγας: -αντας, XIV. 63
γίγνομαι: γένετο, XVIII. 29
γιγνώσκω: γνώσει, V. 3: γνῶν, 152
γλαυκός: -όν, VII. 51: -ᾷ, X. 1: -ον, V. 4
γλυκύδωρος: -ε, III. 3, X. 1: -ον, V. 4
γλυκύς: -ύ, I. 65: -εῖα, V. 151, fr. 16. 1,
    17. 4: -εῖαν, II. 12: -ιστον, III. 47
γλῶσσα: -αν, V. 195, IX. 51
γνάμπτω: ἐγνάμφθη, XII. 52
γνήσιος: γνησίων, VIII. 83
γνώμα: -ᾳ, X. 35: -ας (acc.), III. 79:
    -αισι, fr. 27

γύαλον: -λοις, XIII. 41
γυιαλκής: -έα (sing.), XI. 8: (plur.), VIII.
    38
γυῖον: -ων, XVI. 104: -οις, 124
γυμνάσιον: -ίων, fr. 3. 5
γυνά, V. 139: -αῖκα, fr. 15. 2: -αικός, XII.
    136: -αῖκες, III. 45: -αικῶν, X. 112

Δ

δα-: ἐδάη, V. 64
Δαΐάνειρα: -αν, V. 173: -ᾳ, XV. 24
δαιδαλέος: -ας (gen.), V. 140: -έων, fr.
    3. 3
*δᾳδοφόρος: -όρε, fr. 23. 1
δαΐζω: -ει, XII. 126
δαιμόνιος: -ον, XV. 35
δαίμων, V. 113, 135, VIII. 26, XV. 23, XVI.
    46, fr. 21. 1: -ον, III. 37: -ονος, XIII.
    1: -ονες, XVI. 117: -οσι, VIII. 84
Δαΐπυλος: -ου, V. 145
δαΐς: -τας, fr. 18. 4
δαΐφρων, V. 122, 137
δάκρυ, XVI. 95
δακρύεις, V. 94
δακρύω: -υσα, V. 153
Δάλιος: -ε, XVI. 130
Δαλογενής, III. 58, X. 15
Δᾶλος: -ε, fr. 12
δαμάζω, δάμναμι: δάμασεν, I. 118: δαμά-
    σειας, XVI. 44: δάμναται (midd.), fr. 3:
    ἐδάμησαν, VIII. 64
δάμαλις: -ιν, XVIII. 24
δαμασίμβροτος, XII. 50
δαμάσιππος: -ον, III. 23
*δαμασίχθων: -ονι, XV. 19
Δαμάτηρ: Δάματρα, III. 2
Δαναοί: -οῖς, III. 145
Δαναός: -οῦ, X. 74
δάπεδον: -οις, X. 25
δάπτω: -ομέναν, XV. 14
δάσκιος: -ον, X. 93
δέ, passim (occurring about 160 times;
    cp. καί and τε): as third word of a
    sentence, I. 6, XVII. 47, cp. XII. 127 n.:
    δέ τε, XII. 129, fr. 3. 1: τε..δέ, XII.
    115 n. (?)
δε (enclit.): πόντονδε, XVI. 94: cp. X.
    114 n.
δείδω: ἔδεισεν, XVI. 102: δέδοικα, XVII.
    30
δείκνυμι: δείξομεν, XVI. 46: δεῖξαι, fr.
    11. 4
δειλός: -οῖσιν, I. 51
δειμαλέος: -ᾳ? III. 72 n.
Δεινομένης: -νεος, III. 7, IV. 13: -νευς, V.
    35
δεινός: -οῦ, III. 53
δέκατος: -ον, X. 59: -άτῳ, I. 15
Δελφοί, III. 21: -ῶν, XV. 11
δέμας, V. 147, VIII. 31

Δεξιθέα: -αν, I. 8
‡δεξίστρατος: -ον, XIV. 43
δέος, V. 84
δέρκομαι: -εται, XIV. 51
δέσποινα, X. 117, XII. 95
δεῦρο, V. 8
δέχομαι: ἐδέξατο, VII. 47: δέξατο, XV. 35,
XVI. 85: δέκτο, IX. 31, X. 17
δή, V. 142, 156, X. 95, XI. 4, XII. 121,
193
δῆρις: -ιν, V. 111
διά with gen.: VIII. 47, XII. 52: with
acc.: III. 61, VI. 4, VIII. 30, XII. 156,
XIV. 40
διάγω: -ειν, V. 33
διαιθύσσω: -η, fr. 16. 4
διαΐσσω: -σσεν, III. 54
διακρίνω: -ίνει, VIII. 28, 89: -κεκριμέναι,
fr. 24. 1
διατελέω: -εῖν, fr. 7. 2
διατρέχω: διέδραμεν, XIV. 44
δίδυμος: -ους, III. 78
δίδωμι: ἔδωκε(ν), VIII. 26, X. 39, XII. 80,
fr. 21. 1: δῶκε(ν), XVI. 116: δόσαν, XVI.
37: δοίητε, VIII. 2
διέπω: -ουσι, III. 21
δίζημαι: -ηνται, I. 67: -σθαι, XVII. 60
δικ-: δικών, XVI. 63
δίκα: -ας, X. 26, XVI. 25: -ᾳ, XII. 202:
-ας (acc.), XII. 45, XVII. 42
Δίκα: -ας, IV. 12
δίκαιος: -οι, fr. 18. 4: -ας (acc.), X. 123:
-ων, XIV. 47: -αισι, XIII. 11
δινάεις: -ᾶντα, XII. 165: -ᾶντος, 78
δινέω (-άω): δίνασεν, XVI. 18: δίνηντο,
107
Διονύσιος: -σίοισι, fr. 16. 5
Διόνυσος: -ον, XVIII. 50: Διωνύσου, VIII.
98 (?)
δίς, IX. 27, 29, XVI. 2
δίσκος: -ον, VIII. 32
διχόμηνις: -δος, VIII. 29
διχοστασία: -ίαις, X. 67
διώξιππος: -οι(ο), VIII. 44, X. 75
δνόφεος: -ον, XV. 32
δοιάζω: δοίαξε, X. 87
δοκέω, XVII. 12: -εῖ, fr. 16. 8
δόλιος, XVI. 116
δολιχαύχην: -ενι, XV. 6
δολιχός: -άν, XVII. 16: -ῷ, 45
δολόεις: -εσσα, III. 75
δόμος: -ον, III. 49, XV. 29, XVI. 100: -οι,
III. 40: -ους, XVI. 63: -οις, 111
δονακώδης: -δεα, fr. 22. 2
δόναξ: -ακος, XII. 92
δονέω: -εῖ, V. 67: -έουσι, I. 69: -εῖν, fr.
8. 1
δόξα: -αν, VIII. 1, IX. 18, XII. 61: -ας
(gen.), IX. 37: -ᾳ, XII. 120
δορά: -ᾶς, V. 124
δόρυ, XII. 120, XVI. 90

δράκων, VIII. 13
δράω: δρῶν, III. 83
δρόμος: -ῳ, V. 183: δρόμον, IX. 26
δύα: -ᾳ, p. 439 (I. 79 Blass), fr. 21. 3:
-ᾶν, XIV. 46
δύναμαι: -ται, fr. 7. 2: -το, XVIII. 26
δύναμις: -ιν, XIV. 59
δύνασις: -ιν, IX. 49
δύο, IV. 17, XV. 19, XVII. 46, 49
δύρομαι: -έναις, III. 35
δύσλοφος: -ον, XII. 46
*δυσμάχητος: -τα, fr. 32. 2
δυσμενής, XVII. 6: -έων, V. 133, XII. 208
δύσμορος, XV. 30
δυσπαίπαλος: -α, V. 26
δύστανος: -οιο, X. 102: -ων, V. 63
δῶμα: -ατα, V. 59: -ασι, 173
δῶρον: -α, XVI. 10, 76, 124, VIII. 4, fr.
32. 2: -οις, fr. 16. 5

E

ἑβδομήκοντα, II. 9
Ἕβρος: -ῳ, XV. 5
ἔγγονος: -ων, VIII. 46
ἐγγύθεν, XVI. 128
ἐγκύρω: ἐγκύρσαι, fr. 21. 3
ἐγχέσπαλος: -ου, V. 69
ἔγχος: -εα, fr. 3. 8: -έων, VIII. 43
ἐγώ, V. 127, XII. 221: ἐμέ, XVI. 33 (κἀμέ):
με, XI. 5, XVI. 53: ἐμοί, V. 31, 138,
XII. 226, XV. 2, XVIII. 37: μοι, 151:
ἄμμι, XVI. 25
ἔδος, VIII. 46
ἕδρα: -ας, fr. 11. 1
ἔθειρα: -αν, V. 29: -ας, VI. 8, XII. 197
ἐθέλω: -ει, I. 52, V. 14: ἐθέλων, V. 169:
ἔθελεν, X. 73: cp. θέλω
εἰ, with indic., I. 55, X. 27, XII. 168, 199,
228, XVI. 28 f. (εἰ καί), 57 f. (do.), fr.
7. 2, 29, p. 437 (? I. 9 Blass): with
optat., V. 190: with ellipse of indic.
verb, XI. 4 (εἴ ποτε), XVII. 12 (εἴ τινι).
Cp. αἰ and εἴπερ
εἶδον: εἶδε(ν), V. 40, X. 22, XVI. 109:
ἴδεν, V. 71, XVI. 16: ἰδεῖν, V. 30, XVI.
43: ἴδων, XVI. 72, 101
εἴδωλον, V. 68, V. 25
εἴκοσι, X. 104
εἰλαπίνα: -ας (acc.), XII. 162
εἰμι: ἴμεν, XVII. 12
εἰμί: ἐστί(ν), III. 38, V. 162, 167, XII. 203,
fr. 3. 9, 7. 1, 12. 1: εἰσί, VIII. 88,
fr. 19. 2: εἴη, IX. 12: ἔμμεναι, XVII. 14:
ἔμμεν, V. 144, XVII. 31, 56: εἶμεν, IX.
48: ἐών, I. 56, VII. 46: ἐόντα, IV. 19,
XVIII. 23: εὖντα, III. 78: ἦν, XVII. 21,
XVIII. 15: ἔσεσθαι, XII. 57
εἵνεκεν, XII. 136
εἴπερ, VIII. 86, XVI. 53
εἶπον: εἶπε(ν), III. 48, 77, V. 86, XVI. 47,
LII. 81: εἰπεῖν, VIII. 72, fr. 1. 1

εἰρήνα : -ᾳ, V. 200
Εἰρήνα, fr. 3. 1 : -ᾳ, XII. 189
εἴρω (*dico*) : εἶρεν, XVI. 20, 74
εἰς, XIV. 43 : *see* ἐς
εἷς, fr. 7. 1 : μία, *ib.*, XIII. 8 : ἕνα, I. 45
*εἰσάνταν, V. 110
εἴτε . . ἤ, XV. 5 f. : εἴτ᾽ οὖν . . ἤ ῥα . . ἤ, XVIII. 29 ff.
ἐκ, V. 15, 82, 132, 141, VIII. 35, X. 36, XIII. 8, XVI. 24, 62 (?) : ἐξ, III. 46, V. 61, X. 43, XVI. 122, fr. 4. 1
ἕκαστος : -ῳ, XIII. 16
Ἑκάτα, fr. 23. 1
ἕκατι, I. 6 f., V. 33, VI. 11, IX. 15, X. 9, XVI. 7
ἐκβάλλω : ἐξέβαλεν, XVII. 28
ἔκγονον, XVI. 16
ἐκκαιδέκατος : -αν, VII. 3
ἐκπίμπλημι : ἐκπλήσομεν, XVI. 27
Ἐκτόρεος : Ἑκτορέας (gen.), XII. 154
ἐκτός, IX. 52
Ἕκτωρ : -ορα, XII. 109
ἐλαία : -ας, VII. 52 : -ᾳ, X. 28
ἔλαιον : -ῳ, IX. 23
ἐλαύνω, IX. 51
ἐλαφρός, I. 35 : -όν, fr. 8. 1
ἐλέγχω : -ει, fr. 10. 2
ἐλέφας : -αντι, fr. 16. 9
*ἑλικοστέφανος : -ον, VIII. 62
ἔλλαθι (ἵλημι), X. 8
Ἕλλαν : -άνων, III. 12, V. 111, VIII. 30 : -ασι(ν), VII. 7, IX. 20, XII. 82 : Ἑλλάνεσσιν, 56 f. (?) : Ἕλλανας, VII. 44
Ἑλλάς : -δα, III. 63
ἐλπίς, III. 75, VIII. 18, fr. 16. 4 : -ίδι, I. 54, IX. 40, XII. 220 : -ίσιν, 157
ἔλπομαι, fr. 12
ἐμβάλλω : ἔμβαλεν, X. 54
ἐμός : -ᾶς, XVI. 64 : -ῶν, V. 117 : -αῖς, XII. 229
ἔμπεδον, XII. 178
ἐμπίτνω : -ων, IX. 24
ἔμπορος : -ον, XVII. 36
ἐμπρέπω : ἐνέπρεπεν, VIII. 27
ἐν, II. 6, V. 27, 41, 44, 80, 88, 119, 131, 165, 173, 200, VII. 3, 45, 53, VIII. 22, IX. 19, 29, X. 4, 19, 24, 32, 88, XI. 8, XII. 61, 81, 99, 118, 124, 135, 162, 189, 198, XIII. 15, 41, XVI. 53, XVI. 5, 108, 115, 120, XVII. 23, 45, 49, XVIII. 8, 47, XIX. 1, fr. 3. 6, 15. 1, 17. 5, 21. 2, 32. 1, Epigr. 1. 3 (fr. 33)
ἐναντίος : -ᾱ, V. 76
ἐναρίζω : -ομένων, XII. 151
Ἐνδαῖς : Ἐνδαΐδα, XII. 96
ἔνδοθεν, XVI. 86
ἐνδυκέως, V. 112, 125
ἔνθα, III. 33, V. 63, 107, 127, 182, XIV. 40, XV. 17, XVIII. 42
ἔνθεν, X. 82, 97, 113
ἐννέα, XV. 18

ἐνστάζω : ἐνέσταξεν, XII. 229
ἐντυγχάνω : ἐντυχεῖν, XVII. 44
ἐντύω : ἔντυον, fr. 18. 2
ἐνυφαίνω : -νετε, p. 437 (I. 4 Blass)?
ἔξ, V. 113
ἐξάγω : ἐξαγαγεῖν, X. 103
ἐξαιρέω : -είλετο, V. 74
ἐξαίσιος : -ίοις, XIV. 58
ἐξεναρίζω : -ων, V. 146
ἐξευρίσκω : -ευρεῖν, fr. 4. 3
ἐξικνέομαι : ἐξίκοντο, XII. 132
ἐξόπιν (or ἐξόπιθε), XVI. 91
ἔξοχος : -ον, XVIII. 14
ἑορτά : -αῖς, III. 15
ἐπαθρέω : -ησον, V. 8 (?) : -ήσαις, XII. 227
ἐπαΐσσω : -ων, V. 116
Ἔπαφος : -ον, XVIII. 42
ἐπεί, III. 23, 53, 113, VIII. 2, IX. 25, X. 120, XII. 133, XV. 1, 25, XVI. 43, 93, 121, XVIII. 39
ἔπειμι : ἐπιόντα, XVI. 46
ἔπειτα, V. 74
ἐπέρχομαι : -ονται, fr. 18. 4
ἐπί, with gen., VII. 9, IX. 21, XV. 1 (?), XVI. 83, fr. 3. 3, Epigr. 2. 1 (fr. 34) : with dat., V. 83, 90, 133, VI. 3, VIII. 12, 42, IX. 21, 42, 44, XII. 105, 193, 203, XIII. 16, XV. 34 : with acc., I. 76, VIII. 41, XII. 88, 149, XVII. 37, fr. 18. 1, 20. 3
ἐπιβαίνω : ἐπέβαινε, III. 34 : ἐπέβασε, V. 73
ἐπιγίγνομαι : -γιγνομένοις, VIII. 81
ἐπιδείκνυμι : ἐπεδείξαμεν, II. 9 : ἐπεδείξαο, III. 93
ἐπιδέχομαι : -δέγμενοι, XVI. 96
ἐπίζηλος : -ῳ, V. 52
ἐπικείρω : ἐπέκειρεν, V. 108
ἐπικλώθω : ἐπέκλωσεν, V. 143
ἐπικουρία : -αν, XVII. 13
ἐπιλέγω : -λεξαμένα, V. 136
ἐπίμοιρος : -ον, I. 48
ἐπίμοχθος, I. 71
ἐπινίκιος : -ίοις, II. 13
ἐπισκήπτω : -ων, V. 42, VII. 41
ἐπίσταμαι : -άμαι, IX. 38
ἐπιτάσσω : ἐπέταξε, fr. 9
ἐπιτίθημι : ἐπέθηκεν, XVI. 113
ἐπιτυγχάνω : -τυχόντι, fr. 32. 3
ἐπίφρων : -ονα, XV. 25
ἐπιχθόνιος : -ίων, IV. 15, V. 5, 54 : -ίοις, V. 96, IX. 14
ἐπιχρίμπτω : -ει, fr. 20. 3
ἐπιχωρίαν, XII. 92
ἐποιχνέω : -εῖς, IX. 1 (?)
ἕπομαι : ἕπεται, I. 60 : ἕπεσθαι, V. 194 : ἕσπεο, X. 115
ἐποπτεύω : -εύοις, Epigr. 1. 3 (fr. 33)
ἔπος : -έων, fr. 4. 2
ἑπτά, XVI. 2
ἑπτάπυλος : -οις, XVIII. 47

ἐραννός: -όν, XVI. 42
ἐρατός: -ᾷ, XVI. 129: -ῶν, X. 43, fr. 3. 12: -οῖσιν, XVI. 110
ἐρατύω: ἐράτυεν, XVI. 12
*ἐρατώνυμος, XVI. 31
ἔργμα: -ατι, XIII. 17
ἔργον, VIII. 82, fr. 11. 1: -α, XVII. 18: -οισ(ιν), IX. 44, XII. 203
ἔρδω: -ων, I. 53, V. 36: -οντα, XIII. 18, XVII. 43: ἐργμένον, XII. 207: ἐρχθέντος, XII. 65
ἐρείπω: ἤρειπον, X. 68
*ἐρειψιλάοις, XII. 167 (?)
*ἐρειψιπύλας: -αν, V. 56
ἐρεμνός: -όν, XVI. 116
ἐρέπτω: -ειν, IV. 16: -έψωνται, VIII. 24: ἐρεφθείς, XII. 70
ἐρεύθω: ἔρευθε, XII. 152
Ἐρίβοια, XVI. 14: -ας, XII. 102
ἐριβρύχας, V. 116
ἐρίζω: -ει, I. 58
ἐρικυδής: ἐρικυδέος, XII. 59: ἐρικυδέα (sing.), 190
ἐρισφάραγος: -ου, V. 20
ἔρνος, V. 87
ἐρύκω: -εν (inf.), XVI. 41
ἔρχομαι: ἐρχομένων, XV. 33: ἤλυθεν, I. 4: ἦλθε(ν), V. 184, VIII. 41, XVII. 16, Epigr. 2. 3 (fr. 34): ἔλθῃ, XVI. 28: ἐλθόντα, XI. 7: -ες, X. 78: -ας, fr. 11. 3 f.
ἔρως: ἐρώτων, VIII. 73
ἐς, I. 12, II. 2, III. 59, 62, V. 12, 61, 106, VIII. 17, 20, 34, X. 48, 55, 72, XI. 4, XII. 143, XIII. 8, XIV. 61, XVI. 63, 73, 76, XIX. 10: probably to be inserted in V. 184 and X. 114. See εἰς
ἐσεῖδον: ἐσιδόντες, XII. 139
ἐσθλός: -όν, V. 129, IX. 47 (ἐσελων A), XIII. 3: -ῶν, IV. 20, V. 198, XVI. 132
ἔσχατος: ἔσχατα, VIII. 41
ἔσω, XVI. 22
ἔτερος, IX. 42, fr. 4. 1: -ου, fr. 4. 1: -αν, XVI. 89
ἔτι, III. 31, IV. 1, V. 174, X. 47, fr. 8. 1
ἔτος, X. 59: -εα, III. 81
ἐτύμως, XII. 228
εὖ, I. 41, 53, III. 94, V. 36, 78, 190, VIII. 72, XII. 65, XIII. 1, 18
*εὐαίνετος: -ε, XVIII. 11
εὔανδρος: -ους, VIII. 17
Εὔβοια: -αν, IX. 34
εὔβουλος, XIV. 37: -ου, p. 437 (I. 7 Blass): -ων, IX. 27
*εὔγυιος: -ων, X. 10
εὐδαίδαλος: -ον, XVI. 88, fr. 11. 3
εὐδαιμονία: -ας, V. 186
εὐδαίμων, V. 55
εὔδενδρος: see ἠϋ-
Εὔδημος, Epigr. 2. 1, (fr. 34)
εὔδματος: -ατον, VIII. 54

εὔδοξος, VII. 9: -ον, XIII. 22: -ων, VIII. 21
*εὐεγχής, XII. 147
εὐειδής: -έος, XII. 102
εὐεργεσία: -αν, I. 47
εὐθαλής: -ές, VIII. 5
εὔθρονος, XV. 3
εὐθύδικος: -ον, V. 6
εὐθυμία: -ᾳ, XVI. 125
εὐθύνω: εὔθυνε, imper., XI. 2
εὐκλεής: -έα (acc.), V. 196
εὔκλεια: -ας, I. 74: Εὐκλείᾳ, XII. 183
εὐκλεΐζω: -ξας, VI. 16
Εὔκλειος: Διὸς Εὐκλείου, I. 6
εὐκτίμενος: -αν, V. 149, X. 122, XIV. 10: εὔκτιμέναν, XIX. 10 (?)
ἔϋκτιτος: -ων, III. 46
*εὐμαρέω: -εῖν, I. 65
εὐμαρέως, V. 195
εὐμενής, fr. 17. 3
εὐνά: -αῖς, VIII. 64 (?), XII. 99 (?)
*εὐναής: -εῖ, VIII. 42: -ῇ, p. 439 (I. 75 Blass)
Εὐνομία, XII. 186: -ας, XIV. 55
Εὐξαντίδας: -αδᾶν, p. 437 (I. 9 f. Blass)?
Εὐξάντιος: -ον, I. 15
Εὐξαντίς: -ίδα, II. 8
εὐοχθος: -ους, fr. 18. 4
εὔπακτος: -ων, XVI. 82
εὔπεπλος: -ον, VIII. 61: -οι, X. 42: -οισι, XIV. 49
εὐπλόκαμος, I. 16: -οις, III. 34
εὐποίητος: -ον, V. 177
εὔπρυμνος: -οις, XII. 150
ἔϋπυργος: -ους, V. 184
εὑρίσκω: εὑρήσει, X. 124
*εὐρυάναξ: -ακτος, V. 19
εὐρυβίας, XV. 31: -βία, X. 52: -βίαν, V. 104
*εὐρυδίνας: -αν, III. 7, V. 38
*εὐρυνεφής: -εῖ, XV. 17
εὐρύς: -εῖαν, XIV. 40: -είας, VIII. 47: -είαις, IX. 17
εὐρυσθενής: -έος, XVIII. 17
εὐρύχορος: -ον, IX. 31
Εὐρωπιάδας, I. 14
εὐρώς, fr. 3. 8
εὐσέβεια: -αν, III. 61
εὐσεβής: -έων, XII. 188
εὖτε, I. 73, III. 25, XII. 118, fr. 13. 1
εὔτυκος, VIII. 4
εὔτυκτος: -ον, XVII. 50
εὐτυχία: -ας, fr. 7. 1
εὔυδρος: -ον, X. 119
εὐφεγγής, VIII. 29: -έας, XVIII. 26
εὐφραίνω: εὔφραινε (imper.), III. 83
εὐφροσύνα, III. 87, IX. 53: -ύναι, X. 12
εὐχά: -άν, XVI. 67: -ᾶς, 65: -άς, VII. 50
εὔχομαι: εὔχοντο, XIV. 46: εὐχομένου, X. 107: εὐξαμένῳ, Epigr. 2. 3 (fr. 34)
εὐώδης: -δεα, XIII. 40
ἐφαμέριος: -ίων, III. 76

ἐφάμερος : -ον, III. 73
ἐφίημι: -σι, XII. 48
ἐφίστημι: ἐπιστάσας, III. 55
ἐχθρός: -ά (neut.), III. 47: ἔχθιστος, 52
Ἔχιδνα: -ας, V. 62
ἔχω: -ει, I. 57, X. 124, XIII. 7, fr. 7. 5:
-ουσιν, III. 63: -ειν, I. 50, XVII. 48:
-ων, fr. 7. 2: -οντα, XVII. 32 : ἔσχεν,
V. 104, XII. 106, XVII. 27, 41: ἕξειν,
XII. 163

Z

ζάθεος: -έαν, II. 7: -έας, V. 10: -έοις,
X. 24
ζεύγνυμι: ζεύξασα, X. 46
Ζεύς, III. 55, V. 200, X. 73, XIV. 51, XVI.
68: Ζεῦ, VII. 48, XVI. 53: Ζηνός, III.
11, 26, V. 20, VIII. 5, IX. 29: Ζηνί,
X. 5, XV. 18: Διός, I. 6, III. 70, V. 79,
VI. 1, X. 52, XII. 58, XV. 28, XVI. 20,
30, 75, 86, XVIII. 17: Δία, V. 178
Ζέφυρος: -ου, V. 28: -ῳ, Epigr. 2. 2
(fr. 34)
ζωά: -άν, III. 82: ἇς, V. 144
ζώω: -η, I. 70: -ειν, 57

H

ἤ, 'or,' (1) single, V. 87, VIII. 36, XII.
169: (2) repeated, 'either'...'or,' X.
34, IX. 39–41: (3) after an interrogative,
ἤ..ἤ..ἤ..; XVII. 5–11: πότερα..ἤ..;
XVII. 35: (4) after εἴτε, XV. 6: εἴτ' οὖν
..ἤ ῥα..ἤ.., XVIII. 33–35.—ἤ, 'than,'
IV. 18, fr. 2. 2
ἦ, (1) affirmative, XII. 54, 71, 147, 157,
XVII. 41 : (2) interrogative, XVII. 5
ᾗ, 'where,' V. 9
ἥβα: -αν, III. 90, V. 154
ἤδη, X. 59, XII. 196
ἡδύς. fr. 17. 5 ; cp. ἀδύς
ἤϊθεος: -οι, XVI. 128: -έων, 43, 93
ἥμερος: ἡμέρα, X. 39
ἡμίθεος: -οι, VIII. 10, X. 62: -έοις, XII.
155
ἥμισυς: -υ, I. 9
ἠπιόφρων: -ον (voc.), XII. 78
ἦρα (=χάριν), X. 21
Ἥρα, V. 89, VIII. 8, X. 44, XVIII. 22:
-αν, X. 107
Ἡρακλῆς: -κλεῖ, VIII. 9
ἥρως, V. 71, XIV. 37, XVI. 47, 73, 94: as
voc., 23 : -ω (acc.), VIII. 56, XII. 104 :
-ωες, X. 81
Ἡσίοδος, V. 192
ἠύδενδρος: -ον, XVI. 80
ἦτε, XII. 87

Θ

θαητός: -όν, X. 14, XII. 115
θάλασσα: -ας, XII. 149: θάλασσαν, 181
θάλεια: -ειαν, III. 89

θαλία: -ίας, XII. 187: -ίαις, XIII. 15
θάλλω: -ουσιν, V. 198: -ουσα, XIV. 58:
τέθαλεν, IX. 40
θάλπω: -ει, fr. 3. 11: θάλπῃσι (subjunct.),
fr. 16. 3
θάμα, XII. 193
θαμβέω: θάμβησεν, V. 84
θάνατος: -ον, V. 134: -ου, XIX. 7: -οιο,
XII. 63
θάπτω: -ομεν (impf.), V. 115
θαρσέω: -εῖ, V. 21
θάρσος, XVI. 50
*θατήρ: -ήρων, IX. 23
θαῦμα, XVI. 123
θαυμάζω: -ασθείς, I. 42
θαυμαστός, V. 71: -όν, VIII. 31
θεά, V. 103: -ᾶς, X. 49, XVI. 9
Θεανώ, XIV. 7
θεῖος, VIII. 3
*θελημός: -όν, XVI. 85
*θελξιεπής: -εῖ, XIV. 48
θελξίμβροτος: -ου, V. 175
θέλω: -ει, XII. 51: -η, V. 135: -οιμι,
XVI. 41 : -ων, V. 169, XVI. 69: -ήσει,
III. 64: cp. ἐθέλω
θέμις, III. 88: Θέμιτος, XIV. 55
θεόδματος: -ον, XI. 7, XII. 163 : -οι,
p. 437 (I. 14 Blass): -ους, X. 58
θεόδοτος: -ους, VII. 50
Θεόκριτος, fr. 14
θεόπομπος: -ον, XVI. 132
θεός, V. 36, 50, X. 34, XIII. 18, XVII. 41 :
-όν, III. 21 (bis): -οί, VIII. 50: -ούς, I.
53: -ῶν, III. 38, 57, V. 95, 179, VIII.
63, 89, X. 121, XVI. 24, 100, 124:
-οῖσ(ιν), IV. 18, XII. 138, XIV. 14, 45,
fr. 3. 3
θεοτίματος: -ον, VIII. 98
θεότιμος: -ον, X. 12
θεοφιλής: -ές, X. 60: -λῆ, III. 69 (?)
θεράπων, V. 14
θερμός: -μάν, IX. 22
Θερμώδων: -οντος, VIII. 43
*θερσιεπής, XII. 199
θεσπέσιος: -ίῳ, XII. 108
Θεσσαλία: -ας, XIII. 40 (?)
Θεσσαλός: -άν, XVII. 54
Θέστιος: -ίου, V. 137
θευπροπία: -αν, IX. 41
Θήβα, IX. 30: -ας, VIII. 54
Θῆβαι: -ας, VIII. 20
θηροσκόπος, X. 107
Θησεύς, XVI. 16: -εῦ, 74: -έα, 99
θιγγάνω: θίγεν, XVI. 12
θίς: θῖνα, XII. 149
θνάσκω: θνάσκοντες, XII. 166: θάνῃ, I. 73:
θανεῖν, III. 47
θνατός, I. 56: -όν, III. 78: -ῶν, III. 61,
XVII. 21, fr. 21. 1: -οῖσ(ιν), I. 66, III.
51, 93, V. 160, IX. 52, X. 7, XII. 45,
XIV. 52, XVIII. 45, fr. 3. 1, 9. 1, 20. 1

θοίνα: -as, fr. 18. 2
θοός: θοάν, XVI. 55: θοούς, V. 129: -άs,
   III. 3
θοῶs, XIV. 59, XVI. 98
θράσοs: -ει, XVI. 63; cp. θάρσοs
θρασυκάρδιοs, XIX. 5: -ον, XII. 106
θρασυμέμνων: -ονοs, V. 69
θρασυμήδηs: -εα, XV. 15
θραύς: -ύν, XVII. 39
*θρασύχειρ: θρασύχειροs, II. 4
θροέω: θρόησε, III. 9
θρῴσκω: -ουσα, XII. 90: θόρεν, XVI. 94
θυγάτηρ, V. 124, XVI. 34: θύγατερ, VII. 1,
   XII. 77, fr. 23. 2: θύγατρες, I. 28, X.
   84: -ῶν, V. 167, VIII. 50: -άσι, III. 35
θυμάρμενοs: -ον, XVI. 71
θυμόs, XVI. 82, fr. 17. 3: -όν, I. 33, 69,
   III. 83, V. 80, IX. 45, XII. 220, XVI. 23,
   fr. 7. 2, 16. 3
θυσία: -αισι, V. 101
θύω: θύεν (inf.), XV. 18: θύσω, X. 104

I

ἰαίνω: -ει, XII. 220: ἰανθείς, XVI. 131
ἰάπτω: -εται, fr. 7. 5
ἰατορία: -ᾳ, I. 39
'Ιάων: -όνων, XVI. 3: cp. Ἴων
Ἴδα: -as, V. 66, XVI. 30
ἰδέ (= ἠδέ), XIII. 5 (?)
*ἰδρώεις: -εντα, XII. 57
ἱερόν (subst.): ἱερά, III. 15
ἱερόs: -άν, II. 2, IX. 34: -ᾶν, XVII. 1
'Ιέρων, III. 64, 92: -ωνα, IV. 3, V. 16:
   -ωνοs, III. 4: -ωνι, V. 49, 185, 197
ἴζω: ἐσσαμένων, X. 120
ἵημι: ἵησι, fr. 13. 2: ἱεῖσαι, X. 56: ἵεται,
   V. 48: ἵετο, XVI. 90
'Ιθακήσιος: -ον, fr. 25
ἰθύς: -εῖαν, XIV. 54
ἰθύω: ἰθύσαs, IX. 51
ἱκάνω: ἵκανεν, X. 96: ἵξον, XII. 149
ἵκελοι, fr. 19. 3
ἱκνέομαι: -εῖσθαι, fr. 21. 3: ἵκετο, VIII. 39,
   XV. 16: ἵκῃ, XV. 8: ἱκέσθαι, X. 30
ἵκριον: -ων, XVI. 83
ἵλεωs: -ῳ, X. 15
Ἴλιον: -ου, XII. 115
ἱμείρω: -ει, I. 62
*ἱμεράμπυξ: -πυκοs, XVI. 9
*ἱμερόγυιος: -ου, XII. 137
ἱμερόεις: -εν, X. 118: -εντα, Epigr. 1. 2
   (fr. 33)
ἱμερτός: -άν, I. 13
ἵνα, (1) 'in order that,' IX. 11, p. 437
   (I. 5 Blass): (2) 'where,' X. 79
Ἴναχος: -ου, XVIII. 18
ἰοβλέφαρος: -οι, XVIII. 5: -ων, VIII. 3
'Ιόλα: -αν, XV. 27
ἰόπλοκος: -ον, VIII. 72: -οι, XVI. 37: -ων,
   III. 71

ἰός (' arrow '): ἰόν, V. 75
ἰοστέφανος: -ον, III. 2: -ου, XII. 122: -ων,
   V. 3
ἱππευτάς: -αί, XII. 160
ἵππιος: -ον, XVIII. 15: -ου, XVI. 99
ἱππόβοτος: -ον, X. 80
*ἱπποδίνητος: -ων, V. 2
ἱππόνικος: -ον, XIII. 22 (?)
ἵππος: -ους, III. 4, XIX. 9, p. 437 (I. 19
   Blass): -ων, IV. 6, V. 44
ἱπποτρόφος: -ον, X. 114
*ἱππώκης: -εος, X. 101
ἰσάνεμος: -ους, XIX. 9
'Ισθμιονίκας: -αν, IX. 26
'Ισθμιόνικος: -ον, I. 46
Ἴσθμιος: -ίαν, XVII. 17: -ίας, p. 437
   (I. 6 Blass)
'Ισθμός: -όν, VII. 40: -οῦ, II. 7
ἰσόθεος: -έων, XII. 156
ἰσόρροπος: -ον (neut.), IV. 11 f. (?)
ἴσος, V. 46: ἴσον, I. 62, fr. 2. 2
ἵστημι: ἵσταν (impf.), X. 112: ἔστα, IX.
   23, fr. 18. 1: στᾶθι, V. 80: στᾶσον, 177:
   στασάμεθα, V. 112: σταθείς, XII. 105,
   XVI. 84: σταθέντων, III. 18
ἱστίον, XII. 131
ἱστός: -οί, fr. 3. 7
ἵστωρ: -ορες, VIII. 44
ἰσχυρός: -όν, XVII. 38
ἰσχύς: -ύν, XII. 75: -ύι, V. 22, XVII. 20
ἴσχω: -ουσι, V. 24: ἴσχε (imper.), XVI. 23:
   ἴσχεν (inf.), 88
'Ιτωνία: -as, fr. 11. 2
'Ιφικλος: -ον, V. 128
'Ιώ, XVIII. 41
Ἴων: -ες, fr. 26: -ων, XVII. 2; cp. 'Ιάων

K

Κάδμος, XVIII. 48
κᾶδος: -έων, XVIII. 36
καθαρός: -όν, fr. 27
καί, passim (occurring about 70 times;
   cp. δέ and τε): in crasis, κάμέ, XVI. 33:
   κηΰνυκτον, XVII. 50: χῶτι, III. 81
καιρός: -ῷ, fr. 21. 2
καίω: καῖε, V. 140
κακομάχανος: -οι, XVII. 8
κακόποτμος, V. 138
κακός: -όν (nom. neut.), fr. 2. 2: -ῷ (neut.),
   XVII. 44
καλέω: -ει, II. 11: κέκληται, VII. 9
καλλίζωνος, V. 89
καλλικέρα (fem.): -αν, XVIII. 24. Cp.
   ὑψικέρα
Καλλιόπα, V. 176: -as, XVIII. 13
καλλιπάραος, XIX. 4
*καλλιρόας: -αν, X. 26, 96
καλλίχορος: -ον, V. 106: -ῳ, X. 32
καλός, fr. 14: -όν, VIII. 82, 101: -ῶν,
   I. 146, II. 6, III. 96, V. 51: κᾱλ-,

κρατερός: -όν, XVII. 40: -άν, XII. 143:
-âς, X. 20: -ᾷ, V. 21
κρατέω: -εῦσαν, VI. 7: -ήσας, VI. 15
Κρεμμυῶν: -ῶνος, XVII. 24
Κρέουσα: -ας, XVII. 15
κρέων: κρέουσαν, III. 1
Κρής: -τῶν, I. 5
Κρητικός: -όν, XVI. 4
κρίνω: -εις, X. 6: -ει, V. 131: -ειν, VII. 6:
-εῖ, XVI. 46
Κρίσα: -ας, IV. 14 (?)
κριτός: -οί, VIII. 11
Κροῖσος: -ον, III. 28
Κρονίδας, I. 45, X. 73, XVI. 77: -αν, V.
178: -α (gen.), IX. 29, XVII. 21
Κρόνιος, XVI. 65
κρόταφος: -ον, XVI. 30
κρύπτω: -ειν, III. 14: κρυφθεῖσα, XII. 177
κτείνω: ἔκτανεν, V. 89: κτανεῖν, XVIII. 31
κτίζω: -ειν, X. 72
κτύπος, fr. 3. 9
*κυανανθής: -εῖ, XII. 124
κυάνεος: -ον, XII. 64
κυανοπλόκαμος: -ου, V. 33, VIII. 53: -οι,
X. 83
κυανόπρωρα, XVI. 1
κυανῶπις: -ιδας, XII. 160
κυβερνάω: -ᾷς, XVI. 22: -ᾷ, XII. 160:
-âται, XIII. 10
κυβερνήτας, XI. 1: -αν, V. 47
κῦδος, I. 50, VI. 3, IX. 17
κυδρός: -οτέρᾳ, I. 54
κύκλος: -ον, VIII. 30
Κύκλωψ: -πες, X. 77
κύκνος: -ῳ, XV. 6
κύλιξ: -ίκων, fr. 16. 3
κῦμα: -ατα, V. 26: -ασιν, XII. 125
κυνέα: -αν, XVII. 50
Κύπρις: -δος, V. 175, XVI. 10, fr. 16. 4
κυρέω: -ρῆσαι, III. 8
κύων: κύνα, V. 60
Κωκυτός: -οῦ, V. 64
κῶμος: -οι, X. 12: -ων, fr. 3. 5: -οις, VIII.
103

Λ

λαγχάνω: -νειν, IV. 20: ἔλαχεν, I. 56:
λάχε(ν), 70, VI. 2: λάχῃσι, XVIII. 3:
λαχών, I. 41, III. 11: λαχόντας, X. 70:
λαχοῖσαν, XVIII. 13: λέλογχεν, XII.
187: λελογχώς, IX. 39
λάϊνος: -ον, fr. 18. 1
λαῖς: -δος, XV. 17
λαιψηρός: -ῶν, VII. 6
Λάκαινα: -αν, XVII. 50
Λάμνιος: -ίαν, XVII. 55
λαμπρός: -όν, III. 54
λάμπω: -ει, III. 17, VII. 43: λάμπε
(impf.), XVI. 104, 123: λαμπόμενον, V.
72: -μένα, IX. 3 (?)
Λάμπων, XII. 226: -ωνος, 68

λανθάνω: λαθεῖν, XVIII. 27
Λαομέδων: -οντος, XII. 142
λαός: -ῷ, XII. 231: -ούς, X. 67: -ῶν, I. 9,
VIII. 35, X. 117
λαοφόνος: -ον, XII. 120
λάρναξ: -ακος, V. 141
Λατοΐδας, III. 39
Λατώ: -οῦς, V. 124, X. 16, 98
Λάχων, VI. 1: Λάχωνα, VII. 11
λέγω: -ει, XVII. 18, 32, 47, fr. 29: -ουσι,
V. 57: -ειν, III. 67, V. 164
λείπω: -ει, I. 73: λεῖπον (3rd plur.), XII.
116: λίπον, V. 172: λίπεν, I. 9: λιπεῖν,
XV. 13: λιπών, I. 44: λιποῦσα, XVIII.
15: λιπόντες, II. 8, X. 60, 81, XII. 141:
λιποῦσαι, X. 57: λείπεται, VIII. 87, XII.
64
λείριος: -ων, XVI. 95
λεπτόθριξ: -ιχα, V. 28
*λεπτόπρυμνος: -ον, XVI. 119
λευκός: -όν, XVII. 3: -âν, XVI. 13
λευκώλενος, VIII. 7, XVI. 54: -ε, V. 176:
-ον, XV. 27: -ου, V. 99
λέχος: -ει, VIII. 56, XVI. 30
λέων: -οντα, VIII. 9: -οντος, I. 32: -οντι,
XII. 47
λήγω: λῆξεν, XII. 122, 128
λῃστάς: -αί, XVII. 8
*λιγυκλαγγής: -ῆ, V. 73: -εῖς, XIII. 14
λιγύφθογγος: -ον, IX. 10: -οι, V. 23
λίθος (fem.), fr. 10. 1
λικμάω: -μήσῃ, Epigr. 2. 4 (fr. 34)
λινόστολος: -όλων, XVIII. 43
λιπαρόζωνος: -ων, VIII. 49
λιπαρός: -ά, VII. 1: -όν, XV. 29: -άν, V.
169, X. 38: -âs, p. 437 (I. 13 Blass):
-ῶν, I. 47
λίσσομαι: -όμενος, V. 100: λίσσοντο, X. 69
λόγος, XIV. 44: -ον, XIV. 31: -ων, XIV.
47
λογχωτός: -ά, fr. 3. 8
Λοξίας, XII. 148: Λοξίᾳ, III. 66
Λοῦσοι: -ον, X. 96
λόχος: -ον, XVIII. 32 (?)
Λυγκεύς: -έος, X. 75
λυγρός: -αῖς, X. 68
Λυδία: -ας, III. 24
Λύδιος: -ία, fr. 10. 1
Λύκιος: -ίων, XII. 147
Λυκόρμας: -ᾳ, XV. 34
λύσσα: -ας, X. 102
*Λυταῖος: -ου, XVII. 21
λύω: -ει, fr. 16. 7: ἔλυσεν, I. 43, XII. 113

M

Μαῖα: -ας, XVIII. 25
μαίνομαι: -οιτο, XII. 119
μάκαρ: -ρων, X. 121
Μακελώ, p. 439 (I. 73 Blass)

μακράν (adv.), IX. 51
μάν, XII. 182
μανία: -âν, X. 109
μᾶνις: μᾶνιν, XII. 111
Μαντινεύς: -έες, fr. 6. 2
μανύω: -ύει, fr. 10. 1, 33: -ῦον, IX. 14
μαρμαίρω: -ουσιν, fr. 16. 9
μαρμαρυγά: -αῖς, III. 17
μάρναμαι: -άμεθα, v. 125 (impf.): -αντο, XII. 151
Μάρπησσα: -αν, XIX. 6
ματεύω: -ει, IX. 35
μάτηρ, v. 138: ματρί, III. 50
μάτρως: -ωας, v. 129
μάχα: -αν, XII. 117: -as (gen.), I. 34, II. 4, XVII. 59: -αις, X. 68, XIII. 13
μεγάθυμος, XII. 195
*μεγαίνητος: -νητε, III. 64: -ους, I. 44
*μεγαλοκλεής: μεγαλοκλέας, VII. 49
*μεγαλόκολπος: -ου, fr. 31. 2
μεγαλοσθενής: -σθενές (voc.), XVI. 52
*μεγαλοῦχος: -ον, XVI. 23
μέγαρον, XVI. 100: -ων, III. 46: -οις, v. 119, 165
μέγας: -a, XII. 155: -αν, XVI. 98: -άλου, v. 79: -άλα, fr. 3. 1: -άλαν, IX. 49, XII. 79: -άλας (gen.), v. 24: -άλων, I. 63, XIV. 52: -άλαισιν, XII. 157: μεῖζον, fr. 2. 2: μέγιστον, I. 49, III. 19, fr. 16. 11: -αν, XVIII. 45: -ου, VI. 1, VIII. 55: -ᾱ, III. 61
μεγασθενής, XVI. 67
*μεγιστοάνασσα, XVIII. 21
*μεγιστοπάτωρ, v. 199
μείγνυμι: μειγνύμεν, IX. 65: μειχθεῖσα, XII. 99: μιγεῖσα, XVI. 31
μειλίχιος: -οις, X. 90
μείρομαι: εἱμάρθαι, XIII. 1
μείς: μηνί, I. 16: μῆνες, VII. 2 (?): μῆνας, X. 93
μείων, I. 63
*μελαγκευθής: -ές, III. 55 (?), fr. 25 (?)
μέλαθρον: -ων, X. 44
*μελαμφαρής: -εῖ, III. 13
μελάμφυλλος: -ου, VIII. 33
μέλας: -αινα, XII. 153: -αν, XVI. 17
Μελέαγρος, v. 93: -ου, 77, 171
μελέτα: -αν, XII. 191
μελίγλωσσος: -ου, III. 97: -ων, fr. 3. 2
μέλισσα: -αν, IX. 10
μελίφρων, fr. 3. 10: -ονος, p. 439 (I. 50 Blass)
μέλλω: -ει, v. 164: μέλλον (part.), VIII. 96, IX. 45: -οντος, VIII. 14: -όντων, fr. 7. 4: ἔμελλε, III. 30: μέλλε (impf.), XV. 19: μέλλον (impf.), XII. 164
μέλος, XIX. 3: -έων, XVIII. 2, p. 437 (I. 1 Blass)
μέλπω: -ουσι, XII. 94: -ετε, 190 (imper.)
μέλω: -ει, v. 92: -ειν, fr. 3. 5
Μέμφις: -ιν, fr. 22. 1

μέν, I. 30, III. 15, 63, 85, 90, v. 3, 37, 144, IX. 47, X. 92, XII. 114, 203, XIII. 1, XVI. 1, 24, 75, XVIII. 37, fr. 7. 3, 10. 1, 12, 19. 1, 24. 1
Μένανδρος: -ου, XII. 192
μενέκτυπος: -ον, XVI. 1
Μενέλαος, XIV. 48: -ῳ, 6
μενεπτόλεμος, XVI. 73: -ου, v. 170: -οις, 126
μένος, III. 54
μέριμνα, III. 57, X. 86, XVIII. 11: -αι, I. 69, XVIII. 34: -as (acc.), fr. 16. 6: -âν, v. 7
μέρος, III. 71
μέσος: -ῳ, XIV. 53: -οισι, fr. 32. 1
μετά, with gen., X. 123: with dat., v. 30
Μεταπόντιον, X. 10, 116
μεταπρέπω: μετέπρεπεν, v. 68
μή, III. 13, 68, v. 36, 81, 160, X. 27, XII. 199, XVII. 44
μηδέ, v. 161
μήδομαι: μήσεται, XVII. 42: ἐμήσατο, XV. 30: μησάμενον, IV. 16
μηλόβοτος: -ους, v. 166
*μηλοδαΐκτας: -αν, VIII. 6
μηλοθύτας: -αν, VII. 39
μῆλον: -a, v. 109: -ων, X. 111, XVII. 9
μηλοτρόφος: -ον, X. 95
μήν, see μείς
μῆρα, fr. 3. 4
μῆτις: -ιν, XV. 25, XVI. 29, 52
μιμνάσκω: μεμνᾶσθαι, XVII. 58
μίμνω: -ειν, III. 31: -οντα, XII. 135
μιν, X. 111; cp. νιν
μινύθω: -ει, III. 90 (? μινύνθη), XII. 209
†μίνυνθα, v. 151 (? μινύνθη)
Μίνως, I. 3: -ωϊ, XVI. 8, 68
μίτρα: -αισιν, XII. 196
μοῖρα (fate), v. 121, 143, VIII. 15, XVI. 27, 89: -αν ('portion'), IV. 20, v. 51
Μοῖσα: -âν, v. 4, fr. 27 A 2; cp. Μοῦσα
μολ-: μόλε(ν), XVI. 101, 122: μόλοι, v. 110: μολών, III. 30: μολοῦσα, XIII. 4
μονορχέω: -ήσειν, fr. 16. 8
μόνος, fr. 14: -ου, VIII. 46
*μουνοπάλα: -αν, XI. 8
μοῦνος: -ον, III. 80, IV. 15, v. 156, XVII. 35: -ῳ, fr. 15. 1
Μοῦσα, II. 11, III. 92, XIV. 47, fr. 17. 4: -âν, III. 71, v. 193, VIII. 3, IX. 11, XVIII. 4, Epigr. 1. 3 (fr. 33): cp. Μοῖσα
μῦθος: -ον, XIV. 39: -οισι, X. 90
μύριος: -ία, v. 31, VIII. 48, XVIII. 1: -ίαι, IX. 38, XIII. 8, fr. 24. 2: -ίᾱ, fr. 7. 3: -ίας, X. 126: -ίων, III. 41, XII. 196
μύρω: -ομένοις, v. 163
μυχός: -οῖς, IV. 14
μῶμος, XII. 202

N

ναίω: -εις, X. 116: -ειν, VIII. 99: ναῖον (impf.), X. 61, 80
ναός: -όν, XV. 12, fr. 11. 3: -οῦ, III. 19; cp. νηός
νάπα: -αις, XVII. 23
νασιώτας: -αν, VIII. 77 (?)
νασιῶτις: -ιν, IX. 10
νᾶσος: -ον, II. 8, IX. 35, XI. 6, XII. 75 (?), 182: -ου, V. 11, p. 437 (I. 14 Blass): -οιο, *ib.* (I. 9 Bl.)
ναυβάτας: -αι, XVI. 48
ναῦς, XVI. 1: νᾶα, 89, 119: νᾶες, fr. 16. 11: νᾶας, XII. 74: ναυσί, I. 5, XII. 150
νεανίας: -αι, VI. 9: -αις, fr. 13. 3
νεβρός, XII. 87
νεῖκος, X. 64
Νεῖλος: -ον, XVIII. 40, fr. 22. 2: -ου, VIII. 41
Νεμέα: -έαν, VII. 40: -έᾳ, VIII. 82, XI. 8, XII. 67
Νεμεαῖος: -αίον, VIII. 4
νέμω: νείμῃς, VII. 8: νείμας, I. 12: νέμονται, IX. 33
*νεόκριτος: -ον, p. 475 (fr. of VII.?)
*νεόκροτος: -ον, V. 48
νεόκτιτος: -ῳ, XVI. 126
νέος: -ον (neut.), XVII. 3, 16: -οι, XII. 190, XVI. 129: -ων, X. 11, 12, 91, XVII. 14: -οις, fr. 3. 5
Νέσσος: -ου, XV. 35
νευρά: -άν, V. 73
νέφος, III. 55, XII. 64, fr. 20. 3
νηέω: ναήσατο (Dor.), III. 33
νῆις: νῆιν, V. 174
νηός: νηόν, Epigr. 2. 1 (fr. 34): cp. ναός
Νηρεύς: -έος, XVI. 102: Νηρέος, I. 8
Νηρηΐς: -ῆδος, XII. 123: -ΐδες, XVI. 38
νίζω: νιψάμενος, X. 97
νίκα: -αν, II. 5, V. 49, VIII. 82, X. 39, XII. 190: -ας (gen.), VI. 11, VII. 9, VIII. 67, IX. 52: -ας (acc.), VII. 47: -ᾶν, XII. 205
Νίκα, X. 1, XI. 5, Epigr. 1. 1 (fr. 33): -ας, V. 33, IX. 15: -ᾳ, III. 5
νικάω: -ᾶν, XII. 205: -άσας, V. 183: -άσαντα, 40: -άσαντι, VIII. 25
νιν (sing.), III. 92, IV. 14 (?), V. 24, 43, 78, 159, VIII. 26, IX. 27, X. 15, 22, 86, 89, XII. 230, XIV. 56, XV. 31, XVI. 84, 91, 112, XVIII. 27, 42: (plur.), VIII. 15, p. 439 (I. 76 Blass).—Cp. μιν
νόημα, X. 54
νόος: -ον, V. 95: -ῳ, IV. 9, V. 8
νόσος: -ων, I. 60: cp. νοῦσος
νόσφιν, I. 60
νότος: -ου, XII. 130
νοῦσος: νούσων, fr. 19. 2
νῦν, V. 4, 31, VI. 10, VIII. 25, IX. 9, X. 10, 37, XI. 3, XIII. 20, XVI. 55, fr. 4. 1

νυν (enclitic), XVIII. 8
νύξ: νύκτα, fr. 7. 4: -ός, VIII. 29, 90, XII. 127, 175: -ας, XVIII. 28
Νύξ: Νυκτός, VII. 2, fr. 23. 1
νωμάω: νωμᾶται, V. 26

Ξ

*ξανθοδοδερκής, VIII. 12
ξανθόθριξ: -τριχα, V. 37
ξανθός: -άν, III. 56, VIII. 24, IX. 15: -ᾶς, X. 51, XII. 136: -ᾷ, V. 92, fr. 3. 4: -αί, XIX. 2
ξεῖνος: -ᾶ, X. 85: -ων, I. 40: -οισι, XI. 5
ξενία: -αν, XII. 224
ξένος, V. 11
ξεστός: -ούς, XVII. 49
ξίφος, XVII. 48: -εα, fr. 3. 8
ξουθός: -αῖσι, V. 17
ξύλινος: -ον, III. 49
ξύνειμι: -έασιν, fr. 26
ξυνός: -όν, IX. 6, 12

O

ὁ: (1) As definite article, *passim.* (2) As demonstrative pron., always the first word of the sentence, and (a) often followed by δ(έ): ὁ δέ, XVI. 71: τοῦ δ', X. 106: τῷ δ', V. 76, 111, XVI. 81: τὸν δ(έ), V. 71, 93, 170, X. 85: οἱ δ', IX. 44, and τοὶ δέ, V. 149, fr. 18. 2: ταὶ δ(έ), X. 110, XII. 91: τὰ (nom.) δέ, V. 91: ταῖσιν δέ, V. 68, X. 53: but also (b) with asyndeton, τᾷ ποτ', X. 40: τάν, V. 169: τάς, X. 42: τῶν, XII. 100. (3) As relative pron., in the oblique cases: τοῦ, VIII. 40: τόν, V. 142, VIII. 12, XVI. 115: τάν, XII. 193, 226, 228: τῶν, XII. 67, 168: τοῖσιν, I. 11, V. 135
*ὀβριμοδερκής: -εῖ, XV. 20
*ὀβριμόσπορος: -ου, XVIII. 32
ὅδε: τόνδε, I. 70, XVI. 60, Ep. 2. 1 (fr. 34): τάνδε, XII. 203: τᾷδε, VIII. 89: τάδε, IV. 15, V. 160, 163, 191, XVI. 74: τοῖσδε, fr. 13. 3
ὁδός, fr. 7. 1: -όν, XVI. 89, XVIII. 13: -οῦ, IX. 52
ὀδούς: -όντι, V. 108
ὀδύρομαι: -όμενον, fr. 8. 1
Ὀδυσσεύς: -εῖ, XIV. 5
ὅθεν, XVIII. 46
ὅθι, VIII. 6
οἱ, dat. pron. 3rd pers. (=αὐτῷ), I. 19, 45, X. 110, XVI. 18, 37, 115, XVII. 46, XIX. 9, Ep. 2. 3 (fr. 34)
οἶδα, IX. 49: οἶδε, III. 13, VIII. 53: εἰδώς, V. 78, IX. 42: εἴσεαι, XVI. 64
οἰκεῖος: -ων, I. 57
οἰκέω: -εῦσι, VIII. 43
οἰκίζω: ᾤκισσαν, VIII. 51

'Οϊκλείδας, VIII. 16
οἶκος : -οι, fr. 16. 9
οἰκτίρω : -οντα, V. 158
Οἰνείδας : -αις, IX. 18
Οἰνεύς, V. 97 : -έος, 120: -ῆος, 166
οἶνος, fr. 17. 5
οἶος : -ον, XV. 30: -αν, XII. 46 : οἷα (adv.),
    XVII. 36: οἷά τε, V. 65: -αισιν, XVI.
    120
ὀϊστός : -όν, V. 82
Οἰχαλία : -αν, XV. 14
οἴχομαι : ᾤχετο, I. 12
ὄλβιος, V. 50, fr. 28: -ον, III. 8: -αν,
    XI. 4: -οιο, XVI. 102: -ων, XIV. 56:
    -αις, XVIII. 10
ὄλβος, fr. 20. 2: -ου, III. 92: -ων, 22
ὄλεθρος : -ον, V. 139
*ὀλιγοσθενέω : -ων, V. 139
ὀλκάς : -άδα, XV. 2
ὄλλυμι : ὤλεσε, V. 121: ὤλεσσεν, XIV. 63
ὀλολύζω : ὠλόλυξαν, XVI. 127
ὀλοός : -οά, V. 121
'Ολυμπία : -ᾳ, VI. 6, VII. 3
*'Ολυμπιοδρόμος : -ους, III. 3
'Ολυμπιονίκα : -ας, IV. 17
'Ολύμπιος : -ον, V. 179
"Ολυμπος : -ῳ, X. 4
ὁμιλέω : -εῖ, I. 51
ὅμιλος : -ον, IX. 24: -ῳ, I. 5
ὄμμα, XVI. 18: -άτων, 95, XVII. 54: -ασι,
    XVIII. 19
ὀμφά, XIII. 13
ὀμφαλός : -όν, IV. 4
ὀξύς : -εῖαν, XII. 117
ὀπάζω : ὄπαζε (imper.), XVI. 132: ὤπασεν,
    XIV. 60: ὄπασσας, VII. 50
ὄπα, XVII. 30
ὀπάων : -οσιν, XVII. 35
ὀπίσσω, XII. 53
ὁπλότερος : -ον, X. 71
ὁπότε, I. 143: ὅππστε, XII. 110
ὁράω : ὁρᾷς, fr. 14: ὄψεαι, III. 79
ὀργά : -αί, fr. 24. 1
ὀρέγω : ὄρεξεν, V. 114
ὀρθόδικος : -ου, X. 9, XIII. 23
ὀρθός : -ᾶς, X. 27: ὀρθόν, IV. 11
ὀρθῶς, I. 72, IV. 6
ὀρίνω : ὤρίνατο, XII. 112
ὄριον : -α, XVII. 6
ὁρμά : -άν, IX. 20, XII. 156
ὁρμαίνω : -ει, fr. 16. 12: -οντα, XII. 106
ὁρμάω : -ᾷ, XVII. 41
ὄρνιξ : -ιχες, V. 22
ὄρνυμι : ὦρσαν, XII. 145: ὄρνυο, XVI. 76:
    ὀρνύμενον, V. 45 : -οι, XIV. 41
ὄρος, X. 55
ὄρος, fr. 7. 1: ὅρον, V. 144
ὀρούω : ὄρουσε, XVI. 84
*ὀρσίαλος : -ῳ, XV. 19
*ὀρσιβάκχας : -αν, XVIII. 49
*ὀρσίμαχος : -ου, XIV. 3

ὄρχος : -ους, V. 108
ὅς, relative pron., III. 11, XIII. 23, XIV.
    51, XVII. 20, XVIII. 3, fr. 4. 11, 7. 3:
    ἅ (fem.), VIII. 19, IX. 50, XII. 97, 187,
    XVI. 112, XVIII. 49: ὅν, V. 193: ἇς, IV.
    8: ᾧ, VII. 8: οἵ, VIII. 23, IX. 33, 34, XII.
    114: ἅς, VIII. 50. Also ὅς τε (epic),
    XII. 105, XVII. 39 (?)
ὅς, possessive pron.: ὅν, V. 47
ὅσιος : -ον, XVI. 21: -ιᾶ, III. 83
ὅσος : -οι, III. 63: -αι, VIII. 63: -ᾰ, II. 6.
    Also ὅσσος : -ον, I. 70: -ᾰ, VI. 4,
    IX. 15
ὅστις, III. 67 f., V. 110, X. 124: ὅτι, III.
    57, V. 164, IX. 6 : ὄντινα, I. 68 : ἅντινα,
    IX. 37 : ᾧτινι, V. 50
ὅταν, XII. 63, XVI. 27, p. 439 (I. 37
    Blass)
ὅτε, X. 95, XII. 121, XV. 34, XVIII. 19,
    50, XIX. 4
ὅτι, II. 4, III. 61, 79, 81, VI. 15, XV. 27
ὀτρύνω : ὤτρυνε, VIII. 35, XII. 146
οὐ, οὐκ, οὐχ : I. 36, III. 30, 87, 88, 90, 95,
    V. 24, 53, 84, 122, 129, 136, 162, VIII.
    15, 53, X. 22, XII. 175, XIV. 30, 52,
    XVI. 41, 81, XVII. 43, fr. 3. 9, 11. 1, 12,
    14, 17. 1, 20, 32. 1
οὐδέ, V. 25, XVIII. 25, fr. 3. 10, 4. 2, 11. 1
οὐδείς, fr. 28 : -έν, I. 65, III. 57, XVI. 118,
    fr. 19. 3
οὐδός : -όν, fr. 18. 1
οὐκέτι, XVI. 11, 21
*οὔλιος = οὖλος : -ιον, XVII. 53
οὖλος : -αις, XVI. 113
οὖν, XVIII. 29, 37
οὔπω, V. 43
Οὐρανία, XV. 3 : -ας, V. 13, VI. 11
οὐρανός : -οῦ, XVI. 55
οὔριος : -ία, XII. 130
οὖρος : -ον, XVI. 87
οὔτε .. οὔτε, XVIII. 26 ff.: οὔτε .. οὔτε ..
    οὔτε, fr. 20. 2: οὐ .. οὔτε .. οὔτε (instead
    of οὐδέ), fr. 17. 1 f.
οὔτις, III. 63, VII. 44
οὗτοι, V. 84
οὗτος : τοῦτο, III. 83: τοῦτον, XVII. 31 :
    ταῦτα, V. 136, XVII. 30
ὀφθαλμός : -όν, p. 437 (I. 7 Blass) : -οῖσιν,
    IX. 7
ὄφρα, XVII. 42, Ep. 2. 3 (fr. 34)
ὀφρύς : -ύων, XVI. 17
ὄχθα : -αισιν, VII. 49
ὄψ : ὀπί, XVI. 129, p. 439 (I. 77 Blass)

Π

παγκρατής, X. 44, XVI. 24, fr. 10. 2
παγκράτιον : παγκρατίου, XII. 56
πάγνυμι : πᾶξαι, X. 88
πάγξενος or -ξεινος : παγξείνου, XII. 95 (?) :
    -ένῳ, X. 28

πᾷ, IX. 47
παιανίζω: παιάνιξαν, XVI. 129
παιδικός: -οί, fr. 3. 12
παιηων: -όνων, XV. 8
παῖς, VII. 46: παῖδα, V. 146, 156, X. 14,
   32, XII. 103, XVII. 56, XVIII. 41: -δί,
   VIII. 103, XVI. 70: -δες, V. 36, XIV. 56:
   -δας, I. 43, X. 69, XIV. 63: παῖδας,
   p. 475 (fr. of VII.): -δεσσι, XIV. 39
Πακτωλός, III. 45
πάλα: -ας, VIII. 36, X. 21
πάλαι, fr. 4. 1
παλαιός: -οῦ, VIII. 64
παλαίστρα: -αν, XVII. 26
πάλιν, VIII. 16, XVI. 81
παλίντροπον, X. 54
Πάλλας: -αντος, Ep. 1. 1 (fr. 33)
Παλλάς: -άδος, XIV. 3: -άδι, V. 92
παμμαχία: -ιᾶν, XII. 76
πάμπαν, p. 439 (I. 81 Blass)
*πάμφθερσις, fr. 20. 2
πανδαμάτωρ, XII. 205
πανδερκής: -έα, XVI. 70
Πανδίων: -ονος, XVI. 15, XVII. 15
πάνδωρος, fr. 20. 4
Πανέλλανες: -ων, XII. 198
*πανθᾱλής, XII. 229
πανθᾱλής (Dor. for πανθηλ-): -έων, XII.
   69
Πανθείδας: -α, II. 14: Πανθείδᾳ, I. 37
*πάννικος: -οιο, X. 21
παντᾷ, V. 31, VIII. 48, XIV. 44
παντοδαπός: -ῶν, IV. 19
πάντοθεν, XVIII. 20
παντοῖος: -αισι, XII. 49
παρά, with gen., III. 11, XIII. 1 (?), 10
   (πάρ), XV. 35, XVIII. 3, 13: with dat.,
   III. 20, V. 64, VIII. 84, XII. 150 (παραί):
   with acc., III. 6, IV. 4, V. 38, VIII. 39,
   IX. 29, X. 26, 119, XII. 58, XV. 12,
   XVI. 119, XVIII. 39, fr. 7. 4, 11. 3,
   15. 2
παραπλήξ: -ῆγι, X. 45
παρατρέπω: -τρέψαι, V. 95
παράφρων: see πάρφρων
πάρεδρος: -ον, X. 51
πάρειμι: -εστι(ν), III. 67, IV. 14 (?),
   XVIII. 1, fr. 17. 1
παρηῖς: -ίδων, XVI. 13
παρθενικά: -ᾶς, XVI. 11
παρθένιος: -ίᾳ, X. 47
παρθένος: -ῳ, XV. 21: -οι, III. 50, XII. 94
παρίημι: παρέντα, III. 88
παρίστημι: παρισταμένα, X. 5
πάροιθε(ν), III. 19, VI. 4
πάρος, XI. 4
πάρφρων: -ονος, X. 103
πᾶς: πᾶν, VII. 43: πάντα, V. 55, XIV. 38,
   XVII. 45, fr. 28: πᾶσαν, VIII. 40:
   παντί, I. 58, XII. 231: πάντων, I. 64,
   XVI. 66, Epigr. 2. 2 (fr. 34): πάντεσ-

σι(ν), XII. 81, 203, XVI. 123, fr. 9. 1:
   πᾶσι(ν), XIV. 54, fr. 16. 8
πᾶσις: πάσι, IX. 42 (?)
πασιφανής, XII. 176
πασσυδίᾳ, XII. 141
πατήρ, V. 101, X. 96, XIV. 37, XVI. 78:
   πάτερ, XVI. 53: πατέρα, X. 51: πατρός,
   XVI. 63, 99, 109
πάτρα: πάτραν, X. 30 (?)
πάτριος: -ίων, I. 35
πατρίς: -ίδος, p. 475 (fr. of VII)
πατρῴαν, XII. 74
παῦλα: -αν, IX. 8 (?)
παῦρος: -οισι(ι), VIII. 95, XII. 62, fr. 21. 1:
   παυροτέρων, I. 64
παύω: παύσει, XII. 45: παῦσεν, V. 98,
   X. 108: παῦσαι, 76: παύσασθαι, XIV.
   46
πεδίον, XII. 143: -ῳ, X. 19, XII. 118
*πεδοιχνεῖν, XV. 9
πέδον, VIII. 5
πείθω: πεῖθε (impf.), VIII. 16: πιθοῦσα,
   X. 107: πειθόμεθ', V. 195
πεισίμβροτον, VIII. 2
πέλαγος, XVI. 4, 77
πελάζω: πέλασσεν, X. 33: πελάσσας,
   VIII. 38: πλαθεῖσα, XVI. 35
Πελλάνα: -αν, IX. 33
Πέλοψ: -οπος, V. 181, VII. 53, X. 25,
   p. 437 (I. 13 Blass)
πέλω: πέλονται, IX. 38, fr. 3. 7: ἔπλετο,
   I. 31
πέμπω: -ει, V. 11, XIV. 61, fr. 16. 6: -οι,
   XV. 29: -ειν, V. 197: -εν, VIII. 20:
   ἔπεμψεν, XV. 2: πέμψαι, III. 66:
   πέμψει, V. 91
πενθέω: -εῖν, fr. 2. 2
πενία: -ας, I. 61
πεντάεθλος: -οισιν, VIII. 27
πένταθλον: πεντάθλου, VIII. 104
πέντε, I. 43
πεντήκοντα, I. 5, III. 81, VII. 2
πεπρωμένα: see πορ-
πέπων: -όνων, Ep. 2. 4 (fr. 34)
πέρθω: πέρσαν, X. 122
περί, with gen., V. 124, XVII. 51 (ὕπερ
   MS.): with dat., VII. 50, XII. 55, XVII.
   47
περικλειτός: -έ, fr. 12: -οί, X. 81:
   -κλειτῶν, VIII. 8: -οῖσι(ν), V. 12, IX. 19
Πέρσας: -ᾶν, III. 27
Περσείδας, XII. 48
πέταλον, V. 186
πετάννυμι: πέτασε, XVI. 72
Πετραῖος: -αίου, XIII. 20
Πηλεΐδας, XII. 110
πῆχυς: -υν, fr. 13. 4
πιαίνω: -εται, III. 68
Πιερίδες, XVIII. 35, p. 437 (I. 3 Blass):
   -ων, XVIII. 3
πινυτός. -ᾶς, XIV. 55

πίνω: -οντος, fr. 16. 12
πίπτω: ἔπεσον, X. 20: πεσεῖν, 72: πεσόντα, 23. Cp. πίτνω
Πίσα: -αν, V. 182
πίσυνος: V. 21, XII. 221
Πιτθεύς: -έος, XVI. 34
πίτνω: -νον (impf.), XVI. 6
πιφαύσκω, V. 42: -οι, VIII. 81
πίων: †πιοτάτῳ, Epigr. 2. 2 (fr. 34)
πλαγκτός: -ῷ, VIII. 20 (?)
πλάξιππος, V. 97
πλάσσω: πλᾶξεν, X. 86
πλατύς: -εῖα, fr. 29
Πλεισθενίδας, XIV. 48
*πλείσταρχος: -ον, III. 12
πλείων: -ονα, III. 65: πλεῦνας, VII. 46
Πλευρών: -ῶνα, V. 151, XIX. 10
πλήμμυρις: -ιν, fr. 30
πλημμύρω: -ων, V. 107
πλόκος: -ον, XVI. 114
πλοῦτος, I. 50: -ον, III. 13, XIV. 59, fr. 3. 2, 16. 12: -ου, IX. 49: -ῳ, X. 51
πνέω: -ων, V. 153, IX. 22: -ουσα, XVI. 91
πνοιά: πνοιαῖσιν, V. 28
ποδάνεμος: -ον, VI. 13
ποδάρκης: -εα, XVIII. 30
πόθεν, XVII. 31
ποικίλος: -ον, VII. 43: -αις, X. 33
ποιμήν: -ένων, XVII. 9
ποῖος: -ᾳ, V. 88
*πολέμαιγις: -δος, XVI. 7
πολέμαρχος: -ε, XVI. 39
πολεμήϊος: -αν, XVII. 4: -οις, 33
πόλεμος: -οιο, XII. 121: -ου, XVII. 58: -ῳ, V. 131
πολιοκρόταφος: -ον, fr. 21. 2
πολιός: -όν, III. 88
πόλις: -ιν, I. 13, 29, IV. 2, V. 12, 150, VIII. 54, 66, 98, X. 114, 122, XI. 7, XII. 71, 163, 185, XIV. 41, pp. 437-9 (I. 9, 52 Blass): -ει, X. 78: -ίων, fr. 16. 7
πολυάμπελος: πολυαμπελ-, p. 475 (fr. of VII)
πολυδάκρυος: -ον, III. 30
πολύδακρυς: -υν, XV. 24
πολύζηλος: -ῳ, X. 63
πολυζήλωτος, VII. 10: -ε, VIII. 45: -ον, I. 74, IX. 48
πολυήσατος: -οις, XVIII. 9
πολυκρατής: -ές (voc.), VIII. 15
πολύκρημνος: -ον, I. 11
πολύκριθος: -ον, X. 70
πολυλάϊον, IX. 34
πολύλλιστος: -ον, X. 41
Πολυνείκης: -εϊ, VIII. 20
Πολυπήμων: -ονος, XVII. 27
πολύπλαγκτος: -ον, XII. 181: -οι, X. 35
πολύς: -ύ, X. 50: πολλάν, XVII. 34: πολέες, X. 17: πολλαί, VIII. 89: -έας, Epigr. 1. 3 (fr. 33): -έων, V. 100:

πολλῶν, IX. 48: -οῖς, I. 42, V. 127. Cp. πλείων
πολύστονος: -ον, XVI. 40
*πολύφαντος: -ον, XII. 61
πολύχρυσος: -ῳ, X. 4
πολυώνυμος: -ε, Epigr. 1. 1 (fr. 33)
πόνος: -ον, XII. 54, fr. 7. 5: -ους, fr. 9
πόντιος: -ον, XVI. 84: -ῳ, 35
πόντος, XVI. 128: -ον, XII. 129: -ονδε, XVI. 94: -ου, III. 86, fr. 30: -ῳ, XII. 125
πορ-: ἔπορεν, V. 51: πεπρωμέναν, III. 25, XVI. 26
Πορθανίδας: -δα, V. 70
πόρος: -ῳ, VIII. 42
πόρπαξ: -ξιν, fr. 3. 6
πορσύνω: ἐπόρσυνε, XVI. 89
πορτιτρόφος: -ον, X. 30
πορφύρεος: -εον, XVII. 52: -έαν, XVI. 112: -εοι, fr. 20. 2
*πορφυροδίνας: -αν, VIII. 39
πορφυρόζωνος: -οιο, X. 49
Ποσειδάν, XVI. 79, XIX. 8: -ᾶνος, IX. 19, XIII. 20: -ᾶνι, XVI. 36, 59
Ποσειδάνιος: -ον, fr. 6. 1
ποταίνιος: -αν, XVI. 51
ποταμός: -οῦ, VIII. 65, XII. 77: -ῶν, VIII. 45
ποτέ, III. 23, 72, V. 56, VI. 6, X. 40, XI. 4, XII. 54, XVI. 115, XIX. 1
πότερα, XVI. 133
ποτί, with acc., X. 96, XV. 29: cp. πρός
πότμος: -ον, V. 158
πότνια, XI. 5, Ep. 1. 1 (fr. 33)
που, V. 91: πού, III. 38, 39
πούς: ποδῶν, VII. 6, IX. 20: -εσσι, VI. 2, XII. 86: ποσσί(ν), I. 35, V. 183: ποσίν, XVI. 108, XVII. 17
πρᾶξις, V. 163
πράσσω: -οι, V. 190: -οντας, fr. 21. 2: πράξαντι, III. 94
πρέπω: -ει, XVIII. 12
πρεσβύτατος: -ον, VII. 8
Πρίαμος: -οιο, X. 120: -ῳ, XIV. 38
πρίν, X. 72, XII. 114, XV. 13, XVIII. 38, fr. 21. 3
πρόγονος: -οι, X. 119
πρόδομος: -οις, VI. 14
προΐημι: -ίει, V. 81
Προῖτος: -ου, X. 45, 83: -ῳ, 66
πρόκειμαι: -ται, XIII. 9
Προκόπτας, XVII. 28
προλείπω: -ων, V. 154
πρόξενος: -ον, VIII. 20
προπαροιθε(ν), III. 32, V. 148
προπέμπω: -ε (imperat.), XVI. 55: -πέμπων, VIII. 34
πρόπολος, V. 192
πρός, with dat., X. 23: with acc., V. 45, 149, X. 100
προσεῖδον: προσιδεῖν, V. 161
προσεῖπον: -εν, V. 78

προσεννέπω: προσήνεπεν, XIV. 9
πρόσθε(ν), III. 47, XVI. 45
πρόσπολος, XIV. 2
προστίθημι: προσθέντα, VIII. 72 (?)
πρόσφαμι: προσέφα, V. 93, 171
προσφωνέω: -ει (impf.), or -εῖ, p. 439
(I. 76 Blass)
πρότερος: -ον, XII. 164: -ρων, V. 43
προφαίνω: προφάνη, V. 77
προφανής, III. 51
προφάτας, VIII. 3: -άται, IX. 28
προφέρω: -ειν, X. 51
πρόφρων, Ep. 1. 2 (fr. 33)
προχοά: -αῖς, VI. 3
πρύμνα: -ᾳ, XII. 105
πρύτανις: -ιν, I. 18, XVIII. 43
*πρώθηβος: -ον, XVII. 57
πρών: -ῶνας, V. 67
πρώτιστος: -ον (adv.), VIII. 11
πρῶτος, XIV. 47: -ον, VIII. 9: -οις, I. 58
πτάσσω: -οντι, V. 22: πτᾶσσον, impf.,
XII. 117
πτέρυξ: -ύγεσσι, V. 18
Πυθέας: -έα (gen.), XII. 191
Πυθιόνικος, IV. 5: -ον, X. 13
Πύθιος: -ε, XV. 10: -ίου (neut.), XV. 1 (?)
πυθμήν: -ένες, V. 198
Πυθώ (acc.), III. 62
Πυθών: -ῶνα, VII. 39: -ῶνι, V. 41
πυκινός: -άν, fr. 1. 1
πύλα: -αι, p. 437 (I. 14 Blass): -as (acc.),
fr. 4. 2
πύματος: -ον, V. 153
πυνθάνομαι: πύθετο, XV. 26
πύξ, VI. 7
πῦρ: -ός, III. 53, XVI. 105: -ί, XII. 107,
XV. 14
πυρά: πυράν, III. 31
*πυργοκέρας: -ατα, fr. 31
πύργος: -ων, V. 148
πυργόω: -ωθέντα, III. 13
*πυριέθειρα: -αν, XVI. 56
πυροφόρος: -οι, fr. 16. 10
Πύρριχος: -ου, XIII. 22
πυρσός: -όν, XII. 82
*πυρσόχαιτος: -του, XVII. 51
πω, V. 122; cp. οὔπω
πῶλος: -ον, V. 39
πῶμα, V. 76

Ρ

ῥα, XVIII. 33 (ἤ ῥα)
ῥάδιος: -ον, XVII. 43: ῥᾷστον, fr. 4. 2
ῥέεθρον: -οις, III. 20, V. 64
ῥέπω: -ει, XVI. 25
ῥιπά: -ᾷ, V. 46
ῥίπτω: -ων, VIII. 32
ῥοά: -αῖς, XII. 193
ῥοδοδάκτυλος, XVIII. 18
ῥοδόεις: -εντι, XV. 34

ῥόδον: -οις, XVI. 116
ῥοδόπαχυς: -υν, XII. 96

Σ

σαίνω: -ει, I. 55: -νουσα, p. 439 (I. 77
Blass)
σακεσφόρος: -ον, XII. 104
σάλπιγξ, XVII. 4: -ίγγων, fr. 3. 9
σᾶμα, VIII. 14, XVI. 57
σαμαίνω: σάμαινεν, XIV. 38
σαόφρων, XII. 186
σᾶπω: -εται, III. 87
Σάρδιες, III. 27
σαφής: -ῆ (acc. pl.), XVI. 75
σβέννυμι: σβέννυεν, III. 56
σεισίχθων: -ονος, XVII. 22: -ονι, XVI. 58
σείω: -ων, XII. 120
σελάνα, VIII. 29
σέλας, XVI. 104
Σεμέλα: -αν, XVIII. 48
*σεμνοδότειρα, II. 1
σεμνός: -ά, XII. 195: -άν, XVI. 110: -οῦ,
X. 52: -ᾶς, V. 99
σεύω: σεύοντι (3rd plur.), XVII. 10:
ἔσσευε, V. 104: σευομενᾶν, fr. 16. 3
σθένος, VII. 7, XVII. 40: -ει, V. 107, VIII. 37
σιδαρόδετος: -οις, fr. 3. 6
Σικελία: -as, III. 1
Σικυών, IX. 32
Σίνις: -ιν, XVII. 20
σιωπά, III. 95
Σκάμανδρος: -ον, XII. 165
σκᾶπτρον, III. 70
Σκίρων: -ωνα, XVII. 25
σκοπέω: -εῖς, III. 74
σκότος: -ῳ, III. 14
σκύφος: -οισιν, fr. 17. 5
σμερδαλέος: -έαν, X. 56
σοέω: σόει (impf.), XVI. 90
σός: σόν, XII. 83, XV. 12: σᾶς, VIII. 49:
σῶν, 45: cp. τεός
σοφία, XIV. 31, fr. 10. 2
σοφός, IX. 39, XI. 1, fr. 4. 1: -όν, XII. 201
Σπάρτα: -ᾳ, XIX. 1
στάδιον, VI. 7, 15: -ίου, IX. 21
στάσις, fr. 20. 2
στείχω: -ει, VIII. 47: -ειν, 17, XVII. 36
στέρνον: -οισ(ι), X. 88, XVII. 53
στέφανος: -ῳ, VIII. 23: -οι, X. 19: -ους,
Ep. 1. 4 (fr. 33): -ων, I. 48, III. 8:
-οισ(ιν), II. 10, IV. 16, VI. 8, VII. 11,
XII. 55, 69
στεφανόω: ἐστεφάνωσεν, XII. 197: στεφανωσάμενον, X. 29: -μεναι, XII. 91
στεφαναφόρος: -ων, XVIII. 51 (?)
στῆθος: -έων, V. 15: -εσσι, X. 54
στίλβω: -ειν, XVII. 55
στολά: -άν, XVII. 32
στορέννυμι: στόρεσεν, XII. 129
στραταγέτας, XVII. 7: -αν, XVI. 121

στραταγός: -γέ, V. 2
στρατιά: -άν, XVII. 34
στρατός: -ῷ, III. 27
στρωφάω: -ᾶται, XII. 180
στυγερός: -άν, V. 111: -ῶν, X. 76
σύ, III. 92, VII. 8, XII. 67, XVI. 28 (?), 44, 76, fr. 15. 1: σέο, III. 65: σέθεν, X. 9: σοί (orthot.), V. 168, X. 2, XVI. 54: τίν (orthot.), XVII. 14: τοι (enclit.), X. 104, 118, XII. 79, XVI. 78, XVII. 11: σέ (orthot.), VI. 10, VII. 2, XVI. 58: σε (enclit.), XVI. 29, 39, XVIII. 12, fr. 12
συλάω: -ᾶται, fr. 3. 10
συμπόσιον: -ίων, fr. 3. 12
συμφορά, XIII. 3
σύν, I. 5, II. 10, III. 5, 6, 33, 34, 60, 96, IV. 6, V. 9, 28, 52, 127, VII. 42, VIII. 51, 85, 103, X. 23, 63, 115, 125, XII. 66, 89, 128, 183, 202, XIV. 13, XVI. 125, XVII. 33, 35
συνετός: -ᾷ, III. 85
σύνευνος: -ων, p. 439 (I. 58 f. Blass)?
συνεχέως, V. 113
σύνοικος: -ον, XIV. 56
Συρακόσιος: -ίαν, IV. 1: -κοσίων, V. 1
Συράκοσσαι: -όσσας, V. 184
σῦς, V. 116: σῦν, XVII. 23
σφάζω: σφάξε (impf.), V. 109
σφέτερος: -ον, X. 50: -ας (plur.), III. 36
σφῦρα: -αν, XVII. 28
σχάζω: ἔσχασεν, XVI. 121
σχέτλιος: -ον, XVI. 19
σῶμα, XVI. 63: -τος, XII. 52: -τι, III. 91: -τα, VIII. 38, fr. 17. 1

T

ταινία: -ᾳ, XVI. 107
Ταλαϊονίδας: -αν, VIII. 19
τάλαντον, IV. 12 (?), XVI. 25
ταλαπενθής: -έα (sing.), XV. 26: -έος, V. 157
τάλας: -αινα, XV. 30
τάμνω: -νων, V. 17: τάμνε (impf.), XVI. 4
τανίσφυρος: -ου, V. 59: -οις, III. 60
τανίφυλλος: -ον, X. 55
τανύθριξ: τανυτρίχων, fr. 3. 4
τάπης: -ητες, fr. 17. 2
ταρφέως, XII. 86
ταῦρος: -ους, XV. 18
ταύσιος: -ον, V. 81
ταφ-: τάφεν, XVI. 86: -ον, XVI. 48
τάχα, V. 89
ταχύς: -ύν, XII. 201: -εῖαν, IX. 20: -είαις, V. 18: τάχιστα, Epigr. 2. 3 (fr. 34)
ταχύτας: -ᾶτα, VII. 6
τε (θ'), passim (occurring about 157 times; cp. δέ and καί): fivefold, XVII. 19–27: τε.. καί, III. 79 ff., X. 90 f., fr. 22. 1 f.: τε.. τε καί, VII. 39 f.: δέ τε, XII. 129,

fr. 3. 1: placed after art. and noun, τὸν ὑπέρβιόν τ', XVII. 19; or after prep. and noun, III. 5, σὺν ὑπερόχῳ τε, cp. ib. 6, 34
τέγγω: τέγξαι, V. 157
τέθμιος: -ίου, III. 70 (?)
τεῖχος, X. 77: -εα, XII. 142
τέκνον: -α, X. 102
τέκος, VI. 13, XVIII. 22, fr. 2. 1
Τελαμών: -μῶνα, XII. 98
τελειόω: τελειοῦσαι, III. 26 (?)
τέλεος: -έους, X. 92
τελευτά: -άς, IX. 46
τελευταῖος: -ας (gen.), VIII. 36
τελευτάω: τελευταθεῖσα, I. 72
τελέω: -εῖς (fut.), III. 82: -εῖ (fut.), xVVI. 78: -εῦν (probably fut.), V. 164: τέλεσας, VII. 49: τελεῖται, XVII. 30 (fut.), 45 (pres.)
τέλος, V. 45, X. 6
τέμενος, X. 48, 110, XIII. 21
τεός: τεάν, IX. 13: τεᾶν, XVI. 21: cp. σός
τέρας, XV. 35, XVI. 72
τέρπω: -πον (3rd plur.), XVI. 107: -πόμενος, XV. 7
*τερψιεπής: -εῖς, XII. 230
τερψίμβροτος: -ων, XII. 72
τέρψις, I. 59
τετραέλικτος: -ον, IX. 25 (?)
τεύχος: -εσι, V. 72
τεύχω: -ει, III. 58: τεῦχον (3rd plur.), X. 110
τέχνα: -αις, X. 33, XII. 49
τηλαυγής: -έϊ, XVI. 5
τίθημι: τίθησι, IX. 50: θῆκας, 18: θῆκεν, I. 47: ἔθηκαν, III. 7: θέωσιν, XVI. 118: θέμεν, XVI. 70: θείμαν, V. 169
τίκτω: -ει, IX. 46, fr. 3. 1: ἔτικτε, XII. 97: τίκτε (impf.), XVIII. 50: τέκε(ν), I. 16, V. 119, VIII. 56, XVI. 30, 35, 54
τιμά: -ᾷ, I. 40: -άν, I. 70 f., IX. 39, XII. 80, XIII. 6, XVI. 69, XVIII. 7
τιμάω: -ᾷ, XII. 183: -ῶν, X. 74: -ασεν, XII. 194
Τιμόξενος: -ου, VIII. 102
Τιρύνθιος: -ον, X. 57
Τίρυνς: -θα, X. 71
τίς (interrog.), V. 86, 89, VIII. 53, XIV. 47: τίνα, XVII. 31, 32: τί, IV. 18, IX. 51, XVII. 3, 11, 15, fr. 8
τις (enclit.), III. 21, 97, V. 5, 54, 162, 165, 190, X. 27, XII. 84, XVII. 5, fr. 7. 2: τινί, XVII. 2: τινά, IX. 41, 56, XII. 46, 199, 223, XVI. 43: τί, VIII. 101, XVIII. 9, fr. 11. 4
τιταίνω: -ει, IX. 43
τιτύσκω: -ων, V. 49
τλάμων, V. 153: -ονες, XII. 157 (?)
τόθεν, V. 197
τόθι, III. 7 (?), 19, XVI. 101

516 VOCABULARY.

τοι (particle), I. 58, VIII. 3 (?), 22 : η τοι,
XII. 79. Cp. οὗτοι.—For τοι *tibi*, see
under σύ
τοῖος, VIII. 30: -ον, p. 439 (I. 35 Blass)?
τοιόσδε: -όνδε, XIX. 3: τοιῷδε, VIII. 37
τοιοῦτος: -ον, V. 87
τοξόκλυτος, X. 39
τόξον, IX. 43
τόσος: -ά, III. 48: as relative, I. 37, XV.
11
τότε, III. 58, V. 143, 156, VIII. 19, XV.
23, XVIII. 31
τραχύς: -ύν, V. 82 : -εῖαν, XII. 111
τρέφω: -ει, III. 92, XII. 62: θρέψεν, v.
88, VIII. 7
τρέω: τρέσσαν, XVI. 92
τριέτης: -ει, VIII. 23
τριόδους: -δοντα, fr. 6 2
τρίπους: -όδων, III. 18
τρισευδαίμων, III. 10
τρισκαίδεκα (acc.), X. 92
τρίτατος : -ᾳ, I. 2
τρίτος: -ον, IV. 4
Τροιζήνιος: -ία, XVI. 58
Τροία: -ας, VIII. 46
τροχοειδής: -έα (sing.), VIII. 32
Τρώς: -ῶες, XII. 133, XIV. 50: -ων, XIV.
42
τυγχάνω: τεύξεται, IX. 38: τύχον (1st
pers.), V. 144: τυχών, XII. 67, XVII.
29: τυχόν, VIII. 83: -όντες, XIV. 12
τυφλός: -ά, V. 132
τύχα, IX. 47: -αν, XVI. 132: -ᾳ, V. 52, X.
115: -αις, VIII. 51
τῷ ('therefore'), XVI. 39
τώς, V. 31

Υ

ὕβρις: -ιος, XII. 44: -ιν, XVI. 41
Ὕβρις, XIV. 59
ὑγίεια: -είας, I. 55
ὑγρός: -οῖσιν, XVI. 108
ὕδωρ, III. 36
υἱός, X. 15, XII. 123, XV. 28, XVI. 86,
XVIII. 26: -έ, v. 79, XII. 68, XVI. 20,
XVII. 15: -όν, II. 14, IV. 13, V. 62,
XIX. 11 (?): υἷι, III. 77 (?): υἷας, XII.
100
ὕλα: -αν, X. 93
ὑμέτερος: -αν, V. 11, 32
ὑμνέω: -εῦσι, X. 13: -εῖν, V. 33: -έων,
VII. 40: ὕμνει (imper.), III. 3: ὑμνήσει, III. 97: ὕμνησον, V. 179
*ὑμνοάνασσα, XI. 1
ὕμνος, VI. 11: -ον, V. 10, VIII. 78, p. 475
(fr. of VII)?: -οι, fr. 3. 12: -ους, IV. 10:
-ων, VIII. 83, XII. 223, XV. 4: -οισιν,
XVIII. 8
ὑπαί, with gen., XII. 139
ὑπέρ: see n. on XVII. 51

ὑπεράφανος: -ον, XVI. 49
ὑπέρβιος: -ον, XII. 75, XVII. 19: -ε, III.
37
Ὑπερβόρεοι: -έους, III. 59
ὑπέρθυμος: -ον, XII. 103: -ῳ, VIII. 37
ὑπέροπλος, VIII. 13
ὑπέροχος: -ον, XVI. 68: -ῳ, III. 5, XVIII.
44
ὑπέρτατος: -ον, III. 84, X. 36, XVI. 79
ὑπερφίαλος: -ον, XII. 158: -οι, X. 78:
-ους, XIV. 62
ὕπνος, fr. 3. 10, p. 439 (I. 50 Blass)
ὑπό, with gen., v. 43, IX. 48, XII. 154,
XVI. 17: with dat., III. 17, XII. 125,
166: with acc., XVI. 30. Cp. ὑπαί
ὑπόκλοπος: -ον, XIV. 30
ὑσμίνα: -αν, XII. 144
ὕστερον (adv.), IX. 53, XV. 33
ὑφαίνω: ὕφαινε (impf.), XVI. 51: ὕφαινε
(imper.), XVIII. 8: ὕφανε, XV. 24:
ὑφάνας, v. 9
ὑφαιρέω: -εῖται (midd.), VIII. 18
*ὑψαυχής, XII. 85
*ὑψιάγυια: -αν, XII. 71
*ὑψιδαίδαλτος: -ων, III. 18
*ὑψίδειρος: -ου, IV. 4
ὑψίζυγος, I. 46, X. 3
ὑψικέρα (fem.), -αν, XV. 22. Cp. καλλικέρα
ὑψιμέδων, XIV. 51
ὑψίνοος: -όου, XII. 44
ὑψίπυλος: -ου, VIII. 46
ὑψιφανής: -ῆ, XIII. 5
ὑψοῦ, V. 18, VIII. 84: ὑψοτάτω, fr. 16. 6

Φ

φαεσίμβροτος: -ῳ, XII. 128
φαίδιμος: -ίμοισι, XVII. 47
φαίνω, XII. 224: φαῖνε (impf.), VIII. 31:
φάνη, XVI. 119: ἐφάνη, fr. 2. 2
Φάϊσκος: -ου, X. 14
φάλαγξ: -γγας, XIV. 42
φαμί, I. 49, XII. 54: φασίν, V. 155:
φάμεν (inf.), III. 65: φάσω, I. 49, X.
24: ἔφα, fr. 18. 2: φάτο, V. 84: πέφαται, IX. 52
φάος, III. 80, V. 67, XVI. 43: φάη, VIII.
28
φαρέτρα: -ας, V. 76
φᾶρος: -εΐ, XVI. 5: -εα, IX. 24
φάσγανον, X. 87, XII. 54
φάσκειν: φάσκον (3rd plur.), X. 50
φάτις, VIII. 48
φέγγος, III. 91, V. 162
φεν-: πέφνεν, VIII. 13: ἔπεφνεν, XVII. 17
*φερεκυδής: -έα (sing.), XII. 182: -έϊ,
I. 17
Φερένικος, V. 184: -ον, 37
φερεστέφανος: -οι, XVIII. 6
Φέρης: -ητος, III. 77

φέριστος: -ον (neut.), v. 160
Φερσεφόνα: -as, v. 59
φέρτατος, XVII. 20: -ον (masc.), v. 118, XVI. 33: (neut.), VI. 2: -ου, XVI. 20, XVIII. 17
φέρτερος: -ον (neut.), IV. 18
φέρω: -ει, III. 95, v. 134: -ειν, fr. 32. 3: -ων, III. 59, v. 185: -ουσα, II. 3, XVIII. 41: -οντες, XII. 144: φέρον (impf.), XVI. 97: ἔνεγκε (imper.), XVI. 62
φεῦ, XVI. 119
φεύγω: -εις, fr. 15. 2: φεύγετε, p. 439 (I. 81 Blass): φεύγοντα (neut.), I. 66: φεῦγε (impf.), XVIII. 16: φεῦγον (3rd plur.), v. 150, X. 55, 84, 94: φυγών, XIX. 7, fr. 30
φήμα: -αν, v. 194
Φήμα, II. 1, IX. 1
φθέγγομαι: -ευ, XVII. 12: φθέγξατο, XIV. 49
φθίνω: φθιμένων, v. 83
φθόνος, XII. 200, XV. 31: -ον, v. 188: -ῳ, III. 68
φθόρος: -ον, XIV. 61
φιλάγλαος: -ον, XII. 224: -ους, XVII. 60
φιλαλάκατος? p. 439 (I. 74 Blass)
φιλάνωρ: -ορι, I. 40
φιλέω: -εῖ, IV. 1, XII. 204
φίλιππος: -ον, III. 69
φιλόξεινος: -είνου, XIII. 23: -ῳ, v. 49
φιλοξενία: -as, III. 16
φίλος: -ον (masc.), II. 14, IV. 19, v. 131: -αν, XVI. 109: -ην, fr. 15. 2: -ῳ, XVI. 69: -ᾶ, III. 47: -as (acc.), III. 50
φιλοστέφανος: -ῳ, XII. 184
φιτρός: -όν, v. 142
φλέγω: -ονται, fr. 3. 12
Φλειοῦς: -ντα, VIII. 4
φλόξ: -γί, fr. 3. 4: φλόγα, III. 56, XVII. 56
φοβέω: ἐφόβησε, X. 43
φόβος: -ον, XII. 145: -ῳ, v. 23
φοιβός: -άν, XII. 139
Φοῖβος: -ου, III. 20
*φοινίκασπις: -ιδες, VIII. 10
*φοινικόθριξ: -ότριχας, X. 105
*φοινικοκράδεμνος: -οιο, X. 97: -οισι, XII. 222
*φοινικόνωτος: -ων, V. 102
φοῖνιξ: φοίνισσαν, XVII. 56
Φοῖνιξ: -ικος, XVI. 31
Φοίνισσα, XVI. 54
φοινίσσω: φοινίξειν, XII. 165
φοιτάω: -ᾷ, v. 133
φόνος: -ου, VIII. 14: -ων, III. 52
φορέω: -εῖ, XIV. 30: -εῦντες, fr. 6. 3
φόρμιγξ: -ιγγος, XIII. 13
φραδᾷ: -αῖσι, XVIII. 17
*φρενοάρας: -αις, XVI. 118
φρήν: φρενί, fr. 7. 3: φρένα, v. 6, XV. 7, XVI. 131, fr. 1. 1: φρενῶν, XVI. 22:

φρένεσσιν, XIII. 11: φρασίν, XII. 229(?): φρένας, I. 52, X. 45, XI. 3, fr. 16. 4
φρονέω: -οντι, III. 85
φροντίς: -ίσι, XVI. 120
Φρύγιος: -ίου, VII. 43
φυά: -άν, v. 168
φυλάσσω: -ει, XII. 189: -εν (inf.), XVIII. 25: -ων, v. 47: -ξε, III. 29
φύλλον: -α, v. 65
φυτεύω: -ευσε(ν), XVI. 59, 68: -σαν, XVIII. 35
φύω: ἔφυ, v. 55: φῦναι, v. 160
φωνά: -άν, X. 56
φωνάεις: -άεντα, XIV. 31
φωνέω: φώνησεν, v. 191
φώς: φωτός, v. 158, XVII. 19, 30: φῶτα, XV. 15: φῶτε, XVII. 46: φῶτες, fr. 18. 5: φώτων, XII. 152

X

Χαιρόλας: -αν, p. 475 (fr. of VII)
χαίτα: -αν, X. 28, XII. 70: -αις, XVI. 105
χαλεπός: -όν (neut.), v. 95
χάλκασπις: -ιδες, X. 62
*χαλκεόκρανος: -ον, v. 74
*χαλκεόκτυπος: -ον, XVII. 59
χαλκεομίτραν, XII. 109 (?)
χάλκεος: -εᾶν, fr. 3. 9
χαλκεόστερνος: -ου, v. 34
χαλκοδαίδαλος: -οισιν, fr. 6. 2
χαλκοθώραξ: -ακα, XVI. 14: -άκων, X. 123
χαλκόκτυπος, XIII. 16 (?)
*χαλκοκώδων, XVII. 3
χαλκός, XII. 51
*χαλκοστειχής: -έος, III. 32
χάος: -ει, v. 27
χάρις, III. 38: χάριν, XII. 97, v. 187, VIII. 97, XIII. 19, fr. 7. 4
Χάριτες, VIII. 1, XVIII. 6: -ίτων, I. 41, IX. 39: -ίτεσσι, v. 9: Χάρισσιν, XIV. 49
*χαριτώνυμος: -ον, II. 2
χάρμα, IX. 13
χείμών: -ῶνος, XII. 140
χείρ: χειρός, VIII. 35, XII. 154, XIII. 10, XVI. 61: χέρα, VII. 41: χεῖρα, XII. 49, XVI. 11: χειρῶν, v. 82, 132, X. 36, 91, XVI. 45: χέρεσσι, XVII. 49: χερσίν, v. 189: χέρας, III. 35, XII. 138, XIV. 45: χεῖρας, III. 50, X. 100, XVI. 72
χέρσος: -ον, XII. 132
χέω: χέων, v. 15: χέον (impf.), XVI. 96
χθών: χθονός, IV. 4, XVII. 5: χθονί, v. 88, X. 32: χθόνα, I. 11, VIII. 40, XVI. 80
χιτών: -ῶνα, VIII. 52: -ῶνι, fr. 15. 1
χλαμύς: -ύδα, XVII. 54
χλωραύχην: -ενα, v. 172
χόλος: -ον, v. 99, 104, 123

χολόω: χολώσατο, XVI. 50 (?) : -ωσαμένα,
X. 53
χορός: -ῷ, XVI. 107 : -όν, Epigr. 1. 2 (fr. 33):
-οί, XIII. 14, XV. 11 : -ῶν, XVIII. 51 :
-οῖσι, XVI. 130: -ούς, X. 112
χραίνω: χραῖνον (3rd plur.), X. 111
χρεῖος ('need'), I. 34 (?)
χρέος, VII. 43
χρή, III. 78, V. 164, 187, IX. 56, XIII. 20,
fr. 11. 3
χρηστός: -όν (masc.), IX. 51
χρόνος, XII. 206: -ῳ, VII. 45, X. 120, 125,
XVII. 45: -ον, I. 70, VIII. 80, fr. 21. 1,
28
Χρόνος: -ου, VII. 1
χρύσαιγις: -ιδος, fr. 11. 2
χρυσαλάκατος, X. 38: -οι, VIII. 1
χρυσάμπυξ: -υκος, V. 13
χρυσάορος, III. 28 (?)
χρυσάρματος, XII. 194
χρύσασπις: -ιδος, XIX. 11
*χρυσεόπλοκος, XVI. 106
χρύσεος: -εα (nom.), XVIII. 16; (voc.),
X. 117: -εας (gen.), V. 174; (acc.), XIV.
4: -έᾳ, IX. 40: -εον (masc.), XVI. 60;
(neut.), 36: -έαν, VIII. 72, XII. 61 (?),
XV. 2 (with ῠ̆) : -έοις, IX. 6 (with ῠ̆)
*χρυσεόσκαπτρος: -ου, VIII. 100
χρυσοδίνας, III. 44
χρυσόθρονος? v. 1 of a small fr. numbered
by Kenyon (p. 206) as 22, and referred
by Blass (p. 126) to XIV.
χρυσοκόμας, IV. 2

*χρυσόπαχυς, V. 40
χρυσόπεπλος, XVIII. 22
χρυσός, III. 17, 87, fr. 17. 1: -ῷ, fr. 16. 9
-όν, III. 65, fr. 10. 2, 27
χρώς: χρόα, X. 97
χώρα: -ᾳ, V. 80

Ψ

ψυχά, V. 77, 151, 171 : -ᾷ, X. 48: -αῖσ(ιν),
V. 83, 133: -άς, V. 64

Ω

ὦ, III. 64, VI. 13, VII. 1, 48, VIII. 1, 15,
45, 102, X. 116, XII. 77, 94, 190, XIV.
50, XVI. 15, p. 437 (I. 13 Blass)
ὧδε, XVII. 39, fr. 18. 2
ὠκύμορος: -ον, V. 141
ὠκύπομπος: -ον, XVI. 90
ὠκύπους: ὠκυπόδων, IV. 6
ὠμηστάς: -ᾷ, XII. 40
ὦμος: ὤμοις, XVII. 47
ὡς, (1) 'as,' VIII. 27, XII. 82 (πυρσὸν ὥς):
(2) 'when,' V. 71; (3) 'how,' fr. 6. 1
(unless there the sense was 'when'):
(4) with inf., fr. 1. 1 (ὡς .. εἰπεῖν)
ὥς, 'thus,' V. 84, XII. 133, XVI. 81, fr.
16. 12
ὡσεί, XI. 1
ὥστε, 'as' (= ὡς), XII. 124
ὧτε, 'as,' XVI. 105

519

INDEX.

A

Abas, king of Argos, X. 40

accents, use of, in the Bacchylides papyrus, p. 135: noteworthy, in particular instances, p. 137

accusative, cognate (ἀναδεθεῖσιν ἄνθεα), XII. 59 f.: in apposition with sentence, XII. 93, XIII. 19: double (τὸν δ' εἷλεν ἄχος κραδίαν), X. 85

Achaean settlements in Italy, p. 209, X. 113: ancestry claimed by Ionians, p. 483

Acusilaus, the logographer, X. 50 ff.

adjectives, compound, peculiar to B., pp. 68 ff.: verbal in -τος, of 3 terminations, XII. 181: denoting the parent ('Αλκμήνιος), V. 71: compounded with a noun akin in sense to the subst. (ἀρισταλκὲς σθένος), VII. 7

Adrastus, VIII. 19

Aeacidae, Pindar's tributes to, p. 217

Aegeus and Aethra, legend of, p. 230

Aegina, boxers and wrestlers of, p. 212: festivals at, IX. 3: the nymph, daughter of Asopus, VIII. 55, XII. 77: repute of the island for just dealing, *ib.*, and 182 ff.

aegis of Athena, XVI. 7

Aeolian lyric poetry, p. 29

Aeolic forms, p. 81

Aeschylus, in Sicily, p. 9; his *Aetnaeae*, *ib.*: lyrics of, p. 45: traces of, in the work of B., p. 67: treatment of Io's story, p. 235

'Aetolian' as = 'Elean,' VII. 51

Agelaus, brother of Meleager, V. 117

Agenor, father of Cadmus, p. 235, XVIII. 46

Aglaïa, personified, III. 6

Aiax, p. 206, n. 2: and Hector, XII. 105 ff.

Alcaeus, p. 29: on Apollo's visit to the Hyperboreans, p. 222, XV. 5

Alcman, his partheneia, p. 31

Alexandrian scholia, citations of Bacchylides in, pp. 74 f.: sense of 'dithyramb' in Alexandrian age, p. 39

Althaea's brand, V. 142 ff., pp. 470 f.

Alyattes, father of Croesus, III. 40

Amazons, the, VIII. 43

Amphiaraus, VIII. 16

Amphitrite, her place in the Theseusmyth, p. 222: XVI. 111

Amphitryon, ῑ or ῐ in, V. 156

Anacreon, p. 29

Ancaeus, of Tegea, V. 117

antecedent, to be supplied in dat. (πάρεστι [τούτῳ], ὃς κ.τ.λ.), XVIII. 1 ff.

Antenor, the Trojan, and his sons, pp. 219 f.

aorist partic. after εἶδε, X. 23: infin., as dist. from pres. infin., V. 30, 161, XVI. 43

Aphares, a son of Thestius, V. 129

Apharetidae, the (Idas and Lynceus), Messenian heroes, p. 239

apocope of prep., p. 84

Apollo, bestows the gift of φιλοξενία, I. 40: shepherd to Admetus, III. 77: 'king of the Lycians,' XII. 147 f.: styled Loxias, though he is acting as a war-god, *ib.*: the hunter, XV. 6

apposition, partitive, X. 70 ff.

Archemorus, VIII. 12

Archilochus, his καλλίνικος, p. 36

Arete, personified, XII. 176

Argos, ἱππόβοτον, XVIII. 15

Argus, son of Earth, XVIII. 19, 31

Aristaeus, cult of, p. 428

Aroanian hills in Arcadia, X. 94

Artemis, as a goddess of vegetation, V. 98 f.; of agriculture and cattle-breeding, X. 115 f.: ἀγροτέρα, V. 123, p. 211 n. 1: ἡμέρα ('the soothing'), X. 39, p. 210

Asopus, the Phliasian river, p. 205: his daughters and descendants, p. 206, VIII. 45 ff.

Lightning Source UK Ltd.
Milton Keynes UK
177922UK00001B/37/P